WHAT IS THE INDIE BIBLE

The Indie Bible is a valuable promotional tool for Independent Musicians and Songwriters that lists:

- 4200 publications that will REVIEW your music!
- 3600 radio stations that will PLAY your songs!
- 600 services that will help you to SELL your music!
- 350 sites where you can UPLOAD your band's MP3s or videos!
- and 50 articles that will help your music career to SUCCEED!

ALL styles of music are covered!

Pop, Rock, Hip Hop, Folk, Blues, Classical, Jazz, Punk, ALL Metals, Latin, Indie Rock, Electronic, Experimental, Christian, Dance, World Music, Soul, R&B, Women in Music, Country, Rap, Roots, Bluegrass, Reggae, Ska, Rockabilly, Ambient, Emo, Gothic, Industrial, Progressive Rock, Alternative, Americana, Oi, Jam Band, Hardcore, Garage, Avant-garde, House, Trip Hop, Celtic, EBM, Gospel, Space Rock, Noise, Alt-Country, Children's, New Age, Singer/Songwriter, Trance, Lo-Fi, Funk, Nu-Jazz ...

The Indie Bible also provides you with **50** insightful articles that will help you to succeed!

Articles Include:

- **How to Submit Your Music for Review**
- **How to Get Radio Airplay**
- **Getting Your Music into Film**
- **How to Market Your Music**
- **Why You Need an Entertainment Lawyer**
- **Band and Press Kit Essentials**
- **How Royalties Work**
- **How to Copyright Your Music**

and MANY more!

Professional CD manufacturing:
It's not fast food.

Your prized CD project can't be handled like a "drive through" operation. You need it crafted to *your* specifications, with unusual care, by real artists and real experts. That's an important difference that Oasis has strived to offer musicians on every project. No matter how large or how small. For fifteen years running.

And when we've completed your project—when the pristine sound reproduction, printing, and other painstaking details are all in place—the benefits of being an Oasis client have really just begun. For example, it's a **tremendous** advantage to place your music in the prestigious **OasisSampler radio promotion program**—an exclusive and automatic benefit of working with Oasis. *Your favorite track from your CD will be delivered directly to around 500 of the most relevant radio stations in your pinpointed musical genre—and to our private list of highly connected industry insiders, people who can make a real difference in your career.*

The feedback from these promotional endeavors has been remarkable. Our clients are repeatedly **contacted by radio stations, booking agents, and industry insiders** asking for more material, and some have landed extremely lucrative deals—*like our client whose music was recently purchased for use and played under the credits on Deadwood, HBO's runaway hit series.*

But the Oasis Sampler is only one of a baker's dozen of interrelated **Tools of Promotion (TOP)**. All of our **TOP** services are designed to help independent musicians jumpstart their careers.

Ask your friends. Ask around. Or just pick up the phone and talk with one of our famously friendly Client Advisors. Call **(866) 381-7017** or email **advice@oasisCD.com** and let us know how we can help.

Sincerely,

Micah Solomon, *President and CEO*

www.oasisCD.com/indiebible
(866) 381-7017
info@oasisCD.com

Oasis is the only national disc manufacturing company certified by both The Better Business Bureau and BBBonline.

INCLUDED WITH YOUR CD or DVD PROJECT—THE OASIS TOP™ TOOLS OF PROMOTION:

Your Music on an OasisSampler™ Distributed to Radio Nationwide	Galaris/Oasis CD-ROM with 14,000+ Music Industry Contacts	Distribution for your CD/DVD: **iTunes Music Store** **amazon**.com cdbaby.com **TOWER.COM** **BORDERS**.com **Waldenbooks**.com	A **Full Year** of Electronic Press Kit® Service and Exclusive Live Performance Opportunities: **sonicbids**	SoundScan®, Music-Career Software, Retail Cases, Barcodes	**FREE Website** with the features musicians need!

COVER DESIGN
Warrior Girl Music www.warriorgirlmusic.com based on the acrylic painting " UNDONE " by Gilli Moon www.gillimoon.com

ARTISTS PICTURED and PHOTOGRAPHERS
(top right) Holly Light : www.hollylight.com
Photo by Sharman Petri www.gradientlight.com

(under) Lance Bulen/Kingbaby www.Kingbabymusic.com
Photo by Bernard Baur www.BGOEntNet.com

(mid left) Dig Jelly www.digjelly.com
Photo by Bernard Baur www.BGOEntNet.com

(mid left) Coole High www.coolehigh.com
Photo by Larry Mah (818) 367-3383

(mid left) Denise Vasquez www.myspace.com/denisevasquez
Photo by Bernard Baur www.BGOEntNet.com

(centre) Jacqueline Rendell www.jacquelinerendell.com
Photo by Christina Woerns c_woerns11@hotmail.com

(mid right) Cookie Cutter Girl www.CookieCutterGirl.com
Photo by Frank Douglas (617) 851-7304

(lower right) Justin Winokur www.justinwinokur.com
Photo by Helène Sjöstrand www.fotografhelene.se

(lower left) Gilli Moon www.gillimoon.com
Photo by Ron Wolfson StarPhotg@aol.com

Copyright © 2007 by Big Meteor Publishing

This edition published 2007 by Schirmer Trade Books,
an imprint for the Music Sales Publishing Group

Order No. BM 80000
ISBN 0-9686214-6-5

Exclusive Distributors
Music Sales Corporation
257 Park Avenue South, New York, NY 10010 USA
Music Sales Limited
8/9 Frith Street, London W1D 3JB England
Music Sales Pty. Limited
120 Rothschild Street, Rosebery, Sydney NSW 2018 Australia

Printed in Canada by Bradda Printing

What people are saying about The Indie Bible...

"My press kit is full of positive press from around the WORLD because of The Indie Bible."
**- Terry Christopher,
Award Winning Singer/Songwriter**

"All the artists I work with personally are required to have a copy."
- Tim Sweeney, author of "Tim Sweeney's Guide To Releasing Independent Records"

"The Indie Bible provides a great service for artists and radio programmers."
- Kate Borger, WYEP FM

"I'm getting a nice chunk of radio play for my first CD and just received an label inquiry!"

- John Gordon, Recording Artist

"I can't thank you enough for this amazing summary of all your hard work and dedication. My heartfelt appreciation."

- David Culiner, LovethisLife

"It's great! The articles alone are worth the price."

- Beau Wadsworth, Recording Artist

"I bought the Indie Bible, and am still overwhelmed by it!"

- Michael Grady, The Strange Angels

"I have never seen as much relevent information in one publication. It is every thing I had hoped for!"

- John Morris, Recording Artist

"340 Pages of Pure Gold!"

– Guitar Player Magazine

TABLE OF CONTENTS

Plug into low prices

CDman.com
optical discs & packaging

It burns! It rips!
It has a robotic arm!

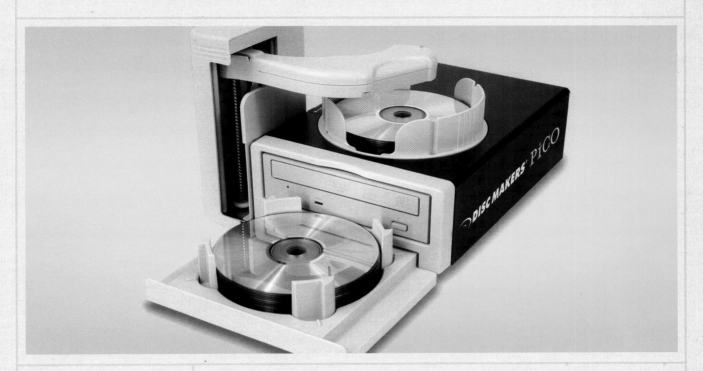

Coolest upgrade ever!

Hands-free ripping of your CD collection to MP3s, FREE – a $99 upgrade! Automatically rips 25 discs at a time into mp3, wav, wma, flac, or aiff formats. Retrieves album, artist, and song title info from the web (PC only).

Disc Makers Pico automated DVD/CD duplicator and MP3 ripper just $699

Don't let its eye-popping price fool you. The Pico delivers easy automated 16x DVD and 48x CD duplication and MP3 ripping (PC only) in the smallest footprint imaginable. Measuring a mere 7.1" x 15.75" and weighing only 6.6 lbs, the Pico features a 25-disc capacity, a built-in 3" disc and CardDisc adapter, and audio and data editing software.

One USB 2.0 connection to your PC or Mac is all you need to start duplicating DVDs or CDs. Includes one-year parts and labor warranty, and free tech support.

CD AND DVD MANUFACTURING MADE EASY

FREE CATALOG Call 1-866-490-7928 or visit www.discmakers.com/indie2 to get your FREE catalog.

TIPS FOR USING THE INDIE BIBLE

How the listings are sorted

a) **TYPE OF SERVICE** (Publication, Radio Station, CD Vendor etc.)

   b) **Genre of Music**

      c) **Geographic Location**

The listings are set up this way so that you can quickly find a *specific* service in a *specific* area for a *specific* style of music. *ie:* Finding a **Hip Hop** magazine in **England** that will **REVIEW** your music.

How the various styles of resources are sorted

1. If a publication welcomes submissions from MANY genres, that publication will be listed in the **Mainstream** section. Publications in the Mainstream section welcome a *wide variety* of genres, but usually nothing too extreme. Common genres in this section are Pop, Rock, Indie Rock etc.

2. There is an unavoidable amount of *Genre Overflow* from section to section. For instance, if you are in a Punk band, you will not only find sites that will review your music in the **Punk** Section, but you will also find several sites that welcome your style of music in the **Metal** and **Goth** Sections.

Most publications review more than one style of music. The sites listed in the Indie Bible are placed in their respective sections based on the musical style that publication lists as their preference. For instance, if a publication states that they welcome Folk, Blues and Jazz music, that publication would be listed in the **Folk Music** section, because "Folk" was the first genre mentioned.

3. Quiz: Where would you find the listing of a magazine that reviews the music of **Christian Women New Age** artists that live in the **Chicago** area? Would you find it in the

   a. Christian Music section?
   b. New Age Music section?
   c. Women in Music section?
   d. The Local Music section under "Chicago"?

The answer is "d", the **Local Music** section. I'm using this example to point out that the LOCAL MUSIC SECTION OVERRIDES all other characteristics of any given resource. If it is a resource that provides a service for a *specific* area (country, city, town, state, province) then that resource is listed in the Local Music section (ie: a resource for Country Music bands based in Montana). The Indie Bible is arranged this way so that you can quickly look at the listings in your area to find out what kind of help is available for you locally. Please make sure to check out the Local Music section for your area (or those places that you will be passing through during your tour). You will be surprised at how many resources there are in your community that are willing to help you out.

4. The majority of the stations listed in the **Mainstream Radio** section are College, University and Community stations that have a weekly show catering to EVERY style of music, both mild and extreme (Country, Pop, Hip Hop, Death Metal, Goth, Classical etc.), so make sure that you CHECK THEM ALL!

About the articles

Before you start contacting the various resources listed in the Indie Bible, I STRONGLY RECOMMEND that you read the articles in **SECTION 7** to better understand how to submit your music for review, radio airplay etc. These articles are written by industry professionals who have a *wealth* of experience. They know what works, what doesn't work – and why. Reading the articles in SECTION 7 will save you an ENORMOUS amount of time and money and will help your career to move in a positive direction. In other words, you won't have to make the same mistakes that I and many others have made while trying to survive in the music business. Please take the time to read these articles. You will be glad that you did!

PLEASE READ THIS!!

I have received several complaints from music reviewers and radio hosts about high number of e-mails and CDs they are receiving **that have nothing to do with the style of music that their publication or show promotes**. PLEASE DO NOT SEND OUT MASS MAILINGS to the sites listed in this book telling them about your new release, latest invention, upcoming shows etc.

Instead of sending your e-mails and CDs out to everyone on the planet, take the time to read through The Indie Bible to find out who is actually looking for your specific style of music. RULE #1: Don't try and convert anyone! Respect that fact that different people have different tastes in music.

Put yourself in the position of a Magazine Editor. Let's say for example you are the Editor of a magazine that covers **Folk Music**. How irritating would it be continually getting blasted with e-mails from artists in **Metal** and **Punk** bands asking you to review their CD? How would you feel each day when you grab the truckload of CDs from your PO Box and find that about 1 in 30 are actually Folk CDs? You're going to feel irritated and frustrated.

Note that there are **50** articles in this edition. You will not find in ANY of the **50** articles a Radio Host or Magazine Editor saying that a *good* way for an artist to make initial contact is by sending out *mass e-mailings*. They all say the same thing, which is "take the time to do some research, and THEN contact the various services personally".

Remember, these are human beings you're dealing with. The recipient of your personalized e-mail or promo package will respect the time you have put in to find out about them and most often will get back to you quickly. On the other hand, a mass mailing is an insult to him/her and your e-mail will be deleted immediately and your CD chucked into the garbage.

The extra time you put in to do a bit of research and to personalize your initial contact will pay off for you in a BIG way in the end!

Final Notes

Please contact me with information on any broken links, outdated sites or mistakes of any kind. They will be addressed right away. Also, feel free to send your comments and suggestions to me. ALL suggestions will be taken into consideration. Thanks to your input, The Indie Bible continues to grow with each new edition.

I hope by utilizing the many contacts found in this book that you make some solid progress with your career. If you feel that you made a worthwhile investment by purchasing The Indie Bible, please tell your friends about it.

Also, remember to sign up for my monthly newsletter. Each month I send out 40 or so new listings of services that can help you to gain more exposure. Simply send an e-mail to **newsletter@indiebible.com** to sign up. Just put "newsletter" in the subject heading.

I wish you the very best with your music!

David Wimble
Editor, The Indie Bible
www.indiebible.com
www.myspace.com/indiebible
Phone: 800-306-8167
david@indiebible.com

SECTION ONE: REVIEWERS OF INDEPENDENT MUSIC

"What impresses me most about an artist is the quality of their music. A very close second is their professionalism and follow through." – **Erik Deckers, Music Reviewer for Indie-Music.com**

Mainstream Publications

Just to clarify, when I say mainstream, I'm not talking about Perry Como music. Mainstream is any sort of music that isn't too far "out there". That's not to say that publications in this section won't listen to all types of music, but they are more likely to enjoy Rock, Pop, Indie Rock etc. They are less likely to go for the Death Metal, Industrial, Hardcore etc….although some will accept those styles.

North America

United States

1340mag.com
PO Box 1347, Fairmont, WV 26555-1347
mark@1340mag.com
www.1340mag.com
We listen to and consider everything received.

20th Century Guitar
135 Oser Ave. Hauppauge, NY 11788
PH: 800-291-9687 FX: 631-434-9057
tcguitar@tcguitar.com
www.tcguitar.com
CD reviews and features.

30music.com
PO Box 3908, Minneapolis, MN 55403-9998
staff@30music.com
www.30music.com
We do our best to review everything received.

75 or Less
23 Laurel Ln. Warren, RI 02885
75orLess@slatch.com
www.75orless.com
Will review anything in less than 75 words.

ADDreviews
PO Box 650113, Sterling, VA 20165-0113
crew@addreviews.com
www.addreviews.com
All music reviews are 20 words or less. It's about brevity. Terseness. Conciseness. You get the idea.

Agouti Music
PO Box 3092, San Leandro, CA 94578
Tom Eppenberger tom@agouti.com
www.agouti.com
Check our site to see if your music fits. It pains us when artists spend good money sending us stuff we'll never review.

alt.culture.guide
PO Box 204, Nolensville, TN 37135
Tommy Hash thash@att.net
www.mondogordo.com
Roots Rock, Punk, Heavy Metal, Prog Rock and Blues.

Altar Magazine
955 Metropolitan Ave. #4R, Brooklyn, NY 11211
info@altarmagazine.com
www.altarmagazine.com
We want to create a space where critical thought and understanding happen simultaneously.

Alternative Addiction
PO Box 531205, Livonia, MI 48153-1541
chad@alternativeaddiction.com
www.alternativeaddiction.com
Helps unsigned bands by offering both CD reviews and the possibility to have your song listed in our Top 10.

Alternative Press
1305 W. 80th St. #2F, Cleveland, OH 44102-1996
PH: 216-631-1510 FX: 216-631-1016
Jonah Bayer editorial@altpress.com
www.altpress.com
News, reviews, new releases etc.

American Songwriter
1303 16th Ave. S. 2nd Fl. Nashville, TN 37212
PH: 615-321-6096 FX: 615-321-6097
info@americansongwriter.com
www.americansongwriter.com
Interviews, writing tips, industry news, reviews, lyric contests and more.

Amplifier
5 Calista Ter. Westford, MA 01886
PH: 978-846-1177
Joe Joyce JoeJ@ AmplifierMagazine.com
www.amplifiermagazine. com
Focuses on Pop, Melodic Rock and Roots Rock.

Angst Magazine
1142 Hayes, Irvine, CA 92620
angstmagazine@ yahoo.com
www.angstmagazine.com
Our contributors are excellent music lovers and have a creative insight into the music scene.

Anthem Magazine
110 W. Ocean Blvd. 10th Fl. Long Beach, CA 90802-4605
info@anthem-magazine.com
www.anthemmagazine.com
Editorial coverage of emerging faces with some of the more well-known icons in film, music and art.

Arthur Magazine
c/o Bull Tongue,
PO Box 627, Northampton, MA 01061
www.arthurmag.com
Our Bull Tongue columnists review the latest emanations from the deep underground.

Aural Minority
PO Box 6681, Oceanside, CA 92052
PH: 714-914-6498
Jeremiah Griffey jeremiahgriffey@gmail.com
www.auralminority.com
We are a weekly online magazine looking to promote innovative and intriguing new artists.

Auralgasms.com
Scott Zumberg szumberg@auralgasms.com
www.auralgasms.com
Reviews, sound samples, bios, discographies, tour dates and links.

The A.V. Club
www.avclub.com/content
Interviews, essays and reviews of movies, music and books.

Babysue
PO Box 3360, Cleveland, TN 37320-3360
lmnop@babysue.com
www.babysue.com
Accepts recordings from major and Indie labels.

BandAttack
125 E. Merritt Isl. Cswy. #209PMB128, Merritt Island, FL 32952
PH: 315-727-9918
rock@bandattack.com
www.bandattack.com
Please visit our contact page if your band or label is interested in submitting.

BandFreaks
138 E. 14th St., Tucson, AZ 85701
PH: 520-867-6686 FX: 216-929-1049
www.bandfreaks.com
Would you like a review of your MP3? Check out our site for submission details.

Bassics
21143 Hawthorne Blvd.
#508, Torrance, CA 90503
PH: 888-223-3340
bassicsrg@aol.com
www.bassics.com
*Each issue includes tracks
from featured artists. All
styles of music are covered.*

BB Gun Magazine
PO Box 5074, Hoboken,
NJ 07030
bbgunmagazine@aol.com
www.bbgun.org
*Alternative literary digest
featuring interviews with
independent musicians.*

BettaWreckonize
the_dogg@
bettawreckonize.com
www.bettawreckonize.com
*Contact us to send about
sending in your CD for
review.*

Better Propaganda
539 Bryant St. #402,
San Francisco, CA 94107
contact@
betterpropaganda.com
www.betterpropaganda.com
*Showcasing truly unique
music.*

Big TakeoverMagazine
249 Eldridge St. #14,
New York, NY 10002-1345
PH: 212-533-6057
Jack Rabid sexton@slf.com
www.bigtakeover.com
*100 pages of Indie music
reviews.*

Billboard
770 Broadway, New York,
NY 10003
PH: 646-654-5549
Jonathan Cohen
jacohen@billboard.com
www.billboard.com
*International news weekly of
music.*

blue coupe
Linda Richards
editor@bluecoupe.com
www.bluecoupe.com
*Open to interviewing you
about your music.*

Bornbackwards.com
2355 NW. 95th Ter.
Coral Springs, FL 33065
submissions@
bornbackwards.com
www.bornbackwards.com
*We'll review just about
anything.*

Buddyhead
PO Box 1268, Hollywood,
CA 90078
FX: 801-684-1387
Travis Keller
travis@buddyhead.com
www.buddyhead.com
*Can't even be defined at this
point in the game.*

buhdge
Alan Haber alan@buhdge.com
www.buhdge.com
*Raging fiercely through the tangled media net to get
to the bottom of that which we hold dear: our
favorite new and old music.*

Buzzine.com
PO Box 18857, Encino, CA 91416-8857
PH: 818-995-6161 FX: 818-995-6136
www.buzzine.com
Interviews, concert reviews and up-to-date news.

CD Babel
Jeff Einowski cdbabel@cdbabel.com
www.cdbabel.com
*We will review anyone's CD so long as it is on CD
Baby. That is our only criteria.*

CD Reviews by You
webmaster@cdreviewsbyyou.com
cdreviewsbyyou.com
*Review any album you like! We're especially looking
to showcase upcoming artists.*

cdreviews.com
1929 Acari Ave. Sacramento, CA 95835
PH: 818-206-4245
www.cdreviews.com
*Are you in a band? Do you have a CD out? If so let
us know.*

The Cheers
thecheers@thecheers.org
www.thecheers.org
Entertainment, opinion, politics, extreme sports.

The ChickenFish Speaks
PO Box 292168, Dayton, OH 45429-0168
PH: 937-609-9913
Grog Grog@theChickenFishSpeaks.com
www.theChickenFishSpeaks.com
*All of our reviewers have eclectic tastes in music...
so send anything and everything!!!*

CinemaBlend
31 Mariners Ln. Stamford, CT 06902
PH: 512-417-0254
Alison Eshelman alisoneshelman@hotmail.com
www.cinemablend.com
*I cover music news and reviews for CinemaBlend's
music section.*

Cityzen Entertainment
Backoffice Box #230, 345 E. 18th St., New York,
NY 10003
PH: 212-260-0086 FX: 212-780-0579
Craig Cook craig@cityzen.tv
www.cityzen.tv
*We're always looking for new and exciting things to
cover.*

CMJ New Music Report
151 W. 25th St. 12th Fl. New York, NY 10001
PH: 917-606-1908 FX: 917-606-1914
www.cmj.com
All styles of music are welcome!

CoffeeHouseTour.com
3615-B St Johns Ct. Wilmington, NC 28403
Attn: CHT Review
PH: 910-793-1507
Annette Warner awarner@coffeehousetour.com
www.coffeehousetour.com
*If you are an act that performs in coffee shops,
forward your CD to the above address.*

"...I Need an Inexpensive, Fast and Affordable Way to Produce My Music or Film..."

Long Run CD/DVD Manufacturing
Short Run On-Demand CD/DVD Duplication
Retail Ready Packages in Runs as Low as 25 pcs.
DVD Authoring and Encoding
Printing, Packaging and Fulfillment
Branded Media (Silkscreened Discs)
Graphic Design
Music Mastering
Barcodes
eCommerce Solutions

Ask about our 'Center Stage' Promotional Package with every order including free hosting on iMuzic.com and AirPlay Direct.

CDDVD Now! is an award winning manufacturing and design company with the flexibility to deliver large and small jobs quickly while maintaining the highest quality standards.

Toll Free: 1.866.945.6800
www.CDDVDNow.com
info@cddvdnow.com

---

cokemachineglow
Scott Reid
promo@cokemachineglow.com
www.cokemachineglow.com
Contact us to get our mailing address. Read our site first, know what we review and, more importantly, how we review.

The Consensus
Andy Chapman
admin@c0nsensus.com
www.c0nsensus.com
Brutally honest music reviews for all genres. Each song gets listened to by five different reviewers.

concertlivewire.com
PO Box 5, Lake Geneva, WI 53147
PH: 262-949-8852
Tony Bonyata
tonyb@concertlivewire.com
www.concertlivewire.com
Brutally honest CD reviews from new artists.

Copacetic Zine
PO Box 17321, Seattle, WA 98127
www.copacetic-zine.com
Please do us both a favor and look around the site before sending us your CD. Make sure your music fits.

Copper Press
PO Box 1601, Acme, MI 49610
steve@copperpress.com
www.copperpress.com
News, reviews, tours etc.

Crazy Talk!
bluegrassroots@hotmail.com
www.crazytalk.org
Features news, reviews, interviews, MP3s etc.

Creem Magazine
Brian BrianJBowe@
CreemMagazine.com
creemmedia.com
News, reviews, interviews and more.

Crud Magazine
crudenquiries@crudmusic.com
www.2-4-7-music.com
All solicited material mailed us will be reviewed and scheduled for inclusion.

Crush Music Magazine
Jason Schleweis
jason.schleweis@
crushmusicmag.com
www.crushmusicmag.com
News, reviews, interviews. To be considered for "Supporting the Scene" visit our website for submission details.

CTG Music Community
www.ctgmusic.com
Write reviews to get your songs listed.

Cut And Paste Magazine
cutandpasterequest@hotmail.com
www.myspace.com/cutandpastemagazine
We believe every artist deserves the opportunity to be exposed.

Daily Vault
PH: 916-335-6548
Jason Warburg dvmailbag@aol.com
www.dailyvault.com
The longest running independent music review site on the web. Reviews music of all genres.

Deep Water Acres
108 Ramblewood Rd. Pennsylvania Furnace, PA 16865
kmm104@psu.edu
www.dwacres.com
News, reviews, interviews and rants.

Demo Universe
c/o Jim Santo, PO Box 4218, Sunnyside, NY 11104
www.demouniverse.com
Send your recording and whatever else.

DemoDaze
2134 Curtis St. Bldg. 1, Denver, CO 80205
yo@demodaze.com
www.demodaze.com
News, reviews, interviews.

demorama
300 Broadway #608, St. Paul, MN 55101
Deneen Gannon quirkell@visi.com
www.demorama.com
We review all genres. We also do online reviews.

Dig This Real
244 5th Ave. #29037, New York, NY 10001-7604
info@digthisreal.com
www.digthisreal.com
Accepts unsolicited material for review.

DiscoveringArtists.com
52 Rogers Ave. 2nd Fl. Manasquan, NJ 08736
dan@discoveringartists.com
www.discoveringartists.com
Giving emerging artists a place to get heard.

Drawer B
PO Box 11726, Columbia, SC 29211-1726
www.drawerb.com
Unsolicited submissions are accepted.

E.O.M Entertainment
1221 E.20th St. #302, Oakland, CA 94606
Maurice Edwards info@eomentertainment.com
eomentertainment.com
Send a copy of your CD, bio and contact info to the above address.

Equal Music
PO Box 456, Marlboro, NJ 07746
PH: 732-580-2537
Danielle Moskowitz danielle@equalmusic.com
www.equalmusic.com
Bands we cover exude elements of originality and passion and possess something that can't be explained—something that sets them apart.

Erasing Clouds
415 S. 46th St. Apt. A, Philadelphia, PA 19143
Dave Heaton erasingclouds@gmail.com
www.erasingclouds.com
Where regular people write about the music.

The road to success can have many twists and turns...

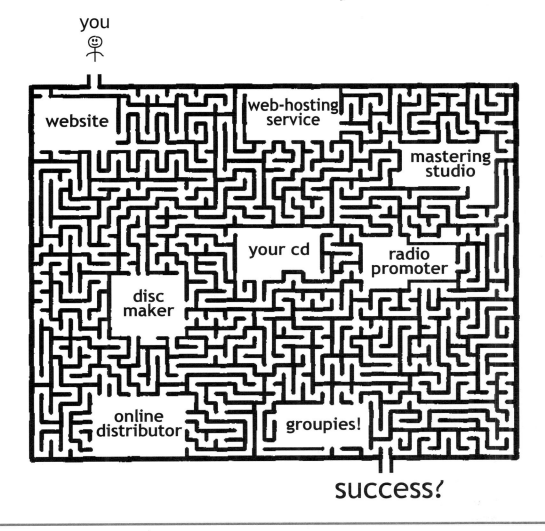

...but it doesn't have to.

PICK GUY

personalized guitar picks and straps

317.698.5141
P.O. Box 70
Westfield, IN 46074

www.PickGuy.com

ExMogul Music
Susan White info@exmogul.com
www.exmogul.com
Do you want us to review your CD? We'll listen and review it for your press kit.

Fader
71 W. 23rd St. #903, New York, NY 10010
PH: 212-741-7100 FX: 212-741-4747
info@thefader.com
www.thefader.com
Digging into the factual experiences of music.

fakejazz
PO Box 9325, New Haven, CT 06533-0325
info@fakejazz.com
www.fakejazz.com
Submit material for review in our publication.

Fifteen Minutes To Live
Michael 15minutestolive@gmail.com
www.15minutestolive.com
Discusses and reviews many forms of popular culture. I am always on the look out for new music.

Figgle
PO Box 1170, Maplewood, NJ 07040-2706
Bruce Hartley info@figgle.com
www.figgle.com
Album reviews and interviews with artists.

Filter Magazine
5908 Barton Ave. Los Angeles, CA 90038
PH: 323-464-4775
info@filtermmm.com
www.filter-mag.com
Exposure for credible artists.

Fingertips
letterbox@
fingertipsmusic.com
www.fingertipsmusic.com
MP3 review site. For a review, you must be "signed", even if it's to a small label.

Firesideometer
823 N. Lesley Ave.
Indianapolis, IN 46219
comments@
firesideometer.com
www.firesideometer.com
Covering Indie bands that make great music.

foxy digitalis
PO Box 700810, Tulsa, OK 74170
foxyd@
digitalisindustries.com
www.digitalisindustries.com/foxyd
Everything received will be reviewed.

Front Row Fanz Magazine
webmaster@
frontrowfanz.com
www.frontrowfanz.com
Interview magazine that will interview Indie artists.

fufkin.com
PO Box 7420,
Fort Lauderdale,
FL 33338-7420
david_fufkin@fufkin.com
www.fufkin.com
Send your CDs to the above address. No need to ask first!

Full Value Review
26489 Ynez Rd. C113, Temecula, CA 92591
PH: 909-318-0686
Bill Gould info@fullvaluereview.com
www.fullvaluereview.com
Our focus is on reviewing food, music, hotels etc. Please send us your CD. We are more than happy to review all genres of music.

GhettoBlaster
392 Central Park W. #5T, New York, NY 10025
info@ghettoblastermagazine.com
www.ghettoblastermagazine.com
Pop culture news, interviews, reviews and MP3s.

Glide Magazine
Reviews Dept. PO Box 716, Bellmore, NY 11710
reviews@glidemagazine.com
www.glidemagazine.com
Submit materials for possible review or feature consideration to the above address.

Groovevolt.com
Chauncy Jackson press@groovevolt.com
www.groovevolt.com
Features Indie and upcoming artists.

Groupeez Magazine
PO Box 220017, Chicago, IL 60622
Mike Matray editor@groupeez.com
www.groupeez.com
Reviews primarily in the area of Rock. Jazz and Hip Hop are also encouraged.

Harp Magazine
8737 Colesville Rd. 9th Fl. Silver Spring, MD 20910-3921
PH: 301-588-4114 FX: 301-588-5531
www.harpmagazine.com
In-depth features and reviews.

Hear/Say
11012 Aurora Hudson Rd. Streetsboro, OH 44241
PH: 330-528-0410 FX: 330-528-0423
jniesel@freetimes.com
www.hearsay.cc
A free music publication for students.

Here and There
19237 Silver Springs Dr. #101, Northville, MI 48167
Michael Sullivan submissions@thehereandthere.net
www.thehereandthere.net
We review everything that comes our way.

High Bias Journal
2200 Willow Creek Dr. #312, Austin, TX 78741
PH: 512-440-1513
Michael editor@highbias.com
community.livejournal.com/highbias
Listening with extreme prejudice.

HITCH Magazine
PO Box 23621, Oklahoma City, OK 73123-2621
R. Lott rod@hitchmagazine.com
www.hitchmagazine.com
The journal of pop culture absurdity. We try to review every CD we receive.

HitSession.com
6453 Pretti Rd. Corunna, MI 48817
dougc@hitsession.com
www.hitsession.com
Small donation to get your music reviewed.

Hot Indie News
269 12th St. #1, Brooklyn, NY 11215-3919
PH: 917-865-2591 FX: 917-591-4846
James Lane HotIndieNews@yahoo.com
www.HotIndieNews.com
Helping artists increase their worldwide exposure. Send CDs and press kits to the above address.

HYBRID Magazine
PO Box 9250, Denver, CO 80209
editor@hybridmagazine.com
www.hybridmagazine.com
We listen to every CD we receive.

ICON Magazine
PH/FX: 425-799-0546
help@icon-magazine.com
www.icon-magazine.com
Features the best independent artists. Contact via phone, fax, or e-mail for press consideration.

Iconoclast Entertainment Group
PO Box 2366, Orange, CA 92859
Attn: CD Reviews
Keavin Wiggins keavin@rocknworld.com
www.ieginc.com
Profiles exciting Indie bands. CD's for reviews and press packs can be sent to the above address.

Idolize Magazine
Yvonne interviews@IdolizeMag.com
idolizemag.com
E-mail me if you would like to book an interview.

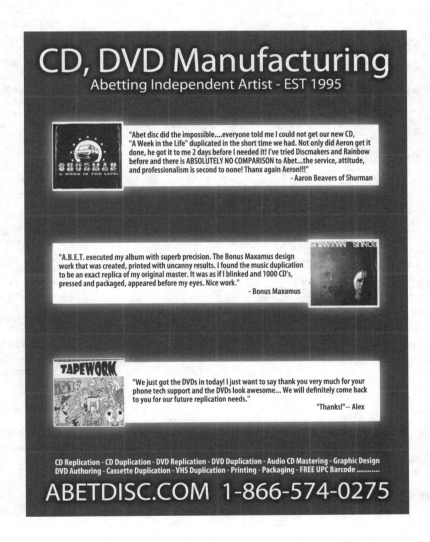

Thank You For Allowing Abet Disc Inc. To Serve You!
- Aeron K. Nersoya

Impact Press
PO Box 361,
10151 University Blvd.
Orlando, FL 32817
PH: 407-263-5504
Craig
editor@impactpress.com
www.impactpress.com
Send your new releases for review.

impose magazine
PO Box 472, Village Stn.
New York, NY 10014
Derek Evers imposeeditor
@hotmail.com
www. imposemagazine.com
Our goal is to articulately illustrate the common sentiment that fans of all genres posses a love of music.

In Music We Trust
1530 SE. Bevington Ave.
Portland, OR 97267-3355
PH: 503-557-9661
FX: 503-650-8365
Alex Steininger
alex@inmusicwetrust.com
www.inmusicwetrust.com
Exposes talented artists to a larger audience.

Independent Songwriter
PO Box 112,
Camden, NY 13316
Jan Best jan@
independentsongwriter.com
www.
independentsongwriter.com
CD reviews, internet radio and much more.

Indie Artist Station
PO Box 212293,
Chula Vista, CA 91921
info@indieartiststation.com
www.indieartiststation.com
Where musicians and industry professionals talk about the business of making music.

Indie-Music.com
PO Box 3339, Cary,
NC 27519-3339
Jennifer Layton
writers@indie-music.com
www.indie-music.com/
reviewpolicy. php
You can request a certain writer, or you can simply submit your package and it will be distributed among our current pool of reviewers.

Indie Pages
757 N. 65th St., Seattle,
WA 98103
chris@indiepages.com
www.indiepages.com
Info about your favorite Indie bands and labels.

The Indie Review
theindiereview.com
Submissions MUST be made through Sonic Bids. Check our website for details.

indieworkshop
1978 NW. 92nd Ct. #1, Clive, IA 50325
Jake info@indieworkshop.com
www.indieworkshop.com
E-mail before submitting items for review.

Ink 19
1161 Sanddune Ln. #306, Melbourne, FL 32935
Julio Diaz julio@ink19.com
www.ink19.com
Accepts CDs and artist bio's for review.

Inquisitor Zine
PO Box 132, New York, NY 10024
www.inquisitor.com
A no-hype rag for the media-saturated masses.

inReview.net
www.inreview.net
We write CD reviews, compose feature articles and conduct interviews with our favorite artists.

Inside Connection
1919 Middle Country Rd. #205, Centereach,
NY 11720
PH: 631-981-8231 FX: 631-981-8424
editor@insidecx.com
www.insidecx.com
New releases from independent bands.

Interlude Magazine
PO Box 261693, San Diego, CA 92196-1693
PH: 601-214-0589
Arlan Hamilton interludemagazine@yahoo.com
www.interlude-magazine.com
Interviews, exclusive performances and more!

InterMixx Magazine
304 Main Ave. PMB 287, Norwalk, CT 06851
PH: 203-483-1798
Noel Ramos MixxMag@InterMixx.com
www.intermixx.com
We help Indies market themselves to consumers!

.ISM quarterly
PO Box 1662, Los Alamitos, CA 90720
PH: 562-458-8899
mail@ismquarterly.com
www.ismquarterly.com
Content is driven by the submissions of our readership, including a free CD in every issue.

Issues Magazine
editors@issues-mag.com
www.issues-mag.com
Reviews any music good enough for radio! Please contact us before sending your CD.

Junk Media
Ben Sterling ben@junkmedia.org
www.junkmedia.org
We strive to highlight music and musicians who have been overlooked by the mainstream music press.

Keyboard Magazine
2800 Campus Dr. San Mateo, CA 94403
PH: 650-513-4300 FX: 650-513-4642
Carl Lumma clumma@cmpinformation.com
www.keyboardmag.com
We are always interested in reviewing music by independent artists and producers.

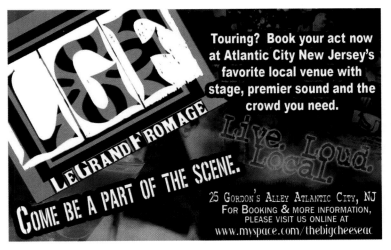

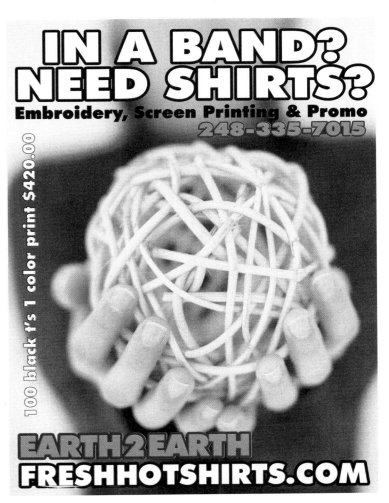

Kitty Magik
PO Box 96, Whitehouse Station, NJ 08889-0096
Marisa Handren marisa@kittymagik.com
www.kittymagik.com
Arts magazine dedicated to covering musicians and artists.

Kludge Magazine
8640 Gulana Ave. #J1014, Playa Del Rey,
CA 90293
PH: 310-710-8831
Arturo Perez arturo@kludgemagazine.com
www.kludgemagazine.com
Features local and up and coming bands.

Kotori Magazine
www.kotorimag.com
Exposing subversive culture and showcasing underground sensations.

Kweevak Music Magazine
38 Oliver Pl. Ringwood, NJ 07456
PH: 973-556-5400
Rich Lynch info@kweevak.com
www.kweevak.com
We now guarantee CD reviews and a full 2-month main page artist spotlight feature for all bands that join our community!

Lab Productions
2350 E. Contour, Baton Rouge, LA 70809
PH: 985-974-0792
albums@labproductions.com
www.labproductions.com
Send your demo to get reviewed/featured.

LooseyLucy's Headquarters
PO Box 13383, Tempe, AZ 85284
PaintedGirlRecords@gmail.com
www.looseylucy.com
We do CD reviews. Each month one person of great achievement is highlighted in the "Under-Hyped" column.

Luminous Flux Records
8 Forest Ave. Glen Cove, NY 11542
webmonkey@fluxnet.com
www.fluxnet.com/submiss.html
Reviews new music from new bands.

Magnet
1218 Chestnut St. #508, Philadelphia, PA 19107
PH: 215-413-8570 FX: 215-413-8569
Matthew Fritch matt@magnetmagazine.com
www.magnetmagazine.com
Gives attention to Indie musicians.

Mean Street Magazine
937 N. Cole Ave. #4, Los Angeles, CA 90038
PH: 323-465-9335 FX: 323-465-9459
hello@meanstreet.com
www.meanstreet.com
Covers the independent music scene.

Metacritic
1223 Wilshire Blvd. #1240, Santa Monica,
CA 90403-5400
www.metacritic.com/music
Reviews your music by assigning it a score.

Modern Drummer
12 Old Bridge Rd. Cedar Grove, NJ 07009-1288
PH: 973-239-4140 FX: 973-239-7139
mdinfo@moderndrummer.com
www.moderndrummer.com
Magazine focusing specifically on drummers.

Modern Fix
3368 Governor Dr. #318, San Diego, CA 92122
PH: 858-650-6885
extra@modernfix.com
www.modernfix.com
Reviews and covers all genres. 20,000 issues a month!

ModaMag.com
editor@modamag.com
www.modamag.com
Will interview up and coming bands.

Mundanesounds.com
PO Box 720, Carthage,
TX 75633
mundane_sounds@yahoo.com
www.mundanesounds.com
Listens to anything that you send in.

The Music Appraisal
matt@themusicappraisal.net
www.themusicappraisal.net
Want your band's CD reviewed? Want to have an interview? We'd love to hear from you!

Music Box
PO Box 3911, Oak Park, IL 60303-3911
editor@musicbox-online.com
www.musicbox-online.com
Concert and album reviews.

Music Connection
16130 Ventura Blvd. #540, Encino, CA 91436
PH: 818-995-0101 FX: 818-995-9235
contactmc@musicconnection.com
www.musicconnection.com
Interviews, reviews, critiques and more!

Music Head
43 Columbine Cir. #102
Newtown, PA 18940
Todd Wojtowicz
musichead@musichead.org
www.musichead.org
Information about the artists making up the realm of today's music.

The Music Issue
Daphne
pinkgerl@yahoo.com
themusicissue.blogspot.com
Freelance music writer for several publications.

Music Korner
PO Box 58095, Charleston,
WV 25358
Geoff musccorn@aol.com
members.aol.com/musccorn
Covers virtually all styles of music.

Music Dish Reviews
editor@musicdish.com
www.musicdish.com
Check our site to find out which reviewer best suits your style of music.

Music Morsels
PO Box 2760, Acworth, GA 30102
PH: 678-445-0006 FX: 678-494-9269
Sandy Serge sergeent@aol.com
www.serge.org
E-zine with independent CD reviews, unsigned band spotlights and an industry profile.

Music Underwater
Kyle Dilla kyle_anderton@cox.net
www.musicunderwater.com
If you want us to review your record, e-mail us.

Musical Taste
jonny@delicado.org
www.musicaltaste.com
A user-driven community with a focus on individual track recommendations.

MuzikReviews.com
PO Box 476, Adams, MA 01220
Keith "MuzikMan" Hannaleck
khannaleck@yahoo.com
www.muzikreviews.com
$50 fee. Keep in mind that your review will be on the MANY sites I post content on.

Nada Mucho
6200 6th Ave. NW. #8, Seattle, WA 98107
Matt editor@nadamucho.com
www.nadamucho.com
Entertaining and educating the MTV generation.

Naughty Secretary Club
PO Box 161702, Austin, TX 78716
info@naughtysecretaryclub.com
www.naughtysecretaryclub.com
Music reviews, interviews, recipes and more!

neumu
Michael Goldberg michael@neumu.net
www.neumu.net
A new alternative pop culture site.

New Artist Radio CD Reviews
17121 Berlin Ln. Huntington Beach, CA 92649
Madmonk mocktudor@socal.rr.com
www.newartistradio.net
Reviews are available to New Artist Radio members only!

New Directions Cello Association
501 Linn St., Ithaca, NY 14850
PH: 607- 277-1686
info@newdirectionscello.com
www.newdirectionscello.com
A network for Alternative or Non Classical cello.

NewBeats
David newbeats1@aol.com
www.newbeats.com
A music magazine that covers all types of music ...the more eclectic the better.

The Night Owl
2804 Woodbridge Estates Dr. St. Louis, MO 63129
PH: 314-846-7551 FX: 314-846-7551
editor@thenightowl.com
www.thenightowl.com
Music reviews covering from Rock to Jazz.

Night Times
PO Box 1747, Maryland Hts, MO 63043
PH: 314-542-9995
Julia Gordon-Bramer wordgirl@nighttimes.com
www.nighttimes.com
Offering CD reviews, show previews and artist interviews. We support local, regional, national and international musicians.

No-Fi Magazine
Attn: Reviews,
1316 El Paso Dr.
Los Angeles, CA 90065
Chris Beyond
nofimag@hotmail.com
www.nofimagazine.com
Generally, we like to receive 2 copies of everything (1 for review and one for possible airplay on No-Fi "Radio"). DO NOT send us MP3s via e-mail!

Norman Famous Rants and Reviews
PO Box 6218, Albany, CA 94706
Norman Famous norman@ normanfamous.com
www.normanfamous.com
I offer online reviews of independent CD releases along with my customary barbed witticisms and wry social comment.

Northeast In-Tune
PO Box 355, Epping, NH 03042-0355
PH: 603-205-5537
Bob Donovan Editor@ northeastintune.com
www.northeastintune.com
We now support and cover Indie music worldwide!

NowOnTour.com
6300 N. Sagewood Dr. #H-533, Park City, UT 84098
Tyler Champley reviews@nowontour.com
www.NowOnTour.com
Tour and show listings, record reviews of Indie bands and more.

Nude as the News
216 Columbia #2A, Brooklyn, NY 11231
Ben French benfrench@aol.com
www.nudeasthenews.com
Focusing on the expansive current state of Rock.

Nuevo Revolution
Staff@NuevoRevolution.com
www.NuevoRevolution.com
Various news, interviews, reviews and downloadable music tracks.

NYLON Magazine
394 W. Broadway 2nd Fl. New York, NY 10012
letters@nylonmag.com
www.nylonmag.com
Consistently features emerging artists and unique talent before they hit the mainstream.

ONE WAY Magazine
311 N. Robertson Blvd. #208, Beverly Hills, CA 90211
PH: 310-275-5141 FX: 310-765-4765
info@onewaymagazine.com
www.onewaymagazine.com
Showcases new music by developing artists.

Sign up for The Indie Contact Newsletter
www.indiebible.com

Online Music Blog
copacetix@gmail.com
www.onlinemusicblog.com
Posts Alternative and independent online music news, reviews and interviews daily.

OnlineRock
2033 Ralston Ave. #50 Belmont, CA 94002
PH: 650-649-2304
Steve Beck info@onlinerock.com
www.onlinerock.com
We offer CD reviews which are perfect for your press kit and website. All types of music accepted.

OpeningBands
c/o Cassie Conner, PO Box 307, Urbana, IL 61802
reviews@openingbands.com
www.openingbands.com/reviews/guidelines.race
Mail 2 copies of your CD (so we can have two people review it). Our address changes often, so please check our site before sending your CD.

Outer Shell
outershel@aol.com
members.aol.com/outershel
Reviews artists in each issue.

OUtlET Magazine
181 Market St., Lowell, MA 01852
PH: 978-328-4466
Mark Henderson outlet@outletzine.org
www.outletzine.org
An independent performance magazine. We accept submissions for review.

Palebear
Attn: Reviews, PO Box 1191, Alhambra, CA 91802
www.palebear.com
We have a love for non-mainstream music. You can either mail your CD or use our e-mail submission form to send us an MP3.

Pathetic Caverns
411A Highland Ave. #404, Somerville, MA 02144
carp@pathetic-caverns.com
www.pathetic-caverns.com
Opinionated and eclectic reviews of music. Please read over our submission guidelines.

Pause & Play
gerry@pauseandplay.com
www.pauseandplay.com
Weekly Pop/Rock artist interview column.

Perfect Sound Forever
perfectsoundweb@furious.com
www.perfectsoundforever.com
Home of musical underdogs of all styles. We respond to every inquiry we get.

Performing Songwriter
2805 Azalea Pl. Nashville, TN 37204
PH: 615-385-7796 FX: 615-385-5637
Abby White abby@performingsongwriter.com
www.performingsongwriter.com
Interviews, reviews, release spotlights and more. Please be patient and continue to send us your new releases.

Pitchfork Media
3147 W. Logan Blvd. #5E, Chicago, IL 60647
mail@pitchforkmedia.com
www.pitchforkmedia.com
Covers all styles and genres of music.

PlatterPicks.com
www.PlatterPicks.com
Reviews covering everything from A Capella to Punk and just about everything in between.

The easiest way to record...

SUPERSCOPE®

- Record directly to CD
- Sing along with CDs
- Change the key of any song
- Built in microphone
- Reduce lead vocals
- Rugged, portable, powerful
- Duplicate CDs on the spot

©2006 MIDS spr60743

TOLL FREE (866)371-4773

PSD300 **$699**

www.superscope.us

You can have it all...

Digital Downloads, Flash Music Players, Blogs, Podcasts, Calendars, Photo Galleries... Forums, Stores, Podcasts, Calendars, Photo Galleries...

WEBSITES THAT KICK ASS

starting at less than

$12/MO.

free trial available!

- ✔ businesses, bands, and solo artists
- ✔ full control over ALL your content!
- ✔ FREE professional designs
- ✔ custom designs available
- ✔ email, webmail, mailing lists, web stats

and much more...

RockAndRollDesign.com

Prefix Magazine
80 Cranberry St. #5A,
Brooklyn, NY 11201
Dave Park
dave@prefixmag.com
www.prefixmag.com
*Reviews CDs and
concerts.*

Prick
PO Box 381,
Tucker, GA 30085
PH: 404-627-7825
Jonathan Williams
music@prickmag.net
www.prickmag.net
*Reviews on regional and
national bands.*

Plug In music
PO Box 4206, Elwyn, PA 19063-4206
Corinne corinne@pluginmusic.com
www.pluginmusic.com
*Band profiles, reviews, interviews and more. Check
our site for submission details.*

Pop Culture Press
PO Box 4990, Austin, TX 78765-4990
Luke editor@popculturepress.com
www.popculturepress.com
Pop and the rest of the musical spectrum.

PopMatters
1555 Sherman Ave. #324, Evanston, IL 60201
Sarah Zupko editor@popmatters.com
www.popmatters.com
CD/concert reviews, artist interview and profiles.

POPsmear
232 N. Almont Dr. Beverly Hills, CA 90211
FX: 310-247-9588
www.popsmear.com
Send us your stuff for review or ridicule.

PopStardom
caiti@popstardom.net
popstardom.net
*Features interviews with established and up and
coming artists of all genres.*

PopZine
8793 Plata Ln. #11, Atascadero, CA 93422
questions@popzineonline.com
www.popzineonline.com
*Reviews, interviews, features and more. Please do
not e-mail us electronic press kits!*

pucknation dot com
4421 Shelbyville Rd. #7, Louisville, KY 40207
pucknation@hotmail.com
www.pucknation.com
Send your demo, CD or comic to review.

RAD Cyberzine
88288 Pond St., Florence, OR 97439-9194
james@radcyberzine.com
www.radcyberzine.com
*We provide CDs to review, concerts to attend and
photo passes with bands.*

The Red Alert
2118 Wilshire Blvd. #680, Santa Monica, CA 90403
Adam McKibbin adam@theredalert.com
www.theredalert.com
*Features interviews, album and concert reviews. See
website for more explicit submission guidelines.*

Red is All the Rage
kim@redisalltherage.com
www.redisalltherage.com
*Let us know you would like to submit your an album
for review by contacting the editor at the
appropriate location.*

RegnYouth Archives
Benjamin Sparano benny@regnyouth.com
www.regnyouth.com
*Provides music related selections and reviews in an
attempt to introduce new and upcoming artists.*

Resonance Magazine
PO Box 95620, Seattle, WA 98145-2620
PH: 206-633-3500
info@resonancemag.com
www.resonancemag.com
*Featuring innovative artists from Indie Rock to the
Avant-garde.*

RetroRadar.com
4230 Fairway Dr. #6210, Carrolton, TX 75010
PH: 972-939-5417
Leslie J. Thompson leslie@retroradar.com
RetroRadar.com
*Swing, Rockabilly, Surf, Lounge, Rock 'n Roll,
Roots/R&B, Blues & Jazz standards. Send 2 copies
of your CD.*

Review You
www.ReviewYou.com
*Have your album reviewed by a professional music
journalist. This is a pay to get reviewed service.*

Rib Magazine
238 1st Ave. S. Franklin, TN 37064
PH: 615-429-0157
Will Jordan rib@ribmag.com
www.ribmag.com
Our objective is simple: to report the truth.

Rikks Revues
Rikk Matheson rikk@rikksrevues.com
rikksrevues.com
A free music revue site focusing on Indie artists.

The Rock and Roll Report
rockandrollreport@hotmail.com
www.rockandrollreport.com
*If you're not sure if your music fits, send me a
couple of MP3s using Dropload.*

Rock Music Review
1009 W. North St., Muncie, IN 47303
PH: 317-345-5986
Jack Shepler indiebible@rockmusicreview.com
www.rockmusicreview.com
*Honest independent CD and concert reviews. We
now accept submissions via Sonicbids.*

RockReviews.net
PO Box 151, Hartland, MI 48353
Shelly Towne shelly@rockreviews.net
www.rockreviews.net
*Specializing in professional Rock, Indie Pop and
other genres of reviews.*

Rocktober Magazine
1507 E. 53rd St. #617, Chicago, IL 60615
Jake Austen editor@roctober.com
www.roctober.com
*Articles on obscure musicians in all genres of
popular music.*

Scram
PO Box 31227, Los Angeles, CA 90031
amscray@gmail.com
www.scrammagazine.com
*Unpopular culture, beatniks, Garage Rock, novelty
acts and anything offbeat.*

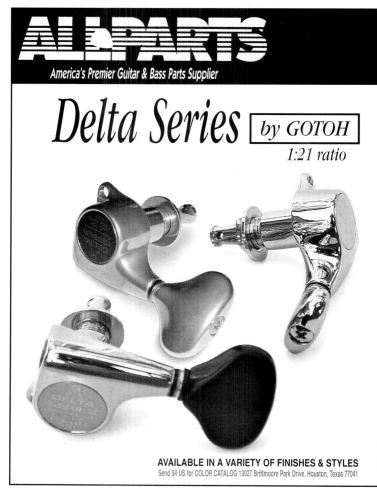

Shotgun Reviews
Troy Brownfield
psikotyk@aol.com
www.shotgunreviews.com
Special emphasis on Hip Hop, Britpop, Electronica and traditional Alternative.

Sing4life.com
464 Rock Glen Dr.
Wynnewood, PA 19096
PH: 610-896-3656
FX: 610-896-6255
Darrell B. Gilbert
supplies4life@net-bizz.com
www.Sing4life.com
Songs from the heart for the heart. A place for the spirit to sing out loud!

Singer Magazine
PO Box 1288,
Harrisburg, VA 22803
PH: 954-973-3555
Greg Tutwiler
SingerMagazine@aol.com
www.singermagazine.com
Inspiring vocal performers and independent recording artists.

Slant Magazine
Sal Cinquemani
sal@slantmagazine.com
www.slantmagazine.com
Featuring reviews, editorials and critiques of a wide array of new and classic music and film.

Smother.Net
c/o Demo Submission,
9237 Berkshire St.,
Manassas, VA 20110
www.smother.net
Covers and reviews all genres of music.

Sound the Sirens
editor@
soundthesirens.com
www.soundthesirens.com
Send your CD in for review.

Soundgenerator
mail@soundgenerator.com
www.soundgenerator.com
Bringing you coverage on many of the best new album, single & DVD releases from every genre.

Southbound Beat
4001 Inglewood Ave.
#101-252, Redondo Beach,
CA 90278
PH: 310-366-7526
FX: 310-366-7432
Ray Carver
southboundbeat@
yahoo.com
www.southboundbeat.com
CD reviews, interviews, columns & more.

SOVIETPANDA
Peter sovietpanda@gmail.com
www.sovietpanda.com
Rock 'n Roll news, reviews etc. Contact me for submission details.

sparkplugg.com
PO Box 5125, Richmond, VA 23220
info@sparkplugg.com
sparkplugg.com
Please send all promotional materials to the above address.

SPIN Magazine
205 Lexington Ave. New York, NY 10016
PH: 212-231-7400 FX: 212-231-7312
spin.com
Bringing you the absolute most in infotainment.

Skuawk!
1133 Broadway #706, New York, NY 10010
FX: 212-465-2516
Marcos Bernal marcos@skuawk.com
www.skuawk.com
A webzine where artists are creatively loud.

Static Multimedia
500 N. Michigan Ave. #300, Chicago, IL 60611
music@staticmultimedia.com
www.StaticMultiMedia.com
If you would like us to review a product, please send it our way.

Stinkweeds Online
1250 E. Apache Blvd. Tempe, AZ 85281-5870
PH: 480-968-9490 FX: 480-968-2131
kimber@stinkweeds.com
www.stinkweeds.com
Reviews of new music added weekly. You'll stay on top of everything Indie.

Stomp and Stammer
PO Box 55233, Atlanta, GA 30308
PH: 404-880-0733 FX: 404-827-0905
www.stompandstammer.com
We cover a wide range of popular and not-so-popular music.

Stylinzine
editor@stylinzine.com
stylinzine.com
For those who are stylin by heart and soul, the individuals who scratch below the superficial surface and embrace the essence of reality.

Stylus Magazine
5091 Station Rd. Box 1394, Erie, PA 16563
Sean Mihlo promos@stylusmagazine.com
www.stylusmagazine.com
Reviews a variety of genres of music.

SugarBuzz
Lucky lucky@sugarbuzzmagazine.com
sugarbuzzmagazine.com
Looking in on today's up and coming Rock 'n Roll artists.

Sure Shot Magazine
8639 B 16th St. #186, Silver Spring, MD 20910
PH: 301-625-0610 FX: 301-625-0611
sureshot@torron.net
www.indiehype.com
An independent music and talent publication that is distributed nationwide.

The Synthesis
210 W. 6th St., Chico, CA 95928
PH: 530-899-7708
bill@synthesis.net
www.thesynthesis.com
Thousands of pages of content, ranging from concert, CD and product reviews to MP3 downloads.

Talent in Motion Magazine
1011 Ave. of the Americas, 4th Fl. New York, NY 10018
PH: 212-354-7189
talentinmotion@mindspring.com
timmag.com
Doesn't do reviews, but does feature a spotlight page on a new artist each issue.

talkbass.com
www.talkbass.com
Interviews for bass players with new releases.

Tangerine Magazine
4821 Maryland Ave. Birmingham, AL 35205
PH: 205-563-9914
Andy acb@tangerinemagazine.com
www.tangerinemagazine.com
For review submission or interview requests contact us.

thepopmanifesto
contact@thepopmanifesto.com
www.thepopmanifesto.com
Quarterly entertainment zine with music news and interviews.

this befuddled universe
1425 Glacier Dr. San Jose, CA 95118-1734
PH: 408-448-7598
Tim Null tim@timnull.com
www.befuddled.org
Services include CD reviews and recorded interviews (MP3).

Tiny Mix Tapes
submissions@tinymixtapes.com
www.tinymixtapes.com
For instructions on how and where to send materials, please e-mail us with a subject that reads "Interested in Submitting."

The Toilet
William H. Club billy@thetoiletonline.com
www.thetoiletonline.com
We welcome bands from all musical genres.

TotalFormat
www.totalformat.com/reviews
Covers a large variety of genres including Pop, Rock, Dance, Indie, Hip Hop, Metal etc.

The Tripwire
info@thetripwire.com
www.thetripwire.com
Supporting music for those in the industry that "genuinely care" and love music as much as we do.

Twee Kitten
1547 Palos Verdes Mall #213, Walnut Creek, CA 94597
PH: 925-947-2842
goldfish@tweekitten.com
www.tweekitten.com
We focus on music possessing beauty, melody, charm etc.

UBO Magazine & Radio
Aaris undergroundbeat69@yahoo.com
www.ubomag.com
Promoting underground artists through media. Hip Hop, Rock, Emo, Punk, R&B, Neo-Soul…

Under the Radar
238 S. Tower Dr. #204, Beverly Hills, CA 90211
PH: 323-653-8705
FX: 323-658-5738
submissions@undertheradarmag.com
www.undertheradarmag.com
We're known for our in-depth and intelligent interviews and for our sharp photo shoots.

UnEarthed.Com
Metalboy
brian@unearthed.com
www.unearthed.com
We get the music that we like heard by the masses.

Unfinished
Hugh Miller
hugh@liepaper.com
www.liepaper.com
I try to review everything I am sent, but cannot guarantee a write-up.

UNSIGNED Music Mag
6980 Roswell Rd. #O6, Atlanta, GA 30328
Ian Cole reviews@unsignedmusicmag.com
www.unsignedmusicmag.com
Our mission is to give artists a venue to let the music buyers of the world know they create, perform and write great music.

Upstage Magazine
PO Box 140, Spring Lake, NJ 07762
PH: 732-280-3305
Gary Wien info@upstagemagazine.com
www.upstagemagazine.com
Frequently features and reviews unsigned/independent artists.

usounds
Erich Redson eredson@usounds.com
www.usounds.com
We embrace the experience of music as well as the music itself.

Varla Magazine
PO Box 65978, Los Angeles, CA 90065-0978
PH: 213-484-6128
music@varla.com
www.varla.com
We cover everything. We will review your CDs.

Vintage Guitar
PO Box 7301, Bismarck, ND 58507
PH: 701-255-1197 FX: 701-255-0250
vguitar@vguitar.com
www.vintageguitar.com
Will review guitar oriented independent CDs.

Weirdearsmag.com
3272 Motor Ave. Ste. I, Los Angeles, CA 90034
PH: 908-309-6716
Lee Wasser Weirdearsmag1@yahoo.com
www.weirdearsmag.com
The best place for Indie-Rock news, under the radar CD reviews, song and video streams.

Whoopsy Magazine
PH: 512-220-7733
Beky Hayes whoopsymail@yahoo.com
www.whoopsymagazine.com
All kinds of music reviews, CD reviews, live show reviews, interviews with local and touring acts etc.

Canada

BangBang
3643 St-Laurent #300 A, Montréal, QC H2X 2V5
PH: 514-845-1658
info@bangbangtemort.com
bangbangtemort.com
Free alternative francophone cultural tabloid which follows both local and international scenes with equal treatment for all.

Being There Magazine
220 Viceroy Rd. #13 Concord, ON L4K 3C2
(US Office): Attn: Russell Bartholomee,
PO Box 172174, Arlington, TX 76003-2174
PH: 647-881-8884 FX: 905-764-8367
Cari Crosby cari@beingtheremag.com
www.beingtheremag.com
An online music & film magazine for the literary minded. We include interviews, features and reviews.

Broken Pencil
PO Box 203, Stn. P, Toronto, ON M5S 2S7
editor@brokenpencil.com
www.brokenpencil.com
We cover zines, books, music, film/video and art produced with an Indie attitude.

the GATE
editor@thegate.ca
www.thegate.ca
Reviews, interviews etc.

Guitar Noise
reviews@guitarnoise.com
www.guitarnoise.com
We review anything guitar related. Check our site for submission guidelines.

Independent Reviewer Sheila Hash
846 Oshawa Blvd. N. Oshawa, ON L1G 5V6
Sheila sheila.hash@sympatico.ca
www.high4records.com
High 4 Records has added a music review section to its website. Please contact me if you would like your CD reviewed.

Indieguitarists.com
PO Box 730 Stn. C Toronto, ON M6J 3S1
Monica Yonge info@indieguitarists.com
www.indieguitarists.com
Contains spotlights, interviews, articles and news.

Indieville
PO Box 91017, 2901 Bayview Ave. Toronto, ON M2K 1H0
PH: 514-262-2711
Matt Shimmer mattshimmer@gmail.com
www.indieville.com
Dedicated to independent music of all sorts. We review everything!

Mote MGZN
PO Box 65026 N. Hill Stn. Calgary, AB T2N 4T6
PH: 403-241-5453
motemgzn@moteinteractive.com
www.moregoatthangoose.com
Reviews, interviews, live reviews etc.

orcasound
5202 Mountain Sights, Montreal, QC H3W 2Y2
PH: 514-483-6722
orcasound@videotron.ca
www.orcasound.com
Reports the hottest musical attractions and recordings.

Soul Shine
20 Gilroy Dr. Scarborough, ON M1P 1Z9
PH: 416-751-3884
Paul Whitfield webmaster@soulshine.ca
www.soulshine.ca
News, features, reviews, gig listings and Indie radio.

Space Junkies Magazine
Wednesday Elektra wednesday@spacejunkies.net
www.spacejunkies.net/ submissions.html
Promoting independent music of all genres. Please check out our "Submissions" page before submitting.

truth explosion magazine
580 Bathurst St., Toronto, ON M5S 2P9
Matthew Parrish matthew@truthexplosion
www.truthexplosion.com
Indie Rock music reviews, interviews, gigs, news etc.

South America

Music Editor Sergio Martorelli
Rua Afonso Pena, 165 casa 5, Rio de Janeiro - Brazil CEP 20270-241
Sergio Martorelli sergio.martorelli@uol.com.br
off-the-press-up-to-date.blogspot.com
I'm the editor of the Brazilian magazine DVD Total/Showtime webmaster/owner of several blog sites.

Super 45
Los Leones 1315 depto 62, Providencia, Chile
www.super45.cl
Música independiente desde 1996.

Velvet Rockmine
Martín Ramos Mejía ak@velvetrockmine.com.ar
www.velvetrockmine.com.ar
Revista virtual de música, cine, arte, moda, teatro y etcéteras (MP3s, videos y especiales muy completos).

Europe

Belgium

The Black Sheep
Sarah Micol
info@sarahmicol.com
www.lilacs-studio.com
I'm Italian and I live in Belgium. I can translate your review into French or English.

Dogmatik
Willy Staeslei 71, 2180 Antwerpen, Belgium
PH: ++32(0)476637033
Joeri De Ren
joeri.de.ren@telenet.be
www.dogmatik.be
Music guide featuring reviews and a band/artist database.

Earfocus
www.earfocus.com
Album and show reviews covering a wide variety of music styles.

Keys & Chords
www.keysandchords.com
Lots of reviews every issue. Covering Rock, Blues, Soul and Modern Jazz.

France

3AM Magazine
12 rue de Tournon, 75006, Paris, France
andrew@3ammagazine.com
www.3ammagazine.com
The hottest in online literature, entertainment and music.

Attica
info@atticawebzine.com
atticawebzine.com
News, reviews, interviews ...

Bokson
44 rue des Pyrénées, 75020 Paris, France
contact@bokson.net
www.bokson.net
Magazine des musiques Rock, Hip Hop Electro, World. Interviews, chroniques, news.

bubblegum perfume
6 rue André Antoine, 75018 Paris, France
Violaine Schütz violaine.schutz@noos.fr
www.bubblegumperfume.ht.st
Fanzine in French about Twee Pop.

Critic Instinct
webmaster@critic-instinct.com
www.critic-instinct.com
Covers Indie music.

Dangerhouse
3 rue Thimonnier, 69001 Lyon, France
PH: 33-0-4-78-27-15-64 FX: 33-0-4-78-39-26-47
dangerhouse@numericable.fr
www.dangerhouse.fr
Comprehensive zine from a record store in France.

Dig It!
32, rue Pharaon, 31000 Toulouse, France
FX: 05-61-14-06-28
digitfanzine@chez.com
www.chez.com/digitfanzine
Rawk 'n' Roll French fanzine!!!

Grandrock
c/o Emmanuel Gathellier, 325 rue de Charenton, 75012 Paris, France
www.grandrock.net
Webzine Rock Indé.

Inrockuptibles
144, rue de Rivoli, 75001 Paris, France
PH: 01-42-44-16-16 FX: 01-42-44-16-00
www.lesinrocks.com
Online music and arts magazine.

Liability Webzine
79, rue Saint Martin, 75004 Paris, France
Dorian Dumont dorian@liabilitywebzine.com
www.liabilitywebzine.com
Pop::Rock::Indé. Nous écoutons 90% des disques que nous recevons.

Nova Planet
33, rue du Faubourg Saint Antoine, 75011 Paris, France
PH: 01-53-33-22-94
redaction@novaplanet.com
www.novaplanet.com
Consortium quotidien de culture underground.

POPnews
8 rue Rosenwald, 75015 Paris, France
Guillaume Sautereau popscene@popnews.com
www.popnews.com
We are very keen on discovering new talents.

positiverage
51, rue Paul Vaillant Couturier, 92240 Malakoff, France
Mathieu Gelézeau positiverage@hotmail.com
www.positiverage.com
Extensive coverage of Indie music.

Premonition
12, rue Lapeyrère, 75018 Paris, France
PH: +33-1-4252-4205
premo@premonition.fr
www.premonition.fr
Our purpose is to give everyone the opportunity to hear independent bands express themselves.

sefronia
info@sefronia.com
www.sefronia.com
Free CD review e-mail magazine.

Speedvibes
26 Ave. de la Cote Bleue -V21,
13960 Sausset Les Pins, France
PH: 06-88-96-49-63 FX: 04-42-44-63-27
niko@speedvibes.com
www.speedvibes.com
Bands from everywhere are welcome to submit.

zicline.com
zicline@zicline.com
www.zicline.com
Each week all music info from Jazz to Heavy Metal.

Germany

CD-KRITIK.DE
Dreibergen 79, 27572 Bremerhaven, Germany
PH: 0471-9-31-34-25 FX: 0471-3-00-61-88
Michael Frost redaktion@cd-kritik.de
www.cd-kritik.de
Wir beschreiben Ihnen die CDs, aber die Wahl haben Sie.

Discover
Im Erpelgrund 80, 13503 Berlin, Germany
PH: +49-30-39932240
André Esch andre@discover.de
www.discover.de
CDs, stories, interviews ...

Flaming Youth
Marceese Trabus info@flamingyouth.de
www.flamingyouth.de
Rock Musik Magazin mit aktuellen album rezensionen und veranstaltungstipps, konzertberichten ...

Guitars Galore
Postfach 41 03 11, 12113 Berlin, Germany
Mike Korbik mail@twang-tone.de
www.twang-tone.de/gg.html
A flyer zine and monthly radio show as well.

indiepoprock.net
wqw wqw@indiepoprock.net
www.indiepoprock.net
Chroniques, interviews, live reports, labels etc.

Kinda Muzik You Like
redactie@kindamuzik.net
www.kindamuzik.net
Giving Underground music the attention it deserves.

The Indie Link Exchange
A new, free and easy way to promote your website
www.indielinkexchange.com/ile

Music-Scan Zine
Hafersteig 57, 12683 Berlin, Germany
PH: +49-7243-572758 FX: +49-7243-572759
Arne Kupetz conczine@aol.com
www.music-scan.de
Tons of news, reviews, interviews, contests, links and information.

Plattentests Online
Bismarckstraße 29, 73084 Salach, Germany
PH: 0176-24432675
Armin Linder armin@plattentests.de
www.plattentests.de
Das Beste aus Rock und independent!

PNG *(Persona Non Grata)*
Postfach 30 14 38, 04254 Leipzig, Germany
PH: 0341-125-72-06
Andreas Richter redaktion@png-online.de
cms.png-online.de
News, reviews, interviews and more.

realmusic.de
Landsberger Allee 171 C, 10369 Berlin, Germany
PH/FX: 49 (0) 700-732568742
Dirk Scheuer ich@dirkscheuer.com
www.realmusic.de
Review and entertainment magazine.

VISIONS.de
Arneckestr. 82-84, 44139 Dortmund, Germany
PH: (0231) 557131-10 FX: (0231) 557131-31
info@visions.de
www.visions.de
Musikmagazin für alternative Musik

Greece

Scream Magazine
Saradaporou 45, 26223 Patra, Hellas, Greece
PH: 2610-422801
Spiros scream_zine@yahoo.com
www.scream.gr
Covers Rock, Jazz and Blues.

Italy

Rockit
Giulio Pons pons@rockit.it
www.rockit.it
Tutta roba Italiana.

Onda Rock
info@ondarock.it
www.ondarock.it
News and reviews.

Sodapop
sodapop@sodapop.it
www.sodapop.it
News, reviews, demos etc.

Three Monkeys
Via Tagliapietre 14, Bologna 40123, Italy
Andy Lawless info@threemonkeysonline.com
www.threemonkeysonline.com
Current affairs/music magazine with interviews and reviews.

The Netherlands

3voor12
3voor12@vpro.nl
www.3voor12.nl
Features, shows, reviews etc.

HEAVEN
bladmanager@heaven.be
www.heaven.be
Popmagazine voor volwassenen.

MusicRemedy.com
Vermeerhof 2, 3862 ZR, Nijkerk, The Netherlands
www.musicremedy.com
Send in your music so we can review it.

OOR
Antwoordnummer 14044, 5126 ZS, Glize,
The Netherlands
PH: 0161-459533 FX: 0161-452913
oor@betapress.audax.nl
www.oor.nl
News, reviews, events calendar and more.

Norway

Luna Kafe
PO Box 2175, Grunerlokka, 0505 Oslo, Norway
luna@fuzzlogic.com
www.fuzzlogic.com/lunakafe
Record reviews, concert reviews, interviews and more.

Spain

BuscaMusica.org
PO Box 440 - Jaen 23080, Spain
Juanma Cantos redaccion@buscamusica.org
www.buscamusica.org
Electronic magazine, band promotion and new Indie label. Upload your music!

eternoViajero.com
info@eternoviajero.com
www.eternoviajero.com
Noticas, fotos, MP3s, cronicas etc.

La Ganzua, Radio Obradoiro
Preguntoiro, 29. 15702, Santiago de Compostela,
A Coruña, Spain
PH: 981-543766-64
laganzua@laganzua.net
www.laganzua.net
E-zine de música independiente con noticias, conciertos, festivales, crónicas, entrevistas, MP3, discos, maquetas ...

Indy Rock
Polígono de Asegra c/Cádiz s/n, 18210 Peligros,
Granada, Spain
PH: 958-809809
info@indyrock.es
www.indyrock.es
News, reviews, concerts, festivals etc.

Manerasdevivir.com
discos@manerasdevivir.com
www.manerasdevivir.com
Punto de ecuentro de todos los amantes del rocanrol. Noticias muy actualizadas, MP3, conciertos, foros ...

Music in a Net
Apdo. de correos 4233, 35080 Las Palmas de G.C.
Las Palmas (Canary Islands), Spain
Héctor Noble Fernández info@music-in-a.net
www.music-in-a.net
We do reviews of absolutely every kind of music. However, it is always best that you contact us before sending anything and tell us what sort of music you would like to send to us.

Muzikalia.com
PO Box 9502, 08012 Barcelona, Spain
PH: 93-415-29-47
Sergio Picón info@muzikalia.com
www.muzikalia.com
Completísima web de música independiente.

El Planeta Amarillo
C/ Carlos III, 38 - 4º C, 30203 Cartagena (Murcia)
Spain
Rafa Skam rafaskam@wanadoo.es
www.yellowmelodies.com/e-zine/Menu.html
Online and print Pop zine with lots of reviews.

pop-page.com
C/ Málaga 11, 18230 Atarfe (Granada), Spain
pop-page.com
E-zine dedicado a la música menos convencional.

RIFF Fanzine
Apartado de Correos 23.114, 08080 Barcelona,
Spain
Pablo Campoy info@riff-fanzine.com
www.riff-fanzine.com
Artículos, discos etc.

Space Rock Heaters
spacerockheaters@hotmail.com
spacerockheaters.com
*Webzine creado en Cáceres con las últimas noticias
sobre conciertos, grupos y festivales.*

thebellemusic.com
contacto@thebellemusic.com
www.thebellemusic.com
*Revista musical Independiente: crónicas de
conciertos, cometarios de discos, novedades
noticias, entrevistas y mucho más.*

Sweden

Indiepop Spinzone
webmeister@indiespinzone.com
www.indiespinzone.com
*Indie music's best friend. Album reviews, interviews,
history and much more!*

melodic.net
Johan Wippsson wippsson@melodic.net
www.melodic.net
Reviews, interviews and "Artist of the Week".

Passagen
Boulevard 40, 169 87 Stockholm, Sweden
passagen@eniro.com
www.passagen.se
Forum for Indie artists.

Revolver
Postfack 180, 116 74 Stockholm, Sweden
farid@revolver.nu
www.revolver.nu
E-zine for Indie artists. Submit your stuff.

United Kingdom

Alternative Music Links
4 Osborne House, St. Mary's Ter. London,
W2 1SG UK
mailbox@alternative-links.co.uk
www.alternative-links.co.uk
Contact us regarding possible gig or album reviews.

AngryApe
603 Lincoln Gate, Lord St., Manchester,
M4 4AD UK
info@angryape.com
www.angryape.com
*Music news, reviews, interviews. Must be NEW
material!*

Artrocker Magazine
info@artrocker.com
artrocker.com
*Rock n' Roll reviews, features, gigs, listings and
MP3s.*

Atomic Duster
nick.j@atomicduster.com
www.atomicduster.com
Music, news, reviews, interviews and competitions.

The Beat Surrender
c/o Kevin Trotter, 77 Smithy Ln. Tingley, Wakefield,
West Yorks, WF3 1QB UK
www.thebeatsurrender.co.uk
Music news, reviews, interviews ...

Beatmag
PO Box 135, Hove BN3 3UG UK
PH: 0044-1273-389178
Thomas H. Green thomas@beathut.com
www.beatmag.net
*The official magazine for Beathut.com the
independent legal MP3 download site.*

between planets
www.betweenplanets.co.uk
*Music news and review site where bands can also
publicize themselves.*

Web Only

Bloodshot Dawn
hello@bloodshotdawn.com
www.bloodshotdawn.com
*Gig reviews and news, plus CD recommendations.
There is good music out there!*

Burn Burn
info@burnburn.com
www.burnburn.com
A community for music fans, bands and artists.

CLUAS
Eoghan O'Neill webmaster@cluas.com
www.cluas.com
Lending an ear to the Irish music scene.

Comfort Comes
John Siwicki info@comfortcomes.com
www.comfortcomes.com
*Would you like your band reviewed on our site?
Send us an e-mail!*

Cool Noise
Richmond Barn, Bayswater Farm Rd. Headington,
Oxford, OX3 8BY UK
Dave Home webmaster@coolnoise.co.uk
www.coolnoise.co.uk
Short reviews, opinions and musings on music.

DirtyZine
dirtyzine@dirtyzine.co.uk
www.dirtyzine.co.uk
*An Alternative Rock zine. Reviews, interviews,
downloads of the month.*

Diskant
Stuart Fowkes newbands@diskant.net
www.diskant.net
*A network of websites by independent fanzines,
bands and record labels.*

Do Something Pretty
dosomethingpretty@hotmail.com
dosomethingpretty.com
Building connections in independent music.

Drowned in Sound
1 Chilworth Mews, London, W2 3RG UK
sean.adams@drownedinsound.com
www.drownedinsound.com
Reviews, gigs, downloads, features and more.

Excellent Online.com
www.excellentonline.com
The home for North American fans of UK music.

Fact Magazine
music@factmagazine.co.uk
www.factmagazine.co.uk
*Provides a platform for talented young musicians,
artists and designers.*

Fast 'n' Bulbous
savand@fastnbulbous.com
www.fastnbulbous.com
*Publishing mainly positive reviews, with the idea
that people should be turned on to the best music.*

Fire Burn Music
fireburnmusic@hotmail.co.uk
www.myspace.com/fireburnmusic
*Reviews of demos/EPs/albums and live
performances. Also a focus on band photography.*

get ready to ROCK!
Neston, Cheshire, CH64 0TD UK
PH/FX: +44-0-845-1665853
www.getreadytorock.com
*Classic and Progressive Rock music news, reviews
and interviews.*

Gigs Unlimited
17 Cromford Ave. Stretford, Manchester,
M32 9RQ UK
info@gigs-unlimited.co.uk
www.gigs-unlimited.co.uk
*Dedicated to promoting fresh new talent to give
them the push they need to be the "Next Big Thing".*

Glasswerk
340A Pinner Rd. Harrow, London, HA1 4LB UK
Jack Cook london@glasswerk.co.uk
www.glasswerk.co.uk
*Promoting the best new music at all levels, locally
and nationally. We'll let you know when your review
is up.*

God Is In The TV Fanzine
Bill godisinthetv2003@yahoo.co.uk
www.godisinthetvzine.co.uk
*An Indie music and culture zine. Features, reviews
and forum.*

Hot Press
13 Trinity St., Dublin 2, UK
feedback@hotpress.com
www.hotpress.com
*The essential guide to Rock, Pop, Dance and
Contemporary music.*

ilikemusic.com *Soundstage*
Unit 5 Belbins Business Park, Cupernham Ln.
Romsey, Hampshire, SO51 7JF UK
PH: +44 (0) 845-430-8651
www.ilikemusic.com
*Reviews of unsigned talent, music promotion
articles, tips and links galore.*

Indiecater Records
indiecater.com
*Not just your average, everyday, ho-hum, so-so, bog
standard Alternative music review website.*

Indigo Flow
www.indigoflow.co.uk
Covers all genres of music.

is this music?
PO Box 13516, Linlithgow, EH49 6AS UK
Stuart McHugh editor@isthismusic.com
www.isthismusic.com
A Scottish music monthly that covers Indie music.

Jamble Magazine
67 Daisy St., Cardiff, CF5 1EQ UK
Ioan Everett info@jamblemag.co.uk
www.jamblemag.co.uk
*Music and travel zine focusing on the best up and
coming acts from around the world.*

Leonard's Lair
leonards.lair@ntlworld.com
www.leonardslair.co.uk
*We're particularly fond of Electronica, Post-Punk,
Post-Rock, Dreampop. It's best to point me out to a
link where I can listen to your music to see if it fits.*

Lost Music
info@lostmusic.co.uk
www.lostmusic.co.uk
*We are constantly searching for new music to give
us that buzz. That thrill. The tingle down the spine.*

Manilla
216 Marton Rd. Middlesbrough, TS4 2ET UK
PH: 01642-228400
info@manillame.com
www.manillame.com
Free mag which promotes unsigned acts.

Mongrel Magazine
10-11 Liffey St. Lower, Dublin 1 Ireland
PH: +353-1-874-7548 FX: +353-1-872-7384
info@mongrel.ie
www.mongrel.ie
*Music and fashion magazine featuring lots of
reviews each month.*

Music 4M
28 Richmond St., Hartlepool, TS25 5SH UK
Sarah Parrott reviews@music4m.com
www.music4m.com
*Reviews and interviews from bands in the UK and
around the world as well as the latest news.*

Music News
17b Charteris Rd. London, N4 3AA UK
Marco Gandolfi marco@music-news.com
www.music-news.com
*News, reviews, interviews and the latest releases &
gossip from the current music scene.*

music week
www.musicweek.com
Music, news, charts, reviews, analysis, features.

MusicOMH.com
unsigned@musicomh.com
www.musicomh.com
*Established reviews and interviews site. Contact us
before you send your music!*

MusicShopper
11 Trout Rd. Haslemere, Surrey, GU27 1RD UK
PH: 44-1428-656878
Stephen Reynolds info@musicshopper.info
www.musicshopper.info
*We review and allow you to promote your music on
our site.*

New Music Express
news@nme.com
www.nme.com
Reviews, interviews, quotes…

Webzy

No Ordinary Music
talent@no-ordinarymusic.com
www.no-ordinarymusic.com
*The UK's best Alternative webzine, brought to you
by lovers of all things musical.*

No Ripcord
76 Heavygate Rd. Sheffield, S10 1PF UK
PH: 44-0114-234-2622
mail@noripcord.com
www.noripcord.com
Reviews and features of Indie/Alternative bands.

Nunuworld
nunununa@nunuworldmusic.co.uk
www.nunuworldmusic.co.uk
Covers Indie music with reviews, photos etc.

The Panhandle
panhandle.co.uk
*Combining recognized and not so well known artists
together without the need for segmentation.*

pennyblackmusic.com
johnclarkson1@hotmail.com
www.pennyblackmusic.com
*Contact to get your promo reviewed in the
magazine.*

PHASE9 Entertainment
FX: 44-0-845-280-1708
Nigel editorial@phase9.net
www.phase9.tv
*Independent site for reviews and information on
music and movies in the UK and USA.*

Pixelsurgeon
Attn: Music Reviews, Flat 2, 50 St Michaels Rd.
Bedford, Beds, MK40 2LU UK
info@pixelsurgeon.com
www.pixelsurgeon.com
We review movies, games and music. Interviews too!

Plan B Magazine
Daniel Trilling daniel@planbmag.com
www.planbmag.com
*Reviews include all the music and culture we love,
not just that being ignored elsewhere.*

PLAYLOUDER
8-10 Rhoda St., London, E2 7EF UK
site@playlouder.com
www.playlouder.com
Bringing you the very best in new music.

Popjustice
31 Chelsea Wharf, Lots Rd. London, SW10 0QJ UK
PH: 020-7352-9444
Peter Robinson MP3s@popjustice.com
www.popjustice.com
*Pop news, MP3s, single features etc. Also a monthly
podcast.*

state51
Rhod·
Pl

rawkstar.net
Bob bob@rawkstar.net
www.rawkstar.net
*Reviews of new releases, demos,
interviews etc.*

Record Scout
374 Victoria Ave. Southend on Sea, Essex,
SS2 6NA UK
www.recordscout.com
*We write music reviews for many magazines around
the country and the bands we review will instantly
receive national publicity.*

Review Centre Indie *Music*
www.reviewcentre.com/products1684.html
*Read about Indie albums and contribute your
comments or reviews, to help others discover new
music.*

reviewed4u.com
PO Box 9749, Birmingham, B28 0WB UK
theteam@reviewed4u.com
www.reviewed4u.com
Music, DVD, gig reviews and music news.

ROCK SOUND
Unit 22, Jack's Pl. 6 Corbet Pl. Spitalfields, London,
E1 6NN UK
Darren darren.taylor@rock-sound.net
www.rock-sound.net
*Bringing you all the best new music from around the
world.*

Rock's Backpages
63 Pont St., London, SW1X 0BD UK
www.rocksbackpages.com
News, reviews and interviews of new artists.

rockcity.co.uk
8 Talbot St., Nottingham, NG1 5GG UK
PH: 0115-9412544 FX: 0115-9418438
boxoffice@rock-city.co.uk
www.rock-city.co.uk
*Reviews of both signed and unsigned recorded
material and live shows.*

RockFeedback.com
PO Box 704, High Wycombe, HP15 7GL UK
press@rockfeedback.com
www.rockfeedback.com
Contact us to get featured on the site.

Russell's Reviews
Russell Barker russ@russellsreviews.co.uk
www.russellsreviews.co.uk
*CD, demo and gig reviews from reviewer based in
Oxford.*

**Shadders Online / Shadders? On me
Lungs?**
16 Woodcock Way, Adwick lE St., Doncaster,
DN6 7UP UK
Colin Newell colinnewell@orange.net
www.shaddersonline.com
*We feature up and coming plus established UK
artists.*

Shindig
64 North View Rd. London, N8 7LL UK
Jon 'Mojo' Mills info@shindig-magazine.com
www.shindig-magazine.com
*Reviews Psych and Garage. No plain ole Indie/
Alt-Rock.*

St., London, E2 7EF UK
. 44-207-729-4343
www.state51.co.uk
Showcasing the best new music in all genres.

Tangents
PO Box 102, Exeter, EX2 4YL UK
editors@tangents.co.uk
www.tangents.co.uk
The home of Un-Popular culture on the web.

Tastyzine
info@tastyfanzine.org.uk
www.tastyfanzine.org.uk
Recommending the soundtrack for the revolution.

TweeNet
c/o Peter Hahndorf at Saltmine Atelier House,
64 Pratt St., London, NW1 0LF UK
PH: 44-7930-283774
www.twee.net
Submit your music and a press release to us.

Uncut Magazine
25th Fl., King's Reach Tower, Stamford St., London,
SE1 9LS UK
PH: 020-7261-6992 FX: 020-7261-5573
www.uncut.co.uk/music
Reviews CDs of major and independent artists.

Whisperin & Hollerin
Cosheen, Schull, Co Cork, Ireland
Tim Peacock tim@whisperinandhollerin.com
www.whisperinandhollerin.com
Music reviews and interviews with an Alternative bias - covers a huge range of genres.

Zap! BANG!
Chico Foley chico@zapbang.org
www.zapbang.org
A zenith for the exposure of the multitude.

Zeitgeist
PO Box 13499, Edinburgh, EH6 8YL UK
www.zeitgeist-scot.co.uk
Reflecting the underground through music.

Australia

Alternate Music Press
PO Box 2286, Ringwood N., VIC 3134 Australia
www.alternatemusicpress.com
Reviews, interviews etc. Please DO NOT send Rock, Alternative or Pop music!

Blunt Review
emily@bluntreview.com
www.bluntreview.com
We review Indie music and interview musicians.

Buzz Magazine
PO Box 55, Dromana, VIC 3936 Australia
PH: 61-3-59812979 FX: 61-3-59861449
psutton@r150.aone.net.au
www.buzzmagazine.com.au
Features interviews with Australian and international artists, reviews and columns.

Long Gone Loser
PO Box 18, Modbury N., SA 5092 Australia
damo@longgoneloser.com
www.longgoneloser.com
Feel free to send anything for review.

Undercover
11-15 Buckhurst St., S. Melbourne, VIC 3205
Australia
PH: +61-3-9686-4800
Tim Cashmere tim@undercover.com.au
www.undercover.net.au
News, reviews, interviews and more!

Asia

BigO
PO Box 784, Marine Parade, Singapore 914410
PH: 63484007 FX: 63480362
singbigo@singnet.com.sg
www.bigo.com.sg
Features more than 150 reviews each issue.

Indie Culture
1217 Leyson St., Talamban, Cebu City, Philippines
PH: 6332-4160333 FX: 6332-4160409
Ian Zafra ian@indiecultureonline.com
www.indiecultureonline.com
Support and nurtures Indie musicians.

Indie's Port
Syuli Firmansyah admin@indiesport.com
www.indiesport.com
Indonesian resource site featuring Indie reviews, music promotion and distribution.

Metropolis
3F Maison Tomoe Bldg. 3-16-1 Minami-Aoyama,
Minato-Ku, Tokyo 107 Japan
PH: 81-3-3423-6932 FX: 81-3-3423-6931
letters@metropolis.co.jp
metropolis.japantoday.com
Japan's #1 English magazine. CD reviews and tour announcements in the music section.

Blues

North America

United States

Blues Blowtorch
RR 2, Box 5, Clinton, IL 61727-9802
PH: 217-935-8603
Frank deltafrank@bluesblowtorch.com
www.bluesblowtorch.com
Promoting the Blues in all its forms.

Blues Music Now!
Jeff Stevens editor@bluesmusicnow.com
www.bluesmusicnow.com
Contact us about sending your CD in for review.

Blues Revue
Rte. 1, Box 75, Salem, WV 26426-9604
PH: 304-782-1971 FX: 304-782-1993
info@bluesrevue.com
www.bluesrevue.com
Artist profiles, interviews, reviews and more.

Blues Bytes
Bruce Coen information@bluenight.com
www.bluenight.com/BluesBytes
A monthly Blues CD review magazine.

Big City Blues
PO Box 1805, Royal Oak, MI 48068
PH: 248-582-1544 FX: 248-582-8242
blues@bigcitybluesmag.com
www.bigcitybluesmag.com
In-depth articles, interviews and CD reviews.

Bluesrockers
Tom Branson tom@bluesrockers.ws
www.bluesrockers.ws
Information and reviews on the best artists and recordings available.

Blueswax.com
www.blueswax.com
Reviews, industry news, interviews and MP3s.

Cross Harp Chronicles
PO Box 6283, Jackson, MI 49204
PH: 517-569-2615 FX: 517-569-8664
Dave King dking@crossharpchronicles.com
crossharpchronicles.com
Interviews with harmonica/Blues movers and shakers, concert news, CD reviews etc.

Electric Blues
PO Box 1370, Riverview, FL 33568-1370
herm@electricblues.com
www.electricblues.com
CD reviews, news and more.

Living Blues Magazine
PO Box 1848, 301 Hill Hall, University, MS 38677
PH: 800-390-3527 FX: 662-915-7842
www.livingblues.com
A bimonthly magazine for the Blues.

Canada

Eddy B's Blueheart Archive
PO Box 458 Stn P, 704 Spadina Ave. Toronto,
ON M5S 2S9
Eddy Brake eddy@blueheartarchive.com
www.blueheartarchive.com
If you have promotional package please send it to me along with your CD.

Real Blues Magazine
PO Box 1201, Victoria, BC V8W 2T6
Andy Griggandy@realbluesmagazine.com
www.realbluesmagazine.com
If you have a CD or DVD you would like considered for review, please send it to me.

Europe

Austria

BluesArtStudio
A-1223 Vienna, PO Box 54, Austria
bluesart@bluesartstudio.at
www.bluesartstudio.at
Supporting and promoting the Blues.

Belgium

Back to the Roots
Knollestraat 1, 8210 Zedelgem, Belgium
PH: 32-0-478-306-325 FX: 32-0-50-27-58-87
backtotheroots.franky@pi.be
www.backtotheroots.be
Is een nederlandstalig magazine voor Blues en aanverwante muziekstijlen.

Germany

Blues News Magazine
Verlag Dirk Föhrs, Freiherr-vom-Stein-Str. 28,
D-58762 Altena, Germany
PH: 0-23-52-21-68-0
Redaktion@Blues-Germany.de
www.blues-germany.de
News, reviews, events etc.

Italy

Blues and Blues
info@bluesandblues.it
www.bluesandblues.it
The Italian Blues website.

The Netherlands

Blue Ears
E. Samsonstraat 5, 1103 MR Amsterdam Z-O,
The Netherlands
info@BlueEars.com
www.blueEars.com
Independent radio station for adventurous Blues (y) music.

Spain

La Hora del Blues Reviews
Apartado de Correos 12.085, 08080 Barcelona,
Spain
Vicente P. Zumel zumel@lahoradelblues.com
www.lahoradelblues.com/criticas.htm
Reviews are done monthly. Send 2 copies.

Sweden

Jefferson
c/o Ingemar Karlsson, Järpegatan 1 C,
SE-664 31 Grums, Sweden
records@jeffersonbluesmag.com
jeffersonbluesmag.com
Administered by the Scandinavian Blues Association.

United Kingdom

Blues In Britain
10, Messaline Ave. London, W3 6JX UK
PH: 44-0-20-8723-7376 FX: 44-0-20-8723 7380
Jon Taylor info@bluesinbritain.org
www.blueprint-blues.co.uk
Blues news, reviews and interviews and a four page gig guide to Blues events in the UK.

Blues Matters!
PO Box 18, Bridgend, CF33 6YW UK
PH: 44-0-1656-743406
Alan 'D' Pearce editor@bluesmatters.com
www.bluesmatters.com
Old, New, Traditional, Nu and any other type of Blues.

Juke Blues
PO Box 1654, Yatton, Bristol, BS49 4FD UK
juke@jukeblues.com
www.bluesworld.com/JukeBlues.html
Interviews, news reviews, gig guide and more.

Children's

Boopadoo
Box 5173, Norwell, MA 02061
www.boopadoo.net
Resources supporting the children's music industry.

Children's Music that Rocks
Warren Truitt paulmccartney@teacher.com
www.kidsmusicthatrocks.blogspot.com
Music for kids that doesn't make adults want to rip their hair out.

Edutaining Kids *Guide to Children's Music*
stephanie@edutainingkids.com
www.edutainingkids.com/music.html
Articles, spotlights, reviews etc.

John Wood Revue
john@kidzmusic.com
www.kidzmusic.com
A great place to find some of the best Children's music.

The Lovely Mrs. Davis Tells You What to Think
Mrs. Davis thelovelymrsdavis@gmail.com.
lovelydavis.blogspot.com
If you have Children's music you would like to submit for a review, please contact me via e-mail.

Zooglobble
Stefan Shepherd zooglobble@earthlink.net
zooglobble.blogspot.com
Children and family music reviews. Music for the kids that parents won't hate.

Christian

North America

United States

BlackChristian.com
PH: 978-590-4609
www.blackchristian.com
Several resources including music reviews.

CatholicMusicNetwork.com
www.catholicmusicnetwork.com
Source for music by today's top Catholic artists.

The Christian Rapper
PO Box 1752, Carrollton, GA 30117
thechristianrapper@yahoo.com
www.thechristianrapper.com
Please send all materials.

Christianity Today
465 Gunderson Dr. Carol Stream, IL 60188
PH: 630-260-6200 FX: 630-260-0114
music@christianitytoday.com
christianmusictoday.com
News, interviews and reviews. We only review the best of what we receive.

Contemporary Christian Magazine
104 Woodmont Blvd. #300, Nashville, TN 37205
www.ccmcom.com
Supporting Indie Christian bands.

CreatorsWeb
Ken Mowery ken@creatorsweb.com
www.creatorsweb.com
Reviews independent musicians.

Godcore.com
12271 Magnolia Way, Brighton, CO 80602
PH: 877-778-4016
www.godcore.com
Helps Christian Rockers gain worldwide exposure.

Gospel Today
286 Hwy. 314 Ste. C, Fayetteville, GA 30214
PH: 770-719-4825 FX: 770-716-2660
gospeltodaymag@aol.com
www.gospeltoday.com
New Gospel CDs, record sales charts etc.

The Gospel Zone
PO Box 5211, Oakland, CA 94605
PH: 510-472-0177
Curtis Jermany info@urbangospelalliance.com
www.thegospelzone.com
Reviews, news, message boards and upcoming events.

GospelFlava.com
info@gospelflava.com
www.gospelflava.com
Reviews new CD and video Gospel releases.

Hammonline.com
4445-B Breton Rd. SE. #196, Kentwood,
MI 49508-8411
Tim Hamm info@hammsterwheel.com
www.hammonline.com
All submissions should include a press kit, or at least a fact sheet pertaining to the release.

Hip Hop For The Soul
TRu bdg@trudatmusic.com
hiphopforthesoul.com
To have your album considered for review, contact me.

HM Magazine
PO Box 367, Hutto, TX 78634
PH: 512-989-7309 FX: 512-670-2764
Doug Van Pelt dvanpelt@hmmagazine.com
www.hmmagazine.com
Features interviews, news and reviews of Hard Music. Send 2 copies (if possible).

Indie Vision Music
PO Box 6305, Laguna Niguel, CA 92607
Brandon Jones brandon@indievisionmusic.com
www.indievisionzine.com
Seeks to bring an independent perspective to issues of faith and entertainment.

Jamsline.com
www.jamsline.com
Weekly single reviews.

Metal for Jesus
Johannes Jonsson johannes@metalforjesus.org
www.metalforjesus.org
If you play in a Christian Metal band, I'll gladly review your CD or demo.

Music Spectrum
619 Pine St., Manitowoc, WI 54220
PH: 920-684-3989
Benjamin Squires benjamin@musicspectrum.org
www.musicspectrum.org
Reviewing music across the spectrum of styles. Connecting secular and Christian music to the Christian faith.

NeuFutur
650 Morris #6, Kent, OH 44243
James McQuiston editor@neufutur.com
www.neufutur.com
Covers anything from Christian praise to Death Metal. Fight on, little ones.

nuthinbutgospel.com
PO Box 30874, Washington, DC 20030-0874
Louis Williams nuthinbutgospel@yahoo.com
www.nuthinbutgospel.com
CONTACT US before you send your music in for review.

Opus' Album Reviews
www.opuszine.com
If you'd like to send in a demo, please contact me. Also, a brief bio about your band, influences etc. would be helpful.

Phantom Tollboth
PO Box 11934, Chicago, IL 60611
PH: 773-274-6413
J. Robert Parks editor@tollbooth.org
tollbooth.org
Album, concert and movie reviews, interviews, features and resource links.

Power Source
PO Box 101336 Nashville, TN 37224
PH: 615- 742-9210 FX: 615-248-8505
Vickie Gardner vickie@powersourcemagazine.com
www.powersourcemusic.com
Official publication of The Christian Country Music Association.

Revolutionary Magazine
1289 Nice Dr. Lexington, KY 40504
PH: 859-699-8986
Timothy Gerst timothygerst@gmail.com
http://www.revolutionarymag.com
We will listen to each and every CD that we receive and will consider it for review.

Singing News Magazine
PO Box 2810, 330 University Hall Dr. Boone, NC 28607
PH: 828-264-3700 FX: 828-264-4621
www.singingnews.com
Concerts, new recordings and the latest chart action.

SouthernGospelNews.com
220 Indian Park Dr. #1501, Murfreesboro, TN 37128 Attn: Reviews
webmaster@sogospelnews.com
sogospelnews.com
News, information, artist interviews, CD reviews and more!

Sphere of Hip Hop
3803 4th Pl. NW., Rochester, MN 55901
Attn: Josh Niemyjski
www.sphereofhiphop.com
Featured items: MP3, reviews, articles and more!

Tastyfresh
4380 Iris Brooke Ln. Snellville, GA 30039
www.tastyfresh.com
Christ centered DJ culture.

Virtuosity
423 Cedar St., Ketchikan, AK 99901
Dave Taylor virtuosity@att.net
home.att.net/~virtuosity
Spiritual Progressive Rock reviews. We play music we review on the radio show "Holy Tsunami" on KRBD.

Wendy V's Christian/Gospel CD spotlight
2136 Ford Pkwy #206, St. Paul, MN 55116
Wendy Vickers wendyv2941@aol.com
www.wendyv.com
E-mail me and tell me about your CD before you send it in!

What's the Word Magazine
200 Rhode Island Ave. NE. #401, Washington, DC 20002
PH: 202-635-8222
info@wtwmagazine.com
www.wtwmagazine.com
New, reviews, interviews, a chat room and message boards.

Canada

FEED
400 Delaney Dr. Ajax, ON L1T 3Y7
PH: 647-722-4306 FX: 866-871-1914
editorial@feedstop.com
www.feedstop.com
Your source for the best in beats, rhymes & light.

GospelCity.com
1410 Stanley, #1020, Montreal, QC H3A 1P8
PH: 514-868-1600 FX: 514-868-1067
michelle@agmediagrp.com
gospelcity.com
News, reviews, articles and more!

E u r o p e

United Kingdom

New Christian Music
PO Box 6207, Leighton Buzzard, Beds. LU7 0WQ UK
Paul Davis enq@newchristianmusic.co.uk
www.newchristianmusic.co.uk
We would like to receive CDs for review.

talkGospel.com
PO Box 13000, London, SW1P 4XP UK
PH: 020-7316-1300 FX: 020-7233-6706
enquiries@talkGospel.com
www.talkgospel.com
Supports the Gospel music scene, particularly British artists.

United by ONE
PO Box 3093, South Croydon, CR2 0YB UK
PH: +44 (0) 20-8681-8339
info@unitedbyone.co.uk
www.unitedbyone.co.uk
Urban Gospel site from the UK to the world.

Classical

N o r t h   A m e r i c a

United States

Bass World
14070 Proton Rd. #100, Dallas, TX 75244
PH: 972-233-9107 x204 FX: 972-490-4219
info@isbworldoffice.com
www.isbworldoffice.com
Reviews recordings and music internationally.

Chamber Music Magazine
305 7th Ave. 5th Fl. New York, NY 10001
PH: 212-242-2022 FX: 212-242-7955
info@chamber-music.org
www.chamber-music.org
Send new CDs and books, as well as press releases by mail.

Classical CD Review
bob@classicalcdreview.com
www.classicalcdreview.com
We review CDs we feel are of particular interest to us and to our readers.

Classicalist.com
support@classicalist.com
www.classicalist.com
Add your review to Classicalist.

Classics Today
David Hurwitz dhurwitz@classicstoday.com
www.classicstoday.com
Five feature reviews per day.

Early Music America
2366 Eastlake Ave. E. #429, Seattle, WA 98102
PH: 206-720-6270 FX: 206-720-6290
info@earlymusic.org
earlymusic.org
Artist profiles, interview and record reviews.

Early Music NEWS
PO Box 544, Pacific Palisades, CA 90272-0544
PH: 310-358-5967
info@earlymusicla.org
www.earlymusicla.org
Features reviews of early music CD recordings.

La Folia
86 Church St., Belfast, ME 04915
PH/FX: 207-338-5585
Mike Silverton editor@lafolia.com
www.lafolia.com
We do review independent CDs. They MUST be Classical, Old and New, or Jazz other than mainstream.

Guitart
guitart@guitart.net
www.guitart.net
Classical guitar magazine blending art and music with a European aesthetic.

The Horn Call
School of Music, W. Michigan U. Kalamazoo, MI 49008
PH: 269-387-4692 FX: 269-387-1113
editor@hornsociety.org
www.hornsociety.org
News, feature articles, clinics, music and reviews.

International Trumpet Guild
PO Box 1308, Westfield, MA 01086-1308
musicreviews@trumpetguild.org
www.trumpetguild.org
Improves communications among trumpet players around the world.

NewMusicBox
30 W. 26th St. #1001, New York, NY 10010
editor@newmusicbox.org
www.newmusicbox.org
Features any new CD that includes repertoire by American composers.

Online Trombone Journal
PO Box 1758, Starkville, MS 39760
PH: 662-325-8021
articles@trombone.org
www.trombone.org
Provides trombonists a place to share information about trombone pedagogy and performance.

Renaissance Magazine
1 Controls Dr., Shelton, CT 06484
PH: 800-232-2224 FX: 800-775-2729
Kim Guarnaccia editor@renaissancemagazine.com
renaissancemagazine.com
We accept music from the Middle Ages and Renaissance time periods for review.

Sequenza21
340 W. 57th St. 12B, New York, NY 10019
Jerry sequenza21@gmail.com
www.sequenza21.com
News, interviews and featured composers.

Strings Magazine
PO Box 767, San Anselmo, CA 94979
PH: 415-485-6946 FX: 415-485-0831
strings@pcspublink.com
www.stringsmagazine.com
For the violin, viola, cello, bass or fiddle.

Violinist.com
c/o Laurie Niles, 315 S. Sierra Madre Blvd. Ste. C,
Pasadena, CA 91107
PH: 626-376-2755
www.violinist.com
*News, reviews and resources. Feel free to promote
your upcoming concerts or CD releases.*

Web Concert Hall
webconcerthall@usa.com
www.webconcerthall.com
Providing artist with a chance to gain exposure.

World Guitarist
1000 W. Foothill Blvd. Glendora, CA 91741
Gunnar Eisel geisel@citruscollege.edu
www.worldguitarist.com
*Daily news coverage for the world Classical Guitar
community.*

Canada

La Scena Musicale
5409 Waverly, Montréal, QC H2T 2X8
PH: 514-948-2520 FX: 514-274-9456
Réjean Beaucage rbeaucage@scena.org
www.scena.org
Publishes reviews from independent artists.

E u r o p e

Czech Republic

Harmonie
Novákovych 8, 180 00 Praha 8, Czech Republic
PH: 266-311-701 FX: 284-820-127
Jana Vondráková info@muzikus.cz
casopisy.muzikus.cz/harmonie
Classical music and Jazz magazine.

His Voice
Besedni 3 118 00 Praha 1, Czech Republic
PH: 420-257-312-422 FX: 420-257-317-424
redakce@hisvoice.cz
www.hisvoice.cz
Festivals and reviews of contemporary music.

France

Avant-Scène Opéra
15, rue Tiquetonne, 75002 Paris, France
PH: 33-1-42-33-51-51 FX: 33-1-42-33-80-91
premieres.loges@wanadoo.fr
www.asopera.com
Publication for professionals and music-lovers.

naïve classique - andante.com
148, rue du Faubourg Poissonnière, 75010 Paris,
France
infos@andante.com
andante.com
News, reviews, concert reviews, essays and more.

Paris Transatlantic.com
47 rue Richer, 75009 Paris, France
Dan Warburton ptmag@club-internet.fr
www.paristransatlantic.com
*Global coverage of New, Classical and Avant-garde
music.*

Germany

Crescendo
Senefelderstraße 14, 80336 München, Germany
PH: 49-0-89-74-15-09-0 FX: 49-0-89-74-15-09-11
crescendo@portmedia.de
www.crescendo-online.de
Deutschlands Klassik Magazin

klassik.com
Dillenburger Strasse 93, D-51105 Köln, Germany
PH: 49-221-240-3856 FX: 49-221-240-4147
redaktion@klassik.com
www.klassik.com
*Klassik-portal mit umfangreichen Informationen zur
Klassischen musik*

Klassik-Heute.com
Jägerstraße 17, Hörgertshausen, 85413, Germany
PH: 49-0-8764-92-09-42 FX: 49-0-8764-92-09-43
info@klassik-treff.de
www.klassik-heute.com
*Musik, Festival, Konzert, Oper, Künstler, CD,
Komponist.*

Online Muzik Magazin
Westkotter Str. 166, 42277 Wuppertal, Germany
PH: 49-0-202-50-63-22 FX: 49-0-202-50-13-23
www.omm.de
*Das erste deutschsprachige Musikmagazin im
internet.*

Oper&Tanz
Brienner Straße 52, 80333 München, Germany
PH: 0941-94-593-12 FX: 0941-94-593-50
redaktion@operundtanz.de
www.operundtanz.de
Zeitschrift für Opernchor und Bühnentanz.

Das Opernglas
Grelckstraße 36, 22529 Hamburg,. Germany
PH: 040-58-55-01 FX: 040-58-55-05
info@opernglas.de
www.opernglas.de
Reviews and information.

Italy

Hortus Musicus
Piazza di Porta Ravegnana 1 - 40126 Bologna, Italy
PH: 051-239295 FX: 051-239295
website@hortusmusicus.com
www.hortusmusicus.com
Italian Early music magazine.

PromArt
36100 Vicenza, contrà san Pietro 21, Italy
PH: 0444-304992 FX: 0444-314320
promart@promart.it
www.promart.it
News, reviews and an artist database.

The Netherlands

Het ORGEL
redactie@hetorgel.nl
www.hetorgel.nl
Europe's oldest magazine on Organ Art.

Spain

FILOMUSICA Classical music and Opera
Daniel Mateos filomusica@terra.es
www.filomusica.com
*We review all kinds of Classical music, including
independent.*

Goldberg
Polígono Talluntxen, Calle A, Nave 24, 31110
Noain, Navarra, Spain
PH: 34-948-250-372 FX: 34-948-196-276
info@goldberg-magazine.com
www.goldberg-magazine.com
We review only CDs of early music before 1750.

Mundo Clasico
admin@mundoclasico.com
www.mundoclasico.com
Articles, interviews, reviews and news.

Ritmo
10 (Oficina95)-28050, Madrid, Spain
PH: 913588774 FX: 91-3588944
correo@ritmo.es
www.ritmo.es
*Disfrute del mundo de la música clásica desde
internet.*

Sweden

Tidskriften OPERA
Box 4038, 102 61 Stockholm, Sweden
PH: 08-643-95-44 FX: 08-442-11-33
info@tidskriftenopera.nu
md.partitur.se
Sweden's foremost Opera magazine!

Switzerland

HarpEvents Magazine
Dorneckstr. 105, CH-4143 Dornach, Switzerland
PH: 41-61-701-88-58
www.harpa.com
News, announcements, CDs and articles.

Musik & Theater
Postfach 1680, CH-8040 Zürich, Switzerland
PH: 41-1-491-71-88 FX: 41-1-493-11-76
musikundtheater@bluewin.ch
www.musikundtheater.ch
*CD-Besprechungen, Musik, Theater, Oper,
Interviews…*

United Kingdom

BBC Music Magazine
BBC Radio 3, London, W1N 4DJ UK
PH: 087-00-100-100
radio3.website@bbc.co.uk
www.bbc.co.uk/music/classical
www.bbc.co.uk/radio3/classical
CD reviews, interviews, features, news etc.

Brass Band World
4th Fl. 117-119 Portland St., Manchester,
M1 6FB UK
PH: 44-0-1298-812816 FX: 44-0-1298-815220
editor@brassbandworld.com
www.brassbandworld.com
An independent monthly magazine for bands.

Classical Guitar Magazine
1 & 2 Vance Ct. Trans Britannia Enterprise Park,
Blaydon on Tyne, NE21 5NH UK
PH: 44-0-191-414-9000 FX: 44-0-191-414-9001
classicalguitar@ashleymark.co.uk
www.classicalguitarmagazine.com
Features, interviews, news and reviews.

Classical Source
31 Great Queen St., London, WC2B 5AE UK
editor@classicalsource.com
www.classicalsource.com
Providing news and reviews.

ClassicalLink *MusicWeb*
40 Portman Sq. 4ᵗʰ Fl. London, W1H 6LT UK
PH: +44 (0) 20-7486-6300
FX: + (44 0) 20-7935-0922
info@classicall.net
www.classicall.net
*We post about 12 new reviews a day. Also live
Classical concerts, Film music and Jazz.*

Double Bassist
c/o Orpheus Publications, 2ⁿᵈ Fl. 30 Cannon St.,
London, EC4M 6YJ UK
PH: 020-7618-3456, FX: 020-7618-3483
www.doublebassist.com
*The music magazine for double bass teachers,
students, players and makers.*

Horn Magazine
CAF Admin Service (6206) Kings Hill,
West Malling, Kent, ME19 4TA UK
mike@british-horn.org
www.british-horn.org
News, views, reviews and The Hornascope.

International Record Review
1 Haven Green, London, W5 2UU UK
PH: 44-0-20-8810-9050 FX: 44-0-20-8810-9081
info@recordreview.co.uk
www.recordreview.co.uk
Actively seeks out CDs for review.

International Trombone Association Journal
1 Broomfield Rd. Coventry, CV5 6JW UK
www.ita-web.org
Trombone news, gigs and record reviews.

MUSIC & VISION
Flat D, 25 Oxford Rd. Ealing, London, W5 3SP UK
PH: +44 (0)20-8840-1564
www.mvdaily.com
*Encouraging and educating young writers about
serious music.*

New Notes
4ᵗʰ Fl. St Margaret's House, 18-20 Southwark St.,
London, SE1 1TJ UK
PH: 020-7407-1640
spnm@spnm.org.uk
www.spnm.org.uk
Promoting new music!

Opera Magazine
36 Black Lion Ln. London, W6 9BE UK
PH: +44 (0)20-8563-8893 FX: +44 (0)20-8563-8635
editor@opera.co.uk
www.opera.co.uk
News, letters, interviews, reviews and more.

Seen and Heard
Marc Bridle SeenandHeard@BTOpenworld.com
www.musicweb.uk.net/SandH
The largest live music review site on the web.

The Strad
PO Box 935, Finchingfield, Braintree, Essex,
CM74LN UK
PH: 44-01371-810433 FX: 44-01371-811065
Peter Quantrill pquantrill@orpheuspublications.com
www.thestrad.com
We review CDs of string music and string musicians.

The Trombonist
1 Broomfield Rd. Coventry, CV5 6JW UK
FX: 44-24-7671-2550
www.trombone-society.org.uk
The magazine of the British Trombone Society.

Australia

Opera~Opera
PO Box R-361, Royal Exchange, NSW 1225
Australia
PH: 61-2-92472264 FX: 61-2-92472269
deg@opera-opera.com.au
www.opera-opera.com.au
*We certainly have no qualms about reviewing
releases emanating from independent quarters.*

New Zealand

The Opera Critic
PO Box 99826, Newmarket, Auckland, NZ
PH: 64-9-525-3996
theoperacritic.com
Reviews, articles and news about opera worldwide.

Asia

CLASSICA JAPAN
iio@tka.att.ne.jp
www.classicajapan.com
Classical music news and links.

Country

*Country, C&W, Americana, Bluegrass, Roots,
Honky Tonk, Alt-Country, Old-Timey and
Rockabilly*

North America

United States

3ʳᵈ COAST MUSIC
237 W. Mandalay Dr. San Antonio, TX 78212
PH: 210-820-3748
John Conquest john@3rdcoastmusic.com
www.3rdcoastmusic.com
I ONLY review Indie releases!

Americana Roots
roots@AmericanaRoots.com
www.americanaroots.com
*If you have a production quality CD (able to sell in
a store) we will review it.*

AngryCountry.com
angrycountry.com
*All Country music related genres are covered
including Bluegrass, Texas Country and Christian
Country.*

Blue Suede News
Box 25E, Duvall, WA 98019
PH: 425-788-2776
shakinboss@aol.com
www.bluesuedenews.com
*We cover the entire spectrum of American Roots
music.*

The Bluegrass Blog
thebluegrassblog.com
*News, interviews and reviews. Send in your news
item, press release, radio update etc.*

Bluegrass Music Profiles
PO Box 850, Nicholasville, KY 40340-0850
PH: 859-333-6465
Kevin Kerfoot info@bluegrassmusicprofiles.com
www.bluegrassmusicprofiles.com
Gettin' personal with Bluegrass music artists!

bluegrass now
PO Box 2020, Rolla, MO 65402
PH: 573-341-7336 FX: 573-341-7352
Deb Bledose bgn@fidnet.com
www.bluegrassnow.com
Reviews, interviews, profiles and more!

Bluegrass Rules
c/o Gary Cook, RR 1, PO Box 112E, Lebanon,
VA 24266
www.bluegrassrules.com
Submit your new release for review.

Bluegrass Unlimited
PO Box 771, Warrenton, VA 20188-0771
PH: 540-349-8181 FX: 540-341-0011
editor@bluegrassmusic.com
www.bluegrassmusic.com
*Promotes Bluegrass and Old-time Country
musicians.*

Bluegrass Works
31 Oakdale Ave. Weston, MA 02493
admin@bluegrassworks.com
www.bluegrassworks.com
*Supports the musicians and other fans who help
make the music.*

BluegrassAmericana.com
PO Box 5202, Concord, NC 28027-5202
PH: 704-788-6789
submissions@GoAmericana.com
www.AmericanaConnect.com
We invite you to send your CDs for review.

Country Interviews Online
PO Box 558, Smyrna, TN 37167
PH: 815-361-3172 FX: 309-273-3965
L. Megan countryinterviewsonline@comcast.net
www.CountryInterviewsOnline.net
*Reviews & interviews with major & Indie label
artists.*

Indie Islands Country Monthly
6470 Glenway Ave. #292, Cincinnati,
OH 45211-5222
TJ Walsh contact@indieislands.com
www.indieislands.com
*We are looking for Country music artists to do
interviews with.*

Country Line Magazine
16150 S. IH-35, Buda, TX 78610
PH: 512-295-8400 FX: 512-295-8600
T.J. Greaney tj@countrylinemagazine.com
www.countrylinemagazine.com
*We are about Country music, born in Texas or
raised in Nashville.*

Country Standard Time
54 Ballard St., Newton Ctr., MA 02459-1251
PH: 617-969-0331
Jeffrey B. Remz countryst@aol.com
countrystandardtime.com
Your guide to Roadhouse, Roots and Rockabilly.

Cybergrass
520 Carved Ter. Colorado Springs, CO 80919
www.cybergrass.com
*News about Bluegrass music, artists and the music
business. Promote your shows!*

Flatpicking Guitar
PO Box 2160, Pulaski, VA 24301
PH: 540-980-0338 FX: 540-980-0557
info@flatpick.com
www.flatpick.com
Presenting the art of flat picking the Acoustic guitar.

Freight Train Boogie
PO Box 4262, Santa Rosa, CA 95402
Bill Frater frater@freighttrainboogie.com
www.freighttrainboogie.com
News and reviews of Roots music.

Hillbilly-Music.com
PO Box 576245, Modesto, CA 95357-6245
Dave webmaster@hillbilly-music.com
www.hillbilly-music.com
We can't promise we'll review everything, but we'll try.

iBluegrass
203 Passage Gate Way, Wilmington, NC 28412
PH: 910-221-9474
Skip Ogden cwo@ibest.net
www.ibluegrass.com
We will accept unsolicited material for review. Check our site for submission details.

Mandolin Magazine
PO Box 13537, Salem, OR 97309
PH: 503-364-2100 FX: 503-588-7707
www.mandolinmagazine.com
We review CDs, books, videos and instruments.

My Kind of Country
100 Sherri Ln. Powhatan Point, OH 44001
Marlene Slater marli@mkoc.com
www.mkoc.com
Country music at its finest.

No Depression
2 Morse Cir. Durham, NC 27713
Peter Blackstock peter@nodepression.net
www.nodepression.net
Covers Alt-Country music (whatever that is).

Old-Time Herald Online
PO Box 51812, Durham, NC 27707
PH: 919-419-1800 FX: 919-419-1881
info@oldtimeherald.org
www.oldtimeherald.org
Celebrates the love of Old-Time music.

Rockabilly Magazine
PO Box 19712, Austin, TX 78760
PH: 888-516-0707 FX: 512-385-4300
Orlando orios@rockabillymagazine.com
www.rockabillymagazine.com
The ultimate source for Rockabilly info.

Roots Music Report
13501 Ranch Rd. 12 #103-327, Wimberley, TX 78676
PH: 877-532-2225
rmr@rootsmusicreport.com
Robert Bartosh rmr@rootsmusicreport.com
www.rootsmusicreport.com
Reviews and articles on Roots music and artists.

Roughstock
rodeo@roughstock.com
www.Roughstock.com
News, reviews, interviews, charts.

TOSSM MUSIC
5605 David Strickland Rd. Fort Worth, TX 76119
Philip Corder philip@tossmmusic.com
www.tossmmusic.com
Home for Texas and Red Dirt music and independent musicians. Reviews, interviews and Artist of the Month.

Western Beat
PO Box 128105, Nashville, TN 37212
PH: 615-248-5026 FX: 615-248-3067
Billy Block billy@westernbeat.com
www.westernbeat.com
A place where musical integrity rules.

Canada

Country Music News
Box 7323, Vanier Stn. Ottawa, ON K1L 8E4
PH: 613-745-6006 FX: 613-745-0576
Larry Delaney larry@countrymusicnews.ca
www.countrymusicnews.ca
Canada's national Country music publication. Now in its 27th year!!

Fiddler Magazine
PO Box 101, N. Sydney, NS B2A 3M1
PH: 902-794-2558
info@fiddle.com
www.fiddle.com
Feature articles, regular columns and more.

Take Country Back
Box 904, Cranbrook, BC V1C 6W4
PH: 250-417-0085
Laurie Joulie laurie@takecountryback.com
www.takecountryback.com
We're very Indie friendly! Americana, Classic and Alt-Country, Bluegrass, Honky Tonk etc.

Europe
Belgium

Rootstime
Generaal De Wittestraat 11, 3545 Halen, Belgium
Freddy Celis rootstime@mail.com
www.rootstime.be
We promote Blues & Roots, Singer/Songwriters, Roots Rock, Americana, Country, Rockabilly, Cajun & Zydeco music.

France

Country Music France
63, rue Victor Hugo, BP 30, 94701 Maisons Alfort, France
pierre@countryfr.com
country-music-france.com
French directory about Bluegrass, Old-Time, Traditional and New Country.

Germany

Country Jukebox
Th. Dombart - Str. 5, 80805 München, Germany
Max W. Achatz info@countryjukebox.de
www.countryjukebox.de
Published monthly in Germany's Country Circle magazine as well as on the web.

CountryHome
Maiselsberger Str. 5, D-84416 Taufkirchen/Vils, Germany
PH: 08084-9166 FX: 08084-9165
iwde@iwde.de
www.countryhome.de
Das online magazin freier fachjournalisten.

The Netherlands

Alt Country NL
dutchtwang@yahoo.com
www.altcountry.nl
Er voor liefhebbers van Americana en Rootsmuziek.

United Kingdom

Americana UK
29 Avonmore Ave. Liverpool, L18 8AL UK
www.americana-uk.com
UK home for Americana, Alt-Country and "No Depression" music. CDs only please. No CDRs or demos.

Country Music People
1-3 Love Ln. London, SE18 6QT UK
PH: 44-020-8854-7217 FX: 44-020-8855-6370
info@countrymusicpeople.com
www.countrymusicpeople.com
Reviews of latest CDs, features and interviews.

Country Music Roundup
PO Box 111, Waltham, Grimsby, DN37 0YN UK
PH: 01522-750150 FX: 01472-821808
countrymusic_ru@hotmail.com
www.cmru.co.uk
Keep up to date on the British Country music scene.

Fiddle On
4 Lee Close, Kidlington, Oxford, OX5 2XZ UK
PH: 01865-374624
Jed Mugford jed@fiddleon.co.uk
www.fiddleon.co.uk
A publication for the UK fiddle players.

Maverick
24 Bray Gardens, Maidstone, Kent, ME15 9TR UK
editor@maverick-country.com
www.maverick-country.com
Changing how Country music is perceived in the UK.

Metro Country
444 Manchester Rd. Astley, Tyldesley, Manchester, M29 7BT UK
Ray Grundy ray@metrocountry.co.uk
www.metrocountry.co.uk
Contact to get your CD reviewed and featured.

Australia

Capital News Country Music
2-6 Lockheed St., PO Box 3520, Tamworth, NSW 2340 Australia
PH: 02-6762-2399 FX: 02-6762 2350
capitalnews@ruralpress.com
www.capitalnews.com.au
Monthly magazine devoted to Country music in Australia.

Dance and Electronic
North America
United States

danceblogga
Dennis Romero chp@earthlink.net
www.dancemusic.blogspot.com
Dance music news and criticism.

DJ Times
25 Willowdale Ave. Port Washington, NY 11050
PH: 516-767-2500 FX: 516-767-9335
Jim Tremayne jtremayne@testa.com
www.djtimes.com
Considered the "bible of the industry" for the professional DJ.

djsinbox.com
807 S. Howard Ave. #211, Tampa, FL 33606
PH: 813-679-4422
Mark Kovach djsinbox@hotmail.com
djsinbox.com
The latest on today's cutting edge music.

Electrocore
PH: 918-852-7973
Andy Khouri andy@electrocore.com
www.electrocore.com
*Your avenue for information on everything
Electroclash / Disko Punk / Electro.*

Faize
info@faizemusic.com
www.faizemusic.com
House and Garage music magazine.

Igloo Magazine!
PO Box 307, Corona, CA 92878
Pietro Da Sacco editor@igloomag.com
www.igloomag.com
Online source for Electronic music coverage.

Iron Feather Journal
PO Box 1905, Boulder, CO 80306
stevyn@ironfeather.com
www.ironfeather.com
*A wicked mega magazine about the subversive HI-
TEK underground, Techno + Jungle scenes.*

Jive Magazine
PO Box 2635, Lilburn, GA 30048
www.jivemagazine.com
*Extensive review section, events and more! Check
our site for submission details.*

Pax Acidus
312 Harvard Ave. E. #105, Seattle, WA 90102
PH: 206-349-1514
www.paxacidus.com
Website for the underground arts of sight and sound.

Progressive Sounds
126 N. Charlotte St., Lancaster, PA 17603
www.progressive-sounds.com
Bringing you the latest in Progressive Trance.

Raves.com
Jennifer Warner jennifer@raves.com
www.raves.com
News, reviews, profiles, shows etc.

Sonic Curiosity
PO Box 28325, Philadelphia, PA 19149
Matt Howarth matt@soniccuriosity.com
www.soniccuriosity.com
Alternative/Electronic music review site.

Canada

Klublife Magazine
1 First Canadian Pl. 37th Fl. Toronto, ON M5X 1K7
PH: 416-644-8681 FX: 416-644-8684
info@klublife.com
www.klublife.com
Up to date music reviews and articles.

Tribe Magazine
PO Box 65053, 358 Danforth Ave. Toronto,
ON M4K 3Z2
PH: 416-778-4115
Alex Dordevic editor@tribe.ca
www.tribemagazine.com
Inspired by the people who go out after dark.

E u r o p e

Belgium

Beyondjazz
Lange Boomgaardstraat 114a, B-9000 Gent,
Belgium
Lennart Schoors office@beyondjazz.net
www.beyondjazz.net
*A Future Jazz community, focusing on the exciting
sounds of Broken Beats, Future Jazz and Space
Funk.*

Estonia

Club Arena
www.clubarena.com
Promos will be reverberated.

Finland

Findance
PH: 040-739-2270
Antti Niemelä antti.niemela@findance.com
www.findance.com
Enimmäkseen muuta kuin kotimaista konemusiikkia.

France

Atome
atome@atome.com
www.atome.com
*Send us your charts, promo-copies, demos, news,
presents.*

IN DA MIX WORLDWIDE
98, rue de Paris, F-94220 Charenton, France
Frederic 'MFSB' Messent
mfsb@indamixworldwide.com
www.indamixworldwide.com
*Send your material (test pressings, vinyl, 12", LP,
CD, CDR) to the above address.*

Novaplanet.com
33, rue du Faubourg Saint Antoine, 75011 Paris,
France
PH: 01-53-33-33-00
redaction@novaplanet.com
www.novaplanet.com
News and reviews.

Yet Another Electro-Webzine?
www.yaew.com
Electronic music news, reviews and interviews.

Germany

BreakBeatz.de
Westerladekop 86a, 21635 Jork, Germany
PH: 0-41-62-91-32-63
www.breakbeatz.de
Your Drum and Bass e-zine.

Couchsurfer.de
Lipowskystr. 4, 81373 Munich, Germany
Michael Kienzler mk@couchsurfer.de
www.couchsurfer.de
*A club culture portal. Send us your promos & mix-
CDs for review.*

Groove
Choriner Straße 82, 10119 Berlin, Germany
PH: 030-44-31-20-22 FX: 030-44-31-20-70
Thilo Schneider thilo@groove.de
www.groove.de
Reviews Electronica, Techno, House etc.

House-Beats.de
mail@house-beats.de
www.house-beats.de
Deutschlands Housemusic community!

Motor
Brunnenstr. 24, 10119 Berlin, Germany
PH: 030-74-7777 FX: 030-74-777-999
webmaster@motor.de
www.motor.de
News, releases, tours, reviews etc.

Samplepoolz
Hollenweg 48, 41515 Grevenbroich, Germany
PH: 0211-58004781
Marc redaktion@samplepoolz.de
www.samplepoolz.de
*Join up and submit your reviews (don't send in your
CD - we don't have the manpower to write extra
reviews).*

Techno Online
Grevener Damm 260, 48282 Emsdetten, Germany
PH: 02572-960690 FX: 02572-9606999
Mirko Seifert info@techno.de
www.techno.de
News, reviews, charts, interviews etc.

Italy

Clubbity.com - The Safe Club Culture Site
www.clubbity.com
*News, reviews, interviews. Most of the music we
promote is by independent artists.*

Disco ID
PH: 39-0541-307333 FX: 39-0541-307335
info@discoid.it
www.discoid.it
Reviews, regular columns, charts etc.

Norway

i:Vibes
Stream stream@ivibes.nu
www.ivibes.nu
*Reviews of all the latest Trance and Electronica
tunes. Interviews with the biggest DJs.*

Portugal

The Connexion Bizarrre
agenda@connexionbizarre
www.connexionbizarre.net
*Electronic music from Synthpop to Noise, touching
everything in between..*

Russia

jungle.ru
info@jungle.ru
www.jungle.ru
News, reviews, artist bio, streaming radio and more.

Sweden

trance.nu
Macman ralf@staff.trance.nu
trance.nu
The biggest Trance community on Earth!

United Kingdom

Blackout Audio
Mark EG info@blackoutaudio.co.uk
www.blackoutaudio.co.uk
Reviews and interviews of new sounds.

Dancemuzik.com
webmaster@dancemuzik.com
www.dancemuzik.com
News, reviews, features etc.

| deephousenetwork |
27 Arasain Na Mara, Lower Salthill, Galway,
Ireland
www.deephousenetwork.com
*Download, mixes, reviews, tracks, charts,
community.*

DJmag
Highbury Lifestyle, Jordan House, 47 Brunswick Pl.
London, N1 6EB UK
PH: 44-0-20-7331-1148 FX: 44-0-20-7331-1115
Helene Stokes editors@djmag.com
www.djmag.com/reviewers.php
Up-front coverage of the Dance music scene.

DogsOnAcid
84 Cavendish Rd. Colliers Wood, London,
SW19 2EU UK
James Shaw james@dogsonacid.com
www.dogsonacid.com
*The world's largest Drum & Bass and Jungle
message board and forum with news, reviews, audio
etc.*

Drum n' Bass Arena
103 Gaunt St., London, SE1 6DP UK
PH: +44 (0) 20-7740-8816
FX: +44 (0) 207-403-5348
info@lists.breakbeat.co.uk
www.breakbeat.co.uk
The latest info on everything to do with D n' B.

Epidemik
PO Box 5180, Chelmsford, Essex, CM3 3QF UK
PH: 07966-491554
Grant Epidemik grant@epidemik.com
www.epidemik.net
Then let them come to you by promoting yourself!

Jon Freer *(Freelance Reviewer)*
14 Flaggwood Ave. Marple, Stockport, Cheshire,
SK6 6HP UK
info@mosoul.co.uk
www.mosoul.co.uk
*I write reviews for magazines such as Blues & Soul,
XLR8R, City Life, Inner Loop, littleplanet.net,
pitchadjust.com, beyondjazz.net,
deephousenetwork.com and skansen.no. I review
everything 'Dance'.*

M8 Magazine
Trojan House, Phoenix Business Pk. Paisley,
PA1 2BH UK
PH: 0141-840-5980 FX: 0141-840-5995
Kevin McFarlane kevin@m8magazine.com
www.m8magazine.com
The latest music reviews and news.

Ministry of Sound
103 Gaunt St., London, SE1 8DP UK
PH: 44-0-20-7740-8600 FX: 44-0-20-7403-5348
arnie@ministryofsound.com
www.ministryofsound.com
Reviews of Dance albums and singles.

mixmag
90/92 Pentonville Rd. London, N1 9HS UK
PH: +207-520-8625 FX: +207 7833 9900
mixmag@mixmag.net
www.mixmag.net
The world's biggest selling clubbing magazine.

Nubreaks.com
e@nubreaks.com
www.nubreaks.com
Helps you get your DJ mix online.

Planetdnb
2nd Fl. 207 Cranbrook Rd. Ilford, Essex,
LG1 4TD UK
PH: 44-0-20-8554-4043 FX: 44-0-20-8554-4043
Andy Rayner mail@planetdnb.com
www.planetdnb.com
One of the leading D n' B resource sites.

Tunes.co.uk
Unit 3E, Oslo House, West Wing, Felstead St.,
London, E9 5LG UK
PH: +44(0)20 8985 8700 FX: +44(0)20 8985 2333
info@tunes.co.uk
www.tunes.co.uk
*Dance music from Soul & Funk to House & Breaks:
reviews, real audio & worldwide mail order.*

Australia

12AM.com.au
PO Box 1212, Windsor, VIC 3181 Australia
12am@12am.com.au
www.12am.com.au
DJ and club e-zine for VIC and NSW.

Resident Advisor
www.residentadvisor.com.au
*Australian/Global Dance news, interviews and
reviews.*

TransZfusion
Level 2, Building 10, 658 Church St., Richmond,
VIC 3121 Australia
www.tranzfusion.net
Trusted voice in Electronica.

Experimental

*Experimental, Electronic, Ambient, Avant-garde,
Noise etc.*

North America

United States

Ambient.us
PO Box 5, Sealston, VA 22547-0005
Dodds Wiley dodds@ambient.us
www.ambient.us
*A positive energy Ambient music guide. Contact me
by e-mail if you would like a review.*

aural innovations
1364 W. 7th Ave. Apt. B, Columbus, OH 43212
Jerry Kranitz jkranitz@aural-innovations.com
aural-innovations.com
Includes Psychedelia and related Electronic music.

Calculated Sound
www.myspace.com/calculatedsound
*Zine and a label dealing with "Experimental
Electronic music". Breakcore, IDM, Glitch, Noise,
Ambient, 8-bit etc.*

The Circular Cosmic Spot
Art Grauer rpt1700@gmail.com
www.myspace.com/cosmicscott
*Electronic/Experimental music reviews and news I
will also accept MP3s for review.*

disquiet.com
marc@disquiet.com
www.disquiet.com
Interviews Ambient/Electronic musicians.

Dream Magazine
PO Box 2027, Nevada City, CA 95959-1941
George Parsons geo@gv.net
www.dreamgeo.com
*Psychedelic (old and new), Experimental, Pop, Jazz,
Folk and more.*

Electro-music.com
944 Flexer Ave. Allentown, PA 18103
admin@electro-music.com
electro-music.com
*Experimental, Electro-Acoustic and Electronic
music.*

Free City Media
90 North Ave. #2C, San Rafael, CA 94903
Heidi@FreeCityMedia.com
www.freecitymedia.com
Psychedelic music and fresh perspectives.

Get Underground
Shlomo Sher sher@getunderground.com
www.getunderground.com
*Writings and arts related to personal impressions
and Experimental visions.*

Innerviews
PO Box 192966, San Francisco, CA 94119-2966
www.innerviews.org
Music without borders.

Modsquare
modsquare@gmail.com
www.modsquare.com
*Arts journal covering the most innovative
developments within Electronic music and its
culture.*

MusicEmissions.com
info@musicemissions.com
www.musicemissions.com
*A music review site that focuses on non-mainstream
music.*

Neumu
PO Box 1948, Sonoma, CA 95476
contact@neumu.net
neumu.net
*Find the work of artists following their creative
vision.*

Ptolemaic Terrascope
PO Box 18841, Oakland, CA 94619-8841
Pat Thomas normalsf@earthlink.net
www.terrascope.org
Unearthing Psychedelic/Folk nuggets.

SIGNAL to NOISE
1128 Waverly St., Houston, TX 77008
Pete Gershon
operations@signaltonoisemagazine.org
www.signaltonoisemagazine.org
The journal of Improvised and Experimental music.

Squid's Ear
160 Bennett Ave. #6K, New York, NY 10040
Kurt Gottschalk kurt@squidco.com
www.squidsear.com
*Experimental, Improvisation, Avant-garde and
unusual musical styles.*

Synthmuseum.com
28 Grenville Rd. Watertown, MA 02472
PH: 617-926-2298
jay@synthmuseum.com
www.synthmuseum.com
Our magazine features reviews of Synth music.

(((Thump))) Radio
FX: 636-216-7865
info@thumpradio.com
www.thumpradio.com
Exposing local talent around the world.

XLR8R
1388 Haight St. #105, San Francisco, CA 94117
Attn: Ken Taylor
PH: 415-861-7583 FX: 415-861-7584
www.xlr8r.com
Over 100 color pages. Internationally distributed.

Canada

Computer Music Journal
School of Fine Art and Music, MacKinnon 214,
U. Guelph, Guelph, ON N1G 2W1
James Harley cmj-reviews@mitpress.mit.edu
mitpress.mit.edu/e-journals/Computer-Music-Journal
Covers digital audio signal processing and Electro Acoustic music. When contacting, include "CMJ" in your Subject line.

musicworks
358-401 Richmond St. W. Toronto, ON M5V 3A8
PH: 416-977-3546 FX: 416-977-4181
sound@musicworks.ca
www.musicworks.ca
Exploration of new music and sound.

Europe

Belgium

l'entrepot
Mesesstraat 6, 2300 Turnhout, Belgium
Tom Wilms tom.wilks@skynet.be
users.skynet.be/entrepot
Resource center for unconventional tunes.

SIDE-LINE
90 rue Charles Degroux, 1040 Brussels, Belgium
PH/FX: 0032-2-732-14-81
info@side-line.com
www.side-line.com
Magazine on the Underground genre.

France

Guts of Darkness
contact@gutsofdarkness.com
www.gutsofdarkness.com
Les archives du sombre et de l'expérimental.

Germany

de:bug
Schwedter Str. 8/9, Haus 9A, 10119 Berlin,
Germany
PH: 030-2838 4458 FX: 030-2838-4459
www.de-bug.de
News and reviews.

dense
Reichenberger Str. 147, 10999 Berlin, Germany
PH: +49 (0)30-616-529-60
FX: +49 (0)30-616-529-46
www.dense.de
Founded in order to promote sound visionaries.
Please CONTACT US before you send material.

Dominion Club
Karl-Schmidt-Str. 26-29, 39104 Magdeburg,
Germany
PH: 0391-4018892 FX: 0391-4082899
info@dominionclub.de
www.dominionclub.de
Events, reviews, news, interview and more.

NMZ
www.nmz.de
*News, reviews, rezensionen, kulturpolitik,
musicwirtschaft, musikforen…*

re.fleXion
Zum Hasenkamp 8, 31552, Rodenberg, Germany
www.re-flexion.de
*Neuigkeiten, kritiken, interviews, kozerte, termine,
bands etc.*

spex
Rolandstrasse 69, 50677 Koln, Germany
PH: 0221-579-7800 FX: 0221-579-7879
www.spex.de
News and reviews.

synthetics
Enzianweg 7, 41836 Huckelhoven, Germany
PH: 02433-95-99-808 FX: 0721-151201169
micha@synthiepop.de
www.synthiepop.de
BODY and SOUL come together.

Westzeit
Holger Seeling, Bahnhofstr. 6, 41334 Nettetal,
Germany
PH: 02157-3858 FX: 02157-1760
info@westzeit.de
www.westzeit.de
Pop auf draht-musik, literatur, kunst und film.

Italy

Neural
a.ludovico@neural.it
www.neural.it
New media art and Electronic music.

The Netherlands

Alfa Report
www.alfacentauri.nl
Leading magazine on Synthesizer based music.

E-dition Magazine
Postbus 2171, 8203 AD Lelystad, The Netherlands
info@e-ditionmag.com
www.e-ditionmag.com
*We will try to review ALL incoming types of
Electronic music.*

United Kingdom

Computer Music
30 Monmouth St., Bath, BA1 2BW UK
PH: 01225-442244 FX: 01225-732353
Ronan MacDonald
ronan.macdonald@futurenet.co.uk
www.computermusic.co.uk
Reviews of the latest gear/news as it happens.

DOT:ALT
xvscott@dot-alt.co.uk
dot-alt.co.uk
Covers progressive, creative music.

Future Music
30 Monmouth St., Bath, BA1 2BW UK
PH: 01225-442244 FX: 01225-732353
andy.jones@futurenet.co.uk
futuremusic.co.uk
Making music at the cutting edge of technology.

Robots and Electric Brains
133 Green End Rd. Cambridge, CB4 1RW UK
Jimmy Possession rebzine@hotmail.com
www.robotsandelectronicbrains.co.uk
*Eclectic zine for music with that extra something
special.*

The Wire
23 Jack's Pl. 6 Corbet Pl. London, E1 6NN UK
PH: +44 (0)20-7422-5014 FX: +44 (0)20-7422-5011
Nick Cain nick@thewire.co.uk
www.thewire.co.uk
*Electronica, Breakbeat, Avant Rock, Free Jazz,
Classical, Global and beyond.*

Australia

Cyclic Defrost
PO Box A2073, Sydney South, NSW 1235 Australia
Sebastian and Dale info@cyclicdefrost.com
www.cyclicdefrost.com
*We cover independent Electronic music, Avant-Rock,
Experimental Sound Art and left field Hip Hop.*

Folk

*Folk, Celtic, Singer/Songwriter, Roots, Acoustic,
Traditional, Maritime*

North America

United States

Acoustic Guitar Magazine
PO Box 767, San Anselmo, CA 94979
PH: 415-485-6946 FX: 415-485-0831
editors.ag@stringletter.com
www.acousticguitar.com
*We only review recordings with widespread
distribution or an established internet distribution
channel.*

CDReviews.com
144 Mead Ln. Middlebury, VT, 05753
Cindy Hill wordwomanvt@yahoo.com
www.cdreviews.com
I do reviews of Folk, Celtic, World and Opera.

Celtic Beat
4 Greenlay St., Nashua, NH 03063
PH: 603-880-3706
celt56@aol.com
www.mv.com/ipusers/celticbeat
Concert and CD reviews galore!

Dirty Linen
PO Box 66600, Baltimore, MD 21239-6600
PH: 410-583-7973 FX: 410-337-6735
info@dirtylinen.com
www.DirtyLinen.com
We welcome submission of audio Roots music.

eFolkMusic
artists@efolkMusic.org
www.efolkmusic.org
*Traditional and Contemporary Folk music from
around the world.*

Folk & Acoustic Music Exchange
82 Leadmine Rd. Nelson, NH 03457
David N. Pyles dnpyles@acousticmusic.com
www.acousticmusic.com/fame/famehome.htm
Submit recordings and artist bio for review.

folklinks.com
David W. Johnson djohnson@ehc.edu
www.folklinks.com
*Web presence for Folk and Acoustic music
performers.*

Folkwax
www.folkwax.com
Weekly Folk music e-zine with reviews.

Green Man Review
82 Rackleff St., Portland, ME 04103
Kim Bates kim@greenmanreview.com
www.greenmanreview.com
*Focus on Folk music in all its aspects. You must
send 2 copies of each CD that you want reviewed.*

Kevin's Celtic & Folk Music CD Reviews
Kevin McCarthy celticfolkmusic@icogitate.com
www.icogitate.com/~celticfolkmusic
Reviewing Celtic, UK Folk and Folk music CDs.

Minor 7th
PO Box 468, Manistee, MI 49660-0468
alan@minor7th.com
www.minor7th.com
*Your CD must prominently feature acoustic guitar
and be a recent release.*

Puremusic
1600 17th Ave. S. Nashville, TN 37212
Frank Goodman frank@puremusic.com
www.puremusic.com
Bringing great music to the masses.

Rambles
1609 Ridgeview Ave. Lancaster, PA 17603
Tom Knapp editor@rambles.net
www.rambles.net
Folk & Traditional music.

Sing Out!
PO Box 5460, Bethlehem, PA 18015
PH: 610-865-5366 FX: 610-865-5129
info@singout.org
www.singout.org
*Articles and interviews, tons of recording and book
reviews.*

thedigitalfolklife.org
John McLaughlin john-mclaughlin@comcast.net
www.thedigitalfolklife.org
Folk interviews, CD and show reviews.

Canada

Celtic Heritage
PO Box 8805, Stn. A, Halifax, NS B3K 5M4
PH: 902-835-6244 FX: 902-835-0080
Alexa Thompson editorial@celticheritage.ns.ca
celticheritage.ns.ca
*Includes reviews of the latest in Celtic music,
including independent labels.*

Independent Reviewer - Paul Emile Comeau
PO Box 142, Saulnierville, NS B0W 2Z0
PH: 902-769-3288
pcm.comeau@ns.sympatico.ca
*I do reviews for Dirty Linen, Penguin Eggs, Global
Rhythm, No Depression, Goldmine and more! I
Review Roots music in a wide sense of the word.*

Penguin Eggs
10942 80th Ave. Edmonton, AB T6G 0R1
PH: 780-433-8287 FX: 780-437-4603
penguineggs@shaw.ca
www.penguineggs.ab.ca
Canada's Folk, Roots and World music magazine.

Europe
France

Trad Magazine
BP 27, 62350 Saint Venant, France
PH: 03-21-02-52-52 FX: 03-21-27-16-70
tradmag@wanadoo.fr
www.tradmagazine.com
*Französisches magazin für Folk und Traditionelle
musik.*

Germany

Folker!
Postfach 1269, 53582 Bad Honnef, Germany
PH: 02224-76510 FX: 02224-71464
info@folker.de
www.folker.de
Das deutsche musikmagazin. Folk, Blues, Cajun ...

FolkWorld
editors@folkworld.de
www.folkworld.de
Contributions from you are welcome!

The Netherlands

Newfolksounds
info@newfolksounds.nl
www.newfolksounds.nl
*Een Nederlands tijdschrift dat één keer in de twee
maanden verschijnt.*

The Real Roots Café
Lincolnstraat 2, 6566 CT Millingen aan de Rijn,
The Netherlands
Jan Janssen rrc@realrootscafe.com
www.realrootscafe.com
*Promotes fabulous American Roots music
musicians.*

United Kingdom

BBC Folk and Acoustic Page
www.bbc.co.uk/radio2/folk
Info, news, reviews, radio, events and more.

Celtic Ways
'Murhy', Keash, Ballymote, Co. Sligo, Ireland
PH: 353-71-918-9377
John Willmott john@celticways.com
celticways.com
*MP3s of Celtic, Folk, World Fusion and World
Tradition music. Free services.*

Folk and Roots
folkandroots@aol.com
www.folkandroots.co.uk
Gigs, reviews, interview featured artists and more.

Folk Roots
PO Box 337, London, N4 1TW UK
PH: 44-020-8340-9651 FX: 44-020-8348-5626
froots@frootsmag.com
www.frootsmag.com
Roots, Folk and World music magazine.

Folking.com
PH: +44 (0) 7956-430-221
Darren Beech folkmaster@folking.com
www.folking.com
Album/gig reviews, CD of the month, MP3s.

RootsMusic.co.uk
PO Box 23911, London, E12 5TD UK
PH/FX: 020-8553-1435
reviews@rootsmusic.co.uk
rootsmusic.co.uk
*Bringing you some the best new and undiscovered
Roots and Acoustic artists.*

Tradition Magazine
9 Burwash, Witnesham, Ipswich Suffolk,
IP6 9EL UK
paul@salmonp56.fsnet.co.uk
www.traditionmagazine.com
Magazine for world custom and tradition.

Trad Music / Music Maker Magazine
28 Grafton Terrace, London, NW5 4JJ UK
PH: 020-7424-0027
Brian Healey tradmusic@btinternet.com
www.tradmusic.net
*Dedicated to the promotion of independent labels,
songwriters & performers. Folk to Country, Rock,
Jazz and World music.*

Australia

Trad&Now
PO Box 17, Albion Park, NSW 2527 Australia
PH: 02-4225-3792 FX: 02-4229-9368
David De Santi david@tradandnow.com
www.tradandnow.com
*Promotes Traditional and Contemporary Folk
music.*

GLBT

365Gay.com
editor@365Gay.com
www.365gay.com/entertainment/MusicChannel/
Musicchannel.htm
*CD reviews and artist profiles are covered in the
music section.*

Chicago Free Press
c/o Gregg Shapiro, 3845 N. Broadway 2nd Fl.
Chicago, IL 60613
gregg1959@aol.com
www.chicagofreepress.com
*I also write for several other publications including
afterelton.com, HX (NYC), Bay Area Reporter (SF),
The Bottom Line (Palm Springs), In Newsweekly
(Boston), Outsmart Magazine (Houston) and many
others!*

Curve Magazine
1479 S. 4th St. #3B, Louisville, KY 40208
PH: 502-636-5194
Margaret Coble "DJ Mags" djmags@gmail.com
www.djmags.com
*Currently my main gig is with Curve Magazine
(though i occasionally still freelance for The
Advocate and Lesbianation.com), so female,
lesbian/bi and trans Indie artists of any genre can
submit their press kits/CDs to me.*

Freelance Reviewer - Jason Victor Serinus
PO Box 3073, Oakland, CA 94609-0073
Jason Victor Serinus healrmn@planeteria.net
www.jasonserinus.com
*Writes and reviews for gay, alternative, New Age
and audiophile publications nationwide.*

gayhiphop.com
mistermaker mister@gayhiphop.com
www.gayhiphop.com
Promoting and featuring both gay and regular artists from the urban scenes around the world equally.

Girlfriends Magazine
3181 Mission St., PMB 30, San Francisco, CA 94110
PH: 415-648-9464
staff@girlfriendsmag.com
www.girlfriendsmag.com
A national monthly magazine for lesbians. We review all kinds of music by women.

Pride Christian Music
PO Box 1083, Farmington, MI 48332
PH: 386-290-3795
email@pridechristianmusic.org
www.pridechristianmusic.org
A FREE networking resource for singers, musicians, & music industry professionals to communicate.

Queerpunks.com
Adam@punkk.com
www.queerpunks.com
Add your news, CD and show reviews etc. Covers Punk and all other Alternative genres.

Velvetpark Magazine
PO Box. 60248, Brooklyn, NY 11206-0248
Kelly McCartney info@velvetparkmagazine.com
velvetparkmagazine.com
Dyke culture in bloom!

Goth

Goth, Industrial, EBM, Ethereal, Synthpop, DeathRock, Darkwave and Pagan.

North America

United States

Absolute Zero Media
magazine@absolutezeromedia.us
magazine.absolutezeromedia.us
Experimental, Dark Industrial/Ambient, Noise and Doom label, mail order, label and zine.

Beautiful Cruelty Magazine
PO Box 605, Round Lake, IL 60073
submissions@beautifulcruelty.com
beautifulcruelty.com
Everything Gothic, Industrial, Grave and beyond. Please CONTACT us before sending any material.

BiteMe!
6038 Hayes Ave. #1A, Los Angeles, CA 90042
PH: 626-359-5338
J j@bitemezine.net
www.bitemezine.net
Interviews, commentary. Also reviews demos.

Black Angel Promotions
6000 Old West Point Rd., LaGrange, GA 30240
blackangelpromotions@gmail.com
www.blackangelpromotions.com
Reviews and interviews.

Chaos Control Digizine
PO Box 1065, Hoboken, NJ 07030
PH: 201-610-0688
Bob Gourley chaoszine@gmail.com
www.chaoscontrol.com
Pioneering online zine focusing on, but not limited to, Electronic music. Features an extensive collection of interviews.

Dark Culture Magazine
PO Box 70112, Pasadena, CA 91107
Cinka info@darkculture.net
www.darkculture.net
An open forum for writers to get their words read.

Dark Realms Magazine
4377 W. 60th St., Cleveland, OH 44144
Music Editor goth@monolithgraphics.com
www.monolithgraphics.com/darkrealms.html
Visit for guidelines to submitting your music.

Dead Angel
PO Box 2434, Austin, TX 78768
monorecs@monotremata.com
www.monotremata.com/dead
E-zine with Underground music reviews.

EsoTerra
5500 Prytania, #216, New Orleans, LA 70115
Chad Hensley hecate999@msn.com
www.esoterra.org
Interviews with musicians, writers and artists existing on society's fringes.

Goth Metal World
chris@gothmetal.net
www.gothmetal.net
Promotes bands in attempts of putting them in the spotlight, giving them a larger fanbase.

Gothic Beauty
4110 SE. Hawthorne Blvd. #501, Portland, OR 97214
FX: 503-249-8844
info@gothicbeauty.com
www.gothicbeauty.com
Send us your press kit.

Grave Concerns
PO Box 692, Valatie, NY 12184
Julie Johnson gothgirl@berk.com
www.graveconcernsezine.com
Gothic and Industrial music resource for CD reviews, interviews etc.

Haunted Attraction *Underground DJ*
PO Box 220286, Charlotte, NC 28222
PH: 704-366-0875 FX: 704-366-0876
info@hauntedattraction.com
www.hauntedattraction.com
Get an expert opinion on the best in Haunted music.

Horror Garage
PO Box 53, Nesconset, NY 11767
Pitch Black HorrorGarage@aol.com
www.horrorgarage.com
Combines he best in original dark fiction with the finest in horrific Rock n' Roll.

Industrial Nation
PO Box 2717, Oakland, CA 94602
PH/FX: 208-575-7234
reviews@industrialnation.com
www.Industrialnation.com
Covers all music Electronic.

Morbid Outlook
Woolsey Stn, PO Box 5043, Astoria, NY 11105
Mistress McCutchan submit@morbidoutlook.com
www.morbidoutlook.com
Feel free to send your CDs and press kits to us

Musicfolio.com
16220 N. 7th St. #3441, Phoenix, AZ 85022
webmaster@musicfolio.com
www.musicfolio.com
Focus on Darkwave, Goth, Ethereal, Synthpop, Industrial etc.

Outburn
PO Box 3187, Thousand Oaks, CA 91359-0187
outburn@outburn.com
www.outburn.com
In-depth interviews with popular musicians and established Underground favorites.

PM Magazine
PO Box 98827, Lakewood, WA 98498-0827
PH: 253-459-3038
Michael A. Cint pmmagazine@pmmagazine.net
www.pmmagazine.net
Looking for reviews for music and print.

Regen Magazine
PO Box 14162, San Francisco, CA 94114-0162
PH: 415-420-8247
Nick Garland submissions@regenmag.com
www.regenmag.com
We feature IDM, Industrial, Goth, Synthpop etc.

Sentimentalist
PO Box 174, Murray Hill Stn. New York, NY 10156
PH: 212-679-1287 FX: 212-679-1287
sentimentalist@asthetik.com
www.asthetik.com/sentimentalist
Alternative music, art, film and fashion magazine.

Swag Magazine
8033 Sunset Blvd. #4500, W. Hollywood, CA 90046
PH: 323-466-3069
submit@SwagMag.com
www.swagmag.com
All about everything the successful Rock stars need.

Vampirefreaks.com
jet@vampirefreaks.com
www.vampirefreaks.com
News about everything Gothic.

VIAL Magazine
PO Box 22514, San Francisco, CA 94122
omen@disinfo.net
www.vialmagazine.com
A dream must accompany your CD.

Voidstar Productions
240 Jackson St. #610, Lowell, MA 01852
David Dodson deftlyd@nauzeeaun.com
www.voidstarproductions.com
Our reviews give constructive criticism directly to the artists.

Canada

Lowlight
360A Bloor St. W., PO Box 68568, Toronto, ON M5S 1X0
submissions@lowlightonline.com
www.lowlightonline.com
Online magazine specializing in Synth-Rock and Electro hybrid projects.

Rue Morgue
PH: 416-651-9675
info@rue-morgue.com
www.rue-morgue.com
Reviews (no demos) Horror related music.

The Temple of Horror
55 Collinsgrove Rd. TH 255, Scarborough,
ON M1E 4Z2
PH: 416-804-8612
Samantha Dennett Slayde@templeofhorror.com
www.templeofhorror.com
Industrial music news, reviews and interviews.

Europe

Belgium

Darker than the Bat
Peter Jan Van Damme pj.vandamme@scarlet.be
www.proservcenter.be/darkerthanthebat
CD reviews, interviews and airplay for Indies.

De Kagan Kalender
Geerdegemstraat 23, 2800 Mechelen, Belgium
PH: +32 (0)15-424363
info@kagankalender.com
www.kagankalender.com
*Each promo is assured to get a review and will be
played on our radio show.*

Croatia

Elektronski Zvuk
info@elektronskizvuk.com
www.elektronskizvuk.com
*We review Electronic music from bands around the
world.*

Czech Republic

teenage.cz
ebm@teenage.cz
teenage.cz
School sucks. Music rocks!

Finland

Kaos Kontrol
Yliopistonkatu 8 D 81, FIN-20100 Turku, Finland
info@kaos-kontrol.org
www.kaos-kontrol.org
Focuses on 'Industrial' sounds.

France

Darkface
postmaster@dark-face.com
dark-face.com
*Se donne le but de faire connaître le mouvement
Electro & Goth, faire circuler le maximum
d'informations.*

D-Side
3 bis, rue Pasteur, 94270 Le Kremlin Bicetre, France
PH: 33-01-47-77-80-28 FX: 33-01-46-77-53-82
Monsieur Bruce ab@d-side.org
www.d-side.org
*Gothic, Rock Metal, Electro, Industrial, Electronica,
Darkwave.*

Germany

Astan Magazine
PF 1247, 48629 Metelen, Germany
astanmagazin@t-online.de
www.astan-magazin.de
Gothic / Electro zine. News, reviews, interviews...

Back Again
Behringstr. 93B, 22763 Hamburg, Germany
Alexander Pohle sam@backagain.de
www.backagain.de
*CD kritiken und interviews aus dem
independentbereich.*

The Black Gift
Ahornweg 25, 50226 Frechen, Germany
PH: 02234-497793 FX: 0721-151 447655
office@the-black-gift.de
www.the-black-gift.de
Gothicmagazin. News, reviews, interviews.

Black Rain
PO Box 300130, 09033 Chemnitz, Germany
FX: 0049-(0)371-3899450
www.blackrain.de
Mail your demos in for review.

The Dark Site
Postfach 1130, 61451 Konigstein im Taunus,
Germany
contact@wavegothic.de
www.wavegothic.de
*Schickt einfach euer Material an unsere Anschrift
und gebt uns ein paar Wochen Zeit (wir müssen die
CDs ja auch intern verteilen).*

Dark Spy Magazine
Demo, Postfach 11 03 01, 46123 Oberhausen,
Germany
PH: +49 (0) 208-635-397-60
FX: +49 (0) 208-635-398-00
info@dark-spy.com
www.dark-spy.com
*Mail your CD or e-mail us with the word "DEMO"
in the subject heading. Stay Dark!*

Darkbeat.Net
Bernadottestr. 84, 60439 Frankfurt, Germany
info@darkbeat.net
www.darkbeat.net
Reviews, events, radio etc.

darkerradio
Ottostrasse 46, 47169 Duisburg, Germany
PH: +49(0)180-5-6-84-30-82-80
FX: +49(0)180-5-6-84-30-80-95
Falk Merten info@darkerradio.com
www.darkerradio.de
Tune in. Turn on. Burn out.

electric diary
Thomas Tröger thomas@electric-diary.com
www.electric-diary.com
*Dark-Alternative Musikmagazin. News, interviews,
reviews, tips etc.*

Electric Tremor
Brolwitzer Str. 14, 06842 Dessau, Germany
contact@electric-tremor.org
www.electric-tremor.de
Home of degenerated music, events and art.

Electricafé
info@electricafe.de
www.electricafe.de
*Fan-E-Zine für Elektronische Musik. Der
Schwerpunkt liegt bei Electro, EBM und Industrial.*

e-lectric.de
Scharrenbroicher Str. 55c, 51503 Rosrath, Germany
Andreas Wolf wolf@e-lectric.de
www.e-lectric.de
*Synthie-Pop und der etwas "härteren" Variante
Future-Pop beschäftigt.*

electrowahn.de
Nachtigallenstr. 26, 41466 Neuss, Germany
demo@electrowahn.de
www.elektrowahn.de
Electro/EBM/Industrial. Includes a "Demo" zone.

elektrauma
Gustav-Heinemann-Ring 64, 81739 Munchen,
Germany
www.elektrauma.de
Musik als therapie für die seele.

Gothic Magazin
Selmastrasse 3, 30451 Hannover, Germany
PH: 0511-261-58-31 FX: 0511-47-333-46
info@schwarze-romantik.com
www.schwarze-romantik.de
Gothic magazin und community.

Gothic Magazine
Konviktstrasse 4, D-72488 Sigmaringen, Germany
Martin Sprissler Martin@dark-media.de
www.gothic-magazine.de
News, reviews, newsletter, links and more!

Gothic Paradise
Birkbuschstraße 76/77, 12167 Berlin, Germany
PH: +49-179-7514371 FX: +49-1212-529-705-763
Freya Diepenbrock info@GothicParadise.de
www.gothicparadise.de
*Gothic, EBM, Alternative, Industrial, Metal,
konzertberichte tourdaten.*

Gothic World
Rainstrasse 3, D-77694 Kehl, Germany
PH: +49 (0)7853-87-34
Sir Ritchie gothicworld@ritchies.de
www.the-gothicworld.de
Unabhängiges internet-magazin für die Gothicszene.

Medienkonverter
Kriegersiedlung 69, D-81369 München, Germany
Bertram Uhner redaktion@medienkonverter.de
www.medienkonverter.de
*Das eZine für die subkulturellen Töne. Darkwave,
Wave, EBM, Gothic, Gothicrock ...*

MeltingClose
Volker Riehl, Waldallee 45, 65817 Eppstein,
Germany
PH: 0177-7134884
darkon@reanimation-club.de
www.meltingclose.de
Eletronic music magazin.

NEROTUNES
3411414, Packstation 101, 30159 Hannover,
Germany
PH/FX: 030-4-84-98-44-97
Jörn Sieveneck info@nerotunes.com
www.nerotunes.com
EBM, Gothic, Industrial music podcast and e-zine.

La Nuit Obscure
Grünhundsbrunnen 2, 96049 Bamberg, Germany
PH: +49-951-519-00-05
Ulrich Herwig uli@subkultur.de
www.lanuitobscure.de
Dark Wave, Gothic, EBM ...

pandaimonix.de
Krokusweg 37, 76199 Karlsruhe, Germany
PH: 0721-98929933
Stefan Thiel public@pandaimonix.de
www.pandaimonix.de
*Provides information about Gothic, Metal and Dark
music. News, reviews, stories...*

Sonic Seducer
Postfach 14 01 54, 46131 Oberhausen, Germany
PH: 0208-699370 FX: 0208-6993715
info@sonic-seducer.de
www.sonic-seducer.de
Musicmagazin: Gothic, EBM, Alternative, Dark.

subKULTur.com
Postfach: 580664 - 10415 Berlin, Germany
PH: 030-446-780-86 FX: +49 (0) 721-151-281-383
redaktion@subKULTur.com
www.subkultur.com
Cd-kritiken, interviews, termine, MP3, galerien.

Zillo Musikmagazin
Sereetzer Weg 20, 23626 Ratekau, Germany
PH: 04504-606680 FX: 04504-60668-10
info@zillo.de
www.zillo.de
Darkwave, Alternative, Industrial music.

Greece

The Enochian Apocalypse
Vassago blackwidow79_drk@yahoo.com
www.enochianapocalypse.com
The best in Electro, EBM, Industrial, Darkwave and Goth music.

Italy

Angelic North-East Alternative Bands Club
info@angelic.it
www.angelic.it
Guide to the Dark Italian scene.

Chain D.L.K.
www.chaindlk.com
We have reviewers for each style and geographic location. Please check our site to see where to send your material.

Kronic.it
info@kronic.it
www.kronic.it
Encouraging music addiction since 2002.

Ver Sacrum
via Rosa Luxemburg 10/P, 56010 Orzignano (PI) - Italy
Marzia Bonato redazione@versacrum.com
www.versacrum.com
Rivista Gotica di letteratura, cinema, musica e arte.

The Netherlands

Funeral Procession
Postbus 5034, 3502 JA Utrecht, The Netherlands
Hans D. hansd@funprox.com
www.funprox.com
Covers all Gothic.

Funprox
Postbus 5034, 3502 JA Utrecht, The Netherlands
info@funprox.com
www.funprox.com
A wide variety of musical styles from Dark Folk to Experimental Electronics.

Norway

Musique Machine
www.musiquemachine.com
Reviews, interviews, editorial columns and MP3s.

Russia

Industrial Onego
Industrial@onego.ru
Industrial.onego.ru
Music reviews archive.

Russian Gothic Page
PO Box 129, Moscow 119331, Russia
coroner@gothic.ru
www.gothic.ru
An underground project promoting Gothic subculture in Russia.

Spain

Sonidobscuro
Pasaje de Briales 9, 2-I, 29009 Málaga, Spain
reviews@sonidobscuro.com
www.sonidobscuro.com
Webzine de musica oscura.

Sweden

Moving Hands
Heleneborgsgatan 6C, SE-117 32 Stockholm, Sweden
Robert Eklind robert.eklind@movinghands.net
www.movinghands.net
We review Synth, Industrial, Electronica, EBM, Postpunk etc.

Release
V Stillestorpsg 23, S-417 Gothenburg, Sweden
PH: 46-31-775-00-83
info@releasemagazine.net
www.releasemagazine.net
Features, reviews, news, classified ads etc.

Switzerland

DARKLIFE fanzine
Gianfranco Sciacca darklifezine@gmx.net
www.darklifezine.org
Gothic/Industrial/Electro/Experimental/Avant-Garde/Ritual music and lifestyles of the current underground scene.

HeAvYmeTaL.ch
Im Trichtisal 12, CH-8053 Zürich, Switzerland
Roderick Zeig rzeig@gmx.ch
www.heavymetal.ch
The Metal / Gothic portal of Switzerland.

Sanctuary
Grand Rue 76, CH-1373 Chavornay, Switzerland
www.sanctuary.ch
Promotes the musical alternative scene.

United Kingdom

DARKLIFE
The Small House, 138b Brownlow Rd. London, GB-N11 2BP UK
Gianfranco Sciacca darklifezine@gmx.de
www.darklifezine.de
All CDs & tapes will be reviewed (Gothic/ Electro/ Industrial/ Experimental/ Avant-garde / Ritual).

DJ Martian's
altmartinuk@excite.com
djmartian.blogspot.com
Delivering cultural sound knowledge for the intelligent generation.

Gutter Glitter.co.uk
queenoftiaras admin@gutterglitter.co.uk
www.gutterglitter.co.uk
An Alternative music e-zine catering to Indie, Electro, Glam & Goth music.

Hard Wired
6 Saxon Ct. Kingsway Gardens, Andover, Hants, SP 10 4BU UK
www.hard-wired.org.uk
Send items for review (demos/albums etc.).

Judas Kiss Magazine
PO Box 44, Gloucester, GL4 5ZA UK
judaskiss@freezone.co.uk
www.judaskissmagazine.co.uk
Capturing the very essence of the post-Industrial scene through the written medium.

MK Magazine
www.mk-magazine.com
News, reviews and interviews. Evil and funny.

Subculture Magazine
Jez Porat jezporat@gmail.com
www.subculturemagazine.com
Alternative music and culture magazine. Dark Electro, EBM, Gothic, Synth and Industrial.

Ukraine

Ukrainian Gothic
stranger@gothic.com.ua
www.gothic.com.ua
Supports the Ukrainian Gothic/Industrial/independent scene.

Hip Hop

North America

United States

AAO Entertainment
PH: 905-730-0644
Wais Yasin aaoent@aaoent.com
www.aaoent.com
We are a 10 year old Hip Hop label. We currently have 4 artists. We also do reviews.

allhiphop.com
PH: 877-499-5111
www.allhiphop.com
Articles, audio, reviews, chat, boards etc.

Altrap.com
PO Box 4075, Tallahassee, FL 32315
A to the L mail@altrap.com
www.altrap.com
News, reviews, interviews and MP3s.

Bombhiphop.com
4104 24th St. #105, San Francisco, CA 94114
Attn: A&R Dept.
PH: 415-821-7965
usa@bombhiphop.com
www.bombhiphop.com
Artists, send in your demos for review.

Bridgez Magazine
480 Broadway 2nd Fl. New York, NY 10013
PH: 646-546-5739 FX: 646-546-5741
info@bridgezmag.com
www.bridgezmag.com
A Hip Hop magazine influenced by Latino culture that caters to everyone.

Coatcheck Magazine
LNMental@coatcheck.net
www.coatcheck.net/
Interviews and reviews with Hip Hop and DnB artists.

Crossover Magazine
PO Box 110708, Cambria Heights, NY 11411
PH: 347-731-0327
Tee tee@crossovermag.com
www.crossovermag.com
An urban magazine whose mission is to bridge the gap between Reggae, Hip Hop and R&B.

DaveyD's Hip Hop Corner
mrdaveyd@aol.com
www.daveyd.com
All the info on the Hip Hop scene.

Dork Magazine
James Oyedijo james@dorkmag.com
www.dorkmag.com
Documenting the mundane, glamorous, funny, disturbing and just plain weird things that define our existence.

eJams
PH: 803-237-3943
sales@ejams.com
www.ejams.com
Let us feature your new CD.

Elemental Magazine
71A Oak St., Brooklyn, NY 11222
PH: 718-218-0077 FX: 718-383-6378
Michael Cusenza mike@elementalmag.com
www.elementalmag.com
True, we never update the site. But we don't care. That's because we run a magazine.

The Elements
PO Box 233, Hollywood, CA 90028-0233
inquiries@hiphop-elements.com
www.hiphop-elements.com
Your #1 source for Hip Hop related issues.

freshsites.com
info@freshsites.com
freshsites.com
Promoting the independent Underground Hip Hop culture.

GlobalHipHop.com
globalhiphop@hotmail.com
www.globalhiphop.com
Reviews, interviews, mix shows & more.

Ground Lift Magazine
PO Box 57278, Chicago, IL 60657
Attn: Reviews
DJ Trew trew@groundliftmag.com
groundliftmag.com
Rare grooves, Hip Hop and Beats. Send your music to the above address for review consideration.

HipHopDX.com
Albert McCluster III editor@hiphopdx.com
www.hiphopdx.com
Hip Hop news, album reviews, links, release dates etc.

HipHopGame
PO Box 337, Manasquan, NJ 08736
730 mr730@tmail.com
www.hiphopgame.com
Daily information from around the world.

HipHopSite.com
4700 S. Maryland Pkwy. #2, Las Vegas, NV 89119
PH: 702-933-2123 FX: 702-947-2290
mistapizzo@hiphopsite.com
www.hiphopsite.com
Reviews and interesting items related to Hip Hop.

Illtip
322 Harbour Way, #18, Richmond, CA 94801
PH: 510-215-6110 FX: 510-215-5112
g-writer@illtipmagazine.com
www.theilltip.com
The last real street magazine.

Insomniac
PO Box 592722, Orlando, FL 32859
PH: 212-629-1797
insom@mindspring.com
www.insomniacmagazine.com
Features interviews, articles and reviews.

Last Word Online
900-306 Summit Walk Dr. Charlotte, NC 28270
PH: 704-364-9222
Mehka mehka_1@hotmail.com
www.lastwordonline.com
We cover Hip Hop topics and music.

Manhunt
info@manhunt.com
www.manhunt.com
News, reviews and artist spotlight.

Murder Dog
164 Robles Dr. #257, Vallejo, CA 94591
PH: 707-553-8191
walkinbuffalo@murderdog.com
www.murderdog.com
America's #1 Rap magazine. Send us 2 copies of your CD for review.

OHHLA
ohhla@pobox.com
www.ohhla.com
Original Hip Hop lyrics archive.

Okay Player
dan@okayplayer.com
www.okayplayer.com
Artists, reviews, insights and much more.

OpenZine
PO Box 562243, Miami, FL 33256
humbyvaldes@openzine.com
www.openzine.com
Submit articles, graffiti art pictures & many other outlets.

Overdue Exposure
256 S. Robertson Blvd. #504, Beverly Hills, CA 90211
PH: 310-285-3148
info@OverdueExposureMag.com
www.OverdueExposureMag.com
The extreme urban-lifestyle magazine.

Ozone Magazine
1310 W. Colonial Dr. #10, Orlando, FL 32804
PH: 407-447-6063 FX: 407-447-6064
Julia Beverly feedback@ozonemag.com
ozonemag.com
The Southern voice of Hip Hop music!

Pass the Mic
4130 Heyward St., Cincinnati, OH 45205
PH: 718-213-4176
www.passthemic.com
Community for independent Hip Hop artists.

Phatmag
thepublisher@phatmag.com
www.phatmag.com
Real news, interviews and reviews.

Rap Scene
rapscene@hotmail.com
www.rapscene.com
Check out our "New Artist Showcase".

RapAttackLives
4750 Kester Ave. #11, Sherman Oaks, CA 91403
PH: 818-917-2217
Nasty-Nes nastynes1@aol.com
www.rapattacklives.com
The true voice of Hip Hop!

RapIndustry.Com
rapindustry.com
Showcase your talent!

Rapmusic.com
www.rapmusic.com
Your total source for Rap/Hip Hop.

Rapnetwork.com
urbanminded@aol.com
www.rapnetwork.com
Source for the hottest Rap music on the planet.

rapreviews.com
PO Box 540938, Omaha, NE 68154
dj.flash@rapreviews.com
www.rapreviews.com
An independent site dedicated to up-and-coming artists.

Raptism.com
Gambler webmaster@raptism.com
www.raptism.com
Reviews, interviews, news etc.

Riot Sound
PO Box 159, Landing, NJ 07850
PH: 973-343-2570
RiotSound@RiotSound.com
www.riotsound.com
Bringing together art, music and information from all corners of the globe in seamless harmony.

Shine Magazine
PO Box 4314, Deerfield Beach, FL 33442
PH: 561-758-7127
editors@planetshine.com
www.planetshine.com
Music, fashion, entertainment and more.

Siccness-Dot-Net
PO Box 106, 5619 Lankershim Blvd. N.
Hollywood, CA 91601
bplease@siccness.net
www.siccness.net
CD Vendors, reviews, interviews etc.

Soundslam
nick@soundslam.com
www.soundslam.com
The latest music news, reviews, artist info, contests and more!

The Source *Unsigned Hype*
info@thesource.com
www.thesource.com
Profiles a talented unsigned artist each month.

Sphere of Hip Hop
3803 4th Pl. NW., Rochester MN 55901
Attn: Josh Niemyjski
www.sphereofhiphop.com
Reviews positive Hip Hop.

Suckarepellent.com
Alexa N. Hernandez alexa_h04@yahoo.com
www.suckarepellent.com
Artist features, Real Audio, fashion and more.

Support Online Hip Hop
PO Box 374, Jersey City, NJ 07303-0374
www.sohh.com
Connect with the online Hip Hop community.

Tha Formula.com
PO Box 385, Gardena, CA 90248
info@thaformula.com
www.thaformula.com
Streaming radio station, news and much more.

THEULTIMATECDLINK.com
ultimatecdlink@yahoo.com
theultimatecdlink.com
Send your CD and promotional materials to us.

Undergroundhip-hop.net
josh@undergroundhip-hop.net
www.undergroundhip-hop.net
Spreading the word about Hip Hop talent.
CONTACT US before you send anything!

The Underwire Interactive Magazine
PH: 602-324-3588 FX: 602-324-3588
Storm info@underwiremagazine.com
www.underwiremagazine.com
An interactive mixtape magazine. The first audio visual media disc publication.

undevco
info@undevco.com
www.undevco.com
We feature real artists with dreams of delivering their unique talents to the world.

Unsigned the Magazine
PO Box 165116, Irving, TX 75016
Robi Wilcox Robi@UnsignedTheMagazine.com
www.unsignedthemagazine.com
Gives unsigned artists and labels maximum exposure.

URB
6300 Wilshire Blvd. #1750, Los Angeles, CA 90048
PH: 323-315-1700
word2urb@urb.com
www.urb.com
Urban alternative culture!

Vice Magazine
97 N. 10th St. #202, Brooklyn, NY 11211
PH: 718-599-3101 FX: 718-599-1769
vice@viceland.com
www.viceland.com
We have offices around the world. Check our site for a contact near you.

The Vinyl Exchange
PO Box 117, 1450 Sutter St., San Francisco, CA 94109
djbooth@vinylexchange.com
www.vinylexchange.com
Please do NOT send CDs for review. We only review vinyl!!

We Eat So Many Shrimp
ManyShrimp@gmail.com
somanyshrimp.com
Blog with Hip Hop news and reviews.

XXL
1115 Broadway, New York, NY 10010
PH: 212-807-7100 FX: 212-620-7787
Leah Rose & Anslem Samuel xxl@harris-pub.com
www.xxlmag.com
Features eye candy, street team, articles and more.

Canada

The CyberKrib.com
Jesse Ohtake info@thecyberkrib.com
www.thecyberkrib.com
Just e-mail me and we'll get you some coverage.

HipHopHotSpot.com
PO Box 35534, Hamilton, ON L8H 7S6
hiphophotspot.com
Free resources to give artists more promotion.

Peace Magazine
PO Box 124, Stn. B, Toronto, ON M5T 2T3
PH: 416-406-2088
info@peacemagazine.com
www.peacemagazine.com
Music. Fashion. Athletics. Lifestyle.

Pound Magazine
675 King St. W. #306, Toronto, ON M5V 1M9
PH: 416-656-7911 FX: 416-656-9388
chris@poundmag.com
www.poundmag.com
Send in all your stuff for review.

ThickOnline.com
3007 W. 7th Ave. Vancouver, BC V6K 1Z7
PH: 778-892-8670 FX: 778-892-8670
info@thickonline.com
www.thickonline.com
Shedding light on unknown talent.

underground sound
PO Box 9622, Saskatoon, SK S7K 7G1
Noyz319@ugsmag.com
www.ugsmag.com
We post/review submitted Hip Hop MP3s.

URBNET.COM
PO Box 10617, Toronto, ON M6H 1L8
PH: 647-271-7736 FX: 647-439-1411
info@urbnet.com
www.urbnet.com
Reviews, CDs and downloads of Techno, House etc.

South America

Equipe AD iretoria
yllwzao@hotmail.com
eadmp3.webcindario.com
O primeiro site da cultura Hip Hop em caldas novas goiás.

Europe

Czech Republic

BBaRák CZ
Pribyslavska 10, 135 00 Praha 3, Czech Republic
PH: +420-222-714-285
info@bbarak.cz
www.bbarak.cz
Reviews local and international artists.

France

Just Like HipHop
97, Ave. Aristide Briand, 92120 Montrouge, France
PH: 33(0)1-58-07-04-85 FX: 33(0)1-58-35-00-53
service-client@justlikevibes.com
www.justlikehiphop.com
News, reviews, interviews, downloads etc.

Germany

Backspin
Winterhuder Weg 29, 22085 Hamburg, Germany
PH: 040-22-92-98-0 FX: 040-22-92-98-50
info@backspin.de
www.backspin.de
Marktplatz, forum, mailorder etc.

Heftig!
Am Holländer 15, 03238 Finsterwalde, Germany
PH: 49-3531-7190500 FX: 49-3531-7190600
Joern-A. Werner einz@heftig.com
www.heftig.com
Reviews, news, release dates, interviews etc.

hamburghiphop.de
Bei der Apostelkirche 26, 20257 Hamburg, Germany
Kristof Maletzke info@hamburghiphop.de
www.hamburghiphop.de
News, reviews, interviews and MP3s.

MK Zwo
Skalitzer Str. 97, 10997 Berlin, Germany
PH: +49 (0)30-616-27-414
FX: +49 (0)30-616-27-415
webmaster@mkzwo.com
www.mkzwo.com
Magazin für Hip Hop, Dancehall und Reggae.

Rap.de
Blucherstr. 22, D-10961 Berlin, Germany
PH: 030-695-972-10 FX: 030-695-972-40
Anne Kummerlöwe anne@rap.de
www.rap.de
Music, radio, video, shop, reviews, interviews.

Truehead.de
webmaster@truehead.de
www.truehead.de
Online community and magazine.

WebBeatz
Auf dem Kamp 13, 42799 Leichlingen, Germany
PH/FX: +49-01212-5-59763024
Daniel Doege info@webbeatz.de
webbeatz.de
Hip Hop promotion platform.

Italy

hotmc.com
Casella 290, Via Valparaiso, 11, 20144 Milano, Italy
s.lippolis@hotmc.com
news.hotmc.com
News, articles and reviews, mainly on the Italian Hip Hop scene.

The Netherlands

Globaldarkness
Postbus 11173, 2301 ED Leiden, Holland
www.globaldarkness.com
Jungle, Electro-Funk, Hip Hop & Reggae.

Hip Hop in je Smoel
yid@hiphopinjesmoel.nl
www.hiphopinjesmoel.nl
Reviews for everything Dutch in Hip Hop.

theBoombap
Postbus 10804, 1001 EV Amsterdam, Netherlands
info2003@theboombap.nl
www.theboombap.nl
Nederlandsch meest gelezen Hip Hop magazine.

Urban Legends
www.urbanlegends.nl
For everything in Dutch Hip Hop. Local artists etc.

Spain

A Little Beat...
Avda.Malvarrosa 106-2 / 46011 Valencia, Spain
PH: 96-3275494
info@alittlebeat.com
www.alittlebeat.com
Hip Hop news, reviews, articles etc.

activohiphop.com
Apartado de correos 171, 28910 Leganés, Madrid,
Spain
activohiphop@activohiphop.com
www.activohiphop.com
*Send information on record launchings, concerts
etc.*

Hip Hop Yaik
siouxlive@gmail.com
www.hiphopyaik.com
Web dedicada al mundo del Hip Hop en Español.

RWHipHop.com
c/ Sant Vicenç Ferrer 37 - 2o 2a, 17300 Blanes -
Girona, Spain
PH: +34-659-51-57-00
webmaster@rwhiphop.com
www.rwhiphop.com
I am Hip Hop, you are Hip Hop, we are Hip Hop.

Sweden

Boom Bap
Hojdvagen 19, 291 41 Kristianstad, Sweden
J. Persson contact@boom-bap.com
www.boom-bap.com
Send your demos to us.

Street Zone
Flottbrovagen 23, 112 64 Stockholm, Sweden
Melin info@streetzone.com
www.streetzone.com
News, reviews, label and more.

Switzerland

Aight-Genossen
Birmensdorferstrasse 67, 8004 Zürich, Switzerland
PH: 41-043-535-31-30
info@aight-genossen.ch
www.aight-genossen.ch
Swiss Hip Hop online.

Cosmic Hip Hop
27 ch. De Champ-Manon, 1233 Bernex, Switzerland
pub@cosmichiphop.com
www.cosmichiphop.com
Web mag exclusively dedicated to Hip Hop.

Urban Smarts
Sturzbuchelstrasse 14, CH-9303 Wittenbach,
Switzerland
PH: 71-298-58-26
get@urbansmarts.com
www.urbansmarts.com
*Sheds light on independent Hip Hop artists from all
coasts and continents.*

United Kingdom

Big Smoke Magazine
PO Box 38799, London, E10 5UZ UK
PH: 44-0-7966472051
Dirty Harry dirtyharry@bigsmokelive.com
www.bigsmokelive.com
Interviews, reviews, events, competitions and more!

Invincible Magazine
Unit 107, 203 Mare Studio, London, E8 3QE UK
PH: 0044 (0) 208-525-4131
FX: 0044 (0)207-493-4935
adverts@invinciblemag.com
www.invinciblemag.com
Covering Urban music and lifestyle.

Knowledge
1 Trafalgar Mews, Eastway, London, E9 5JG UK
PH: 0-208-533-9300 FX: 0-2008-533-9320
Colin Steven editor@knowledgemag.co.uk
www.knowledgemag.co.uk
*The magazine for D n' B, Jungle, Hip Hop,
Breakbeat and urban culture.*

RAGO Magazine
PO Box 1668, Wolverhampton, WV2 3WG UK
info@ragomagazine.com
www.ragomagazine.com
*Interviews, features, news and mixed tape, album,
single & video reviews.*

spinemagazine
16 Kingly St., London, W1B 5PT UK
PH: +44 (0) 20-7494-4401
FX: +44 (0) 20-7494-4402
Zaid zaid@spinemagazine.com
www.spinemagazine.com
In-depth music reviews.

Australia

Stealth
PO Box 666, Sydney, NSW 2001 Australia
info@stealthmag.com
www.stealthmag.com
Australia's premier Hip Hop magazine.

StreetHop.com
PO Box 2102, Salisbury Downs, Adelaide, SA 5108
Australia
www.streethop.com
*Promoting the Hip Hop culture: news, interviews,
artist directory, music reviews ...*

Africa

Africasgateway
PO Box 1087, Woodstock, 7915, South Africa
FX: 086-670-9873
info@africasgateway.com
www.africasgateway.com
*Africa's largest platform for independent artists and
record labels.*

Jam Band

An Honest Tune
PO Box 1362, Oxford, MS 38655
PH: 662-281-0753
Tom Speed tspeed@anhonesttune.com
www.AnHonestTune.com
*Mostly Jam bands, Americana, Alt-Country & Roots
music.*

ebong.org
info@ebong.org
ebong.org
*We are an international collective of "special folk"
who wish to provide a venue for creativity.*

Glide Magazine
PO Box 716, Bellmore, NY 11710
Eric Ward reviews@glidemagazine.com
www.glidemagazine.com
Covering today's most innovative artists.

High Times
419 Park Ave. S. 16th Fl. New York, NY 10016
PH: 212-387-0500 x 249
www.hightimes.com
Presenting the true independent voice of today.

Hittin' the Note
PH: 770-640-1124
info@hittinthenote.com
www.hittinthenote.com
Americana sounds of Blues, Rock & Jazz.

Honest Tune Magazine
PO Box 1362, Oxford, MS 38655
Tom Speed tspeed@honesttune.com
honesttune.com
The American journal of Jam and Roots music.

JamBands.com
Dean Budnick dean@jambands.com
www.jambands.com
*An online web zine devoted to Improvisational
music.*

Jammed Online
www.jammedonline.com
*A place for people to read reviews and interviews
about their favorite artists and music.*

KyndMusic
6304 Tall Trees Ln. #T2, Springfield, VA 22152
Attn: Reviews
bandsubmittal@kyndmusic.com
www.kyndmusic.com
*We cover the national and regional Jam scene as
well as Folk, World, Indie Rock, Jazz and Blues.*

Relix Magazine
104 W. 29th St. 11th Fl. New York, NY 10001
PH: 646-230-0100 FX: 646-230-0200
Steve Bernstein steve@relix.com
www.relix.com
Covering other, non-mainstream, types of music.

Jazz

North America

United States

ABYSS Jazz Magazine
8947 Washington Ave. Jacksonville, FL 32208
PH: 904-264-4642 FX: 904-264-4667
River Homes mailbox@abyssjazz.com
www.abyssjazz.com
Free Jazz publication distributed by Jazz radio stations and festivals across the country.

All About Jazz
761 Sproul Rd. #211, Springfield, PA 19064
PH: 610-690-0326
Michael Ricci mricci@allaboutjazz.com
www.allaboutjazz.com
Jazz & Blues magazine/resource.

All About Jazz Italian Version
302A W. 12th St. #204, New York, NY 10014
PH: 610-690-0326 FX: 240-359-2349
aajitalia@allaboutjazz.com
italia.allaboutjazz.com
All the info on the Italian Jazz scene.

American Rag
20137 Skyline Ranch Dr. Apple Valley, CA 92308
PH: 760-247-5145 FX: 760-247-5145
don@americanrag.com
www.americanrag.com
Commentary, news, articles of interest and reviews.

Contemporary Jazz
PO Box 16671, Chattanooga, TN 37416
Terrill J. Hanna Terrill@contemporaryjazz.com
www.contemporaryjazz.com
News, reviews, interviews and release listings.

Culturekiosque
164 Madison Ave. 5th Fl. New York, NY 10016-5411
editors@culturekiosque.com
www.culturekiosque.com
Worldwide A&E guide. We do Jazz and Classical music reviews.

Down Beat
102 N. Haven Rd. Elmhurst, IL 60126
editor@downbeat.com
www.downbeat.com
Send in your material for review.

Independent Reviewer - Frank Matheis
frank@matheisproductions.com
www.frankspicks.com
Writes a weekly column as music critic for Taconic Press.

Jazz & Blues Report
19885 Detroit Rd. #320, Rocky River, OH 44116
PH: 216-651-0626 FX: 440-331-0886
Bill Wahl billwahl@jazz-blues.com
www.jazz-blues.com
Features show listings and reviews.

Jazz Improv
PO Box 26770, Elkins Park, PA 19027
PH: 215-887-8808
jazz@jazzimprov.com
www.jazzimprov.com
100 detailed Jazz CD reviews in each issue.

Jazz Now
PO Box 19266, Oakland, CA 94619-0266
jazznow@sbcglobal.net
www.jazznow.com
Covering the hottest up-and-coming stars.

Jazz Online
contact@jazzonline.com
www.jazzonline.com
Fresh reviews of fresh Jazz music.

Jazz Times
8737 Colesville Rd. 9th Fl. Silver Spring,
MD 20910-3921
PH: 301-588-4114 x511 FX: 301-588-2009
www.jazztimes.com
World's leading Jazz publication.

Jazz USA
2613 NE. MLK Blvd. Ste. B, Portland, OR 97212
jazzusa.com
Submit music that you would like reviewed.

Jazziz
2650 N. Military Trail, Fountain Sq. II Bldg. #140,
Boca Raton, FL 33431
PH: 561-893-6868 x303 FX: 561-893-6867
www.jazziz.com
The voice of a new Jazz culture.

JazzPolice
301 Oak Grove St. #101, Minneapolis, MN 55403
Don Berryman editor@jazzpolice.com
www.jazzpolice.com
If you would like your CD featured, send a copy to be reviewed and another copy for our give-away.

JazzReview.com
10033 W. Ruby Ave. Milwaukee, WI 53225
www.jazzreview.com
Promotes all styles of Jazz music.

The Mississippi Rag
9448 Lyndale Ave. S. #120, Bloomington,
MN 55420
PH: 952-885-9918 FX: 952-885-9943
editor@mississippirag.com
www.mississippirag.com
New bands are highlighted in each issue.

Saxophone Journal
www.dornpub.com/saxophonejournal.html
Publishes reviews that are positive in nature. Visit our site to find which reviewer covers your style of music.

Turbula.net
PO Box 3497, Escondido, CA 92033
Jim Trageser editor@turbula.net
www.turbula.net
Talented people seem strangely compelled to send us interesting works for others to enjoy.

Canada

eJazzNews
news@ejazznews.com
www.ejazznews.com
News, profiles, interviews, reviews and more.

Smooth Jazz Now
main@smoothjazznow.com
SmoothJazzNow.com
News, reviews and interviews. Also covers New Age music.

Europe

Austria

jazzeit.at
Große Sperlgasse 2, A-1020 Wien, Austria
PH: 01-532-8560 FX: 01-532-8561
jazzzeit@jazzzeit.at
www.jazzzeit.at
Information and CD reviews.

Belgium

Dragon Jazz
Ave. du Forum n°17 / boîte 39, B-1020 Bruxelles,
Belgium
Pierre Dulieu pierre.dulieu@skynet.be
users.skynet.be/sky19290
Accent mis sur les productions Européennes et Belges en particulier. Jazz, Blues, Avant-garde, Fusion, World Jazz, Jazz Européen ...

Denmark

JAZZ SPECIAL
Havnegade 41, DK-1058 K, Denmark
PH: 45-33-33-87-60 FX: 45-33-33-87-30
maiken@jazzspecial.dk
www.jazzspecial.dk
The world's most distributed Jazz magazine!

France

Citizen Jazz
127, Ave. Marcel ouvrier, 91550 Paray Vieille Poste,
France
PH: 33-01-69-38-06-26
redaction@citizenjazz.com
www.citizenjazz.com
CD review, articles, interviews, audio and radio.

Jazz Break
info@jazzbreak.com
www.jazzbreak.com
Covers the worldwide Jazz scene.

Jazz Hot
BP 405, 75969 Paris 20, France
PH: 33-01-43-66-74-88 FX: 33-01-43-66-72-60
jazzhot@wanadoo.fr
www.jazzhot.net
La revue internationale du Jazz depuis 1935.

Jazz Magazine
63 ave. des Champs-Elysées 75008 Paris, France
PH: +33 (0)1-56-88-17-79
info@jazzmagazine.com
www.jazzmagazine.com
Interviews, articles, exhibitions, concert dates, news reviews etc.

Germany

Jazz Pages
Friedrich Ebert Str 75, 69239 Neckarsteinach,
Germany
PH: 06229-28-20-7 FX: 06229-28-20-8
Frank Schindelbeck jazz@jazzpages.com
www.jazzpages.com
All about Jazz in Germany.

Jazz Thing
Verlag Azel Stinshoff, Sulzburgstr. 74, 50937 Koln,
Germany
PH: 0221-941-488 FX: 0221-413-166
redaktion@jazzthing.de
www.jazzthing.de
Die Zeitschrift für weltoffene Musikliebhaber von heute.

Jazzdimensions
Postfach 36 03 10, 10973 Berlin, Germany
PH: 49-30-612-850-68 FX: 49-30-695-08-273
info@jazzdimensions.de
www.jazzdimensions.de
News, reviews, interviews and articles.

Italy

CiaoJazz
www.ciaojazz.com
Artist bios, MP3s and much, much more.

Italian Jazz Musicians
PH: 39-080-3929215
www.ijm.it
News, reviews, MP3s and online CD sales.

Russia

Jazz News
home.nestor.minsk.by/jazz
A monthly magazine on Jazz and Blues.

Spain

Cuaderno de Jazz
S.L. Hortaleza, 75, 2° dcha. 28004 Madrid, Spain
PH: 91-308-03-02 FX: 91-308-05-99
cuadernos@cuadernosdejazz.com
www.cuadernosdejazz.com
Articles about Jazz musicians.

Switzerland

Smooth Jazz Vibes
Blattenstr. 8, Postfach 55, 9450 Altstätten,
Switzerland
PH: 41-71-755-07-90
Peter Böhi pboehi@boehi.ch
www.smoothvibes.com
Please visit the site for submission details.

United Kingdom

Jazzwise
2B Gleneagle Mews, Ambleside Ave. London,
SW16 6AE UK
PH: 44-020-8664-7222 FX: 4-020-8677-7128
Jon Newey jon@jazzwise.com
www.jazzwise.com
From cutting-edge to Jazz club crossover and World Jazz.

Asia

CyberFusion
webmaster@jazzfusion.com
jazzfusion.com
CD reviews, interviews, live reports.

Warta Jazz.com
info@wartajazz.net
www.wartajazz.com
The ultimate source for Indonesian Jazz lovers.

Latin

La Banda Elástica
PO Box 2608, West Covina, CA 91793-2608
rock@labandaelastica.com
www.labandaelastica.com
Latin Alternative music magazine.

BoomOnline.com
PO Box 398752, Miami Beach, FL 33239
PH: 305-718-3612 FX: 305-468-1983
Gustavo Albán gustavo.alban@boomonline.com
www.boomonline.com
The community site for Latin Rock and Pop.

brazilica
brazilkitchen@hotmail.com
www.brazilica.nl
Bringing you news and fresh sounds directly from the Brazilian underground music scene.

Brownpride Online
PO Box 3852, Fullerton, CA 92834
FX: 714-792-3806
info@digitalaztlan.com
www.brownpride.com
Everything about the Latino scene.

La Factoria del Ritmo
Apd. 647. CP 39080, Santander - Cantabria, Spain
info@lafactoriadelritmo.com
www.lafactoriadelritmo.com
El primer magazine musical en Español vía internet.

Flamenco-world.com
Huertas 62, local, 28014 Madrid, Spain
PH: + (34) 913600865 FX: + (34) 91 3690244
magazine@flamenco-world.com
www.flamenco-world.com
Your one stop shop for anything and everything Flamenco!

HispanicOnline.com
www.hispaniconline.com
Does reviews and has an artist-of-the-month feature.

Latin Beat Magazine
15900 Crenshaw Blvd. #1-223, Gardena, CA 90249
PH: 310-516-6767 FX: 310-516-9916
rudy@latinbeatmagazine.com
latinbeatmagazine.com
If you're a new singer or group, here's a chance for some FREE publicity.

MUSICA SALSA
Schomburgstr. 54 a, D- 22767 Hamburg, Germany
Stefan stefan.renz@salsayazucar.com
www.musicasalsa.de
Events and Latin-American culture in Germany, Colombia and more...

'LA'Ritmo.com
info@laritmo.com
www.laritmo.com
Interviews and reviews of established and up-and-coming artists.

SalsaPower.com
Jacira Castro & Julián Mejía jacira@salsapower.com
www.salsapower.com
We only review artists who do Salsa, Timba and other related Afro-Cuban rhythms.

Timba.com
6800 Bird Rd. #267, Miami, FL 33155
mail@timba.com
www.timba.com
News, some independent reviews and concert information.

Metal

All styles of Metal as well as Hard Rock, Modern Rock and Stoner Rock

North America

United States

666metal.com
metal@popstar.com
www.666metal.com
If you are interested in reviews/interviews, please contact the author whose tastes you think matches your style the most.

Absolut Metal
editor@absolutmetal.com
www.absolutmetal.com
Reviews, local tour dates/shows and more.

Adrenalin Metal Fanzine
PO Box 296, Waunakee, WI 53597
Mike Burmeister mike@adrenalinfanzine.com
www.adrenalinfanzine.com
Promotes bands of the various Metal styles.

AllThingsMetal.net
108 St. Michelle, Apt G, Hawk Point, MO 63349
Jennifer Shipley jenn@allthingsmetal.net
www.allthingsmetal.net
We are bringing them together...the signed & the unsigned.

The Atomic Chaser
theatomicchaser@yahoo.com
atomicchaser.journalspace.com
Great music hiding beyond what the mega-power radio stations want you to hear.

Aversion Online
PO Box 5084, Richmond, VA 23220
andrew@aversionline.com
www.aversionline.com
Exposure for all forms of Extreme/Underground music.

BallBusterHardMUSIC.com
PO Box 58368, Louisville, KY 40268-0368
PH: 502-447-2568 FX: 502-447-2568
ballbusterhard@webtv.net
www.ballbusterhardmusic.com
Without prejudice, 100% lead for your head!

The Beer Pit
God of Metal godofmetal@thebeerpit.com
www.thebeerpit.com
To be considered for inclusion, please fill out our online form and let us know what your poison is.

Blabbermouth.net
PO Box 8234, White Plains, NY 10602
bmouth@bellatlantic.net
www.blabbermouth.net
All the latest Heavy Metal / Hard Rock news and reviews. Updated daily

Bleeding for Metal US
120 Rising Trail Dr. Middletown, CT 06457
Christopher McGirr galahad@bleeding.de
www.bleeding.de
Please address demos, promo-materials etc. to the above address.

Chronicles of Chaos
NorthAmerica@ChroniclesOfChaos.com
Europe@ChroniclesOfChaos.com
RestOfTheWorld@ChroniclesOfChaos.com
www.chroniclesofchaos.com
Extreme music webzine. Updated daily! Contact the reviewer in your region for our mailing address.

Crave Magazine
1013 NE. 68th St., Vancouver, WA 98665
PH: 360-991-9332 FX: 501-694 8061
Robin Steeley robin@portlandmusicians.com
www.cravemagazine.com
Your guide to extreme culture.

The Cutting Edge
tkscutedge@aol.com
www.thecutting-edge.net
Rock's finest web magazine!

DigitalMetal.com
PO Box 295, Drexel Hill, PA 19026
FX: 610-734-3716
submissions@digitalmetal.com
www.digitalmetal.com
News, reviews and interviews.

The Edge
5555 Rangeland, San Antonio, TX 78247
PH: 210-564-0088 FX: 210-655-6586
Toni Torres edgemag@satx.rr.com
www.theedgemagazine.com
Supports national and unsigned bands.

FUELMYPAIN.COM
W2433 Twin Pine Ln. Porterfield, WI 54159
Ben Steimle admin@fuelmypain.com
www.fuelmypain.com
Heavy Metal, Hard Rock community.

The Gauntlet
174 W. Foothill Blvd. #235, Monrovia, CA 91016
PH: 310-909-8514 FX: 310-492-5172
www.thegauntlet.com
Metal Indie musicians, bi-weekly mailing list, reviews, videos and more.

Glam-Metal.com
Thomas S. Orwat glammetal@adelphia.net
glam-metal.com
Bringing you the most updated information on the best Hard Rock bands on the face of the planet.

The Grimoire of Exalted Deeds
PO Box 1987, Clifton, NJ 07011
PH: 973-478-3743
masterzebub@aol.com
www.thegrimoire.com
A Death Metal magazine for assholes, by assholes.

Hammerhead
hamhedzine@aol.com
hammer.hammerheadzine.com
Resource of Metal music and more.

The Hard Rock Society
2621 14th St. S. #4, Fargo, ND 58103
mmd@hardrocksociety.com
www.hardrocksociety.com
A Hard Rock/Heavy Metal site with reviews.

Hardrock Haven
John Kindred webmaster@hardrockhaven.net
www.hardrockhaven.net
Contact us about submitting your material for review.

HMAS.org *Heavy Metal Appreciation Society*
374 1st St. N. Huntingdon, PA 15642
John Brighenti
webmaster@hmas.org
www.hmas.org
We review ONLY Heavy Metal and its various sub genres.

Hyperblast
Cleric Curst
chris@hyperblastmetal.com
www.hyperblastmetal.com
Heavy Metal news, CD reviews, show reviews etc.

In Depth
Anthony concertrag@aol.com
www.indepthzine.com
Show and album reviews and live pictures.

Inside Metal
Sam Humphreys info@insidemetal.net
www.insidemetal.net
Reviews and promotes independent bands and labels.

Into Obscurity
4807 Chester Ave. #208, Philadelphia, PA 19143
PH: 215-724-9838
Death Metal Dan bane@into-obscurity.com
www.into-obscurity.com
Reviews, interviews, tour dates, events and more!

Jen's Metal Page
www.jensmetalpage.com
News, reviews, interviews, MP3s etc.

Justin's Heavy Metal Site
Justin "Battle Angel" Harvey
thelearning@comcast.net
justinsmetalwebsite.com
Reviews all kinds of Metal music.

lambgoat.com
PO Box 15106, Reading, PA 19612
info@lambgoat.com
www.lambgoat.com
News, reviews, interviews, audio samples and more.

Live 4 Metal US
5837 SW. 24th Ter. Topeka, KS 66614
Scott Alisoglu Live4Metal68@yahoo.com
www.live4metal.com
The best of the Metal world.

Loudside
1549 Burnside Ave. Ventura, CA 93004 Attn: Jono
Jono jon@loudside.com
www.loudside.com
Send in your stuff for review.

Maelstrom
3234 Clay St., San Francisco, CA 94115
Roberto Martinelli giorgio75@hotmail.com
www.maelstrom.nu
Live/album reviews, interviews and more.

Maximum Metal
6305 Greenway Dr. Roanoke, VA 24019
Frank Hill news@maximummetal.com
www.maximummetal.com
We will review every promo and demo we receive!

Metal Core
PO Box 622, Marlton, NJ 08053
metalczine@aol.com
www.metalcorefanzine.com
Review section for signed and unsigned bands.

Metal Coven
PO Box 580326, Houston, TX 77258
Angel Bollier webmistress@metalcoven.com
www.metalcoven.com
Extremely informative webzine promoting the Heavy and Underground Metal scene.

Metal Crypt
michelr@metalcrypt.com
www.metalcrypt.com
Submit your Metal CDs/demos for review.

Metal Fanatix
70 Patrick Cir. Fulton, NY 13069
Jeffrey Adkins LEGION59@aol.com
www.metalfanatix.com
News, reviews, interviews of Metal music.

Metal Hordes
www.metalhordes.com
Extreme Metal community. profiles, reviews, interviews.

Metal Judgement
PO Box 979, Santa Monica, CA 90406-0979
info@metaljudgment.com
www.metaljudgment.com
In-depth reviews on the world of Heavy Metal.

Metal Maniacs
PO Box 263, Denton, MD 21629
Attn: Label consideration
metalmaniacsnews@aol.com
www.metalmaniacs.com
News, reviews etc.

Metal Meltdown
3605 W. 50th St., Cleveland, OH 44102
Dr. Metal metalmeltdownshow@mac.com
www.metalmeltdown.com
Metal interviews, radio, reviews, news and pictures.

Metal Reigns *Unsigned Artist page*
PO Box 989, Burnet, TX 78611
crusher@metalreigns.com
www.metalreigns.com
You can learn about up and coming metal bands, or just hear some cool new metal music.

Metal Reviews
contact@metalreviews.com
www.metalreviews.com
Loads of reviews. Updated weekly!

Metal Sludge
PO Box 371202, Reseda, CA 91337-1202
Donna Anderson metalsludge@metalsludge.tv
www.metalsludge.tv
The minimum number of CDs we need is TWO.
Don't send just one!

MetalReview.com
PO Box 25097, Woodbury, MN 55125
www.metalreview.com
Album reviews, concert reviews, band interviews.

metalunderground.com
9008 Harris St., Frederick, MD 21704
metalunderground.com
Send promo CDs, demos, stickers, t-shirts etc.

Midwest Metal Magazine
PO Box 612, Downers Grove, IL 60516
Mauricio Mauricio@midwestmetalmagazine.com
www.midwestmetalmagazine.com
Send CDs, cassettes, vinyl and contact/photos.

MidwestMetal.info
Review Dept. PO Box 39023, St. Louis, MO 63139
Maggot maggot@midwestmetal.info
www.midwestmetal.info
Mail your demo/CD to us. Please include your
band's name, website & e-mail address.

Neo-Zine
PO Box 144, Asheville, PA 16613
neo-zine@earthlink.net
www.Neo-Zine.com
We are involved in all kinds of Noise, Death Metal,
Black Metal, Punk etc.

On Track Magazine
1752 E. Ave. J #243, Lancaster, CA 93535
David Priest priest@ontrackmagazine.com
www.ontrackmagazine.com
Coverage of your favorite Hard music bands.

Pit Magazine
PO Box 9545, Colorado Springs, CO 80932
PH: 719-633-5752 FX: 719-633-8081
everything@pitmagazine.com
www.pitmagazine.com
The Extreme music magazine.

PiTRiFF Online
PO Box 1101, Twinsburg, OH 44087
PH: 206-202-5013
pitriffmail@gmail.com
www.pitriff.com
News, reviews, radio etc.

Pivotal Rage
665 S. Banana River Dr. Merritt Island, FL 32952
Leevan Macomeau leevan@pivotalalliance.com
with
webzine.pivotalalliance.com
www.pivotalrage.com
If you can send extra CDs or merch we will use
them for giveaways on our website.

Raginpit Magazine
PH: 209-203-0002
John Southworth edge@raginpit.com
raginpit.com
The world's loudest magazine. Heavy Metal and
Hardcore CD reviews, interviews, show reviews,
MP3s and more ...

Revolver
1115 Broadway, New York, NY 10010
PH: 212-807-7100
www.revolvermag.com
The world's loudest Rock magazine!

RIFTrock
Jason Lutjen jason@riftrock.com
www.riftrock.com
Rock promotion and daily news.

Rock and a Hard Place Zine
812 Countryside Pk. Fargo, ND 58103
Torch douggroff@clearchannel.com
www.rockhardplace.com
CD reviews, independent Rock, Metal and AOR.

Rock My Monkey
PO Box 828, Olympia, WA 98507
PH: 360-789-0703
www.rockmymonkey.com
Covers any and all forms of abrasive Rock.

Rocknation
info@rocknation.tv
www.rocknation.tv
Reviews and interviews. Demos accepted.

RockNet Webzine
1565 W. Main St. Ste. 208 #169, Lewisville,
TX 75067
Angela rocknetwebzine@earthlink.net
www.Rocknetwebzine.com
I am a huge fan of Rock and Metal music. One thing
I enjoy doing is going out to shows and meeting
people.

Rough Edge
PO Box 5160, Ventura, CA 93005
PH/FX: 805-293-8507
info@roughedge.com
www.roughedge.com
CD and live reviews, news, photos and more.

Score! Music Magazine
Bands@ScoreMusicMagazine.com
www.scoremusicmagazine.com
To get your CD reviewed, fill out the submissions
form on our website.

Screachen Publications
PO Box 16352, Phoenix, AZ 85011-6352
Editor@Screachen.com
www.screachen.com
Hard Rock news, interviews, reviews and more.

Silent Uproar
5614 Split Oak Dr. Raleigh, NC 27609
info@silentuproar.com
www.silentuproar.com
We cover a wide range of Alternative, Metal,
Hardcore music.

siN's Metal News
Aidan aidan@SMNnews.com
www.smnnews.com
News, reviews, interviews.

Sleazegrinder
PO Box 51446, Boston, MA 02205
sleazegrinder@gmail.com
www.sleazegrinder.com
Preservation of full-tilt, high octane, blistering Rock!

Soul Killer
neil@soulburn3d.com
www.soulkillerwebzine.com
The very best in Death, Grind, Classic and New
Metal.

stonerrock.com
PO Box 78, Carmen, ID 83462
El Danno dan@stonerrock.com
www.stonerrock.com
News, reviews, interviews etc. We don't want your
MP3s!

Strigl's Music News
PO Box 4112, New York, NY 10163
Mark Strigl mark@captaint.com
striglsmusicnews.com
Please send GUITAR ROCK ONLY - Metal, Punk,
Glam, Emo, Grunge etc.

Tad Loud Productions
PMB 226, 5815 82nd St. #145, Lubbock, TX 79424
PH: 505-762-7346
Sean Pruitt tadloudrocks@door.net
www.tadloudrocks.com
Helping to promote Indie artists by posting links,
articles, CD reviews, interviews, news and more.

Theundergroundscene.net
28 Brookside Ave. Boylston, MA 01505
Michael Byrne mike@theundergroundscene.net
www.theundergroundscene.net
Send your album our way and we'll see what we can
do.

Transcending the Mundane
5 Hudson Ave. Bohemia, NY 11716
Ladd Everitt ladddc@aol.com
tmetal.com
Quality reviews of newly-released Heavy Metal
albums.

Ultimate Metal Reviews
info@metal-reviews.com
www.metal-reviews.com
Small fee required with your CD/promo kit.

UltimateMetal.com
mail@ultimatemetal.com
www.ultimatemetal.com
Supporting the Metal underground. Forums,
discussion, interviews, reviews.

Unchain the Underground
PO Box 15, Stony Point, NY 10980
Al Kikuras al@unchain.com
www.unchain.com
Reviews and interviews of all forms of Extreme
music.

Uranium Music
Mike Smathers smathers@uraniummusic.com
www.uraniummusic.com
Covering bands that don't receive the attention they
deserve. Reviews/interviews/tour sponsors for Metal
and Rock bands.

Vibrations of Doom
PO Box 1258, Suwanee, GA 30024-0963
Steven Cannon vibrationsofdoom@hotmail.com
vibrationsofdoom.com
Resource for Metal artists and fans.

VM Underground
Vic Mendoza vm7573@hotmail.com
www.v-m-u.com
CD reviews and interviews of independent artists
and other special features like "Artist of the
Month".

VOXonline.com
PO Box 712412, Los Angeles, CA 90071
vox@voxonline.com
www.voxonline.com
We will listen to all submissions and publish reviews for those that we favor.

Worm Gear
PO Box 426, Mayfield, MI 49666
Marty Rytkonen korgull@chartermi.net
www.crionicmind.org/wormgear
Interviews, news, reviews, merchandise and more.

Canada

Blistering.com
43 Samson Blvd. #322, Laval, QC H7X 3R8
PH/FX: 450-689-7106
Rob Cotter rob@blistering.com
www.blistering.com
Submit your CDs and demos. Bands can sell their CDs at our store. We also feature downloads.

Brave Words and Bloody Knuckles
368 Yonge St., Toronto, ON M5B 1S5
PH: 416-229-2966 FX: 416-586-0819
bwbk@bravewords.com
www.bravewords.com
Metal news, features, columns, reviews...

Caustic Truths
POB 1190, Stn. A, Toronto, ON M5W 1G6
PH: 416-703-6429
www.caustictruths.com
Heavy Metal news, Metal reviews and other Hard Rock.

The Metal Observer
770 Sherbrooke W. #1750, Montréal, QC H3A 1G1
Mark McKenna mark@metal-observer.com
www.metal-observer.com
Contact us about sending your promo/demo/CD in for review.

Metallian.com
34 Okanagan Dr. #1129, Richmond Hill, ON L4C 9R8
metallian@canada.com
www.metallian.com
Promotes all sub-genres of Heavy Metal.

PureGrainAudio.com
59 Duncannon Dr. Toronto, ON M5P 2M3
PH: 416-723-3911 FX: 905-640-1490
mail@puregrainaudio.com
www.puregrainaudio.com
We are looking for any Heavy music bands to send us their material so that we may offer them some free press. No demos please!

theprp.com
wookubus@theprp.com
www.theprp.com
We work relentlessly all year round providing news, reviews and uncovering the very latest acts.

Sleaze Roxx
PO Box 142, Minto, MB R0K 1M0
Skid skid@sleazeroxx.com
www.sleazeroxx.com
Your Hard Rock and Heavy Metal resource.

Stoner Rock Chick
201 Sherbourne St. #2209, Toronto, ON M5A 3X2
Deanna St.Croix deanna@stonerrockchick.com
www.stonerrockchick.com
Bands and Labels, send your CDs for review.

Strutter Magazine
4001 Bayview Ave. #214, Toronto, ON M2M 3Z7
PH: 416-985-6609
info@struttermagazine.com
www.struttermagazine.com
As North America's LOUDEST music magazine we enter the Rock, Rock n' Roll, Punk and Heavy Pop scene with a fresh, aggressive and enjoyable format.

UNRESTRAINED!
5625 Glen Erin Dr. #57, Mississauga, ON L5M 6V2
PH: 416-483-7917
Adam Wasylyk info@unrestrainedmag.com
www.unrestrainedmag.com
Every demo is taken into review/interview consideration.

South America

himnosrituales
PO Box 1451, Popayan, Colombia
Jimmy Ruiz himnosrituales@yahoo.com
www.himnosrituales.com
Please send in only Metal!!!

Kuravilu
PO Box 548, Valdivia, Chile
carlos@kuravilu.cl
www.kuravilu.cl
Reviews, videos, interviews etc.

Music Extreme
Billinghurst 2380 2-A, (C1425DTV) Buenos Aires, Argentina
Federico Marongiu info@musicextreme.com
www.musicextreme.com
Lots of new reviews every month!

Roadie Crew
metal@roadiecrew.com
www.roadiecrew.com
A revista de Heavy Metal do Brasil.

Valhalla
Rua Luzerne Proenca Arruda, 128 Sorocaba, SP
CEP: 18081-021, Brazil
PH: +55-15-3212-4364 FX: +55-15-3211-1621
Eliton Tomasi valhalla@valhalla.com.br
www.valhalla.com.br
A revista Underground mais Metal do Brasil.

Europe

Austria

Arising Realm
Sechshauserstr. 59/6, A-1150 Vienna, Austria
PH: 0043-1-9665357
redaktion@arisingrealm.at
www.arisingrealm.at
Reviews, interviews etc.

DarkScene
Gumppstr. 77/21, 6020 Innsbruck, Austria
Thomas Kernbichler t.kernbichler@inode.at
www.darkscene.at
Metal and Gothic magazine with interviews, reviews and more!

deathmetal.at
Markus [h3ll] h3ll@deathmetal.at
www.deathmetal.at
Brutal Death Metal zine.

Resurrection
www.resurrection.at
News, reviews, interviews, tour dates and more.

Belgium

BMU
Temsestraat 27, 9150 Rupelmonde, Belgium
bmu.lasseel.be
Promoting the underground in Belgium.

The Dark Towers of Lugburz
info@lugburz.be
www.dma.be/p/lugburz
A support site for Belgian Black & Death Metal bands.

Denmark

Antenna
Lerbjergvej 9, 2650 Hvidovre, Denmark
PH: +45-36-77-37-27
Lars Lolk lolk@antenna.nu
www.antenna.nu
News, reviews, interviews ...

Intromental Webzine
Nørrebrogade 200B, 4tv, DK-2200 Copenhagen N, Denmark
PH/FX: +45-38344833
Claus Jensen webzine@intromental.com
www.intromental.com/webzine
Send us your Metal and Hard Rock related titles for review and interview.

RevelationZ Magazine
Gebauersgade 2, 4. sal, -3, 8000 Aarhus C, Denmark
Steen Jepsen steen@revelationz.net
www.revelationz.net
Your Heavy Metal and Hard Rock resource.

Finland

Imperiumi
tiedotteet@imperiumi.net
www.imperiumi.net
Visit our website to see which reviewer covers your particular style of Metal.

Lamentations of the Flame Princess Weekly
Seriegatan 15 P 5, 65320 Vasa, Finland
James Edward Raggi IV lotfp@lotfp.com
www.lotfp.com
Our interviews are as informative and in-depth as any ever done on Planet Earth.

meteli.net
tapahtumat@meteli.net
www.meteli.net
Metal in Finland.

RockUnited.Com *A&R Dept.*
Urban Wallström urban@rockunited.com
rockunited.com
We review demos or independent releases of unsigned bands looking for promotion.

France

Burn Out
2, rue de la Colinette, 51110 Bourgogne, France
PH: 33-0-326-892-668
Phil Kieffer burn.out@wanadoo.fr
www.burnoutzine.net
Chroniques, interviews, concerts, distro ...

Decibels Storm
38 cours Gambetta 69007 Lyon, France
Christophe Noguès decibelsstorm@free.fr
decibelsstorm.free.fr
Le site de Metal par les fans, pour les fans.

Heavy Metal Universe
c/o Ludovic Castelbou, 343, chemin de la Treille, 83500 la Seyne-sur-mer, France
www.heavymetaluniverse.com
Please CONTACT US before you send in your music.

Leprozy.com
webmonster@leprozy.com
www.leprozy.com
Send us news, tour dates, CDs etc. Contact us for our mailing address.

Lords of Winter
lord-of-winter@wanadoo.fr
lordsofwinter.free.fr
News, reviews, articles etc.

Metalorgie.com
11 rue Sully, Apt. 5, 44 000 Nantes, France
Eric Cambray bacteries@metalorgie.com
www.metalorgie.com/metal
Metal and Punk webzine.

ObsküR[e]
Emmanuel H. emmanuel.obskure@gmail.com
www.obskure.com
Metal Gothique, Electro, Indus, Death, Black, Progressif, Ambient, Heavy.

Santagore
10 rue pierre Bouvier, 69270 Fontaines sur Saône, France
Pierre Noel pierrot@santagore.com
www.santagore.com
Chroniques, interviews, photos ...

Spirit of Metal
Kivan kivan@spirit-of-metal.com
www.spirit-of-metal.com
Reviews, biographies, reports etc.

La Terre Des Immortels
The Lord lordlatem@netcourrier.com
www.metal-immortel.com
Metal, Rock Prog etc.

Snakepit
La Calloterie, 72210 Voivres Les Le Mans, France
Laurent Ramadier snakepit2@free.fr
truemetal.org/snakepit
Around 200 reviews per issue.

Underground Society
181 Rue Des Messanges, Résidence Les Vignes, Apt. N°15, 40990 Saint Paul Les Dax, France
Philippe Duarte duarteph@wanadoo.fr
undersociety.free.fr
News, reviews, interviews and video clips.

Versus Magazine
1, boulevard de Strasbourg, 75010 Paris, France
PH: 01-53-34-66-45 FX: 01-53-34-66-46
www.versusmagazine.net
Magazine mensuel spécialisé dans tous les Rock.

Germany

21st Century Metal Net
webmaster@21stcenturymetal.net
www.21stcenturymetal.net
Heavy Metal, Hard Rock, Thrash, Black, Death ...

Allschools Network
PO Box 911116, 30431 Hannover, Germany
Torben Utecht torben@allschools.de
www.allschools.net
Online Hardcore fanzine. Send demos to the above address.

Amboss
Postfach 1119, 32001 Herford, Germany
info@amboss-mag.de
www.amboss-mag.de
Heavy Metal and Gothic music magazine.

Ancient Spirit
Burdastr. 4, 77656 Offenburg, Germany
info@ancientspirit.de
www.ancientspirit.de
News, interviews, tour dates, live/CD reviews.

Bleeding for Metal
contact@bleeding.de
www.bleeding.de
Please address demos, promo-materials etc. to the above address.

Bloodchamber
Scharnhorststr. 7, 04275 Leipzig, Germany
Christian Rosenau info@bloodchamber.de
www.bloodchamber.de
CD and DVD reviews, interviews and MP3s.

BloodDawn.de
Kleine Mantelgasse 18, 69117 Heidelberg, Germany
Julian Strube gevatter.tod@blooddawn.de
www.blooddawn.de
News, reviews and featured bands.

Bright Eyes
Grunewaldstraße 49b, 22149 Hamburg, Germany
PH: +49 (0)40-69667832
info@brighteyes.de
www.bright-eyes.de
Updates, interviews, reviews, tour dates, festival-news und vieles mehr ...

Carnage
Herderstr. 76, D - 28203 Bremen, Germany
Leif Timm leif@carnagedeathmetal.de
carnagedeathmetal.de
Death Metal fanzine.

Daredevil
Kantstr. 31, 68723 Oftersheim, Germany
Ralf Burkart daredevil-mag@web.de
www.daredevil.de
If you want your stuff reviewed just send it to us.

echoes-online.de
Klauprechtstr. 21, 76137 Karlsruhe, Germany
Julian Finn redaktion@echoes-online.de
www.echoes-online.de
Metal review blog.

Eternity
StraBmannstr. 49, 10249 Berlin, Germany
redaktion@eternitymagazin.de
eternitymagazin.de
News, interviews, specials, diskussionen, festivalberichte, dates ...

Evil Rocks Hard
Groß-Gerauer-Str. 6, 65468 Trebur, Germany
Nils Manegold evilrockshard@web.de
www.evilrockshard.de
Wir sind ein Musik-Magazin für Hard-Rock, independent, Metal, Punk & Ska!

Evilized
Geusaer Straße 88 - WH12, 06217 Merseburg, Germany
Markus Wirth markus.wirth@evilized.de
www.evilized.de
Death Metal, Swedish Metal, Melodic Death Metal.

FFM-Rock.de
www.ffm-rock.de
Interviews, CD reviews, live reviews etc.

Heavy-Magazine.de
Nürnbergerstr.2, 85134 Stammham, Germany
M. Stenner webmaster@heavy-magazine.de
www.heavy-magazine.de
Habt Ihr Info Material , eine Promo CD , einen Song oder ein neues Album? Dann nehmt Kontakt per E-Mail.

Heavy-Metal.de
Amtsgerichtstr 10, 47119 Duisburg, Germany
PH: 49-0203-666-804 FX: 49-0203-66-93-253
mail@heavy-metal.de
www.heavy-metal.de
News, reviews, interviews, festival/tour dates...

Home of Rock
Kolumbusstr 17, 81543 München, Germany
Fred Schmidtlein webmaster@home-of-rock.de
www.home-of-rock.de
Rock, Heavy Metal news, reviews etc.

Lärmbelästigung
Marienstrasse 67, 21073 Hamburg, Germany
Karim Daire laermbelaestigung@gmx.de
www.laermbelaestigung.net
News, reviews, interviews. Death-Metal, Grind.

Metal District
Nürnberger Straße 33, 96114 Hirschaid, Germany
Patrick Weinstein redaktion@metal-district.de
www.metal-district.de
We review all styles of Metal.

Metal-Dungeon.de
c/o Marco Bianchi, Theodor-Billroth-Straße 19, 28277 Bremen, Germany
www.metal-dungeon.de
Metalheadz meet Metalheadz.

Metal Inside
www.metal-inside.de
News, reviews, interviews, tour dates & more.

METALMESSAGE.de
Brückenring 39a, 86916 Kaufering, Germany
PH: +49 (0)8191-6970
Markus Eck info@metalmessage.de
www.metalmessage.de
Reviews and Interviews in German & English.

Metal1.info
Eidinghausener Str. 168, 32549 Bad Oeynhausen, Germany
Andi Althoff webmaster@metal1.info
www.metal1.info
Reviews, interviews und biografien aus der szene!

Metal2Metal
Jahnstr. 7, 46145 Oberhausen, Germany
Dennis Hemken ambiguity@metal2metal.de
www.metal2metal.de
The ultimate (online) Metal-fanzine / magazin.

Metal.de
Postfach 11 30, 6141 Konigstein im Taunus, Germany
PH: 06174-2939849
contact@metal.de
metal-online.de
The dark site.

Metalglory
Im Moore 16 A, 30167 Hannover, Germany
metal@metalglory.de
www.metalglory.de
Heavy, Thrash, Black, Doom Metal reviews,
interviews ...

Metalius Multizine
Postfach 7110, 24171, Kiel, Germany
multizine@metalius.de
www.metalius.de
Reviews of band CDs and videos.

Metalnews
Metzstrasse 64, 24116, Kiel, Germany
Christian Wenzel premutos@metalnews.de
www.metalnews.de
Metal, Heavy Metal, Blackmetal, Deathmetal,
Darkmetal, Gothicmetal etc.

Morrigan's Pit
PO Box 1720, 33247 Guetersloh, Germany
Silkie Gerold morrigan@morrigans-pit.org
www.morrigans-pit.org
You might want to check with us first to make sure
your music fits.

MyRevelations.de
www.myrevelations.de
Don't spit on those who chose to pose!

NecroSlaughter
Christian Schmitz wurst@necroslaughter.tk
www.necroslaughter.tk
We review only Death Metal, Thrash Metal, Grind
Core or a comparable style.

Nocturnal Hall
Schmale Strasse 8, 48149 Muenster, Germany
PH: +49 (0) 251-867493
Dajana Winkel office@nocturnalhall.com
www.nocturnalhall.de
We use a scale from 1 to 10 (1 = biggest crap ever
to 10 = fucking brilliant).

Powermetal.de
Oberpforte 22, 61200 Wölfersheim, Germany
Alex Straka info@powermetal.de
www.powermetal.de
CD and show reviews and interviews.

Rock Hard Online
Postfach 11 02 12, 44058 Dortmund, Germany
PH: 0231-56-20-14-0 FX: 0231-56-20-14-13
Holger Stratmann Megazine@RockHard.de
www.rockhard.de
Ist sowohl in der Printausgabe als auch online das
groesste Rock- und Metal-Magazin Europas.

Rock It!
Seilandstr. 40, 59379 Selm, Germany
PH: 02592-918-599 FX: 02592-918-598
www.rock-it-magazine.de
*Das AOR * Hard Rock * Metal Magazin.*

Schweres-Metall.de
Hochwaldstraße 23, D-66954 Pirmasens, Germany
Sandy Cutter sandy@schweres-metall.de
www.schweres-metall.de
Das Onlinemagazin für Rock und Metal.

Sonny's Rock & Metal Heaven
webmaster@sonny1968.de
www.sonny1968.de
If you want to send me a copy of your CD for
review/ interview, please contact me.

Sounds Of Eternal War
soew_webzine@web.de
www.soew-webzine.de.vu
Dedicated to all fucking, true Black, Death, Thrash
Metal and Grindcore maniacs out there! Contact us
for submission details.

Tiefgang
Paulusstr. 8, 33602 Bielefeld, Germany
Marius Neugebauer info@tiefgang-online.de
www.tiefgang-online.de
News, interviews, MP3s, tour dates, reviews etc.

Tinnitus
Spannskanmp 26, 22527 Hamburg, Germany
Haiko Nahm haiko@tinnitus-mag.de
www.tinnitus-mag.de
Für adressen für demos und promos bitte die
entsprechenden mitarbeiter kontaktieren.

Underground Empire Metal Magazine
Seufzerweg 5, D - 66877 Ramstein-Miesenbach,
Germany
Stefan Glas stefan@underground-empire.com
www.underground-empire.de
Prasentiert Deutschlands fuhrendes Metal e-mag.

Underground Empire the Online Empire
Postfach 1602, D - 72006 Tübingen, Germany
Stefan Glas redaktion@underground-empire.com
www.underground-empire.com
News, interviews, reviews etc.

Vampster
Reichenberger Strasse 9, 71711 Steinheim, Germany
PH: 49-7144-894099 FX: 49-7144-894088
Andrea Veyhle andrea@vampster.com
www.vampster.com
Bands! labels! veranstalter! schickt daten, promos,
demos etc.

vampyria
Bergstrasse 2, 27367 Sottrum, Germany
Guido J. Schroeder contact@vampyria.de
www.vampyria.de
The Northern Metal site. Send CDs, demos, promos
etc. to the above address.

Voices from the Darkside
www.voicesfromthedarkside.de
The magazine for brutal Death, Thrash and Black
Metal!

Whiskey Soda
Postfach 42 01 02, 12061 Berlin, Germany
PH: 030-75-76-59-52
Sascha & Jens info@whiskey-soda.de
www.whiskey-soda.de
Alternative Rock/Metal music community.

Greece

Metal Eagle
Kerasouintos St. 33-35, Nea Smirni, 17124,
Athens, Greece
Konstantinos battlerager@metaleagle.com
www.metaleagle.com
News, reviews, interviews and more.

Metal Temple
www.metal-temple.com
Check our website for details on where to send your
music.

Italy

Babylon Magazine
www.babylonmagazine.net
Covering the Metal underground.

Shapeless Zine
PO Box 113, 20030 Senago (MI), Italy
Carlo Paleari hellvis@shapeless.it
www.shapeless.it
We review all Metal bands except nu-Metal bands.

Silent Scream
Via Benedettina Inferiore, 1, 98050 - Terme
Vigliatore (ME), Italy
Fulvio Adile industry@silentscreamzine.com
www.silentscreamzine.com
Metal and Alternative music site.

The Netherlands

Aardschok
PO Box 7, 5690 AA Son, The Netherlands
FX: 0499-475945
www.aardschok.com
You can send all CDs, demos and bios.

Blackfuel
www.blackfuel.nl
Metal & Hardcore e-zine.

Brutalism
Markiezaatpad 5, 5628 BR Eindhoven,
The Netherlands
PH: +31-6-231-33-859 FX: +31 (0) 847-16-59-67
Twan Sibon twan@brutalism.com
www.brutalism.com
Interviews, reviews etc. You can also have your
band/label promoted on our site for free!

Lords of Metal
Postbus 756, 1780 AT Den Helder, The Netherlands
Horst Vonberg lordsofmetal@quicknet.nl
www.lordsofmetal.nl/english
CD reviews, gig reviews and new interviews.

Rock-E-Zine
Klaproos 16, 4102HN, Culemborg, The Netherlands
info@rockezine.com
www.rockezine.net
It's all about Rock n' Roll but we like it hard. Up to
date interviews, concert reviews and CD reviews of
all genres!

Vampire Magazine
Kapittelhof 34, 4841 GX Prinsenbeek,
The Netherlands
Ricardo Mouwen ricardo@vampire-magazine.com
vampire-magazine.com
Covering the world of Underground Metal. Please
send your promos, demos and other material to us
for a fair review.

Norway

Beat the Blizzard
Ostover, N-2730 Lunner, Norway
AJ Blisten aj@beattheblizzard.com
www.beattheblizzard.com
Labels and bands are welcome to ship CDs for
review.

Enslaved by Metal
Erling Høviks veg 21, 7058 Jakobsli, Norway
Ole Markus contact@enslavedbymetal.com
www.enslavedbymetal.com
If you want us to review a demo/promo, contact us.

Metal Express Radio Show
Ovrefoss 14, N-0555 Oslo, Norway
Stig. G. Nordahl stig@metalexpressradio.com
www.metalexpressradio.com
Streaming radio, news, reviews, interviews...

Scream Magazine
scream@scream.no
www.screammagazine.com
Norway's biggest Metal magazine!

The Streets
Renvikveien 47, 8160 Glomfjord, Norway
PH: 480-93-990
Even Knudsen even@streetswebzine.com
www.streetswebzine.com
Dedicated to Heavy Metal music.

Poland

diabolous.com
Lord Darnok darnok@diabolous.com
diabolous.com
*Before sending any promo materials please
CONTACT us.*

Multum In Parvo
Ul. Zagorna 17, 05-230 Kobylka, Poland
PH: 0-691-34-89-20
Mariusz mechatronika@interia.pl
www.mip.av.pl/mip
MP3, zdjecia, ogloszenia, konkursy...

rockmetal.pl
rockmetal@rockmetal.pl
www.rockmetal.pl
Rock i Metal po polsku.

Russia

totalmetal.net
info@totalmetal.net
www.totalmetal.net
Russian's #1 Heavy Metal site.

Spain

Alfa:Omega
C/Pintor Balaca,5 1º A, 30205 -Cartagena (Murcia),
Spain
PH: 679397683
Jose E. Ricondo correo@alfaomega.info
www.alfaomega.info
*Webzine musical indpependente para metnes
inquietas.*

Basa Rock
Rafa Basa info@rafabasa.com
www.rafabasa.com
Portal en Castellano dedicado al Heavy Metal.

Canedo Rock
Apartado de Correos: 1027, 32001 - Ourense, Spain
canedorock@canedorock.com
www.canedorock.com
*Webzine dedicado al Rock en todas sus variantes
Metal, Heavy, Punk etc.*

Cuerdas de Acero
contacto@cuerdasdeacero.com
www.cuerdasdeacero.com
Tu portal de Rock Nacional.

Heavy Weight
Aptdo. Correos 541, 11200 Cádiz, Spain
Rodrigo infoheavyweight@ono.com
www.truemetal.org/heavyweight
Reviews, interviews, demos, news and more.

Inside Out Webzine
correo@insideoutwebzine.com
www.insideoutwebzine.com
*Musica, Metal, Rap-Metal, Nu-Metal, noticias,
conciertos, discos, listas ...*

The Metal Circus
Sergi Ramos sergi@themetalcircus.com
www.themetalcircus.com
Tu webzine de Metal.

Portaldelrock.com
comentariosportal@gmail.com
www.portaldelrock.com
Un portal de musica Rock y Metal.

Rock Circus
APDO. 146, 28820, Madrid, Spain
Iván Ortega rockcircus@arrakis.es
www.rockcircus.net
Tu revista de Rock en internet.

ROCK ESTATAL
rockestatal@rockestatal.com
rockestatal.com
Rock nacional estatal Heavy Metal y Punk.

XTREEM MUSIC
PO Box 1195, 28080, Madrid, Spain
info@xtreemmusic.com
www.xtreemmusic.com
Portal devoted to Extreme music.

Sweden

Close Up
PO Box 4411, SE-102 69, Stockholm, Sweden
PH: 46-8-462-02-14 FXA: 46-8-462-02-15
mail@closeupmagazine.net
www.closeupmagazine.net
A forum for all types of Extreme and Heavy music!

Metal Heart
Skivyxvägen 19, 723 53 Västerås, Sweden
Övrigt noak@metalheart.se
www.metalheart.se
Mainly focused on Metal and Hard Rock.

metal-only
Tvistevägen 9A Läg 106, 90729 Umeå, Sweden
Jan-Erik Nyman demo@metal-only.com
www.metal-only.com
*Review, interviews, write your own review or read
the latest Metal news.*

Swedish Metal
Olstorpsvägen 4, 616 30 ÅBY, Sweden
Fredrik Kreem fredrik@swedishmetal.net
www.swedishmetal.net
News, reviews, interviews, downloads etc.

Tartarean Desire
Rydsvagen 218A, S-584 32 Linkoping, Sweden
Vincent Eldefors tartareandesire@yahoo.com
www.tartareandesire.com
Metal and Dark music with reviews, interviews etc.

Switzerland

Schwermetall
info@schwarzmetall.ch
www.schwarzmetall.ch
Dark, Black, Trash Metal etc.

Swiss Metal Factory
PO Box 809, 5401 Baden, Switzerland
PH: 41-0-79-638-1021
metal@metalfactory.ch
www.metalfactory.ch
Reviews, interviews, concerts etc.

United Kingdom

Black Velvet
336 Birchfield Rd. Webheath, Redditch, Worcs,
B97 4NG UK
editor@blackvelvetmagazine.com
www.blackvelvetmagazine.com
Features Glam, Punk, Rock, Metal and more.

Burn Magazine
PO Box 350, Dover, Kent CT17 0WF UK
info@burnmag.co.uk
media21c@aol.com
www.burnmag.co.uk
The magazine without fear!

doom-metal.com
122 Colwith Rd. London, W6 9EZ UK
reviews@doom-metal.com
www.doom-metal.com
Please see submission guidelines before sending.

Justin-Case.co.uk
PO Box 1055, Market Harborough, Leicestershire,
LE16 7ZL UK
PH: 0116-858464678
justin@justin-case.co.uk
www.justin-case.co.uk
Rock album reviews.

Kerrang! Magazine
Mappin House, 4 Winsley St., London,
W1W 8HF UK
PH: 020-7436-1515
kerrang@emap.com
www.kerrang.com
The world's biggest selling weekly Rock magazine.

Live 4 Metal
6 Kingston House, 232-234 Imperial Dr. Rayners
Ln. Harrow, Middlesex, HA2 7HJ UK
Pete Woods kutulu666@hotmail.com
www.live4metal.com
The best of the Metal world.

Metal Hammer
1 Balcombe St., London, NW1 6NA UK
Attn: Reviews editor
PH: +44 (0)870-444-8649
Jamie Hibbard jamie.hibbard@futurenet.co.uk
www.metalhammer.co.uk
Send a copy of your latest demo.

Metal Mayhem
Chris Rogers chris@metal-mayhem.co.uk
www.metal-mayhem.co.uk
Please contact us for the address to send stuff to.

New Breed
newbreed@newbreedonline.co.uk
newbreedonline.co.uk
*Promoting signed and unsigned bands. Features CD
reviews, live reviews and interviews.*

Planet-Loud
PO Box 2581, Reading, Berks, RG1 7GT UK
info@planet-loud.com
www.planet-loud.com
The loudest music site on the net!

Powerplay
PO Box 227, Manchester, M22 4YT UK
PH: 0161-4914211
Mark Hoaksey
mark@powerplaymagazine.freeserve.co.uk
www.powerplaymagazine.co.uk
Hard, Heavy, Power, Prog, Progressive, Speed,
AOR, FM, Death, Extreme and Black.

Raw Nerve Promotions
24 Brooklyn Ter. Armley, Leeds, W. Yorkshire,
LS12 2BX UK
Paul Priest paulrawnerve@ntlworld.com
www.rawnervepromotions.co.uk
News, interviews, reviews, articles, profiles, shows,
gigs etc.

Rock Midgets.com
www.rockmidgets.com
We focus on Rock, Metal and Punk.

ROCK SOUND
#22, Jack's Pl., 6 Corbet Pl., Spitalfields, London,
E1 6NN UK
Darren darren.taylor@rock-sound.net
www.rock-sound.net
Monthly music magazine in the UK.

ROCKREVIEW.co.uk
Liam Martin liam@rockreview.co.uk
www.rockreview.co.uk
News and reviews from the world of Rock and
Metal.

Terrorizer
#36, 10-50 Willow St., London, EC2A 4BH UK
PH: 44-20-7729-7666 FX: 44-20-7739-0544
Jonathan Selzer editorial@terrorizer.com
www.terrorizer.co.uk
Magazine for Extreme music of ANY kind.

Australia

The Buzz
PO Box 55, Dromana, VIC 3936 Australia
PH: 61-3-59812979 FX: 61-3-59861449
psutton@r150.aone.net.au
www.ozonline.com.au/buzz
CD reviews, interviews and coverage of local
artists.

FasterLouder.com.au
PO Box 1964, Strawberry Hills, NSW 2012
Australia
PH: 02-8353-7070 FX: 02-8353-7099
www.fasterlouder.com.au
Gig info, interviews, reviews etc.

MelodicRock.com
GPO Box 1770, Hobart, TAZ 7001 Australia
PH: +61-3-6229-3113
Andrew J. McNeice ajm@melodicrock.com
www.melodicrock.com
Reviews Melodic and Hard Rock.

PyroMusic
PO Box 6016, Marrickville South, NSW 2204
Australia
pyromusic@pyromusic.net
www.Pyromusic.net
If you're Metal we're happy to receive your material
for review.

TheSharpEndZine
PO Box 1581, Coorparoo DC, QLD 4151 Australia
Sean thesharpendfanzine@yahoo.com
www.myspace.com/thesharpendfanzine
A Hardcore and Metal orientated black and white
zine.

Asia

HeavyMetal.co.il
www.heavymetal.co.il
Supporting the Israeli Metal scene.

New Age

Amazing Sounds
Apartado de Correas 727, PO Box 08220, Tarrasa,
Barcelona, Spain
amazingsounds@amazings.com
www.amazings.com
News, articles, interviews, album reviews…

Ambient Visions
PO Box 539, Lucas, OH 44843
Michael Foster editor@ambientvisions.com
www.ambientvisions.com
Reviews and interviews of Ambient, New Age,
Electronica and Techno music.

Awareness Magazine
446 S. Anaheim Hills Rd. #183, Anaheim,
CA 92807
PH: 714-283-3385 FX: 714-283-3389
info@awarenessmag.com
www.awarenessmag.com
Holistic magazine with music and video reviews.

EarthLight Magazine
111 Fairmount Ave. Oakland, CA 94611
PH: 510-451-4926
klauren@earthlight.org
www.earthlight.org
We do very occasional CD reviews.

The Harp Column
2101 Brandywine, #200B, Philadelphia, PA 19130
Attn: Jan Jennings,
PH: 800-582-3021 FX: 215-564-3518
www.harpcolumn.com
Reviews, news, forum and announcements regarding
the harp.

Innerchange
1602 S. Wade Ave. Garner, NC 27529
PH: 919-661-2282 FX: 919-779-9136
Karen Newton editor@innerchangemag.com
innerchangemag.com
Magazine website with music reviews.

Kindred Spirit
Sandwell Barns, Harberton, Totnes, Devon,
TQ9 7LJ UK
PH: 01803-866686 FX: 01803-866591
web@kindredspirit.co.uk
www.kindredspirit.co.uk
The UK's leading guide for body, mind and spirit.

Magical Blend
PO Box 600, Chico, CA 95927-0600
PH: 530-893-9037 FX: 530-893-9076
info@magicalblend.com
www.magicalblend.com
An entertaining and thoroughly unique look at the
modern spiritual lifestyle.

Mysteries Magazine
PO Box 490, Walpole, NH 03608-0490
PH: 603-352-1645 FX: 603-352-0232
Kim Guarnaccia editor@mysteriesmagazine.com
www.MysteriesMagazine.com
We review CDs of World music, New Age music,
healing/meditation/yoga music etc.

New Age Retailer
2183 Alpine Way, Bellingham, WA 98226
PH: 800-463-9243 FX: 360-676-0932
www.newageretailer.com
Two independent music review columns.

New Age Reporter
650 Poydras #2523, New Orleans, LA 70130
www.newagereporter.com
We will review New Age, World, Celtic, Folk and
Neo-Classical works.

New Renaissance
3A Cazenove Rd. London, N16 6PA UK
PH: +44-20-88064250
newren@ru.org
www.ru.org
Reviews of books, recordings and events.

Solo Piano Publications
Kathy Parsons kathypiano@comcast.net
www.solopianopublications.com
Helping to promote New Age and Classical piano
music in hopes of reaching new ears and audiences.

Spirit of Change
PO Box 3073, Oakland, CA 94609
Jason Serinus jserinus@planeteria.net
www.spiritofchange.org
Welcomes independent music reviews and all music
releases.

Writings by Serge Kozlovsky
PO Box 410, 220050 Minsk, Belarus
serge_kozlovsky@tut.by
mkmk.com/kozlovsky
Articles, interviews and reviews.

Yoga Journal
475 Sansome St. #850, San Francisco, CA 94111
PH: 415-591-0555 FX: 415-591-0733
Kaitlin Quistgaard editorial@yogajournal.com
www.yogajournal.com
The voice of yoga online.

Yoga Magazine
26 York St., London, W1U 6PZ UK
PH: 44-020-7729-5454 FX: 44-020-7739-0025
www.yogamagazine.co.uk
Willing to listen to anything you send.

Progressive Rock

Progressive Rock, AOR, Jazzrock, Melodic
Rock, Progressive Metal, Spacerock,
Krautrock, Psychedelic and Improvisational
Rock

North America

United States

Exposé
6167 Jarvis Ave. #150, Newark, CA 94560-1210
ptlk@expose.org
www.expose.org
Focuses on Progressive and Experimental Rock.

ghostland.com
chad@ghostland.com
ghostland.com
*Your source for Progressive Rock on the web.
Contact us for mailing address.*

Ground and Sky
1820 Ontario Pl. Washington, DC 20009
webmaster@progreviews.com
www.progreviews.com
*Please do not e-mail us asking if it's OK to send us
your CD. Just send it in and we'll make the
judgment based on the music.*

Music Street Journal
Gary Hill
musicstreetjournal@musicstreetjournal.com
www.musicstreetjournal.com
News, reviews, interviews ...

Prog Archives
www.progarchives.com
Post your reviews on our site.

Prog4you.com
PO Box 687, Coatesville, PA 19320
info@prog4you.com
www.prog4you.com
*We are always looking for new material, that we can
listen to and review.*

ProGGnosis
PO Box 27226, Golden Valley, MN 55427-0226
webmaster@proggnosis.com
www.proggnosis.com
*Our goal is to further the success of Progressive and
Fusion music genres.*

Progression Magazine
PO Box 7164, Lowell, MA 01852
PH: 978-970-2728 FX: 978-970-2728
progzine@aol.com
www.progressionmagazine.com
News, reviews, interviews and features.

Progressive Ears
1594 6th St., Trenton, NJ 08638
Floyd Bledsoe floyd@progressiveears.com
progressiveears.com
Progressive Rock discussion, polls and reviews.

ProgressiveWorld.net
Stephanie sollows@progressiveworld.net
www.progressiveworld.net
*Check our site to find out which reviewer accepts
your style of Prog music.*

ProgNaut.com
PO Box 266, Santa Monica, CA 90406-0266
reviews@prognaut.com
www.prognaut.com
Vessel for Southern California Progressive music.

ProgScape.Com
www.progscape.com
Get your CD or DVD reviewed.

Sea of Tranquility
53 Old Country Rd. Monroe, NY 10950
www.seaoftranquility.org
Journal of Fusion and Progressive Rock.

Ytsejam.com
www.ytsejam.com
We try to review all CDs we receive.

South America

Planeta-Rock
info@planeta-rock.com.ar
www.planeta-rock.com.ar
New, reviews, radio etc.

Progressive Rock & Progressive Metal
Rua Tailandia 426, Bras de Pina, Cep 21011350, Rio
de Janeiro, Brasil
Carlos Vaz carlosvaz@br.inter.net
www.progressiverockbr.com
Reviews, interviews and much more.

Europe

Belgium

Prog Nose
Beekstraat 1, 2640 Mortsel, Belgium
Claeskens Jany info@prog-nose.org
www.prog-nose.be
Promoting Progressive Rock in general.

Prog-résiste
Ave de l'Equinoxe, 8, B-1300, Wavre, Belgium
PH: 32-0-10-41-35-71 FX: +32-0-10-41-05-49
Gilles Arend webmaster@progresiste.com
www.progresiste.com
*We publish (in French only) a quarterly, 132 pages
magazine with reviews, news, rumors, events ...*

Rock Report
Collegestraat 129, B-8310 Assebroek, Belguim
PH: 32-050-35-87-72 FX: 32-050-35-87-72
info@rockreport.be
www.rockreport.be
A new medium, totally dedicated to AOR.

France

AmarokProg
webmaster@amarokprog.net
www.amarokprog.net
*All about Progressive Rock, Metal, Alternative Rock
and Electro with band pages, concert guides, news,
reviews and much more!*

Big Bang
17 ave. de la Monta, 38120 St. Egreve, France
PH: 33-04-76580290 FX: 33-04-76580290
redaction@bigbangmag.com
www.bigbangmag.com
*Une revue Français consacrée aux musiques
Progressives.*

KOID'9
51, ave. Wilson, 45500 Gien, France
koid9@club-internet.fr
koid9.fanzine.free.fr
*Un fanzine trimestriel très complet, réalisé par des
passionnés, traitant avec humour de l'actualité du
Rock Progressif, Metal Progressif et Rock Alternatif.*

Progressia.net
promotion@progressia.net
www.progressia.net
*Rock Progressif, Metal Progressif, Jazz
Expérimental, Fusion, Post-Rock.*

somethingprog.com
webmaster@somethingprog.com
www.somethingprog.com
*Rock Progressif, Métal Progressif, Death Metal,
Doom ...*

Traverses
c/o Stéphane Fougère, 16, ave. d'Alfortville, 94600
Choisy le Roi, France
traversesmag.org
*Musiques presque nouvelles et autrement Progressia
neogressives.*

Germany

AOR Heaven
Landshuter Strasse 11, 84051 Altheim, Germany
PH: 49-8703-8517 FX: 49-8703-8568
georg.siegl@aorheaven.com
www.aorheaven.com
If you have a demo feel free to contact us.

Babyblaue Prog-Reviews
Grünwalder Straße 117, D-81547 München,
Germany
PH: 089-64260946
Udo Gerhards promos@babyblaue-seiten.de
www.babyblaue-seiten.de
Die Prog-Enzyklopädie der mailing liste.

Bright Eyes
Grunewaldstraße 49b, 22149 Hamburg, Germany
PH: +49 (0)40-69667832
info@brighteyes.de
www.brighteyes.de
*Interviews und reviews aus der Metal und HardRock
szene.*

Progressive Newsletter
Postfach 1806, D-71208 Leonberg, Germany
Kristian Selm Kristian@Progressive-Newsletter.de
www.progressive-newsletter.de
Reviews, interviews, gig dates etc.

Italy

Arlequins
Via Paparoni 6, 53100 Siena, Italy
Alberto Nucci info@arlequins.net
www.arlequins.it
Covers the Progressive Rock underground scene.

MovimentiPROG
staff@movimentiprog.net
www.movimentiprog.net
Riflessioni scritte sulla musica che evolv.

The Netherlands

Axiom of Choice
PO Box 80-089, 3508TB Utrecht, The Netherlands
Jurriaan Hage jur@cs.uu.nl
www.cs.uu.nl/people/jur/progrock.html
Progressive Rock music and related genres.

Background Magazine
PO Box 3155, 1620 GD Hoorn, The Netherlands
info@backgroundmagazine.nl
www.backgroundmagazine.nl
*High quality information on Progressive Rock and
closely related music on an international level.*

The Dutch Progressive Rock Page
29 Lutton Cres. Billingham, TX22 5DZ UK
B. Mulvey dprp@vuurwerk.nl
www.dprp.vuurwerk.nl
Internet magazine on Progressive Rock.

The iO Pages
Postbus 67, 2678 ZH De Lier, The Netherlands
FX: +31-174-51-12-13
iopages@iopages.nl
www.iopages.nl
*Magazine devoted to Progressive Rock and all its
related genres.*

Prog Visions
Laan van de Mensenrechten 180. 7331 VV
Apeldoorn, The Netherlands
www.progvisions.net
Center of information about Progressive Rock.

Progwereld
Postbus 7069, 2701 AB Zoetermeer,
The Netherlands
Maarten Goossensen info@progwereld.org
www.progwereld.org
News, reviews, interviews, columns etc.

Psychedelic Music Database
webmaster@psychedelic-music.net
www.psychedelic-music.net
Submit reviews, information on your band etc.
Contact us before you send your music.

Norway

Tarkus
Mollefaret 48B, N-0750 Oslo, Norway
Sven Eriksen sven@tarkus.org
www.tarkus.org
We cover a wide spectrum of Progressive music.

Portugal

Prog PT
Travessa de Monserrate N 32, 3 Dto. 4450-199
Matosinhos, Portugal
Spulit info@prog-pt.com
www.prog-pt.com
Promoting Progressive music in all of its sub-genres.

United Kingdom

Acid Attack
19 Belper Row, Dudley W. Midlands, DY2 9LP UK
Martyn Jones acidattack.music@virgin.net
www.acidattackmusic.co.uk
Reviews and news on mostly independent music.

Mood Swings
nigel@mswings.com
www.mswings.com
News, links, interviews, reviews etc.

New Horizons
feedback@elrose.demon.co.uk
www.elrose.co.uk
Progressive, Classic and Melodic Rock on the web.

Uzbekistan

ProgressoR
PO Box 4065, Tashkent, 700100, Uzbekistan
Vitaly Menshikov vitt@glb.net
www.progressor.net
Send your CDs to us for review. Please, no demos!

Punk

Punk, Hardcore, Emo, Oi, Garage and Anti-Folk

N o r t h   A m e r i c a

United States

A Thousand Apologies
Brian Roberts brian@athousandapologies.com
www.athousandapologies.com
Interviews, reviews, bad ass music news and info!

Absolute Punk
jason.tate@absolutepunk.net
www.absolutepunk.net
Submit your demo, album or EP to us.

Acclaimed Punk
Derek Clement derek@acclaimedpunk.com
AcclaimedPunk.com
Music news, interviews, reviews and more.

Alarm Press
53 W. Jackson Blvd. #1256, Chicago, IL 60604
music@alarmpress.com
www.alarmpress.com
Bi-monthly magazine. Covers Northeast concerts.

All Ages Zine.com
Jeffrey Kurtis allageszine@allageszine.com
www.AllAgesZine.com
Dedicated to music of all kinds. We do reviews,
interviews, post tour dates, band information…

American Music Press
PO Box 1070, Martinez, CA 94553
Scoot@ampmagazine.com
ampmagazine.com
Interviews, reviews, columns, articles etc.

Askew Reviews
PO Box 684, Hanover, MA 02339
denis@askewreviews.com
www.askewreviews.com
We cover, review and promote music.

Aversion.com
PO Box 271556, Fort Collins, CO 80527-1556
PH: 970-493-0585
info@aversion.com
www.aversion.com
Submit your press kits and demos. Rock, Punk and
Indie.

Burning Angel
c/o reviews, PO Box 111014, Brooklyn, NY 11211
www.burningangel.com
*Labels, send your newest releases.*Site contains*
ADULT content.

Bystander Fanzine
PO Box 10392, Albany, NY 12201
PH: 518-369-8759
Scott bystanderfanzine@gmail.com
www.bystanderfanzine.com
Covering the Hardcore scene.

centerfuse.net
reviews@centerfuse.net
www.centerfuse.net
Dedicated to the independent music scene.

Chain-Whipped Magazine
2976 Washington Blvd. Cleveland Heights,
OH 44118
PH: 216-397-1191
Warren Davis chain-whipped@chain-whipped.com
www.chain-whipped.com
Born in the back alleys of Tokyo and spreading like
a virus worldwide.

Chaos and Fruit Punch
PO Box 13380, Mill Creek, WA 98082
Adam Chaos adam@operationphoenixrecords.com
www.operationphoenixrecords.com/zine.html
Reviews music while publishing personal stories.

Chord Magazine
PO Box 56821, Sherman Oaks, CA 91413
PH: 818-905-9347
Gus Peña gus@chordmagazine.com
www.chordmagazine.com
National magazine published 6 times a year.
Features Emo, Punk, Metal, Hardcore …

The Continental Magazine
PO Box 4336, Bellingham, WA 98227-4336
Sean Berry records@dblcrown.com
www.dblcrown.com
Surf/Instrumental and Garage Rock n' Roll.

Corn 'Zine
PO Box 321, Huntington, WV 25708
www.cornzine.com
Covering Hardcore, Punk, Ska, Indie, Emo etc.

Culture Bunker
PO Box 480353, Los Angeles, CA 90048
culturebunker@culturebunker.com
www.culturebunker.com
Indiscriminate, wholesale, erotic, power-mad killing.

Da' Core
4407 Bowes Ave. W. Mifflin, PA 15122
PH: 412-462-0203
E. Corbin ecorbin@dacorerecords.com
www.da-core.com
A Hardcore label and magazine.

Dagger Zine
PO Box 820102, Portland, OR 97282-1102
daggerboy@prodigy.net
www.indiepages.com/dagger
Interviews, articles and hundreds of reviews.

Deadtide.com
4950 N. Kimball Ave. #2E, Chicago, IL 60625
Jason Muxlow info@deadtide.com
www.deadtide.com
We'll review your album. Send it to the above
address.

Decoy Music Magazine
PO Box 6078, Atascadero, CA 93423
www.decoymusic.com
Covering everything from Punk to Metal to Indie to Hip Hop. Industry revealing interviews and more.

Delusions of Adequacy
PO Box 23558, Rochester, NY 14692
doa@adequacy.net
www.adequacy.net
Music reviews, interviews, concert reviews and more.

Dick Snot! Fanzine
PO Box 228, Centereach, NY 11720
PH: 347-886-9378
Chris Manic manic@dicksnot.net
www.dicksnot.net
DSF stands as a key example of all that can go wrong in print.

emotionalpunk.com
PO Box 11052, Glendale, CA 91226
Andrew Martin andrew.martin@emotionalpunk.com
www.emotionalpunk.com
If you are an artist or promoter and want a "guaranteed" review, be sure to e-mail me first.

Empyre Lounge
11 Parker St. 3rd Fl. Malden, MA 02148
label@empyrelounge.com
www.empyrelounge.com
Protecting endangered music.

hardcorewebsite.net
nycore@hardcorewebsite.net
www.hardcorewebsite.net
I only support bands that support our scene.

How's Your Edge?
72 Rockland Rd. Auburn, MA 01501
Brian Murphy murphy@howsyouredge.com
www.howsyouredge.com
News, reviews, shows etc.

ihateyour.com
560 Pine Ct. Sequim, WA 98382
John Himmelberger contact@ihateyour.com
www.ihateyour.com
Send us your press kit, along with your latest release.

Independent Clauses
8820 S. 75th E. Ave. Tulsa, OK 74133
IndependentClauses@hotmail.com
www.independentclauses.com
Dedicated to the reviewing of unknown music, be it independent or 'signed'. We want to hear your band.

Juice
1924 Vera Ct. Wilmington, NC 28403
PH: 910-313-6986 FX: 910-313-1082
Terri Craft JuiceMag@aol.com
www.juicemagazine.com
Sounds, surf and skate.

Laminated
1134 22nd St. #6, San Pedro, CA 90731
Dustin Pryor email@laminated.org
www.laminated.org
CD/show reviews, interviews and photographs.

The Lance Monthly
PO Box 613, Sandia Park, NM 87047
Dick Stewart rvstewartproductions@yahoo.com
www.lancerecords.com
'60s Surf and Garage band music.

Lollipop
PO Box 441493, Boston, MA 02144
PH: 617-623-5319
Scott Hefflon scott@lollipop.com
www.lollipop.com
We cover all that fiercely Alternative music.

Music Spork
PO Box 27883, Los Angeles, CA 90027-0883
Aerin Wilson editor@musicspork.com
www.musicspork.com
Guide to new Indie Rock, Garage, Electronica etc.

Neu Futur
650 Morris #6, Kent, OH 44243
James McQuiston editor@neufutur.com
www.neufutur.com
I review anything that comes across my desk.

Paranoize
PO Box 15554, New Orleans, LA 70175-5554
Bobby Bergeron paranoize@hotmail.com
www.paranoizenola.com
Covers Sludge, Grindcore, Hardcore, Extreme Metal, Stoner Rock and non-Pop/Ska influenced Punk.

pastepunk
9126 Huber Ct. Burke, VA 22015
Jordan A. Baker jordan@pastepunk.com
www.pastepunk.com
Tons of reviews, interviews and columns.

Psychobilly Homepage
roy@wreckingpit.com
www.wreckingpit.com
Concerts, news, reviews interviews and more.

Punk Globe
1626 N. Wilcox Ave. #256, Hollywood, CA 90028
Ginger Coyote ginger@punkglobe.com
www.punkglobe.com
News, interviews, music & show reviews.

Punk Magazine
PO Box 675, 200 E. 10th St., New York, NY 10003
Editor@punkmagazine.com
www.punkmagazine.com
Send all promo material, CDs and other hard copy to us.

Punk-it.net
sev@punk-it.net
www.punk-it.net
Interviews, show and CD reviews, columns ...

Punkmusic.com
Neal Ganslaw neal@punkmusic.net
www.punkmusic.com
News, interviews, reviews, links and more.

punknews.org
39 Greenhaven Dr. Port Jefferson Stn., NY 11776
Attn: Brian Shultz
www.punknews.org
Submit your material for review.

punkplanet.com
4229 N. Honore, Chicago, IL 60613
PH: 773-248-7172 FX: 773-248-7189
letters@punkplanet.com
www.punkplanet.com
We will make every attempt to include you in our reviews section.

punkrockreviews.com
4133 W. Melrose St., Chicago, IL 60641-4641
Bart Niedzialkowski info@punkrockreviews.com
www.punkrockreviews.com
Accepts all your material. No MP3s!

READ Magazine
PO Box 3437, Astoria, NY 11103
editor@readmag.com
www.readmag.com
Want to send us something? We review everything!

Redefine Magazine
PO Box 95219, Seattle, WA 98145-2219
Vivian Hua letters@redefinemag.com
www.redefinemag.com
An online magazine dedicated to Rock music, art and social commentary.

Redstar Magazine
PO Box 536811, Orlando, FL 32853
PH: 407-497-9793
skweels@redstarmag.com
www.redstarmag.com
Online magazine supporting music and modeling. New, reviews, interviews ...

Reviewer Magazine
PO Box 87069, San Diego, CA 92138
PH: 619-694-6680
Rob editor@reviewermagazine.com
www.reviewermag.com
We cover Indie and Punk Rock, social issues etc.

Rock n Roll Purgatory
PO Box 276258, San Antonio, TX 78227
rocknrollpurgatory@yahoo.com
www.rocknrollpurgatory.com
We review Rockabilly, Surf, Punk, Oi, Swing, Psychobilly and then some ...

Ska, Punk and Other Junk
407 Regency Ct. Middletown, NY 10940
Bryan Kremkau
webmaster@skapunkandotherjunk.com
www.skapunkandotherjunk.com
CD, DVD, concert reviews, interviews etc.

Skratch Magazine
17300 17th St. J-123, Tustin, CA 92780
www.SkratchMagazine.com
Covers Garage Rock, Punk, Hardcore and Emo.

Skyscraper
PO Box 486, Mamaroneck, NY 10543
skyscraperzine@hotmail.com
www.skyscrapermagazine.com
Music, print, live reviews and more.

Soundnova.com
PH: 410-627-1733
Corey Evans info@soundnova.com
www.Soundnova.com
Covering mainstream and underground acts.

soundriot
sara@sound-riot.com
www.sound-riot.com
News, reviews, interviews and more!

Stand Up Jack zine
13545 S. Horrell Rd. Fenton, MI 48430
John McKay StandUpJackzine@aol.com
www.StandUpJack.net
We make an attempt to review all submissions, as well as do interviews/features.

Status Magazine
PO Box 1300, Thousand Oaks, CA 91358
statusmagazine@gmail.com
www.statusinc.com/magazine
Free magazine covering Alternative, Hardcore, Emo, Indie Rock, Pop Punk ...

Super Bitch Magazine
PO Box 973, Royal Oak, MI 48068
John Davies superbitchmagazine@yahoo.com
www.superbitchmagazine.com
Dedicated to girls, booze, music ...and more girls. Music reviews that don't follow the norm.

Switch Magazine
PO Box 3623, Myrtle Beach, SC 29578
switchmagazine.com
We do mostly Punk and Hip Hop reviews.

The Toilet
Ralph W. Llama ralph@thetoiletonline.com
www.thetoiletonline.com
Submit anything you have to offer.

Tragic Endings
2 Stephanie Ln. Lakeville, MA 02347
Stephanie DeMoura stephanie@tragicendings.net
www.tragicendings.net
We're not about money or being into the 'scene' or any of that nonsense. We love to help out the bands.

truepunk.com
301 E. 34th St. #103, Austin, TX 78705
staff@truepunk.com
www.truepunk.com
News, reviews, interviews and a message board.

Tweed Magazine
312 Humboldt St. #3, Brooklyn, NY 11211
Stewart Smith stewart@tweedmag.com
tweedmag.com
Interviews with bands, artists, and other influential members of society.

UsedWigs
Russ Starke russ@usedwigs.com
www.usedwigs.com
Current Indie, Punk and other assorted quality music reviews.

Canada

Ambush The Night
15 Waterbridge Way, Toronto, ON M1C 5C5
info@ambushthenight.com
www.ambushthenight.com
Send your CD in for review!

Edge of Summer
71 Elliott St., London, ON N5Y2E6
Ashley ashlee@edgeofsummer.net
www.edgeofsummer.net
Punk and Indie Rock zine. Send your CDs to the above address.

Flex Your Head
11067 146 A St., Surrey, BC V3R 3V3
info@flexyourhead.net
www.flexyourhead.net
Reviews, audio samples, interviews, links and more.

punkhardcore.com
PO Box 25442, London, ON N6C 3P5
Ryan Izzard ryan@punkhardcore.com
www.punkhardcore.com
Up to date news, interviews, CD reviews and more.

SHZine
Stu Hood stuart@shzine.com
www.shzine.com
Get in touch and we'll send you our mailing address. If possible, please include a link to where a sample of your band can be heard or read about.

Scene It All
20355 Erie Peat Rd. Port Colborne, ON L3K 5V4
PH: 905-835-0355
Louie Baribeau louey@sceneitall.net
sceneitall.net
Built to better serve the music scene with CD reviews, interviews, MP3 teasers, live footage etc.

Europe

Belgium

High Heels Slut
Oude Tramweg 50, 8560 Moorsele, Belgium
PH: ++32-(0)56-42-66-90
Wim 'Retard' Cottenier cottenier.wim@yucom.be
www.myspace.com/highheelsslut
Coverage on any kind of true and wild R'n'R. Punk, Garage, Surf, HC ...

Mashnote.Magazine
Asstraat 4/2, 2400 Mol, Belgium
Jim Faes info@mashnote.net
www.mashnote.net
Interviews, reviews, news and more. Contact us before sending in your music.

Nameless
Rue de Warnoumont, 53, 4140 Sprimont, Belgium
weare@webzinenameless.net
www.webzinenameless.net
News, reviews, interviews and more.

Punk Updates
St-Hubertusplein 52/1, 3290 Schaffen, Belgium
Hein Terweduwe hein@punkupdates.com
www.punkupdates.com
Send in stuff for review or put up links.

PunkRockTheory
PO Box 79, Mechelen, Belgium 2800
PH: 0032-479-232-680
Thomas Dumarey thomas@punkrocktheory.com
www.punkrocktheory.com
We have tons of reviews, interviews, MP3s and label profiles.

Finland

Hardcoresounds
Kauppapuistikko 24 B 22, 65100 Vaasa, Finland
Arto Mäenpää crew@hardcoresounds.net
hardcoresounds.net
Send us an album or other material for review.

France

Kill...What?
9 Ave. de la Gare, 34440, Nissan, France
Kelly Saux kelly@killwhat.com
www.killwhat.com
Send in your promo material.

Metalorgie.com
djou@metalorgie.com
www.metalorgie.com/punk
There are different contacts covering the various sub-genres of Punk.

Punk (is) For Dummies
anne@punk4dummies.com
punk4dummies.com
News, reviews, interviews, MP3s ...

Sans Tambour ni Trompette
9, rue Bartholdi, 56700 Hennebont, France
info@stnt.org
www.stnt.org
Interactive ezine & radio show from France with news (a lot!), reviews, links, interviews...

Germany

Allschools Network
PO Box 911116, 30431 Hannover, Germany
Torben Utecht torben@allschools.de
www.allschools.de
Network Hardcore eZine.

Between Evil And Peace
info@beap.de
www.beap.de
Stoner Rock, Psychedelic Rock ...

Broken Violence
Hofstattstr. 36, 70825 Munchingen, Germany
www.brokenviolence.de
E-Zine für Hardcore, Punk, Indie und Metal.

CORE Ground
RehmstraBe 119, #501, 49080 Osnabruck, Germany
Holger Straede holger@coreground.de
www.coreground.de
Hardcore fanzine. Send in your material.

Daredevil Magazine
Kantstr. 31, 68723 Oftersheim, Germany
Ralf Burkart daredevil-mag@web.de
www.daredevil.de
Send in your material to get reviewed.

Enough
PO Box 12 07 50, 68058 Mannheim, Germany
info@enoughfanzine.com
www.enoughfanzine.com
DIY punk/HC/Ska/Indie e-zine for the scene!

FetzOrDie.com
Werner-Bock Str 9, D- 33602, Bielefeld, Germany
Raphael Gutberlet information@fetzordie.com
www.fetzordie.com
Send all CDs, tour information etc. to the above address.

In-Your-Face
Postfach 65 71, D- 30065, Hannover, Germany
Ralf Sonnenberg redaktion@in-your-face.de
www.in-your-face.de
Punk, Hardcore, Emo, Metal, Nu Metal ...

Konzi-Tip.de
Schopenhauer Strasse 31, D-14467 Potsdam, Germany
PH: 030-70301911 FX: 0331-7482913
Martin R. Woicke webmaster@konzi-tip.de
www.konzi-tip.de
Punk, Emo, Hard Rock, Gothic ...

Moloko Plus
Feldstr 10, 46286 Dorsten, Germany
info@moloko-plus.de
www.moloko-plus.de
News, dates, gigs, zines and more.

Online Zine
Aulgasse 131, 53721 Seigburg, Germany
Savage Alex savage_alex@onlinezine.de
www.onlinezine.net
The voice of subculture. Reviews, news and more.

Ox Fanzine
PO Box 102225, 42766 Haan, Germany
PH: +49 (0)2104-810-828 FX: +49 (0)2104-810-830
Joachim Hiller mail@ox-fanzine.de
www.ox-fanzine.de
Germany's biggest Punk Rock & Hardcore zine.

Plastic Bomb
Postfach 100205, 47002 Duisburg, Germany
PH: 0203-730613 FX: 0203-734288
info@plastic-bomb.de
www.plastic-bomb.de
News, reviews, interviews and much more.

purerock.de
Diesterwegstr. 9c, 10405 Berlin, Germany
PH: 030-420-22-917 FX: 030-420-22-917
Steffen Lehmann webmaster@purerock.de
www.purerock.de
Your Alternative Rock community.

Scarred For Life
www.scarred-for-life.de
Punk, Oi, Ska, Metal reviews, interviews etc.

Trust Fanzine
Postfach 11 07 62, 28087 Bremen, Germany
PH: 0421-49-15-88-0 FX: 0421-49-15-88-1
Dolf Hermannstädter dolf@trust-zine.de
www.trust-zine.de
Online resource for Hardcore, Punk Rock and Emo.

Waste of Mind
Oranienstr. 6, 10997 Berlin, Germany
Kai Wydra wom@wasteofmind.de
www.wasteofmind.de
News, reviews, tour dates, MP3s and much more.

XSEBX.com
www.xsebx.com
Contact us via our online form before sending in your music.

Italy

Be Nice to Mommy
theguru@benicetomommy.com
www.benicetomommy.com
Fanzine Italiana dedicata al Punk-Rock.

Freak Out
43, 80059, Torre Del Greco, Napoli, Italy
FX: 0039-081-8822687
Vittorio Emanule freakout@libero.it
www.freakout-online.com
Independent music magazine. Postrock Noise, Emo, Metal ...

In Your Eyes
Via N. Cantalupo 15h/5b, 17019 Varazze (SV) Italy
Simone Benerecetti simone@iyezine.com
www.iyezine.com
About what we think and what we feel.

komakino
Paolo yrkomakino@gmail.com
www.inkoma.com
If you can direct me to a couple of MP3s, I'll check them out and get in touch.

The Netherlands

Asice.net
W. Kluinveenweg 28, 7641 AR Wierden,
The Netherlands
David Brinks info@asice.net
www.asice.net
Get your stuff reviewed, promoted or whatever!

Norway

punkbands.com
Haldensvingen 31, 1387 Asker, Norway
Carsten Jacobsen reviews@punkbands.com
www.punkbands.com
Promotes Punk/Ska/Oi bands from all over the world.

Spain

I wanna.
PO Box 156.103, 28080, Madrid, Spain
www.ipunkrock.com
Online Punk- Rock n' Roll zine in Spanish.

iPunkRock
c/o Rafael Peláez, PO Box 156.103, 28080 -
Madrid, Spain
www.ipunkrock.com
Punk, Punk Rock, Garage, PowerPop, Rock n' Roll.

RockCore
www.rockcore.com
Hardcore, Rock, Metal y Punk.

Sweden

Doomsday Magazine
Gamlestadsvägen 19F, 41502 Göteborg, Sweden
Andreas Hedberg doomsday@home.se
www.doomsdaymag.com
News, interviews, reviews and more.

Happy as Raw Sewage *(HARS)*
Vallavagen 8.213, SE-582 Linkoping, Sweden
Hjertstrand contact@happyasrawsewage.com
www.happyasrawsewage.com
Covers Ska, Swing, Punk, Emo and Hardcore.

United Kingdom

Brain Love
brain.love@btinternet.com
www.brainlove.co.uk
Interviews, news, reviews and much, much more.

Bubblegum Slut
27 Stores Ln. Tiptree, Essex, CO5 0LH UK
bubblegumslutzine@gmail.com
www.bubblegumslutfanzine.1hwy.com
A glammy / sleazy / punky / gothy fanzine! This is NOT the place for Emo, Grunge and things ending in 'core' okay.

Courage to Care
9 Welton Mount, Hyde Park, Leeds, LS6 1ET UK
K. Thompson kittyxcore@gmail.com
www.couragetocare.co.uk
Hardcore news, reviews and interviews.

FiveMilesHigh
www.fivemileshigh.net
Rock n' Roll / Punk / Rock. Sadly we do not have the time to respond to every demo we are sent. Rest assured, if we like you, we will be in touch!

FREE-Magazine
Victoria McNaught-Davis editor.free@gmail.com
www.free-magazine.co.uk
Send in any demos, photos or reviews that you have. Indie and Punk music only. Contact me for submission details.

Hardcore Times
Papion, Erskine Ave. Grestones, Co. Wicklow,
Ireland
Shay Murphy info@hardcore-times.com
www.hardcore-times.com
News, reviews, interviews, listings and more.

Kudos Magazine
Footloose Farm, Crediton Devon, EX17 4RX UK
www.kudosmagazine.com
Send promos and any other promotional materials.

Organ Zine
c/o The Old Gramophone Works, 326 Kensal Rd.
London, W10 5BZ UK
Sean organ@organart.demon.co.uk
www.organart.com
We're mostly interested in Punk/Metal/Alternative/Prog and music of a left field guitar nature.

Punktastic.com
91 Gloucester Ave. Grimsby, NE. Lincs,
DN34 5BU UK
ben@punktastic.com
www.punktastic.com
Send any goodies / releases / promos (no horses' heads please) to the above address.

Real Overdose
64 Chatsworth Dr. Rushmere Park, Ipswich, Suffolk,
IP4 5XD UK
tard@realod.com
www.realod.com
Always review a ton o' wax, a heap o' zines and a stack o' shows.

R*E*P*E*A*T Online
PO Box 438, Cambridge, CB4 1FX UK
rosey@repeatfanzine.co.uk
www.repeatfanzine.co.uk
Focuses on the Underground music scene.

Suspect Device
PO Box 295, Southampton, SO17 1LW UK
suspectdevicehq@hotmail.com
www.suspectdevicehq.co.uk
We have diverse tastes and cover most styles of Punk Rock.

trakMARX.com
1st St. NAC Coventry, CV8 2LZ UK
PH: 07786-261821
wastebin@trakMARX.com
www.trakmarx.com
We bring you the juice on young upstarts.

vanity project
43 Hartley Cr. Woodhouse, Leeds, LS6 2LL UK
skif@vanityproject.co.uk
www.vanityproject.co.uk
Informative interviews, reviews and articles.

Sign up for
The Indie Contact Newsletter
www.indiebible.com

Africa

zapunx.com
Matt matt@zapunx.com
www.zapunx.com
Alternative music community website. Share your views on CDs, EPs, LPs, VHS Tapes, DVDs, anything!

Reggae

Reggae, Ska, Rocksteady, Dancehall and Caribbean.

The Beat Magazine
PO Box 65856, Los Angeles, CA 90065
PH: 818-500-9299 FX: 818-500-9454
Chuck Foster editor@getthebeat.com
www.getthebeat.com
A bimonthly publication of Reggae, African, Caribbean and World music, providing information, news, reviews, interviews etc.

DerDude Goes SKA.de
Emser Straße 18, 56076 Koblenz, Germany
derdude@derdude-goes-ska.de
www.derdude-goes-ska.de
Ska nicht einfach eine muzik!

Dizzybeat *Australia*
dizzybeat.com
Ska, Reggae, Punk, Life. We encourage people to contribute photos, reviews, news and articles.

JahWorks.org
PO Box 9207, Berkeley, CA 94709
editor@jahworks.org
jahworks.org
Portrays Caribbean and African-based music and culture with enthusiasm and integrity.

Jammin Reggae
4584 G. W. Pt. Loma Blvd. San Diego, CA 92107
PH: 619-226-6108 FX: 619-226-6108
eznoh@niceup.com
niceup.com
The gateway to Reggae music on the internet!

Reggae in Germany
Bremer Str. 16, D-45481 Mülheim / Ruhr, Germany
Peter Beckhaus node@reggaenode.de
www.reggaenode.de
News, reviews, forums etc.

Reggae in Rio
www.reggaeinrio.com.br
Reggae in Rio de Janeiro-Brazil.

Reggae News
18 Dalberg Rd. Brixton, London, SW2 1AN UK
info@reggaenews.co.uk
www.reggaenews.co.uk
We review a very wide selection of Reggae music.

Reggae Report
21300 NE. 24 Ct. Miami, FL 33180
PH/FX: 305-933-9918
newreleases@reggaereport.com
www.reggaereport.com
All the info on the Reggae scene.

The Reggae Source
655 Deerfield Rd. #100-336, Deerfield, IL 60015
PH/FX: 773-785-7536
service@reggaesource.com
www.reggaesource.com
Solid information on this crucial music form.

Reggae Train.com
info@reggaetrain.com
reggaetrain.com
Comprehensive Reggae music portal on the web.

Reggae Vibes
Pieter Brueghelstraat 5, 6181 DJ Elsloo,
The Netherlands
PH: 31-46-4373228 FX: 31-46-4376427
info@reggae-vibes.com
www.reggae-vibes.com
Spread the "Reggae vibes"...anyway & anywhere!

Reggaefrance.com
33, rue de Trévise, 75009 Paris, France
redaction@reggaefrance.com
www.reggaefrance.com
Retrouvez la référence Reggae Dancehall, nombreuses interviews d'artistes Jamaïquains & Français.

Roots Garden Promotions
3 Kings Mews, Hove, BN3 2PA UK
info@rootsgarden.com
www.rootsgarden.com
We specialise in playing and promoting strictly conscious Reggae and Dub music new and old.

RudeGal.com
rudegal@rudegal.com
www.rudegal.com
Dancehall Reggae music - the internet resource.

The Ska Tipz
skatipz@neoska.com
neoska.com
A site for Japanese Ska bands and other Ska music.

Ska Wars
Forskarbacken 9/0604, 104 05 Stockholm, Sweden
Karl Peterz johan@skawars.nu
www.skawars.nu
Guide to Ska, Reggae and Rocksteady.

Surforeggae
contato@surforeggae.com.br
www.surforeggae.com.br
All the info on the Reggae scene.

Soul / R&B

United States

Black Macon
PO Box 1013, Macon, GA 31202
PH: 478-464-0074
Editor-in-Chief editor@blackmaconweb.com
www.blackmaconweb.com/entertainment.html
We'll review CDs from African American artists of any genre.

Gedup.com
info@gedup.com
www.gedup.com
We like artists who have more noble goals than just becoming celebrities.

RHYTHMflow.net
PO Box 130, Bronx, NY 10467
editor@rhythmflow.net
www.rhythmflow.net
If you are an artist and would like to have your project considered for an upcoming issue, please e-mail us your info.

Soul Strut
PO Box 174, Sellersville, PA 18960
ish411@soulstrut.com
www.soulstrut.com
All promotional material in the Hip Hop, Jazz, Funk, R&B vein can be sent to the above address. No MP3s!!

Soul Tracks
chris@soultracks.com
www.soultracks.com
Reviews, biographies and group updates.

Viqi French Fever
Viqi French info@viqifrench.com
ViqiFrenchFever.blogspot.com
Covers Jazz, Neo Soul, Hip Hop and Acid Groove.

Finland

Soul Express
Box 105, 02101 ESPOO, Finland
soulexpress@kolumbus.fi
PH: 358-9-759-40401
www.kolumbus.fi/soulexpr
Music Magazine specialising in real Soul and Funk.

Germany

Groove Attack Magazine
Von-Huenefeld-Str. 2, 50829 Cologne, Germany
PH: +49 (0) 221-990750 FX: +49 (0) 221-99075990
info@grooveattack.com
www.grooveattack.com
News, new releases and profiles. We also deal with distribution and promotion.

Jazz not Jazz
Chateauneufstrasse 5, 20535 Hamburg, Germany
PH: +49-40-41260844
Dirk Binsau jnj@jazz-not-jazz.com
blog.jazz-not-jazz.com
Specialising in Neo-Soul and quality Indie Soul releases. Please CONTACT me prior to sending anything.

SoulSite.de
Westring 249, 55120 Mainz, Germany
FX: +49 (0)6131-26-87-64
info@soulsite.de
www.soulsite.de
The home of Soul in Germany.

The Netherlands

Soul of Amsterdam
2e Oosterparkstraat 59-D, 1091 HW Amsterdam,
The Netherlands
PH: +31-6-165-22229
Andreas Hellingh
andreas@thesoulofamsterdam.com
thesoulofamsterdam.com
Resource centered around Soul music. We also provide coverage of R&B, Urban, Disco, Funk, Gospel and Jazz.

United Kingdom

Blues & Rhythm
82 Quenby Way, Bromham, Bedfordshire,
MK43 8QP UK
PH: +44 (0)123-482-6158
Tony Burke tonyburke@bluesandrhythm.co.uk
www.bluesandrhythm.co.uk
Europe's leading Blues, R&B and Gospel mag.

Blues & Soul Magazine
153 Praed St., London, W2 1RL UK
Bob Kilbourn bob@bluesandsoul.com
www.bluesandsoul.com
Covers all the latest UK and US Urban music info,
including news, charts, reviews, events and clubs, as
well as in-depth interviews

funkjunkiez.biz
www.funkjunkiez.biz
Soul, R&B, Urban music etc. Reviews of the latest
albums, singles and even live gigs.

futureboogie
PO Box 2051, Bristol, BS6 9ZY UK
demos@futureboogie.com
www.futureboogie.com
Soul & Funk news, reviews and interviews. Send
your demos to us (no attachments please).

In The Basement Magazine
193 Queens Park Rd. Brighton, E. Sussex,
BN2 9ZA UK
PH: 00-44-1273-601217 FX: 00-44-1273-601217
David Cole inthebasement@btinternet.com
www.basement-group.co.uk
60's, 70's-style Soul music specialist magazine.
Happy to receive CDs for review.

Life & Soul Promotions
PH: +44 (0)1934-642121
Mike Ashley mike@lifeandsoulpromotions.co.uk
indiesoulnews.blogspot.com
www.lifeandsoulpromotions.co.uk
mikeashley.blogspot.com
Independent Soul news and reviews.

Soul Sorts
dodger@soulsorts.plus.com
www.soulsorts.co.uk
News, reviews and events.

Straight No Chaser
17D Ellingfort Rd. London, E8 3PA UK
PH: +44-020-8533-9999 FX: +44-020-8985-6447
Paul Bradshaw info@straightnochaser.co.uk
straightnochaser.co.uk
We review mostly "music from the African
diaspora" - Jazz, Hip Hop, Latin etc.

VIBIN
info@vibinmusic.co.uk
www.vibin.co.uk
Submitting your work for the unsigned artist
section:
Our Unsigned Artist section is designed to showcase
up & coming artists on the R&B scene.

Write On Point!
Janice Spence janice@writeonpoint.co.uk
www.writeonpoint.co.uk
Features and interviews from within the world of
black entertainment on both sides of the Atlantic.

Women in Music

Most of the publications in the section review
exclusively Women's music. Solo artists, bands
or female fronted bands.

United States

3BlackChicks Review
PO Box 871883, New Orleans, LA 70187-1883
Cassandra Henry cass@3blackchicks.com
www.3blackchicks.com
Interested in submissions from Black artists.

Bamboo Girl
PO Box 507, New York, NY 10159-0507
BambooGirl@aol.com
www.bamboogirl.com
Reviews Indie/Progressive/Hip Hop female music.

Bitch
1611 Telegraph Ave. #515, Oakland, CA 94612
PH: 510-625-9390
Lisa Jervis lisa@bitchmagazine.com
www.bitchmagazine.com
Covers all female music/musicians.

CandyforBadChildren.Com
PO Box 51446, Boston, MA 02205
Stacey Dawn
staceydawn@candyforbadchildren.com
www.candyforbadchildren.com
Send us press kits, promos and screeners for review.

Cha Cha Charming
284 Lafayette St. #5D, New York, NY 10012
editor@chachacharming.com
www.chachacharming.com
Covering female Pop stars from Tokyo to Paris.

Collected Sounds
3010 Hennepin Ave. S. #630, Minneapolis,
MN 55408
www.collectedsounds.com
A site dedicated to women in music.

Cool Grrrls
PO Box 186, Balboa Island, CA 92662
PH: 714-960-2650 FX: 714-532-6829
Melody Licious editors@coolgrrrls.com
www.coolgrrrls.com
Show & CD reviews, interviews and more.

Crash Zine
PO Box 20455, Newark, NJ 07101
Shay shay@crashzineonline.net
www.crashzineonline.net
Feminist pop culture and politix for the rest of us.
Punk, Punk Pop, Rock etc.

Cutting Edge Voices
c/o Reviews Editor, PO Box 539, Lucas, OH 44843
Michael Foster editor@cuttingedgevoices.com
www.cuttingedgevoices.com
Promoting female vocalists from around the world.
Interviews, reviews, news …

Daily Diva
2794 Seabreeze Dr. Fairfield, CA 94533
PH: 916-821-0773
helpdesk@dailydiva.com
www.dailydiva.com
Fashion, music, culture and fine women of color. We
review independent music.

Ectophile's Guide
PO Box 30187, Seattle, WA 98113-0187
Neile Graham neile@sff.net
www.ectoguide.org
Submit your material for reviews.

Female Musician
PO Box 623, Northport, NY 11768
Tj Orlando tj@femalemusician.com
www.femalemusician.com
Interviews & CD reviews with independent artists.

Female Musicians Online
1341 Rosecrans St. #3, San Diego, CA 92106
femalemusiciansonline.com
Supporting only the best female bands, musicians,
composers, songwriters in the music industry!

Gilded Serpent
PO Box 1928, San Anselmo, CA 94979
PH: 415-455-8455
editor@gildedserpent.com
www.gildedserpent.com
Digital community for Middle Eastern performers
and other adventurers.

Girlposse
www.girlposse.com
We review independent artists from time to time.

GirlPunk.Net
PO Box 177, Roebling, NJ 08554
FX: 609-298-6566
jessica@girlpunk.net
www.girlpunk.net
News, reviews, articles, featured bands etc.

Girly Thing
christina@girlything.com
www.girlything.com
Entertainment news with a touch of all things girly.

GoGirlsMusic.com
PO Box 16940, Sugar Land, TX 77496-6940
Madalyn Sklar info@gogirlsmusic.com
www.gogirlsmusic.com
Promoting women in music. You must be a GoGirls
Elite member to get your CD reviewed. Info at
www.gogirlselite.com.

Heartless Bitches International
bitchsupreme@heartlessbitches.com
www.heartless-bitches.com
Music for the heartless bitch in all of us.

Lilith's Child
44 Rooney St. #2, Clifton, NJ 07011
PH: 973-272-8050
Erin P. Capuano info@lilithschild.com
www.lilithschild.net
We're always looking for female artists or female
fronted bands to cover. Articles, interviews, concert
& CD reviews.

MS. Magazine
433 S. Beverly Dr. Beverly Hills, CA 90212
www.msmagazine.com
We do publish music reviews, but not in every issue.

musical discoveries
rwelliot@hotmail.com
www.musicaldiscoveries.com
Reviews of Contemporary, Progressive and
Crossover recordings.

Purple Pyjamas
Martine editor@purplepjs.com
www.purplepjs.com
Reviews CDs, musical shows and concerts.

Rockrgrl
3220 1st Ave. S., #203, Seattle, WA 98134
PH: 206-624-7131 FX: 206-624-7037
info@rockrgrl.com
www.rockrgrl.com
For women involved in music.

She Caribbean
PO Box 1146, Castries, St. Lucia, WI
PH: 758-450-7827 FX: 758-450-8694
waynem@candw.lc
www.shecaribbean.com
We are only interested in Caribbean labels or
artists, especially women.

Venus Magazine
2000 W. Carroll #402, Chicago, IL 60612
PH: 312-738-3701 FX: 312-738-3702
feedback@venuszine.com
www.venuszine.com
Women in music, art, film and more.

Women of Country
www.womenofcountry.com
Features undiscovered female Country musical gems.

xsisterhoodx.com
1430 Ella T. Grasso Blvd. New Haven, CT 06511
kelly@xsisterhoodx.com
www.xsisterhoodx.com
Promotes girls in Hardcore and Straightedge.

Germany

Melodiva Net Club
Roßdorfer Str. 24, D-60385 Frankfurt/M, Germany
PH: 69-4960-848 FX: 69-4960-800
musik@melodiva.de
www.frauenmusikbuero.de
News, reviews, interviews etc.

The Netherlands

Metal Maidens
PO Box 230, 4140 AE Leerdam, The Netherlands
metalmaid@globalxs.nl
www.metalmaidens.com
CDs, seven inches, demo tapes and concert reviews and dates.

Reviews of Women Composers
Patricia Werner Leanse patricia@dds.nl
www.patricia.dds.nl/cds.htm
Does reviews of Classical music CDs by women.

United Kingdom

AMP: IT'S THE TITS!
PO Box 30639, London, E1 6GA UK
amp@ampnet.co.uk
www.ampnet.co.uk
For chicks and dicks and ... just about anybody, really.

Celestial Voices Reviews
16 Atlantic House, Waterson St., Shoreditch, London, E2 8HH UK
www.loobie.com
Promoting ethereal female vocals on the internet.

wears the trousers
Commonwealth House, 1 New Oxford St., London, WC1A 1NU UK
Alan Pedder unzipped@thetrousers.co.uk
www.thetrousers.co.uk
A resolutely anglocentric peek at the world of women in music. We are very happy to receive discs for review.

Australia

Femail Magazine
8 E. Concourse, Beaumaris, VIC 3193 Australia
Michelle Warmuz michelle@femail.com.au
femail.com.au
Please try to assist us by including a subject heading in your enquiry, ie: product reviews, competitions etc.

World Music

Allafrica.com
920 M St. SE.,
Washington, DC 20003
PH: 202-546-0777
FX: 202-546-0676
allafrica.com/music
Distributor of African news/music worldwide.

Global Rhythm
PH: 212-868-4354
edit@globalrhythm.net
www.globalrhythm.net
World music, culture & lifestyle.

globalvillageidiot.net
c.nickson@tiscali.co.uk
www.globalvillageidiot.net
Find the latest news in World music.

Jewish Entertainment Resources
PO Box 12692, Alexandria, LA 71315
PH: 318-442-3346
FX: 318-442-3356
info@jewishentertainment.net
www.jewishentertainment.net
Jewish music resources. Get your music reviewed.

Klezmer Shack
ari@ivritype.com
www.klezmershack.com
Good Klezmer and the music inspired by it.

Mondomix
9, Cité Paradis, 75010 Paris, France.
PH: + 33 (0)1-56-03-90-89
FX: + 33 (0)1-56-03-90-84
info@mondomix.com
www.mondomix.com
The electronic media of reference for World music.

Musical Traditions
1 Castel St., Stroud, Glos, GL5 2HP UK
PH: 01453-759475
Rod Stradling rod@mustrad.org.uk
www.mustrad.org.uk
Traditional music throughout the world.

The Piper & Drummer
editor@piperanddrummer.com
www.piperanddrummer.com
Devoted solely to piping and drumming.

Whispering Wind Magazine
PO Box 1390, Folsom, LA 70437-1390
PH: 985-796-5433 FX: 985-796-9236
www.whisperingwind.com
We offer Native American musicians a place to get their Indie music reviewed.

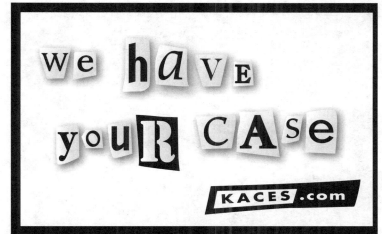

World Music Central
552 Parkview Dr. Burlington, NC 27215-5036
info@worldmusiccentral.org
www.worldmusiccentral.org
We accept news stories/articles/reviews, and other contributions. There is an online form that you need to fill.

World Music Magazine
Via Alfiera 19, 10121 Torino, Italy
PH: +39-011-5591849 FX: +39-011-2307034
www.worldmusiconline.it
Since 1991, the only World music magazine in Italy.

World Music Site at About.com
4203 Poydras Hwy. Breaux Bridge, LA 70517
PH: 337-332-1478
Megan Romer worldmusic.guide@about.com
worldmusic.about.com
I review all areas of World music, including Cajun/Zydeco, Celtic, African, Reggae, Caribbean etc.

www.indielinkexchange.com/ile

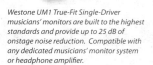

SECTION TWO: "REGIONAL" PUBLICATIONS AND RESOURCES

"Getting that first article written about you can be quite a challenge. Two great places to start are your local town papers and any local fanzine" – **Ariel Hyatt, Ariel Publicity**

The resources listed in this section can help you to gain exposure in your local area, whether it be a CD review, allowing you to post information about your band, post info on a new release, upcoming shows etc. Most of the organizations listed (Folk, Jazz, Blues etc.) publish a newsletter that will review your CD. Note that many of these resources will promote music from outside of their region, but give preference to local talent.

United States

boulevards.com / Associated Cities
www.boulevards.com
In the music and nightlife section you can find out about bars in most major cities.

Citysearch
www.citysearch.com
Extensive coverage of the local music scene of all major cities. Post your shows and events.

Craigslist
www.craigslist.org
Now available for communities all over the world. Get the word out about your music, gigs etc.

donewaiting.com
2648 Deming Ave. Columbus, OH 43202
Robert Duffy bobduffy1@yahoo.com
www.donewaiting.com
We currently have nine writers writing about their local scenes.

Home Town News
www.hometownnews.com
Providing direct links to more than 2,600 daily and weekly U.S. newspapers!

ListeningRoomTour.com
3615-B St Johns Ct. Wilmington, NC 28403
Annette Warner awarnerentertainment@ec.rr.com
ListeningRoomTour.com
Dedicated to building and maintaining a database of 'Listening Room' atmospheres for live music, poetry and stand-up comedy acts.

Local Band Network
John Fitzgerald fitz@localband.net
www.localband.net
Information about local bands and music venues ...no matter where "local" is to you.

Local Music Now
localmusicnow@gmail.com
www.localmusicnow.net
Fostering community through music ...one city at a time. Get your band listed. Submit your gigs.

Localeyez
fye.com
FYE, Strawberries, Coconuts, Spec's Music and Planet Music are giving local artists the opportunity to be seen & heard in our stores.

LocateBands.com
contact@locatebands.com
www.locatebands.com
A leader in connecting musicians and those who love them.

Loose Record
532 La Guardia Pl. #371, New York, NY 10012
oops@looserecord.com
www.looserecord.com
Focuses on the local scene of various cities. Please send all CDs and promotion materials to the above address.

MusicJamCentral.com
kevin@musicjamcentral.com
MusicJamCentral.com
A state-by-state listing of bands. Submit yours!

MYLOCALBANDS.com
bands@mylocalbands.com
www.mylocalbands.com
Add information about your band as well as your MP3s. Sign up to play at local venues.

NewsDirectory College Newspapers
www.newsdirectory.com/college_news.php
Links to hundreds of college newspapers.

Newspaper & News Media Guide
www.abyznewslinks.com
Links to over 12,000 newspapers worldwide.

openmikes.org
comments@openmikes.org
www.openmikes.org
A listing of music open-mike nights in the US and Canada.

Podbop
Taylor McKnight podbop@gmail.com
podbop.org
Fans type in a city, get MP3s, discover a band they like and go see them.

Spins.US
spins.us
An Electronic Dance music information resource and events calendar covering communities throughout the US.

United States Newspapers and News Media Database
www.abyznewslinks.com/unite.htm
Links to hundreds of US newspapers.

US Newspaper List
www.usnpl.com
Links to newspapers throughout the country.

YourLocalHipHop
yourlocalhiphop.com
A network of nationwide Hip Hop sites. Submit the details on MC Battles, B Boy Competitions and Hip Hop artist showcases near you.

Alabama

al.com
www.al.com/music
Online presence for the Birmingham News, Huntsville Times and Mobile Register. Local music section.

Alabama Bluegrass Music Association
PO Box 220, Leeds, AL 35094
www.alabamabluegrass.org
Promoting Bluegrass music in the state of Alabama.

Alabama Blues Project
www.alabamablues.org
Dedicated to the preservation of Blues music as a traditional American art form.

Bama Hip Hop
2216 Christine Ave. Anniston, AL 36207
PH: 256-282-0799 FX: 925-475-7458
bamahiphop@hotmail.com
bamahiphop.homestead.com
Lists your bio, company profile, concert/festival schedule, release dates and booking contacts.

Birmingham Buzz
PO Box 660686, Vestavia Hills, AL 35266
PH: 205-602-6872
Tim Taylor timt@bhambuzz.com
bhambuzz.com
Dedicated to covering the local Rock music scene in Birmingham.

Black & White
2210 2nd Ave. N. 2nd Fl. Birmingham, AL 35203
PH: 205-933-0460
www.bwcitypaper.com
Birmingham's city paper. Events, concerts and live music sections.

Cajun-Zydeco Connection of Huntsville
www.czdance.com
Dedicated to Cajun and Creole music, dancing and culture in the North Alabama area.

Crimson White
PO Box 2389, Tuscaloosa, AL 35403-2389
PH: 205-348-7845 FX: 205-348-8036
www.cw.ua.edu
University of Alabama newspaper.

fleabomb.com
www.fleabomb.com
Promotes local bands in Birmingham. We cover Punk, Grindcore, Indie Rock/Pop, Emo and Hip Hop.

Indie Community
9495 Brook Forest Cir. Helena, AL 35080
PH: 205-492-3284
Jennifer McConnell info@indiecommunity.com
www.indiecommunity.com
Alabama's network for independent Christian bands and artists.

Magic City Blues Society
PO Box 55895, Birmingham, AL 35255
PH: 205-822-7387
www.magiccityblues.org
Encourages the performances of the Blues and develops an appreciation within the community.

MobileSucks
webmaster@mobilesucks.net
www.mobilesucks.net
Covering the Punk scene in Mobile.

Alaska

AK Ink
PO Box 244235, Anchorage, AK 99524
jennink@gmail.com
www.geocities.com/akinkzine
Anchorage based Punk zine covering local and international bands.

AK This Month
PO Box 202941, Anchorage, AK 99520
akthismonth@hotmail.com
www.alaskathismonth.com
Free guide to entertainment in the 49th State!

Alaskan Folk Music And More!
gary@alaskafolkmusic.org
alaskafolkmusic.org
Comprehensive source for local and statewide Folk music happenings.

The Anchorage Press
PO Box 241841, Anchorage, AK 99524-1841
PH: 907-561-7737
info@anchoragepress.com
www.anchoragepress.com
An A&E weekly newspaper.

YourAnchorageRadio.com
webmaster@youranchorageradio.com
youranchorageradio.com
An online music community. Post shows, reviews, events etc.

Arizona

Acoustic Music Arizona
PO Box 1554, Queen Creek, AZ 85242
PH: 480-888-1692
info@acousticmusicaz.com
www.acousticmusicaz.com
Promoting Acoustic music and Arizona based Acoustic musicians.

The AMAZ Store
PO Box 1554, Queen Creek, AZ 85242
PH: 480-888-1692
Chris Masters info@theamazstore.com
www.theamazstore.com
Sells Acoustic music from Arizona artists.

Arizona Bluegrass Association
PO Box 8139, Glendale, AZ 85312-8139
www.azbluegrass.org
Up-to-date information about news, events, festivals and Bluegrass bands.

Arizona Irish Music Society
9867 Roundup Ct. Sun City, AZ 85373
www.azirishmusic.com
News, events, listings etc.

Arizona Music Club
9920 S. Rural Rd. #108, Tempe, AZ 85284
PH: 480-206-3435 FX: 480-753-7021
music@blackdogpromotions.com
www.arizonamusicclub.com
Help us spread the word about the great music of Arizona!

Arizona Old-Time Fiddlers Association
7470 Derryberry Dr. Flagstaff, AZ 86004
www.arizonaoldtimefiddlers.org
Created to preserve and promote the art of Old-Time fiddling.

Arizona Open Mics
chris@azopenmic.com
azopenmic.com
Includes pictures and artist profiles.

ASU Web Devil
PH: 480-727-6941
webdevil@asu.edu
www.statepress.com
Arizona State University online publication.

AZPunk.com
PO Box 64862, Phoenix, AZ 85082-4862
Chris Lawson chris@azpunk.com
www.AZPunk.com
Arizona's #1 source for Punk Rock!

CollectiveUnderground.com
www.collectiveunderground.com
Dedicated to Arizona's heaviest music.

Desert Bluegrass Association
www.desertbluegrass.org
Developing and promoting Bluegrass music in the Greater Tucson area.

Phoenix Band Guide
Melissa Ostrow mp3@phx.com
phoenixbandguide.com
Post your band info, Take advantage of our services including unlimited downloads of MP3s.

Phoenix Blues Society
www.phoenixblues.org
Promotes and perpetuates local and national Blues music.

Phoenix Early Music Society
www.pems.org
Keeps you up to date on local events from the Medieval, Renaissance and Baroque eras.

Phoenix New Times
PO Box 2510, Phoenix, AZ 85002
PH: 602-271-0040 FX: 602-253-4884
www.phoenixnewtimes.com
Free weekly alternative paper. Thursday has local reviews.

Prescott Jazz Society
www.pjazz.org
Presenting, promoting and celebrating Jazz performance and education in Northern Arizona.

Rock in Phoenix
PO Box 61432, Phoenix, AZ 85082
info@rockinphoenix.org
www.rockinphoenix.org
A Spanish Rock/Punk/Metal website dedicated to the Spanish Rock scene in Phoenix.

RockThis.net
nikki@rockthis.net
www.rockthis.net
Serving Bullhead City, Kingman and Lake Havasu City. Local musicians forums, chat room, articles, photos and more!

So Much Silence
somuchsilence@gmail.com
somuchsilence.blogspot.com
MP3 blog covering the Arizona music scene.

SouthWestHipHop.com
PO Box 57917, Phoenix, AZ 85017
southwesthiphop.com
Album reviews, artist interviews, monthly features and more!

Tucson Guitar Society
www.tucsongs.org
Organizes classic guitar concerts in the Tucson area for local, national and international talent.

Tucson Friends of Traditional Music
www.tftm.org
Sponsors and promotes concerts, dances, workshops and informal music sessions.

Tucson Jazz Society
www.tucsonjazz.org
Promotes Jazz across Southern AZ with concerts, festivals and media activities.

Tucson Weekly
PO Box 27087, Tucson, AZ 85726-7087
PH: 520-792-3630 FX: 520-792-2096
Stephen Seigel musiced@tucsonweekly.com
www.tucsonweekly.com
Free weekly paper. Indie record reviews. Publish the annual "Tucson Musician's Register".

Zia Record Exchange
1940 W. Indian School Rd. Phoenix, AZ
PH: 602-241-0313
www.ziarecords.com
Can set you up with a consignment arrangement.

Arkansas

Delta Boogie
1710 Henry St., Jonesboro, AR 72401
www.deltaboogie.com
Information about music, art and entertainment in NE Arkansas and the Mississippi Delta.

Fayetteville Free Weekly
PO Box 843, Fayetteville, AR 72702
PH: 479-521-4550
www.freeweekly.com
Entertainment weekly. Covers local music.

Little Rock Hardcore
Dustin Weddle dustin@LittleRockHardcore.com
www.littlerockhardcore.com
Interviews, concert and album reviews, downloads etc.

Little Rock Scene
www.littlerockscene.com
Improving our local music scene. News, reviews, gallery etc.

Midsouth Metal Society
midsouthmetal.com
Online community where you can post shows, news, releases etc.

Nightflying
PO Box 250276, Little Rock, AR 72225
PH: 501-354-8577 FX: 501-354-1994
pr@nightflying.com
www.nightflying.com
Free monthly alternative magazine. Live music guide, CD reviews, features and previews.

Ozark Blues Society
www.ozarkblues.com
Promoting public knowledge of local, national and international Blues music.

Spa City Blues Society
www.spacityblues.com
Preserving and promoting Blues music and musicians.

Under the Ground
gforce@undertheground.com
www.undertheground.com
Covering the Little Rock Hip Hop scene.

The Indie Link Exchange
www.indielinkexchange.com/ile

California

The (916) Magazine
5001 Freeport Blvd. Sacramento, CA 95822
PH: 916-452-2482
the916@comcast.net
www.the916.com
Hip Hop magazine providing information about the best in local talent in Northern CA.

All Access Magazine
15981 Yarnell St. #122, Rancho Cascades, CA 91342
PH: 818-833-8852
allaccessmgzn@aol.com
www.allaccessmagazine.com
A free bi-weekly music and entertainment publication. Keeping the local music alive!

Amoeba Music *Home Grown*
www.amoebamusic.com
Our Home Grown artists are nominated by Amoeba staff and must be local to Berkeley, Hollywood or San Francisco.

American Guitar Society
library.csun.edu/igra/ags
Provides an opportunity for you to perform before an appreciative audience.

Bakotopia / BakersfieldBands.com
PO Box 2454, Bakersfield, CA 93303
PH: 661-395-7660
spud@bakotopia.com
www.bakotopia.com
www.bakersfieldbands.com
Covering the latest and greatest music in Bakersfield.

Barflies.net
PO Box 1367, Orange, CA 92856-1367
www.barflies.net
Weekly concert calendar, weekly CD/show reviews and a bi-monthly features magazine.

Butte Folk Music Society
www.bfms.freeservers.com
Supports traditional and Folk music through concert venues and other music-related activities.

CaBands.com
PO Box 661254, Sacramento, CA 95866
PH: 916-247-9024
Robert Michael Lockwood II robert@cabands.com
www.cabands.com
We do concert and CD reviews and list over 7,000 local CA bands.

California Aggie
25 Lower Freeborn, 1 Shields Ave. Davis, CA 95616
PH: 530-752-0208
www.californiaaggie.com
UC Davis Student paper is distributed free on the UC Davis campus and in the Davis community.

California Bluegrass Association
www.cbaontheweb.org
Dedicated to the furtherance of Bluegrass, Old-Time and Gospel music.

California Hardcore
nick@calihardcore.com
www.calihardcore.com
The latest information on the bands, zines, record labels, distros and more from the Bay area.

California Lawyers for the Arts
cla@calawyersforthearts.org
www.calawyersforthearts.org
Provides lawyer referrals, dispute resolution services, publications and a resource library.

California State Old-Time Fiddler's Association
www.fiddle.com/calfiddle
Dedicated to the preservation of Old-Time fiddle music.

California Traditional Music Society
www.ctmsfolkmusic.org
Dedicated to the preservation and dissemination of traditional Folk music and related Folk arts

California Newspapers
www.usnpl.com/canews.html
www.usnpl.com/canews2.html
Links to newspapers throughout the state.

Carmel Classic Guitar Society
www.starrsites.com/CarmelClassicGuitar
Promotes the Classical guitar through education, recitals and gatherings.

The Catalyst
PO Box 279214, Sacramento, CA 95827
submissions@thecatalystonline.com
thecatalystonline.com
Monthly art culture and political newspaper geared to provide fresh perspectives.

CentralCali.com
www.centralcali.com
Covers the Hip Hop scene in California, featuring message boards and news on local events.

Chico News and Reviews
353 E. 2nd St., Chico, CA 95928
PH: 530-894-2300 FX: 530-894-0143
www.newsreview.com/chico/home
Provides extensive coverage of grassroots issues and the local music scene.

chico underground show info
chicolist@synthesis.net
www.chicolist.com
Promotes the local Indie/Punk/Hardcore scene in the Chico area. Emphasize unity in the scene.

CRIMEZINE
PO Box 2533, Lompoc, CA 93436
Barnz barnz@crimezine.com
www.crimezine.com
Punk zine focusing on the Central Coast, but not limited just that area. Calendar, shows, reviews etc.

DIG Music
1831 V St., Sacramento, CA 95818
PH: 916-442-5344 FX: 916-442-5382
ben@digmusic.com
www.digmusic.com
Independent record label and artist management company. We mainly have relationships with local/regional acts.

East Bay Express
1335 Stanford Ave. Emeryville, CA 94608
PH: 510-879-3700 FX: 510-601-0217
David.Downs@eastbayexpress.com
www.eastbayexpress.com
Extensive coverage of local music including weekly reviews and gig listings.

The Fresno Bee
1626 E. St., Fresno, CA 93786-0001
PH: 559-441-6356 FX: 559-441-6457
features@fresnobee.com
www.fresnobee.com
Central California's leading daily newspaper. Local entertainment section.

Fresno Folklore Society
home.pacbell.net/ckjohns
Preserves Folk arts, especially traditional music, in California's San Joaquin Valley.

Good Times
PO Box 1885, Santa Cruz, CA 95061
PH: 831-458-1100 x223 FX: 831-458-1295
Damon Orion dorion@gtweekly.com
www.gdtimes.com
Santa Cruz news and entertainment weekly. Extensive coverage of the local music scene.

HDBands.com
PH: 760-963-6516
contact@hdbands.com
www.HDBands.com
Covering the High Desert Punk scene. Specializing in photography, reviews, interviews and more!

Humboldt Folklife Society
www.humboldtfolklife.org
Working to bring together Folk dancers, musicians and music lovers.

HumboldtMusic.com
mike@humboldtmusic.com
www.humboldtmusic.com
Provides an extensive and searchable directory of local musicians and music resources.

inTUNE: SoCal Bluegrass News
www.socalbluegrass.org
Profiles regional Bluegrass folks. The DISCoverings column lets you know which CDs to buy.

Jazz Connection
jazzconnection@hotmail.com
jazzconnectionmag.com
Celebrating the fine art of Jazz music in Northern CA.

Jazz Society of Santa Cruz County
santacruzjazz.org
Promotes Jazz with a bulletin board, musician's directory service and news and views of Jazz.

JeRQ THIS
PH: 916-308-0593
Jon Robert Quinn jonrobertquinn@excite.com
www.JeRQ-THIS.com
Features the best music Sacramento has to offer.

The List
skoepke@stevelist.com
jon.luini.com/thelist
stevelist.com
Features SoCal Funk-Punk-Thrash-Ska upcoming shows of interest.

The Living Tradition
PH: 949-559-1419
livingtradition@hotmail.com
www.thelivingtradition.org
Sponsors regular contra dances, Folk music concerts and Folk music jams in Bellflower and Anaheim.

Mach Turtle
FX: 305-768-6224
agentwahine@yahoo.com
www.machturtleprods.com
Listing of live Surf music events in Southern CA.

MetroSantaCruz
115 Cooper St., Santa Cruz, CA 95060
PH: 831-457-9000 FX: 831-457-5828
www.metcruz.com
Free weekly alternative paper. Indie music reviews.

Modesto Area Musician Association
4300 Finch Rd. Modesto, CA 95357
FX: 209-572-0221
mama@modestoview.com
www.modestoview.com/mama
News, reviews, MP3s etc.

Moshking.com
PO Box 1605, Glendora, CA 91740
moshking@moshking.com
www.moshking.com
Info on all Metal and Hard Rock concerts, events and bands in the SoCal area.

New Times
505 Higuera St., San Luis Obispo, CA 93401
PH: 805-546-8208 FX: 805-546-8641
www.newtimes-slo.com
San Luis Obispo County's news & entertainment weekly.

North Bay Bohemian
216 E. St., Santa Rosa, CA 95404
FX: 707-527-1288
www.metroactive.com/sonoma
Arts and entertainment weekly. Covers the local music scene.

Northern California Metal Underground
Klaudia webmaster@ncmu.com
www.ncmu.com
100% uncompromised Underground Metal.

OC Punk
www.ocpunk.com
A resource for Orange County Punk bands and their fans.

OC Weekly
1666 N. Main St. #500, Santa Ana, CA 92701-7417
PH: 714-550-5950 FX: 714-550-5903
Chris Ziegler submissions@ocweekly.com
www.ocweekly.com
Orange County A&E weekly. Lots of local music coverage.

Open Mikes in California
www.openmikes.org/calendar/CA

Orange County Bands
admin@ocbands.com
www.ocbands.com
Band listings, post gigs, find band members or clubs that need bands.

The Orion
CSU, Chico, CA 95926-0600
PH: 530-898-5625 FX: 530-898-4799
www.orion-online.net
California State U. Chico's student publication.

Pacific Sun
PO Box 8507, San Rafael, CA 94915
PH: 415-485-6700 FX: 415-485-6226
www.pacificsun.com
North Bay's weekly paper.

Palo Alto Weekly
Box 1610, Palo Alto, CA 94302
PH: 650-326-8210 FX: 650-326-3928
Rebecca Wallace editor@paweekly.com
www.paloaltoonline.com
Semi-weekly newspaper. Post your events online.

PARADIGM magazine
PO Box 9541, Brea, CA 92835
Kari Hamanaka ParadigmMag@aol.com
www.myspace.com/paradigmmagazine
Distributed to records stores throughout SoCal. Half of the zine is devoted to interviews of local, unsigned bands.

Pasadena Weekly
50 S. DeLacey Ave. #200, Pasadena, CA 91105
PH: 626-584-1500 FX: 626-795-0149
Julie Riggott julier@pasadenaweekly.com
www.pasadenaweekly.com
Pasadena's A&E weekly. Lists gigs by local bands, reviews CDs, writes features etc.

Powerslave.com
1610 Blossom Hill Rd. #7F, San Jose, CA 95124
PH: 408-266-0300 FX: 408-266-0303
info@powerslave.com
www.powerslave.com
NoCal underground Metal scene with show and album reviews.

Reviewer Magazine
PO Box 87069, San Diego, CA 92138
PH: 619-992-9211
Kent Manthie music@reviewermagazine.com
www.reviewermagazine.com
Southern California music, entertainment and lifestyle magazine.

Rose Street Music
1839 Rose St., Berkeley, CA 94703
PH: 510-594-4000
rosestbooking@yahoo.com
www.rosestreetmusic.com
A Berkeley house concert venue featuring women musicians and songwriters.

Sacramento Guitar Society
www.sacguitar.com
Provides education and performance opportunities to all cultures, ages, abilities and economic means.

Santa Barbara Blues Society
www.sbblues.org
Dedicated to keeping the African-American Blues tradition alive in the Santa Barbara area.

Santa Barbara Choral Society
www.sbchoral.org
Provides qualified singers with an opportunity to study and perform great works of music.

Santa Barbara Independent
122 W. Figueroa St., Santa Barbara, CA 93101
PH: 805-965-5205 FX: 805-965-5518
www.independent.com
The county's news and entertainment paper.

Santa Clara Valley Fiddlers Association
www.scvfa.org
Dedicated to the preservation of traditional American music such as Old-Time, Bluegrass and Gospel.

Santa Clarita Valley Blues Society
www.home.earthlink.net/%7Escvblues
Preserving and promoting Blues music.

Santa Cruz Sentinel
207 Church St., Santa Cruz, CA 95060
PH: 831-423-4242
www.santacruzsentinel.com
Entertainment section includes a calendar of music events.

Seven South Record Shop
382 N. La Cumbre Rd. Santa Barbara, CA 93110
PH: 805-898-0710
recordshop@sevensouth.com
sevensouth.com
Sell recordings at our shop if you're from the Santa Barbara / Ventura area.

Skinnie
10184 6th St. Ste. A Rancho Cucamonga, CA 91730
PH: 909-476-0270 FX: 909-476-5931
Ramon Gonzalez ramon@skinniemagazine.com
www.skinniezine.com
A monthly entertainment and lifestyles magazine based out of Rancho Cucamonga.

Socal-Breaks Community
Robtronik robtronik@robtronik.com
www.socal-breaks.com
News, promotion, events etc.

Sonoma County Blues Society
www.sonomacountybluessociety.org
Interviews and CD reviews in our monthly newsletter.

Sonoma Tunes
webmaster@sonomatunes.com
www.sonomatunes.com
Dedicated to live Blues in Northern CA in general and Sonoma County in particular.

Southern California Blues Society
www.socalblues.org
Presentation of Blues music through teaching, publications, festivals and concerts.

Southern California Early Music Society
www.earlymusicla.org
Supports the study, performance and enjoyment of Medieval, Renaissance, Baroque and Classical music.

Southland Blues
6475 E. Pacific Coast Hwy. #397, Long Beach, CA 90803
PH: 562-498-6942 FX: 562-498-6946
info@southlandblues.com
www.southlandblues.com
The hub of the Blues in Southern CA.

SouthWest Bluegrass Association
www.s-w-b-a.com
Bi-monthly newsletter with information about festivals and house jams. Members get free web page.

Supergiant Productions
2109 W. St. #4, Sacramento, CA 95818
PH: 916-501-4799
Gina Azzarello gina@supergiantproductions.com
www.supergiantproductions.com
We promote and book bands in the Sacramento area.

The Switchboard
Lady Noir ladynoir@socalgoth.com
www.socalgoth.com
Southern California Goth directory. Contact us to be included on the site.

Top Secret Records
mike@humboldtmusic.com
www.humboldtmusic.com/tsr
Owned by musicians solely to produce music under the total control of the musicians themselves.

Valley Scene Magazine
6520 Platt Ave. #336, West Hills, CA 91307
PH: 818-888-2114 FX: 818-888-7142
contact@valleyscenemagazine.com
www.valleyscenemagazine.com
Provides the most current information on entertainment, restaurants, retail, services and more.

Ventura Reporter
4840 Market St. Ste. D, Ventura, CA 93003
PH: 805-658-2244 FX: 805-658-7803
Stephanie stephanie@vcreporter.com
www.vcreporter.com
Ventura County's news and entertainment weekly. Covers local music with articles and show listings.

webookbands.com
7095 Hollywood Blvd. #794, Hollywood, CA 90028
PH: 323-651-1582 FX: 323-651-2643
info@webookbands.com
www.webookbands.com
Books talent and promotes for over 30 venues, both club and theatre, in California and Seattle.

West Coast Performer
475 Haight St. #4, San Francisco, CA 94117
PH: 415-255-6567
Kjersti Egerdahl wcpeditorial@performermag.com
www.performermag.com/wcperformer.php
Want your CD reviewed? Send your CDs and press releases.

Westcoast Worldwide
Mike xhatex@earthlink.net
www.westcoastworldwide.com
Covers the Punk/Hardcore scene. Has a message board, zine, CD reviews, gig listings, bookings etc.

Wild Iris Productions
Diane Hering info@wildirisfolkfestival.org
www.wildirisfolkfestival.org/
Wild_Iris_Productions.html
Providing performance opportunities for local musicians as well as world class Folk artists to Mendocino County.

Your Best Bet Magazine
PO Box 1062, Lake Isabella, CA 93240
YourBestBet4oc@hotmail.com
yourbestbet4oc.tripod.com
Serving the Southern CA area. Looking for bands to interview and to help spread the word on up and coming local bands.

Your Music Magazine
105 Pioneer St. Ste. I, Santa Cruz, CA 95060
PH: 831-465-1305
mikelyon@yourmusicmagazine.com
www.yourmusicmagazine.com
Metal magazine distributed throughout SoCal.

The Bay Area

Bay Area Blues Society
www.bayareabluessociety.net
Dedicated to the preservation, promotion and representation of Blues, Jazz and Gospel.

Bay Area Bunch Newsletter
bab_news@yahoo.com
www.geocities.com/SunsetStrip/Venue/9842
Highlights live Acoustic music performed by women singer-songwriters in the Bay Area.

Bay Area Ska Page
PO Box 3092, San Leandro, CA 94578
info@bayareaska.com
www.bayareaska.com
Reviews are broken up between albums or demos by a band, compilations and shows.

baymusicscene.com
633 Renfrew Rd. El Sobrante, CA 94803
PH: 925-768-6994
www.baymusicscene.com
Provides free resources for musicians including an online store, show listings and club information.

BayProg
don@till.com
www.bayprog.org
San Francisco area Progressive Rock community.

Bluegrass by the Bay
134 Serrano Dr. San Francisco, CA 94132
deirdre@deirdre-cassandra.com
www.scbs.org/bbb.htm
Contains reviews and articles about shows, venues, albums, artists and upcoming Bluegrass event.

Cruzin' the Bluz
Onnie Heaney cruzinbluz@earthlink.net
www.cruzinbluz.com
Blues news and reviews from Santa Cruz and the Bay Area.

Dub Beautiful Collective
Maer Ben-Yisrael maer@dub-beautiful.org
www.dub-beautiful.org
Presents live Electronic music events. We record all of our shows and stream the best recordings.

East Bay Recorder Society
www.sfems.org/ebrs
Hosts monthly meetings for amateur recorder players to play Renaissance and Baroque music.

Flavorpill SF
985 Howard St. San Francisco, CA 94103
sf_editor@flavorpill.net
sf.flavorpill.net
A publishing company that seeks out the best in arts, music and culture and delivers its findings.

illstatic
Selino Valdes selino@illstatic.com
www.illstatic.com
Focused on bringing the current listings in Hip Hop, Dirty House, Electro, DnB, Indie, DIY and more. Post your events!

KFOG's Local Scene
55 Hawthorne St. #1000, San Francisco, CA 94105
PH: 415-817-5364 FX: 415-995-6867
kfog@kfog.com
www.kfog.com/music/local_scene
Turning the spotlight on up and coming Bay Area musicians.

KUSF Entertainment Calendar
2130 Fulton St., San Francisco, CA 94117
kusf@usfca.edu
kusf.org/calendar.shtml
Please send only calendar listings to this address.

Laughing Squid
PO Box 77633, San Francisco, CA 94107
hello@laughingsquid.com
www.laughingsquid.org
An online resource for underground art and culture of San Francisco and beyond.

Mesh Magazine
617 Oak St., San Francisco, CA 94117
PH: 415-845-9979
Brian Brophy info@meshsf.com
www.meshsf.com
Free entertainment magazine. Our musical coverage focuses on independent Rock, Hip Hop and Punk.

Metro San Jose
550 S. 1st St., San Jose, CA 95113
PH: 408-298-8000 FX: 408-298-0602
www.metroactive.com/metro
Silicon Valley's leading weekly newspaper.

No Left Turn Records
633 Renfrew Rd. El Sobrante, CA 94803
PH: 925-768-6994
John Maddox john@nolefturnrecords.com
www.nolefturnrecords.com
We search for the best talent in California for record contracts and compilation albums.

North Bay Music
info@northbaymusic.com
www.northbaymusic.com
An online guide to live music in the San Francisco area.

On The Tip of My Tongue
Cecilia Gin ceemoon@yahoo.com
www.tipofmytongue.net
We produce a cable video show in San Francisco that focuses on local Bay Area talent.

Outsound
www.outsound.org
Tries to raise public awareness of music by presenting public performance, promotion and education.

The Owl Mag
829 27th Ave. #206, Oakland, CA 94601
info@theowlmag.com
theowlmag.com
Written specifically for the Bay Area's vibrant and diverse music scene.

Pacific Noise Video Podcast
pacificnoise@gmail.com
www.pacificnoise.com
Each week we capture some element of San Francisco's hidden art and music scene and broadcast it.

Redwood Bluegrass Associates
www.rba.org
Serving the Bay area to promote Bluegrass and related Acoustic music through concerts and workshops.

Royal Ark Music
13763 Campus Dr. Oakland, CA 94605-3833
PH: 510-867-8902
Dejah Fortune blakkbuddha@aol.com
www.royalarkmusic.com
We provide promotion for Hip Hop artists in the SF Bay area.

San Francisco Bay Area Early Music Concert Listings
1071 Blair, Sunnyvale, CA 94087
FX: 408-245-6901
Jonathan Salzedo listings@albanyconsort.com
www.albanyconsort.com/concerts
A resource for working musicians and concert-goers.

San Francisco Classical Guitar Society
www.sfcgs.org
Promoting the awareness, understanding and appreciation of the Classical guitar.

San Francisco Classical Voice
225 Bush St. #500, San Francisco, CA 94104
Editor@SFCV.org
www.sfcv.org
The Bay Area's website journal of Classical music criticism. Features reviews of musical performances.

San Francisco Early Music Society
www.sfems.org
Creates a supportive environment for the performance of Medieval, Renaissance and Baroque music.

San Francisco Traditional Jazz Foundation
www.sftradjazz.org
Helps foster live, high quality traditional Jazz, regionally and worldwide.

San Jose Jazz Society
www.sanjosejazz.org
Presents free concerts, festivals, hands-on workshops, clinics and master classes.

San Jose Mercury News
750 Ridder Park Dr. San Jose, CA 95190
PH: 408-920-5027 FX: 408-288-8060
Ron Kitagawa rkitagawa@mercurynews.com
www.mercurynews.com
Entertainment section covers the local music scene.

SF Bay Guardian
135 Mississippi, San Francisco, CA 94107-2536
PH: 415-255-3100 FX: 415-255-8762
www.sfbg.com
Free weekly alternative paper. Local Indie music, concert reviews and artist interviews.

SF JAZZ
www.sfjazz.org
Devoted to Jazz at the highest level, with concert performers ranging from acknowledged masters to the newest and most promising talents.

SF Weekly
185 Berry #3800, San Francisco, CA 94107
PH: 415-536-8100 FX: 415-541-9096
Jennifer Maerz feedback@sfweekly.com
www.sfweekly.com
San Francisco's smartest publication. Local music section.

SFBAYou
sfbayou@sfbayou.com
www.sfbayou.com
Will keep you informed on Bay Area events, new CDs and books and Cajun-Zydeco news.

SFBlues.net
Rich Piellisch peach@sfblues.net
www.sfblues.net
Your source of information on San Francisco's Blues scene.

sfcelticmusic.com
jim@sfcelticmusic.com
www.sfcelticmusic.com
Traditional Celtic music of Ireland, Scotland, Cape Breton and Brittany in the Bay Area.

sfgoth.com
www.sfgoth.com
Provided for free to the SF net.goth community for hosting Gothic or Industrial club pages.

SFMPB.com
e@sfmpb.com
www.sfmpb.com
Exists to promote Brazilian music in the San Francisco Bay Area.

sfstation.com
3528 17th St., San Francisco, CA 94110
PH: 415-552-5588 FX: 415-552-5587
www.sfstation.com
San Francisco's independent information resource.

Sister SF
PO Box 6, 1001 Page St., San Francisco, CA 94117
www.sistersf.com
Providing a supportive, friendly platform for any female DJ, MC or live performer.

South Bay Folks
contact-sbf@SouthBayFolks.org
www.SouthBayFolks.org
Dedicated to promoting Folk music in the greater San Jose area.

South Bay Guitar Society
www.sbgs.org
Promotes Classical and related guitar music by providing performance opportunities to professional and amateur musicians.

Thrasher Magazine
1303 Underwood Ave. San Francisco, CA 94124
PH: 415-822-3083 FX: 415-822-8359
greg@thrashermagazine.com
www.thrashermagazine.com
Covers SF Punk and Hardcore music scene.

Transbay Creative Music Calendar
1510 8th St., Oakland, CA 94607
PH: 510-893-2840
mail@transbaycalendar.org
transbaycalendar.org
Concert listings for non-commercial, adventurous new music in the Bay Area.

True Skool
Ren dj_ren@true-skool.org
true-skool.org
Dedicated to preserving Hip Hop and Funk. Covering the Bay Area's musicians and events.

urban delicious
Alex Pleasant alex@urbandelicious.com
www.urbandelicious.com
San Francisco event calendar.

West Coast Songwriters
1724 Laurel St. #120, San Carlos, CA 94070
PH: 650-654-3966 FX: 650-654-2156
info@westcoastsongwriters.org
www.westcoastsongwriters.org
Promotes, educates and provides tools and opportunities to songwriters from Alaska to California.

Zero Magazine
12 S. 1st St. #300, San Jose, CA 95113
PH: 408-971-8511
Larry Trujillo larry@zero.cc
www.zeromag.com
Alternative record reviews & interviews. Please CONTACT me before sending your music.

Los Angeles

The Americana Music Circle
Lauren Adams americanacircle@yahoo.com
www.americanacircle.com
A place for songwriters to enjoy themselves, stretch out and meet new comrades each month.

AOL City Guide Los Angeles *Music*
home.digitalcity.com/losangeles
Contains feature articles plus highlights, a running music poll and interactive message board.

Flavorpill LA
la_events@flavorpill.net
la.flavorpill.net
A publishing company that seeks out the best in arts, music and culture and delivers its findings.

folkWorks
PO Box 55051, Sherman Oaks, CA 91413
PH: 818-785-3839
mail@folkworks.org
www.folkworks.org
A newspaper dedicated to promoting Folk music, dance and other folk arts.

hollywoodband.com
2510-G Las Posas Rd. #200, Camarillo, CA 93010-3496
PH: 805-322-4265
www.hollywoodband.com
Underground band directory. Rock, Pop, Punk, Metal etc. Reviews, news, shows ...

JesusJams.com
PH: 301-289-5635
news@jesusjams.com
www.jesusjams.com
L.A. area Christian music concerts and events.

Jointz Magazine
1800 S. Robertson #0420, Los Angeles, CA 90035
PH: 213-351-1006 FX: 323-417-4977
listings@jointzmag.com
www.jointzmag.com
Provides expansive coverage of club listings and events, as well as trends in music.

la-underground: los angeles loves you
losanjealous@gmail.com
la-underground.blogspot.com
Music, art, film, culture.

LA Weekly
PO Box 4315, Los Angeles, CA 90078
PH: 323-465-9909
www.laweekly.com
LA arts and entertainment. Local music coverage includes spotlight artists, reviews and gig listings.

LAmusic.com
dean@lamusic.com
www.lama.com
Promotes artists with little or no access to airwaves due to economic rather than creative reasons.

LAReggaeClubs.com
10008 National Blvd. #144, Los Angeles, CA 90034
White Lightning admin@lareggaeclubs.com
www.lareggaeclubs.com
Your one stop for Reggae entertainment in Los Angeles.

LOL Records
PO Box 5148, Beverly Hills, CA 90209
PH: 310-790-5689 FX: 208-460-2903
Gerry Davies info@lolrecords.com
www.lolrecords.com
A record label gearing up to sign more music and help Indie artists get their careers off the ground.

Los Angeles Goes Underground
lagu.somaweb.org
Showcasing Los Angeles based Underground, Alternative & Indie Rock bands.

Los Angeles Jazz Society
www.lajazzsociety.org
Keeps its members informed through its quarterly newsletter, "Quarter Notes."

Los Angeles Gothic-Industrial Network
help@lagoth.net
www.lagoth.net
If you are in a Goth/Industrial/Deathrock band and are local to LA/OC, then submit a band form.

Los Angeles Songwriters' Network
PH: 626-818-0047
Jimi Yamagishi, jimi@songnet.org
www.songnet.org
Career-minded artists supporting each other through network events, seminars and collaboration.

The Los Angeles Swing Times
www.nocturne.com/swing
Covering all things Swing in L.A.

Los Angeles Times
202 W. 1st St., Los Angeles, CA 90012
PH: 213-237-5000
www.latimes.com
Covers local and national music scene.

LosAngeles.com
www.losangeles.com/music
Our insider's look at the L.A. music scene.

Music Glob
Dan info@musicglob.com
www.musicglob.com
An MP3 blog about Rock music. E-mail me MP3s, videos etc. you would like to share.

Music Plus TV
517 N. Alvarado St., Los Angeles, CA 90026
PH: 213-572-0240 FX: 213-572-0241
Marc Cubas marc@musicplustv.com
www.musicplustv.com
We air undiscovered and Indie artists of all genres 24/7 on our cable and web TV stations.

Planet Shark Productions
333 N. Hayworth Ave. Los Angeles, CA 90048
Sally sohosharky@aol.com
www.planetsharkproductions.com
Produces, markets and promotes film, record and DVD release parties & other industry events.

Rock City News
7030 De Longpre Ave. Hollywood, CA 90028
PH: 323-461-6600 FX: 323-461-6622
Ruben webmaster@rockcitynews.com
www.rockcitynews.com
Covering local bands, clubs and other social gatherings.

Rock Insider
PO Box 1314, Hollywood, CA 90078
JAX jax@rockinsider.com
www.rockinsider.com
A Hollywood music scene MP3 blog. News, downloads, concerts etc.

TheSceneLA.com
editor@thescenela.com
www.thescenela.com
Articles, reviews, release information ...

Venice Magazine
PO Box 1, Venice, CA 90294-0001
venicemag@venicemag.com
www.venicemag.com
Los Angeles A&E magazine.

Webookbands.com
7095 Hollywood Blvd. #794, Hollywood, CA 90028
PH: 323-651-1582 FX: 323-651-2643
info@webookbands.com
www.webookbands.com
A booking service giving local unsigned talent easy access to clubs throughout Los Angeles.

WHERE Magazine
3679 Motor Ave. #300, Los Angeles, CA 90034
PH: 310-280-2880 FX: 310-280-2890
art@wherela.com
www.wherela.com
List your upcoming events.

You Set the Scene
Duke dukeufo@hotmail.com
yousetthescene.blogspot.com
Keeping track of the massive Los Angeles music scene. Primarily focusing on Indie Rock.

YourLocalScene.com Los Angeles
PO Box 41669, Long Beach, CA 90853
Eric eric@yourlocalscene.com
la.yourlocalscene.com
Los Angeles' home on the internet for local music information, bands, venues and more!

San Diego

Accretions
PO Box 81973, San Diego, CA 92138
PH: 619-299-5371
sounds@accretions.com
www.accretions.com
An artist-based label with an ear towards Experimental, Improvisational and Global sounds.

Blues Lovers United of San Diego
www.blusd.org
Presenting and supporting local and national Blues artists and culture.

Fox Rox
foxrox@fox6.com
www.fox6.com/foxrox
San Diego's only local music TV show. Gives the lowdown on new releases and local shows.

Imperfekshun Magazine
5106 Federal Blvd. #105, San Diego, CA 92105
PH: 619-527-0710
info@imperfekshun.com
www.imperfekshun.com
Multi-cultural publication servicing San Diego and its immediate surrounding towns.

Lo-CaL
info@lo-cal.com
www.lo-cal.com
Supporting the San Diego music scene. News, concerts, MP3s ...

Oly's San Diego Open Mic Schedule
PH: 720-985-7423
Scott "Oly" Olson olyjams@yahoo.com
webspawner.com/users/sdopenmic
A comprehensive list of various open mic events in the San Diego area.

San Diego Acoustic Music Scene
Kelley Martin kelley@acousticpie.com
www.acousticpie.com/SanDiego.html
San Diego is becoming a hotbed of Acoustic Singer/Songwriters and a springboard for national talent.

San Diego CityBEAT
3550 Camino Del Rio N. #207, San Diego, CA 92108
PH: 619-281-7526 FX: 619-281-5273
www.sdcitybeat.com
Has "locals only" section.

San Diego Early Music Society
www.sdems.org
Showcasing the musical treasures of Europe's Medieval, Renaissance and Baroque periods.

San Diego Local Metal
raymond@sdmetal.com
www.sdmetal.com
Presenting the best of San Diego's local Metal bands.

San Diego Magazine
1450 Front St., San Diego, CA 92101
PH: 619-230-9292 FX: 619-230-0490
www.sandiego-online.com
We welcome information on upcoming events in the San Diego area.

San Diego Musicians Network
PH: 858-344-2294
info@sdmusicnet.com
www.sdmusicnet.com
Featured artists section plus show dates, new bands and new projects by your favorite artists.

San Diego NSAI
EAxford@aol.com
www.pianopress.com/nsai.htm
We do writing exercises as well as group song critiques. Every month we feature our "Night of Original Songs" Showcase at Claire de Lune.

San Diego Reader *Hometown CDs*
c/o Music Editor, PO Box 85803, San Diego, CA 92186
PH: 619-235-3000 FX: 619-231-0489
e-music@sdreader.com
www.sdreader.com/ed/calendar/music.html
Does reviews of local artists.

San Diego Songwriter's Guild
3368 Governor Dr. #F-326, San Diego, CA 92122
sdsongwriters@hotmail.com
www.sdsongwriters.org
Exposing original songs to the recording, TV and movie industries via pitch sessions with entertainment professionals.

San Diego Swings
PO Box 460084, Escondido, CA 92046-0084
FX: 760-740-1732
www.sandiegoswings.com
Your source for Swing and Big Band music in America's finest city.

San Diego Troubadour
sdtroubadour@yahoo.com
gothere.com/sandiego/Troubadour
A free publication specializing in Alt-Country, Folk, Gospel and Bluegrass.

San Diego Union-Tribune *Under the Radar*
PO Box 120191, San Diego, CA 92112-0191
PH: 619-718-5200 FX: 619-260-5081
Anna Maria Stephens
annamaria.stephens@uniontrib.com
entertainment.signonsandiego.com/section/music
Takes a look at the independent arts and music scene.

SanDiegoPunk.com
Joel Scheingross joel@sandiegopunk.com
www.sandiegopunk.com
Coverage includes show listings, pictures, interviews, places to hang out and buy records and more.

sdmetal.org
webmaster@sdmetal.org
www.sdmetal.org
San Diego's online realm for Metal.

Colorado

Black Rose Acoustic Society
www.blackroseacoustic.org
Dedicated to the education, performance and preservation of all types of traditional music.

Boulder Weekly
690 S. Lashley Ln. Boulder, CO 80303
PH: 303-494-5511 FX: 303-494-2585
www.boulderweekly.com
Free weekly alternative paper. CD and concert reviews, club listings.

Classical Guitar Society of Northern Colorado
www.coloradoguitar.com
Brings both Classical and Acoustic guitar players and friends together each month in a pleasant cafe.

Colorado Art Rock Society
www.coloradoprog.com
A society for like minded and intelligent odd-metered music connoisseurs.

Colorado Arts Net
Box 300-245, Denver, CO 80203
letters@coarts.net
www.coloradoarts.net
The most informative exciting tool for any local fan of the arts.

Colorado Bluegrass Music Society
www.coloradobluegrass.org
Promotes and encourages the development, performance and preservation of Bluegrass.

Colorado Blues Society
www.coblues.com
Creating a wider appreciation of the American indigenous art form, the Blues.

Colorado Friends of Cajun/Zydeco Music and Dance
cfcz.org
Your guide for the best in Cajun and Zydeco music in the front range area of Colorado.

Colorado Music Association *(COMA)*
www.coloradomusic.org
Presents music festivals showcasing and celebrating local talent.

Colorado Springs Independent Newsweekly
235 S. Nevada, Colorado Springs, CO 80903
PH: 719-577-4545 FX: 719-577-4107
www.csindy.com
Colorado Springs weekly A&E paper.

ColoradoRock.com
webmaster@coloradorock.com
www.coloradorock.com
Resource site and TV show.

Commotion Music Promotion
PH: 303-921-5271
www.commotionpromotion.com
We offer you a full range of internet and traditional publicity services.

Fort Collins Music Index
studio@seldomfed.com
www.seldomfed.com/fcmusic.htm
We list musician's pages, artists, music projects, venues, stores and more. Learn about the music biz.

GJLive.com
PH: 800-340-6545
Sean Gibbs info@GJLive.com
www.GJLive.com
Your source for the latest on the Grand Junction music scene!

Hapi Skratch Entertainment
1151 Eagle Dr. #324, Loveland, CO 80537-8020
PH: 970-613-8879 FX: 775-256-2501
info@hapiskratch.com
www.hapiskratch.com
Offers a complete line of service essential to the growth and development of any band.

Independent Records and Video
3030 E. Platte Ave. Colorado Springs, CO 80909
PH: 719-473-0882
independent@beindependent.com
www.beindependent.com
Since 1978, fulfilling Southern Colorado's music needs.

Kaffeine Buzz
PO Box 181261, Denver, CO 80218
PH: 303-394-4959
bands@kaffeinebuzz.com
www.kaffeinebuzz.com
An online music and entertainment source for Colorado and beyond.

KGNU's Bluegrass Calendar
Cuz'N Nickles bluegrass@kgnu.org
www.kgnu.org/bluegrass
List your upcoming Bluegrass event.

KTCL Local Access
4695 S. Monaco St., Denver, CO 80237
PH: 303-713-8000
www.area93.com
Streaming music from some of Colorado's best bands.

MileHighMusicStore.com
1151 Eagle Dr. #324, Loveland, CO 80537-8020
PH: 970-613-8879
info@milehighmusicstore.com
MileHighMusicStore.com
We want to sell all CDs that have a Colorado and Rocky Mountain connection.

Rock on Colorado!
1550 Larminer St. #608, Denver, CO 80202
David Webmaster@RockOnColorado.com
www.rockoncolorado.com
A celebration of Colorado's music scene!

Scene Magazine
PO Box 489, Fort Collins, CO 80522
PH: 970-490-1009 FX: 970-490-1266
Danielle Cunningham editor@scenemagazine.info
www.scenemagazine.info
Ft. Collins arts and music information covering local and national acts. Profiles bands and reviews CDs.

Denver

Creative Music Works
PO Box 5, Denver, CO 80201
PH: 303-960-5372
info@creativemusicworks.org
creativemusicworks.org
Provides educational and performance opportunities for Jazz and other contemporary music.

DenverBoulderMusic.com
info@denverbouldermusic.com
www.denverbouldermusic.com
The finest site on the web to find the best music in Denver, Boulder and all over Colorado.

DenverMix.com
PO Box 11081, Englewood, CO 80151
PH: 303-722-6322
submit@denvermix.com
denver.mixliving.com
Denver's hippest online entertainment guide. Submit your band's information and website address.

KTCL's Locals Only Calendar
4695 S. Monaco St., Denver, CO 80237
PH: 303-713-8000
www.area93.com
Post your upcoming shows.

Swallow Hill Music Association
www.swallowhill.com
Denver's home for Folk and Acoustic music. Publishes the Swallow Hill Quarterly.

Underground Network
www.undergroundnet.net
Submit events, club nights, links, event reviews, CD or DJ reviews and much more.

Westword
PO Box 5970, Denver, CO 80217
PH: 303-296-7744 FX: 303-296-5416
www.westword.com
Denver free weekly alternative paper. Reviews CDs and normally does a full bio on one local band each week.

Connecticut

Club CT Live Bands
24 Wilfred Rd. Manchester, CT 06040
PH: 860-680-4756
clubct2@clubct.com
www.clubct.com/bands.htm
Submit your band if playing in Connecticut. Also contains a band of the month feature.

Connecticut Area Blues Bands and Musicians
www.megablues.com/conn.htm
Features local band links, photos, area venues and more!

Connecticut Bluegrass Music Association
www.ctbluegrass.org
Preserves Bluegrass music in Connecticut and the surrounding area.

Connecticut Blues Society
www.ctblues.org
Promoting a sense of community through our newsletters and special events.

Connecticut Classical Guitar Society
www.ccgs.org
Serving Classical guitarists by providing a forum for listening, learning, performing and teaching.

Connecticut Songwriters Association
PO Box 511, Mystic, CT 06355
Bill Pere bill@billpere.com
www.ctsongs.com
Weekly newsletter full of helpful information, news, classified ads and upcoming events.

CT Punx
www.ctpunx.com
News, reviews, profiles and MP3s.

CT Ska Productions
33 Central Ave. Naintic, CT 06357
info@ctska.com
www.ctska.com
Working to supply CT with quality information on the state's Ska scene.

CTFolk.com
www.ctfolk.com
Current info on the Connecticut Folk music scene.

CTMusic.com
Keith Wilkinson email@ctmusic.com
www.ctmusic.com
Connecticut's definitive music web resource.

CTMusicians.org
PO Box 779, Windsor, CT 06095
PH: 860-298-8689
Tomaca Govän info@ctmusicians.org
ctmusicians.org
Featuring musicians and bands from the greater Connecticut area.

entertainment.ctcentral.com
Weekend, New Haven Register, 40 Sargent Dr.
New Haven, CT 06511
FX: 203-865-7894
entertainment.ctcentral.com
CTCentral's hub for entertainment news. Phone or fax your shows. Do not send by e-mail!

Fairfield County Weekly
350 Fairfield Ave. #605, Bridgeport, CT 06640
PH: 203-382-9666 FX: 203-382-9657
www.fairfieldweekly.com
Free weekly paper. CD and concert reviews, previews shows, interviews bands.

Hartford Advocate
121 Wawarme Ave. 1st Fl. Hartford, CT 06114
PH: 860-548-9300 FX: 860-548-9335
www.hartfordadvocate.com
CD reviews. Local Bands and Happenings. Updated every Thursday.

Hartford Courant
285 Broad St., Hartford, CT 06115
PH: 860-241-6200
www.ctnow.com
Accepts CD for review if playing in Connecticut. Previews shows and interviews bands.

Hartford Jazz Society
www.hartfordjazzsociety.com
Improves Jazz as America's gift to the music world and fosters an appreciation and love for Jazz.

Media Factory TV / Media Factory Radio Show
718 Enfield St. Space B, Enfield, CT 06082
PH: 860-741-8801
netshows@aol.com
www.netshows.us
TV and radio shows. Musicians, send us your videos and music CDs.

New Haven Advocate
900 Chapel St. #1100, New Haven, CT 06510
PH: 203-789-0010 FX: 203-787-1418
www.newhavenadvocate.com
New Haven's weekly newspaper. Local bands and happenings, updated every Thursday.

openmikeonline.com
www.openmikeonline.com
Features pictures and news from CT open mics. Site includes a "featured artist".

Soundwaves
PO Box 710, Old Mystic, CT 06355
PH: 860-572-5738 FX: 860-572-5738
David L. Pottie editor@swaves.com
www.swaves.com
Southern New England's entertainment guide. In-depth band & club info.

Delaware

Brandywine Friends of Old-Time Music
www.brandywinefriends.org
Preserving and presenting traditional American music.

Delaware Friends of Folk
www.delfolk.org
Furthering the cause of Folk music and Folk musicians in our area.

DelawareOnline
PO Box 15505, Wilmington, DE 19850
PH: 302-324-2500
www.delawareonline.com/entertainment
Concerts, clubs and local nightlife around Delaware and Philadelphia.

Delaware Today
3301 Lancaster Ave. #5-C, Wilmington, DE 19805
PH: 302-656-1809 FX: 302-656-5843
www.delawaretoday.com
List your upcoming events.

Diamond State Blues Society
www.diamondstateblues.com
Supporting local Blues artists as well as to bring national acts to the Diamond State.

freedelaware.com
PH: 302-421-9377 FX: 302-421-8365
info@freedelaware.com
freedelaware.com
Includes a message board, MP3 service area and search engine.

Newark Arts Alliance
100 Elkton Rd. Newark, DE 19711
PH: 302-266-7266
info@newarkartsalliance.org
www.newarkartsalliance.org
Community A&E calendar accepts events.

Project Unity
PO Box 129, Hockessin, DE 19707
xprojectunityx@hotmail.com
www.projectunity.cjb.net
We have a spot for local up and coming bands to play and gain exposure.

Florida

AM Marketing/AM Publications
PO Box 20044, St. Petersburg, FL 33742
PH: 727-577-5500
Al Martino AMPUBS@aol.com
www.ampubs.com
Entertainment magazine in Central Florida. Covers many Indie CDs.

Axis Magazine
116 S. Orange Ave. Orlando, FL 32801
PH: 407-839-0039
www.axismag.com
Orlando's A&E magazine.

Broward Folk Club
www.browardfolkclub.com
Promotes Folk and Acoustic music.

City Link
PO Box 14426, Fort Lauderdale, FL 33302
PH: 954-356-4943
www.citylinkmagazine.com
Your link to news, A&E in Broward & Palm Beach County.

Coffee Stain
PO Box 50802, Sarasota, FL 34232
PH: 941-323-2545
joe@coffeestain.com
www.coffeestain.com
Band news, reviews, interviews, listings etc.

Country Grapevine
PO Box 380219, Murdock, FL 33938
PH: 941-625-8486 FX: 941-625-1172
Roxanne Moore roxanne@countrygrapevine.com
www.countrygrapevine.com
A grassroots newspaper concerning Country music, dance and fun.

Fla.vor Alliance
7809 N. Orleans Ave. Tampa, FL 33604
PH: 813-935-8887 FX: 813-935-0535
info@flavoralliance.com
www.flavoralliance.com
Supports local Christian Hip Hop music and artists.

Florida Harpers and Friends
www.florida.harper.org
An organizing force for Florida harpers and other instrumentalists.

Florida State Fiddlers Association
www.nettally.com/fiddler
Hold a yearly convention and fiddle contest.

FloridaLocalMusic.Com
jared@schoolnightrecords.com
www.floridalocalmusic.com
Find information on the Florida local music scene.

Folio Weekly
9456 Philips Hwy. #11, Jacksonville, FL 32256
PH: 904-260-9770 FX: 904-260-9773
www.folioweekly.com
Jacksonville free weekly alternative paper with complete concert calendar.

Fort Pierce Jazz Society
www.jazzsociety.org
A cultural, educational and entertainment resource for Jazz.

Friends of Florida Folk
www.foff.org
Publicizes, sponsors and produces newsletters, film, records, festivals and other events.

Gainesville Band Family Tree
donundeen@yahoo.com
www.gainesvillebandfamilytree.com
A list of every band that has ever been in Gainesville.

Gainesville Friends of Jazz and Blues
www.gnvfriendsofjazz.org
Promotes and supports Jazz and Blues music in Gainesville and surrounding area.

Girlz Like Us
PH: 407-929-4348
Lil lil@girlzlikeus.com
www.girlzlikeus.com
Produces and promotes events for lesbians throughout central Florida. Post your event.

Gulf Coast Bluegrass Music Association
www.gcbma.org
Bringing Bluegrass music to Northwest Florida and Southern Alabama.

Gulf Jazz Society
www.gulfjazzsociety.com
Sponsors Jazz clinics, awards music scholarships and stages Jazz festivals and concerts.

Heat Beat
3100 Boca Raton Blvd. #201, Boca Raton, FL 33431
PH: 877-525-0052 FX: 561-826-0338
info@heatbeat.com
www.heatbeat.com
Florida's entertainment magazine for over 10 years!

Hiphopelements
PH: 954-977-7886 FX: 775-249-0062
webmaster@hiphopelements.com
www.hiphopelements.com
Supporting the Florida Hip Hop scene.

TheIndieOutie.com
admin@theindieoutie.com
theindieoutie.com
Selling the music of Central Florida artists.

JaxBands
PO Box 14315, Jacksonville, FL 32238-1315
webmaster@JaxBands.com
www.jaxbands.com
Dedicated to supporting Jacksonville local bands!

Jazz Club of Sarasota
www.jazzclubsarasota.com
Provides Jazz and community programs for Florida's West Coast.

JungleTV
info@jungletv.com
www.jungletv.com
TV program featuring the best in South Florida music.

localrocksite.com
localrock@cfl.rr.com
localrocksite.com
Local live music schedules, venues and band bios covering Brevard County.

METAL MASTERS
2780 E. Fowler Ave. #224, Tampa, FL 33612
Tom Riley info@metalmasters.net
www.metalmasters.net
A one hour video/interview show, showcases top names and up and coming new artists.

Movement Magazine
1650-302 Margaret St. PMB 132, Jacksonville, FL 32204
movementmagazine@aol.com
www.movementmagazine.com
Underground music magazine. Interviews with local and world renowned musicians.

MusicPensacola.com
tiger@gulfbreeze.net
www.musicpensacola.com
Pensacola's weekly live entertainment guide. Local artists, concerts, festivals and services.

New Times Broward Palm Beach
PO Box 14128, Ft. Lauderdale, FL 33302-4128
PH: 954-233-1600 FX: 954-233-1521
www.newtimesbpb.com
Weekly paper with local music coverage. Reviews and previews bands playing the area.

North Florida Bluegrass Association
www.nfbluegrass.org
Promotes and preserves Bluegrass music.

Orlando Weekly
100 W. Livingston St., Orlando, FL 32801
PH: 407-377-0400 FX: 407-377-0420
www.orlandoweekly.com
Free weekly alternative paper. Covers local music scene, reviews new CD releases.

OrlandoCityBeat.com
www.orlandocitybeat.com/citybeat/music
The definitive guide to the Orlando music scene.

OrlandoSwing.com
swing-info@orlandoswing.com
www.orlandoswing.com
Delivers the latest swing news and events.

Rag Magazine
8930 State Rd. 84 #322, Ft. Lauderdale, FL 33324
PH: 954-234-2888 FX: 954-727-1797
info@ragmagazine.com
www.ragmagazine.com
South Florida's music magazine.

Realitysnap.com
5401 65th Ter. N. Ste. A, Pinellas Park, FL 33781
PH: 727-520-7540
Ken Thomas Ken@realitysnap.com
www.realitysnap.com
A comprehensive Tampa Bay music resource.

Rivot Rag
www.myspace.com/rivotrag
Tampa Bay's ONLY Underground Metal magazine.

South Florida Blues Society
www.soflablues.org
Promoting, teaching and advancing the Blues through networking with fans and musicians.

Space Coast Jazz Society
www.spacecoastjazzsociety.com
Promotes, preserves and educates Jazz-music lovers and Jazz-music makers.

Suncoast Blues Society
www.suncoastblues.org
Dedicated to upholding the traditions of the Blues.

Swept Away TV
4915 Oxford Cr. Boca Raton, FL 33434
PH: 561-241-9110 FX: 561-241-4422
www.sweptawaytv.com
A TV program that airs in more than 60 markets. We are now accepting electronic submissions from unsigned artists to be featured on our show. You MUST submit your press kit electronically through Sonic Bids www.sonicbids.com

Tampa Bay Entertainment Guide
PO Box 17674, Clearwater, FL 33762
tampabayentertainment.com
Promoting Tampa Bay's entertainment industry.

TampaBayMusician.com
admin@tampabaymusician.com
www.tampabaymusician.com
Resources for Tampa Bay area musicians.

tampahiphop.com
kramtronix@tampahiphop.com
www.tampahiphop.com
Covering the local scene.

We Are the Scene
www.wearethescene.com
Keeping you up to date with the happenings in the local music scene.

Weekly Planet
810 N. Howard Ave. Tampa, FL 33606
PH: 813-739-4800 FX: 813-739-4801
scott.harrell@weeklyplanet.com
www.weeklyplanet.com
Tampa free weekly alternative paper. Covers local scene and reviews Indie CD releases.

Miami

CityLink Online
PO Box 14426, Fort Lauderdale, FL 33302
PH: 954-356-4943
www.citylinkonline.com
South Florida's alternative news magazine.

CLOSER Magazine
520 Clematis St., West Palm Beach, FL 33401
Steve Rullman steve@thehoneycomb.com
www.closermagazine.com
Networks for you. Meet artists from Palm Beach to Miami.

GoPBI.com
2751 S. Dixie Hwy. West Palm Beach, FL 33405
PH: 561-820-3700 FX: 561-820-3722
Leslie Gray Streeter lstreeter@pbpost.com
www.gopbi.com/events/music
Music guide for the Palm Beaches and South Florida.

Miami New Times Online
PO Box 011591, Miami, FL 33101-1591
PH: 305-576-8000 FX: 305-571-7677
www.miaminewtimes.com
Online paper with local music section.

Slammie Productions
PO Box 5891, Lake Worth, FL 33461
PH: 954-532-4333
feedback@slammie.com
www.Slammie.com
An independent concert promoter presenting club shows in South Florida.

South Florida's Entertainment News & Views
www.entnews.com
Miami's premiere A&E weekly.

South Florida Jams
13855 Langley Pl. Davie, FL 33325
PH: 954-424-8728 FX: 954-424-8902
ethanschwartz@southfloridajams.com
www.southfloridajams.com
Bringing the best live music to South Florida.

South Florida Zydeco Society
www.soflozydeco.com
Educating and encouraging Zydeco music in South Florida.

TheHoneyComb.com
623 Selkirk St., West Palm Beach, FL 33405
Steven Rullman steven@thehoneycomb.com
thehoneycomb.com
This site is an "underground" resource module for the So-Fla area.

Georgia

Athens Exchange
196 Alps Rd. #2-133, Athens, GA, 30606
editor@athensexchange.com
www.athensexchange.com
Online A&E magazine.

Athens Folk Music and Dance Society
www.uga.edu/folkdance
Promotes Folk music by providing an opportunity to perform in the area.

Augusta Goth
triplespiral@hotmail.com
www.angelfire.com/sc2/nocturn
Info on the Goth scene in Augusta, Georgia.

Connect Savannah
1800 E. Victory Dr. #7, Savannah, GA 31404
PH: 912-231-0250 FX: 912-231-9932
www.connectsavannah.com
Weekly news, A&E publication. Extensive coverage of local music.

Georgia Music Industry Association
www.gmia.org
Educates the songwriter and performer on all aspects of the music industry.

Georgia Music Magazine
329 Cotton Ave. Macon, GA 31201
PH: 478-744-9955 FX: 678-559-0263
info@georgiamusicmag.com
www.georgiamusicmag.com
Profiles of the state's artists, pioneers and colorful characters related to music.

Gospel Music Productions
PO Box 7317, Warner Robins, GA 31095
PH: 478-997-1734 FX: 478-218-2720
www.gospelmusicproductions.net
Provides aspiring local Gospel artists the opportunity to use their gifts and promote their musical talents.

Lokal Loudness
734 Hickory Oak Hollow,
Augusta, GA 30901
PH: 706-836-5683
John "Stoney" Cannon
info@lokalloudness.com
www.lokalloudness.cjb.net
Covering the Augusta music scene.

Metropolitan Spirit
700 Broad St., Augusta,
GA 30901
PH: 706-738-1142
FX: 706-733-6663
Andy Stokes
andy.stokes@metrospirit.com
www.metrospirit.com
Augusta's most popular newsweekly.

Nuçi's Space
396 Oconne St., Athens,
GA 30601
PH: 706-227-1515
FX: 706-227-1524
space@nuci.org
www.nuci.org
A resource center for musicians.

redandblack.com
540 Baxter St., Athens, GA 30605
PH: 706-433-3000 FX: 706-433-3033
www.redandblack.com
U. Georgia's student publication.

Savannah Underground
Jon jkolko@gmail.com
www.savannahunderground.com
The definitive resource for the Savannah music scene.

Southeast Performer
449½ Moreland Ave. #206 Atlanta, GA 30307
PH: 404-582-0088
Susan Wile Schwarz
sepeditorial@performermag.com
www.performermag.com
Want your CD reviewed? Do you have news on your band? Send your CDs and press releases.

South Eastern Bluegrass Association
www.sebabluegrass.org
Promotes Bluegrass activities through a newsletter.

Technique
353 Ferst Dr. Atlanta, GA 30332-0290
Evan Zasoski entertainment@technique.gatech.edu
cyberbuzz.gatech.edu/nique
Georgia Tech's student newspaper.

Whatz Happenin' TV
1529 Spring Rd. Ste. E, Smyrna, GA 30080
PH: 770-437-0002 FX: 770-319-6694
info@whtv1.com
www.whtv1.com
TV program on broadcast television that has videos and interviews.

Atlanta

Art Rock in Atlanta
www.gnosisarts.org/aria
News, references and resources for the Atlanta Art Rock community.

Atlanta Blues Society
www.atlantablues.org
Keeping the Blues alive.

Atlanta Journal
PH: 404-522-4141
www.accessatlanta.com
Arts and entertainment online resource.

Atlanta Magazine
260 Peachtree St. #300, Atlanta, GA 30303
PH: 404-527-5500 FX: 404-527-5575
www.atlantamagazine.com
List your upcoming events online.

Atlanta Music Guide
878 Peachtree St. NE. #504, Atlanta, GA 30309
PH: 404-892-1533 FX: 404-254-2749
info@atlantamusicguide.com
www.atlantamusicguide.com
Atlanta bands, news, concerts, reviews, venues and radio stations.

AtlantaJamz.com
4514 Chamblee Dunwoody Rd. #279, Atlanta,
GA 30338
PH: 678-476-3726
info@atlantajamz.com
atlantajamz.com
Online store, full service promotion and marketing.

AtlantaJazz Discussion Group
groups.yahoo.com/group/AtlantaJazz
Supports and encourages the proliferation of Jazz music.

atlantashows.com
shows@atlantashows.com
www.atlantashows.com
Information on how to get recognition for your band.

atlantashows.org
darian@atlantashows.org
www.atlantashows.org
Listing of Metro Atlanta and surrounding area shows.

Cable and Tweed
cableandtweed@gmail.com
cableandtweed.blogspot.com
MP3 blog with news and reviews. Submissions are welcome, especially from Atlanta/Athens bands.

Creative Loafing Atlanta
384 Northyards Blvd. #600, Atlanta,
GA 30313-2454
PH: 404-688-5623 FX: 404-614-3599
Heather Kuldell
heather.kuldell@creativeloafing.com
www.atlanta.creativeloafing.com
Free weekly alternative paper. Covers local music scene and reviews CDs.

DryerBuzz
PH: 770-912-2217 FX: 877-576-1895
support@dryerbuzz.com
www.dryerbuzz.com
Atlanta's Urban entertainment magazine.

Jamgrrl.com
Jamgrrl gencole@gmail.com
www.jamgrrl.com
Supporting Atlanta's Jam scene.

LA Alliance
c/o Demos, #231, 6555 Sugarloaf Pkwy. #307,
Duluth, GA 30097
PH: 800-407-5893 x4
demo@laalliance.net
www.laalliance.net
21ˢᵗ century marketing for your album. R&B, Pop, Hip Hop, Holy Hip Hop, Gospel and Christian.

Sounds Atlanta
PO Box 49266, Atlanta, GA 30359
PH: 404-329-9438 FX: 404-325-8401
Bill Tullis SoundsAtlanta@aol.com
soundsatlanta.com
Studio & remote recording - mastering.

Undaground ATL Magazine
PO Box 370216, Decatur, GA 30037
PH: 678-905-6747
Nate Short undagroundatl@yahoo.com
www.undagroundatl.com
Atlanta's hardest hustlin', Hip Hop promotin', interactive CD-Magazine. We provide independent Hip Hop and Urban artists with CD reviews.

Hawaii

808shows.com
PO Box 11871, Honolulu, HI 96828
Jason Miller hwnexp@aol.com
www.808shows.com
Bands can list their upcoming shows on this site.

Aloha Joe
PO Box 4777, Lakewood, CA 90711
PH: 562-925-3711
alohajoe@alohajoe.com
www.alohajoe.com
Will review or play any music created on the Island.

BuyHawaiianMusic.com
1145 Kilauea, Hilo, HI 96720
PH: 888-652-2212 FX: 808-935-7761
info@buyhawaiianmusic.com
www.buyhawaiianmusic.com
All your favorite Hawaiian CDs and new releases.

Hawaiian Steel Guitar Association
www.hsga.org
Promotes traditional Hawaiian music.

HawaiiEventsOnline.com
www.hawaiieventsonline.com
Includes listings of live shows going on throughout Hawaii.

Honolulu Advertiser *TGIF*
PO Box 3110, Honolulu, HI 96802
PH: 808-525–8056 FX: 808-525–8037
tgif@honoluluadvertiser.com
www.honoluluadvertiser.com/tgif
Weekly arts section. Covers local music and events.

Honolulu Weekly
1200 College Walk #214, Honolulu, HI 96817
PH: 808-528-1475 FX: 808-528-3144
www.honoluluweekly.com
Honolulu's A&E weekly.

Maui Time Weekly
33 Market St. #201, Wailuku, HI 96793
PH: 808-661-3786 FX: 808-661-0446
www.mauitime.com
Maui weekly A&E paper.

mele.com
PO Box 223399, Princeville, HI 96722
www.mele.com
The internet's largest in-stock catalog of Hawaiian music CD titles.

Idaho

The Arbiter
1910 University Dr. Boise, ID 83725
PH: 208-345-8204 FX: 208-426-3198
www.arbiteronline.com
Boise State U's student newspaper.

Argonaut
301 Student Union, Moscow, ID 83844
PH: 208-885-8924 FX: 208-885-2222
Tara Roberts arg_arts@sub.uidaho.edu
www.argonaut.uidaho.edu
U. of Idaho's student paper.

Boise Blues Society
www.boiseblues.org
Promoting the Blues as an American art form.

Idaho Bluegrass Association
www.smithfowler.org/bluegrass/IdahoBGindex.htm
Promoting Bluegrass music in Idaho.

Zidaho
www.zidaho.com
Everything in Idaho from A to Z. Add your event listing.

Illinois

Blues Blowtorch Society
www.bluesblowtorch.com/society
Promotes local artists as well as regional and national talents.

Central Illinois Jazz Society
www.midil.com/cijs.html
Provides opportunities for Jazz artists to play.

Fox Valley Blues Society
www.foxvalleyblues.org
Promotes the Blues through festivals, CD reviews etc.

Illinois Times
PO Box 5256, Springfield, IL 62705
PH: 217-753-2226 FX: 217-753-2281
www.illinoistimes.com
Springfield's A&E weekly.

Northern Illinois Bluegrass Association
www.nibaweb.org
Promotes Bluegrass music by sponsoring events.

Peoria Shows
Melvin Malone peoriashows@hotmail.com
www.peoriashows.net
Everything you need to know about the Peoria music scene.

River City Blues Society
www.rivercityblues.com
Submit news items, CD reviews and articles for the newsletter.

Southern Illinois Music E-Zine
Tad VanDyke ld_manager45@hotmail.com
www.sime-zine.com
Submit your gig and information online.

Tank's Place
Jerry Pfeiffer tanksplace@insightbb.com
www.tanksplace.com
Promoting live music entertainment in Central Illinois.

Chicago

American Gothic Productions
PMB 258, 2506 N. Clark St., Chicago, IL 60614
PH: 773-278-4684
scaryladysarah@aol.com
www.americangothicprod.com
Send your recordings for review.

AOL City Guide Chicago *Music*
home.digitalcity.com/chicago
Weekly feature articles plus weekend entertainment highlights.

Association for the Advancement of Creative Musicians
aacmchicago.org
Dedicated to nurturing, performing and recording serious, original music.

Barbershop Hip Hop
3452 W. Irving Park Rd. Chicago, IL 60618
Kevin Slimko
slimthebarber@barbershophiphop.com
barbershophiphop.com
TV program showcasing the finest talent in Chicago's underground Hip Hop scene.

Bluegrass Chatterbox Discussion Group
launch.groups.yahoo.com/group/bgrass-chatbox-illinois
Join for info on bands, musicians, festivals, jam sessions, concerts and more.

Centerstage Chicago
3540 N. Southport Ave. #280, Chicago, IL 60657
PH: 847-784-0095 FX: 773-442-0190
centerstage.net
Find and post gigs, announce auditions, buy & sell gear!

chi-improv Discussion Group
launch.groups.yahoo.com/group/chi-improv
Discussion about the Chicago creative and Improvised music scene.

Chicago Cajun Connection
PH: 708-361-2321
cajunconnx@earthlink.net
home.earthlink.net/~cterra440
Lists local events featuring traditional Cajun and Zydeco music.

Chicago Classical Guitar Society
www.chicagoclassicalguitarsociety.org
Sponsors recitals, master classes, evaluated recitals and lectures.

Chicago Flame
222 S. Morgan #3E, Chicago, IL 60607
PH: 312-421-0480 FX: 312-421-0491
chicagoflame@chicagoflame.com
www.chicagoflame.com
Independent student newspaper of the U. Illinois.

Chicago Harmony and Truth
PO Box 578456, Chicago, IL 60657
www.chatmusic.com
Creates a more hospitable music business environment.

Chicago Jazz Magazine
PO Box 737, Park Ridge, IL 60068
PH: 847-322-3534
reviews@ChicagoJazz.com
www.chicagojazzmagazine.com
News, reviews, shows etc.

Chicago Music Guide
chicago.citysearch.com
Extensive coverage of local music. Post your shows and events.

Chicago Reader
11 E. Illinois St., Chicago, IL 60611
PH: 312-828-0350
musiclistings@chicagoreader.com
www.chicagoreader.com
Free weekly paper. Chicago's essential music guide.

Chicago Singer Spotlight
www.singerspotlight.com
Produces three singer showcases in the Chicago area.

Chicago Songwriter's Collective
chicagosongwriters.com
Our purpose is to work for the community of artists by networking, showcases and educational seminars.

Chicago Stoner Rock
1573 N. Milwaukee Ave. PMB 488, Chicago, IL 60622
PH: 773-276-4474
www.chicagostonerrock.com
Reviews Heavy, Stoner, Drug Metal and Space Rock CDs and live shows.

ChicagoAfterhours.com
PH: 312-286-3832 FX: 413-691-4783
info@chicagoafterhours.com
www.chicagoafterhours.com
Provides information on Chicago's brightest night clubs, DJ's and artists.

ChicagoGigs.com
PO Box 2419, Palatine, IL 60078-2419
contact@chicagogigs.com
www.Chicagogigs.com
Covers both local and national touring acts.

ChicagoGroove.com
2318 S. Oakley, #3, Chicago, IL 60608
info@chicagogroove.com
www.chicagogroove.com
Pics and audio sets from local DJs.

ChicagoJazz.com
Contact@ChicagoJazz.com
www.chicagojazz.com
Online version of Chicago Jazz Magazine.

ChiCds.com
980 N. Michigan Ave. One Magnificent Mile, #1400, Chicago, IL 60611
PH: 800-683-8200
chiradio@hotmail.com
www.chicds.com
Rap and Soul online CD store.

Early MusiChicago
www.earlymusichicago.org
Covering this captivating but strangely under-appreciated art form that we call Early music.

Entertainment Law Chicago
PO Box 558023, Chicago, IL 60655
PH: 773-882-4912 FX: 708-206-1663
info@entertainmentlawchicago.com
www.entertainmentlawchicago.com
Entertainment, music and intellectual property legal issues.

Gothic Chicago
davidb@gothicchicago.com
www.gothicchicago.com
We want to be your resource to events in the Chicago Gothic community.

Illinois Entertainer
124 W. Polk St., Chicago, IL 60605
Attn: CD Reviews
PH: 312-922-9333 FX: 312-922-9369
service@illinoisentertainer.com
www.illinoisentertainer.com
Chicago A&E weekly. Loads of local music coverage!

Jazz Institute of Chicago
410 S. Michigan Ave. Chicago, IL 60605
PH: 312-427-1676 FX: 312-427-1684
www.JazzInstituteOfChicago.org
Preserving and perpetuating Jazz.

JstreetZine.com
PO Box 126, Waukegan, IL 60079
PH: 847-589-1396
Jesse Mendoza jesse@jstreetzine.com
www.jstreetzine.com
Focuses on unsigned, talented, hardworking artists.

Live Music Chicago
webmaster@livemusicchicago.com
www.livemusicchicago.com
The premier source for Chicago live music entertainment and DJs for all occasions.

Love, Chicago
3042 N. Christiana #2, Chicago, IL 60618
Erica Burke reviews@lovechicago.org
lovechicago.org
Our mission is to enhance readers' awareness about remarkable independent artists.

MODchicago
Eric ericcolin@modchicago.com
www.modchicago.com
Featuring music and events, Chicago's MOD history, MP3s and everything modern.

Newcity Chicago
770 N. Halsted #306, Chicago, IL 60622
www.newcitychicago.com
Chicago's free A&E publication.

Oh My Rockness Chicago
chicago@ohmyrockness.com
chicago.ohmyrockness.com
Your one-stop shop for Indie Rock show listings in Chicago. If you think people should know more about you e-mail us and tell us.

Revolutionslive.com
2521 N. Artesian Ave. #2, Chicago, IL 60647
Sean seanorr@revolutionslive.com
www.revolutionslive.com
Online provider of tour dates , show reviews, venue info and more for the Chicago area.

Rock Out Chicago
pete@rockoutchicago.com
www.rockoutchicago.com
Chicago's premier online music community.

Silver Wrapper Productions
5352 N. Lockwood Ave. Chicago, IL 60630
heynow@silverwrapper.com
www.silverwrapper.com
Concerts, Jazz, Funk, Electronic, Creole and Soul music.

Start A Revolution
1635 W. Julian, Chicago, IL 60622
www.startarevolution.com
Focuses on the Chicago Jam Band and Prog Rock scene.

Suburban NiteLife
PO Box 428, W. Chicago, IL 60186
PH: 800-339-2000 FX: 630-653-2123
www.nitelife.org
Chicago entertainment magazine.

Triple Dot MAS
2549 Waukegan Rd. # 178, Bannockburn, IL 60015-1510
PH: 312-223-0088
Davan Sand davan@3dmas.com
www.3dmas.com
A movement towards unity and harmony amongst creative people through our multimedia events.

UR Chicago Magazine
213 W. Institute Pl. #305, Chicago, IL 60610
PH: 312-238-9782 FX: 312-238-9838
editorial@urchicago.com
www.urchicago.com
New releases, local shows and more.

Windy City Media Group
1940 W. Irving Park Rd. Chicago, IL 60657
www.wctimes.com
The voice of Chicago's gay, lesbian, bisexual and transgender community. Has a music section. Post your upcoming shows.

Windyhop
www.windyhop.org
Covering the Chicago swing scene.

Women With Guitars
contact@womenwithguitars.com
www.womenwithguitars.com
Submit your promotional materials to be considered for a WWG showcase slot.

Indiana

BandNut
www.bandnut.com
Local band connection for the Evansville Tri-State area local bands.

Central Indiana Folk Music & Mountain Dulcimer Society
www.indianafolkmusic.org
Promoting and preserving American Folk music and Acoustic instruments.

Crush Entertainment
booking@crushentertainment.com
www.crushentertainment.com
We are your promotional hand in the Indianapolis metropolitan area!

Empress Alyda Productions
PO Box 421302, Indianapolis, IN 46242
Alyda Stoica empress@alyda.com
www.alyda.com
Books Goth, Industrial, Alternative Pop and Rock and Worldbeat bands in Indianapolis.

EvansvilleScene.com
Adam Ferguson webmaster@evansvillescene.com
www.evansvillescene.com
Promoting local talent in the area.

FortWayneMusic.com
feedback@fortwaynemusic.com
www.fortwaynemusic.com
Exposing as many people as possible to the excellent Fort Wayne music scene.

Indiana SKAlendar
thomska@yahoo.com
php.indiana.edu/~tgatkins/ska.html
Upcoming Ska shows in the Indiana area.

Indianapolis Musicians
www.indymusicians.com
Promoting the music profession in Indiana.

IndianapolisMusic.net
5260 Hinesley Ave. Indianapolis, IN 46208
Matt Fecher imn@indianapolismusic.net
indianapolismusic.net
Sparking interest in local music. Features Indy MP3 project.

IndianaRap.com
604 W. Taylor St. #201, Kokomo, IN 46901
Alex Clark reviews@indianarap.com
www.IndianaRap.com
If you would like your music reviewed, send 2 CDs to the above address.

Liquid Magazine
1601 E. Bowman St., South Bend, IN 46613
PH: 574-310-3789
Jedediah Walls dej_llaws@yahoo.com
www.myspace.com/liquidmagazine
Michiana's most popular free magazine for local music and culture. Promoting Michiana talent!

Midwest BEAT Magazine
2613 41st St., Highland, IN 46322
PH: 219-972-9131
Tom Lounges tom@midwestbeat.com
www.midwestbeat.com
A&E weekly publication throughout the Midwest.

MidWestBands.com
PO Box 558, Owensville, IN 47665
PH: 877-731-1081 FX: 509-351-9927
mwbcontact@midwestbands.com
www.midwestbands.com
Provides a wealth of resources to aid bands and individuals.

Naptown Reggae
the_lioness@naptownreggae.com
www.naptownreggae.com
Covering the Indianapolis Reggae scene.

Northern Indiana Bluegrass Association
www.bluegrassusa.net
Info on Bluegrass and all Acoustic music in a 200 mile radius of Fort Wayne.

NUVO Newsweekly
3951 N. Meridian St., Indianapolis, IN 46208
PH: 317-254-2400 FX: 317-254-2405
www.nuvo.net
Indianapolis free weekly alternative paper. Covers local music scene!

NWiLive.com
PO Box #551, Schererville, IN 46375
admin@nwilive.com
www.nwilive.com
Northwest Indiana's premium source for local music info.

TheMuncieScene.com
PH: 765-215-5440
Phantom phantom@TheMuncieScene.com
themunciescene.com
Assisting local artists in the creation and distribution of their music.

Whatzup Magazine
2305 E. Esterline Rd. Columbia City, IN 46725
PH: 260-691-3048
whatzup@whatzup.com
www.whatzup.com
Indianapolis based entertainment magazine. Show listings and reviews of local bands.

Iowa

515 Crew/ Iowa Hardcore
4710 Steinbeck #103, Ames, IA 50014
Greg Rice greg@ttecore.com
www.515crew.com
Covering the Iowa Hardcore scene. News, shows, band listings etc.

Central Iowa Blues Society
www.cibs.org
Keeping the Blues alive through appreciation and education.

Des Moines Register
PO Box 957, Des Moines, IA 50304-0957
PH: 515-284-8000
www.desmoinesregister.com
Daily A&E paper. Covers new music and Indie bands.

Iowa HomeGrown Music
PO Box 23265, Nashville, TN 37202
PH: 615-244-0570 FX: 615-242-2472
bronson@iowahomegrown.com
www.iowahomegrown.com
Represents songwriters and artists with a variety of musical styles.

Linn County Blues Society
www.lcbs.org
Preserving Blues music in Eastern Iowa.

Lizard Creek Blues Society
www.lizardcreekblues.org
Promoting the local Blues scene.

Mississippi Valley Blues Society
www.mvbs.org
Educating the general public about the Blues through performances.

Mushroom Cloud Records
3006 46th St., Des Moines, IA 50310-3530
PH: 515-278-4485
Rob Nowadzky rob@mushroomcloudrecords.com
www.mushroomcloudrecords.com
Providing an outlet for artists to have their music heard and seen.

River Cities' Reader
532 W. 3rd St., Davenport, IA 52801
PH: 563-324-0049 FX: 563-323-3101
www.rcreader.com
Davenport news & entertainment weekly.

Kansas

F5
322 S. Mosley, Wichita, KS 67202
PH: 316-263-0548
pr@F5Wichita.com
www.f5wichita.com
Wichita's alternative news magazine.

hiphopkc.com
hiphopkc@gmail.com
www.lawrencehiphop.com
Uniting Hip Hop artists in the KC area.

Kansas Prairie Pickers Association
www.accesskansas.org/kppa
Preserving Bluegrass and Old-Time Acoustic music.

Lawrence.com
645 New Hampshire St., Lawrence, KS 66044
PH: 785-832-7270
www.lawrence.com
Good coverage of local music scene.

Manhattan Mercury
PO Box 787, Manhattan, KS 66505
PH: 785-776-8808 FX: 785-776-8807
www.themercury.com
Contact us if you would like your band showcased.

Pipeline Productions
c/o The Bottleneck, 737 New Hampshire St.,
Lawrence, KS 66044
Julie music@pipelineproductions.com
www.pipelineproductions.com
Presents concerts in Lawrence & Kansas City. Visit our site for submission details.

RockKansas.com
www.RockKansas.com
Band directory, calendar etc.

Kentucky

Amplifier
PO Box 27, Dunbar, KY 42219
PH/FX: 270-526-2987
Don Thomason don@amplifier.ky.net
amplifier.ky.net
Bowling Green monthly music & entertainment magazine.

Kentuckiana Blues Society
kbsblues.org
Accepts and lists CDs from local acts.

Leobeat.com
640 S. 4th St. #100, Louisville, KY 40402
leobeat@leoweekly.com
www.leobeat.com
Your complete guide to the city's musical goings-on.

Louisville Music Industry Alliance
www.lmiacentral.com
Supporting and furthering of the Louisville original music scene.

Louisville Music News
3705 Fairway Ln. Louisville, KY 40207
PH: 502-893-9933 FX: 502-721-7482
www.louisvillemusic.com
Free monthly music paper. Covers regional music scene.

Louisville Scene
www.louisvillescene.com
Extensive music review section.

Louisiana

Cajun French Music Association
www.cajunfrenchmusic.org
Preserves and promotes traditional French Cajun music.

Cajunfun.com
www.cajunfun.com
List your show or event.

Cox.net NewOrleans.com *Music*
neworleans.cox.net
Got a show? Let us know!

Gambit Weekly
www.bestofneworleans.com
New Orleans' alternative weekly magazine.

girl gang productions
4523 Iberville St., New Orleans, LA 70119
Margaret Coble info@girlgangproductions.com
www.girlgangproductions.com
Promoting live music shows, drag king shows, dance parties, for and about women and GLBT performers.

Gumbo Pages
www.gumbopages.com
Dedicated to the music and culture of New Orleans.

HisMusic.com
PH: 985-781-0830
David Grant info@HisMusic.com
www.hismusic.com
Provides Christian concert listings for New Orleans.

Lafayette Local Entertainment
www.lafayettelocalentertainment.com
Features Lafayette area acts who are producing original material and are presenting it live.

LiveNewOrleans.com
jason@liveneworleans.com
www.LiveNewOrleans.com
Dedicated to covering the New Orleans music scene with reviews and photographs.

Louisiana Blues Preservation Society
www.geocities.com/Bluespreserve
Preserving and supporting Blues music throughout.

Louisiana Folk Roots
www.lafolkroots.org
Nurturing the unique Folk art scene in Louisiana.

Louisiana Music Factory
210 Decatur St., New Orleans, LA 70130
PH: 504-586-1094
info@louisianamusicfactory.com
www.louisianamusicfactory.com
Resources for artists in Louisiana.

Louisiana Songwriters Association
www.lasongwriters.org
Holds workshops to increase understanding of the music industry.

MojoNO.com
PH: 504-914-6860
staff@mojono.com
www.mojono.com
Free band listings and personal gig calendar.

Mothership Entertainment
1403 Annunciation St., New Orleans, LA 70130
PH: 504-488-3865 FX: 504-488-1574
funk@mothershipentertainment.com
www.MotherShipEntertainment.com
Aids artists by building a strategy designed for success.

New Orleans Bands.com
1609-D Hesiod St., Metairie, LA 70005
Thaddeus Frick thaddeus@nolabands.com
www.neworleansbands.com
Providing a network to help New Orleans talent become successful.

New Orleans Bands.net
4453 E. Falk St., New Orleans, LA 70121
www.neworleansbands.net
Bringing a new dimension to the local music scene in the Big Easy.

New Orleans Blues Project
1112 9th St., New Orleans, LA 70115
PH: 504-895-0739 FX: 504-895-6070
contact@bluesproject.com
www.bluesproject.com
Promotes communication, dialogue and understanding of the Blues.

New Orleans Live
jdonley@nola.com
www.nolalive.com/music
News and reviews of local music.

NewOrleansOnline.com
www.neworleansonline.com/neworleans/music
Extensive coverage of local music.

NOLA Life
nolalife@yahoo.com
www.nolalife.com
Where New Orleans talent networks online!

Offbeat
4211 Frenchmen St. #200, New Orleans,
LA 70116-2506
PH: 504-944-4300 FX: 504-944-4306
offbeat@offbeat.com
www.offbeat.com
Louisiana's music and entertainment magazine.

Pershing Well's South Louisiana Music Site
150 Shady Arbors Cr. #17-D, Houma, LA 70360
PH: 985-209-2229
info@pershingwells.com
www.pershingwells.com
Provide free listings for Louisiana artists.

Satchmo.com
Greg Hardison gregh@satchmo.com
www.satchmo.com
New Orleans & Louisiana music news, CD reviews, listings etc.

Shrevepunx
www.shrevepunx.com
Post pictures and info on your upcoming shows.

South Louisiana Bluegrass Association
www.southlouisianabluegrass.org
Promoting and preserving Bluegrass music.

Times of Acadiana
221 Jefferson St., Lafayette, LA 70501
PH: 337-289-6300 FX: 337-289-6443
Arsenio Orteza arsenioort@aol.com
www.timesofacadiana.com
Lafayette's A&E weekly.

T.R.E.A.L News
PO Box 63082, Lafayette, LA 70506
PH: 337-234-1526
trealnews@aol.com
www.trealnews.com
Helping to market Hip Hop artists in the Dirty South.

Where y'at Magazine
5500 Prytania St. #248, New Orleans, LA 70115
PH: 504-891-0144 FX: 504-891-0145
Billy Thinnes billy@whereyat.net
www.whereyatnola.com
New Orleans' monthly entertainment magazine.

Maine

Bluegrass Music Association of Maine
www.bmam.org
Supports local Bluegrass musicians.

Entertainment in Maine Today.com
390 Congress St., Portland, ME 04104
PH: 207-822-4060 FX: 207-879-1042
entertainment.mainetoday.com
Maine music resource including reviews and previews.

Maine Songwriters Association
www.mesongwriters.com
Supporting songwriters and their art.

MaineList.com
www.mainelist.com
Submit your Maine-based website.

MaineMusic.Org
997 State St., Bangor, ME 04401
PH: 207-775-9056
www.mainemusic.org
Supporting artists of all genres throughout Maine.

Partridge Records and Music
Jeffrey Thibeault jthibeault@partridgemusic.com
www.partridgerecords.com
Established to support independent artists and song writers in the local New England market.

Portland Maine Music
anton@portlandmainemusic.com
www.portlandmainemusic.com
Supports original music created in Maine.

Portland Phoenix
16 York St. #102, Portland, ME 04101
PH: 207-773-8900 FX: 207-773-8905
www.portlandphoenix.com
Local band coverage including MP3s from locally based musicians.

Maryland

Baltimore Blues Society
www.mojoworkin.com
Reviews CD releases by national, regional and local artists.

The Baltimore Buzz
reviews@buzz-magazine.com
www.buzz-magazine.com
Accepts submissions for the genres of Rock and Metal music. Contact us for our mailing address.

Baltimore City Paper
812 Park Ave. Baltimore, MD 21201
PH: 410-523-2300 FX: 410-523-2222
www.citypaper.com
Baltimore's weekly news and entertainment paper. Covers local music.

Baltimore Classical Guitar Society
www.bcgs.org
Organizes concerts for local and national Classic guitarists.

BaltimoreBands.com
www.baltimorebands.com
Classifieds, gigs, plus the ultimate list of Baltimore and Maryland's finest music makers.

Cajun/Zydeco in the Mid-Atlantic Region
Pat Yaffe patyaffe@yahoo.com
www.wherewegotozydeco.com
Cajun and Zydeco music and dance guide for the Baltimore-Washington area.

Frederick Blues Society
www.frederickblues.org
Supporting the Blues in the Frederick area.

Maryland Night Life.com
PH: 410-239-2817
www.marylandnightlife.com
Free online entertainment guide with local music section.

MarylandParty.com
409 Lee Dr. Baltimore, MD 21228
PH: 410-869-9348 FX: 443-697-0210
www.mdparty.com
Guide to live music in Maryland and surrounding states.

Music Monthly
2807 Goodwood Rd. Baltimore, MD 21214
PH: 410-426-9000 FX: 410-426-4100
musicmonthly@comcast.net
www.musicmonthly.com
Baltimore monthly music magazine. Register your band.

Potomac River Jazz Club
www.prjc.org
Encouraging and promoting traditional Jazz.

StatiQ Records
11221 Grouse Ln. Hagerstown, MD 21742
PH: 301-992-9889
Natasha A. Smith-Hazzard tasha@statiqrecords.ws
www.statiqrecords.ws
Record company with virtual music recording studio, music production & publishing and video production.

Tri-State Bluegrass Association
www.tri-statebluegrass.com
Promotes interest in Bluegrass and Old-Time music.

Walther Productions
PO Box 116, Jefferson, MD 21755
FX: 301-834-3373
info@walther-productions.com
www.walther-productions.com
Hosts tons of awesome Jam Band shows in the Baltimore & DC areas.

Massachusetts

Cambridge Society for Early Music
www.csem.org
Enlightening, educating and promoting the rich musical culture of five centuries.

capecodmusic.com
info@capecodmusic.com
www.capecodmusic.com
Extensive listing of events in the area. Post yours.

Concert and Venue Listings for New England
www.geocities.com/concertlistings
Listings of hundreds of venues in MA, CT, NH, ME, RI and VT.

Country Dance and Song Society
www.cdss.org
Celebrating English and Anglo-American Folk dance and music.

Folk Arts Center of New England
www.facone.org
Promoting traditional Dance, music and related Folk arts.

Link2Rock
22 Bridge St., Wilbraham, MA 01095
PH: 413-543-2022
Kingkevinis@hotmail.com
www.link2rock.com
Focuses on the Western Mass Indie Rock scene.

MassConcerts
MassMediaGirl@aol.com
www.massconcerts.com
Find information about music and entertainment events in the Northeast US.

Music For Robin
www.music-for-robin.org
Folk & Celtic resources covering Mass.

NBVIP.org
4 Kimberly Way, Acushnet, MA 02743
Eric Marcelino booking@nbvip.org
www.nbvip.org
Brings you the hot shows and dance parties in New Bedford area.

New England Country Music Club
www.necmc.homestead.com
Promoting Country music and local talent!

New England Entertainment Digest
PO Box 88, Burlington, MA 01803
Julie Ann Charest jacneed@aol.com
www.jacneed.com
Covering all of New England and New York.

New England Jazz Alliance
www.nejazz.org
Celebrating and perpetuating the tradition of Jazz in New England.

NewEARS
www.newears.org
A community dedicated to sharing and promoting Progressive Rock in the New England area.

newenglandrock.com
www.newenglandrock.com
New England area live entertainment resource.

NoMaSoNHa
friekman@hotmail.com
www.nomasonha.com
Greater Merrimack Valley music magazine with coverage from Lowell, MA to Manchester, NH and from Nashua, NH to Salem, NH ...and beyond.

Northeast Performer
285 Washington St., Somerville, MA 02143
PH: 617-627-9200
Kerianne Murphy nepeditorial@performermag.com
www.performermag.com
Want your CD reviewed? Send your CDs and press releases.

PACE Arts Center
pioneerarts.org
Supporting the arts in Massachusetts.

Skope Magazine
PO Box 231179, Boston, MA 02123
www.skopemagazine.com
Taking local music global!

TRP/NME Wreckidz
9 Hutchins Ct. Gloucester, MA 01930
PH: 978-394-0751
Mr. Dilligence mrdilligence@aol.com
www.NMEwreckidz.com
Indie record label/grassroots distributor for Massachusetts (and beyond) Rappers/R&B singers.

Valley Advocate
116 Pleasant St., Easthampton, MA 01027
PH: 413-529-2840 FX: 413-529-2844
www.valleyadvocate.com
Springfield free weekly alternative paper. Local bands and happenings section.

Worcester County Jazz Scene
Don Ricklin don@donricklin.com
www.donricklin.com/worcjazz
Everything you want to know about Jazz in Worcester County.

Wormtown
www.wormtown.org
Info on the Worcester, MA scene. Free listings.

Boston

Boston Beats
PO Box 1243, Allston, MA 02134
PH: 781-381-2856 FX: 206-237-2473
artists@bostonbeats.com
www.bostonbeats.com
Your guide to Boston's music scene.

Boston Bluegrass Union
www.bbu.org
Promoting and supporting the wealth of regional bands.

Boston Blues Society
www.bostonblues.com
Preserving and promoting the Blues.

Boston Classical Guitar Society
www.bostonguitar.org
Bimonthly newsletter. Submit your info to get posted.

The Boston Hip-Hop Alliance
askdarcie@hotmail.com
bostonhha.tripod.com
Helping to make the experience of Hip Hop artists, producers, promoters etc. better in the city of Boston.

Boston Jazz Fest
Chris Allen centralarteryproject@yahoo.com
bostonjazzfest.com
Promoting Jazz in the Boston area.

Boston Phoenix
126 Brookline Ave. Boston, MA 02215
PH: 617-536-5390 FX: 617-536-1463
www.bostonphoenix.com
Entertainment magazine covering the New England region.

Boston Society of Mechanics
www.bsm.us
Contains every resource artists need.

BostonNoise.org
1200 Massachusetts Ave. #28W, Cambridge, MA 02138
Karl Giesing submit@bostonnoise.org
bostonnoise.org
Submit your Noise act and MP3s to our site. It's best to contact us first.

BostonRap.com
www.bostonrap.com
Covering the Boston Rap scene. New releases, downloads, videos etc.

Exploit Boston!
343 Medford St. #2A, Somerville, MA 02145
PH: 781-420-9660
Susan Kaup contact@exploitboston.com
www.exploitboston.com
Event calendar and guide to interesting happenings around Boston: art, books, music, theater etc.

Folk Song Society of Greater Boston
www.fssgb.org
Providing opportunities for everyone to make, enjoy and support this music.

GyrlsRock Boston
1238 Comm Ave. #36, Boston, MA 02134
Sara Hamilton webmaster@gyrlsrock.com
www.gyrlsrock.com
100% devoted to female musicians in Boston.

Improper Bostonian
142 Berkeley St., Boston, MA 02116
PH: 617-859-1400
music@improper.com
www.improper.com
Boston's A&E magazine.

The Noise
74 Jamaica St., Boston, MA 02130
PH: 617-524-4735
www.thenoise-boston.com
If you're a New England band, we'll review your music!

On the Download
onthedownload@phx.com
thephoenix.com/onthedownload
The Phoenix's MP3 blog with hundreds of downloads plus news, reviews and scene reports.

Onward Charles
onward.charles@gmail.com
onwardcharles.blogspot.com
MP3 blog covering the local scene.

Purerockfury.com
Deek deek@purerockfury.com
www.purerockfury.com
Covering the Hard Rock/Metal scene. Includes a local band spotlight.

SalsaBoston.com
salsaboston.com
Boston's premiere Latin music and dance website.

thewicked
Ashley Wicked ashley@the-wicked.org
www.the-wicked.org
Listing of upcoming Boston gigs.

WBUR Online Arts
890 Commonwealth Ave. 3rd Fl. Boston, MA 02215
PH: 617-353-0909
Bill Marx bmarx@wbur.bu.edu
www.wbur.org/arts/archive/music
Covers the local Boston music scene.

Michigan

Ann Arbor Classical Guitar Society
www.society.arborguitar.org
Bringing performances of Classical guitar music to Michigan.

Ann Arbor Council for Traditional Music and Dance
thedance.net/~aactmad
Dedicated to the promotion and preservation of Acoustic Folk, Traditiona and Ethnic music only.

The Ark
316 S. Main St., Ann Arbor, MI 48104
PH: 734-761-1818
www.theark.org
Presenting and encouraging Folk, Roots and Ethnic music.

Capital Area Blues Society
www.cabsblues.org
Reviews of new album releases every month.

Current Magazine
212 E. Huron St., Ann Arbor, MI 48104
PH: 734-668-4044 FX: 734-668-0555
music@sgipub.com
ecurrent.com
Free monthly A&E magazine. Covers local music scene, news and reviews.

Flint Folk Music Society
www.flintfolkmusic.org
Promoting Folk music through performances and workshops.

Folk Alliance Region Midwest
www.farmfolk.org
Promotes the growth of Folk music and dance.

From the Garage
Sarah Morgan reviews@fromthegarage.com
www.fromthegarage.com
This site lists Punk, Ska, Emo, & Hardcore bands and shows from all over Michigan.

Grand River Folk Arts Society
www.grfolkarts.org
Contact to perform in West Michigan.

Great Lakes Acoustic Music Association
www.greatlakesacoustic.org
Promoting Bluegrass and Acoustic music.

Hearts On Fire Records
PO Box 852, Marshall, MI 49068
PH: 800-381-1063
www.heartsonfirerecords.com
Kalamazoo, Michigan Rock!

Kalamazoo Valley Blues Association
www.kvba.org
Preserving Blues music around Kalamazoo.

K'zoo Folklife Organization
www.geocities.com/Vienna/Studio/5893
Promotes multi-cultural, traditional and contemporary Folk music.

Magazine of Country Music
PO Box 1412, Warren, MI 48090
PH: 586-755-0471
countrymusicmag@yahoo.com
www.magazineofcountrymusic.com
Monthly publication. Features national and local Country music.

Michigan Artists
contactus@michiganartists.com
www.michiganartists.com
Supporting Michigan artists with postings of history, bios, pictures and more!

Michigan Bands dot Com
www.michiganbands.com
Submit news and press releases and add links to your band page.

The Michigan Musician's Network
www.mimusicnet.com
Resources for up-and-coming working singers, musicians, bands, songwriters, producers, managers etc.

Michigan Television Network
PO Box 765, Royal Oak, MI 48068-0765
PH: 248-376-4162
MichiganTV@hotmail.com
mitvnet.tripod.com/home.html
Increasing public awareness of Michigan's homegrown talent.

MichiganMetal
webmaster@michiganmetal.com
www.michiganmetal.com
Michigan's Heavy Metal resource. Downloads, gigs and more!

MLive
www.mlive.com
Michigan's home on the net. CD and concert reviews, music news.

Northern Express
PO Box 209, Traverse City, MI 49685-0209
PH: 231-947-8787 FX: 231-947-2425
www.northernexpress.com
Covering Northern Michigan. Does features on local musicians.

Northern Michigan Update
northernmichiganupdate.com
Any new CD releases, Big events, you would like me to promote?

Southeast Michigan Jazz Association
www.semja.org
Monthly newsletter and free online listings.

State News
435 E. Grand River Ave. East Lansing, MI 48823
PH: 517-432-3000
www.statenews.com
Michigan State U's student paper.

Tawas Bay Blues Society
www.bluesbythebaytawas.com
Promoting and preserving Blues music and culture.

West Michigan Blues Society
www.wmbs.org
Promotes Blues appreciation by sponsoring concerts, festivals and community events.

West Michigan Jazz Society
www.wmichjazz.org
Promotes numerous events and local artists.

West Michigan Music
listen@westmichiganmusic.com
www.westmichiganmusic.com
The area's one-stop place for the best information on the unique and exciting West Michigan music scene.

WGRD Local Music Page
PO Box 96, Grand Rapids, MI 49501
PH: 616-451-4800 FX: 616-451-4807
grdbrian@yahoo.com
www.wgrd.com/localmusic
Helping Western Michigan bands promote themselves and to keep fans up to date on local happenings.

Wheatland Music Organization
www.wheatlandmusic.org
Resource center for the preservation and presentation of traditional music and arts.

Detroit

DetMusic.com
www.detmusic.com
A local artist boards community. Promote your CD or upcoming shows.

Detroit Blues Society
home.flash.net/~dbsblues
Promotes the Blues to the general public.

Detroit Metro Times
733 Saint Antoine, Detroit, MI 48226
PH: 313-961-4060 FX: 313-961-6598
www.metrotimes.com
Free weekly alternative. CD reviews, concert reviews and previews.

DetroitCountryMusic.com
11449 Fleming St., Hamtramck, MI 48212
larry@detroitcountrymusic.com
www.detroitcountrymusic.com
Promotes and showcases local talent.

Motor City Rocks
PH: 313-982-0607 FX: 313-982-0607
Gary Blackwell gary@motorcityrocks.com
www.motorcityrocks.com
Our mission is to promote Detroit musicians and Detroit music venues.

Nestor in Detroit
hectop@peoplepc.com
www.nestorindetroit.com
News, releases and show reviews of the local Punk scene.

Online Bands
joe@onlinebands.com
www.onlinebands.com
Visit our site where you will find exciting fresh music from Detroit area bands.

Real Detroit Weekly
359 Livernois Ave. 2nd Fl. Ferndale, MI 48220
PH: 248-591-7325 FX: 248-544-9893
B.J. Hammerstein bj@realdetroitweekly.com
www.realdetroitweekly.com
Detroit's entertaining source for music, nightlife, movies and all other things under the pop culture umbrella.

Sign up for
The Indie Contact Newsletter
www.indiebible.com

Renaissance Soul Detroit
PMB #323, 23205 Gratiot Ave. Eastpointe, MI 48021
Kelly "K-Fresh" Frazier djkfresh@rensoul.com
rensoul.com
The Detroit Urban alternative. Dedicated to Detroit Hip Hop.

Minnesota

Christian World Today Television
Joseph Mckenzie ntwbroadcasting@msn.com
www.christianworldtodaytelevision.net
Gives Christian artists exposure in the Minneapolis and Midwest area.

City Pages MN Music Directory
401 N. 3rd St. #550, Minneapolis, MN 55401
PH: 612-372-3792
Lindsey Thomas lthomas@citypages.com
www.citypages.com/mmd
Magazine resource for local musicians.

KXXR's Loud & Local Page
2000 SE. Elm St., Minneapolis, MN 55414
PH: 612-617-4000
Patrick loudandlocal@93xrocks.com
www.93x.com/loudnlocal.asp
Submit news on your local band.

Midwest Movement
2520 Silver Ln. NE. #205, Minneapolis, MN 55421
PH: 651-308-1469
info@midwestmovement.com
www.midwestmovement.com
Covering the Midwest Punk scene. Reviews, interviews, spotlight bands etc.

Minnesota Bluegrass and OT Music Association
www.minnesotabluegrass.org
Host's Bluegrass and Old-Time music events and celebrations.

Minnewiki
mail@mpr.org
minnewiki.publicradio.org/index.php/Minnewiki_Home
An online reference about music-related artists, groups and venues that have a connection to Minnesota.

MusicScene
1998 Bluestem Ln. Shoreview, MN 55126-5013
PH: 612-747-0894 FX: 612-605-1299
Conal "Reverend Gonzo" Garrity
gonzo@musicscene.org
www.musicscene.org
Submit your band, gig, news etc. Send your demos and CDs for review.

Springboard for the Arts
www.springboardforthearts.org
Provides affordable management information for Indie artists.

TCElectronica
admin@tcelectronica.com
www.tcelectronica.com
A networking site for Electronic musicians in Minnesota and beyond.

Minneapolis/St.Paul

Blues On Stage
PO Box 582983, Minneapolis, MN 55458-2983
Ray Stiles mnblues@aol.com
www.mnblues.com
Covering Blues in the Twin Cities & around the world. Send 2 copies of your CD for review.

Dinosaur in Trouble
Lee@dinosaurintrouble.com
www.dinosaurintrouble.com
Proudly serving Twin City music geeks!

Downtown Journal
1115 Hennepin Ave. S., Minneapolis, MN 55403
PH: 612-825-9205 FX: 612-825-0929
www.downtownjournal.com
Covers the Twin Cities music scene.

D.U. Nation Underground Hip Hop
PH: 612-770-8357
www.dunation.com
Provides info about upcoming concerts and local events.

More Cowbell
kyle@morecowbell.net
www.morecowbell.net
Covering the Twin Cities' scene.

Pulse of the Twin Cities
3200 Chicago Ave. S., Minneapolis, MN 55407
PH: 612-824-0000 FX: 612-822-0342
Steve McPherson musiceditor@pulsetc.com
pulsetc.com
Weekly alternative paper. CD reviews and concert previews.

Rake Magazine
800 Washington Ave. N. #504, Minneapolis, MN 55401
PH: 612-436-2880 FX: 612-436-2890
www.rakemag.com
Provides entertaining reading for the Twin Cities.

Sick and Wrong
Sven sickandwrong@musician.org
sickandwrong.blogspot.com
A blog set up to comment on live music in the Minneapolis and St. Paul area.

Twin Cities Acoustic Music Calendar
www.tcacoustic.com
Includes major events in the upper Midwest, including Wisconsin, Iowa, ND and SD.

Twin Cities Jazz Society
www.tcjs.org
Sponsors local Jazz concerts, workshops and education programs.

Twin Cities Music Network
23 SE. 4th St. #213, Minneapolis, MN 55414
PH: 612-605-7960
email@tcmusic.net
www.tcmusic.net
List performances, band info and sell your CDs online.

Mississippi

blues.ms
blues.ms
Mississippi's Blues news.

The Burger
PO Box 1169, Hattiesburg, MS 39403-1169
PH: 601-529-9993
editor@theburger.org
www.theburger.org
Hattiesburg's one and only alternative press!

Dead Man Dancing Promotions
201A S. 14th Ave. Hattiesburg, MS 39401
PH: 601-466-5861
TC Byrd deadmandancing@gmail.com
www.deadmandancing.com
Source for the Hattiesburg music scene.

Magnolia State Bluegrass Association
www.geocities.com/magnoliabluegrass
Promotes Bluegrass music in the Deep South.

Mississippi Link
2659 Livingston Rd. Jackson, MS 39213
PH: 601-355-9103 FX: 601-355-9105
www.mississippilink.com
Jackson weekly paper.

Mississippi Old Time Music Society
www.fiddlemania.com/motmsweb
Sponsors several events and jams throughout the state.

Planet Weekly
PH: 601-714-4719
feedback@planetweekly.com
www.planetweekly.com
A&E section covers the local music scene.

The Reflector
www.reflector-online.com
Mississippi State U's student paper.

Missouri

Blues Society of the Ozarks
www.ozarksblues.org
Encourages performance of the Blues at clubs, at festivals and on radio.

CapeScene.com
scott@capescene.com
www.capescene.com
Covering upcoming events in the Cape Girardeau music scene.

Central Plains Jam Band Society
www.cpjs.org
Promotes the arts, music and spirit of Jam Band music.

Columbia360.com
www.columbia360.com
List your band, event, news etc.

COMOmusic
admin@comomusic.com
www.comomusic.com
Columbia's definitive guide to local music. Post your profile, CD and show reviews etc.

Heavy Frequency
13415 15th St., Grandview, MO 64030
PH: 816-995-0460
Heather Bashaw
heather.bashaw@heavyfrequency.com
www.heavyfrequency.com
Features promising Heavy Metal and Hardcore acts emerging from the depths of the Midwest underground.

Maneater
214 Brady Commons, Columbia, MO 65211
PH: 573-882-5500
www.themaneater.com
Student newspaper of the U. Missouri - Columbia.

Missouri Area Bluegrass Committee
www.bluegrassamerica.com
Promoting Bluegrass music across the US.

MO Blues Association
www.moblues.org
Artist photos, merchandise, CD reviews and more!

MOHeads.com
brooks@moheads.com
www.moheads.com
Post your news, listings, events etc.

MOrawk.com
318½ Park Central W. #204, Springfield, MO 65806
PH: 417-832-9795
aaron@morawk.com
www.morawk.com
Supporting independent music in Missouri.

Springfield Music Scene
3055 S. Lakeside Ave. Springfield, MO 65804
James Kavanaugh james@gufbal.com
springfieldmusicscene.com
Springfield's source for live music and music hosting.

Tri-State Bluegrass Association
k0bkl.org/tristate.htm
Publishes both a yearly festival guide and quarterly newsletter.

Unsigned Hype
PH: 206-984-4973
info@unsignedhype.org
unsignedhype.stlhiphop.com
Hip Hop artist promotion and services.

Voxmagazine
320 Lee Hills Hall, Columbia, MO 65211
PH: 573-882-6432 FX: 573-884-1870
vox@missouri.edu
www.voxmagazine.com
Columbia's weekly guide to area new, arts and entertainment.

Kansas City

Banzai Magazine
PO Box 7522, Overland Park, KS 66207
PH: 913-642-2262
Jim Kilroy banzaimagazine@hotmail.com
www.banzaimagazine.net
Kansas City's Rock n' Roll headquarters.

eKC online
Brandon Whitehead kinginyellow@juno.com
www.kcactive.com
Metro Kansas City news and entertainment.

Heart of America Bluegrass and Old-Time Music
www.banjonut.com/habot
Performances, jam sessions, newsletter, gigs etc.

hiphopkc.com
hiphopkc@gmail.com
www.hiphopkc.com
The virtual Hip Hop community of Kansas City.

Kansas City Blues Society
www.kcbluessociety.com
Keeping the Blues alive.

Kansas City Concert Page
concerts@hearditontheradio.com
www.hearditontheradio.com/concerts.aspx
Submit your Kansas City concert.

Kansas City Guitar Society
www.kansascityguitarsociety.org
Encourages artistry of the Classical guitar.

Kansas City Infozine
PO Box 22661, Kansas City, MO 64113
PH: 913-432-2661
www.infozine.com
Post your show information on the music page.

Kansas City Jazz Ambassadors
PO Box 36181, Kansas City, MO 64171
info@jazzkc.org
www.jazzkc.org
Publishes Jam Magazine. Submit CDs for review.

Kansas City Music
2510 Grand Ave. #603, Kansas City, MO 64108
PH: 816-520-8430
valentine@boxofchalk.com
www.kansascitymusic.com
Find musicians, their gigs, as well as posting your own.

KC Christian Music
17300 Gray Dr. Pleasant Hill, MO 64080
Connie Whitlock info@kcchristianmusic.com
www.kcchristianmusic.com
KCCM is about artists coming together to help each other grow in our ministries.

KCLocalBands
kclocalbands.com
News, interviews, forums, radio etc.

Pitch Weekly
1701 Main St., Kansas City, MO 64108
PH: 816-561-6061 FX: 816-756-0502
Jason Harper jason.harper@pitch.com
music.pitch.com
Kansas City free weekly alternative. Reviews new CD. Focuses on local music scene.

Songwriters Circle of Kansas City
www.songwriterscircle.org
Supporting local Indie songwriters.

St. Louis

Entertainment St. Louis
PO Box 1354, St. Louis, MO 63188
PH: 314-771-0200 FX: 314-771-0300
editor@slfp.com
www.slfp.com/Entertainmentstl.html
A St. Louis internet-only publication. Post your event.

gtp-inc.com
shaunbrooks@gtp-inc.com
www.gtp-inc.com
Dedicated to the St. Louis music scene.

playback
PO Box 9170, St. Louis, MO 63117
PH: 314-952-6404 FX: 877-204-2067
Laura Hamlett editor@playbackstl.com
www.playbackstl.com
St. Louis pop culture. Send your info and news.

Riverfront Times
6358 Delmar Blvd. #200, St. Louis, MO 63130-4719
PH: 314-754-5966 FX: 314-754-5955
Annie Zaleski Annie.Zaleski@riverfronttimes.com
www.rftstl.com
St. Louis free weekly A&E paper. Covers local music scene.

Spin City Record
748 N. Hwy. 67 #279, Florissant, MO 63031
PH: 314-839-4443
spincityrecordz@spincityrecordz.com
www.spincityrecordz.com
Record label formed to market Hip Hop artists from St. Louis.

St. Louis Donna Page
o2bkjn@swbell.net
home.swbell.net/o2bkjn
Featuring this weeks Cajun and Zydeco music and dance events.

St. Louis Gothic
stlouisgothic@yahoo.com
www.stlouisgothic.com
Your source for St. Louis Darkwave events and information!

St. Louis Magazine
1034 S. Brentwood Blvd. #1220, St. Louis, MO 63117
PH: 314-727-0900
www.stlmag.com
What's happening in the arts, music, politics, the media and more.

St. Louis Punk Page
PO Box 63207, St. Louis, MO 63163
jerome@stlpunk.com
www.stlpunk.com
Post your band info and events.

STLBlues
11469 Olive Blvd. #163, St. Louis, MO 63141
publisher@stlblues.net
www.stlblues.net
E-mail us to get your band listed here!

STLScene
PO Box 300575, St. Louis, MO 63130
info@stlscene.com
www.stlscene.net
Connecting the St. Louis local music scene.

STLtoday.com
www.stltoday.com/entertainment
Extensive local music coverage. News, reviews, spotlights etc. Submit your band's info.

The Uncle Rudy Show
Uncle Rudy Unclerudy@stlbackout.com
stlblackout.com/therudyshow/realrudy.html
I am looking for family friendly kinds of videos. The show runs on public access in St. Louis.

Montana

Exponent
www.asmsuexponent.com
Montana State U.'s student newspaper.

Lively Times
1152 Eagle Pass Trail, Charlo, MT 59824
PH: 406-644-2910
www.livelytimes.com
Montana's complete A&E calendar.

Missoula Folklore Society
www.montanafolk.org
Preserving contemporary and traditional music.

Missoula Independent
115 S. 4th St. W., Missoula, MT 59801
PH: 406-543-6609 FX: 406-543-4367
Skylar Browning arts@missoulanews.com
www.missoulanews.com
Free weekly alternative paper. CD and concert reviews, interviews and previews.

Montana Kaimin
Journalism 206, U. Montana, Missoula, MT 59801
PH: 406-243-6541 FX: 406-243-4303
www.kaimin.org
U. Montana's student paper.

Nebraska

Blues Society of Omaha
www.bluesgroup.com
Promoting Blues music in the greater Omaha-Lincoln area. News, reviews, newsletter, upcoming shows...

Great Plains Bluegrass & Old-Time Music Association
gpbotma.homestead.com
Promoting Bluegrass and Old-Time music in and around Omaha.

Homer's Music & Gifts
info@homersmusic.com
www.homersmusic.com
Several stores throughout Nebraska that promote local artists. Runs an online shop as well.

Lazy-i
743 J.E. George Blvd. Omaha, NE 68132
Tim McMahan timmymac29@aol.com
www.timmcmahan.com/lazyeye.htm
Interviews and band profiles, reviews and hype.

OMAHAMUSIC.com
4535 Leavenworth St., Omaha, NE 68106
PH: 402-553-5818 FX: 402-553-5819
oma@omahamusic.com
www.omahamusic.com
Official website of the Omaha Musician's Association. Band and event listings.

The Reader
5015 Underwood Ave. #101, Omaha, NE 68132
PH: 402-341-7323 FX: 402-341-6967
www.thereader.com
Alternative news zine. Submit your info/events.

SLAM Omaha
PO Box 391264, Omaha, NE 68139-1264
mick@slamomaha.com
www.slamomaha.com
Local music, featured bands, new releases etc.

Starcityscene.com
Tery info@astropopweb.com
www.starcityscene.com
Your guide to the Lincoln music scene.

Nevada

Las Vegas

Guitar Society of Las Vegas
www.gslv.org
Promoting the art of Acoustic guitar.

Jazzlasvegas.com
jazzlasvegas@mediaband.net
www.jazzlasvegas.com
Emphasis on Jazz in the Las Vegas area.

Las Vegas City Life
1385 Pama Ln. #111, Las Vegas, NV 89119
PH: 702-871-6780
Mike Prevat mprevatt@lvcitylife.com
www.lvcitylife.com
Extensive music section with profiles and reviews of musicians.

Las Vegas Jam Band Society
www.lvjbs.org
Creating a supportive music community in Southern Nevada for the musicians of the Jam Band genre.

Las Vegas Jazz Society
www.vegasjazz.org
Publishes and reviews concerts, club dates and special events.

Las Vegas Weekly
PO Box 230040, Las Vegas, NV 89123-0011
PH: 702-990-2411 FX: 702-990-2400
www.lasvegasweekly.com
Extensive coverage of both local and touring bands.

Neon
1111 W. Bonanza Rd. PO Box 70, Las Vegas, NV 89125
PH: 702-383-0211
www.reviewjournal.com/neon
Entertainment section of the Las Vegas Review-Journal.

onethirtyeight.org
PH: 702-759-4138
Gilbert Estrada ge138@onethirtyeight.org
onethirtyeight.org
Devoted to the REAL Las Vegas Punk Rock scene.

Reno

Reno Blues Society
www.renoblues.org
One stop source for the Blues in Reno.

Reno News & Review
708 N. Center St., Reno, NV 89501
PH: 775-324-4440 FX: 775-324-4572
Kat Kerlin katk@newsreview.com
www.newsreview.com
Reno's news and entertainment weekly.

New Hampshire

Blues Audience Newsletter
www.bluesaudience.com
Supports New England's fine Blues musicians and clubs.

Foster's Online *Showcase Magazine*
333 Central Ave. Dover, NH 03820
showcase@fosters.com
www.fosters.com
Dover weekly A&E magazine.

Monadnock Folklore Society
www.monadnockfolk.org
Offering support to local musicians' projects.

Peterborough Folk Music Society
www.acousticmusic.com/pfms/index.htm
Supporting musicians in the Monadnock region.

Spotlight Magazine
spotlight@seacoastonline.com
www.seacoastonline.com/calendar/nightlife.htm
Portsmouth's A&E magazine.

New Jersey

All-Access-Minus
87 Gless Ave. 2nd Fl. Belleville, NJ 07109
PH: 732-266-9828
M. Pimentel minus@minusp.com
www.minusp.com
Site for upcoming Hip Hop artists in the Tri-State area.

Aquarian Weekly
52 Sindle Ave. PO Box 1140, Little Falls, NJ 07424
PH: 973-812-6766 FX: 973-812-5420
www.theaquarian.com
Covers the area of New York, New Jersey and Connecticut.

Basically-HipHop.Com
PO Box 7093-WOB, West Orange, NJ 07052
Max-Jerome maxjerome@basically-hiphop.com
www.basically-hiphop.com
Represents Underground music, artists and MCs.

Blow Up Radio
PO Box 664, Old Bridge, NJ 08857
lazlo@blowupradio.com
BlowUpRadio.com
Posts news, reviews, downloads and concert listings.

Central NJ Song Circle
www.jerseysongs.com
A friendly, in-the-round get-together for testing out new songs.

Chorus and Verse
editor@chorusandverse.com
www.chorusandverse.com
Provides exposure and insight into the New Jersey scene.

Composers Guild of New Jersey
www.cgnj.org
Focuses on local contemporary music.

Create A Vibe
booking@createavibe.com
www.createavibe.com
Northern NJ Jam music promoters. Send information, MP3s, videos etc.

Crooked Beat
feedback@crooked-beat.com
www.crooked-beat.com
Band pages and gig listings for NY and NJ bands.

Eastside
Cherry Hill HS East, 1750 Kresson Rd.
Cherry Hill, NJ 08003
Sam Katz entertainmenteditors@yahoo.com
www.eastside-online.org
We're seeking Indie CDs to review and publicize in our paper.

Folk Project
www.folkproject.org
Sponsors Folk music and dance activities in the NJ area.

Le Grand Fromage
PO Box L, Atlantic City, NJ 08401
Michael Messina thebigcheeseac@msn.com
www.myspace.com/thebigcheeseac
Atlantic City venue trying to build the local scene. If you would like to book your band at the club, send us an e-mail.

Jersey Beat
418 Gregory Ave. Weehawken, NJ 07086
info@jerseybeat.com
www.jerseybeat.com
Will accept all CDs, but local releases get the highest priority.

Jersey Jam
www.@jerseyjam.com
www.jerseyjams.com
We'll visit your website, listen to your music, see what you're up to and decide if you should be the "SpotLight Artist of the Month"!

Jersey Shore Jazz and Blues Foundation
www.jsjbf.com
Formed to preserve, promote and perpetuate Jazz, Blues and other indigenous music forms in New Jersey.

JERSEYMUSIC.COM
jerseymusic.com
Connect to the local music scene.

JerseyShoreRocks
1137 Hope Rd. Asbury Park, NJ 07712-3162
PH: 732-542-2688
info@JerseyShoreRocks.com
www.jerseyshorerocks.com
Lists bands, bars, clubs and venues.

New Jersey Jazz Society
www.njjs.org
Monthly magazine with feature articles, reviews and event calendar.

Night & Day
PO Box 202, Spring Lake, NJ 07762
PH: 732-974-0047 FX: 732-974-0163
info@ndmag.com
www.ndmag.com
Covers movies, concerts, local bands and more.

NJ State of Music
128 Louisville Ave. Neptune, NJ 07753
PH: 908-433-8963
nj.stateofmusic.com
Will stream your demo, post shows, news and sell merchandise.

Princeton Folk Music Society
www.princetonol.com/groups/pfms
Encourages the growth of Folk music.

SouthJerseyClubs.com
300 N. Broadway, Gloucester City, NJ 08030
PH: 856-456-8080
info@southjerseyclubs.com
www.southjerseyclubs.com
Info on clubs, events and local bands.

Steppin' Out Magazine
381 Broadway, Westwood, NJ 07675
stepoutmag@aol.com
www.steppinoutmagazine.com
North Jersey/NYC music weekly.

TheNJScene.com
mike@thenjscene.com
thenjscene.com
Info site for fans and bands alike.

Tri-State Punk
Stumpy stumpy@tristatepunk.com
www.tristatepunk.com
Informing the tri-state area about all musical events.

Upstage Magazine
PO Box 140, Spring Lake, NJ 07762
PH: 732-280-3305
Gary Wien info@upstagemagazine.com
www.upstagemagazine.com
Supporting the original arts scene of Central NJ.

New Mexico

Albuquerque Live Music
info@albuquerquemusicscene.com
www.abqlivemusic.com
The hottest place on the web to find where your favorite band is playing.

Albuquerque Music Scene
500 Tyler NE., Albuquerque, NM 87113
PH: 505-341-3916
info@albuquerquemusicscene.com
www.albuquerquemusicscene.com
Band listings, websites, promotion and lots of music!

Alibi
2118 Central Ave. SE. #151, Albuquerque, NM 87106-4004
PH: 505-346-0660 x260 FX: 505-256-9651
Laura Marrich lauram@alibi.com
alibi.com
Albuquerque's weekly A&E paper. Extensive local music coverage.

Hyper Active Music Magazine
11024 Montgomery PMB 253, Albuquerque, NM 87111
PH: 505-293-0594
Erin Barnes erin@hyperactivemusicmag.com
hyperactivemusicmag.com
Catering to the hungry ears of Southwesterners. We support national bands that are from, or are touring through the Southwest.

Mitch's New Mexico Music Connection
Mitch Mitch@NMMusic.com
www.nmmusic.com
Band listings, events, classifieds etc.

New Mexico Folk Music & Dance Society
www.folkmads.org
Promoting and teaching traditional music and dance.

NewMexicoEvents.com
5104 Gaviota NW., Albuquerque, NM 87120
FX: 505-922-8775
Mark Hendricks mark@nmevents.com
www.newmexicoevents.com
Submit events and band info to get listed.

Santa Fe Reporter
132 E. Marcy St., Santa Fe, NM 87504
PH: 505-988-5541 x217 FX: 505-988-5348
Trisha Sauthoff culture@sfreporter.com
www.sfreporter.com
Weekly news and culture paper. Covers local music scene.

Southwest Traditional and Bluegrass Music Association
www.southwestpickers.org
Promoting Acoustic music through jams and workshops.

New York

A Place for Jazz
1221 Wendell Ave. Schenectady, NY 12308
jerrygordon@juno.com
timesunion.com/communities/jazz
Supports Jazz through concerts and workshops.

AlmostPunk NY
almostpunkny@hotmail.com
www.almostpunkny.com
Promoting local Punk Rock bands in the area.

Artvoice
810-812 Main St., Buffalo, NY 14202
PH: 716-881-6604 FX: 716-881-6682
editorial@artvoice.com
www.artvoice.com
Buffalo free weekly A&E paper. Reviews album releases and profiles new bands.

Bands of New York State
ableals@juno.com
www.yrbook.com/music
Supporting upstate NY groups and artists.

The Blues Society of Western New York
www.wnyblues.org
Promoting Blues events, record releases and club scenes.

Buffalo Music Online
www.wnymusic.com
Submit your band news, info and events.

Buffalobarfly.com
info@buffalobarfly.com
www.buffalobarfly.com
Promoting nightlife and entertainment in the Buffalo area.

BuffaloBluegrass.com
www.buffalobluegrass.com
Dedicated to promoting Bluegrass music in the Buffalo area.

Bushwick is Beautiful
bushwickisbeautifulblog@yahoo.com
bushwickisbeautiful.blogspot.com
Covering the Bushwick, NY music scene.

Capital Region Unofficial Musicians and Bands Site
Andy andy.gallo@att.net
www.crumbs.net
Online music resource for the Albany area.

Central New York Bluegrass Association
www.cnyba.com
News, calendar, classifieds, jams, festivals etc.

Central New York Friends of Folk
www.folkus.org/fof
Supporting Folk and Acoustic music.

Central New York Music
PO Box 1526, Auburn, NY 13021
PH: 315-255-4650
Steve Johnson cnymwebmaster03@cnymusic.com
www.cnymusic.com
Promoting and supporting live music in and around Central NY.

Folkus Project
712 1st St., Liverpool, NY 13088
PH: 315-457-2290
joe@folkus.org
www.folkus.org
Presents Folk and Acoustic music. Includes artist spotlight.

Freetime Magazine
850 University Ave. Rochester, NY 14607
PH: 585-473-2266
freetime@frontiernet.net
www.freetime.com
Rochester A&E mag. Covers local and national music.

Garagista Music
PO Box 238, Dobbs Ferry, NY 10522
www.garagistamusic.com
Our mission is to showcase Rivertown artists through online and local distribution.

Golden Link
www.goldenlink.org
Rochester publication containing everything about Folk music.

Hudson Valley Bluegrass Association
www.hvbluegrass.org
Contains Bluegrass news, show schedules, CD reviews, newsletter etc.

Hudson Valley Folk Guild
www.hvfg.org
Produces events and nurtures new Folk artists.

INSIDEOUT Magazine
PH: 845-255-6500 FX: 845-255-5533
Linda Boyd Kavars lk@insideouthv.com
www.insideouthv.com
The Hudson Valley magazine for the GLBT community.

Ithaca Times
PO Box 27, Ithaca, NY 14851
PH: 607-277-7000 FX: 607-277-1012
Jessica del Mundo jdelmundo@ithacatimes.com
www.ithacatimes.com
Free weekly alternative paper. Local concert reviews, accepts CDs for review.

Metroland
419 Madison Ave. Albany, NY 12210
PH: 518-463-2500 FX: 518-463-3712
Shawn Stone sstone@metroland.net
www.metroland.net
Albany's alternative newsweekly.

Mohawk Valley Bluegrass Association
www.mvbga.org
Building a base of members in an area that is rich in musicians.

Music 315
PO Box 4796, Rome, NY 13442
FX: 866-851-3851
Zoe zoe@music315.com
www.music315.com
Area code 314 bands contact us to get your site listed.

MyRochester.com
www.myrochester.com
Rochester's ultimate online music guide.

Nadeau Music
PO Box 6511, Watertown, NY 13601
PH: 315-785-8484
nadeaumusic@aol.com
www.nadeaumusic.net
Promoting local, independent and international Blues and Rock artists.

New York Newspapers
www.usnpl.com/nynews.html
Links to newspapers throughout the state.

New York Open Mikes
www.openmikes.org/calendar/NY

New York/Tri-State Area Bluegrass/ Old Time Music Scene
www.banjoben.com
Send details of your gig to get posted.

Northeast Blues Society
www.timesunion.com/communities/nebs
Exposing regional Blues talent to the largest possible audience.

Prog 90
3150 Weidrick Rd. Walworth, NY 14568
www.prog90.com
Gives Progressive Rock bands in NY support with gigs, contact, recording and promotional outlets.

The Pulse
www.thepulse.com
City Guide for Utica. Post your gigs.

PRIMO PR 716
59 Cimarand Dr. Buffalo, NY 14221
Mark Weber primopr716@adelphia.net
www.primopr.com
Specializes in getting the word out to Buffalo and beyond about upcoming concerts and events put on by Christian artists.

The Refrigerator
dearrefrigerator@therefrigerator.net
www.therefrigerator.net
Rochester A&E online zine.

Rkstar.com
1699 W. Glenville Rd. Amsterdam, NY 12010
Dan Goodspeed editor@rkstar.com
www.rkstar.com
Covering the capital district of NY and the national music scenes. All genres.

Rochester Groove
7758 Newco Dr. Hamlin, NY 14464
webmaster@rochestergroove.com
www.rochestergroove.com
An effort to promote local Groove/Jam Bands who are making the effort & playing around the region.

Rochester Music Coalition
PO Box 26378, Rochester, NY 14626
rochestermusiccoalition.org
Supports and promotes artists of all genres.

The Stencil
dude@thestencil.com
www.thestencil.com
MP3 blog covering Buffalo music and upcoming shows.

Syracuse New Times
1415 W. Genesee St., Syracuse, NY 13204-2156
PH: 315-422-7011 FX: 315-422-1721
newtimes.rway.com
Provides extensive A&E information for the Syracuse area.

Syracuse Ska scene
danny@wxxe.org
syracuseska.com
Shows, classifieds, MP3s and more!

Tribal Jams Magazine
stepheninfo@tribaljams.com
www.tribaljams.com
Information on festivals and venues for the "tie-die" Jam Band music in the NE U.S.

TriStateBands.com
PH: 917-232-4624
Kevin Rath kevin@tristatebands.com
www.TriStateBands.com
For NY, NJ and CT bands. List your band, bio and other info.

Underground Music Television
PO Box 2441, Liverpool, NY 13089
PH: 315-652-9383
Rich Stahle rich@umtv.info
umtv.info
A TV show that features local, unsigned and underground artist's music videos.

Upstate NY Reggae
Ras Adam Simeon rasadam@yahoo.com
go.to/NYreggae
Postings for concerts, radio shows, shops, venues, contacts etc.

Western New York / S. Ontario Raves
www.wnysor.net
Promoting all upcoming events.

Long Island

AOL CityGuide Long Island *Music*
home.digitalcity.com/longisland
Regional music column and forum.

AURAL FIX
PO Box 6054, North Babylon, NY 11703
PH: 631-943-3213
Mike Ferrari auralfix@optonline.net
www.auralfix.com
We are the ONLY publication that covers the Long Island music scene exclusively!!!

Club Long Island
info@clublongisland.com
www.clublongisland.com
Has a Local Band feature.

The Improper Magazine
59A W. Montauk Hwy.
Westhampton, NY 11977
PH: 631-288-9555
FX: 631-898-0214
Darren Paltrowitz
music@theimproper.com
www.theimproper.com
Free magazine that covers the arts, culture and lifestyles of Long Island and NYC with an irreverent, yet sophisticated edge.

Island Songwriter Showcase
www.islandsongwriters.org
Support original music through workshops and showcases.

Long Island Blues Society
www.liblues.org
Band listings, newsletter, events etc.

Long Island Classical Guitar Society
www.licgs.us
Hosts a quarterly mixer to showcase local talent.

Long Island Metal
metalfan@limetal.com
limetal.com
Our main goal is to re-unite the Metal culture.

Long Island Press
1103 Stewart Ave. Garden City, NY 11530
PH: 516-629-4327 FX: 516-992-1801
www.longislandpress.com
Bi-weekly A&E paper. Reviews concerts, profiles and interviews bands.

Long Island Punx
admin@lipunx.com
www.lipunx.com
Covering the Long Island scene. News, reviews, gig calendar.

LongIsland.com *Nightlife*
nightlife.longisland.com
Long Island band pages, calendar, interviews, bulletin boards and more.

longislandmusicscene
groups.yahoo.com/group/longislandmusicscene
Discussing the LI original music scene.

longislandmusicscene.com
PO Box 417, E. Rockaway, NY 11518-0417
PH: 516-887-0923 FX: 516-887-0923
webguy@longislandmusicscene.com
www.longislandmusicscene.com
Provides free exposure and resources for musicians.

New York City

5th Floor Artist Management
Jen Carlson info@5thFloor.org
5thFloor.org
Are you a band in need of management, booking and PR?

Acoustic Live!
51 MacDougal St. PO Box #254, New York, NY 10012
riccco@earthlink.net
www.acousticlive.com
Monthly newsletter showcasing all Acoustic performances in NY.

Antifolk.net
PO Box 20469, Tompkins Sq. Stn. New York, NY 10009
info@antifolk.net
www.antifolk.net
The home for the NYC Antifolk scene.

AOL CityGuide New York *Music*
home.digitalcity.com/newyork
Regional music column and forum.

Associated Musicians of Greater New York
www.local802afm.org
Musicians union fighting for your well-being.

BadmintonStamps
SkinnySlim skinnyslim@badmintonstamps.com
www.badmintonstamps.com
Covering the NYC music scene.

Big Apple Jazz
Gordon Polatnick gordon@bigapplejazz.com
www.bigapplejazz.com
Reinvigorating the Jazz scene in NYC, by introducing fans to the more authentic and hidden Jazz events that occur.

Black Rock Coalition
PO Box 1054, Cooper Stn. New York, NY 10276
PH: 212-713-5097
Earl Douglas edouglas@blackrockcoalition.org
www.blackrockcoalition.org
Represents a united front musically and politically progressive Black artists and supporters.

Brooklyn Bodega
info@brooklynbodega.com
www.brooklynbodega.com
Covering the Hip Hop scene. The Brooklyn Bodega crew will do their best to serve it up to you daily.

Brooklyn Vegan
brooklynvegan@hotmail.com
www.brooklynvegan.com
Music, photos & news from a vegan in Brooklyn.

Cari Cole Voice Studios
401 E. 34th St. #N91K, New York, NY 10016-4951
PH: 212-532-0828
Cari Cole cariacole@aol.com
www.vocalmag.com
Specializes in private vocal technique, vocal problems, keeping singers healthy on tour and contemporary styling. Our studio has one of the very finest methodologies available for building, toning, strengthening and repairing voices. Get your voice in the best shape of your career!

CelticTV.com
7 Sterling Pl. Edgewater, NJ 07020
PH: 201-491-4055 FX: 419-781-0744
William A. Phillips celtictv@yahoo.com
www.celictv.com
All things Celtic Rock and Irish music in NYC.

Chicks With Guitars
PH: 917-969-6409
Jeanette Palmer info@chickswithguitars.com
chickswithguitars.com
Provides publishing and performing opportunities for emerging and established musicians.

Coolfer
coolfer@coolfer.com
www.coolfer.com
Music and the industry in NYC.

Crackers United
crackersunited@gmail.com
crackersunited.com
Covers NYC music scene. We welcome records and promotional materials for consideration.

Crashin' In
204 Powers St. #1, Brooklyn, NY 11211
Lio dj@crashinin.com
www.crashinin.com
For reviews, interviews, online listening parties and all other inquiries, send us an e-mail.

Daily Refill
Jen C. dailyrefill@gmail.com
dailyrefill.blogs.com/daily
I also write about music for The Villager, run 5th Floor Artist Management and write and edit the arts + events section of gothamist.com.

The Deli
info@thedelimagazine.com
www.thedelimagazine.com
Provides news, reviews and in-depth interviews with local bands, analyses of where the scene is headed.

Elizabeth Records
PO Box 22049, Brooklyn, NY 11202
PH: 212-330-7082
info@elizabethrecords.com
www.elizabethrecords.com
Promotes Indie Folk artists.

Fearless Music TV Show
mail@fearlessmusic.tv
www.fearlessmusic.tv
Weekly show featuring Indie bands.

Flavorpill NYC
594 Broadway #1212, New York, NY 10012
PH: 212-253-9309 FX: 212-313-9833
nyc_events@flavorpill.net
flavorpill.net
A publishing company with a weekly e-mail events list.

Free Williamsburg
311 Graham Ave. Brooklyn, NY 11211
www.freewilliamsburg.com
Providing you with cutting edge music.

GigApple.com
www.gigapple.com
The place to find out where to go and see and listen to live independent music in NYC.

Gothamist
jencarlson@gothamist.com
www.gothamist.com
A website about NYC and everything that happens in it.

GothamJazz
www.gothamjazz.com
Shedding light on lesser known, Indie performers.

Greenwich Village Gazette
PO Box 1023 Island Hts., NJ 08732
www.nycny.com
Complete listing of NYC Jazz, Folk and Rock events.

HelloBrooklyn.com
PH: 917-754-3537
info@hellobrooklyn.com
www.hellobrooklyn.com
Send your calendar listings by e-mail.

HUGE!
hugemassif@gmail.com
www.hugemassif.com
Focuses on the NYC rave scene.

i rock i roll
irockiroll@gmail.com
irockiroll.blogspot.com
NYC blog about music, gigs and other assorted stuff.

Indie Sounds NY
indiesoundsny.com
We cover the people that make up one of the most creative and vibrant artistic communities on the planet.

JACKMUSIC
332 Bleecker St. G7, New York, NY 10014
PH: 212-279-3941
info@jack-music.com
www.jack-music.com
We represent the music of NYC's best small label and unsigned talent.

Jazz Clubs in Brooklyn and Queens
www.ny.com/clubs/jazz/brooklyn&queens.html

Jazz Clubs in Manhattan
www.ny.com/clubs/jazz

The L Magazine
20 Jay St. #207, Brooklyn, NY 11201
PH: 718-596-3462
editor@thelmagazine.com
thelmagazine.com
A distillation of the best music and special events the city has to offer.

Mass Appeal
976 Grand St., Brooklyn, NY 11211
PH: 718-858-0979 FX: 347-365-2159
Gavin Stevens gavin@massappealmag.com
www.massappealmag.com
Focuses on urban culture, music, art and fashion.

melodynelson.com
Audrey audrey@melodynelson.com
www.melodynelson.com
Information about the NYC music scene.

Metal Injection
hatemail@metalinjection.net
www.metalinjection.net
TV show representing Metal and Hardcore in its truest nature.

The Modern Age
Miss Modernage edit@themodernage.org
www.themodernage.org
A cheat sheet for those who can only pretend they're cool enough to live in Williamsburg, Brooklyn.

More in the Monitor
Amy sonikgurl@hotmail.com
moreinthemonitor.blogspot.com
This is what happened at various shows around NYC. We swear.

Music Snobbery
musicsnobbery@comcast.net
www.musicsnobbery.com
I go to gigs, interview bands and musicians. I like Brit Pop, but will check out most styles of music.

Neatness.com
www.neatness.com
Music resource for the NYC area. Photos, calendar and more!

New York Blues and Jazz Society
www.nybluesandjazz.org
Blues news, reviews, listings etc.

New York Blade
333 7th Ave. 14th Fl. New York, NY 10001
PH: 212-268-2701 FX: 212-268-2069
www.nyblade.com
A weekly newspaper covering the New York Gay communities.

New York City Area Bluegrass Music Scene
banjoben.com
A calendar of Bluegrass events. Submit your info.

New York City Classical Guitar Society
www.nyccgs.com
Providing a dynamic community for Classical guitarists in New York City.

New York Cool
Wendy R. Williams wendy@newyorkcool.com
www.newyorkcool.com
Entertainment site that gives great coverage of local musicians and events.

New York Metro
444 Madison Ave. 4th Fl. New York, NY 10022
www.newyorkmetro.com/arts/theweek/music
A&E magazine. Covers local music.

New York Metropolitan Country Music Assc.
www.nymcma.org
We produce a series of free concerts in public parks during the summer. These concerts feature at least one local band.

New York Music Guide
newyork.citysearch.com
Extensive coverage of the local music scene. Post your shows and events.

New York Musician
PH: 917-576-3745
William J. Taylor listing@newyorkmusician.com
www.newyorkmusician.com
Free guide to NYC music industry.

New York Pinewoods Folk Music Club
www.folkmusicny.org
Concerts and events plus a monthly newsletter.

New York Press
333 7th Ave. 14th Fl. New York, NY 10001
PH: 212-244-2282 FX: 212-244-9864
listings@nypress.com
www.nypress.com
Free weekly A&E paper. Reviews CDs and concerts by Indie artists.

New York Times *Music Section*
directory@nytimes.com
www.nytimes.com/pages/arts/music
Send a blank e-mail for an automated response including mailing address and departmental e-mail addresses.

New York Underbelly
RSVP@NewYorkUnderbelly.com
www.newyorkunderbelly.com
DJ events and live music shows around the city.

NewYorkCity.com
235 Pinelawn Rd. Melville, NY 11747-4250
PH: 516-843-2000
ndstaff@newsday.com
www.nyc.com
Guide to New York music and clubs.

Notorious Marketing & Promotion
31-15 30th St. #3R, Astoria, NY 11106
PH: 718-545-9816
Notorious L.I.Z. notorious@notoriousradio.com
www.notoriousradio.com
Promotes Alternative/Rock Indie bands and artists.

NY JAZZ REPORT
WillWolf@NYJazzReport.com
www.nyjazzreport.com
News and links about jazz in NYC. Musicians, clubs, concerts, poetry, music, interviews etc.

NY Rock
PO Box 563, Gracie Stn. New York, NY 10028
PH: 212-426-4657
www.nyrock.com
Reviews full length CDs.

NY Waste
PO Box 20005, W. Village Stn. New York, NY 10014
FX: 212-243-7252
info@newyorkwaste.com
www.newyorkwaste.com
New York's Punk Rock newspaper. News, reviews and attitude.

NYC Gothic Events
nygothic@razorwire.com
anon.razorwire.com/events
Add your news or upcoming events.

NYC Music Places
61 W. 23rd St. 4th Fl. New York, NY 10010-4205
PH: 212-886-2503 FX: 212-737-1496
info@nycmusicplaces.org
www.nycmusicplaces.org
Find rehearsal and performance spaces in NYC.

NYC Reggae
Ras Adam rasadam@yahoo.com
web.syr.edu/~affellem/nycshows.html
Covering concerts, shows and dances in the NYC area.

Oh My Rockness
PO Box 720337, Jackson Heights, NY 11372
shows@ohmyrockness.com
ohmyrockness.com
Your one-stop shop for Indie Rock show listings in NYC. If you think people should know more about you, e-mail us and tell us.

One Louder
onelouder@gmail.com
www.oneloudernyc.com
Does interviews and reviews of local shows.

Other Music NYC
15 E. 4th St., New York, NY 10003
PH: 212-477-8150
www.othermusic.com
An unparalleled selection of Underground and Experimental music. We are all about supporting independent music, so we do consign the music of NYC artists.

PAPERMAG
365 Broadway, New York, NY 10013
PH: 212-226-4405 FX: 212-226-0062
edit@papermag.com
www.papermag.com
Guide to urban culture, events, people, news and entertainment.

Popular Music Venues in NYC
www.ny.com/clubs/pop
The city's Rock clubs have a history of discovering and showcasing new acts.

Product Shop NYC
www.productshopnyc.com
Blog covering NYC entertainment. Local shows, articles etc.

punkcast.com Podcast
POB 2016 Madison Sq. Stn. New York, NY 10159-2016
PH: 212-608-1334
joly@dti.net
punkcast.com
Videos of the NYC underground music scene.

Real Magic TV
PO Box 264, Bedford Hills, NY 10507-0264
PH: 917-495-0741
Music@RealMagicNY.com
www.realmagictv.com
Send your band's material in for a chance to get booked.

Roulette Television
228 W. Broadway, New York, NY 10013
PH: 212-219-8242 FX: 212-219-8773
infoo@roulette.org
www.roulette.org
Presents New Jazz, World Music, Experimental Rock, Improvisation, Traditional and Hybrid ensembles from NYC and around the world.

SHOWLIST.org
info@showlist.org
www.showlist.org
NYC/New Jersey shows e-mailed weekly to industry people. Visit our site to add your show dates!

The Simple Mission
Elliot Aronow elliot@thesimplemission.com
www.thesimplemission.com
Blog about the NYC music scene.

So More Scene
Miss Modernage edit@somorescene.com
www.somorescene.com
It's so more scene than you'll ever be.

Songwriter's Beat
PO Box 20086, W. Village Stn. New York, NY 10014
songwritersbeat.com
Create an environment where musicians can share their experiences.

SoundArt
PO Box 70, Stottville, NY 12172
PH: 518-828-0131
soundarts@soundart.org
www.soundart.org
New York City's source for information on concerts of contemporary music.

StereoactiveNYC
info@thedelimagazine.com
stereoactivenyc.com
We focus on bands we have seen live. Please DO NOT SEND US MASS E-MAILS — contact us directly about sending CDs, or attending shows.

stereogum
info@stereogum.com
www.stereogum.com
MP3 blog with local band news, tracks etc.

subinev blog
bryan@subinev.com
www.subinev.com
Bands! Get in touch! If I like what I hear and plan on checking you out I'll add your shows here.

Sucka Pants
sucka@suckapants.com
suckapants.com
MP3 blog from Brooklyn. If you would like to send music, contact me via e-mail.

The Swift Chancellor Report
Wes Jack info@brooklynbodega.com
swiftchancellor.blogspot.com
Observations, reviews and ramblings about Hip Hop culture.

This Twilight Garden
chris@thechristophereffect.com
thistwilightgarden.blogspot.com
Musical adventures in New York City.

Time Out New York
475 10th Ave. 12th Fl. New York, NY 10018
PH: 646-432-3000 FX: 646-432-3010
music@timeoutny.com
www.timeoutny.com
The obsessive guide to impulsive entertainment.

Tiswas Records
332 Bleecker St. #G11, New York, NY 10014
tiswasrecords@aol.com
www.tiswasnyc.com
Exposing exciting NYC music to a larger audience and growing their fan base.

UMO Music
www.umo.com
Provides online artist promotional accounts, live music events and compilation CDs.

Underrated Magazine
Rachael Darmanin
rdarmanin@underratedmagazine.com
www.underratedmagazine.com
New York City's independent music magazine!

Urban Folk
www.myspace.com/urbanfolkzine
Stories of the bohemians, bums and poet troubadours out there trying to explain the universe or at least entertain it for awhile.

VICIOUS NYC
booking@melodynelson.com
jenyk.com/VICIOUS.htm
Showcasing new local bands with the most potential and finding the city's best kept musical secrets.

Video City TV
PO Box 1607, New York, NY 10013
Attn: A&R Department
212-613-0072
videocitytv@aol.com
www.videocity.tv
Cable show that spotlights Indie music.

The Village Broadsheet
302 E. 3rd St. #5A, New York, NY 10009
www.villagebroadsheet.com
CD and show reviews.

Village Indian
417 E. 6th St. #20, New York, NY 10009
Amrit villageindian@gmail.com
www.villageindian.com
Musings on music, art and life in the East Village. Send in your music!

Village Voice
36 Cooper Sq. New York, NY 10003
PH: 212-475-3333
www.villagevoice.com
Alternative weekly newspaper. Extensive A&E section.

Vocal Area Network
890 West End Ave. #11B, New York,
NY 10025-3521
www.van.org
Dedicated to the advancement of vocal ensemble music in the New York City area.

Volunteer Lawyers for the Arts
1 E. 53rd St. 6th Fl. New York, NY 10022-4201
PH: 212-319-2787 FX: 212-752-6575
www.vlany.org
Pro bono legal services for artists.

Webtunes
39-37 50th St., Woodside, NY 11377
FX: 718-426-6346
John Elder tunemaster@webtunes.com
www.webtunes.com
New York City's premier music guide.

ZydecoRoad.com
2450 Marshall Ave. North Bellmore, NY 11710
PH: 516-643-7231
K-Paule Pachter zydecoroad@yahoo.com
www.zydecoroad.com
Covering Zydeco and Cajun music in NYC and Long Island.

North Carolina

A. Warner Entertainment
3615-B St Johns Ct. Wilmington, NC 28403
Annette Warner awarnerentertainment@ec.rr.com
www.awarnerentertainment.com
Catering to a variety of up and coming local and regional Singer/Songwriters, bands and entertainers.

Amps 11
David Kiser david@ampseleven.com
www.ampseleven.com
Taking Charlotte's music scene to the next level!

Asheville Citizen Times
PO Box 2090, Asheville, NC 28802
PH: 828-232-5855
tkiss@citizen-times.com
www.citizen-times.com
Reviews CDs and interviews bands if playing in the area.

Banjo in the Hollow
banjointhehollow.org
Preserving and promoting Bluegrass and Old-Time music.

Blues Society of the Lower Cape Fear
www.capefearblues.org
Welcomes listeners, musicians and Blues enthusiasts.

Central Carolina Songwriters Association
www.ccsa-raleigh.com
Promotes songwriting and music in NC.

Charlotte Blues Society
www.charlottebluessociety.org
Presents Blues concerts, forums, workshops and educational programs.

Charlotte Chapter NSAI
www.secondwindmusic.com/NSAICLT
Supporting songwriters through workshops, festivals and concerts.

Charlotte Folk Society
www.folksociety.org
Promoting contemporary Folk music, dance and crafts.

Charlotte Live Music.com
PO Box 34726, Charlotte, NC 28234-4726
PH: 704-248-8104
www.charlottelivemusic.com
Guide for live music, bands, venues and the local music scene.

Creative Loafing Charlotte
820 Hamilton St. #C-2, Charlotte, NC 28206
PH: 704-522-8334 FX: 704-522-8088
charlotte.creativeloafing.com
Free weekly alternative paper. Covers local and national music.

Dalloway Records
PO Box 4751, Greensboro, NC 27404 Attn: A & R
Christina Lewis clewis@dallowayrecords.com
www.dallowayrecords.com
Headed by a lawyer and a shrink - we've found that both professions are much needed in the industry.

East Carolinian
2nd Fl. Old Cafeteria Complex, Greenville,
NC 27858
PH: 252-328-6366 FX: 252-328-6558
www.theeastcarolinian.com
East Carolina U's student paper.

Encore
PO Box 12430, Wilmington, NC 28405
PH: 910-791-0688 FX: 910-791-9177
www.encorepub.com
Covers local music with interviews, previews and reviews.

Fiddle & Bow Society
www.fiddleandbow.org
Preserving Folk music, dance and related arts.

goTriad.com
www.gotriad.com
Covering A&E in Greensboro.

Guitartown
webmaster@guitartown.org
www.guitartown.org
Features news of the thriving NC Roots music scene.

Independent Weekly
PO Box 2690, Durham, NC 27715
PH: 919-286-1972 FX: 919-286-4274
indyweek.com
Interviews bands, previews and reviews CDs and concerts.

Lumber River Regional Bluegrass Association
www.lrrba.com
Keeping alive the Bluegrass traditions of our country.

Mountain Xpress
PO Box 144, Asheville, NC 28802
PH: 828-251-1333 FX: 828-251-1311
mountainx.com/ae/music.php
Has music section covering the Asheville area music scene.

musicomet
PO Box 31725, Charlotte, NC 28231
PH: 704-527-7570
Samir Shukla cometriderx@yahoo.com
www.musicomet.com
I am the current listing editor and music writer for Creative Loafing (Charlotte).

NC Goth DOT COM
steve@ncgoth.com
www.ncgoth.com
All the info on the NC Goth scene.

NCMusic.com
PO Box 17383, Winston-Salem, NC 27116-7383
noel@ncmusic.com
www.ncmusic.com
Opinions and reviews about music in NC.

NCScene.com
63 John Lewis Rd. Walstonburg, NC 27888
webmaster@ncscene.com
www.ncscene.com
Rock, Metal Hardcore and more!

North Carolina Songwriters Co-op
www.ncsongwriters.org
Promoting songwriters in NC.

Nothing but Drums
John Ehlers john@nothingbutdrums.net
www.nothingbutdrums.net
A Charlotte TV show featuring local area drummers.

Piedmont Blues Preservation Society
www.piedmontblues.org
Preserving the fine art of American Blues.

Queen City Independent
2600 Duncan Ave. Charlotte, NC 28205
Brian McKinney brian@queencityindie.com
www.queencityindie.com
We book bands that play original music in the Charlotte area.

Raleigh Underground
dj-joey@raleighunderground.com
www.raleighunderground.com
Lists info on Raleigh's Underground music scene.

Raleighmusic.com
joanna@raleighmusic.com
www.raleighmusic.com
Marketing local artists to a regional audience.

SleeplessInCharlotte.com
www.sleeplessincharlotte.com
Information on artists, events, venues etc. in Charlotte. Send us your photos, flyers, events listing.

SongwritersSoapbox.com
3615-B St Johns Ct. Wilmington, NC 28403
PH: 910-793-1507
Annette Warner awarnerentertainment@ec.rr.com
www.SongwritersSoapbox.com
Creating the perfect ambiance for listening and enjoying a songwriter in their rawest form.

Up & Coming Magazine
PH: 910-484-6200
www.upandcomingmag.com
Weekly A&E paper. Artist interviews, CD and concert reviews.

Village Idiot Magazine
205 E. 5th St., Greenville, NC 27858
PH: 252-341-6457 FX: 252-758-4439
Eric Walls expressions.g-vegas@cox.net
the-village-idiot.com
All bands/labels looking for exposure in NC, whether your from here or are just passing through you need to get up with us.

Wilkes Acoustic/Folk Society
www.wilkesfolks.com
Educating the public in music appreciation.

WilmingtonNCMusic.com
3615-B St Johns Ct. Wilmington, NC 28403
Annette Warner awarnerentertainment@ec.rr.com
wilmingtonncmusic.com
We provide venue and musician pages, free musician and venue listings, CD reviews, press releases and articles.

ZSpotlight
PH: 919-215-5000
www.zspotlight.com
Information on who's playing where in the Triangle.

North Dakota

BUSTHQ.com
busthq.fargousa.com
Supporting independent music in the Northern Plains!

North Dakota State U. Spectrum
www.ndsuspectrum.com
Campus publication. Covers local music.

Saboingaden.com
www.saboingaden.com
Fargo Electronica community & center of the Electronica earth. Dedicated to news and events in the ND and MN region.

Ohio

Athens Musician's Network
amn@frognet.net
www.athensmusician.net
Covers the local music scene around Athens.

BGMusicians.com
www.bgmusicians.com
Covering the Bowling Green music scene.

Blues, Jazz & Folk Music Society
www.bjfm.org
Promoting Blues, Jazz & Folk music in the Mid-Ohio Valley.

Central Ohio Bluegrass Association
www.centralohiobluegrass.com
Preserving Bluegrass in the central Ohio area.

CowTownMusic.com
PO Box 144, Orient, OH 43146
sixis@columbus.rr.com
www.cowtownmusic.com
Source for live entertainment in central Ohio.

Highlands of Ohio Folk & Celtic Music Society
www.highlandsofohio.com
Keeps the local community informed of Celtic concerts and other events.

M Class Recordings
4302 Colby Ave. Columbus, OH 43227
PH: 614-256-3051
Duane Anderson m_classrecordingsllc@yahoo.com
www.mclassrecordings.com
Our mission is to discover, develop, create and distribute quality music from the Columbus area.

Midwest Mixtapes
mixtapes@midwestmixtapes.com
midwestmixtapes.com
Bringing you the hottest mixtapes from the Midwest.

Ohio Bands Online
PH: 330-206-0564
ohiobandsonline@yahoo.com
www.ohiobandsonline.com
A listing of Ohio bands by city and genre.

Ohio Hystairical Musick Society
ohms.nu
We list the shows and venues where bands can get gigs. Send in your band and gig info.

Ohio Online Magazine
Peanuts hostofthenorthcoast@yahoo.com
www.ohioonline.com
Supporting the local music scene.

OhioRap.com
PH: 330-338-4348
T cr4zyt@ohiorap.com
www.ohiorap.com
A free website designed for artists and fans. Our goal is to help put Ohio on the map.

T-TownMusic.com
Scott Stampflmeier scott-stamp@t-townmusic.com
www.t-townmusic.com
Covering NW Ohio's Hip Hop scene.

Utter Trash
PO Box 771021, Lakewood, OH 44107
trashmag@uttertrash.net
www.uttertrash.net
Covering the best underground entertainment in Northeast Ohio and beyond.

Cincinnati

Cincinnati CityBeat
811 Race St. 5th Fl. Cincinnati, OH 45202
PH: 513-665-4700 FX: 513-665-4368
Brian Baker letters@citybeat.com
www.citybeat.com
Covers news, A&E, reviews CDs and posts gigs.

Cincinnati Music Online
PO Box 54096, Cincinnati, OH 45254
cincymusic.com
Free promotion of Cincinnati artists and music.

Cincinnati Shows
PO Box 42815, Cincinnati, OH 45242-0815
cincyshows@niceguyrecords.com
www.cincinnatishows.com
Show listings, downloads, links, pictures etc. of Cincinnati bands.

Cincinnatibands.com
cincinnatibands.com
Covering everything about local bands.

Greater Cincinnati Blues Society
www.cincyblues.org
Advancing the culture and tradition of Blues music.

Greater Cincinnati Guitar Society
www.cincinnatiguitarsociety.org
Get in touch with the local Acoustic scene.

LocalMetal.com
localmetal@gmail.com
www.localmetal.com
Supporting the Cinci Metal scene.

Cleveland

ClePunk
clepunk@gmail.com
www.clepunk.com
All the info on the local Punk scene.

Cleveland Composers Guild
my.en.com/~jaquick/ccg.html
Promoting the music of composers living in Northeast Ohio.

Cleveland Free Times
800 W. St. Clair Ave. 2nd Fl. Cleveland, OH 44113-1266
PH: 216-479-2033
Jeff Niesel jniesel@freetimes.com
www.freetimes.com
Covers local music scene. CD and concert previews and reviews.

Cleveland Metal Connection
jjodon@clevmetalconn.org
www.clevmetalconn.org
Connect to the Metal scene. Features a band of the month.

Cleveland Scene
PO Box 15029, Cleveland, OH 44115-0029
PH: 216-241-7550 FX: 216-802-7212
Chris Parker chris.parker@clevescene.com
www.clevescene.com
Alternative news weekly.

Cleveland.com
www.cleveland.com/music
Create a free website for your band.

Domain Cleveland
6571 Liberty Bell Dr. #216, Brookpark, OH 44142
www.domaincleveland.com
Your source for Indie news, reviews, interviews, photos and more!

The North Coast STARS
c/o MAPATV, PO Box 111285, Cleveland,
OH 44111
visitor@ncstars.tv
www.ncstars.tv
Video magazine that showcases original material submitted by artists.

Starvation Army Zine
11124 Clifton Blvd. #9, Cleveland, OH 44102
starvationarmyzine@yahoo.com
groups.myspace.com/starvationarmyzine
All things in the DIY world!!! Mostly Cleveland shite.

Columbus

Columbus Alive
62 E. Broad St., Columbus, OH 43215
PH: 614-221-2449 FX: 614-221-2456
www.columbusalive.com
Covers local Indie music with concert previews and reviews.

Columbus Blues Alliance
www.colsbluesalliance.org
Encourages ties between traditional and electric Blues.

ColumbusArts.com
www.columbusarts.com
Resource for Central Ohio culture and arts.

columbusound.com
www.columbusound.com
Central Ohio's #1 music directory!

Cringe
PO Box 10276, Columbus, OH 43201
PH: 614-421-7589
webmaster@cringe.com
www.cringe.com
Accepts nearly all submissions from the Columbus area.

musicohio
5579 Valencia Park Blvd. Hilliard, OH 43026
PH: 614-771-4243
Jason Perlman jason@musicohio.com
www.musicohio.com
Un-known artists get recognition. Covers mostly the Columbus area.

The Other Paper
5255 Sinclair Rd. Columbus, OH 43229
PH: 614-847-3800 FX: 614-848-3838
www.theotherpaper.com
Covers Indie music with band interviews, CD and concert previews and reviews.

U Weekly
46-A E. 8th Ave. Columbus, OH 43201-2550
PH: 614-291-0732 FX: 614-291-0732
Brian O'Neill d6ua5pp02@sneakemail.com
www.uweekly.com
If you are a local band or in a band coming through Columbus, get in touch.

Dayton

Dayton Band Resource Page
1408 Poplar Dr. Fairborn, OH 45324
PH: 937-878-4937
Tony Hurley info@DaytonBands.com
www.daytonbands.com
Helping Indie local musicians become successful.

H.M.D. Music Resource Guide
251 W. Central Ave. #292, Springboro,
OH 45066-1103
PH: 937-746-4426
Sonny Thomas contact@thehmd.com
www.thehmd.com
Gem City resource where "unsigned" means you're a star here!

NiteOnTheTown.com
3430 S. Dixie Dr. #200, Dayton, OH 45439
PH: 937-297-3052 FX: 937-293-4523
www.niteonthetown.com
Guide to local nightlife. Includes local music listings.

WXEG's Local Band Page
101 Pine St., Dayton, OH 45402
PH: 937-224-1137 FX: 937-224-9965
Jericho jericho@wxeg.com
www.wxeg.com/pages/local_bands.html
Always keeping you up to date on the music that you love.

Toledo

MWO Entertainment
www.myspace.com/mwotoledo
Our evolution has laid the ground work for our own concert promotion and design services.

Toledo Jazz Society
www.toledojazzsociety.org
Increasing the appreciation of Jazz.

The Toledo Wire
thetoledowire.com
Created to connect Toledo's underground music and art communities, promote awareness, growth and interest.

T-townmusic.com
Scott scott-stamp@t-townmusic.com
www.t-townmusic.com
Your source for Northwest Ohio and Southeast Michigan's local music scene.

Oklahoma

Bartlesville Music Scene
Bridgetkt Bridgetkt@cableone.net
bartlesvillemusic.blogspot.com
Promotes local bands in and around Bartlesville. Interviews, photos, blog, calendar etc. for all in the community to use.

BestofTulsa.com *Music*
4821 S. Sheridan #228, Tulsa, OK 74145
PH: 918-632-0000
info@bestoftulsa.com
bestoftulsa.com/html/music.shtml
Listings, spotlights, events etc.

Green Country Bluegrass Association
www.gcba.homestead.com
Promoting Bluegrass in Northeast OK.

MidwestVenues.com
Pat O'Reilly Midwestvenues@aol.com
www.midwestvenues.com
Providing the music community with info on thousands of venues in the greater Midwest region.

NormanMusicScene.com
511 Highland Pkwy. Norman, OK 73069
pchelp@normanmusicscene.com
www.normanmusicscene.com
Linking local musical artists, events & venues.

NormanNow.com
www.normannow.com
Post your band info and upcoming shows.

OKC Live
PH: 405-410-7360
info@okclive.com
www.okclive.com
Oklahoma City's online entertainment source.

Oklahoma Blues Society
www.okblues.org
CD reviews, news, gig listings etc.

Oklahoma Bluegrass Events
myweb.cableone.net/cdonaghe/bgrassfest.htm
Add information about your upcoming shows.

Oklahoma City Traditional Music Association
www.octma.org
Learning, teaching and playing Acoustic Folk music.

Oklahoma Country Music Association
www.oklahomacma.com
Created to promote and advance Country & Western music and its artists in Oklahoma.

Oklahoma Music Guide
author@oklahomamusicguide.com
www.oklahomamusicguide.com
Up to date news about the local music scene.

OklahomaPunkscene.com
Barb spano25@hotmail.com
www.oklahomapunkscene.com
Articles, interviews, photos, reviews and more!

OklahomaRock.com
Ryan LaCroix ryan@oklahomarock.com
www.oklahomarock.com
Helping others to realize what great talents are out there in Oklahoma. News, reviews etc.

Payne County Line Promotions
3333 E. 68th St., Stillwater, OK 74074
PH: 405-612-5477
Stan Moffat stan@paynecountyline.com
www.paynecountyline.com
Working hard to support Oklahoma live music!

Southwest Songwriters Association
www.swsongwriters.com
Place for musicians looking for bands, or bands looking for musicians.

Stillwater Scene
916 N. Duck, Stillwater, OK 74075
PH: 405-762-9733
www.stillwaterscene.com
Magazine with local music news, reviews, interviews etc.

Tulsa Music Pulse
www.tulsamusicpulse.com
Tulsa Bands heard here. Cuz every band was local at some point. Protect endangered music.

Tulsa Rock 'n' Roll
8530 E. 131st St. S., Bixby, OK 74008
Emmett Lollis Jr. emmett@tulsarocknroll.com
www.tulsarocknroll.com
If you would like to be considered for a CD review or interview please mail us your press kit .

TulsaBands.com
tulsabands.com
Oklahoma's #1 website for Tulsa Bands and Music!!!

tulsajazz.com
www.tulsajazz.com
Providing an online portal to the activities of the Tulsa Jazz community.

TulsaMusicScene.com
www.tulsamusicscene.com
Showing the world the sea of musical talent that Tulsa has to offer.

Urban Tulsa Weekly
710 S. Kenosha, Tulsa, OK 74120
PH: 918-592-5550 FX: 918-592-5970
urbantulsa@urbantulsa.com
www.urbantulsa.com
Free weekly A&E paper. Covers local music scene.

Oregon

Cascade Blues Association
www.cascadeblues.org
Promoting Blues and Roots music in the Northwest.

Creative Music Guild
PO Box 40564, Portland, OR 97240-0564
PH: 503-772-0772
www.creativemusicguild.org
Promotes new music that advances the art of composition.

Early Music Guild of Oregon
www.emgo.org
Bulletin board of news and events related to Early music.

Eugene Weekly
1251 Lincoln, Eugene, OR 97401
Melissa Bearns melissa@eugeneweekly.com
www.eugeneweekly.com
Eugene's A&E publication.

IndieAvenue.com
8152 SW. Hall Blvd. #103, Beaverton, OR 97008
PH: 503-961-2998 FX: 717-828-8257
Boyd Martin boyddrums@indieavenue.com
www.indieavenue.com
Database of Northwest musicians, bands and venues.

Jazz Society of Oregon
www.jsojazzscene.org
Promotes Jazz musicians, Jazz education and Jazz appreciation.

Kingbanana
kingbanana@kingbanana.net
www.kingbanana.net
Covering the Portland Punk/Hardcore/Metal scene.

NAIL Distribution
14134 NE. Airport Way, Portland, OR 97230
PH: 888-6245-462 FX: 503-257-9061
info@naildistribution.com
www.naildistribution.com
Placing independent music in Northwest stores.

Nexus Underground
Jeremy Dietz jeremy@nexusunderground.com
www.nexusunderground.com
Indie distribution center offering free distribution, MP3s and more.

Northeast Oregon Folklore Society
www.neofs.us
Promotes traditional forms of music and dance.

Oregon Bluegrass Association
www.oregonbluegrass.org
Promotes, encourages, fosters and cultivates bluegrass. The Bluegrass Express is our bi-monthly newsletter.

Oregon Live
www.oregonlive.com/music
All the info on the Oregon music scene.

PDX Bands.com
matt@pdxbands.com
pdxbands.com
What Portland sounds like.

Portland Folklore Society
www.portlandfolklore.org
Promoting Folk music and arts in the greater Portland area.

Portland Mercury
605 NE. 21st Ave. #200, Portland, OR 97232
PH: 503-294-0840 FX: 503-294-0844
www.portlandmercury.com
Portland's A&E weekly. Submit your info.

Portland Songwriters Association
www.portlandsongwriters.org
Developing the talents of our members.

portlandmusicians.com
www.portlandmusicians.com
Your online connection to the Portland music scene.

Two Louies Magazine
2745 NE. 34th, Portland, OR 97212
PH: 503-284-5931
twolouie@aol.com
www.twolouiesmagazine.com
Portland monthly music paper. CD and concert reviews.

Willamette Week
2220 NW. Quimby, Portland, OR 97210
PH: 503-243-2122 FX: 503-243-1115
Mark Baumgarten mbaumgarten@wweek.com
www.wweek.com
A weekly calendar of live music in venues throughout the city.

Pennsylvania

AK Music Scene
Bill Domiano bill@akmusicscene.com
www.akmusicscene.com
Based in the Alle-Kiski Valley, we provide free resources to help promote unsigned bands, including: show calendar, an affiliation with Indie Band Radio and much more!

AudioXposure
616 W. Schuylkill Rd. #359, Pottstown, PA 19465
Jennifer Mattern reviews@audioxposure.com
audioxposure.com
Promoting musicians in Southeastern and Southcentral PA. We also highlight select non local artists each month.

Berks Tonight
1527 Kenhorst Blvd. Kenhorst, PA 19607
info@berkstonight.com
www.berkstonight.com
The source for what's happening in Reading PA and Berks County.

Billtown Blues Association
www.billtownblues.org
Providing opportunities for area residents to experience Blues music. Our newsletter is the Blues Note.

Bucks County Blues Society
www.bucksbluessociety.com
Keeping the Blues alive in Bucks County!

Bucks County Folk Song Society
www.bucksfolk.org
Furthering the interest and appreciation of Folk music.

Central PA Friends of Jazz
www.pajazz.org
Presenting and promoting local and national Jazz artists.

Central Pennsylvania Blues Calendar
www.delta-blues.com/PABLUES.HTM
Listing Blues events in & around central PA.

ErieShows.com
Mike Torti miketorti@erieshows.com
www.erieshows.com
Covering the Erie Punk scene.

Fly Magazine
22 E. McGovern Ave. Lancaster, PA 17602
PH: 717-293-9772 FX: 717-295-7561
info@flymagazine.net
www.flymagazine.net
Central PA's most complete guide to entertainment.

Gallery of Sound
www.galleryofsound.com
Monthly publication reviewing CDs plus interviews with new musicians.

Harrisburg Online
4401 N. 6th St. #222, Harrisburg, PA 17110
PH: 717-231-7019
info@hbgonline.com
www.hbgonline.com
Central PA's entertainment guide.

Lehigh Valley Blues Network
www.lvbn.org
Promoting the Blues in the Lehigh Valley area.

Lehigh Valley Folk Music Society
lvfolkmusicsociety.org
Promoting the appreciation of the Old-Time American Folk music.

Merge
101 N. 6th St., Allentown, PA 18101
PH: 610-508-1555
www.mergedigital.com/music
Your weekly guide to the Lehigh Valley.

Northeast Gospel Music
www.northeastgospelmusic.net
Dedicated to promoting Gospel music in the Northeast US.

Out On the Town
100 Temple Blvd. Palmyra, NJ 08065
PH: 856-786-1600 FX: 856-786-1450
Michael Vagnoni ootme2@aol.com
www.ootweb.com
Entertainment trade paper covering PA and NJ.

PABands.com
info@pabands.com
www.pabands.com
Sign your band up today. Free unlimited listing.

PaMidstate
www.pamidstate.com
Your A&E guide to the Midstate region of PA.

Patriot News
2214 Market St., Camp Hill, PA 17011-4600
PH: 717-255-8161 FX: 717-255-8456
www.patriot-news.com
Interviews bands, previews and reviews CDs and concerts.

PaXposure
1278 W. Liberty Rd. Reynoldsville, PA 15851
PH: 814-894-5570
mail@paxposure.com
www.paxposure.com
Your most extensive source for PA's best Indie artists.

Pennsylvania Arts & Music
www.artsandmusicpa.com
Guide to the arts, music and local cultures of PA.

Pennsylvania Musician Forum
PH: 717-506-4700
msa1663@adelphia.com
www.pa-musician.com
Our ultimate goal is to provide a home for all walks of musicians and to build a support community that is beneficial for all.

Pennsylvania Musician Magazine
PO Box 362, Millerstown, PA 17062
PH: 717-444-2423
Deanna Trio dtrio1974@hotmail.com
www.pamusician.net
Guide and marketing tool for the entertainment industry in PA.

Pocono Bluegrass and Folk Society
www.poconobluegrass.org
Dedicated to the promotion and preservation of authentic Acoustic music.

Pulse Weekly
930 N. 4th St. #205, Allentown, PA 18102
PH: 610-437-7867 FX: 610-437-7869
Michael Faillace michaelf@pulseweekly.com
www.pulseweekly.com
Covering the A&E scene in the Lehigh Valley and beyond.

Rock in PA
www.rockinpa.com
Information about local bands, concerts, clubs etc.

ROCKPAGE
www.rockpage.net
We're doing our best to serve the local and regional music community here in PA. Set up your own band page, list gigs etc.

Seven Mountains Bluegrass Association
www2.epix.net/~7mtns
Preserving and promoting Bluegrass music.

Susquehanna Folk Music Society
www.sfmsfolk.org
Preserving and encouraging the traditional arts in Central PA.

The Weekender
15 N. Main St., Wilkes-Barre, PA 18711
PH: 570-829-7101
www.timesleader.com
Free weekly A&E paper. Interviews bands and previews concerts.

Philadelphia

BadmintonStamps Philadelphia
Philabuster philabuster@badmintonstamps.com
www.badmintonstamps.com
Covering the Philly music scene.

Call me Mickey
callmemickey@gmail.com
callmemickey.blogspot.com
MP3 blog covering the local music scene.

Ch8slittle.com
252 Rosemar St., Philadelphia, PA 19120-1415
PH: 215-438-4370
info@ch8slittle.com
www.ch8slittle.com
We are a management group promoting R&B, Hip Hop and Alternative acts in Philadelphia.

Her Jazz
Maria T Sciarrino maria@plainparade.org
herjazz.org/maria
Music blog. From time to time I enjoy sharing music from Philadelphia bands in MP3 format.

Jazzmatazz
4 E. Mt. Pleasant Ave. Philadelphia, PA 19119
Alan Lankin jazzmatazz@att.net
www.Jazzmatazz.info
I concentrate on Jazz and Jazz-related releases. List of upcoming shows.

maneo.com
www.maneo.com
Philadelphia's online nightlife guide. Spotlights local bands. Local events guide.

Origivation Magazine
PO Box 1412, Havertown, PA 19083
Anthony info@origivation.com
www.origivation.com
All original music publication and hosts Philadelphia's most popular message board.

Philadelphia Ambient Consortium
www.simpletone.com
Unifying the city's Ambient, Chill, D n' B, intelligent community.

Philadelphia City Paper
123 Chestnut St. 3rd Fl. Philadelphia, PA 19106
PH: 215-735-8444
pat@citypaper.net
citypaper.net
Free weekly alternative paper. Covers all music styles.

Philadelphia Classical Guitar Society
www.phillyguitar.org
Encouraging Classical guitar activities in the area.

Philadelphia Songwriters Project
www.phillysongwriters.com
Local artists can showcase their music and advance their career.

Philadelphia Weekly
1500 Sansom St. 3rd Fl. Philadelphia, PA 19102
PH: 215-563-7400
Neil Ferguson nferguson@philadelphiaweekly.com
www.philadelphiaweekly.com
Free weekly alternative paper. Does CD reviews.

Philebrity
tips@philebrity.com
www.philebrity.com
A city blog covering the arts, gossip and media in Philadelphia. We'll be here long after you move back to New York.

Philly Blues
phillyblues@comcast.net
www.phillyblues.com
A comprehensive list of Blues bands, events and websites.

Philly Future
www.phillyfuture.org
Information about local shows in the music section.

Philly Goth
1429 Locust St., Norristown, PA 19401
jules@fusion-web.org
www.fusion-web.org/phillygoth
All the info on the local Goth scene.

Philly Local Concert Listings
online@xpn.org
www.xpn.org/concerts.php
Submit your concert & event information. Be sure to include the date, artist, time, venue and hyperlink information.

Philly Prog Rock Connection
PO Box 687, Coatesville, PA 19320
George george@pprcmusic.com
www.pprcmusic.com
Dedicated to bringing Progressive and intense music to the forefront.

phillymusic.com
www.phillymusic.com
All the latest on the Philly music scene.

tbtmo.com
PO Box 63619, Philadelphia, PA 19147
info@tbtmo.com
www.tbtmo.com
Covering the Philadelphia Electronic music scene.

Urban Web Link
PO Box 38922, Philadelphia, PA 19104
PH: 888-628-2618
www.urbanweblink.com
Your source for Urban Christian events in the Philadelphia area.

Wonkavision Magazine

PO Box 63680, Philadelphia, PA 19147
PH: 215-413-2136 FX: 775-261-5247
Jeff Meyers jeff@wonkavisionmagazine.com
www.wonkavisionmagazine.com
Entertainment magazine covering Rock and Punk in the Philly area.

WXPN Musicians On Call

Attn: Volunteer Musicians, 216 W. 18th St. #201B,
New York, NY 10011
www.xpn.org/moc.php
Brings live music to the bedsides of patients in healthcare facilities throughout the region.

P i t t s b u r g h

Flidop

info@flidop.com
www.flidop.com
Our mission is to revive the Pittsburgh music scene by providing a resource for local bands to post gigs, upload MP3s and communicate through our message board.

pghgoth.com

Boo Radley de la Raphrat raphrat@tyranny.com
www.pghgoth.com
Covering the local Goth scene.

PghLocalMusic.com

PO Box 17970, Pittsburgh, PA 15235
info@pghlocalmusic.com
www.pghlocalmusic.com
All the info on the local music scene.

pittpunk.com

2803 Fitzhugh Way, Pittsburgh, PA 15226
Adam Rahuba adam.rahuba@gmail.com
www.pittpunk.com
CD and show reviews, event calendar and MP3s.

Pittsburgh Beat.com

www.pittsburghbeat.com
Discussion board for all things music in Pittsburgh

Pittsburgh City Paper

650 Smithfield St. #2200, Pittsburgh, PA 15222
PH: 412-316-3342 FX: 412-316-3388
Aaron Jentzen ajentzen@steelcitymedia.com
www.pghcitypaper.com
Free weekly A&E paper.

Pittsburgh Folk Music Society

www.calliopehouse.org
Promotes traditional and contemporary Folk music.

Pittsburgh Jazz Society

www.pittsburghjazz.org
Preserving and perpetuating local Jazz music.

Pittsburgh Live Music

mediawebsource@yahoo.com
www.mediawebsource.com/pittsburghlive
Band websites, event and concert listings, venue directory etc.

Renaissance and Baroque Society of Pittsburgh

www.rbsp.org
Presents performances of the music of the middle ages.

WebJHN.com

PH: 877-726-1786
info@webjhn.com
webjhn.com
Taking Hip Hop entertainment in Pittsburgh to the next level.

Rhode Island

Basement Elevation Magazine

PO Box 81019, Warwick, RI 02888
Tassia Joseph basement_elevation@yahoo.com
www.basementelevation.i8.com
Underground Hip Hop music magazine with a focus on RI, MA and CT artists. To be considered for promotion and CD reviews please send us a press kit.

Lotsofnoise

chris@lotsofnoise.com
www.lotsofnoise.com
Devoted to Providence-area Indie shows, leaning towards Noise and Punk Rock.

Rhode Island Songwriters Association

www.risongwriters.com
An organization dedicated the art of songwriting.

South Carolina

Charleston City Paper

1049 B Morrison Dr. Charleston, SC 29403
PH: 843-577-5304 x118 FX: 843-853-6899
T. Ballard Lesemann
ballard@charlestoncitypaper.com
www.charlestoncitypaper.com
Free weekly A&E paper. CD and concert previews and reviews.

columbiatunes

PO Box 1333, Columbia, SC 29202
PH: 803-771-6161
Otis Taylor Jr. otaylor@thestate.com
www.columbiatunes.com
Covers local music scene with interviews, previews and reviews.

Free Times

6904 N. Main St., Columbia, SC 29203
PH: 803-765-0707 FX: 803-765-0727
music@free-times.com
www.free-times.com
Free A&E paper. CD and concert previews and reviews.

Greenville Chapter NSAI

www.nsaigreenville.com
Learn about songwriting and find out how the music business works.

GRITZ

24 Vardry St. #101-G, Greenville, SC 29601
PH/FX: 864-467-1699
Michael Buffalo Smith editor@gritz.net
www.gritz.net
A national print magazine with a sister e-zine. We review CDs, DVDs, books - all Southern flavored.

Rivertown Bluegrass Society

www.rivertownbluegrasssociety.com
Supports local Bluegrass musicians/events.

South Carolina Bluegrass and Traditional Music Assoc.

expresswebs.com/scbtma
Host's Bluegrass concerts and workshops to promote the art.

Southeastern Bluegrass Association of South Carolina

www.sebga.org
Preserving the love of Bluegrass music.

South Dakota

C-Sharp Productions

421 N. Edgerton, Mitchell, SD 57301
PH: 605-996-0232
live@sharpmusic.com
www.sharpmusic.com
Production company and label that signs and develops acts.

Rapid City Journal

507 Main St., Rapid City, SD 57701
PH: 605-394-8300
www.rapidcityjournal.com
Covers local music scene with CD and concert reviews.

Sioux Falls Jazz and Blues Society

www.sfjb.org
Promoting Jazz and Blues through events and education.

South Dakota Friends of Traditional Music

www.fotm.org
Promoting traditional music for generations of South Dakotans.

Wipe Your Eyes and Face the Day

811 S. Minnesota, Sioux Falls, SD 57104
PH: 605-728-4635
jayson jweihs@hotmail.com
wye.slyink.com/board
Report of the local Punk scene.

Tennessee

BlueHighways TV

111 Shivel Dr. Hendersonville, TN 37075
PH: 866-454-2488
feedback@bluehighwaystv.com
bluehighwaystv.com
Fresh and original Roots music that combines new faces and places with our library of original programming.

BlueSpeak

25 Linden Ave. Memphis, TN 38103
info@bluespeak.com
www.bluespeak.com
Features and reviews of Memphis music and related information.

Down-South.com

www.down-south.com
Reviews local and major Hip Hop albums.

Enigma Online

PO Box 825, Chattanooga, TN 37401
PH: 423-267-6072 FX: 423-265-0120
enigmathemagazine@yahoo.com
www.enigmaonline.com
We support the local Indie music scene.

jungleroom.com

www.jungleroom.com
Memphis local music notes. Post news about your upcoming release.

Knoxville Metro Pulse

602 S. Gay St., Knoxville, TN 37902
PH: 865-522-5399 FX: 865-522-2955
Molly Kincaid mkincaid@metropulse.com
www.metropulse.com
A&E section allows local bands to list info and post MP3s.

KnoxShows
info@knoxshows.com
www.knoxshows.com
Post band info, upcoming events, links etc.

Live From Memphis
PH: 901-523-9763
Christopher Reyes info@livefrommemphis.com
www.livefrommemphis.com
We support and promote local musicians, filmmakers and artists who are the lifeblood of the Memphis creative scene.

Memphis Acoustic Music Association
www.mamamusic.org
Sponsors Acoustic music, both American Folk and Celtic.

Memphis Area Bluegrass Association
www.memphis-bluegrass.org
Info on the Bluegrass scene. Reviews CDs.

Memphis Commercial Appeal
495 Union Ave. Memphis, TN 38103
PH: 901-529-2345
www.commercialappeal.com
Covers the tri-state music scenes. Profiles touring bands, reviews CDs.

Memphis Flyer
460 Tennessee St., Memphis, TN 38103
PH: 901-521-9000 FX: 901-521-0129
Chris Herrington herrington@memphisflyer.com
www.memphisflyer.com
Free weekly paper. Covers local scene and bands playing the area.

The Memphis Mojo
www.memphismojo.com
Focusing on local music, where it's played and by whom.

Memphis Music Commission
47 Union Ave. Memphis, TN 38103
PH: 901-543-5334 FX: 901-543-5351 |
www.memphismusic.org
A community for the people who play music and the people who appreciate it.

Memphis Songwriters Association
www.memphissongwriters.org
All the resources local songwriters need.

MemphisRap.com
PO Box 30337, Memphis, TN 38130
PH: 901-332-3504
feedback@memphisrap.com
www.MemphisRap.com
Artists can submit news, links, demos, audio files and more!

Rebourne Entertainment
1102 Llano Cove, Memphis, TN 38134-7908
PH: 901-388-2988
Bill & Holly Simmers simmers@rebourne.net
www.rebourne.net
A network of bands, vocalists, musicians and songwriters who are committed to using their talents to make a positive impact on the world around them.

Smoky Mountain Blues Society
www.smokymountainblues.com
Serving Maryville, Knoxville and all of East Tennessee.

Tennessee Jazz & Blues Society
www.jazzblues.org
Submit news, articles, CDs for review and more.

Tennessee Songwriters Association
www.clubnashville.com/tsai.htm
Educating, assisting and representing all songwriters.

Nashville

American Music Showcase
9 Music Sq. S. #210, Nashville, TN 37203
ams@nashvilleconnection.com
www.americanmusicshowcase.com
Promote your music on Comcast 75 TV.

Music City Blues
www.musiccityblues.org
Hosts performances and programs to sustain this music.

Music Row
1231 17th Ave. S., Nashville, TN 37212
PH: 615-321-3617 FX: 615-329-0852
David M. Ross ross@musicrow.com
www.musicrow.com
Nashville's music industry publication.

Nashville Ear
4636 Lebanon Pike #144, Hermitage, TN 37076
Steve McNaron smac@NashvilleEar.com
NashvilleEar.com
A venue for songwriters and singers to get their music out on the internet to gain exposure.

Nashville Gothic
djneph@nashvillegothic.com
www.nashvillegothic.com
Serving the needs of the Gothic community in the area.

Nashville OnStage TV Show
923 Kipling Dr. Nashville, TN 37217
PH: 615-367-2803
Debbie & Ernie Simms dsimms55@comcast.net
www.nashvilleonstage.com/about.html
Play your songs in front of a live audience. Great exposure, reaches 3 million viewers. Country, Pop, Folk, Country Rock, Americana.

Nashville Scene
2120 8th Ave. S., Nashville, TN 37204-2204
PH: 615-244-7989
Tracy Moore editor@nashvillescene.com
www.nashscene.com
Free weekly alternative paper. Covers local music scene.

Nashville Songwriter's Association International *(NSAI)*
www.nashvillesongwriters.com
Protecting the rights and serving songwriters in all genres.

NashvilleConnection.com
9 Music Sq. S. #210, Nashville, TN 37203
PH: 615-826-4141
info@nashvilleconnection.com
www.NashvilleConnection.com
Your source for info about the business of music in Nashville.

NashvilleRock.net
PH: 615-319-1773
Jerry Work jwork@workmedia.net
nashvillerock.net
The latest local Rock news, reviews and concert information.

The Rage
1100 Broadway, Nashville, TN 37203
PH: 615-664-2270 FX: 615-664-2280
www.nashvillerage.com
Nashville free A&E weekly.

Tunesmith
info@tunesmith.net
www.tunesmith.net
Presents some of Nashville's best undiscovered songwriting!

Writer/Artist Showcase
PO Box 1346, Hendersonville, TN 37077
PH: 615-826-9550
Jack Scott mail@writerartist.com
www.writerartist.com
A tool for success for aspiring songwriters and artists.

Texas

The All-You-Can-Eat Texas Music Cafe
TMC/Media Communications 3801 Campus Dr.
Waco, TX 76705
Paula Unger texasmusiccafe@hot.rr.com
www.texasmusiccafe.com
Variety music television and radio program.

CD TEX
8806 Lockway, San Antonio, TX 78217
PH: 210-654-8773 FX: 210-654-8895
contact@bgmnetwork.com
www.cd-tex.com
CD store for Texas and Americana Music.

Central Texas Bluegrass Association
www.centraltexasbluegrass.org
Post events and get your CD reviewed.

corpusmusic.com
corpusmusic.com
Band information, show dates and song downloads of local artists.

Country Line Magazine
16150 IH 35, Buda, TX 78610
PH: 512-295-8400 FX: 512-295-8600
TJ Greaney tj@countrylinemagazine.com
www.countrylinemagazine.com
A Country Music magazine distributed throughout Texas. Special ad rates for Indies.

Denton Rock City
www.dentonrockcity.com
An information source for Denton musicians, bands, venues and music writers.

diy-danna publishing
PO Box 3296, Cedar Park, TX 78630
Danna submissions@diy-danna.com
www.diy-danna.com
Are you a solo musician or band in the Austin/Central Texas area? I write music reviews for Hyperactive Music Magazine, INsite's "Local Trax", Kill Your FM and Whoopsy! Magazine.

East Texas Gig Guide
www.easttexasgigguide.com
A resource for finding live entertainment and fun things to do throughout the Arklatex region.

El Paso Scene
PO Box 13615, El Paso, TX 79913
PH: 915-542-1422 FX: 915-542-4292
Brian Chozick epscene@epscene.com
www.epscene.com
Free monthly A&E paper. Concert previews and CD reviews.

ElDoradoUnderground.com
www.eldoradounderground.com
Resource for the local music scene. Post your news, MP3s etc.

Gruene With Envy
1215 W. Slaughter Ln. #2513, Austin, TX 78748
Katie Ross katie@415e.com
www.gruenewithenvy.com
Texas/Americana music reviews plus a radio show.

Harmonica Organization of Texas
www.hoottexas.com
Promoting the art of playing the harmonica.

HillCountryScene.com
PH: 702-340-6748
Roy Al Rendahl royalrendahl@thefaro.com
www.thefaro.com/hillcountryscene.html
Covering the Central Texas Hill Country scene - music and arts.

The Juice
210 S. Grimes #108, San Antonio, TX 78203
PH: 210-226-1939 FX: 866-378-1258
Carl Booker avista@thejuiceonline.com
www.thejuiceonline.com
San Antonio's A&E magazine.

Left Ear Entertainment
2611 N. Beltline Rd. #111, Sunnyvale, TX 75182
PH: 469-233-9563
Chaz@HearLeftEar.com
www.myspace.com/texasradio1
Dedicated to supporting local music from The Lone Star State!

Lone Star Music
1243 Gruene Rd. New Braunfels, TX 78130
PH: 830-627-1992 FX: 830-624-0976
customerservice@lonestarmusic.com
www.lonestarmusic.com
Reviews, tour dates, contests, prizes and much more.

MyTexasMusic.com
PO Box 148, Linden, TX 75563
PH: 903-756-8944 FX: 888-693-9379
Lucky Boyd MyTexasMusic@aol.com
www.mytexasmusic.com
We are doing more for musicians in Texas than other online vendors could ever pretend to do.

musicTX.com
musictx.com
Show postings for Texas Underground/Alternative bands.

SA Music Scene
PH: 210-367-2572
www.samusicscene.net
Promotes Texas bands and all acts touring through there.

SAMPLE Press
PO Box 471159, Fort Worth, TX 76147
Jason Manriquez jason@samplepress.com
samplepress.com
Features independent Rock bands, primarily (but not entirely) from Texas.

San Antonio Blues Society
www.sanantonioblues.com
Preserving various styles of Blues music.

San Antonio Rocks
www.sanantoniorocks.fr.st
Covering the local Christian Rock scene.

San Antonio Weekly Music News
PO Box 201090, San Antonio, TX 78220
PH: 210-227-4821 FX: 210-225-5009
editor@sambe.org
sambe.org
An online newsletter with all that's going on in the SA music scene.

Spring Creek Bluegrass Club *(SCBC)*
www.springcreekbluegrass.com
An organization dedicated to preserving the wonderful tradition of Bluegrass music.

State of Texas Gospel Announcers Guild
www.texasgag.com
Increasing the penetration of Gospel music in cities in America.

Texarkana Blues Society
www.texarkanablues.com
Preserving Blues history, supporting Blues education and promoting the ongoing development of Blues music.

Texarkanarocks.com
webmaster@texarkanarocks.com
www.texarkanarocks.com
Providing useful information about music related issues and events in and around Texarkana.

Texas Music Chart
2500 Tanglewilde #106, Houston, TX 77063
PH: 713-952-9221 FX: 713-952-1207
katie@shanemedia.com
www.texasmusicchart.com
The industry standard weekly compilation of radio airplay for Texas artists and their fans.

Texas Music Magazine
PO Box 50273, Austin, TX 78763
PH: 512-472-6630 FX: 208-485-0347
info@txmusic.com
www.txmusic.com
Promoting original Indie Texas music.

Texas Music Round-Up
PO Box 49884 Austin, TX 78765-9884
PH: 512-480-0765 FX: 512-499-0207
info@texasmusicroundup.com
www.texasmusicroundup.com
Your independent Texas music superstore!

Texas Talent Register
www.governor.state.tx.us/music
Listing of Texas born or based recording artists.

texasmetalundeground.com
www.texasmetalundeground.com
Band profiles, interviews, articles etc.

TexasMusicGuide.com
PO Box 2032, Allen, TX 75013-0036
www.texasmusicguide.com
Texas music festivals, events, venues, CD releases and artist links.

TexasReggae.org
www.texasreggae.org
Covering all things Reggae in Texas.

This Is Texas Music
2311 Westforest Dr. Austin, TX 78704
PH: 512-638-6410
Patrick Nichols patrick@thisistexasmusic.com
www.thisistexasmusic.com
Reviews, profiles, interviews etc.

Austin

Austin 360 *Ultimate Austin Band List*
PO Box 670, Austin, TX 78767
PH: 512-912-2591 FX: 512-912-2926
Steven Smith ssmith@statesman.com
www.austin360.com
List your band, events etc.

Austin Celtic Association
www.austincelts.org
Promoting Celtic culture through music, dance and the arts in Central Texas.

Austin Classical Guitar Society
www.austinclassicalguitar.org
Link between amateur and professional guitarists and the community.

Austin Friends of Traditional Music
www.main.org/aftm/aftmhome.htm
Preserving all genres of traditional music.

Austin Metro Entertainment
PO Box 1583, Pflugerville, TX 78691-1583
PH: 512-251-1882 FX: 512-251-1909
info@austinmetro.com
www.austinmetro.com
An entertainment guide for Austin and Central Texas.

Austin Music Foundation
www.austinmusicfoundation.org
Professional development and economic advancement of local musicians.

INsite Magazine
1704½ S. Congress Ste. J, Austin, TX 78704
PH: 512-462-9260 FX: 512-326-4923
mail@insiteaustin.com
www.insiteaustin.com
Features with local up-in-coming acts.

Jupiter index
PO Box 2024, Austin, TX 78768-2024
Gabrielle Burns mail@jupiterindex.com
www.jupiterindex.com
Helping musicians by connecting them with a wider audience.

MusicAustin
www.musicaustin.com
A catalog of the Austin music scene.

Dallas/Fort Worth

Dallas Hardcore
www.dallashardcore.com
Promoting the Hardcore scene.

Dallas Music Guide
660 Preston Forest Ctr. #218, Dallas, TX 75230
PH: 214-739-5300 FX: 214-696-6249
Paul Salfen psalfen@dallasmusicguide.com
www.dallasmusicguide.com
Online music magazine in the Dallas/Ft. Worth area.

Dallas Songwriter's Association
www.dallassongwriters.org
Enhancing the overall personal growth and professionalism of our members.

dallas.com
www.dallas.com
The Dallas area music scene: clubs, concerts, bars, nightlife and a local band directory.

dallasmusic
4912 Wedgeview Dr. Hurst, TX 76053
Darin Wakely dallasmusic@hotmail.com
www.dallasmusic.com
Live reviews, CD reviews, interviews and more!

Dallas Observer
PO Box 190289, Dallas, TX 75219-0289
Sam Machkovech
sam.machkovech@dallasobserver.com
www.dallasobserver.com
Night & Day section covers the local music scene.

DFW Hip Hop Society
dfwhiphopsociety.com
Covering Hip Hop events in Dallas/ Ft. Worth.

Fort Worth Songwriters Association
www.fwsa.com
Improving musical work through fellowship, workshops and education.

Fort Worth Weekly
1204-B W. 7th St. #201, Fort Worth, TX 76102
PH: 817-321-9700 FX: 817-335-9575
www.fwweekly.com
Fort Worth's A&E weekly.

ftworthmusic.com
1912 River Bend Rd. Arlington, TX 76104
ftworthmusic@hotmail.com
ftworthmusic.com
Live reviews, CD reviews, interviews and more!

GuideLive.com
508 Young St., Dallas, TX 75202
PH: 214-977-8861 FX: 214-977-8177
www.guidelive.com
Covers the local music scene. Post your shows and events.

Harder Beat
PO Box 59711, Dallas, TX 75229
PH/FX: 972-484-8030
Linda Hollar linda@harderbeat.com
www.harderbeat.com
Local band features, show and CD reviews and more.

Southwest Blues
PO Box 710475, Dallas, TX 75371
PH: 214-887-1188 FX: 972-642-6999
southwestblues@aol.com
www.southwestblues.com
We feature and spotlight Blues artists that deserve the recognition.

Spune Productions
1009 Andrew Dr. Burleson, TX 76028
PH: 817-426-0264
info@spune.com
www.spune.com
Promotes quality artists. Reviews demos, posts events and more.

TexasGigs.com
8140 Walnut Hill Ln. #605, Dallas, TX 75231
PH: 214-363-9304
listings@pegasusnews.com
www.texasgigs.com
Promoting and supporting the Dallas-area music scene.

Houston

Bay Area Bluegrass Association
www.bayareabluegrass.org
Promotes Bluegrass music in the Houston area and beyond.

Best In Texas Magazine
2500 Tanglewilde, #106, Houston, TX 77063
PH: 713-952-9221
Ed Shane smsofc@shanemedia.com
www.bestintexasonline.com
News, reviews and profiles, plus reports on new releases, live shows, events etc.

Guitar Houston
www.guitarhouston.org
Supports developing artists through free concerts.

Houston Band Coalition
www.hbclive.com
Includes a forum for musicians, fans and industry pros.

Houston Beat
www.houstonbeat.com
List your bands, shows and special events.

Houston Blues Society
www.houstonbluessociety.org
Blues education, special events and a monthly jam session.

Houston Folklore & Folk Music Society
www.houstonfolkmusic.org
Promoting folklore and Folk music.

Houston/Fort Bend Songwriters Association
www.hfbsa.org
Supports and encourages the art and craft of songwriting.

Houston Press
1621 Milam, #100, Houston, TX 77002
PH: 713-280-2400 FX: 713-280-2444
John Nova Lomax john.lomax@houstonpress.com
www.houstonpress.com
Major news and entertainment weekly.

houstonbands.net
10250 Lands End #304, Houston, TX 77099
Mark Landrum webmaster@houstonbands.net
www.houstonbands.net
The network for Houston bands on the internet. Send your CDs for review.

Jazz Houston
Kelly kel@jazzhouston.com
www.jazzhouston.com
Gig listings, profiles, recordings, news and more.

Space City Rock
PO Box 541010, Houston, TX 77254
gaijin@spacecityrock.com
www.spacecityrock.com
Covering the Houston music scene.

Utah

Draztikbeatz.net
www.draztikbeatz.net
The Hip Hop/Rap resource for the Salt Lake City area!

The Echo TV
c/o KCSG TV, 845 E. Red Hill Pkwy. St. George, UT 84770
theecho@kcsg.com
www.myspace.com/theechotv
TV show dedicated to showcasing independent music. Send in your video for airplay or your CD for background music during interviews.

Intermountain Acoustic Music Association
www.iamaweb.org
Preserving Acoustic music, including Bluegrass, Folk etc.

LDS Music World
www.ldsmusicworld.com
News, reviews, features, music downloads, internet radio and more.

LDSMusicians.com
www.ldsmusicians.com
Discussion forum for LDS musicians and fans.

The Rock Salt
therocksalt@gmail.com
www.therocksalt.com
Bringing you the Rock from the Great Salt Lake.

Salt Lake City Weekly
248 S. Main St., Salt Lake City, UT 84101
PH: 801-575-7003
www.slweekly.com
Free weekly alternative paper. Band interviews, CD and concert previews and reviews.

Salt Lake Under Ground (SLUG)
351 W. Pierpont Ave. 4B, Salt Lake City, UT 84101
PH: 801-487-9221 FX: 801-487-1359
info@slugmag.com
www.slugmag.com
Covers local music scene with concert and Indie CD reviews.

Utah Blues
info@utahblues.com
www.utahblues.com
Information, news, gigs etc.

UtahBands.com
info@fungusent.com
www.utahbands.com
Music posting service for band members to promote their concerts.

Vermont

Deerfield Valley News
events@vermontmedia.com
www.dvalnews.com
Southern Vermont's source for entertainment.

Early Music Vermont
www.earlymusicvermont.org
Connecting artists and fans of Early music.

Seven Days
PO Box 1164, Burlngton, VT 05402
PH: 802-864-5684 FX: 802-865-1015
Casey Rea casey@sevendaysvt.com
www.sevendaysvt.com
Weekly A&E paper. Accepts CDs for review.

Vermont Music Shop
PO Box 428, Burlington, VT 05402
PH: 800-3033-1590 FX: 802-865-6200
musicshop@bigheavyworld.net
www.vermontmusicshop.com
Selling local musicians CDs. Consign your CDs with us.

The Indie Link Exchange
A new, free and easy way to promote your website.

www.indielinkexchange.com/ile

Virginia

Americana Rhythm
PO Box 450, Dayton, VA 22821
PH: 540-746-0360
Greg E. Tutwiler greg@americanrhythm.com
www.americanrhythm.com
Reviews CDs of regional artists and those touring through the area. Americana, Roots, Bluegrass and Folk.

Bluegrass Connection
9908 Brightlea Dr. Vienna, VA 22181
PH: 703-927-1875
pmilano@bgstate.com
www.gotech.com
Band, performer and festival home pages for the Virginia area.

The Breeze
G1, Anthony-Seeger Hall, MSC 6805, Harrisonburg, VA 22807
PH: 540-568-3151
breezearts@hotmail.com
www.thebreeze.org
James Madison U. student paper.

C-Ville Weekly
106 E. Main St., Charlottesville, VA 22902
PH: 434-817-2749 FX: 434-817-2758
music@c-ville.com
www.c-ville.com
Charlottesville free weekly paper. Covers local music scene.

Cavalier Daily
PO Box 400703, Charlottesville, VA 22904-4703
PH: 434-924-1086 FX: 434-924-7290
www.cavalierdaily.com
U. Virginia's student newspaper.

Charlottesville Monthly
301 E. Market St., Charlottesville, VA 22902
PH: 804-295-9004 FX: 434-293-5618
artsmonthly.com
Monthly A&E magazine. Covers local music scene.

Dan River Region Blues and Folk Society
www.danriverregion.com/bluessociety
Supports local artists. Gig calendar, artist info etc.

Fredericksburg Songwriters' Showcase
122 Laurel Ave. Fredericksburg, VA 22408
PH: 540-898-0611
Bob Gramann showcase@bobgramann.com
www.webliminal.com/songwrite
A forum for local songwriters with monthly showcases.

GetRockedOut.com
www.getrockedout.com
Helping the music scene in Blacksburg and surrounding areas. Shows, band listings etc.

HamptonRoads.com
PH: 757-446-2989
www.hamptonroads.com
News, information, calendars, reviews and more.

The Hook
100 2nd St., Charlottesville, VA 22902
PH: 434-295-8700 FX: 434-295-8097
www.readthehook.com
A&E weekly. Covers local music scene.

James River Blues Society
www.jamesriverblues.org
Promoting and preserving Blues music in the area.

MEONA
meona@verizon.net
www.meona.net
Supporting the local music scene in the SE Virginia area.

Natchel Blues Network
www.natchelblues.org
Blues newsletter, reviews, gig listings and a "spotlight artist" feature.

NorVaGoth.Net
shawn@norvagoth.net
www.norvagoth.net
The Norfolk/Tidewater area Goth/Industrial guide.

Phat Cats Entertainment
6483 Fenestra Ct. #100, Burke, VA 22015
PH: 202-415-9268
Enrique Lopez bookings@phatcats.com
www.phatcats.com
Management/entertainment company that brings the best talent to the DC, MD and VA area.

Reload
3729 Colonial Pkwy. Virginia Beach, VA 23452
Don Womack webmaster@710.com
www.710.com/reload
Promoting the local talent of Hampton Roads and Richmond.

Richmond.com
1427 W. Main St., Richmond, VA 23220
PH: 804-355-4500 FX: 804-355-3110
www.richmond.com
Online guide to Richmond events. Submit your gig.

Richmond Jazz Society
www.vajazz.org
Promotes Jazz through performances, lectures and workshops.

Richmond Music Journal
PO Box 8372, Richmond, VA 23226
PH: 804-569-6283 FX: 804-569-6284
Mariane Matera rmjournal@mindspring.com
www.mindspring.com/~rmjournal
Covering local music in Richmond. Please do NOT send us CDs if you are not from Richmond!

River City Blues Society
www.rivercityblues.com
Educating and enlightening the metropolitan area on the Blues.

Roanoke Fiddle & Banjo Club
www.roanokefiddleandbanjoclub.org
Fostering and preserving Old-Time and Bluegrass music.

Roanoke Times
201 W. Campbell Ave. PO Box 2491, Roanoke, VA 24010-2491
PH: 800-346-1234
jeff.debell@roanoke.com
www.roanoke.com
Covers Southern Virginia music scene.

RVA
3512 Floyd Ave. #1, Richmond, VA 23221
PH: 804-349-5890
R. Anthony Harris content@rvamag.com
www.rvamag.com
We are a magazine focused on showing you Richmond's progressive arts and culture.

SevenZeroThree
info@sevenzerothree.com
www.sevenzerothree.com
Raising awareness about the local music scene.

Style Weekly
1707 Summit Ave. #201, Richmond, VA 23230
PH: 804-358-0825 FX: 804-358-1079
Carrie Nieman carrie.nieman@styleweekly.com
www.styleweekly.com
Richmond's magazine of news, culture and opinion.

Tidewater Classical Guitar Society
www.tcgs.cx
Concert schedule features local performers.

Tidewater Friends of Folk Music
www.tffm.org
Promotes traditional and contemporary Folk music in SE Virginia.

Tidewater Rocks!
edrocker@tidewaterrocks.net
www.tidewaterrocks.net
Get the lowdown on Hampton local bands.

VaRockBands.com
812 Moorefield Park Dr. #300, Richmond, VA 23236
Jason Smith staff@varockbands.com
www.myspace.com/varockbands
Linking fans with Virginia's best bands.

Virginia Organization of Composers and Lyricists
www.vocalsongwriter.org
Promoting the art and craft of songwriting and musical composition.

The Undersound
AlexWinfield@theundersound.com
theundersound.com
Virginia Beach local music scene. Punk, Hardcore ...all types of music.

Wadi Magazine
PO Box 70129, Richmond, VA 23255
www.wadimagazine.com
Virginia's freaky bi-weekly. Send us your CDs!

Washington

Bellingham Independent Music Association
www.bima.com
Independent musicians and music supporters promoting local arts.

Blues to Do
PO Box 22950, Seattle, WA 98122-0950
PH: 206-328-0662
info@bluestodo.com
www.bluestodo.com
Source of information about live Blues in the Northwest!

ForceWeb.com
www.forceweb.com
Puget Sound Live Music.

Inland Empire Blues Society
www.ieblues.org
Promoting the Blues in the Northwest.

Inland Northwest Bluegrass Association
www.spokanebluegrass.org
Host's Bluegrass concerts, jams, festivals and other events.

Northwest Artist Management
PH: 503-774-2511
www.nwmusicpro.com
Represents the best artists in the Northwest.

Northwest Dance Music Association
www.nwdma.org
The premier record pool covering the Pacific Northwest.

Northwest Folklife
www.nwfolklife.org
The most visible advocate of the traditional arts in the Northwest region.

Northwest Music Network
PO Box 46401, Seattle, WA 98146
info@northwestmusic.net
www.northwestmusic.net
Online guide to all things musical in the Northwest!

Northwest Tekno
www.nwtekno.org
Electronic music community.

NWBlues.com
PO Box 551, Stanwood, WA 98292
PH: 360-629-8027
Carol nwblues1@msn.com
www.nwblues.com
Promoting Blues and Blues artists in the Northwest.

Old Time Music in Portland
www.bubbaguitar.com
Lists Old-Time music gigs and music gatherings in the Portland area.

Olymusic.com
www.olymusic.com
Site for Olympia musicians.

Pacific Northwest Inlander
1020 W. Riverside Ave. Spokane, WA 99201
PH: 509-325-0638
www.theinlander.com
Spokane weekly that reviews and covers local music.

Songwriters of the Northwest Guild
www.songnw.com
Helps songwriters define and pursue their artistic goals.

Spokanebands.com
PH: 509-701-0333
Dan info@spokanebands.com
www.spokanebands.com
Events, bands, news, forums, venues and much more.

Three Rivers Folklife Society
www.3rfs.org
Promoting Folk music in the Tri-Cities area.

Walla Walla Blues Society
www.wwbs.org
Keeping the public in touch with our American musical heritage.

Washington Bluegrass Association
www.washingtonbluegrassassociation.org
Promotes understanding and enjoyment of Bluegrass and other closely related music.

Washington Blues Society
www.wablues.org
News, CD reviews, classifieds etc.

Seattle

Early Music Guild of Seattle
www.earlymusicguild.org
Supports Early music artists through concerts and programs.

Earshot Jazz
www.earshot.org
Supports Jazz and increases awareness in the community.

Gospel Music Workshop of America Pacific
www.pacificnwchapter.com
Promoting Gospel and all its beliefs in the community.

KMTT Local Access
1100 Olive Way #1650, Seattle, WA 98101
PH: 206-233-8984 FX: 206-233-8979
studio@kmtt.com
www.kmtt.com/mountainmusicinfo.asp
Each month we will feature a local band with links to music, pictures, bios and schedules of upcoming shows.

KNDD Seattle Music Page
1100 Olive Way #1650, Seattle, WA 98101
PH: 206-622-3251
www.1077theend.com/seattlemusic.asp
Find out about the best bands in Seattle - pictures, bios and music.

Seaspot.com
info@seaspot.com
www.seaspot.com
Covering the entertainment scene in the Seattle area.

Seattle Classic Guitar Society
www.seattleguitar.org
Events calendar, local news, articles of interest and more.

Seattle Composer's Alliance
www.seattlecomposers.org
Uniting Seattle composers to share ideas.

Seattle Drummer
Aaron aarongrey@seattledrummer.com
www.seattledrummer.com
Helping musicians achieve their personal and professional goals.

Seattle Folklore Society
seafolklore.org
Promoting Folk and traditional arts in the Seattle area.

Seattle Gay News
1605 12th Ave. #31, Seattle, WA 98122
PH: 206-324-4297 FX: 206-322-7188
sgn2@sgn.org
www.sgn.org
Post your shows and events.

Seattle Weekly
1008 Western Ave. #300, Seattle, WA 98104
PH: 206-623-0500 FX: 206-467-4338
www.seattleweekly.com
Covers local music scene with artist interviews, CD and concert previews and reviews.

The Stranger
1535 11th Ave. 3rd Fl. Seattle, WA 98122
PH: 206-323-7101 FX: 206-323-7203
www.thestranger.com
Seattle free weekly alternative paper. Covers local music with concert previews and CD reviews.

Three Imaginary Girls
PO Box 20428, Seattle, WA 98102
TIG@threeimaginarygirls.com
www.threeimaginarygirls.com
Seattle's sparkly Indie Pop press.

Washington DC

AOL CityGuide Washington *Music*
home.digitalcity.com/washington
Regional music column and forum.

DC Bluegrass Union
www.dcbu.org
Promoting and supporting Bluegrass music in the area.

DC Blues Society
www.dcblues.org
Dedicated to preserving and promoting the Blues.

DC Hip Hop Network
launch.groups.yahoo.com/group/dchiphopnetwork
Share music, drop rhymes, post show info and more.

DC Music Net
info@dcmusicnet.com
www.dcmusicnet.com
Washington's scene for local talent.

DCGoGo.COM
5814 Clay St. NE. Washington, DC 20019
PH: 202-257-7992 FX: 202-398-8299
www.dcgogo.com
Source for Go Go music in our nations capital.

DCjazz.com
PH: 202-882-6573
www.dcjazz.com
MP3s, videos, CD store and more!

dcMusicNews
www.dcmusicnews.com
Resource sites for independent musicians in the area.

DCShows.net
www.dcshows.net
Local Punk, Metal and Hardcore shows for the mid-Atlantic.

dcska.com
www.dcska.com
Reviews, show dates, interviews, multimedia and more.

Exotic Fever Records
PO Box 297, College Park, MD 20741-0297
Sara sara@exoticfever.com
www.exoticfever.com
Supports local and regional independent music/writing/art.

Folklore Society of Greater Washington
www.fsgw.org
Promoting the traditional Folk music and folklore of the American people.

House of Musical Traditions
7040 Carroll Ave. Takoma Park, MD 20912
PH: 301-270-9090 FX: 301-270-3010
hmtmail@hmtrad.com
www.hmtrad.com
We have one of the most extensive collections of recordings done by musicians local to the DC area.

Mantis Magazine
PO Box 9566, Silver Spring, MD 20916
submissions@mantismagazine.com
www.mantismagazine.com
Promoting local artists and writers. E-mail us to let us know you've sent your music.

Metro Distortion
metrodistortion@hotmail.com
www.metrodistortion.blogspot.com
Providing reviews and news on the DC, Baltimore and NYC live music scene.

MetroMusicScene.com
Jeff Campagna jeffc@lastsecondcomeback.com
www.metromusicscene.blogspot.com
A source for music news and community for the DC metro area.

On Tap
4238 Wilson Blvd. #3078, Arlington, VA 22203
PH: 703-465-0500 FX: 703-465-0400
Chris Connelly
christopher.connelly@ontaponline.com
www.ontaponline.com
Arts & entertainment magazine for the DC area.

Pheer.com
pablo@pheer.com
www.pheer.com
Shows listing for Punk/Hardcore bands. Post your MP3s.

Seeking Irony
seeking_irony@yahoo.com
www.seeking_irony.blogspot.com
DC music news, shows, release parties etc.

Society of Art Rockers
www.dc-soar.org
Promoting the musical form called Art Rock or Progressive Rock in the Metropolitan Washington, DC area.

Songwriters' Association of Washington
saw.org
Resource for professional songwriters to further their careers.

Washington Area Lawyers for the Arts
901 New York Ave. NW. Ste. P-1,
Washington DC 20001-4413
PH: 202-289-4440 FX: 202-289-4985
legalservices@thewala.org
www.thewala.org
Provides legal service to the arts community.

Washington Area Music Association
wamadc.com
Promotes local music regardless of genre.

Washington City Paper
2390 Champlain St. NW., Washington, DC 20009
PH: 202-332-2100 FX: 202-332-8500
www.washingtoncitypaper.com
Covers the local music scene and previews upcoming A&E events.

Washington Post
1150 15th St. NW., Washington, DC 20071
PH: 202-334-7582
www.washingtonpost.com
Considers Indie albums for review. Covers local music scene.

washingtonpost.com MP3
mp3@wpni.com
mp3.washingtonpost.com
Self-publishing by and for the Metro region's music community.

West Virginia

304live.com
303 Del Ray Dr. St. Albans, WV 25177
www.304live.com
Accepts CDs from local Hip Hop artists.

The Daily Athenaeum
1374 VanVoorhis Rd. Lot D14, Morgantown, WV 26505
www.da.wvu.edu
West Virginia U's daily paper. We're always looking for new things to write about. My next article could be your CD review!

Graffiti
519 Juliana St., Parkersburg, WV 26101
PH: 304-485-1891
www.grafwv.com
Covers local music scene with interviews, concert and CD reviews.

Wisconsin

Brave the Cold
Dawn dawners13@gmail.com
www.myspace.com/bravethecold
Supporting local/regional music in the Midwest area and beyond. What do you need??? We can hook you up or get it done for you.

Cty Murph's Music Page
ctymurph@netwurx.net
www.ctymurph.com
Listing of Wisconsin bands and show dates.

FolkLib Index
PO Box 1447, Oshkosh, WI 54903-1447
henkle@pobox.com
www.folklib.net/index/wi
Information of Wisconsin Folk, Bluegrass, Celtic, Acoustic and Blues artists.

Fondy Acoustic Music Alliance
www.fondyacoustic.org
Providing listening and playing opportunities for fans of Acoustic music.

Isthmus
101 King St., Madison, WI 53703
PH: 608-251-5627
Dean Robbins robbins@isthmus.com
www.thedailypage.com
Madison's news & entertainment weekly.

mad.city.hard.core
www.MadHC.com
A Madison/Milwaukee area music site focusing on Punk, Metal, Hardcore and Rock.

Madison Blues Society
www.madisonbluessociety.com
Keeping the Blues alive in the Madison area.

Madison Folk Music Society
www.madfolk.org
Dedicated to fostering Folk Music in the Madison area.

Madison Jazz Society
www.madisonjazz.com
Preserving and promoting Jazz music.

MadisonSongwriters.com
www.madisonsongwriters.com
Provides education and networking opportunities within the music business.

MadisonMusicians.Net
admin@madisonmusicians.net
www.madisonmusicians.net
Connect with the local music scene.

Maximum Ink
PH: 608-245-0781 FX: 608-245-0782
Rokker Rokker@maximumink.com
www.maximumink.com
Music magazine featuring interviews/stories, CD reviews, events and more.

Milwaukee-Hardcore.com
xbaxterx@hotmail.com
www.milwaukee-hardcore.com
Covering the Milwaukee Punk/Hardcore scene.

The Music Review
Elvis Aaron Presley Sheehan
the.music.review@gmail.com
www.myspace.com/themusicreview
Helping local Rock, Jam and Metal bands spread original music and live concerts. Check our website for submission details!

Muzzle of Bees
uwmryan@yahoo.com
www.muzzleofbees.com
Blog covering the Madison music scene.

OnMilwaukee.com
1930 E. North Ave. 2nd Fl. Milwaukee, WI 53202
PH: 414-272-0557
www.onmilwaukee.com
Milwaukee music guide. Add your band to our local music database.

OnWisconsin.com Live: Music and Night Life
www.onwisconsin.com/music
Your LIVE guide for Wisconsin music.

Rick's Cafe
836 E. Johnson St., Madison, WI 53703
PH: 608-250-2565
Rick Tvedt rick@rickscafe.org
www.rickscafe.org
A local music newspaper near Madison. CD and live show reviews.

The Scene
PO Box 462, Hilbert, WI 54129
PH: 920-853-7500 FX: 920-853-7506
www.valleyscene.com
Appleton A&E weekly.

Shepherd Express
207 E. Buffalo St. #410, Milwaukee, WI 53202
PH: 414-276-2222 FX: 414-276-3312
www.shepherd-express.com
Milwaukee free daily alternative paper. Covers local music scene.

Southern Wisconsin Bluegrass Music Association
www.swbmai.org
News about Bluegrass events, profiles of area bands and reviews.

Up the Downstair
bish_tim_archer@yahoo.com
www.upthedownstair.net
MP3 blog focussing on the Madison music scene.

WISCONLINE
www.wisconline.com
Everything Wisconsin. Submit your music event.

Wisconsin Area Music Industry
www.wamimusic.com
Our purpose is to educate and recognize the achievements and accomplishments of individuals in the Wisconsin music industry.

Wisconsin Musical Groups
regent@execpc.com
www.execpc.com/~regent
Wisconsin's music resource! Submit your band/gig info.

Wyoming

Jackson Hole Online
610 W. Broadway, WY 83001
PH: 377-733-5681
www.jacksonholenet.com
Entertainment section covers local music.

Canada

A Better World
601 Magnetic Dr. # 8, Toronto, ON M3J-3J2
mastermail@abetterworld.ca
www.abetterworld.ca
Created to encourage artists to convey 'Better World' themes through their art form.

Association of Canadian Women Composers
www.acwc.ca
Active in the promotion of music written by Canadian women composers and endeavors to help these composers achieve a higher profile in the community.

AtlanticSeabreeze.com
283 Valermo Dr. Toronto, ON M8W 2L2
PH: 416-255-3127 FX: 416-255-8192
info@AtlanticSeabreeze.com
www.atlanticseabreeze.com
Supports Celtic, East Coast and Country music in Canada.

BandMix.ca
bandmix.ca
We promote your music. Make a profile and get exposure from our daily traffic. Post your gigs on your calendar.

Bedlam Society
Joel Carriere joel@bedlamsociety.com
www.bedlamsociety.com
Emo, Rock, Punk ...from BC to PEI, we've got you covered! Find local show listings, read reviews, or just turn your mind to mush on the message board!

Borealis Recording Company
225 Sterling Rd. #19, Toronto, ON M6R 2B2
PH: 416-530-4288 FX: 416-530-0461
info@borealisrecords.com
www.borealisrecords.com
The best in Canadian Folk music.

Bullfrog Music
PO Box 5036, 1625 Fort St., Victoria, BC V8R 6N3
PH: 250-370-5448
jeremiah@bullfrogmusic.com
www.bullfrogmusic.com
Bringing self-produced Canadian music to the world.

Canada.com
www.canada.com
Post your event news! (check for the contact e-mail for your city).

Canada Noise
canadanoise.com
Everything related to the Canadian independent music scene. Be it news, reviews, interviews ...you name it.

Canadian Academy of Recording Arts and Sciences (CARAS)
355 King St. W. #501, Toronto, ON M5V 1J6
PH: 416-485-3135 FX: 416-485-4978
info@carasonline.ca
www.carasonline.ca
Development of opportunities to showcase and promote Canadian artists and music.

Canadian Amateur Musicians
www.cammac.ca
Creating opportunities for musicians of all levels.

Canadian Celtic Music
Kimberley kimberley@islandviewcreations.com
members.shaw.ca/kimberleyw/canadacelticmusic
Musician's websites, tour date, news and more.

Canadian Copyright Act
webadmin@justice.gc.ca
laws.justice.gc.ca/en/C-42
Important information on the Canadian copyright act.

Canadian Country Music Association
www.ccma.org
Developing Canadian Country music.

Canadian Cowboy Country Magazine
#4, 9343- 50th St., Edmonton, AB T6B 2L5
PH: 800-943-7336
www.canadiancowboy.ca
Features a Country music review in each edition.

Canadian Electroacoustic Community
cec.concordia.ca
Network for the flow and exchange of information and ideas.

Canadian Gospel Music Association
www.cgmaonline.com
Promoting the growth and ministry of the Christian music arts in Canada.

Canadian Guitar Players Association
www.guitarassociation.org
Sharing information and helping one another in developing individual talents.

Canadian Intellectual Property Office
50 Victoria St. Rm. C-229, Gatineau, QC K1A 0C9
PH: 819-953-7620
cipo.contact@ic.gc.ca
strategis.gc.ca/sc_mrksv/cipo
Responsible for intellectual property (copyright and trademarks) in Canada.

Canadian Music Center
20 St. Joseph St., Toronto, ON M4Y 1J9
PH: 4160961-6601 FX: 416-961-7198
info@musiccentre.ca
www.musiccentre.ca
Collecting, distributing and promoting music by Canada's composers.

Canadian Music Creators Coalition
musiccreators@gmail.com
www.musiccreators.ca
Sharing the common goal of having our voices heard about the laws and policies that affect our livelihoods.

Canadian Musical Reproduction Rights Agency (CMRRA)
56 Wellesley St. W. #320, Toronto, ON M5S 2S3
PH: 416-926-1966 FX: 416-926-7521
inquiries@cmrra.ca
www.cmrra.ca
Represents the vast majority of music copyright owners (usually called music publishers) doing business in Canada. Issues licenses and collects royalties for the use of music on CDs and other products.

Canadian Musician
23 Hannover Dr. #7, St., Catharines, ON L2W 1A3
PH: 905-641-3471 FX: 905-641-1648
mail@nor.com
www.canadianmusician.com
Showcases unsigned Canadian acts.

Canadian Newspaper and News Media Database
www.abyznewslinks.com/canad.htm
Links to hundreds of Canadian newspapers.

Canadian Society for Traditional Music
www.yorku.ca/cstm
Articles, notices and reviews on all aspects of Canadian Folk music.

CanadianBands.com
#17-5612 53rd Ave. Cold Lake, AB T9M 1R7
canconrox@excite.com
www.canadianbands.com
Submit band info, gigs, reviews etc.

canEHdian.com
PO Box 119, Heatherton, NS B3M 4H4
info@canehdian.com
www.canehdian.com
Everything music for Canada. Professional review site.

Canuck Blues
admin@canuckblues.ca
www.canuckblues.ca
Created for the promotion of Canuck Blues music.

CBC Records
PO Box 500 Stn. A, Toronto, ON M5W 1E6
PH: 416-555-1212 FX: 416-205-2139
www.cbcrecords.cbc.ca
Making the music of Canadian performers available to music lovers around the world.

Chart Magazine
41 Britain St. #200, Toronto, ON M5A 1R7
PH: 416-363-3101 FX: 416-363-3109
chart@chartattack.com
www.chartattack.com
Canadian college radio and retail charts, reviews and lots more.

Choose The Blues Productions
65 Williams St. W., Smiths Falls, ON K7A 1N5
PH: 613-283-8830 FX: 613-283-3273
info@choosetheblues.ca
choosetheblues.ca
Bringing you the best in the Blues with a focus on Canadian talent. Artist management, event production etc.

COBA Collective Of Black Artists
610 Queen St. W. 2nd Fl. Toronto, ON M6J 1E3
PH: 416-658-3111 FX: 416-658-9980
info@cobainc.com
www.cobainc.com
Dedicated to the creation and production of dance and music while preserving cultural traditions of the African Diaspora.

Coffeehouse Arts & Culture
SpiceTea@coffeehouse.ca
www.coffeehouse.ca
Networking the artist, their community of friends, audience and venues where they meet.

Concept Entertainment Ltd.
20421 89A Ave. Langley, BC V1M 1A9
PH: 604-882-6908 FX: 604-882-6928
Mario Brox mario@conceptentertainment.net
www.conceptentertainment.net
West Coast based promotion agency featuring Canadian talent in Europe.

Earshot Concerts
23 Herman Ave. Toronto, ON M6R 1Y1
PH: 416-538-2006
Scott Good ad@earshotconcerts.ca
www.earshotconcerts.ca
Produces concerts of new Canadian Art music.

EventInfo.ca
email@eventinfo.ca
www.eventinfo.ca
We'll list any type of event in Canada for free. We also list artist profiles, venue locations, event promoter profiles etc.

!*@# Exclaim!
7-B Pleasant Blvd. #966, Toronto, ON M4T 1K2
PH: 416-535-9735
Ian Danzig ian@exclaim.ca
www.exclaim.ca
Coverage of new music across all genres of Canadian cutting-edge artists.

Federation of Canadian Music Festivals
www.fcmf.org
An umbrella organization for 230 local and provincial festivals.

Festival Distribution
1351 Grant St., Vancouver, BC V5L 2X7
PH: 604-253-2662 FX: 604-253-2634
fdi@festival.bc.ca
www.festival.bc.ca
Distributor of Canadian Indie music of all genres.

Folk Alliance Canada
info@folkalliancecanada.org
www.folkalliancecanada.org
Helps you create, perform and market your Folk music here and internationally.

GuitarsCanada
www.guitarscanada.com
Helps out any up and coming Canadian bands. Submit your info.

HERIZONS
PO Box 128, Winnipeg, MB R3C 2G1
PH: 888-408-0028
Penni Mitchell editor@herizons.ca
www.herizons.ca
Feminist magazine. We focus on Canadian female Indie musicians.

hiphopcanada.com
532 Montreal Rd. #493, Ottawa, ON K1K 4R4
PH: 613-749-7777 FX: 613-747-9317
submissions@hiphopcanada.com
www.hiphopcanada.com
Send artist press kits, new updates etc.

Indie Band Canada
162 St. John's Rd. Toronto, ON M6P 1T9
Winston So webmaster@indiebandcanada.com
www.indiebandcanada.com
Community for bands to network and display their music. Free artist website and internet radio exposure.

Indie Can Music
301 Dupont St., Toronto, ON M5R 1W1
PH: 416-239-8737
Joe Chisolm info@indiecan.com
www.indiecan.com
Online community where fans, bands and industry insiders meet.

Indie Pool
118 Berkeley St., Toronto, ON M5A 2W9
PH: 416-424-4666 FX: 416-424-4265
mail@indiepool.com
www.indiepool.com
Provides an affordable distribution alternative.

jambands.ca
www.jambands.ca
Bringing together great bands and appreciative fans.

JamHub.ca
www.jamhub.ca
Canada's online Jam Bands community.

Jazz Canadiana
bebop@sympatico.ca
www.jazzcanadiana.on.ca
For people everywhere who enjoy Jazz and the artists who make it happen.

JazzPromo.com
650 Dupont St. #503, Toronto, ON M6G 4B1
jazz@jazzpromo.com
www.jazzpromo.com/canadajazz.php
Showcasing Canadian artists. Artist of the Month feature.

Linear Reflections
B-2837 Peatt Rd. Victoria, BC V9B 3V5
PH: 250-474-0692
Naomi de Bruyn nai@shaw.ca
www.linearreflections.com
An arts review e-zine, which deals with all genres of music.

LiveTourArtists
1451 White Oaks Blvd. Oakville, ON L6H 4R9
PH: 905-844-0097 FX: 905-844-9839
info@livetourartists.com
www.livetourartists.com
International booking agency representing talented artists.

MapleMusic
230 Richmond St. W. 11th Fl. Toronto, ON M5V 3E5
PH: 877-944-5144 FX: 416-961-1040
justcurious@maplemusic.com
www.maplemusic.com
Submit your info, gigs, sell your CD from our site and more.

Music By Mail Canada
rob_mcintyre@excite.com
www.musicbymailcanada.com
Canadian source for music.

Music is My Business
music.gc.ca
We'll help you better understand the inner workings of the Canadian music industry.

New Music Canada
PO Box 4600, Vancouver, BC V6B 4A2
PH: 877-955-6565 FX: 604-662-6594
mymusic@newmusiccanada.com
www.newmusiccanada.com
Send us your MP3s and we put it up on the site.

Opera.ca
www.opera.ca
Keeps members abreast of issues relating to artistic quality and creativity, education and audience development.

Orchestras Canada
www.oc.ca
The national service organization for all Canadian orchestras.

PhemPhat
Ebonnie Rowe phemphat@hotmail.com
www.phemphat.com
Created to foster the growth, education and promotion of women in all aspects of the Canadian Urban entertainment scene.

SMASHING LUMBER.COM
40 Baif Blvd. #313, Richmond Hill, ON L4C 5M9
info@smashinglumber.com
www.smashinglumber.com
Created to provide exposure opportunities for Canadian artists and help them navigate the tricky waters of the music business.

Songwriters Association of Canada
26 Soho St. #340, Toronto, ON M5T 1Z7
PH: 416-961-1588 FX: 416-961-2040
sac@songwriters.ca
www.songwriters.ca
Exclusively for Canadian composers, lyricists and songwriters.

stillepost.ca
stillepost.ca
Online music community with information from cities across Canada.

Supernova.com
PH: 416-635-8885 x333 FX: 416-638-6333
Kevin Bunting kevin@supernova.com
www.supernova.com
Free service where Canadian bands upload their music and create profiles.

Urban Music Association of Canada
www.umac.ca
Domestic and international promotion and development of Canadian Urban music.

UrbanFLOWcase
211 Yonge St., Toronto, ON M5B 1M4
PH: 416-214-5000
Aisha Wickham aisha@flow935.com
www.urbanflowcase.com
FLOW FM is committed to fostering Canadian artists who create music that reflects the station's unique Urban format.

The Wedge
muchmail@muchmusic.com
www.muchmusic.com/tv/thewedge
A weekly showcase of Alternative/Indie music videos on MuchMusic.

Words & Music
socan@socan.ca
www.socan.ca
SOCAN's publication. Music news and bios are done on a few members each month. New releases are also listed.

Zone Francophone
450, rue Rideau, bureau 405, Ottawa, ON K1N 5Z4
PH: 613-241-8770 FX: 613-241-6064
fccf@zof.ca
www.francoculture.ca
A site dedicated to francophone culture and arts.

Zoilus.com
c/o The Globe and Mail, 444 Front St. W., Toronto, ON M5V 2S9
Carl Wilson caligariscabinet@gmail.com
www.zoilus.com
I am an editor and critic at the Toronto Globe & Mail. My music column Overtones appears there every Saturday. Send me your CDs for review.

Alberta

2nd Floor Music Management
5739-68 St. NE., Calgary, AB T3J 1W1
PH: 403-285-3047
Chris Perrault chris@2ndfloor.ca
www.2ndfloor.ca
Management company assisting artists with direction and development.

ALBERTA Metal
64261-5512 4th St. NW., Calgary, AB T2K 6J0
Christine Garton admin@albertametal.net
www.albertametal.net
Canadian Metal bands may submit a profile and MP3.

ALTAsound Independent Bands Site
webmaster@altasound.com
www.altasound.com
A site for Alberta bands with MP3s, charts, spotlights, band stores, biographies, contacts ...

Bignote Entertainment
87 Tuscany Springs Way NW., Calgary, AB T3L 2N4
PH: 403-668-0880 FX: 403-286-5773
Jim Samuelson jim@bignote.net
bignote.net
Our mission is simple: to bring audiences and artists together in the creation of great musical experiences!

CalgaryPlus.ca
PH: 403-228-1800 FX: 403-240-5669
www.calgaryplus.ca
Post your music events.

Dark Calgary
webmaster@darkcalgary.com
www.darkcalgary.com
A means for local Goth artists and organizers to promote their creations.

Dose Calgary
www.dose.ca/calgary
A free daily online magazine. One of the key areas of our website is promotion of Indie bands.

Dose Edmonton
www.dose.ca/edmonton
A free daily online magazine. One of the key areas of our website is promotion of Indie bands.

Edmonton Composers' Concert Society
www.eccsociety.com
Our vision is to ensure that the musical works of composers from Edmonton, as well as Alberta, Canada and the rest of the world, are made fully accessible to and for the Canadian public.

EdmontonPlus.ca
PH: 403-228-1800 FX: 403-240-5669
www.edmontonplus.ca
Online A&E magazine covering the local music scene.

FFWD
1902-B 11th St. SE. Calgary, AB T2G 3G2
PH: 403-244-2235 FX: 403-244-1431
Kirsten Kosloski kkosloski@ffwd.greatwest.ca
www.ffwdweekly.com
Calgary's news and entertainment weekly.

Foothills Bluegrass Music Society
www.melmusic.com/fbms
Promoting Bluegrass music in Calgary.

The Gauntlet
RM. 319, MacEwan Students' Ctr.
2500 University Dr. NW., Calgary, AB T2N 1N4
PH: 403-220-4376
entertainment@gauntlet.ucalgary.ca
gauntlet.ucalgary.ca
U. of Calgary's student paper. Large music section.

Megatunes
CAL: customer.service@megatunes.com
EDM: edmt.customer.service@megatunes.com
www.megatunes.com
An independent music store located in Calgary and Edmonton.

SEE Magazine
10275 Jasper Ave. #200, Edmonton, AB T5J 1X8
PH: 780-430-9003 FX: 780-432-1102
info@see.greatwest.ca
www.seemagazine.com
Edmonton's weekly source for news, arts and entertainment.

British Columbia

B.C. Country Music Association
www.bccountry.com
Promotes the BC Country music community.

BC Touring Council
PO Box 547, Nelson, BC V1L 5R3
PH: 250-352-0021 FX: 250-352-0027
fyi@bctouring.org
www.bctouring.org
Expands touring opportunities for artists.

Brand X Media
106-715 Vancouver St., Victoria, BC V8V 3V2
Jesse Ladret jesse@brandxmedia.ca
www.brandxmedia.ca
Reviews music predominantly from Western Canada, covering all genres of music.

Cd Isle
1527 Extension Rd. Nanaimo, BC V9X 1A6
PH: 250 754-3170
Ric Lafontaine info@cdisle.ca
www.cdisle.ca
A CD store & archive of artists living on Vancouver Island, the Sunshine Coast and all islands in BC.

CFOX New Music Page
#2000-700 W. Georgia, Vancouver, BC V7Y 1K9
PH: 604-684-7221 FX: 604-331-2755
webmaster@cfox.com
www.cfox.com/shows/indie_night.cfm
Are you a local band looking for some exposure? Got some songs we can put up? Contact us!

Cosmic Debris
PO Box 90, Duncan, BC V9L 3X1
Guy Langlois cosmic@cvnet.net
www.cvnet.net/cosmic
Entertainment magazine covering the local music scene.

Cowichan Folk Guild
www.folkfest.bc.ca
Preserves and promotes local Folk artists.

Gothic BC
www.gothic.bc.ca
British Columbia's Gothic source.

Hornby Island Blues Society
www.hornby-blues.bc.ca
Connects listeners and players of Blues music.

KelownaGigs
www.kelownagigs.com
Your local, up to date concert listings.

liquidbeat.com
www.liquidbeat.com
Underground Dance community site catering to the BC interior.

Monday Magazine
818 Broughton, Victoria, BC V8W 1E4
PH: 250-382-6188 x132
John Threlfall johnt@mondaymag.com
web.bcnewsgroup.com/portals/monday
Victoria's weekly entertainment magazine.

The Nerve Magazine
508-825 Granville St., Vancouver, BC V6Z 1K9
PH: 604-734-1611 FX: 604-684-1698
info@thenervemagazine.com
www.thenervemagazine.com
The Northwest's Rock n' Roll magazine.

Okanagan Music Online
4140 Hwy. 6, Lumby, BC V0E 2G7
PH: 250 547-2312
info@okanaganmusic.ca
www.okanaganmusic.com
The largest and most established music website in the Okanagan Valley.

The Pacific Music Industry Association
www.musicbc.org
Supports and promotes the spirit, development and growth of the BC music community.

Rave Victoria
thefolks@ravevictoria.com
www.ravevictoria.com
Provides DJ sets for download by the community.

SaltSpringMusic.Com
328 Lower Ganges Rd. Salt Spring Island, BC V8K 2V3
PH: 250-475-5896 FX: 250-537-2613
info@saltspringmusic.com
www.saltspringmusic.com
We have begun to expand to take in other Western Canadian artists.

Victoria Fiddle Society
www.bckitchenparty.com
A fiddle community for all persons interested in fiddle music in the Victoria region.

Victoria Jazz Society
www.vicjazz.bc.ca
Presenting high quality Jazz to the community.

West Kootenay Bluegrass Site
pickingrinin@shaw.ca
www.westkootenaybluegrass.com
All the info on the local Bluegrass scene.

Vancouver

Beyond Robson
beyondrobson.com/music
Blog covering Vancouver arts and entertainment.

Coastal Jazz & Blues Society
www.jazzvancouver.com
Covering the Jazz scene both locally and nationally.

DISCORDER
c/o CITR, #233-6138 SUB Blvd. Vancouver,
BC V6T 1Z1
PH: 604-822-3017 x3
discorder.citr.ca
An Indie review magazine published by CITR FM.

Dose Vancouver
www.dose.ca/vancouver
A free daily online magazine. One of the key areas of our website is promotion of Indie bands.

From Blown Speakers
Quinn quinn.omori@gmail.com
itcameoutmagical.blogspot.com
MP3 blog covering the Vancouver and Pacific NW music scene.

Live Music In Vancouver
Kristine Morrison
kristine@livemusicinvancouver.com
www.livemusicinvancouver.com
The main focus of the website is photos of local bands.

Rogue Folk Club
www.roguefolk.bc.ca
Vancouver area folk dancing, jam sessions etc.

Georgia Straight
1701 W. Broadway, Vancouver, BC V6J 1Y3
PH: 604-730-7000 FX: 604-730-7010
www.straight.com
Mag covering the active urban West Coast lifestyle.

LiveMusicVancouver.com
PH: 604-871-0477
Sati Muthanna sati@LiveMusicVancouver.com
livemusicvancouver.com
Covering local music with news, gigs, resources etc.

oscillations.ca
comments@oscillations.ca
oscillations.ca
The source for New Music events and performances in Vancouver and the surrounding region.

Pacific Bluegrass and Heritage Society
www.pacificbluegrass.bc.ca
Host's jams, workshops, concerts and other special events.

Spawner Records
PO Box 93046, Langley, BC V3A 8H2
staff@spawnerrecords.com
www.spawnerrecords.com
Label run by bands for bands from Vancouver.

VanCityBands.com
www.vancitybands.com
Showcasing unsigned Vancouver Indie music!

Vancouver Courier
1574 W. 6th Ave. Vancouver, BC V6J 1R2
PH: 604-738-1411
www.vancourier.com
Vancouver news and entertainment. Covers local music.

vancouverJazz.com
www.vancouverjazz.com
Reviews, news, interviews etc.

Vancouver World Music Collective
www.vancouverworldmusic.org
Promoting our music and city internationally.

Westender
1490 W. Broadway #200, Vancouver, BC V6H 4E8
PH: 604-742-8686
www.westender.com
Vancouver's urban voice. Covers local music.

Western Front Society
303 E. 8th Ave. Vancouver, BC V5T 1S1
PH: 604-876-9343 FX: 604-876-4099
Debbie Boyko music@front.bc.ca
www.front.bc.ca
Produces and promotes contemporary media.

Manitoba

Backstage Winnipeg
500 Carlaw Ave. Winnipeg, MB R3L 0V1
Kristie Allen info@backstagewinnipeg.com
www.backstagewinnipeg.com
Dedicated to promoting the Indie scene. We offer monthly interviews, show reviews, CD reviews and more!

Blues Music in Winnipeg
webmaster@winnipegblues.com
www.winnipegblues.com
Blues reviews, news, previews and more.

Manitoba Audio Recording Industry Association
www.manitobamusic.com
Helps anyone involved with music in Manitoba.

Manitoba Blues Society
www.mbblues.mb.ca
Promotes, fosters and supports the Blues in Manitoba.

Manitoba OldTyme & Bluegrass Society
www.manitobabluegrass.ca
All the info on the local Bluegrass scene.

Musicians Network
90 Greensboro Sq. Winnipeg, MB R3T 4L1
Mike Garbutt riffvandal@mts.net
www.bytes4u.ca
Join a band, form a band, tour, record or jam and more.

Uptown Magazine
1465 St. James St., Winnipeg, MB R3H 0W9
PH: 204-949-4370 FX: 204-949 4376
www.uptownmag.com
Winnipeg's online source for arts, entertainment & news.

Winnipeg Classical Guitar Society
www.winnipegclassicalguitarsociety.org
Promoting the Classical guitar in Winnipeg.

Winnipeg Early Music Society
www.mts.net/~mhultin/wems.htm
Gives members opportunities to perform.

Winnipeg Metal
winnipegmetal.cjb.net
Online Metal community. Post shows, reviews, news etc.

New Brunswick

Argosy
152 Main St., Sackville, NB E4L 1B3
PH: 506-364-2236
argosy@mta.ca
argosy.mta.ca
Mount Allison U. independent student journal.

canadaeast.com
www.canadaeast.com
Local music covered in the entertainment section.

giraffecycle.com
webmaster@giraffecycle.com
www.giraffecycle.com
Dedicated to the Saint John Hardcore music scene.

Maritime Metal
www.discorporatemusic.com/MessageBoard
A forum is meant exclusively for Maritime Metal bands.

monctonlocals.com
admin@monctonlocals.com
www.monctonlocals.com
Covering the local music scene. Post your info!

Music New Brunswick
www.musicnb.org
Promoting and developing the New Brunswick music industry.

Newfoundland

AtlanticCanadianMusic.com
PO Box 847, Mount Pearl, NL A1N 3C8
PH: 709-744-5037 FX: 709-737-0912
info@atlanticcanadianmusic.com
www.atlanticcanadianmusic.com
We offer over 300 titles of music and audio books from Atlantic Canada.

Bluegrass and Oldtime Country Music Society of NFLD & Labrador
www.bluegrass-nl.ca
Fosters the awareness, development and growth of Bluegrass & Oldtime Country music in the province.

Music Industry Association of NFLD & Labrador
www.mia.nf.ca
Provides opportunities for local bands to grow. Our newsletter, "The Measure" features local artists.

nflocals.com
Dan Murray admin@nflocals.com
www.nflocals.com
The very best in underground culture.

Nova Scotia

Castlebay Music
904 Castlebay Rd. Cape Breton, NS B1T 1J6
PH: 902-379-2343
tracey@castlebaymusic.com
www.castlebaymusic.com
Cape Breton and East Coast music.

cblocals.com
Eli Richards bands@cblocals.com
www.cblocals.com
Covering the Cape Breton underground culture.

Celtic Music Interpretive Centre
www.celticmusicsite.com
Promoting the traditional music of Cape Breton Island through education and performance.

The Coast
5435 Portland Pl. Halifax, NS B3K 6R7
PH: 902-422-6278 FX: 902-425-0013
Tara Thorne tarat@thecoast.ca
www.thecoast.ca
Submit info about your event, performance or gig to us.

East Coast Catalogue Company Ltd.
45 Madeira Cr. Dartmouth, NS B2W 6G7
PH: 800-461-3361 FX: 902-492-8770
www.eastcoastcatalogue.com
Mail order retailer of Atlantic Canadian products.

Halifamous Music Forum
2570 Sherwood St., Halifax, NS B3L 3G8
PH: 902-499-4682
Greg Bates greg@halifamous.com
www.halifamous.com
Hip Hop community where you can post music, images, lyrics etc. for evaluation by other members.

halifaxlocals.com
Sean MacGillivray admin@halifaxlocals.com
www.halifaxlocals.com
Connect to the Halifax underground culture.

JazzEast
PO Box 33043, Halifax, NS B3L 4T6
PH: 902-492-2225
www.jazzeast.com
Presents live Jazz concerts and workshops.

Maritime Metal
www.maritimemetal.net
Atlantic Canada's Metal community.

Music Industry Association of Nova Scotia
www.mians.ca
Promotes the local music industry in Nova Scotia.

Nova Scotia Punk Resource
www.punk.hfxns.org
Post your shows, news etc.

Rock In Halifax
www.rockinhalifax.net
News, updates, show listings etc.

Ontario

Barrie Folk Society
www.barriefolk.com
Supports artistic talent, style and creative vision.

BayToday.ca
664 Sherbrooke St., North Bay, ON P1B 2C6
PH: 705-497-9619 FX: 705-497-9671
Robert Palangio robert@rpkma.com
www.baytoday.ca
North Bay A&E publication. Post your news and events.

Brantford Folk Club
www.brantford.folk.on.ca
Keeping the tradition alive!

Brock Press
www.brockpress.com
Brock U. campus paper.

Canada South Blues Society
www.bluessociety.ca
Helping to keep the Blues alive in SW Ontario.

Cornwall Underground
The_Nads@hotmail.com
www.geocities.com/cornwallunderground
The best website for all the latest news in the Cornwall music scene.

Cuckoo's Nest Folk Club
www.cuckoosnest.folk.on.ca
Promoting traditional Folk music in London.

Dogbus Music
14 Oak St., Lindsay, ON K9V 5K4
Ryan Oliver ryanoliver@dogbusonline.com
www.dogbusonline.com
We're always looking for new Punk bands to support and help grow their message.

ECHO Weekly
19 King St. E. 2nd Fl. Kitchener, ON N2G 2K4
PH: 519-220-1594 FX: 519-743-7491
www.echoweekly.com
Weekly alternative magazine covering the greater Kitchener/Waterloo/Cambridge/Guelph area.

The Ford Plant
1 King St., Brantford, ON N3R 3V9
PH: 519-754-4859
thefordplant@gmail.com
www.thefordplant.ca
Founded to help re-vitalize Brantford's struggling art and music community.

Grand River Blues Society
www.grandriverblues.org
Encouraging a greater appreciation of the music being created in our community.

Imprint
Student Life Center, Rm. 1116, U. Waterloo,
Waterloo, ON N2L 3G1
PH: 519-888-4048 FX: 519-884-7800
Margaret Clark arts@imprint.uwaterloo.ca
imprint.uwaterloo.ca
U. Waterloo's student paper.

The Journal
272 Earl St., Kingston, ON K7L 2H8
PH: 613-533-2800 FX: 613-533-6728
journal_ae@ams.queensu.ca
www.queensjournal.ca
Queens U.'s student paper.

Kingston Jazz Society
kingstonjazz.com
Preserving Jazz music in the Limestone City.

London INDIE
www.londonindie.com
We are attempting to re-establish the London scene.

London Hardcore
www.londonhardcore.com
Local discussion board. Talk about upcoming shows, reviews, news etc.

The London Musicians' Association
www.londonmusicians.com
Benefits include our Booking Referral Service.

London Ontario Rox
930 N. Park Rd. PO Box 33044, Brampton,
ON L6S 3Y0
Josie info@londonontariorox.com
www.londonontariorox.com
Advertise your band, post your events.

LondonPunkRock.Kicks-Ass.org
Laurie ljwedge@shaw.ca
londonpunkrock.kicks-ass.org
If you would like to submit photos, add a link, promote a band, a CD or an upcoming gig, get in touch with us.

MyGigList.com
Box 1883, London, ON N6A 5J4
PH: 519-670-5066
Cora Linden webmistress@mygiglist.com
www.mygiglist.com
Promoting gigs, artists and venues in Southwestern Ontario... for free!

Niagara Blues & Jazz Society
www.niagarabluesandjazz.com
Enriching lives through a mutual appreciation of Blues and Jazz music and the preservation of its roots.

The Northern Bluegrass Committee
www.northernbluegrass.com
Promoting the local Bluegrass scene.

Northern Blues
225 Sterling Rd. #19, Toronto, ON M6R 2B2
PH: 416-536-4892 FX: 416-536-1494
info@northernblues.com
www.northernblues.com
Bringing you the best in world class Blues.

Ontario Council of Folk Festivals
www.ocff.ca
Website includes a list of upcoming Folk festivals.

Ontario Metal Pages
Tina tina@ontariometal.net
www.ontariometal.net
The ultimate authority on Metal in Ontario!

ontariopunk.com
PH: 416-499-3079
Shane Macaulay shane@ontariopunk.com
www.ontariopunk.com
News, reviews, interviews, contests etc.

Open Mics in Ontario
www.openmikes.org/calendar/ON

Orillia Folk Society
www.geocities.com/liveatjives/ofs1.html
Focus on local contemporary and traditional Folk music.

overhear
490 Castlefield Ave. Toronto, ON M5N 1L6
PH: 416-480-0788
webmaster@overhear.com
www.overhear.com
Listings for Ontario Indie artist and bands.

PartyInKingston.com
www.partyinkingston.com
Submit gig info, album reviews etc.

Pulse Niagra
243 Church St. #208, St. Catharines, ON L2R 3E8
PH: 905-682-5999 FX: 905-682-1414
www.pulseniagara.com
The Niagra region's weekly alternative paper.

Rock Crew Productions
14 Garrett St., Kingston, ON K7L 1H6
PH: 613-539-8438
chris@rockcrew.ca
www.rockcrew.ca
Presenting local, Canadian and international talent in Kingston's premier live venues.

royalcitymusic.ca
info@royalcitymusic.ca
www.royalcitymusic.ca
An online community for artists and fans from a variety of genres in the Guelph area.

Scene Magazine
PO Box 2302, London, ON N6A 4E3
PH: 519-642-4780 FX: 519-642-0737
music@scenemagazine.com
www.scenemagazine.com
London arts & entertainment magazine.

Scotia Entertainment
PH: 519-895-2723
104 Pattandon Ave. Kitchener, ON N2M 3S5
admin@scotiaentertainment.com
www.scotiaentertainment.com
Artist management & bookings, showcase events and event planning.

Steel City Music
www.steelcitymusic.ca
Website dedicated to the promotion of the Hamilton, Ontario music scene.

tbshows.com
www.tbshows.com
Covering the Thunder Bay Punk scene.

Thunder Bay Blues Society
www.thunderbaybluessociety.ca
Supports local, national and international Blues artists.

Traditions Folk Club
www.acoustictraditions.com/folkclub.html
Showcases local performers.

The Underground
1265 Military Trail, Rm. 207, Students Ctr.
Scarborough, ON M1C 1A4
PH: 416-287-7054 FX: 416-287-7055
info@the-underground.ca
the-underground.ca
U of T Scarborough student publication.

Upfront Magazine
325 Chatham St. W., Windsor, ON N9A 5M8
PH: 519-254-5268 FX: 519-254-6110
info@upfrontwindsor.com
www.upfrontwindsor.com
Windsor's independent news, music and art culture magazine.

VIEW Magazine
20 Jackson St. #300, Hamilton, ON L8P 1L2
PH: 905-527-3343 FX: 905-527-3721
www.viewmag.com
Greater Hamilton's weekly alternative.

Wow! Sudbury
info@wowsudbury.com
www.wowsudbury.com
Sudbury's entertainment website. Covers local music.

Ottawa

The Bear's Soundcheck
PH: 613-225-1069 x168 FX: 613-226-3381
soundcheck@thebear.fm
www.thebear.fm/content/soundcheck
Classified ads for musicians in Ottawa.

Blues4U
67 North St., Gatineau, QC J9H 2W8
steam@allblues4u.com
www.allblues4u.com
Covering the Ottawa Blues scene.

Dark Ottawa
darkottawa@gmail.com
community.livejournal.com/darkottawa
An alternative guide to Canada's capital.

Dose Ottawa
www.dose.ca/ottawa/music
A free daily online magazine. One of the key areas of our website is promotion of Indie bands.

Dummy Cream
Clem Lee dummycream@hotmail.com
myspace.com/dummycream
Local Punk zine full of local events, music reviews, poetry, stories, interviews and just any kind of crap I come up with.

The Humm
PO Box 1391, Almonte, ON K0A 1A0
editor@thehumm.com
www.thehumm.com
Ottawa Valley's arts, entertainment & ideas monthly newspaper.

National Capital Rock
Andrew Carver andcarver@hotmail.com
www.natcaprock.blogspot.com
I work on the opinion pages and review music for The Ottawa Sun, as well as take photographs at local gigs.

Ottawa Blues, Jazz and Swing Guide
bu932@ncf.ca
ottawabluesjazz.ca
Ottawa's one-stop Blues and Jazz event site.

Ottawa Blues Society
www.ottawabluessociety.com
Concert reviews and information on the scene.

Ottawa Chamber Music Society
www.chamberfest.com
Dedicated to presenting Chamber music of the highest possible artistic standard.

Ottawa Metal
Eric Mulligan ottawametal@hotmail.com
www.ottawametal.com
Covering Metal music in the Ottawa/Gatineau region.

The Ottawa Musician
www.theottawamusician.com
With continuing support, The OM site has a NEW feature promoting talented artist MP3s from the greater Ottawa area.

Ottawa Underground
ottawaunderground@yahoo.com
www.geocities.com/ottawaunderground
Covering the Ottawa Punk scene.

Ottawa Valley Bluegrass Music Association
www.valleygrass.ca
Promotes and publicizes Bluegrass music and activities.

Ottawa XPress
396 Cooper St. #204, Ottawa, ON K2P 2H7
PH: 6133-237-8226 FX: 613-237-8220
www.ottawaxpress.ca
Weekly paper. Coverage of local music.

OttawaJazz.com
kgrace@entrenet.com
www.ottawajazz.com
Lists upcoming gigs and special events.

OttawaMusicScene.Com
OttawaMusicScene.Com
Promotes the Ottawa area music scene.

OttawaPlus.ca
www.ottawaplus.ca
Online A&E guide. Submit your info.

OttawaStart
ottawastart.com
Add your events for free to our calendar.

punkottawa.com
PO Box 57043, 163 Bell St., Ottawa, ON K1R 6P0
PH: 613-234-7869
info@punkottawa.com
www.punkottawa.com
Covers the local Punk scene.

VOIR Ottawa/Gatineau
396 Cooper #204, Ottawa, ON K2P 2H7
PH: 613-237-8226 FX: 613-237-8220
www.voir.ca
A&E magazine. In French.

Toronto

10:51am Toronto
travis@1051am.com
www.toronto.1051am.com
Music & pop culture and other random wonderfulness from Toronto.

2 The Beat
161 Spadina Ave. Toronto, ON M5V 2L6
PH: 416-598-8120 FX: 416-598-9031
brian@2thebeat.com
2thebeat.com
Offers Electronic/Techno physical and online sales.

The Ambient Ping
2141 Kipling Ave. PO Box 30119, Etobicoke, ON M9W 6T1
info@theambientping.com
www.theambientping.com
Weekly musical performance event. Ambient, Soundscapes, Downtempo etc.

Are You Familiar?
areyoufamiliar@hotmail.com
areyoufamiliar.blogspot.com
MP3 blog with upcoming gigs, news and reviews.

ARRAYMUSIC
60 Atlantic Ave. #218, Toronto, ON M6K 1X9
PH: 416-532-3019 FX: 416-532-9797
info@arraymusic.com
www.arraymusic.com
Site for composers of all levels.

blogTO
info@blogto.com
www.blogto.com/music
Covers Toronto music, film, the arts, bars, restaurants, people, places and more.

Citygigs *Toronto*
#2 116 Pembroke St., Toronto, ON M5A 2N8
PH: 416-926-3711 FX: 416-926-3711
toronto@citygigs.com
www.citygigs.com
Reviews, interviews, concert previews and more!

Classic Jazz Society of Toronto
www.classicjazztoronto.com
Promotes the original form of Jazz.

Daughters of Invention
Jaime sin.jaime@gmail.com
daughtersofinvention.blogspot.com
MP3 blog with tracks, news and upcoming shows.

Dose Toronto
1450 Don Mills Rd. Toronto, ON M3B 2X7
info@dose.ca
www.dose.ca/toronto
A free daily online magazine. One of the key areas of our website is promotion of Indie bands.

eye
625 Church St. 6th Fl. Toronto, ON M4Y 2G1
PH: 416-596-4393
www.eye.net
Toronto's A&E weekly. Local music covered.

The Eyeopener
Student Campus Ctr. 55 Gould St. 2nd Fl. Toronto, ON M5B 1W7
PH: 416-979-5262 x2342
entertainment@theeyeopener.com
www.theeyeopener.com
Ryerson's independent student newspaper.

Flying Cloud Folk Club
www.flyingcloudfolk.ca
Information about the Toronto Folk music scene.

Guitar Society of Toronto
www.guitar-toronto.on.ca
Promoting the Classical guitar and artists.

Jazz in Toronto
3 St. Patrick St., Toronto, ON M5T 1T9
PH: 416-599-5486
jazz@jazzintoronto.com
www.jazzintoronto.com
The official guide to Jazz in Toronto.

kid with camera
David Waldman david@kidwithcamera.com
www.kidwithcamera.com
Print and online zine. Chronicle of photography and journal entries covering the Toronto Punk scene.

Maple Blues
www.torontobluessociety.com/maple.htm
Toronto Blues Society's magazine promoting local artists.

Music Gallery
www.musicgallery.org
Center for new and unusual music.

New Adventures in Sound Art
401 Richmond St. W. #358, Toronto, ON M5V 3A8
PH: 416-910-7231 FX: 905-454-7662
Nadene naisa@soundtravels.ca
www.soundtravels.ca
Produces performances and installations spanning the entire spectrum of Electroacoustic and Experimental Sound Art.

Nocturnal
info@nocturnalmagazine.net
www.nocturnalmagazine.net
Guide to the music and artists of Toronto.

NOW
189 Church St., Toronto, ON M5B 1Y7
PH: 416-364-1301
Sarah Liss sarahl@nowtoronto.com
www.nowtoronto.com
Extensive coverage of local music.

Rotate This
620 Queen St. W., Toronto, ON M6J 1E4
ilovespam@rotate.com
www.rotate.com
One of Toronto's best known independent record stores. We stock new releases from independent bands and artists from around the world.

Small World Music
29 Gwynne Ave. Toronto, ON M6K 2C2
PH: 416-536-5439 FX: 416-536-2742
Alan Davis alan@smallworldmusic.com
www.smallworldmusic.com
Created to promote World Music activity in Toronto.

Spill
3055 Harold Sheard Dr. Mississauga, ON L4T 1V4
PH: 905-677-8337 FX: 905-677-9705
info@spillmagazine.com
www.spillmagazine.com
Concert listings, show and CD reviews and more.

Toronto Blues Society
www.torontobluessociety.com
Promoting and preserving the Blues.

Toronto Downtown Jazz
82 Bleecker St., Toronto, ON M4X 1L8
PH: 416-928-2033 FX: 416-928-0533
tdjs@tojazz.com
www.torontojazz.com
Our missions is to promote the art of Jazz. Devoted to year round activities and initiatives.

Toronto Early Music Players Organization
www.chass.utoronto.ca/~dresher/TEMPO
Nurtures and encourages all early music.

Toronto-goth.com
tg@toronto-goth.com
www.toronto-goth.com
Resource for Toronto's Gothic/Industrial scene.

Toronto Hip Hop Online
RR #3, Parkhill, ON N0M 2K0
FX: 519-238-1224
Matt Eagleson matt@megacityhiphop.com
www.megacityhiphop.com
Gets exposure for your work. Reviews CDs.

ToRonTo HisPaNo.com
PH: 416-694-1834
info@torontohispano.com
www.torontohispano.com
Covering music in the Toronto Hispanic community.

Toronto Musicians' Association
www.torontomusicians.org
Our experience and support can help you achieve your goals.

toronto.com
www.toronto.com
Covers the local music scene.

The Varsity
21 Sussex Ave. Toronto, ON M5S 1J6
PH: 416-946-7600 x205
Jordan Brimm review@thevarsity.ca
www.thevarsity.ca
U. Toronto's student newspaper.

Wavelength
PO Box 86010, 670 Bloor St. W., Toronto, ON M6G 1L2
howdy@wavelengthtoronto.com
www.wavelengthtoronto.com
Underground music from Toronto and beyond.

Word Magazine
4-2880 Queen St. E. #123, Brampton, ON L6S 6H4
PH: 905-799-1630 FX: 905-799-2788
happenings@wordmag.com
www.wordmag.com
Toronto's Urban culture magazine.

Prince Edward Island

Alchemy Music
www.alchemymusic.net
PEI's leading music news and discussion website.

The Buzz
PO Box 1945, Charlottetown, PE C1A 7N5
PH: 902-628-1958 FX: 902-628-1953
buzzon@isn.net
www.buzzon.com
What's going on in the lively cultural scene of PEI.

East Coast Music Association
www.ecma.ca
Promote/celebrates music locally and globally.

peilocals.com
admin@peilocals.com
www.peilocals.com
The very best in the PEI underground scene.

Quebec

33-MTL.com
info@33-mtl.com
www.33mtl.com
Covering the Montreal Urban music scene.

Bandeapart.fm
1400 boul. Rene-Levesque E. 8E etage Montreal, QC H2L 2M2
PH: 514-597-5909 FX: 514-597-7373
bap@radio-canada.ca
www.bandeapart.fm
Magazine internet sur les musiques Alternatives francophones.

FOLQUÉBEC
www.folquebec.com
Increases recognition of Québéc's Folk music and dance culture.

Hour
355 W. St. Catharine 7th Fl. Montreal, QC H3B 1A5
PH: 514-848-0777 FX: 514-848-9004
info@hour.ca
www.hour.ca
Weekly news. Extensive coverage of local music.

Le Kop Shop
111 Roy E., Montreal, QC H2W 1M1
info@lekopshop.com
lekopshop.com
The freshest in fresh street art, ill tunes and all the things we love.

Midnight Poutine
midnightpoutine.ca/music
Blog covering the Montreal arts and entertainment scene.

Montreal Mirror
465 McGill St. 3rd Fl. Montreal, QC H2Y 4B4
PH: 514-393-1010 FX: 514-393-3173
www.montrealmirror.com
Weekly A&E paper. Covers local music.

Montreal Stage Show
PH: 514-831-4413
southriversiderecords@yahoo.ca
www.montrealstagereview.com
To help bands gain recognition through networking and simply getting you out on stage and into the public eye.

Montrealgroove
3750 Cremazie E. #305, Montreal, QC H2B 1A6
PH: 514-727-2737 FX: 514-727-2737
info@montrealgroove.com
www.montrealgroove.com
CD vendor for local Montreal artists.

MontrealMusicScene.com
info@montrealmusicscene.com
www.montrealmusicscene.com
Informing locals about the Montreal music scene.

MontrealPlus.ca
english.montrealplus.ca
Online A&E magazine covering the local music scene.

Quebec Hardcore
c/o Jeff Lambert, 898 Short #2 Sherbrooke, QC J1H 2G2
www.qchc.com
Promoting local bands, labels and organizations.

Quebec Punk Scene
660 Ave. Chouinard #4, Quebec City, QC G1S 3E4
info@quebecpunkscene.net
www.quebecpunkscene.net
La source #1 de la scène Punk Québécoise.

QuebecPlus.ca
www.quebecplus.ca
Online A&E magazine covering the local music scene.

Rimouski Metal
106 St. Germain E. #16, Rimouski, QC G5L 1A6
www.rimouskimetal.net
News, reviews, gig dates etc.

Sang Frais
C.P. Saint-Andre, B.P. 32111, Montreal, QC H2L 4Y5
info@sangfrais.com
www.sangfrais.com
Le 'zine Métal Québécoise 100% francophone.

SOPREF
info@sopref.org
www.sopref.org
Société pour la promotion de la relève musicale de l'espace francophone.

SubQuebec.com
186 Boul. Indutriel #201, Saint-Eustache, QC J7R 5C2
PH: 450-974-9339
www.subquebec.com
Covering the Hard Music scene in Quebec.

Sur Scene
www.surscene.qc.ca
Quebec music and arts scene.

TechnoQuebec.com
www.technoquebec.com
La porte d'entrée la plus électronique du web.

Thirty Below
1108 rue Dollar, Val-Belair, QC G3K 1W6
FX: 418-847-9815
thirtybelow@trentesouszero.com
www.trentesouszero.com
Quebec traditional and Folk music site.

Trois-Rivieres Metal
584 rue Principale, St-Boniface, QC G0X 2L0
PH: 819-535-3777
info@troisrivieresmetal.com
www.troisrivieresmetal.com
Ce site est une référence Metal pour la région de Trois-Rivières.

Velvetpanda
info@velvetpanda.com
www.velvetpanda.com
Montreal based podcast that videotapes the lives of cultural icons in their natural habitats and distributes this content via the internet.

Voir
internet@voir.ca
www.voir.ca
A&E magazine with editions for Montreal and Quebec City.

Vu d'ici / Seen From Here
Marie-Chantale Turgeon m-c@mcturgeon.com
www.mcturgeon.com/blog
Blogging about Montreal, music, the arts and pop culture.

Saskatchewan

The Carillon
RM. 227 Riddell Ctr., U. Regina, SK S4S 0A2
PH: 306-586-8867 FX: 306-586-7422
www.carillon.uregina.ca
U. Regina's student publication.

Regina Jazz Society
www.reginajazz.ca
Our newsletter covers local Jazz events.

Saskatchewan Country Music Association
www.scma.sk.ca
Promoting Saskatchewan Country music.

Saskatchewan Recording Industry Association
www.saskrecording.ca
The sound recording industries of Saskatchewan.

The Saskatoon Blues Society
www.saskatoonbluessociety.ca
Celebrates Blues music throughout Saskatchewan.

Saskatoon Jazz Society
www.jazzbassment.com
Jazz Rag newsletter covers local music events.

Saskmetal.com
www.saskmetal.com
Online Metal community. Post shows, reviews, news etc.

The Sheaf
93 Campus Dr. Rm. 108 Memorial Bldg. Saskatoon, SK S7N 5B2
PH: 306-966-8668 FX: 306-966-8699
www.thesheaf.com
U. Saskatchewan students' newspaper.

Threeohsix.org
PH: 306-880-3440
threeohsix.org
A cross-genre Underground music webzine.

Yukon

Jazz Society of Yukon
www.jazzyukon.ca
Our mandate is to develop, promote and present jazz in Yukon.

MusicYukon
www.musicyukon.com
Formed to help promote Yukon recording artists and help them get themselves export ready.

United Kingdom

AFunk
info@afunk.co.uk
www.afunk.co.uk
Interviews and reviews with UK Urban artists.

antifolk.co.uk
info@antifolk.co.uk.
www.antifolk.co.uk
Dedicated to the Antifolk scene in the UK.

Association of British Orchestras
www.abo.org.uk
Exists to support, develop and advance the interests and activities of the orchestras in the UK.

Association of Independent Music
www.musicindie.org
Designed to increase the market share & business potential of the UK independent Music Industry.

BandBase Online
bandbase.co.uk
Promote your band, up-to-the-minute "Gig Guide" and more!

Big-Gig Guide to Live Music
3 Eastbourne Gate, Taunton, Somerset, TA1 1SZ UK
PH: 01823-353-608
www.big-gig.co.uk
A music events guide, UK festival guide and live music forum section.

BIRDpages Record Review
www.birdpages.co.uk
Your online gateway to UK record dealers, record shops.

Blues Connection
john@bluesconnections.com
www.bluesconnections.com
Will write short reviews. Lists local UK Blues venues and other Blues information.

BritCaster.com
britcaster.com
Lists and forums on various podcasts based in the UK.

British Horn Society
www.british-horn.org
Dedicated to the art, craft and fun of horn playing.

British Music Information Centre (*BMIC*)
www.bmic.co.uk
Information on composers, live events programs and more.

British Musician's Union
www.musiciansunion.org.uk
Loads of resources and benefits for members.

BritishHipHop.co.uk
info@britishhiphop.co.uk
www.britishhiphop.co.uk
Showcases unknown Hip Hop acts from the UK.

Country Music In Britain
info@cmib.co.uk
www.cmib.co.uk
All the info on the Country music scene in the UK.

Entertainment Live UK
11, Ballam Close, Upton, Poole, Dorset,
BH16 5QU UK
PH: +44 (0)1202-621574
Simon Thomson entertainmentliveuk@eluk.co.uk
www.eluk.co.uk
Promoting, assisting and encouraging new and used bands. Profile page with graphics, MP3s, news etc.

falmusic.co.uk
PH: +44 (0)20-8816-8374
Rob info@falmusic.co.uk
www.falmusic.co.uk
Forum for musicians and venues near Falmouth.

Federation of Guitar Societies
www.federationofguitarsocieties.org.uk
Promoting the Classical guitar and related instruments.

Jazz Services / Jazz UK
26 The Balcony, Castle Arcade, Cardiff,
CF10 2BY UK
PH: 029 2066 5161 FX: 029-2066-5160
jazzuk.cardiff@virgin.net
www.jazzservices.org.uk
Supporting the UK Jazz scene.

lovealbatross
albatross@lovealbatross.com
www.lovealbatross.com
Free promotion for unsigned bands in the UK.

M. J. MusicShop
PH: 01553-617546
Merv J. Flutter admin@mjmusicshop.co.uk
www.mjmusicshop.co.uk
Are you a British Country artist? Would you like us to sell your CDs?

Music Jobs UK
PH: 020-7253-8581
uk.music-jobs.com
The UK's Music Industry central point for employment seekers & employers.

Musician-Online.com
29-33 Berners St., London, W1T 3AB UK
www.musician-online.com
Advertise yourself, your band and concerts for free.

musicians-web.co.uk
webmaster@musicians-web.co.uk
www.musicians-web.co.uk
Connect with musicians across the land.

nuArts
14 King St. Glasgow, G1 5QP UK
PH: 0141-552 8641
kate@nuarts.co.uk
www.nuarts.co.uk/music
Provides video, photographic and graphic artwork services ideal for emerging acts.

OurBand.net
Studio 2, Keystone House, Exeter Rd.
Bournemouth, BH2 5AR UK
PH: 01202-298882 FX: 01202-298883
Bob bob@ourband.net
www.ourband.net
Promotion service for local bands.

Profile Heaven Music
www.profileheaven.com
A leading conduit between bands and fans in the UK.

PromoteMyGig.com
www.PromoteMyGig.com
A fast, reliable and efficient service to get gigs promoted easily.

Real UK Music
www.realukmusic.co.uk
Resource for events, venues, festivals, clubs performers, concerts studios etc.

shoegaze.co.uk
www.shoegaze.co.uk
Forum for lovers of Shoegazer and Dream Pop worldwide.

Society for the Promotion of New Music
(*spnm*)
www.spnm.org.uk
Promotes music composed by musicians born in the UK.

soundsxp
30 Somerville Rd. London, SE20 7NA UK
submissions@soundsxp.com
www.soundsxp.com
Push your product. Indie, Punk and Electronica. UK releases only!

swampmusic
PO Box 94, Derby, DE22 1XA UK
chrishall@swampmusic.co.uk
www.swampmusic.demon.co.uk
Guide to all things Cajun & Zydeco in the UK.

The Talent Scout
PO Box 10349, London, NW1 9WJ UK
PH: 0207-864-1300
info@thetalentscout.co.uk
www.thetalentscout.co.uk
Gives unsigned bands the chance to get recognized.

talentSTAR
PO Box 111, Derwentside, DH9 8YR UK
PH: 0800-043-6990
info@talentstar.net
www.talentstar.net
Giving opportunities through performing and promotion to up and coming music performers.

Tommy Shots
Adam cubak@hotmail.com
tommyshots.blogspot.com
Takes the best of new UK music and puts it to people everywhere.

Traffic Online
6 Stucley Pl. London, NW1 8NS UK
teams@trafficonline.net
www.trafficonline.net
We build, maintain and coordinate street teams in the UK for bands and record labels.

tourdates.co.uk
www.tourdates.co.uk
Listings of all major local upcoming events.

UK-Flava (*Strictly UK*)
5 Florence Nightingale House, London, N1 2PL UK
hello@uk-flava.com
www.uk-flava.com
Working with local artists. Accepts demos.

UK Gospel
www.ukgospel.com
Reviews some of the best Urban projects in the country.

UK Metal Underground
16D Grahams Rd. Falkirk, FK1 1HS UK
Lisa Coverdale lisa@ukmetalunderground.com
www.myspace.com/ukmetalunderground
We support and promote the UK Metal scene both within the UK and abroad.

UK Mix
webmaster@ukmix.net
www.ukmix.net
Your guide to the UK music scene starts here.

UK Newspaper and News Media Database
www.abyznewslinks.com/uking.htm
Links to hundreds of UK newspapers.

UKbands.net
www.ukbands.net
THE one-stop music promotion portal for UK artists.

ukevents.net
PH: 07733-295387
www.ukevents.net
Guide to music events in the UK.

ukhh.com (*UK Hip Hop*)
PO Box 49654, London, N8 7YB UK
info@ukhh.com
www.ukhh.com
A chance to gain exposure for all UK Hip Hop acts.

UKMusic.com
management@ukmusic.com
www.ukmusic.com
We have the perfect mix of music news, features, interviews and reviews from all your favourite UK artists!

UKmusicsearch
PO Box 176, Tavistock, PL19 1AP UK
Mike Bond mike@ukmusicsearch.co.uk
www.ukmusicsearch.co.uk
News, reviews and more. Send us your music!

Venuesandbands.com
PO Box 37, Ottery St. Mary, EX11 1WW UK
PH: 01404-814521
venuesandbands.com
Provides the tools for venues and bands to fully interact with each other.

England

AcoustiCity.co.uk
21 Constantine Rd. Colchester, Essex,
CO3 3DU UK
info@acousticity.co.uk
www.acousticity.co.uk
Reviews, links & listings for local Acoustic based music.

Alternative Devon
tom@alternativedevon.co.uk
www.alternativedevon.co.uk
A free MP3 hosting service for bands from the Southwest.

AuralVox
8-10 Fore St., Newquay, Cornwall, TR7 1LN UK
PH: 07837448345
atekdave@auralvox.co.uk
auralvox.co.uk
Music promotion for bands and artists in Cornwall.

Barratt Folk
www.barrattfolk.co.uk
Focusing on Folk Music around the Central South Coast of England.

BEDFORD METAL
bedfordmetal@hotmail.com
www.Bedfordmetal.co.uk
Promote the Rock, Punk, Goth and Metal scene in the Bedford & surrounding area.

Bedford Unplugged
music@bedfordunplugged.co.uk
www.bedfordunplugged.co.uk
If you want your Bedford area 100% live music listed FREE, please send us an e-mail.

Birmingham Jazz
www.birminghamjazz.co.uk
Providing the best in Jazz and contemporary music.

Birmingham Music Network
www.birminghammusicnetwork.co.uk
Promotes all related music businesses operating within the region.

Bowlie
www.bowlie.com
Indie Pop online community, covering gigs, club nights, record releases, current affairs ...

Bromley Guitar Society
www.bromleyguitarsociety.org.uk
Created to encourage local interest in the Classical guitar.

Concrete Chaos
info@concretechaos.co.uk
www.concretechaos.co.uk
News, reviews, interviews etc. covering the Buckingham scene.

Devon Folk Music
www.devonfolk.co.uk
Serving the whole of Devon in all aspects of Folk.

Dorset Blues Society
www.bluesnights.co.uk
For Blues lovers everywhere.

Dorset Guitar Society
www.dorsetguitarsociety.org.uk
Promoting music via solo and ensemble performances, master classes, workshops and concerts.

English Folk Dance & Song Society
www.efdss.org
Provides support and assistance to anyone interested in the Folk arts.

Essex Folk Association *efn Magazine*
37 Sidwell Ave. Benfleet, Essex, SS7 1LF UK
PH: 44-01268-793905
www.pvcw.freeserve.co.uk
Folk articles, record reviews, songs and tunes.

Fat Northerner Records
Langley Lane Farm, Middleton, Manchester,
M24 5LJ UK
PH: 0161-610-7516
staff@fatnortherner.com
www.fatnortherner.com
Developing and releasing music by good musicians from the North of England.

Folk Around Bristol
folkaroundbristol.co.uk
Gives local and new Folk bands a chance.

Folk London
4A Kenilworth Rd. Petts Wood, Kent, BR5 1DY UK
PH: 44-01-689-825-263
Sheila Finn folklondon@hotmail.com
www.grove-cottage.demon.co.uk/folklon
Folk clubs and events in London and the Southeast of England.

Folk North West
7, Sunleigh Rd. Hindley, Wigan, Lancashire,
WN2 2RE UK
webmaster@folknorthwest.co.uk
www.folknorthwest.co.uk
News, reviews of live events, CDs & more.

Folk Talk
57, Lloyds Ave. Scunthorpe N. Lincolnshire,
DN17 1BY UK
PH: 01724-844241
Jim Hancock Jim@folktalk.co.uk
www.folktalk.co.uk
The magazine for Folk music in Lincolnshire & East Yorkshire.

Folkus
55 The Strand, Fleetwood, Lancs, FY7 8NP UK
PH: 01253-872317 FX: 01253-878382
www.folkus.co.uk
Deals with local and international talent.

Fresh Sounds
PO Box 2760, Caterham, CR3 6WW UK
PH: 0870-609-3683 FX: 0870-486-0348
Michael East contact@fresh-sounds.co.uk
www.fresh-sounds.co.uk
Showcases unsigned bands in Britain.

Gigwise
4th Fl. Gostins Bldg. 32-34 Hanover St., Liverpool,
L1 4LN UK
andy@gigwise.com
www.gigwise.com
Covering the Liverpool music scene. Gigs, reviews, news etc.

GlassWerk Media
www.glasswerk.co.uk
The Northwest's premier website for unsigned musical artists. Visit our website for the contact information in your area.

Greenwood Classical Guitar Society
www.greenwoodgs.org.uk
Encouraging and developing Classical guitar playing.

Herts & Essex Live Band Photos
livebandphotos@gmail.com
www.livebandphotos.co.uk
Live bands, pubs & music venues in the Herts & Essex Area. Includes Herts & Essex area band news.

¡JAMMING!
Tony Fletcher tony@ijamming.net
www.ijamming.net
A music and lifestyle website hosted by author, journalist and DJ Tony Fletcher.

irLondon
PH: 07717-798-483
matty@irLondon.co.uk
www.irlondon.co.uk
Online club/gig guide as well as reviews & news.

josaka
www.josaka.com
Supporting live music in Berkshire. Gig and CD reviews, venue information, news and a lot more.

Kent and East Sussex Gig Guide
chris@kentgigs.com
kentgigs.com
Listings are updated every week!

leeds music scene
PH: 07005-964-458
info@leedsmusicscene.net
www.leedsmusicscene.net
Includes an extensive CD review, live, news and interview archive, gig guide and previews.

Lemonrock
editor@lemonrock.com
www.lemonrock.com
The live music guide for London and the Southeast. Gig listings, MP3 clips and gig reviews.

Live Circuit
14 John Barker Pl. Hitchin, Hertfordshire, S
G5 2PE UK
Roger roger@livecircuit.net.
www.livecircuit.net
Dedicated to providing facilities to nurture Hertfordshire's up and coming original music talent.

London Gig Guide
Ms. Tricitybendix tricity@howdoesitfeel.co.uk
www.howdoesitfeel.co.uk/londongigguide.html
If you have a show that you'd like to submit for inclusion, e-mail us.

London Musicians Collective
www.l-m-c.org.uk
Promotes Improvised and Experimental music via concerts and an annual festival.

londonimprov.com
admin@londonimprov.com
www.londonimprov.com
Home for the London Improv scene.

LondonNet *London Music Guide*
www.londonnet.co.uk
News and reviews of local music.

Low Life Records
19 Devonshire St., London, W1G 7AH UK
PH: 44-208-324-2400
info@lowliferecords.co.uk
www.lowliferecords.co.uk
The place to check for quality British Rap.

manchestermusic.co.uk
PO Box 1977, Manchester, M26 2YB UK
enquiries@music-dash.co.uk
www.manchestermusic.co.uk
Information regarding local music and bands.

Midnight Mango
21 Kings Dr. Westonzoyland, TA7 OHJ UK
PH: 07779723061
gigs@midnightmango.co.uk
www.midnightmango.co.uk
Covers all things to do with local bands.

North West Bluegrass News
1 Woodlands Rd. Saltney, Chester, CH4 8LB UK
PH: 01244-683563
www.nwbn.freeserve.co.uk
British Bluegrass magazine. Photos, reviews, tabs etc.

Northampton Bands
www.northamptonbands.co.uk
Bands can use our site as an information source for their fans.

nwdnb.co.uk
www.nwdnb.co.uk
Central hub of information for D n' B in Liverpool and Manchester.

Peterborough Folk Diary
www.fenfolk.glowinternet.net
Your guide to music and Folk events in Peterborough.

Punk & Oi in the UK
PO Box 158, Leeds, LS27 7XP UK
rebecca@punkoiuk.co.uk
www.punkoiuk.co.uk
Information on the current Punk & Oi scene.

Rhythm and Booze
32 Barnes Way, Worcester, WR5 3AP UK
PH/FX: 01905-731615
chrisbennion@netbreeze.co.uk
www.rhythmandbooze.net
Covering the Birmingham music scene.

Sandman Magazine
www.sandmanmagazine.co.uk
The North's free monthly music magazine. Check our website for the contact in your area.

South Riding Folk Network
www.folk-network.com
Maintaining the strength and vibrancy of the Folk arts.

South Yorkshire Folk
editor@syfolk.co.uk
www.syfolk.co.uk
News, festivals and CD reviews.

Southampton Classical Guitar Society
www.scgs-guitar.org.uk
Focal point for those playing the Classical guitar in South Hampshire.

Southern Country
53 Windsor Rd. Alresfor, Hants, SO24 9HU UK
PH: 0044-0-1962-734401
SueMac@southerncountry.fsnet.co.uk
angelfire.com/sd/scountry
Reviews, news, features and articles on related subjects.

Stirrings
11 Ratcliffe Rd. Sheffield, S11 8YA UK
PH: 0114-26611582
stirrings@taproot.demon.co.uk
www.stirrings.co.uk
Folk, Roots and Acoustic music in South York and beyond.

Sussex Folk Guide
whatson.brighton.co.uk/folk
Free publication listing Folk events in Brighton and Hove.

The Swish Blog
the.swish.blog@gmail.com
www.swishblog.co.uk
An MP3 blog generally about London-based Alternative music.

This is Wiltshire
www.thisiswiltshire.co.uk
Covers local bands and events.

totallywired
PO Box 70, Brighton, BN1 1YJ UK
PH: 01273-244144
mod@totallywired.co.uk
www.totallywired.co.uk
Covering the Brighton music scene.

The Virtually Acoustic Club
www.viac.co.uk
Open mic listings for many clubs in London and the UK.

Wiltshire Folk Association
www.wiltsfolka.fsnet.co.uk
All the info on the local Folk music scene.

Ireland

IrishUnsigned.com
Ron Healy ron@irishunsigned.com
www.irishunsigned.com
A cross-genre, nationwide showcase and resource for all new or unsigned Irish acts.

Australia

Arts Law Centre of Australia
www.artslaw.com.au
Advice and information for all artists.

Association of Independent Record Labels
www.air.org.au
Largest Australian music online database. New releases and back catalogue info. If you're an Oz Indie label, join us.

Ausradiosearch Distribution
PO Box 532, Newcastle, NSW 2300 Australia
PH: 61-02-49270290
www.isonliveradio.com
We can get your film clips aired on Aussie TV.

Australian Christian Artists Network
PO Box 636, Greensborough, VIC 3088 Australia
PH: 1300-138-826
nationaloffice@acan.org.au
www.acan.org.au
Bringing you Australia's finest Christian artists.

Australian Copyright Council
www.copyright.org.au
Technical info on the music business.

Australian Music Association
www.australianmusic.asn.au
Furthering the interests of the music industry.

Australian Music Online
PO Box 2227, Sydney, NSW 2001 Australia
PH: 61-2-8353-6900 FX: 61-2-8353-6999
info@amo.org.au
www.amo.org.au
Promotes all new Australian music.

Australian Music Radio Airplay Project
(AMRAP)
PO Box 564, Alexandria, NSW 1435 Australia
PH: (02) 9310-2999 FX: (02) 9319-4545
amrap@cbaa.org.au
amrap.org
Works with musicians and community broadcasters to create increased radio airplay opportunities for contemporary Australian music.

Australian Music Website
www.amws.com.au
Resource for tracking down anything to do with Australian music.

Australian Songwriters Association
www.asai.org.au
Supports and promotes developing Australian songwriters.

BAR Promotions
PO Box 68, Darlington, WA 6070 Australia
PH: 0011-61-8-9255-3336
FX: 0011-61-8-9255-3395
Melanie DeCull
office@bluesandrootspromotions.com
www.bluesandrootspromotions.com
Promoting Australian Blues & Roots music globally.

Blues Oz
www.bluesoz.com
Includes an e-mail forum and chat site for the discussion of the local Blues scene.

The Blurb Magazine
PO Box 3038, Norman Park, QLD 4170 Australia
feedback@theblurb.com.au
www.theblurb.com.au
A&E magazine featuring new releases and music events.

Bombshell Zine
PO Box 8032, Werrington County, NSW 2747 Australia
info@bombshellzine.com
www.bombshellzine.com
News, reviews, MP3s etc.

Buywell.com
PO Box 1010, Willagee Central, WA 6156 Australia
www.buywell.com
We sell Classical music CDs produced in Australia.

ChaosMusic
45 Collins St., E. Melbourne, VIC 3000 Australia
PH: 61-3-9654-1144 FX: 61-3-9654-2333
info@chaos.com
www.chaosmusic.com
Promotes local music to a global audience.

Country Music Association of Australia
www.countrymusic.asn.au
Promotes all aspects of the Australian Country music industry.

Country Music Store
GPO Box 3000, Brisbane, QLD 4001 Australia
PH: 07-3221-3000 FX: 07-3221-3983
cmstore@countrymusic.com.au
www.countrymusic.com.au
Online resource for all your Australian Country Music.

Folk Alliance Australia
www.folkalliance.org.au
Preserving the Folk arts. Reviews CDs of members.

Folk Australia
PO Box 3100, East Blaxland, NSW 2774 Australia
thefolk@folkaustralia.com
www.folkaustralia.com
Promoting Folk music in Australia.

Indie-CDs
85 Oakfords Rd. Wattle Grove, TAS 7109 Australia
PH: 03-6295-0735 FX: 03-6295-0835
www.indie-cds.com
Music by independent Australian artists.

inthemix.com.au
PO Box 1964, Strawberry Hills, NSW 2012 Australia
PH: 02-9282 4000 FX: 02-9282-4099
www.inthemix.com.au
Covering the Australian Dance music scene. News, reviews, events etc.

Loud! Online
23 Yester Rd. Wentworth Falls, NSW 2782 Australia
Brian Fischer-Giffin annex@bigpond.net.au
www.geocities.com/SunsetStrip/Stage/4599
Promotion and exposure for Australian Heavy Metal music in all its forms.

Mediasearch
PO Box 132 Melbourne, VIC 3001 Australia
PH: 61-3-9282-4841
info@mediasearch.com.au
www.mediasearch.com.au
Music, film and fashion in Australia.

Middle Eight Music
PO Box 9337, South Yarra, VIC 3141 Australia
PH/FX: (03) 9866-1222
www.middle8.com
Australia's premiere Show Music store.

Move Records
1 Linton St., Ivanhoe, VIC 3079 Australia
PH: 03-9497-3105 FX: 03-9497-4426
move@move.com.au
www.move.com.au
Independent Classical label supporting Australian composers and performers.

MP3.com.au
Level 2, Bldg. 10, 658 Church St., Richmond, VIC 3121 Australia
PH: 03-8415-9111 FX: 03-8415-9100
www.mp3.com.au
The primary focus of this network is to provide artists the opportunity to get music heard.

musicworldonline.com.au
musicworldonline.com.au
Australian music community. Search for all your Australian music needs.

New Music Network
www.newmusicnetwork.com.au
Hosts performances of new Australian music.

Oz Music Central
PO Box 559, Toronto, NSW 2283 Australia
PH: 0417-275-042
ozmusic-central@bigpond.com
www.ozmusic-central.com
Australian music resource. Reviews, featured artists and more!

OzBlues.net
PO Box 1921, Launceston, TAZ 7250 Australia
Fred Davis ozblues@hotmail.com
www.ozblues.net
Australian Blues music resource. Clubs, shows, festivals etc.

OzRock.com
PO Box 7227, Baulkham Hills, NSW 2153 Australia
www.ozrock.com
Independent, unsigned and undiscovered artists, bands and music.

Rockus
PO Box 2221, Warwick, WA 6024 Australia
PH: 0403-223-012
Steph Edwardes mail@rockus.com.au
www.rockus.com.au
Specializing in the Indie, Pop and Rock genres. Australian artists only!

SCALA News
www.scala.org.au
Provides info and support for songwriters in Australia.

Tamworth Songwriters' Association Inc.
www.tsaonline.com.au
Represents Australian Country music songwriters.

themusic.com.au
PH: 02-9557-7766
Phil Tripp tripp@themusic.com.au
www.themusic.com.au
The ultimate Australian music business portal with news, resources and links.

What Was That
#276 - 189 Queen St., Melbourne, VIC 3000 Australia
PH: 03-9018-9497 FX: 03-9012-4205
Craig craig@whatwasthat.com.au
www.whatwasthat.com.au
We offer a promotional tool for musicians and artists to help promote their gigs for free. Australian artists only please!

New South Wales

3D World Magazine
Level 2, 25 Cooper St., Surry Hills, NSW 2010 Australia
PH: 612-9211-1222 FX: 612-9281-4193
www.threedworld.com.au
Free circulating street press music magazine.

Bathhurst After Dark
bathurstafterdark.com
Promote local music. MP3s, gig guide and more!

Canberra Blues Society
www.canberrabluessociety.com
Our aim is to provide regular music jams, Blues events and Blues-related social activities.

CanberraRootsMusic.com
webmaster@CanberraRootsMusic.com
www.canberrarootsmusic.com
Dedicated to promoting Roots music venues, gigs and musicians in the Canberra region.

Corporate News Jazz n' Blues
PH: 0412-199-818
enquiries@corporatenews.com.au
www.corporatenews.com.au
Covering the Sydney Jazz and Blues scene. Artist profiles, gigs guide, interviews, CD reviews, radio guide and festivals.

JAM - Folk Federation of NSW
38 Alleyne Ave., North Narrabeen, NSW 2101 Australia
Wayne Richmond inquiries@folkfednsw.org.au
jam.org.au
Presents & supports Folk music, song and dance.

I-94 Bar
PO Box 105, Mortdale, NSW 2223 Australia
barman@i94bar.com
www.i94bar.com
Covers the Rock action in the area.

Newcastle Music
PO Box 985, Newcastle, NSW 2300 Australia
contact@newcastlemusic.net
www.newcastlemusic.net
Covers the Newcastle music scene. Bands, albums, downloads, gigs etc.

Sydney Blues Society
www.sydneyblues.org
Our monthly Newsletter "The Blues Times" does CD / DVD reviews of mainly Australian Blues artists.

Sydney Friction
info@sydneyfriction.com
www.sydneyfriction.com
Sydney Drum'n'Bass resource.

Sydney Music Guide
sydney.citysearch.com.au
Extensive coverage of the local music scene. Post your shows and events.

Queensland

Blues Association of South East Queensland
baseq.tripod.com
Promoting local Blues musicians locally and globally.

brispop.com
PO Box 103, Spring Hill, QLD 4004 Australia
PH: 61-0409-204-424
admin@brispop.com
www.brispop.com
Portal for local bands, gigs and more.

Time Off
PO Box 515, Brisbane, QLD 4001 Australia
PH: 07-3252-9666 FX: 07-3252-9761
timeoff@timeoff.com.au
www.timeoff.com.au
Queensland's leading street press.

South Australia

MusicSA
Music House, Level 1, Corner North Tce & Morphett St., Adelaide, SA 5000 Australia
PH: 08-8218-8404 FX: 08-8218-8122
Elizabeth Reid info@musicsa.com.au
www.musicsa.com.au
Offering South Australian artists free listings (including space for MP3s & video clips), reviews and other free promotional opportunities.

Rip it Up
93 King William St., Kent Town, SA 5067 Australia
PH: 08-8132-7000 FX: 08-8363-4190
maryanneagostino@ripitup.com.au
www.ripitup.com.au
Adelaide's leading street press magazine.

South Australian Roots 'n Blues
53 Cooinda Ave. Redwood Park, SA 5097 Australia
PH: 0408-085-821
David Stoeckel sablues@sablues.org
www.sablues.org
Promoting the Blues in SA.

Victoria

Beat Magazine
3 Newton St., Richmond, Melbourne, VIC 3121
Australia
PH: 613-9428-3600 FX: 613-9428-3611
info@beat.com.au
www.beat.com.au
Free weekly paper. Focus on local music.

Cheap Thrills
PH: 03-8486-2157 FX: 03-8486 2121
info@cheapthrills.com.au
cheapthrills.com.au
Supporting Melbourne artists, musicians, business and anything funky!

Early Music Society of Victoria
home.vicnet.net.au/~emsv
Promotes the performance of Early music.

GrooveOn.com.au
PO Box 7572, Melbourne, VIC 8004 Australia
www.grooveon.com.au
R&B / Hip Hop / Latin news, events, clubs and more.

MELBAND
1/43-45 Melverton Dr. Hallam, VIC 3803 Australia
PH: 03-9702-3244
Geoff Mison info@melband.com.au
www.melband.com.au
Listing of all things music in Melbourne.

Melbourne Blues Appreciation Society
www.mbas.org.au
We feature CD reviews, a monthly newsletter, workshops, jams and clinics.

MelbourneMuso.com
dave@melbournemuso.com
www.melbournemuso.com
Site focussing on music in Melbourne, has gig, venue and artist information, MP3 downloads, fan forum and community.

Victorian Folk Music Club
users.bigpond.net.au/vfmc
Folk music organization in Australia.

The Indie Link Exchange
A new, free and easy way to promote your website
www.indielinkexchange.com/ile

Western Australia

Perth Blues Club
www.perthbluesclub.org.au
Supporting local & international Blues & Roots music.

Scoop Magazine
#3-266 Hay St., Subiaco, WA 6008 Australia
PH: 08-9388-8188 FX: 08-9388-8199
editorial@scoop.com.au
www.scoop.com.au
Western Australian lifestyle magazine.

Western Front
Clay clay@wf.com.au
www.wf.com.au
Info on Western Australia's Metal music scene.

XPress Magazine
73 Railway Parade, City W. Business Cn. W. Perth,
WA 6872 Australia
PH: 6618-9213-2888 FX: 618-9213-2882
Mike Wafer localmusic@xpressmag.com.au
www.xpressmag.com.au
Interviews, reviews and news on the local music scene.

Zebra Magazine
Mike Wafer localmusic@zebramag.com.au
www.zebramag.com.au
A&E publication that covers the Perth music scene.

SECTION THREE: RADIO STATIONS AND SHOWS THAT ARE WILLING TO PLAY INDEPENDENT MUSIC

*"Following a DJ's set list is **mandatory**. I find it annoying when someone contacts me asking if I have received their CD, when I have already played them once or twice. It shows me that they would rather bother me than do the work to find out themselves."* – **Angela Page, Host of Folk Plus on WJFF Radio**

Promotional Services

United States

Advanced Alternative Media
7 W. 22nd St. 4th Fl. New York, NY 10010
PH: 212-924-3005 FX: 212-929-6305
justin@aaminc.com
www.aampromo.com
The number one choice in independent marketing and college radio promotions nationwide since 1982.

AirPlay Direct
Music Upload Ctr. 200 Corporate Lake Dr. Columbia, MO 65203-7172
support@airplaydirect.com
www.airplaydirect.com
A cost effective way to securely deliver your music to radio industry professionals across the world.

Backstage Entertainment
2530 Atlantic Ave. Ste. C, Long Beach, CA 90806
PH: 310-325-9997
www.backstageentertainment.net
A marketing information company which focuses its management abilities throughout all aspects of the music industry.

Bill Wence Promotions
PO Box 39, Nolensville, TN 37135
PH: 615-776-2060 FX: 615-776-2181
Bill Wence info@billwencepromotions.com
www.billwencepromotions.com
Hundreds of singles and albums have been charted for our clients.

Bryan Farrish Radio Promotion
1828 Broadway, 2nd Fl. Santa Monica, CA 90404
PH: 310-998-8305 FX: 310-998-8323
airplay@radio-media.com
www.radio-media.com
Indie airplay promotion to commercial, commercial specialty and college radio stations in the U.S. and Canada.

Creativity In Music
PO Box 3481, Bridgeport, CT 06605
Gi Dussault npsfunk@optonline.net
www.creativityinmusic.com
Radio Promotion of all genres, concert promotion and submission of press releases.

Engine That Could Promotions
PO Box 5550, Berkeley, CA 94705-0550
PH: 510-547-2521
Seth Lepore info@enginethatcouldpromotions.com
www.enginethatcouldpromotions.com
College radio promotion, mainline distribution, national press releases to over 15,000 music publications.

Howard Rosen Promotion
5605 Woodman Ave. #206, Van Nuys, CA 91401
PH: 818-901-1122 FX: 818-901-6513
musicsubmissions@howiewood.com
www.howiewood.com
We are a full service radio promotion company that has been in business since 1985.

IndiePodcasting.com
314 Centre St., South Orange, NJ 07079
PH: 973-763-9215
Tony Alexander webmaster@indiepodcasting.com
www.indiepodcasting.com
Promoting artists using a combination of podcasting technology, syndication and viral marketing.

Jerome Promotions & Marketing
2535 Winthrope Way, Lawrenceville, GA 30044
PH: 770-982-7055 FX: 770-982-1882
Bill Jerome hitcd@bellsouth.net
www.jeromepromotions.com
We call the music directors and program directors of over 250 stations several times a week in order to help our artists get airplay and the recognition that they deserve with the goal of helping them make a deal with a major label.

Jerry Lembo Entertainment Group
742 Bergen Blvd. 2nd Fl. Ridgefield, NJ 07657
PH: 201-840-9980 FX: 201-840-9921
Jerry Lembo jerry@lemboentertainment.com
www.lemboentertainment.com
Specializing in radio promotion, artist management, music publishing and publicity.

KDM Promotion
4002 SW. Webster St., Seattle, WA 98136
PH: 206-938-6679
FX: 206-938-6379
Kathleen Monahan kdmpromo@mindspring.com
www.mc-kdm.com
We introduce new music and artists to radio stations focusing on Jazz, Blues, World, Celtic, Ambient, Acoustic and Folk programming.

Loggins Promotion
2530 Atlantic Ave. Ste. C, Long Beach, CA 90806
PH: 310-325-2800
promo@logginspromotion.com
www.logginspromotion. com
Most advanced system for tracking radio airplay.

Mediaguide
1000 Chesterbrook Blvd. #150, Berwyn, PA 19312
music@mediaguide.com
www.mediaguide.com
Music monitoring company that provides radio airplay information products on nearly 2,500 stations.

MiaMindMusic
259 W. 30th St. #12FR, New York, NY 10001-2809
PH: 212-564-4611 FX: 212-564-4448
MiMiMus@aol.com
www.miamindmusic.com
Radio tracking and working with CMJ and R&R surveyed radio stations.

Nice Promotion
PO Box 352, Portland, OR 97207
PH: 503-848-9976
info@nicepromo.com
www.nicepromo.com
Providing college radio promotion to labels and Indie musicians alike. Genres: Alternative, Rock, Pop, Electronic and more!

Pirate! Promotion and Management
145 Columbia St., Cambridge, MA 02139
PH: 617-354-5200 FX: 248-694-2949
radio@piratepirate.com
www.piratepirate.com
Services college and non-commercial radio stations across North America to gain airplay for our artists.

Planetary Group
PO Box 52116, Boston, MA 02205
PH: 617-451-0444 FX: 617-451-0888
www.planetarygroup.com
Full promotional services as well as targeted radio mailing services.

Powderfinger Promotions
47 Mellen St., Framingham, MA 01702
PH: 800-356-1155 x.234
powderspam@aol.com
nimbit.com/promo
We have solid connections at over 500 college and AAA stations across the U.S. and Canada and hundreds of press contacts.

Radio & Retail Promotions
PH: 323-876-7027
Jon Flanagan promotions@radioandretail.com
www.radioandretail.com
Build a fan base through radio airplay and retail promotion.

RadioSubmit.com
13501 Ranch Rd. 12 #103-327, Wimberley, TX 78676
PH: 866-432-7965
Robert Bartosh rs@radiosubmit.com
www.radiosubmit.com
Allows artists to submit their music directly to radio stations around the world.

RadioWave
radiowavemonitor@radiowavemonitor.com
www.radiowavemonitor.com
A suite of services that will help you to get your music heard by potentially thousands of internet radio listeners.

RAM *(Realtime Airplay Metrics)*
151 W. 25th St. 12th Fl. New York, NY 10001
PH: 917-606-1908 FX: 917-606-1914
ram@cmj.com
www.cmj.com/ram
A revolutionary airplay tracking service.

Space 380
2008 Swindon Ave.
Columbia,
MO 65203-8985
PH: 573-446-7221
FX: 309-210-9037
Mat Matlack
indiebible@space380.com
www.space380.com
We develop name recognition for independent artists & labels of ALL genres.

The Syndicate
1801 Willow Ave.
Weehawken,
NJ 07086-6614
PH: 201-864-0900
Matt college@thesyn.com
musicsyndicate.com
We work mainly with artists and labels that are completely ready, with all the puzzle-pieces in place.

Tinderbox Music
3148 Bryant Ave. S.,
Minneapolis, MN 55408
PH: 612-375-1113
FX: 612) 341-3330
Krista Vilinskis
krista@tinderboxmusic.com
www.tinderboxmusic.com
Music promotion and distribution company.

Triplearadio.com
228 Commercial St., Nevada City, CA 95959-2507
PH: 530-477-2224 FX: 530-477-5599
Dave Chaney dave@triplearadio.com
www.triplearadio.com
Helps anyone who will be working their music to Triple A radio.

TRS Music Promotion
36625 N. 7th St. Bldg. 4, Phoenix, AZ 85086
PH: 800-616-3270 FX: 602-465-0395
TRS@radiopromo.com
www.radiopromo.com
Makes sure your music is getting attention.

Twin Vision
261 5th Ave. #1F, Brooklyn, NY 11215
PH: 718-369-1370
Peter Hay TwinVision@aol.com
twinvision.net
Radio promotion with proven strategies that create exposure with national audiences.

Canada

ANR Lounge
www.mincanada.com
Promote CDs through e-mail to stations across Canada.

dB Promotions & Publicity
1365 Yonge St. #204, Toronto, ON M4T 2P7
PH: 416 928 3550 FX: 416 928 3401
Dulce Barbosa info@dbpromotions.ca
www.dbpromotions.ca
National radio promotion and artist publicity.

RadioDirectX
650 Dupont St. #503, Toronto, ON M6G 4B1
PH: 888-746-7234
info@radiodirectx.com
www.radiodirectx.com
We've focused on developing a service that offers artists the opportunity to gain an international listening audience.

Spincycle Direct
1187 W. 16th Ave. Vancouver, BC V6H 1S8
Geoff Goddard geoff@spincycledirect.com
www.spincycledirect.com
Service provider for artists to securely distribute singles to radio for airplay consideration.

United Kingdom

Anglo Plugging
www.angloplugging.co.uk
Radio, television and internet promotion for bands and artists.

Matchbox Recordings
33 Bath St., Abingdon, Oxfordshire, OX14 3RH UK
info@matchboxrecordings.co.uk
www.matchboxrecordings.co.uk
Plugging dept specializes in delivering and plugging new release singles and albums to alternative/ specialist DJ's in the U.K.

Sign up for The Indie Contact Newsletter
www.indiebible.com

Stations that Play a Variety of Genres

*Most stations listed in the Variety section have weekly shows that cater to every style of music – Pop, Rock, Folk, Jazz, Various Metals, Punk, Goth, Industrial, Electronic, Hip Hop, Country, Blues etc. As one Music Director pointed out, when contacting these stations, it is **crucial** to add: **ATTENTION - MUSIC DIRECTOR** in the Subject: heading of your e-mail, as well as on the **package** you mail to the station.*

North America

United States

Alabama

WALW
531 Walnut St., Moulton AL 35650
PH: 256-905-4400
Jason Wells jason@walw.org
www.walw.org

WBLZ *U. Alabama*
HUC 151, 1530 3rd Ave. S., Birmingham, AL 35294-1150
PH: 205-975-9259 FX: 205-975-9261
blazeradio.newsroom.uab.edu

WEGL
116 Foy Union Blvd. Auburn U. AL 36849-5231
PH: 334-844-4113 FX: 334-844-4118
wegl@auburn.edu
wegl.auburn.edu

WLJS *Jacksonville State U.*
700 Pelham Rd. N. Jacksonville, AL 36265
PH: 256-782-5571 FX: 256-782-5645
www.jsu.edu/92j

WUAL
PO Box 870370, Tuscaloosa, AL 35487-0370
PH: 205-348-6644 FX: 205-348-6648
apr@apr.org
www.wual.ua.edu

WVUA *U. Alabama*
PO Box 870152, Tuscaloosa, AL 35487
PH: 205-348-6461
wvuamusic@sa.ua.edu
www.newrock907.com

Alaska

KBBI
3913 Kachemak Way, Homer AK 99603
PH: 907-235-7721
Paulette Wellington paulette@kbbi.org
www.kbbi.org

KBRW
PO Box 109, Barrow, AK 99723
PH: 907-852-6811
info@kbrw.org
www.kbrw.org

KCAW
2 Lincoln St. Ste. B, Sitka, AK 99835
PH: 907-747-5877 FX: 907-747-5977
ravenradio@ak.net
www.ravenradio.org

KCHU
PO Box 467, Valdez, AK 99686
PH: 800-478-5080
kchu@cvinternet.net
www.kchu.org

KEUL
PO Box 29, Girdwood, AK 99587
PH: 907-754-2489
radio@glaciercity.us
glaciercity.us

KHNS
PO Box 1109, Haines, AK 99827
PH: 907-76-2020 FX: 907-766-2022
khns@khns.org
www.khns.org

KMXT
620 Egan Way, Kodiak, AK 99615-6487
PH: 907-486-5698 FX: 907-486-2733
Mike Wall gm@kmxt.org
www.kmxt.org

KRUA *U. Alaska Anchorage*
PSB Rm. 254, 3211 Providence Dr. Anchorage,
AK 99508
PH: 907-786-6805
aykrua1@uaa.alaska.edu
www.uaa.alaska.edu/krua

KSTK
PO Box 1141, Wrangell, AK 99929
PH: 907-874-2345 FX: 907-874-3293
www.kstk.org

KSUA *U. Alaska Fairbanks*
PO Box 750113, Fairbanks, AK 99775
PH: 907-474-5782 FX: 907-474-6314
ksuamusic@uaf.edu
ksua.uaf.edu

KTOO
360 Egan Dr. Juneau, AK 99801-1748
PH: 907-586-1670 FX: 907-586-3612
www.ktoo.org

KUHB
PO Box 905, St. Paul, AK 99660
PH: 907-546-2254 FX: 907-546-2367
Josh Krohn gm@kuhb.org
www.kuhb.org

Arizona

KAMP *U. Arizona*
PO Box 3605, Tucson, AZ 85722
Attn: Music Director
PH: 520-626-4460 FX: 520 626-5986
headmd@kamp.arizona.edu
kamp.arizona.edu

KASC *Arizona State U.*
Stauffer Hall A231, Tempe, AZ 85287-1305
PH: 480-965-4163
www.theblaze1260.com

KFHX
12645 E. Saguaro Blvd. PO Box 17228,
Fountain Hills, AZ 85269
PH: 602-260-1620 FX: 480-837-2820
info@kfhx.org
www.kfhx.com

KJACK *N. Arizona U.*
PO Box 5619, Flagstaff, AZ 86011
PH: 928-523-4554 FX: 928-523-1505
www.jackcentral.com/kjack

KPRP *Radio Free Bisbee*
63C Brewery Gulch, PO Box 1501, Bisbee,
AZ 85603
PH: 520-432-1400
kbrp@cableone.net
www.kbrpradio.com

KRIM
HC4 Box 4C, Payson, AZ 85541
PH: 928-468—5746 FX: 928-468-5746
LeiLani Dawn krimfm@cbiwireless.com
www.krim-fm.com

KWSS
PH: 480-551-1067
radioinfo@kwss1067.com
www.kwss1067.com

KXCI
220 S. 4th Ave. Tucson, AZ 85701
PH: 520-622-5924
kxcimd@kxci.org
www.kxci.org

Arkansas

KABF
2101 S. Main St., Little Rock, AR 72206
PH: 501-372-6119 FX: 501-376-3952
kabf@acorn.org
www.kabfradio.org

KHDX *Hendrix College*
506 Oak St., Conway, AZ
PH: 501-327-8129 FX: 501-327-5073
khdx@hendrix.edu
students.hendrix.edu/orgs/khdx

KSWH *Henderson State U.*
HSU Box 7872 Arkadelphia, AR 71999
PH: 870-230-5185
kswh@hsu.edu
stuwww.hsu.edu/kswh

KUAF *U. Arkansas*
747 W. Dickson St., Fayetteville, AR 72701
PH: 479-575-6574 FX: 479-575-8440
PJ Robowski pjrobows@uark.edu
www.kuaf.com

KXUA *U. Arkansas*
A665 Arkansas Union, Fayetteville, AR 72701
PH: 479-575-5883
charts@uark.edu
www.kxua.com

Live at Acoustic Sounds Cafe *KUAR*
2801 S. U. Little Rock, AR 72204
PH: 501-569-8485 FX: 501-569-8488
Joe.Henry@AcousticSoundsCafe.org
www.acousticsoundscafe.org/radioshow.htm
*It's not a drop-in, just-show-up, open-mic kind of
situation. We book 6-12 months in advance.*

California

Demolisten *KXLU*
1 LMU Dr. Los Angeles, CA 90045
PH: 310-338-5958 FX: 310-338-5959.
www.kxlu.com
*Submit your homemade music on cassettes and
CDRs. We expose the unexposable.*

Free Radio San Diego
PO Box 33430, San Diego, CA 92163-3430
Attn: (name of DJ)
PH: 619-544-0918
www.pirate969.org
*Just burn MP3s onto a CD and mail it to whatever
DJ you think will care and want to play it.*

Free Radio Santa Cruz
PO Box 7507, Santa Cruz, CA 95061
PH: 831-427-3772
frsc@freakradio.org
www.freakradio.org

Indie 103
5700 Wilshire Blvd. #250, Los Angeles, CA 90036
PH: 877-452-1031
feedback@indie1031.fm
indie1031.fm

iRADIO Los Angeles
PO Box 1403, Covina, CA 91722
PH: 626-780-6323 FX: 626-974-4776
Mark Maverick info@iradiola.com
www.iradiola.com
*The #1 Indie radio station, playing 100% Indie
bands on REAL RADIO!*

KALX *U. California Berkeley*
26 Barrows Hall #5650, Berkeley, CA 94720-5650
PH: 510-642-1111
kalxmail@media.berkeley.edu
kalx.berkeley.edu

KAPU *Azusa Pacific U.*
PO Box 9521, #5168 Azusa, CA 91702
music@kapuradio.com
kapu.apu.edu

KAZU
PO Box 210, 167 Central Ave. Pacific Grove,
CA 93950
PH: 831-375-7275 FX: 831-375-0235.
www.kazu.org

KBeach
1212 Bellflower Blvd. USU #110, Long Beach, CA 90815
PH: 562-985-1624
musicdirector@kbeach.org
www.kbeach.org

KCPR *California Poly State U.*
Graphic Arts Bldg. 26 #201, San Luis Obispo, CA 93407
PH: 805-756-2965
kcprmd@kcpr.org
www.kcpr.org

KCR *San Diego College*
5200 Campanile Dr. San Diego, CA 92182
PH: 619-594-7014 FX: 619-594-6092
md.kcr.sdsu@gmail.com
kcr.sdsu.edu

KCRW
1900 Pico Blvd. Santa Monica, CA 90405
PH: 310-450-5183 FX: 310-450-7172
music@kcrw.org
www.kcrw.org

KCSB *U. California*
PO Box 13401, Santa Barbara, CA 93107-3401
PH: 805-893-3757
internal.music@kcsb.org
www.kcsb.org

KCSC *Cal State U. Chico*
Chico, CA 95929
PH: 530-898-6229
kcscradio.com

KCSN *Cal State U. Northridge*
18111 Nordhoff St., Northridge, CA 91330-8312
PH: 818-677-3090
www.kcsn.org

KCSS *Cal State U. Stanislaus*
801 W. Monte Vista Ave. Turlock, CA 95380
PH: 667-3378 FX: 667-3901
www.kcss.net

KCXX
242 E. Airport Dr. #106, San Bernardino, CA 92408
PH: 909-384-1039 FX: 909-888-7302
www.x1039.com

KDVS *U. California*
14 Lower Freeborn, Davis, CA 95616
PH: 530-752-7777
musicdept@kdvs.org
www.kdvs.org

KFCF
PO Box 4364, Fresno, CA 93744
PH: 559-233-2221
kfcf@kfcf.org
www.kfcf.org

KFJC
12345 El Monte Rd. Los Altos Hills, CA 94022
PH: 650-949-7260 FX: 650-948-1085
music@kfjc.org
www.kfjc.org

KFOK
PO Box 4238, Georgetown, CA 95634
PH: 530-333-4300
info@kfok.org
www.kfok.org

KFSR *Cal State Fresno*
Mail Stop SA #119, 5201 N. Maple, Fresno, CA 93740
PH: 559-278-4082 FX: 559-278-6985
kfsr_musicdirector@yahoo.com
www.csufresno.edu/kfsr

KGFN *Grossmont College*
8800 Grossmont College Dr. El Cajon, CA 92020
PH: 619-644-7287
kgfnfm@yahoo.com
www.grossmont.net/kgfn

KHUM *Humboldt State U.*
PO Box 25 Ferndale, CA 95536
PH: 707-786-5104 FX: 707-786-5100
info@khum.com
www.khum.com

KISL
PO Box 1980, Avalon, CA 90704
PH: 310-510-7469 FX: 310-510-1025
contact@kisl.org
www.kisl.org

KITS *Soundcheck*
865 Battery St. 2nd Fl. San Francisco, CA 94111
PH: 415-478-5483
www.live105.com

KKSM *Palomar College*
1140 W. Mission Rd. San Marcos, CA 92069
PH: 760-744-1150 x2183
www.palomar.edu/kksm

KKUP
933 Monroe St., PMB 9150, Santa Clara, CA 95050
PH: 408-260-2999
admin@kkup.org
www.kkup.com

KMUD
PO Box 135, 1144 Redway Dr. Redway, CA 95560-0135
PH: 707-923-2513 x109 FX: 707-923-2501
Kate Klein md@kmud.org
kmud.org

KNAB *Chapman U.*
1 University Dr. Orange, CA 92866
PH: 714-516-5622
musicdirector@chapmanradio.com
www.ChapmanRadio.com

KOZT
110 S. Franklin St., Fort Bragg, CA 95437
PH: 707-964-7277 FX: 707 964-95FM
thecoast@kozt.com
www.kozt.com

KPCC *Pasadena City College*
1570 E. Colorado Blvd. Pasadena, CA 91106-2003
PH: 626-585-7000
mail@kpcc.org
www.kpcc.org

KPFA
1929 MLK Jr. Way Berkeley, CA 94704
PH: 510-848-6767 FX: 510-848-3812
info@kpfa.org
www.kpfa.org

KQRP
PO Box 612, Salida, CA 95368
kqrp1061@yahoo.com
www.myspace.com/kqrpradio

KRBS
PO Box 9, Oroville, CA 95965
PH: 530-534-1200
krbs@cncnet.com
www.radiobirdstreet.org

KRCB
5850 Labath Ave. Rohnert Park, CA 94928
PH: 707-585-8522 FX: 707-585-1363
listener@krcb.org
www.krcb.org/radio

KRFH *Humboldt State U.*
c/o Dept. of Journalism, HSU, Arcata, CA 95521
PH: 707-826-6077
krfh@humboldt.edu
www.humboldt.edu/~krfh

KRSH
3565 Standish Ave. Santa Rosa, CA 95407
PH: 707-588-9999
studio@krsh.com
www.krsh.com

KSAK *Mt. San Antonio College*
1100 N. Grand Ave. Walnut, CA 91789
PH: 909-594-5611 x5725
ksak@mtsac.edu
www.ksak.com

KSCR *U. Southern California*
STU 404, Los Angeles, CA 90089-0895
PH: 213-740-1486
music@kscr.org
www.kscrradio.com

KSCU *Santa Clara U.*
SCU 3207, 500 El Camino Real, Santa Clara, CA 95053
PH: 408-554-5728
music@kscu.org
www.kscu.org

KSDT *U. California San Diego*
9500 Gilman Dr. #0315, La Jolla, CA 92093-0315
PH: 858-534-5738
scw.ucsd.edu

KSFS *San Francisco State U.*
1600 Holloway Ave. San Francisco, CA 94132
PH: 415-338-1532
ksfs@sfsu.edu
ksfs.sfsu.edu

KSJS *San Jose State U.*
Hugh Gillis Hall #132, San Jose, CA 95192-0094
PH: 408-924-5757 FX: 408-924-4558
ksjs@ksjs.org
www.ksjs.org

Kspaz Radio / Kspaz Productions
715 N. Broadway #31, Escondido, CA 92025
PH: 760-294-4008
Richard Spasoff kspazradio@cox.net
www.kspazradio.com
A zany mix of comedy, music and celebrities ...and "would you believe" inspiring stories?

KSPB *Stevenson H.S.*
3152 Forest Lake Rd. Pebble Beach, CA 93953
PH: 831-625-5078
Matty Wolowodiuk music@kspb.org
www.kspb.org

KSPC *Pomona College*
Thatcher Music Bldg. 340 N. College Ave. Claremont, CA 91711
PH: 909-621-8157 FX: 909-607-1269
www.kspc.org

KSSU *California State U.*
c/o ASI, 6000 J St., Sacramento, CA 95819
PH: 916-278- 3666 FX: 916-278-6278
music@kssu.com
www.kssu.com

KSUN *Sonoma State U.*
1801 E. Cotati Ave. Rohnert Park, CA 94928
PH: 707-664-2623
www.sonoma.edu/ksun

KUCI *U. California*
PO Box 4362, Irvine, CA 92616
PH: 949-824-6868
music@kuci.org
www.kuci.org

KUCR *U. California*
Riverside, CA 92521
PH: 951-827-3838
www.kucr.org

KUSF *U. San Francisco*
2130 Fulton St., San Francisco, CA 94117
PH: 415-386-5873
kusfmusic@yahoo.com
www.kusf.org

KUSP
203 8th Ave. Santa Cruz, CA 95062
PH: 831-476-2800
kusp@kusp.org
kusp.org

KVMR
401 Spring St., Nevada City, CA 95959
PH: 530-265-9555 FX: 530-265-9077
office@kvmr.org
www.kvmr.org

KWMR
PO Box 1262, 11431 State Rt. One #8,
Point Reyes Station, CA 94956
PH: 415-663-8492
music@kwmr.org
www.kwmr.org

KXLU *Loyola - Marymount U.*
1 LMU Dr. Los Angeles, CA 90045
PH: 310-338-5958 FX: 310-338-5959
www.kxlu.com

KZFR
PO Box 3173, Chico, CA 95927
PH: 530-895-0131 FX: 530-895-0775
music@kzfr.org
www.kzfr.org

KZSC *U. California*
1156 High St., Santa Cruz, CA 95064
PH: 831-459-5972 FX: 831-459-4734
kzscmusic@gmail.com
kzsc.org

KZSU *Stanford U.*
PO Box 20510, Stanford, CA 94309
PH: 650-723-9010 FX: 650-725-5865
music@kzsu.stanford.edu
kzsu.stanford.edu

KZYX
PO Box 1, Philo, CA 95466
PH: 707-895-2451 FX: 707-895-2554
musicdir@kzyx.org
www.kzyx.org

Morning Becomes Eclectic *KCRW*
1900 Pico Blvd. Santa Monica, CA 90405
PH: 310-450-5183 FX: 310-450-7172
Nic Harcourt music@kcrw.org
www.kcrw.com/show/mb
*We attempt to mark the next new sound and bring to
the public eye a range of music and artists.*

New Ground *KCRW*
1900 Pico Blvd. Santa Monica, CA 90405
PH: 310-450-5183 FX: 310-450-7172
James Combs newgroundmail@aol.com
www.kcrw.com/show/gz
*Host Chris Douridas features the best new music in
current and forthcoming releases.*

Penguin Radio *Dominican U. California*
50 Acacia Ave. San Rafael, CA 94901
PH: 482-3587
radio.dominican.edu

Pirate Cat Radio
1598 Custer Ave. San Francisco, CA 94124
PH: 415-970-0698
piratecatradio@yahoo.com
www.piratecatradio.com

Play it as it Lays *KUCI*
PO Box 4362, Irvine, CA 92616
PH: 949-824-5824
Sean Boy Walton playit889@yahoo.com
playit.blogspot.com
Indie-Hip-Pop-Rock 'n' Soul.

Proper Social Etiquette *KSCU*
DJ Bardot dj_bardot@hotmail.com
soundinwater.blogspot.com
*Indie, Lounge/Electronica, No Wave, New Wave,
Synthpop and whatever suits my fancy.*

Titan Radio *California State U.*
PO Box 6868, Fullerton, CA 92834-6868
PH: 714-278-5505 FX: 714-278-5514
titanradio@fullerton.edu
tir.fullerton.edu

UCLA Radio
118 Kerckhoff Hall, 308 Westwood Plaza,
Los Angeles, CA 90024
PH: 310-825-9999
music@UCLAradio.com
www.uclaradio.com

Western Addition Radio
www.westaddradio.com
Features shows covering a variety of genres.

WPMD *Cerritos College*
11110 Alondra Blvd., Norwalk, CA 90650
PH: 562-860-2451 x2626 FX: 562-467-5005
wpmd@cerritos.edu
www.cerritos.edu/wpmd

Colorado

etown
207 Canyon #302, Boulder, CO 80302
PH: 303-443-8696 FX: 303-443-4489
Nick & Helen Forster info@etown.org
www.etown.org
*Syndicated show featuring a variety of musical
styles. Live performances and interviews.*

iSAMI
1420 Austin Bluffs Pkwy. PO Box 7150,
Colorado Springs, CO 80933-7150
radio.uccs.edu

KAFM
1310 Ute Ave. Grand Junction, CO 81501
PH: 970-241-8801 x5 FX: 970-241-0995
md@kafmradio.org
www.kafmradio.org

KASF *Adams State*
110 Richardson Ave. Alamosa, CO 81102
PH: 719-587-7871
kasf.asf.adams.edu

KBUT
PO Box 308, Crested Butte, CO 81224
PH: 970-349-5225 x15 FX: 970-349-6440
music@kbut.org
kbut.org

KCSU *Colorado State U.*
Student Ctr. Box 13, Lory Student Ctr. Fort Collins,
CO 80523
PH: 970-491-7611 FX: 970-491-7612
kcsumusic@gmail.com
kcsufm.com

KDNK
PO Box 1388, Carbondale, CO 81623
PH: 970-963-0139 FX: 970-963-0810
Luke Nestler luke@kdnk.org
www.kdnk.org

KDUR *Ft. Lewis College*
1000 Rim Dr. Durango, CO 81301
PH: 970-247-7628
kdur_pd@fortlewis.edu
www.kdur.org

KGNU
4700 Walnut St., Boulder, CO 80301
PH: 303-449-4885
Elaine C. Erb music@kgnu.org
www.kgnu.org

KMSA *Mesa State College*
1100 N. Ave. Grand Junction, CO 81501-3122
PH: 970-248-1718
www.mesastate.edu/kmsa

KOTO
PO Box 1069, 207 N. Pine St., Telluride, CO 81435
PH: 970-728-4334 x2
koto.org

KRCC *Colorado College*
912 N. Weber St., Colorado Springs, CO 80903
PH: 719-473-4801
Jeff Bieri jeff@krcc.org
www.krcc.org

KRCX *Regis U.*
3333 Regis Blvd. Denver, CO 80221
PH: 303-964-5396
krcx@regis.edu
academic.regis.edu/krcx

KSRX *U. Northern Colorado*
928 20th St., Greeley, CO 80639
PH: 970-351-1256 FX: 305-489-8256
uncstudentradio@yahoo.com
www.unco.edu/ksrx

KTSC *U. Southern Colorado*
2200 Bonforte Blvd. Pueblo, CO 81001
719-549-2820
rev89@colostate-pueblo.edu
www.colostate-pueblo.edu/rev89

KVCU *U. Colorado*
Campus Box 207, Boulder, CO 80309
PH: 303-492-7405 FX: 303-492-1369
dj@radio1190.org
www.colorado.edu/StudentGroups/KVCU

KVDU *U. Denver*
2055 E. Evans Ave. Denver, CO 80208
PH: 303-871-2020
kvdu.du.edu

KVNF
PO Box 1350, Paonia, CO 81428
PH: 970-527-4868 FX: 970-527-4865
kvnf@kvnf.org
www.kvnf.org

KWSB *Western State College*
Taylor Hall, Rm. 111, Gunnison, CO 81230
PH: 970-943-3033
www.kwsb.org

Connecticut

Offbeat *WPKN*
244 U. Ave. Bridgeport, CT 06604
PH: 203-331-9756
Rich Kaminsky wpkn@wpkn.org
www.wpkn.org
Reviewing sounds and styles that fly just beneath the radar of commercial radio stations.

Upper Room with Joe Kelley
PO Box 3481, Bridgeport, CT 06605
Gi Dussault or Joe Kelley npsfunk@optonline.net
www.upperroomwithjoekelley.com
Interviews, in-house concert series and support of Indie artists of all genres. E-mail us before sending a CD.

WACC *Asnuntuck College*
170 Elm St., Enfield, CT 06082
PH: 860-253-9222
waccfm@yahoo.com
www.acc.commnet.edu/WACC

WCNI *Connecticut College*
PO Box 4972, 270 Mohegan Ave. New London, CT 06320
PH: 860-439-2850 FX: 860-439-2805
wcni_music@yahoo.com
www.wcniradio.org

WECS *Eastern Connecticut State U.*
83 Windham St., Willimantic, CT 06226
PH: 860-456-2164
WECS@hotmail.com
www.easternct.edu/depts/wecs

WESU *Wesleyan U.*
222 Church St., Middletown, CT 06459
PH: 860-685-7700 FX: 860-704-0608
wesu@wesufm.org
www.wesufm.org

WFCS *Central Connecticut State U.*
1615 Stanley St., New Britain, CT 06050
PH: 860-832-1077 FX: 860-832-3757
WFCS1077@yahoo.com
clubs.ccsu.edu/wfcs

WHUS *U. Connecticut*
1501 Storrs Rd. Storrs, CT 06269-3008
PH: 860-429-9487
whus.musicdirector@gmail.com
whus.org

WNHU *U. New Haven*
300 Boston Post Rd. West Haven, CT 06516
PH: 203-479-8801 FX: 203-931-6055
newmusic@wnhu.net
www.newhaven.edu/wnhu

WPKN
244 U. Ave. Bridgeport, CT 06604
PH: 203-331-9756
wpkn@wpkn.org
www.wpkn.org

WRTC *Trinity College*
300 Summit St., Hartford, CT 06106
PH: 860-297-2450
www.wrtcfm.com

WSIN *Southern Connecticut State U.*
Student Ctr. Rm. 210, 501 Crescent St., New Haven, CT 06456
PH: 203-392-5353
wsin1590@gmail.com
radio.southernct.edu

WVOF *Fairfield U.*
1073 N. Benson Rd. Box R, Fairfield, CT 06430-5195
PH: 203-254-4144 FX: 203-254-4224
wvofmusicdirector3@yahoo.com
www.wvof.org

WWEB *Choate Rosemary Hall*
333 Christian St., Wallingford, CT 06492
wweb@chaote.edu
student.choate.edu/wweb

WWUH *Hartford U.*
200 Bloomfield Ave. West Hartford, CT 06117
PH: 860-768-4701 FX: 860-768-5701
wwuh@hartford.edu
www.wwuh.org

WXCI *Western Connecticut State U.*
181 White St., Danbury, CT 06811
PH: 203-837-9924
wxcimd@hotmail.com
www.myspace.com/wxci

Delaware

WVUD *U. Delaware*
Perkins Student Ctr. Newark, DE 19716
PH: 302-831-2701 FX: 302-831-1399
wvudmusic@udel.edu
www.wvud.org

Florida

Pop Garden Radio *WMEL*
Adam Waltemire adam@popgardenradio.com
www.PopGardenRadio.com
3 hours of great Pop music from all ends of the genre.

WBUL *U. South Florida*
4202 E. Fowler Ave. CTR 2487, Tampa, FL 33620
PH: 813-974-3285
wbul_md@yahoo.com
www.ctr.usf.edu/wbul

WERU *Embry-Riddle Aeronautical U.*
SGA Office, 600 S. Clyde Morris Blvd. Daytona Beach, FL 32114
PH: 386-226-6272 FX: 386-226-6083
general@eaglesfm.com
www.eaglesfm.com

WFCF *Flagler College*
PO Box 1027, St. Augustine, FL 32085-1027
PH: 904-829-6940
wfcf@flagler.edu
www.flagler.edu/news_events/wfcf.html

WGKN *U. Central Florida*
PO Box 161344, Orlando, FL 32816-1344
PH: 407-823-4151 FX: 407-823-6360
wgknwebmaster@yahoo.com
wnsc.ucf.edu

WKNT *U. Central Florida*
PO Box 163230, Orlando, FL 32816
PH: 407-823-4584 FX: 407-823-5899
Carmen Serrano spincycleradio@hotmail.com
www.knightcast.org

WMNF *Tampa College*
1210 E. MLK Blvd. Tampa, FL 33603-4449
Attn: Music Director <your genre>
PH: 813-238-9663 FX: 813-238-1802
wmnf@wmnf.org
www.wmnf.org

WNSU *Nova Southeastern U.*
3301 College Ave. Ft. Lauderdale, FL 33314
PH: 954-262-8457 FX: 954-262-3928
wnsu@nova.edu
radiox.nova.edu

WOSP *U. North Florida*
4567 St. John's Bluff Rd. S., Jacksonville, FL 32224
PH: 904-620-2908 FX: 904-620-1560
Chris Lloyd chrisel@gmail.com
www.unf.edu/groups/wosp

WOWL *Florida Atlantic U.*
777 Glades Rd. U. Ctr. #207D, Boca Raton, FL 33431
PH: 561-297-2842 FX: 561-297-3771
wowl@fau.edu
wowl.fau.edu

WPBZ *Smith College*
701 Northpointe Pkwy. #500, West Palm Beach, FL 33407
PH: 561-616-4600
www.buzz103.com

WPRK *Rollins College*
1000 Holt Ave. 2745, Winter Park, FL 32789
PH: 407-646-2915 FX: 407-646-1560
wprkfm@rollins.edu
www.rollins.edu/wprk

WRGP *Florida International U.*
11200 SW. 8th St., U. Park, GC 319, Miami, FL 33199
PH: 305-348-3575 FX: 305-348-6665
wrgp@fiu.edu
wrgp.fiu.edu

WSLR
PO Box 2540, Sarasota, FL 34230
PH: 941-894-6469
info@wslr.org
www.wslr.org

WVFS *Florida State U.*
420 Diffenbaugh Bldg. Tallahassee, FL 32306-1550
music@wvfs.fsu.edu
www.wvfs.fsu.edu

WVUM *U. Miami*
PO Box 248191, Coral Gables, FL 33124
PH: 305-284-3131 FX: 305-284-3132
info@wvum.org
wvum.org

Georgia

BritPopTarts *SCAD Radio*
www.myspace.com/britpoptarts
*Indie, Alternative and Powerpop. The fab radio
show that digs you the most, baby!*

Just Off the Radar *WUGA*
U. Georgia, 1197 S. Lumpkin St., Athens, GA 30602
PH: 706-542-9842 FX: 706-542-6718
Joe Silva justofftheradar@yahoo.com
justofftheradar.com
*The best of Folk to Techno and everything in
between.*

SCAD Radio *Savannah College of
Art and Design*
Student Media Ctr. PO Box 3146, Savannah,
GA 31402
PH: 912-525-5541 FX: 912-525-5509
radiomd@scad.edu
www.scadradio.org

WMRE *Emory U.*
PO Drawer AG, Atlanta, GA 30322
PH: 404-727-9673 FX: 404-712-8000
www.wmre.org

WRAS *Georgia State U.*
PO Box 4048, Atlanta, GA 30302-4048
PH: 404-651-4488 FX: 404-463-9535
www.wras.org

WREK *Georgia Tech*
350 Ferst Dr. NW. #2224, Atlanta, GA 30332-0630
PH: 404-894-2468 FX: 404-894-6872
music.director@wrek.org
www.wrek.org

WRFG
1083 Austin Ave. NE., Atlanta, GA 30307-1940
PH: 404-523-8989
info@wrfg.org
www.wrfg.org

WUOG *U. Georgia*
Box 2065 Tate Student Ctr. Athens, GA 30602
PH: 706-542-8466 FX: 706-542-0070
md@wuog.org
wuog.org

WVVS *Valdosta State U.*
Valdosta, GA 31698
PH: 229-333-7314
www.valdosta.edu/wvvs

WWGC *West Georgia U.*
1600 Maple St., Carrollton, GA 30118
PH: 770-836-6500
wwgc@westga.edu
www.westga.edu/~wwgc

Hawaii

KKCR
PO Box 825, Hanalei, HI 96714
PH: 808-826-7771
kkcr@kkcr.org
www.kkcr.org

KTUH *U. Hawaii*
2445 Campus Rd. Hemenway Hall #203,
Honolulu, HI 96822
PH: 808-956-7261 FX: 808-956-5271
music@ktuh.org
ktuh.hawaii.edu

Idaho

KRFP
#201-116 E. 3rd St., Moscow, ID 83843
PH: 208-892-9200
info@radiofreemoscow.com
www.radiofreemoscow.com

KISU *Idaho State U.*
Campus Box 8014, Pocatello, ID 83209
PH: 208-282-5939
kisufm91@isu.edu
www.kisu.org

KUOI *U. Idaho*
3rd Fl. Student Union Bldg. Campus Box 444272,
Moscow, ID 83844-4272
PH: 208-885-6433 FX: 208-885-2222
kuoi@uidaho.edu
kuoi.asui.uidaho.edu

Illinois

Jstreet Radio
PO Box 126, Waukegan, IL 60079
PH: 847-546-9757
radio@jstreetzine.com
www.jstreetzine.com/radio
*Spinning independent music, on-air interviews and
more!*

The Perfect Face for Radio *WLUW*
6525 N. Sheridan Rd. Chicago, IL 60626
PH: 773-508-0590 FX: 773-508-8082
Nicole mcnicole@gmail.com
www.theperfectfaceforradio.com
Music and interviews. The best in Indie Rock.

SHINE.fm *Olivet Nazarene U.*
1 University Ave. Bourbonnais, IL 60914-2345
PH: 800-987-9668 FX: 815-939-5087
shine@olivet.edu
www.shine.fm

UIC Radio *U. Illinois Chicago*
750 S. Halsted, Rm. 386, 118 M/C, Chicago,
IL 60607
PH: 312-413-2191
uicradio@uic.edu
uicradio.pages.uic.edu

WAUG *Augustana College*
639 38th St., Rock Island, IL 61201
PH: 309-794-7512
waug@augustana.edu
waug.augustana.edu

WCSF *U. St. Francis*
500 N. Wilcox St., Joliet, IL 60435
PH: 815-740-3217
www.stfrancis.edu/theedge
Rock/Alternative format.

WCRX *Columbia College*
600 S. Michigan Ave. Chicago, IL 60605
PH: 312-344-8160
www.colum.edu/crx/snoble

WDBX
224 N. Washington St., Carbondale, IL 62901
PH: 618-457-3691 FX: 618-529-5900
Brian Powell wdbx@globaleyes.net
www.wdbx.org

WEFT
113 N. Market St., Champaign, IL 61820
PH: 217-359-9338
weft@weftfm.org
www.weft.org

WEIU *Eastern Illinois U.*
PH: 217-581-6116
hitmix@weiu.net
www.weiufm.org

WESN *Illinois Wesleyan U.*
PO Box 2900, Bloomington, IL 61701
PH: 309-556-2949 FX: 309-556-2949
wesn@iwu.edu
www.iwu.edu/~wesn

WHPK *U. Chicago*
5706 S. U. Ave. Chicago, IL 60637
PH: 773-702-8424 FX: 773-834-1488
whpk-sm@uchicago.edu
whpk.uchicago.edu

WIDB *Southern Illinois U.*
Mailcode 4428, Carbondale, IL 62901
PH: 618-536-2361
pd@widb.net
www.widb.net

WIIT *Illinois Inst. Tech*
3300 S. Federal St., Chicago, IL 60616
PH: 312-567-3088 FX: 312-567-7042
md.wiit@iit.edu
radio.iit.edu

WIUS *Indiana U.*
326 Sallee Hall, Macomb, IL 61455
PH: 309-298-3218
wiusmusicdirector@yahoo.com
www.wiu.edu/thedog

WJMU *Millikin U.*
1184 W. Main St., Decatur, IL 62522
PH: 217-424-6377
wjmu@mail.millikin
www.millikin.edu/wjmu

WLKL *Lake Land College*
5001 Lake Land Blvd. Mattoon, IL 61938
PH: 217-234-5373
themax_llc@yahoo.com
www.themaxradio.com

WLTL *Lyons Township H.S.*
100 S. Brainard Ave. La Grange, IL 60525
PH: 708-482-9585 FX: 708-482-7051
www.wltl.net

WLUW *Loyola U.*
6525 N. Sheridan Rd. Chicago, IL 60626
PH: 773-508-0590 FX: 773-508-8082
musicdept@wluw.org
www.wluw.org

WMCR *Monmouth College*
700 E. Broadway Monmouth, IL 61462
PH: 309-457-3060 FX: 309-457-2141
department.monm.edu/wmcr

WNTH *New Trier H.S.*
385 Winnetka Ave. Winnetka, IL 60093
PH: 847-501-6457
wnth@newtrier.k12.il.us
www.wnth.org

WNUR *Northwestern U.*
1920 Campus Dr. Evanston, IL 60208-2280
PH: 847-491-7102 FX: 847-467-2058
rock-md@wnur.org
www.wnur.org

WONC *North Central College*
30 N. Brainard St., Naperville, IL 60540-4690
PH: 630-637-5969 FX: 630-637-5900
feedback@wonc.org
www.wonc.org

WPCD *Parkland College*
2400 W. Bradley Ave. Champaign, IL 61821
PH: 217-373-3790
www.parkland.edu/wpcd

WQNA *Springfield*
2201 Toronto Rd. Springfield, IL 62712
PH: 217-529-5431 x164 FX: 217-529-7861
info@wqna.org
www.wqna.org

WQUB *Quincy U.*
1800 College Ave., Quincy, IL 62301-2699
PH: 217-228-5410
www.quincy.edu/wqub

WRDP *DePaul U.*
2250 N. Sheffield Ave. #317, Box #640, Chicago,
IL 60614
PH: 773-325-7341 FX: 773-325-7399
wrdpmusic@hotmail.com
radio.depaul.edu

WRRG *Triton College*
2000 5ᵗʰ Ave., River Grove, IL 60171
PH: 708-583-3110
info@wrrg.org
www.wrrg.org

WRSE *Elmhurst College*
190 Propect Ave. Elmhurst, IL 60126
PH: 630-617-5683
webmaster@wrse.com
www.wrse.com

WSIE *S. Illinois U.*
0141 Dunham Hall, Box 1773, Edwardsville,
IL 62026
PH: 618-650-2228
www.siue.edu/WSIE

WVJC *Wabash Valley College*
2200 College Dr. Mount Carmel, IL 62863
PH: 618-262-8989 FX: 618-262-7317
www.iecc.cc.il.us/wvjc

WVKC *Knox College*
PO Box K-254 2 E. S. St., Galesburg, IL 61401
PH: 309-341-7441
ebyng@knox.edu
deptorg.knox.edu/wvkc

WXAV *St. Xavier U.*
3700 W. 103ʳᵈ St., Chicago, IL 60655
PH: 773-298-3386 FX: 773-298-3381
wxavmusic@yahoo.com
web.sxu.edu/wxav

WZND *Illinois State U.*
007 Fell Hall, Normal, IL 61790-4481
PH: 309-438-5490 FX: 309-438-2652
z106music@hotmail.com
www.wznd.com

WZRD *Northeastern Illinois U.*
5500 N. St. Louis Ave. Chicago, IL 60625-4699
PH: 773-442-4578 FX: 773-442-4665
wzrd@neiu.edu
www.WZRDChicago.com

Indiana

City of Music
7399 N. Shadeland Ave. #284, Indianapolis,
IN 46250
PH: 317-471-3333
information@cityofmusic.com
www.cityofmusic.com

WBAA *Purdue U.*
712 3ʳᵈ St., W. Lafayette, IN 47907-2005
PH: 765-494-5920
www.purdue.edu/wbaa

WBDG *Ben Davis H.S.*
1200 N. Girls School Rd. Indianapolis, IN 46214
PH: 317-244-9234 FX: 317-243-5506
www.wayne.k12.in.us/bdwbdg

WBKE *Manchester College*
MC Box 19, North Manchester, IN 46962
PH: 260-982-5272 FX: 260-982-5043
Steve Grubb WBKEmusic@gmail.com
wbke.manchester.edu

WCCR *Purdue U.*
Box M, 1016 W. Stadium Ave. West Lafayette,
IN 47906-4243
PH: 765-494-9773
wccr@ics.purdue.edu
purdue.edu/wccr

WCRD *Ball State U.*
BC 132, Muncie, IN 47306
PH: 765-285-2473
wcrd@bsu.edu
wcrd.net

WECI *Earlham College*
801 National Rd. W. Dr. 45, Richmond, IN 47374
md@weciradio.org
PH: 765-983-1246 FX: 765-983-1641
www.weciradio.org

WFHB
PO Box 1973, Bloomington, IN 47402
PH: 812-323-1200 FX: 812-323-0320
music@wfhb.org
www.wfhb.org

WGCS *Goshen College*
1700 S. Main St., Goshen, IN 46526
PH: 574-535-7488 FX: 574-535-7293
globe@goshen.edu
www.goshen.edu/wgcs

WGRE *DePauw U.*
609 Locust St., Greencastle, IN 46135
PH: 765-658-4637
wgre@depauw.edu
www.depauw.edu/univ/wgre

WISU *Indiana State U.*
217 Dreiser, Terre Haute, IN 47809
PH: 812-237-FM90 FX: 812-237-8970
Dave Sabaini MrRadio@indstate.edu
wisu.indstate.edu

WMHD *Rose-Hulman Inst. Tech*
5500 Wabash Ave. Terre Haute, IN 47803
PH: 812-877-8350
indie@wmhdradio.org
wmhdradio.org

WNDY *Wabash College*
301 W. Wabash Ave. Crawfordsville, IN 47933
PH: 765-361-6038
www.wabash.edu/orgs/wndy

WPUM *St. Joseph's College*
US Hwy. 231, PO Box 870, Rensselaer, IN 47978
PH: 219-866-6000 x6905
wpum@saintjoe.edu
www.saintjoe.edu/~wpum

WQHU *Huntington College*
2303 College Ave. Huntington, IN 46750
www.wqhu.net

WUEV *U. Evansville*
1800 Lincoln Ave. Evansville, IN 47722
PH: 812-479-2020 FX: 812-479-2320
wuevfm@evansville.edu
wuev.evansville.edu

WVFI *U. Notre Dame*
200 LaFortune Hall, Notre Dame, IN 46556
PH: 574-631-6400
wvfi@nd.edu
www.nd.edu/~wvfi

WVUR *Valparaiso U.*
32 Schnabel Hall, 1809 Chapel Dr. Valparaiso,
IN 46383
PH: 219-464-6683
www.valpo.edu/student/wvur

Iowa

KALA *St. Ambrose U.*
518 W. Locust St., Davenport, IA 52803
PH: 563-333-6216 FX: 563-333-6218
kala@sau.edu
sau.edu/kala

KBVU *Buena Vista U.*
610 W. 4ᵗʰ St., Storm Lake, IA 50588
PH: 712-749-1234 FX: 712-749-2037
KBVU@bvu.edu
edge.bvu.edu

KDPS *Grand View College*
1200 Grandview Ave. Des Moines, IA 50309
PH: 515-263-2985
kdpsradio@gvc.edu
www.kdpsradio.com

KICB *Iowa Central College*
330 Ave. M, Fort Dodge, IA 50501
PH: 515-576-0099 ext. 2353
www.iccc.cc.ia.us/kicb

KMSC *Morningside College*
1501 Morningside Ave. Sioux City, IA 51106
PH: 712-274-5331
kmscmusic@morningside.edu
webs.morningside.edu/masscomm/KMSC

KRNL *Cornell College*
810 Commons Cir. Mount Vernon, IA 52314
PH: 319-895-5765
www.cornellcollege.edu/krnl

KRUI *U. Iowa*
379 IMU, Iowa City, IA 52242
PH: 319-335-8970
www.uiowa.edu/~krui

KULT *U. Northern Iowa*
L045 Maucker Union, Cedar Falls, IA 50614
PH: 319-372-5858
kult@uni.edu
www.uni.edu/kult

KURE *Iowa State U.*
1199 Friley Hall, Ames, IA 50012
PH: 515-294-9292 FX: 515-294-4332
music@kure885.org
www.kure885.org

KWAR
100 Wartburg Blvd. Waverly, IA 50677
PH: 319-352-8306
theone@kwar.org
www.kwar.org

KWLC *Luther College*
700 College Dr. Decorah, IA 52101-1045
PH: 563-387-1571 FX: 563-387-2158
kwlcam@luther.edu
kwlc.luther.edu

KZOW *Waldorf College*
106 S. 6th St., Forest City, IA 50436
PH: 515-923-3210
www.kzowfm.com

Kansas

KBCU *Bethel College*
PO Box 88, North Newton, KS 67117
PH: 316-284-5228
kbcu@bethelks.edu
www.bethelks.edu/KBCU

KFHS *Fort Hays State U.*
600 Park St., Hays, KS 67601
PH: 785-628-4198
kfhs@fhsu.edu
www.fhsu.edu/int/kfhsradio

KJAG
624 Sonora Dr. McPherson, KS 67460
PH: 620-960-4929
airplay@kjagradio.com
www.kjagradio.com

KJHK *U. Kansas*
1301 Jayhawk Blvd. Kansas Union, Rm. 427,
Lawrence, KS 66045
PH: 785-864-5483
kjhkmusic@ku.edu
kjhk.org

KSDB *Kansas State U.*
105 Kedzie Hall, Manhattan, KS 66506-1501
PH: 785-532-0919
radio@k-state.edu
wildcatradio.ksu.edu

Kentucky

The Indie Connection *WKMS*
2018 University Stn. Murray, KY 42071
PH: 270-762-4359
John Gibson john.gibson@gmail.com
www.myspace.com/indieconnection
*Focusing on independent and local bands. You
MUST e-mail me first with a link to your music.*

WFPK
619 S. 4th St., Louisville, KY 40202
PH: 502-814-6500
studio@wfpk.org
www.wfpk.org

WMMT
91 Madison St., Whitesburg, KY 41858
PH: 606-633-1208
wmmtfm@appalshop.org
www.appalshop.org/wmmt

WRFL *U. Kentucky*
777 U. Stn. Lexington, KY 40506-0025
PH: 859-257-4636 FX: 859-323-1039
music@wrfl881.org
wrfl881.org

WWHR *Western Kentucky U.*
College Heights, 1 Big Red Way, Bowling Green,
KY 42101
PH: 270-745-5350
info@revolution.fm
www.wku.edu/revolution917

Louisiana

KGRM *Grambling U.*
Dunbar Hall, Rm. 220, PO Box K, Grambling,
LA 71245
PH: 318-274-6343 FX: 318-274-3245
Joyce Evans evansjb@gram.edu
www.gram.edu/kgrm

KLPI *Louisiana Tech*
PO Box 8638, Tech Stn. Ruston, LA 71272
PH: 318-257-4851 FX: 318-257-5073
www.latech.edu/tech/orgs/klpi

KLSP *Louisiana State Penitentiary*
Angola, LA 70712
www.corrections.state.la.us/LSP/KLSP.htm
*The only licensed radio station to operate from
within a prison by inmate DJs.*

KLSU *Louisiana State U.*
B-39 Hodges Hall, Baton Rouge, LA 70803
PH: 225-578-4620 FX: 225-578-1698
music.director@klsu.fm
www.klsu.fm

KSCL *Centenary College*
2911 Centenary Blvd. Shreveport, LA 71104
PH: 318-869-5296
www.centenary.edu/life/kscl

KSLU *Southern Louisiana U.*
D. Vickers Rm. 112, SLU 10783, Hammond,
LA 70402
PH: 985-549-5758 FX: 985-549-3960
kslu@selu.edu
www.selu.edu/kslu

KXUL *U. Louisiana*
130 Stubbs Hall, 401 Bayou Dr. Monroe,
LA 71209-8821
PH: 318-342-5662
kxul.com

WTUL
Tulane U. Ctr., New Orleans, LA 70118
PH: 504-865-5885 FX: 504-463-1023
md1@wtul.fm
www.wtul.fm

Maine

WBOR *Bowdoin College*
Smith Union, Brunswick, ME 04011
PH: 207-725-3210
wbor@bowdoin.edu
studorgs.bowdoin.edu/wbor

WERU
PO Box 170, 1186 Acadia Hwy., East Orland,
ME 04431
PH: 207-469-6600 FX: 207-469-8961
info@weru.org
www.weru.org

WHSN *Husson College*
1 College Cir. Bangor, ME 04401
PH: 207-941-7116 FX: 207-947-3987
whsn@nescom.edu
www.whsn-fm.com

WMEB *U. Maine*
5748 Memorial Union, Orono, ME 04469-5748
PH: 207-588-2333 FX: 207-581-4343
wmeb_feedback@umit.maine.edu
www.umaine.edu/wmeb

WMHB *Colby College*
4000 Mayflower Hill, Waterville, ME 04901
PH: 207-872-3686
wmhb@colby.edu
www.colby.edu/wmhb

WMPG *U. Southern Maine*
96 Falmouth St., Portland, ME 04104-9300
PH: 207-780-4976
musicdepartment@wmpg.org
www.wmpg.org

WRBC *Bates College*
Lewiston, ME 04240
PH: 207-777-7532 FX: 207-795-8793
www.bates.edu/people/orgs/wrbc

WUMF *U. Maine*
111 South St., Farmington, ME 04938
PH: 207-777-7353 FX: 207-778-7113
wumf@umf.maine.edu
wumf.umf.maine.edu

WUPI *U. Maine Presque Isle*
PO Box 525, 181 Main St., Presque Isle, ME 04769
PH: 207-768-9742
stationmanager@wupiradio.com
www.umpi.maine.edu/~wupi

Maryland

URSCENE Internet Radio/TV
8452 Ardwick Ardmore Rd. Landover,
MD 20785-2306
PH: 301-806-3740
Pharice Brown pmarissabrown@hotmail.com
www.urscene.com
*Features the performances of Indie artists. We also
play Indie artists on our internet/TV show.*

WFWM *Frostburg State U.*
Frostburg, MD 21532
PH: 301-687-7096
wfwm@frostburg.edu
www.wfwm.org

WMBC *U. Maryland*
U. Ctr. 101, 1000 Hilltop Cir. Baltimore, MD 21250
PH: 410-455-26582 FX: 410-455-3067
indie@wmbc.umbc.edu
wmbc.umbc.edu

WMUC *U. Maryland*
3130 S. Campus Dining Hall, College Park,
MD 20742-8431
PH: 301-314-7868
www.wmuc.umd.edu

WXSU *Salisbury U.*
PO Box 3151 Salisbury, MD 21801
PH: 410-548-4760
wxsu@salisbury.edu
orgs.salisbury.edu/wxsu

XTSR *Towson U.*
8000 York Rd. Media Ctr. Rm. 005, Towson, MD 21252
PH: 410-704-5309
xtsr@hotmail.com
wwwnew.towson.edu/xtsr
Towson's commercial free Rock station.

Massachusetts

Three Ring Circus *WMBR*
3 Ames St., Cambridge, MA 02142
PH: 617-253-8810
Joan Hathaway circus@wmbr.org
wmbr.mit.edu
Roots Rock, Indie, Blues, Garage, Surf/instro and all the billies (Rocka, Hill and Psycho).

WAMH *Amherst College*
AC #1907 Campus Ctr. Amherst, MA 01002-5000
PH: 413-542-2288
wamh@amherst.edu
wamh.amherst.edu

WAVM *Maynard H.S.*
1 Tiger Dr. Maynard, MA 01754
PH: 978-897-5179
studio@wavm.org
www.wavm.org

WBIM *Bridgewater College*
109 Campus Ctr. Bridgewater, MA 02325
PH: 508-531-1303 FX: 508-531-1786
wbimmd@hotmail.com
www.bridgew.edu/wbim

WBRS *Brandeis U.*
Shapiro Campus Ctr. 415 South St., Waltham, MA 02453-2728 Attn: (genre)
PH: 781-736-4785
music@wbrs.org
www.wbrs.org

WBTY *Bentley College*
175 Forest St., Waltham, MA 02452
PH: 781-891- 3473
www.wbty.com

WCCH *Holyoke College*
303 Homestead Ave. Holyoke, MA 01040
www.wcch.blogspot.com

WCFM *Williams College*
Baxter Hall, Williamstown, MA 01267
PH: 413-597-2373 FX: 413-597-2259
wcfmbd@wso.williams.edu
wcfm.williams.edu

WCHC *College of the Holy Cross*
1 College St., Worcester, MA 01610
PH: 508-793-2474
wchc@holycross.edu
college.holycross.edu/wchc

WCUW
910 Main St., Worcester, MA 01610
PH: 508-753-2274
wcuw@wcuw.com
www.wcuw.com

WDOA
128 Mechanic St., Spencer, MA 01562
FX: 253-323-1606
wdoainfo@wdoa.com
www.wdoa.com

WERS *Emerson College*
120 Boylston St., Boston, MA 02116
PH: 617-824-8084
music@wers.org
www.wers.org

WHHB *Holliston H.S.*
370 Hollis St., Holliston, MA 01746
PH: 508-429-0681
ProgramDirector@whhbfm.com
www.whhbfm.com

WIQH
500 Walden St., Concord, MA 01742
PH: 978-369-2440
wiqh@colonial.net
www.colonial.net/wiqh

WMBR *Mass Inst. Technology*
3 Ames St., Cambridge, MA 02142
PH: 617-253-7777
music@wmbr.org
wmbr.mit.edu

WMFO *Tufts U.*
PO Box 65, Medford, MA 02155
PH: 617-627-3800
md@wmfo.org
www.wmfo.org

WMHC *Mt. Holyoke College*
Blanchard Student Ctr. South Hadley, MA 01705
PH: 413-538-2044 FX: 413-538-2431
www.mtholyoke.edu/org/wmhc

WMUA *U. Massachusetts*
105 Campus Ctr. Amherst, MA 01003
PH: 413-545-3691 FX: 413-545-0682
music@wmua.org
wmua.org

WMWM *Salem State College*
352 Lafayette St., Salem, MA 01970-5353
PH: 978-745-9170
wmwmsalem@gmail.com
www.wmwmsalem.com

WOMR
494 Commercial St., Provincetown, MA 02657
PH: 508-487-2619
www.womr.org

WOZQ
Campus Ctr. Northampton, MA 01063
PH: 413-585-4977
sophia.smith.edu/org/wozq

WPAA *Phillips Academy*
180 Main St., Andover, MA 01810
PH: 978-749-4384
WPAA@aol.com
users.aol.com/wpaa

WRBB *Northeastern U.*
360 Huntington Ave. Boston, MA 02115
PH: 617-373-4339 FX: 617-373-5095
wrbbradio.org

WRNX
98 Lower Westfield Rd. Holyoke, MA 01040
PH: 413-536-1009 FX: 413-536-1153
www.wrnx.com

WRSI
15 Hampton Ave. PO Box 268, Northampton, MA 01060
PH: 413-585-8939 FX: 413-585-8501
Johnny Memphis johnny@wrsi.com
www.wrsi.com

WSFR *Suffolk U.*
41 Temple St., Boston, MA 02114
PH: 617-305-8324
radio@suffolk.edu
www.suffolk.edu/radio

WSHL *Stonehill College*
320 Washington St., North Easton, MA 02357
PH: 508-565-1913 FX: 508-565-1974
wshl@stonehill.edu
wshl.stonehill.edu

WSKB *Westfield State College*
577 Western Ave. Westfield, MA 01086
PH: 413-572-5579 FX: 413-572-5625
ninjadonkey2001@yahoo.com
www.wsc.ma.edu/wskb

WSMU *U. Mass/Dartmouth*
285 Old Westport Rd., North Dartmouth, MA 02747
PH: 508-999-8150 FX: 508-999-8173
wsmu@umassd.edu
www.wsmu.org

WTBU *Boston U .*
640 Commonwealth Ave. Boston, MA 02215
PH: 617-353-6400 FX: 617-353-6403
www.wtburadio.com

WTCC *Springfield Tech*
#1, PO Box 9000, Springfield, MA 01102-9000
PH: 413-736-2781 FX: 413-755-6305
musicwtcc@stcc.edu
www.wtccfm.org

WUML *U. Massachusetts*
1 U. Ave. Lowell, MA 01854
PH: 978-934-4975
md@wuml.org
wuml.org

WWPI *Worcester Polytechnic Inst.*
100 Institute Rd. Worcester, MA 01609
PH: 508-831-5956
radio@wpi.edu
radio.wpi.edu

WXOJ
140 Pine St., Florence, MA 01062
PH: 413-585-1033
vfrprogramming@gmail.com
info@valleyfreeradio.org
www.valleyfreeradio.org

WXPL *Fitchburg State*
160 Pearl St., Fitchburg, MA 01420
PH: 978-665-4848
falcon.fsc.edu/~wxpl

WZBC *Boston College*
McElroy Commons, 107 Chestnut Hill, MA 02467
PH: 617-552-4686 FX: 617-552-1738
wzbcmusic@gmail.com
www.wzbc.org

WZLY *Wellesley College*
Schneider Ctr. 106 Central St., Wellesley, MA 02481
PH: 781-283-2690
md@wzly.net
wzly.net

Michigan

Lake FX Radio *Muskegon College*
221 S. Quarterine Rd. Muskegon, MI 49437
PH: 231-777-0330
lakefxradio.com

WCBN *U. Michigan*
530 Student Activities Bldg. Ann Arbor,
MI 48109-1316
PH: 734-763-3501
music@wcbn.org
www.wcbn.org

WHFR *Henry Ford College*
5101 Evergreen Rd. Dearborn, MI 48128
PH: 313-845-9783 FX: 313-317-4034
whfr-md@hfcc.edu
whfr.hfcc.net

WIDR *Western Michigan U.*
1501 Faunce Student Service Bldg. Kalamazoo,
MI 49008-6301
PH: 269-387-6306
widr-music@groupwise.wmich.edu
www.widr.org

WKUS *Kettering U.*
1700 W. 3rd Ave. Flint, MI 48504
PH: 810-762-9725
www.wkus.org

WLBN *Albion College*
611 E. Porter St., Albion, MI 49224
PH: 517-629-1000
wlbn@albion.edu
www.albion.edu/wlbn

WLSO *Lake Superior State U.*
680 W. Easterday Ave. Sault Ste. Marie, MI 49783
PH: 906-635-2107 FX: 906-635-2111
wlso@lssu.edu
www.lssu.edu/wlso

WMHW *Central Michigan U.*
183 Moore Hall Mt. Pleasant, MI 48859
PH: 989-774-7287
wmhw@cmich.edu
www.bca.cmich.edu/WMHW

WMTU *Michigan Tech U.*
G03 Wadsworth Hall, 1703 Townsend Dr. Houghton
MI 49931-1193
PH: 906-487-2333 FX: 906-483-3016
wmtu@mtu.edu
wmtu.mtu.edu

WNMC *NW Michigan College*
1701 E. Front St., Traverse City, MI 49686
PH: 231-995-1135
wnmc@nmc.edu
www.wnmc.org

WOES *Ovid-Elsie Area Schools*
8989 Colony Rd. Elsie, MI 48831
PH: 989-862-4237
woes@oe.k12.mi.us
oe.edzone.net/~woes

WQAC *Alma College*
614 W. Superior St., Alma, MI 48801
PH: 989-466-4359
wqaccharts@blazemail.com
students.alma.edu/organizations/wqac

WUMD *U. Michigan Dearborn*
4901 Evergreen Rd. Dearborn, MI 48128
PH: 313-593-5167 FX: 313-593-3503
wumd_music_director@hotmail.com
www.umd.umich.edu/wumd

WUPX *Marquette U.*
1204 U. Ctr. Marquette, MI 49855
PH: 906-227-1844 FX: 906-227-2344
www.wupx.com

WXOU *Oakland U.*
69 Oakland Ctr. Rochester, MI 48309
PH: 248-370-2845 FX: 248-370-2846
wxoumusic@yahoo.com
www.oakland.edu/org/wxou

WYCE
711 Bridge St. NW., Grand Rapids, MI 49504
PH: 616-459-4788 FX: 616-742-0599
Pete Bruinsma pete@wyce.org
www.wyce.org

Minnesota

KAXE
260 NE. 2nd St., Grand Rapids, MN 55744
PH: 218-326-1234 FX: 218-326-1235
kaxe@kaxe.org
www.kaxe.org

KBSB *Bemidji State U.*
1500 Birchmont Dr. NE., Bemidji, MN 56601-2699
PH: 218-755-4120 FX: 218-755-4048
fm90@bemidjistate.edu
www.fm90.org

KFAI
1808 Riverside Ave. Minneapolis, MN 55454
PH: 612-341-3144 x20 FX: 612-341-4281
kfaimusicdept903@hotmail.com
www.kfai.org

KGSM *Gustavus Adolphus College*
800 W. College Ave. St. Peter, MN 56082
PH: 507-933-8000 x8783.
www.gac.edu/oncampus/orgs/kgsm

KJNB *College of St. Benedict*
37 S. College Ave. St. Joseph, MN 56374
PH: 320-363-3379
kjnb@csbsju.edu
www.csbsju.edu/kjnb

KMSC *Minnesota State U. Moorhead*
Owens Hall Box 138, Moorhead, MN 56563
PH: 218-477-2116
kmsc1500am@yahoo.com
www.dragonradio.org

KMSU *Minnesota State U.*
AF 205, Mankato, MN 56001
PH: 507-389-5678 FX: 507-389-1705
Shelley Pierce shelley215@juno.com
www.mnsu.edu/kmsufm

KORD *Concordia College*
901 8th St. S., Moorhead, MN 56562
www.cord.edu/dept/kord

KQAL
PO Box 5838, Winona, MN 55987
PH: 507-453-5229 FX: 507-457-5226
www.kqal.org

KRLX
300 N. College St., Northfield, MN 55057
PH: 507-646-4127
recordlibrary@krlx.org
www.krlx.org

KSMR *St. Mary's U.*
2500 Park Ave. Minneapolis, MN 55404-4403
PH: 507-457-1613
ksmr@smumn.edu
www2.smumn.edu/studorg/~ksmr

KSTO *St. Olaf College*
1500 St. Olaf Ave. Northfield, MN 55057
PH: 507-646-3603
ksto@stolaf.edu
www.stolaf.edu/orgs/ksto

KUMM *U. Minnesota*
600 E. 4th St., Morris, MN 56267
PH: 320-589-6076
kumm@kumm.org
www.kumm.org
Hard Alternative music.

KUOM *U. Minnesota*
610 Rarig Ctr. 330 21st Ave. S., Minneapolis,
MN 55455
PH: 612-625-5304 FX: 612-625-2112
music@radiok.org
www.radiok.org

KVSC *Saint Cloud State U.*
720 4th Ave. S. 27 Stewart Hall, St. Cloud, MN
56301-4498
PH: 320-308-3126 FX: 320-308-5337
music@kvsc.org
www.kvsc.org

Radio Rumpus Room *KFAI*
1808 Riverside Ave. Minneapolis, MN 55454
PH: 612-341-3144 FX: 612-341-4281
rumpus2@bitstream.net
www.radiorumpusroom.com
*Surf, Hot Rod, Rockabilly, '60s Garage, Hillbilly,
Psychedelia, Back-to-the-Roots Country…*

WELY
133 E. Chapman St., Ely, MN 55731
PH: 218-365-4444
www.wely.com

WMCN *Manchester College*
1600 Grand Ave. Saint Paul, MN 55105
PH: 651-696-6082
wmcn@macalester.edu
www.macalester.edu/wmcn

WTIP
PO Box 1005, Grand Marais, MN 55604
PH: 218-387-1070 FX: 218-387-1120
info@wtip.org
wtip.org

Mississippi

WMSV *Mississippi State U.*
PO Box 6210 Student Media Ctr. MS 39762-6210
PH: 662-325-8034 FX: 662-325-8037
wmsv@msstate.edu
www.wmsv.msstate.edu

WUMS *U. Mississippi*
PO Box 1848, UM, 38677-1848
PH: 662-915-5395
www.olemiss.edu/orgs/wums

Missouri

3WK Undergroundradio
PO Box 160161, St. Louis, MO 63116.
Wanda wandagm@3wk.com
www.3wk.com

The Growl
901 S. National, Springfield, MO 65804
PH: 417-836-6286
Ben Craig bengrowl@gmail.com
thegrowl.missouristate.edu

KCFV *Florissant Valley College*
3400 Pershall Rd. St Louis, MO 63135-1499
PH: 414-595-4463 FX: 314-595-4217
stew8@hotmail.com
www.stlcc.cc.mo.us/fv/kcfv

KCLC
209 S. Kings Highway, St Charles, MO 63301
PH: 636-949-4880
fm891@lindenwood.edu
www.891thewood.com

KCOU *U. Missouri*
101F Pershing Hall, Columbia, MO 65201
PH: 573-882-7820
kcou.missouri.edu

KDHX
3504 Magnolia, St. Louis, MO 63118
PH: 314-664-3955 x301 FX: 314-664-1020
musicdepartment@kdhx.org
www.kdhx.org

KGLX *Webster U.*
470 E. Lockwood, St. Louis, MO 63119
PH: 314-968-7162
www.kglx.org

KKFI
PO Box 32250, Kansas City, MO 64171
PH: 816-931-3122 x106
www.kkfi.org

KMNR *U. Missouri*
113E U. Ctr. W. 1870 Miner Cir. Rolla,
MO 65409-1440
PH: 573-341-4273 FX: 573-341-6021
kmnr@umr.edu
marconi.kmnr.umr.edu/kmnr-web

KOPN
915 E. Broadway St., Columbia, MO 65201
PH: 573-874-1139 FX: 573-499-1662
mail@kopn.org
www.kopn.org/artist_sub.htm

KSLU *St. Louis U.*
20 N. Grand Blvd. St. Louis, MO 63108
PH: 314-977-1574 FX: 314-977-1579
kslu@slu.edu
kslu.slu.edu

KTBG
Wood 11, Warrensburg, MO 64093
PH: 660-543-4491
Jon Hart jhart@ktbg.cmsu.edu
ktbg.fm

KTRM *Truman State U.*
100 E. Normal St., Student Union Bldg. LL,
Kirksville, MO 63501
PH: 660-785-5876 FX: 660-785-7261
ktrm.truman.edu

KWUR *Washington U.*
Campus Box 1205, 1 Brookings Dr. St. Louis,
MO 63105
PH: 314-935-5952
info@kwur.com
www.kwur.com

KYMC
PO Box 4038, Chesterfield, MO 63006
PH: 636-532-6515 x256
Natalie Hall nhall@ymcastlouis.org
www.kymcradio.netfirms.com

KZLX *NW Missouri State*
800 University Dr. Maryville, MO 64468
PH: 660-562-1162
KZLX@excite.com
info.nwmissouri.edu/~KDLX

Retro Red-Eye Express *KKFI*
PO Box 32250, Kansas City, MO 64171-2250
Attn: Sunshine
Sunshine retroredeye@gmail.com
www.myspace.com/retrosunshine
retroredeye.blogspot.com
*If your music fits the type of music I play on my
show (see profile), please send your CD.*

Sonic Spectrum *KCUR*
4825 Troost Ave. #202, Kansas City, MO 64110
PH: 816-235-2869
Robert Moore moorerb@umkc.edu
www.kcur.org/sonicspectrum.html
Blues to Drum n' Bass, Indie Rock to Honky Tonk.

Montana

KBGA *U. Montana*
U. Ctr. Rm. 208, Missoula, MT 59812
PH: 406-243-5715
kbgamd@kbga.org
www.kbga.org

KDWG
Campus Box 119, 710 S. Atlantic St., Dillion,
MT 59725
PH: 406-683-7394
www.umwestern.edu/kdwg

KGLT
MSU Box 17424, Bozeman, MT 59717-4240
PH: 406-994-6483 FX: 406-994-1987
wwwkglt@montana.edu
www.kglt.net

KMSM *Montana Tech*
1300 W. Park St. #117, Butte, MT 59701
PH: 406-496-1071 FX: 406-496-4702
kmsm@mtech.edu
www.mtech.edu/kmsm

Nebraska

KDNE *Doane College*
1014 Boswell Ave. Crete, NE 68333
PH: 402-826-8677
kdne@doane.edu
webcast.doane.edu

KLPR *U. Nebraska*
109 Thomas Hall, Kearney, NE 68849
PH: 308-865-8217
klpr.unk.edu

KRNU *U. Nebraska*
147 Andersen Hall, PO Box 880466, Lincoln,
NE 68588-0466
PH: 402-472-8277
krnu-music@unl.edu
krnu.unl.edu

KZUM
941 "O" St., Lincoln, NE 68508
PH: 402-474-5086 FX: 402-474-5091
programming@kzum.org
www.kzum.org

New Hampshire

Radio SNHU *S. New Hampshire U.*
2500 N. River Rd. Manchester, NH 03106-1045
PH: 603-629-4695
radiosnhu@snhu.edu
radio.snhu.edu

WDCR *Dartmouth College*
theradio@dartmouth.edu
www.dartmouth.edu/~wdcr

WKNH *Keene State College*
229 Main St., Keene, NH 03435
PH: 603-358-2420
music@wknh.org
www.wknh.org

WPCR *Plymouth State College*
17 High St., Plymouth, NH 03264
PH: 603-535-2242
mindwarp.plymouth.edu

WSCA
PO Box 6532, Portsmouth, NH 03802
PH: 603-430-9722 FX: 603-430-9822
music@portsmouthcommunityradio.org
www.wscafm.org

WSCS *Colby-Sawyer College*
541 Main St., New London, NH 03257
PH: 603-526-3443
wpeters@colby-sawyer.edu
www.colby-sawyer.edu/wscs

WUNH *U. New Hampshire*
MUB Durham, NH 03824
PH: 603-862-2222
music@wunh.org
wunh.org

New Jersey

All Mixed Up *WDHA*
55 Horsehill Rd. Cedar Knolls, NJ 07927
Jim Monaghan AllMixedUpRadio@aol.com
www.AllMixedUpRadio.com
*A little Rock, Folk, Country, Soul, Jazz - all custom-
blended for your Sunday morning.*

Carnival of Song *WFDU*
Metropolitan Campus, 1000 River Rd. Teaneck,
NJ 07666
Lynn Crystal lynncrystal@carnivalofsong.com
carnivalofsong.com
*I play music from artists who deserve to be heard
because of the emotional honesty of their work.*

WBZC *Burlington County College*
601 Pemberton Browns Mills Rd. Pemberton,
NJ 08068-1599
PH: 609-894-9311 x1592 FX: 609-894-9440
mail@z889.com
staff.bcc.edu/radio

WFDU *Fairleigh Dickinson U.*
Metropolitan Campus, 1000 River Rd. Teaneck,
NJ 07666
PH: 201-692-2806 FX: 201-692-2807
Barry Sheffield barrys@fdu.edu
wfdu.fm

WFMU
PO Box 5101, Hoboken, NJ 07030
PH: 201-521-1416
www.wfmu.org

WGLS *Rowan U.*
201 Mullica Hill Rd. Glassboro, NJ 08028
PH: 856-863-9457 FX: 856-256-4704
wgls@rowan.edu
wgls.rowan.edu

WJTB *New Jersey Inst. of Tech.*
323 MLK Blvd. Newark, NJ 07102
PH: 973-596-5816
www.wjtb.org

WMCX *Monmouth U.*
400 Cedar Ave. W. Long Branch, NJ 07764
PH: 732-571-5229 FX: 732-263-5145
wmcxradio@monmouth.edu
hawkmail.monmouth.edu/~wmcx

WMSC *Montclair State U .*
1 Normal Ave. Upper Montclair, NJ 07043
PH: 973-655-4587 FX: 973-655-7433
www.montclair.edu/orgs/WMSC

WNTI *Centenary College*
400 Jefferson St., Hackettstown, NJ 07840
PH: 908-979-4355
Amanda Socko wntimd@aol.com
www.wnti.org

WPRB *Princeton U.*
030 Bloomberg Hall, Princeton, NJ 08544
PH: 609-258-3655 FX: 609-258-1806
music@wprb.com
www.wprb.com

WRNU *Rutgers U.*
350 MLK Blvd. Rm. 315 Newark, NJ 07102
PH: 973-353-5746 FX: 973-353-5187
staff@wrnu.net
wrnu.net

WRPR *Ramapo College*
505 Ramapo Valley Rd. Mahwah, NJ 07430
WRPR@Ramapo.edu
orion.ramapo.edu/~wrpr

WRSU *Rutgers U.*
126 College Ave. New Brunswick, NJ 08901
PH: 732-932-7800 x23 FX: 732-932-1768
music@wrsu.org
wrsu.rutgers.edu

WSOU *Seton Hall U.*
400 S. Orange Ave. South Orange, NJ 07079
PH: 973-761-7546 FX: 973-761-7593
wsou@shu.edu
www.wsou.net

WTSR *College of New Jersey*
Kendall Hall, PO Box 7718, Ewing, NJ 08628
PH: 609-771-2420 FX: 609-637-5113
music@wtsr.org
www.wtsr.org

WVPH *Rutgers U. Livingston*
#117 Student Ctr. 84 Joyce Kilmer Ave. Piscataway,
NJ 08854
PH: 732-445-4100
Peter Slocum rockrlc@gmail.com
www.thecore.rutgers.edu

WVRM
615 Valley Rd. Upper Montclair, NJ 07043
PH: 973-746-4999 FX: 973-746-4749
info@villageradio.com
www.villageradio.com

New Mexico

KRUX *New Mexico State U.*
Corbett Ctr. Box 30004, Las Cruces, NM 88003
PH: 505-646-4640 FX: 505-646-5219
music@kruxradio.com
www.krux.nmsu.edu

KTEK *New Mexico Tech.*
SAC Rm. 219, 801 Leroy Place, Socorro,
NM 87801
PH: 505-835-6013
ktek@nmt.edu
infohost.nmt.edu/~ktek

KUNM *U. New Mexico*
MSC06 3520, Onate Hall 1, Albuquerque,
NM 87131-0001
PH: 505-277-5615
music@kunm.org
www.kunm.org

New York

106 VIC *Ithaca College*
118 Roy H. Park Hall, Ithaca, NY 14850
PH: 607-274-1059
vic@ithaca.edu
www.ithaca.edu/radio/vic

Emotional Rescue *WJFF*
4765 State Rt. 52, PO Box 546, Jeffersonville,
NY 12748
PH: 845-482-4141 FX: 845-482-9533
Kae Kotarski rescue@wjffradio.org
www.wjffradio.org
A weekly, 90 minute music show covering most genres.

Fast Forward Reverse *East Village Radio*
TimmyG fastfwdrev@yahoo.com
www.myspace.com/fastforwardreverse
Shoegaze, Indie Rock/Pop, BritPop, Dreampop, Post Punk/New Wave, Altrock ...

Fredonia Radio *SUNY Fredonia*
115 McEwen Hall, Fredonia, NY 14063
PH: 716-673-3420
www.fredoniaradio.com

The Indie Show *WBER*
2596 Baird Rd. Penfield, NY 14526
PH: 585-381-4353 FX: 585-419-8191
Joey wber@monroe.edu
wber.monroe.edu
2 hours of music exclusively from independent labels.

Radio Liberation Front *WXXE*
826 Euclid Ave. Syracuse, NY 13210
PH: 315-455-5624 FX: 315-701-0303
Dale R. Gowin dale@wxxe.org
www.wxxe.org
Featuring a mix of explicitly political music from many genres.

RocklandWorldRadio.com
1 Wood Ln. Suffern, NY 10901
PH: 845-364-9473
www.RocklandWorldRadio.com
Download our release form and send it with your CD.

Sandy Acres Sound Lab *East Village Radio*
DJ Matilda von Crumbcake sugartown@gmail.com
girljukebox.typepad.com
Indie, New Wave, Post Punk & more!

The Tuesday Night Rock & Roll Dance Party *WUSB*
Stony Brook Union 266, Stony Brook,
NY 11794-3263
PH: 631-632-6501 FX: 631-632-7182
music@wusb.fm
wusb.fm
Contact us to lay down a set of music.

WAIH *SUNY Potsdam*
9050 Barrington Dr. Potsdam, NY 13676
PH: 315-267-2511
stationmanager@theway903.com
www2.potsdam.edu/WAIH

WALF *Alfred U.*
1 Saxon Dr. Alfred, NY 14802
PH: 607-871-2200 FX: 607-871-2287
walfmusicdirector@hotmail.com
jobs.alfred.edu/~walf

WAMC
PO Box 66600, Albany, NY 12206
PH: 518-465-5233 FX: 518-432-6974
mail@wamc.org
www.wamc.org

WBAI
120 Wall St.10th Fl. New York, NY 10005
PH: 212-209-2800 FX: 212-747-1698
info@wbai.org
www.wbai.org

WBAR *Barnard College*
3009 Broadway, New York, NY 10027-6598
PH: 212-854-6538 FX: 601-510-7683
wbar@columbia.edu
www.wbar.org

WBER *Monroe College*
2596 Baird Rd. Penfield, NY 14526
PH: 585-419-8190 FX: 585-419-8191
wber@monroe.edu
wber.monroe.edu

WBMB *Baruch College*
1 Bernard Baruch Way, #3-280, New York,
NY 10010
wbmbonline@gmail.com
wbmbradio.com

WBNY *Buffalo State U.*
1300 Elmwood Ave. Buffalo, NY 14222
PH: 716-878-3080 FX: 716-878-6600
wbny@buffalostate.edu
www.wbny.org

WBSU *SUNY Brockport*
135 Seymour Union, Brockport, NY 14420
PH: 716-395-2580 FX: 585-395-5534
bestmusic@891thepoint.com
www.891thepoint.com

WCDB *U. Albany*
Campus Ctr. 316 1400 Washington Ave. Albany,
NY 12222
PH: 518-442-5262 FX: 518-442-4366
wcdbpd@gmail.com
www.albany.edu/~wcdb

WCWP *Long Island U.*
720 Northern Blvd. Brookville, NY 11548-1300
PH: 516-299-2627 FX: 516-299-2767
wcwp@cwpost.liu.edu
www.liu.edu/cwis/cwp/radio/wcwp

WDFH
21 Brookside Ln. Dobbs Ferry, NY 10522
PH: 914-674-0900
music@wdfh.org
wdfh.org

WDST
PO Box 367, Woodstock, NY 12498
PH: 845-679-7266 x13 FX: 845-679-5395
Rick Schneider ricks@wdst.com
www.wdst.com

WDYN
2844-46 Dewey Ave. Rochester, NY 14616
PH: 585-621-6270 FX: 585-621-6278
wdyn@wdyn.net
dynamicradio.net

WERW *Syracuse U.*
Schine Student Ctr. Rm. 126G, 303 University Pl.
Syracuse, NY 13210
PH: 315-443-2021
md@werw.syr.edu
werw.syr.edu

WETD *Alfred State College*
10 Upper Campus Dr., Alfred NY 14802
PH: 607-587-2907
wetd@alfredstate.edu
web.alfredstate.edu/wetd

WFNP *SUNY*
SUB 413, New Paltz, NY 12561-2443
PH: 845-257-3041 FX: 845-257-3099
wfnp@newpaltz.edu
www.newpaltz.edu/wfnp

WFUV *Fordham U.*
Bronx, NY 10458
PH: 718-817-4550 FX: 718-365-9815
www.wfuv.org

WGFR *Adirondack College*
640 Bay Rd. Queensbury, NY 12804
PH: 518-743-2300 x2376
www.wgfr.org

WGSU *SUNY Geneseo*
Blake B 104, 1 College Cir. Geneseo, NY 14454
PH: 585-245-5488
wgsumd@geneseo.edu
onesun.cc.geneseo.edu/~wgsu

WHCL *Hamilton College*
198 College Hill Rd. Clinton, NY 13323
PH: 315-859-4200
mngrwhcl@hamilton.edu
www.whcl.org

WHPC *Nassau College*
1 Education Dr. Garden City, NY 11530-6793
PH: 516-572-7438 FX: 516-572-7831
whpc@ncc.edu
www.sunynassau.edu/dptpages/whpc/whpc.htm

WICB *Ithaca College*
118 Park Hall, Ithaca, NY 14850
PH: 607-274-1040 FX: 607-274-1061
wicb@ithaca.edu
www.ithaca.edu/radio/wicb

WITR *Rochester Institute of Tech.*
32 Lomb Memorial Dr. Rochester, NY 14623-0563
PH: 585-475-5643 FX: 585-475-4988
musicdirector@modernmusicandmore.com
www.modernmusicandmore.com

WJFF
4765 State Rt. 52, PO Box 546, Jeffersonville,
NY 12748
PH: 845-482-4141 FX: 845-482-9533
wjff@wjffradio.org
www.wjffradio.org

WKRB *Kingsborough College*
2001 Oriental Blvd. Brooklyn, NY 11235
PH: 718-368-4572 FX: 718-368-4776
gm@wkrb.org
www.wkrb.org

WKZE
7392 S. Broadway, Red Hook, NY 12571
PH: 845-758-9811 FX: 845-758-9819
info@wkze.com
www.wkze.com

WLIX
PO Box 594, Ridge, NY 11961
PH: 631-345-3946
programming@radiox.fm
www.radiox.fm

WMAR *Marist College*
3399 North Rd. Poughkeepsie, NY 12601
PH: 845-575-3132
www.maristradio.com

WNYO *SUNY Oswego*
9B Hewitt Union, Oswego, NY 13126
PH: 315-312-2101 FX: 315-312-2907
wnyo@oswego.edu
www.oswego.edu/~wnyo

WNYU *New York U.*
194 Mercer St. 5th Fl. New York, NY 10012
PH: 212-998-1660 FX: 212-998-1652
music@wnyu.org
www.wnyu.org

WONY *SUNY Oneonta*
Alumni Hall, Oneonta, NY 13820
PH: 607-436-2712
wony@oneonta.edu
organizations.oneonta.edu/wony

WQKE *Plattsburgh State U.*
110 Angell College Ctr. Plattsburgh, NY 12901
PH: 518-564-2727
chia1230@mail.plattsburgh.edu
clubs.plattsburgh.edu/wqke

WRAJ *Bohemia*
FX: 413-521-5976
www.wrajradio.com

WRCU *Colgate U.*
13 Oak Dr. Hamilton, NY 13346
PH: 315-228-7901 FX: 315-228-7028
wrcu@mail.colgate.edu
wrcu.colgate.edu

WRHO *Hartwick College*
1 Hartwick Dr. Oneonta, NY 13820O
PH: 607-431-4555 FX: 607-431-4064
wrho@hartwick.edu
users.hartwick.edu/wrho

WRHU *Hofstra U.*
Rm. 127, Hempstead, NY 11549-1000
PH: 516-463-3674
WRHUmusic@wrhu.org
www.wrhu.org

WRPI *Rensselaer Polytechnic Inst.*
1 WRPI Plaza, Troy, NY 12180
PH: 518-276-2648 FX: 518-276-2360
wrpi-md@rpi.edu
www.wrpi.org

WRUB *SUNY U. Buffalo*
174/175 MFAC. Buffalo, NY 14261
PH: 716-645-3370
WRUBmusic@hotmail.com
www.subboard.com/new_wrub

WRUC *Union College*
Reamer Campus Ctr. Schenectady, NY 12308
PH: 518-388-6151
wruc.union.edu

WRUR *U. Rochester*
PO Box 277356, Rochester, NY 14627
PH: 585-275-6400 FX: 585-256-3989
Meggan Patterson mpatterson@wrur.org
wrur.rochester.edu

WSBU *St. John's U.*
Drawer O, St. Bonaventure, NY 14778
PH: 716-375-2322 FX: 716-375-2583
wsbumusic@yahoo.com
wsbufm.net

WSIA *College of Staten Island*
2800 Victory Blvd. Rm. 1C-106, Staten Island,
NY 10314
PH: 718-982-3057 FX: 718-982-3052
music@wsia.csi.cuny.edu
wsia.fm

WSPN *Skidmore College*
815 N. Broadway, Saratoga Springs, NY 12866
PH: 518-580-5787
wspn@skidmore.edu
www.skidmore.edu/~wspn

WSUC *SUNY Cortland*
PH: 607-753 2936
wsucsecretary@yahoo.com.
web.cortland.edu/wsuc

WTSC *Clarkson U.*
PO Box 8743, Potsdam, NY 13699
PH: 315-268-7658
radio@clarkson.edu
radio.clarkson.edu

WUSB *SUNY Stoneybrook*
Stony Brook Union 266, Stony Brook,
NY 11794-3263
PH: 631-632-6501 FX: 631-632-7182
music@wusb.fm
wusb.fm

WVBR
957 Mitchell St. Ste. B, Ithaca, NY 14850
PH: 607-273-4000 FX: 607-273-4069
www.wvbr.com

WVKR *Vassar College*
Box 726, 124 Raymond Ave. Poughkeepsie,
NY 12604
PH: 845-437-5476 FX: 845-437-7656
music@wvkr.org
www.wvkr.org

WXXE
826 Euclid Ave. Syracuse, NY 13210
PH: 315-455-0850 FX: 315-701-0303
music@wxxe.org
www.wxxe.org

WYDN
2844-46 Dewey Ave. Rochester, NY 14616
PH: 585-621-6270 FX: 585-621-6278
wdyn@wdyn.net
www.dynamicindieradio.com
When you send your CD, please include the form found at our website.

North Carolina

The New Music & Indie Label Show
801 Wood Ridge Ctr. Dr. Charlotte, NC 28217
PH: 704-714-9444
Divakar 90minutes@1065.com
www.1065.com
Features new music & bands from all over the country.

Wake Radio *Wake Forest U.*
PO Box 7760, Winston-Salem, NC 27109
PH: 336-758-4894 FX: 336-758-4562
radio.wfu.edu

WASU *Appalachian State U.*
Wey Hall #332, Boone, NC 28608
PH: 828-262-3170 FX: 828-262-2543
music@wasurocks.com
www.wasurocks.com

WCOM
201 N. Greensboro St., Carrboro, NC 27510
PH: 919-929-9601
volunteer@communityradio.coop
www.communityradio.coop

WDCC *Central Carolina College*
1105 Kelly Dr. Sanford, NC 27330
PH: 919-718-7257
bfreeman@cccc.edu
www.wdccfm.com

WKNC *North Carolina State U.*
Mail Ctr. Box 8607, Raleigh, NC 27695-8607
PH: 919-515-2401 FX: 919-213-2353
wknc.org

WNCW *Isothermal College*
PO Box 804, Spindale, NC 28160
PH: 828-287-8000 x349
info@wncw.org
www.wncw.org

WPVM
75 Haywood St., Asheville, NC 28801.
PH: 828-258-0085 FX: 828-350-7853
www.wpvm.org

WQFS *Guilford College*
17714 Founders Hall, 5800 W. Friendly Ave.
Greensboro, NC 27410
PH: 336-316-2352
wqfs@guilford.edu
www.guilford.edu/wqfs

WSGE *Gaston College*
201 Hwy. 321 S. Dallas, NC 28034
PH: 704-922-6552 FX: 704-922-2347
www.wsge.org

WSOE *Elon College*
Campus Box 2700, Elon, NC 27244
PH: 336-278-7211 FX: 336-278-7298
wsoe@elon.edu
www.elon.edu/wsoe

WUAG *U. North Carolina Greensboro*
PO Box 26170, Greensboro, NC 27402
PH: 336-334-5688
wuagmd@hotmail.com
www.uncg.edu/wua

WVOD
637 Harbor Rd. Wanchese, NC 27981
PH: 252-475-1888
www.wvod.com

WXDU *Duke U.*
PO Box 90689, Duke Stn. Durham, NC 27708
PH: 919-684-2957
music_director@wxdu.org
www.wxdu.duke.edu

WXYC *U. North Carolina*
CB 5210 Carolina Union, Chapel Hill, NC 27599
PH: 919-962-7768
md@wxyc.org
www.wxyc.org

WZMB *East Carolina U.*
Mendenhall Basement, Greenville, NC 27858
PH: 252-328-4751 FX: 252-328-4773
wzmb@mail.ecu.edu
wzmb.ecu.edu

Ohio

ACRN *Ohio U.*
9 S. College St. #315, Athens, OH 45701
PH: 740-593-4910
music@acrn.com
www.acrn.com

BearCast Radio *U. Cincinnati*
2217 Mary Emery Hall, PO Box 210003,
Cincinnati, OH 45221
PH: 513-556-6578
bearcastprogramming@gmail.com
www.bearcast.uc.edu

KBUX *Ohio State U.*
1739 N. High St. #15-S, Columbus, OH 43210
PH: 614-688-3780 FX: 614-688-5788
www.underground.fm

Radio U *Westerville*
PO Box 1887, Westerville, OH 43086
PH: 614-890-9977 FX: 614-839-1329
www.radiou.com

WAIF
1434 E. McMillan Ave. Cincinnati, OH 45206
PH: 513-961-8900
www.waif883.org

WBGU *Bowling Green State U.*
120 West Hall, Bowling Green, OH 43403
PH: 419-372-2820 FX: 419-372-9449
music@wbgufm.com
www.wbgufm.com

WBWC *Baldwin-Wallace College*
275 Eastland Rd. Berea, OH 44017
PH: 440-826-2145 FX: 440-826-3426
contact@wbwc.com
www.wbwc.com

WCSB *Cleveland State U.*
Rhodes Tower 956, 2121 Euclid Ave. Cleveland,
OH 44115-2214
PH: 216-687-3721 FX: 216-687-2161
musicdirector@wcsb.org
wcsb.org

WCWS *College of Wooster*
Wishart Hall, Wooster, OH 44691
PH: 330-263-2240 FX: 330-263-2690
wcws_music@wooster.edu
www.wooster.edu/wcws

WGXM *U. Dayton*
300 College Park, Dayton, OH 45469-2060
PH: 937-229-2774
flyer-radio.udayton.edu

WJCU *John Carroll U.*
20700 N. Park Blvd. U. Heights, OH 44118
PH: 216-397-4437 FX: 216-397-4438
directors@wjcu.org
www.wjcu.org

WKCO *Kenyon College*
Student Activities Ctr. Gambier, OH 43022
PH: 740-427-5411
wkco@kenyon.edu
wkco.kenyon.edu

WKSR *Kent State U.*
C306 Music & Speech, Kent, OH 44242
PH: 330-672-2131
Rock@KentBSR.com
www.kentbsr.com

WLHS *Lakota H.S.*
6840 Lakota Ln. Liberty Township, OH 45044
PH: 513-759-4864
requests@wlhsradio.com
www.wlhsradio.com

WMCO *Muskingum College*
163 Stormont St., New Concord, OH 43762
PH: 740-826-8907
wmco@muskingum.edu
muskingum.edu/~wmco

WMSR *Miami U.*
221 Williams Hall, Oxford, OH 45056
PH: 513-529-1985
miamiradio@gmail.com
www.orgs.muohio.edu/wmsr

WOBC *Oberlin College*
Wilder Hall 319, 135 W. Lorain St., Oberlin,
OH 44074
PH: 440-775-8107 FX: 440-775-6678
music.wobc@oberlin.edu
www.wobc.org

WOBO
PO Box 338, Owensville, OH 45160
PH: 513-724-3939
www.wobofm.com

WONB *Ohio Northern U.*
Freed Ctr., Ada, OH 45810
PH: 419-772-1194 FX: 419-772-2794
wonb@onu.edu
www.onu.edu/wonb

WOXY
5120 College Corner Pike, Oxford, OH 45056
PH: 513-523-4114
Matt Shiv shiv@woxy.com
www.woxy.com

WRDL *Ashland U.*
401 College Ave. Ashland, OH 44805
PH: 419-289-5678 FX: 419-289-5329
wrdl@ashland.edu
personal.ashland.edu/~wrdl

WRMU *Mount Union College*
1972 Clark Ave. Alliance, OH 44601
PH: 800-992-6682, ext. 3777 FX: 330-823-4913
wrmu@muc.edu
www.muc.edu/wrmu

WRUW *Case Western Reserve U.*
11220 Bellflower Rd. Cleveland, OH 44106
PH: 216-368-2207 FX: 216-368-5414
md@wruw.org
www.wruw.org

WSLN *Ohio Wesleyan U.*
HWCC Box 1366, Delaware, OH 43015
PH: 740-368-2239
wslntheline@gmail.com
wsln.owu.edu

WUDR *U. Dayton*
300 College Park K.U. #215, Dayton, OH 45409
PH: 937-229-3058
flyer-radio.udayton.edu

WWCD *Independent Playground, Indie Playground Deux*
503 S. Front St. #101, Columbus, OH 43215
PH: 614-221-9923 FX: 614-227-0021
Tom Butler tbutler@cd101.com
www.cd101.com
Award winning independent music shows.

WWSU *Wright State U.*
W010 Student Union, Dayton, OH 45435
PH: 937-775-5554 FX: 937-775-5553
wwsuprogramming@yahoo.com
www.wright.edu/studentorgs/wwsu

WXUT *U. Toledo*
2801 W. Bancroft, SU2515, Toledo, OH 43606
PH: 419-530-4172 FX: 419-530-2210
wxut.utoledo.edu

WZIP *U. Akron*
302 E. Buchtel Ave. Akron, OH 44325-1004
PH: 330-972-7105 FX: 330-972-5521
wzip@uakron.edu
www.wzip.fm

Oklahoma

KRSC *Rogers State U.*
1701 W. Will Rogers Blvd. Claremore, OK 74017
PH: 918-343-7913
rsuradio@hotmail.com
www.rsu.edu/krsc/fm

WIRE *U. Oklahoma*
860 Van Vleet Oval, Norman, OK 73019
PH: 405-325-0121 FX: 405-325-7565
wiremusic@ou.edu
wire48.ou.edu

Oregon

KBVR *Oregon State U.*
210 Memorial Union E. Corvallis, OR 97331
PH: 541-737-6323 FX: 541-737-4545
kbvrfmprogdir@oregonstate.edu
oregonstate.edu/dept/kbvr/html

KEOL *Eastern Oregon State College*
1 University Blvd. La Grande, OR 97850
PH: 541-962-3698
keol@eou.edu
www3.eou.edu/~keol

KLC *Lewis and Clark College*
0615 SW. Palatine Hill Rd. Portland, OR 97219
PH: 503-768-7132 FX: 503-768-7130
klcmusic@lclark.edu
www.lclark.edu/~klc

KPSU *Portland State U.*
PO Box 751-SD, Portland, OR 97207
PH: 503-725-4071 FX: 503-725-4079
music@kpsu.org
www.kpsu.org

KRVM *Eugene*
1574 Coburg Rd. PMB 237, Eugene, OR 97401
PH: 541 687-3370
www.krvm.org

KSLC *Linfield College*
900 SE. Baker St. #A498, McMinnville, OR 97128
PH: 503-883-2666 FX: 503-883-2665
kslc@linfield.edu
www.linfield.edu/kslc

KTEC
PO Box 2009, Klamath Falls, OR 97601
PH: 541-885-1840 FX: 541-885-1857
ktec@oit.edu
www.oit.edu/d/ktec

KWVA *U. Oregon*
PO Box 3157, Eugene, OR 97403
PH: 541-346-4091 FX: 541-346-0648
kwva@uoregon.edu
www.kwvaradio.org

Pennsylvania

Musician Showcase with Sherri Mullen
PO Box 177, Middletown, PA 17057
Sherri musicshowcase@sherrimullen.com
www.sherrimullen.com/musicshowcase
Attention ALL-INDIE artists!!!! Get YOUR music heard!

Radio Show Host Stewart Brodian
PO Box 1253, Easton, PA 18044
Stewart Brodian sbrodian@yahoo.com
www.webspawner.com/users/brodianpage
I am a radio DJ at three area radio stations: WDIY (+WXLV 90.3 FM) Allentown, WMUH Allentown and WLVR Bethlehem. Check my playlists to see if your music fits!

UArts Radio *U. of the Arts*
320 S. Broad St., Philadelphia, PA 19102
PH: 800-616-2787
radio@uarts.edu
www.cmacradio.org

WARC *Allegheny College*
520 N. Main St. Box C, Meadville, PA 16335
PH: 814-332-3376
warc@allegheny.edu
warc.allegheny.edu

WBUQ *Bloomsburg U.*
1250 McCormick Ctr. 400 E. 2nd St.,
Bloomsburg, PA 17815
PH: 570-389-4686 FX: 570-389-2718
orgs.bloomu.edu/wbuq

WCLH *Wilkes U.*
84 W. South St., Wilkes Barre, PA 18766
PH: 570-408-2908 FX: 570-408-5908
wclh@wclh.org
wclh.org

WCUR *West Chester U.*
237 Sykes Student Union, West Chester, PA 19383
PH: 610-436-2478
WCURMD@gmail.com
www.wcur.fm

WDCV *Dickinson College*
PO Box 1773, Carlisle, PA 17013
PH: 717-245-1444
usherh@dickinson.edu
omega.dickinson.edu/~wdcv

WDIY
301 Broadway, Bethlehem, PA 18015
PH: 610-694-8100 FX: 610-954-9474
info@wdiyfm.org
www.wdiyfm.org

WDNR *Widener U.*
Box 1000, 1 University Pl. Chester, PA 19013
PH: 610-499-4000
wdnr895@mail.widener.edu
www.wdnr.com

WDSR *Duquesne U.*
1345 Vickroy St., CMC #2500500, Pittsburgh,
PA 15219
PH: 412-396-5085
wdsr97@yahoo.com
www.wdsr.org

WEHR *Penn State*
120 S. Burrowes St. Box 30, U. Park, PA 16801
PH: 814-865-0897
www.clubs.psu.edu/wehr

WERG *Gannon U.*
University Sq. Erie, PA 16541
PH: 814-871-5841
werg@gannon.edu
www.wergfm.com

WESS *East Stroudsburg U.*
200 Prospect St., E. Stroudsburg, PA 18301-2999
PH: 570-422-3512
wess@esu.edu
www.esu.edu/wess

WFSE *Edinboro U. of Pennsylvania*
Edinboro, PA 16444
PH: 814-732-2888 FX: 814-732-2427
wfse@flashmail.com
piper.edinboro.edu/cwis/wfse

WHRC *Haverford College*
370 Lancaster Ave. Haverford, PA 19041
PH: 610-896-2920
whrc@haverford.edu
www.whrcradio.com

WIUP *U. Pennsylvania*
121 Stouffer Hall, Indiana, PA 15705
PH: 724-357-7971
www.coe.iup.edu/wiupfm

WIXQ *Millersville U.*
Student Memorial Ctr. Millersville, PA 17551-0302
PH: 717-872-3333 FX: 717-872-3383
music.director@wixq.com
www.wixq.com

WJRH *Lafayette College*
Farinon Ctr., PO Box 9473, Easton, PA 18042
PH: 610-330-5316 FX: 610-330-5318
www.lafayette.edu/~wjrh

WKDU *Drexel U.*
3210 Chestnut St., Philadelphia, PA 19104
PH: 215-895-2580
musicdir@wkdu.org
www.wkdu.org

WKPS *Penn State U.*
125 HUB-Robeson Ctr. U. Park, PA 16802-6600
PH: 814-865-7983 FX: 814-865-2751
LION-Radio@psu.edu
www.lion-radio.org

WKVR *Juniata College*
1005 Juniata College, Huntingdon, PA 16652
PH: 814-641-3341 FX: 814-643-4477
wkvr@juniata.edu
clubs.juniata.edu/wkvr

WLVR *Lehigh U.*
39 University Dr. Bethlehem, PA 18015
PH: 610-758-3000
inwlvr@lehigh.edu
www.wlvr.org

WMSS *Middletown HS*
214 N. Race St., Middletown, PA 17057-2242
PH: 717-948-9136
www.wmssfm.com

WMUH *Muhlenberg College*
2400 Chew St., Allentown, PA 18104
PH: 484-664-3239 FX: 484-664-3539
wmuh@muhlenberg.edu
www.muhlenberg.edu/cultural/wmuh

World Café *WXPN*
3025 Walnut St., Philadelphia, PA 19104
David Dye wxpndesk@xpn.org
worldcafe.org
Daily interviews and live in-studio performances featuring Blues, Rock, Folk and Alt-Country. Send TWO CDs!

WPPJ *Point Park College*
201 Wood St., Pittsburgh, PA 15222
PH: 412-392-4724
wppjradio@hotmail.com
www.pointpark.edu/default.aspx?id=350

WPTC *Pennsylvania College of Tech.*
DIF 48, 1 College Ave. Williamsport, PA 17701
PH: 570-326-3761 x7214
wptc@pct.edu
www.pct.edu/wptc

WPTS *U. Pittsburgh*
411 William Pitt Union, Pittsburgh, PA 15260
PH: 412-648-7990 FX: 412-648-7988
wptsmusicdirector@hotmail.com
www.wpts.pitt.edu

WPUR *Philadelphia U.*
School House Ln. Philadelphia, PA 19144-5494
PH: 215-951-2728
wpur@philau.edu
orgs.philau.edu/wpur

WQHS *U. Pennsylvania*
Rm. 504 Hollenback Ctr. 3000 South St.,
Philadelphia, PA 19104
PH: 215-898-3500
music@wqhs.org
www.wqhs.org

WQSU *Susquehanna U.*
514 University Ave. Selinsgrove, PA 17870
PH: 570-372-4030
pulserequest@susqu.edu
www.susqu.edu/wqsu-fm

WRCT *Carnegie Mellon U.*
1 WRCT Plaza, 5000 Forbes Ave. Pittsburgh,
PA 15213
PH: 412-621-0728
intmusic@wrct.org
www.wrct.org

WRFT *Temple U.*
580 Meetinghouse Rd. Ambler, PA 19002
PH: 215-283-1280
www.temple.edu/wrft

WRLC *Lycoming College*
700 College Pl. Williamsport, PA 17701
PH: 570-321-4054
wrlc@lycoming.edu
www.lycoming.edu/orgs/wrlc

WRKC *Kings College*
133 N. Franklin St., Wilkes Barre, PA 18711
PH: 570-208-5931
wrkc@kings.edu
www.kings.edu/wrkc

WRSK *Slippery Rock U.*
C-211 U. Union, Slippery Rock, PA 16057
PH: 724-738-2931 FX: 724-738-2754
www.wrsk.org

WSRN *Swarthmore College*
500 College Ave. Swarthmore, PA 19081
PH: 610-328-8335
wsrn.swarthmore.edu

WSYC *Shippensburg U.*
3rd Fl. CUB, 1871 Old Main Dr. Shippensburg,
PA 17257
PH: 717-532-6006 FX: 717-477-4024
wsyc@wsyc.org
www.wsyc.org

WUSR *U. Scranton*
800 Linden St., Scranton, PA 18510
PH: 570-941-7648 FX: 570-941-4628
academic.uofs.edu/organization/wusr

WVBU *Bucknell U.*
Box C-3956, Lewisburg, PA 17837
PH: 570-577-1174
www.orgs.bucknell.edu/wvbu

WVMW *Marywood U.*
2300 Adams Ave. Scranton, PA 18509-1514
PH: 570-348-6202 FX: 570-961-4769
webmaster@vmfm917fm.com
www.vmfm917fm.com

WVYC *York College*
Country Club Rd. York, PA 17405-7199
PH: 717-815-1932 FX: 717-849-1602
music@wvyc.org
www.ycp.edu/wvyc

WXPN *U. Pennsylvania*
3025 Walnut St., Philadelphia, PA 19104
PH: 215-898-6677 FX: 215-898-0707
wxpndesk@xpn.org
xpn.org

WXVU *Villanova U.*
210 Dougherty Hall, 800 Lancaster Ave. Villanova,
PA 19085-1699
PH: 610-519-7200
wxvu.villanova.edu

WYBF *Cabrini College*
610 King of Prussia Rd. Radnor, PA 19087
PH: 610-902-8457
modernrock@wybf.com
www.wybf.com

WYEP
67 Bedford Sq. Pittsburgh, PA 15203
PH: 412-381-9131 FX: 412-381-9126
info@wyep.org
www.wyep.org

Rhode Island

WBRU *Brown U.*
88 Benevolent St., Providence, RI 02906-2046
PH: 401-272-9550 FX: 401-272-9278
wbru.com

WBSR *Brown U.*
PO Box 1930, Providence, RI 02912
PH: 401-863-9600
music.director@bsrlive.com
www.bsrlive.com

WDOM *Providence U.*
549 River Ave. Providence, RI 02918-0001
PH: 401-865-2460 FX: 401-865-2822
wdomdj@yahoo.com
studentweb.providence.edu/~wdom

WJMF *Bryant U.*
Box 6, 1150 Douglas Pike, Smithfield, RI 02917
PH: 401-232-6150
www.wjmf887.com

WQRI *Roger Williams U.*
1 Old Ferry Rd. Bristol, RI 02809-2923
PH: 401-253-9774
musicdirector_wqri@rwu.edu
wqri.rwu.edu

WRIU *U. Rhode Island*
326 Memorial Union, Kingston, RI 02881
PH: 401-874-4949 FX: 401-874-4349
rock@wriu.org
www.wriu.org

WXHQ
PO Box 3541, Newport, RI 02840
PH: 401-847-1955
info@radionewport.org
www.radionewport.org

WXIN *Rhode Island College*
600 Mt. Pleasant Ave. Providence, RI 02908
PH: 401-456-8541 FX: 401-456-1988
tom_remington@ricradio.org
www.ricradio.org

South Carolina

WSBF *Clemson U.*
210 Hendrix Ctr. Clemson, SC 29634
PH: 864-656-4010 FX: 864-656-4011
music@wsbf.net
wsbf.clemson.edu

WSSB *South Carolina State U.*
PO Box 7619, Orangeburg, SC 29117
PH: 803-536-8196
www.scsu.edu/Services/Radio

WUSC *U. South Carolina Columbia*
RHUU Rm. 343, 1400 Greene St., Columbia,
SC 29208
PH: 803-777-5124
wuscmd@gwm.sc.edu
wusc.sc.edu

South Dakota

KBHU *Black Hills State U.*
1200 University St. #9000, Spearfish, SD 57799
PH: 605-642-6265
KBHUFM@gmail.com
www.bhsu.edu/studentlife/organizations/kbhu

KCFS *U. Sioux Falls*
1101 W. 22nd St., Sioux Falls, SD 57105
PH: 605-331-6691 FX: 605-331-6615
kcfs@usiouxfalls.edu
www.thecoo.edu/campus/radio

KTEQ *SD School of Mines and Tech.*
Surbeck Ctr. 501 E. St. Joseph St., Rapid City,
SD 57701
PH: 605-394-2231
kteq@sdsmt.edu
www.hpcnet.org/kteq

Tennessee

Eclectic Cuts *WMTS*
PO Box 331775, Murfreesboro, TN 37133-1775
Jane Elizabeth jep2a@mtsu.edu
sites.kindweb.com/eclecticcuts
Features interviews and CD reviews. Focuses on a different genre each show.

WAWL *Chattanooga State Tech*
4501 Amnicola Hwy. Chattanooga, TN 37406-1097
Don Hixson don.hixson@chattanoogastate.edu
www.wawl.org

WEVL
PO Box 40952, Memphis, TN 38174
PH: 901-528-0560
wevl@wevl.org
wevl.org

WMTS *Middle Tennessee State U.*
Box 58, 1301 E. Main St., Murfreesboro, TN 37132
PH: 615-898-2636 FX: 615-898-5682
music@wmts.org
www.wmts.org

Writer's Block *WDVX*
PO Box 18157, Knoxville, TN 37928
PH: 865-494-2020
Karen E. Reynolds writersblockinfo@aol.com
www.writersblockonline.com
Interviews, a new live performance series and in studio performances.

WRLT
1310 Clinton St. #200, Nashville, TN 37203
PH: 615-242-5600 FX: 615-523-2199
www.wrlt.com

WRVU *Vanderbilt U.*
PO Box 9100, Stn. B, Nashville, TN 37235
PH: 615-322-3691 FX: 615-343-2582
wrvu@vanderbilt.edu
wrvu.org

WTTU *Tennessee Tech.*
1000 N. Dixie Ave. UC Rm. 376, Cookeville,
TN 38505
PH: 931-372-3688
wttu@tntech.edu
www.tntech.edu/wttu

WUMC
PO Box 9, Milligan College, TN 37682
PH: 423-461-8464
WUMC@milligan.edu
www.milliganradio.com

WUTK *U. Tennessee*
P103 Andy Holt Tower, Knoxville, TN 37996-0333
PH: 865-974-2229 FX: 865-974-2814
wutk@utk.edu
www.wutkradio.com

WUTM *U. Tennessee*
220 Gooch Hall, U. St. Martin, TN 38238
PH: 731-587-7000
wutm@utm.edu
www.utm.edu/~wutm

WUTS *Sewanee U.*
735 University Ave. Sewanee, TN 37383
PH: 931-598-1206
wuts@sewanee.edu
www.wuts913.org

WVCP *Volunteer State College*
1480 Nashville Pike, A-201, Gallatin,
TN 37066-3188
PH: 615-230-3618 FX: 615-230-4803
holly.nimmo@volstate.edu
www2.volstate.edu/wvcp

Texas

Frequency Down *KNTU*
PO Box 310881, Denton, TX 76203-0881
Frank Hejl frequencydown@unt.edu
www.kntu.fm/frequencydown
Features Indie and Alternative music. PLEASE check the past playlists in the blogs to see what kind of music we play!

KACC
3110 Mustang Rd. Alvin, TX 77511
PH: 281-756-3897
comments@kaccradio.com
www.kaccradio.com
Rock format.

KACV *Amarillo College*
PO Box 447, Amarillo, TX 79178
PH: 806-371-5222
kacvfm90@actx.edu
www.kacvfm.org

KANM *Texas A&M U.*
Student Services Bldg. 1236 TAMU,
College Station, TX 77843-1236
PH: 979-862-2516 FX: 979-847-8854
md@kanm.tamu.edu
kanm.tamu.edu

KEOS *College Station*
PO Box 78, College Station, TX 77841
PH: 979-779-5367 FX: 979-779-7259
John Roths jroths@mail.tca.net
www.keos.org

KFAN
PO Box 311, Fredericksburg, TX 78624
PH: 830-997-2197 FX: 830-997-2198
musicandprogramming@ctesc.net
www.texasrebelradio.com

KGSR
8309 N. IH 35, Austin, TX 78753
PH: 512-832-4000 FX: 512-908-4902
Susan Castle scastle@kgsr.com
www.kgsr.com

KNON
PO Box 710909, Dallas, TX 75371
PH: 214-828-9500 x234
md@knon.org
www.knon.org

KOOP
PO Box 2116, Austin, TX 78768-2116
PH: 512-472-1369 FX: 512-472-6149
music@koop.org
www.koop.org

KPFT
419 Lovett Blvd. Houston, TX 77006
PH: 713-526-4000 x313 FX: 713-526-5750
music@kpft.org
www.kpft.org

KRTU *Trinity U.*
One Trinity Pl. San Antonio, TX 78212
PH: 210-999-8313
KRTU@trinity.edu
www.krtu.org

KSAU *Stephen F. Austin State U.*
1936 North St., Nacogdoches, TX 75961
PH: 936-468-4000
ksaumusic@yahoo.com
www.sfasu.edu/ksau

KSHU *Sam Houston State U.*
PO Box 2207, Huntsville, TX 77341
PH: 936-294-1111
thekatkshu@yahoo.com
www.kshu.org

KTAI *Texas A&M U.*
Campus Box 178, Kingsville, TX 78363
PH: 361-593-5824 FX: 361-593-3402
ktai@tamuk.edu
www.tamuk.edu/ktai

KTCU *Texas Christian U.*
Box 298020, Fort Worth, TX 76129
PH: 817-257-7631
ktcu@tcu.edu
www.ktcu.tcu.edu

KTRU *Rice U.*
PO Box 1892, Houston, TX 77251
PH: 713-348-5878
noise@ktru.org
www.ktru.org

KTSW *Southwest Texas State U.*
601 University Dr. Old Main Rm. 106, San Marcos,
TX 78666
PH: 512-245-3485
ktswmusic@txstate.edu
www.ktsw.net

KTXT *Texas Tech*
PO Box 43081, Lubbock, TX 79409
PH: 806-742-3916 FX: 806-742-3906
ktxtfm@yahoo.com
www.ktxt.net

KUT/KUTX *U. Texas*
1 University Stn. A0704, Austin, TX 78712
PH: 512-471-1631 FX: 512-471-3700
music@kut.org
www.kut.org

KVRX *U. Texas/Austin*
PO Box D, Austin, TX 78713-7209
PH: 512-471-5431
music@kvrx.org
www.kvrx.org

KWTS *West Texas A & M U.*
2501 4th Ave. Canyon, TX 79016-0001
PH: 806-651-2000
kwts@mail.wtamu.edu
www.wtamu.edu/kwts

KYSM *San Antonio College*
1300 San Pedro Ave. San Antonio, TX 78212
PH: 210-733-2800
ksym@accd.edu
www.ksym.org

Utah

KAGJ *Snow College*
150 E. College Ave. Ephraim, UT 84627
PH: 435-283-7007
thekagj@yahoo.com
www.snow.edu/~kage

KPCW
PO Box 1372, Park City, UT 84060
PH: 435-645-7629
letters@kpcw.org
www.kpcw.org

KRCL
1971 W. N. Temple, Salt Lake City, UT 84116
PH: 801-363-1818 FX: 801-533-9136
Gianni Ellefsen gianni@krcl.org
www.krcl.org

KSUU *Southern Utah U.*
351 W. Ctr. Cedar City, UT 84720
PH: 435-865-8224 FX: 435-865-8352
ksuu@suu.edu
www.suu.edu/ksuu

KUTE *U. Utah*
200 S. Central Campus Dr. #418A, Salt Lake City,
UT 84112
PH: 801-581-7981 FX: 801-581-7527
kutemusic@gmail.com
www.kute.org

KWCR *Weber State U.*
Ogden, UT 84408
PH: 801-626-6450
organizations.weber.edu/kwcr

KZMU
PO Box 1076, 1734 Rocky Rd. Moab, UT 84532
PH: 435-259-8824 FX: 435-259-8763
music-director@kzmu.org
www.kzmu.org

Vermont

Download *WEQX*
PO Box 102.7 Manchester, VT 05254
PH: 802-362-4800 FX: 802-362-5555
Alex Taylor alext@weqx.com
www.weqx.com
3 Hours of the new music every Sunday night!

Early Warning *WBTZ*
PO Box 999, Burlington, VT 05402
PH: 877-893-2899
mailbag@999thebuzz.com
www.999thebuzz.com
New music from new artists and unheard of bands.

radio free brattleboro
PO Box 1951, Brattleboro, VT 05302
PH: 802-258-9879
rfb@sover.net
www.rfb.fm

WGDR *Goddard College*
PO Box 336, Plainfield, VT 05667
PH: 802-454-7367
wgdrmusic@goddard.edu
www.wgdr.org

WJSC *Johnson State College*
337 College Hill, Johnson, VT 05656
PH: 802-635-1355 FX: 802-635-1202
WJSC907@hotmail.com
www.wjsc.findhere.org

WNCS
169 River St. Montpelier, VT 05602
PH: 802-223-2396 FX: 802-223-1520
feedback@pointfm.com
www.pointfm.com

WRMC *Middlebury College*
Middlebury, VT 05753
PH: 802-443-6324 FX: 802-443-5108
music@wrmc.middlebury.edu
wrmc.middlebury.edu

WRUV *U. Vermont*
Billings Student Ctr. UVM Burlington, VT 05405
PH: 802-656-0796
wruv@wruv.org
www.wruv.org

WVTC *Vermont Tech College*
Randolph Ctr., VT 05061-0500
PH: 800-442-8821
www.wvtc.net

WWPV *Saint Michael's College*
Box 274, Winooski Park, Colchester, VT 05439
PH: 802-654-2334 FX: 802-654-2336
wwpv@smcvt.edu
personalweb.smcvt.edu/wwpv

Virginia

The Bopst Show *WCLM*
3165 Hull St., Richmond, VA 23224
PH: 804-231-7685
Chris Bopst bopst@mindspring.com
www.wclmradio.com/pages/bopst.html
*Fighting the scrooge of corporate mandated
playlists and genre specific formatting.*

The Electric Croude *WCVE*
23 Sesame St., Richmond, VA 23235
PH: 804-560-8172
George Maida George_Maida@wcve.pbs.org
www.wcve.org/wcvefm
*As far as music goes, the show is very eclectic.
I play both acoustic and electric. The only genre
I don't play is Rap.*

WCWM *College of William and Mary*
Campus Ctr. PO Box 8793, Williamsburg, VA 23186
PH: 757-221-3287 FX: 757-221-2118
wcwmmd@wm.edu
www.wcwm.org

WDCE
Box 85, U. Richmond, VA 23173
PH: 804-289-8698 FX: 804-289-8996
wdce@richmond.edu
www.student.richmond.edu/~wdce

WEBR
2929 Eskridge Rd. Ste. S, Fairfax, VA 22031
PH: 703-573-8255 FX: 703-573-1210
webr@fcac.org
www.fcac.org/webr

WFFC *Ferrum College*
Ferrum, VA 24088
PH: 540-365-4483
wffc@ferrum.edu
www.ferrumradio.com

WGMU *George Mason U.*
4400 University Dr. MS4B7, Fairfax,
VA 22031-4444
PH: 703-993-2940 FX: 703-993-2941
programming@wgmuradio.com
www.wgmuradio.com

WLUR *Washington & Lee U.*
Early-Fielding Ctr. 204 W. Washington St.,
Lexington, VA 24450-2116
PH: 540-458-4995 FX: 540-458-4079
wlur@wlu.edu
wlur.wlu.edu

WMWC *Mary Washington College*
Box WMWC, 1301 College Ave. Fredericksburg,
VA 22401
PH: 540-654-1152
station@wmwc.org
www.wmwc.org

WNRS
2250 Old Ivy Rd. #2, Charlottesville, VA 22903
PH: 434-979-0919 FX: 434-971-6562
wnrsmd@sbc.edu
wnrs.sbc.edu

WODU *Old Dominion U.*
2102 Webb Ctr. Norfolk, VA 23529
PH: 757-683-3441
manager@woduradio.com
www.woduradio.com

WRIR *Richmond Indie Radio*
PO Box 4787, Richmond, VA 23220
PH: 804-649-9737 FX: 804-622-1436
music@wrir.org
wrir.org

WTJU *U. Virginia*
PO Box 400811, Charlottesville, VA 22904-4811
PH: 434-924-0885 FX: 434-924-8996
wtju@virginia.edu
wtju.net

WUVT *Virginia Tech*
350 Squires Student Ctr. Blacksburg,
VA 24061-0546
PH: 540-231-9880 FX: 208-692-5239
wuvt-music@vt.edu
www.wuvt.vt.edu

WVCW *Virginia Commonwealth U.*
PO Box 842010, Richmond, VA 23284-2010
PH: 804-828-1058
wvcw@hotmail.com
www.wvcw.cc

WVRU *Radford U.*
PO Box 6973, Radford, VA 24142
PH: 540-831-6059 FX: 540-831-5893
wvru@radford.edu
www.runet.edu/~wvru

WWHS *Hampden-Sydney College*
PO Box 128, Hampden-Sydney, VA 23943
PH: 434-223-6009
programs@wwhsfm.org
www.wwhsfm.org

WXJM *James Madison U.*
MSC 6801 Seeger Hall, Harrisonburg, VA 22807
PH: 540-568-7939 FX: 540-568-7907
wxjm@jmu.edu
www.jmu.edu/wxjm

Washington

KAOS *Evergreen State College*
CAB 301 2700 Evergreen Pkwy. Olympia,
WA 98505
PH: 360-867-6896
kaos_music@evergreen.edu
www.kaosradio.org

KBCS
3000 Landerholm Cir. SE. Bellevue,
WA 98007-6484
PH: 425-564-2424
office@kbcs.fm
kbcs.fm

KCCR *Pacific Lutheran U.*
Pacific Lutheran U. Tacoma, WA 98447
PH: 253-535-8860
kccr@plu.edu
www.plu.edu/~kccr

KCWU *Central Washington U.*
400 E. U. Way, Ellensburg, WA 98926-7594
PH: 509-963-2283 FX: 509-963-1688
md@cwu.edu
www.881theburg.com

KEXP *U. Washington*
113 Dexter Ave. N., Seattle, WA 98109
PH: 206-520-5833 FX: 206-520-5899
info@kexp.org
www.kexp.org

KGRG *Green River College*
12401 SE. 320th St., Auburn, WA 98092-3699
PH: 253-833-9111 ext.2192 FX: 253-288-3439
music@kgrg.com
www.kgrg.com

KNDD
1100 Olive Way #1650, Seattle, WA 98101
PH: 206-622-3251
www.1077theend.com
Rock format.

KOHO
7475 KOHO Place, Leavenworth, WA 98826
PH: 509-548-1011 FX: 509-548-3222
www.kohoradio.com

KSER
2623 Wetmore Ave. Everett, WA 98201
PH: 425-303-9070 FX: 425-303-9075
www.kser.org

KSUB *Seattle U.*
901 12th Ave. PO Box 222000, Seattle WA 98122
PH: 206-296-2255
ksubmd@seattleu.edu
www.seattleu.edu/ksub

KSVR *Skagit Valley College*
2405 E. College Way, Mount Vernon, WA 98273
PH: 360-416-7711
mail@ksvr.org
www.ksvr.org

KUGS *Western Washington U.*
700 Viking Union MS 9106, Bellingham, WA 98225
PH: 360-650-2936
music@kugs.org
www.kugs.org

KUPS *U. Puget Sound*
1500 N. Warner, Tacoma, WA 98416
PH: 253-879-2974
kupsmusic@ups.edu
kups.ups.edu

KVTI *Clover Park College*
4500 Steilacoom Blvd. SW., Lakewood,
WA 98499-4098
PH: 253-589-5884 FX: 253-589-5797
i-91fm@cptc.edu
www.i91.ctc.edu

KWCW *Whitman College*
200 E. Boyer Ave. Walla Walla, WA 99362.
PH: 509-527-5285
music@kwcw.net
www.kwcw.net

KWRS *Whitworth College*
300 W. Hawthorne Rd. Spokane, WA 99251
PH: 509-777-4575
kwrsmd@whitworth.edu
www.whitworth.edu/KWRS

KYVT
1116 S. 15th Ave. Yakima, WA 98902
PH: 509-573-5013.
Ryan ricigliano.ryan@ysd.wednet.edu
kyvtradio.com
Rock format.

KZUU *Washington State U.*
CUB Rm. 311, Pullman, WA 99164
PH: 509-335-2208
md@kzuu.org
www.kzuu.org

Nite Life *KEXP*
113 Dexter Ave. N., Seattle, WA 98109
PH: 206-520-5833 FX: 206-520-5899
DJ Michele michele@kexp.org
www.myspace.com/djmichele
*Features Alt-Rock, Brit Pop, Trip-Hop, Soul, Indie,
Pop…*

Rainy Dawg Radio *U. Washington*
SAO 254, Box 352238, Seattle, WA 98195
PH: 206-543-7675
www.rainydawg.org
*Visit our website to find the e-mail address for your
style of music.*

Washington DC

Radio CPR
radiocpr@riseup.net
www.radiocpr.com

WCUA *Catholic U. America*
129 Pryzbyla Ctr. Washington, DC 20064
PH: 202-319-5106
cua-radio@cua.edu
wcua.cua.edu

WGTB *Georgetown U.*
432 Leavey Ctr. Washington, DC 20057
PH: 202-687-3702 FX: 202-687-8940
wgtb.music@gmail.com
georgetownradio.com

WRGW *George Washington U.*
800 21st St. NW. #G02, Washington, DC 20052
PH: 202-994-7554 FX: 202-994-4551
music@gwradio.com
www.gwradio.com

WVAU *American U.*
Mary Graydon Ctr. 256, 4400 Massachusetts Ave. NW.,
Washington, DC 20016
PH: 202-885-1212
hey@wvau.org
www.wvau.org

West Virginia

WMUL *Marshall U.*
1 John Marshall Dr. Huntington, WV 25755-2635
PH: 304-696-2295 FX: 304-696-3232
wmul@marshall.edu
www.marshall.edu/wmul

WSHC *Shepherd U.*
PO Box 3210, Shepherdstown, WV 25443
PH: 304-876-5369 FX: 304-876-5405
wshc@shepherd.edu
www.897wshc.org

WVBC *Bethany College*
PO Box 507, Bethany, WV 26032-0507
PH: 304-829-7881
www.bethanywv.edu/wvbc

WVWC *West Virginia Wesleyan*
Box 167, 59 College Ave. Buckhannon,
WV 26201-2999
PH: 304-473-8292
office@wvwc.edu
www.wvwc.edu/c92

WWVU *West Virginia U.*
PO Box 6446, Morgantown, WV 26506-6446
PH: 304-293-3329 FX: 304293-7363
u92@mail.wvu.edu
www.wvu.edu/~u92

Wisconsin

KUWS *U. Wisconsin*
PO Box 2000, Superior, WI 54880
PH: 715-394-8530 FX: 715-394-8404
JMunson@uwsuper.edu
kuws.fm

Power 100 *U. Wisconsin*
137 MSC, 302 10th Ave. Menomonie, WI 54751
PH: 715-232-2332
power100@uwstout.edu
www.power100.uwstout.edu

WBCR *Beloit College*
Box 39, 700 College St., Beloit, WI 53511
PH: 608-363-2402 FX: 608-363-2718
wbcr@www.beloit.edu
www.beloit.edu/~wbcr

WCCX *Carroll College*
100 N. East Ave. Waukesha, WI 53186
PH: 262-524-7355
wccx@cc.edu
wccx.cc.edu

WIPZ *U. Wisconsin*
900 Wood Rd. Kenosha, WI 53141
PH: 262-595-2527
www.uwp.edu/clubs/wipz

WLFM *Appleton*
Music Ctr. 420 E. College Ave. Appleton, WI 54911
PH: 920-832-6567 FX: 920-832-6904
www.lawrence.edu/sorg/wlfm

WMMM
7601 Ganser Way, Madison, WI 53719
PH: 608-826-0077 FX: 608-826-1245
1055triplem@entercom.com
www.1055triplem.com

WMSE *Milwaukee School of Engineering*
1025 N. Broadway, Milwaukee, WI 53202
PH: 414-277-6942 FX: 414-277-7149
Mike Bereiter bereiter@msoe.edu
www.wmse.org

WMUR *Marquette U.*
1131 W. Wisconsin Ave. #421 Milwaukee,
WI 53233
PH: 414-288-7541 FX: 414-288-0643
marquetteradio.mu.edu

WORT
118 S. Bedford St., Madison, WI 53703-2692
PH: 608-256-2001 FX: 608-256-3704
musicdir@wort-fm.org
www.wort-fm.org
*Our Friday afternoon show features interviews with
independent artists.*

WRFW *U. Wisconsin*
306 N. Hall, 410 S. 3rd St., River Falls, WI 54022
PH: 715-425-3689 FX: 715-425-3532
www.uwrf.edu/wrfw

WRPN *Ripon College*
300 Seward St., Ripon, WI 54971
PH: 920-748-8147 FX: 920-748-7243
wrpn.fm@gmail.com
www.ripon.edu/students/Orgs/wrpn

WSRI *U. Wisconsin Eau Claire*
132 Davies Ctr. UWEC Eau Claire, WI 54702
PH: 715-836-5819
sri@uwec.edu
sri.uwec.edu

WSUM *U. Wisconsin Madison*
PO Box 260020, Madison, WI 53726-0020
PH: 608-262-1206
music@wsum.wisc.edu
wsum.wisc.edu

WSUP *U. Wisconsin Platteville*
42 Pioneer Tower, 1 U. Plaza, Platteville, WI 53818
PH: 608-342-1165 FX: 608-342-1290
music@wsup.org
www.wsup.org

WSUW *U. Wisconsin Whitewater*
1201 Anderson Library, Whitewater, WI 53190
PH: 262-472-1323 FX: 262-472-5029
wsuw@uww.edu
www.wsuw.org

WWSP *U. Wisconsin Steven's Point*
105 CAC Reserve St., Stevens Point, WI 54481
PH: 715-346-4722 FX: 715-346-4012
wwsp@uwsp.edu
www.uwsp.edu/stuorg/wwsp

Canada

Canadian Satellite Radio
161 Bay St. #2300, PO Box 222, Toronto,
ON M5J 2S1
PH: 416-203-6666 x2219
Richard Rotman rrotman@wilcoxgroup.com
www.cdnsatrad.com
*Formed to provide subscription-based satellite radio
service to Canadians.*

Creative Radio
431 Barton St. E., #3, Hamilton, ON L8L 2Y5
PH: 905-540-8366
cradio@creativeradiocentral.com
www.creativeradiocentral.com
Get the exposure you deserve.

Galaxie - The Continuous Music Network
PO Box 3220, Stn. C, Ottawa, ON K1Y 1E4
PH: 877-425-2943 FX: 613-562-8889
information@galaxie.ca
www.galaxie.ca
*We recognize Canadian talent by supporting the
development and promotion of our home-grown
musicians. Our "Rising Stars" program encourages
Canada's up-and-coming stars.*

radioKAOS
1067 Bruce Ave. Windsor, ON N9A 4Y1
PH: 519-984-2377
radio@radiokaos.com
radiokaos.com
*Featuring many live shows and welcomes requests
24/7.*

RadioMOI
#1-1555 Dublin Ave. Winnipeg, MB R3E 3M8
PH: 204-786-3994 FX: 204-783-5805
www.radiomoi.com
We accept submissions from independent artists.

Alberta

CJSR *U. Alberta*
0-09 Students' Union Bldg. Edmonton, AB T6G 2J7
PH: 780-492-2577 x232 FX: 780-492-3121
Jay Hannley wormsnot@cjsr.com
www.cjsr.com

CJSW *U. Calgary*
#127 MacEwan Hall, Calgary, AB T2N 1N4
PH: 403-220-3085 FX: 403-289-8212
cjswfm@ucalgary.ca
www.cjsw.com

CKXU *U. Lethbridge*
SU 164, 4401 University Dr. W., Lethbridge,
AB T1K 3M4
PH: 403-329-2335 FX: 403-329-2224
www.ckxu.com

CKUA
10526 Jasper Ave. Edmonton, AB T5J 1Z7
PH: 780-428-7595 FX: 780-428-7624
music.director@ckua.org
www.ckua.org

British Columbia

CFBX *U. College of the Cariboo*
900 McGill Rd. House 8 Kamloops, BC V2C 5N3
PH: 250-377-3988 FX: 250-372-5055
radio@cariboo.bc.ca
www.thex.ca

CFML *BC Inst. Tech*
Building SE-10, 3700 Willingdon Ave. Burnaby,
BC V5G 3H2
PH: 604-432-8510
allofus@radiocfml.com
www.radiocfml.com

CFRO
110-360 Columbia St., Vancouver, BC V6A 4J1
PH: 604-684-8494 x250
music-department@coopradio.org
www.coopradio.org

CFUR *UNBC*
3333 University Way, Prince George, BC V2N 4Z9
PH: 250-960-7664
music@cfur.ca
www.cfur.ca

CFUV *U. Victoria*
PO Box 3035, Victoria, BC V8W 3P3
PH: 250-721-8704
cfuvmd@uvic.ca
cfuv.uvic.ca

CHET
PO Box 214, Chetwynd, BC V0C 1J0
PH: 250-788-9452 FX: 250-788-9402
info@peacefm.ca
www.chetradio.com

CHLS
Box 2124, Lillooet, BC V0K 1V0
PH: 250-256-2457 FX: 250-256-7405
www.lss.sd74.bc.ca/chls

CHLY *Malaspina U. College*
#2-34 Victoria Rd. Nanaimo, BC V9R 5B8
PH: 250-716 3410
music@chly.ca
www.chly.ca

CITR
#233-6138 SUB Blvd. Vancouver, BC V6T 1Z1
PH: 604-822-8733 FX: 604-822-9364
citrmusic@club.ams.ubc.ca
www.citr.ca

CJLY
Box 767, Nelson, BC V1L 5R4
PH: 250-352-9600 FX: 250-352-9653
music@kootenaycoopradio.com
www.kics.bc.ca/kcr

CJSF *Simon Fraser U.*
TC 216, Burnaby, BC V5A 1S6
PH: 604-291-3076 FX: 604-291-3695
cjsfmusc@sfu.ca
www.cjsf.bc.ca

CKMO *Camosun College*
3100 Foul Bay Rd. Victoria, BC V8P 5J2
PH: 250-370-3658 FX: 250-370-3679
Doug Ozeroff doug@village900.ca
www.village900.ca

CVUE
PO Box 2288, Sechelt, BC V0N3A0
PH: 604-885-0800 FX: 604-885-0803
cvuemail@yahoo.ca
www.civu.net

Manitoba

CJUM
Rm. 308 U. Ctr. Winnipeg, MB R3T 2N2
PH: 204-474-7027 FX: 204-269-1299
cjum@cjum.com
www.umfm.com

CKIC *Red River College*
W-106, 160 Princess St., Winnipeg, MB R3B 1K9
rick@kick.fm
www.kick.fm

CKUW *U. Winnipeg*
Rm. 4CM11, 515 Portage Ave. Winnipeg,
MB R3B 2E9
PH: 204-786-9998 FX: 204-783-7080
ckuw@uwinnipeg.ca
www.ckuw.ca

Native Communications Inc.
1507 Inkster Blvd. Winnipeg, MB R2X 1R2
PH: 204-772-8255 FX: 204-779-5628
info@ncifm.com
www.ncifm.com
*An Aboriginal service organization offering radio
programming throughout Manitoba.*

New Brunswick

CHMA *Mount Allison U.*
152-A Main St. #303, Sackville, NB E4L 1B4
PH: 506-364-2269
chma@mta.ca
www.mta.ca/chma

CHSR *U. New Brunswick*
PO Box 4400, Fredericton, NB E3B 5A3
PH: 506-453-4985 FX: 506-453-4999
chsrmd@unb.ca
www.unb.ca/web/chsr

CJPN
715 rue Priestman, Fredericton, NB E3B 5W7
PH: 506-454-2576 FX: 506-453-3958
direction.cjpn@nb.aibn.com
www.centre-sainte-anne.nb.ca/cjpn

CJSE
96 rue Providence, Shédiac, NB E4P 2M9
PH: 506-532-0080 FX: 506-532-0120
cjse@cjse.ca
www.cjse.ca

CKUM *U. Moncton*
Centre Etudiant, Moncton, NB E1A 3E9
PH: 506-858-5772
musique@radioj935.com
www.radioj935.com

Newfoundland

CHMR *Memorial U. Newfoundland*
Box A-119 St. John's, NL A1C 5S7
PH: 709-737-4777 FX: 709-737-7688
chmr@mun.ca
www.mun.ca/chmr

The Songwriters *CHMR*
Box A-119 St. John's, NL A1C 5S7
PH: 709-744-3429
Terry Parsons t.parsons@roadrunner.nf.net
www.geocities.com/chmrshows
If you are a Singer/Songwriter and would like to be a guest, contact me.

Nova Scotia

CFXU *St. Francis Xavier U.*
PO Box 948, Antigonish, NS B2G 2X1
PH: 902-867-2321
thefox@stfx.ca
www.cfxu.ca

CKDU *Dalhousie U.*
Dalhousie Stud. Union Bldg. 6136 U. Ave. Halifax, NS B3H 4J2
PH: 902-494-6479
Jessica Whyte jessica@ckdu.ca
www.ckdu.ca

Ontario

C101.5 *Mohawk College*
135 Fennell Ave. W. PO Box 2034, Hamilton, ON L8N 3T2
PH: 905-575-2175 FX: 905-575-2385
www.mohawkcollege.ca/msa/cioi

CFBU *Brock U.*
500 Glenridge Ave. St. Catharines, ON L2S 3A1
PH: 905-346-2644
md@cfbu.ca
www.cfbu.ca

CFFF *Trent U.*
715 George St., N., Peterborough, ON K9H 3T2
PH: 705-748-4761
info@trentradio.ca
www.trentu.ca/trentradio

CFMU *McMaster U.*
Student Ctr. Rm. B119, Hamilton, ON L8S 4S4
PH: 905-525-9140 x22053
cfmumusic@msu.mcmaster.ca
cfmu.mcmaster.ca

CFRC *Queens U.*
Carruthers Hall Kingston, ON K7L 3N6
PH: 613-533-2121 FX: 613-533-6049
cfrcmusic@ams.queensu.ca
www.cfrc.ca

CFRE
3359 Mississauga Rd. Mississauga, ON L5L 1C6
PH: 905-569-4712 FX: 905-569-4713
www.cfreradio.com

CFRL *Fanshawe College*
1460 Oxford St. E, London, ON N5V 1W2
PH: 519-453-2810 x201
music@1069fm.ca
www.1069fm.ca

CFRU *U. Guelph*
U.C. Level 2 Guelph, ON N1G 2W1
PH: 519-824-4120 x56919 FX: 519-763-9603
music@cfru.ca
www.cfru.ca

CHRW *U. Western Ontario*
Rm. 250, UCC, UWO, London, ON N6A 3K7
PH: 519-661-3601 FX: 519-661-3372
chrwmp@uwo.ca
www.chrwradio.com

CHRY *York U.*
Rm. 413, Student Ctr. Toronto, ON M3J 1P3
PH: 416-736-5145 FX: 416-650-8052
chrymd@yorku.ca
www.yorku.ca/chry

CHUO *U. Ottawa*
65 University Pvt. #0038, Ottawa, ON K1N 9A5
PH: 613-562-5800 x2720 FX: 613-562-5969
music@chuo.fm
www.chuo.fm

CILU *Lakehead U.*
955 Oliver Rd. Rm. UC2014A, Thunder Bay, ON P7B 5E1
PH: 807-766-7207
info@luradio.ca
www.luradio.ca

CIUT *U. Toronto*
91 St. George St., Toronto, ON M5S 2E8
PH: 416-978-0909 x214 FX: 416-946-7004
Ron Burd r_burd@ciut.fm
www.ciut.fm

CJAM *U. Windsor*
401 Sunset Ave. Windsor, ON N9B 3P4
PH: 519-253-3000 ext.2527 FX: 519-971-3605
progcjam@uwindsor.ca
www.uwindsor.ca/cjam

CJIQ *Conestoga College*
Rm. 3B15, 299 Doon Valley Dr. Kitchener, ON N2G 4M4
PH: 519-748-5220 x3223
Mike Thurnell mthurnell@conestogac.on.ca
www.cjiq.fm

CJLX *Loyalist College*
PO Box 4200, Belleville, ON K8N 5B9
PH: 613-966-0923 FX: 613-966-1993
91xmusic@loyalistmail.ca
cjlx.loyalistc.on.ca

CKCU *Carleton U.*
Rm. 517 U. Ctr., 1125 Colonel By Dr. Ottawa, ON K1S 5B6
PH: 613-520-2898
music@ckcufm.com
www.ckcufm.com

CKDJ *Algonquin College*
PH: 613-727-4723 x7740
www.algonquincollege.com/ckdj

CKHC *Humber College*
205 Humber College Blvd. Toronto, ON M5W 5L7
PH: 416-675-6622 x4913
ckhc@humber.ca
radio.humberc.on.ca

CKLN *Ryerson*
55 Gould St. 2nd Fl. Toronto, ON M5B 1E9
PH: 416-979-5251 FX: 416-595-0226
music@ckln.fm
www.ckln.fm

CKLU *Laurentian U.*
935 Ramsey Lake Rd. Sudbury, ON P3E 2C6
PH: 705-673-6538 FX: 705-675-4878
music@cklu.ca
www.cklu.ca

CKMS *U. Waterloo*
200 University Ave. W., Waterloo, ON N2L 3G1
PH: 519-886-2567x204 FX: 519-884-3530
www.ckmsfm.ca

CKRG *Glendon College*
2275 Bayview Ave. Toronto, ON M4N 3M6
PH: 416-487-6739
www.ckrg.org

CKON *Akwesasne Mohawk Nation Radio*
PO Box 1496, Cornwall, ON K6H 5V5
PH: 613-575-2100 FX: 613-575-2566
ckon@ckonfm.com
www.ckonfm.com

CKVI *Kingston Collegiate*
235 Frontenac St., Kingston, ON K7L 3S7
PH: 613-544-7864 FX: 613-544-8795
ckvi@limestone.on.ca
www.thecave.ca

CKWR
375 University Ave. E. Waterloo, ON N2K 3M7
PH: 519-886-9870 FX: 519-886-0090
general@ckwr.com
www.ckwr.com

CSCR *U. Toronto*
1265 Military Trail, Scarborough, ON M1C 1A4
PH: 416-287-7049
programmanager@fusionradio.ca
www.fusionradio.ca

Indie Hour *CFNY*
PH: 416-408-3343 FX: 416-847-3300
Dave Bookman INDIEHOUR@edge.ca
www.edge102.com/station/sp_indie_hour.cfm
We do NOT ACCEPT CDs anymore. Send us one MP3 for the show.

Kangar Radio International
216 Cook St. #11, Barrie, ON L4M-4H5
PH: 866-838-0537
Andrew Allan kangarradio@hotmail.com
www.kangarradio.com
*Bringing you the best new groups and solo artists
from around the globe.*

Off the Beaten Track *CKCU*
Rm. 517 U. Ctr., 1125 Colonel By Dr. Ottawa,
ON K1S 5B6
PH: 613-520-2898
Dave Aardvark daardvark@yahoo.com
www.offthebeatentrackradio.com
*Far reaching Underground Rock based, general
music show with an emphasis on "organic" sounds.*

Radio Laurier
3rd Fl. Fred Nichols Campus Ctr. WLU, 75
University Ave. W., Waterloo, ON N2L 3C5
PH: 519-884-0710 x2192
Kat Lourenco katlourenco@gmail.com
www.radiolaurier.com

Spirit Live Radio *Ryerson Polytechnic U.*
350 Victoria St., Toronto, ON M5B 2K3
PH: 416-979-8151 FX: 416-979-5246
www.spiritlive.net

Up for Sale *CHRY*
Rm. 413, Student Ctr. Toronto, ON M3J 1P3
PH: 416-736-5656 FX: 416-650-8052
Daria info@upforsaleradio.com
www.upforsaleradio.com
*Indie Rock show. Feel free to drop me a line, or
send your music to the station!*

Quebec

CFAK *U. Sherbrooke*
2500, boul. de l'Université, Sherbrooke,
QC J1K 2R1
PH: 819-821-8000 poste 2693 FX: 819-821-7930
musik@cfak.qc.ca
www.cfak.qc.ca

CFLX
67, rue Wellington nord, Sherbrooke, QC J1H 5A9
PH: 819-566-2787 FX: 819-566-7331
cflx@cflx.qc.ca
www.cflx.qc.ca

CFOU
3351, boul. des Forges, Trois-Rivières,
QC G9A 5H7
PH: 819-376-5184 FX: 819-376-5239
cfou@uqtr.ca
www.cfou.ca

CHAA
91, rue St. Jean, Longueuil, QC J4H 2W8
PH: 450-646-6800 FX: 450-646-7378
info@fm1033.ca
www.fm1033.ca

CHGA
163 Laurier, Maniwaki, QC J9E 2K6
PH: 1-819-449-3959 FX: 819-449-7331
www.chga.qc.ca

CHYZ *U. Laval*
Local 0236, Pavillon Pollack, QC G1K 7P4
PH: 418-656-2131 FX: 418-656-2365
chyz-fm@public.ulaval.ca
www.chyz.qc.ca

CIBL
1691, boul Pie IX, Montréal, QC H1V 2C3
PH: 514-526-2581 FX: 514-526-3583
info@cibl.cam.org
www.cibl.cam.org

CISM *U. de Montréal*
2332 Edouard Montpetit, C-1509 C.P. 6128,
Montréal, QC H3C 3J7
PH: 514-343-CISM FX: 514-343-2418
musique@cam.org
www.cismfm.qc.ca

CJLO
7141 Sherbrooke St. Ouest, #CC-430, Montreal,
QC H4B 1R6
PH: 514-848-8663 FX: 514-848-7450
program@cjlo.com
www.cjlo.com

CJMQ *Bishops U.*
Box 2135, Lennoxville, QC J1M 1Z7
PH: 819-822-9600 ext. 2689
cjmqmusicdirector@yahoo.ca
www.cjmq.uni.cc

CKRL *Québec City*
405, 3e Ave. Québec City, QC G1L 2W2
PH: 418-640-2575 FX: 418-640-1588
studio@ckrl.qc.ca
www.ckrl.qc.ca

CKUT *McGill U.*
3647 U. St., Montreal, QC H3A 2B3
PH: 514-398-6787 FX: 514-398-8261
music@ckut.ca
www.ckut.ca

Muzik Paradise
C.P. 151, Bromont, QC J2L 1A9
www.muzikparadise.org
La radio internet du top chrétien francophone!

Saskatchewan

CFCR
PO Box 7544, Saskatoon, SK S7K 4L4
PH: 306-664-6678
tracking@cfcr.ca
www.cfcr.ca

Six Strings & A Million Possibilities
PO Box 334 Stn. Main, Regina, SK S4P 3A1
Bob Evans SixStrings@BobEvansGuitar.com
www.bobevansguitar.com/six_strings.html
*I'm open to almost anything where the guitar is the
featured instrument.*

Mexico

e-reverenc!a
ereverencia@gmail.com
www.e-reverencia.net
*Para quienes expresarse no es una falta de respeto
(New Rock, Alternative, Indie).*

Eufonia Radio
Postal 2146 Sucursal de Correos "J" 64841
Monterrey, N.L. México
PH: 5281-8387-0665
programa@eufonia.net
www.eufonia.net
*2hrs weekly of Indie Rock and other non
commercial genres.*

XHUG *Radio U. de Guadalajara*
#976, PISO 12A.P. 4-29 C.P. 44100 Guadalajara,
Jalisco, México
PH: 0133-3825-6000 FX: 0133-3826-1848
server.radio.udg.mx

E u r o p e

Austria

FM4 *Linz U.*
A-1136 Wien, Austria
PH: +43-1-505-22-55 FX: 01-50101-16449
fm4.orf.at

Freier Rundfunk Oberösterreich
GmbH Kirchengasse 4 A-4040 Linz, Austria
PH: 43-732-71-72-77 FX: 43-732-71-72-77 -155
fro@fro.at
www.fro.at

Orange 94.0 *Free Radio in Wien*
Klosterneuburger Str. 1, A-1200 Wien, Austria
PH: 43-1-3190999 FX: 43-1-3190999-14
musikarchiv@o94.at
www.orange.or.at

Radio 1476
ORF, 1476 Argentinierstr. 30a A-1040 Wien, Austria
1476@orf.at
1476.orf.at

UniRadio Salzburg *U. Salzburg*
Rudolfskai 42, 5020 Salzburg, Austria
www.unitv.sbg.ac.at/uniradio/mambo

Belgium

Belgischer Rundfunk
Kehrweg 11, 4700 Eupen, Belgium
PH: 087-591111 FX: 087-591199
musik@brf.be
www.brf.be

FM Brussel
Eugène Flageyplein 18, Bus 18 - 1050 Elsene,
Belgium
PH: 02-800-0-808 FX: 02-800-0-809
muziekredactie@fmbrussel.be
www.fmbrussel.be

Kinky Star Radio
Vlasmarkt 9 9000 Gent, Belgium
PH: +32-9-223-48-45
Sebbe d'Hose sebbe@kinkystar.com
www.kinkystar.com
Features Indie music, news and reviews.

Radio 1
Auguste Reyerslaan 52 1043, Brussels, Belgium
PH: 02-741-38-93-kantooruren FX: 02-736-57-86
info@radio1.be
www.radio1.be

Radio 101
PO Box 2, B-4851 Gemmenich, Belgium
radio101.de

Radio Campus Bruxelles
cp 166/21 22 av. Paul Héger 1000 Bruxelles,
Belgium
PH: 32-2-640-87-17 FX: 32-2-650-34-63
rcampus@ulb.ac.be
radiocampus.ulb.ac.be

Radio Panik
Rue Saint Josse, 49, 1210 Bruxelles, Belgium
PH/FX: +32 (0)2-732-14-45
cp@radiopanik.org
www.radiopanik.org

Radio Scorpio
Naamsestraat 96, 3000 Leuven, Belgium
PH: 32-016-222-300
programname@radioscorpio.com
www.radioscorpio.com

RUN
OREFUNDP ASBL, Rue du Séminaire,
22/15 5000 Namur, Belgium
run@fundp.ac.be
www.run.be

Urgent FM *U. Ghent*
Sint-Pietersnieuwstraat 43, 9000 Gent, Belgium
PH: 09-264-79-09
muziek@urgent.fm
urgent.fm

Czech Republic

THC Radio
submit@thcradio.net
www.thcradio.net

Denmark

DR Barometer
TV Byen, Pavillion 22, 2860 Søborg, Denmark
barometer@dr.dk
www.dr.dk/skum/barometer
Danmark's Alternative radio channel.

Station 10
Stationsvej 10 9400 Nørresundby, Denmark
PH: 98-19-47-91
kristian@station10.dk
www.station10.dk

Universitetsradioen Nalle Kirkväg
Krystalgade 14, 1172 København K, Denmark
PH: 35-32-39-39 FX: 35-32-39-38
info@universitetsradioen.dk
www.uradio.ku.dk

Radio Østsjælland
Vinkældertorvet 2A Postboks 34 4640 Fakse,
Denmark
PH: 56-71-30-03 FX: 56-71-39-51
fakse@lokalradio.dk
www.lokalradio.dk

Finland

Radio Robin Hood
Itäinen Rantakatu 64 20810 Turku, Finland
PH: 02-2773-666 FX: 02-2500-905
info@radiorobinhood.fi
www.radiorobinhood.fi/rrh

France

Alternantes FM
19, rue de Nancy, BP 31 605, 44 316 Nantes 3,
France
PH: 02-40-93-26-62 FX: 02-40-93-04-98
musique@alternantesfm.net
www.alternantesfm.net

Le Biplan
19 rue Colbert 59000 Lille, France
PH: 33-03-20-420-227
lebiplan.programmation@wanadoo.fr
www.lebiplan.org

Canal B Rennes
BP 7147, 35171 Bruz, France
PH: 33-0-2-99-52-77-66 FX: 33-0-2-99-05-39-07
canalb@rennet.org
www.rennet.org/canalb

Coloriage
Ferme de la Vendue 21500 Fain les Moutiers,
France
PH: 03-80-96-40-76 FX: 03-80-96-34-99
coloriage@free.fr
coloriage.free.fr

Couleur 3 Lausanne
Av. du Temple 40, case postale 78, CH-1010
Lausanne, France
PH: +41-21-318-15-42
www.couleur3.ch

C'rock radio
BP 231, 38201 Vienne, France
PH: 04-74-53-28-91 FX: 04-74-31-59-07
www.crockradio.com

L'Eko des Garrigues
BP5555 34070 Montpellier 3, France
PH: 04-67-70-80-86 FX: 04-67-70-93-65
www.ekodesgarrigues.com

FMR
9 bd. Minimes, 31200 Toulouse, France
PH: 05-61-58-35-12 FX: 05-61-58-37-04
www.radio-fmr.net

JetFM
11 rue de Dijon 44800 St., Herblain, France
PH: 02-40-58-63-63 FX: 02-40-43-68-05
contact@jetfm.asso.fr
www.jetfm.asso.fr

Ocean Radio
2, place du Foirail 81220 St Paul Cap de Joux,
France
eole@ocean-music.com
www.ocean-music.com

Planet Claire
denis@planet-claire.org
planet-claire.org

Planet of Sound
planet_of_sound@lemoneyes-radio.com
www.lemoneyes-radio.com/music

Radio 666
BP 666, 14201 Hérouville Saint Clair, France
PH: 02-3194-6666
radio666@radio666.com
www.radio666.com

Radio Alpine Meilleure
Rue du Sénateur Bonniard 05 200 Embrun, France
PH: 04-92-43-37-38 FX: 04-92-43-54-43
ram05@wanadoo.fr
perso.wanadoo.fr/jb.oury/RAM.htm

Radio Beton
90, ave. Maginot, 37100 Tours, France
PH: 02-47-51-03-83
info@radiobeton.com
www.radiobeton.com

Radio Campus
16 rue degeorges 63000 Clermont-FD, France
PH: 04-73-140-158 FX: 04-73-902-877
clermont@radiocampus.org
clermont.radio-campus.org

Radio Campus Grenoble
av. Centrale Domaine universitaire 38402 Saint
Martin d'Hères, France
PH: 04-56-52-85-20
contact@campusgrenoble.org
www.grenoble.radio-campus.org

Radio Campus Lille
campus@campuslille.com
www.campuslille.com

Radio Campus
50, rue des Tournelles, 75 003 Paris, France
PH: 01-49-96-65-45
www.radiocampusparis.org

Radio Canut
24, rue Sergent Blandan 1er arrdt - BP 1101 - 69201
Lyon, France
PH: 04-78-39-18-15 FX: 04-78-29-26-00
radio@radiocanut.org
regardeavue.com/radiocanut

Radio Dio
BP 51, 42002 St-Etienne, France
PH: 0477250594 FX: 0477417916
radiodio.org

Radio En Construction
BP124, 67069 Strasbourg, France
PH: 33-0-3-88-600-915
contact@radioenconstruction.com
www.recfm.com

Radio Grenouille
41, rue Jobin, 13003 Marseille, France
PH: 04-95-04-95-15 FX: 04-95-04-95-00
radio.grenouille@lafriche.org
www.lafriche.org/grenouille

Radio Grésivaudan
94, rue du Brocey, 38920 Crolles, France
PH: 04-76-08-91-91
webmaster@radio-gresivaudan.org
www.radio-gresivaudan.org

Radio Pluriel
BP 106 69801 Saint-Priest, France
PH: 04-78-21-83-49 FX: 04-78-21-46-58
prog@plurielfm.org
www.plurielfm.org

Radio Primitive
13, rue. Flodoard BP 2169 51081 Reims, France
PH: 33-03-26-02-33-74 FX: 33-03-26-02-68-30
radio.primitive@wanadoo.fr
perso.wanadoo.fr/primitive

Radio Pulsar
15, rue. des Feuillants 86035 Poitiers, France
PH: 05-49-88-33-04 FX: 05-49-88-07-99
info@radio-pulsar.org
www.radio-pulsar.org

RCT
BP 2001-69603 Villeurbanne, France
PH: 33-04-78-89-59-48 FX: 33-04-72-44-34-42
rctworld@radio-rct.com
www.radio-rct.com

RCV
41 Bis Bd Vauban, 59046 Lille, France
PH: 33-03-20-54-12-11 FX: 33-03-20-30-40-51
rcv.lille@wanadoo.fr
www.rcv-lille.com

Sauvagine
15 rue Rode, 33000 Bordeaux, France
PH: 05-56-00-87-00 FX: 05-56-90-07-57
info@radio-sauvagine.com
www.radio-sauvagine.com

Germany

Alooga Radio
Westerwaldstr.35, D-53489 Sinzig, Germany
PH: +49-2642-43385 FX: +49-30-484983193
Gerd Hoeschen aka DJ Ottic info@alooga.de
www.alooga.de
Features Alternative music.

ALPHAbeat Radio
Westerwaldstr.35 D-53489 Sinzig, Germany
PH: 49-2642-43385 FX: 49-30-484983193
DJ Ottic info@ottic.de
www.ottic.de

Bayerischer Rundfunk
Rundfunkplatz 1 80300 München, Germany
PH: (089) 59-00-01
info@br-online.de
www.br-online.de

Campus-Welle Köln
Albertus-Magnus-Platz 50923 Köln, Germany
PH: 0221-470-4831 FX: 0221-470-6712
musik@koelncampus.com
www.koelncampus.com

coloRadio
Jordanstraße 5 01099 Dresden, Germany
PH: 0351-317-9227 FX: 0351-317-9226
www.freie-radios.de/coloradio

Eins live
WDR, 50600 Köln, Germany
PH: 0180-5678-111
einslive@wdr.de
www.einslive.de

elDOradio!
Vogelpothsweg 74, 44227 Dortmund, Germany
PH: 0231-755-7474 FX: 0231-755-7476
musik@elDOradio.de
www.eldoradio.de

Freies Radio für
Rieckestr. 24 70190 Stuttgart, Germany
PH: 0711-64-00-444 FX: 0711-64-00-443
info@freies-radio.de
www.freies-radio.de

FRITZ Radio
Postfach 90 9000 14439 Potsdam, Germany
PH: 0331-70-97-110 FX: 0331-731-39-83
fritz@fritz.de
www.fritz.de

HSF Studentenradio
e.V. Postfach 100 565 D-98684 Ilmenau, Germany
PH: 49-3677-694-222 FX: 49-3677-694-216
info@radio-hsf.de
www.hsf.tu-ilmenau.de

ju: N ai
UNI, radio über Otto-von-Guericke-Universität PF
4120 39016 Magdeburg, Germany
uni-radio@uni-magdeburg.de
www.uni-magdeburg.de/uniradio

Kontrast Radio
Postfach 36 03 36, 10973 Berlin, Germany
PH: +49-30-61107895
info@kontrastradio.net
www.kontrastradio.net
Berlin's finest Alternative radio. Does reviews too.

Lord Litter's Radio Show
Pariser Str. 63, 10719 Berlin, Germany
LordLitter@LordLitter.de
www.lordlitter.de/radioshow.html
*Indie bands-submit your music for worldwide
airplay.*

M945
Schwere-Reiter-Str. 35 Gebäude 40a 80797
München, Germany
PH: 089-360-388-0 FX: 089-360-388-59
info@m945.de
m945.afk.de/m

Oldenburg Eins
Bahnhofstr.11 26 122 Oldenburg, Germany
PH: 0441 21-888-44 FX: 0441 21-888-40
info@oeins.de
www.oeins.de

POPSCENE with J*A*L*A*L
Elisabethstr.120, 28217 Bremen, Germany
info@popscenewithjalal.com
www.popscenewithjalal.com
One of the leading Indie radio shows in Europe.

QUERFUNK
Steinstraße 23 76133 Karlsruhe, Germany
PH: 0721 38-50-30 FX: 0721 38-50-20
info@querfunk.de
www.querfunk.de

Radio 19/4
Vennheideweg 49 D-48165 Münster, Germany
PH: 0049-251-13-66-855
andy@radio19-4.de
www.radio19-4.de

Radio Blau
V.i.S.d.P Paul-Gruner-StraBe 62 04107 Leipzig,
Germany
PH: 0341-301-00-97 FX: 0341-301-00-07
musik@radioblau.de
www.radioblau.de

Radio C.T.
Ruhr-Universität 44780 Bochum, Germany
PH: 0234-971-90-80 FX: 0234-971-90-82
info@radioct.de
www.radioct.de

Radio Dreyeckland
Betriebs GmbH Adlerstr. 12, D - 79098 Freiburg,
Germany
PH: 0761-31028 FX: 0761-31868
verwaltung@rdl.de
www.rdl.de

radioeins
Marlene-Dietrich-Allee 20, 14482 Potsdam -
Babelsberg, Germany
PH: 0331-70-99-888 FX: 0331-70 99 333
www.radioeins.de

Radio Flora
Zur Bettfedernfabrik 1 30451 Hannover, Germany
PH: 0511-219-79-0 FX: 0511-219-79-19
postbox@radioflora.de
radioflora.apc.de

Radio Mittweida
Leisniger Straße 9, 09648 Mittweida, Germany
PH: 03727-581022 FX: 03727-581454
musik@radio-mittweida.de
www.radio-mittweida.de

Radio Neckarburg
August-Schuhmacher-Straße 10,
78664 Eschbronn-Mariazell, Germany
PH: 07403-8000 FX: 07403-8002
info@radio-neckarburg.de
www.radio-neckarburg.de

Radio Rheinwelle
Postfach 49 20 65039 Wiesbaden, Germany
PH: 0611-609-9333 FX: 0611-609-9334
musik@radio-rheinwelle.de
www.radio-rheinwelle.de

Radio SIRUP
AVMZ Adolf-Reichwein-Str.2 57068 Siegen,
Germany
PH: 0271-2-383-666 FX: 0271-740-25-26
musik@radio-sirup.de
www.radio-sirup.de

Radio T
Karl-Liebknecht-Str. 19 09111 Chemnitz, Germany
PH: 0371-350-235 FX: 0371-350-234
info@radiot.de
www.radiot.de

Radio Wüste Welle
Hechingerstr. 203, 72072 Tübingen, Germany
PH: 07071-760204 FX: 07071-760347
info@wueste-welle.de
www.wueste-welle.de

RadioActiv
Rhein-Neckar e.V.U. Mannheim Schloß, Postfach
144 68131 Mannheim, Germany
PH: 0621-1-81-18-11 FX: 0621-1-81-18-12
musikred@radioaktiv.org
www.radioaktiv.org

recordcaster
Mahnkopfweg 12-14 13595 Berlin, Germany
PH: 01805-227-11-777-0 FX: 01805-227-11-777-1
info@recordcastergroup.de
www.recordcaster.de

uniRadio
Malteser Str. 74-100/ Haus M 12249 Berlin,
Germany
PH: 030-841-727-101 FX: 030-841-727-109
redaktion@uniradio.de
www.uniradio.de

Uniwelle Tübingen
Gmelinstr. 6/1 72076 Tübingen, Germany
PH: 07071-297-7688 FX: 07071-29-5881
uniradio@uni-tuebingen.de
www.uni-tuebingen.de/uniradio

YOU FM
60222 Frankfurt a.M. Germany
PH: 069-55-30-40 FX: 069-55-88-06
studio@you-fm.de
www.youfm.de

Greece

ERA Aigaiou
nk@aegean.gr
www.aegean.gr/era_aegean

Hot Station
info@hotstation.gr
www.hotstation.gr

Rhodes Radio *Rhodes U.*
PH: 0241-99090
radio@Rhodes.aegean.gr
www.rhodes.aegean.gr/radio.htm

Hungary

Tilos Rádió
1462 Budapest, Pf: 601, Hungary
radio@tilos.hu
tilos.hu

Italy

Kristall Radio
Via Ludovico Il Moro 165 - 20142 Milano, Italy
PH: 0039-02-8912 FX: 0039-02-0212
info@kristallradio.it
www.kristallradio.it

Novaradio
PH: 055-3215143
musica@novaradio.info
www.novaradio.fol.it

Radio Beckwith
PH: 0121-954194
redazione@rbe.it
www.rbe.it

radiocitta'fujiko
PH: +39051346458
rc103@rc103.it
radiocittafujiko.it

RadioLina
PH: 0817340853
radiolina@bastardi.net
www1.autistici.org/radiolina

Radio Onda d'Urto
via Luzzago 2/b, 25126 Brescia, Italy
PH: 026692519
info@radiondadurto.org
www.radiondadurto.org

Radio Onda Rossa
Via dei Volsci 56 00185 Rome, Italy
PH: 06-491-750 FX: 06-446-3616
www.ondarossa.info

Luxembourg

Eldoradio Dortmund
B.P. 1344 L-1013, Luxembourg
PH: 352-409-509-1 FX: 352-409-509-509
program@eldoradio.lu
www.eldoradio.lu

Radio ARA
3, rue principale, L-9183 Schlindermanderscheid,
Luxembourg
radioara@mindless.com
www.ara.lu

The Netherlands

3FM
Postbus 26444 1202 JJ Hilversum, The Netherlands
3fm.omroep.nl

3voor12
Postbus 6, 1200AA Hilversum, The Netherlands
3voor12lokaal@vpro.nl
3voor12.vpro.nl

B92
Bulevar AVNOJ-a 64 11000 Beograd,
The Netherlands
PH: 381-11-301-2000 FX: 381-11-301-2001
www.b92.net

PopScene Radio
PH: 31-0-6-5264-1135
Nicole Blommers nicole@popscene.nl
www.popscene.nl
Dutch Indie radio show.

Radio Patapoe
patapoe@freeteam.nl
freeteam.nl/patapoe

Radio Winschoten
Mr. D.U. Stikkerlaan 39, 9675 AA Winschoten,
The Netherlands
PH: 0597-424200 FX: 0597-424221
info@radiowinschoten.nl
www.radiowinschoten.nl

A Shake Of Music
Vreelust 26, 2804 LJ Gouda, The Netherlands
Sjaak Sekeris sjajol@planet.nl
www.realrootscafe.com/shakeofmusic.html
A lot of different styles like Pop, R&B, Country-
Rock, Symphonic Rock, Soul, Gospel etc.

StadsRadio Almere
Edestraat 18, 1324 KB Almere Stad,
The Netherlands
PH: 036-534-15-02 FX: 036-534-43-79
info@StadsOmroep-almere.nl
www.stadsomroep-almere.nl/radio

Stadsomroep
Edestraat 18, 1324 KB Almere Stad,
The Netherlands
PH: 036-534-15-02 FX: 036-534-43-79
info@StadsOmroep-almere.nl
www.stadsomroeparnhem.nl

Norway

Independentradio.no
info@independentradio.no
www.independentradio.no
Listen to the best from the Norwegian independent
scene.

Radio Nova
Slemdalsveien 15, Postboks 1162 Blindern,
0317 Oslo, Norway
PH: 22-85-70-00 FX: 22-84-41-94
tips@radionova.no
www.radionova.no

Radio Tango
Hegdehausveien 24, 0352 Oslo, Norway
PH: 23-33-35-76 FX: 23-33-35-71
www.radiotango.no

Studentradioen i Bergen
Parkveien 1, 5007 Bergen, Norway
PH: 47-55-54-51-29 FX: 47-55-32-84-05
musikkredaktor@srib.no
studentradioen.uib.no

Studentradio'n i Trondheim
Elgesetergt. 1 7030 Trondheim, Norway
PH: 47-73-51-88-88 FX: 47-73-89-96-69
post@studentradion.no
www.studentradion.no

Poland

Radio Akademickie
INDEX ul. Podgórna 50 DS 1 65-246 Zielona Góra,
Poland
PH: 0-68-328-22-25 FX: 0-68-324-55-93
muzyczna@index.zgora.pl
www.index.zgora.pl

Radio Sfera
U. Mikolaja Kopernika Rozglosnia U. Gagarina 17,
87-100 Torun', Poland
PH: 48-56-611-49-00 FX: 48-56-611-45-84
redakcja@sfera.umk.pl
www.sfera.umk.pl

Portugal

Rádio Universitária do Minho
apartado 3061, 4711-906 braga, Portugal
PH: 351-253-200-630
rum@rum.pt
www.rum.pt

Tráfico Alternativo *Viriato FM*
Rua Prof. Aristides Amorim Girão Lote 70, 2ºdir,
Moinho de vento, 3500-041 Viseu, Portugal
Nuno Polónio trafico@viriatofm.com
www.viriatofm.com
Special attention on international independent
releases, new bands and live acts.

Viriato FM
Rua Prof. Aristides Amorim Girão Lote 70, 2ºdir,
Moinho de vento, 3500-041 Viseu, Portugal
PH: 232-085-965 FX: 232-183-223
inforadio@viriatofm.com
www.viriatofm.com

Romania

Radio DELTA RFI
OP 32 - CP 108, Bucuresti, Romania
PH: 021-318-40-44 FX: 021-319-31-99
office@rfi.ro
www.deltarfi.ro

Russia

Special Radio
PO Box 424, Moscow, 119017, Russia
admin@specialradio.ru
www.specialradio.ru

Serbia and Montenegro

Alternatives Show Radio 021
Brace Ribnikar, 65a, 21000 Novi Sad, Serbia &
Monte Negro
Predrag Strazmester silver@ns.sbb.co.yu
www.radio021.info
I have been promoting independent music for over
10 years.

Radio FEDRA
infofedra@sezampro.yu
www.fedraradio.org.yu

Slovakia

Radio Mars
Gosposvetska cesta 83, 2000 Maribor, Slovakia
PH: 386-2-228-19-20 FX: 0386-2-25-25-489
urednistvo@radiomars.si
www.radiomars.si

Slovenia

Radio Student Ljubljana
PO Cesta 27. aprila 31 1000 Ljubljana, Slovenia
PH: 386-1-24-28-800 FX: 386-1-24-28-808
www.radiostudent.si

Spain

Radio Contadero
C/ Granada 45, 18198 Huétor Vega, Granada, Spain
PH: 958-301048
radiocontadero@huetorvega.com
www.radiocontadero.com

Ràdio Despí
Avda. Barcelona, 64, 08970 Sant Joan Despí,
Barcelona, Spain
PH: 93-373-43-40 FX: 93-373-87-54
radiodespi@infonegocio.com
www.radiodespi.com

Radio PICA
PO Box 9242, 08080 Barcelona, Spain
pica@gracianet.org
www.radiopica.net

Sweden

DemoRadio
Eklandagatan 54 D, 412 61 Göteborg, Sweden
info@voolife.se
www.voolife.se

K103 Göteborgs Studentradio
Götabergsgatan 17, 411 34 Göteborg, Sweden
PH: 031-182250
k103@k103.se
www.k103.se

Radio AF
Sandgatan 2 223 50 Lund, Sweden
PH: 046-14-60-00 FX: 046-14-60-01
radioaf@radioaf.com
radio.af.lu.se

Rocket Radio
THS 10044 Stockholm, Sweden
PH: 468-790-9869
eric@rocket.fm
www.rocket.fm

Umeå Studentradio
Box 7652 907 13 Umeå, Sweden
PH: 090-786-90-40 FX: 090-13-09-28
musikchef@umeastudentradio.se
www.umeastudentradio.se

Switzerland

Frequence Banane
Centre Est, EPFL 1015 Lausanne, Switzerland
PH: 41-0-21-693-40-25 FX: 41-0-21-693-40-24
programmation@frequencebanane.ch
fbwww.epfl.ch

Radio Lora
Militärstrasse 85a, 8004 Zürich, Switzerland
PH: 044-567-24-10 FX: 044-567-24-17
musik@lora.ch
www.lora.ch

radio RaBe
Randweg 21 Postfach 297 3000 Bern 11,
Switzerland
PH: 031-330-99-90 FX: 031-330-99-92
rabe@rabe.ch
www.rabe.ch

United Kingdom

2010fm.com
PO Box 212, Baldock, SG7 6ZR UK
info@2010fm.com
www.2010fm.com
Live webcasts of unsigned bands and DJs.

209radio
Citylife House, Sturton St., Cambridge,
CB1 2QF UK
PH: 01223-488418 FX: 01223-488419
getinvolved@209radio.co.uk
www.209radio.co.uk

BBC Radio 1 *Indie*
www.bbc.co.uk/radio1/alt
*Home page of the BBC Radio 1's various Indie
music shows. Info, shows, contacts etc.*

BBC Radio 2 *Rock and Pop*
www.bbc.co.uk/radio2/r2music/rockandpop
*Home page of the BBC Radio 2's various Rock and
Pop shows. Info, shows, contacts etc.*

BCB Radio
11 Rawson Rd. Bradford, West Yorkshire,
BD1 3SH UK
PH: 01274-771677 FX: 01274-771680
info@bcb.yorks.com
www.bcb.yorks.com

BLAST 1386 *Thames Valley U.*
Thames Valley U., Crescent Rd. Reading,
Berkshire RG1 5RQ UK
PH: 0118-967-5090 FX: 0118-967-5083
music@blast1386.com
www.blast1386.com

Cambridge U. Radio
Churchill College, Cambridge, CB3 0DS UK
PH: 01223-501004 FX: 01223-336180
music@cur1350.co.uk
new.cur1350.co.uk

Celtica Radio Wales
PO Box 48, Bridgend, CF32 9ZY UK
PH: 07005-963770
info@celticaradio.com
www.celticaradio.com
*A platform for artists who have been denied
elsewhere.*

Clare FM
Abbeyfield Ctr. Francis St. Ennis, Co. Clare,
Ireland UK
PH: 353-0-65-68-28-888 FX: 353-0-65-68-29-392
info@clarefm.ie
www.clarefm.ie

Diversity Radio *St. Martins College*
PH: 01524-383394
postmaster@dfmradio.com
www.dfmradio.com

Downtown Radio
Kiltonga Ind. Est. Newtownards County Down,
BT23 4ES UK
PH: 028-9181-5555 FX: 028-9181-5252
www.downtown.co.uk

Earwax
PO Box 155, Sidcup, DA15 8XT UK
info@wax-music.com
www.wax-music.com
*Focused on bringing you the best in new and local
talent as well as tracks from more established
artists.*

Ellesmere Radio
PH: 07813-724082
studio101@ellesmereradio.co.uk
www.ellesmereradio.co.uk
Playing the best of the unknown.

Web Only (handwritten note)

Forest of Dean Radio
1 Berisford Ct. Cinderford, Gloucestershire,
GL14 2BS UK
PH: 01594-820722 FX: 01594-820724
contactus@fodradio.org
www.fodradio.org

Fresh Air FM
5/2 Bristo Sq. Edinburgh, EH8 9AL UK
PH: 44-0-131-650-2656 FX: 44-0-131-668-4177
music@freshair.org.uk
www.freshair.org.uk

HFM Radio
PO Box 1055, Market Harborough, Leicestershire,
LE16 7ZL UK
PH: 01858-464666 FX: 01858-464678
info@harboroughfm.co.uk
www.harboroughfm.co.uk

Imperial College Radio
Beit Quad Prince Consort Rd. S. Kensington,
London, SW7 2BB UK
PH: 020-7594-8100 FX: 020-7594-8101
manager@icradio.com
icradio.su.ic.ac.uk

Indiepop Radio
dan@indiepopradio.co.uk
www.indiepopradio.co.uk
*I am always happy to receive CDs for review. Before
getting in touch, please have a listen to the station
to get a feel for the music.*

Jimmy Possession's Radio Show
c/o r+eb 133 Green End Rd. Cambridge,
CB4 1RW UK
rebzine@hotmail.com
www.robotsandelectronicbrains.co.uk
*Band demos, unreleased tracks and (as yet)
undiscovered bands from all over the world.*

jockrock radio
PO Box 13516, Linlithgow, EH49 6WB UK
FX: 070-92-011-439
jockrock@vacant.org.uk
www.vacant.org.uk/jockrock/jockrock.html

Junction11 *U. Reading*
Reading, Berkshire, RG6 6AZ UK
PH: 0118-986-5159
www.1287am.com

KCC Live *Knowsley College*
Rupert Rd. Liverpool, Lancashire, L36 9TD UK
PH: 0151-477-5080
studio@kcclive.com
www.kcclive.com

Kick FM
The Studios 42 Bone Ln. Newbury Berkshire,
RG14 5SD UK
PH: 01635-841600 FX: 01635-841010
mail@kickfm.com
www.kickfm.co.uk

Kooba Radio
54 Maltings Pl. 169 Tower Bridge Rd. London,
SE1 3LJ UK
submissions@koobaradio.co.uk
www.KoobaRadio.co.uk
Internet radio exclusively for the unsigned.

KUSU *Keele U.*
Newcastle-under-Lyme, Staffordshire, ST5 5BH UK
PH: 01782-583700 FX: 01782-712671
www.kusu.net

Last.fm
86C Greenfield Rd. London, E1 1EJ UK
PH: +44-20-7247-0292
labels@last.fm
www.last.fm/labels
The listeners decide what's great music and what's rubbish.

LCR *Loughborough U.*
Union Bldg. Ashby Rd. Loughborough,
LE11 3TT UK
studio@lcr1350.co.uk
www.lcr1350.co.uk

LIPA Radio *Liverpool Inst. Performing Arts*
1 Mount St., Liverpool,Merseyside, L1 9HF UK
lipa.radio@lipa.ac.uk
radio.lipa.ac.uk

LiveIreland
www.liveireland.com
Five stations that play Irish influenced music.

Livewire *U. East Anglia*
Union House, Norwich, Norfolk, NR4 7TJ UK
PH: 01603-592512
www.livewire1350.com

LSR FM *Leeds U.*
PO Box 157, Leeds, LS1 1UH UK
PH: 0113-380-1280 FX: 07845-13-83-16
info@lsrfm.com
www.lsrfm.com

LUSHRADIO *U. Leicester*
Students Union Bldg. University Rd. Leicester,
Leicestershire, LE1 8RH UK
PH: 0116-231223 FX: 07977-223179
lush@le.ac.uk
www.lushradio.co.uk

Luton FM *U. Luton*
Rm. A315, U. Luton, Park Sq., Park St., Luton,
Bedfordshire, LU1 3JQ UK
PH: 015-82-703-020
lutonfm@hotmail.co.uk
www.lutonfm.net

NEAR FM
Northside Civic Ctr. Bunratty Rd. Dublin 17 Ireland
www.nearfm.ie

Northern Broadcasting *Halifax*
feedback@northernbroadcasting.co.uk
www.northernbroadcasting.co.uk

OneMusic *BBC Radio 1*
London, W1A 7WW UK
onemusic@bbc.co.uk
www.bbc.co.uk/radio1/onemusic
Resources for unsigned bands – articles, downloads, radio shows etc.

Oxide Radio *Oxford U.*
Thomas Hull House, 1 New Inn Hall St., Oxford,
Oxfordshire, OX1 2DH UK
PH: 01865-288-458
music@oxideradio.co.uk
www.oxfordstudentradio.com

Phantom FM
12 Camden Row, Dublin 8 Ireland
PH: 353-1-478-0363 FX: 353-1-476-2138
music@phantomfm.com
www.phantomfm.com

Phoenix FM
Unit 333 The Blanchardstown Centre,
Blanchardstown, Dublin 15 Ireland
PH: 822-72-22
phoenixfm@iolfree.ie
www.iolfree.ie/~phoenixfm

Phoenix FM
Hutton Poplars Lodge, Rayleigh Rd. Hutton,
Brentwood, CM13 1BA UK
PH: 01277-234555 FX: 0870-706-1174
www.phoenixfm.com

Pipeline Radio
pipelineradio.org
Shows featuring Rock, Pop, Soul, Jazz, Funk ...

Priory FM *Grantham*
studio@prioryfm.co.uk
www.prioryfm.co.uk

PuLSE Radio
LSE Houghton St., London, WC2A 2AE UK
PH: 44-0-20-7405-7686
pulsedj@lse.ac.uk
www.pulsefm.co.uk
Playing independent music over the net.

Pulse Unsigned
Enterprise House, Woodgreen Industrial Estate,
Salhouse, Norwich, NR13 6NY UK
PH: +44 (0) 870-1423456 FX: +44 (0) 1603-735160
info@pulseunsigned.com
www.pulseunsigned.com
You must fill out our online submission pack to be considered for airplay.

PURE FM *Portsmouth U.*
Student Ctr. Cambridge Rd. Portsmouth,
PO1 2EF UK
PH: 02392-84-3987
live.studio@purefm.com
purefm.com

QualityBeatsRadio UK
#11E The Wren Centre, Westbourne Rd. Emsworth,
Hants, PO10 7SU UK
PH: 01243-373660
alexschindler6@msn.com
www.qualitybeatsradio.com
Providing quality DJs and shows of all genres.

Queens Radio *Queens U.*
Students' Union, University Rd. Belfast,
Ireland BT7 1NF
PH: (028) 90-97-1065
music@queensradio.org
queensradio.org

Radio Gets Wild
16 Parkside, Sedgeford, Hunstanton,
Norfolk, PE36 5NE UK
Tim Daymond tim@radiogetswild.com
www.radiogetswild.com
Indie artists interviewed live on air. Visitors can vote and comment on the music they hear.

Radio Six International
PO Box 600, Glasgow, G41 5SH, Scotland
Music@radiosix.com
www.radiosix.com

Radio Telefís Éireann
Donnybrook, Dublin 4, Ireland
PH: 353 (0) 1-208-3111
radio1@rte.ie
www.rte.ie/radio
The Irish national public service broadcasting organization.

Radio Warwick *U. Warwick*
Student's Union Coventry, CV4 7AL UK
PH: 024-765-73077
studio@radio.warwick.ac.uk
www.raw.warwick.ac.uk

RadioReverb
170 North St., Brighton, East Sussex, BN1 1EA UK
PH: +44 (0) 1273-323-040
office@radioreverb.com
radioreverb.com

RamAir
Communal Bldg. U. Bradford, BD7 1DP UK
PH: 01274-233267
studio@ramair.co.uk
www.ramairfm.co.uk

rare FM
UCL Union 25 Gordon St., London,
WC1H 0AY UK
PH: 44-020-7679-2509
hom.rarefm@ucl.ac.uk
www.rarefm.co.uk

Reptor Productions Radio
PO Box 198, Abergele, Conwy, LL22 9WZ UK
PH: 44-0-1745-343-777
Dug submissions@reptorproductions.co.uk
www.reptorproductions.co.uk
We offer radio play online to UK and US artists.

Shock Radio *U. Salford*
University House, Salford, Manchester,
M5 4WT UK
PH: 0161-295-6303 FX: 07765-65-38-62
music@shockradio.co.uk
www.shockradio.co.uk

Sin Radio *Southampton Solent U.*
Students Union Bldg. East Park Ter. Southampton,
Hampshire, SO14 0YN UK
PH: 023-80319920 FX: 07845-61-22-33
music@sinradio.co.uk
www.sinradio.co.uk

Smoke Radio *U. Westminster*
Students Union, Harrow Campus, London,
HA1 3TP UK
PH: 020-79115000 x4413
programming@smokeradio.co.uk
smokeradio.co.uk

Spirit FM
9-10 Dukes Ct. Bognor Rd. Chichester,
West Sussex, PO19 8FX UK
PH: 01243-539000 FX: 01243-786464
www.spiritfm.net

Star FM *St. Andrews U.*
Students Union, St. Mary's Pl, KY16 9UZ Scotland
radio@st-andrews.ac.uk
standrewsradio.com

Subcity Radio *Glasgow U.*
John McIntyre Bldg. University Ave. Glasgow,
G12 8QQ Scotland
PH: 0141-341-6222 FX: 0141-337-3557
music@subcity.org
subcity.org

Sure Radio *U. Sheffield*
University House, Western Bank, Sheffield,
S10 2TG UK
PH: 0114-2228750
music@sureradio.com
www.sureradio.com

SURGE *U. Southampton*
Students' Union, Southampton, SO17 1BJ UK
PH: 023-8059-8852 FX: 023-8059-5252
studio@surgeradio.co.uk
surgeradio.co.uk

Tapp Out Radio
submissions@tappoutradio.co.uk
www.tappoutradio.co.uk
We cover many genres from Hip Hop and R&B right through to Rock and Alternative.

thesunmachine.net Radio
234/5 Marionville Rd. Edinburgh, Midlothian,
EH7 6BE UK
www.thesunmachine.net/radio
Discover a whole new world of music.

Today FM
124 Upper Abbey St., Dublin 1, Ireland
PH: 01-8049000
www.todayfm.com

totallyradio
170 North St., Brighton, BN1 1EA UK
www.totallyradio.com
Packed with new music across the board.

Tube Radio *Thames Valley U.*
TC 308, St. Mary's Rd. Ealing, London,
W5 5RE UK
PH: 020-8758-8500
tuberadio_studios@hotmail.com
www.tuberadio.co.uk

UCA Radio *U. Paisley*
U. Campus Ayr, Beech Grove,
Ayr KA8 0SR Scotland
PH: 01292-886385
Marcus.Bowman@paisley.ac.uk
www.ucaradio.paisley.ac.uk

U. Radio York
c/o Vanbrugh College, U. York, Heslington,
York, YO10 5DD UK
PH: 01904-433840 FX: 01904-433840
ury@york.ac.uk
ury.york.ac.uk

URB *U. Bath*
Students' Union, Claverton Down, Bath,
BA2 7AY UK
PH: 01225-38-66-11 FX: 07890-160-839
urb-music@bath.ac.uk
www.1449urb.com

URF *U. Sussex*
Norwich House, Falmer, Brighton,
Sussex BN1 9QS UK
PH: 01273-678-999
music@urfonline.com
www.urfonline.com

URN *U. Nottingham*
Students Union U. Park Nottingham, NG7 2RD UK
PH: 0115-846-8722 FX: 0115-846-8801
music@urn1350.net
urn1350.net

URY *U. York*
Vanbrugh College, Heslington, York,
YO10 5DD UK
PH: 01904-433840 FX: 01904-433840
ury@york.ac.uk
ury.york.ac.uk

The Vibe *U. Radio York*
c/o Vanbrugh College, Heslington, York,
YO10 5DD UK
PH: 01904-433840 FX: 01904-433840
James Brookes ury@york.ac.uk
ury.york.ac.uk/microsite/thevibe
A new music review show. Also includes music news, interviews and gig guide.

Vic McGlynn Show *Spare Room Music*
Rm. 540, Western House, 99 Great Portland St.,
London, W1A 1AA UK
Vic McGlynn vic.6music@bbc.co.uk
www.bbc.co.uk/6music/shows/vic_mcglynn
The only submission policy being, it must be produced by yourself, in your spare room. Genius.

WCR *Wolverhampton College*
Newhampton Ctr. Newhampton Rd. E.,
Wolverhampton, WV1 4AP UK
PH: 01902-572257 FX: 01902-572261
www.wcr1350.co.uk

Wired Radio *Goldsmiths College*
Student's Union, Lewisham Way, New Cross,
SE14 6AH UK
PH: 020-7717-2220
www.wired.gold.ac.uk

XFM
30 Leicester Sq. London, WC2H 7LA UK
PH: 020-7766-6000
xfm.co.uk

XFM Scotland
The Four Winds Pavilion, Glasgow, G51 1EB UK
www.xfmscotland.co.uk

Xpress Radio *Cardiff U.*
Students Union, Park Place, Cardiff, Wales
CF10 3QN
PH: 02920-781530 FX: 07722-263888
info@xpressradio.co.uk
www.xpressradio.co.uk

Xpression *U. Exeter*
c/o Devonshire House, Stocker Rd. Exeter, Devon,
EX4 4PZ UK
PH: 01392-26-3568
music@xpressionfm.com
xpression.ex.ac.uk

Xtreme Radio *Swansea U.*
Union House, Singleton Park, Swansea,
SA2 0AE UK
uwsradio@hotmail.com
www.xtremeradio.org

The Zone *Runshaw College*
Langdale Rd. Leyland, Lancashire, PR25 3DQ UK
studio@zoneradio.net
zoneradio.net

Yugoslavia

Radio Free Belgrade
B92 Bulevar AVNOJ-a 64 11000 Beograd,
Yugoslavia
PH: 381-11-301-2000 FX: 381-11-301-2001
www.b92.net

Australia

1ART
PO Box 3573, Manuka, ACT 2603 Australia
PH: 02-6295 8444 FX: 02-6295 8499
onair@artsoundfm.asn.au
www.artsoundfm.asn.au

1VFM
Post: PO Box 112, Erindale, ACT 2903 Australia
PH: 041-775-2494 FX: 02-6292-0332
valleyfm895@optusnet.com.au
www.valleyfm.com

2AAA
PO Box 2019, Wagga Wagga, NSW 2650 Australia
PH: 61-02-6925-3000 FX: 61-02-6925-2300
fm107@2aaafmradio.org.au
www.2aaafmradio.org.au

2ARM
PO Box 707, Armidale, NSW 2350 Australia
PH: 6772-1486
2arm@northnet.com.au
users.northnet.com.au/~2arm

2BAY
PO Box 1003, Cleveland, QLD 4163 Australia
PH: 07-3821-0022 FX: 07-3286-9166
bayfm@bayfm.org.au
www.bayfm.org.au

2BBB
PO Box 304, Bellingen, NSW 2454 Australia
PH: 02-6655-0718 FX: 02-6655-1888
2bbb@midcoast.com.au
www.2bbb.midcoast.com.au

2BCR
PO Box 659, Padstow, NSW 2211 Australia.
PH: 02-9771-2846 FX: 02-9774-5292
bfm1009@bigpond.net.au
www.2bfm.com

2BLU
PO Box 64 Katoomba, NSW 2780 Australia
PH: 02-4782 2490 FX: 02-4782 6699
info@blufm.org.au
blufm.org.au

2CBD
PO Box 129, Glen Innes, NSW 2370 Australia
PH: 02-67321270
webmaster@2cbd.org.au
www.2cbd.org.au

2CCC
PO Box 19, Gosford, NSW 2250 Australia
PH: 02-4322-0072 FX: 02-4322-0075
twoccc@tac.com.au
www.2ccc.net

2CCR
PO Box 977, Baulkham Hills, NSW 1755 Australia
PH: 9686-3888 FX: 9639-5618
mail@2ccr-fm.com
www.2ccr-fm.com

2CHY
30 Orlando St., Coffs Harbour, NSW 2450 Australia
PH: 02-6651-1104 FX: 02-66513-100
radiochyfm@hotmail.com
www.chyfm.midcoast.com.au

2EAR
PO Box 86, Moruya, NSW 2537 Australia
PH: 02-4474-3443 FX: 02-4474-3500
earfm@earfm.com
www.earfm.com

2FBI
PO Box 1962, Strawberry Hills, NSW 2012
Australia
PH: 02-8332-2999 FX: 02-8332 2901
info@fbi.org.au
www.fbi.org.au

2GLF
306 Macquarie St., Liverpool, NSW 2170 Australia
PH: +61-2-9822 8893 FX: +61-2-9602-3232
office@893fm.com.au
www.893fm.com.au

2MCE
Panorama Ave. Bathurst, NSW 2795 Australia
PH: 02-6338-4790 FX: 02-6338-4402
2mce@csu.edu.au
www.2mce.org

2MCR
PO Box 1420, Campbelltown, NSW 2560 Australia
PH: 02-4625 2768 FX: 02-4627 0670
feedback@2mcr.org.au
www.2mcr.org.au

2MIA
Groongal Ave. Griffith, NSW 2680 Australia
PH: 02-69641033 FX: 02-69644046
2miafm@dragnet.com.au
www.2mia.dragnet.com.au

2NCR
PO Box 5123, E. Lismore, NSW 2480 Australia
PH: 02-66203-929 FX: 02-66-203884
fm2ncr@scu.edu.au
www.2ncr.org.au

2NSB
PO Box 468, Chatswood, NSW 2057 Australia
PH: 02-9419-6969 FX: 02-9413-1684
James Vyver jamesv@fm993.com.au
www.2nsb.org.au

2NUR *U. Newcastle*
University Dr. Callaghan, NSW 2308 Australia
PH: 61-2-4921-5555 FX: 61-2-4921-7158
contact@2nurfm.com
2nurfm.com

2RRR
PO Box 644, Gladesville, NSW 1675 Australia
PH: 61-29816-2988 FX: 61-2-9817-1048
www.2rrr.org.au

2SER
PO Box 123, Broadway, NSW 2007 Australia
PH: 61-2-9514-9514 FX: 61-2-9514-9599
info@2ser.com
www.2ser.com

2TEN
PO Box 93, Tenterfield, NSW 2372 Australia
PH: 02-6736-3444 FX: 02-6736-2197
twotenfm@halenet.com.au
www.halenet.com.au/~twotenfm

2UNE
UNE, Armidale, NSW 2351 Australia
PH: 02-677-323-99 FX: 02-677-27-633
airtime@tunefm.une.edu.au
2une.une.edu.au

2UUU
PO Box 884, Nowra, NSW 2541 Australia
PH: 02-4422-1045 FX: 02-4421-8222
jukebox@shoalhaven.net.au
www.shoalhaven.net.au/jukebox

2VOX
PO Box 1663, Wollongong, NSW 2500 Australia
PH: 02-4227-3436 FX: 02-4226-5922
vox@1earth.net
www.vox.1earth.net

2VTR
11 Fitzgerald St., Windsor, NSW 2756 Australia
PH: 02- 45-775-662 FX: 02-45-878-865
www.hawkradio.org.au

2XX
PO Box 812, Canberra, ACT 2601 Australia
PH: 02-6230-0100 FX: 02-6248-5560
info@2xxfm.org.au
www.2xxfm.org.au

3CR
PO Box 1277, Collingwood, Melbourne,
VIC 3065 Australia
PH: 03-9419-8377 FX: 03-9417-4472
programming@3cr.org.au
www.3cr.org.au

3MBR
PO Box 139, Murrayville, VIC 3512 Australia
PH: 03-5095-2045 FX: 03-5095-2346
3mbr@riverland.net.au
www.riverland.net.au/~3mbr

3MGB
PO Box 555, Mallacoota, VIC 3892 Australia
PH: 03-5158-0929 FX: 03-5158-0079
cootafm@vicnet.net.au
home.vicnet.net.au/~cootafm

3ONE
Box 6824, Shepparton, VIC 3632 Australia
PH: 03-5831-7282 FX: 03-5831-2722
music@fm985.com.au
www.onefm.com.au

3PBS
PO Box 2917 Fitzroy MDC, VIC 3065 Australia
PH: 61-3-8415-1067 FX: 61-3-8415-1831
peter@pbsfm.org.au
www.pbsfm.org.au

3RIM
PO Box 979, Melton, VIC 3337 Australia
PH: 03-9747-8500 FX: 03-9747-0405
info@979fm.net
www.979fm.net

3RPP
PO Box 602, Somerville, VIC 3912 Australia
PH: 03-5978-8200 FX: 03-5978-8551
rpp@peninsula.hotkey.net.au
www.3rpp.asn.au

3RRR
25 Victoria St. PO Box 304, Fitzroy,
VIC 3065 Australia
PH: 61-3-9419-2066 FX: 61-3-9417-1841
3rrr@rrr.org.au
www.rrr.org.au

3SCB
PO Box 2132, Moorabbin, VIC 3189 Australia
PH: 03-9553-5444 FX: 03-9553-5244
info@southernfm.org.au
www.southernfm.org.au

3SER
PO Box 977 Cranbourne DC, VIC 3977Australia
PH: 03-5996-6977 FX: 03-5996-6900
David Lentin dlentin@3ser.org.au
www.3ser.org.au

3WAY
PO Box 752 Warrnambool, VIC 3280 Australia
PH: 03-55612666 FX: 03-55612585
3wayfm@hotkey.net.au
www.3wayfm.org.au

4CCR
PO Box 300m Manunda, QLD 4870 Australia
PH: 61-7-4053-6891 FX: 61-7-4053-2085
info@cairnsfm891.org
www.4ccr-fm.org.au

4CLB
PO Box 2101 Logan City DC, QLD 4114 Australia
PH: 07-3808-8101 FX: 07-3808-7787
admin@101fm.asn.au
www.101fm.asn.au

4CRM *Mackay*
PO Box 1075, Mackay, QLD 4740 Australia
PH: 07-49531411
Allan Berry allan.berry@4crm.com.au
www.4crm.com.au

4RED
PO Box 139, Redcliffe, QLD 4020 Australia
PH: 07-3284-5000 FX: 07-3283-4527
www.red997.com.au

4ZZZ
PO Box 509, Fortitude Valley, QLD 4006 Australia
PH: 07-3252-1555 FX: 07-3252-1950
music@4zzzfm.org.au
www.4zzzfm.org.au

5PBA
PO Box 433 Salisbury, SA 5108 Australia
PH: 61-8-8250-3735 FX: 61-8-8281-7495
pbafm@pbafm.org.au
www.pbafm.org.au

5UV
228 N. Terrace, Adelaide, SA 5000 Australia
PH: 61-8-8303-5000 FX: 61-8-8303-4374
Jane Costessi jane.costessi@adelaide.edu.au
radio.adelaide.edu.au

6KCR
PO Box 916, Kalamunda, WA 6076 Australia
PH: 08-9293-0548 FX: 08-9293-0549
committee@kcr-fm.com
www.kcr-fm.com

96.5 Family FM
PO Box 965, Milton BC, QLD 4064 Australia
PH: 07-3217-5999 FX: 07-3217-5888
www.96five.org.au

ABC Radio
www.abc.net.au/radio
*Produces national shows as well as local shows
throughout the network.*

Bondi FM
PO Box 7588 Bondi Beach, NSW 2026 Australia
PH: 61-0-2-9365-55-88
team@bondifm.com.au
www.bondifm.com.au

Boost Digital Indie Radio
PO Box 1398, Rozelle, NSW 2039 Australia
PH: +61-2-9460-1400 FX: +61-2-9460-0044
Ian MacRae newmusic@boostdigital.com
www.boostdigital.com
*Dedicated to giving independent artists a platform
to expose their talent. Please include a copy of our
online submission form.*

City Park Radio
PO Box 1501, Launceston, TAS 7250 Australia
PH: 03-6334-7429
cityparkradio@cityparkradio.com
www.cityparkradio.com

Contact! *2RDJ FM*
contact2001@bigpond.com
www.users.bigpond.com/celt1969
*International Indie/Alternative/New Wave Pop,
broadcast across Australia. Demos too.*

fat planet *FBI*
Stuart Buchanan mail@fatplanet.com.au
www.fatplanet.com.au/blog
*We LOVE getting new music, so please do feel free
to send material our way.*

ISON Live Radio
PO Box 532, Newcastle, NSW 2300 Australia
PH: 6102-49270290 FX: 6102-49270290
Sean Ison info@isonliveradio.com
www.isonliveradio.com

JOY Melbourne
PO Box 907, S. Melbourne, VIC 3205 Australia
PH: 61-03-9699-2949 FX: 61-03-9699-2646
pm@joy.org.au
www.joy.org.au

QBN FM
PO Box 984, Queanbeyan, NSW 2620 Australia
PH: 02-6299-6899 FX: 02-6299-6804
admin@qbnfm.com.au
www.qbnfm.com.au

RTR FM
PO Box 842, Mt. Lawley, WA 6929 Australia
PH: +61-8-9260-9200 FX: +61-8-9260-9222
rtrfm@rtrfm.com.au
www.rtrfm.com.au

Sub Fm *La Trobe U.*
Union Bldg. VIC 3086 Australia
PH: 613-03-9479-3835
Simon Knight s.knight@latrobe.edu.au
www.subfm.org

Three D Radio
PO Box 937, Stepney, SA 5069 Australia
PH: 61-8-83633937
mail@threedradio.com
www.threedradio.com

TiN Radio
#7, Level 1, Civic Arcade, 401 Hunter St.,
Newcastle, NSW 2300 Australia
PH: 02-49271668
music@tin.org.au
www.tin.org.au

Triple H *Sydney*
PH: 9476-0105 FX: 9482-1662
programming@hhhfm.org.au
www.hhhfm.org.au

Triple J
PO Box 9994, Canberra, NSW Australia
PH: 1300-0555-36
www.abc.net.au/triplej

Triple U
PO Box 884, Nowra, NSW 2541 Australia
PH: 02 4422-1193 FX: 02 4421-8222
pres@tripleu.org.au
www.tripleu.org.au

UMFM
217 Rear Commercial Rd. South Yarra, VIC 3141
Australia
Sea radio@umfm.net
www.umfm.net
*If you are a band, musician, DJ, producer or other
musical artist, we would love to hear your music.*

WOW FM
PO Box 1041, St. Marys, NSW 1790 Australia
PH: 9833-1444 FX: 9833-4539
www.wowfm1007.com.au

WYN
PO Box 155, Werribee, 3030 VIC Australia
PH: 9216 8089
wynfm@wynfm.org.au
www.wynfm.org.au

New Zealand

95b FM
PO Box 4560 Shortland St., Auckland 1001
New Zealand
PH: 64-9-309-4831 FX: 64-9-366-7224
95bfm@95bfm.com
www.95bfm.co.nz

Radio Active
PO Box 11-971 Wellington, New Zealand
PH: 64-4-801-9089
agency@radioactive.co.nz
www.radioactive.co.nz

Radio Kidnappers
PO Box 680, Hastings, New Zealand
PH: 06-876-6914 FX: 06-876-6914
David Teesdale kidnap.am@xtra.co.nz
www.radiokidnappers.org.nz

Radio One
PO Box 1436, Dunedin, New Zealand
PH: 03-477-1969
Tom Bell tom@r1.co.nz
www.r1.co.nz

RDU *U. Canterbury*
PO Box 31-311, Ilam, Christchurch, New Zealand
PH: 03-348 8610 FX: 03-364-2509
station@rdu.org.nz
www.rdu.org.nz

Asia

music-islands.com web-radio
2-19-20-603 Mizusawa, Miyamae, Kawasaki,
Kanagawa 216-0012 Japan
PH: 044-979-1124 FX: 044-979-1124
Masayoshi Yamamiya fishthemusic@gmail.com
music-islands.com/radio
Playing a variety of styles.

Radio Oxigen
Emin Vafi Korusu Muallim Naci cad. No 61/5
Ortaköy 80840, Turkey
PH: 0212-236-5436 FX: 0212-236-5440
info@radiooxigen.com
www.radiooxigen.com

Web only

Yellow Beat *Shonan Beach FM*
Gremlin and Baby Magic
ciao_babies@yellowbeat.net
www.yellowbeat.net
*We can be a key step to introducing your into the
Japanese market.*

Sign up for
*The Indie Contact
Newsletter*
www.indiebible.com

Internet Radio and Syndicated Shows

12StepRadio.com
11452 El Camino Real, #401, San Diego, CA 92130
info@12stepradio.com
www.12stepradio.com/submitsongs.asp
*We are always looking for new recovery oriented
music suitable to play on the "air". We are very
selective.*

24-7 Indie Radio
www.247indie.com
Want to be heard on 24-7 New Artist? Contact us.

247 On-Air
PH: 519-742-6907 FX: 519-742-0992
Sandra Mitchell sandra@lucasgaye.com
*Indie artists must sign an artist agreement in order
to get airplay.*

2kool4radio
music@2kool4radio.com
www.2kool4radio.com
Alternative, Indie, Punk, Hip Hop and more.

440MUSIC.COM
1042 W. Barry Ave. Ste. B, Chicago, IL 60657-4344
Tom Cramer samples@440music.net
www.440music.com
*We play only original music from independent
bands. Please fill out our online submission form.*

AccuRadio
119 W. Hubbard #4E, Chicago, IL 60610
PH: 312-527-3879
artist-contact@accuradio.com
www.accuradio.com
Featuring over 280 channels of really cool music.

Airbubble
info@airbubble.com
www.airbubble.com
Free form radio covering various genres of music.

Alexa Digital Internet Radio
webmaster@alexadigitalmusic.com
alexadigitalmusic.com
The best mix of Indie music on the web.

All Songs Considered *NPR*
635 Mass. Ave. NW., Washington, DC 20001
Bob Boilen allsongs@npr.org
www.npr.org/programs/asc
*Full versions of the music snippets played on NPR's
afternoon news program. Check our site for
submission details.*

All Songs Considered *Open Mic*
NPR, Attn. Robin Hilton, 635 Mass. Ave. NW.,
Washington, DC 20001
www.npr.org/programs/asc
*A showcase for independent artists. Print, fill out
and sign the online submission form and send it in
along with your CD.*

Allan Handelman Show
PH: 800-762-5825
Allan ahshow@vnet.net
ifitrocks.com
*Rock n' Roll and the Rock culture. The talk show
that rocks!*

Alloy Radio
Schram Studios, 202 W. 24th St. #706, New York, NY 10011
email@alloyradio.com
www.alloyradio.com
You'll receive a confirmation e-mail when we receive your submission and a notice if and when your music is added to the radio.

Altrok Radio
www.altrok.com
We're paying attention to scenes all over the world, watching the energy build and waiting to see what it creates.

American Radio Network *ARN*
5287 Sunset Blvd. Hollywood, CA 90027
PH: 323-464-4580
kclafm@kclafm.com
www.kclafm.com

Angry Coffee Radio Show
hello@angrycoffee.com
www.angrycoffee.com
We will compliment online marketing efforts to Indie and major record labels alike.

ArtistFirst Internet Radio
1062 Parkside Dr. Alliance, OH 44601
PH: 330-823-2264
info@artistfirst.com
www.artistfirst.com
If you have a CD, you can have a 1hr prime-time radio show here.

Artists International Independent Radio
www.aiiradio.net
Featuring worldwide independent recording artists.

AudioRealm.Com
504 N. Hockley Main, Ropesville, TX 79405
PH: 806-562-3838
www.audiorealm.com
Operates the AudioRealm Broadcast Network with currently over 800 active stations.

ArtistLaunch.com
14852 Dasher Allen Park, MI 48101
PH: 313-492-5657
www.artistlaunch.com
Live showcases, internet and real-world radio outlets, reviews and artist pages.

Artists Without a Label Radio
PO Box 879, Ojai, CA 93024
PH: 805-640-7399 FX: 805-646-6077
info@awal.com
www.awal.com
Discover great new music and artists.

Audio Independence
PO Box 73193, Metairie, LA 70033-3193
Wesley Clark wesley@wesleyclark.com
www.audioindependents.com
Features a new independent artist each week for a one hour show.

Audio Style
PO Box 13526, Macon, GA 31208-3526
Joey Stuckey stuckey2003@msn.com
www.audio-style.com
Submit your CDs to us for airplay consideration to the above address.

AURICAST
235 W. 56th St. #31D, New York, NY 10019
PH: 212-307-1333 FX: 212-246-2329
info@auricast.com
www.auricast.com
Would you like your sound in rotation at thousands of retail locations?

BAGeL Radio
209 11th Ave. San Francisco, CA 94118-2101
Ted feedback@bagelradio.com
www.bagelradio.com
Playlists include Indie & Alternative Rock and Noisy Pop. Mostly guitar music ...no testosterock.

Big Dumb Fun Show
PH: 888-832-7561
Venkman, Frank and Aaron
info@bigdumbfunshow.com
www.bigdumbfunshow.com
You can submit your songs to us in MP3 format to the above address. If we use your music, we will let you know.

BlackLight Radio
11975 Gun Smoke Dr. Collinsville, OK 74021
Gene Savage postmaster@blacklightradio.com
www.blacklightradio.com
We WILL play independent artists and if requested we can review CDs. We welcome submissions in all genres.

Brainwave Radio
943 Old Mars Hill Hwy. #5, Weaverville, NC 28787
musicdirector@brainwaveradio.com
indieartistradio.com
A mix of Indie, Alternative, Rock and Punk that brings you the perfect balance of music that will get your brain moving.

Cactus Radio
411 W. Buena Vista Dr. Tempe, AZ 85284-5221
www.cactusradio.com
Shows featuring Power Pop, Emo and otherwise Alternative artists. Visit our website for submission details.

CoolStreams
www.CoolStreams.com
You must fill out our online artist submission form before sending your CD.

Craig's Music
PH: 631-458-1130
Craig Manganello craig@craigsmusic.net
www.craigsmusic.net
Syndicated program featuring Indie music and interviews.

Crossfire Radio
www.myspace.com/crossfireradio
Play music of all genres from around the world!

Cygnus Radio
SwanSpirit swannie@cygnusradio.com
www.cygnusradio.com
Bringing the best of independent music to a wider audience.

DaNawlinzGroove
9310 Starcrest Dr. #5, San Antonio, TX 78217
PH: 504-232-3353
Tabitha/SunShyne danawlinzgroove@yahoo.com
www.danawlinzgroove.com
Features Indie artists of all genres.

Dark Side of the Radio
2288 Sharon Depoy Rd. Greenville, KY 42345
hollywood@kih.net
www.dsotr.8m.com/indy.htm
No MP3s. See submission guidelines.

D'Art Radio
PO Box 303, W. Long Branch, NJ 07764
Arlene Smith dartradio@mail.com
www.dartradio.com
Playing Rock, Techno, Pop, R&B, Rap and Hip Hop. An artist may submit one MP3 for free.

Desperate Radio
620 R St. NW., Washington, DC 20001
djdesperate@desperateradio.com
www.desperateradio.com
Internet station for Britpop and new Indie Rock.

Drama Free Radio
PH: 877-891-3117
Laneeka content@dramafreeradio.com
www.dramafreeradio.com
Your favorites styles of music, talk and news without the drama!

Elvii Radio
PO Box 272014 Columbus, OH 43227
email@elvii.com
www.Elvii.com
Upload your MP3s for airplay.

eoRadio
PO Box 441234, Aurora, CO 80014-1234
PH: 303-808-8140
Ryan Smith webmaster@eoradio.com
www.eoradio.com
The best free music from unsigned artists from around the globe.

The Epicenter
PO Box 90440, Tucson, AZ 85752
contact@vivaldimedia.com
www.TheEpicenterRocks.com
THE source for the best of the best in independent music. You love music and we love you for it.

erika.net
PO Box 7858, Ann Arbor, MI 48107
programming@erika.net
erika.net
Sounds and styles you won't hear on other radio stations.

Evolving Artist
18 Mill St., Southbridge, MA 01550-2757
Programming Dept. CODE: EA
PH: 508-764-9500 FX: 508-764-9501
info@evolvingartist.com
evolvingartist.com
Submit your CDs and MP3s to ENGAGE internet Radio. Submit your DVDs to Evolving Artist internet TV.

Excellent Radio Online
www.excellentonline.com
The home for North American fans of UK music.

ExtraPlay.com Radio
www.extraplay.com
If you'd like to make your sound available and broadcast on our radio, register today.

eXtreme Indie Radio
joshua@extremeindieradio.com
www.extremeindieradio.com
Unsigned music without Limits! Playing the best in the independent and unsigned music.

FatCat Radio Network
FatCat_Radio@ieatcatsforfun.com
www.freewebs.com/fatcatradio
Submit via our online submission form. Your music must come from a funender.com site. (No exceptions. It's the OMD that powers our station). Must be lo-fi (48kbps max.).

FindingYourMusic.com
370 N. East Camano Dr. #5 -153, Camano Island, WA 98282-7279
PH: 425-931-8777
Ava avaanddennis@msn.com
www.FindingYourMusic.com
Bringing original music to the world from an ocean of untapped talent.

FlagAss Radio!
PO Box 297, Frankenmuth, MI 48734
PH: 989-652-9520
Dan Coleman submit@flagass.com
www.FlagAssRadio.com
Promoting ALL genres of music. You can even produce your own radio show!

Following My Fish
info@followingmyfish.com
www.followingmyfish.com
An eclectic mix of Indie, Punk, Soul, Blues and anything else that I think is worth hearing.

FreeWorldRadio.com
152 Meads Cross Rd. Stormville, NY 12582
PH: 800-259-7130
FreeWorldRadio.com
Music news, artist bios, album reviews, exclusive interviews and performances.

FreshBlend Radio
PO Box 85, Bell Buckle, TN 37020
requests@freshblendradio.com
www.freshblendradio.com
The latest music from a variety of styles.

Garage Radio
John Foxworthy roadrash@garageradio.com
www.garageradio.com
Promoting independent artists via internet radio stream. Please visit our site for submission details.

Get Indie Radio
4080 Paradise #242, Las Vegas, NV 89109
PH: 702-880-5717 FX: 702-248-8564
www.getindie.com/indexlowhigh.cfm
22 different radio stations in one location.

Global Pop Conspiracy
ilovecalculator@globalpopconspiracy.com
www.globalpopconspiracy.com
Pop and Rock internet station.

Web only

GotRadio
8100 Mulrany Way, Antelope, CA 95843
programmer@gotradio.com
www.gotradio.com
Send your CD to our address and mention the STATION you are contacting ie: "New Age".

Growth House Radio
Package Receiving, 2215-R Market St. #199, San Francisco, CA 94114
PH: 415-863-3045
info@growthhouse.org
www.growthhouse.org
Created to improve the quality of compassionate care for people who are dying. We offer several different channels with music and easy-listening education features on end-of-life care.

Harris Radio
www.harrisradio.com
Created to offer "Intelligent music for Intelligent Minds".

The Heterogeneous Mezzanine *Sidewok Radio*
Antonic & The Mohawkian Princess
thmezzanine@sidewok.com
www.myspace.com/thmezzanine
From Punk to Hawaiian, from Indie Rock to Hall & Oates, we've got it all covered. Other features: The Cover Corner and The Local Artist Spotlight.

IMC Radio
PO Box 2366, Madison, MS 39130-2366
PH: 601-605-9691
Duane Lamb braintrust@imcradio.com
www.imcradio.com
Open format internet radio station. The home of "The Better Music Mix"!

Independent Nation
www.independentnation.net
Great independent music, interviews and some really off beat comedy.

Indie Band Radio
indiebandradio.com
All unsigned. All the time!

Indie Limelight
James St. James info@iarnetworks.com
indieartistradio.com
Each week the show brings over 1.3 million listeners music and interviews from the best independent music from around the world.

www.indielinkexchange.com/ile

The Indie Show

Beau beau@theindieshow.com
www.theindieshow.com
Broadcasting live every Sunday morning from the entertainment capital of the world, Las Vegas.

Indie-Unsigned

Desmond desmond.grundy@indie-unsigned.com
www.indie-unsigned.com
We also occasionally post reviews of the music we play.

IndieEARadio

141 Nanoke Ln. Carencro, LA 70520
PH: 337-442-6644
Joie Chauitn guitarmoses_619@yahoo.com
www.myspace.com/guitarmoses
Features unique artists playing new Blues to Alternative Metal.

InRadio

PO Box 6882, Minneapolis, MN 55406
PH: 612-332-9606 FX: 612-338-6043
info@inradio.net
www.inradio.net
Encourages music and ideas not found on mainstream FM radio.

Insomnia Radio Network

www.insomniaradionetwork.com
Our hosts scour the independent music scene discovering unknown artists.

The Jaci Rae Show *ArtistFirst Radio*

PO Box 1118, Felton, CA 95018
PH: 727-443-7115
Jaci Rae info@jacirae.com
jacirae.com/jacishow.html
Weekly talk show covering various aspects of the music business. Often interviews Indie artists.

Jack and Jill Radio

PO Box 450967, Sunrise, FL 33345
PH: 954-741-7233
Grant Porter djradiojack@jackandjillradio.com
www.jackandjillradio.com
Acoustic, Folk, Blues, Bluegrass, Country and Light Pop.

JeRQ THIS Radio

Jon Robert Quinn jonrobertquinn@excite.com
www.JeRQ-THIS.com
Providing Rock, Alternative and Hip Hop music. Visit our website for submission details.

Jolt Radio

joltradio@gmail.com
www.jolt-radio.com
We play all types of music.

Kill Radio

c/o Robin Torres (and show name if any),
3806 Beverly Blvd. #201, Los Angeles, CA 90004
PH: 310-737-9148
info@killradio.org
www.killradio.org
Anti corporate internet radio.

K-IRB

www.K-IRB.com
Ninja pirate radio!

Kool Rock Radio

kool@koolrockradio.com
www.koolrockradio.com
Formed by international DJs. Featuring the best Underground radio shows with the best Indie music.

Kulak's Woodshed

5230½ Laurel Canyon Blvd., North Hollywood, CA 91607
PH: 818-766-9913
Paul Kulak paulkulak@earthlink.net
www.kulakswoodshed.com
Live internet video webcasts and Acoustic music showcases.

Kweevak Music Magazine

38 Oliver Pl. Ringwood, NJ 07456
PH: 973-556-5400
Rich Lynch info@kweevak.com
www.kweevak.com
A weekly, 1-hour syndicated program now on five stations and growing.

Lime Light Radio

PH: 609-424-4556
Nick Willever admin@limelightradio.com
www.limelightradio.com
We play only unsigned, Indie music on our station. Includes public profiles and a lot more.

Liquid Radio Live

New Music Dept. 1490 Lafayette St. #203,
Denver, CO 80218
PH: 303-839-9400
lrl@liquidcompass.net
www.liquidradiolive.com
A free service allowing online listeners to access new, independent artists!

Little Radio

558 Westminster Ave. Venice, CA 90291
questions@littleradio.com
littleradio.com
A variety of shows that welcome submissions.

Live365.com

950 Tower Ln. #400, Foster City, CA 94404
PH: 323-469-4582 FX: 650-345-7497
www.live365.com
Over 3 million visitors per month and 5,000 radio stations.

Live Net Music

livenetmusic@gmail.com
www.livenetmusic.com
We're always interested in finding out about new sources of live music online.

LuxuriaMusic

PO Box 26290, San Francisco, CA 94126-6290
lux_feedback@luxuriamusic.com
www.luxuriamusic.com
Featuring Outré Lounge and Latin Jazz, breezy swinging instrumentals and vocals, groovy 60's Go-Go, Psychedelia etc.

M3 Radio

259 W. 30th St. 12th Fl. New York, NY 10001
PH: 917-351-1021
Tony-O m3newmusic@yahoo.com
www.m3radio.com
Gets independent musicians airplay.

M4 Radio

463 Boxwood Ct. Kissimmee, FL 34743
PH: 407-344-1902
Banzai banzai@m4radio.com
www.m4radio.com
All Indie music. The invasion continues!

The Michael Anthony Show

PO Box 1284, Hillsville, VA 24343
Michael Anthony
michael@michaelanthonyshow.com
www.michaelanthonyshow.com
We play, review and promote every genre of music (except religious oriented music).

Mighty Field of Vision Radio

805 Prospect Dr. Decatur, AL 35601
PH: 256-351-7835
John D. Wyker wyker@mightyfieldofvision.com
www.mightyfieldofvision.com
Providing a real avenue of radio exposure for Indie artists.

Monks Media Radio Network

44 N. 9th St. #202, Noblesville, IN 46060
PH: 317-776-4127 FX: 317-776-4128
Jeffrey S. Monks jeff@monksmedia.com
www.monksmedia.com
A weekly show that showcases Indie artists.

MUSIC CHOICE

Attn: Unsigned Material:
328 W. 34th St., New York, NY 10001
www.musicchoice.com
44 genre specific non-stop digital quality music channels.

Music Highway Radio with Sheena Metal

15030 Ventura Blvd. #843, Sherman Oaks, CA 91403
PH: 818-785-7144
Sheena Metal sheena@musichighwayradio.com
www.musichighwayradio.com
The playlist is 100% fan/listener requested. That means that an artist's fans will be responsible for picking the show's music each week. Visit our website for submission details.

Music Places

200A Linville St., Morganton, NC 28655
Wayne Fetherbay wayne@fetherbay.com
www.musicplaces.com
Our free music promotion will stream your music worldwide.

Musical Justice

justice@musicaljustice.com
www.MusicalJustice.com
We welcome your submissions. Please note that we prefer to get CDs or links to MP3s. E-mailing us MP3 files just fills up our in-box and makes us grumpy.

Musicians.net

1000 Singleton Blvd. Dallas, TX 75212
peri@musicians.net
www.musicians.net
Provides independent artists and musicians all of the tools to get their music heard.

MyRealBroadcast

myrealtalent.com
Talk and music radio shows promoting undiscovered talent.

NEKKID Radio

nekkidradio@gmail.com
www.nekkidradio.com
DJs from around the world and the widest mix of music anywhere on the NET!

NeverEndingWonder Radio
16 SW. 3rd #18, Portland, OR 97204
PH: 503-219-6741
Lee Widener uncleozma@neverendingwonder.com
www.neverendingwonder.com/radio.htm
*Plays a wide variety of music & comedy. NOT
interested in Rap, Hip Hop or Dance.*

New Artist Radio
70 W. Hale Dr. Pleasant Grove, UT 84062
PH/FX: 801-796-0504
info@newartistradio.net
www.newartistradio.net
*A FREE service offered to bands & new artists that
would like to get their music heard worldwide on a
Top 40 show & 8 other radio shows.*

No-Fi Radio
1316 El Paso Dr. Los Angeles, CA 90065
nofiradio@nofimagazine.com
www.nofiradio.com
*Featuring independent music for independent
people! DO NOT send us MP3s via e-mail.*

On The Horizon *New Artist Radio*
490 S. Main Pleasant Grove, UT 84062
PH: 801-380-0215 FX: 801-785-2157
www.theothnetwork.com
*A weekly show that plays independent music and
interviews independent artists.*

Outsight Communications
5224 Shoreline Blvd. Waterford, MI 48329-1670
PH: 248-842-5850
Tom Schulte outsight@usa.net
www.new-sounds.com
Brings to light non-mainstream music.

Pandora
Attn: Music Genome Project Indie Submission,
360 22nd St. #390, Oakland, CA 94612
pandora-support@pandora.com
www.pandora.com
*A music discovery service designed to help clients
find and enjoy music that they love. Along with your
CD, send in your bio, tour dates, press clippings etc.*

PittRadio
PH: 202-483-6864
pittradio.bottomlesspitt.com
*Streaming the cutting edge artistry of the
independents. Upload your music today!*

Popbang.com
PO Box 6522, St. Paul, MN 55106
Jay Anderson jay@popbang.com
www.popbang.com
Newer power Pop and other Rock!

Pulse Now
6133 Bristol Pkwy. #175, Culver City, CA 90230
PH: 310-216-9047
music@pulsenowmail.com
www.pulsenow.com
*Print & complete our online submission pack and
send it in along with your CD.*

Radio Artistopia
PO Box 6691, Woodbridge, VA 22195
info@artistopia.com
radio.artistopia.com
*To have your music aired you will need to begin by
establishing your presence on Artistopia.com, which
is free as well.*

Radio Contraband
Steve Walker steve@radiocontraband.com
www.radiocontraband.com
*We are continuously looking for new artists to
feature on our music streams and podcasts.*

Radio Crystal Blue
3655 Shore Pkwy. #1F, Brooklyn, NY 11235
PH: 718-646-0158
Dan Herman cblue456@optonline.net
www.radiocrystalblue.com
*Featuring the best of the independents. Send your
latest CD to the above address.*

Radio Free Tunes
PH: 412-818-1131
Paul Carosi radiofreetunes@yahoo.com
www.radiofreetunes.com
*I promote Indie musicians from around the world
from a wide range of genres.*

Radio Free World
PO Box 444, Idyllwild, CA 92549
information@radiofreeworld.com
www.radiofreeworld.com
Almost 12 hrs of Indie music per day.

Radio Indie
info@radioindie.com
www.radioindie.com
*Independent, streaming radio station dedicated to
your music and your fans.*

Radio Indie Pop
175 E. 2nd St. #1B New York, NY 10009
Rob Sacher LunaSeaRecords@nyc.rr.com
www.radio-indie-pop.com
*Music by independent label artists with no
commercial radio airplay.*

Radio Muse
1111 Davis Dr. #1-456, Newmarket, ON L3Y 9E5
Jodi Krangle jodi@musesmuse.com
www.musesmuse.com/radiomuse.html
*Bringing together the very best Indie music. Please
visit our site for submission details!*

Radio Nowhere
Christopher radionowhere@hotmail.com
www.radionowhere.org
Alternative, Electro and Indie music show.

Radio Paradise
PO Box 3008, Paradise, CA 95967
bill@radioparadise.com
www.radioparadise.com
We welcome CDs from artists & record labels.

Radio X
PO Box 42448, Middletown, OH 45042
PH: 513-273-4459
promos@usradiox.com
www.usradiox.com
We are Indie music friendly!

RadioAid.com
1006 Banister Ln. #1101, Austin, TX 78704
Rob Vining support@radioaid.com
www.RadioAid.com
*Artists upload their music on our site and select
which songs they want to appear in our streaming
radio player.*

RadioINDY.com
PO Box 230581, Encinitas, CA 92023
support@radioIndy.com
www.radioindy.com
Home for independent music on the web.

radioio
1015 Atlantic Blvd. #303, Atlantic Beach, FL 32233
PH: 800-884-8634
www.radioio.com
*Alternative Rock, cutting-edge Pop, contemporary
Folk, Blues and Jazz.*

RadioMike
PO Box 2631, Austin, TX 78768-2631
Mike Perazzetti
galahad@thefeveredbrainofradiomike.com
www.thefeveredbrainofradiomike.com
*Our mission is to make the world safe for good
music.*

RadioMojo
radiomojo.com
*Modern and Alternative Rock with some
Rap/Electronica mixed in for good measure.*

RadioU
PO Box 1887, Westerville, OH 43086
PH: 614-890-9977
radiou.com
We play the stuff corporate radio doesn't.

RadioXY
Chaos aceking@pobox.com
radioxy.com
Underground Alternative music.

RelaxRadio
43 Federal St., Karlgarin, WA 6358 Australia
PH: 618-98895050
Ron Trigwell music_submission@esat.net.au
www.relaxradio.net.au
Supporting independent artists worldwide. We play most genres of music except Heavy Alternative.

((revolving radio))
PO Box 478487, Chicago, IL 60647
dj@revolvingradio.net
www.revolvingradio.net
Review our artists list to see if you fit the format. Please do not e-mail MP3s directly.

Rock Solid Pressure *KWTF*
4254 Whistlewood Cir. Lakeland, FL 33811
Patty Yagtu rocksolidpressure@yahoo.com
rocksolidpressure.com
The only independent music game show on the net! Focusing exclusively on 'Rock' music.

Rule Radio
1114 Magnolia St. 2ⁿᵈ Fl. Greensboro, NC 27401
PH: 336-324-6784 FX: 336-274-5431
theruler@ruleradio.com
ruleradio.net
Paid service. An affordable and powerful way to get exposure.

SayHy Radio
111 N. Michigan Ave. Howell, MI 48843
PH: 517-861-9380
Ron Howard info@sayhyradio.com
www.sayhyradio.com
Plays only Indie and unsigned music 24/7 365!

Scrub Radio
info@scrubradio.com
www.scrubradio.com
A station dedicated to unsigned artists.

Shredding Radio
PO Box 2271, San Rafael, CA 94912
shreddingpaper@netscape.net
www.shreddingradio.com
Underground Pop, Britpop, J-Pop, New Wave, Riot Grrrl and Shoegazer!

Sirius Satellite Radio
1221 Ave. of the Americas, New York, NY 10020
PH: 212-584-5100
www.siriusradio.com
The best music you've ever heard and never heard.

Sloth Radio
slothdog@gmail.com
www.slothradio.com
Playing the best in modern and classic Synthpop and New Wave.

SomaFM
1594 Treat Ave. San Francisco, CA 94110
Attn: (channel name)
shawn@somafm.com
www.somafm.com
Internet broadcasts that reach around the world.

Songtiger.com
6415 Oliver Ave. S., Richfield, MN 55423
PH: 952-200-6255
Mike Johnson webmaster@songtiger.com
www.songtiger.com
Covers most genres of music.

SongPlanet Radio
www.songplanet.com
You'll be amazed at the quality of music that the major labels don't want you to hear.

The Sound of Young America
Jesse Thorn splangy@splangy.com
www.splangy.com
Syndicated show with in-depth discussions with personalities from the world of entertainment. If you think that you would fit, get in touch. We're all ears!

Spider Bite Radio
435 Elm S. Manchester, NH 03101
PH: 603-645-1449 FX: 603-657-7202
PB Kidd pbkidd@spiderbiteradio.com
www.spiderbiteradio.com
Independent music from around the globe!

StardustRadio.com
stardust@stardustradio.com
www.stardustent.com
Internet radio supporting the US troops. All genres welcome.

StreetBlast Radio
www.streetblastradio.com
Underground music, popular culture, rants and raves.

SubZero
admins@subzeroradio.com
www.subzeroradio.com
We would love to play some of your songs on air. Please e-mail us an MP3 of your music. Put in subject "be heard".

Texas Online Radio
music@texasonlineradio.com
www.texasonlineradio.com
We're not limited to Texas artists! We support the growth and promotion of new artists everywhere!

The Trans-Atlantic Underground
www.myspace.com/transatlanticunderground
Takes you around the world of Shoegaze, Indie, Psychedelia and other movements within a vast body of Underground music.

Tyrus Indie Radio
201 S. Mill St., Lewisville, TX 75057
PH: 972-353-2763
Scotty Owen info@thetyrusmusiciansgroup.com
www.TheTyrusMusiciansGroup.com
We help Indie artists any way we can.

Unsigned Band Radio
www.unsignedbandradio.com
Send us your CD or latest demo and we'll play it for you for free!!

Virtual Party Zone Radio
PO Box 912, Woodbury, CT 06798-0912
PH: 203-405-2239
eutche eutche@vpzradio.com
www.vpzradio.com
Supports and works with Indie artists to get there music exposed to the world.

Way Out There Radio
info@wayoutthere.net
www.wayoutthere.net
You can be sure to hear our DJs play local bands and unsigned artists from their area and everywhere.

WCH Radio
GW Carver House, 3035 Bell Ave. St. Louis, MO 63106
PH: 314-718-7143 FX: 270-682-9474
John ODay wchradio1@lycos.com
wchradio.com
We try to play as much Indie music as possible.

WebRadioPugetSound.com
PO Box 1801, Eatonville, WA 98328
wrps1@comcast.net
www.webradiopugetsound.com
See website for submission guidelines/forms.

Wild Side Radio
10662 De La Roche, Montreal, QC H2C 2P5
Station@WildSideRadio.com
www.WildSideRadio.com
A variety of shows featuring the best in Indie music. Send in a CD or a link to your music.

Whole Wheat Radio
PO Box 872, H St., Talkeetna, AK 99676
www.wholewheatradio.org
We play independent music exclusively.

WSVN Radio
PO Box 132, Thornton, IL 60476-0132
wsvnradio@yahoo.com
www.wsvnradio.net
Send your CD and additional info.

X-Site Radio
4200 Arch Dr. Ste. XMLA, Studio City, CA 91604
818-985-2464
Ten ten@xmradio.la
www.xsiteradio.com
Upload your music. The world is listening!

XM Satellite Radio
1500 Eckington Place NE., Washington, DC 20002-2194
Attn: Billy Zero
FX: 202-380-4065
Billy Zero yzero@xmradio.com
radiounsigned.com
unsigned.xmradio.com
Submit your CD with genre labeled. No MP3s.

XMU *XM Radio*
Tobi xmu@xmradio.com
xmu.xmradio.com
We play what's next ...now! It's Indie Pop, Indie Rock, Electronic, Down Tempo and Underground Hip Hop!

XND Radio
PH: 360-488-0460
Joshua Morgan joshua@xndradio.com
www.xndradio.com
24/7 internet radio station playing the best in independent music.

Xradio.biz
90 Stowell St., Upland, CA 91786
info@enexes.com
www.Xradio.biz
Official Indie music supporter!

YourOnLive.com
Jim theshow@youronlive.com
www.youronlive.com
Rock and talk only the internet can handle.

Zero Art Radio
2809 Galesburg Dr. Nashville, TN 37217
www.zeroartradio.com
A consortium of Alternative musicians, artists and people in general who are enthused by creativity and free thought.

Podcasts

Podcasts listed in this section feature a variety of musical styles. Other more genre-specific podcasts can be found in the appropriate sections of this book. Most podcasters don't mind if you send MP3s via e-mail, but there are some will DELETE any attachments sent to them and insist that you send a LINK to your song file. So just to be safe, make sure to check the submission details for each show.

Many podcasts feature what is called "podsafe music". To find out what podsafe music is, read the article in SECTION SEVEN of this book called "What is Podsafe Music?"

United States

75 Minutes
PH: 801-784-1337
Mike & Lyssa 75minutes@gmail.com
www.75minutes.com
We scour the earth looking for the best of the independent music world, no matter the language, style or level of presumed hipness.

Absolutely Kosher Records Podcast
1412 10th St., Berkeley, CA 94710-1512
Cory Brown macher@absolutelykosher.com
absolutelykosher.blogspot.com
A look at life's little idiosyncrasies and quirks and a ton of cool music.

Accidental Hash
PO Box 367, Milford, MA 01757
C.C. Chapmanaccidenthash@gmail.com
www.accidenthash.com
Playing the best in podsafe music Visit the website for submission details.

Adam Curry's Daily Source Code
adam@podshow.com
www.dailysourcecode.com
Podfather Adam Curry scours the globe for the hottest new mashups, podcast highlights and podsafe music.

Adzuki Bean Stash
Cchang cchang@math.utexas.edu
adzukipodcast.blogspot.com
Monthly podcasts from my stash of music.

Alaska Podshow
PO Box 221856, Anchorage, AK 99522-1856
Scott Slone media@alaskapodshow.com
www.alaskapodshow.com
Local news, events and introducing independent music from artists around the world.

American Cliche
PH: 206-203-3425
Scott
TheAmericanCliche@gmail.com
americancliche.net
Bizarre news stories, politics and undiscovered music all served up with a heaping dose of sarcasm. We want to hear from you!

America Unsigned
americaunsigned.com
Featuring the best independent musicians in the country. Send us an e-mail with a short bio and the names of the songs you would like played.

Amplified Podcast
PO Box 151, Seattle, WA 98111
Eric Hoglund
eric@amplifiedpodcast.com
www.amplifiedpodcast.com
Podcasting great Indie bands from around the globe.

Ash Radio
PH: 203-389-1736
csr@froppo.com
www.ashradio.com
Dedicated to giving you the best exposure we possibly can. Visit our site for submission details.

Association of Music Podcasting (AMP)
PO Box 463, Williamsville, IL 62693
PH: 217-899-3512
FX: 217-899-3512
Matt Galligan
matt.galligan@musicpodcasting.org
musicpodcasting.org
Consider submitting your music to AMP's music library, which our members use to fill their unique podcasts with hot new acts.

ATW1
Greg Johnson gregj013@yahoo.com
www.ATW1.tk
Alternative Pop radio. We play music from unknown Rock bands at no cost.

Audio Popcorn
PH: 763-390-5051
audiopopcorn@gmail.com
www.audiopopcorn.net
Small musical shows focusing on one artist or group.

Audiocrush
PH: 425-969-5502
hello@audiocrush.us
audiocrush.us
About confessions, music and everything else.

Bald Guy Show
PH: 651-204-9032
baldguyshow@gmail.com
www.baldguyshow.com
Playing great podsfafe music. We talk about music, politics, relationships and other stuff too!

Bandtrax

c/o Produktion, 1617 W. Jefferson St., Boise, ID 83702
feedback@bandtrax.net
www.bandtrax.net
If you've got music, we'd love to play it in our podcast and give you a chance to sell your CDs in our online store.

Band Weblogs Podcast

Jenny & Dave info@bandweblogs.com
www.bandweblogs.com/podcastshow.html
Playing podsafe and independent music with the occasional special guest dropping by.

Bands Under the Radar

kami@viperroom.com
bandsundertheradar.com
Featuring unsigned bands and Indie artists.

Barefoot Radio

PO Box 351979, Westminster, CO 80234
PH: 888-640-5899
paul@barefootradio.com
barefootradio.com
Nobody does more to promote independent bands and musicians. We work hard to sell your music.

BFNinYourEars.com

Bob Dubilina bob@bfninyourears.com
www.bfninyourears.com
Bold declarations, risky propositions, dark humor, angry rants, wild interviews and great music!

Big Daddy Dan Podcast

PH: 206-202-3557
dannyt@hintonet.net
okieradio.com
Podsafe music, random banter, humor, technology, events.

The Bitterest Pill

PH: 206-309-7455
Dan Klass pill@danklass.com
www.thebitterestpill.com
Commentary and music from a stay-at-home dad/shut in.

The Bottom40 Rock Show

3664 St. Johns Ave. Jacksonville, FL 32205
Adam Hartmann adam@hartmanndesign.net
www.bottom40rockshow.com
I like everything from Bluegrass to Heavy Metal to Punk. I don't like pop Country. Really old Country is ok.

Buckeye Drive Time

buckeyedrivetime@gmail.com
www.buckeyedrivetime.com
A drive time alternative. 3 Songs, 3 Promos, no idiots!

The Buddy Culver Show

Darren Proctor darrenproctor@gmail.com
www.buddyculver.com
Coming to you from the bowels of a basement in Dearborn, MI. Highlighting Indie bands from all decades.

BZoO HomeGrown Radio

cafeRg@gmail.com
www.splashhall.org/blog
Where political pundits, artists, poets and fans play!

C.C. Chapman's U-Turn Cafe

PO Box 367, Milford, MA 01757
PH: 206-984-2233
C.C. Chapman uturncafe@gmail.com
u-turncafewp.podshow.com
A special focus on mellow, chilled Acoustic music. Grab a seat and enjoy!

Chillcast

375 Redondo Ave. #326, Long Beach, CA 90814
Anji Bee anjibee@gmail.com
thechillcast.podshow.com
Music ranging from Downtempo to Deep House, Trip Hop to Dream Pop, Electro Lounge to old school Jazz and Blues.

The Closet Geek Show

Brent closetgeekshow@gmail.com
www.closetgeekshow.com
A mix of Trance, D n' B, Rock, Metal and mashups that will make you want to dance, mosh or both at once.

CoolerPodcasts.com

PO Box 26272, Akron, OH 44319
PH: 330-807-5236
Dave Jackson musicianscooler@gmail.com
www.coolerpodcasts.com
Where musicians come to trade advice and music.

Coverville

PMB 12, 15400 W. 64th Ave. #E-9, Arvada, CO 80007
PH: 206-222-2683
Brian Ibbott coverville@gmail.com
www.coverville.com
A podcast that focuses on new renditions of previously recorded songs.

Cream of the Crop

creamofthecrop.cc
A musical competition hosted by Doug DeLong. Featuring the very best independent music available today. Be part of the fun by voting each week for your favorite contestant!

Creot Radio

www.creotradio.net
Weekly show featuring artists from around the globe. The show is hosted by musicians in a new city each week and features that city's local artists.

Dailysonic

73-23 194th St., Flushing, NY 11366
PH: 877-766-4254
Aaron Taylor Waldman music@dailysonic.com
www.dailysonic.com/main
Discusses news, independent music, fringe culture, arts, technology, lifestyle, activism etc.

Deliberate Noise

www.deliberatenoise.com
Music from independent record labels and unsigned artists.

The Desperate Housewife

Tracey Auer thedesperatehousewife@gmail.com
thedesperatehousewife.libsyn.com
Finally a podcast for women who are tired of losing their husbands and boyfriends to this new podcasting world! Indie music is featured each show.

Digital Detroit Radio

Matt digitaldetroitradio@gmail.com
www.digitaldetroitradio.com
Our mission is to promote independent bands that aren't associated with the RIAA. I love spreading the word about Indie bands that people might not have heard of yet.

DigiVegas

Paulie Podcaster submit@digivegaspodcast.com
www.digivegaspodcast.com
Bringing you the very best Indie music from Las Vegas, as well as from all over the world.

Eclectic Mix

eclecticmix@gmail.com
eclecticmix.com
Offers the best from a mixture of musical styles. A single artist will be highlighted during each show so that the listener can absorb what is offered.

Electric LarryLand

podcast@electriclarryland.com
www.electriclarryland.com
Podcast of video and audio production techniques. Accepts music for airplay. Visit site for details.

Flow Music

www.getyourflow.com
Features live music performances from hot NYC venues as well as music videos submitted by independent artists from all over the world.

Get Jacked!

getjacked@hanamas.com
getjacked.hanamas.com
I play what I like. Say what I like. Show up when I like.

High Orbit

matthewebel.com/podcast
Music, news and feedback from all over the quadrant with Matthew Ebel.

The Home Made Hit Show

Tony Butterworth homemadehitshow@gmail.com
www.homemadehitshow.com
Featuring exciting and original Rock, Acoustic, Blues and Pop music made by home based artists.

Illinoise!

PH: 512-533-0655
Just Pete & NASA Janet noise@illinoise.net
www.illinoise.net
Join us for Robot Theatre, Haiku Reviews and the Karaoke Challenge!

IndependentCast

JBU Box 3466, 2000 W. University St., Siloam Springs, AR 72761
PH: 530-632-3673
James Smith james@independentcast.com
www.independentcast.com
A weekly half-hour podcast featuring the best independent artists from around the globe.

Indie Eye

Dave Phillips dphillips@fivemasks.com
www.indierelease.com
We close our show each week with an independent music clip. A great way to get your music to new ears.

Indie Interviews

indieinterviews@indieinterviews.com
indieinterviews.com
Weekly podcast of interviews with Indie artists.

Indie-Music.com Podcast

PO Box 602, Columbus, IN 47202
Suzanne Glass suzanne@indie-music.com
www.impodcast.com
Create a free online press kit at www.indie-music.com/join and automatically be considered.

IndieFeed
Chris MacDonald info@indiefeed.com
www.indiefeed.com
*Your music must be unique, high impact, high
energy and compelling. Your songs must push the
envelope and resonate, stimulate and perhaps even
challenge the audience.*

IndiePodcasting.com
Tony Alexander pd@indiepodcasting.com
www.indiepodcasting.com
*A service that promotes Indie artists using a
combination of podcasting, syndication, webcasting
and viral marketing.*

Inside the Music Business Radio
PH: 510-213-2446
Troy Ewing troy@insidethemusicbusiness.com
www.imbradio.com
*Who better to get advice from than artists,
managers, labels execs, attorneys and other industry
power players.*

Insomnia Radio
765 Mesa View Dr. #128, Arroyo Grande,
CA 93420
PH: 805-709-1551
Jason Evangelho jason@insomniaradio.net
insomniaradio.net
*Consistently delivering the best music you've never
heard. Business Week calls it one of their Top 8
podcasts in the world.*

Jason Knows
knows.jason@gmail.com
www.jasonknows.com
Deals in Indie music and interviews.

The Jersey Toddshow
Jerseytoddshow@gmail.com
www.jerseytoddshow.com
The hardest working lawyer in podcasting.

King Bonk's Campfire Cast
kingbonk@gmail.com
www.kingbonk.libsyn.com
A periodic setting of sound and story.

The Lee Show
Lee Harris juvenilehi@gmail.com
www.theleeshow.com
*A bi-weekly hodgepodge of music and fun for
everyone.*

Looking out the Window
PH: 206-600-5665
artist@lookingoutthewindow
lookingoutthewindow.com
*Highlights the inspiration behind the music. Peak
inside the musicians studio and you just may be
inspired yourself!*

Love House Radio
PH: 206-222-1905
PD Love LoveHouseRadio@gmail.com
www.lovehouseradio.com
Fresh music and personal interviews.

Lunatic Radio
theshow@lunaticradio.com
lunaticradio.com
Interviews with independent artists and their music.

Lying Media Bastards
PO Box 4705, San Diego,
CA 92164
Jake lmbradio@gmail.com
www.lyingmediabastards.com
*Couples excellent music
with angry news
commentary (and the
occasional interview). If
you've got songs for us
send MP3s via e-mail.*

Mashup of the Week
mashuptown@gmail.com
www.mashuptown.com
*Promoting the brilliance,
creativity and hard work of
DJs, producers, Mashup
artists and the original
artists whose music is
mashed.*

MFJ: Rocket Sauce
3491 Holiday Rd. #102,
Traverse City, MI 49686
PH: 231-645-0271
Julie Olson
juliepaloo@monkeypup.org
musicforjerks.com
*Focusing on the most kick-
ass, cream your jeans Rock
music we can find.*

Most People Are DJs
PO Box 1231,
Union Lake, MI 48387
PH: 206-202-2643
Mikel O.D.
mostpeoplearedjs@
gmail.com
mostpeoplearedjs.libsyn.com
Send me stuff for my show!!

Music 4 iPods
www.music4ipods.com
*Featuring music from
independent bands.
Submissions are accepted
through Sonicbids
www.sonicbids.com*

Music For Jerks
3491 Holiday Rd. #102,
Traverse City, MI 49686
PH: 231-645-0270
Joshua Olson monkeypup@
monkeypup.org
www.musicforjerks.com
*A rock-your-socks-off Indie
Rock podcast. You want the
goods? I got the goods.*

MusiciansCast.com
info@musicianscast.com
podcast.musicianscast.com
*Professional musician Jonn
Savannah, legendary
recording engineer Shelly
Yakus and communications
guru Peter Bowman team
up to bring you a free daily
podcast that really informs
and entertains with hard-
hitting topics all about the
music business and getting
ahead in today's music
industry.*

musicNerve.com Weekly Podcast
PO Box 67405, Albuquerque, NM 87193-7405
Peter Mezensky misspeter@gmail.com
www.musicnerve.com
We seek out the best Indie Rock, the weirdest outsider music and the most ground breaking of the Experimental and Avant-garde.

MusicRebellion.com
Paul Mahern paulm@musicrebellion.com
www.musicrebellion.com
Our podcasts feature information about up and coming artists.

Next Big Hit
30 Magaw Pl. #1D, New York, NY 10033
PH: 646-345-3433
submissions@nextbighit.com
www.nextbighit.com
Submit your music for us to consider for our podcast programming and for Indie Airplay Internet Radio!

Notes From The Underground
music@notesunderground.com
notesunderground.com
New music recommendations, music news, film reviews and more.

The Nothing War
PH: 206-203-4869
Jeff & Patrick admin@thenothingwar.com
thenothingwar.com
We play music. The good stuff along with some talk, yes the good talk.

The Obtuse Angle
Steve Dupont obtuseangle@stevedupont.com
obtuseangle.libsyn.com
Brought to you by the hardest working brain cell in America!

Off the Beat-n-Track
offthebeatntrack.libsyn.com
The best in Indie music from across the country and beyond. Live performances, interviews, CD spotlights and more.

The Open Mic
PH: 206-338-2577 FX: 704-843-5396
Tyler McKenzie openmicpod@gmail.com
www.openmicpodcast.com
Features music and information on independent artists.

Pancake Radio
www.myspace.com/pancakeradio
If you have anything you want to share: obscure gems, your band's new demo, recordings of your parents making whoopee, feel free to drop us a line and we'll make the arrangements.

PEACEPOD
PH: 213-417-8838
Jason Brock peacepod@songserverworldwide.com
www.songserverworldwide.com
A cutting edge way for activists, artists and the audience to connect. For music submissions please sign the guest book with a link to your music.

The PhiLL(er)
podcast@thephiller.com
www.thephiller.com/podcast
Weekly independent music showcase.

Phonograph
www.ph0n0graph.com
The show provides an outlet for independent musicians as well as musicians that may have gone unnoticed in the past.

PinkBeltRage
Joy pinkbelt@pinkbeltrage.com
outloud.pinkbeltrage.com
I love music more than anything in the world!

Planet Moonbeam
moonbeam@podomatic.com
moonbeam.podomatic.com
On a quest to find the best Indie music we can.

PMC Top10
6130 Bryant Pond, Houston, TX 77041
Chris Doelle pmctop10@gmail.com
www.podmusiccountdown.com
A weekly countdown show featuring the top tunes being spun by podcasters.

The Podcast Network
podnet@principius.com
www.thepodcastnetwork.com
One of the best resources for quality audio content that people can listen to when they want, where they want and on any device they want.

The Podcast Network's Rock Show
Ewan ewanspence@gmail.com
rock.thepodcastnetwork.com
Walking the dark corners of the internet to find the best underground and unnoticed Rock bands.

Podsafe Music Daily
Blaze podsafemusicdaily@gmail.com
podsafemusicdaily.podomatic.com
Your daily dose of 100% podsafe music to make your day go by just that much faster.

podsafe music network
music.podshow.com
The best in new music and music podcasts. Submit your music and watch your fans and CD sales grow!

Podshow Music Rewind
Marcus Couch podshowmusicrewind@gmail.com
rewind.podshow.com
The best independent music from the best independent music podcasts.

Podshow Radio
PH: 213-291-6892
podshowradio@gmail.com
www.podshowradio.com
Where we talk about music and more!

Preying Lizard Podcasts
101 Hodgesville Rd. L-50, Dothan, AL 36301
preyinglizard@netscape.net
www.preyinglizardmusic.com
Check our various podcasts for one that features your style of music.

Pure Brilliant
Hugh Morrison purebrilliantpodcast@gmail.com
www.purebrilliantpodcast.blogspot.com
Featuring bands covering a wide variety of genres.

Radio Guitarhoo!
Furbelly furbelly@guitarhoo.com
www.radioguitarhoo.com
Spotlights, interviews, features and loads of music from Heavy Metal, Punk, Jazz, Blues, Flamenco, Experimental and beyond!

Radio QRM
PH: 206-337-0776
radioqrm@gmail.com
radioqrm.com
Noise traditional radio can't ignore.

Radio.Speljamr
303 Hyland Ave. Depew, NY 14043
PH: 716-698-8426
Timothy Finucane radiospeljamr@gmail.com
radio.speljamr.com
A podcast featuring independent music of all genres.

Random Signal
Jason randomsignal@gmail.com
randomsignal.libsyn.com
Tangential transmissions from a disorganized mind.

The Riverbend
theriverbend@gmail.com
theriverbendpodcast.com
The next generation of radio is here!

Rock and Roll Geek Indie Show
PH: 706-621-7625
Michael Butler rockandrollgeek@podshow.com
www.rockandrollgeek.org
Playing the best in podsafe Indie and unsigned Rock.

Rock and Roll Jew Show
David Jacobs rockandrolljew@gmail.com
www.rockandrolljew.com
The best Indie Rock 'n Roll from all over the world. A special spotlight is put on bands from Israel or with Jewish heritage.

rudeboy podcast
rudeboypodcast@gmail.com
www.rudeboypodcast.com
An eclectic blend of podsafe music, exclusive mixes and other audio randomness.

The RuckuS PodcasT
theruckuspodcast@gmail.com
theruckus.blogspot.com
A blend of tunes as eclectic as the blend-er himself. Served with fresh new flavors every episode.

Scotch on the Rocks
scotchrocker@gmail.com
www.scotch-rocks.com
The best independent bands in a show dedicated to a genre, feel or style. You can't get less specific than that!

Shifted Sound
www.shiftedsound.com
Showcasing great independent and small label music.

Sleephouse Radio
sleephouseradio@gmail.com
www.sleephouse.blogspot.com
Our mission is simply to spread the word of good music - music that gets scant little representation elsewhere.

Sonic Playground
Lynn Bernardi sonicplayground@gmail.com
sonicplayground.libsyn.com
Independent music podcast featuring Indie Rock, Shoegaze, Lo-Fi, Dream Pop, Euro Pop and anything along those lines. Contact me for my mailing address.

The Sonic Spotlight
War-N Harrison sonicspotlight@gmail.com
www.sonicspotlight.com
Features interviews with bands, solo artists and people behind the scenes of the music business.

The Sounds in My Head
daniel@thesoundsinmyhead.com
www.thesoundsinmyhead.com
A weekly show featuring songs and bands you might have missed.

TBA (chicago)
Robert renglish@tbachicago.com
www.tbachicago.com
Supporting emerging music from around the world.

This Is Our Music
thisisourmusic@mtvne.com
www.thisisourmusic.tv
The show that travels around the world to discover new artists and bring them to light.

Tracks Up the Tree
contact@upthetree.com
www.upthetree.com
We play artists we connect to, so bio's and photographs are strongly suggested. I also post reviews occasionally.

The Tripwire
info@thetripwire.com
www.thetripwire.com/podcast
We always aim to support and highlight music for those in the industry that "genuinely care" and love music as much as we do.

UC Radio
PH: 323-319-4230
Mike ucradio@gmail.com
www.ucradiopodshow.com
Always on the look out for anything that is good and that hasn been tainted by corporate baggage.

The Unharshed Mellow
Seuss & BJ theunharshedmellow@gmail.com
www.theunharshedmellow.com
Like a wet willy of independent music.

Ultimatemix
ultimatemix@gmail.com
www.ultimatemix.i12.com
If you want your music to be played, contact us in time for the next podcast.

Unsigned at The Podcast Brewery
hello@podcastbrewery.com
www.podcastbrewery.com
Looking to help get some more exposure, awareness and increase your listenership? Then you can become part of our growing niche podcasts.

Unsigned Underground
230 S. Main St., Newtown, CT 06470
PH: 203-426-2030 FX: 203-426-2036
Darryl Gregory info@unsignedunderground.net
www.unsignedunderground.net
Features independent CDs and interviews with artists. Great free exposure!

Uwe Hermann's Music Podcast
uwe@hermann-uwe.de
www.hermann-uwe.de/podcast
Playing freely available (podsafe) music by various artists and from most music genres.

Viva Podcast
PH: 206-339-8482
Lisa & Greg mail@vivapodcast.com
www.vivapodcast.com
The first podcast in the state of New Mexico!

Well-Rounded Radio
59 Forest Hills St., Jamaica Plain, MA 02130-2933
PH: 617-233-6613
Charlie McEnerney charlie@wellroundedradio.net
www.wellroundedradio.net
An interview program that finds what inspires and influences artists work.

WHYME
seth@whymepodcast.org
www.whymepodcast.org
The magic's in the music and the music's on WHYME, the Worst Music You've Ever Heard.

Xero Bubble Radio
Hunter xero.bubble@gmail.com
xerobubble.blogspot.com
Weekly show featuring new artists.

Zaldor's World
www.zaldor.com
Detroit based show playing a wide variety of music.

Canada

Audio Popcorn
14 St-Georges St., Oka, QC J0N 1E0
PH: 514-758-5503
Krash Coarse audiopopcorn@gmail.com
audiopopcorn.net
Featuring a single artist (2-3 songs) per program. Maximum tunes, minimum "blabla".

mostlytunes.com
PO Box 87, Ste-Marthe-sur-le-Lac, QC J0N 1P0
PH: 267-220-3701
music@mostlytunes.com
www.mostlytunes.com
We're always looking for new music!

Space Junk Radio
506-60 Windward St., St. Catharines, ON L2M 4H2
filmjunk@gmail.com
www.spacejunk.org
News and reviews from the world of movies and pop culture plus the best in Indie Rock and Electronic music.

France

Meltingpod
Annie Viglielmo meltingpod@free.fr
meltingpod.free.fr
A melting pot of music, colors and cultures.

Germany

Blade Radio
bladeradio@gmx.de
blade-radio.podspot.de
Das hier ist der Podcast für alle Leute die Spaß an guter Musik und unterhaltsamen Themen haben.

Italy

RockCast Italia
dok@rockcastitalia.com
www.rockcastitalia.com
Il podcast n°1 per gli amanti del rock in Italia.

Portugal

Safecast
Vitor Fernandes vmlf@sapo.pt
safecast.vmlf.net
Each show focuses on a particular style of music.

United Kingdom

Bite Size Bonus
Ground Fl. 75 Newry St., Holyhead Anglesey, LL65 1HR UK
PH: +441407-765014
GD greendragonmedia@gmail.com
www.greendragononline.co.uk
One of the UK's most popular podcasts playing and supporting independent artists worldwide.

Bitjobs for the Masses!
54 Briery Rd. Halesowen, West Mids, B63 1AS UK
PH: 07790068549
Phil Coyne phil@bitjobs.net
www.bitjobs.net
An independent music podcast playing the very best music from around the world.

CrApJunkie Unsigned!
Mosherant mosherant@crapjunkie.com
www.crapjunkie.com
Searching through garages the world over to bring you the very best in unsigned, Alternative music!!!

Dark Compass
Rowland darkcompass@gmail.com
www.darkcompass.com
With the knowledge that regular radio will almost never play or support Indie music, we are giving you a free and valuable service.

Darkhorse Radio
darkhorse@podomatic.com
www.darkhorseradio.co.uk
Plays only the BEST independent music from around the world - no fillers, just great music.

The Flashing 12
55 Marlborough Pk. Ave. Sidcup, Kent, DA15 9DL UK
PH: 07767-443536
Paul & Janet Parkinson flashing12@gmail.com
www.theflashing12.com
We are known as "The Richard and Judy of podcasting". We both talk about stuff and nonsense and tech and anything else that drifts past the window.

Homegrown
Nic Treadwell nic@homegrownpodcast.co.uk
homegrown.libsyn.com
Music, poetry and prose featuring an ecclectic mix of artists from all over the world.

The Kaflooey
159 Cherry Tree Rd. Blackpool, Lancashire, FY4 4PQ UK
PH: 07712045613
Chris Sherry kaflooey@gmail.com
www.kaflooey.com
A comedy and music podcast featuring comedy sketches and independent podsafe music.

Monochrome Museum
Moll the Bat & John Mono
john@monochromemuseum.co.uk
www.monochromemuseum.co.uk
We try to help unsigned bands from around the world. We also feature artist interview and get out to see as many live bands as possible.

My Silver Mount Zion
12 St Michael's Mount, Northampton, NN1 4JH UK
PH: 206-888-6769
Rob & Steve mysilvermountzion@gmail.com
robular.libsyn.com
We welcome you to something you haven't heard before.

NonStuff
brothers@nonstuff.com
www.nonstuff.com
We will listen to any music you'd like to send in.

Not Your Usual Bollocks
www.notyourusualbollocks.squarespace.com
An on-demand refuge from main-stream radio featuring the best independent artists from the Rock and Electronic music genres.

popHOLE
Dan dan.klyn@gmail.com
www.pophole.com
I'm a pretty big fan of Pop music. In fact, I need Pop music.

Radio Clash
PH UK: 07005-850-524 PH US: 206-202-5274
radioclash@mutantpop.net
www.mutantpop.net/radioclash
From remixes to DJ mixes, bootlegs to Electronica, Indie and cutups/Experimental weirdness to aural oddities and insane covers.

Reaching for Lucidity
PH US: 985-878-5161
ebancrawford@gmail.com
reachingforlucidity.net
The condom for your ears in the fight against STD's (sonically transmitted diseases).

Rock On London
rockonlondon@gmail.com
www.rockonlondon.com
Most of the music chosen is by unknown independent artists and I just want to expose more people to cool music.

Short Attention Span Radio
shortattentionspan_radio@yahoo.co.uk
sasradio.blogspot.com
If you hear your favourite bands on here, let us know - well see it doesn't happen again.

$talker Radio Show
1 Belmont Hall Ct. Belmont Grove, London, SE13 5DU UK
PH: 07787-514763
lizzie@stalkerrecords.co.uk
www.stalkerrecords.co.uk
The best in independent and unsigned music, brought to you courtesy of DJ Lucky Face and his multiple personalities.

Take Your Medicine
mikesmithmikesmith@gmail.com
www.take-your-medicine.co.uk
Showcasing the best in Indie, Folk, Lo-Fi, Hi-Fi, Eclectic and Electric music every week.

TheDogBox
Bruce woof@thedogbox.info
www.thedogbox.info
A regular round-up of motorsport news plus great music.

Three From Leith
Grant Mason threefromleith@gmail.com
www.threefromleith.com
Send an e-mail submission, attaching a track or two, along with a few paragraphs about yourself or the band.

Tunetrader
PO Box 647, Portsmouth, PO1 2ZT UK
PH: 0845-2262162
Nick Hooper enquiries@tunetrader.com
www.tunetrader.com/about.asp
A periodic half-hour podcast featuring the best independent artists from around the world.

Xan Phillips Presents
admin@xan.co.uk
www.xan.co.uk
Due to the high volume of excellent new music we are being sent we have put them into a half-hour show called The New Music Collection.

Hong Kong

Panda's Hideout!!
pandashideout@gmail.com
fiercepandaaa.blogspot.com
Focusing on quirky Electronica, dancable Indie Pop, Chill-Out Acoustic and rockable...Rock.

Japan

...My cup of tea...
mail@mycupoftea.cc
www.mycupoftea.cc
Music, talk, creative commons and more.

podshower.com
2-19-20-603 Mizusawa, Miyamae, Kawasaki, Kanagawa 216-0012 Japan
PH: 044-979-1124 FX: 044-979-1124
Masayoshi Yamamiya info@fishthemusic.com
www.podshower.com/pod
Podcast for Japanese music made in Japan.

Blues Radio

Internet, Syndicated Shows and Podcasts

United States

Bandit Blues Radio
3586 Ridgefield Dr. Murfreesboro, TN 37129
mgr@banditbluesradio.com
www.banditbluesradio.com
We are willing to help new and up coming artists gain exposure. We also do reviews.

Beale Street Caravan
66 Monroe Ave. #101, Memphis, TN 38103
PH: 901-527-4666 FX: 901-529-4030
info@bealestreetcaravan.com
www.bealestreetcaravan.com
Aired weekly on over 280 public, community and college radio stations nationwide.

Blue Icewater Radio
DJ Smilestir smilestir@blueicewater.com
www.blueicewater.com
Plays an eclectic blend of swampy, Jazzy, Rock, Acoustic and spiritual Blues.

Blues Before Sunrise
PO Box 272, Forest Park, IL 60130
Steve Cushing
steve.cushing@bluesbeforesunrise.com
www.bluesbeforesunrise.com
Nationally syndicated public radio program explores, preserves and popularizes the various eras and genre of Blues heritage.

The Blues Shop
Josh Jones josh@thebluesshoppodcast.com
www.thebluesshoppodcast.com
Podcast dedicated to playing the best independent Blues.

Cybro Radio
460 Cypress Ln. El Cajon, CA 92020
PH: 619-590-1569 FX: 619-460-5749
Larry Lowe info@cybroradio.us
www.cybroradio.com
Broadcasting Blues, Jazz, Country Gospel and Hip Hop music and featuring emerging new stars.

ElectricBlues Radio
PO Box 1370, Riverview, FL 33568-1370
GoodBlues@ElectricBluesRadio.com
web.tampabay.rr.com/ebradio
Sizzlin' electric Blues guitar.

Murphy's Saloon
murphyssaloon@gmail.com
www.murphyssaloon.com
Podcast home of the Blues!

The Roadhouse
Tony Steidler-Dennison steidler@gmail.com
www.roadhousepodcast.com
A weekly podcast of great Blues music by unknown artists. The finest Blues you've never heard!

Smokestack Lightnin' WUCF
200 Shell Point W., Maitland, FL 32751
blues@smokestacklightnin.com
www.smokestacklightnin.com
Syndicated show playing Blues, Rhythm & Blues, Soul, Funk, Blues/Rock and Zydeco.

California

Ann the Raven's Blues Show KCSN
18111 Nordhoff St., Northridge, CA 91330-8312
PH: 818-885-5276
Ann the Raven anntheraven@aol.com
www.kcsn.org/programs/anntheraven.html
Delivering the best Blues sounds in Southern CA for over 20 years.

Blues Evening Train KKUP
933 Monroe St., PMB 9150, Santa Clara, CA 95050
PH: 408-260-2999
www.kkup.org/dj/conductor.html
The Conductor hips listeners to the best in Blues, whether it's hot off the presses or a scratchy vinyl LP.

Damn Traffic! KKUP
933 Monroe St., PMB 9150, Santa Clara, CA 95050
PH: 408-260-2999
Jammin Jim jammin_jim@comcast.net
www.kkup.org/dj/farris.html
Features up-and-coming Blues artists, the Youngbloods of the Blues.

Rollin' and Tumblin / Two Steps from the Blues KUSP
PO Box 423, Santa Cruz, CA 95061
PH: 831-476-2800 FX: 831-476-2802
kusp@kusp.org
www.kusp.org
Send any promotional items for airplay, giveaway or review.

Colorado

Strictly Blues 103.5 The Fox
4695 S. Monaco, Denver, CO 80237
www.thefox.com/pages/strictlyblues-index.html
Host Kai Turner features the best of national, international & local Blues as well as interviews and live in-studio performances.

Connecticut

Sunday Night Blues WCCC
1039 Asylum Ave. Hartford, CT 06105
Beef Stew beefstew@wccc.com
www.megablues.com/program.htm
Six hours of ass kickin' Blues!

Illinois

Basement of Blues *WMKB*
Chicago Slim chicagoslim@basementofblues.com
www.basementofblues.com
Blues from classic artists to current local talents.

Indiana

The Blues Revue *WVPE*
2424 California Rd. Elkhart, IN 46514
PH: 888-399-9873
Ole Harv oleharv@worldnet.att.net
www.wvpe.org/blues_revue.html
Celebrating over 20 years of the Blues!

Minnesota

Rollin & Tumblin *KFAI*
1808 Riverside Ave. Minneapolis, MN 55454
PH: 612-341-3144
Jacquie Maddix diamondblue@qwest.net
www.kfai.org/programs/roll_tum.htm
A synthesis of Blues and Big Band.

Mississippi

WMPR
1018 Pecan Park Cir. Jackson, MS 39286
PH: 601-948-5950 FX: 601-948-6162
wmpr@wmpr901.com
www.wmpr901.com
Blues and Gospel station.

Nebraska

Mystic Mile *KZUM*
941 "O" St., Lincoln, NE 68508
PH: 402-474-5086 FX: 402-474-5091
Mike Flowers mflowers@lps.org
www.kzum.org/mystic
Nothing but the very best of Blues with the classics and new releases.

New York

Across the Tracks *WFDU*
Metropolitan Campus, 1000 River Rd. Teaneck, NJ 07666
PH: 201-692-2806 FX: 201-692-2807
Richy Harps richyharps@aol.com
wfdu.fm
Blends both classic Blues and Soul with new artists who perform in the traditional style.

Bad Dog Blues Radio Show *WITR*
32 Lomb Memorial Dr. Rochester, NY 14623-0563
PH: 585-475-2271 FX: 585-475-4988
Gary & Jeff info@baddogblues.com
www.baddogblues.com
We span the history of the Blues bringing you everything from Barrelhouse Piano to searing Electric Blues.

Sunday Night Blues *WAER*
795 Ostrom Ave. Syracuse, NY 13244-4601
PH: 315-443-4021 FX: 315-443-2148
Tom Townsley waer@syr.edu
waer.org/blues.html
For over 12 years supplying Blues fans a healthy dosage of both national and local Blues talent.

Texas

The Casbah *KYSM*
1300 San Pedro Ave. San Antonio, TX 78212
PH: 210-733-2800
Brian Parrish casbahradio@yahoo.com
www.ksym.org
Featuring Surf-Instrumentals, Garage, Blues and more!!

On the Roadside *KMBH*
PO Box 2147, Harlingen, TX 78551
PH: 800-839-6771 FX: 956-421-4150
Chris Maley kmbhkhid@aol.com
www.kmbh.org/radio/roadside.htm
The best in classic & latest Blues.

Virginia

Blues Valley *WMRA*
PO Box 1292, Harrisonburg, VA 22803
PH: 540-568-6221 FX: 540-568-3814
Gregory Versen versengr@cisat.jmu.edu
www.jmu.edu/wmra/blues.html
I accept Indie releases, give them a listen and if it fits, I play it.

Canada

At the Crossroads
PO Box 20027, Stn. Sahali Mall, Kamloops, BC V2C 6X1
Brant Zwicker brant@atcblues.ca
www.atcblues.ca
A syndicated program that focuses upon Blues music and many various genres – Soul, R&B, Swing, Delta, Zydeco etc.

BluesfestRadio.com
103 - 1501 Howard Ave. Windsor, ON N8X 3T5
PH: 519-253-0352 FX: 519-253-0362
artists@BluesfestRadio.com
bluesfestradio.com
Send in your music and be heard around the world by devoted Blues fans.

Eclectic Blues *CFBU*
500 Glenridge Ave. St. Catharines, ON L2S 3A1
PH: 905-346-2644
Debbie Cartmer pd@cfbu.ca
www.cfbu.ca
A fusion of Blues blending Chicago, Delta, Jump, Memphis, Louisiana, Folk, Rock, Country and Punk Blues. A special focus on homegrown talent and Canadian women in Blues.

Natch'l Blues *CKUA*
10526 Jasper Ave. Edmonton, AB T5J 1Z7
PH: 780-428-7595 FX: 780-428-7624
Holger Petersen holger.petersen@ckua.org
www.ckua.org
Canada's longest running Blues program. Over 33 years old!

Saturday Night Blues *CBC*
PO Box 555, Edmonton, AB T5J 2P4
PH: 780-468-7472
www.cbc.ca/snb
Host Holger Petersen presents concerts, interviews, artist features and new releases.

France

Midnight Special Blues Radio
Paul Bondarovski, 14, rue Olier, 75015 Paris, France
PH: +33-1-45323893 FX: 2062030639
www.ms-blues.com
Host Paul Bondarovski provides support for independent artists. Keeping the Blues alive!

The Netherlands

Blue Ears
E. Samsonstraat 5, 1103 MR Amsterdam Z-O, The Netherlands
info@BlueEars.com
www.blueEars.com
Independent radio station for adventurous Blues (y) music.

Blueprint
Tjariet 34, 9642 KD Veendam, The Netherlands
Thomas Kaldijk thomasharm@planet.nl
www.realrootscafe.com/blueprint.html
Honest and genuine music styles like Southern Soul, Blues, Country and Rock n' Roll. Roots music from past and present with heart and soul.

Spain

La Hora del Blues *Radio PICA*
Apartado de Correos 12.085, 08080 Barcelona, Spain
Vicente P. Zumel zumel@lahoradelblues.com
www.lahoradelblues.com
Each CD received is listed and rated on our website.

United Kingdom

The Raven 'n' the Blues
Koraki, Taggs Island, Hampton, TW12 2HA UK
Dave Raven dave@raven.dj
www.bfbs2.com/rnb.html
60 minutes of the best in Blues, every Saturday evening.

Australia

Blues Oz Radio
radio@bluesoz.com
www.bluesoz.com
Supporting Australian Blues. Write us to find out how to get your music into rotation.

BluesBeat *5EFM*
PO Box 1008, Victor Harbor, SA 5211 Australia
Geoff Pegler bluesbeat@waltech.com.au
www.bluesbeatradio.com
Labels & Indie artists CDs welcome for airplay.

Salty Dog Blues n Roots Podcast
saltyblues@gmail.com
www.salty.com.au
Playing Blues, Roots and Alt-Country.

Children's Radio

Alphabet Soup *WBRS*
Shapiro Campus Ctr. 415 South St., Waltham, MA 02453-2728
PH: 781-736-4785
music@wbrs.org
www.wbrs.org
The best Children's music on the airwaves.

Boost Digital Kids Radio
36 Emmett St., Crows Nest, NSW 2065 Australia
PH: +61-2-9460-1400 FX: +61-2-9460-0044
Graeme Logan kids@boostdigital.com
www.boostdigital.com
Please send your submission to the above address. Make sure to include a completed copy of our online submission form.

CBC 4 Kids Music
PO Box 500 Stn. A, Toronto, ON M5W 1E6
PH: 866-306-4636
kids@cbc.ca
www.cbc.ca/kids
Features interviews and music from Canadian music stars.

Children's Corner *KUFM*
MPR, 32 Campus Dr. U. Montana, Missoula,
MT 59812-8064
PH: 406-243-4931 FX: 406-243-3299
www.kufm.org
Delightful stories and music for children.

Children's Hour *KRZA*
528 9th St., Alamosa, CO 81101
PH: 719-589-8844
programming@krza.org
www.krza.org

Children's Hour *KUNM*
MSC06 3520, Onate Hall, 1 UNM, Albuquerque,
NM 87131-0001
PH: 505-277-5615
kunmkids@unm.edu
www.kunm.org
Music and stories for children of all ages.

Children's Stories & Music *KMUD*
PO Box 135, 1144 Redway Dr. Redway,
CA 95560-0135
PH: 707-923-2513 FX: 707-923-2501
Kate Klein md@kmud.org
www.kmud.org
An inspirational blend of stories and music for children of all ages.

Christian Pirate Radio Kids Show
701 N. Brand Blvd. #550, Glendale, CA 91203
PH: 888-321-2469 FX: 818-956-7030
ahoy@mycpr.com
www.mycpr.com
Programs for kids and kids at heart.

HIS KIDS RADIO
PO Box 151515, Grand Rapids, MI 49515-1515
mail@HisKidsRadio.net
hiskidsradio.gospelcom.net
A Christian station for the young heart.

Kids Corner *WXPN*
3025 Walnut St., Philadelphia, PA 19104
PH: 215-898-6677 FX: 215-898-0707
Robert Drake robert@kidscorner.org
kidscorner.org
Entertaining and educational programming for children.

Kids Play *WLUW*
6525 N. Sheridan Rd. Chicago, IL 60626
PH: 773-508-8080 FX: 773-508-8082
Sheila Donlan kidsplay@wluw.org
wluw.org
Features new and old releases of Kids' music.

Kid's Radio *KDPS*
1200 Grandview Ave. Des Moines, IA 50309
PH: 515-263-2985
Crazy Dave kidsradio@gvc.edu
www.kdpsradio.com/kidsradio
The most mixed-up, crazy kid-fun anywhere on the planet.

Pea Green Boat *KUFM*
MPR, 32 Campus Dr. Missoula, MT 59812-8064
PH: 406-243-4931 FX: 1-406-243-3299
www.kufm.org
Stories, songs, poetry and special guests for kids.

Radio Lollipop
6 St Andrew St., London, EC4A 3LX UK
PH: 44-0-208-661-0666
info@radiolollipop.org
www.radiolollipop.org
Providing smiles and laughter to children during their stay in the hospital.

Spare the Rock, Spoil the Child
140 Pine St., Florence, MA 01062
Bill Childs show@sparetherock.com
sparetherock.com
Kid-friendly music that wont make parents gouge out their ears.

Tell Us a Tale *WTJU*
PO Box 7344, Charlottesville, VA 22906-7344
Attn: Review
PH: 434-978-3603 FX: 434-978-4935
Peter@tellusatale.com
www.tellusatale.com
Send us your CDs for radio airplay consideration or review.

We Kids Radio
PO Box 444, Paradise, CA 95969
Mr.Nick@WeKids.org
www.wekids.org
Pointing little people and their families to God.

We Like Kids! *KTOO*
360 Egan Dr. Juneau, AK 99801-1748
PH: 907-463-6425 FX: 907-586-3612
Jeff Brown jbrown@alaska.net
www.ktoo.org
Weekly Children's music show.

Yes All Ages Radio *WBCR*
PO Box 152, Great Barrington, MA 01230
Scott Marks listlessscott@gmail.com
legovan.com/yes
A weekly kid-focused radio show.

Christian Radio

Promoters

HMG-Nashville Radio Promotions
PO Box 100584, Nashville, TN 37224
PH: 615-248-8105 FX: 615-248-8505
Jason Higgins info@powersourcemusic.com
ccma.cc/hmg
Country, Christian Country, Southern Gospel, Bluegrass & Bluegrass Gospel etc.

Stations and Shows

United States

Abundant Life Radio
300 Euclid Sq. Mall, Euclid, OH 44132
PH: 216 767-0000
info@abundantlifeccci.org
www.abundantlifeccci.org
If you're an artist that needs exposure and wants to sell albums, we would love to interview you.

After Midnight *WQME*
1100 E. 5th St. Anderson, IN 46012
PH: 765-641-3800
www.myspace.com/aftermidnight987
We play the best in Christian Rock/Hardcore/Emo/Hip Hop.

Air 1
5700 W. Oaks Blvd. Rocklin, CA 95765
PH: 888-937-2471 FX: 888-329-2471
www.AIR1.com
If you have something with exceptional sound quality, contact us.

Almighty Metal Radio
Steve Roush steve@almightymetalradio.com
www.almightymetalradio.com
The finest Christian Metal, classic Christian Rock and rockin' Blues in a unique new mix!

Arraz Radio
240 Fleetwood Dr. Hot Springs, AR 71913
PH: 501-844-7748
Andrew Bonds bonds@arraz.net
arraz.net
Playin' GODCORE music for a HARDCORE world. 24/7 Christian: Rock, Metal, & Rap.

Bigloo Christian Radio
Attn: Louis Rivera, PO Box 182, West Chester,
OH 45071
www.biglooradio.com
A mix from the best contemporary Christian to Christian Rock to Inspirational to the best in Christian Indie artists!

The Bored-Again Christian Podcast
Just Pete boredagainchristian@gmail.com
www.boredagainchristian.com
Christian music for people who are tired of Christian music.

Bread-n-Jam *WRXV*
Erik Lane erik@breadnjam.net
www.breadnjam.net
Rock n' Roll 2 feed your soul!

Black Gospel Radio
4142 Ogletown-Stanton Rd. #138, Newark,
DE 19713
PH: 215-227-5026
Alicia Hall dj@blackgospelradio.net
www.blackgospelradio.net
Playing the best in Black Gospel music on the internet.

ChargeRadio.com
PO Box 671, Lebanon, OH 45036
PH: 513-255-8477
chargemail@chargeradio.com
www.chargeradio.com
We are a Christian CHR station with a sound that is competitive with a mainstream Top 40 station.

Christian Blues Radio
37637 Five Mile Rd. #218, Livonia, MI 48154-1543
CustomerService@ChristianBlues.net
www.christianblues.net
The web's most complete resource for Christian Blues music and Christian Blues artists.

Christian Pirate Radio
701 N. Brand Blvd. #550, Glendale, CA 91203
PH: 888-321-2469 FX: 818-956-7030
Ahoy@mycpr.com
www.mycpr.com
Playing independent artists, modern Rock and contemporary Christian music.

Christian Rock Radio
online@christianrockradio.com
www.christianrockradio.com
We also do album and concert reviews.

ChristianRock.net
333 Park Central E. #610, Springfield, MO 65806
PH: 417-865-1283 x41 FX: 417-865-9062
mail@christianrock.net
www.christianrock.net
Listen to what they play on the station and only send it if it matches the style.

Classic Christian Rock Radio
mrbill@classicchristianrock.net
www.classicchristianrock.net
Features Rock music from artists who proclaim themselves to be Christians and who have demonstrated Christian attributes in their lives.

CMRadio.Net
PO Box 687, Allentown, PA 18105-0687
FX: 610-746-4053
musicmakers@cmradio.net
www.cmradio.net
Worldwide source of Christ inspired music.

The Corner Church Podcast
Rick Massey masseysmusic@podomatic.com
masseysmusic.podomatic.com
A varied collection of locally based independent Christian artists. No big names here!! Just great music.

Cornerstone *KXUL*
130 Stubbs Hall, ULM Monroe, LA 71209-8821
PH: 318-342-5662
kxul.com
A non-sectarian presentation of contemporary Christian music.

Creative Soul Radio
creativesoul@charter.net
www.creativesoulradio.com
Tired of the same old Christian songs played over and over on regular radio? You'll never find that here. Contact us for submission details.

Daily Devotions
1 Congress Sq. Portland, ME 04101
PH: 207-523-2945 FX: 207-828-6620
Peter Panagore info@dailydevotions.org
www.dailydevotions.org
The music we play is eclectic and falls generally into the category of "music I like."

DeltaWav
c/o WEJF Radio, 2824 Palm Bay Rd. Palm Bay, FL 32905
Rick & Kevin info@deltawav.com
deltawav.com
Dedicated to playing Indie artists. We are bringing Indie Christian music to the air waves.

Effect Radio
PO Box 271, Twin Falls, ID 83301
PH: 208-734-2049 FX: 208-736-1958
www.effectradio.com
We play music as led by the spirit of the living God of the Bible.

En Sound
PO Box 319, Bronx, NY 010453
PH: 718-741-3271 FX: 801-340-1126
Delroy ensound@ensoundentertainment.com
ensoundentertainment.com/radio.htm
News, interviews and reviews of Gospel music.

FaithRock Radio
www.FaithRock.org
Today's home for the best mix of Christian music.

The Fish 95.9
PO Box 29023, Glendale, CA 91209
PH: 818-956-5552
fishfeedback@thefish959.com
www.TheFish959.com
The hottest Christian radio station on the planet!

GNX The Next Nivel *Miami*
www.myspace.com/gnx883
www.883fm.org
Offering a message of hope and grace using radio airwaves as our medium. Features Rock, Hip Hop, Trance etc.

The Gospel Connection *WRBB*
360 Huntington Ave. #174, Curry Student Ctr. Boston, MA 02115
PH: 617-373-4339 FX: 617-373-5095
wrbbradio.org
The longest running Gospel show in Boston!

The Gospel Experience *KPFA*
1929 MLK Jr. Way Berkeley, CA 94704
PH: 510-848-4425 FX: 510-848-3812
Emmit Powell emmitap@aol.com
www.epgospelelites.com/radio.htm
One of the longest running Gospel music shows in the Bay Area.

Gospel Harmony Mix *KSGM*
1023 N. Pine St., DeRidder, LA 70634
PH: 337-463-2040
ghm.ksgm@cox.net
www.ksgm.com
A nice blend of Southern Gospel music and Country Gospel music.

The Gospel Hiway
PO Box 34321, Houston, TX 77234-4321
Attn: Music Director
dj@thegospelhiway.org
www.thegospelhiway.org
Submissions must be on CD, professionally produced along with a bio on the group or artist so we can know more about you.

Gospel House Music Radio
PO Box 583151, Minneapolis, MN 55458
thomas@gospelhousemusic.com
www.gospelhousemusic.com
Your original source for Gospel House music.

Gospel Jazz Podcast
21901 Mada Ave. Southfield, MI 48075
PH: 734-658-9482 FX: 248-356-2021
Norvell Molex Jr. mo131@gospeljazzsite.com
gospeljazzsite.mypodcasts.net
Giving the Lord praise through Jazz music and poetry.

Gospel Jazzations *WFDU*
Metropolitan Campus, 1000 River Rd. Teaneck, NJ 07666
PH: 201-833-0694
Tony Smith gospeljazzations@yahoo.com
www.gospeljazzations.com
Focuses on the instrumental side of Gospel Jazz.

Gospel Revelations *WFDU*
Metropolitan Campus, 1000 River Rd. Teaneck, NJ 07666
PH: 201-692-2806 FX: 201-692-2807
Stacy Wendell gospelrevelations@yahoo.com
www.wfdu.fm
Bringing you the very best variety of Traditional Gospel music.

The Gospel Sound
1023 N. Pine St., DeRidder, LA 70634
PH: 337-463-2040
soul.ksgm@cox.net
thegospelsound.com
Southern Gospel music featuring quartet-style singing and close harmony.

The Gospel Truth *WNCW*
PO Box 804, Spindale, NC 28160
PH: 828-287-8000 x328 FX: 828-287-8012
www.wncw.org
programming@wncw.org
Bluegrass Gospel. Send 2 CDs to the attention of the music director. Make sure to include a one-sheet bio.

Gospel Twang
1023 N. Pine St., DeRidder, LA 70634
PH: 337-463-2040
gtr.ksgm@cox.net
gospeltwang.com
A nice blend of Christian Country and Bluegrass Gospel music.

The Gospel Vault
1343 Clipper Heights Ave. Baltimore, MD 21211
PH: 443-690-0749 FX: 312-277-8670
info@thegospelvault.com
www.thegospelvault.com
Weekly show syndicated on multiple radio stations and online.

Gospel Vibrations *WFDU*
114 Shepard Ave. Teaneck, NJ 07666
PH: 201-833-0694
Floyd Cray GospelVibrations@aol.com
www.gospelvibrations.org
Features a large variety of contemporary Gospel music.

Gospel's Glory Road *KOHO*
7475 KOHO Place, Leavenworth, WA 98826
PH: 509-548-1011 FX: 509-548-3222
www.kohoradio.com
Host John T. Humphreys presents an exciting blend of music and artists.

HCJB World Radio
PO Box 39800, Colorado Springs, CO 80949-9800
PH: 719-590-9800 FX: 719-590-9801
info@hcjb.org
www.hcjb.org
Broadcasts the Gospel in nearly 120 languages.

Holy Culture Radio
2249A Otero Loop, Holloman AFB, NM 88330
DJ MVP mvp@holycultureradio.com
www.holycultureradio.com
The platform for Holy Hip Hop. Your chances of getting rotation increase dramatically by sending your music to all of our mixshows.

Holy Hip Hop Radio
PO Box 1023, Pine Lake, GA 30072
www.holyhiphop.com/radio
Over 200 domestic & international markets. Please send 2 CDs!

HOPE 107.9
PO Box 278, Albany, OR 97321
PH: 541-926-2431
Paul Hernandez paul@hope1079.com
www.hope1079.com

Indie Rock Show / Indie Rock Show Xtreme
PO Box 120358, Clermont, FL 34712-0358
theindierockshow@yahoo.com
www.theindierockshow.com
www.theindierockshow.com/irsx.shtml
Home of the hottest Indies on the Planet! Please fill out our online submission form.

Indy Live
PO Box 2552, Lakeside, AZ 85929
Bill Freeland kwkmbillman@yahoo.com
indylive.gq.nu
We only air positive mindset, non-degrading, or Christian-Spiritual based materials.

Intense Radio
PO Box 1477, Mt. Juliet, TN 37121-1477
www.IntenseRadio.com
Christian Rock. Programs, great music, interviews and more.

KCMS
19319 Fremont Ave. N., Seattle, WA 98133
PH: 206-546-7350 FX: 206-546-7372
Sarah Taylor sarah@spirit1053.com
www.spirit1053.com

KCWJ
4240 Blue Ridge Blvd. #530, Kansas City, MO 64133
PH: 816-313-0049 FX: 816-313-1036
Paul Van Sickle Paul@1030thelight.com
www.1030thelight.com

Kingdom Keys Network
PO Box 8088, Amarillo, TX 79114-8088
PH: 806-359-8855 FX: 806-354-2039
kjrt@kingdomkeys.org
www.kingdomkeys.org
Teaching, preaching, music, news, talk and commentaries.

KJTX
PO Box 150151, Longview, TX 75615
PH: 903-759-1243
KJTXLR@juno.com
www.kjtxgospel.com
High energy Gospel. We do play independent artists.

KLRC *John Brown U.*
2000 W. University, Siloam Springs, AR 72761
PH: 479-524-7101 FX: 479-524-7451
klrc@klrc.com
www.klrc.com

KOBC *Ozark Christian College*
1111 N. Main Joplin, MO 64801
PH: 417-781-6401 FX: 417-782-1841
kobc@kobc.org
www.kobc.org

Krunk-Radio
PO Box 669, Tomball, TX 77377
info@krunk-radio.com
www.krunk-radio.com
Home of tha krunkest Christian music on tha planet!

KTIS *Northwestern College*
3003 Snelling Ave. N., Saint Paul, MN 55113-1598
PH: 651-631-5000
studio@ktis.org
www.ktis.org

KTCU *Texas Christian U.*
TCU Box 298020, Fort Worth, TX 76129
PH: 817-257-7631
ktcu@tcu.edu
www.ktcu.tcu.edu/ktcu

KWCB
1905 10h St., Floresville, TX 78114
PH: 830-393-4703
kwcb89fm@yahoo.com
www.wcn-online.com/kwcb

Lifespring!
PH: 206-350-2255
steve.lifespring@gmail.com
lifespringpodcast.com
Christian talk and music podcast. Blues to Classical to Folk to Rock 'n Roll.

New Release Tuesday Podcast
info@newreleasetuesday.com
www.newreleasetuesday.com
Updates you every Tuesday on what's new in Christian music.

Nightowl Radio *WIOJ*
10055 Beach Blvd. Jacksonville, FL 32246
PH: 904-641-1010 FX: 9046411022
wioj@wioj.net
www.wioj.net
Christian Rock, Punk, Electronic and Techno show.

Power FM
11061 Shady Trail, Dallas, TX 75229
PH: 214-353-8970
Drue Mitchell drue@kvrk.com
897powerfm.com
A full time Christian Rock station in North Texas.

The Praise House
PO Box 1113, Conley, GA 30288
PH: 404-381-0755
praisehouse@comcast.net
www.thepraisehouse.com
Gospel webcast network.

Rapture Radio
1932 E. Lindsey #212, Norman, OK 73071
Cindy cinflames@cox.net
www.raptureradio.net
The best in Christian Metal. We support Indie artists 100%!!!!!

Rawk 'N Review *WTBN*
RJ & Strick RawkNReview@gmail.com
www.myspace.com/rawknreview
Music and reviews of lesser known Christian artists.

Rebourne Radio
1102 Llano Cove, Memphis, TN 38134
PH: 901-388-2988
Bill Simmers radio@rebourne.net
www.rebourneradio.com
Indie positive CD submissions are welcome!

Reign Radio
PO Box 10252, Daytona Beach, FL 32120-0252
md@reignradio.com
www.reignradio.com
Christian Rock. Helping Christian artists get heard!

Renegade Radio
PO Box 490, Wadsworth, NV 89442
PH: 775-575-7777 FX: 775-575-7737
William E. Bauer email@renegaderadio.org
www.renegaderadio.org
Christian Rock, Hip Hop, Metal and Electronic Beat. We accept MP3s, but please contact us BEFORE you send an attachment.

RevFM
925 Houserville Rd. State College, PA 16801
PH: 814-867-1922
info@revfm.net
www.revfm.net
Encouraging believers to grow spiritually and to share the message of Jesus with unbelievers.

The Rezdog *KNNB*
PO Box 1613, Whiteriver, AZ 85941
PH: 928-338-6197
rezdog.org/aym/knnb.htm
Playing the best in Christian music.

Sacred Heart Radio
e@sacredheartradio.net
sacredheartradio.net
All styles of Catholic music welcome!

Savagerock
PH: 866-868-9824
Shane Timson shane@savagerock.com
savagerock.com
Our goal is to provide the world with great Hard Rock focused on Jesus Christ.

Serious Comedy Radio
1023 N. Pine St., DeRidder, LA 70634
PH: 337-463-2040
scr.ksgm@cox.net
Family-friendly comedy featuring many Christian artists.

sglive365.com
903 Rogers St., Clinton, TN 37716
chuckpeters@sglive365.com
www.sglive365.com
Southern Gospel radio. Feel free to send us your music!

SGM Radio
rob@sgmradio.com
www.sgmradio.com
Today's best Southern Gospel and Christian Country music. We'll also review your album.

Silent Planet Radio *WCLH*
11 Catherine St., Plains, PA 18705
PH: 570-417-3818
Mark Blair mark@silentplanetradio.com
www.silentplanetradio.com
Progressive Christian music.

Slice of Heaven *KULV*
1950 3rd St., La Verne, CA 91750
PH: 909-593-3511 x 4777 FX: 909-392-2706
www.ulv.edu/kulv
Christian music show hosted by Frank Melia Jr.

Solid Gospel
402 BNA Dr. #400 Nashville, TN 37217
PH: 615-367-2210 FX: 615-367-0758
info@solidgospel.com
www.solidgospel.com

Southern Fried Gospel *WDCB*
College of DuPage, 425 Fawell Blvd. Glen Ellyn, IL 60137
PH: 630-942-4200 FX: 630-942-2788
Harry Rohde RohdeH@wdcb.org
wdcb.org
Reflecting a branch of the rich Southern culture.

Spin 180
6400 N. Beltline Rd. #210, Irving, TX 75063
Matt Mungle info@spin180.net
www.spin180.net
Submit your CD, bio and lyric sheet to the above address. Christian Rock and Alternative only.

The Spirit Radio
PO Box 245, Pendleton, IN 46064
PH: 317-501-2242 FX: 317-428-4675
info@thespiritradio.com
www.thespiritradio.net
Christian artists ranging from Easy Listening to Heavy Metal.

Spiritco1.com Radio
6178 Oxon Hill Rd. #101, Oxon Hill, MD 20745
PH: 301-567-5349
Henry W. Harris hharris@spiritco1.com
www.spiritco1.com
Spreading the Gospel ministry of music and messages to the internet radio community.

Star93fm.com
PO Box 4048, Clinton, MS 39058
PH: 601-925-3548 FX: 601-925-3337
www.star93fm.com

Sunday Night Gospel Show
PO Box 1184, Crockett, TX 75835
PH: 936-546-8291 FX: 270-837-1977
submissions@24hourgospelnetwork.org
www.24hourgospelnetwork.org
Accepting Black Gospel and Gospel Jazz music for airplay consideration.

Three Angels Broadcasting Network
PO Box 220, W. Frankfort, IL 62896
PH: 618-627-4651 FX: 618-627-2726
www.3abn.org

Train to Glory *KUNM*
MSC06 3520, Onate Hall 1 U. New Mexico,
Albuquerque, NM 87131-0001
PH: 505-277-5615
music@kunm.org
www.kunm.org
Black Gospel music featuring traditional, contemporary and local church choirs.

Uncle Samoo's Zoo *WITR*
998 Beaver Creek Dr. Webster, NY 14580
PH: 585-475-2271 FX: 585-475-4988
Pastor Samme sammep@aol.com
www.thelivingrock.com
Featuring independent & import artists from all around the globe!

Uneon Entertainment
PH: 310-384-0386
Bryant Johnson info@uneonentertainment.com
www.uneonentertainment.com
Spiritual Hip Hop.

WAY-FM
1012 McEwen Dr. Franklin, TN 37067
PH: 615-261-9293 FX: 615-261-3967
waym.wayfm.com
We use radio to encourage youth and young adults in their Christian walk.

WBCS *Bethel College*
3900 Bethel Dr. St. Paul, MN 55112-6999
PH: 651-638-6283
wbcs@bethel.edu
www.bethel.edu/Majors/Communication/wbcs

WCDR *Cedarville College*
PO Box 601, Cedarville, OH 45314
PH: 800-333-0601 FX: 937-766-7927
www.cdrradio.com

WCNO
2960 SW. Mapp Rd. Palm City, FL 34990
PH: 772-221-1100 FX: 772-221-8716
wcno@wcno.com
www.wcno.com
Adult Contemporary Christian music and programming.

WCSE
126 Sharp Hill Rd. Uncasville, CT 06382
PH: 860-848-7400
info@wcse.org
www.wcse.org
A Christian station that plays the music of independent artists.

wePRAISE.fm
7101 Deshon Bend Cove, Lithonia, GA 30058
PH: 678-526-0592 FX: 678-526-2533
Winston A. Walker admin@wepraise.fm
www.wePRAISE.fm
We play Gospel videos and songs that we feel uplifts and edifies the body of Christ.

WETN *Wheaton College*
501 College Ave. Wheaton, IL 60187
PH: 630-752-5074
wetn@wheaton.edu
www.wheaton.edu/wetn

WFAR
25 Chestnut St., Danbury, CT 06810
PH: 203-748-0001 FX: 203-746-4262
www.radiofamilia.com
Christian and Ethnic radio.

WFCA *French Camp Academy*
Rte. 1, Box 12, French Camp, MS 39745
PH: 662-547-6414 FX: 662-547-9451
events@wfcafm108.com
www.wfcafm108.com
All Southern Gospel radio.

WGEV *Geneva College*
c/o Dept. of Communication, 3200 College Ave.
Beaver Falls, PA 15010
PH: 724-846-5100
thughes@geneva.edu
www.wgev.net

WGTS *Columbia U. College*
7600 Flower Ave. Takoma Park, MD 20912
PH: 301-270-1800 FX: 301-270-9191
wgts@wgts919.com
www.wgts.org

WGVR
1343 Clipper Heights Ave. Baltimore, MD 21211
airplay@wgvr.com
www.wgvr.com
Please notify us via the form on our contact page that you will be sending music.

What's the Buzz *WCNI*
247 Haley Rd. Ledyard, CT 06339
PH: 860-572-2705
John the Baptist buzzradiowcni@aol.com
www.wcniradio.org
Christian Rock, Pop & Hip Hop. I am happy to play the music of independent artists.

Whitedove Radio
HCR 82 Box 62-A, Salem, MO 65560
Crystal Clear crystalclear@whitedoveradio.com
www.whitedoveradio.com
Featuring Christian music of all styles.

WMHK *Columbia International U.*
PO Box 3122, Columbia, SC 29230
PH: 803-754-5400 FX: 803-714-0849
wmhk@wmhk.com
www.wmhk.com

WOCG *Oakwood College*
7000 Adventist Blvd. Huntsville, AL 35896
PH: 256-726-7420 FX: 256-726-7417
wocg@wocg.org
www.wocg.org

WRCM *Columbia International U.*
PO Box 17069, Charlotte, NC 28227
PH: 704-821-9293 FX: 704-821-9285
info@newlife919.com
www.newlife919.com
Featuring family friendly Christian music.

WRVL *Liberty U.*
1971 U. Blvd Lynchburg, VA 24502
PH: 434-582-3688 FX: 434-582-2994
wrvl@liberty.edu
www.liberty.edu/wrvl

WSAE *Spring Arbor College*
106 E. Main St., Spring Arbor, MI 49283
PH: 517-750-9723 FX: 517-750-6619
info@home.fm
www.home.fm

WTBC
PO Box 36474, Panama City, FL 32412
E. L. Jones tb1@wtbcradio.com
www.wtbcradio.com
Gospel and Holy Hip Hop. Please submit your music using Sonic Bid www.sonicbids.com.

Canada

CHRI
1010 Thomas Spratt Pl. #3, Ottawa, ON K1G 5L5
PH: 613-247-1440 FX: 613-247-7128
chri.ca

eJNM.net
6550 Maurice-Duplessis, Montréal-Nord,
QC H1G 6K9
PH: 514-324-2190
Gene Kelley englishprogram@ejnm.net
eJNM.net
A source of blessing for independent Christian artists. We have programming in English, French, Italian & Spanish.

The MAD Christian Radio Show
42 Moneta Ave. Timmins, ON P4N 7R6
Kristen McNulty madradioshow@hotmail.com
www.madradioshow.net
A syndicated youth radio show that is making a difference in the lives of youth around the world. Christian Rock artists can send their material to the above address.

United Kingdom

Branch FM
PH: 01924-465600
studio@branchfm.co.uk
www.branchfm.co.uk
Christian music 24/365 available across the globe.

Cross Rhythms Radio
PO Box 1110, Stoke on Trent, ST1 1XR UK
PH: 44-8700-118-008 FX: 44-8700-117-002
radio@crossrhythms.co.uk
www.crossrhythms.co.uk/radio
Predominantly contemporary Christian music.

Australia

Rhema FM
PO Box 886, Belmont, VIC 3216 Australia
PH: 61-3-5241-6550 FX: 61-3-5241-6552
rhema@rhemafm.org.au
www.rhemafm.org.au
A station that can change lives for good and the promotion of family values.

Classical Radio

North America

United States

Adventures in Good Music *WITF*
1982 Locust Ln. PO Box 2954, Harrisburg,
PA 17105-2954
PH: 717-236-6000
Karl Haas fm@witf.org
www.witf.org
Heard on over 180 stations. Glad to receive CDs for consideration on the program.

Brass Band Podcast
Peter brasscast@gmail.com
www.brasscast.com
Produced for your entertainment and to keep you informed of events in the world of Brass Band music.

Classical Excursions *KTCU*
TCU Box 298020, Fort Worth, TX 76129
PH: 817-257-7631
Rosemary Solomons R.Solomons@tcu.edu
www.ktcu.tcu.edu/ktcu/html/classical_excursions.html
Two uninterrupted hours of music from the Baroque to the present.

ClassicalGuitar.cc
Michael Cervane info@classicalguitar.cc
ClassicalGuitar.cc
Music for the Classical guitar, including solos, chamber pieces and concertos.

ClassicalMusicAmerica.com
PH: 248-324-2600 FX: 248-324-0439
Pat McElroy
patmcelroy@classicalmusicamerica.com
www.classicalmusicamerica.com
Local events, music and recording artists are prominent in the mix.

Colorado Public Radio
7409 S. Alton Ct. Centennial, CO 80112
PH: 303-871-9191 FX: 303-733-3319
cpr.org
Presents the full range of Classical music.

The Composer's Voice *MPR*
45 E. 7th St. Saint Paul, MN 55101
PH: 651-290-1212
John Zech mail@mpr.org
music.minnesota.publicradio.org/programs/composersvoice
The program that asks current composers: Who are you? What does your music sound like? Why does it sound the way it does?

Contemplation Connection *KKUP*
933 Monroe St., PMB 9150, Santa Clara, CA 95050
PH: 408-260-2999
Roger Werner wernerr@pacbell.net
www.kkup.com
Visionary and Classical music for contemplation. Quotes for self-awareness.

From the Top
295 Huntington Ave. Boston, MA 02115
PH: 617-437-0707 FX: 617-262-4267
www.fromthetop.org
Showcases the nation's most exceptional pre-college age Classical musicians.

Harmonia *WFIU*
1229 E. 7th St., Bloomington, IN 47405
PH: 812-855-1357
Emily Blacklin harmonia@indiana.edu
www.indiana.edu/~harmonia
Brings the music of these earlier periods to life.

Here of a Sunday Morning *WBAI*
120 Wall St., New York, NY 10005
PH: 212-209-2900
Chris Whent mail@hoasm.org
www.hoasm.org
The very best in Early music.

KANU
1120 W. 11th St., U. Kansas, Lawrence, KS 66044
PH: 785-864-4530 FX: 785-864-5278
Rachel Hunter rhunter@ku.edu
kanu.ku.edu
We do play music by independent Classical musicians.

KBIA
409 Jesse Hall, Columbia, MO 65211
PH: 573-882-3431 FX: 573-882-2636
kbia@kbia.org
www.kbia.org
We love to play music from new and independent Classical artists.

KBPS
515 NE. 15th Ave. Portland, OR 97232
PH: 503-916-5828 FX: 503-916-2642
music.info@allclassical.org
www.allclassical.org
Happy to receive any CDs by Indie performers of standard Classical.

KBYU *Brigham Young U.*
2000 Ironton Blvd. Provo, UT 84606
PH: 800-298-5298
www.kbyu.org
New material is reviewed and aired if deemed appropriate.

KCME
1921 N. Weber St., Colorado Springs, CO 80907
PH: 719-578-5263 FX: 719-578-1033
jazz@kcme.org
www.kcme.org
We play independent labels Classical and Jazz music.

KCSC *U. Central Oklahoma*
100 N. University Dr. Edmond, OK 73034
PH: 405-974-3333 FX: 405-974-3844
kanderson@kcscfm.com
www.kcscfm.com

KDFC
201 3rd St. #1200, San Francisco, CA 94103
PH: 415-764-1021
rmalone@kdfc.com
www.kdfc.com
We don't discriminate against struggling musicians!

KEDM
ULM 225 Stubbs Hall Monroe, LA 71209-6805
PH: 318-342-5565 FX: 318-342-5570
classical@kedm.org
kedmjazz@ulm.edu
www.kedm.org
We do play Classical and Jazz music by independent musicians/composers/producers.

KFUO
85 Founders Ln. St. Louis, MO 63105
PH: 314-725-0099 FX: 314-725-3801
John Roberts jroberts@classic99.com
www.classic99.com

KING
10 Harrison St. #100, Seattle, WA 98109
PH: 206-691-2981 FX: 206-691-2982
Tom Olsen tomo@king.org
www.king.org
We do air independent musician's recordings.

KNAU *Northern Arizona U.*
Bldg. 83 Box 5764, Flagstaff, AZ 86011
PH: 928-523-5628
knauradio.org

KNPR *Nevada Public Radio*
1289 S. Torrey Pines Dr. Las Vegas, NV 89146
PH: 702-258-9895 FX: 702-258-5646
Florence Rogers flo@knpr.org
www.knpr.org
I try to play as many independents as I can.

KRPS
PO Box 899, Pittsburg, KS 66762
PH: 620-235-4288
Tim Metcalf tmetcalf@pittstate.edu
www.krps.org
Any music received is first reviewed by our program director.

KSUI
710 S. Clinton St., Iowa City, IA 52242-1030
PH: 319-335-5746 FX: 319-335-6116
Joan Kjaer Kirkman joan-kirkman@uiowa.edu
ksui.uiowa.edu
We welcome the music of independent Classical musicians.

KUAT
PO Box 210067, Tucson, AZ 85721-0067
PH: 520-621-5828 FX: 520-621-3360
www.kuat.org
A "serious" Classical station. NO recordings from New Age noodlers.

KUFM *Morning Classics*
U. Montana, Missoula, MT 59812-8064
PH: 406-243-4931 FX: 406-243-3299
www.kufm.org
We play a wide variety of Classical music.

KUHF
4343 Elgin, Fl. 3 Houston, TX 77204-0887
PH: 713-743-0887 FX: 713-743-0868
www.kuhf.org
As long as your performances and recordings are of professional quality, we'll play 'em.

KUSC
PO Box 77913, Los Angeles, CA 90007-0913
PH: 213-225-7400
kusc@kusc.org
www.kusc.org
Making Classical music a more important part of more people's lives.

KWAX *U. Oregon*
Agate Hall, Eugene, OR 97403
PH: 541-345-0800
kwax@qwest.net
www.kwaxradio.com
Classical music 24-hour a day.

KWIT *West Iowa Tech College*
4647 Stone Ave. PO Box 5199, Sioux City,
IA 51106
PH: 712-274-6406 FX: 712-274-6411
www.kwit.org

KXMS *Missouri Southern State U.*
75 Centennial Loop, Eugene, OR 97401
PH: 417-625-9356 FX: 417-625-9742
kxms@mssu.edu
www.kxms.org
*Happy to highlight independent Classical CDs.
Please send only Classical music!*

Millennium of Music
2775 S. Quincy St., Arlington, VA 22206
radman@weta.com
www.classicstoday.com/mom
*Features the evolution of Sacred music, East and
West. Our one-hour national weekly program is
heard on over 190 public radio stations across the
country.*

Modern Masterpieces *WBHM*
650 11th St. S. Birmingham, AL 35294
PH: 205-934-2606 FX: 205-934-5075
Alan Chapman info@wbhm.org
www.wbhm.org
*Features music by acknowledged Classical masters
as well as emerging composers of merit.*

A Musical Meander *KRCU*
1 University Pl. Cape Girardeau, MO 63701
PH: 573-651-5070 FX: 888-651-5070
Alan Journet ajournet@semo.edu
www.semo.edu/sepr
*The basic theme is Classical music in the broadest
sense.*

The New Edge *WMBR*
3 Ames St., Cambridge, MA 02142
PH: 617-253-8810
Ken Field newedge@wmbr.org
newedge.home.att.net
*Creative and innovative, mostly instrumental new
music, composed and improvised at the intersection
of Classical, Jazz and World styles.*

New Sounds *WNYC*
1 Centre St. 24th Fl. New York, NY 10007
PH: 212-669-3333 FX: 212-669-3312
John Schaefer newsounds@wnyc.org
www.wnyc.org/shows/newsounds
*New works from the Classic and Operatic to Folk
and Jazz.*

Pipedreams *MPR*
480 Cedar St., Saint Paul, MN 55101-2217
PH: 651-290-1212
Michael Barone mail@americanpublicmedia.org
pipedreams.mpr.org
The finest organ music from around the world.

Saint Paul Sunday *MPR*
480 Cedar St., Saint Paul, MN 55101-2217
PH: 651-290-1212
www.stpaulsunday.org
*Host opens the studio to the world's best Classical
artists.*

Sound and Spirit *PRI*
125 Western Ave. Boston, MA 02134
PH: 617-300-4415
Ellen Kushner spirit@pri.org
www.wgbh.org/wgbh/pages/pri/spirit
Blends Classical, Traditional and World music.

Sunday Baroque *WSHU*
5151 Park Ave. Fairfield, CT 06825
PH: 203-365-6604
Suzanne Bona sundayb@wshu.org
www.sundaybaroque.org
An exploration of Baroque and Early music.

Taste of Classics *WBCX*
Brenau U., 500 Washington St. SE., Gainesville,
GA 30501
PH: 770-538-4744
Vanessa Hyatt vhyatt@brenau.edu
www.brenau.edu/about/wbcx/Taste-of-Classics.htm
*Promotes "local" artists or anyone of quality and
would like some air time.*

Thursday Evening Classics *WWUH*
Attn: Music Director, 200 Bloomfield Ave.
West Hartford, CT 06117
PH: 860-768-4701 FX: 860-768-5701
Steve Petke sdpetke@snet.net
www.wwuh.org
*Offers a broad range of music from the Middle Ages
to the present, highlighting Renaissance Choral
music and lesser-known works by familiar and
obscure composers.*

WBJC
6776 Reisterstown Rd. #202, Baltimore, MD 21215
PH: 410-580-5800
wbjcinformation@wbjc.com
www.wbjc.com
The Baltimore region's only Classical music station.

WCLV
26501 Renaissance Pkwy. Cleveland, OH 44128
PH: 216-464-0900
wclv@wclv.com
www.wclv.com
Spotlights new Classical CDs.

WCNY *Syracuse*
506 Old Liverpool Rd. Liverpool, NY 13088-6259
www.wcny.org/classicfm
*Features performances by numerous local musical
institutions.*

WCPE
PO Box 897, Wake Forest, NC 27588
PH: 919-556-5178
William Woltz music@TheClassicalStation.org
www.wcpe.org
Makes great Classical music available to the public.

WDAV
PO Box 7178, 423 N. Main St., Davidson,
NC 28035-7178
PH: 704-894-8900 FX: 704-894-2997
wdav@davidson.edu
www.wdav.org
*We have numerous independently produced
recordings as part of its regular music rotation.*

WDIY
301 Broadway 3rd Fl. Bethlehem, PA 18015
PH: 610-694-8100 FX: 610-954-9474
info@wdiyfm.org
www.wdiyfm.org
*We will certainly consider the efforts of independent
musicians!*

WDPR
126 N. Main St., Dayton, OH 45402
PH: 937-496-3850 FX: 937-496-3852
Charles Wendelken-Wilson cww@dpr.org
dpr.org
*The voice for our region's performing and fine arts
organizations.*

WETA
2775 S. Quincy St., Arlington, VA 22206
PH: 703-998-2600 FX: 703-998-3401
www.weta.org
Feel free to submit your music.

WFCR *U. Massachusetts*
Hampshire House, 131 County Cir. Amherst,
MA 01003-9257
PH: 413-545-0100 FX: 413-545-2546
John Montanari jm@wfcr.org
www.wfcr.org

WFMR
5407 W. McKinley Ave. Milwaukee,
WI 53208-2540
PH: 414-978-9000 FX: 414-978-9001
Steve Murphy smurphy@wfmr.com
www.wfmr.com

WFMT
5400 N. St. Louis Ave. Chicago, IL 60625-4698
PH: 773-279-2020
www.wfmt.com
We do play some self-produced CDs.

WGMS
3400 Idaho Ave. NW., Washington, DC 20016
PH: 202-895-5000
www.wgms.com

WHRO
5200 Hampton Blvd. Norfolk, VA 23508
PH: 757-889-9400 FX: 757-489-0007
info@whro.org
www.whro.org
*Will consider any independent Classical recordings
for possible airplay.*

WILL
Campbell Hall 300 N. Goodwin Ave. Urbana,
IL 61801-2316
PH: 217-333-0850 FX: 217-244-9586
willamfm@uiuc.edu
www.will.uiuc.edu
*Send us your Classical, Jazz and Traditional/Ethnic
music.*

WITF
1982 Locust Ln. PO Box 2954, Harrisburg,
PA 17105-2954
PH: 717-236-6000
fm@witf.org
www.witf.org
Offering Classical music and news.

WKAR *Michigan State U.*
283 Communication Arts Bldg. East Lansing,
MI 48824-1212
PH: 517-432-9527 FX: 517-353-7124
mail@wkar.org
wkar.org/90.5

WKSU *Kent State U.*
PO Box 5190, Kent, OH 44242–0001
PH: 330-672–3114 FX: 330-672–4107
letters@wksu.org
www.wksu.org

WMNR
PO Box 920, Monroe, CT 06468
PH: 203-268-9667
info@wmnr.org
www.wmnr.org
Non-commercial Classical and Fine Arts music.

WMRA *James Madison U.*
983 Reservoir St., Harrisonburg, VA 22801
PH: 540-568-6221 FX: 540-568-3814
wmra@jmu.edu
www.jmu.edu/wmra
Interested in hearing contemporary composer's music.

WMUH *Muhlenberg College*
2400 Chew St., Allentown, PA 18104-5586
PH: 484-664-3239 FX: 484-664-3539
wmuh@muhlenberg.edu
www.muhlenberg.edu/cultural/wmuh
We play independent Classical 4 hrs/week.

WNPR
1049 Asylum Ave. Hartford, CT 06105
PH: 860-278-5310 FX: 860-244-9624
info@wnpr.org
www.wnpr.org
We welcome the music of independent Classical musicians.

WQED
4802 5th Ave. Pittsburgh, PA 15213
PH: 412-622-1300 FX: 412-622-1488
music@wqed.org
www.wqed.org
You are more than welcome to send CDs for consideration.

WQXR
122 5th Ave. New York, NY 10011
PH: 212-633-7600 FX: 212-633-7730
listener.mail@wqxr.com
www.wqxr.com
Welcomes submissions from independent artists.

WRTI
1509 Cecil B. Moore Ave. 3rd Fl. Philadelphia, PA 19121-3410
PH: 215-204-3393 FX: 215-204-7027
Jack Moore jack@wrti.org
www.wrti.org
Plays some Classical/Jazz independent music.

WSCL
PO Box 2596, Salisbury, MD 21802.
PH: 410-543-6895
prd@salisbury.edu
publicradiodelmarva.net
Will accept quality Indie submissions.

WWFM
PO Box B, Trenton, NJ 08690
PH: 609-587-8989 FX: 609-586-4533
wwfm@mccc.edu
www.wwfm.org
Playing the finest Classical music available.

WXPR
303 W. Prospect St., Rhinelander, WI 54501
PH: 715-362-6000 FX: 715-362-6007
wxpr@wxpr.org
www.wxpr.org

WXXI
280 State St. PO Box 30021, Rochester, NY 14603-3021
PH: 585-258-0200
wxxi@wxxi.org
www.wxxi.org
We do play the music of independent artists.

Yellowstone Public Radio
1500 U. Dr. Billings, MT 59101
PH: 406-657-2941 FX: 406-657-2977
mail@ypradio.org
www.yellowstonepublicradio.org

Canada

Music Around Us *CBC*
PO Box 500, Stn. A, Toronto, ON M5W 1E6
www.cbc.ca/musicaroundus
Host Keith Horner presents concerts recorded across Ontario.

Northern Lights *CBC*
PO Box 160, Winnipeg, MB R3C 2H1
radio.cbc.ca/programs/northernlights
Host Andrea Ratuski sometimes plays independent Classical artists.

Shades of Classics *CKUW*
Rm. 4CM11 U. Winnipeg, 515 Portage Ave.
Winnipeg, MA R3B 2E9
PH: 204-774-6877 FX: 204-783-7080
John Iverson shades@mts.net
www.jliverson.com/ckuw
Promoting the music of local musicians/ensembles.

Symphony Hall *CBC*
PH: 403-521-6109 FX: 403-521-6232
www.cbc.ca/symphonyhall
Host Katherine Duncan presents a showcase for Canadian orchestras and their musicians.

Two New Hours *CBC*
CBC Radio, Box 500, Stn. A, Toronto, ON M5W 1E6
PH: 416-205-8577 FX: 416-205-6040
www.cbc.ca/2newhours
Host Larry Lake brings you the world of New Concert music by Canadian and international composers.

Europe

Czech Republic

Cesky rozhlas 3 - Vltava
Vinohradská 12 120 99 Prague, Czech Republic
PH: 420-221-552-647 FX: 420-221-552-676
info@rozhlas.cz
www.rozhlas.cz/vltava
Live broadcasts Opera, Classical music and Jazz from all over the world.

The Netherlands

AVRO Klassiek
klassiek@avro.nl
klassiek.avro.nl

Classic FM
Postbus 1088 1400 BB Bussum, The Netherlands
PH: 035-699-79-99 FX: 035-699-79-98
classicfm@classicfm.nl
www.classicfm.nl

The Concertzender
www.concertzender.nl
Presenting remarkable programs with lots of genuine Jazz and Classical music.

Norway

NRK - NRK Alltid Klassisk
PH: 815-65-900
info@nrk.no
www.nrk.no/kanal/nrk_alltid_klassisk
The Classical station of the Norwegian Public Radio.

Portugal

antena2
Ave. Marechal Gomes da Costa, 37, 1849-030 Lisbon, Portugal
PH: 00-351-217-947-000 FX: 00-351-217-947-570
www.rdp.pt
Broadcasting Classical music from all epochs and styles.

United Kingdom

BBC Radio 3 *Classical*
www.bbc.co.uk/radio3/classical
Home page of the BBC Radio 3's various Classical shows. Info, shows, contacts etc.

BBC Radio 2 *Easy Listening and Classical*
www.bbc.co.uk/radio2/r2music/easy
Home page of the BBC Radio 2's various Easy Listening and Classical shows. Info, shows, contacts etc.

BBC Radio 3
London, W1N 4DJ UK
PH: 087-00-100-100
www.bbc.co.uk/radio3/classical
The mother of all Classical radio stations!

Hear and Now *BBC*
Radio 3, London, W1N 4DJ UK
PH: 087-00-100-100
www.bbc.co.uk/radio3/hearandnow
Features live concerts, studio sessions from the best new music groups.

Lyric FM
Cornmarket Sq. Limerick, Ireland
PH: 353-0-61-207300 FX: 353-0-61-207390
lyric@rte.ie
www.lyricfm.ie
Irish Classical music station.

Australia

2MBS
76 Chandos St., St Leonards, NSW 2065 Australia
PH: 9439-4777 FX: 9439-4064
admin@2mbs.com
www.2mbs.com
Programs of Classical, Jazz and Contemporary music.

ABC Classical Music
PO Box 9994, Melbourne, VIC 3001 Australia
PH: 03-9626-1600 FX: 03-9626-1633
www.abc.net.au/classic
Programs that feature new Australian Classical music.

**Direct traffic to your website
www.indielinkexchange.com/ile**

Country Radio

Radio Promoters

Bill Wence Promotions
PO Box 39, Nolensville, TN 37135
PH: 615-776-2060 FX: 615-776-2181
Bill Wence info@billwencepromotions.com
www.billwencepromotions.com
Hundreds of singles and albums have been charted for our clients.

Billy James Productions
PO Box 5496, Deptford, NJ 08096
PH: 856-468-7889
Billy billyjames@wnjc1360.com
www.wnjc1360.com/Shows/Billy_James/
billy_james.html
We offer promotion for artists and bands.

E. H. King Music
PO Box 40, Santa Fe, TX 77517
PH: 409-925-4539
Ed & Barbara Ekingehk@cs.com
www.wingnut.net/ehk.htm
We'll mail out your CDs for you!! We get airplay!!

Jerry Duncan Promotions
PO Box 40471, Nashville, TN 37204
www.duncanpromo.com
Has successfully promoted 60 #1 country hits including breakthrough singles for some of today's biggest stars including Tim McGraw, Toby Keith, Martina McBride, Brad Paisley and Alison Krauss.

Marco Promotions
PO Box 24454, Nashville, TN 37202
PH: 615-269-7071 FX: 615-269-0131
info@marcopromo.com
www.marcopromo.com
Our radio marketing strategy provides the artist an opportunity to make an impact at secondary country radio by establishing an audience base and creating product awareness in targeted sales markets.

NorthAmerica

United States

Internet, Syndicated Shows and Podcasts

Abbott's Bluegrass Habit
PO Box 54668, Cincinnati, OH 45254-0668
Vicki Abbott abbottsbluegrasshabit@yahoo.com
www.geocities.com/abbottsbluegrasshabit
Do you have material that you would like to be considered for airplay? Contact me!

Alt Country Opry!
brenthoodenpyle.com/alt-country-podcast.htm
Monthly podcast. Hear songs, interviews and commentary from up and coming Indie Alt-Country artists.

Americana Roots Review
roots@AmericanaRoots.com
www.americanaroots.com
Podcast featuring music from some great unsigned Americana artists.

Blue Wave Bluegrass
783 E. King St., Strasburg, VA 22657
Bill Foster foster.bill@verizon.net
www.bluewavebluegrass.com
Artists, send your music in to the above address.

Bluegrass Review
PH: 651-690-1508
Phil Nusbaum pnusbaum@bitstream.net
www.bluegrassreview.com
Includes Bluegrass classics as well as the current wave.

Bluegrassbox
admin@bluegrassbox.com
www.bluegrassbox.com
We encourage visitors to purchase the releases of the bands represented here.

BluegrassRadio.org
293 JC Saunders Rd. Moultrie, GA. 31768
Clyde Scott controlroom@bluegrassradio.org
bluegrassradio.org
If you would like to have your project considered for "wire play" please submit it to the above address.

Cowboy Cultural Society
1110 Main St. #16, Watsonville, CA 95076
Laura Ellen laura@cowboyculturalsociety.com
www.cowboyculturalsociety.com
No great social upheaval or revolutionary insights, just classic Cowboy music.

The Doo Wop Cafe Radio
furjack@iname.com
www.doowopcaferadio.com
Dedicated to preserving the best music that there is, vocal group harmony.

Frank's Americana
frank@franksamericana.com
www.franksamericana.com
Cooking the music of the world in the melting pot of American life!

Gruene With Envy Radio
1215 W. Slaughter Ln. #2513, Austin, TX 78748
Dave Lytle dave@415e.com
www.gruenewithenvy.com
Playing music from all of your favorite Texas and Americana artists.

Independent Country Artists Radio
2010 Ashford Ln. Midlothian, TX 76065
PH: 866-631-5118 FX: 972-775-8527
music@originalcountryradio.com
www.originalcountryradio.com/indie.html
Hosts Bluegrass, Country and Country Gospel shows.

Independent Music Network
8424 Santa Monica Blvd. S. #776, West Hollywood, CA 90069
PH: 323-654-2182
Gary Hendrix gary@independentmusicnetwork.com
independentmusicnetwork.com
Featuring the best independent artists in the universe!

Into the Blue
Attn: Programming,
PO Box 112000, Nashville, TN 37222
www.bluegrassradio.com
Longest running commercial Bluegrass syndication in the country.

Kicker Country *525.com*
contact525@525.com
www.525.com/kicker-country.htm
Featuring the best in Country music old and new.

Moozikoo Radio
PO Box 50322, Nashville, TN 37205-0322
Anthony Bates anthony@moozikoo.com
www.MoozikooRadio.com
The best music from today's independent artists. We focus on music in the Americana, Alt-Rock, Bluegrass, Blues and Alt-Country genres.

Muldoon in the Afternoon *World Wide Bluegrass Radio*
PO Box 95, Marathon, OH 45145
PH: 513-724-1440
Gracie Muldoon gracie@worldwidebluegrass.com
www.freewebs.com/muldoon_til_noon
www.worldwidebluegrass.com
Do you have material that you would like to be considered for airplay? Contact us!

The Nashville Nobody Knows
Candace Corrigan candace@candacecorrigan.com
www.nashvillenobodyknows.com
Interview and performance podcast featuring Country, Folk, Acoustic and Roots artists. Great music and in depth interviews.

Olde Surber Station
3578 Old Rail Rd. Eagle Rock, VA 24085
PH: 540-567-2000
Jack W. Lewis JackLewis@surberstation.com
www.surberstation.com/radio
Music and interviews covering Bluegrass, Old-Time and Gospel music.

Pickin' in the Pines
203 Passage Gate Way, Wilmington, NC 28412
PH: 910-221-9474
Skip Ogden cwo@ibest.net
www.pickininthepines.com
Bluegrass radio. Please check the site for submission details.

Psychobilly Deluxe
psychoads@gmail.com
www.psychobillydeluxe.com
Playing the best Psycho/Rockabilly, Alt-Country, Cow Punk, Surf and even some Bluegrass.

RAM Radio
Pam McCluskey pam@ramradio.net
www.ramradio.net
Playing the legends of Country as well as today's vibrant independent artists.

Roots Rock Radio
PO Box 397, Sykesville, MD 21784
Richard Taylor rt@rrradio.com
RRRadio.com
Showcases the best Indie Roots Rock, Americana, Alt-Country, Indie Pop/Rock etc.

Skydog's Red Dirt Radio
2579 Hwy. 252, Laurens, SC 29360
PH: 513-255-8477
Joe (Skydog) Clem skydog@skydogmusic.com
www.RedDirtRadio.net
We're searching for the BEST new Red Dirt music to add to our playlist.

Sugar in the Gourd
4639 Hazel Ave. Philadelphia, PA 19143-2103
John Salmon john@sugarinthegourd.com
sugarinthegourd.com
Bluegrass and Old-Time music. View the website for submission details.

Taproot Radio
Calvin Powers director@TaprootRadio.com
www.taprootradio.com
A blend of Alt-Country, Roots Rock, 60's era Soul and deep Blues. Contact us for our mailing address.

Traditional Country Music Radio
Dusty Owens dusowens@hotmail.com
www.tcmradio.com
Presents the most qualified work from artists.

Twang City
programming@twangcity.com
www.twangcity.com
Alt-Country, Bluegrass, Folk, Honky Tonk, Zydeco, Blues, Folk ...

Twangtown USA
Dick Shuey dick@dickshuey.com
www.twangtownusa.com
Broadcasting a variety of Country music shows.

Western Beat Radio
PO Box 128105, Nashville, TN 37212
PH: 615-248-5026 FX: 615-248-3067
Billy Block billy@westernbeat.com
www.westernbeat.com
The only nationally syndicated program devoted to the Americana side of the Country spectrum.

X Country *XM Radio*
PH: 866-964-8439
xcountry@xmradio.com
xcountry.xmradio.com
Honors the roots of Country while infusing a sonic personality that is unmistakably NOW!

Alaska

The Arctic Cactus Hour *KNBA*
818 E. 9th Ave. Anchorage, AK 99501
Eric Smith & Jim Stratton stratto@alaska.net
www.alaska.net/~stratto
Covering all that Rocks and honky tonks.

Arizona

M-PAK Radio
PO Box 3262, Gilbert, AZ 85299-3262
Mike Mikels mikemikels@cox.net
www.mpakproductions.com
Plays Country/Texas Country/and Americana artists. We also review or recommend certain CDs.

California

Bluegrass, Etc. *KCSN*
18111 Nordhoff St., Northridge, CA 91330-8312
PH: 818-885-5276
Frank Hoppe fhoppe@kcsn.org
kcsn.org/programs/bluegrassetcetera.html
Features traditional Bluegrass, Old-Time and Early Country music to move your heart and your feet.

Bluegrass Signal *KALW*
500 Mansell St., San Francisco, CA 94134
PH: 415-841-4121 FX: 415-841-4125
Peter Thompson bgsignal@comcast.net
www.kalw.org
A unique synthesis of Blues and Old-Time Country music, with elements of Celtic, Jazz and a variety of Folk music.

Boot Liquor Radio
32 Park Groton Pl. San Jose, CA 95136-2519
Roy Batchelor roy@bootliquor.com
bootliquor.com
American Roots music for saddle-weary drunkards.

Carefree Highway *KVMR*
401 Spring St., Nevada City, CA 95959
PH: 530-265-9555 FX: 530-265-9077
Gary Harrison carefreehighway@kvmr.org
www.kvmr.org/personalities/g_harrison.html
Folk, Americana, Cowboy & Native American. Send 2 CDs (one is for our library).

Cupertino Barndance *KKUP*
933 Monroe St., PMB 9150, Santa Clara, CA 95050
Stompin' Steve Hathaway steve@westernswing.com
www.westernswing.com/barndance.html
Classic Country, Honky Tonk, Western Swing, Bluegrass and Rockabilly. The middle hour features a current release of either a new artist or reissue.

Down Home *KCSN*
18111 Nordhoff St., Northridge, CA 91330-8312
PH: 818-885-5276
Chuck Taggart chuck@downhome.org
www.downhome.org
Folk, Roots, Traditional base and beyond.

Down On the Pataphysical Farm *KUSP*
203 8th Ave. Santa Cruz, CA 95062
PH: 831-476-2800
Leigh Hill bluegrass@kusp.org
www.kusp.org/playlists/pharm
If it's good, Acoustic and Country I'll play it.

Freight Train Boogie Radio
PO Box 4262, Santa Rosa, CA 95402
Bill Frater frater@freighttrainboogie.com
www.freighttrainboogie.com
An emphasis on Alt-Country or Americana music. Please send 2 copies of your CD.

Howdylicous!
PO Box 4362, Irvine, CA 92616
PH: 949-824-6868
Wanda wanda@kuci.org
www.howdylicious.com
The best in new and old Twangy music.

Lunch on the Back Porch *KZYX*
PO Box 1, Philo, CA 95466
PH: 707-895-2324 FX: 707-895-2451
Diane Hering gm@kzyx.org
kzyx.org/show_profiles/lunch_on_porch.htm
Traditional and contemporary Bluegrass.

Semi-Twang
59 36th Way, Sacramento, CA 95819
Paul A. Hefti semitwang@yahoo.com
www.angelfire.com/indie/semitwang
Classic Country show.

Sunny Side Up *KZSU*
PO Box 20510, Stanford, CA 94309
PH: 650-723-9010 FX: 650-725-5865
Bruce Ross country@kzsu.org
kzsu.stanford.edu
Features Bluegrass and Old-Time music.

Tangled Roots *KCSN*
18111 Nordhoff St., Northridge, CA 91330-8312
PH: 818-885-5276
Pat Baker pat@kcsn.org
kcsn.org/programs/tangledroots.html
Alt-Country, Folk, Folk/Rock, Gospel, Blues and music from the Singer/Songwriter tradition.

Trolling for Trout *KFOK*
PO Box 4238, Georgetown, CA 95634
PH: 530-333-4300
Gary Oswald oztown1@yahoo.com
www.kfok.org
Submerged in a fishy emulsion based on a redneck/hippy/hillbilly perspective.

Wildwood Flower *KPFK*
3729 Cahuenga Blvd. W., North Hollywood, CA 91604
PH: 818-985-2711 FX: 818-763-7526
Ben Elder weissenben@earthlink.net
www.kpfk.org
Your music MUST be Bluegrass, Old-Time or Traditional Country to be considered for airplay.

Colorado

The Conman Radio Show
9697 E. Mineral Ave. Englewood, CO 80112
Chris Conn conman@jonesradio.net
www.countrydj.com/conman
Bar Bands & Basement Tapes is one our special features.

Honky Tonk Heroes / Old Grass GNU Grass
4700 Walnut St., Boulder, CO 80301
PH: 303-449-4885
music@kgnu.org
www.kgnu.org
Old and new Country & Western music!

KCUV
1201 18th St. #250, Denver, CO 80202
PH: 303-296-7025
www.kcuvradio.com
Americana music.

KSUT
PO Box 737, 123 Capote Dr. Ignacio, CO 81137
PH: 970-563-0255 FX: 970-563-0399
www.ksut.org
An eclectic Triple A and Americana music mix.

Connecticut

Go Kat Go! *WNHU*
PO Box 5392, Milford, CT 06460
PH: 203-934-9296
Michelle gokatgo13@hotmail.com
www.gokatgoradio.com
Spinning the latest and greatest Rockabilly and Psychobilly.

Swingin' West *WVOF*
Fairfield U. 1073 N. Benson Rd. Fairfield, CT 06824
PH: 203-254-4000
mike@swinginwest.com
www.swinginwest.com
Western Swing and Western music (not Country).

U-H Radio Bluegrass *WWUH*
200 Bloomfield Ave. West Hartford, CT 06117
PH: 860-768-4701 FX: 860-768-5701
Kevin Lynch KLbgrass@aol.com
www.wwuh.org
Traditional to contemporary Bluegrass music as well as occasional live performances.

Delaware

Rural Free Delivery *WVUD*
Perkins Student Ctr. U. Delaware, Newark, DE 19716
PH: 302-831-2701 FX: 302-831-1399
Suzi Wollenberg rivrhors@dca.net
www.wvud.org
Devoted to Bluegrass, Old-Time and Classic Country music.

Florida

CountryBear.com
PO Box 758, Lake Placid, FL 33862
PH: 863-531-0102 FX: 863-531-0103
sbc48@hotmail.com
www.countrybear.com
All material must be licensed through one of the licensing companies.

This is Bluegrass *WMNF*
1210 E. MLK Blvd. Tampa, FL 33603-4449
PH: 813-238-9663 FX: 813-238-1802
Tom Henderson wmnf@wmnf.org
www.wmnf.org
Old and new Bluegrass.

Sonic Detour *WMNF*
1210 E. MLK Blvd. Tampa, FL 33603-4449
PH: 813-238-9663 FX: 813-238-1802
Denny Reisinger wmnf@wmnf.org
www.wmnf.org
Roots Rock, Rockabilly, Zydeco, Blues and Honky Tonk.

Illinois

Live-N-Kickin Bluegrass *WLUW*
6525 N. Sheridan Rd. Chicago, IL 60626
PH: 773-508-8080 FX: 773-508-8082
Billy J. Ivers BillyJ@wluw.org
www.wluw.org
Recorded and live Bluegrass music in the studio with featured artist.

Southbound Train *WNUR*
1920 Campus Dr. Evanston, IL 60208-2280
PH: 847-491-7102 FX: 847-467-2058
www.wnur.org
Americana, Roots …

Strictly Bluegrass *WDCB*
College of DuPage, 425 Fawell Blvd. Glen Ellyn, IL 60137
PH: 630-942-4200 FX: 630-942-2788
Larry Robinson RobinsonL@wdcb.org
wdcb.org
Presenting the music I love, along with information on local groups and Bluegrass concerts.

WWHP
407 N. Main St., Farmer City, IL 61842
PH: 309-928-9876 FX: 309-928-3708
wwhp@farmwagon.com
www.wwhp.com
Blues, Bluegrass, Rock, Gospel and American Roots music.

Iowa

High Plains Hootenanny *KRUI*
379 IMU, Iowa City, IA 52242
PH: 319-335-8970
Rob highplainshoot@yahoo.com
www.avalon.net/~rrussell
Alt and Insurgent Country and anything else Rootsy.

Kansas

Rockabilly Mood Swing *KKFI*
PO Box 9332, Shawnee Mission, KS 66201
PH: 816-931-5534
Lynne Greenamyre kcrockabilly@yahoo.com
launch.groups.yahoo.com/group/KCRockabilly
A revved up trip down the Rockabilly speedway! With side trips to Jump Blues, Psychobilly, Punk, Hillbilly and Old-Time Country Twang.

Trail Mix *KPR*
1120 W. 11th St. U. Kansas, Lawrence, KS 66044
PH: 785-864-4530 FX: 785-864-5278
Bob McWilliams radiobob@ku.edu
kpr.ku.edu/trailmix.shtml
Celtic, Folk, Old-Time and Bluegrass.

Kentucky

Americana Crossroads *WMKY*
UPO Box 903, MSU, Morehead, KY 40351
PH: 606-783-2001 FX: 606-783-2335
Jonese Franklin wmky@moreheadstate.edu
www.wmkyradio.com
Blending Folk, Bluegrass, Alt-Country and Acoustic Blues in a music format known as Americana.

Barren River Breakdown *WKYU*
W. Kentucky U., 1906 College Heights Blvd. #11035, Bowling Green, KY 42101-1035
PH: 800-599-9598 FX: 270-745-6272
Erika Brady & Mark Hayes wkyufm@wku.edu
www.wkyufm.org
The best of American music with roots, including plenty of Bluegrass.

Blue Yodel # 9 *WRFL*
PO Box 777, University Stn. Lexington, KY 40506-0025
PH: 859-257-4636 FX: 859-323-1039
Joe Takacs shadygrove@prodigy.net
wrfl881.org
Country and Americana.

The Cecilian Bank Bluegrass Hour *WLVK*
519 N. Miles St. PO Box 2087, Elizabethtown, KY 42702-2087
PH: 270-766-1055
theboman@theboman.com
www.theboman.com/cecilian.html
Once Bluegrass music gets into your body, life as you know it will change forever.

H. Perkins Bluegrass *WBRT*
106 S. 3rd St., Bardstown, KY 40004
Howard Perkins h.perkins@juno.com
I play a lot of independent music. I have live bands drop by as well.

Roots n' Boots *WFPK*
619 S. 4th St., Louisville, KY 40202
PH: 502-814-6500
Michael Young myoung@wfpk.org
www.wfpk.org/programs/rootsandboots.html
There's room for outlaws, preachers, rockers and prophets.

Sunday Bluegrass *WFPK*
619 S. 4th St., Louisville, KY 40202
PH: 502-814-6500
Berk Bryant bbryant@wfpk.org
www.wfpk.org/programs/bluegrass.html
If it fits the format of the show, I'll play it.

WHAY
PO Box 69, Whitley City, KY 42653
PH: 606-376-2218 FX: 606-376-5146
whayradio@highland.net
www.hay98.com

Louisiana

American Routes
501 Basin St. Ste. D, New Orleans, LA 70112
Nick Spitzer mail@amroutes.org
amroutes.org
Presenting a broad range of American music – Blues, Jazz, Gospel, Soul, Old-Time Country, Zydeco …

Old Time Country and Bluegrass *WWOZ*
PO Box 51840, New Orleans, LA 70151-1840
Hazel The Delta Rambler hazeldelt@yahoo.com
www.wwoz.org

Maine

The Blue Country *WMPG*
96 Falmouth St., Portland, ME 04104-9300
PH: 207-780-4909
Blizzard Bob blizbob@maine.rr.com
www.wmpg.org
Where the Bluegrass grows high, under a clear country sky.

Maryland

Rockabilly Radio
PO Box 5046, Baltimore, MD 21220
www.rockabillyradio.net
The voice of independent Rockabilly artists.

Massachusetts

American Primitive *WMBR*
3 Ames St., Cambridge, MA 02142
PH: 617-253-8810
Jay Beek primitive@wmbr.org
wmbr.mit.edu
Some Gospel for you sinners. Not the same old Blues crap.

Bluegrass Junction *WICN*
6 Chatham St., Worcester, MA 01609
PH: 508-752-0700 FX: 508-752-7518
Tom tbanyai@worldnet.att.net
www.bluegrassjunction.org
Back to days when the radio was the center of family entertainment.

Bradford Street Bluegrass *WOMR*
494 Commercial St., Provincetown, MA 02657
PH: 508-487-2619
Bob Seay bob@womr.org
www.womr.org

Hillbilly at Harvard *WHRB*
389 Harvard St., Cambridge, MA 02138
PH: 617-495-4818
mail@whrb.org
www.whrb.net
The best Country/Western show in New England.

Lost Highway *WMBR*
3 Ames St., Cambridge, MA 02142
PH: 617-253-8810
Doug Gesler highway@wmbr.org
wmbr.mit.edu
Americana, Alt-Country, Blues, Bluegrass, Cajun, Zydeco and Hawaiian.

Michigan

Progressive Torch and Twang *WDBM*
G-4 Holden Hall, MSU East Lansing, MI 48824
PH: 517-353-4414
Doug Neal nealdoug@msu.edu
www.msu.edu/~depolo
Home of hip-shakin', soul-swayin' music!

Minnesota

Good 'n' Country *KFAI*
1808 Riverside Ave. Minneapolis, MN 55454
PH: 612-341-0980
Ken Hippler vintagecountry@hotmail.com
www.kfai.org/programs/goodnc.htm
One of KFAI's oldest programs.

The Other Side of Country *WMGT*
104 N. Main St., Stillwater, MN 55082
PH: 651-439-5006
Jack K. Sparks othersideofcountry@hotmail.com
www.othersideofcountry.com
Alt-Country and Hillbilly music.

Missouri

Bluegrass Breakdown *KDHX*
3504 Magnolia St. Louis, MO 63118
PH: 314-664-3688 FX: 314-664-1020
Walter & Willa Volz bluegrassbreakdown@kdhx.org
www.kdhx.org/programs/bluegrassbreakdown.htm
Part of each show will be dedicated to Homegrown Grass.

Country Function Bluegrass Junction *KDHX*
3504 Magnolia, St. Louis, MO 63118
PH: 314-664-3688 FX: 314-664-1020
Gene & Larry cfandbj@kdhx.org
www.kdhx.org/programs/countryfunctionbluegrassju
nction.htm
Featuring local artists and unknown artists.

Down Yonder *KDHX*
3504 Magnolia St. Louis, MO 63118
PH: 314-664-3688 FX: 314-664-1020
Keith Dudding, downyonder@kdhx.org
www.kdhx.org/programs/downyonder
Bluegrass and Old-Time music.

Fishin' with Dynamite *KDHX*
3504 Magnolia St. Louis, MO 63118
PH: 314-664-3688 FX: 314-664-1020
Fred Friction fishinwithdynamite@kdhx.org
www.kdhx.org/programs/fishinwithdynamite.htm
Features the finest Alt-Country, Cow-Punk and Roots Rock.

New Jersey

Burlington County Bluegrass *WBZC*
601 Pemberton Browns Mills Rd. Pemberton, NJ 08068-1599
PH: 609-894-9311 x1592 FX: 609-894-9440
Nancy Longenecker clongen@aol.com
staff.bcc.edu/radio
Bluegrass with a mixture of Celtic fiddle tunes and Folk music mixed with African rhythms. Welcomes projects by independent artists!

Honky Tonk Roadhouse *WDVR*
PO Box 191, Sergeantsville, NJ 08557
PH: 609-397-1620 FX: 609-397-5991
Ted Lyons tlyons@blast.net
www.wdvrfm.org

Trash, Twang and Thunder *WFMU*
PO Box 5101, Hoboken, NJ 07030
PH: 201-521-1416
www.wfmu.org/playlists/MO
Twang Rock for now cowboys. Lots of live music too.

WDVR
PO Box 191 Sergeantsville, NJ 08557
PH: 609-397-1620 FX: 609-397-5991
host@wdvrfm.org
www.wdvrfm.org
Quite a few of the DJ's play Indie artists.

New Mexico

Green Chile Revival & Medicine Show *KGLP*
200 College Rd. Gallup, NM 87301
PH: 505-863-7626 FX: 505-863-7633
www.kglp.org/chile
An eclectic mix of Country, Blues, Zydeco, Tex -Mex, Folk. In short - Roots music.

The Santa Fe Opry *KSFR*
PO Box 31366, Santa Fe, NM 87504-1366
PH: 505-428-1527 FX: 505-428-1237
Stephen W. Terrell robotclaww@msn.com
steveterrell.blogspot.com
Hardcore, Alternative, Outlaw, Insurgent, No Depression.

New York

All Together Now *WBNY*
1300 Elmwood Ave. Buffalo, NY 14222
PH: 716-878-3080 FX: 716-878-6600
Al Riess riessaf@buffalostate.edu
www.wbny.org
All styles of Country, Folk and Bluegrass.

Bluegrass Ramble *WCNY*
PO Box 2400, Syracuse, NY 13220-2400
Bill Knowlton udmacon@aol.com
www.wcny.org/classicfm
www.fmhs.cnyric.org/notes/knowlton-bio.html

The Bristol Brothers Show *WDYN*
2844 Dewey Ave. Rochester, NY 14616
Brother Don drk@dynrec.com
dynrec.com/bristolbrothers
Old-Time Bluegrass music. I play independent artists only.

Salt Creek Show *WVBR*
957 Mitchell St., Ithaca, NY 14850
PH: 607-273-2121 FX: 607-273-4069
wvbr.com/salt.html
Old-Time, Bluegrass, Old and Alt-Country with a sprinkling Cajun, Blues and Gospel.

String Fever *NCPR*
St. Lawrence U. Canton, NY 13617-1475
PH: 315-229-5356 FX: 315-229-5373
Barb Heller barb@ncpr.org
www.northcountrypublicradio.org/programs/local/
string.html
Instrumental finger picking guitar for GREAT musicians.

North Carolina

The Goat Show
Jim Magaw jim.magaw@gmail.com
www.thegoatshow.com
If you are an Old-Timey musician with a CD you would like me to play, please contact me for my mailing address.

The Good-Tyme Bluegrass Show *WFSS*
1200 Murchison Rd. Fayetteville, NC 28301
PH: 910-672-1919 FX: 910-672-1964
Bob and Sara Barden monkous@nc.rr.com
www.wfss.org

This Old Porch *WNCW*
PO Box 804, Spindale, NC 28160
PH: 828-287-8080 FX: 828-287-8012
Joe Cline kilocycles@carolina.rr.com
www.wncw.org
Features classic music from the Old-Time Country music tradition.

The Wrecking Ball *WCOM*
201 N. Greensboro St., Carrboro, NC 27510
Jayson miamimystic23@yahoo.com
www.geocities.com/miamimystic23/wreckingball
Roots, Americana, Alt-Country etc. If yours is a CD that might fit the format of my show, send it to me for review.

Ohio

D28+5 *WOUB*
9 S. College St., Athens, OH 45701
PH: 740-593-1771 FX: 740-593-0240
radio@woub.org
woub.org/bluegrass
Bluegrass Roots radio for SE Ohio.

Roots 'n' Offshoots *WCBE*
540 Jack Gibbs Blvd. Columbus, OH 43215
PH: 614-365-5555 FX: 614-365-5060
Maggie Brennan mbrennan@wcbe.org
www.wcbe.org
Folk, Bluegrass, Rockabilly and more.

Oregon

Early Morning Gumbo *KBOO*
20 SE. 8th Ave. Portland, OR 97214
PH: 503-231-8187 FX: 503-231-7145
Diane Karl dkarl@ipns.com
www.kboo.fm
Features Acoustic Blues, Texas Folk, Cajun, Old-Time, Bluegrass etc.

The Long & Dusty Road *KBOO*
20 SE. 8th Ave. Portland, OR 97214
PH: 503-231-8187 FX: 503-231-7145
Don Jacobson donj@dslnorthwest.net
www.kboo.fm
Americana, Alt-Country, Roots etc.

Pennsylvania

The Bluegrass Jam Session *WYEP*
67 Bedford Sq. Pittsburgh, PA 15203
PH: 412-381-9900 FX: 412-381-9126
Bruce Mountjoy mtjoypgh@aol.com
www.wyep.org
Explores Bluegrass music from its 1940's creation by Kentuckian Bill Monroe into the new century.

Mountain Folk
PO Box 2266, Sinking Spring, PA 19608
mtnfolk@aol.com
www.mountainfolk.com
Indie artists are encouraged to send material.

Pure as Stone Country Music Jamboree *WQSU*
Susquehanna U. 514 U. Ave. Selinsgrove, PA 17870
PH: 570-372-4030
www.susqu.edu/wqsu-fm
Traditional Country & Western music.

Roots and Rhythm Mix *WYEP*
67 Bedford Sq. Pittsburgh, PA 15203
PH: 412-381-9900 FX: 412-381-9126
Kate Borger kateb913@hotmail.com
www.wyep.org
As well as playing Roots and Alt-Country, I'm also in to any regional rhythms - Tex-Mex, New Orleans, Cajun and Zydeco, Latin etc.

Traditional Ties *WYEP*
67 Bedford Sq. Pittsburgh, PA 15203
PH: 412-381-9900 FX: 412-381-9126
John Trout johntrout91@hotmail.com
www.wyep.org
New Bluegrass releases and old favorites.

South Carolina

The Bluegrass Sound *ETV*
1101 George Rogers Blvd. Columbia,
SC 29201-4761
PH: 803-737-3420
www.etvradio.org/bgs
Host Larry Klein presents a mix of both traditional and contemporary Bluegrass music, some occasional Old-Time Mountain music.

Tennessee

Bluegrass Breakdown *WPLN*
630 Mainstream Dr. Nashville, TN 37228-1204
PH: 615-760-2903 FX: 615-760-2904
Dave Higgs bluegrass@wpln.org
www.wpln.org/bluegrass
Our goal is to edify, educate and entertain. We leave no instrument unpicked, no song unsung and no interview undone.

The Bluegrass Special *WDVX*
PO Box 18157 Knoxville, TN 37928
PH: 865-494-2020
Alex Leach alex899@comcast.net
www.wdvx.com/programs/bluegrassspecial.html
The best in Bluegrass music, old and new.

Clinch River Breakdown *WDVX*
PO Box 27568, Knoxville, TN 37927
PH: 865-494-2020
Amy Campbell campbellcreative@charter.net
Charlie Lutz charlie_lutz@comcast.net
www.wdvx.com/Programs/Clinch.html
Bluegrass, Old-Time and Classic Country.

Cumberland Sunday Morning *WDVX*
PO Box 27568, Knoxville, TN 37927
PH: 865-494-2020
Mike Kelly bluegrassmike@hotmail.com
www.wdvx.com/programs/Cumberland.html
The best in Bluegrass Gospel. I enjoy spreading the word about musicians that folks may not be familiar with.

WDVX
PO Box 27568, Knoxville, TN 37927
PH: 865-494-2020
mail@wdvx.com
www.wdvx.com
We play all types of Country, Celtic and Folk.

Texas

The Bluegrass Zone *KPFT*
419 Lovett Blvd. Houston, TX 77006
PH: 713-526-5738 FX: 713-526-5750
Chris Hirsch cshirsch@alltel.net
www.bluegrasszone.com
Houston's Bluegrass radio program.

The LoneStar JukeBox *KPFT*
620 W. 21st St., Houston, TX 77008
PH: 713-526-5738
Rick Heysquierdo rick@lonestarjukebox.com
www.lonestarjukebox.com
Promotes Americana and Alt-Country genres.

Third Coast Music Network *KSYM*
7519 Dell Oak, San Antonio, TX 78218-2634
PH: 210-733-2800
David Ludwig ihod7519@yahoo.com
www.accd.edu/tcmn

TOSSM Radio
5605 David Strickland Rd. Fort Worth, TX 76119
Philip Corder philip@tossmmusic.com
www.tossmradio.com
If you would like your music played on our station, contact us.

Variety96 Country
PO Box 304, Dale, TX 78616
www.variety96.com
We offer airplay to as many artists as possible and will consider all music submitted.

Utah

The Amarillo Highway *KZMU*
PO Box 1076, 1734 Rocky Rd. Moab, UT 84532
PH: 435-259-5968 FX: 435-259-8763
Professor Purple music-director@kzmu.org
www.kzmu.org
Hillbilly, Alt-Country, Alterna-Twang, No Depression, Country, Honky Tonk.

Monday Breakfast Jam *KRCL*
1971 W. North Temple, Salt Lake City, UT 84116
PH: 801-359-9191 FX: 801-533-9136
Doug Young dougy@krcl.org
www.krcl.org
Eclectic mix of Insurgent Country, contemporary Singer/Songwriter, Folk and Rock.

Virginia

Allegheny Mountain Radio
users.htcnet.org/wvls/AMR.html
Country, Bluegrass, Gospel, Rock, Classical and Jazz.

Bluegrass Sunday Morning *WNRN*
2250 Old Ivy Rd. #2, Charlottesville, VA 22903
PH: 434-979-0919
wnrn.rlc.net
Host Scott Buchanan features 4 hours of Bluegrass music.

WGRX
4414 Lafayette Blvd. #100, Fredericksburg,
VA 22408
PH: 540-891-9696 FX: 540-891-1656
Stephanie Taylor staylor@thunder1045.com
www.thunder1045.com
We air an Americana/Bluegrass/Texas Country show on Sunday nights that incorporates independent artists.

TwangCast Radio
PO Box 1702, Georgetown, TX 78627
twangradio@takecountryback.com
www.twangcast.com
We play independent artists of several genres.

Washington

Front Porch Bluegrass *KPBX*
2319 N. Monroe St., Spokane, WA 99205
PH: 509-328-5729 FX: 509-328-5764
Kevin Brown bluegrass@kpbx.org
www.kpbx.org/programs/frontporch
Classic Bluegrass and its progressive offshoots.

Road Songs *KBCS*
3000 Landerholm Cir. SE., Bellevue,
WA 98007-6484
Attn: Music Director
PH: 425-564-2424
Hal Durden asubdude@att.net
kbcs.fm
A journey down the highways of Alt-Country, Folk, Classic Country and Country Rock.

Washington DC

Bluegrass Overnight *WAMU*
A.U. 4400 Mass. Ave. NW., Washington,
DC 20016-8082
PH: 202-885-1200
Lee Michael Demsey demsey@wamu.org
www.wamu.org
Six lively hours of Bluegrass every week.

bluegrasscountry.org
4000 Brandywine St. NW., Washington, DC 20016
bluegrasscountry.org
Traditional and contemporary Bluegrass.

The Ray Davis Show *WAMU*
A.U. 4400 Mass. Ave. NW., Washington,
DC 20016-8082
PH: 202-885-1200
feedback@wamu.org
www.wamu.org/programs/rd
Traditional and Gospel Bluegrass.

Stained Glass Bluegrass *WAMU*
A.U. 4400 Mass. Ave. NW., Washington,
DC 20016-8082
PH: 202-885-1200
Red Shipley rs@ns.gemlink.com
www.wamu.org/programs/sgbg
Receives and considers material from anyone.

WAMU *American U.*
4400 Mass. Ave. NW., Washington, DC 20016-8082
PH: 202-885-1200
feedback@wamu.org
www.wamu.org

West Virginia

Sidetracks
151 S. Mineral St., Keyser, WV 26726
PH: 304-788-7878
Ed McDonald sidetracks@eioproductions.com
www.wvpubcast.org/radio/sidetracks
A weekly syndicated program of Bluegrass, Folk, Country, Blues and related styles of contemporary Acoustic music.

Wisconsin

Bluegrass on Saturday *WXPR*
303 W. Prospect Ave. Rhinelander, WI 54501
PH: 715-362-6000 FX: 715-362-6007
Henry Galvin wxpr@wxpr.org
www.wxpr.org/program/bluegrass.cfm
Four big hours of Bluegrass every Saturday afternoon.

Canada

Angel Radio Bluegrass
Stormin Norman norm@angelradio.net
angelradio.net
Bluegrass old and new.

The Back Forty *CKCU*
56-121 Buell St., Ottawa, ON K1Z 7E7
PH: 819-827-0068
Ron Moores ron.moores@back40.ca
www.back40.ca
Traditional Country, Western and Bluegrass music.

Brave New Frontiers Podcast
radio.weblogs.com/0146182
Host Randall Cousins presents a weekly peek into the on-the-edge Country influenced Indie scene.

Daybreak In Dixie CJAM
401 Sunset Ave. Windsor, ON N9B 3P4
PH: 519-253-3000 ext.2527 FX: 519-971-3605
David Blakney daybreakindixie@hotmail.com
www.uwindsor.ca/cjam
Bluegrass music.

Dagwood Country Radio
Cluade Camacho rambler@dagwoodradio.com
dagwoodradio.com
Blue jeans, guitars, NASCAR. Two-steppin' fools and yahoos. Hell Yeah!! Today's Country Rocks!!

Fire on the Mountain CKUA
10526 Jasper Ave. Edmonton, AB T5J 1Z7
PH: 780-428-7595 FX: 780-428-7624
Craig Korth craig.korth@ckua.com
www.ckua.org
From the roots of Bluegrass to the new Acoustic frontier.

Good 'n Country CFFF
715 George St. N., Peterborough, ON K9H 3T2
PH: 705-748-4761
Barb Holtmann restorix@nexicom.net
www.trentu.ca/trentradio
Blending the old, the new and the unusual in Country music. News, views and interviews with local and area artists.

Pacific Pickin' CITR
#8-700 St. Georges Ave., North Vancouver, BC V7L 4T1
PH: 604-822-2487
Arthur & Andrea Berman aberman@telus.net
www.citr.ca
Bluegrass, Old-Time music and its derivatives.

Radio Boogie CKLN
55 Gould St. 2nd Fl. Toronto, ON M5B 1E9
PH: 416-979-5251 FX: 416-595-0226
Steve Pritchard s.pritchard1@sympatico.ca
www.ckln.fm
Bluegrass, Old-Tyme, Acoustic and Traditional Country.

Six Strings & A Million Possibilities CJTR
PO Box 334 Stn. Main, Regina, SK S4P 3A1
PH: 306-525-7274 FX: 306-525-9741
Bob Evans SixStrings@BobEvansGuitar.com
www.bobevansguitar.com/six_strings.html
Primarily, but not exclusively, instrumental.

Spirit of the West
Lot 1, Hyas Lake Rd. Pinantan, BC V0E 3E1
PH: 250-573-5731 FX: 250-573-5731
Hugh_McLennan@telus.net
www.cowboylife.com
Features talented independent artists. The show is heard around the world.

Wide Cut Country CKUA
10526 Jasper Ave. Edmonton, AB T5J 1Z7
PH: 780-428-7595 FX: 780-428-7624
Allison Brock allison.brock@ckua.org
www.ckua.com
Traditional Hillbilly to Pop Country of today.

Europe

Austria

Archangel's Country Club
Wienerbruckstr. 87, A-2344 Maria-Enzersdorf, Austria
Kurt K. Gabriel archangel-country@kabsi.at
Weekly Country music show.

Go West Go Country Radio Ostttirol
Amlacher Str. 2, A-9900 Lienz, Austria
Hans Mair hans.mair@hella.co.at
www.radio.osttirol.net/gowest.htm
Send your promotional CDs to the above address.

Denmark

Absolute Country
Gammel Strandvej 426, 3060 Espergaerde, Denmark.
Per Kildahl per-kildahl@adslhome.dk
www.radiohelsingor.dk
A mix of old and new Country music.

BJ the DJ
Radio Sindals, Her bor vi. Norgesgade 1 9870 Sindal, Denmark
bj-the-dj@mail.dk
www.dj.1go.dk
Playing independent artists from all over the world.

Bornholms Stemme
Gammeltoft 36 – 25, 3790 Hasle, Bornholm, Denmark
Lulu and Arne Andersen arne_lulu@country-vaerkstedet.dk
www.country-vaerkstedet.dk
On the local radio we air Country music 2 hours a week, plus entertain every second Saturday with mixed music for 3 hours.

Radio Oestsjaelland
Vinkældertorvet 2A Postboks 34 4640 Fakse, Denmark
PH: 56-71-30-03 FX: 56-71-39-51
Hans-Henrik Thamdrup country@lokalradio.dk
www.lokalradio.dk/voresprg/countrymusic
A lot of the Indie music is at least as good as the music of famous artists.

Estonia

Bluegrass Radio 108
bluegrassradio@hot.ee
www.hot.ee/bluegrassradio
Devoted to the American Bluegrass and Grassroots music.

Germany

Country Special Radio Countrymusic24
Verantwortlicher i. S. d. P., Birgit Walter, Hildburghauser Str. 35 in 12279 Berlin, Germany
wunsch@countrymusic24.com
www.countrymusic24.com
A weekly show that plays independent Country music.

Hillbilly Boogie
Saarstraße 8, 72070 Tübingen, Germany
PH: +49(0)7073-2250 FX: +49(0)7073-2134
Rainer Zellner zellner@musiccontact.com
www.musiccontact.com
We cover many musical genres related to Country or Hillbilly.

Hillbilly Jukebox Radio Rhein Welle
Hauptstrasse 62, 65396 Walluf, Germany
FX: 012-126-744-372-84
Rolf Hierath cashville@gmx.de
www.cashville.de

Hillbilly Rockhouse Countrymusic24
PO Box 1130, 49836 Lengerich, Germany
PH: (0) 5904-9383-13 FX: (0) 5904-9383-82
DJ Gerd Stassen g.stassen@t-online.de
www.countrymusic24.com

Luxembourg

Country Club Music Show
2, rue de la Boucherie, L-1247 Luxembourg
Mam Lexy lexyzen@pt.lu
www.ara.lu

Country Music Show Radio Ara
3, rue principale, L-9183 Schlindermanderscheid, Luxembourg
Willie Jervis radioaracountryshow@yahoo.com
www.ara.lu
If you send us your Country and Folk CDs, we'll play them!

The Netherlands

Alt Country Cooking
Gasthuislaan 31, 9671 JC Winschoten, The Netherlands
Theo Oldenburg
altcountrycooking@radiowinschoten.nl
www.realrootscafe.com/altcountrycooking.html
Features Americana, Folk, Alt-Country, Blues, Roots-Rock and Singer/Songwriter music.

B.R.T.O.
Burgemeester van Hasseltstraat 7, 4611 BG Bergen op Zoom, The Netherlands
redactie@brto.nl
www.brto.nl
Bluegrass, Gospel, Cajun, Zydeco, Tex Mex, Rockabilly and Modern Country.

Country Express Radio Rucphen
Zwaard 27 4871 DL Etten Leur, The Netherlands
Ries & Johan verwijmerenries@zonnet.nl
www.home.zonnet.nl/verwijmerenries
Please send me material (CDs & Bio) for my show.

Countryland Radio Barneveld
p/a Valkhof 63, 3772 EC Barneveld, The Netherlands
PH: 0342-422-411
Dick Brink & Timen van Ark
countryland@radiobarneveld.nl
www.radiobarneveld.nl
Bluegrass, Old-Time Country, New Country, aandacht aan de Nederlandse artiesten en in mei geen artiest van de maand, maar Bluegrass maand!!

The Long Distance
Schout 48, 1625 BP Hoorn, The Netherlands
Nico Druyf nicodr@hetnet.nl
www.realrootscafe.com/longdistance.html
All kinds of Roots styles like Alt-Country, Cajun, Blues, Tex-Mex, Rockabilly, Singer/Songwriter, Zydeco etc.

PeelGrass
Akelei 10 5803 CA Venray, The Netherlands
Rein Wortelboer peelgras@xs4all.nl
www.xs4all.nl/~peelgras
Send a promotional CD for review and possible airplay.

proRadio4
Postbus 86, 5900 AB Venlo, The Netherlands
PH: 01805-7834-24001 FX: 001831-677-9141
Dean Grunwald info@proradio4.com
www.proradio4.net
Playing high quality independent music of all genres, with a particular emphasis on Country, Rock and Dance music.

Norway

Radio Risor
Klingra, Gjernes, N-4990 Sondeled, Norway
PH: 47-3715-4528 FX: 47-3715-2022
Dagfinn M. Pedersen dagfinn@bluegrass.no
www.bluegrass.no
All types of Bluegrass, including Gospel, Roots and music on the edges.

Spain

La Diligència
Gran Via Jaume I, 29, 2ⁿᵈ Fl. E-17001 Girona, Spain
Jesús Garcia & Lluís Sala
diligenciaARROBAonamusica.com
members.fortunecity.com/lsala66/dilig.htm
El programa de música Country d'Ona musica.

United Kingdom

Bob Harris Country *BBC 2*
PH: 08700-100-200
www.bbc.co.uk/radio2/shows/bobharriscountry
The best in Country, from cowboy classics to the newest sounds coming out of Nashville.

Bop 2 B
55B Occupation Ln. Sheffield S12 4PS UK
Dave Brighton info@thisgigguide.fsnet.co.uk
www.dbrighton.rockabillyradio.net
Various Rockin' styles ranging from Rockabilly through Jump-Blues and Doo-Wop.

Country Corner Radio Show *Claire FM*
Abbeyfield Ctr. Francis St. Ennis Co Clare, Ireland
PH: 353-0-65-682-8888 FX: 353-0-65-682-9392
Mike Gardiner mgardiner@clarefm.ie
www.clarefm.ie
Features Irish, American and European Country music, new and old.

Metro Country
ray@metrocountry.co.uk
www.metrocountry.co.uk
E-mail to submit your material.

Twangfest *U. Radio York*
10 Heworth Hall Dr. Heworth, York, Yorkshire
YO31 1AQ UK
Allan Nelson allan@allan70.wanadoo.co.uk
ury.york.ac.uk
Roots, Americana, Folk, Country etc.

A u s t r a l i a

Bay Breeze Country *Bay FM*
PO Box 1003, Cleveland, QLD 4163 Australia
Bob Atkins bob_atkins@iprimus.com.au
www.bayfm.org.au
Weekly show featuring independent artists.

Cool Country Radio
PO Box 2, The Entrance, NSW 2261 Australia
PH: 0415-616-431
941fm@coolcountry.com.au
www.coolcountry.com.au

Make Mine Country *WYN*
PO Box 1011, St. Albans, VIC 3021 Australia
PH: +61-3-9364-0817
Trudy trudy-burke@bigpond.com
www.wynfm.org.au
You will hear some Australian, some overseas major label artists and a whole lot of independent Country music artists from around the world.

MCR Radio
PO Box 1420, Campbelltown, NSW 2560 Australia
PH: 02-4625-2768 FX: 02-4627-0670
feedback@2mcr.org.au
2mcr.org.au/country
Our station features a variety of Country music shows.

Music from Foggy Hollow *Hawk Radio*
20 Hale Cres. Windsor, NSW 2756 Australia
PH: 02-45-775-662
Mike Kear foggyhollow@bluegrass.org.au
www.hawkradio.org.au/bluegrass
Our show is a new releases Bluegrass show.

Saturday Night Country *ABC*
PO Box 694 Townsville, QLD 4810 Australia
PH: +61-7-4722-3050 FX: 07-4722-3099
John Nutting snc@your.abc.net.au
www.abc.net.au/snc
Your gateway to the best in Australian Country music.

Slinga's Independent Country *WYN*
PO Box 4221 MDC, Hoppers Crossing,
VIC 3029 Australia
PH: 61-1-03-9742-1868 FX: 61-1-03-9742-1868
Tony Slinga slinga1@slinga.com
slinga.com
Indie Country music from all over the world!

Stone Cold Country *Yarra Valley FM*
85 Rathmullen Rd. Boronia, VIC 3155 Australia
PH: 61-0419-346230
Rod Bradey rod@austadhesives.com.au
Featuring mainly independent Country music artists.

New Zealand

Alison on WHP
Rural Delivery 9 D, Oamaru 8921, New Zealand
Alison Paulsen alip51@yahoo.co.uk
Please send music for airplay to the above address.

Best of Bluegrass *Radio Kidnappers*
PO Box 680, Hastings, New Zealand
PH: 06-876-6914 FX: 06-876-6914
Trevor Ruffell comus@xtra.co.nz
www.radiokidnappers.org.nz
Two hours of contemporary and Old-Time Bluegrass music.

New Zealand Country Music Network
PO Box 352, Stratford, Taranaki 4352 New Zealand
contact@countrymusic.net.nz
www.nzcountrymusic.net
We welcome CDs from most sources for air play on the five LPFM stations we currently operate in.

Dance and Electronic Radio

N o r t h   A m e r i c a

United States

1groovE.com
1groove@icebergradio.com
1groove.icebergradio.com
D n' B, Electronica, House etc.

Absolute Technoise Radio
www.technofor.us
Techno radio and online community.

Abstract Science *WLUW*
Kim Schlechter kim@abstractscience.net
abstractscience.net
Explores what we refer to as 'future music' - the constant evolution of modern Electronic music in its varied forms, to its roots in Funk, Jazz, Dub and Soul.

astralwerks Radio
A+R Dept. 104 W. 29ᵗʰ St. 4ᵗʰ Fl. New York,
NY 10001
a&r@astralwerks.net
www.astralwerks.com
Limit your demo to your 3 best tracks. Please, no phone calls!

BassDrive
info@bassdrive.com
www.bassdrive.com
The best of D n' B & Jungle music.

Beats in Space *WNYU*
194 Mercer Str. 5ᵗʰ Fl. New York, NY 10012
PH: 212-998-1660 FX: 212-998-1652
Tim Sweeney tim@beatsinspace.net
www.beatsinspace.net
The sounds you'll hear are not limited to one style.

Bentwave *WNYU*
Trent Wolbe trent@bentwave.org
www.bentwave.org
Brings the experimental side of Electronic music to radio in a format you can dance to.

ClubNetRadio.com
c/o Alden Gillespy, 6511-A Centerwalk Dr.
Winter Park, FL 32792-8319
www.clubnetradio.com
We are always accepting submissions by artists, DJs and record labels who would like us to review their material for possible airing on our station.

Beta Lounge Radio Show
1072 Illinois St., San Francisco, CA 94107
feedback@betalounge.com
www.betalounge.com
Send a sample of your material.

Darkside Radio Internet Program *(DRiP)*
PO Box 1905, Boulder, CO 80306
Stevyn stevyn@ironfeather.com
www.ironfeather.com
We welcome Dance & Electronica CDs, demos etc.

Dave's Lounge
daveslounge@gmail.com
www.daveslounge.com
A weekly podcast that showcases the best in Chillout, Trip Hop and Downtempo Electronica. If you make any of these styles of music e-mail your artist info and MP3 files (or links to MP3 files) to me.

Digitally Imported Radio
demos@di.fm
www.di.fm
E-mail to get submission instructions.

djmixed.com
BPM Magazine, 6725 Sunset Blvd. St. 320,
Los Angeles, CA 90028
PH: 310-360-7170 x107 FX: 310-360-7171
feedback@djmixed.com
www.djmixed.com
DJ culture and the Electronic music lifestyle.

dnbradio.com
info@dnbradio.com
www.dnbradio.com
D n' B, Jungle and Liquid Funk. If you would like to submit your work, please contact us.

dublab Radio
707 Ridgewood Pl #201, Los Angeles, CA 90038
support@dublab.com
www.dublab.com
Positive, Freeform music.

Future Breaks FM *KUSF*
2130 Fulton St., San Francisco, CA 94117
PH: 415-751-5873
dj PUSH djpush@futurebreaks.fm
www.futurebreaks.fm
21st Century Breakbeat music, pioneering Underground music and DJ culture on the airwaves.

Gruvsonic Dance Radio
720 Two Mile, Wisconsin Rapids, WI 54494
info@gruvsonic.com
www.gruvsonic.com
Willing to spin any Dance material via live mix shows.

The Hitchhiker's Dance Guide *WEVL*
518 S. Main Memphis, TN 38103
PH: 901-528-1990
prmmgr@wevl.org
www.wevl.org
Guest hosts present Progressive to Breaks, House to Trip Hop and just about everything in between.

Limbik Frequencies
320 E. Buffalo St. #605, Milwaukee, WI 53202
djsam@limbikfreq.com
www.limbikfreq.com
Our mix of Ambient, Downtempo, Ethereal, Industrial and intelligent Techno, is an active exploration into deep and uncharted modes of existence.

KNHC *Nathan Hale H.S.*
10750 30th Ave. NE., Seattle, WA 98125
PH: 206-421-8989 FX: 206-252-3805
www.c895fm.com
A recognized leader in Dance music.

LYME.fm
www.lyme.fm
Love your music everywhere!

Metropolis *KCRW*
1900 Pico Blvd. Santa Monica, CA 90405
PH: 310-450-5183 FX: 310-450-7172
Jason Bentley metroweb@kcrw.org
www.kcrw.org/show/mt
The hypnotic pulse of modern city life.

milk.audio
gani@milkaudio.com
www.milkaudio.com
If you would like to send CDs or vinyl, e-mail me.

Mixin' It Up
DJ Baddog djbaddog@mixinitup.com
www.myspace.com/djbaddog
A showcase for signed & unsigned artists alike. Latin beats & rhythms, Hip Hop, Dance, House, Club music & all its many genres.

Modsnap Radio *KSYM*
724 E. Grayson, San Antonio, TX 78208-1015
PH: 210-473-3377
Cornflakes cornflakes@modsnap.com
modsnap.com/audio.htm
Trance - Progressive - Bossa Nova - Downtempo.

Phuture Frequency Radio
www.pfradio.com
Online music community & D n' B radio station.

Proton Radio
Jay Epoch jason@protonradio.com
www.protonradio.com
The internet's gold standard for underground Dance music. Visit our site for submission details.

SectionZ Radio
Joshua 'Z' Hernandez, 2513 W. Superior St. 1st Fl. Chicago, IL 60612
www.sectionz.com
We have a bunch of different DJs hand picking the tracks for the wirewaves. Upload all the tracks you want and get feedback from thousands of other artists.

The "So Very" Show *KTUH*
Honolulu, Hemenway Hall #203, 2445 Campus Rd. Honolulu, HI 96822.
PH: 808-956-7261 FX: 808-956-5271
Ms. Angel thesoveryshow@gmail.com
ktuh.org/sovery
Groove to the sounds of Deep House.

Sovereign Glory! *KDHX*
3504 Magnolia St. Louis, MO 63118
PH: 314-664-3688 FX: 314-664-1020
Li'l Edit sovereignglory@kdhx.org
www.kdhx.org/programs/sovereignglory.htm
Li'l Edit spins beat music live without a net.

Streetbeat *WNUR*
1920 Campus Dr. Evanston, IL 60208-2280
PH: 847-866-9687 FX: 847-467-2058
streetbeat-md@wnur.org
streetbeat.wnur.org
Dance music that doesn't get exposure elsewhere.

Technodrome *KUCI*
PO Box 4362, Irvine, CA 92616-4362
www.technodromeweb.com
Trance, Techno, Electronica, House, Progressive etc.

Technomusic.com Radio
www.technomusic.com
Broadcasting live DJ Mixes, 24/7. Also does music reviews.

Trance Lab Radio
DJ Lord Bass lordbass@trancelab.com
www.trancelab.com
Podcast featuring new flavors of German Tech-House, Glitch and fuzzy Electro grooves with an interest in exposing new music and dusting off old cuts.

The Underground Sounds Show *KTUH*
PO Box 12073, Honolulu, HI 96828-1073
PH: 808-591-3500
info@double-o-spot.com
www.double-o-spot.com
The hottest and latest Dance tracks with a mix of past recordings, combining House, Trance, D n' B, Trip Hop etc.

Universal Vibes
info@universalvibes.com
www.universalvibes.com
Hosts a variety of shows. Has interviews and guest DJs.

Untamed Tongues Poetry Lounge Radio Show
7575 W. Washington Ave. #127-171 Las Vegas, NV 89128
PH: 702-644-4688 FX: 702-474-4688
www.untamedtongues.com
The right blend of music and Spoken Word. We feature Neo-Soul, Jazz, Hip Hop and Funk fusions.

VoyagerRadio
547 Gayley Ave. #1, Los Angeles, CA 90024
Harold J. Johnson voyagerradio@gmail.com
www.voyagerradio.com
The only internet radio station in the known universe webcasting Downtempo from outer space. Send your demos to the above address.

WMPH *Mt. Pleasant H.S.*
5201 Washington St. Ext. Wilmington, DE 19809
PH: 302-762-7199 FX: 302-762-7042
www.wmph.org
We accept Indie releases.

XTC Radio
2508 Constance St., Atlanta, GA 30344
www.xtcradio.com
Trance, Hard and Acid Trance etc.

ZM Radio *KUCI*
PO Box 4362, Irvine, CA 92616
PH: 949-824-6868
Ziba ziba@kuci.org
www.myspace.com/zmradio
Dance dance dance to the radio!

Canada

The Groove *CKCU*
Rm. 517 U. Ctr. 1125 Colonel By Dr. Ottawa, ON K1S 5B6
PH: 613-520-2898
Elorius Cain music@ckcufm.com
www.ckcufm.com
Canada's longest running Disco show playing every variation.

Higher Ground *CIUT*
Jason Palma jasonpalma@rogers.com
www.highergroundradio.com
Along with the music I love, we also feature information on upcoming events.

Radio Free Polygon *CKDU*
Dalhousie Stud. Union Bldg. 6136 U. Ave. Halifax, NS B3H 4J2
PH: 902-494-6479
radiofreepolygon@gmail.com
www.radiofreepolygon.net
Focusing on the local and international Indie Electronic music scene.

Techno Prisoners
DJ Tykx tykxboy@hotmail.com
www.techno-prisoners.com
Techno, Hard House and Electronica.

Tongue and Groove *CKUA*
10526 Jasper Ave. Edmonton, AB T5J 1Z7
PH: 780-428-7595 FX: 780-428-7624
Kevin Wilson kevin.wilson@ckua.org
www.ckua.com
Oasis of everything that grooves.

Tuned In Radio *The New Rhythm Of The Nation*
68 Walmer Rd. Richmond Hill, ON L4C 3X1
PH: 905-883-5773 FX: 905-883-4337
tunedin@tunedinradio.com
www.tunedinradio.com
Always looking for 'radio friendly' recording artists to interview.

South America

Grooveland
R. Dr. Jorge Winther - 736, AP.22, Centro - Taubaté,
São Paulo - Brazil
PH: 12010-150
grooveland@grooveland.com.br
www.grooveland.com.br
*Nujazz, broken beat, Brazilian music, Latin & Afro
beats, Deep Jazz and soulful House.*

Europe

Belgium

Beyondjazz Radio Show
Lange Boomgaardstraat 114a, b9000 Gent, Belgium
Jurriaan Persyn office@beyondjazz.net
www.beyondjazz.net
*We play, review and discuss on the show whatever
we like and love. Broken Beats, Future Jazz, Space
Funk ...*

Grimelock
grimelock@boup.com
grimelock.com
*Podcast with nasty mixes and tunes from the best
Grime and Dubstep producers!*

Denmark

beats.dk
PH: 45-702-334-56
info@beats.dk
www.beats.dk
A funky LIVE and on demand musical website.

France

Galaxie Radio
BP 21-59392 Wattrelos, France
PH: 03-20-83-57-57 FX: 03-20-75-09-87
info@galaxiefm.com
www.galaxiefm.com

MaXXima
contact@maxxima.org
www.maxxima.org
*Electronic, NuJazz, Lounge, Downtemp,
DeepHouse, House, TekHouse ...*

Radio FG Paris
PH: 0892-69-1000
team@radiofg.com
www.radiofg.com
Broadcasting a variety of Dance music shows.

Radio Nova
33, rue du Faubourg Saint Antoine, 75011 Paris,
France
PH: 01-53-33-33-15
radionova@radionova.com
www.novaplanet.com
*Broadcasting on various stations throughout
France.*

Germany

Back to the Basics
NDR, Rothenbaumchaussee 132 20149 Hamburg,
Germany
PH: 040-41-56-2788 FX: 040-41-56-3018
web@vinylizer.net
www.vinylizer.net
*Presents new releases and exclusively recorded
sessions by DJs from all over the world.*

Klub Radio
Caseler Str. 4A, 13088 Berlin, Germany
PH: 030-27-59-60-41
kontakt@klubradio.de
www.klubradio.de
*Brings you the worlds best DJs live from the best
clubs in Germany.*

Nova Radio
Postbox 40 13 51, 80713 Munich, Germany
PH: 089-3715645-67 FX: 089-3715645-27
www.novaradio.de
Club sound network.

Radio Quintessenz
Lörenskogstr. 4, 85748 München/Garching,
Germany
PH: +49 (0)89-24408713 FX: +49 (0)89-24408712
Wolfgang Droszczack wolfgang@quintessenz-
muenchen.de
www.quintessenz-muenchen.de
*Videostream of Electronic music live in the Mix.
Party.*

Techno Paradise FM
Quedlinburger Str.30, PLZ: 12627 Berlin, Germany
PH: +49-030-240-33-171 FX: +49-030-240-33-170
info@technoparadise.fm
www.technoparadise.fm
Dance, Trance, Techno, Hardstyle ...

The Netherlands

Radio X-Clusief
Reepstraat 33, 2583 XG 'S-Gravenhage,
The Netherlands
PH: +316-12136870
info@exclusieffm.nl
www.exclusieffm.nl
The #1 Trance-station of the Hague.

Switzerland

Basic.ch
Boulevard St-Georges 21 PO Box 166, CH1211
Geneva 8, Switzerland
PH: 41 22 800 22 32 FX: 41 22 800 22 33
basic@basic.ch
live.basic.ch
Covering quality Electronic music and more.

lounge-radio.com
Haegelerstrasse 75, CH-5400 Baden, Switzerland
PH: 0041-79-681-73-92
Thomas Zumbrunnen dj@lounge-radio.com
www.lounge-radio.com
*Fresh beats of NuJazz - dipped with a smile of
Brazil and served with a breath of Ambient. We play
lot of stuff from independent artists.*

Radio Couleur 3
Av. du Temple 40, Case Postale 78, CH-1010
Lausanne, Switzerland
PH: +41-21-318-15-42
www.couleur3.ch

SwissGroove
Spyristrasse 48, CH 8044 Zürich, Switzerland
Patrik Jungo mail@swissgroove.ch
swissgroove.ch
*Our sound is a mix of Acid, Nu, Smooth-Jazz, Trip
Hop, Funk, Soul, R&B, Lounge & Latin.*

United Kingdom

B2B Radio
PO Box 41, Tipton, DY4 7YT UK
PH: +44 (0) 7946-768-278
JB & Spice back2basicsrecordings@hotmail.com
www.back2basicsrecords.com
The best in up front D n' B.

BBC Radio 1 *Dance Music*
www.bbc.co.uk/radio1/dance
*Home page of the BBC Radio 1's various Dance
music shows. Info, shows, contacts etc.*

BBC Radio 1xtra *Drum & Bass*
www.bbc.co.uk/1xtra/drumbass
*Home page of the BBC 1xtra's various D n' B
shows. Info, shows, contacts etc.*

BBC Radio 1xtra *Garage*
www.bbc.co.uk/1xtra/garage
*Home page of the BBC 1xtra's various Garage
shows. Info, shows, contacts etc.*

Breaks FM
www.breaksfm.com
*Playing host to the worlds leading breaks DJs/labels
& artists.*

freakin
freakininfo@gmail.com
www.freakin.org
Underground House music.

lukashopwood.co.uk
Lukas Hopwood lukas@lukashopwood.co.uk
www.lukashopwood.co.uk
*Podcast featuring mixes of old/new,
Pop/Underground.*

ministryofsound radio
103 Gaunt St., London, SE1 6DP UK
PH: 44-0-20-7740-8600 FX: 44-0-20-7403-5348
label@ministryofsound.com
www.ministryofsound.com/radio
The biggest digital dance floor on the planet.

Power FM
68 Parkwest Enterprise Ctr. Dublin 12 Ireland
PH: 353-76-6700883 FX: 353-16296085
info@powerfm.org
www.powerfm.org
Streaming live Dance music from Dublin.

Radio Magnetic
Argyle House, 16 Argyle Ct. 1103 Argyle St.,
Glasgow, Scotland, G3 8ND
PH: 44-141-226-8808 FX: 44-141-226-8818
studio@radiomagnetic.com
www.radiomagnetic.com
Covers the UK and Scottish Dance music scenes.

UK Rumble
info@ukrumble.com
www.ukrumble.com
Webcasting a varied style of Dance music.

UrbanBreakzFM.com
3 Bolshaw Close, Leighton, Crewe, Cheshire,
CW1 3WX UK
PH: 07969-164390
www.urbanbreakzfm.com
*Playing a whole spectrum of music from Funky
House to Speed Garage.*

Vibe FM
www.vibefm.co.uk
England's #1 Dance music radio station.

Australia

Australian Underground Dance Station
Ison Live Radio, PO Box 532, Newcastle,
NSW 2300 Australia
PH: 6102-49270290 FX: 6102-49270290
Sean Ison info@isonliveradio.com
www.isonliveradio.com
*Underground Dance music from all around the
world!*

Fresh FM
Unit Level 2, 230 Angas St., Adelaide,
SA 5000 Australia
PH: 08-8232-7927 FX: 08-8224-0922
reception@freshfm.com.au
www.freshfm.com.au
The rhythm of Adelaide's youth.

In the Mix Podcast
PO Box 1964, Strawberry Hills, NSW 2012
Australia
PH: 02-9282-4000 FX: 02-9282-4099
www.inthemix.com.au/podcast
Features cutting edge Dance music tracks.

Mix Up
PO Box 9994, Sydney, NSW 2001 Australia
www.abc.net.au/triplej/mixup/default.htm
*Grab your clubbin' outfit, your water bottle and
jump into your fav dancing shoes.*

PsyKe Out
www.psykeout.net
All the very best and latest Psy-Trance.

Spraci
PH: 61-0-402-605-188 FX: 1-603-691-5915
support@spraci.com
spraci.cia.com.au
*An extensive list of weekly Dance music radio shows
heard around the Sydney area.*

Experimental Radio

North America

United States

420 Train Wreck
Rocksanne@420TrainWreck.com
www.420trainwreck.com
Psychedelic, Stoner Rock, Space & Heavy Groove.

Aural Innovations SpaceRock Radio
1364 W. 7th Ave. Ste. B, Columbus, OH 43212
jkranitz@aural-innovations.com
www.aural-innovations.com/radio/radio.html
*Space Rock, Psychedelia and eclectic forms of
Progressive Rock.*

Blue Distortion Podcast
www.bluedistortion.com
*Dedicated to Experimental and Underground music
and artwork. Send us a link to your MP3.*

Bohemian Radio
BohemianRadio@comcast.net
www.bohemianradio.com
*An eclectic selection of Electronic music, mixed in
with Sci-Fi tunes.*

Cyberage Radio *KUNM*
237 Cagua NE., Albuquerque, NM 87108
PH: 505-277-5615
Tommy T tommyt@dsbp.cx
www.cyberage.cx
Electronic music and Underground sounds.

Dr. Demento On the Net
PO Box 884, Culver City, CA 90232
DrDemento@drDemento.com
www.drdemento.com
*Mad music and crazy comedy heard on over 100
stations coast to coast. It's a free-wheeling
unpredictable mix of music and comedy.*

Electronic Periodic Podcast
www.electronicperiodic.com
*Mixes and live recordings of Ambient, IDM, Electro,
Trance and Experimental music. Fill out our online
submission form.*

Esoterica *WQNA*
PO 1233, Springfield, IL 62705
PH: 217-528-8466
Ted Keylon eted@blowingthewhistle.org
www.thespectra.net/esoterica
Experimental, Electronica, unsigned and unusual.

Galactic Travels *WDIY*
PO Box 632, Nazareth, PA 18064-0632
Bill Y. Fox billyfox@soundscapes.us
wdiy.org/programs/gt
*An Electronic, Ambient, Progressive and Space
music show. Inquire by e-mail before submitting
music! I just want to make sure your music is one of
the above genres.*

The Greatest Show From Earth *WWUH*
Attn: Music Director, 200 Bloomfield Ave. West
Hartford, CT 06117
PH: 860-768-4701 FX: 860-768-5701
Mark DeLorenzo teltanman@cox.net
www.teltan.org
*Focuses on Psychedelic, Electronic and Progressive
music.*

marvin suicide podcast
marvin@marvinsuicide.org
marvinsuicide.org
*Do you like the smell of goats? Spend every day
thinking about fun? Don't like using public toilets?
Then try listening our 30 minutes of eclectic music.*

Music For Nimrods *KXLU*
1 LMU Dr. Los Angeles, CA 90045
PH: 310-338-5958 FX: 310-338-5959
Reverend Dan ReverendDan@Hotmail.com
www.musicfornimrods.net
Looking for degenerate music of all styles.

The Musical Transportation Spree *KFAI*
316 Hennepin Ave. #300, Minneapolis, MN 55414
Chris Waterbury mts@mtsradio.com
www.mtsradio.com
We prefer home recordings.

New Dreamers *KLCC*
Lane College 4000 E. 30th Ave. Eugene,
OR 97405-0640
PH: 541-726-2212 FX: 541-744-3962
Kent Willocks klcc@lanecc.edu
www.klcc.org
*Electronic and Synthesized sounds from this world
and beyond. The full spectrum of Electronic music,
from Classical to Progressive Rock, Avant-garde to
Spacemusic.*

No Pigeon Holes Radio Show *KKUP*
933 Monroe St., PMB 9150, Santa Clara, CA 95050
PH: 408-260-2999
Don Campau campaudj@jps.net
lonelywhistle.tripod.com/playlists
I accept all styles of music for airplay.

Other Music *KZUM*
941 "O" St., Lincoln, NE 68508
PH: 402-474-5086 FX: 402-474-5091
Thad, Erik, Malcom & Jeff om_kzum@yahoo.com
www.kzum.org
*We mostly delve into Experimental types of Jazz,
Electronica, Rock, Spoken Word and Freeform
Improvisation.*

Press the Button *WRUW*
11220 Bellflower Rd. Cleveland, OH 44106
PH: 216-368-2208 FX: 216-368-5414
info@pressthebutton.com
pressthebutton.com
An Experimental radio show of found sound collage.

Psych-Out *WREK*
350 Ferst Dr. NW. #2224, Atlanta, GA 30332-0630
PH: 404-894-2468 FX: 404-894-6872
oncomouse@gmail.com
www.wrek.org
*Specializing in the best Psychedelic music from
around the globe.*

Pushing The Envelope *WHUS*
1501 Storrs Rd. Storrs, CT 06269-3008
PH: 860-429-9487
Joel Krutt whus.musicdirector@gmail.com
www.whus.org
The finest in Avant Ephemera.

Some Assembly Required
3010 Hennepin Ave. S. #145, Minneapolis,
MN 55408
PH: 612-990-0460
Jon Nelson assembly@detritus.net
www.some-assembly-required.net
*Focuses exclusively on "tape manipulations, digital
deconstruction and turntable creations."*

Something Else *WLUW*
PO Box 667, Chicago, IL 60690
PH: 773-508-8080 FX: 773-508-8082
Philip von Zweck somethingelse@wluw.org
www.wluw.org
*A weekly radio program of Sound Art & New/
Experimental music.*

Spartacus Roosevelt Podcast
Spartacus spartacus@spartacusroosevelt.com
www.spartacusroosevelt.com/podcast.php
*Obscure Noise, glitchy Electropop, fake nostalgia,
bastardized Exotica, tweaky Lounge, creepy Ambient
and musical non sequitors.*

Strange Music in Small Doses
inkxpotter.libsyn.com
*Podcast featuring a three cut collision to the avant
extremes of sound.*

Transfigured Night *WKCR*
2920 Broadway Mailcode 2612, New York,
NY 10027
PH: 212-854-9920
newmusic@wkcr.org
www.wkcr.org
*An overnight exploration of Experimental music,
with an emphasis on Electronic works*

Ultra Radio *KVMR*
401 Spring St., Nevada City, CA 95959
PH: 530-265-9555 FX: 530-265-9077
Kevin Kormylo ultraradio@kvmr.org
www.ultraradio.org
Bringing new music, sound sculptures and rarely heard recordings together into a seamless flow of electrifying radio experience.

Weirdsville!
PO Box 936, Northampton, MA 01061
weirdo@weirdsville.com
www.weirdsville.com
We are constantly on the hunt for strange, bizarre and righteous music to blow your minds.

Canada

Adventures In Plasticland *CKWR*
19 Norfolk Ave. Cambridge, ON N1R 3T5
Spaceman Stan spacedman40@hotmail.com
www.romislokus.com/eng/stan.html
Progressive, Acid, Stoner, Psychedelic, Garage, Indie and Rock music of the 60's up to now.

Brave New Waves Radio Show *CBC*
PO Box 6000, Montreal, QC H3C 3A8
PH: 514-597-5923
Patti Schmidt bnw@cbc.ca
www.bravenewwaves.ca
Anything from Indie Rock to Dance, Experimental Electronic and more.

Cranial Explosions: Sounds That Blow Minds! *CJTR*
PO Box 334 Stn. Main, Regina, SK S4P 3A1
PH: 306-525-7274 FX: 306-525-9741
kcolhoun@cjtr.ca
www.cjtr.ca
Submit your impacting music to us and if it moves us, we will play it on our show!!

Do Not Touch This Amp *CFBX*
House 8, U. College of the Cariboo, 900 McGill Rd.
Kamloops, BC V2C 5N3
PH: 250-377-3988 FX: 250-372-5055
Steve Marlow dntta@yahoo.ca
www.geocities.com/dntta
An Experimental/Electronic/Industrial program that runs every Friday night.

Le Navire Night
navire@radio-canada.ca
radio-canada.ca/radio/navire
Electro-Acoustique, expérimentation.

Two New Hours *CBC*
PO Box 500, Stn. A Toronto, ON M5W 1E6
PH: 416-205-8577 FX: 416-205-6040
www.radio.cbc.ca/programs/2newhours
We're always interested in discovering new composers. Hosted by Larry Lake.

Europe
Germany

Radio Future 2
RadioFuture2@t-online.de
www.radiofuture2.purespace.de
Electro, Industrial, Crossover, Darkwave...

The Netherlands

MeMbus
info@membus.nl
www.membus.nl
Podcast featuring Soundscapes, Rough Radio, Tape Distortion.

United Kingdom

BBC Radio 3 *New Music*
www.bbc.co.uk/radio3/newmusic
Home page of the BBC Radio 3's various New Music shows. Info, shows, contacts etc.

Flat four radio
14 Torrington Park, London, N12 9SS UK
dan@flatfourradio.co.uk
www.mcld.co.uk/flatfour
We broadcast Indie and Experimental music. We like to support independent-minded artists - so send us your stuff!

Resonance FM
9 Denmark St., London, WC2H 8LS UK
PH: 020-7836-3664
Ed Baxter info@resonancefm.com
www.resonancefm.com
Radio art station, brought to you by London Musicians' Collective.

Xfm Dublin
PO Box 200, Dublin 1, Ireland UK
www.xfmdublin.com

Australia

Sound Quality *ABC*
PO Box 9994, Canberra, Australia
PH: 02-8333-2051 FX: 02-8333-1381
www.abc.net.au/rn/music/soundqlt
Host Tim Ritchie presents the interesting, the evolutionary, the inaccessible and the wonderful.

Folk Radio
North America
United States

Internet, Syndicated Shows and Podcasts

Acoustic Café
PO Box 7730, Ann Arbor, MI 48107-7730
Rob Reinhart rob@acafe.com
www.acafe.com
Rare Acoustic cuts and classic tracks with a strong commitment to Indies. Heard on 60+ stations.

Acoustic Pie Radio
Kelley Martin kelley@acousticpie.com
www.acousticpie.com/Radio.htm
Devoted to Acoustic Singer/Songwriters.

Art of the Song
PO Box 2913, Taos, NM 87571
John & Viv jv@johnandviv.com
www.artofthesong.org
Syndicated show with music and interviews exploring inspiration and creativity through songwriting and other art forms.

Celtic Music News Podcast
www.celticmusicnews.com
From Celtic Rock to very mellow relaxed Celtic music.

The Folk Sampler
PO Box 520, Siloam Springs, AR 72761
Mike Flynn mike@folksampler.com
www.folksampler.com
Folk, Traditional, Bluegrass and Blues.

FolkScene
PO Box 707, Woodland Hills, CA 91365
PH: 818-883-7557
Roz & Howard folkscene@folkscene.com
www.folkscene.com
Live music, interviews and remote recordings.

GidaFOLK
multithd@hotmail.com
gida.tzo.net/RadioDB
Playing whatever sounds good.

Grassy Hill Radio
c/o Submissions Mgr., PO Box 160, Lyme, CT 06371
radio@grassyhill.org
radio.grassyhill.org
Streaming lesser known/self released songs.

Highlander Radio
www.CelticRadio.net
Scottish, Irish and Celtic music.

Hober Radio
PO Box 5748, Takoma Park, MD 20913
PH: 301-270-1734
hober.com
An attempt to bring human warmth to the computer environment. Hober brings unvarnished sounds into a glossy space.

Internet Folk Festival
PO Box 331173, Elmwood, CT 06133-1173
feedback@internetfolkfestival.com
www.internetfolkfestival.com
Send your CDs and information to us.

Online Folk Festival
580 E. Town St. #101, Columbus, OH 43215
PH: 614-224-2906
Greg Grant greg@onlinefolkfestival.com
www.onlinefolkfestival.com
Freeform Folk and Folk related music.

radiowayne
PO Box 17742, Shreveport, LA 71138
Wayne Greene radiowayne@att.net
www.radiowayne.com
An eclectic mix of Folk, Singer/Songwriter, Acoustic, Swing and more.

Renradio
800 W. Basse Rd. #109, San Antonio, TX 78212
Michael Harris rengeek@renradio.com
renradio.com
The music and spirit of Renaissance and Celtic Festivals.

Singer Magazine's Indie Artists Showcase
PO Box 1288, Harrisburg, VA 22803
Greg Tutwiler greg@singermagazine.com
www.live365.com/stations/singermagazine
The voice of the independent musician and songwriter. It's the new American music revolution!

Songs to Hang on Stars *XM*
1325 Corcoran St. NW., Washington, DC 20009
Mary Sue Twohy
marysue@songstohangonstars.com
songstohangonstars.com
The best songs of the contemporary Folk scene.

Whole Wheat Radio
PO Box 872 H St., Talkeetna, AK 99676
www.wholewheatradio.org
We focus on independent music. Do not ask if you can send your music – JUST SEND IT!

Woodsongs Old-Time Radio Hour
PO Box 200, Lexington, KY 40588
Attn: Submissions
FX: 859-225-4020
radio@woodsongs.com
www.woodsongs.com/wotrh.html
Exploring the beautiful world of Folk, Bluegrass and Songwriting. Submit TWO CDs and a press kit with a brief cover letter.

Your Folk Connection *KRCU*
1 U. Plaza, Cape Girardeau, MO 63701
PH: 573-651-5070 FX: 888-651-5070
comments@yourfolkconnection.org
www.yourfolkconnection.org
Folk artists, performers and songwriters.

Alaska

Acoustic Accents
PO Box 89, Tok, AK 99780
Bud Johnson info@acousticaccents.net
www.acousticaccents.net
In-depth interviews and songs from some of the best performers around.

It's All Folk *KEUL*
PO Box 29, Girdwood, AK 99587
PH: 907 754-2489
Karen Rakos keulkaren@hotmail.com
www.glaciercity.us
I play Folk, Roots, Bluegrass and Old-Time music.

Arkansas

From Albion and Beyond *KUAR*
2801 S. University, Little Rock, AR 72204
PH: 501-569-8485 FX: 501-569-8488
Len Horton lholton@swbell.net
home.swbell.net/lholton/fromalbionandbeyond.html
Traditional, revival and contemporary Folk music.

California

A Patchwork Quilt *KALW*
500 Mansell St., San Francisco, CA 94134
PH: 415-841-4121 FX: 415-841-4125
Kevin Vance kevin_vance@yahoo.com
www.kalw.org
A program of Celtic and other traditional music.

Celtic Quest
6872 Panamint Row #4, San Diego, CA 92139
PH: 619-475-4484
Doug Shaw info@celticquest.info
www.celticquest.info
Playing traditional and contemporary music from Scotland, Ireland, other Celtic regions of the world.

Cool As Folk *KDVS*
14 Lower Freeborn Hall, UC, Davis, CA 95616
PH: 530-752-0728
Michael Leahy coolasfolk@hotmail.com
www.coolasfolk.com
Folk, Bluegrass, Americana, Indie Singer/ Songwriter and other Acoustic based music. I also welcome weekly in-studio guests.

Desert Highway Radio
1015 Gayley Ave. #1115, Los Angeles, CA 90024
info@deserthighwayrecords.com
deserthighwayradio.com
Features Roots music (Blues, Folk Rock, Rock, Country, Gospel, or any combination of these terms).

Don't Get Trouble on Your Mind *KMUD*
PO Box 135, 1144 Redway Dr. Redway,
CA 95560-0135
PH: 707-923-2513 FX: 707-923-2501
Ed Denson md@kmud.org
www.kmud.org
Each show I play 25 or so Folk and Blues songs.

Don't Panic (It's Just Us Folks) *KKUP*
933 Monroe St., PMB 9150, Santa Clara, CA 95050
PH: 408-260-2999
Lisa Atkinson latkinson@rcn.com
www.kkup.com
Folk, Country, Bluegrass, Irish and Blues.

Folk Music & Beyond *KALW*
500 Mansell St., San Francisco, CA 94134
PH: 415-841-4121 FX: 415-841-4125
JoAnn & Bob kalwfolk@rahul.net
www.kalwfolk.org
Folk, traditional and original music.

Folk Roots *KSBR*
34031 Calle de Bonanza, #1, San Juan Capistrano,
CA 92675
Marshall Andrews tomarshall@aol.com
www.ksbr.net
A wide range of Bluegrass, Old-Time, Celtic, Gospel and Folk.

KPIG
1110 Main St. #16, Watsonville, CA 95076
PH: 831-722-9000
sty@kpig.com
www.kpig.com
Great music and serious fun - Folk, Rock, Acoustic, Roots, Blues.

Heaven's Bar 'n Grill *KZSC*
1156 High St., Santa Cruz, CA 95064
PH: 831-459-5972 FX: 831-459-4734
Clytia Fuller clytia@cruzio.com
members.cruzio.com/~clytia
Showcases live guests playing in the area.

Music Along The Feather *KRBS*
PO Box 9, Oroville, CA 95965
PH: 530-534-1200
Erv krbs@cncnet.com
www.radiobirdstreet.org
Contemporary Folk. Bluegrass, Country and new Folk.

Music Without Boundaries *91X*
PO Box 60427, San Diego, CA 92166
PH: 619-226-1174 FX: 619-226-1181
Kenny Weissberg otissing@aol.com
members.aol.com/mwb98
Healthy doses of R&B, Folk, Blues, Gospel and more.

Nevada City Limits *KVMR*
401 Spring St., Nevada City, CA 95959
PH: 530-265-9555 FX: 530-265-9077
Dennis Brunnenmeyer dennisb@kvmr.org
www.kvmr.org
Americana and Folk with occasional journeying into Celtic, Old-Time & Bluegrass. Please send 2 CDs.

New Brick Road *KVMR*
401 Spring St., Nevada City, CA 95959
PH: 530-265-9555 FX: 530-265-9077
Laurie DesJardins lauriedj@pacbell.net
www.kvmr.org
Contemporary and traditional Folk music.

New Wood *KKUP*
933 Monroe St., PMB 9150, Santa Clara, CA 95050
PH: 408-260-2999
Peter Schwarz schwarz@almaden.ibm.com
www.kkup.com
American, Celtic and Bluegrass. Find your roots.

Ordinary Town Folk Show *KFOK*
PO Box 462, Garden Valley, CA 95633
PH: 530-333-4300
Cindy Hayden cindy@qnoteproductions.com
www.kfok.org
Featuring traditional and contemporary Folk, Americana, Bluegrass, & Celtic music.

Wild River Radio *KMUD*
PO Box 135, 1144 Redway Dr. Redway,
CA 95560-0135
PH: 707-923-2513 FX: 707-923-2501
Kate Klein md@kmud.org
www.kmud.org
Sometimes you can hear independent Folk artists. Looking for songs promoting social justice.

Colorado

The Folk Show *KRFC*
619 S. College Ave. #4, Fort Collins, CO 80524
PH: 970-221-5065
Leonard Epstein lsepstein2@aol.com
krfcfm.org
Send your music in!

Connecticut

AcousticConnections *WSHU*
5151 Park Ave. Fairfield, CT 06825
PH: 203-365-6604
Walt Graham graham@wshu.org
www.wshu.org
Acoustic music, Folk, Celtic and Bluegrass.

Caterwaul *WWUH*
Attn: Music Director, 200 Bloomfield Ave. West
Hartford, CT 06117
PH: 860-768-4701 FX: 860-768-5701
Ed McKeon emckeon@aol.com
www.wwuh.org
The "Father" of the Folk Next Door concert series. Our most unusually progressive and eclectic Folk show.

Harmony Junction *WKZE*
Oblong Books & Music, PO Box 482, Rhinebeck,
NY 12572
Dick Hermans dickhermans@taconic.net
www.wkze.com
Review and promotional copies are welcomed. Please send to the above address.

Profiles in Folk *WSHU*
5151 Park Ave. Fairfield, CT 06825-1000
PH: 203-330-6203 FX: 203-365-0425
Steve Winters winters@wshu.org
wshuweb.wshu.org/profiles/prindex.php
Traditional and Celtic Folk with Bluegrass.

Sunday Night Folk Festival
Box U-3008, U. Connecticut, Storrs,
CT 06269-3008
PH: 860-429-9487
Susan Forbes Hansen flkczarina@aol.com
whus.org

Florida

Acoustic Highways *WPRK*
4041 Lake Forest, Mount Dora, FL 32757
PH: 407-646-2915 FX: 407-646-1560
Rich Pietrzak rapietrzak@hotmail.com
www.rollins.edu/wprk
A free-wheeling show devoted to bringing Folk music, performing songwriters and other guitar-based acoustic music to the airwaves.

Folk & Acoustic Music *WLRN*
172 NE. 15th St., Miami, FL 33132
PH: 305-995-2207 FX: 305-995-2299
Michael Stock mstock@wlrn.org
www.wlrn.org/radio/folkacoustic
Playing songs ignored by other stations.

Folk, Bluegrass and More *WFIT*
150 W. University Blvd. Melbourne, FL 32901-6975
PH: 321-674-8140 FX: 321-674-8139
Bill Stuart ukidnme@aol.com
www.wfit.org
Weekly Acoustic music show.

Georgia

Fox's Minstrel Show
182 Elizabeth St. NE., Atlanta, GA 30307
Harlon Joye sheartfiel@aol.com
www.wrfg.org
A mixture of Folk, Blues, Country, some Rock and even some early Jazz.

Green Island Radio Show *WSVH*
12 Ocean Science Cir. Savannah, GA 31411
PH: 912-598-3300 FX: 912-598-3306
Harry O'Donoghue wsvhirish@earthlink.net.
www.wsvh.org/giarchive.htm
The very best Irish and Celtic music.

Illinois

Celtic Connections *WSIU*
Southern Illinois U. Carbondale, IL 62901-6602
PH: 618-453-1884
Bryan Kelso Crow bcrow@siu.edu
www.celticconnectionsradio.org
The finest selections from new releases.

Continental Drift *WNUR*
1920 Campus Dr. Evanston, IL 60208-2280
PH: 847-491-7102 FX: 847-467-2058
Raysh Weiss drift-producer@wnur.org
www.wnur.org/drift
Roots and Folk music of cultures around the world.

Folk Fiasco *WDBX*
224 N. Washington St., Carbondale, IL 62901
PH: 618-529-5900 FX: 618-529-5900
Randy Auxier drauxier@yahoo.com
www.wdbx.org
Weekly Singer/Songwriter show.

Midnight Special *WFMT*
PO Box 58, Mahomet, IL 61853
PH: 773-509-1111
www.midnightspecial.org
Host Rich Warren presents Folk music with a sense of humor.

Somebody Else's Troubles *WLUW*
1137 Noyes St., Evanston, IL 60201
PH: 847-475-1615,
Tom Jackson musicdept@wluw.org
www.wluw.org
Open to all kinds of Acoustic music.

Indiana

The Back Porch *WVPE*
2424 California Rd. Elkhart, IN 46514
PH: 888-399-9873
Norm Mast nmast@wvpe.org
www.wvpe.org/backporch.html
The best of Folk and Bluegrass.

Crossings *WGCS*
1700 S. Main St., Goshen, IN 46526
PH: 574-535-7488 FX: 574-535-7293
globe@goshen.edu
www.goshen.edu/wgcs
Folk music show, 10 years strong. Features live in studio performances.

Roots For Breakfast *WFHB*
PO Box 1973, Bloomington, IN 47402
Mark Richardson polskacat@hotmail.com
www.wfhb.org
The usual assortment of Old-Time, Blues, Alt-Country, Bluegrass and Folk songs/tunes are played.

Iowa

KUNI's Folk Music
U. Northern Iowa, Cedar Falls, IA 50614-0359
PH: 319-273-6400 FX: 319-273-2682
www.kuniradio.org/kufolk.html
Traditional and contemporary Acoustic music.

Louisiana

Hootenanny Power *WRKF*
3050 Valley Creek Dr. Baton Rouge, LA 70808
Taylor Caffery tlcaffery@yahoo.com
www.hootenannypower.com
Folk and Acoustic music.

Maine

Us Folk *WMPG*
96 Falmouth St., Portland, ME 04104-9300
PH: 207-780-4909
Chris ctdarlin@maine.rr.com
www.wmpg.org
Promotes independent Folk artists from around the world.

Maryland

Detour *WTMD*
Towson U. 8000 York Rd. Towson, MD 21252
Paul Hartman wtmd@towson.edu
www.charm.net/~dirtylin/detour.html
An eclectic blend of Folk and World music.

Just Folks *WSCL*
PO Box 2596, Salisbury, MD 21802
PH: 410-543-6895 FX: 410-548-3000
John Kalb jdkalb@salisbury.edu
www.wscl.org
Contemporary Folk music (mostly Acoustic).

Roots and Wings *WMUC*
3130 S. Campus Dining Hall, College Park, MD 20742-8431
PH: 301-314-7868
John McLaughlin john-mclaughlin@comcast.net
thedigitalfolklife.org
Folk and Bluegrass.

Massachusetts

A Celtic Sojourn *WGBH*
125 Western Ave. Boston, MA 02134
PH: 617-300-4415
Alice Abraham alice_j_abraham@wgbh.org
www.wgbh.org
Traditional and contemporary music from the Celtic countries.

Against The Grain *WICN*
6 Chatham St., Worcester, MA 01609
PH: 508-752-0700 FX: 508-752-7518
David Ritchie david@wicn.org
www.wicn.org
Folk, Blues, traditional and Alt-Country, Roots, World music and more.

Celtic Twilight *WUMB*
U. Mass, 100 Morrissey Blvd. Boston, MA 02125-3393
PH: 617-287-6900 FX: 617-287-6916
Gail Gilmore gail.gilmore@wumb.org
www.wumb.org
Contemporary and traditional music from the British Isles.

The Fiddle & the Harp *WOMR*
494 Commercial St., Provincetown, MA 02657
PH: 508-487-2619
Dinah Mellin dinah164@capecod.net
www.womr.org
Irish, Scottish and Canadian Maritime music.

Folk 'n Good Music Show *WMFO*
PO Box 65 Medford, MA 02155
PH: 617-625-0800
Morgan Huke morganhuke@yahoo.com
www.wmfo.org
An experience of Acoustic and Electric tunes live from our studios. Features up and coming artists.

Folk is a Four Letter Word *Creative Radio*
PO Box 441444, Somerville, MA 02144
Sarah Woolf sarahw@sarahwoolf.com
www.sarahwoolf.com/4folk.htm
Please don't send photos or elaborate press kits. I don't care what you look like or where you have performed.

Folk on WGBH
125 Western Ave. Boston, MA 02134
PH: 617-300-4415
Alice Abraham alice_j_abraham@wgbh.org
www.wgbh.org
New and traditional Folk music by local and national musicians.

The Old Songs' Home *WOMR*
PO Box 2171, Orleans, MA 02653
Bob Weiser theoldsongshome@hotmail.com
www.womr.org
I will gladly review CDs for airplay. Folk and Acoustic music, traditional and contemporary.

Sounds of Erin Radio
Box 12, Belmont, MA 02428
soundoferinradio@comcast.net
soundoferinradio.com
Features interviews, music, book reviews, sports and other items of interest for the world-wide Celtic community.

Watch City Coffeehouse *WBRS*
PO Box 2171, Orleans, MA 02653
Bob Weiser theoldsongshome@hotmail.com
www.wbrs.org
I will gladly review CDs for airplay. Folk and Acoustic music, traditional and contemporary.

WUMB *U. Mass Boston*
100 Morrissey Blvd. Boston, MA 02125-3393
PH: 617-287-6900 FX: 617-287-6916
wumb@umb.edu
www.wumb.org
The only full-time listener funded Folk station in the US.

Michigan

Folks Like Us *WEMU*
4600 Cass Ave. Detroit, MI 48201
PH: 313-577-1019
Matt Watroba matt@watrobanetwork.com
www.folkslikeus.org
Traditional and contemporary Folk music.

The Folk Tradition *WKAR*
283 Comm Arts Bldg. Michigan State U.
East Lansing, MI 48824-1212
PH: 517 432-9527 FX: 517-353-7124
Bob Blackman blackman@wkar.org
wkar.org/folktradition
Traditional Folk songs, Celtic tunes and more.

Old Front Porch *WXOU*
2360 Oaknoll, Auburn Hills, MI 48326
Maggie Ferguson marmikdj@yahoo.com
www.oakland.edu/org/wxou/maggie.html
Pioneering progressive Folk, holding fast to Traditional Roots. We promote and support Michigan and regional artists.

Minnesota

Folk Migrations *KUMD*
Duluth Ent. Convention Ctr. 350 Harbor Dr.
Duluth, MN 55802
Bryan French bfrench@decc.org
www.kumd.org
If you would like your CDs considered for airplay, please send them to me at the above address.

Urban Folk *KFAI*
1808 Riverside Ave. Minneapolis, MN 55454
PH: 612-341-3144 x20 FX: 612-341-4281
Beth Shaw xafolk@yahoo.com
www.kfai.org/programs/urb_folk.htm
Folk, Bluegrass, Blues and international Roots music.

Missouri

The Acoustic Edge *KRFC*
1731 B. S. 11th St., St. Louis, MO 63104-3459
PH: 314-588-9255
Naomi & Terry nstm1@yahoo.com
www.geocities.com/nstm1/acousticedge.html
Cool tunes each Sunday.

Blue Highways/No Limit *KOPN*
110 E. Hubbell Dr. Columbia, MO 65201
PH: 573-874-5676 FX: 573-499-1662
Clint Harding thevoice@coin.org
www.kopn.org
We cruise the back roads to track down great Folk, Jazz, Blues and Rock music. Please e-mail me before you send in your material.

Family Reunion *KDHX*
3504 Magnolia, St. Louis, MO 63118
PH: 314-664-3688 FX: 314-664-1020
Judy Stein ashehi@kdhx.org
www.kdhx.org/programs/familyreunion.htm
Often featuring artists who will be performing locally.

Sunday Morning Coffeehouse *KOPN*
1907 Juniper Dr. Columbia, MO 65201-3862
PH: 573-874-5676 FX: 573-499-1662
Steve Jerrett sjerrett@coin.org
www.smchouse.org
Traditional Folk, Bluegrass, Country, Celtic and Singer/Songwriter expressions of the ever-evolving Folk process.

Montana

The Folk Show *KUFM*
MPR, 32 Campus Dr. U. Montana, Missoula, MT 59812-8064
PH: 406-243-4931 FX: 406-243-3299
www.kufm.org
Host Beth Anne Austein presents a potpourri of Folk music from around the world.

New Hampshire

The Folk Show *NHPR*
207 N. Main St., Concord, NH 03301-5003
PH: 603-228-8910 FX: 603-224-6052
Kate McNal folkshow@nhpr.org
www.nhpr.org
Traditional and contemporary Acoustic and Folk music. In-studio guests as well.

Writers in the Round *WSCA*
c/o Portsmouth Radio, PO Box 6532, Portsmouth, NH 03802
PH: 603-430-9722 FX: 430-9822
Deidre Randall WITR@deidrerandall.com
www.deidrerandall.com
A weekly showcase of live music with two songwriters and one poet.

New Jersey

The Legacy Program *WTSR*
Kendall Hall, PO Box 7718, Ewing, NJ 08628
PH: 609-771-2554 FX: 609-637-5113
Peter Kernast wtsrlegacy1@cs.com
www.wtsr.org
Folk and New World music. Features live guests.

Music You Can't Hear On the Radio *WPRB*
79 Rittenhouse Rd. Stockton, NJ 08559
PH: 609-258-3655 FX: 609-397-9016
John Weingart VerySeldom@aol.com
www.veryseldom.com
Folk music, String Band music, Bluegrass, Blues and humor.

The Roots Rock Review *WBZC*
601 Pemberton Browns Mills Rd. Pemberton, NJ 08068-1599
PH: 609-894-9311 x1592 FX: 609-894-9440
Greg Gaughan no9mngmt@enter.net
staff.bcc.edu/radio
This show mixes Rock n' Roll, Folk, Blues, Bluegrass, even Country.

Traditions *WFDU*
Metropolitan Campus, 1000 River Rd. Teaneck, NJ 07666
Ron Olesko sundaysession@aol.com
wfdu.fm
Sharing the unique and expansive world of Folk music. Continuing its long "tradition" of introducing new artists to its audience.

New York

A Thousand Welcomes *WFUV*
Fordham U. Bronx, NY 10458
PH: 718-817-4550 FX: 718-365-9815
Kathleen Biggins kathleenbiggins@wfuv.org
www.wfuv.org/wfuv/kathleen.html
Celtic traditional music.

After Midnight *WXXE*
PO Box 35091, Syracuse, NY 13235
info@luminist.org
luminist.org/radio
An eight-hour Roots and Acoustic music program.

Bound for Glory *WVBR*
957 B Mitchell St., Ithaca, NY 14850
PH: 607-273-2121
www.wvbr.com/bfg.html
Host Phil Shapiro provides free, live Folk concerts.

Common Threads *WAER*
795 Ostrom Ave. Syracuse, NY 13244-4601
PH: 315-443-4021 FX: 315-443-2148
Larry Hoyt waer@syr.edu
waer.org/threads.html
Traditional Folk and Acoustically-based music.

Dancing on the Air *WAMC*
PO Box 66600, Albany, NY 12206
PH: 800-323-9262 FX: 518-432-6974
Jay Ungar & Molly Mason mail@wamc.org
dancingontheair.com
Live musical performances. Folk, Celtic, Swing, Cajun, Old-Time Country, Bluegrass and more.

Folk Plus *WJFF*
45 Dwyer Ave. Liberty, NY 12754
Angela Page folkplus@wjffradio.org
www.wjffradio.org/FolkPlus
I explore the music and artists that I call FOLK.

Folk, Rock & Roots *WVKR*
Box 726, Vassar College, 124 Raymond Ave.
Poughkeepsie, NY 12604
PH: 845-437-5476 FX: 845-437-7656
Andrew Tokash aptokash@aol.com
members.aol.com/aptokash/vkr-frr.html
Playing Folk, Alt-Country, Rock, Blues, guitar instrumentals and Roots Rock.

The Folk Show *WSLU*
St. Lawrence U. Canton, NY 13617
PH: 315-229-5356 FX: 315-229-5373
Mike Alzo folkshow@ncpr.org
www.northcountrypublicradio.org/programs/local/folk.html
Traditional and contemporary Folk music.

Hootenanny Cafe *WTBQ*
62 N. Main St., Florida, NY 10921
PH: 845-651-1110 FX: 845-651-1025
Jon Stein musicnow@frontiernet.net
www.wtbq.com
Acoustic music show.

Hudson River Sampler *WAMC*
PO Box 66600, Albany, NY 12206
PH: 800-323-9262 FX: 518-432-6974
Wanda Fischer wanda@wamc.org
www.wamc.org/hurisam.html
Folk, Bluegrass and Blues.

It's For Folks *WBNY*
Buffalo State College, 1300 Elmwood Ave. Buffalo, NY 14222
PH: 716- 673-3260
Ken "Dr. K" Nagelberg kenfolkdj@yahoo.com
www.wbny.org
Features Folk and Acoustic Singer/Songwriters on independent and self-published labels.

Light Show *WBAI*
120 Wall St. 10th Fl. New York, NY 10005
PH: 212-209-2917 FX: 212-747-1698
Evan Ginzburg lightshow@wbai.org
www.wbai.org
Folk songs, tale of struggle, people's poetry, drama, liturgy, theology, professional wrestling — narrative forms that proclaim the values of a civilization striving to be born.

Nonesuch *WVBR*
957 Mitchell St. Ste. B, Ithaca, NY 14850
PH: 607-273-2121 FX: 607-273-4069
nonesuch@wvbr.com
wvbr.com/nonesuch.html
Music in the Folk tradition.

Sunday Street *WUSB*
Stony Brook Union 266, Stony Brook, NY 11794-3263
PH: 631-632-6501 FX: 631-632-7182
Charlie Backfish cbackfish@aol.com
wusb.fm
An Acoustic-oriented program on the air since 1978.

A Variety of Folk *WRUR*
PO Box 277356, Rochester, NY 14627
PH: 585-275-6400 FX: 585-256-3989
Tom Bohan tombohan@rochester.rr.com
home.rochester.rr.com/bohan
Folk, Bluegrass, Old-Time, Singer/Songwriter etc.

North Carolina

Back Porch Music *WUNC*
120 Friday Ctr. Dr. Chapel Hill NC 27517
PH: 919-966-5454 FX: 919-966-5955
Freddy Jenkins fjenkins@wunc.org
www.wunc.org/backporchmusic
A wide range of Acoustic-based Folk music.

Ohio

Below the Salt *WOUB*
9 S. College St., Athens, OH 45701
PH: 740-593-1771 FX: 740-593-0240
Keith Newman belowthesalt@woub.org
woub.org/belowthesalt
An eclectic mix of Folk music.

The Dear Green Place *WYSO*
795 Livermore St., Yellow Springs, OH 45387
PH: 937-767-6420
Cindy Funk wyso@cindyfunk.com
cindyfunk.com
Top names in the world of Celtic music, as well as local acts and performers you've never heard of ...but need to meet.

Detours *WYSO*
795 Livermore St., Yellow Springs, OH 45387
PH: 937-767-6420
Norm Whitman nwhitman@msn.com
www.wyso.org/detours.htm
Mainly Folk and Celtic music, but sometimes I throw in a bit from some other genre.

FolkAlley.com
1613 E. Summit St., Kent, OH 44242-0001
letters@folkalley.com
www.folkalley.com
The online gateway to the world of Folk music!

Folk Music *WKSU*
PO Box 5190, Kent, OH 44242-0001
PH: 330-672-3114 FX: 330-672-4107
letters@wksu.org
www.wksu.org/folk
We air 13 hours of Folk music weekly!

Toss the Feathers *WCBE*
540 Jack Gibbs Blvd. Columbus, OH 43215
PH: 614-365-5555 FX: 614-365-5060
Doug Dickson ddickso1@insight.rr.com
www.tossthefeathers.org
Featuring the best of Celtic and British Folk - Rock.

Visiting The Folks *WJCU*
7666 N. Gannett, Sagamore Hills, OH 44067
PH: 216-397-4937 FX: 216-397-4438
Fred Dolan dolan@en.com
www.wjcu.org
Folk, Acoustic, Celtic, Classic Country, & Bluegrass vocals.

Oklahoma

Folk Salad *KWGS*
U. Tulsa, 600 S. College Ave. Tulsa, OK 74104
PH: 918-836-4354
Richard & Scott folksalad@kwgs.org
kwgs.org/folksalad.html
Contemporary and traditional offerings in Folk.

Oregon

The Saturday Cafe *KLCC*
PO Box 50698, Eugene, OR 97405
Frank Gosar fgosar@efn.org
www.klcc.org
Mostly Acoustic, Folk and Singer/Songwriter music.

Pennsylvania

In The Tradition *WDIY*
3681 Huckleberry Rd. Allentown, PA 18104
PH: 610-395-5908
Tom Druckenmiller littlecat@enter.net
www.wdiy.org
Features traditional based North American and Celtic music.

Roots *WVUD*
PO Box 701, Unionville, PA 19375
PH: 302-831-2701 FX: 302-831-1399
Todd Tyson folkbloke@kennett.net
www.wvud.org
All kinds of Folk, for all kinds of folks.

The Saturday Light Brigade *WRCT*
PO Box 100092, Pittsburgh, PA 15233
PH: 412-761-5144 FX: 412-761-3625
slb@slbradio.com
www.slbradio.com
Acoustic music and family fun.

Transitions Radio Magazine *KBAC*
17 Alondra Rd. Santa Fe, NM 87508
Alan Hunter & Elizabeth Rose
hosts@transradio.com
www.transradio.com
Music crosses over typical industry classifications to provide a wide range of vocals and instrumentals, Acoustic and Electronic styles, from the familiar to the unique.

Rhode Island

Traditions *WRIU*
326 Memorial Union, Kingston, RI 02881
PH: 401-874-4949 FX: 401-874-4349
folk@wriu.org
www.wriu.org
The place to hear new Folk & Roots releases.

Texas

Folk Fury *KTEP*
500 W. U. Ave. #200, El Paso, TX 79968-0001
PH: 915-747-5152 FX: 915-747-5641
Dan Alloway ktep@utep.edu
www.ktep.org
Unique blends of Bluegrass, Blues, Western Swing, Progressive Country and, of course, Folk music.

Folkways *KUT*
1 University Stn. A0704, Austin, TX 78712
PH: 512-471-2345 FX: 512-471-3700
Ed Miller edmiller@io.com
www.kut.org
Six hours of assorted Folk music.

Some Call it Folk *KEDT*
4455 S. Padre Island Dr. #38, Corpus Christi, TX 78411-4481
PH: 361-855-2213 FX: 361-855-3877
Pam Stakes prstakes@aol.com
www.kedt.org/fm/pamstakesbio.htm
Featuring today's Singer/Songwriters and yesterday's Folk legends.

Utah

Fresh Folk *UPR*
Utah State U. Logan, UT 84322-8505
Blair Larsen blair@mfire.com
www.upr.org/folk.html
Folk, Blues, Bluegrass and Celtic new releases.

Saturday Sagebrush Serenade *KRCL*
1971 W. N. Temple, Salt Lake City, UT 84116
PH: 801-359-9191 FX: 801-533-9136
Dave davesa@krcl.org
www.krcl.org/programs/satsage.htm
Folk and Acoustic Rock to ease you from your morning cup of coffee through your Sunday afternoon.

Sunday Sagebrush Serenade *KRCL*
1971 W. North Temple, Salt Lake City, UT 84116
PH: 801-359-9191 FX: 801-533-9136
Phil phill@krcl.org or Lori lorir@krcl.org
www.krcl.org/programs/sunsage.htm
Folk and Acoustic Rock every Sunday.

Thursday Breakfast Jam *KRLC*
1752 S. 600 E., Salt Lake City, UT 84105
PH: 801-359-9191 FX: 801-533-9136
Susanne Millsaps susannem@krcl.org
www.krcl.org/~susannem
Folk, Jazz, World, Eclectic mix.

Vermont

All the Traditions *Vermont Public Radio*
20 Troy Ave. Colchester, VT 05446
PH: 802-655-9451 FX: 802-655-2799
www.vpr.net/music/traditions.shtml
Host Robert Resnik plays Folk, Country, Old-Time etc.

Crossroads *WNCS*
169 River St. Montpelier, VT 05602
PH: 802-223-2396 FX: 802-223-1520
Tim Downey & Todd Tyson
crossroads@pointfm.com
www.pointfm.com
Traditional and contemporary Folk, Bluegrass,
Gospel and Blues.

The Folk Show *WWPV*
St. Michael's College, Box 274, Winooski Park,
Colchester, VT 05439
PH: 802-654-2334 FX: 802-654-2336
John Sheehey wwpv@smcvt.edu
personalweb.smcvt.edu/wwpv
Contemporary Folk, Celtic, Blues and more.

Virginia

Acoustic Café *WMRA*
PO Box 1292, Harrisonburg, VA 22803
PH: 540-568-6221 FX: 540-568-3814
Tom DuVal duvalte@jmu.edu
www.jmu.edu/wmra/folk.html
Cover up and coming artists.

Out O' the Blue Radio Revue *WCVE*
PO Box 1117, Mechanicsville, VA 23111-6117
PH: 804-559-8855 FX: 804-559-0516
Page Wilson page@pagewilson.com
www.pagewilson.com/ootbrr.html
Folk, Blues, Bluegrass, Country, Cajun/Zydeco,
Rock n' Roll, Irish and more.

Sunset Road *WTJU*
PO Box 400811, U. Virginia, Charlottesville,
VA 22901-4811
Terry Carpenter etc56@aol.com
wtju.net
Folk show featuring local, regional, national and
international artists. Also, what's happening at local
and regional venues, new releases, interviews,
featured artists and more.

Washington

Inland Folk *KWSU*
PO Box 2184-CS, Pullman, WA 99165
PH: 509-332-5047
Dan Maher dmaher@wsu.edu
www.kpbx.org/programs/inlandfolk.htm
Music of local and national Folk artists.

Lunch With Folks *KBCS*
3000 Landerholm Cir. SE. Bellevue,
WA 98007-6484
PH: 425-564-2424
John Sincock john.sincock@verizon.net
kbcs.fm
Every weekday a different host features 3 hours of
flavorful Folk music.

Our Saturday Tradition *KBCS*
3000 Landerholm Cir. SE., Bellevue,
WA 98007-6484
PH: 425-564-2424
Hal Durden asubdude@att.net
kbcs.fm
Traditional Folk music including Bluegrass, Old-
Time, British and American contemporary.

Sunday Brunch *KMTT*
1100 Olive Way #1650, Seattle, WA 98101
PH: 206-233-1037 FX: 206-233-8978
Drew Dundon adundon@entercom.com
www.kmtt.com
Selections from the lighter side of the music library.

Washington DC

Traditions *WETA*
2775 S. Quincy St., Arlington, VA 22206
PH: 703-998-2600 FX: 703-998-3401
Mary Cliff traditions@weta.com
www.marycliff.net
A mix of traditional, revival, Singer/Songwriter,
Ethnic and World music.

Wisconsin

Acoustic Revival *WWSP*
105 CAC UWSP Reserve St., Stevens Point,
WI 54481
PH: 715-346-4029 FX: 715-346-4012
Granddad granddad90fm@hotmail.com
www.uwsp.edu/stuorg/wwsp/AR_Main.htm
The best selections of Acoustic music in Central
Wisconsin.

Diaspora *WORT*
118 S. Bedford St., Madison, WI 53704
PH: 608-256-2695 FX: 608-256-3704
Terry O'Laughlin diaspora@terryo.org
diaspora.terryo.org
Folk and World music.

Folkways *WOJB*
13386 W. Trepania Rd. Hayward, WI 54843
PH: 715-634-2100 FX: 715-634-4070
Mark Pedersen pedersen@chibardun.net
www.wojb.org
From American Roots music to contemporary
Singer/Songwriters.

Northwoods Cafe *WXPR*
303 W. Prospect Ave. Rhinelander, WI 54501
PH: 715-362-6000 FX: 715-362-6007
Marcia Barkus wxpr@wxpr.org
www.wxpr.org/program/northcafe.cfm
Folk, Roots, World, Blues, Cajun, Zydeco...

Simply Folk *Wisconsin Public Radio*
821 University Ave. Madison, WI 53706
PH: 800-747-7444
Tom Martin-Erickson martin-erickson@wpr.org
www.wpr.org/simplyfolk
Bringing you concerts recorded here in Wisconsin.

Wyoming

Morning Music With Don Woods *WPR*
U. Wyoming, Dept: 3984 1000 E. U. Laramie,
WY 82071
PH: 307-766-4240 FX: 307-766-6184
Don Woods dwoods@uwyo.edu
uwadmnweb.uwyo.edu/wpr/mm
Daily 3 hour show.

US Virgin Islands

The Doug Lewis Show *WVGN*
PO Box 6786, St. Thomas, VI 00804-6786
PH: 340-777-6035
Doug Dick cddick@viaccess.net
www.wvgn.org
Blues, Folk, Classic Rock n' Roll and Country.

Sign up for
The Indie Contact
Newsletter
www.indiebible.com

Canada

Acoustic Roots *CHUO*
65 University Pvt. #0038, Ottawa, ON K1N 9A5
PH: 613-729-1106
L.J. Bouchard ljbouchard@rogers.com
www.chuo.fm
We play acoustic guitar-focused Singer/Songwriters,
traditional music from Celtic to Americana, Acoustic
Blues, Old-Timey music, World music - on occasion,
Newgrass, Bluegrass, (some) Country.

Acoustic Routes *CKLN*
168 Combe Ave. Toronto, ON M3H 4K3
PH: 416-979-5251 FX: 416-595-0226
Joel Wortzman jwortzman@sympatico.ca
www.ckln.fm
Contemporary Acoustic Singer/Songwriter.

The Celtic Show *CKUA*
10526 Jasper Ave. Edmonton, AB T5J 1Z7
PH: 780-428-7595 FX: 780-428-7624
Andy Donnelly andy.donnelly@ckua.org
www.ckua.com
Traditional ballads to hard-driving Rock tunes.

Edge On Folk *CITR*
#233-6138 SUB Blvd. Vancouver, BC V6T 1Z1
PH: 604-822-2487
Steve Edge steveedgeonfolk@telus.net
www.citr.ca
Send me a link with samples I can check it out. If I
like what I hear I'll request a copy of your CD.

Folk Roots/Folk Branches *CKUT*
235 Metcalfe Ave. #402, Westmount, QC H3Z 2H8
PH: 514-398-4616 FX: 514-398-8261
Mike Regenstreif mike@ckutfolk.com
www.ckutfolk.com
Broadly-defined Folk-oriented program.

Folk Routes *CKUA*
10526 Jasper Ave. Edmonton, AB T5J 1Z7
PH: 780-428-7595 FX: 780-428-7624
Tom Coxworth tom.coxworth@ckua.org
www.ckua.org
Tracing Folk music from around the world.

For the Folk *CHRW*
Rm. 250, UCC, UWO, London, ON N6A 3K7
PH: 519-661-3600 FX: 519-661-3372
chrwradio.com
Host Allison Brown plays Folk, Roots, Traditional,
Celtic and Singer/Songwriter.

Freewheeling Folk Show *CFMU*
16 Penlake Ct. Hamilton, ON L9C 5Y7
Jim Marino jlmarino@mountaincable.net
cfmu.mcmaster.ca
Folk and Celtic music with a touch of Bluegrass and
an emphasis on local talent.

Jigs and Reels *CKWR*
6-130 Columbia St. W., Waterloo, ON N2L 3K9
PH: 519-886-9870 FX: 519-886-0090
Dean Clarke general@ckwr.com
www.ckwr.com
East Coast style music show.

Prairie Ceilidh *CKJS*
96 Erlandson Dr. Winnipeg, MB R3K 0G8
Lyle Skinner pceilidh@shaw.ca
members.shaw.ca/pceilidh
Traditional and contemporary Celtic music.

Regina's Mighty Shores *CJTR*
PO Box 334, Stn. Main, Regina, SK S4P 3A1
Roman & Brenda Tacik mightyshores@hotmail.com
regie2.phys.uregina.ca
Featuring Folk, Roots, Celtic, Bluegrass etc.

Roots and Wings *CBC*
PO Box 500, Stn. A, Toronto, ON M5W 1E6
PH: 416-205-3700 FX: 416-205-6040
radio.cbc.ca/programs/roots
Hosted by Philly Markowitz. Send in any and all music.

Roots & Writers *UMFM*
153 Emerson Ave. Winnipeg, MB R2G 1E8
Len Osland lennytunes@shaw.ca
www.umfm.com
A weekly cocktail of Roots/Blues/Country & rockin' Folk tunes served up by artists you may never have heard of before.

Steel Belted Radio
126 Meadow Lake Dr. Winnipeg, MB R2C 4K3
PH: 204-224-1663
steelbeltedradio@shaw.ca
www.steelbeltedradio.com
Specializing in Roots, Country and all the down and dirty stuff those wimps at other radio stations won't play!

Sunday Coffee House *CJLX*
PO Box 4200, Belleville, ON K8N 5B9
PH: 613-966-2559 FX: 613-966-1993
Greg Schatzmann sundaycoffeehouse@yahoo.ca
www.cjlx.fm
Folk/Acoustic/Celtic/Roots music & beyond.

Tell the Band to Go Home
A-136 Spence St., Winnipeg, MB R3C 1Y3
Jeff Robson bandgohome@shaw.ca
www.tellthebandtogohome.com
Weekly Singer/Songwriter radio show. I also review CDs and write music articles for local publications.

Waxies Dargle *UMFM*
Rm. 308 U. Ctr. Winnipeg, MB R3T 2N2
PH: 204-474-7027 FX: 204-269-1299
Lyle Skinner waxies@shaw.ca
www.umfm.com
Traditional and Contemporary Celtic-edged Folk/Pop/Rock music from near and afar.

Window of Opportunity *CKCU*
61 Highmont Ct. Kanata, ON K2T 1B2
Laurie-Ann Copple lcopple@ncf.ca
www.ncf.ca/~eh202/window.html
We support up-and-coming Folk, Blues and Jazz artists. Bluegrass, Celtic and World artists are often featured as well.

Europe

Belgium

Psyche van het Folk
PO Box 28, 2570 Duffel, Belgium
PH: 0472-769207
Gerald Van Waes
psychevanhetfolk@radiocentraal.be
psychevanhetfolk.homestead.com
World progressive music, Acoustic crossovers, Acid Folk ...

Germany

Keine Heimat *Radio Dreyeckland*
Lehener Str. 31, 79098 Freiburg, Germany
PH: 49-761-35329 FX: 49-761-35329
Christian Rath info@keine-heimat.de
www.keine-heimat.de
The Euro-Folk-show.

Radio ISW
Mozartstraße 3a, 84508 Burgkirchen/Alz, Germany
PH: 08679-9827-0 FX: 08679-9827-30
info@inn-salzach-welle.de
www.inn-salzach-welle.de
Folk & Country music.

Radio ZuSa
Scharnhorststr. 1, 21335 Lueneburg, Germany
Juergen Kramer j.kramer@zusa.de
www.zusa.de
Folk, Acoustic and Traditional music from around the world.

Italy

"Highway 61" and "Un Mondo Di Musica"
PO Box 12, 15040 San Michele, Alessandria, Italy
PH: 39-131-225791 FX: 39-131-225791
Massimo Ferro highway61@interfree.it
www.highway61.it
Highway 61 plays Folk, Country, Bluegrass, Blues, Roots Rock, Americana, Alt-Country etc. Un Mondo Di Musica deals with every form of Folk, Roots & World music.

The Netherlands

Crossroads Radio *BRTO*
Smitsstraat 13, 4623 XP Bergen op Zoom,
The Netherlands
Jos van den Boom crossroadsradio@home.nl
www.crossroadsradio.nl
Roots and Singer/Songwriter music. Once a month musicians from all over the world are invited to record an acoustic session in front of an audience of about 50 people.

Landslide
Tarwestraat 99, 1446 CC Purmerend,
The Netherlands
PH: 00-31-0-299-463138
Michael van Bruggen landslide@planet.nl
www.realrootscafe.com/landslide.html
Country, Folk, Blues, Singer/Songwriters, Cajun, Zydeco etc. We're always looking for new talent!

Under the Tree
Hoogewaard 39, 2396AC Koudekerk aan den Rijn,
The Netherlands
PH: 00-31-0-713-414-647
Hans Hoogeveen hanshoogeveen@planet.nl
www.realrootscafe.com/underthetree.html
Folk, Singer/Songwriters, a little Blues, Americana & Country, some World music and sip of Pop and Rock every now and then.

United Kingdom

BBC Radio 2 *Folk and Acoustic*
www.bbc.co.uk/radio2/r2music/folk
Home page of the BBC Radio 2's various Folk and Acoustic shows. Info, shows, contacts etc.

BBC Radio 2 *Folk and Country*
www.bbc.co.uk/radio2/r2music/folkandcountry
Home page of the BBC Radio 2's various Folk and Country shows. Info, shows, contacts etc.

The Late Session *RTÉ*
PH: 01-2082040 FX: 01-2083092
Áine Hensey brownep@rte.ie
www.rte.ie/radio1/thelatesession
Irish traditional and Folk music.

The Miller Tells Her Tale
Karen karen@themillertellshertale.co.uk
www.themillertellshertale.co.uk
Singer/Songwriter, Alt-Country, Americana, Contemporary Folk, Power Pop and some Blues. PLEASE e-mail me before you send any music!

Roots Around the World *Spirit FM*
The Barn, Fordwater Ln. Chichester, W. Sussex,
PO19 6PT UK
PH: 01243-774641 FX: 01243-789787
rootsaroundtheworld@btopenworld.com
rootsaroundtheworld.info
The best in Folk, Blues, World and Country music, including the latest gig news, exclusive airplays and interviews.

Australia

A Dog's Breakfast
Glenn Morrow glen@saturdaybreakfast.com
saturdaybreakfast.com
Playing a mixture of Blues, Folk, Roots, Country and World music.

Celtic World
PO Box 9014, Deakin, ACT 2600 Australia
postmaster@celtic-world.net
www.celtic-world.net
Today's top performers, from the traditional to the very modern.

Come All Ye *2MCE*
Panorama Ave. Bathurst, NSW 2795 Australia
PH: 02-6338-4790 FX: 02-6338-4402
Bruce Cameron cameron@ix.net.au
www.2mce.org
The longest running Folk program on Australian radio. Preview CDs are welcomed.

Folk till Midnight / Good Morning Folk *5EB*
10 Byron Pl. Adelaide, SA 5000 Australia
FX: 8231-1456
Henk de Weerd hdeweerd@hotkey.net.au
www.5ebi.com.au
Please send in your promotional CDs.

Grassroots Australia *2Air FM*
PO Box 226, Woolgoolga, NSW 2456 Australia
Jennifer Flux grassroots2air@yahoo.com.au
Contemporary and Traditional Folk. Roots and World music.

Northside Folk *Triple H*
26 Awatea Rd. St Ives, NSW 2075 Australia
Jude & Mart Fowler fowlermj@bigpond.net.au
www.hhhfm.org.au
Promotional material welcome. Please send to the above address.

On the Right Track *KLFM*
PO Box 2997, Bendigo, VIC 3554 Australia
Phil Knipe phillipknipe@aapt.net.au
www.klfm.com.au
Featuring a selection of the best Roots Rock, C&W, Blues, Folk, Gospel and more.

New Zealand

Folk on Sunday
1214 Louie St., Hastings, New Zealand 4201
PH: 64-6-8785395
Mitch and Robyn Park mfpark@xtra.co.nz
www.radiokidnappers.org.nz
Ballads, Shanties, Blues, Gospel, Bluegrass etc.

Town & Country
21 Redvers Dr. Belmont, Lower Hutt 6009,
New Zealand
Eddie O'Strange blue.smoke@actrix.gen.nz
Folk and Roots music.

GLBT Radio

After Hours *KPFT*
400 Westmoreland #2, Houston, TX 77006
PH: 713-526-5738 FX: 713-526-5750
Jimmy Carper afterhours@kpft.org
www.kpft.org
Queer weekly variety show, generally 6-8 GLBT songs per show.

All Thangs Queer *WSLR*
PO Box 10763, Bradenton, FL 34282-0763
Billi & Patti billiandpatti@tampabay.rr.com
www.billiandpatti.com/songlist.htm
We like to celebrate independent "out" queers.

Amazon Country *WXPN*
3025 Walnut St., Philadelphia, PA 19104
PH: 215-898-6677. FX: 215-898-0707
Debra D'Alessandro amazon@xpn.org
www.xpn.org/amazon.php
One of the longest-running gay and lesbian/feminist radio shows in America.

Audiofile
PO Box 66648, Houston, TX 77006
info@audiofile.org
www.audiofile.org
The monthly radio review of new music of interest to the gay, lesbian, bisexual and transgender communities. .

Bear Radio Network
261 W. Squire Dr. #1, Rochester, NY 14623-1735
Joe Maulucci Poetbear@BearRadio.net
www.BearRadio.Net
We're looking for submissions from artists in the GLBT community and those musicians who are gay friendly.

Beat FM
PH: 02-9516-1771
music@beatfm.com.au
www.beatfm.com.au
The very best gay programming and even better Dance music!

Dykes on Mics *3CR*
PO Box 1277, Collingwood, Melbourne,
VIC 3065 Australia
PH: 03-9419-8377 FX: 03-9417-4472
programming@3cr.org.au
www.3cr.org.au

Dykes On Mykes *4ZZZ*
PO Box 509, Fortitude Valley, QLD 4006 Australia
dykesonmykes@hotmail.com
www.queerradio.org/dykesonmykes.html
100% women-presented and women-focused.

Dykes on Mykes *CKUT*
3647 U. St., Montreal, QC H3A 2B3
PH: 514-398-4616 FX: 514-398-8261
music@ckut.ca
www.ckut.ca
Dyke radio for everyone. Even Barbie listens.

Face the Music *WCUW*
910 Main St., Worcester, MA 01610
PH: 508-753-1012
wcuw@wcuw.com
www.wcuw.com
Syndicated lesbian/feminist music program.

Fresh Fruit *KFAI*
1808 Riverside Ave. Minneapolis, MN 55454
PH: 612-341-3144 x842
Leigh Combs peaceluv@bitstream.net
www.kfai.org/programs/frshfrut.htm
Interviews with activists, authors and musicians from all over the country. It offers recorded music, live music, news and more.

Gay Spirit *WWUH*
200 Bloomfield Ave. West Hartford, CT 06117
PH: 860-768-4701 FX: 860-768-5701
wwuh@hartford.edu
www.wwuh.org
Greater Hartford's only gay news program featuring contemporary issues, music and special guests.

GaydarRadio.com
PH: +44-700-4429-327
studio@gaydarradio.com
www.gaydarradio.com
Featuring great music and interviews.

Generation Q *WRSU*
126 College Ave. New Brunswick, NJ 08901
PH: 732-932-8800 FX: 732-932-1768
Pedro Serrano gd4nuttin@operamail.com
wrsu.rutgers.edu
Out music, interviews & conversation. On the air for over 25 years!

Highest Common Denominator *WRSU*
126 College Ave. New Brunswick, NJ 08901
PH: 732-932-8800 FX: 732-932-1768
Bill Stella realman@att.net
wrsu.rutgers.edu
Champions great under appreciated musicians. Gay/Queer/Out music + political & passionate songs.

Homo Radio *WRPI*
51 Park Ave. Albany, NY 12202-1722
PH: 518-225-0931 FX: 518-276-2360
Sean McLaughlin HomoRadio@yahoo.com
www.myspace.com/homoradio
Mix of talk and music by GLBT artists of all genres.

Homophobic *PlanetOut Radio*
PO Box 500, San Francisco, CA 94104-0500
PH: 415-834-6500 FX: 415-834-6502
www.planetout.com/pno/radio
A music show bringing you interesting, hip and relevant artists from the past, present and future.

IMRU Radio *KPFK*
11333 Moorpark St. PMB 456, Studio City,
CA 91602
imru@kpfk.org
www.imru.org
Focusing on issues affecting the GLBT community in SoCal. We welcome CD submissions from all "out" LGBT artists. We do CD reviews as well.

Lesbian Radio
PO Box 13-0021, Christchurch, New Zealand
info@lesbianradio.org.nz
www.lesbianradio.org.nz
A weekly half-hour magazine that is primarily focused on lesbians and queer women. Usually 3 songs per show but every few weeks a whole show is dedicated to new and old music.

Out, Loud, & Queer *WJFF*
4765 State Rt. 52, PO Box 546, Jeffersonville,
NY 12748
PH: 845-482-4141 FX: 845-482-9533
Kathy Rieser kathy@trashq.com
www.wjffradio.org
Showcasing local talent and issues whenever possible.

PCM Radio
PO Box 1083, Farmington, MI 48332
PH: 386-290-3795
ilisten@pcmradio.com
www.pcmradio.com
The voice of Pride Christian music!

PrideNation
pridenation.com/radio.htm
24 hour Dance music with Trance, House, Techno and more.

Queer Ear for Far and Near *KZYX*
2000 Grand View Dr. Redwood Valley, CA 95470
Lark Letchworth LarkLet@Lycos.com
www.kzyx.org
I'm very interested in Indie art, but only the queer kind for our radio show.

Queer Corps *CKUT*
3647 U. St., Montreal, QC H3A 2B3
PH: 514-398-4616 FX: 514-398-8261
music@ckut.ca
www.ckut.ca

Queer Radio *4ZZZ*
82 Main Ave. Wavell Heights, QLD 4012 Australia
PH: +61-7-3350-1562
John Frame jvframe@ozemail.com.au
www.queerradio.org
Support, talk, music and news for GLBT.

Queer Voices *KPFT*
PO Box 66075, Houston, TX 77266-6075
PH: 713-526-5738 FX: 713-529-6929
JD Doyle jack@queervoices.org
www.queervoices.org
It's a public affairs show but that doesn't stop me from slipping in a number of new songs each week.

Queer Waves *KOOP*
2819 Foster Ln. F122, Austin, TX 78757
PH: 512-472-1369 FX: 512-472-6149
Taylor Cage cagetaylor@aol.com
www.koop.org
A weekly showcase for GLBT and just plain queer musicians.

Q'zine *WXPN*
3025 Walnut St., Philadelphia, PA 19104
PH: 215-898-6677. FX: 215-898-0707
Robert Drake qzine@xpn.org
www.xpn.org/qzine.php
Celebrates queer arts and culture with a mix of interviews, commentary and music from out artists worldwide.

Rainbow World Radio
len@stonewallsociety.net
www.rainbowworldradio.com
Promoting GLBT artists, GLBT music and the GLBT community with music choices and interviews!

SIRIUS OutQ
1221 Ave. of the Americas, New York, NY 10020
PH: 212-584-5334 FX: 212-584-5200
Charlie Dyer cdyer@siriusradio.com
www.sirius.com/outq
America's only 24/7 radio station for the gay, lesbian, bisexual and transgender community. Provocative, entertaining-even titillating! Plus news, interviews and music from GLBT recording artists.

Think Pink *WLUW*
6525 N. Sheridan Rd. Chicago, IL 60626
PH: 773-508-8080 FX: 773-508-8082
Erik & Ali thinkpink@wluw.org
www.wluw.org
Focuses on music made by the GLBT community but will also include music with queer themes and music targeting the queer audience.

This Way Out
PO Box 38327, Los Angeles, CA 90038-0327
PH: 818-986-4106
tworadio@aol.com
www.thiswayout.org
Internationally syndicated news magazine. Plays music between segments. Particularly interested in "out" songs that are relevant to current events.

Tranny Wreck
trannywreck@gmail.com
www.trannywreck.com
I do occasional comedy skits, interviews and play a good dose of podsafe music.

Windy City Queercast *WCKG*
5443 N. Broadway, Chicago, IL 60640
PH: 773-871-7610 FX: 773-871-7609
Hosts: Amy Matheny & Peter Mavrik
www.windycityqueercast.com
A fun program that allows for a new and creative outlet to cover the GLBT community.

Womanist Power Authority *KFAI*
Box 70, 1808 Riverside Ave. Minneapolis, MN 55454
PH: 612-341-3144 x20 FX: 612-341-4281
womanistpowerauthority@yahoo.com
kfai.org/programs/l_p_a.htm
Lesbian music, interviews, announcements ...

Goth Radio

North America

United States

A Feast Of Friends *KTUH*
Hemenway Hall #203, 2445 Campus Rd.
Honolulu, HI 96822
PH: 808-956-7261 FX: 808-956-5271
Nocturna feast@ktuh.org
www.myspace.com/djnocturna
Features Gothic, Industrial, Ethereal, Darkwave, Death Rock and Dark Narrative Rock music. The music is dark and we de our best to keep it there.

ampedOut
Stoicite stoic@ampedout.net
ampedout.net
A source for music other than the pre-fab radio bullshit.

Bats in the Belfry *WMBR*
3 Ames St., Cambridge, MA 02142
PH: 617-253-8810
Mistress Laura bats@wmbr.org
wmbr.mit.edu
Moody, dark and atmospheric – beginning with ancient music and chant, to the newest Gothic Rock, Darkwave, Goth-Industrial and Dark-Ambient.

The Black Cauldron *KUCI*
PO Box 4362 Irvine, CA 92616
PH: 949-824-6868
Dr. Raven morven@byz.org
www.kuci.org/~mbrown/cauldron.html
Goth, Industrial, Pagan, Ethereal, Electronica and Darkwave.

Cathedral #13
c13@cathedral13.com
www.cathedral13.com
Goth, Deathrock, Darkwave, Postpunk.

Circle of Souls Pagan Radio
3045 W. Beech Ave. Visalia, CA 93277
www.circleofsouls.net
A means to promote the efforts of musical artists who put a bit of a Pagan flavor into their music.

Closed Caskets for the Living Impaired
KUCI
PO Box 4362 Irvine, CA 92616
PH: 949-824-5824
Dach dach@kuci.org
www.closedcaskets.com
The most popular Goth radio show of all time.

Dark Horizons *WMNF*
6006 N. Branch Ave. Tampa, FL 33604
PH: 813-238-9663
darkhorizons@wmnf.org
www.darkhorizonsradio.com
Ethereal, Gothic, Industrial and Synthpop bands.

Dark Nation Radio
DJ Cypher cypher@bound.org
www.darkwavelounge.com/dnr.html
Features a mix of Gothic, Industrial, Deathrock and Ambient.

Detroit Industrial Underground
brian@detroitIndustrial.org
www.detroitIndustrial.org
Questions, comments and playlist suggestions are always welcome. Free CDs from bands and labels are even more welcome.

Digital Gunfire
shirow@digitalgunfire.com
www.digitalgunfire.com
Industrial, EBM and Electronic. Please submit our online release form with your music.

EBM-Radio.com
Catatonic catatonic@ebm-radio.com
www.ebm-radio.com
The best Industrial, EBM, Futurepop, Synthpop, Darkwave, Goth and Dark Electronic.

Escape From Noise
David Vesel efn@purplenote.com.
efn.purplenote.com
Featuring genres such as Synthpop, Electropop, Industrial, Darkwave, EBM etc. Fill out our online permission form in order to get airplay.

Factory 911 *WEGL*
116 Foy Union Bldg. Auburn U., AL 36849-5231
PH: 334-844-4113 FX: 334-844-4118
Robert Dykes wegl@auburn.edu
wegl.auburn.edu
An Industrial and Electronic show.

Generation Death *KSPC*
Thatcher Music Bldg. 340 N. College Ave.
Claremont, CA 91711
PH: 909-626-5772 FX: 909-621-8769
Wednesday gendeath@excite.com
www.kspc.org/shows/generationdeath
Gothic, Industrial, Ethereal, Darkwave and Shoegazer.

GotBlack.com Radio
5501 N. 7th Ave. PMB 721, Phoenix, AZ 85013
joe@gotblack.com
www.gotblack.com/radio
Plays Gothic, Industrial and Electronic music. We are currently accepting CDs and press kits.

Goth Metal Radio
chris@gothmetal.net
www.gothmetal.net/radio
20,000 listeners per day. When did your band last get a chance to play for an audience like this?

Goth Nights Podcast
E.Barbarella & Distilled1
ebarbarella@gothnights.com
www.gothnights.com
We are always looking for good Dark, Goth/Synth, Pop/Industrial and Metal tunes to add to rotation.

Gothic Paradise Radio
jacob001@comcast.net
www.Gothicparadise.com
Gothic, Industrial, Darkwave, EBM, Ethereal and Synthpop.

In Perpetual Motion Radio
314 Kensington Ave. Ferndale, MI 48220-2359
G. R. Perye III ipm@ipmradio.com
www.ipmradio.com
Indie artists of the Gothic, Industrial and Electronic genres.

Industrial Radio
industrialradio.org
Podcast featuring the very best Industrial music, news and interviews.

The Industrial Factory *WZBC*
Boston College 107, Chestnut Hill, MA 02467
PH: 617-552-4686 FX: 617-552-1738
Brian Industrialfactory@hotmail.com
www.wzbc.org
Underground Cyber-Electro Industrial music.

Lance and Graal Podcast
info@lanceandgraal.com
www.lanceandgraal.com
Pagan talk radio with attitude! Has yearly music awards show.

Morgue Radio
Dr. Millay morgueradio@thecountymorgue.com
www.thecountymorgue.com
Various shows playing Ethereal, Darkwave, Gothic ...

Nevermind Radio
nemesis2207@attbi.com
www.live365.com/stations/nemesis2207
A mix of Gothic, Synthpop, Industrial, EBM and the occasional strange song you can't really classify!

Pagan Pentagram Radio
paganpentagram@comcast.net
home.comcast.net/~paganpentagram
Pagan, Celtic, New Age etc.

Pagan Radio Network
PH: 651-457-0912
Paul Ieson arizonatramp@hotmail.com
paganradio.thewitchesbrew.net
Pagan Rock with attitude. PLEASE, send only PAGAN music!

Plagued By Rhythm
1515 W. Veterans Pkwy. Marshfield, WI 54449
www.plastiksickness.com
Host DJ I.Z. features Industrial/Darkwave bands. I'm always accepting promos and demos to use in my DJing.

Radio Free Abattoir
PO Box 190792, Miami Beach, FL 33119-0792
PH: 305-434-8651 FX: 305-531-5609
Sam Bradford radiofreeabattoir@slaghuis.net
www.radiofreeabattoir.com
Gothic, Darkwave and Industrial.

Radio Free Satan
Matt G. Paradise matt@purgingtalon.com
www.radiofreesatan.com
Corrupting the minds of the youth since 2000.

Radio Satan 666
www.radiosatan666.com
Various shows including Goth, Metal etc.

Reform Radio
DJ Reform reformradio@reformatory.us
reformradio.com
EBM, Industrial, Goth, Noize.

Regen Podcast
PO Box 14162, San Francisco, CA 94114-0162
PH: 415-420-8247
Nick Garland submissions@regenmag.com
www.regenmag.com
Playing the best in IDM, Industrial, Goth and Darkwave.

Seismic Radio
Teri teri@comcast.net
www.seismicradio.com
Have your band featured/interviewed.

Sounds and Visions of Tomorrow Today
PO Box 54771, Philadelphia, PA 19148
losafa@aol.com
www.drugmusic.com
Drug and Drone music.

sursumcorda Radio
5115 Excelsior Blvd. #235, Minneapolis, MN 55416
FX: 612-677-3272
inquiry@sursumcorda.com
www.sursumcorda.com
New directions in Electronic organic groove.

This is Corrosion
4317 Harlem Rd. Amherst, NY 14226
legion@thisiscorrosion.com
www.thisiscorrosion.com
Please send only CDs.

Tin Omen *WMTS*
Box 58, 1301 E. Main St., Murfreesboro, TN 37132
PH: 615-898-2636 FX: 615-898-5682
www.myspace.com/tinomenwmts
I play the greatest in Dark Ambient, Darkwave, Goth Rock, Goth Metal, Industrial and Black Metal. Not for people who hang out at the mall!

Vampture Radio
DJ Traumatic webmaster@vampture.com
www.vampture.com
The best from the Underground! Darkwave, Goth, both new and classic Gothic/Industrial.

The Vapour Treatment *WUSB*
Stony Brook Union 266, Stony Brook, NY 11794-3263
PH: 631-632-6501 FX: 631-632-7182
DJ Datura vapourtreatment@yahoo.com
www.geocities.com/radiovt
Modern Electronic music, Industrial, New Wave, Synth Pop, Electro and more.

WPBN
1544 S. Vaughn Cir. Aurora, CO 80012
Hawks hawk@tekneek.com
www.tekneek.com/wpbn
The witchcraft pagan broadcast network.

Canada

The Alcove *CKCU*
PO Box 24052, Hazeldean RPO, Kanata, ON K2M 2C3
PH: 613-520-2528
Nikki info@thealcove.ca
www.thealcove.ca
Ottawa's only Gothic/Industrial radio show.

Distorted Circuitry
RaZoRGrrL info@razorgrrl.com
www.razorgrrl.com
The best in crunchy and harder-edged Industrial and EBM.

EBM *CIUT*
91 St. George St., Toronto, ON M5S 2E8
PH: 416-978-0909 x214 FX: 416-946-7004
Sophia & Burt ebm@ciut.fm
www.ciut.fm
Electronic music for the body and mind. Industrial/Noise, EBM, Synth-Pop, Darkwave and Gothic.

The Electric Front
djlee@theelectricfront.com
www.theelectricfront.com
Industrial, Electronic, Synth, Goth and Dark-Rock songs.

Electrosynthesis
promo@electrosynthesis.ca
www.electrosynthesis.ca
Goth, Industrial, Experimental, Ambient, Techno...

Les Mouches Noires *CISM*
1094 Martial, Laval, QC H7P 1E5
Francois Richer lesmouchesnoires@videotron.ca
www.lesmouchesnoires.com
Send your press kit and CD or demo to us.

RantRadio
Box 18121, 1215-C 56 St., Delta, BC V4M 2M4
info@rantradio.com
www.rantradio.com
Industrial and Punk station. Visit our website for submission details (Industrial music has a different contact address).

Real Synthetic Audio
2515 Bathurst St. #B01, Toronto, ON M6B 2Z1
Todd Clayton todd@synthetic.org
www.synthetic.org
The most listened to Industrial net-radio show.

Rue Morgue Radio
2926 Dundas St. W., Toronto, ON M6P 1V8
Tomb Dragonmir tomb@ruemorgueradio.com
www.ruemorgueradio.com
Sounds of Horror.

What The...? *CHUO*
65 University Pvt. #0038, Ottawa, ON K1N 9A5
PH: 613-562-5800 x2720 FX: 613-562-5969
The Thorn what-the@email.com
www.myspace.com/the_thorn
The purpose of the show is to expose listeners to artists or material they wouldn't otherwise discover.

Europe

Belgium

Darker than the Bat
ZRO, Pierets-De Colvenaerplein 7a, 9060 Zelzate, Belgium
PH: 32-0-9-345-54-55 FX: 32-0-9-342-99-38
DJ Peter-Jan pj.vandamme@scarlet.be
www.proservcenter.be/darkerthanthebat/radio.html
Featuring Gothic, Industrial, Electro, EBM ...

Kagan *Radio Scorpio*
Geerdegemstraat 23, 2800 Mechelen, Belgium
PH: +32 (0)15-424363
Wim Troost radio@kagankalender.com
www.kagankalender.com
Wave, Gothic, Electro, Industrial. Each promo is assured a review and airplay.

France

Coquille Felee Radio
Jeckel jeckel@coquille-felee.net
coquille-felee.net
Goth, Industrial and Electronica music.

Meiose
Meiose RCT, BP 2001 69603 Villeurbanne, France
PH: 04-78-94-37-37
kb69@free.fr
meiose.free.fr
Industriel, Gothique, Expérimental, Electro Dark, Dark Folk, Médiéval.

Schizophonia
24 rue Pasteur, 51000 Châlons en Champagne, France
Philippe Chrétien schizophonia@duskofhope.com
schizophonia.duskofhope.com
Industrial, Neofolk, Rhythmic Electronics & Noise.

Germany

Black Channel Radio Show
An der Lehmgrube 4, D-79312 Emmendingen, Germany
PH: 49-160-8532545 FX: 49-7641-9373-13
Tobias Kuechen info@blackchannel.org
www.blackchannel.org
Wave, Gothic, Industrial, Dark Techno, Electro, Ritual etc.

Dead or Alive *Radio R1live*
PF: 837 121, D-90255 Nürnberg, Germany
PH: 49-0-175-703-706-1 FX: 012-12-5-110-23-008
info@r1live.de
www.r1live.de
Darkwave & Gothic radio.

(((EBM Radio)))
Kleine Düwelstrasse 13a, 30171 Hannover, Germany
Michael Stoll radiomaster@ebm-radio.de
www.ebm-radio.de
Strange music 4 strange people.

Radio Morituri
Sundische Straße 84, 18356 Bart, Germany
PH: 038231-45088
Vlad Tepecz vlad.tepecz@radio-morituri.de
radio-morituri.de
Featuring Goth and Industrial music.

Ultra Dark Radio
Lievelingsweg 129, D-53119 Bonn, Germany
PH: 0178-378-29-03
webmaster@ultra-dark-radio.com
www.ultra-dark-radio.com
Dark, Indie, Elektro, New Wave, Darkwave, Industrial ...

Italy

Chain the Door Radio Show
c/o Ferruccio Milanesi, Via G. Jannelli 45/D, 80131 Napoli, Italy
www.chaindlk.com
Promote your music through our show.

Radio Blackout
via Antinori 3 10129 Torino, Italy
PH: 39-011-580-68-88
blackout@ecn.org
www.ecn.org/blackout
L'unica Radio libera In piemonte. Sostieni la frequenza libera!

United Kingdom

DARKLIFE Podcast
The Small House, 138b Brownlow Rd. London, GB-N11 2BP UK
Gianfranco Sciacca darklifezine@gmx.de
www.darklifezine.de
Spreading the latest sounds pertinent to the varied world of Dark and Experimental music.

Spiderpower Sounds
4, Ballyoran Pk. Portadown, County Armagh, N. Ireland BT62 1JN
www.spiderpower.co.uk
Send me demos, talk to me. Let me promote YOU!!!

TotalRock
1 Denmark Pl. London, WC2H 8NL UK
info@totalrock.com
www.totalrock.com
Featuring Rock, Metal and Industrial releases.

Australia

Darkwings Radio Show *RTR*
PO Box 842, Mt. Lawley, WA 6929 Australia
PH: +61-8-9260-9210 FX: +61 8 9260 9222
rtrfm@rtrfm.com.au
www.rtrfm.com.au
For all your Industrial and Gothic wants.

Dawntreader *RTR*
PO Box 842, Mt. Lawley, WA 6929 Australia
PH: +61-8-9260-9210 FX: +61 8 9260 9222
rtrfm@rtrfm.com.au
www.rtrfm.com.au
Post-Punk, Industrial and more.

Sacrament *2RRR*
PO Box 644 Gladesville, NSW 1675 Australia
PH: +61-2-9816-2938 FX: 61-2-9817-1048
info@sacramentradio.org
www.sacramentradio.org
Gothic music & information program.

Hip Hop Radio
Radio Promoters

Mo' Better Music
77 Bleecker St. #C115, New York, NY 10012
PH: 212-388-0597 FX: 212-388-0592
retail@mobettermusic.com
www.mobettermusic.com
A National marketing and promotion company.

Insomniac Media & Promotions
PO Box 592722, Orlando, FL 32859
PH: 212-629-1797
insom@mindspring.com
www.insomniaconline.com/services
Get your Hip Hop release on radio stations nationally.

Looking4airplay
PO Box 630372, Houston, TX 77263
PH: 281-277-6626 FX: 281-277-6626
Michael Matthews support@looking4airplay.com
www.looking4airplay.com
Urban radio & record pool marketing (Rap/Hip-Hop/R&B Format). We will digitally deliver your next hit directly to radio today!

Raw Talent
rawtalent@hiphopdx.com
PH: 888-753-6291 x0
www.rawtalentdx.com
We can get you the exposure you crave through radio airplay, record distribution, showcases and even recording deals.

Shocksoundpromotions.com
3840 E. Robinson Rd. #200, Amherst, NY 14228
PH: 716-578-0097
shocksoundpromo@yahoo.com
www.shocksoundpromotions.com
National radio promotions, event consulting etc.

Stations and Shows
North America
United States

Apex Express *KPFA*
1929 MLK Way, Berkeley, CA 94704
PH: 510-848-4425
apex@apexexpress.org
apexexpress.org
If you have music that you'd like featured on our show, HOLLA!!! Preferably music created by Asian/Pacific Islanders.

The Bassment Online Radio
1112 Montana Ave. #122, Santa Monica, CA 90403
DJ Spider djspider@thebassment.com
www.thebassment.com
Send us your music!

The Beat Kitchen *Sidewok Radio*
mixshow@sidewok.com
www.sidewok.com
Featuring live interviews of Hip Hop artists with special guest DJs.

The Beat Suite *Sidewok Radio*
beatsuite@sidewok.com
www.sidewok.com
We promote local independent Hip Hop artists and DJs/Turntablists.

Beatsauce *KUSF*
2130 Fulton St., San Francisco, CA 94117
PH: 415-386-5873
J. Boogie justin@jboogie.com
www.kusf.org
San Francisco's premier Underground Hip Hop mix show. We create a positive vibe for local and out of town artists to showcase their talent and promote their skills for the entire Bay Area and beyond.

Blazin' Mics FM
PO Box 25668, Baltimore, MD 21224
Hector Rivera blazinmicsfm@yahoo.com
www.blazinmicsfm.com
#1 unsigned hype internet station. 24/7 365 days of non stop music!

BMS Radio
PH: 815-918-4267
webmaster@blackmsusic-spot.com
www.bmsradio.com
Featuring unsigned artist and dope Hip Hop!

Chiradio.com
980 N. Michigan Ave. 1 Magnificent Mile #1400, Chicago, IL 60611
PH: 312-214-3521 FX: 775-264-7137
www.chiradio.com
Features a Rap and Soul station.

Cipha Sounds
DJ Cipha Sounds djcipha@ciphasounds.com
www.ciphasounds.com
DJ Cipha Sounds is one of the select few trailblazers with the natural ability to discover and develop new talent.

The City *XM Radio*
PH: 866-388-6767
thecity@xmradio.com
thecity.xmradio.com
The hottest Hip Hop, Reggae and R&B from your favorite artists and the newcomers to watch.

Dedicated *WNUR*
Campus Dr. Evanston, IL 60208-2280
PH: 847-491-7102 FX: 847-467-2058
dj3rdrail@dj3rdrail.com
dj3rdrail@dj3rdrail.com/main.htm
www.wnur.org
To those who continue to represent Hip Hop.

The Difference
5555 Wissahickon Ave. #L8, Philadelphia, PA 19144
Statik info@illvibe.net
illvibe.net
You can expect to hear anything from Funk to Traditional Jazz, from Hip Hop to Bossanova and Soulful House.

DREADXX.com
PO Box 647, Boynton Beach, FL 33425
PH: 561-503-1513
Wilfrid Antoine willydread@yahoo.com
dreadxx.com
A Hip Hop station that also promotes music through different record pools and A&R.

Earthbound Radio
PH: 858-366-4327
info@twelvez.com
www.twelvez.com
From Hip Hop to Jazz and Acoustic to Electronic.
No limits and no boundaries.

ExtravaGangsta Radio
ras@enemymindz.com
extravagangstaradio.blogspot.com
Featuring some of the hottest music in Underground
Hip-Hop, Reggaeton and R&B.

The Fresh Connection *KPSU*
1825 SW. Broadway #443 Portland, OR 97201
PH: 503-725-5945 FX: 503-725-4079
DJ Fresh fresh3122000@yahoo.com
freshconnection.cjb.net
Portland's hottest Hip Hop show!

GMS Radio
16100 Van Aken Blvd. #207, Cleveland, OH 44120
PH: 216-798-4199
James Thomas marketing@gmsradio.com
www.gmsradio.com
We feature unsigned artists and post Hip Hop
events.

Hip Hop FundaMentalz Radio
4940 Merrick Rd. # 311, Massapequa Park,
NY 11762 - 3803
PrizMatiK info@hiphopfundamentalz.com
www.hiphopfundamentalz.com
Streaming Hip Hop 24/ 7. Send all promo material
to the above address.

Hoodhype.com
PO Box 1453, Brighton, MI 48116
music@hoodhype.com
www.HoodHype.com
An all Urban podcast focusing on underground
artists.

Hot City Radio
28870 US 19 N. 3rd Fl. Clearwater, FL 33761
PH: 727-417-6838
Maurice info@hotcityradio.com
www.HotCityRadio.com
Whatever you say is what we play. Indie friendly.
R&B and Hip Hop.

KMEL
340 Townsend St. 4th Fl. San Francisco, CA 94107
Big Von Johnson vonjohnson@clearchannel.com
www.106kmel.com
Plays both independent and mainstream music.

The Last Hip-Hop
c/o Jerome Ford , PO Box 7093-WOB,
West Orange, NJ 07052
PH: 973-720-2738
www.basically-hiphop.com/lastshow
Submit your music.

The Mixtape Show
kucrdex@gmail.com
www.mixtapeshow.net
This is your opportunity to be featured right next to
some heavy hitters.

Movement Radio
steppa@movementradio.com
www.movementradio.com
We have 3 streams featuring the best in
Underground Hip Hop, Reggae and Jungle/D n' B.

NashvilleRap.Com
PO Box 1507, Goodlettsville TN 37070-1507
PH: 615-260-7636
Robert Grady info@nashvillerap.com
www.NashvilleRap.com
Our mission is to expose both local and
international artists.

Outside The Box Radio
530 Main St. #653, New Rochelle, NY 10801
PH: 914-879-8837
ty@otbradio.com
www.otbradio.com
The tri-states' #1 station for Underground and
unsigned Hip Hop.

Planet X Radio
1011 NE. 109th St., Portland, OR 97218
nbnusa@hotmail.com
www.planetxradio.com
Underground Hip Hop sounds. Download the
release form from our website and send it in with
your CD.

The Pro Flow Fa-Sho Show
PO Box 8287, Akron, OH 44320
PH: 330-431-1680
MaD MaXxx M3@maxheat.com
maxheat.com
The show has a strong Hip Hop origin.

RAW *XM Radio*
PH: 866-280-4729
Leo G. 66raw@xmradio.com
raw.xmradio.com
All about living on the cutting edge of today's Hip
Hop scene.

SOL of HIPHOP Radio *TIR*
PO Box 6868, Fullerton, CA 92834-6868
PH: 714-278-5505 FX: 714-278-5514
DJ Buddhabong buddhabong@solofhiphop.com
www.solofhiphop.com
Streamin' live every Friday 4-7 PM pst.

Spinatiks Radio
PO Box 51815. San Jose, CA 95151
PH: 866-767-5269
DJ Spindizzy info@spinatiks.com
www.spinatiks.com
We are in search for artists to play live on our show
in the genres of Rap, Hip Hop, R&B and Dance.

Starving Artist *WBCR*
Rm. 306, Whitehead Hall, 2900 Bedford Ave.
Brooklyn, NY 11210
PH: 718-951-4515
brooklyncollegeradio@gmail.com
brooklyncollegeradio.org
Introduces those that are ambitious and are trying it
to make a breakthrough in the music industry.

Sunday Night Jams *KTXT*
Texas Tech U. PO Box 43081, Lubbock, TX 79409
PH: 806-742-3916 FX: 806-742-3906
ktxtfm@yahoo.com
www.ktxt.net
The #1 rated Urban show in Lubbock!!

The SureShot *iLLVIBE Radio*
5555 Wissahickon Ave. #L8, Philadelphia, PA 19144
Statik statik@illvibe.net
illvibe.net
A taste of new Underground Hip Hop, mixed with
some classics, some Funk, exclusives and whatever
else we think is dope!

Tables of Content *KCSN*
18111 Nordhoff St., Northridge, CA 91330-8312
PH: 818-885-5276
Anthony Valadez antonio.valadez@kcsn.org
www.kcsn.org/programs/tablesofcontent.html
Transcends mainstream so-called Hip Hop stations
by exposing listeners to non-corporate motivated
musical acts.

Third Floor Radio
PO Box 6868, Fullerton, CA 92834-6868
Roslynn thirdfloorla@yahoo.com
ThirdFloorRadio.com
A journey through Hip Hop's past, present and
future.

True Unda-ground *WCSB*
Rhodes Tower 956, 2121 Euclid Ave. Cleveland,
OH 44115-2214
PH: 216-687-3721 FX: 216-687-2161
DJ Doc doc@liquid.web.com
www.wcsb.org
Alien Hip Hop - most of these groups you can only
hear HERE!

The Twiglet Zone *WBCR*
Rm. 306, Whitehead Hall, 2900 Bedford Ave.
Brooklyn, NY 11210
PH: 718-951-4515
TheTwigletZone@gmail.com
brooklyncollegeradio.org
Dedicated to playing the good, the weird and the
wonderful.

The Underground Railroad *WBAI*
120 Wall St., 10th Fl. New York, NY 10005
PH: 212-209-2800 x2931
Jay Smooth jsmooth@hiphopmusic.com
www.hiphopmusic.com/radio.html
The first DJ on radio to explore mixing classic Jazz
cuts with the latest underground Hip Hop.

Unified Sounds
www.unifiedbeats.com
Supports Underground music. Get recognition!

The UnSung Radio Show
7575 W. Washington Ave. #127-171, Las Vegas,
NV 89128
PH: 702-644-4688
Warrick Roundtree untamedtongues@yahoo.com
www.untamedtongues.com
This is where Spoken Word meets real music. Send 4
CDs along with press kits to the above address.

WBCR *Brooklyn College*
Rm. 306, Whitehead Hall, 2900 Bedford Ave.
Brooklyn, NY 11210
PH: 718-951-4515
brooklyncollegeradio@gmail.com
brooklyncollegeradio.org

WFNK
requests@wfnk.com
wfnk.com/radio
Covering every aspect of Alternative Black music.

W.I.N.D. IndieStreet Radio
DJ Suave wind@indiestreetent.com
www.indiestreetent.com/underground.html
Showcasing underground talent from around the
globe.

WKXN
PO Box 369, Greenville, AL 36037
PH: 334-286-9301 FX: 334-382-7770
Roscoe Miller wkxn@wkxn.com
www.wkxn.com
Hip Hop, Gospel and R&B.

Canada

Hip Hop 101 *UMFM*
Rm. 308 U. Ctr. Winnipeg, MB R3T 2N2
PH: 204-474-7027 FX: 204-269-1299
Kinetik kinetikaljoints@frozenbroccoli.com
www.frozenbroccoli.com/hiphop101.htm
*The best in independent and underground Hip Hop.
Constantly introducing the city to brand new artists
and flavas!*

in over your head
PH: 206-202-3291
inoveryourhead@gmail.com
inoveryourhead.net
Hip Hop podcast, culture and wrath from Montreal.

Keep it Surreal *CJUM*
Rm. 308 U. Ctr. Winnipeg, MB R3T 2N2
PH: 204-474-7027 FX: 204-269-1299
DJ Brace dj.brace@gmail.com
www.djbrace.com
*An eclectic mix of turntable related music. From
breaks to the music that sampled them. Focusing
heavily on turntablism galore, breaking it down and
playing it.*

The Lounge *CKUW*
Rm. 4CM11, 515 Portage Ave. Winnipeg,
MB R3B 2E9
PH: 204-774-6877 FX: 204-783-7080
thelounge@mailcity.com
www.ckuw.ca
*Online radio show playing Hip Hop, R&B and
Dancehall Reggae.*

Off the Hook *CKUT*
3647 U. St., Montreal, QC H3A 2B3
PH: 514-398-4616 FX: 514-398-8261
music@ckut.ca
www.myspace.com/offthehookradio
*Montreal's Underground + independent Hip Hop
source.*

The Wax Jungle *CKMS*
200 University Ave. W., Waterloo, ON N2L 3G1
PH: 519-886-2567 FX: 519-884-3530
www.ckmsfm.ca
The show focuses on Hip Hop and R&B beats.

E u r o p e

France

Skyrock
Skyrock.com, 37 bis rue Grenéta 75002 Paris,
France
www.skyrock.com
Rap, Hip Hop, R&B...

Norway

Goodshit Radio
c/o Noregs Rap og Småtaggarlag, Postboks 9110
Grønland, 0133 Oslo Norway
www.goodshitradio.com
*Our policy is that we only play good shit, hence the
name.*

Sweden

P3 Hip-Hop
Sveriges Radio, 211 01 Malmö, Sweden
www.sr.se/p3/hiphop
*Y'all need to peep this, because it's slammin! Nuff
said!*

United Kingdom

BBC Radio 1xtra *Hip Hop*
www.bbc.co.uk/1xtra/hiphop
*Home page of the BBC 1xtra's various Hip Hop
shows. Info, shows, contacts etc.*

BBC Radio 1 *Urban Music*
www.bbc.co.uk/radio1/urban
*Home page of the BBC Radio 1's various Urban
music shows. Info, shows, contacts etc.*

Big Bang Theory
www.myspace.com/bigbangtheoryradioshow
*If you feel your shit is good enough (check the
influence list for standards) then holla at me on the
messages and send that shit!!*

Conspiracy UK
montana1099@hotmail.com
www.conspiracyuk.com
*Hip Hop, Old Skool, Jungle, DnB, Garage, Tekno,
Soul, Reggae and much much more!*

Grand Theft Audio
PH: 07919-437120
info@grandtheftaudio.co.uk
grandtheftaudio.co.uk
*An urban internet radio station that plays Hip Hop,
D n' B, Garage etc. Providing an opportunity for
producers and DJs to have their talents displayed.*

Innacity Radio
dubs@innacityfm.com
innercityfm.com
*Only a few of us have any real heart , any real
intention of making a chance or trying to make a
difference. Only a few of us understand what it's all
about.*

A u s t r a l i a

Open Source *2SER*
U. Tech. Sydney, Level 26, Building 1, 1 Broadway,
Ultimo, NSW 2007 Australia
PH: 02-9514-9500 FX: 61-2-9514-9599
Dan Collins opensource@2ser.com
www.2ser.com/programs/shows/opensource
Electronic and Hip Hop.

New Zealand

True School Hip Hop Show *95bFM*
PO Box 4560, Shortland St., Auckland 1001
New Zealand
PH: 64-9-309-4831 FX: 64-9-366-7224
music@95bfm.com
www.95bfm.co.nz
*The phattest coverage of local and international Hip
Hop.*

A f r i c a

Bay FM
PO Box 70371, Greenacres 6000 South Africa
PH: 041-363-6788 FX: 041-363-7085
info@bayfm.co.za
www.bayfm.co.za
Have regular Hip Hop shows.

Jam Band Radio

Dead to the World *KPFA*
484 Lake Park Ave. #102, Oakland CA 94610-2730
PH: 510-848-4425
David Gans david@trufun.com
dttw.gdhour.com
*A mix of various Americana and Jam Bands in the
second hour.*

Finding The Groove *KUMD*
U. Minnesota, 130 Humanities, 1201 Ordean Ct.
Duluth, MN 55812
PH: 218-726-7181 FX: 218-726-6571
kumd@kumd.org
www.kumd.org
*A collection of Jam Bands from all over the U.S. &
the world.*

Home Grown Radio
PO Box 340, Mebane, NC 27302
PH: 919-563 4923
leeway@homegrownmusic.net
www.homegrownmusic.net/radio.html
Discover new bands and kind music.

Honest Tunes Radio Show *KXUA*
618 E. Edna St., Fayetteville, AR 72703
Daniel Gold goodgold@gmail.com
www.dgold.info/radio
*Covering a wonderful array of Songwriters, Jam
Bands and Roots music, including Blues, Jazz,
Bluegrass, Folk, Improv and live Electronic. Please
send CD's and press kits.*

Jam Band Extravaganza *KIWR*
2700 College Rd. Council Bluffs, IA 51503
PH: 712-325-3254 FX: 712-325-3391
Brock Turner jamband897@gmail.com
www.897theriver.com/jam.asp
*Specializing in automated hydro phonic growing
systems and the cutting edge of Rock.*

Jambana *WPGU*
#107, 24 E. Green St., Champaign, IL 61801
PH: 217-244-3000 FX: 217-244-3001
music@wpgu.com
www.wpgu.com
Jam Band music.

Jamnation *WXPN*
3025 Walnut St., Philadelphia, PA 19104
PH: 215-898-6677. FX: 215-898-0707
Bruce Warren online@xpn.org
www.xpn.org/jamnation.php
*Dedicated to the broad variety of musical output
often grouped under the "Jam Band" umbrella.*

The Music Never Stops *KPFK*
c/o Nomenclature Records, 419 N. Larchmont Blvd.
#15, Los Angeles, CA 90004
Barry Smolin shmo@well.com
www.mrsmolin.com/radio.php
*Contemporary Jam-Rock and miscellaneous
Psychedelia.*

The Side Trip *WQNR*
6622 Vermont Ave. 1st Fl. St. Louis, MO 63111
PH: 314-832-5529
James Mullin jamesm@thesidetrip.com
www.thesidetrip.com
Groove and Jam music.

Sign up for The Indie Contact Newsletter
www.indiebible.com

Stumble In The Dark *KDHX*
3504 Magnolia St. Louis, MO 63118
PH: 314-664-3688 FX: 314-664-1020
James Mullin volunteerdj@stumbleinthedark.com
www.stumbleinthedark.com
An eclectic mix of Rock, Jazz, Funk and Bluegrass.
Features some of the best live music from today's
best Jam Bands.

The Wildman Steve Show *WQNR*
2514 S. College St. #104, Auburn, AL 36830
Wildman Steve wildmansteve@wildmansteve.com
www.WildmanSteve.com
An eclectic mix of deep-catalog Classic Rock and
new 'good' music.

Jazz Radio

North America

Promotional Services

United States

Lisa Reedy Promotions
275 Bonnie Briar Pl. Reno, NV 89509
PH: 775-826-0755
Lisa Reedy reedylm@aol.com
www.jazzpromotion.com
A full-service radio promotions company that
specializes in Jazz and related music.

Internet, Syndicated Shows and Podcasts

aTTeNTioN sPaN raDiO
www.attentionspanradio.net
The hippest, coolest mix of Jazz, Funk and Rock
instrumentals available.

BendingCorners
PO Box 1955, San Mateo, CA 94401
bendingcorners@gmail.com
www.bendingcorners.com
Podcast featuring Jazz and Jazz-inspired grooves. If
you enjoy the groove side of all things "Jazz", this
is your thang.

Big Band Jump
PH: 800-377-0022 FX: 404-231-7990
Don Kennedy don@bigbandjump.com
www.bigbandjump.com
Featuring both original and later Swing music.

Broke N' Beat Radio
2217 Fitzwater St #2, Philadelphia, PA 19146
brokenbeatradio@gmail.com
www.brokenbeatradio.com
Podcast featuring the latest Broken Beat and Nu
Jazz sounds.

Cat Galaxy
catprotector@catgalaxymedia.com
www.catgalaxymedia.com
It is my hope that all of you cats and your humans
will enjoy this station. Smooth Jazz, Classic Rock,
Alternative, Funk, R&B and Swing.

Chill With Chris Botti
Chris info@chillwithchrisbotti.com
www.chillwithchrisbotti.com
Syndicated show playing NY Chill music. Chris also
posts recommended CDs on his website.

Coastal Jazz Radio
188 Summerlake Dr. SW., Marietta, GA 30060
PH: 770-438-7780
Eliott James ej@eliottjames.com
www.eliottjames.com/coastaljazzradio.html
Internet Jazz radio station. Submit CDs for
consideration.

Cobalt Stream 59
kirk.jackson@gmail.com
www.cobaltstream59.com
Kicking off an abstract mix of dangerously sexy
music featuring Down Tempo, Jazz, Trip Hop, Nu
Jazz and Funk.

Icy Hot Jazz *525.com*
contact525@525.com
www.525.com/icy-hot-jazz.htm
Featuring the best in Jazz old and new.

Jazz After Hours
729 N. 66th St., Seattle, WA 98103
Jim Wilke jim@jazzafterhours.org
www.jazzafterhours.org
New and well-established Jazz artists regularly drop
in for a chat.

The Jazz Suite
21901 Mada Ave. Southfield, MI 48075
PH: 734-658-9482 FX: 248-356-2021
Norvell Molex Jr. nmolexjr@comcast.net
thejazzsuite.mypodcasts.net
Podcast playing Contemporary, Progressive & Acid
Jazz from independent artists.

Jazz, Then and Now *Healthy Life Radio*
PH: 949-231-8476
Bill Tannebring biltan@usa.net
www.healthylife.net
Showcases mainstream Jazz of all genres from
around the world. I also invite established and up
and coming players to talk about their careers and
their music.

Jazz with Bob Parlocha
1216 Post St., Alameda, CA 94501
bob@jazzwithbobparlocha.com
www.jazzwithbobparlocha.com
Information about Jazz recordings, publications,
musicians and live gigs.

JazzSet
Dee Dee Bridgewater jazzset@npr.org
www.npr.org/programs/jazzset
Jazz radio series presenting today's artists.

Jazztrax
611 S. Palm Canyon Dr. #7-458, Palm Springs,
CA 92264-7402
PH: 760-323-1171 FX: 760-323-5770
jazztrax@jazztrax.com
www.jazztrax.com
The very best songs, from the very best Smooth Jazz
albums.

LuxuriaMusic.com
PO Box 26290, San Francisco, CA 94126-6290
support@luxuriamusic.com
www.luxuriamusic.com
Outré lounge and Latin Jazz, breezy swinging
instrumentals and vocals, Psychedelia, quirky
oddities, Retro Pop and Surf music.

New Orleans Radio
inquiry@lagniappe.la
www.neworleansradio.com
Produces and delivers regional custom music.

NPR Jazz
635 Massachusetts Ave. NW., Washington,
DC 20001
nprjazz@npr.org
www.nprjazz.com
Submit your CD for review consideration.

Quietmusic.com
www.quietmusic.com
Host Nick Francis brings you Smooth Jazz.

OverXposure.FM
overxposure.fm
Looking for Downtempo, Chillout, Modern lounge,
Electro Jazz, Nu Jazz. Please visit our site to see if
your music fits our formats. No Smooth Jazz.

Smoothjazz.com
PO Box 982, Pacific Grove, CA 93950
feedback@smoothjazz.com
www.smoothjazz.com
For on-air consideration, record representatives
may e-mail our music department.

SmoothNetRadio.com
adultmix@hotmail.com
smoothnetradio.com
A mix of Smooth Jazz blended with soulful Slow
Jams.

SoulfulSmoothJazz.com Radio
PO Box 660-100, Flushing, NY 11366
Blackwell contact@SoulfulSmoothJazz.com
www.SoulfulSmoothJazz.com
The world's hot spot for Soulful Smooth Jazz &
R&B where you can request your music and hear it
instantly. Commercial free all day, every day!

WCJZ World's Cool JazZ
www.wcjz.com
Our goal is to help the new Jazz artists get exposure
for their music. Submit your info via our online
"Artists Music Submission" form.

WNJL.com
1040 Riverview Dr. Florence, NJ 08518
PH: 609-922-1620 FX: 609-499-1971
wnjl@wnjl.com
www.wnjl.com
The home of Smooth Jazz On the internet.

Alabama

Alabama Public Radio Evening Jazz
PO Box 870370, Tuscaloosa, AL 35487-0370
PH: 205-348-6644 FX: 205-348-6648
Alisa Beckwith abeckwith@apr.org
www.apr.org

WJAB *Alabama A&M*
PO Box 1687, Normal, AL 35762
Ellen C. Washington ewashington@aamu.edu
www.aamu.edu/wjab

WVSU *Samford U.*
Birmingham, AL 35229-2301
PH: 205-726-2934 FX: 205-726-4032
wvsu@samford.edu
www.samford.edu/groups/wvsu

Arizona

KJZZ
2323 W. 14th St., Tempe, AZ 85281
PH: 480-834-5627 FX: 480-774-8475
mail@kjzz.org
www.kjzz.org

KYOT
PH: 480-966-6236
www.kyot.com
Featuring lots of known & unknown Jazz artists.

Arkansas

KASU *Arkansas State U.*
PO Box 2160, State U. AR 72467
PH: 870-972- 2200
www.kasu.org

KXRJ
Hwy 7 N., Russellville, AR 72801
PH: 479-964-0806 FX: 479-498-6024
broadcast.atu.edu/broadcasting.shtml

California

Capital Public Radio
7055 Folsom Blvd. Sacramento, CA 95826
PH: 916-278-8900 FX: 916-278-8989
jazz@capradio.org
www.capradio.org

FreeFall *KUSF*
111 Laidley St., San Francisco, CA 94131
PH: 415-386-5873
David Bassin playlist@freefallradio.com
www.freefallradio.com
A mix of Future Jazz, Soul, Abstract Beats & World Rhythms.

Horizons *KIFM*
1615 Murray Canyon Rd. #710, San Diego,
CA 92108-4321
PH: 619-297-3698 FX: 619-543-1353
Kelly Cole kelly@kifm.net
www.kifm.com
An hour-long listen to the artists and music breaking ground in Smooth Jazz. Join me for a serious sampling of what's on the horizon.

In the Groove *KUSP*
203 8th Ave. Santa Cruz, CA 95062
PH: 831-476-2800
Mike Lambert kusp@kusp.org
www.kusp.org/playlists/synch
Send any promotional items for airplay, giveaway or review.

In Your Ear *KPFA*
1929 MLK Jr. Way, Berkeley, CA 94704
PH: 510-848-4425 FX: 510-848-3812
Art Sato music@kpfa.org
www.kpfa.org
A cool fusion of Jazz and Latin music, giving voice to musicians deserving wider recognition.

KCBX
4100 Vachell Ln. San Luis Obispo, CA 93401
PH: 805-549-8855
kcbx@kcbx.org
www.kcbx.org

KCLU *California Lutheran College*
60 W. Olsen Rd. #4400, Thousand Oaks, CA 91360
PH: 805-493-3900
Jim Rondeau jrondeau@clunet.edu
www.kclu.org

KCSM
1700 W. Hillsdale Blvd. San Mateo, CA 94402
PH: 650-524-6945
Jesse Varela jesse_varela@kcsm.net
www.kcsm.org/jazz91.html
E-mail Jesse to set up submissions etc.

KKJZ *California State U.*
1288 N. Bellflower Blvd. Long Beach, CA 90815
PH: 562-985-5566 FX: 562-597-8453
info@kkjz.org
www.kkjz.org

KKSF
340 Townsend St., San Francisco, CA 94107
Attn: Music Director
PH: 415-975-5555 FX: 415-975-5573
Ken Jones comments@kksf.com
www.kksf.com
Send your CD to the music director at the above address. You will notified if we add it to rotation.

KPFK
3729 Cahuenga Blvd. W., North Hollywood,
CA 91604
PH: 818-985-2711 FX: 818-763-7526
Armando Gudiño pd@kpfk.org
www.kpfk.org

KRVR
961 N. Emerald Ave. Ste. A, Modesto, CA 95351
PH: 209-544-1055
theriver@krvr.com
www.krvr.com

KSBR *Saddleback College*
28000 Marguerite Pkwy. Mission Viejo, CA 92692
PH: 949-582-4228 FX: 949-347-9693
Vienna Yip jazziegirl.ksbr@gmail.com
www.ksbr.net

KSDS
1313 Park Blvd. San Diego, CA 92101
PH: 619-388-3068 FX: 619-230-2212
Joe Kocherhans joek@jazz88online.org
www.jazz88online.org

Madly Cocktail *KCSN*
18111 Nordhoff St., Northridge, CA 91330-8312
PH: 818-885-5276
Kat Griffin madlycocktail@aol.com
www.kcsn.org/programs/madlycocktail.html
An excellent mix of Cocktail Jazz, Latin Soul and Big Band mayhem all done up with a healthy dose of class.

Radio Sausalito
PO Box 397, Sausalito, CA 94966
PH: 415-332-5299
info@radiosausalito.org
www.radiosausalito.org
Several locally produced, Jazz oriented programs every week.

Tony Palkovic's Jazz Show *KSPC*
Thatcher Music Bldg. 340 N. College Ave.
Claremont, CA 91711-6340
PH: 909-626-5772 FX: 909-621-8769
Tony tpjazzshow@cs.com
www.kspc.org
A mix of Jazz-Fusion, Straight Ahead and Latin.

Colorado

KAJX
110 E. Hallam #134, Aspen, CO 81611
PH: 970-925-6445 x19 FX: 970-544-8002
Mike Rosenbaum music@kajx.org
www.kajx.org

KCME
1921 N. Weber St., Colorado Springs, CO 80907
PH: 719-578-5263 FX: 719-578-1033
Lenny Mazel jazz@kcme.org
www.kcme.org

KRFC
1705 Heatheridge D303, Fort Collins, CO 80525
PH: 970-221-5075
Louis Fowler musicdirector@krfcfm.org
krfcfm.org

KRZA
528 9th St., Alamosa, CO 81101
PH: 719-589-8844 FX: 719-587-0032
Mike Sisneros music@krza.org
www.krza.org

KUNC *U. Northern Colorado*
822 7th St. #530, Greeley, CO 80631-3945
PH: 970-350-0808 FX: 970-378-2580
Kyle Dyas kyle.dyas@kunc.org
www.kunc.org

KUVO
PO Box 2040, Denver, CO 80201-2040
PH: 303-480-9272 x17
Arturo Gomez arturo@kuvo.org
www.kuvo.org

Connecticut

In The Groove, Jazz and Beyond *WHUS*
1501 Storrs Rd. Storrs, CT 06269
Ken Laster ken@lasternet.com
www.lasternet.com/inthegroove
From Jazz masters of past and present to emerging new artists performing Jazz, Fusion and Funk.

Out Here & Beyond *WWUH*
200 Bloomfield Ave. West Hartford, CT 06117
PH: 860-768-4701 FX: 860-768-5701
Chuck Obuchowski cobuchow@aol.com
www.wwuh.org
I attempt to capture the diversity of the modern Jazz realm. I frequently feature interviews with the music-makers.

Florida

WDNA
PO Box 558636, Miami, FL 33255
PH: 305-662-8889 FX: 305-662-1975
feedback@wdna.org
www.wdna.org
Send in your serious Jazz.

WFIT *Florida Tech*
150 W. University Blvd. Melbourne, FL 32901
PH: 321-674-8949 FX: 321-674-8139
Todd Kennedy tkennedy@fit.edu
www.wfit.org

WLOQ
2301 Lucien Way #180, Maitland, FL 32751
PH: 407-647-5557 FX: 407-647-4495
Brian Morgan bmorgan@wloq.com
www.wloq.com
CD Reviews- 'Smooth Jazz' shows all day.

WLRN
172 NE. 15th St., Miami, FL 33132
PH: 305-995-2207 FX: 305-995-2299
info@wlrn.org
www.wlrn.org

WSJT
9721 Executive Ctr. Dr. N. #200, St. Petersburg,
FL 33702-2439
PH: 727-563-8830 FX: 727-568-9758
Kathy Curtis kcurtis@wsjt.com
wsjt.com
CD Reviews, concerts, interviews. Note that it's more difficult to get music on the air if you don't have any representation.

WUCF *U. Central Florida*
PO Box 162199, Orlando, FL 32816-2199
PH: 407-823-0899
Dave Martin dpmartin@mail.ucf.edu
wucf.ucf.edu

WUFT *U. Florida*
PO Box 118405, Gainesville, FL 32611
PH: 352-392-5200 FX: 352-392-5741
radio@wuft.org
www.wuft.org/fm

Georgia

The Jazz Spot *Georgia Public Radio*
260 14th St. NW., Atlanta, GA 30318
PH: 404-685-2400 FX: 404-685-2684
Masani jazz@gpb.org
www.gpb.org/public/radio/jazzspot
Mainstream and progressive contemporary impressions of Jazz music.

WBCX *Brenau U.*
PH: 770-538-4744
Scott Fugate wbcx@hotmail.com
www.brenau.edu/about/wbcx
Promotes and supports local Jazz musicians.

WCLK *Clark Atlanta U.*
111 James P. Brawley Dr. SW., Atlanta, GA 30314
PH: 404-880-8273
John Armwood armwood@armwood.com
www.wclk.com

Hawaii

Jazz with Don Gordon *KIPO*
738 Kaheka St., Honolulu, HI 98614
PH: 808-955-8821 FX: 808-942-5477
Don Gordon dgordon@hawaiipublicradio.org
dongordon.net/archive.htm
Jazz is a very thick tree with deep roots and many branches and I try to cover the gamut.

The Real Deal *KIPO*
738 Kaheka St. #101, Honolulu, HI 96814
PH: 808-955-8821 FX: 808-942-5477
Seth Markow realdeal@lava.net
www.hawaiipublicradio.org
I do play independent music, namely Jazz (likely to expand soon to include more diverse Roots music).

Idaho

BSU Radio Network *Boise State U.*
1910 University Dr. Boise, ID 83725-1915
PH: 208-947-5660 FX: 208-344-6631
radio.boisestate.edu
Radio Vision and Idaho's Jazz station.

Illinois

Extensions *WBEZ*
CPR, Navy Pier, 848 E. Grand Ave. Chicago, IL 60611-3462
PH: 312-948-4855
Sarah Toulousemusic@wbez.org
www.wbez.org
I explore the Jazz sounds of local, national and international artists, creating original, daring and diverse music.

New Vintage *WDCB*
College of DuPage, 425 Fawell Blvd. Glen Ellyn, IL 60137
PH: 630-942-4200 FX: 630-942-2788
Bill O'Connell OConnellB@wdcb.org
wdcb.org
Celebrating the many successes of today's band leaders dedicated to furthering and promoting America's greatest contribution to world music history.

WBEZ
Navy Pier, 848 E. Grand Ave. Chicago, IL 60611-3462
PH: 312-948-4855
music@chicagopublicradio.org
www.wbez.org

WDCB *College of DuPage*
425 Fawell Blvd. Glen Ellyn, IL 60137
PH: 630-942-4200 FX: 630-942-2788
wdcb.org
We're known for our eclectic music programming.

WGLT
8910 Illinois State U. Normal, IL 61790-8910
PH: 309-438-7871 FX: 309-438-7870
Jon Norton j.norton@ilstu.edu
www.wglt.org

WILL *U. Illinois*
Campbell Hall, 300 N. Goodwin Ave. Urbana, IL 61801-2316
PH: 217-333-0850 FX: 217-244-9586
willamfm@uiuc.edu
www.will.uiuc.edu
Send us your Classical, Jazz and Traditional/Ethnic music.

Indiana

Jazz By The Border *WVPE*
2424 California Rd. Elkhart, IN 46514
PH: 888-399-9873
Lee Burdorf lburdorf@wvpe.org
www.wvpe.org/border.html
We love to receive music from independent artists!

WBAA AM *Purdue U.*
712 3rd St. W. Lafayette, IN 47907-2005
PH: 765-494-3961
David Bunte dpbunte@wbaa.org
www.purdue.edu/wbaa

WFIU *Indiana U.*
1229 E. 7th St., Bloomington, IN 47405
PH: 812-855-1357
wfiu@indiana.edu
www.indiana.edu/~wfiu

WSND *U. Notre Dame*
315 LaFortune Student Ctr. Notre Dame, IN 46556
PH: 574-631-4069
wsnd@nd.edu
www.nd.edu/~wsnd

Iowa

KCCK *Kirkwood College*
6301 Kirkwood Blvd. SW., Cedar Rapids, IA 52406
PH: 319-398-5446 FX: 319-398-5492
Bob Stewart bobs@kcck.org
www.kcck.org

KHKE *U. Northern Iowa*
U. Cedar Falls, IA 50614-0359
PH: 319-273-6400 FX: 319-273-2682
kuni@uni.edu
www.khke.org

WOI *Iowa State U.*
2022 Comm. Bldg. Iowa State U. Ames, IA 50011-3241
PH: 515-294-2025 FX: 515-294-1544
info@woi.org
www.woi.org

Kansas

Jazz in the Night *U. Kansas*
1120 W. 11th St. U. Kansas, Lawrence, KS 66044
PH: 785-864-4530 FX: 785-864-5278
Bob McWilliams radiobob@ku.edu
kpr.ku.edu/Jazz

KMUW *Wichita State U.*
3317 E. 17th St. N., Wichita, KS 67208-1912
PH: 316-978-6789
info@kmuw.org
www.kmuw.org

Kentucky

WKMS *Murray State U.*
2018 U. Stn. Murray, KY 42071
PH: 270-809-4744 FX: 270-762-4667
Mark Welch mark.welch@murraystate.edu
www.wkms.org

WMKY *Morehead State U.*
132 Breckinridge Hall, Morehead, KY 40351
PH: 606-783-2001 FX: 606-783-2335
wmky@moreheadstate.edu
www.wmkyradio.com

WNKU *Northern Kentucky U.*
PO Box 337, Highland Heights, KY 41076
PH: 859-572-6500 FX: 859-572-6604
radio@nku.edu
www.wnku.org

Louisiana

KRVS *U. Southern Louisiana*
PO Box 42171, Lafayette, LA 70504
PH: 337-482-5787 FX: 337-482-6101
David Spizale dspizale@krvs.org
www.krvs.org

WWOZ
1008 N. Peters St., New Orleans, LA 70116
wwoz@wwoz.org
www.wwoz.org

Maryland

WTMD *Towson U.*
8000 York Rd. Towson, MD 21252
PH: 410-704-8938
wtmd@towson.edu
wwwnew.towson.edu/wtmd

WYPR *Johns Hopkins U.*
2216 N. Charles St., Baltimore, MD 21218
PH: 410-235-1660 FX: 410-235-1161
Andy Bienstock bienstock@wypr.org
www.wypr.org

Massachusetts

Jazz Safari *WFCR*
Hampshire House, U. Mass, 131 County Cir. Amherst, MA 01003-9257
PH: 413-545-0100 FX: 413-545-2546
Kari Njiiri kari@wfcr.org
www.wfcr.org
African, Afro-Latin, Afro-Caribbean and other international Jazz styles.

WGBH
PO Box 200, Boston, MA 02134
PH: 617-300-4415
www.wgbh.org

WHRB *Harvard U.*
389 Harvard St., Cambridge, MA 02138
PH: 617-495-4818
mail@whrb.org
www.whrb.net

WICN *Worcester*
50 Portland St., Worcester, MA 01608
PH: 508-752-0700 FX: 508-752-7518
Tyra Penn tyra@wicn.org
www.wicn.org
Many hours of Jazz, CD release parties and more!

Michigan

Nightside Jazz and Blues *CMU Public Radio*
1999 E. Campus Dr. Mt. Pleasant, MI 48859
PH: 989-774-3105 FX: 989-774-4427
John Sheffler sheff1j@cmich.edu
www.wcmu.org/radio/cmuradioproductions/
nightside.html
Artists/labels submit your music for airplay.

WDET *Wayne State U.*
4600 Cass Ave. Detroit, MI 48201
PH: 313-577-4146 FX: 313-577-1300
wdetfm@wdetfm.org
www.wdetfm.org

WEMU *Eastern Michigan U.*
PO Box 980350, Ypsilanti, MI 48198
PH: 734-487-2229
www.wemu.org

WGVU
301 W. Fulton Ave. Grand Rapids, MI 49504-6492
PH: 616-331-6666
music@wgvu.org
www.wgvu.org/radio

WLNZ *Lansing College*
400 N. Capitol, #001, Lansing, MI 48933
PH: 517-483-1710 FX: 517-483-1894
Lyn Peraino lyn@wlnz.org
www.lcc.edu/wlnz

Minnesota

Great Blend of Watercolors *KFAI*
1808 Riverside Ave. Minneapolis, MN 55454
PH: 612-341-3144
Dee Henry Williams deelin1@juno.com
www.kfai.org/programs/watercol.htm
Jazz, Blues, Rhythm & Blues, great interviews and mo' fun.

KBEM
1555 James Ave. N., Minneapolis, MN 55411
PH: 612-668-1752 FX: 612-668-1766
Kevin O'Connor kevino@jazz88fm.com
www.jazz88fm.com

One Final Note *KFAI*
1808 Riverside Dr. Minneapolis, MN 55454
PH: 612-341-0980
Scott Hreha scott@onefinalnote.com
onefinalnote.com/radio
The latest in Jazz and Improvised music.

Mississippi

WJSU *Jackson State U.*
PO Box 18450, Jackson, MS 39217
PH: 601-979-2140 FX: 601-979-2878
Bobbie Trussell Bobbie.Walker@jsums.edu
www.wjsu.org

WUSM *U. Southern Mississippi*
118 College Dr. #10045, Hattiesburg, MS 39406
PH: 601-266-4287 FX: 601-266-4288
wusmmik@yahoo.com
www-dept.usm.edu/~wusm

Missouri

KSMU
901 South National, Springfield, MO 65804-0089
PH: 417-836-5878 FX: 417-836-5889
ksmu@missouristate.edu
www.ksmu.missouristate.edu

KWWC *Stephens College*
1200 E. Broadway, Columbia, MO 65215
PH: 573-876–7272
Jonna Wiseman jwiseman@stephens.edu
www.stephens.edu/campuslife/kwwc

Nebraska

KIOS
3230 Burt St., Omaha, NE 68131
PH: 402-557-2777 FX: 402-557-2559
Mike Jacobs mike.jacobs@ops.org
www.kios.org

Nevada

KUNV *U. Nevada Las Vegas*
1515 E. Tropicana Ave. #240, Las Vegas, NV 89119
PH: 702-798-8797
Frank Mueller frank.mueller@unlv.edu
kunv.unlv.edu

New Jersey

The Groove Boutique
41 Watchung Plaza #387, Montclair, NJ 07042
Rafe Gomez music@thegrooveboutique.com
www.thegrooveboutique.com
An exhilarating listening experience that melds vibrant Jazz musicianship with dynamic, irresistible rhythms.

WBGO
54 Park Pl. Newark, NJ 07102
PH: 973-624-8880 FX: 973-824-8888
www.wbgo.org

WBJB *Brookdale College*
765 Newman Springs Rd. Lincroft, NJ 07738
PH: 732-224-2492
www.wbjb.org

New Mexico

KGLP
200 College Rd. Gallup, NM 87301
PH: 505-863-7626 FX: 505-863-7633
www.kglp.org

KRWG *New Mexico State U.*
PO Box 3000, Las Cruces, NM 88003-3000
PH: 505-646-4525 FX: 505-646-1974
krwgfm@nmsu.edu
www.krwgfm.org

KSFR *Santa Fe College*
PO Box 31366, Santa Fe, NM 87504-1366
PH: 505-428-1527 FX: 505-428-1237
info@ksfr.org
www.ksfr.org

New York

WAER
795 Ostrom Ave. Syracuse, NY 13244-4610
PH: 315-443-4021 FX: 315-443-2148
Eric Cohen escohen@syr.edu
www.waer.org

WBFO *U. Buffalo*
205 Allen Hall, 3435 Main St., Buffalo,
NY 14214-3003
PH: 716-829-6000
Bert Gambini bgambini@wbfo.org
www.wbfo.buffalo.edu

WDWN *Cayuga County College*
197 Franklin St., Auburn, NY 13021
PH: 315-255-1743 x2284 FX: 315-255-2690
wdwn@hotmail.com
www.wdwn.fm

WEOS *Hobart and William Smith Colleges*
300 Pulteney St., Geneva, NY 14456
PH: 315-781-3812 FX: 315-781-3916
Peter Rountree weosmusic@hws.edu
www.weos.org

WFNP *SUNY New Paltz*
SUB 413, New Paltz, NY 12561-2443
PH: 845-257-3041 FX: 845-257-3099
wfnpmusic@newpaltz.edu
www.newpaltz.edu/wfnp

WGMC
1139 Maiden Ln. Rochester, NY 14615
PH: 585-966-2404 FX: 585-581-8185
Derrick Lucas derrick@jazz901.org
www.jazz901.org

WLIU *Long Island U.*
239 Montauk Hwy. Southampton, NY 11968
PH: 631-591-7005 FX: 631-287-8392
Bonnie Grice bonnie@wliu.org
www.wliu.org

WQCD
395 Hudson St. 7th Fl. New York, NY 10014
PH: 212-352-1019 FX: 212-929-8559
cd1019@cd1019.com
www.cd1019.com
Playing NY Chill. CD reviews, live events and concert series.

WSKG/WSQX
PO Box 3000, Binghamton, NY 13902-3000
PH: 607-729-0100 FX: 607-729-7328
mail@wskg.pbs.org
www.wskg.com/radiowskg.htm

North Carolina

WSHA *Shaw College*
118 E. South St., Raleigh, NC 27601
PH: 919-546-8430 FX: 919-546-8315
wsha@shawu.edu
www.wshafm.org

WZRU
232 Roanoke Ave. Roanoke Rapids, NC 27870
PH: 252-308-0885 FX: 252-537-3333
Allen Garrett agarrett.wzru@charter.net
www.wzru.org

Ohio

The Fusion Show *WCSB*
2121 Euclid Ave. Cleveland, OH 44115-2214
PH: 216-687-3515 FX: 216-687-2161
Randy Allar fusion893@earthlink.net
thefusionshow.com
Fusion, Progressive, Instrumental music.

Mama Jazz *WMUB*
Williams Hall, Miami U. Oxford, OH 45056
PH: 513-529-5885 FX: 513-529-6048
Phyllis Campbell mamajazz@yahoo.com
www.wmub.org/mamajazz
The best in Jazz from the classics to today.

WAPS
65 Steiner Ave. Akron, OH 44301
PH: 330-761-3098 FX: 330-761-3240
Bill Gruber billgruber@913thesummit.com
www.wapsfm.com

WJZA
4401 Carriage Hill Ln. Columbus, OH 43220
PH: 614-451-2191 FX: 614-451-1831
www.columbusjazz.com
Live Jazz concerts listing, lots of Jazz programming.

WMUB *Miami U.*
Williams Hall, Miami U. Oxford, OH 45056
PH: 513-529-5885 FX: 513-529-6048
wmub@wmub.org
www.wmub.org

WNWV
PO Box 4006, Elyria, OH 44036
PH: 440-236-9283 FX: 440-236-3299
Bernie Kimble wavecontact@elbc.net
www.wnwv.com
Great Jazz and local concert listings for the area.

WYSO *Antioch U.*
795 Livermore St., Yellow Springs, OH 45387
PH: 937-767-6420
Greg Hil greghill@wyso.org
www.wyso.org

WYSU *Youngstown State U.*
1 University Plaza, Youngstown, OH 44555
PH: 330-941-3363
info@wysu.org
www.wysu.org

Oregon

Jazz Show *Radio Tierra*
PO Box 859, Hood River, OR 97031
PH: 541-387-3772 FX: 510-740-3637
John Metta jazz@jmetta.com
www.radiotierra.org
Send me your Jazz or Blues CD and I'll get your music on the air.

KLCC
4000 E. 30th Ave. Eugene, OR 97405-0640
PH: 541-463-6000 FX: 541-463-6046
klcc@lanecc.edu
www.klcc.org

KMHD *Mt. Hood College*
26000 SE. Stark St., Gresham, OR 97030
PH: 503-491-7633 FX: 503-491-6999
Greg Gomez music_director@kmhd.fm
www.kmhd.org

KMUN
PO Box 269, Astoria, OR 97103
PH: 503-325-0010
music@coastradio.org
www.kmun.org

Pennsylvania

WDUQ *Duquesne U.*
Pittsburgh, PA 15282
PH: 412-396-6030 FX: 412-396-5061
music@wduq.org
www.wduq.org

WPSU *Pennsylvania State U.*
102 Wagner Bldg. University Park, PA 16802
PH: 814-865-9778 FX: 814-865-3145
Kristine Allen kta1@outreach.psu.edu
wpsu.org/radio

WRDV
PO Box 2012, Warminster, PA 18974
PH: 215-674-8002
info@WRDV.org
www.wrdv.org
Jazz, Big Band, R&B.

Tennessee

WETS *East Tennessee State U.*
PO Box 70630, Johnson City, TN 37614-1709
PH: 423-439-6440 FX: 423-439-6449
www.wets.org

WFHC *Freed-Hardeman U.*
158 E. Main St., Henderson, TN 38340
PH: 731-989-6691
wfhu@fhu.edu
www.fhu.edu/radio

WFSK *Fisk U.*
Nashville, TN 37208-3051
PH: 615-329-8754
Xuam Lawson xlawson@fisk.edu
www.fisk.edu/wfsk

WMOT *Middle Tenn. State U.*
PO Box 3, Murfreesboro, TN 37132
PH: 615-898-2800 FX: 615-898-2774
Greg Lee Hunt ghunt@mtsu.edu
www.wmot.org

WUMR *U. Memphis*
PH: 901-678-2766
WUMRJazz@memphis.edu
www.people.memphis.edu/~wumrjazz

WUOT *U. Tennessee*
209 Comm. Building, U. Tennessee, Knoxville, TN 37996.
PH: 865-974-5375 FX: 865-974-3941
wuot@utk.edu
sunsite.utk.edu/wuot

WUTC *U. Tennessee*
104 Cadek Hall, Dept. 1151, 615 McCallie Ave. Chattanooga, TN 37403
PH: 423-265-9882 FX: 423-425-2379
Mark Colbert mark-colbert@utc.edu
www.wutc.org

Texas

KACU *Abilene Christian U.*
PO Box 27820, Abilene, TX 79699
PH: 325-674-2441
info@kacu.org
www.kacu.org

KNTU *U. North Texas*
PO Box 310881, Denton, TX 76203
PH: 940-565-3688 FX: 940-565-2518
kntu@unt.edu
www.kntu.unt.edu

KTXK *Texarkana College*
2500 N. Robison Rd. Texarkana, TX 75599
PH: 903-838-4541 x3269 FX: 903-832-5030
Jerry Atkins jbbop@aol.com
www.tc.cc.tx.us/ktxk

KVLU *Lamar U.*
PO Box 10064, Beaumont, TX 77710
PH: 409-880-8164
Joe Elwell elwelljc@hal.lamar.edu
dept.lamar.edu/kvlu

KWBU *Baylor U.*
1 Bear Pl. #97296, Waco, TX 76798-7296
PH: 254-710-3472 FX: 254-710-3874
www.baylor.edu/kwbu/index.php

Morning Jazz *KTEP*
500 W. University Ave. Cotton Memorial #203,
El Paso, TX 79968
PH: 915-747-5152 FX: 915-747-5641
www.ktep.org
Mainstream Jazz, Big Band, Traditional and up and coming Jazz artists.

Utah

KUER *U. Utah*
101 S. Wasatch Dr. Salt Lake City, UT 84112
PH: 801-581-4997
Steve Williams swilliams@media.utah.edu
www.kuer.org

Virginia

Soundwaves *WDCE*
PO Box 85, U. Richmond, VA 2317
PH: 804-289-8790 FX: 804-289-8996
Herb King wdce@richmond.edu
www.student.richmond.edu/~wdce
Purist prepare for an expansive look at the Jazz idiom.

Washington

KEWU *Eastern Washington U.*
104 R-TV Bldg. Cheney, WA 99004-2431
PH: 509-359-4282
jazz@mail.ewu.edu
www.kewu.ewu.edu

KPLU
12180 Park Ave. S., Tacoma, WA 98447-0885
PH: 253-535-7758 FX: 253-535-8332
Joey Cohn cohnjt@plu.edu
www.kplu.org

Washington DC

WPFW
2390 Champlain St. NW. 2nd Fl. Washington, DC 20009
PH: 202-588-0999 x357
Yolanda Turner turner_yolanda@wpfw.org
www.wpfw.org

Wisconsin

WOJB *Lac Courte Oreilles Ojibwa College*
13386 W. Trepania Rd. Hayward, WI 54843
PH: 715-634-2100 FX: 715-634-4070
Nicky Kellar programdirector@wojb.org
www.wojb.org

Wisconsin Public Radio *WPR*
821 University Ave. Madison, WI 53706
PH: 800-747-7444
Vicki Nonn NonnV@wpr.org
www.wpr.org/regions

Canada

African Rhythms Radio *CITR*
319 W. Hastings St., Vancouver BC V6B 1H6
PH: 604-488-1234
David Jones david@africanrhythmsradio.com
www.africanrhythmsradio.com
Jazz, Nu Jazz, Soul, Latin, Hip Hop.

After Hours *CBC*
PO Box 160, Winnipeg, MB R3C 2H1
www.cbc.ca/afterhours
*Entertaining, informing and challenging Jazz lovers
with host Andy Sheppard.*

Café Jazz Radio Show
669 Fairmont Rd. Winnipeg, MB R3R 1B2
PH: 204-777-5200 FX: 204-777-5323
ted@jazzlynx.net
www.jazzlynx.net
*Exposes and support new artists from around the
world.*

In a Mellow Tone *CKCU*
Rm. 517, U. Ctr., 1125 Colonel By Dr. Ottawa,
ON K1S 5B6
PH: 613-520-2898
Ron Sweetman ronsweetman@canada.com
www.ckcufm.com/inamellowtone.html
Jazz from every era and in every style.

Jazz Beat *CBC*
PO Box 6000, Montreal, PQ H3C 3A8
PH: 416-205-3700
radio.cbc.ca/programs/JazzBeat
*Concert recordings and studio sessions, current and
classic CD releases with host Katie Malloch.*

jazz for a sunday night *CHRW*
Rm. 250, UCC, UWO, London, ON N6A 3K7
PH: 519-661-3600 FX: 519-661-3372
Barrie Woodey jazz4a@yahoo.ca
chrwradio.com/shows/jazz.htm
Covers the whole spectrum of Jazz.

JAZZ.FM91
4 Pardee Ave. #100, Toronto, ON M6K 3H5
PH: 416-595-0404 FX: 416-595-9413
info@jazz.fm
www.jazz.fm
Latest Jazz and Blues styles, artists and their music.

Silence...on Jazz! *CBC*
PH: 604-662-6167 FX: 604-662-6161
Andre Rheaume silenceonjazz@vancouver.radio-
canada.ca
radio-canada.ca/regions/colombie-
britannique/Radio/silenceonjazz.shtml
*Concerts from across the country, new CD releases
and anecdotes.*

SkyJazz Radio
8-1288 Ritson Rd. N. #314, Oshawa, ON L1G 8B2
info@skyjazz.com
www.skyjazz.com
Hear great Jazz from new and undiscovered artists.

Swing is in the Air *CKCU*
Jacques Émond jre@radiojazz.ca
www.radiojazz.ca
*On the air for over 20 years. Featuring a wide
spectrum of Jazz, including Traditional, Blues, Bop,
Latin as well as Contemporary Jazz.*

Time for Jazz *CKUA*
10526 Jasper Ave. Edmonton, AB T5J 1Z7
PH: 780-428-7595 FX: 780-428-7624
Roger Levesque roger.levesque@ckua.com
www.ckua.com
Blending all eras of popular Jazz into three hours.

Europe

Belgium

The Global Jazz Scene
Peter Maguire pmaguire@jazz-clubs-
worldwide.com
www.jazz-clubs-
worldwide.com/netradio/jazzhalfhour.htm
*Please e-mail me and I will send you submission
details.*

Germany

department deluxe
Blutenburgstraße 82, d-80636, Munich, Germany
PH: +49 (0) 170-14-77-039
Jan Siegmund info@department-deluxe.org
www.department-deluxe.org
*NuJazz and Freestyle with a touch of Jazz. I always
request some MP3 samples to see if your music fits
our format.*

jazz-network.com
Hohnerstr. 23, 70469 Stuttgart, Germany
PH: 49-711-3966294 FX: 49-711-3966295
info@jazz-network.com
www.jazznradio.com
*Traditional to modern, mainstream to Blues and
World music.*

JazzRadio.net
Kornaue 1, 14109 Berlin, Germany
PH: 030-80692050 FX: 030-80692051
info@jazzradio.net
www.jazzradio.net
*Covering the world of Jazz - from Jazz news and
reviews to the Jazz lifestyle.*

Late Night Lounge *radioeins*
Liegnitzer Str. 15, D-10999 Berlin, Germany
Stephan Karkowsky kkowsky@lycos.de
www.radioeins.de
*Chill-Out, Folk-Lounge, New-Jazz, Downbeat or
Acoustic lounge show. No heavy beats!*

The Netherlands

Jazz & Blues Tour
PO Box 471, 2400 Al Alphen a/d Rijn,
The Netherlands
Joost van Steen jazzbluestour@alphenstadfm.nl
www.jazzbluestour.nl
Send any promotion material for airplay.

NPS Radio
www.omroep.nl/nps/output
Jazz, World and beyond.

Portugal

The Jazz Picante Radio Show
Largo dos Fornos - nº3 - 2ºESQ, Paço de Arcos -
2770-067 Portugal
Daniel info@jazzpicante.com
www.jazzpicante.com
Broken Beat, Nu Jazz, Nu Soul, Hip Hop ...

nujazzsoul.com
Av. D. Afonso Henriques, 276, 4814-515
Guimaraes, Portugal
Joao Cari jcari@nujazzsoul.com
www.nujazzsoul.com
*Nu Jazz, Broken Beats, Soul, Funk, Hip Hop, House
music and anything with a groove.*

Spain

All that Jazz Radio
Apartado de Correos 445, San Pedro de Alcantara,
29670, Malaga, Spain
PH: 34-95-278-56-16 FX: 34-95-278-39-04
Brian Parker bp@jazz-radio.fm
www.jazz-radio.fm
*Online 24 HOURS A DAY with the best Jazz on the
net.*

United Kingdom

BBC Radio 2 *Jazz and Big Band*
www.bbc.co.uk/radio2/r2music/jazz
*Home page of the BBC Radio 2's various Jazz and
Big Band shows. Info, shows, contacts etc.*

BBC Radio 3 *Jazz*
www.bbc.co.uk/radio3/jazz
*Home page of the BBC Radio 3's various Jazz
shows. Info, shows, contacts etc.*

JazzDJ Podcast
PO Box 2119, Leigh on Sea, SS9 LWJ UK
pod@jazzdj.co.uk
www.jazzdj.co.uk
*Explorations in Jazz. Exploring the many essences
of that Jazz juice groove!*

Jazz FM
26-27 Castlereagh St., London, W1H 5DL UK
www.jazzfm.com
Latin Jazz, world Jazz, fusion, vocalists and more.

Australia

3MBS
146 Cotham Rd. Kew, VIC 3101 Australia
PH: 03-9816-9355 FX: 03-9817 3777
info@3mbs.org.au
www.3mbs.org.au
Jazz and Classical music.

ozzyjazz.com
bob@ozzyjazz.com
www.ozzyjazz.com
Features live Jazz recorded around the world.

Latin Radio

100% Salsa Radio
PH: 910-797-4357
www.100-PercentSalsa.com
*We play all styles of Salsa old and new. We also do
CD reviews.*

Al Lado Latino *KBCS*
3000 Landerholm Cir. SE., Bellevue,
WA 98007-6484
PH: 425-564-2424
Johnny Conga kbcsdj@ctc.edu
kbcs.fm
*A lively fusion of Latin music showcasing the
diversity of the Latin music community of yesterday
and today.*

Alma del Barrio *KXLU*
1 LMU Dr. Los Angeles, CA 90045
PH: 310-338-5958 FX: 310-338-5959
www.kxlu.com
Authentic and traditional Latin music.

Alma Latina *KDHX*
3504 Magnolia, St. Louis, MO 63118
PH: 314-664-3688 FX: 314-664-1020
Lydia and Carlos almalatina@kdhx.org
www.kdhx.org/programs/almalatina.htm
Caribbean beats, classic boleros and Latin-style Rock 'n Roll.

Arriba *WDVR*
PO Box 191 Sergeantsville, NJ 08557
PH: 609-397-1620 FX: 609-397-5991
Carla Van Dyk carla@carlavandyk.com
www.wdvrfm.org
Featuring Latin rhythms.

Bachata 106
PH: 866-562-1866
bachata106@aol.com
www.bachata106.com
Mixing new and classic Latin music.

Batanga.com
2007 Yanceyville St., Greensboro, NC 27405
Attn: Programming
www.batanga.com
Plays several Hispanic genres.

The Best of Brazil *KZUM*
941 "O" St., Lincoln, NE 68508
PH: 402-474-5086 FX: 402-474-5091
Randy Morse somdobrasil@alltel.net
www.kzum.org/brazil
Featuring Brazilian musicians and composers.

Cafe Brasil *WDNA*
PO Box 558636, Miami, FL 33255
PH: 305-662-8889 FX: 305-662-1975
Gene de Souza feedback@wdna.org
www.wdna.org
Brazilian Jazz/Bossa Nova music in all styles , interviews and special in-studio musical guests.

Canto Tropical *KPFK*
3729 Cahuenga Blvd. W., North Hollywood, CA 91604
PH: 818-985-2711 FX: 818-763-7526
Hector Resendez hector@westsiderc.org
www.kpfk.org
Focusing on Salsa, Mambo, Afro-Cuban, & Latin Jazz from around the world.

Chicano Radio Network
7336 Santa Monica Blvd. #800, Hollywood, CA 90046
PH: 480-636-8853 FX: 612-465-4500
info@crnlive.com
www.crnlive.com
Submit your recordings to be included for possible rotation.

Con Clave *KPOO*
PO Box 423030, San Francisco, CA 94142
PH: 415-346-5373 FX: 415-346-5173
Chata Gutierrez conclave@kpoo.com
www.kpoo.com
Celebrating 30 years of Salsa music on the airwaves.

Con Sabor *KPFA*
1929 MLK Jr. Way, Berkeley, CA 94704
PH: 510-848-4425 FX: 510-848-3812
Luis Medina music@kpfa.org
www.kpfa.org
Afro-Caribbean Dance music. A mix of Salsa, Afro-Cuban and Latin Jazz.

Con Salsa *WBUR*
890 Commonwealth Ave. 3rd Fl. Boston, MA 02215
PH: 617-353-0909
Jose Masso jmasso@consalsa.org
www.consalsa.org
Afro-Cuban music, Salsa, Latin-Jazz, Merengue, Nueva Trova and World music.

Corriente *KGNU*
4700 Walnut St., Boulder, CO 80301
PH: 303-449-4885
music@kgnu.org
www.kgnu.org
Music, news, poetry and features.

Dimension Latina *WLUW*
6525 N. Sheridan Rd. Chicago, IL 60626
PH: 773-508-8080 FX: 773-508-8082
musicdept@wluw.org
wluw.org
Four hours of Latin music with occasional news.

El Viaje *WRTI*
1509 Cecil B. Moore Ave. 3rd Fl. Philadelphia, PA 19121-3410
PH: 215-204-3393 FX: 215-204-7027
David Ortiz davidortiz@phillysalseros.com
www.wrti.org
Spinning the classics alongside the currents in the ever-growing field of Latin Jazz.

Encanto Latino *WBEZ*
CPR, Navy Pier, 848 E. Grand Ave. Chicago, IL 60611-3462
PH: 312-948-4855
Catalina Maria Johnson music@wbez.org
www.wbez.org
Reaching back to classic recordings and looking ahead for some of the best of today's emerging sounds.

EnFiltro.com
enfiltro@gmail.com
www.enfiltro.com
Podcast featuring independent music from around the globe.

Esencia Latina *WGMC*
1139 Maiden Ln. Rochester, NY 14615
PH: 585-966-5299 FX: 585-581-8185
Javier Rivera javier@jazz901.org
www.jazz901.org
The best in Afro Caribbean music, Latin Jazz and Salsa.

Horizontes *KUT*
1 University Stn. A0704, Austin, TX 78712
PH: 512-471-2345 FX: 512-471-3700
Michael Crockett mcrockett@caravanmusic.com
www.kut.org
Travel the musical airways of Latin America.

Jazz on the Latin Side *KKJZ*
1288 N. Bellflower Blvd. Long Beach, CA 90815
PH: 562-985-5566 FX: 562-597-8453
Jose Rizo info@kkjz.org
www.kkjz.org

Jazz Tropicale *WDCB*
College of DuPage, 425 Fawell Blvd. Glen Ellyn, IL 60137
PH: 630-942-4200 FX: 630-942-2788
Marshall Vente VenteM@wdcb.org
wdcb.org
From traditional to contemporary and Brazilian to Caribbean. It's a Jazz show with palm trees.

KDNA
121 Sunnyside Ave. PO Box 800, Granger, WA 98932
PH: 509-854-1900
info@kdna.org
kdna.org
Addressing the needs and interests of Spanish speaking audiences.

KHDC
5005 E. Belmont, Fresno, CA 93727
PH: 559-455-5777 FX: 559-455-5778
www.radiobilingue.org
The only national distributor of Spanish-language programming in public radio.

Latin Aura *WCLK*
111 James P. Brawley Dr. SW., Atlanta, GA 30314
PH: 404-880-8273
Tomás Algarín wclkfm@cau.edu
www.wclk.com
Afro-Latin Jazz and Salsa that is free of time, type and music genre mandates.

The Latin Connection *KUNV*
1515 E. Tropicana Ave. #240, Las Vegas, NV 89119
PH: 702-798-8797
kunv.unlv.edu
Host Rae Arroyo hosts TLC so that Latin artists have a chance to be heard.

The Latin Train/El Tren Latino *CHUO*
65 University Pvt. #0038, Ottawa, ON K1N 9A5
PH: 613-562-5967 FX: 613-562-5969
Michael Bongard latintrain@yahoo.com
www.chuo.fm
Weekly show featuring Latin Jazz, Salsa, Timba and Cuban Son.

Latina Del Swing *WGMC*
1139 Maiden Ln. Rochester, NY 14615
PH: 585-966-5299 FX: 585-581-8185
Eugenio Marlin eugenio@jazz901.org
www.jazz901.org
Latin Pop music show.

Latino 54 *WMNF*
2815 3rd Ave. N., St. Petersburg, FL 33713
PH: 813-239-9663
Franco Silva dj@wmnf.org
www.wmnf.org
A worldwide journey through Latin culture.

Latino America Sonando *KMUD*
PO Box 135, 1144 Redway Dr. Redway, CA 95560-0135
PH: 707-923-2513 FX: 707-923-2501
Kate Klein md@kmud.org
www.kmud.org
The latest in Salsa, Songo, Latin Jazz, Afro-Cuban Folkloric, music from all over Latin America, plus interviews and other specials.

Latino Time Radio Oxigen
Emin Vafi Korusu Muallim Naci cad. No 61/5 Ortaköy 80840, Turkey
PH: 0212-236-5436 FX: 0212-236-5440
Ayhan Sicimoglu info@radiooxigen.com
www.radiooxigen.com

The Mambo Machine *WKCR*
2920 Broadway, Mailcode 2612, New York, NY 10027
PH: 212-854-9920
Jose "Cheo" Diaz latin@wkcr.org
www.columbia.edu/cu/wkcr
The longest running Salsa show in New York City.

Muszik 4 All
11221 Grouse Ln. Hagerstown, MD 21742
PH: 301-991-6724
Natasha A. Smith-Hazzard tasha@statiqrecords.ws
www.live365.com/stations/muszik4all
Fuzion Latino, Spanish Rap, Reggaeton, Salsa, Latin Jazz.

Noche de Ronda *KCSN*
18111 Nordhoff St., Northridge, CA 91330-8312
PH: 818-885-5276
Betto Arcos betto@kcsn.org
kcsn.org/programs/nochederonda.html
Covering the vast territory of Latin music in a weekly 3-hour show.

Onda Nueva *WUSB*
Stony Brook Union 266, Stony Brook, NY 11794-3263
PH: 631-632-6501 FX: 631-632-7182
Felix Palacios music@wusb.fm
wusb.fm
Everything from Sun to Salsa, Plena, Afro-Antillean, Latin-American music, interviews, history, live in-studio jams and critique.

Que Viva La Musica *WFDU*
Metropolitan Campus, 1000 River Rd. Teaneck, NJ 07666
PH: 201-692-2806 FX: 201-692-2807
Vicki Sola quevivalamusica@yahoo.com
wfdu.fm
Salsa and Latin Jazz of famous performers, plus artists rarely heard on commercial stations.

Radio Tierra
PO Box 859, Hood River, OR 97031
PH: 541-387-3772 FX: 510-740-3637
Hugo Florez hugo@radiotierra.org
www.radiotierra.org

Raices *KUNM*
MSC06 3520, Onate Hall, 1 U. NM, Albuquerque, NM 87131-0001
PH: 505-277-5615
Henry Gonzales music@kunm.org
www.kunm.org
All genres of Hispanic music.

Raizes Radio Show *KBCS*
3000 Landerholm Cir. SE., Bellevue, WA 98007-6484
PH: 425-564-2424
Paula Maya paulamaya@yellowhouserecords.us
kbcs.fm
Explores the music and culture of Brazil and its neighbors.

The Red Zone Indie *103.1*
Cha Cha theredzone@cookman.com
www.myspace.com/theredzone
Spins the hottest music being made by Latin artists from around the globe - spanning the alternative, Rock, Hip Hop, Punk, Ska, Electronic, Reggae and other cool music genres.

Ritmo Latino
www.ritmolatino.org
An hour of eclectic Latin music that will leave you shaking your booty and speaking in tongues. (Really.)

Ritmos Latinos *KRBS*
PO Box #9, Oroville, CA 95965
Mike Coranado krbs@cncnet.com
www.radiobirdstreet.org
Music from The Americas, Europe and the Caribbean.

Rock Sin Anestesia *WLUW*
6525 N. Sheridan Rd. Chicago, IL 60626
PH: 773-508-8080 FX: 773-508-8082
spanishrock@wluw.org
wluw.org
Latin Alternative radio show featuring Indie-Rock, Electronica, Surf, Fusion, Ska and more!

Sabor Tropical *KIPO*
738 Kaheka St. #101, Honolulu, HI 96814
PH: 808-955-8821 FX: 808-942-5477
Ray Cruz salsaymas@aol.com
www.hawaiipublicradio.org
Tropical programming with emphasis on Salsa, Afro-Cuban & Latin Jazz.

The Salsa and Latin Jazz Show *KVMR*
401 Spring St., Nevada City, CA 95959
PH: 530-265-9555 FX: 530-265-9077
Leon Reyes elleon7993@aol.com
www.kvmr.org
The best in Salsa, Salsa Jazz, Latin Jazz and those other Latin musical surprises.

Salsa Sabrosa *KUNM*
MSC06 3520, Onate Hall, 1 U. New Mexico, Albuquerque, NM 87131-0001
PH: 505-277-5615
Wellington Guzman music@kunm.org
www.kunm.org
Friday nights are hot hot hot!

Son de Cuba *WRTU*
PO Box 21305, San Juan, Puerto Rico 00931-1305
PH: 787-763-8500
Elmer González sondecuba2007@hotmail.com
www.wrtu.org
Afro-Cuban, Cuban Jazz, Timba.

Son del Caribe *WRTU*
PO Box 21305, San Juan, Puerto Rico 00931-1305
PH: 787-763-8500
Elmer González sondelcaribe@hotmail.com
www.wrtu.org
Afro-Caribbean, Latin Jazz, Salsa.

Son Pacifica *KPFT*
419 Lovett Blvd. Houston, TX 77006
PH: 713-526-5738
Alfonso Rivera alfonso@sonpacifica.com
www.sonpacifica.com
The best of independent Latino music!

The Sounds of Brazil
5250 Grand Ave. 14/111, Gurnee, IL 60031
PH: 847-855-8546 FX: 240-358-3096
www.connectbrazil.com
The best and the latest sounds from Brazil.

¡Tertulia! *WFCR*
Hampshire House, U. Mass, 131 County Cir. Amherst, MA 01003-9257
PH: 413-545-0100 FX: 413-545-2546
Luis Meléndez melendezl@acad.umass.edu
www.wfcr.org
Latin Jazz, Boleros, Salsa, Merengue, Nueva Trova, Tango and Folk music.

Tiene Sabor *WWOZ*
PO Box 51840, New Orleans, LA 70151-1840
www.wwoz.org
Host Yolanda Estrada wants to be the first to play a new record!

Viejoteca *CFRU*
U.C. Level 2 Guelph, ON N1G 2W1
PH: 519-837-2378 FX: 519-763-9603
DJ Gury Gury djgurygury@yahoo.ca
www.cfru.ca
The best in old school Salsa, along with the hottest new performers. Que Viva la Salsa!

La Voz Hispana *WWGC*
State U. W. Georgia, 1600 Maple St., Carrollton, GA 30118
PH: 770-836-6500
wwgc@westga.edu
www.westga.edu/~wwgc
Spanish news, music and information are featured.

WHCR
138th & Convent, Nac Building, Rm. 1515, New York, NY 10031
PH: 212-650-7481
whcr903fm@yahoo.com
www.whcr.org
Hosts many Latin music shows.

WKCR *Columbia U.*
2920 Broadway, Mailcode 2612, New York, NY 10027
PH: 212-854-9920
latin@wkcr.org jazz@wkcr.org
www.wkcr.org
A leader in Latin and Jazz music broadcasting.

WRTE *Mexican Fine Arts Center*
1401 W. 18th St., Chicago, IL 60608
PH: 312-455-9455 FX: 312-455-9755
www.wrte.org
Bilingual youth-operated, urban, community radio.

Metal Radio
Radio Promoters

McGathy Promotions
119 W. 23rd St. #609, New York, NY 10011
PH: 212-924-7775 FX: 212-691-8303
www.mcgathypromotions.com
Works with Commercial and Modern Rock. Also develops radio concerts, tours, promotions and more.

Skateboard Marketing
1150 Agnes Ct. Valley Stream, NY 11580
Attn: Munsey Ricci
PH: 516-328-1103 FX: 516-328-1293
Munsey excuseking@aol.com
www.skateboard-marketing.com
Street marketing & commercial specialty shows, active Rock & college Metal radio promotion.

Stations and Shows

North America
United States

4Q Radio
PH: +44-7793868611
andy@4qradio.com
www.4qradio.com
Station with a Metal and Punk Rock show.

Auditory Demise *WBGU*
120 West Hall, Bowling Green, OH 43403
PH: 419-372-8657 FX: 419-372-9449
www.myspace.com/auditorydemise
Steve Lazenby plays the latest and best of the Metal genre plus interviews with some up-and-coming bands.

The Autopsy Report
Gramie Pompous.Brit@gmail.com
theautopsyreport.heavymetalradio.net
If you are heavy, true and seriously minded, you WILL be played. I will contact you if you are good enough for the show. Send a CD/bio. Good MP3s are perfectly acceptable.

Axecaliber *WITR*
32 Lomb Memorial Dr. Rochester, NY 14623-0563
PH: 585-475-2271 FX: 585-475-4988
geno@heavyrock.com
www.heavyrock.com/radioshow.html
Promotes undiscovered Heavy Rock artists.

Bad Attitude Radio
PO Box 604, Kewaskum, WI 53040
cormws@charter.net
www.kissthis.com
Send your music and info and a written letter stating that you give us permission to air your music.

Bieber Labs Podcast
Ron ron@bieberlabs.com
podcast.bieberlabs.com
Highlighting independent instrumental Guitar Rock in the Steve Vai, Joe Satriani and Steve Morse vein.

Beyond the Grave *WKNH*
Attn: Paul Weston, 229 Main St., Keene, NH 03435
PH: 603-358-8863
www.btgrave.com
Weekly Metal show.

Brutality Radio
36804 Farmbrook Dr. B13, Clinton Twp. MI 48035
www.xwarp.net
Host Laura Walters plays only the most brutal Death Metal from around the world!!!

CottonRock Radio Podcast
PO Box 3646, Meridian, MS 39303-3646
www.myspace.com/cottonrock
Gives exposure to some of the best Rock, Hard Rock, Metal and Indie bands.

ChroniX Radio
www.chronixradio.com
Metal/Hard Rock/Alternative internet radio station.

Dementia Radio
www.dementiaradio.com
We encourage Indies to submit their music to us.

Doom Metal Radio
info@doom-metal.com
www.doom-metal.com/radio.html
All Doom and closely related music 24 hours a day, 7 days a week.

Electric Eye Radio
PH: 914-925-3443
Ed Glass eemb1@i-2000.com
www.electriceyeradio.com
Classic, Hard and Modern Rock, Heavy Metal, Goth and Punk.

Embrace of the Darkness & Metal *WMUA*
105 Campus Ctr. U. Mass, Amherst, MA 01003
PH: 413-545-3691 FX: 413-545-0682
DJ Solveig embraceofthedarkness@yahoo.com
www.embraceofthedarkness.com
European Metal (Death, Black etc.) Sunday nights.

From the Depths *KTRU*
PO Box 1892, Houston, TX 77251
PH: 713-348-5878
Wes Weaver fromthedepths666@hotmail.com
www.myspace.com/fromthedepths
Extreme Death and Black Metal radio program.

Havok Radio
1150 Fairview Ave. #205, Arcadia, CA 91007
PH: 888-295-9773
havokradio@hotmail.com
havokradio.com
Death, Black and Extreme Metal from around the world!

HeavyMetalRadio.com
Marc Schoech webmaster@heavymetalradio.com
www.heavymetalradio.com
The loudest site on the internet!!!

HoTMetaLradio
www.hotmetalradio.com
We play the music that YOU want to hear.

Into the Pit *KUPD*
c/o Marcus Meng, 1900 W. Carmen, Tempe, AZ 85283
www.98KUPD.com
The shit your mama don't want you to hear.

K666 Radio /StonerRock.com
PO Box 4, Tendoy, ID 83468
El Danno dan@stonerrock.com
www.stonerrock.com
If you're disgusted with the pathetic state of popular music, you've come to the right place. Please send TWO copies of your CD.

The Last Exit for the Lost *WVBR*
PO Box 224, Ovid, NY 14521-0224
PH: 607-273-2121 FX: 607-273-4069
lastexit@thelastexit.org
www.thelastexit.org
Supports Indie Metal, Goth, Punk, Industrial etc.

Livehardrock.com
livehardrock@livehardrock.com
www.livehardrock.com
Carries Hard Rock shows with DJs from around the world.

Maddog Rock Radio
www.heavymetalradio.net
Broadcasting from Kailua, Hawaii, but hey, even in paradise, we need to crank up the amps to 11 once in awhile! Check out the site for submission details.

Metal Reigns Live *LV ROCKS*
PO Box 989, Burnet, TX 78611
crusher@metalreigns.com
www.metalreigns.com
Tune in to hear the latest Metal releases.

The Metal Show
PH: 216-373-2304
Warlock and Chris Akin metal@themetalshow.com
www.themetalshow.com
Metal music podcast.

Metalradio.com
1321 Campbell Ave. La Salle, IL 61301
FX: 815-780-6001
webmaster@metalradio.com
www.metalradio.com
The only station for a Metal nation! Send us your demos or press releases and we'll get 'em up on the site.

Power Tracks *525.com*
contact525@525.com
www.525.com/power-tracks.htm
Featuring the best in Hard Rock.

PulverRadio.com
115 Broadhollow Rd. #225, Melville, NY 11747
PH: 631-961-8998 FX: 631-293-3996
programming@pulverradio.com
www.pulverradio.com
We're ready to blast your eardrums with cutting edge tunes from the world of in-your-face, up-all-night, guitar smashing Rock!

Rampage Radio *KUSF*
2130 Fulton St., San Francisco, CA 94117
Dirty Sanchez rampageradio@hotmail.com
www.rampageradio.com
The Bay Area's heaviest radio show since 1981. Please send any promo CDs to the address above. If your band wants to be interviewed on the show, e-mail me.

RIFF Radio
2621 14th St. S. #4, Fargo, ND 58103
Dan mmd@hardrocksociety.com
www.hardrocksociety.com
New, reviews and new releases are posted.

Rock Hard Place Radio Show
812 Countryside Park, Fargo, ND 58103
Torch rockhardtorch@hotmail.com
www.rockhardplace.com
Looking for new Rock, Metal, Industrial, Punk, Goth and other loud music!

The Root Of All Evil *KFAI*
1808 Riverside Ave. Minneapolis, MN 55454
PH: 612-341-3144
Earl Root root@rootofallevil.com
www.rootofallevil.com
Molten Metal meltdowns, demented and deranged. Totally tasteless. Rotten mean and nasty.

Rough Edge Radio
PO Box 5160, Ventura, CA 93005
PH/FX: 805-293-8507
R. Scott Bolton info@roughedge.com
roughedgeradio.com
Features 2 weekly Metal shows.

Scene Zine Podcast
Marcus Couch thescenezine@gmail.com
www.thescenezine.com
Featuring independent Hard Rock artists.

Snakenet Metal Radio
Jerry "Snake" Storch snake@snakenet.com
www.snakenetmetalradio.com
Contact to send CDs/promotional material.

Sound of the Fury *WLUW*
6525 N. Sheridan Rd. Chicago, IL 60626
PH: 847-424 1931
Kimberly Tester kim@uraniummusic.com
www.soundofthefury.com
The best in Death, Black, Power, Thrash, Hardcore and Progressive Metal.

Spread Radio Live
Dave Navarro spreadradiolive@6767.com
www.spreadradiolive.com
We play anything and everything we think is good!
Alternative, Electro, Metal, Punk and Goth.

STEEL 93
adamz@steel93.com
www.steel93.com
All forms of Rock. Hard, Metal, Punk, Glam etc. We
would love to play your songs!

StrongArm Radio *WRBB*
www.strongarmradio.com
www.myspace.com/strongarmradio
Loud, heavy and all about the local and
underground. If your band wants to be played, let us
know and send us some music.

Sudden Death Overtime *WITR*
32 Lomb Memorial Dr. Rochester, NY 14623-0563
PH: 585-475-2271 FX: 585-475-4988
ron@suddendeathovertime.com
suddendeathovertime.com
Every sub-genre is represented: Death, Thrash,
Power, Traditional, Doom and more! Just send you
music to us!

Thunderground Radio
1964 W. Acacia Ave. #56, Hemet, CA 92545
Rich Gardner rich@thundergroundradio.com
www.thundergroundradio.com
Featuring the BEST independent bands we can find!
Our primary genres are Hard Rock/Metal. We also
play Modern Rock, Industrial and anything that
ROCKS!

The Tink's Metal Show *WVUD*
PO Box 9284, Wilmington, DE 19809
PH: 302-798-0144
The Tink tink@thetinksinc.com
www.thetinksinc.com
The TINK is metal incarnate. Radio. Video. Online.
And, In Person. He is the Godfather. He is the man,
the myth, the legend and the entity that makes it
possible for the rest of us to be metal.

Vomit Radio
PO Box 93006, Albuquerque, NM 87199-3006
vomitbag@vomitradio.com
vomitradio.com
Heavy and uncensored 24 hours a day!

WGCC
1College Rd. Batavia, NY 14020
PH: 585-343-0055 x6420
Jared Ingersoll Ingus18@yahoo.com
wgcc-fm.com
A mixture of Rock, Metal and Punk programming.

Canada

Bourreau Metallique *CIBL*
1691, boul Pie IX, Montréal, QC H1V 2C3
PH: 514-526-2581 FX: 514-526-3583
bourreaumetallique@hotmail.com
www.sangfrais.com/bourreau

The Darkest Hours
Patrick Dumas info@thedarkesthours.com
www.thedarkesthours.com
Send us your demos, promos & press kit!

Feel The Rage *CJIQ*
Rm. 3B15, 299 Doon Valley Dr. Kitchener,
ON N2G 4M4
PH: 519-748-5220 x3223
Dan Kieswetter rage@gto.net
www.cjiq.fm/feeltherage.jsp
Weekly Heavy Metal radio show featuring all sub-
genres of Metal!

Hard Beyond Driven
PO Box 47665, 939 Lawrence Ave. E., Don Mills,
ON M3C 3S7
metalmike@hardbeyonddriven.com
www.hardbeyonddriven.com
Heavy Metal bands send your promos/CDs to us.

Metal Canvas *CHUO*
65 University Pvt. #0038, Ottawa, ON K1N 9A5
PH: 613-562-5967 FX: 613-562-5969
metalcanvas@yahoo.com
www.chuo.fm
If you send it, Metal Canvas will broadcast it!

Métal Pesant *CFLX*
67 rue Wellington nord, Sherbrooke, QC J1H 5A9
PH: 819-566-2787 FX: 819-566-7331
metalpesant@hotmail.com
www.cflx.qc.ca
Where the word Metal finds all its meaning.

MetalNetRadio.com
1 Selkirk Rd. W., Lethbridge, AB T1K 4N4
programdirector@metalnetradio.com
www.metalnetradio.com
We maintain our independence and play only what
we think is good and what our listeners think is
good.

Metalurgy's "Live Evil" *CFCR*
PO Box 21068, Grosvenor Park, Saskatoon,
SK S7H 5N9
PH: 306-664-5002
Larry Lava metalurgy@shaw.ca
members.shaw.ca/metalurgy/main.htm
The most extreme & brutal radio show to be heard
on the Canadian airwaves.

Midnight Metal *CHET*
PO Box 1325, Chetwynd, BC V0C 1J0
PH: 250-788-1663
Metal Mike mike@midnightmetal.com
www.midnightmetal.com
Get your album reviewed, sampled and played.

Mind Compression *CJSR*
Rm. 0-09 Students' Union Bldg. U. Alberta,
Edmonton, AB T6G 2J7
PH: 780-492-2577 x232 FX: 780-492-3121
Hosts: Metal John & DJ Temptress
www.cjsr.com
Canada's longest running Heavy Metal show! Metal
John plays Old School Metal, Hardcore, Classic
Metal and anything else he wants.

Pure Grain Audio Radio
59 Duncannon Dr. Toronto, ON M5P 2M3
PH: 416-723-3911
radio@puregrainaudio.com
www.puregrainaudio.com
Send us an e-mail and we'll arrange to have your
music featured on our amazing Indie show or all of
our weekly shows.

Space in Your Face *CKMS*
200 University Ave. W., Waterloo, ON N2L 3G1
PH: 519-886-2567 FX: 519-884-3530
siyf@gto.net
ckmsfm.uwaterloo.ca
Features Metal news, interviews, giveaways and
more!

Mexico

Mi Mama Me Mima
losmimados@gmail.com
www.mimamamemima.com.mx
Internet radio with a Rock format.

Europe

Andorra

KWFM.net
c/o Prat De La Creu, 16 - AD500 Andorra La Vella,
Andorra
J-E je.henley@kwfm.net
www.kwfm.net
International Rock and Metal radio. All submissions
are welcome without restriction of country and
language!

France

Kerosene Radio
6 bis, rue d'Echange, 35000 Rennes, France
kfuel@kfuel.org
www.kfuel.org
Rock, Noise, Hard/Emo Core, Experimental, Punk,
Pop ...

Rock'One
Poste Restante Paris beaubourg, 90 rue St. Denis,
75001 Paris, France
Emma emma@rockone.fr
www.rock-1.com
La webradio Rock.

Germany

InfraRot
Amtsgericht HRA 10032 Memmingen, Germany
PH: 49-0-8333/93113 FX: 49-0-8333/93114
Jörg Wolfgram gott@infrarot.de
www.infrarot.de
Fresh music for rotten people.

Radio Melodic
Postfach 3144, 70777 Filderstadt, Germany
PH: +49-7158-956611 FX: +49-7158-956611
radio@radiomelodic.de
www.radiomelodic.de
Each show is full of new CDs, news, interviews,
concert reports and more.

Rock of Ages *Bermuda-Funk*
Georg Lögler georg.loegler@web.de
www.bermudafunk.org
All styles of Rock/Metal. No Death Metal. My
emphasis is on UNKNOWN bands.

Rock Station Kiel
von Lüttwitz-Heinrichstr. 18, 24802 Emkendorf,
Germany
Heiko Mangels rockstation@kielfm.de
www.rockstationkiel.de
We play all styles from AOR to Metal in 2 shows.
Please send promotional stuff to the above address.

Rockin` Radio
Banderbacher Str. 24, 90513 Zirndorf, Germany
PH/FX: 0911-60-95-95
info@rockin-radio.de
www.rockin-radio.de
Das beste fur franken in Sachen Rock.

Stahlwerk-Hannover *Radio Flora*
Zur Bettfedernfabrik 1, D-30451 Hannover,
Germany
PH: 49-511-219790 FX: 49-511-2197919
info@stahlwerk-hannover.de
www.stahlwerk-hannover.de
Different bands without a recent record deal are featured.

Portugal

S.O.S Heavy Metal Radio Show
PO Box 408, 4703 Braga Codex, Portugal
PH: +351-919051581
Filipe Marta mail@sosradio.online.pt
www.sosradio.online.pt
Online and screaming fucking loud!

United Kingdom

One Louder Radio UK
richard@oneloudermedia.com
www.OneLouderRadio.co.uk
If you do not have any MP3s, you can e-mail us for our mailing address.

The Rock Show
Ewan Spence ewanspence@gmail.com
rock.thepodcastnetwork.com
If you think you should be in a future show, then you need to let me know. I'll be happy with a URL pointing to a demo or even a small MP3 file.

Sex to 9 with María *TotalRock*
1 Denmark Pl. London, WC2H 8NL UK
maria@sexto9.com
www.sexto9.com
Rock and Metal like you've never heard it before ...with a touch of exotic Latin passion.

Zed's Psycholopedia of Rock *TotalRock*
1 Denmark Pl. London, WC2H 8NL UK
Zaid 'Zed' Couri zed@psycholopedia.co.uk
www.psycholopedia.co.uk
A kick-arse Rock/Heavy Metal show.

A u s t r a l i a

Critical Mass Radio Show *RTR FM*
PO Box 949, Nedlands, WA 6909 Australia
PH: 08-9260 9210
Dysie & Killmachine c_mass@bigpond.com
www.wf.com.au/criticalmass
Stay Heavy Metal and bang your heads.

Full Metal Racket *Triple J*
GPO Box 9994, Melbourne , VIC 3000 Australia
PH: 1-800-0555-36
Andrew Haug fullmetalracket@triplej.abc.net.au
www.triplej.abc.net.au/racket
Covering a wide range of the latest and greatest heavy sounds with news updates, interviews, local and international tour announcements and tonnes more. Send in your demo CDs and tapes.

New Age Radio

United States

Alpha Rhythms *WYSO*
795 Livermore St., Yellow Springs, OH 45387
PH: 937-767-6420
Lori ltaylor@uc-council.org Jerry
allank@earthlink.net
www.wyso.org/alpharhythms.htm
4 hours of Ambient and New Age music.

Ambience *WWUH*
200 Bloomfield Ave. West Hartford, CT 06117
PH: 860-768-4701 FX: 860-768-5701
Susan teltanman@cox.net
www.teltan.org
Ambient and Atmospheric Electronic music to drift into Sunday morning with.

AM/FM *WMUH*
PO Box 632, Nazareth, PA 18064-0632
Bill Y. Fox billyfox@soundscapes.us
soundscapes.us/amfm
Electronic, Ambient, Space, Acoustic, Electric, Pop, New Age and whatever strikes my fancy. Inquire by e-mail BEFORE submitting your music!

Astreaux World
www.astreauxworld.com
Ambient/ New Age / Space music. Visit our website to find out submission details.

Audioscapes *KCPR*
Graphic Arts Bldg 26, Rm. 201, CPSU
San Luis Obispo, CA 93407
PH: 805-756-2965
audioscapes@yahoo.com
www.geocities.com/audioscapes
A Classical, Electronic and Progressive music merge.

Audiosyncracry *KTEP*
500 W. University Ave. Cotton Memorial #203,
El Paso, TX 79968
PH: 915-747-5152 FX: 915-747-5641
www.ktep.org
Host Jamey Osborne covers a wide range of music, from Acoustic to Electronica. A good deal of Jazz and Classical is played with an occasional dash of World music.

Bodies at Rest
1515 Ygnacio Valley Rd. Ste. C, Walnut Creek,
CA 94598
PH: 925-250-2805
Celestial Dancer celdancer@yahoo.com
www.bodiesatrestonline.com
Offers relaxing music and spoken word poetry by Indie artists to soothe you into momentary bliss.

BRAINWAVES *KXCI*
220 S. 4th Ave. Tucson, AZ 85701
PH: 520-623-1000
Doug Wellington brainwaves@kxci.org
www.brainwavesradio.com
New Age, Ambient, Experimental, Electro-Acoustic Classical, World music.

CheezMuzik *WTUL*
177 Chatsworth St., Baton Rouge, LA 70802
PH: 504-865-5887 FX: 504-862-3072
Chris Albright cheez_director@hotmail.com
www.wtul.fm
One of the longest running shows in New Orleans' radio history. Over 30 years & still going strong!

Cosmic Island
kevin@thecosmicisland.com
TheCosmicIsland.com
The best mix of New Age and Ambient music. Please do NOT send MP3s!

The Crystal Ballroom *NetRadioLink.com*
info@netradiolink.com
www.netradiolink.com/id1.html
Quiet Brilliance! Piano, Keyboard and Progressive Electronic music.

Different Standards *KMBH*
PO Box 2147, Harlingen, TX 78551
PH: 956-421-4111 FX: 956-421-4150
Kim Menard kmbhkhid@aol.com
www.kmbh.org/radio
Instrumental and Ambient music from the classic sounds right up to the newest releases.

Earth Tones *KVLU*
PO Box 10064, Beaumont, TX 77710
PH: 409-880-8164
Elizabeth French kvlu@hal.lamar.edu
dept.lamar.edu/kvlu
Two hours of New Age, Acoustic, Ambient and World music.

Echoes
PO Box 256, Chester Springs, PA 19425
FX: 610-827-9614
echoes@echoes.org
www.echoes.org
Send submissions for airplay (CDs only). Do NOT attach MP3s!

ethnosphere *KRCL*
450 S. 300 West, Salt Lake City, UT 84101
PH: 801-359-9191 FX: 801-533-9136
Sohrab Mafi sohrabm@krcl.org
www.krcl.org/programs/ethnosphere.htm
A meditative journey into the world of consciousness through music.

Galactic Voyager *KCSN*
18111 Nordhoff St., Northridge, CA 91330-8312
PH: 818-885-5276
Meishel Menachekanian meishel@kcsn.org
www.kcsn.org/programs/galacticvoyager.html
A blend of Electronic and New Age music.

Gift of Peace *WJFF*
4765 State Rt. 52, PO Box 546, Jeffersonville,
NY 12748
PH: 845-482-4141 FX: 845-482-9533
Lisa Brody jimandlisa@pronetisp.net
www.wjffradio.org
The New Age music has to have a certain feel to it. I guess you could call it spiritual, but not sappy. The World music is usually very mellow.

Hearts of Space Radio
454 Las Gallinas #333, San Rafael, CA 94903
PH: 415-499-9902 FX: 415-499-9903
radio@hos.com
www.hos.com/radio.html
Submit your music, send CD & promo info.

Idyllic Music
idyllicmusic@cox.net
www.idyllicmusic.com
Podcast featuring Trip Hop, Ambient, Jazz, Dub and Downtempo songs by outstanding bands from around the globe.

Inner Visions *WNMC*
1701 E. Front St., Traverse City, MI 49686
PH: 231-995-2562
www.wnmc.org
A mix of sounds and textures that could not be more appropriate for a Sunday morning.

Instrumental Saturdays *WMSE*
1025 N. Broadway, Milwaukee, WI 53202
PH: 414-277-6942 FX: 414-277-7149
Mary Bartlein meab@execpc.com
my.execpc.com/~meab
New Age, Ambient and World music.

Iridium Radio *KZYX/KZYZ*
PO Box 1, Philo, CA 95466
Kitty & Creek Iridiumradio@starband.net.
www.iridiumradio.com
Currently we are interested in exploring your offerings in New Age, World and Cool Jazz.

The Lighthouse *KCHO*
Cal State U. Chico 95929-0500
PH: 530-898-5896 FX: 530-898-4348
info@kcho.org
www.kcho.org
Mellow and uplifting music.

Lucid Sounds *WZBC*
Boston College, McElroy Commons 107,
Chestnut Hill, MA 02467
PH: 617-552-4686 FX: 617-552-1738
Victor wzbcmusic@gmail.com
www.wzbc.org
Expanding awareness.

Midnight Light *KKUP*
933 Monroe St., PMB 9150, Santa Clara, CA 95050
PH: 408-260-2999
Joseph Leight kkup.folk@gmail.com
www.kkup.com
Soundscapes, spoken words, occasionally taped interviews with the thoughts to foster peaceful states of mind

Morning Breeze *KSBR*
28000 Marguerite Pkwy. Mission Viejo, CA 92692
PH: 949-582-4221
Donna Jo Thornton themorningbreeze@gmail.com
www.ksbr.net
A mixture of New Age, World, Acoustic Instrumental and Spacey Electronic music.

The Morning Fog *WVUD*
Perkins Student Ctr. U. Delaware, Newark, DE 19716
PH: 302-831-2701 FX: 302-831-1399
Gary Dunham morningfogman@yahoo.com
www.wvud.org
Early morning Ambience for sleeping or waking.

Music From Beyond the Lakes *WDBX*
224 N. Washington St., Carbondale, IL 62901
PH: 618-457-3691
Jerry & Namdar wdbx@globaleyes.net
www.wdbx.org
New Age music show.

Music from the Cosmic Wheel *WSCS*
Postmaster, E. Andover, NH 03231
PH: 603-735-5586
Brad Hartwell brad@cosmicwheel.net
www.cosmicwheel.net
New Age, Ambient/Electronic/Space, World Fusion, Native, Celtic etc. Taped interviews and live performances are an occasional feature.

Music of the 21ˢᵗ Century with Chris Hickey *WXXI*
280 State St. PO Box 30021, Rochester, NY 14603-3021
PH: 585-258-0200
wxxi.org
New Age, Celtic, Jazz and World music that is energetic, rhythmic and melodic. It is a journey through a pleasing, surprising and sometimes startling musical landscape.

Musical Starstreams
Forest & Madison info@starstreams.com
www.starstreams.com
Mid to Downtempo, exotic Electronica. If you think your stuff fits, send your release on regular CD only (no MP3s) to our mailing address and then watch our playlists to see if it worked for us.

Mystic Music *KKUP*
933 Monroe St., PMB 9150, Santa Clara, CA 95050
Eric Mystic admin@kkup.com
www.kkup.com/ericm.html
Something special and out of the ordinary. Lifts and awakens you above normal consciousness.

Mystic Soundscapes
PO Box 50128, Albuquerque, NM 87181-0128.
www.mysticsoundscapes.com
We make it our mission to promote your music to our large listener base. If your music fits the New Age, World music, Celtic, Ambient or Instrumental genre, we'd love to hear from you.

Neptune Currents *KKUP*
933 Monroe St., PMB 9150, Santa Clara, CA 95050
Steve Davis & Carol Joyce
neptuneradio@earthlink.net
www.kkup.org
Tranquil, expressive, meditative. Emphasis on electronic & Electro-Acoustic music, plus music of the Far East and other World music.

New Age Collage *SDPR*
555 Dakota St. PO Box 5000, Vermillion, SD 57069
PH: 800-456-0766
Jerry Cooley programming@sdpb.org
www.sdpb.org/radio/newage
2 hours of modern instrumental music.

New Age Sampler *WWSP*
105 CAC Reserve St., Stevens Point, WI 54481
PH: 715-346-2696 FX: 715-346-4012
BEAR nasbear@bearheartltd.com
www.bearheartltd.com/nas
Ambient, Celtic, Instrumental, New Age, Orchestral, Smooth Jazz, Space & World music.

The New Edge *WMBR*
3 Ames St., Cambridge, MA 02142
PH: 617-253-8810
Ken Field newedge@wmbr.org
wmbr.mit.edu
Mostly instrumental creative new music, composed and improvised at the intersection of Classical, Jazz and World styles.

New Frontiers *WXDU*
PO Box 90689, Duke Stn. Durham, NC 27708
Attn: Marty
PH: 919-684-2957
music_director@wxdu.org
www.wxdu.duke.edu
Two hours of Space music. Almost Ambient, almost Trance & almost Folk.

New Music Gallery *WMNR*
PO Box 920, Monroe, CT 06468
PH: 203-268-9667
info@wmnr.org
www.wmnr.org

Night Breeze *KCCK*
6301 Kirkwood Blvd. SW., Cedar Rapids, IA 52406
PH: 319-398-5446 FX: 319-398-5492
Mark Jayne nightbreeze@kcck.org
www.kcck.org
The most relaxing evening in radio. An exotic blend of mellow Jazz with new Instrumental and Ambient sounds.

Night Tides *KCUR*
4825 Troost Ave. #202, Kansas City, MO 64110
PH: 816-235-1551 FX: 816-235-2864
Renee Blanche blanchea@umkc.edu
www.kcur.org/nighttides.html
Instrumental & Electronic music that combines upbeat grooves and dubs with soothing melodies that whisper (softly) to the soul.

Nightcrossings *Radio Kansas*
815 N. Walnut #300, Hutchinson, KS 67501-6217
PH: 620-662-6646
Sara Sayers comments@radiokansas.org
www.radiokansas.org/nc.cfm
New Age music with light Jazz and Classical.

Nightstreams *KASU*
PO Box 2160, State University, AR 72467
PH: 870-972- 2200
Marty Scarbrough kasu@astate.edu
www.kasu.org
Relaxing, contemporary instrumental music.

Nocturnes *KEDM*
ULM 225 Stubbs Hall, Monroe, LA 71209-6805
PH: 318-342-5556 FX: 318-342-5570
Adrainne LaFrance classical@kedm.org
kedm.ulm.edu
Mixes Acoustic and Classical music forms.

Oasis *Montana Public Radio*
U. Montana, Missoula, MT 59812-8064
PH: 406-243-4931 FX: 406-243-3299
www.mtpr.net
Electronic and Acoustic New Age music with host Joan Richarde.

Open Space District *KRCB*
5850 Labath Ave. Rohnert Park, CA 94928
PH: 707-585-8522 FX: 707-585-1363
John Katchmer listener@krcb.org
www.krcb.org/radio
A weekly slide through the dreamy, dopey, sexy world of contemporary Electronica.

The Riverbank
Mudgie DaOtter mudgie@riverotter.net
www.riverotter.net/riverbank.html
Playing a mix of New Age, Ambient and Electronic music.

Solitudes *WXPR*
303 W. Prospect Ave. Rhinelander, WI 54501
PH: 715-362-6000 FX: 715-362-6007
wxpr@wxpr.org
www.wxpr.org
An hour of New Age or "Space" music.

Soundscape *WSKG*
PO Box 3000, Binghamton, NY 13902
PH: 607-729-0100 x315
Crystal Sarakas Crystal_Sarakas@wskg.pbs.org
wskg.com/Soundscape/soundscape.htm
New Age & World music.

Star's End *WXPN*
PO Box 22, Upper Darby, PA 19082-0022
Chuck van Zyl info@starsend.org
www.starsend.org
A non-stop drifting blend, drawing from many genres including Ambient, Spacemusic, Chillout, New Age etc.

Sunday CD Spotlight *WSHU*
5151 Park Ave. Fairfield, CT 06825
PH: 203-365-6604
Julie Freddino jfred@wshu.org
wshuweb.wshu.org/spotlight/spotlight.php
New Age and Space music.

Sunday Session *WKZE*
7392 S. Broadway, Red Hook, NY 12571
PH: 845-758-9811 FX: 845-758-9819
Steve Utterback info@wkze.com
www.wkze.com
An interesting mix of Contemporary Jazz, Native, World Beat and New Age music.

Sunday Sunrise *KRVR*
961 N. Emerald Ave. Ste. A, Modesto, CA 95351
PH: 209-544-1055
Jim Bryan theriver@krvr.com
www.krvr.com
Acoustic, New Age and World music.

Sunrise *WUTC*
615 McCallie Ave. Dept. 1151, Chattanooga, TN 37403
PH: 423-265-9882 FX: 423-425-2379
Rabbit rabbit@celticradio.org
www.wutc.org
Soothing Acoustic, New Age and World music. Quiet and reflective moments provide an opportunity to begin your weekend with a peaceful atmosphere of relaxing music.

Tangents *KALW*
82 Valmar Ter. San Francisco, CA 94112-2156
PH: 415-841-4134 FX: 415-841-4125
Dore dore@tangents.com
www.tangents.com
A program that explores the bridges connecting various styles of music, such as World and Roots music and creative Jazz hybrids.

Tonal Vision *WICN*
6 Chatham St., Worcester, MA 01609
PH: 508-752-0700 FX: 508-752-7518
Karen Mungal karen@wicn.org
www.wicn.org
New Age, Acoustic, Ambient and World music.

Visionary Activist *KPFA*
PO Box 94, Cabin John, MD 20818
PH: 510-848-4425 FX: 510-848-3812
Caroline W. Casey info@visionaryactivism.com
www.visionaryactivism.com/radioshow.htm
Insights on the nature of magic and reality.

Canada

Deep Intense Radio *CHLY*
c/o Music Dept. #242, 1-5765 Turner Rd. Nanaimo, BC V9T 6M4
www.deepintense.com
We're looking for Downtempo Electronica music artists to submit their music for airplay.

Germany

Sounds of Syn
Steffen Thieme redaktion@sounds-of-syn.de
www.sounds-of-syn.de
A program for Synthesizer music.

The Netherlands

Time Trek
Jelke Bethlehem jelkeb@xs4all.nl
timetrek.nl
Het programma neemt u mee op een ontspannende reis door de wereld van de New Age muziek.

Sound Sounding
Ronald promotiekk@boortman.presenteert.nl
boortman.presenteert.nl
Smooth moods, which one can bring spiritual emotions.

Spain

Musical Trip Radio Iliberis
Plaza Los Caquis Nº1, Maracena, GranadaI CP 18200, Spain
PH: +34-958-420310
Miguel Angel Espigares Flores
yoparoeltiempo@terra.es
otrasmusicas.net
We want to be the first in discovering it. New Age, Symphonic Rock, Jazz Fusion, Soundtracks, Lounge and Contemporary Electronic music.

Australia

Ultima Thule *2MBS*
PO Box 633, Potts Point, NSW 1335 Australia
information@ultimathule.info
www.ultimathule.info
Enthralling audiences with a unique, entrancing melange of Ambient and Atmospheric music from around the world.

Japan

Earth Feeling *Love FM*
2-18-1-501 Kusagae, Chuo-ku, Fukuoka, 810-0045, Japan
PH/FX: 81-92-716-8848
Jeffrey Martin earthfeeling@yahoo.com
www.lovefm.co.jp
Features relaxing kinds of sounds that is described in Japan as "healing music," known more popularly in Europe and America as New Age.

Progressive Rock Radio

North America

United States

Afterglow *WMUH*
PO Box 632, Nazareth, PA 18064-0632
Bill Fox billyfox@soundscapes.us
soundscapes.us/afterglow
I host a mixed bag of Acoustic, Electric, Pop, New Age and Progressive Rock. Inquire by e-mail before submitting music. I just want to make sure your music is one of the above genres.

Aural Moon
Davin Flateau avian@auralmoon.com
www.auralmoon.com
A large portion of our playlist is from independent artists.

The Canvas Prog Hour
411 Lorraine Blvd. Pickerington, OH 43147
Matt Sweitzer canvas@insight.rr.com
www.canvasproductions.net
We welcome promos that fall under the rather broad category of Jazz Fusion, Prog and/or Art Rock.

Delicious Agony
Don Cassidy dcass21@optonline.net
deliciousagony.com
We have added more live DJs and many live shows, each with a different flavor.

Dreams Wide Awake *WOSP*
11800 UNF Dr. HB #2565, Jacksonville, FL 32224
Jason Ellerbee jeller@unf.edu
www.unf.edu/~jeller/dreams.html
Features Progressive Rock and related music.

Epic Prog with The Lurker
6237 Bent Pine Dr. #610A, Orlando, FL 32822
Michael Citro michael@thedividingline.com
thedividingline.com/ep.html
I'm always looking for great new artists!

Epic Rock Radio
Kailef kailef@epicrockradio.com
www.epicrockradio.com
We regularly feature independent artists, as long as the style (Symphonic / Melodic / Power Metal) matches with what we play.

FesterHead Radio
www.festerhead.com
A wealth of Prog shows broadcasting out of Hawaii.

Gagliarchives *WBZC*
645 S. Forklanding Rd. #18, Maple Shade, NJ 08052
PH: 609-332-2019 FX: 609-894-9440
Tom Gagliardi gagliarchives@yahoo.com
gagliarchives.com
A Progressive and Art Rock program.

Groove Traffic Control *WHCL*
198 College Hill Rd. Clinton, NY 13323
Sean stice@hamilton.edu
www.whcl.org
New and up-coming jam oriented music.

Koolkat's Odd Sky
Koolkat koolkat14215@hotmail.com
groups.msn.com/KoolkatsOddSky
Prog Rock internet station.

Newgrass, Prog & More!
HCR 66, Box 1999, Mathews, VA 23109
Steve Sikes-Nova MFSB@safe-mail.net
www.progressiveradiocat.com
The best in Newgrass, Progressive Rock, Indie & Alternative. musicians are welcome to submit CDs.

Night Vision *WITR*
32 Lomb Memorial Dr. Rochester, NY 14623-0563
PH: 585-475-2271 FX: 585-475-4988
Jack Luminous jluminous@hotmail.com
www.modernmusicandmore.com
The best in Progressive Rock from all across the globe! If you have a band looking for a new audience, get in touch with us about airplay.

The Pit *WYBF*
610 King of Prussia Rd. Radnor, PA 19087
PH: 610-902-8457
Joe Stevenson loudrock@wybf.com
www.wybf.com
The authority on Progressive Rock, Jazz, Jam and New Age music.

Planet Prog
PO Box 04512, Milwaukee, WI 53204
Mark Krueger markakrueger@hotmail.com
planetprog.com
You are invited to send your promotional discs and information for airplay consideration to the above address.

Prog Palace Radio
PO Box 441431, Kennesaw, GA 30160
Greg Stafford gregstaf@progpalaceradio.com
www.progpalaceradio.com
If you feel your music fits our format, send us your CD.

Progged Radio
6435 W. Wenden Way, Tucson, AZ 85743
Chan Weinmeister chan@proggedradio.com
www.proggedradio.com
Focuses on the harder edge of Progressive music.

progradio.com
pdirector@progradio.com
www.progradio.com
Progressive music for your mind!

Progressive Positivity Radio
3301 Claymore Dr. Plano, TX 75075
moses@progpositivity.com
www.progpositivity.com
We are very proud to feature the best (and most positive) independent Progressive Rock.

The Progressive Rock Radio Network
Jon Yarger jon@progradio.net
www.progradio.net
Discover the joys of Progressive music.

Progressive Soundscapes Radio
artist-contact@progressivesoundscapes.com
progressivesoundscapes.com
Supports independent or signed to small labels bands.

ProgRockRadio
PO Box 8335, Red Bank, NJ 07701
www.progrockradio.com
Send a CD with press kit to the above address.

ProgScape Radio
www.progscaperadio.com
Host Michael Ostrich exposes listeners to music that they simply wouldn't hear anywhere else.

The Prog-Rock Diner *WEBR*
2929 Eskridge Rd. Ste. S, Fairfax, VA 22031
PH: 703-573-8255 FX: 703-573-1210
Debbie Sears webr@fcac.org
www.fcac.org/webr
Prog from all over the world.

progrock.com
www.progrock.com
Can only accept Ogg Vorbis files with the quality set to 5 for playback.

Progulus Radio
1135 Valley Dr. Windsor, CO 80550
Mike Klemmer progulus@comcast.net
www.progulus.com
Poised to make a name for ourselves in the Progressive / Metal arena.

The Radiant Flow
Bill Hammell bill@progrock.org
www.theradiantflow.com
We believe firmly in playing new artists! Each host is responsible for their own show's content.

Rogues' Gallery
Frans Keylard frans@thedividingline.com
www.thedividingline.com/rg.html
A wide swath of Progressive-influenced music from the unknown to the infamous.

The Trip *WRFL*
U. Kentucky, PO Box 777, Lexington,
KY 40506-0025
Clay Gaunce thetrip@uky.edu
www.uky.edu/~wrfl/trip/trip.html
Send us your music.

WEER Radio
John W. Patterson eermusic@nc.rr.com
www.JazzRock-Radio.com
Jazz Rock Fusion show. Each show is guaranteed as good or better than the show aired last week!

Canada

The Dividing Line
#593 - 1027 Davie St., Vancouver, BC V6E 4L2
Rene Young promotions@thedividingline.com
www.thedividingline.com
Promotes artists by playing their music and broadcasting interviews.

La Villa Strangiato *CHUO*
Gary Lauzon & Gilles Potvin lavilla@yantz.com
www.yantz.com/lavilla
Are you in a Prog band wanting airplay on the radio to get the recognition you deserve? Drop me an e-mail and I will be glad to give you my address and play your material on my show!

South America

The Musical Box *Argentina*
eventos@themusicalbox.com.ar
www.themusicalbox.com.ar
Progressive Rock radio show.

Europe

France

Instinct Progressif
226 rue de Bordeaux, 16021 Angoulême, France
Arnaud metalnono@free.fr
instinct.prog.free.fr
Pour les groupes qui souhaiterais être diffusés durant l'émission, vous pouvez nous envoyer vos démos à l'adresse de la radio, accompagnées d'une petite biographie du groupe.

Germany

Progdependent *Rockin` Radio*
Banderbacher Str. 24, 90513 Zirndorf, Germany
PH/FX: 0911-60-95-95
progdependent@rockin-radio.de
www.rockin-radio.de

The Netherlands

Mark From Holland Radio Show
Simon van Haerlemstraat 34, 1962 VC Heemskerk,
The Netherlands
PH: ++31-251-246497
Mark C. Deren mcd@wanadoo.nl
www.markfromholland.com
It is recommended to "follow-up" submissions of music with a request via e-mail for a Sunday night "on air" interview. The conversations usually last 5-7 minutes.

Paperlate
Boompjesdijk 102, 4671 PT Dinteloord,
The Netherlands
PH: 31-0-167566111 FX: 31-0-167566111
Andre Steijns paperlte@westbrabant.net
www.paperlate.nl
Concentrates on Classic, Progressive and Psychedelic Rock.

Psychedelicatessen Radio Patapoe
Feddo Renier f.renier@kennisnet.nl
launch.groups.yahoo.com/group/psychedelicatessen
Psychedelic and Progressive music show.

Symfomania
symfomania@xs4all.nl
home.wanadoo.nl/symfomania
Progressive, Symphonic & Melodic Rock show. If you have new material that you would like us to play, get in touch!

United Kingdom

Rush Radio
NMB, City Campus, Pond St., Sheffield,
South Yorkshire S1 2BW UK
Ken Shipley ken@rushradio.org
www.rushradio.org

Punk Radio

North America

United States

alt FM
info@alt.fm
www.alt.fm
All Alternative. Alternative, Punk, Indie, New Rock, Nu, Post-Punk ...

American Underground *WKNT*
PO Box 163230, Orlando, FL 32816
PH: 407-823-4585 FX: 407-823-5899
Josh Evans americanunderground@hotmail.com
www.knightcast.org
Everything Punk and Ska.

@ntiRADIO *KGNU*
Sin bleedingright@gmail.com
www.myspace.com/antiradio
Features everything from old-school Punk and 80's New Wave to Goth and Horror-Punk, Hardcore, Metal, Industrial, Lounge.

The Anti-Emo Empire! *WNHU*
PO Box 5392, Milford, CT 06460
PH: 203-934-9296
Jeff Terranova theantiemoempire@earthlink.net
www.theantiemoempire.com
Spinning the best rare old school and new school Hardcore/Punk.

AudibleRecon
punkasfuck@cox.net
audiblerecon.com
Podcast featuring the best in Rock, Punk, Indie, Alternative, Emo and whatever else the kids are calling it these days.

The Bitter Sky Tonight *WBWC*
275 Eastland Rd. Berea OH, 44017
PH: 440-826-2145 FX: 440-826-3426
contact@wbwc.com
www.wbwc.com
3 hours of Rock influenced Emo, Indie and Emo-Hardcore.

Bottom 40 Radio
www.myspace.com/bottom40radio
Playing the best in Punk, Emo, Hardcore and Nerd Rock.

ceremony *Western Addition Radio*
www.myspace.com/ceremonyradio
Post-Punk, New Wave, Indie etc. with an emphasis on underground songs you may otherwise never hear.

On Christmas Eve 1982, Bad Brains began their 3-day stint at a Hardcore Festival hosted by legendary CBGB. This DVD represents the very best of these shows, culled from over 4 hours of footage.

800.888.0486 | www.DVDNote.com

MVDvisual
A DIVISION OF MVD ENTERTAINMENT GROUP

DVD VIDEO

First Bad Brains home video EVER!

The Cherry Blossom Clinic *WFMU*
PO Box 5101, Hoboken, NJ 07030
www.wfmu.org/playlists/TT
Hosted by Terre T. Please DON'T send any attached files of any type (no flyers, MP3s etc.). Also, DON'T contact me and ask if I played your CD or demo. Check my playlist to find out.

Coffee n' Smokes *WMFO*
PO Box 65, Medford, MA 02153
PH: 617- 625-0800
coffeensmokes@verizon.net
coffeensmokes.freeservers.com
Garage/Punk, Surf, Psychedelic, Rockabilly, Pop obscurities ...

Cry Baby Emo Kids
PH: 650-456-2235
crybabyemokids@gmail.com
www.crybabyemokids.com
A podcast made by teenagers from around the world. Along with the best in Emo/independent artists.

DIY Radio *WAPS*
444 Lodi St., Akron, OH 44305
PH: 330-761-3099 FX: 330-761-3240
Ron Mullens submissions@diyradio.net
www.diyradio.net
A Punk Rock radio show.

Etiquette of Violence *KDHX*
3504 Magnolia, St. Louis, MO 63118
PH: 314-664-3688 FX: 314-664-1020
Cricket O'Neill etiquetteofviolence@kdhx.org
www.kdhx.org/programs/etiquetteofviolence.htm
A tasteful array of Pop/Rock/Punk/Country.

Extra Super Action Show
Big Mike
bigmike@extrasuperactionshow.com
www.extrasuperactionshow.com
Files you send in (using our online form) must be in .wav or .mp3 format. Alternative, Indie and Punk.

GaragePunk.com Podcast
PH: 206-339-8979
Kopper
kopper@garagepunk.com
www.garagepunk.com
Bands and labels, submit material for airplay.

Get The Fuck Up!
KillRadio
Aaron
aaron@GTFUradio.com
www.GTFUradio.com
A mix of band interviews, live musical performances and prank calls, all masked under the clever disguise of being drunken fools.

Hussieskunk
PO Box 1599,
Reynoldsburg, OH 43068
Matt
mattg@hussieskunk.com
www.hussieskunk.com
Every CD we receive is reviewed and promoted on our site, as well as featured on our show.

idobi.com Radio
1825 New Hampshire Ave. #407, Washington, DC 20009
music@idobi.com
www.idobi.com/radio
Broadcasts Alternative Rock and Punk music. We are committed to bringing you the best of the known (and not-so-well-known) artist from around the world.

Mohawk Radio
10862 Coronel Rd. Ste. B, Santa Ana, CA 92705
Rich Z. richz@mohawkradio.com
www.mohawkradio.com
Hundreds of Punk MP3s for download. Check our website for submission guidelines.

Music to Spazz By *WFMU*
PO Box 5101, Hoboken, NJ 07030
PH: 201-521-1416
www.wfmu.org/~spazz
Host Dave the Spazz presents this Punk Rock R n' B Surf Garage radio show!

The Next Big Thing *KALX*
26 Barrows Hall #5650, Berkeley, CA 94720-5650
PH: 510-642-1111
Marshall Stax robins@ix.netcom.com
kalx.berkeley.edu
Showcase for demo and pre-released music. I want Punk, Hardcore, Emocore ...anything with an edge, passion or purpose.

The No Show *KDHX*
3504 Magnolia, St. Louis, MO 63118
PH: 314-664-3688 FX: 314-664-1020
Brett Underwood noshow@kdhx.org
www.kdhx.org/programs/noshow.htm
Punk, Post-Punk, Noisy & No-Wave and more.

Planet Verge
15 Albert Terrace, Bloomfield, NJ 07003
PH: 973-338-0560
editorial@planetverge.com
www.planetverge.com
Interviews up-and-coming Punk/Rock bands.

Punk University *WSOU*
400 S. Orange Ave. South Orange, NJ 07079
PH: 973-761-9768 FX: 973-761-7593
wsou@shu.edu
www.wsou.net
Underground Punk and Ska.

Punk Up the Volume *KIWR*
2700 College Rd. Council Bluffs, IA 51503
PH: 712-325-3337
KC Jones riverpunk897@yahoo.com
www.897theriver.com/punk.asp
Punk music every Sunday night!

Rock Hell Radio
104 Lake Ct. Chapel Hill, NC 27516
James Saltzman rockhellradio@yahoo.com
www.rockhellradio.com
We play Street, Oi, Oldschool, Hardcore, Thrash and other Punk indiscretions.

Sonic Overload
PO Box 2746, Lynn, MA 01903
Al sonicoverload@earthlink.net
sonicoverload.moocowrecords.com
Punk, Hardcore, Garage and other loud music from the past and present.

Super Fun Happy Hour *KDHX*
3504 Magnolia, St. Louis, MO 63118
PH: 314-664-3688 FX: 314-664-1020
Tim, Matt & Heather superfunhappyhour@kdhx.org
www.kdhx.org/programs/superfunhappyhour.htm
Punk Rock from the 70's to the latest independent and major label releases of today.

The Super Rock Fun Show
PO Box 6868, Fullerton, CA 92834-6868
Dave thesuperrockfunshow@excite.com
www.thesuperrockfunshow.com
Punk Rock internet radio show. E-mail me your info and an MP3. If you send it, I'll play it.

The Tragically Nameless Podcast
PH: 206-350-3935
denbez@gmail.com
tnppodcast.libsyn.org
Want your music played on the show? Send me an email with a couple MP3s!

Under the Big Top *WMUA*
105 Campus Ctr. U. Mass, Amherst, MA 01003
PH: 413-545-3691 FX: 413-545-0682
Jerod Weinman music@wmua.org
www.wmua.org
Punk to Ska, Emo to Hardcore and more.

UsedWigs Radio
Jeff Lyons jeff@usedwigs.com
www.usedwigs.com
Satiric stories and news, celebrity interviews, music and movies reviews and pop-culture-based columns.

The Wayback Machine *KDHX*
3504 Magnolia, St. Louis, MO 63118
PH: 314-664-3688 FX: 314-664-1020
Kopper kopper@garagepunk.com
www.garagepunk.com
Bands and labels, submit material for airplay.

WDOA.com
128 Mechanic St., Spencer, MA 01562
FX: 253-323-1606
Mike Malone wdoainfo@wdoa.com
wdoa.com
We actively encourage independent bands and artists to send us their music.

Canada

Danko Radio
240 Clayton St. E., Listowel, ON N4W 2G1
Paul Cardiff admin@danko-radio.com
danko-radio.com
Home of the best underground Punk, Metal, Rock and whatever else we feel like playing.

Equalizing X Distort *CIUT*
35 Raglan Ave. #204, Toronto, ON M6C 2K7
PH: 416-978-0909 FX: 416-946-7004
Stephe Perry equalizingxdistort@ciut.fm
www.exd.sohc.org
Dedicated to the underground Hardcore Punk scene.

Flex Your Head Radio Show *CITR*
#233-6138 SUB Blvd. Vancouver, BC V6T 1Z1
PH: 604-822-2487 FX: 604-822-9364
info@flexyourhead.net
www.flexyourhead.net
Long running Hardcore/Punk radio program.

Generation Annihilation *CiTR*
PO Box 48116, 595 Burrard St., Vancouver, BC V7X 1N8
Aaron Kid & Andy Grotesque
crashnburnradio@yahoo.ca
streetpunkradio.com
Punk and Hardcore, both old and new.

Punk Pod Radio
Info@PunkPodRadio.Com
www.punkpodradio.com
Featuring the best Punk, Hardcore, Psychobilly and oi bands out there today. Do NOT send MP3s to our e-mail. Send us a LINK where we can download it.

PunkRadioCast
6-295 Queen St. E. #388, Brampton, ON L6W 4S6
PH: 905-495-6003
info@punkradiocast.com
www.punkradiocast.com
Features a variety of Punk related shows.

E u r o p e

Austria

Chilibox Rocks! *Radio Orange*
Klosterneuburger Strasse 1, A-1200 Wien, Austria
PH: 01-319-09-99
chilibox@gmx.at
www.chilibox.net
Punk, Ska and Hardcore.

France

Ecrasons La Vermine *Radio Campus Lille*
59656 Villeneuve d'Ascq, France
chpunk@chpunk.org
chpunk.org
Punk, Hardcore, Oi, Crust, Ska ...

Germany

new/noise/edition
newnoiseedition.podspot.de
Punk, Hardcore, Emo and Metal podcasting since 2004.

Italy

dirtywaves radio *Radio Onda d'Urto*
c\o cs Leoncavallo via Watteau 7, 20125 Milano, Italy
dirtywaves@hotmail.it
dirtywaves.blogspot.com
Music, interviews etc.

United Kingdom

Hardcore Street Sounds *TotalRock*
1 Denmark Pl. London, WC2H 8NL UK
Anne Maria annmahss@aol.com
www.hardcorestreetsounds.com
Punk and Hardcore with Oi, Ska and Metal.

hungbunny podcast
satanicholiness@hotmail.com
www.hungbunny.co.uk
Fisting your ears with my noise.

Punky
PH: 07939-081-391
Paul & Tony info@lastminutecomedy
www.lastminutecomedy.com/punky
Podcast featuring tracks you've never heard before, expressions you've never heard before and jokes you'll never want to hear again.

Australia

Blackmarket Radio *5UV*
228 N. Terrace, Adelaide, SA 5000 Australia
PH: 61-8-8303-5000 FX: 61-8-8303-4374
www.myspace.com/blackmarketrad
Punk/Hardcore/Ska radio show. Feel free to send us CDs etc.

Reggae Radio

United States

Beast Reggae *KTUH*
Hemenway Hall #203, 2445 Campus Rd. Honolulu, HI 96822.
PH: 808-956-7261 FX: 808-956-5271
Big Bar bigbar@ktuh.org
ktuh.org/beastreggae
Roots Reggae show. Our "Progression Session" segment features all new releases.

BigUp Radio
US: PO Box 20650, Oakland, CA 94620
UK: PO Box 2821, Reading, RG1 9EH UK
info@bigupradio.com
www.bigupradio.com
If you want airplay on our Roots or Dancehall stations please forward us your CD for consideration.

Dub Mixture *KDHX*
3504 Magnolia, St. Louis, MO 63118
PH: 314-664-3688 FX: 314-664-1020
DJ Ranx dubmixture@kdhx.org
www.kdhx.org/programs/dubmixture.htm
The hottest Reggae in the classic Dub style with DJ Ranx.

Dub Session
DJ Chill Will dubsession@gmail.com
www.dubsession.com
Podcast of progressive Reggae, Dub and Downtempo grooves.

Everything Off Beat *WLUW*
6525 N. Sheridan Rd. Chicago, IL 60626
PH: 773-508-8080 FX: 773-508-8082
DJ Chuck Wren wluwradio@wluw.org
wluw.org
The world's premier Ska oriented radio show.

Ithaska *WVBR*
957 Mitchell St. Ste. B, Ithaca, NY 14850
PH: 607-273-2121 FX: 607-273-4069
ithaska@ithaska.com
ithaska.com
Despite our name, we play all sorts of music.

Jammin Reggae Radio
eznoh@niceup.com
niceup.com
The Gateway to Reggae music on the internet!

Kingston Beat *WXXE*
826 Euclid Ave. Syracuse, NY 13210
PH: 315-455-5624 FX: 315-701-0303
wxxe.org
Explorations in Ska, Rock Steady and Reggae, with an emphasis on new interpretations of the more traditional Jamaican forms.

The Night Shift *KDHX*
3504 Magnolia, St. Louis, MO 63118
PH: 314-664-3688 FX: 314-664-1020
Kevin Straw roots@kdhx.org
www.kdhx.org/programs/nightshift.htm
Reggae, Dub and Groove.

Play I Some Music *WXXE*
826 Euclid Ave. Syracuse, NY 13210
PH: 315-455-5624 FX: 315-701-0303
Papa Andy playisomemusic@email.com
wxxe.org
The best in Reggae, African and Caribbean music, covering all eras and styles.

Positive Vibrations *KDHX*
3504 Magnolia, St. Louis, MO 63118
PH: 314-664-3688 FX: 314-664-1020
Professor Skank pskank@kdhx.org
Michael Kuelker positivevibes_michael@kdhx.org
www.kdhx.org/programs/positivevibrations.htm
For the latest - and the greatest - in Reggae music.

Puffcast
Dr. Puff puffcast@yahoo.com
www.puffcast.com
Reggae and Dub wrapped up in homemade Electronica. Featuring independent artists from around the world.

Raw Roots Podcast
badgals-radio.com
Interviews, reviews and great Reggae, Dancehall, Funk and R&B.

Reggae Rhythms *WAPS*
412 Bettie St. Ste. A, Akron, OH 44306-1212
PH: 330-761-3099 FX: 330-761-3240
B. E. Mann theenergymanbe@yahoo.com
www.bemann.com/reggaerhythms.htm
Reggae music from the US and abroad.

The Reggae Ride *WDNA*
PO Box 558636, Miami, FL 33255
PH: 305-662-8889 FX: 305-662-1975
Flagga Dupes flagga@wdna.org
www.wdna.org
Authentic Reggae music from Ska (60's) to present.

The Reggae Train *KRBS*
PO Box #9, Oroville, CA 95965
PH: 530-534-1200
krbs@cncnet.com
www.radiobirdstreet.org
Classic Roots Reggae music.

reggaemania.com
rnelson@reggaemania.com
www.reggaemania.com
Discover the pulse of the dancehall.

Rocket Ship Ska Trip *KFAI*
1808 Riverside Ave. Minneapolis, MN 55454
PH: 612-341-3144
Capt. 2much FREETIME capt2much@yahoo.com
www.kfai.org/programs/rocketst.htm

Roots, Rock, Reggae *KUSP*
203 8th Ave. Santa Cruz, CA 95062
PH: 831-476-2800
Lance & Jeff kusp@kusp.org
www.kusp.org/playlists/rrr
The best from the Reggae world.

sakapfet.com
PO Box 66-9303, Miami, FL 33166
PH: 305-599-8060 FX: 305-599-1005
www.sakapfet.com
Your cyber-highway to Haiti.

Saturday's a Party *WUSB*
Stony Brook Union 266, Stony Brook, NY
11794-3263
PH: 631-632-6501 FX: 631-632-7182
Lister Hewan-Lowe music@wusb.fm
wusb.fm
*The longest-running Reggae-politics mix (RPM) in
the USA. Den de Dubwise playyyyyyy, it play, it
play!!!*

Ska's The Limit *KDHX*
3205 Pestalozzi Ave. St. Louis, MO 63118
PH: 314-664-3688 FX: 314-664-1020
Paul Stark stlska@mindspring.com
home.mindspring.com/~stlska/ska.htm
A weekly all-Ska radio show.

Tropical Reggae *KGLP*
200 College Dr. Gallup, NM 87301
PH: 505-863-7626 FX: 505-863-7633
Steve Buggie buggie@unm.edu
www.kglp.org/tropicalreggae
*You'll hear the finest in Reggae music from the
Caribbean, Africa or elsewhere.*

Tunnel One *WNYU*
194 Mercer St. 5th Fl. New York, NY 10012
PH: 212-998-1660 FX: 212-998-1652
DJ Mush1 tunnelone@wnyu.org
www.wnyu.org
Old school, Rocksteady and third wave Ska.

Vibes of the Time *KRUA*
PO Box 20-2831, Anchorage, AK 99520
PH: 907-223-4531
Ras Jahreal dready@gci.net
reggaealaska.com/jahreal
*Featuring Roots Reggae, Dancehall Dub and Lovers
Rock.*

West Indian Rhythms *WWUH*
200 Bloomfield Ave. West Hartford, CT 06117
PH: 860-768-4701 FX: 860-768-5701
Philip Mitchell pearl286@aol.com
www.wwuh.org
*A blend of music and information straight from the
Caribbean. A rich mixture of Calypso and Reggae.*

Canada

Caribbean Linkup *CJSW*
DJ Leo C caribbeanlinkup@shaw.ca
members.shaw.ca/caribbeanlinkup
*Dedicated to the Caribbean - news, views and
music. E-mail for address to submit.*

Reggae in the Fields *CKCU*
U. Ctr. Rm. 517, 1125 Colonel By Dr. Ottawa,
ON K1S 5B6
PH: 613-520-2898
Junior Smith reggaeinthefields@canada.com
www.cyberus.ca/%7Eacdas/Reggae.html
The longest-running Reggae program in Canada.

Scratch
scratch@azevedo.ca
www.azevedo.ca/scratch
*Early-1960's Ska, through Rocksteady, Reggae and
on to modern-day Dub.*

Ska Party *CIUT*
91 St. George St., Toronto, ON M5S 2E8
PH: 416-978-0909 x214 FX: 416-946-7004
DJ Skip skaparty@ciut.fm
www.skapages.com/skip
*Features interviews, news, reviews and some
schmooze. How can we spread the word if we don't
know about it? Send your goods and info!*

Jamaica

IrieFM.net
Coconut Grove, Ocho Rios, St. Ann, Jamaica
PH: 876-974-5051 FX: 876-974-5943
customerservice@iriefm.net
www.iriefm.net
24-hour all-Reggae station.

Belgium

Reggae Connection
68 rue de Roux. 6140 Fontaine l'Evêque, Belgium
PH: 32-0-498-339112
Salvatore Baldacchino reggaeconnection@be.tf
www.reggaeconnection.be.tf
*If you have new promo releases press info, send
them to the above address.*

France

Dance Hall Style *Radio Mega*
DJ Prince Thierry princethierry@wanadoo.fr
www.dancehallstyle.net
*All styles of Reggae with a little bit emphasis on
Roots, Oldies and Dub.*

Dub Action *Radio Canut*
24, rue Sergent Blandan 1er arrdt - BP 1101 - 69201
Lyon, France
PH: 04-78-39-18-15 FX: 04-78-29-26-00
Bassta bassta69@hotmail.com
regardeavue.com/radiocanut
*Ici toute les composantes de la musique jamaïcaine
sont d'actualité: du Mento, du Ska, du Rock Steady,
du Reggae etc.*

Germany

Freedom Sounds *Radio Flora*
Radio Flora, Zur Bettfedernfabrik 1, 30451
Hannover, Germany
Peter Roth info@freedomsounds.de
www.freedomsounds.de
Ska, Reggae and Rocksteady.

United Kingdom

BBC Radio 1xtra *Dancehall*
www.bbc.co.uk/1xtra/dancehall
*Home page of the BBC 1xtra's various Dancehall
shows. Info, shows, contacts etc.*

Israel

Reggae Power
Dr. Reggae drreggae@irielion.com
www.irielion.com/israel/reggae_power.htm
The best Reggae vibes from the best radio station!

Soul / R&B Radio

Radio Promotion

Monet Radio Promotions
PO Box 560526, The Colony, TX 75056
PH: 832-545-0998
Arsdale Harris monetproductions@comcast.net
www.monetproductionsinc.com/
monetradiopromo.html
*Over 100 radio program directors and DJs in our
contact database.*

Stations

United States

African New Dawn *WRSU*
126 College Ave. New Brunswick, NJ 08901
PH: 732-932-8800 FX: 732-932-1768
Alvin Fair wrsu@wrsu.rutgers.edu
wrsu.rutgers.edu
*Promotes new, unknown and un(der)exposed music
artists and music companies.*

blackmusicamerica.com
support@bossnetworks.com
www.blackmusicamerica.com
*Music, information, culture and entertainment for
the Black community.*

BlakeRadio.com
PO Box 403, Massapequa Park, NY 11762
PH: 866-269-7197
RainbowSoul@BlakeRadio.com
www.blakeradio.com
R&B, Jazz, Soul and Reggae slow jams.

Chocolate City *KCRW*
1900 Pico Blvd. Santa Monica, CA 90405
PH: 310-450-5183 FX: 310-450-7172
Garth Trinidad garth.trinidad@kcrw.org
www.kcrw.org
*A progressive mix of Soul, Hip Hop and World
Rhythms.*

City Sounds Radio
Dick Fairchild citysounds@citysounds.biz
www.citysounds.biz
*Welcomes R&B, Smooth Jazz, Southern Soul and
Blues for possible airplay. We will help to promote
you however we can.*

Etherbeat Radio
14781 Memorial Dr. #1791, Houston, TX 77079
PH: 713-344-1562
www.etherbeat.com
Funk, Soul, Jazz, Latin, World, Afro, Reggae.
Charges a FEE for airplay.

Fusebox *WRSU*
14 Easton Ave. #250, New Brunswick,
NJ 08901-1918
PH: 732-932-8800 FX: 732-932-1768
DJ Fusion djfusion@exit9hiphop.com
www.Exit9HipHop.com
Supports new and un(der)exposed artists. Soul,
Funk, R&B, Hip Hop etc.

The Half Show
PH: 206-600-4253
Me-saj & Jason thehalf@thehalfshow.com
www.thehalfshow.com
Podcast featuring an undiscovered star on the rise
in genres such as music, comedy, acting and
literature.

KBBG
918 Newell St. Waterloo, IA 50703
PH: 319-235-1515
management@kbbg.org
www.kbbgfm.org
R&B, Jazz, Gospel, Blues etc.

KJLU
PO Box 29, Jefferson City, MO 65102
PH: 573-681-5301 FX: 573-681-5299
www.lincolnu.edu/pages/504.asp

KPOO
PO Box 423030, San Francisco, CA 94142
PH: 415-346-5373 FX: 415-346-5173
info@kpoo.com
www.kpoo.com
Specializes in Jazz, Reggae, Salsa, Blues, Gospel
and Hip Hop.

KPVU *Prairie View A&M U.*
PO Box 519, Prairie View, TX 77446-0519
PH: 936-857-3311
kpvu_fm@pvamu.edu
www.pvamu.edu/kpvu

KTSU *Texas Southern U.*
3100 Cleburne, Houston, TX 77004
PH: 713-313-4354
www.ktsufm.org

Liquid Sound Lounge *WBAI*
120 Wall St., 10th Fl. New York, NY 10005
PH: 212-209-2800 x2931
radio@liquidsoundlounge.com
www.liquidsoundlounge.com
Devoted to exposing Soul infused grooves of all
persuasions.

The Listening Lounge with Alysia Cosby
WEIB
Alysia weibfm@aol.com
www.weibfm.com
A hip and groovy mix of Chillout, Jazz, Soul,
Brazilian, Latin and World rhythms.

Love Radio
238 Auburn Ave. Atlanta, GA 30303
PH: 404-523-2656
Dr. Love tdavis@dr-love.com
www.dr-love.com
We are looking for Soul. R&B, Hip Hop and Reggae
artists to play on our shows. We also offer
opportunities to play at our events in Atlanta.

The Love Zone *WHCR*
1026 6th Ave. #301 S., New York, NY 10018
PH: 917-545-2169
Maurice Watts maurice@mauricewatts.com
www.mauricewatts.com
For over 23 years playing some of the best R&B
love songs of the past and present.

LoveZone247.com
1026 6th Ave. #301 S., New York, NY 10018
PH: 917-545-2169
Maurice Watts maurice@mauricewatts.com
www.lovezone247.com
24 hour Old School, Soul and R&B station host by
legendary radio host Maurice "The Voice" Watts.

The Michael Baisden Show / B-Side
14902 Preston Rd. #404-1022, Dallas, TX 75254
pye@michaelbaisden.com
www.MichaelBaisden.com
Breaking new and undiscovered artists! Songs
MUST fit the Love, Lust and Lies format, Old
school, R&B and Neo Soul. No Hip Hop or Rap!
Check site for submission details.

projectVIBE
submissions@projectvibe.net
projectvibe.net
From Neo-Soul rhythms to Deep House, from Jazz
to Classic R&B. Visit our site for submission details.

RadioBlack.com
www.radioblack.com
A guide to radio stations around the world catering
to Urban America.

RHYTHMflow Radio
PO Box 130, Bronx, NY 10467
rhythmflowradio@rhythmflow.net
www.rhythmflow.net/Radio.html
We're always looking for R&B, Jazz, Gospel and
other neglected music genres (sorry, no Rap or Hip
Hop) to add to our playlist.

Slow Jam
1528 6th St. #501, Santa Monica, CA 90401
Kevin James slowjam@verizon.net
www.slowjam.com
The best R&B slow jams, both old & new. I do mix
in some independent music.

The Smooth Groovers Review Podcast
www.smoothgroovers.com
In addition to Smooth Jazz we love Jazz-Funk, Funk
and Soul.

smoothbeats.com
www.smoothbeats.com
Streaming non-stop beats 24 hours a day.

Soul Music of The World Podcast
LRMC-CMR 402, Box 999, APO AE 09180
PH: 011-49-16091790264
DJ Come of Age djcomeofage@yahoo.com
djcoa.libsyn.com
Features independent Soul artists from all over the
world.

Soul Patrol Radio
PH: 609-351-0154
Bob Davis earthjuice@prodigy.net
www.soul-patrol.com
A celebration of great Black music from the ancient
to the future.

SoulSis Radio
stephanie@soulsis.net
www.soulsis.net/radio.html
Ranges from R&B to Hip Hop to Jazz. I will
eventually incorporate some Gospel!

Southern Exposure *KRUA*
PSB Rm. 254, 3211 Providence Dr. Anchorage,
AK 99508
PH: 907-786-6805
Marcus lrd47@hotmail.com
www.uaa.alaska.edu/krua
Rap and R&B by a lot of artists outside of the
Top 20.

Urban Landscapes
1029 Southwood Dr. Ste. D, San Luis Obispo,
CA 93401
Velanche Stewart mail@urbanlandscapes.org
www.urbanlandscapes.org
Funk & Soul (old school & new sounds),
Latin/Brazilian, Soulful House.

WHCR *City College of New York*
138th & Convent Ave. Nac Building, Rm. 1/513,
New York, NY 10031
PH: 212-650-7481
whcr903fm@whcr.org
www.whcr.org

WMOC
info@mocradio.com
www.mocradio.com
R&B to Hip Hop to Old School to House music.

WNAA *North Carolina A & T State U.*
c/o D. Cherie'Lofton,
200 Price Hall, Greensboro, NC 27411
PH: 336-334-7936 FX: 336-334-7960
wnaafm@ncat.edu
wnaalive.ncat.edu

WNSB *Norfolk State U.*
700 Park Ave. Norfolk, VA 23504
PH: 757-823-9110
www.nsu.edu/wnsb
A unique blend of R&B, Jazz, Hip-Hop, Gospel and
Reggae.

World Dynamic Radio
1055 Lancashire Cir. #B4, Stone Mountain,
GA 30083
Carla P. Jewel worlddynamicradio@yahoo.com
www.WorldDynamicRadio.com
Features Jazz, Pop, Sacred Gospel and R&B.

WURC *Rust College*
150 Rust Ave. Holly Springs, MS 38635
PH: 662-252-5881 FX: 662-252-8869
Wayne A. Fiddis, Sr. wfiddis@rustcollege.edu
www.wurc.org
Jazz, Gospel, Blues, Reggae, R&B.

WVSD *Mississippi Valley U.*
14000 Hwy. 82, Box 7221, Itta Bena, MS 38941
PH: 662-254-3612
wvsd@mvsu.edu
www.mvsu.edu/917FM
Jazz, Gospel and R&B.

Canada

FLOW 93.5
211 Yonge St. #400, Toronto, ON M5B 1M4
PH: 416-214-5000 FX: 416-214-0660
info@flow935.com
www.flow935.com
An Urban music mix that primarily includes R&B
and Hip Hop. We also feature Reggae, Soca and
Gospel music.

The Grooveyard *CKIC*
W-106, 160 Princess St., Winnipeg, MB R3B 1K9
K-Berries kberries@kick.fm
www.kick.fm
Blues, Trad R&B, Soul and Funk.

The X, Urban FM *Fanshawe College*
1460 Oxford St. E, London, ON N5V 1W2
PH: 519-453-2810 x201
music@1069fm.ca
www.1069fm.ca

France

Right On FM
7 Rue du Stade, 57050 Longeville -
Les - Metz, France
PH/FX: +33 (0) 3-87-63-86-54
contact@righton-fm.com
www.righton-fm.com
A melting pot of Jazz, Soul, Funk, DnB, NuJazz etc.

Touchofsoul
touchofsoul.free.fr
Afrobeat, Electro, Broken Beat, Soul and Funk.

The Netherlands

Royal Groove
royalgroove@royalgroove.org
www.royalgroove.org
Starting with Funk and Soul and going from Jazz to Bossa Nova, from Hip Hop to Latin, Afro-Beat and everything in between.

SaveOurSoul
saveoursoul.nl
Playing the best in today's R&B and Classic Soul. We also review and interview some of the artists we play.

The Soul of Amsterdam Radio Show
2e Oosterparkstraat 59-D, 1091 HW Amsterdam,
The Netherlands
PH: +31-6-165-22229
Andreas Hellingh
andreas@thesoulofamsterdam.com
thesoulofamsterdam.com
Show centers around Soul music. We also play R&B, Urban, Disco, Funk, Gospel and Jazz.

United Kingdom

Basic Soul
www.basic-soul.co.uk
Syndicated show broadcasting through various stations online.

BBC Radio 1xtra *RnB*
www.bbc.co.uk/1xtra/rnb
Home page of the BBC 1xtra's various R&B shows. Info, shows, contacts etc.

BBC Radio 2 *Blues, Soul and Reggae*
www.bbc.co.uk/radio2/r2music/blues
Home page of the BBC Radio 2's various Soul and Reggae shows. Info, shows, contacts etc.

Choice FM
PO Box 969, London, WC2H 7BB UK
PH: 0207 378 3969 FX: 0207 378 3911
des.paul@choicefm.com
www.choicefm.net
The future of Urban music radio & culture.

Invincible Radio
#107, 203 Mare Studios, London, E8 3QE UK
PH: +44-0208-525-4131
adverts@invinciblemag.com
www.invincibleradio.com
The world's market-leading radio station for new music, bringing you the future today.

Solar Radio
PH: +44-8707-451-879
info@solarradio.com
www.solarradio.com
The best in Soul, Jazz, Funk and other related music.

Starpoint Radio
46 Jasper Rd. Upper Norwood, London,
SE19 1SH UK
PH: +44 (0) 20-8659-7581
info@starpointradio.com
www.starpointradio.com
The real alternative for Soul music on the internet.

Women in Music Radio

North America

United States

Acoustic Songbird / AcoustiNation Radio
416 W. Pike St., Morrow, OH 45152
PH: 513-899-4463
Liz Zorn admin@acousticsongbird.com
www.acousticsongbird.com
Female, Acoustic and acoustic based performing songwriters.

All Girls Slumber Party *KLSU*
B-39 Hodges Hall, LSU, Baton Rouge, LA 70803
PH: 225-578-4620 FX: 225-578-1698
music.director@klsu.fm
www.klsu.fm
All female artists ranging from all girl bands to Country to Hip Hop to Jazz.

Amazon Radio Show *WPKN*
PO Box 217, New Haven, CT 06513
Pamela S. Smith psmith@amazonradio.com
www.amazonradio.com
Welcomes music from women everywhere, all styles.

Assorted Women *WDIY*
301 Broadway, Bethlehem, PA 18015
PH: 610-694-8100 FX: 610-954-9474
info@wdiyfm.org
www.wdiyfm.org
From Folk-Rockers to Jazz greats, from soul divas to torch singers: It's not just chicks with guitars...

Bread & Roses *KBOO*
20 SE. 8ᵗʰ Ave. Portland, OR 97214
PH: 503-231-8187 FX: 503-231-7145
www.kboo.fm
Public Affairs radio produced and engineered by women.

Bunch of Betty's Podcast
Betty serafinafly@hotmail.com
www.bunchofbettys.blogspot.com
My specialties of knowledge are: women vocalists, current and past Folk music, Britpop and really anything unique and strange ...like ME!

Church of Girl Radio
1405 SE. Belmont #65, Portland, OR 97214-2669
PH: 503-819-9201
Mary Ann Naylor radiogirl@churchofgirl.com
www.churchofgirl.com
Featuring 14 different rotations of lady-made music. Interviews too!

Circle of Women *KBOO*
20 SE. 8ᵗʰ Ave. Portland, OR 97214
PH: 503-231-8187 FX: 503-231-7145
Annelise Hummel annelieseh99@yahoo.com
www.kboo.fm
Covering women's issues and all genres of music.

Diva Radio *KUSF*
2130 Fulton St., San Francisco, CA 94117
PH: 415-386-5873
kusfmusic@yahoo.com
www.kusf.org
A focus on women's independently produced music.

Divalicious
PO Box 15739, Boston, MA 02215
info@podgrrls.net
www.podgrrls.net/divalicious
Amazing Ambient, tasty Trance and groovy Global Beats. Please fill out our online release form.

Dreamboat Radio *WRUW*
11220 Bellflower Rd. Cleveland, OH 44106
PH: 216-368-2207 FX: 216-368-5414
Monica Ionescu dreamboatradio@gmail.com
dreamboatradio.tripod.com
Showcases the work of women artists in Old-Time, Bluegrass and mostly traditional Acoustic music.

The Eclectic Woman *WTJU*
PO Box 400811, Charlottesville, VA 22904-4811
PH: 434-924-0885 FX: 434-924-8996
wtju.net
Showcases female Singer/Songwriters.

Enchantress Radio *Radio Free Tunes*
Paul Carosi radiofreetunes@yahoo.com
www.artistlaunch.com/enchantressradio
An online streaming music station that features female artists

Eve Out Loud *WICB*
118 Park Hall, Ithaca, NY 14850
PH: 607-274-3217 FX: 607-274-1061
wicb@ithaca.edu
www.ithaca.edu/radio/wicb
We're ALWAYS looking to promote new artists!

Every Womon Radio *WAIF*
PO Box 23065, Cincinnati, OH 45223
Lauren everywomon@yahoo.com
www.everywomanradio.com
We currently are accepting CDs for potential airplay. Visit our site for more information.

The Ezone *KWJG*
PO Box 1121, Kasilof, AK 99610
Chick tracey.tideswell@gmail.com
www.ezonechick.net
Dedicated to women in music.

Face the Music *KZFR*
PO Box 3173, Chico, CA 95927
PH: 530-895-0131 FX: 530-895-0775
Terre Reynolds ponderosagal@yahoo.com
kzfr_facethemusic.tripod.com
Tilts the scales in the opposite direction with music performed, written and arranged by women.

The Female Form *KBGA*
U. Ctr. Rm. 208, Missoula, MT 59812
PH: 406-243-5715
kbgamd@kbga.org
kbga.org
All female artists and bands: from Country to Punk.

FEMALE FRONT
DJ Arhythmius arhythmius@hotmail.com
www.femalefront.com
Most of the music falls under the mega heading of "Alternative". That means very little Pop, R&B, Hip Hop or Folk.

FemFrequency
PO Box 15739, Boston, MA 02215
info@podgrrls.net
www.podgrrls.net/ff
Amazing, rocking musical talent from the women your mother warned you about. Please fill out our online release form.

The Feminine Groove
Barb Hill brnshuga61@yahoo.com
www.cyberstationusa.com
The best music, from today's women artists.

Feminist Magazine *KPFK*
3729 Cahenga Blvd. W., North Hollywood, CA 91604
feministmagazine@yahoo.com
www.feministmagazine.org
Public affairs show that eagerly spotlights the work of women in all walks of life.

La Femme Fatale *WBRS*
Shapiro Campus Ctr. 415 South St., Waltham, MA 02453-2728
PH: 781-736-4785
music@wbrs.org
www.wbrs.org
Dedicated to dangerous women and their music.

Femme FM *KUT*
1 University Stn. A0704, Austin, TX 78712
PH: 512-471-2345 FX: 512-471-3700
Teresa Ferguson sanferg@austin.rr.com
www.kut.org
Music performed by women artists of all genres.

Grrrlville *WIDR*
1511 Faunce Student Service Bldg. Kalamazoo, MI 49008-6301
PH: 269-387-6305
widr-music@groupwise.wmich.edu
www.widr.org
Delivering a diverse mix of female-fronted bands and Singer/Songwriters.

Global Women Radio Collective *Radio CPR*
radiocpr@riseup.net
www.radiocpr.com
Voices and music from women in our community and from around the world.

Her Infinite Variety *WORT*
118 S. Bedford St., Madison, WI 53703-2692
PH: 608-256-2001 FX: 608-256-3704
www.wort-fm.org
Showcases women in all genres/styles of music.

In Other Words *KUFM*
MPR, 32 Campus Dr. U. Montana, Missoula, MT 59812-8064
PH: 406-243-4931 FX: 406-243-3299
www.kufm.org
Women's program of music, international news…

Instrumental Women *KSDS*
1313 Park Blvd. San Diego, CA 92101
PH: 619-234-1062 FX: 619-230-2212
Janine Harty j9blue@yahoo.com
www.jazz88online.org
Highlights women in Jazz.

Into the Light *KMFA*
3001 N. Lamar #100, Austin, TX 78705
PH: 512-476-5632 FX: 512-474-7463
Kathryn Mishell kmishell@austin.rr.com
www.kmfa.org
Devoted to the music of Classical women composers.

Moving On *KBOO*
PO Box 10652, Portland, OR 97296
PH: 503-231-8187 FX: 503-231-7145
L.C. Hansen lchansen@spiritone.com
www.kboo.org
Political, feminist, Folk music.

Murphy's Magic Mess *KZUM*
941 "O" St., Lincoln, NE 68508
PH: 402-474-5086 FX: 402-474-5091
Nadine Murphy programming@kzum.org
www.kzum.org
Alternative spirituality, New Age and Women's music.

Nette Radio
10455 N. Central Expwy. #109-503, Dallas, TX 75231
FX: 267-851-3130
Annette Conlon submit@netteradio.com
www.netteradio.com/submit.html
From Piano to Punk - it's great music by fab women artists. You MUST mail or fax our release form with your music.

Nowhere To Go Radio
814 N. 15th St., San Jose, CA 95112
Ursula Romanowski ursula@ntgradio.com
www.ntgradio.com
We play strictly women artists, both Indie and mainstream. Please visit our website for submission details.

Odd Man Out *WUOG*
Box 2065 Tate Student Ctr. Athens, GA 30602
PH: 706-542-7100 FX: 706-542-0070
DJ Molly mollycoddle@gmail,com
wuog.org
From Hardcore to Riot Grrrl, Punk to Ambient and soothing melodies.

Other Voices *WORT*
118 S. Bedford St., Madison, WI 53703-2692
PH: 608-256-2001 FX: 608-256-3704
wort@terracom.net
www.wort-fm.org
Women composers, performers and conductors.

Rebel Grrrls Radio *WMTS*
Box 58, 1301 E. Main St., Murfreesboro, TN 37132
PH: 615-898-2636 FX: 615-898-5682
www.myspace.com/rebelgrrrlsradio
A show featuring women artists or bands with women in them. From every time period and every genre.

The Red Spot *KCPR*
Graphic Arts Bldg 26, Rm. 201, CPSU San Luis Obispo, CA 93407
PH: 805-756-2965
Bobbie Sox kcprMD@kcpr.org
www.kcpr.org
Featuring women in music of all genres.

Rubyfruit Radio
rubyfruitradio@gmail.com
rubyfruit.libsyn.com
Podcast featuring the best Indie female artists. All girls all the time!

Sing it Sister *KRZA*
528 9th St., Alamosa, CO 81101
PH: 719-589-8844
programming@krza.org
Music featuring women artists.

Sirens' Muse *WEVL*
PO Box 40952, Memphis, TN 38174
PH: 901-528-0560
Lea lea@wevl.org
wevl.org
A variety of genres of contemporary music by women.

Sister Sound *KAOS*
CAB 301, 2700 Evergreen Pkwy. Olympia, WA 98505
PH: 360-867-6896
Jan O. TowandaJT@aol.com
www.kaosradio.org
We are always looking for ways to promote women musicians, especially lesbians.

Sisters *KLCC*
4000 E. 30th Ave. Eugene, OR 97405-0640
PH: 541-463-6000 FX: 541-463-6046
Nanci LaVelle lavellen@comcast.net
www.klcc.org
Features the best of female performances in virtually every genre of music.

Sisters *KVSC*
720 4th Ave. S., 27 Stewart Hall, St. Cloud, MN 56301-4498
PH: 320-308-3126 FX: 320-308-5337
Laura & Emily music@kvsc.org
www.kvsc.org
Women's music Sundays from 2-5pm.

SmartWomen Internet Radio
551 Valley Rd. Upper Montclair, NJ 07043
Patti patti@smartwomen.org
www.smartwomen.org/onair.htm
We are accepting CDs for airplay.

Something About the Women *WMFO*
PO Box 65 Medford, MA 02155
PH: 617-625-0800
info@satwomen.com
www.satwomen.com
The voices of woman artists in all genres.

The Sound Job *WNCI*
PO Box 4972, 270 Mohegan Ave. New London, CT 06320
PH: 860-439-2850 FX: 860-439-2805
wcni_music@yahoo.com
www.wcniradio.org
All styles, all eras. Music by women only - so leave your dick at home.

Stroke the Goddess *WMHB*
Colby College, 4000 Mayflower Hill, Waterville, ME 04901
PH: 207-872-3686
Annie aandandy@somtel.com
www.colby.edu/wmhb
A show devoted to music by female artists.

Suffragette City *KDHX*
3504 Magnolia, St. Louis, MO 63118
PH: 314-664-3688 FX: 314-664-1020
René Saller suffragette@kdhx.org
www.suffragettecity.org
The mood and pace? Challenging but not jarring; beautiful but not sappy; fun but not mindless.

T.G.I. Femmes *KZUM*
941 "O" St., Lincoln, NE 68508
PH: 402-474-5086 FX: 402-474-5091
Tad Frazier programming@kzum.org
www.kzum.org
An eclectic selection of women's music: Folk, Rock and fun.

Under the Skirt *WDBX*
224 N. Washington St., Carbondale, IL 62901
PH: 618-457-3691
wdbx@globaleyes.net
www.wdbx.org
Playing women vocalists (Jazz, Rock, Indie etc.)

Venus Rising *KRBS*
PO Box #9, Oroville, CA 95965
PH: 530-534-1200
Marianne krbs@cncnet.com
www.radiobirdstreet.org
Music by women. Local and underplayed.

Voices of Women *WRIU*
326 Memorial Union, Kingston, RI 02881
PH: 401-874-4949 FX: 401-874-4349
Toni, Beth & Jo comments@wriu.org
www.wriu.org/voicesofwomen

Wild Women Radio *WNHU*
300 Boston Post Rd. West Haven, CT 06516
PH: 203-479-8801 FX: 203-931-6055
newmusic@wnhu.net
www.newhaven.edu/wnhu

The Wimmin's Music Program *KKUP*
933 Monroe St., PMB 9150, Santa Clara, CA 95050
PH: 408-260-2999
Laura Testa rinaldi@cruzio.com
www.kkup.com
Music by, about and for women.

The Wimmin's Show *KZUM*
941 "O" St., Lincoln, NE 68508
PH: 402-474-5086 FX: 402-474-5091
thewimminsshow@hotmail.com
www.kzum.org
WANTED: Recorded music by, for and about women.

Woman Song *KKFI*
PO Box 32250, Kansas City, MO 64171
PH: 816-931-3122 x106
www.kkfi.org
Host Linda Wilson presents music by women for women.

Woman Voices *KUNV*
1515 E. Tropicana Ave. #240, Las Vegas, NV 89119
PH: 702-798-8797
kunv.unlv.edu
Want to hear some singing women? Hosted by Gerrie Blake.

Womanotes *KBCS*
3000 Landerholm Cir. SE., Bellevue, WA 98007-6484
PH: 425-564-2424
Mary & Tracey kbcsdj@ctc.edu
kbcs.fm
Enjoy Jazz music by women.

Womanwaves *WFPK*
619 S. 4th St., Louisville, KY 40202
PH: 502-814-6500
www.wfpk.org
Female artists (or fronted bands) send your stuff.

Women Hold Up Half the Sky *KALX*
26 Barrows Hall #5650, Berkeley, CA 94720-5650
PH: 510-642-1111
kalxmail@media.berkeley.edu
kalx.berkeley.edu
Talk radio and music by and about women.

Women in the 3rd Decade *KRCL*
1971 W. North Temple, Salt Lake City, UT 84116
PH: 801-359-9191 FX: 801-533-9136
Babs DeLay babs@urbanutah.com
www.krcl.org/programs/women3rd.htm
News, information and mainly music by women.

Women in the Arts *KALX*
26 Barrows Hall #5650, Berkeley, CA 94720-5650
PH: 510-642-1111
kalxmail@media.berkeley.edu
kalx.berkeley.edu
Interviews, reviews, roundtables, music, artist spotlight segments.

Women In Music *NPR*
PO Box 15465, Boston, MA 02215
Laney Goodman WomenOnAir@aol.com
www.womenonair.com
Looking for exciting new female talent to add to our playlists!

Women In Music *WERS*
120 Boylston St., Boston, MA 02116
PH: 617-824-8891
womeninmusic@wers.org
www.wers.org

Women in Music *KRVM*
1574 Coburg Rd. PMB 237, Eugene, OR 97401
PH: 541 687-3370
Leigh wimusic@hotmail.com
www.myspace.com/womeninmusic
www.krvm.org
From Blues to New Wave to the most current to the obscure.

Women in Music *KSLC*
900 SE. Baker St. #A498, McMinnville, OR 97128
PH: 503-883-2666
kslc@linfield.edu
www.linfield.edu/kslc
We pay tribute to the awesome contributions of women in the music world.

Women In Music *WTIP*
PO Box 1005, Grand Marais, MN 55604
PH: 218-387-1070 FX: 218-387-1120
info@wtip.org
wtip.org
A new perspective to women and their music, featured artists and interviews.

Women in Rock *KUGS*
700 Viking Union MS 9106, Bellingham, WA 98225
PH: 360-650-2936
music@kugs.org
www.kugs.org
Weekly show for women that rock!

Women in Rock *WEFT*
113 N. Market St., Champaign, IL 61820
PH: 217-359-9338
weft@weftfm.org
www.weft.org

Women of Jazz *KEWU*
E. Washington U. 104 R-TV Bldg. Cheney, WA 99004-2431
PH: 509-359-4282
jazz@mail.ewu.edu
www.kewu.ewu.edu
Three hours of music from dazzling divas.

Women on Wednesday / One of Her Voices *KMUD*
PO Box 135, 1144 Redway Dr. Redway, CA 95560-0135
PH: 707-923-2513 FX: 707-923-2501
Kate Klein md@kmud.org
www.kmud.org
Women's voices, women's issues and women's music.

Women on Women Music Hour *WLUW*
6525 N. Sheridan Rd. Chicago, IL 60626
PH: 773-508-8080 FX: 773-508-8082
wowmusichour@wluw.org
wluw.org
Focusing on female musicians from all genres.

Women's Blues and Boogie *KZUM*
941 "O" St., Lincoln, NE 68508
PH: 402-474-5086 FX: 402-474-5091
Carol Griswold cbluelf@aol.com
www.kzum.org
Legendary and contemporary female vocals.

Women's Collective *KVMR*
401 Spring St., Nevada City, CA 95959
PH: 530-265-9555 FX: 530-265-9077
womenscollective@kvmr.org
www.kvmr.org/programs/women
A group of broadcasters dedicated to bringing women's voices and women's experiences to the airwaves.

Women's Independent Music Show
1940-2 Harrison St., Hollywood, FL 33020
Diane Ward wims@wims.ws
www.wims.ws
Turning listeners on to great independent music.

Women's Music *KMUN*
PO Box 269, Astoria, OR 97103
PH: 503-325-0010
music@coastradio.org
www.kmun.org

Women's Music Hour *WXPN*
3025 Walnut St., Philadelphia, PA 19104
PH: 215-898-6677. FX: 215-898-0707
wxpndesk@xpn.org
xpn.org
Sixty minutes devoted to women's music.

Women's Music Radio *WMSE*
1025 N. Broadway, Milwaukee, WI 53202
PH: 414-799-1917
Jenny, Maria & Rose
musicwomen91_7@hotmail.com
www.geocities.com/musicwomen91_7
www.wmse.org
Every week we do our best to bring you the best in music from a wide variety of women artists!

Women's Music Show *KUMD*
130 Humanities, 1201 Ordean Ct. Duluth, MN 55812
PH: 218-726-7181 FX: 218-726-6571
kumd@d.umn.edu
www.kumd.org
Music by women in all genres, with local interviews and information.

Womens' Prerogative *KTOO*
360 Egan Dr. Juneau, AK 99801-1748
PH: 907-586-1670 FX: 907-586-3612
www.ktoo.org
Music by, for and about women with host Lise Paradis.

Women's Radio
2121 Peralta St. #138, Oakland, CA 94607
PH: 510-891-0004 FX: 510-891-0003
www.womensradio.com
The music of every woman artist your heart desires.

The Women's Show *WMNF*
1210 E. MLK Blvd. Tampa, FL 33603-4449
PH: 813-238-9663 FX: 813-238-1802
Arlene Engelhardt arlene@wmnf.org
www.wmnf.org
An eclectic feminist/womanist radio magazine.

Women's Voices *KZYX*
PO Box 1, Philo, CA 95466
PH: 707-895-2451 FX: 707-895-2554
musicdir@kzyx.org
www.kzyx.org

Women's Windows *WERU*
PO Box 170, 1186 Acadia Highway E. Orland, ME 04431
PH: 207-469-6600 FX: 207-469-8961
Magdalen & Linda info@weru.org
www.weru.org

Womenfolk *KFAI*
1808 Riverside Ave. Minneapolis, MN 55454
PH: 612-341-3144
Ellen Stanley womenfolk@earthlink.net
www.kfai.org/programs/womenflk.htm
Bringing you the best in women's Folk & Acoustic music.

Womansoul *KBOO*
20 SE. 8th Ave. Portland, OR 97214
PH: 503-231-8187 FX: 503-231-7145
Annelise Hummel annelieseh99@yahoo.com
www.kboo.fm
Women's music with rotating hosts.

Womyn Making Waves *WEFT*
113 N. Market St., Champaign, IL 61820
PH: 217-359-9338
weft@weftfm.org
www.weft.org
Features live interviews and performances with local women as well as women from around the world. All genres of music are played.

Womyn's Rock *KBVR*
210 Memorial Union E. Corvallis, OR 97331
PH: 541-737-6323
kbvrfmrock@oregonstate.edu
oregonstate.edu/dept/kbvr/html

World Woman *KOPN*
915 E. Broadway, Columbia, MO 65201
PH: 573-874-5676 FX: 573-499-1662
Leigh & Kay mail@kopn.org
www.kopn.org
Playing local artists and women's music from around the globe.

Canada

Audible Woman *CIUT*
91 St. George St., Toronto, ON M5S 2E8
PH: 416-978-0909 x214 FX: 416-946-7004
Sarah Peebles speeb@sympatico.ca
www.sarahpeebles.net/audwoman.htm
Explore Avant-garde music & performance. Please send in TWO copies of your CD!

Babae(h) Mama *CIUT*
91 St. George St., Toronto, ON M5S 2E8
PH: 416-978-0909 x214 FX: 416-946-7004
Danielle & Donna babaehmama@yahoo.ca
www.ciut.fm
Local and global feminist perspectives.

Big Broad Cast *CFUV*
PO Box 3035, Victoria, BC V8W 3P3
PH: 250-721-8702
cfuvwoa@uvic.ca
cfuv.uvic.ca/women

Broadly Speaking *CHRW*
Rm. 250, UCC, UWO, London, ON N6A 3K7
PH: 519-661-3600 FX: 519-661-3372
broadlyspeaking@chrwradio.com
www.chrwradio.com
Occasional shows on women musicians and have then play a song or two.

Hersay *CKUT*
3647 U. St., Montreal, QC H3A 2B3
PH: 514-398-4616 FX: 514-398-8261
music@ckut.ca
www.ckut.ca
Transister radio.

A Madwoman's Underclothes *CFRU*
U.C. Level 2, Guelph, ON N1G 2W1
PH: 519-837-2378 FX: 519-763-9603
Lori music@cfru.ca
www.cfru.ca
Words and music made mostly by women.

The Neo Brideshead *CHLY*
#2-34 Victoria Rd. Nanaimo, BC V9R 5B8
PH: 250-716 3410
Elle J & Mel neobrideshead@chly.ca
www.chly.ca/the_neo_brideshead.php
Female emPOWERed music.

Radio Active Femminism *CKLN*
55 Gould St. 2nd Fl. Toronto, ON M5B 1E9
PH: 416-979-5251 FX: 416-595-0226
radioactivefeminism@ckln.fm
www.ckln.fm
A news program for and about issues that concern women and feminism.

She Stuff *CKXU*
SU 164, 4401 University Dr. W., Lethbridge, AB T1K 3M4
PH: 403-329-2335 FX: 403-329-2224
www.ckxu.com
Features the female voice, energy and creative juices.

Women of the 90's (and today) *Live365*
PH: 440-228-6479
Mark Collins mmzjm@centurytel.net
www.geocities.com/missmarcym/WOT90s.html
Features the music of women from the 90's to today.

Women on Air *CFUV*
PO Box 3035, Victoria, BC V8W 3P3
PH: 250-721-8702
cfuvwoa@uvic.ca
cfuv.uvic.ca/women
Music, news and interviews on diverse women's voices.

Womyn's words *CHRY*
Rm. 413, Student Ctr. Toronto, ON M3J 1P3
PH: 416-736-5656 FX: 416-650-8052
chrymd@yorku.ca
www.yorku.ca/chry
International documentaries on women and feminism.

The XX Show *CIOI*
135 Fennell Ave. W. PO Box 2034, Hamilton, ON L8N 3T2
PH: 905-575-2175 FX: 905-575-2385
www.mohawkcollege.ca/msa/cioi
Music written and performed by women.

France

Babes in Boyland *Clapas FM*
195 bd de l Aeroport Int. Le Polynice Bat B, Appt 48, 34000 Montpellier, France
babes@babesinboyland.info
www.babesinboyland.info
Entirely dedicated to women in music, especially "Rock" but it nevertheless remains open to any digression. Feel free to send us stuff.

panx radio
BP 5058, 31033 Toulouse, France
PH: 33-0-561612145 FX: 33-0-561114895
infos@panx.net
www.panx.net
Hardcore, Punk, CyberThrash, Grindcore, TechnoBruit, Crades Mélodies.

The Netherlands

Radio Monalisa Amsterdam FM
Patricia Werner Leanse monalisa@dds.nl
www.radiomonalisa.nl
A weekly program of women's Classical music.

United Kingdom

Girls and Guitars *Forest of Dean Radio*
1 Berisford Ct. Cinderford, Gloucestershire GL14 2BS UK
PH: 01594-820722
Sue Brindley contactus@fodradio.org
www.fodradio.org
Featuring female Singer/Songwriters.

Australia

3RPP Women's Music Programming
PO Box 602, Somerville, VIC 3912 Australia
PH: 03-5978-8200 FX: 03-5978-8551
programming@3cr.org.au
www.3rpp.asn.au
We feature a DOZEN shows that help to promote women artists.

Behind the Lines, Frock Off, Women with Attitude *2XX*
PO Box 812, Canberra, ACT 2601 Australia
PH: 02-6247-4400 FX: 02-6248-5560
info@2xxfm.org.au
www.2xxfm.org.au
Programs that endeavour to give a fair representation to performances by women.

Burning Down The House / Drastic On Plastic *RTR FM*
PO Box 842, Mt. Lawley, WA 6929 Australia
PH: +61-8-9260-9210 FX: +61 8 9260 9222
rtrfm@rtrfm.com.au
www.rtrfm.com.au
Women's issues and music from all genres.

Girly is Good *3CR*
PO Box 1277, Collingwood, Melbourne, VIC 3065 Australia
PH: 03-9419-8377 FX: 03-9417-4472
Emily Hayes girlyisgood@today.com.au
www.3cr.org.au
Featuring women musicians, visual artists ....basically any art form that is girly.

The Grrrly Show *2RRR Sydney*
PO Box 644 Gladesville, NSW 1675 Australia
PH: 61-29816-2988 FX: 61-2-9817-1048
Giselle & Alison thegrrrlyshow@coolgrrrls.com
www.2rrr.org.au
Riot Grrrl to Indie Pop, Electronica and Folk, interspersed with music news, interviews and artist info.

MegaHerz *4ZZZ*
4ZZZ, PO Box 509, Fortitude Valley, QLD 4006
Australia
PH: 07-3252-1555 FX: 07-3252-1950
info@4zzzfm.org.au
www.4zzzfm.org.au
Women's issues and music.

Women on Waves *JOY Radio*
PO Box 907, S. Melbourne, VIC 3205 Australia
PH: 61-03-9699-2949 FX: 61-03-9699-2646
womenonwaves@joy.org.au
www.joy.org.au/womenwaves
The latest and best eclectic mix of basically Alternative "women's music".

New Zealand

Girl School *RDU*
PO Box 31-311, Ilam, Christchurch, New Zealand
PH: 03-348 8610 FX: 03-364-2509
Missy G. station@rdu.org.nz
www.rdu.org.nz
It's all about the ladies!

World Radio

United States

Afrodicia
PO Box 19866, Los Angeles, CA 90019
PH: 323-938-0720 FX: 206-279-3020
afrodicia@yahoo.com
www.afrodicia.com
African music, Afrobeat, Afropop and World music.

Afropop Worldwide
688 Union St. Storefront, Brooklyn, NY 11215
www.afropop.org/radio
Dedicated to African music and the music of the African Diaspora. Does CD reviews too.

alterNATIVE Voices *KUVO*
PO Box 2040, Denver, CO 80201-2040
producer@alternativevoices.org
www.alternativevoices.org
We entertain, educate and generally promote positive excellence and appropriate role models by and for, American Native people.

The American Indian Radio
PO Box 83111, Lincoln, NE 68501
airos@unl.edu
airos.org
A national distribution system for Native programming to Tribal communities and to general audiences.

Café LA *KCRW*
1900 Pico Blvd. Santa Monica, CA 90405
PH: 310-450-5183 FX: 310-450-7172
Tom Schnabel cafe@kcrw.org
www.kcrw.com/show/cl
Emphasis on new Brazilian, European, African and Tropical Latin music. There are also frequent guests and live performances.

Confundable Willows *Sidewok Radio*
www.myspace.com/confundablewillows
We just kinda play whatever we like, specifically up & coming Asian Pacific Islander musicians, bands, vocalists, poets and producers!

Culture Cafe *WWUH*
200 Bloomfield Ave. West Hartford, CT 06117
PH: 860-768-4701 FX: 860-768-5701
Brian Grosjean abgrosjean@earthlink.net
www.wwuh.org
Folk music from the rest of the world - African, Latin, Flamenco, Native American, Asian music and much more.

Desi Live Radio
www.desiliveradio.com
Featuring Bollywood, Hindi and Bhangra songs.

Earthsongs
818 E. 9th Ave. Anchorage, AK 99501
PH: 907-258-8880 FX: 907-258-8914
Shyanne Beatty feedback@knba.org
www.earthsongs.net
Exploring the Native influences that help shape and define contemporary American music.

Folks of the World *KDHX*
3504 Magnolia, St. Louis, MO 63118
PH: 314-664-3688 FX: 314-664-1020
Harriet Shanas folksoftheworld@kdhx.org
www.kdhx.org/programs/folksoftheworld.htm
A wealth of old and new ethnic music from Asia, Europe and the Mid East.

Giramondu *KUSP*
203 8th Ave. Santa Cruz, CA 95062
PH: 831-476-2800
Gypsy Flores gypsy_flores@yahoo.com
www.kusp.org
An eclectic blend of music from everywhere.

The Global Hit Podcast
theworld@pri.org
www.theworld.org/globalhits
A daily spotlight on international musical artists or trends.

The Indestructible Beat *WITR*
32 Lomb Memorial Dr. Rochester, NY 14623-0563
PH: 585-475-2271 FX: 585-475-4988
Terry Lindsey
musicdirector@modernmusicandmore.com
www.modernmusicandmore.com
Devoted to World music. A wide range of sound, from early 20th Century field recordings to the latest cutting edge world fusions.

International Pulse! *WVKR*
Box 726, Vassar, 124 Raymond Ave. Poughkeepsie, NY 12604
PH: 845-437-5476 FX: 845-437-7656
Michel Joseph msanonjoseph@hotmail.com
www.wvkr.org
The rhythmic music of Afro-Caribbean, South/Central America and Eurasia.

Island Time *KMXT*
620 Egan Way, Kodiak, AK 99615-6487
PH: 907-486-5698 FX: 907-486-2733
Russ Josephson russ_josephson@yahoo.com
www.kmxt.org
Polynesian, Caribbean, other islands traditional music.

Joyous Noise Radio
20644 Keeney Mill Rd. Freeland, MD 21053
PH: 410-329-8304
John Madill jmadill@joyousnoise.com
www.joyousnoise.com/radio
Didjeridu music.

KIDE *Hoopa Radio*
PO Box 1220, Hoopa, CA 95546
PH: 530-625-4245
kide@hoopa-nsn.gov
www.hoopa-nsn.gov/departments/kide.htm
Tribally owned and operated community radio.

KILI
PO Box 150, Porcupine, SD 57772
www.lakotamall.com/kili
Largest native owned and operated public radio station in America.

Kindbeat *KGLP*
200 College Dr. Gallup, NM 87301
PH: 505-863-7626 FX: 505-863-7633
www.kglp.org/moon
Host Lester Kien honors cultural diversity and a strong commitment to community awareness of social concerns.

KLND
11420 SD Hwy. 63, McLaughlin, SD 57642
PH: 605-823-4661 FX: 605-823-4660
www.klnd.org
Bringing forth tradition for Native people through educational and cultural programming.

KNBA
3600 San Jeronimo Dr. #480, Anchorage, AK 99508
PH: 907-279-5622 FX: 907-793-3536
feedback@knba.org
www.knba.org
Native American music.

KUYI
PO Box 1500, Keams Canyon, AZ 86034
PH: 928-738-5525 FX: 928-738-5501
kuyihopiradio@yahoo.com
www.kuyi.net
Native American public radio.

KWRR
PO Box 396, Fort Washakie, WY 82514
PH: 307-335-8659 FX: 307-335-8740
admin@kwrr.net
kwrr.net
Native American radio at its best!

KWSO
PO Box 489, Warm Springs, OR 97761
PH: 541-553-1968 FX: 541-553-3348
info@kwso.org
www.kwso.org
Native American radio.

Morning Breeze *KSBR*
28000 Marguerite Pkwy. Mission Viejo, CA 92692
PH: 949-582-4221 FX: 949-347-9693
Donna Jo Thornton themorningbreeze@gmail.com
www.ksbr.net
World / New Age music.

**The Motherland Influence /
Ambiance Congo** *WRIR*
1311 Wentbridge Rd. Richmond, VA 23227
David Noyes davidn4010@yahoo.com
www.motherlandinfluence.com
The best of African, Latin & Caribbean music.

Music From Everywhere But Here *WBGU*
120 West Hall, BGSU, Bowling Green, OH 43403
PH: 419-372-8657 FX: 419-372-9449
David Sears dsears@bgnet.bgsu.edu
www.wbgufm.com
Weekly World music show.

Music of the World *KEUL*
Glacier City Radio, PO Box 29, Girdwood,
AK 99587
PH: 907 754-2489
Karen Rakos keulkaren@hotmail.com
www.glaciercity.us
Get ready to dance to the beat of the latest World music.

Native Music Hours *KANW*
2020 Coal Ave. SE., Albuquerque, NM 87106
PH: 505-242-7848
www.kanw.com
Join Beulah Sunrise for an adventure of the best Native American music.

New World Buzz Radio
116 Farmcrest Dr. Oakdale, PA 15071-9332
info@newworldbuzz.com
www.newworldbuzz.com
Provides a showcase to promote the composers, artists and performers of music genres from all over the world.

Passport *WBEZ*
CPR, Navy Pier, 848 E. Grand Ave. Chicago,
IL 60611-3462
PH: 312-948-4855
Chris Heim music@wbez.org
www.wbez.org
Your musical ticket to exciting sounds from around the globe.

Planet Waves *KZFR*
PO Box 3173, Chico, CA 95927
PH: 530-895-0131 FX: 530-895-0775
Sister Shoshana rootsandcultureradio@yahoo.com
www.kzfr.org
Rhythmic music from around the planet and beyond.

Radio Afrodicia
PO Box 19866, Los Angeles, CA 90019
PH: 323-938-0720 FX: 206-279-3020
Nnamdi & Donna nnamdi@afrodicia.com
www.afrodicia.com
Afrobeat, Afropop, World and Fuji music.

Sound Travels *WERU*
PO Box 170, 1186 Acadia Hwy., East Orland,
ME 04431
PH: 207-469-6600 FX: 207-469-8961
Joe & Tim info@weru.org
www.weru.org
World music show.

Spin the Globe *KAOS*
CAB 301, Evergreen State College, Olympia,
WA 98505
PH: 360-867-6896
Scott Stevens spintheglobe@earball.net
www.earball.net/spintheglobe
World music news and reviews.

Sunday Simcha *WFDU*
Metropolitan Campus, 1000 River Rd. Teaneck,
NJ 07666
Bill Hahn billh891@optonline.net
www.wfdu.fm
Traditional & contemporary Jewish music.

Vibe FM
KujA Moto, 29193 Northwestern Hwy. #605,
Southfield, MI 48034-1023
PH: 248-358-8702 FX: 248-358-8702
www.vibefm.com.gh
The music of Ghana.

World Fusion Radio
1452 Oak Ave. #2S, Evanston, IL 60201
worldfusionradio.com
We play only certain genres of music that fit under the "World Fusion" or "World Beat" umbrella. PLEASE read our submission policy! Hosted by DJ ProFusion.

The World Music Show *WTUL*
Tulane U. Ctr. New Orleans, LA 70118
PH: 504-865-5887 FX: 504-862-3072
Neema Nazem world@wtul.fm
www.wtul.fm

World Party *KEWU*
E. Washington U. 104 R-TV Bldg. Cheney,
WA 99004-2431
PH: 509-359-4282
jazz@mail.ewu.edu
www.kewu.ewu.edu
Music from around the globe: Latin, Brazilian, African, European, Hawaiian, Reggae and others.

Worldbeat Transfusion *KEDT*
4455 S. Padre Island Dr. #38, Corpus Christi,
TX 78411-4481
PH: 361-855-2213 FX: 361-855-3877
W. C. Welz wcwelz@kedt.org
www.kedt.org/fm/Worldbeat.htm
Tastes of Middle Eastern, Ethno-Ambient, Latino Salsa, Celtic and Light Fusion musical selections.

Canada

CKMO
3100 Foul Bay Rd. Victoria, BC V8P 5J2
PH: 250-370-3658 FX: 250-370-3679
feedback@village900.ca
www.village900.ca
Our music programming is a format called Global Roots, a contemporary mix of Folk, Roots and World Beat music.

Espace Musique *CBC*
Pierre Fortier pierre_fortier@radio-canada.ca
www.radio-canada.ca/folkalliance
Canada's leading broadcaster of World music. We're always on the look-out for new talent.

Global Village *CBC*
PO Box 500, Stn. A, Toronto, ON M5W 1E6
PH: 416-205-3700 FX: 416-205-6040
www.radio.cbc.ca/programs/global
Host Jowi Taylor reports on musical life from 305 places in 108 countries.

Italy

World Music FM
Elisa Semprini info@worldmusicfm.it
www.worldmusicfm.it
Podcast featuring the Afro sounds and rhythms evolution up to the present World music.

United Kingdom

BBC Radio 3 *World Music*
www.bbc.co.uk/radio3/worldmusic
Home page of the BBC Radio 3's various World music shows. Info, shows, contacts etc.

Front-ears *U. Radio York*
c/o Vanbrugh College, Heslington, York,
YO10 5DD UK
PH: 01904-433840 FX: 01904-433840
Eddie Ferrero ury@york.ac.uk
ury.york.ac.uk/microsite/frontears
The absolute best in International music.

Australia

4EB
PO Box 7300, East Brisbane, QLD 4169 Australia
PH: 07-3240-8600 FX: 07-3240-8633
admin@4eb.org.au
www.4eb.org.au
Sharing the World with you!

Israel

Worldwaves *Radio Upper Galilee*
Nimron 2, Katzrin 12900, Israel
Menachem Vinegrad menny2@yahoo.com
A weekly program of eclectic Folk and World music, sending a message of peace through good music for all to enjoy.

South Africa

Channel Africa
PO Box 91313, Auckland Park 2006 South Africa
PH: +27-11-7144541 FX: +27-11-7142072
David Moloto molotod@sabc.co.za
www.channelafrica.org
Music from all the continents including exceptional, underexposed artists.

Radio Shows that Spotlight Local Musicians

"Local" is a relative term. For some stations, "Local" is defined as any artist who lives within the city limits. Others consider "Local" to be anyone that lives within the listening area. There are many shows that consider "Local" to be musicians from anywhere within the state, province or territory, while others consider "Local" to be artists from the host country. If you're not sure whether you qualify for airplay with a particular show, get in touch with the station (or host) and in most cases they will happily respond and clarify what they consider to be "Local" talent.

North America

United States

Alabama

WBHM *Tapestry*
650 11th St. S., Birmingham, AL 35294
PH: 205-934-2606 FX: 205-934-5075
info@wbhm.org
www.wbhm.org/Tapestry
Music magazine that has a segment featuring local musicians.

WEGL *Homegrown Show*
116 Foy Union Bldg. Auburn U. AL 36849-5231
PH: 334-844-4114 FX: 334-844-4118
wegl@auburn.edu
wegl.auburn.edu

WVUA *Loud and Local*
PO Box 870152, Tuscaloosa, AL 35487
PH: 205-348-6461
wvuamusic@sa.ua.edu
www.newrock907.com
From garage bands to headliners, it's all local all the time.

Alaska

The ANC Podcast
theancpodcast@gmail.com
theancpodcast.blogspot.com
Featuring local Anchorage musicians and music.

KRUA *Locals Only*
PSB Rm. 254, 3211 Providence Dr. Anchorage, AK 99508
Dave Waldron aykrua9@uaa.alaska.edu
PH: 907-786-6805
www.uaa.alaska.edu/krua
An eclectic mix of Anchorage-area and statewide music.

KWJG *Local Expressions*
PO Box 1121, Kasilof, AK 99610
PH: 907-260-7702
Holly akhollybear@hotmail.com
www.ezonechick.net/local_expressions.html
Live music by Alaskan artists.

Arizona

KEDJ *Local Frequency*
7434 E. Stetson Dr. #265, Scottsdale, AZ 85251
Gadger gadger@theedge1039.com
www.theedge1039.com
Three songs from Arizona's best local bands every week night at midnight!

KXCI *Locals Only*
220 South 4th Ave. Tucson, AZ 85701
PH: 520-623-1000
www.myspace.com/kxci
Host Don Jennings features music and live performances from local artists.

KZGL *Local Z*
2690 E. Huntington Dr. Flagstaff, AZ 86004
www.radioflagstaff.com/kzgl/ZHome.htm
Airing the best Arizona has to offer!

Radio Arizona
nitish@radioaz.net
radioaz.net
Supporting the Arizona music scene.

WWJD
10953 N. Frank Lloyd Wright Blvd. #110, Scottsdale, AZ 85259
producer1@arizonamusicradio.com
www.kaltaz.com
Showcases AZ's best local Christian bands. Please fill out our online submission form.

Arkansas

KXUA *NW Arkansas Local*
A665 Arkansas Union, Fayetteville, AR 72701
PH: 479-575-5883
charts@uark.edu
www.kxua.com
Bringing you the best in local and regional music.

WXFX *The Fox Consumer Guide to New Rock*
1 Commerce St. #300, Montgomery, AL 36104
PH: 334-240-9274 FX: 334-240-9219
Rick Hendrick thefox@wxfx.com
www.wxfx.com/guide
Playing the best new Rock.

California

Buck City Podcast
N.L. Belardes contact@nlbelardes.com
nlbelardes.com/musicrev.html
Hear local music, get book talk and interviews from Bakersfield artists.

dnbradio.com *916Junglist*
Billy Lane 916junglist@916junglist.com
www.916junglist.com
Promoting Sacramento based D n' B artists.

Insomnia Radio: San Francisco
PH: 206-203-1275
scott@insomniaradio.net
sf.insomniaradio.net
Podcast featuring the best Alt-Rock and Indie Noise from the Bay.

KALX *KALX Live!*
26 Barrows Hall #5650, Berkeley, CA 94720-5650
PH: 510-642-1111
kalxlive@kalx.berkeley.edu
kalx.berkeley.edu
Musicians of varied styles perform at the beginning of the show, then at around 10:30 PM, the will be a live broadcast from a local club.

KCSB *Bring It Up!*
PO Box 13401, Santa Barbara, CA 93107-3401
PH: 805-893-3757
internal.music@kcsb.org
www.kcsb.org
An eclectic program with an emphasis on showcasing local artists.

KIOZ *Local Music*
9660 Granite Ridge Dr. San Diego, CA 92123
PHH 858-292-2000
rock1053@clearchannel.com
www.kioz.com
San Diego bands, send us an e-mail and tell us about your band.

KKUP *Bajaba On Jazzline*
933 Monroe St., PMB 9150, Santa Clara, CA 95050
PH: 408-260-2999
Afrikahn Jahmal Dayvs jzzline@yahoo.com
www.kkup.com
The evolution of the Blues from Bebop to Hip Hop featuring Bay Area Jazz and Blues artists.

KOZT *Local Licks*
110 S. Franklin St., Fort Bragg, CA 95437
PH: 707 964-7277 FX: 707-964-9536
thecoast@kozt.com
www.kozt.com/LocalLicksInfo.htm
Mendocino County musicians playing a variety of music.

KRCK
73-733 Fred Waring Dr. #201, Palm Desert, CA 92260
PH: 760-341-0123 FX: 760-341-7455
The Big KC kc@krck.com
www.krck.com
We support local talent and encourages independent artists. Rock & Alternative format.

KRQR
856 Manzanita Ct. Chico, CA 95926
15minutes@zrockfm.com
www.z-rock.com/localmusic.shtml
Local music Monday through Friday from 9:05 pm to 9:20 pm.

KRXQ *Local Licks*
5345 Madison Ave. Sacramento, CA 95841
PH: 916-334-7777 FX: 916-339-4293
www.krxq.net
The best local bands in Sacramento along with the occasional interview and special in-studio guest.

KSDS *Local Jazz Corner*
1313 Park Blvd. San Diego, CA 92101
PH: 619-234-1062 FX: 619-230-2212
www.jazz88online.org
Host Cynthia Hammond features Jazz from local artists.

KULV *Backstage Pass*
1950 3rd St., La Verne, CA 91750
PH: 909-593-3511 x 4777 FX: 909-392-2706
Erica Pembleton pembleto@ulv.edu
www.ulv.edu/kulv
Get a backstage pass to meet the local bands!

KZFR *ChicoButta*
PO Box 3173, Chico, CA 95927
PH: 530-895-0131 FX: 530-895-0775
DJX wordgroove@podomatic.com
wordgroove.podomatic.com
Features music/poetry/sounds produced in the northern fertile Sacramento valley of CA.

KZFR *LA Sounds*
PO Box 3173, Chico, CA 95927
PH: 530-895-0131 FX: 530-895-0775
Señor Felipe DJSrFelipe@aol.com
www.kzfr.org
East LA Cholo. Soul, R+B, Blues, Latin, Folk and Gospel.

KZSU *Wednesday Night Live*
PO Box 20510, Stanford, CA 94309
PH: 650-723-9010 FX: 650-725-5865
music@kzsu.stanford.edu
kzsu.stanford.edu
In studio performances and interviews.

SOSD Radio
c/o Marc Balanky, PO Box 122512, San Diego, CA 92112
entertainment.signonsandiego.com/section/music
San Diego bands and national touring acts, send us your CDs!

Sound Pollution Podcast
soundpollution@gmail.com
www.soundpollution.info
Music and interviews with local Fresno bands. We also rant, rave and review.

Sound Scene Revolution Podcast
Rich soundscenerevolution@gmail.com
www.soundscenerevolution.com
Music and interviews with local bands in the SF Bay Area. We also review new music.

West Coast Live
2124 Kittredge Ave. #350, Berkeley, CA 94704
PH: 415-664-9500 x2
producers@wcl.org
www.wcl.org
Music, ideas and humor from a rich mix of musicians, writers and thinkers from the Bay Area and around the country.

XTRA *Loudspeaker*
9660 Granite Ridge Dr. San Diego, CA 92123
www.91x.com
Our local show featuring bands from and in San Diego.

Colorado

KCSU *The Local Show*
Student Ctr. Box 13, Lory Student Ctr. Fort Collins, CO 80523
PH: 970-491-7611 FX: 970-491-7612
kcsumusic@gmail.com
www.kcsufm.com

KVCU *Basementalism*
Campus Box 207, Boulder, CO 80309
PH: 303-492-3243
us@basementalism.com
www.basementalism.com
We are a strong supporter of the Colorado Hip Hop Scene.

KVCU *Local Shakedown*
Campus Box 207, U. Colorado, Boulder, CO 80309
PH: 303-492-5031 FX: 303-492-1369
dj@radio1190.org
www.radio1190.org

Connecticut

WKZE *Off the Beaten Track*
7392 S. Broadway, Red Hook, NY 12571
PH: 845-758-9811 FX: 845-758-9819
Todd Mack info@wkze.com
www.wkze.com
The show spotlights artists residing within the WKZE listening area.

WPLR *Local Band Show*
PO Box 6508, Whitneyville, CT 06517
Rick Allison rick@thelocalbandsshow.com
www.thelocalbandsshow.com
We listen to everything that comes from the WPLR listening area.

Delaware

WSTW *Hometown Heroes*
PO Box 7492, Wilmington, DE 19803
Johnny B. johnnyb@wstw.com
www.wstw.com
Spotlighting the best music from the Delaware Valley! We'll even bring some of the artists into the studio to perform live on the air.

Florida

97X *Local Motion*
11300 4th St. N. #300, St. Petersburg, FL 33716
localmotion@97xonline.com
97xonline.com
The best and brightest of our local music scene. Check out who's been in the studio, who's playing where, submit a gig...

All Florida Indies Podcast
PO Box 560727, Orlando, FL 32856
Bing Futch bing@jobentertainment.com
allflorida.blogspot.com
Here's to hoping that you'll discover what a diverse music scene we have here in Florida.

Orlando Underground Radio Network
orlandoundergroundradio@yahoo.com
www.thefuzionradio.com
Various shows featuring local artists.

Rock 104 *Locals Only*
PO Box 14444, Gainesville, FL 32604
PH: 352-392-0771 FX: 352-392-0519
Philip Nyguen pandamight@hotmail.com
www.rock104.com/locals.asp
Exploring the Gainesville music scene, featuring music by local and regional bands.

Sunday Blues *The Local Set*
WKPX, 8000 NW. 44th St., Sunrise, FL 33351
DAR dar@blueatheart.com
www.blueatheart.com
Local Blues bands, send in your CDs!

WJRR *Native Noise*
2500 Maitland Center Pkwy. #401, Maitland, FL 32751
PH: 407-916-7800
DJ dj@realrock1011.com
www.wjrr.com
Join DJ as he brings you the best from the local music scene.

WMNF *Live Music Showcase*
1210 E. MLK Blvd. Tampa, FL 33603-4449
PH: 813-238-9663 FX: 813-238-1802
Bill & Chris livemusic@wmnf.org
www.wmnf.org
Features live performances by local and national musicians.

WPBZ *Local Band Of The Month*
701 Northpointe Pkwy. #500, West Palm Beach, FL 33407
PH: 561-616-4600
www.buzz103.com
A local band from South Florida visits the Buzz studios to perform.

WPRK *Local Music*
1000 Holt Ave. 2745, Winter Park, FL 32789
Attn: Russell
PH: 407-646-2915 FX: 407-646-1560
wprkfm@rollins.edu
www.rollins.edu/wprk
This is your opportunity to get: airplay, exposure and most importantly—your music heard!

WVFS *Hootenanny*
420 Diffenbaugh Bldg. Tallahassee, FL 32306-1550
music@wvfs.fsu.edu
www.wvfs.fsu.edu
Local music, interviews and live performances.

Georgia

Joe Stevenson Music / Homegrown
2536 Henry St. Augusta, GA 30904
PH: 706-364-7614 FX: 706-790-6857
info@joestevensonmusic.com
www.joestevensonmusic.com
We produce 95 Rock's Homegrown radio program, featuring the Southeast US's best up and coming artists.

SLAB Radio *(Southern Local Area Bands)*
3340 Haverhill Rowe, Lawrenceville, GA 30044
Chris Horton info@slabmusic.com
www.slabmusic.com
Playing the music of bands from the Southeast United States.

WPUP *Local Noise*
1010 Tower Place, Bogart, GA 30622
PH: 706-549-6222 FX: 706-353-1967
Chris Brame brame@rock1037.com
www.rock1037.com
Three hours of the best in local music.

WRAS *Georgia Music Show*
PO Box 4048, Atlanta, GA 30302-4048
PH: 404-651-4488 FX: 404-463-9535
www.wras.org
If you "used" to live in Georgia and now live elsewhere, you are no longer local.

WREK *Live at WREK*
350 Ferst Dr. NW. #2224, Atlanta, GA 30332-0630
PH: 404-894-2468 FX: 404-894-6872
music.director@wrek.org
www.wrek.org
Music you don't hear on the radio.

Hawaii

The DoctorTrey.com Podcast
PH: 206-350-8739
podcast@doctortrey.com
www.doctortrey.com
Dedicated to the Hawaiian music industry.

KIPO *Aloha Shorts*
738 Kaheka St. #101, Honolulu, HI 96814
PH: 808-955-8821 FX: 808-942-5477
Cedric Yamanaka hprmusic@hawaiipublicradio.org
www.hawaiipublicradio.org/alohashorts.htm
A program of local literature, local authors, local actors and local music.

KTUH *Monday Night Live*
2445 Campus Rd. Hemenway Hall #203, Honolulu, HI 96822
PH: 808-956-5288 FX: 808-956-5271
live@ktuh.org
ktuh.hawaii.edu/shows.php?mnl
Featuring occasional interviews with the band du jour. At 10pm is Monday Night Live proper, featuring an hour of original music from one of Hawaii's best local bands.

Illinois

ChiRap.com
staff@chirap.com
www.ChiRap.com
Listen to tha hottest Rap acts outta tha Chicago area!!!

Mac and Slater *Fearless Radio*
401 W. Ontario #150, Chicago, IL 60610
PH: 312-224-8270 FX: 312-423-6598
www.fearlessradio.com
A Chicago based show hosted by Mac and Slater that features local personalities.

TwangOff
flamethrower@twangoff.com
www.twangoff.com
A once-a-month battle of the bands show that takes place at Martyrs' in Chicago. Alt-Country, Americana etc.

WDCB *Folk Festival*
College of DuPage, 425 Fawell Blvd. Glen Ellyn, IL 60137
PH: 630-942-4200 FX: 630-942-2788
Lili Kuzma KuzmaL@wdcb.org
wdcb.org
Music in the Folk tradition with live performances and interviews with local and regional artists.

WEFT *Local Music / Live Local Music*
113 N. Market St., Champaign, IL 61820
PH: 217-359-9338
weft@weftfm.org
www.weft.org
Two shows featuring local artists.

WKQX *Local 101*
230 Merchandise Mart, Chicago, IL 60654
PH: 312-527-8348 FX: 312-527-8348
Chris Payne Chris@Q101.com
www.q101.com/local101
Airplay and reviews of Chicago artists.

WLUW *Radio One Chicago*
6525 N. Sheridan Rd. Chicago, IL 60626
PH: 773-508-8080 FX: 773-508-8082
Mike Gibson mike@lovehasnologic.com
wluw.org
Interviews, music and guests explore Chicago's independent music scene.

WONC *Local Chaos*
30 N. Brainard, PO Box 3063, Naperville, IL 60566
PH: 637-5965 x 3 FX: 630-637-5900
www.wonc.org
Local music every Sunday night.

WPGU *Inner Limits*
#107, 24 E. Green St., Champaign, IL 61801
PH: 217-244-3000 FX: 217-244-3001
DrewPatterson1071@yahoo.com
www.wpgu.com
One hour of local music.

WXAV *The A & J Show*
3700 W. 103rd St., Chicago, IL 60655
PH: 773-298-3376 FX: 773-298-3381
Jim and Chris AandJShow@aandjshow.com
aandjshow.com
We've had several Chicago bands visit us in the studio over the years.

WXRT *Local Anesthetic*
4949 W. Belmont Ave. Chicago, IL 60641
PH: 773-777-1700 FX: 773-777-5031
Richard Milne rankenter@aol.com
www.wxrt.com
WXRT will only accept recorded materials that are clearly labeled as such. Any packages with hand written "send to" or "received from" information will not be accepted into the station.

Indiana

IndianaRap.com
www.indianarap.com
Listen to tha hottest Rap acts outta tha Indiana area!!!

One Kind Radio *Independent & Local Show*
PO Box 127, Hobart, IN 46342
John Bowles jbowles@onekindradio.com
www.onekindradio.com/indie
A mixture of local and Indie music from Chicagoland and beyond.

WFHB *The Local Show*
PO Box 1973 Bloomington, IN 47402
PH: 812-323-1200 FX: 812-323-0320
music@wfhb.org
www.wfhb.org

Iowa

KAZR *Local Licks*
1416 Locust St., Des Moines, IA 50309
PH: 515-280-1350
Suzi suzi@lazer1033.com
www.lazer1033.com
If your band is releasing a CD, send me an e-mail with all of the info.

KIWR *New Day Rising*
2700 College Rd. Council Bluffs, IA 51503
PH: 712-325-3254 FX: 712-325-3391
Dave & Beau ndrdave@cox.net
www.897theriver.com/new.asp
The best in fresh, new Rock before you will hear it anywhere else.

KIWR *Planet O!*
2700 College Rd. Council Bluffs, IA 51503
PH: 712-325-3254 FX: 712-325-3391
Kady & James planeto897@yahoo.com
www.897theriver.com
Omaha's longest running local music show! Accept NO substitute!!!!

KUNI *Live from Studio One*
U. Northern Iowa, Cedar Falls, IA 50614-0359
PH: 319-273-6400 FX: 319-273-2682
Karen Impola karen.impola@uni.edu
www.kuniradio.org/kustud.html
Unique weekly live broadcast featuring local and national artists.

Kansas

KJHK *Plow the Fields*
1301 Jayhawk Blvd. Kansas Union, Rm. 427, Lawrence, KS 66045
PH: 785-864-5483
Caterina kjhkproduction@ku.edu
kjhk.org
Celebrate the area's fertile musical heritage. Indigenous harmonies from all genres. Local music submissions always accepted and appreciated as well.

KLZR *Local Lazer Music*
3125 W. 6th St., Lawrence, KS 66049
Newman newman@lazer.com
www.lazer.com
Wanna be on the radio? Send those CDs and concert updates to us. If you have an MP3, you can e-mail it to me.

Kentucky

WWHR *Local Shots*
College Heights, 1 Big Red Way, Bowling Green, KY 42101
PH: 270-745-5350
Koufax localshots@revolution.fm
www.myspace.com/localshots
Features artists from Bowling Green and the surrounding areas.

Louisiana

KBON
109 S. 2nd St., Eunice, LA 70535
PH: 337-546-0007 FX: 337-546-0097
101.1@KBON.com
www.kbon.com
About 70% of the music on KBON is the music of Louisiana recording artists.

KLRZ *Rajun' Cajun*
11603 Hwy. 308, PO Drawer 1350, Larose, LA 70373
PH: 985-798-7792 FX: 985-798-7793
klrz@mobiletel.com
www.klrzfm.com
All Louisiana, all the time!

KLSU *Saturated Neighborhood*
B-39 Hodges Hall, LSU, Baton Rouge, LA 70803
PH: 225-578-4620 FX: 225-578-1698
music.director@klsu.fm
www.klsu.fm
Music and interviews with Louisiana bands of all styles.

New Orleans Radio
inquiry@lagniappe.la
www.lagniappe.la
We've now built the site to allow for MP3 uploads of music or syndicated shows.

WTUL *Local Music Show*
Tulane U. Ctr. New Orleans, LA 70118
PH: 504-865-5887 FX: 504-862-3072
Liz localmusic@wtul.fm
www.wtul.fm

Maine

WCLZ *Greetings From Area Code 207*
One City Ctr. Portland, ME 04101
PH: 207-774-6364
Charlie Gaylord charlie.gaylord@citcomm.com
989wclz.com/gfac207_main.html
Featuring live interviews and new music from the best local musicians.

WMPG *Local Motives*
96 Falmouth St., Portland, ME 04104-9300
PH: 207-780-4909
Jan Wilkinson localmotives@yahoo.com
www.localmotives.org
Every Friday night, we bring a the sounds of a local Portland band.

WMPG *The Locals*
96 Falmouth St., Portland, ME 04104-9300
PH: 207-780-4909
Isaac Shainblum ishainblum@cs.com
www.wmpg.org
Highlights local acts, singers, bands and producers who are some how, some way local.

Maryland

98 Rock *Noise in the Basement*
3800 Hooper Ave. Baltimore, MD 21211
PH: 410-481-1098 FX: 410-467-3291
Matt David mattdavis@hearst.com
www.98online.com
Baltimore's local music outlet. For airplay consideration send your material to the above address.

WWDC *Local Lix*
1801 Rockville Pike #405, Rockville, MD 20852
Roche roche@dc101.com
dc101.com
Devoted to the many great local bands in the DC metropolitan area.

Massachusetts

Boston Beats Radio
PO Box 1243, Allston, MA 02134
PH: 781-381-2856 FX: 206-237-2473
radio@bostonbeats.com
www.bostonbeats.com/Radio/Radio.htm
The best way to find out what's going on in the Boston music scene is to hear it for yourself.

Exploit Boston! Radio
PO Box 1243, Allston, MA 02134
PH: 781-420-9660
contact@exploitboston.com
www.exploitboston.com
Regional and national acts coming to town should contact us.

Folkadelica Radio
2 Northwood Ter. Haverhill, MA 01830
PH: 978-373-9199 FX: 978-373-9359
Shawna Torres Shawna@folkadelica.com
folkadelica.com
Plays local RI and Massachusetts Singer/ Songwriters.

WAAF *Bay State Rock*
20 Guest St. 3rd Fl. Boston, MA 02135-2040
PH: 617-931-1112 FX: 617-931-1073
Carmelita baystaterocklistings@yahoo.com
www.baystaterock.com
Playing the music of bands from the Boston area. We feature 4 song acoustic sets from bands at 11:30 each Sunday night.

WAMH *Live @ WAMH*
AC #1907 Campus Ctr. Amherst, MA 01002-5000
PH: 413-542-2288
Mike & Zachary wamh@amherst.edu
wamh.amherst.edu

WATD *Tomorrow's Dreams*
Box 284, 1271-A Washington St., Weymouth, MA 02189-2316
Steve & Bobbie Sands
tomorrowsdreams@comcast.net
www.tomorrowsdreamsshow.com
Spotlighting New England talent. No Heavy Rock or Rap. Most everything else goes.

WBCN *Boston Emissions*
83 Leo M. Birmingham Pkwy. Boston, MA 02135
PH: 617-746-1400
Dan O'Brien dobrien@wbcn.com
www.wbcn.com
Features local artists plus a band of the month.

WBRS *Watch City Coffeehouse*
Shapiro Campus Ctr. 415 South St., Waltham, MA 02453-2728
PH: 781-736-4785
music@wbrs.org
www.wbrs.org

WFNX *New England Product*
25 Exchange St., Lynn, MA 01901
PH: 781-595-6200
fnxradio@fnxradio.com
www.myspace.com/newenglandproductfnx
Live in-studio performances and interviews. We focus on bringing you the best up-and-coming acts.

WICN *Jazz New England*
6 Chatham St., Worcester, MA 01609
PH: 508-752-0700 FX: 508-752-7518
Tyra Penn tyra@wicn.org
www.wicn.org
Music from regional artists, conversations about their music.

WICN *The Contemporary Café*
6 Chatham St., Worcester, MA 01609
PH: 508-752-0700 FX: 508-752-7518
Nick DiBiasio nick@wicn.org
www.wicn.org
The finest acoustic performances of Folk, Blues and Americana music by the biggest names in New England and around the world.

WICN *Live From Café Fantastique*
6 Chatham St., Worcester, MA 01609
PH: 508-752-0700 FX: 508-752-7518
www.wicn.org
Some of the best local and nationally acclaimed musicians in Folk, Blues and Country music.

WMBR *Pipeline!*
3 Ames St., Cambridge, MA 02142
PH: 617-253-8810
DJ Cottonlicker pipeline@wmbr.org
wmbr.mit.edu
Proof that there are geographical solutions to emotional problems! Local bands and a live in-studio performance every single week.

WMVY *The Local Music Cafe*
PO Box 1148, Tisbury, MA 02568
PH: 508-693-5000 FX: 508-693-8211
www.mvyradio.com/local_musicafe
Music from some of the best local musicians on Cape Cod and the Islands of Martha's Vineyard and Nantucket.

WPXC *Homegrown*
154 Barnstable Rd. Hyannis, MA 02601
PH: 800-445-7499 FX: 508-790-4967
Suzanne Tonaire rockbabe@pixy103.com
www.pixy103.com
Cape Cod's original local artists showcase. Includes band of the month.

WUML *Live from the Fallout Shelter*
1 University Ave. Lowell, MA 01854
falloutshelter@wuml.org
fallout.wuml.org
A variety of Indie, Punk, Alt-Country, Jazz and any and all other Underground music.

WZBC *Boston Jukebox*
BC, McElroy Commons 107, Chestnut Hill, MA 02467
www.myspace.com/bostonjukebox
Each month Tracey Stark spins local music and video. Local musicians are welcome to bring their own band's CDs, demos and videos.

WZBC *Mass. Avenue and Beyond*
BC, McElroy Commons 107, Chestnut Hill, MA 02467
PH: 617-552-4686 FX: 617-552-1738
Tracey wzbcmusic@gmail.com
www.wzbc.org
Local Rock, focusing on new music. Includes interviews from local musicians, artists etc.

Michigan

Bar Hop Sessions
PH: 206-333-1997
barhopsessions@gmail.com
www.barhopsessions.com
Podcast bringing you artists who I've seen perform or would like to see perform live in the Detroit-Ann Arbor area.

CJAM *Sox at Seven*
www.myspace.com/11196992
Host Andrea Sox plays music from Detroit area artists. From Punk to Hip Hop and everything in between.

Detroit Jazz Stage
jazzstage@gmail.com
jazzstage.us
A monthly podcast featuring the best talent from the Detroit Jazz scene.

The Plan Nine Rock Show
6037 Voerner St., Warren, MI 48091
PH: 586-757-9378
Jasper p9print@sbcglobal.net
www.plannineprint.com
Podcast featuring Underground Rock, primarily from the Detroit area.

WCBN *The Local Music Show*
530 Student Activities Bldg. Ann Arbor, MI 48109-1316
PH: 734-763-3501
localmusic@wcbn.org
www.wcbn.org/lms
A weekly 2 hour broadcast of music from Ann Arbor and the surrounding area.

WRIF *Motor City RIFFS*
Attn: Shaffee, 1 Radio Plaza, Detroit, MI 48220
PH: 248-547-0101 FX: 248-542-8800
Doug and Jay jay@wrif.com
www.wrif.com/motorcityriffs
WRIF puts the local scene in the spotlight every Sunday night.

Minnesota

Independent Stream
Gary Holdsteady
independentstream@podomatic.com
www.independentstream.podomatic.com
Podcast supporting the Minnesota music scene.

KFAI *Local Sound Department (LSD)*
1808 Riverside Ave. Minneapolis, MN 55454
PH: 612-341-3144
lsdkfai@yahoo.com
www.kfai.org/programs/lsd.htm
Dedicated to playing music created by Minnesota artists.

KQRS *KQ Homegrown*
2000 SE. Elm St., Minneapolis, MN 55414
PH: 612-617-4000 FX: 612-623-9292
www.radiohomegrown.com
Music, interviews and in studio performances by your favorite local groups.

KTCZ *Minnesota Music*
1600 Utica Ave. S. #400, St. Louis Park, MN 55416
PH: 952-417-3000
Jason Nagle jason@cities97.com
www.cities97.com/pages/mnmusic.html
In addition to playing local artists' tunes throughout the week, we dedicate a full hour to them Sunday nights.

KVSC *Monday Night Live*
720 4th Ave. S. 27 Stewart Hall, St. Cloud, MN 56301-4498
PH: 320-308-5337 FX: 320-308-5337
info@kvsc.org
www.kvsc.org
Every Monday it's an hour of live music from our studio featuring the best in Minnesota music.

KXXR *Loud & Local*
2000 SE. Elm St., Minneapolis, MN 55414
PH: 612-617-4000
Patrick loudandlocal@93xrocks.com
www.93x.com
Send in info on your band.

KUOM *Off the Record*
610 Rarig Ctr. 330 21st Ave. S., Minneapolis, MN 55455
PH: 612-625-3500 FX: 612-625-2112
music@radiok.org
www.myspace.com/otrhatesu
Local music and a live band in Studio K.

WHMH *MN Homegrown*
1010 2nd St. N. Sauk Rapids, MN 56379
Tim Ryan tim@rockin101.com
www.rockin101.com
If you have a band and want some exposure send CDs and bios to us.

Minneapoliscast
4044 13th Ave. S., Minneapolis, MN 55407
www.minneapoliscast.com
A podcast featuring independent Minnesota artists. Send me your CD and bio.

MPR *The Current*
PH: 651-989-4893
mail@mpr.org
minnesota.publicradio.org/radio/services/the_current
*Features performances by the outstanding artists of
our region alongside recordings by the world's finest
music makers.*

MPR *The Local Show*
Chris Roberts mail@mpr.org
minnesota.publicradio.org/radio/programs/
local_show
*The show explores the Twin Cities local music
scene, both past and present.*

Mississippi

WMSV *Homegrown*
PO Box 6210 Student Media Ctr. Mississippi State,
MS 39762-6210
PH: 662-325-8034 FX: 662-325-8037
www.wmsv.msstate.edu
Host April Wallace features music from local artists.

Missouri

KKFI *The KC Spotlight Sessions*
PO Box 32250, Kansas City, MO 64171
PH: 816-931-3122 x106
aoxman@sbcglobal.net
www.kcspotlightsessions.com
*Kansas City's music show. Do you have a CD and
would like to be on the show? Send us an e-mail.*

KPNT *The Local Show*
800 Union Stn. Powerhouse Bldg, St. Louis,
MO 63103
PH: 314-231-1057 FX: 314-621-3000
www.kpnt.com
*Get in on STL's bitchin' local scene and hear the
Indie bands that might become tomorrow's Rock
superstars.Hosted by Cornbread.*

WVRV *The River Homegrown*
11647 Olive Blvd. St. Louis, MO 63141
PH: 314-983-6000
Ken Williams ken.williams@wvrv.com
www.wvrv.com
*We feature the best talent coming from the STL
region.*

Montana

KUFM *Musician's Spotlight*
32 Campus Dr. U. Montana, Missoula,
MT 59812-8064
PH: 406-243-4931 FX: 406-243-3299
www.kufm.org
*Montana and regional musicians performing in
KUFM's studios or in area theaters or clubs.*

Nebraska

KEZO *Z-92's Homegrown*
c/o Scott Murphy, 11128 John Galt Blvd. #192,
Omaha, NE 68137
PH: 402-592-5300 x5316
www.z92.com
*Features the best music from local Rock bands every
Sunday night.*

KIBZ *Local Bandwidth*
4630 Antelope Creek Rd. Lincoln, NE 68506
PH: 402-484-8000 FX: 402-483-9138
Luna luna@kibz.com
www.kibz.com
Featuring the music of local acts.

KRNU *Heresy*
147 Andersen Hall, PO Box 880466, Lincoln,
NE 68588-0466
PH: 402-472-8277
Robert Haisch krnu_heresy@yahoo.com
krnu.unl.edu
*My radio show is strictly for Metal and Hardcore
music. The unsigned bands I play are from the
Lincoln/Omaha area.*

KZUM *Alive in Lincoln*
941 "O" St., Lincoln, NE 68508
PH: 402-474-5086 FX: 402-474-5091
Hardy strawberry67@neb.rr.com
www.kzum.org
Variety of local artists of all genres.

KZUM *River City Folk*
941 "O" St., Lincoln, NE 68508
PH: 402-474-5086 FX: 402-474-5091
Tom May programming@kzum.org
www.kzum.org
Interviews and regional Folk artists.

Nebraska Public Radio *Live From the Mill*
1800 N. 33rd St., Lincoln, NE 68583
PH: 402-472-2200 FX: 402-472-2403
William Stibor wstibor2@unl.edu
netnebraska.org/radio
*Discussion and performances with featured guests
representing a broad range of arts topics, including
writing, dance, music and theatre.*

Nevada

KTHX
300 E. 2nd, 14th Fl. Reno, NV 89501
PH: 775-333-0123 FX: 775-333-0110
info@globalstudio.com
www.kthxfm.com
*We play local music every night at 10pm and have
Acoustic performances on several of our shows.*

KXTE *It Hurts When I Pee*
6655 W. Sahara Ave. #C-202, Las Vegas, NV 89146
homie@xtremeradio.com
www.myspace.com/ithurtswhenipeemusic
*The new music show with a really goofy name.
Local and Indie bands.*

LV Rocks *Sounds of Sin*
PH: 866-587-6257
www.myspace.com/localmusicmama
*Host Miss Amber features interviews and live
performances from some of Vegas' hottest musicians
& bands.*

New Hampshire

WSCA *Hear Us Out*
PH: 603-430-9722 FX: 603-430-9822
PO Box 6532, Portsmouth, NH 03802
Steve & Paul
music@portsmouthcommunityradio.org
www.wscafm.org
Features New Hampshire artists.

New Jersey

WDHA *Homegrown Spotlight*
55 Horsehill Rd. Cedar Knolls, NJ 07927
PH: 973-455-1055 x1345 FX: 973-538-3060
Tony Paige tpaige@greatermedianj.com
www.wdhafm.com
Weeknights at 7:30.

WDVR *Heartlands Hayride*
PO Box 191, Sergeantsville, NJ 08557
PH: 609-397-1620 FX: 609-397-5991
Chris Val lcvillano@aol.com
www.wdvrfm.org/hayride.htm
*Live Country music show. The show invites
participation to new and upcoming local talent who
would not ordinarily have access to performing on
the radio.*

WSOU *Street Patrol*
400 S. Orange Ave., South Orange, NJ 07079
PH: 973-761-9768 FX: 973-761-7593
wsou@shu.edu
www.wsou.net
*Highlighting the area's top local Hard Rock acts. We
also feature regular interviews and live
performances.*

New Mexico

KANW *New Mexico Spanish Music*
2020 Coal Ave. SE., Albuquerque, NM 87106
PH: 505-242-7848
www.kanw.com
*This program has truly become a part of the rich
tradition and culture that is New Mexico.*

New York

Brooklyn Heights Radio
smetrick@aol.com
www.brooklynheightsradio.com
*To those artists and musicians in Brooklyn, who
struggle to have their efforts heard THIS IS FOR
YOU.*

Bumpskey.com
jerry@bumpskey.com
www.Bumpskey.com
*Live show featuring all independent music and in
studio performances.*

East Village Radio
19 1st Ave. New York, NY 10003
PH: 212-420-5908
Veronica veronica@eastvillageradio.com
www.eastvillageradio.com
*We are supporters of the movement of free radio and
are interested in providing a forum for obscure
music as well as a platform for local DJs and
personalities.*

Radio Free Ithica
Mike Levy mlevy4@twcny.rr.com
www.radiofreeithaca.net
*Comprised solely of Ithaca-based bands and
musicians.*

WBAB *The Homegrown Show*
555 Sunrise Hwy. West Babylon, NY 11704
PH: 631-587-1023 FX: 631-422-1023
Fingers fingers@cox.com
wbab.com/homegrown
*For over 20 years WBAB has supported the local
Long Island music scene, playing Long Island's best
bands.*

WBNY *The Local Show*
1300 Elmwood Ave. Buffalo, NY 14222
PH: 716-878-3080 FX: 716-878-6600
wbny@buffalostate.edu
www.wbny.org

WCWP *Aural Fix Transmission*
PO Box 6054, North Babylon, NY 11703
PH: 631-943-3213
Mike Ferrari auralmail@aol.com
www.auralfix.com
Features artists from the Long Island, New York region. Don't ask for permission…just SEND YOUR MUSIC IN!

WICB *Home Brew*
118 Park Hall, Ithaca, NY 14850
PH: 607-274-3217 FX: 607-274-1061
Kris Capulet wicb@ithaca.edu
www.ithaca.edu/radio/wicb
Join Taz for local music news and in studio performances.

WLIR *Tri-State Sound*
3075 Veterans Memorial Hwy. #201, Ronkonkoma, NY 11779
www.wlir.fm
Host Harlan Friedman showcases the best up and coming musicians from Long Island, NYC, CT and NJ.

WUSB *Local Insomniac Music*
Stony Brook Union 266, Stony Brook, NY 11794-3263
PH: 631-632-6501 FX: 631-632-7182
music@wusb.fm
wusb.fm
The best in original local music from the Tri-State area, in a variety of genres.

WUSB *LOCAL LIVE*
Stony Brook Union 266, Stony Brook, NY 11794-3263
PH: 631-632-6501 FX: 631-632-7182
Bill Frey longislandmusiclive@yahoo.com
wusb.fm
Radio show featuring Long Island musicians in a live performance & interview format.

WVKR *Scene Unseen*
Box 726, Vassar College, 124 Raymond Ave. Poughkeepsie, NY 12604
PH: 845-437-5476 FX: 845-437-7656
music@wvkr.org
www.wvkr.org
Featuring bands and music artists from the listening area. Local music news, interviews and live musical performances.

North Carolina

WEND *90 Minutes*
801 E. Morehead St. #200, Charlotte, NC 28202
PH: 704-376-1065
Divakar 90minutes@1065.com
www.1065.com/pages/90minutes.html
The ONLY place for local & regional music in Charlotte.

WGWG *Carolina Drive*
PO Box 876, Boiling Springs, NC 28017
info@wgwg.org
www.wgwg.org
Spotlighting artists of all styles across the Carolinas. Rock, Country, Blues, Bluegrass, Gospel, Classical, Jazz. Anything goes!

WPVM *Be Here Now*
75 Haywood St., Asheville, NC 28801.
PH: 828-258-0085 FX: 828-350-7853
www.wpvm.org
Features new and exciting regional music. Live in-studio performances each week.

WSGE *Complex Radio*
236 Hickory Hill Ln. Stanley, NC 28164
Andrew Webster andrew@complexradio.com
www.complexradio.com
Playing the music of Charlotte artists.

WSQL *Southern Exposure*
PO Box 1240, Brevard, NC 28712
PH: 828-877-5252 FX: 828-877-5253
aandl@citcom.net
www.wsqlradio.com
Summer show featuring live performances by local musicians.

Ohio

Audio Gumshoe
PH: 888-223-5108
talent@audiogumshoe.com
www.richpalmer.com/podcasts
A Miami Valley podcast that features the people in SW Ohio that keep music interesting.

Constant Columbus
constantcolumbus@gmail.com
www.constantcolumbus.com
Podcast dedicated to Columbus music. We try to play as much as we can get our hands on.

OhioRap Radio
PH: 330-338-4348
cr4zyt@ohiorap.com
www.ohiorap.com
Listen to tha hottest Rap acts outta tha Ohio area!!!

WAIF *Kindred Sanction / Live City Licks, Spin Cincinnati*
PO Box 6126, Cincinnati, OH 45206
PH: 513-961-8900
www.waif883.org
Local, regional music and interviews.

WAPS *DIY Radio*
65 Steiner Ave. Akron, OH 44301
PH: 330-761-3099 FX: 330-761-3240
Ron & Ed diy@diyradio.net
www.diyradio.net
Two hours of Punk Rock, past and present, with spotlights on the local music scene.

WCSB *Blue Monday*
Rhodes Tower 956, 2121 Euclid Ave. Cleveland, OH 44115-2214
PH: 216-687-3721 FX: 216-687-2161
John Veverka musicdirector@wcsb.org
www.wcsb.org
The finest local and national Blues artists are heard.

WYSO *Banks of the Ohio*
795 Livermore St., Yellow Springs, OH 45387
PH: 937-767-6420
Fred Bartenstein banksoftheohio@aol.com
www.wyso.org/banksohio.htm
Features Bluegrass from Ohio artists.

Oklahoma

KITX *Home Grown*
1600 W. Jackson, Hugo, OK 74743
PH: 580-326-2555 FX: 580-326-2623
homegrown@k955.com
www.k955.com
Nightly show featuring local artists.

KMYZ *HomeGroan*
5810 E. Skelly Dr. #801, Tulsa, OK 74135
PH: 918-665-3131 FX: 918-663-6622
www.myspace.com/z1045homegroan
Featuring local and regional talent.

Tulsa Music Pulse Radio
Jordan Hiteshew jordanius@tulsamusicpulse.com
www.tulsamusicpulse.com
Contact me about getting your music played online.

Oregon

JamminFM.com *Tha Undaground Show*
0234 SW. Bancroft, Portland, OR 97201
PH: 503-243-7595 FX: 503-417-7653
StarChile starchile@jamminfm.com
www.jamminfm.com
Portland'z #1 ALL Hip Hop show!!!! This is the ONLY show the gives MAJOR LUV 2 Northwest artists!!!

KBPS *Played in Oregon*
515 NE. 15th Ave. Portland, OR 97232-2897
PH: 503-916-5828 FX: 503-916-2642
Robert McBride robert@allclassical.org
www.allclassical.org
There needs to be some Oregon connection and it needs to be "Classical" music.

KBVR *Locals Live*
210 Memorial Union E., Corvallis, OR 97331
PH: 541-737-6323 FX: 541-737-4545
oregonstate.edu/dept/kbvr/html
A 2 hour show that gives local musicians the chance to perform live on KBVR.

KINK *Local Spotlight*
1501 SW. Jefferson, Portland, OR 97201
PH: 503-517-6000 FX: 503-517-6100
Kevin Welch kwelch@kink.fm
www.kinkfm102.com
Tuesday through Friday at 9:20 pm we spotlight a couple of tracks from a local artist or group.

KLCC *Friends and Neighbors*
4000 E. 30th Ave. Eugene, OR 97405-0640
PH: 541-463-6000 FX: 541-463-6046
Kobi Lucas klcc@lanecc.edu
www.klcc.org
Very Acoustic Folk music. A focus on new releases and local music, both recorded and live.

KLRR *Homegrown Music Showcase*
711 NE. Butler Market Rd. Bend, OR 97701
PH: 541-389-1088 FX: 541-388-0456
Dori Donoho dori@clear1017.fm
www.klrr.com
A full hour of music you won't hear anywhere else. If you are a musician or band from Oregon, we want to hear from you.

KMHD *Home Grown Live*
26000 SE. Stark St., Gresham, OR 97030
PH: 503-661-8900 FX: 503-491-6999
Mary Burlingame burlingm@mhcc.edu
www.kmhd.org
Featuring the music of Oregon artists.

KNRK *Get Local*
0700 SW. Bancroft St., Portland, OR 97305
PH: 503-733-5470
Jaime Cooley jaime@947.fm
www.knrk.com
I play a local band every weeknight at 8pm.

KNRQ *Native Noise*
1200 Executive Pkwy. #440, Eugene, OR 97405
PH: 541-684-0979
Derrick dlau@nrq.com
www.nrq.com
Featuring the music of Oregon Rock bands.

NW-Radio.com
8992 SW. Gravenstein Ln. Tigard, OR 97224
donovan@prepaidfriends.com
www.nw-radio.com
Dedicated to bands from the NW US and Lower West Canada. If you're interested in being featured, fill in the form on our website.

PDXBluescast
letters@pdxbluescast.com
www.pdxbluescast.com
Podcast showcasing great Blues music originating from Portland and surrounding areas.

Pennsylvania

Coal Cracker Radio
coalcrackerradio@gmail.com
www.coalcrackerradio.net
Music and interviews with some of NE Pennsylvania's best independent artists.

Indie Band Radio *The Pennsylvania Rock Show*
bill@akmusicscene.com
www.parockshow.info
Featuring the best unsigned Rock Pennsylvania has to offer.

Local Support
www.citypaper.net/podcast
Philadelphia City Paper's bi-weekly local music podcast.

Old School House Radio
201 Ross Ave. Ste. B, New Cumberland, PA 17070
PH: 717-920-0905
info@OSHRadio.com
www.oshradio.com
Reviews, interviews and you can also post your MP3s. Several shows covering the Harrisburg entertainment scene.

PaXposure Radio
320 Jackson St., Reynoldsville, PA 15851
xposureradio@paxposure.com
www.paxposure.com
Playing PA's best Indie artists. Send us a copy of your CD. NO attachments!

The Phil Stahl Show *WXLV*
PO Box 231, Pennsburg, PA 18073
PH: 610-799-1145
Phil phil@philstahl.com
philstahl.indiegroup.com
Features unsigned local music acts only.

WBXQ *The Backyard Rocker*
PH: 814-944-9320
www.wbxq.com
A 2 hour weekly local music program.

WPTS *Live Show*
411 William Pitt Union, Pittsburgh, PA 15260
PH: 412-648-7990 FX: 412-648-7988
wptsmusicdirector@hotmail.com
www.wpts.pitt.edu

WQXA *Under the Radar*
919 Buckingham Blvd. Elizabethtown, PA 17022
Maria maria@1057thex.com
1057thex.com
Local and regional music. Send your music in. No phone calls, please!

WRVV *Open Mic Night*
600 Corporate Cir. Harrisburg, PA 17110
PH: 717-671-9973
Michael Anthony Smith
requestsomething@yahoo.com
www.river973.com
Join us every Sunday nights for 2 hours of the best local and regional Rock n' Roll.

WXPN *Philly Local*
3025 Walnut St., Philadelphia, PA 19104
PH: 215-898-6677. FX: 215-898-0707
Helen Leicht phillylocal@xpn.org
www.xpn.org/phillylocal.php
Each weekday at 1 pm I put the spotlight on one song from an up and coming local artist. Please do not send your bios, demos etc. by e-mail!

WYBF *The Local Show*
610 King of Prussia Rd. Radnor, PA 19087
Bobby Maro localshow@wybf.com
www.wybf.com
Contact me by e-mail to get your music played.

The WYEP 10 O'clock Local News
67 Bedford Sq. Pittsburgh, PA 15203
PH: 412-381-9131 FX: 412-381-9126
Kyle Smith kyle@wyep.org
www.wyep.org
Highlighting new local CD releases and up and coming talent from the Pittsburgh and surrounding region. Check our site for formats we play. CD must be available locally in stores and not a demo recording.

WZZO *Backyard Bands*
1541 Alta Dr. #400, Whitehall, PA 18052-5632
PH: 610-720-9595 FX: 610-434-9511
Brother Joel wzzobyb@aol.com
www.wzzo.com
Eastern PA's #1 radio showcase for regional unsigned bands.

Rhode Island

WBRU *Home BRU'd*
88 Benevolent St., Providence, RI 02906-2046
PH: 401-272-9550 FX: 401-272-9278
homebrud@wbru.com
wbru.com
We play stuff hot off the local music presses, chat about gigs around the area and dish out the latest in local music news.

WHIY *Soundcheck*
75 Oxford St., Providence, RI 02905
PH: 401-224-1994 FX: 401-467-1103
Big Jim bigjim@whjy.com
www.whjy.com
Our local music show.

WRIU *Vocalists & Localists*
326 Memorial Union, Kingston, RI 02881
PH: 401-874-4949 FX: 401-874-4349
jazz@wriu.org
www.wriu.org
A showcase for the many talented Jazz artists who call New England home.

WXHQ *Digging It Up In New England*
PO Box 3541, Newport, RI 02840
PH: 401-847-1955
info@radionewport.org
www.radionewport.org
Focusing on local New England artists and recordings and featuring independent labels, live recordings and demos.

South Carolina

WUSC *Locals Only*
RHUU Rm. 343, 1400 Greene St., Columbia, SC 29208
PH: 803-777- 9872
wuscmd@gwm.sc.edu
wusc.sc.edu
Featuring the music of SC artists.

Tennessee

WDVX *Live At Laurel*
PO Box 18157, Knoxville, TN 37928
PH: 865-494-2020
Brent Cantrell cantrellb@netstarcomm.net
www.wdvx.com
Performances recorded Live directly from the historic Laurel Theater in Knoxville.

WEVL *The Memphis Beat*
PO Box 40952, Memphis, TN 38174
PH: 901-528-0560
wevl@wevl.org
www.myspace.com/memphisbeat
There are a lot of talented musicians in Memphis and we love to show them off!

WMTS *Fascination Street Radio*
Box 58, 1301 E. Main St., Murfreesboro, TN 37132
PH: 615-898-2636 FX: 615-898-5682
DJ Steve music@wmts.org
www.myspace.com/fascinationstreetradio
I interview local artists and sometimes have them play an acoustic song or two live on the air.

WRLT *Local Lightning Spotlight*
1310 Clinton St. #200, Nashville, TN 37203
lightning100@wrlt.com
www.wrlt.com/music/local-lightning.cfml
Features two different local artists each week. Send in your music and bio. Please, no phone calls!

WQOX *Juke N Jamm*
3634 Lynchburg, Memphis, TN 38135
Bob Holden bob@jukenjamm.com
www.jukenjamm.com
Playing Memphis music. Contact us if you would like to plug a gig or be interviewed.

Texas

Girls Gone Radio Show
2611 N. Beltline Rd. #111, Sunnyvale, TX 75182
PH: 469-233-9563
Chaz Chaz@HearLeftEar.com
www.myspace.com/girlsgoneradio
Gossip about the local scene. Guests include Texas Alternative Rock bands performing right after the podcast.

KACV *TexTunes*
PO Box 447, Amarillo, TX 79178
PH: 806-371-5222
kacvfm90@actx.edu
www.kacvfm.org
Sunday mornings, it's all about Texas music. Join Marcie Lane for three hours of tunes from artists who live and rock in the Lone Star State.

KBXX
24 Greenway Plaza, #900 Houston, TX 77046
latinagirl1979@yahoo.com
www.kbxx.com
#1 for Hip Hop and R&B. We meet with local artists/labels on Monday's between 1 pm-3 pm at the KBXX offices.

KCUB
471 Harbin Dr. #102, Stephenville, TX 76401
PH: 254-968-7459 FX: 254-968-6258
Pamela Hollinger pamela@texas98.com
www.texas98.com
A unique blend of Traditional Country and Texas music geared to music fans of the Lone Star State.

KFAN *Texas Six Pack / The Texas Lady's Spotlight*
PO Box 311, Fredericksburg, TX 78624
PH: 830-997-2197 FX: 830-997-2198
musicandprogramming@ctesc.net
www.texasrebelradio.com
Daily segments featuring unsigned local and regional Texas musicians.

KISS *Texas Traxx*
8930 Four Winds Dr. #500, San Antonio, TX 78239
PH: 210-646-0105 FX: 210-871-6116
Randy Bonillas randy.bonillas@coxradio.com
www.kissrocks.com
Weekly show featuring local music from the state of Texas.

KOOP *Around the Town Sounds*
PO Box 2116, Austin, TX 78768-2116
PH: 512-472-1369 FX: 512-472-6149
Charlie Martin charliemuz@aol.com
www.koop.org
Covering the many genres and ethnic shades of the contemporary local club scene.

KOOP *ATX Live*
PO Box 2116, Austin, TX 78768-2116
PH: 512-472-1369 FX: 512-472-6149
Andrew Dickens music@koop.org
www.koop.org
Local artists offer up live performances, album previews, interviews and more.

KPFT *Spare Change*
419 Lovett Blvd. Houston, TX 77006
PH: 713-526-5738 FX: 713-526-5750
lcw90@juno.com
www.kpft.org

KPLX *The Front Porch*
3500 Maple Ave. #1600, Dallas, TX 75219
PH: 214-526-2400 FX: 214-520-4343
Justin Frazell Justin@995thewolf.com
www.995thewolf.com/porch.html
Proud and honored to play TEXAS MUSIC.

KSTV *Texas Style Saturday Night*
PO Box 289, Stephenville, TX 76401
PH: 254-968-2141
Shayne Hollinger shayneholl@yahoo.com
www.kstvfm.com
Music and interviews with local artists.

KSTX *Sunday Nite Session*
8401 Datapoint Dr. #800, San Antonio,
TX 78229-5903
PH: 210-614-8977
David Furst sns@tpr.org
www.tpr.org/programs/sns.html
Features interviews, live music and recordings of contemporary musicians from San Antonio and around Texas.

KTRU *The Local Show*
PO Box 1892, Houston, TX 77251
PH: 713-348-KTRU
noise@ktru.org
www.ktru.org
Featuring the music of area artists.

KUT/KUTX *Live Set*
1 University Stn. A0704, Austin, TX 78712
PH: 512-471-2345 FX: 512-471-3700
Larry Monroe music@kut.org
www.kut.org
Some of the best darned music you'll hear anywhere on the planet!

KVRX *Local Live*
PO Box D, Austin, TX 78713-7209
PH: 512-495-5879
local_live@kvrx.org
www.kvrx.org/locallive
Handmade according to an ancient Austin recipe, using only the choicest barley, hops and spring water.

Texas Blues Cafe
PH: 206-337-0285
texasblues@podomatic.com
texasblues.podomatic.com
We promote the Blues featuring as many local and regional independent blues artists as we can.

Texas Radio 1
2611 N. Beltline Rd. # 111 Sunnyvale, TX 75182
PH: 972-203-8886
www.texasradio1.com
Features music, interviews and LIVE performances from Texas artists.

Utah

Live in the Lobby
2835E 3300ᵗʰ St. S., Salt Lake City, UT 84109
Brian Baldwin brian@liveinthelobby.com
liveinthelobby.com
Each show features local music plus an in-studio guest that is involved with Utah's music scene.

provoPODCAST.com
submit@provopodcast.com
www.provopodcast.com
Each week we pack up our gear and go hunting for the coolest local Provo artists.

Utah Out Loud
Ryan Bradshaw utahoutloud@gmail.com
www.utahoutloud.com
The premier place for local Utah music. Check site for submission details.

UTPodcasts
utpodcasts@gmail.com
www.utpodcasts.com
A collection of podcasts from Utah that pulls together 27 feeds into a single address.

Vermont

WBTZ *Buzz Homebrew*
255 S. Champlain St., Burlington, VT 05401
Attn: Homebrew Crew
mailbag@999thebuzz.com
www.999thebuzz.com
A show for local acts to prove that good music comes in all forms and genres.

WEQX *EQX-Posure!!*
PO Box 1027, Manchester, VT 05255
PH: 802-362-4800
Jason Irwin eqx@capital.net
www.weqx.com
The BEST local/regional music!

Virginia

WCFS
3540 Holland Rd. #113 PMB 103, Virginia Beach, VA 23452
PH: 757-651-5063 FX: 757-468-6988
indiebible@wcfsradio.us
www.wcfsradio.us
Non stop broadcasting of local bands.

WNOR *Homegrown*
870 Greenbrier Cir. #399, Chesapeake, VA 23320
PH: 757-366-9900 FX: 757-366-9870
Shelley shelley@fm99.com
www.fm99.com/homegrown.asp
Featuring local and regional bands, plus live interviews and performances.

WRIR *Locals Only*
PO Box 4787, Richmond, VA 23220
PH: 804-649-9737 FX: 804-622-1436
Scott Burger music@wrir.org
wrir.org
Featuring music from Virginia.

Washington

The KCDA Local Lounge
808 E. Sprague, Spokane, WA 99202
Stella Mar stellamar@clearchannel.com
www.myspace.com/kcdalocallounge
I hand the KCDA studio and the station over to a new band each week.

KCMS *Local Music Project*
19319 Fremont Ave. N., Seattle, WA 98133
PH: 206-546-7350 FX: 206-546-7372
Sarah Taylor sarah@spirit1053.com
www.spirit1053.com
Every weekday at 5:30 we feature the music of a local Puget Sound Christian artist.

KNDD *The Young & The Restless*
1100 Olive Way #1650, Seattle, WA 98101
PH: 206-622-3251
www.1077theend.com/seattlemusic.asp
Two hours of Northwest bands.

KPLU *Jazz Northwest*
1010 S. 122ⁿᵈ St., Tacoma, WA 98447-0885
PH: 253-535-7758 FX: 253-535-8332
Jim Wilke kplu@plu.edu
kplu.org/jandb/wilke.html
Focuses on the regional Jazz scene from Portland to Vancouver.

KUGS *Local Music Show*
700 Viking Union MS 9106, Bellingham, WA 98225
PH: 360-650-2936
music@kugs.org
www.kugs.org

Rainy Dawg Radio *Local Joe*
SAO 254, Box 352238, Seattle, WA 98195
PH: 206-543-7675
www.rainydawg.org
Joe Milan plays a wide variety of local music from the Northwest. From Punk, to Electronic and everything in between.

West Virginia

Bluegrass Preservation Society Radio Show
94 Beech St., Gassaway, WV 26624
Ewell Ferguson ewell@bluegrasspreservation.org
www.bluegrasspreservation.org
We only play what we record locally. You won't hear any slick, studio recordings here.

WAMX *Loud and Local*
134 4th Ave. Huntington, WV 25701
PH: 304-525-7788 x143 FX: 304-525-3299
Brandon Woolum
brandonwoolum@clearchannel.com
www.myspace.com/x1063local
The original local & regional Rock show.

WWVU *The Morgantown Sound*
PO Box 6446, Morgantown, WV 26506-6446
PH: 304-293-3329 FX: 304293-7363
Orville Weale oweale@yahoo.com
www.wvu.edu/~u92
The exclusive source of live local music in the area.

Wisconsin

MusicMadeInMadison.com
PO Box 259424, Madison, WI 53725-9424
PH: 608-835-5415
jjohnson@musicmadeinmadison.com
www.musicmadeinmadison.com
We are passionate about the Madison music scene!

WMSE *Midnight Radio*
1025 N. Broadway, Milwaukee, WI 53202
PH: 414-277-6942 FX: 414-277-7149
Hosts: Bob & Dave
www.wmse.org

WWSP *Club Wisconsin*
105 CAC Reserve St., Stevens Point, WI 54481
PH: 715-346-2696 FX: 715-346-4012
Jeff clubwi@hotmail.com
www.uwsp.edu/stuorg/wwsp
The best in Moo-town music. Local concert information and interviews of bands playing in the area.

Canada

120 Seconds *CBC*
Box 4600, Vancouver, BC V6B 4A2
PH: 877-955-6565 FX: 604-662-6594
info@120seconds.com
www.120seconds.com
A showcase for the latest in Canadian bite-sized entertainment. Videos, spoken word, music and film.

All Axis Radio
PO Box 51073, RPO Beddington, Calgary,
AB T3K 3V9
PH: 206-339-2947
AllAxisRadio@gmail.com
allaxisradio.com
100% Canadian music podcast. We feature great new Indie music, a few anecdotes and the odd interview with Canadian musicians.

Bandwidth *CBC*
PO Box 3220, Stn. C, Ottawa, ON K1Y 1E4
PH: 613-562-8570
www.cbc.ca/bandwidth
Host Amanda Putz features an eclectic mix of Canadian music.

calls to nothing
www.calls-to-nothing.com
MP3 blog and podcast promoting female Canadian artists.

Canada Noise Podcast
brendan@canadanoise.com
canadanoise.com
Music and interviews with some of your favorite Canadian bands.

CIUT *Back To The Sugar Camp*
100 Bain Ave. 19 The Lindens, Toronto,
ON M4K 1E8
PH: 416-465-9464
Steve steve@backtothesugarcamp.com
www.backtothesugarcamp.com
Weekly radio show featuring Canadiana music.

CKCU *Canadian Spaces*
Rm. 517, U. Ctr. 1125 Colonel By Dr. Ottawa,
ON K1S 5B6
PH: 613-520-2898
Chopper McKinnon chopper@nutshellmusic.com
www.ckcufm.com
Canada's most respected Folk and Roots music and interview show.

Definitely Not the Opera *CBC*
Box 160, Winnipeg, MB R3C 2H1
PH: 204-788-3182
www.cbc.ca/dnto
Host Sook-Yin Lee likes to play Canadian Indie bands on the show and is always looking for new music.

Free Canada Radio
Peter freecanadaradio@shaw.ca
www.freecanadaradio.ca
Independent Canadian music, lively current events and illuminating articles.

Indie Night in Canada *CFOX*
#2000-700 W. Georgia, Vancouver, BC V7Y 1K9
PH: 604-684-7221 FX: 604-331-2755
webmaster@cfox.com
www.cfox.com/shows/indie_night.cfm
Independent bands from Vancouver and across the country plus interviews and special live performances.

Madly Off in All Directions *CBC*
PO Box 500 Stn. A, Toronto, ON M5W 1E6
PH: 416-205-6103
Frank Opolko frank_opolko@cbc.ca
radio.cbc.ca/programs/madlyoff
Music, improvisation and satirical stand-up from all across Canada.

Roots Music Canada *CBC*
PO Box 4600, Vancouver, BC V6B 4A2
PH: 604-662-6790 FX: 604-662-6594
info@rootsmusiccanada.com
www.rootsmusiccanada.com
Features Canadian Roots and Folk music.

Sirius Satellite *Iceberg Radio*
2 St. Clair Ave. We. 2nd Fl. Toronto, ON M4V 1L6
PH: 416-323-5220
Liz Janik ljanik@sri.ca
www.sirius.ca
Offers an eclectic blend of Canadian Rock, Pop, Alternative, Folk and R&B musical styles. We devote 25% of our broadcast time to new artists.

Soul Shine Indie Radio
20 Gilroy Dr. Scarborough, ON M1P 1Z9
PH: 416-751-3884
info@soulshine.ca
www.soulshine.ca/radio
The best in Canadian Indie. If you'd like to be heard, contact us.

Sounds Like Canada *CBC*
Box 4600, Vancouver, BC V6B 4A2
PH: 604-662-6608 FX: 604-662-6025
www.cbc.ca/soundslikecanada
Our goal is to drench the airwaves with voices and sound from all over the country. Hosted by Shelagh Rogers

The Sunday Edition *CBC*
PO Box 500 Stn. A, Toronto, ON M5W 1E6
PH: 416-205-3700 FX: 416-205-6461
radio.cbc.ca/programs/thismorning/sunday.html
Here you will also find a particularly eclectic mix of music. Hosted by Michael Enright.

TheSoundRadio
#204 - 10138 81 Ave. Edmonton, AB T6H 1X1
PH: 780-702-2907
www.thesoundradio.com
A place for rising artists to host their MP3s and build a fan base.

Vinyl Café *CBC*
PO Box 500 Stn. A, Toronto, ON M5W 1E6
PH: 416-205-3700
www.cbc.ca/vinylcafe
Host Stuart McLean features music, both live and recorded.

Waxing Deep *CKUT*
235 Metcalfe Ave. #402, Westmount, QC H3Z 2H8
PH: 514-398-4616 FX: 514-398-8261
Daniel daniel.zacks@mail.mcgill.ca
www.waxingdeep.org
Specializes in Canadian and Quebecois Bossa, Jazz, Funk, Breaks, Soul, Disco, Latin and everything in between.

Alberta

CBC *Our Music*
PH: 403-521-6241
www.cbc.ca/ourmusic
Host Catherine McClelland presents the best of Alberta's many talented Classical musicians.

CFBR *Red, White & New*
#100-18520 Stony Plain Rd. Edmonton,
AB T5S 2E2
PH: 780-486-2800 FX: 780-489-6927
Park Warden park@bear.fm
www.TheBearRocks.com
The latest, greatest Canadian Rock from homegrown to our international superstars.

Key of A *CBC*
PH: 780-468-7472 FX: 780-468-7468
www.cbc.ca/keyofa
Host Katherine Duncan goes behind the scenes with performers from across Alberta.

British Columbia

CBC *Westcoast Performance*
Box 4600, Vancouver, BC V6B 4A2
PH: 604-662-6076
www.cbc.ca/wcp
Host Michael Juk presents the finest BC Classical and World music artists.

CVUE *The All Canadian Show*
PO Box 2288, Sechelt, BC V0N3A0
PH: 604-885-0800
Mike oceanviewaudioworks@hotmail.com
www.civu.net
Fabulous Canadian music from 'then' & 'now' with lots of music by local musicians & other artists from around BC.

North by Northwest *CBC*
Box 4600, Vancouver, BC V6B 4A2
PH: 604-662-6089
www.cbc.ca/nxnw
Host Sheryl MacKay presents creative people and what they create.

On the Island *CBC*
1025 Pandora Ave. Victoria, BC V8V 3P6
PH: 250-360-2227 FX: 250-360-2600
www.cbc.ca/ontheisland
Host Paul Vasey presents a lively blend of news, reviews and interviews.

Radio Bandcouver
#110, 360 Columbia St., Vancouver, BC V6A 4J1
Mark Bignell mark@bandcouver.com
www.bandcouver.com
Artists & bands send your CDs and press kits in.

Suburban Transpondency
PH: 206-203-4250
suburban@transpondency.com
transpondency.com
Podcast with an earful of suburban culture and Indie music from BC and beyond.

The Zone's Band of the Month
The Zone, Top Fl. 2750 Quadra St., Victoria,
BC V8T 4E8
PH: 250-475-6611
James Sutton james@TheZone.fm
www.thezone.fm
Our featured band will be highlighted in a mini audio bio that will air between five and seven times each day.

Manitoba

CKIC *HomeSpun*
W-106, 160 Princess St., Winnipeg, MB R3B 1K9
benny@kick.fm
www.kick.fm
Featuring music made in Manitoba.

CKUW *Beer For Breakfast*
1 Neptune Bay, Winnipeg, MB R3T 0Z6
PH: 204-774-6877
Broose & Gavin beerradio959@gmail.com
beerradio959.blogspot.com
I only play local or visiting artists. We always have time for live interviews.

Weekend Morning Show *CBC*
PH: 204-788-3612 FX: 204-788-3674
www.cbc.ca/weekendmorning
Host Ron Robinson presents eclectic music, comedy and special features.

New Brunswick

Shift *CBC*
PO Box 2358, Saint John, NB E2L 3V6
PH: 506-632-7743 FX: 506-632-7761
www.cbc.ca/shift
Host Paul Castle connects people in NB with the events of the day and with each other.

Newfoundland

CHMR *Upon this Rock*
Box A-119 St. John's, NL A1C 5S7
PH: 709-737-4777 FX: 709-737-7688
Kevin Kelly thekmaster@yahoo.com
www.mun.ca/chmr
Two hours of the best in Newfoundland and Labrador music. From Traditional to Alternative.

MUSICRAFT *CBC*
PO Box 12010, Stn. A, St. John's, NL A1B 3T8
www.cbc.ca/musicraft
Host Francesca Swann presents musical events from across the province and discussions with the people who bring the music to life.

On the Go *CBC*
PO Box 12010, Stn. A, St. John's, NL A1B 3T8
PH: 709-576-5270
www.cbc.ca/onthego
Host Ted Blades presents a lively package of news, interviews and the best in local music.

The Performance Hour *CBC*
PO Box 12010, Stn. A, St. John's, NL A1B 3T8
www.cbc.ca/performancehour
Newfoundland's finest Singers and Songwriters recorded live at the LSPU Hall in St. Johns.

Republic of Avalon Radio
PO Box 5851, St. John's, NF A1C 5X3
Jim Fidler republicofavalonradio@gmail.com
www.republicofavalonradio.com
Newfoundland's first podcast. A bit of everything from the heart of Avalon.

Nova Scotia

All The Best *CBC*
PO Box 30000, Halifax, NS B3J 3E9
PH: 902-420-4426 FX: 902-420-4089
www.cbc.ca/allthebest
Host Shauntay Grant presents music ranging from Classical through classic Jazz to traditional.

Atlantic Airwaves *CBC*
PO Box 3000, Halifax, NS B3J 3E9
PH: 902-420-4426 FX: 902-420-4089
www.cbc.ca/atlanticairwaves
Host Stan Carew presents profiles of music makers from Canada's four Atlantic Provinces as well as national and international artists appearing throughout the region.

CIGO *East Coast Rising*
11 MacIntosh Ave. Port Hawkesbury, NS B9A 3K4
PH: 902-625-1220 FX: 902-625-2664
1015thehawk@1015thehawk.com
www.1015thehawk.com/ecr.asp
Tune in to get updates on the East Coast music scene!!

CIGO *Highland Fling*
11 MacIntosh Ave. Port Hawkesbury, NS B9A 3K4
PH: 902-625-1220 FX: 902-625-2664
1015thehawk@1015thehawk.com
www.1015thehawk.com/highland.asp
Committing to focus on Cape Breton fiddle, piano, Gaelic song and bagpipes.

CKDU *The One Inch Punch*
Dalhousie Stud. Union Bldg. 6136 U. Ave. Halifax,
NS B3H 4J2
PH: 902-494-6479
Derrick & Louie music@ckdu.ca
www.ckdu.ca
Punk focusing on the local scene.

CKDU *Saturday Morning Musical Box*
Dalhousie Stud. Union Bldg. 6136 U. Ave. Halifax,
NS B3H 4J2
PH: 902-494-6479
Walter Kemp music@ckdu.ca
www.ckdu.ca
Classical music. Interviews with local performers.

Connections *CBC*
PO Box 30000, Halifax, NS B3J 3E9
PH: 902-420-4248 FX: 902-420-4089
www.cbc.ca/connections
Host Olga Milosevich presents an uplifting mixture of music - largely Maritime and ranging from Classical to Folk, Jazz, Pop and World Beat.

MainStreet Halifax *CBC*
PO Box 3000, Halifax, NS B3J 3E9
PH: 902-420-4378 FX: 902-420-4357
www.cbc.ca/mainstreetns
Host Carmen Klassen brings you the latest on the news of the day ...and of course, some great music.

WEEKENDER
PO Box 3000, Halifax, NS B3J 3E9
PH: 902-420-4378 FX: 902-420-4357
www.radio.cbc.ca/programs/weekender
Host Peter Togni features music that's engaging, fun and played by the best in the business.

Ontario

All in a Day *CBC*
PO Box 3220, Stn. C, Ottawa, ON K1Y 1E4
PH: 613-562-8442 FX: 613-562-8810
www.cbc.ca/allinaday
In any given program, you're likely to hear Rock, Jazz, Pop, World Beat, Classical or Blues. Hosted by Adrian Harewood

CFFF *Smooth Operator*
715 George St. N., Peterborough, ON K9H 3T2
PH: 705-748-4761
trentradio@trentu.ca
www.trentu.ca/trentradio
Listen to local music along with interviews with interesting people from the Peterborough area.

CHUO *L'Express Country*
65 University Pvt. #0038, Ottawa, ON K1N 9A5
PH: 613-562-5967 FX: 613-562-5969
Robert Guindon webmestre@transcontinental.ca
groups.msn.com/RobertGuindonAnimateur
Musique Country francophone d'artistes connus dans la région.

CJLX *The Spin on Quinte*
PO Box 4200, Belleville, ON K8N 5B9
PH: 613-966-2559 FX: 613-966-1993
91x@loyalistmail.ca
www.cjlx.fm
Each week we spin some of the best music Quinte has to offer.

CKCU *Ottawa Live Music*
Rm. 517 U. Ctr. 1125 Colonel By Dr. Ottawa,
ON K1S 5B6
PH: 613-520-2898
Charles Anthony music@ckcufm.com
www.ottawalivemusic.com
Artists perform live on the air in the CKCU studios. Listeners call in with questions.

Fresh Air *CBC*
PO Box 500, Stn. A, Toronto, ON M5W 1E6
PH: 416-205-3700
www.cbc.ca/freshair
Host Jeff Goodes presents a variety of music and stories. It's like sitting around the kitchen table with old friends.

Ottawa Morning
PO Box 3220, Stn. C, Ottawa, ON K1Y 1E4
PH: 613-562-8442 FX: 613-562-8810
www.cbc.ca/ottawamorning
Matthew Crosier is your ear on entertainment and the local music scene.

Sunday night Soul *AM1430*
Johnny Max johnnymaxband@rogers.com
www.sundaynightsoul.com
I love promoting the amazing talent pool that the Toronto region has. Canadian Blues, Soul, Roots, whatever, I play the music that we love.

Toronto Independent Music Podcast
musicface.com/tim
If you are in a Toronto area band and would like to have a song considered for the show, please fill out our online form.

Toronto Indie Scene
301 Dupont St., Toronto, ON M5R 1W1
PH: 416-239-8737
Joe Chisolm info@indiecan.com
www.indiecan.com
Includes live music, recorded music and interviews from bands and industry insiders.

Prince Edward Island

Island Music Radio
PO Box 2000, Charlottetown, PE C1A 7N8
PH: 902-368-6176 FX: 902-368-4418
peiarts@peiartscouncil.com
www.gov.pe.ca/radio
Please fill out our online form and send it in with your CD.

Quebec

A Propos *CBC*
Box 6000, Montreal, QC H3C 3A8
PH: 514-597-6000 FX: 514-597-4423
www.cbc.ca/apropos
Host Jim Corcoran features the most popular tunes coming out of Quebec.

Saskatchewan

Morning Edition *CBC*
2440 Broad St., Regina, SK S4P 4A1
PH: 800-661-7540 FX: 306-347-9797
www.cbc.ca/morningedition
Host Sheila Coles features music and a good sprinkling of humour.

Europe

United Kingdom

BBC Radio Scotland
Rm. 206, Music Dept. Queen Margaret Dr. Glasgow,
Scotland, G12 8DG
enquiries.scot@bbc.co.uk
www.bbc.co.uk/scotland/music

Fuse FM *Homegrown Beats*
Students Union, Oxford Rd. Manchester,
M13 9PR UK
music@fusefm.co.uk
www.fusefm.co.uk
The best in UK Hip Hop.

LCR *Gigged*
Loughborough U., Union Bldg. Ashby Rd.
Loughborough, LE11 3TT UK
studio@lcr1350.co.uk
www.lcr1350.co.uk
Great music from bands in the East Midlands.

Phoenix FM *Phoenix Unplugged*
Unit 333 The Blanchardstown Centre,
Blanchardstown, Dublin 15 Ireland
PH: 822-72-22
phoenixfm@iolfree.ie
www.iolfree.ie/~phoenixfm
We're interested in hearing from new bands particularly from the Dublin 15 area.

The Problem With Scene Points
podcast@theproblemwithscenepoints.com
www.theproblemwithscenepoints.com
Featuring Punk, Emo, Metal and Hardcore bands from The UK.

Radio Free MK
PO Box 3595, Newport, Pagnell, Bucks,
MK16 0BF UK
live@radiofreemk.co.uk
www.radiofreemk.co.uk
Our aim is to provide a station for music from Milton Keynes and its so-called 'catchment area'.

Rock3.co.uk
4 Sturdee, Frimley, Surrey GU16 8DL UK
info@rock3.co.uk
www.rock3.co.uk
We review and play new and unsigned bands from the British Isles.

The tartanpodcast
tartanpodcast@gmail.com
www.tartanpodcast.com
Podcast playing Scottish artists. E-mail us 2 or 3 MP3 files and a paragraph about your band.

Vic's Demo Derby *BBC*
Radio 1 Scotland, Queen Margaret Dr. Glasgow,
Scotland G12 8DG
Vic Galloway vic@bbc.co.uk
www.bbc.co.uk/radio1/vicgalloway/demoderby.shtml
Every week, two Scottish bands square up to one another.

XFM Scotland *X-Posure*
Four Winds Pavilion 1a Pacific Quay Glasgow,
G51 1EB UK
Jim Gellatly jim@xfm.co.uk
www.myspace.com/xposurescotland
Scotland's leading showcase for new bands.

Australia

2RRR *Sydney Sounds*
PO Box 644 Gladesville, NSW 1675 Australia
PH: 61-29816-2988 FX: 61-2-9817-1048
www.2rrr.org.au
Interviews and music by Garage/Surf/Punk & Power Pop bands from around Sydney.

2SER *Electro-plastique*
U. Tech. Sydney, Level 26, Building 1, 1 Broadway,
Ultimo, NSW 2007 Australia
PH: 61-2-9514-9514 FX: 61-2-9514-9599
info@2ser.com
www.clananalogue.org
A policy of playing 100% Australian Electronic music.

2VOX *Australian Independent Music Show*
PO Box 1663, Wollongong, NSW 2500 Australia
PH: 02-4227-3436 FX: 02-4226-5922
Ben Hession vox@1earth.net
www.vox.1earth.net
Promoting local artists.

3CR *Local and Live*
PO Box 1277, Collingwood, Melbourne,
VIC 3065 Australia
PH: 03-9419-8377 FX: 03-9417-4472
programming@3cr.org.au
www.3cr.org.au
Featuring music and interviews with local musicians, live-to-air performances and gig guides.

3D *Local and Live*
48 Nelson St., Stepney, SA 5069 Australia
PH: 08-8363-3937 FX: 08-8362-6937
www.threedradio.com
All the best local music!

3RRR *Local and or General*
PO Box 2145, Brunswick East, VIC 3057 Australia
Ryan Egan localgeneral@hotmail.com
www.myspace.com/packingdeath
Live-to-air performances and interviews.

5PBA *Max Radio*
PO Box 433 Salisbury, SA 5108 Australia
PH: 61-8-8250-3735 FX: 61-8-8281-7495
www.pbafm.org.au/max
Live bands, interviews, feature albums, laughter and more.

5UV *Adelaide Concert Hour*
228 N. Terrace, Adelaide, SA 5000 Australia
PH: 61-8-8303-5000 FX: 61-8-8303-4374
Alastair Mackintosh radio@adelaide.edu.au
radio.adelaide.edu.au
Local Classical music performances recorded live.

5UV *Local Noise*
228 N. Terrace, Adelaide, SA 5000 Australia
PH: 61-8-8303-5000 FX: 61-8-8303-4374
Andrew Turner andrew.j.turner@adelaide.edu.au
radio.adelaide.edu.au
Local bands live to air from Studio 1.

92.9 *Australian First*
PO Box, Fox FM, St. Kilda, 3182 VIC Australia
www.929.com.au
Send your demo CD/tape for consideration on our "Thrown in the Deep End" segment.

ABC Backyard *Local Radio Music*
Bill Riner riner.bill@abc.net.au
www.abc.net.au/backyard/rinermusic.htm

Aussie Bar-B-Que *4ZZZ*
PO Box 509, Fortitude Valley, QLD 4006 Australia
PH: 07-3252-1555 FX: 07-3252-1950
Tracey traceyn@4zzzfm.org.au
www.myspace.com/aussiebarbque4zzz1021fm
100% Australian artists and bands.

Bay FM *Australian Music*
PO Box 1003 Cleveland, QLD 4163 Australia
PH: 07-3821-0022 FX: 07-3286-9166
bayfm@bayfm.org.au
www.bayfm.org.au

City Park Radio *OZ Muster*
PO Box 1501, Launceston, TAS 7250 Australia
PH: 03-6334-7429 FX: 03-6334-3344
country@cityparkradio.com
www.cityparkradio.com
All Australian Country music.

Heartland FM
PO Box 277, Ashmore, QLD 4214 Australia
PH: 07-5597-0282 FX: 07-5597-0282
admin@heartlandfm.com
www.heartlandfm.com
Independent Australian artists are a daily feature.

Music Deli *ABC*
PH: 03-9626-1623 FX: 03-9626-1621
Paul Petran musicdeli@your.abc.net.au
www.abc.net.au/rn/musicdeli
Folk, Traditional and Acoustic music and what is commonly known as World music. There's a strong emphasis on Australian performances.

PBS FM *No Frills*
PO Box 2917, Fitzroy MDC, VIC 3065 Australia
PH: 61-3-8415-1067 FX: 61-3-8415-1831
Claire Stuchbery claire@pbsfm.org.au
www.pbsfm.org.au
Showcasing the hard working, often under represented sector of the Australian music industry.

RTR FM *Homegrown*
PO Box 842, Mt. Lawley, WA 6929 Australia
PH: +61-8-9260-9210 FX: +61 8 9260 9222
rtrfm@rtrfm.com.au
www.rtrfm.com.au
Local music scene news, reviews and interviews

Triple H *HOME BREW*
4, Florence Gardens, 48-50 Florence St., Hornsby,
NSW 2077 Australia
www.homebrewradio.com.au
Host Phil Bromley plays 100% Australian music

Triple J *Home and Hosed*
GPO Box 9994 Canberra, NSW Australia
www.abc.net.au/triplej/homeandhosed
Australian music from all over. Music, interviews, chat, news live sounds and much more.

SECTION FOUR: SERVICES THAT WILL HELP YOU TO SELL YOUR MUSIC

"You must believe in yourself. Realize that you don't need a label to be a success. Don't be egotistical, but be confident. Be optimistic – believe you are good enough and can get what you want. If you don't have faith in yourself – no one else will."
– Bernard Baur, Music Connection Magazine

Promotional Services

United States

+1 Management & Public Relations
242 Wythe Ave. Studio 6, Brooklyn, NY 11211
PH: 718-599-3740 FX: 718-599-0998
Ashley Purdum ashley@plusonemusic.net
www.plusonemusic.net
If you have a demo you think we might like, send it with a bio and any press clips to our address.

2 Generations SPA Music Management
300 E. 34th St. #28B, New York, NY 10016
PH: 212-842-8478
Aimee aimee@2generations.com
www.2generations.com
Consulting company representing unsigned bands/artists.

Allure Artist Management
102C W. Germantown Pk. #302, Norristown, PA 19401
www.allureinc.com
Works with, counsels and advises artists to promote and advance their music careers.

The Almighty Institute of Music Retail
11724 Ventura Blvd. Ste. B, Studio City, CA 91604
PH: 323-851-2430 FX: 815-642 0806
Clark Benson clark@almightyretail.com
www.almightyretail.com
Services record labels and youth culture companies looking to promote their product in record stores and other outlets that sell prerecorded music.

AlphaMusicGroup
1133 Broadway #706, New York, NY 10010
PH: 212-696-7934
info@alphamusicgroup.com
www.alphamusicgroup.com
A selective independent A & R company that strives to be the most reliable source for unsigned artists/bands looking for help in getting a record deal.

American Voices
404 CordellSt., Houston, TX 77009
PH/FX: 713-862-7125
John Ferguson john.ferguson@americanvoices.org
www.americanvoices.org
Furthering the appreciation and understanding of American music, especially in developing countries.

AMP3
PH: 646-827-9594
info@artist-media.com
Artist-Media.com
A boutique PR firm specializing in arts & entertainment publicity for lifestyle brands.

ANDARO Entertainment & Media Corp.
1000 S. Mitchell Ste. D, Warrensburg, MO 64093
PH: 877-826-3276 FX: 877-826-3276 x006
Deacon deacon@andarorecords.com
www.andarorecords.com
A talent management, promotion and development group with over 30 years major(s) experience. Home to ANDARO Records.

Ariel Publicity Artist Relations and Cyber Promotions
325 W. 38th St. #505, New York, NY 10018
PH: 212-239-8384 FX: 212-239-8380
Ariel Hyatt ariel@arielpublicity.com
www.arielpublicity.com
Professional promotional services for Indie artists.

Arrow/ATM Distributing Company
1373 Grandview Ave. #212, Columbus, OH 43212
PH: 800-552-3472 FX: 877-249-6787
Matt E. Earley mee@arrdis.com
www.arrdis.com
National distribution of college music to retailers, bookstores & mass merchants. Specializing in East Coast and Midwest distribution.

Art Attack Promotions
2414 Elmglen Dr. Austin, TX 78744
PH: 512-445-7117 FX: 512-447-2493
Gigi Greco info@artattackpromotions.com
www.artattackpromotions.com
Full service entertainment marketing company specializing in grassroots marketing, online promotions, lifestyle campaigns and street team development.

Baker/Northrop Media Group
501-I S. Reino Rd. #380, Thousand Oaks, CA 91320
PH: 805-498-5880
FX: 805-498-5246
Sheryl Northrop sheryl@bakernorthrop.com
bakernorthrop.com
Providing creative, thoughtful press campaigns for a diverse client roster ranging from high-profile artists to independent musicians.

bandpromote.com
PO Box 4102, Hollywood, CA 90078
PH: 323-276-1000
FX: 323-276-1001
Mike Galaxy mgalaxy@bandpromote.com
www.bandpromote.com
Distribute your music to thousands of record execs.

Believe In Magic
1834 Cole Rd. Biscoe, NC 27209
FX: 440-860-3732
Amy Priest amy@believeinmagic.net
www.believeinmagic.net
Specializing in press kits, online promotion, CD art, posters and identity packages.

Bill Wence Promotions
PO Box 39, Nolensville, TN 37135
PH: 615-776-2060 FX: 615-776-2181
Bill Wence info@billwencepromotions.com
www.billwencepromotions.com
Hundreds of singles and albums have been charted for our clients.

Black & Blue Star
1410 Wellesley Ave. #106, Los Angeles, CA 90025
PH: 310-924-5651 FX: 253-830-0840
Mindi Sue Meyer mindi@blackandbluestar.com
www.blackandbluestar.com
Independent record label giving talented artists an avenue to have their voices and masterpieces heard.

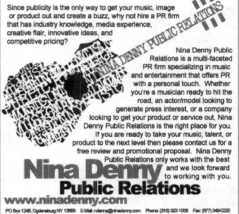

Jerome Promotions & Marketing

Always looking for new talent

Radio Promotion is our specialty

Office: 770.982.7055
Fax: 770.982.1882

2535 Winthrope Way
Lawrenceville, GA 30044
email: hitcd@bellsouth.net

www.jeromepromotions.com

Blackcat Entertainment/ Publishing
PO Box 26174, El Paso, TX 79926
David O. Samaniego info@blackcattalent.com
www.blackcattalent.com
BC Talent is a management company, BC Music Pub. handles publishing, licensing and representation and BC Music Group is an Indie label.

Broken Record Productions
PO Box 969, Katy, TX 77492
PH: 832-457-7790
Devon Mikeska
devon@brokenrecordproductions.com
www.brokenrecordproductions.com
We are an artist development company helping bands with radio, booking, PR and management.

BTM Communications
1325 Corcoran St. NW., Washington, DC 20009
PH: 202-483-1105
Mary Sue Twohy marysue@buildthemountain.com
www.buildthemountain.com
We offer publicity services for the touring artist including press and radio advance work, press release writing and launch and ensuring posters and photos are sent to venues in a timely fashion to further your career.

Canary Promotion + Design
PO Box 4377, Philadelphia, PA 19118-8377
PH: 215-242-6393
Megan Wendell megan@canarypromo.com
www.canarypromo.com
Publicity and graphic design services for web and print.

CD Register
PO Box 182492, Shelby Twp., MI 48318
PH: 586-480-3000
Terrance info@cdregister.com
cdregister.com
Do you currently have a CD available? Get your music in the hands of DJs, magazine writers, film & TV producers and A&R staff from around the world.

conqueroo
13351-D Riverside Dr. #655, Sherman Oaks, CA 91423-2450
PH: 818-501-2001
Cary Baker
cary@conqueroo.com
conqueroo.com
A music industry publicity firm started up in 2004 by an ex label executive.

Crash Avenue
120 Webster St. #215, Louisville, KY 40206
PH: 502-640-2251
Jeffrey Smith jeffrey@crash-avenue.com
www.crash-avenue.com
An Indie publicity and radio promotion company.

Deluxxe Media & Management
PH: 503-236-0796
Barbara Mitchell cocktailhr@gmail.com
Publicity and management firm. Also handles national and tour press.

Dream Relations: Divine Relationships in Entertainment & Media
PH: 347-715-4921
Daw Michelle dreamrelations@yahoo.com
I am a publicist and marketing consultant.

Drophit.com
3205 Brookline Dr. Wilmington, DE 19808
www.drophit.com
Artist Booking - Publicity - Radio - Public Relations. Guaranteed the lowest prices in the industry!

Fanatic Promotion
135 W. 29th St. #1101, New York, NY 10001
PH: 212-616-5556
Josh Bloom josh@fanaticpromotion.com
www.fanaticpromotion.com
Our goal is to turn on the world to talented new artists.

Foley Entertainment
PO Box 358, Greendell, NJ 07839
PH: 908-684-9400
Eugene Foley EugeneFoleyMusic@aol.com
FoleyEntertainment.com
Providing a wide range of music industry disciplines, including artist development, marketing, promotion, advertising, songwriting, composing, arranging, intellectual property, publishing, touring, distribution, producing and merchandising.

Fusent Entertainment
130 Church St. #166, New York, NY 10007
PH: 212-812-5432 FX: 212-812-5432
Don DeSalvo fusent@fusententertainment.com
www.fusententertainment.com
Artist management, development, promotions and creative concepts.

The Gate Media Group
1270 Springbrook Rd. Ste. H, Walnut Creek, CA 94597-3995
PH: 925-256-1770 FX: 925-256-1774
sales@gatemedia.com
www.gatemedia.com
Develops successful Indie music promotional campaigns.

Green Galactic
1680 N. Vine St. #211, Los Angeles, CA 90028
PH: 323-466-5141 FX: 866-703-5344
Lynn Hasty lynn@greengalactic.com
www.greengalactic.com
A marketing and production media company specializing in youth culture.

Head First Entertainment
1146 N. Mesa Dr. #102-103, Mesa, AZ 85201
PH: 480-827-8686 FX: 480-733-7870
Dave Tedder dave@headfirstentertainment.com
www.headfirstentertainment.com
An independent management, marketing and publicity firm.

Head to the Ground Entertainment
29 Chestnut Dr. Newnan, GA 30263
PH: 770-377-9843 FX: 770-599-3622
Shannon Scott sdselt@yahoo.com
www.htgentertainment.com
Booking and promotions agency. Also offers photography and video recording for musicians looking to take it to the next level.

The Hennessy Group
4236 Franklin Ave. Hollywood, CA 90027
PH: 323-371-2895 FX: 323-953-8592
Tom tom@thehennessygroup.net
www.thehennessygroup.net
Talent management for bands and solo artists. Management and promotions tailored to your needs.

Holiday Matinee
920 E. St. #301, San Diego, CA 92101
www.holidaymatinee.com
Campaigns that produce increased exposure, profitability and brand awareness.

Impact Entertainment
1640 W. Oak Knoll Cir. Fort Lauderdale, FL 33324
PH: 954-370-7000 FX: 954-370-7005
Rob Cohen impactent@aol.com
www.impactentertainmentgrp.com
Full service artist management for unsigned artists.

In House Booking
PH: 650-585-2239
info@inhousebooking.com
www.InHouseBooking.com
A new approach to booking and securing performances. We make the calls, you play the halls!

The Indie Edge
8130 La Mesa Blvd. #142, La Mesa, CA 91941
PH/FX: 619-567-5146
www.theindieedge.com
Artist management, guerrilla marketing and PR for the Indie artist.

indie911.com
8949 Sunset Blvd. #201, West Hollywood,
CA 90069
PH: 310-943-7164 FX: 310-919-3091
Justin Goldberg justin@indie911.com
www.indie911.com
*Label and management company. Helps Indie
musicians and labels sustain their livelihoods and
increase their revenues by managing their most
valuable asset, their own music.*

The Industry Resource
101 W. 23rd St. #2152, New York, NY 10011
PH: 800-878-6113 FX: 800-878-6114
www.theindustryresource.com
*Home to today's top industry professionals from
management companies, booking agents, labels and
publishing firms. These executives are actively
seeking new and exciting talent.*

IRL Music Group
31441 Santa Margarita Pkwy. #A366,
Rancho Santa Margarita, CA 92688
PH: 949-766-7979
Johnny Mendola jmendola@earthlink.net
www.johnnyrock.com/join
*Get exposed to over 3,500 labels worldwide! Free
online service. Join now!*

Kari Estrin Artist Career Consulting
PO Box 60232, Nashville, TN 37206
PH: 615-262-0883
kari@kariestrin.com
www.kariestrin.com
Consulting, artist services and special projects.

Kari-On Productions
PO Box 436, Evans, GA 30809
PH: 706-294-9996 FX: 706-210-9453
Kari Gaffney karionprod@knology.net
www.karigaffney.com/publicity.html
*Solicits all major magazines, network television
morning/weekend news programming, online
publications & critics for reviews, interviews and
appearances. Creates online image awareness.*

Last Call Agency
26 Church St. #300, Cambridge, MA 02138
PH: 781-922-1238
Susan Scotti susan@lastcallagency.com
www.lastcallagency.com
Offers booking, publicity and promotional services.

Luck Media & Marketing
8900 Olympic Blvd. Beverly Hills, CA 90211
PH: 310-860-9170
Steve Levesque steve@luckmedia.com
luckmedia.com
*Our staff has a well-deserved and well-earned
reputation as one of the most creative, productive
and successful PR organizations.*

Massive Music America
1227 Perry St., Denver, CO 80204
PH: 877-571-4521
questions@massivemusicamerica.com
www.massivemusicamerica.com
*Independent promotions company that offers radio,
media/print, internet and tour support.*

Mazur Public Relations
PO Box 2425, Trenton, NJ 08607-2425
PH: 609-890-4550 FX: 609-890-4556
Michael Mazur michael@mazurpr.com
www.mazurpr.com
Full service PR company that represents all genres.

MC-Input.com
499 N. Canon Dr. 4th Fl. Beverly Hills, CA 90210
PH: 310-926-7232
Gingio Muehlbauer info.us@mc-input.com
www.mc-input.com
*Helps artists recognize their potential and assists
them by giving useful tips and connections to
succeed in the industry.*

Mi2N PR Syndicate
www.mi2n.com/prsyndicate
*We'll syndicate your press release across the web,
getting your announcement in front of industry and
friends.*

Milestone Agency
PH: 972-977-8663 FX: 877-822-0643
D. Dumais ddumais@milestoneagency.com
www.milestoneagency.com
*National booking/college agency. Committed to
providing each client with opportunities to enter
new markets for optimal success. Please contact us
for our mailing address.*

M-Squared Productions
PO Box 1331, Oklahoma City, OK 73101
PH: 405-601-1479
Mark Maxey m-squared@m-squared.org
m-squared.org
*Graphic designs, photography, public relations and
marketing. Over 20 years experience in the arts
industry.*

MusicSUBMIT
650 Pennsylvania #25, Miami Beach, FL 33139
PH: 888-476-8745 FX: 303-444-9122
support@musicsubmit.com
www.MusicSUBMIT.com
*Promotes your music to the decision makers at
internet radio stations, music blogs, online music
magazines and more, AND we give you a full report
of everything we do for you!*

New Game Media
332 N. La Brea Ave. Los Angeles, CA 90036
PH: 949-650-6229
Ken Tamplin Ken@NewGameMedia.Com
www.NewGameMedia.com
*A strategic entertainment marketing investment
company focussing on talent with pre-exiting fan
bases and taking them to the next level. We look for
exceptional Indie artists that we can help with
corporate endorsements, TV, film etc.*

Nina Denny Public Relations
PO Box 1248, Ogdensburg, NY 13669
PH: 315-323-1058 FX: 877-349-0225
www.ninadenny.com
*PR with a personal touch, affordable rates and
music expertise.*

Notch Music Group
1570 C. Malcolm Ct. Fairborn, OH 45324
PH: 314-369-4867
Ronnie Notch producer.notch@gmail.com
www.notchmusicgroup.com
*We offer high quality production and management to
artists that are working hard to establish a
recording contract.*

Omni Entertainment/Caprice Records
5919 Greenville Ave. #361, Dallas, TX 75206
PH: 214-452-3726 FX: 214-452-3726
Don Brooks info@omnicaprice.com
www.omnicaprice.com
*A full service management, booking, marketing and
promotions company.*

On Target Media Group
6464 W. Sunset Blvd. #829, Hollywood, CA 90028
PH: 323-461-4230 FX: 323-461-4229
www.ontargetmediagroup.com
*Internet marketing, publicity and promotion, music
video and EPK editing as well as DVD authoring.*

On That Note Entertainment
141 New Rd. #1J, Parsippany, NJ 07054
PH: 973-486-0867 FX: 973-486-0875
Dan Balassone dan@onthatnote.net
www.onthatnote.net
*A full service booking agency working with national
and regional acts of all types and genres.*

Paperwork Media
2248 W. Belmont Ave. #3700, Chicago, IL 60618
Jill jill@paperworkmedia.com
www.paperworkmedia.com
*A one-stop music boutique that represents bands &
artists. We remove the hassles of everyday business-
related paperwork and allow clients to focus solely
on their music.*

Posse Up Entertainment
24451 Lake Shore Blvd. #1601, Cleveland,
OH 44123
PH: 216-373-2398 FX: 440-269-8344
Jessica Hollenbach jessica@posseupent.com
www.PosseUpEntertainment.com
*We are full service Management and publicity firm
specializing in press kit design, radio promotion and
more. We will get the "Buzz" going for up and
coming talent and established artists.*

The PR Muse
31 Mariners Ln. #2, Stamford, CT 06902
PH: 512-417-0254
Alison alison@theprmuse.com
www.theprmuse.com
*I specialize in publicity for Indie musicians looking
to move their music forward.*

PR That Rocks
Christopher Buttner rockme@prthatrocks.com
prthatrocks.com
*Public relations and marketing services for
musicians.*

The Press House
302 Bedford Ave. #13, Brooklyn, NY 11211
PH: 718-302-1522 FX: 718-302-1522
Dawn Kamerling dawn@thepresshouse.com
www.thepresshouse.com
*Full service media relations company specializing in
music of all genres.*

Prototype Entertainment
24-21 27th St. #2-B, Astoria, NY 11102
PH: 973-715-1101
Don Di Napoli don@prototypeentertainment.com
www.prototypeentertainment.com
*Full service artist development company that
handles all aspects from production to publicity.*

Rainmaker Talent Group
8127 Mesa Dr. PO Box 206-74, Austin, TX 78759
PH: 512-485-3170 FX: 512-485-3171
info@rainmaker-talent.com
www.rainmaker-talent.com
*Provides management, booking, promotional and
financial support.*

Randolphe Entertainment Group
738 Main St. #454, Waltham, MA 02451
PH: 781-983-4120
Serge Randolphe, Jr. serge@randolphe.com
www.randolphe.com
We work harder to connect artists to their fans!
College radio promotion, tour promotion,
distribution and more.

Raspberry Art Music Group
341 Barclay Ave. Pittsburgh, PA 15221
PH: 412-913-0876
Ron raspberryart@gmail.com
myspace.com/raspberryartmusicgroup
Promotion group that can get your music in the
hands of many press, radio and other promotional
outlets.

Serge Entertainment Public Relations
PO Box 2760, Acworth, GA 30102
PH: 678-445-0006 FX: 678-494-9269
Sandy Serge SergeEnt@aol.com
www.serge.org/pr
The honest PR people. No spin, no speculation; only
the raw facts and the naked truth.

Sevier Productions
3110 West End Cir. #4, Nashville, TN 37203
PH: 615-500-4411
Chris Sevier chris.sevier@vanderbilt.edu
www.sevierproductions.com
Artist development and A&R outsourcing. We help
deserving artists make a record and build their team
for success.

Smash Publicity
683 S. Main St., Corona, CA 92882
PH: 951-737-3938
Michele Weber smashpublicity@sbcglobal.net
www.smashpublicity.com
A full service public relations firm for bands. We
also offer website design services at reasonable
prices.

Space 380
2008 Swindon Ave. Columbia, MO 65203-8985
PH: 573-446-7221 FX: 309-210-9037
www.space380.com
Creates name recognition for independent artists of
all genres.

Spygirl Productions
PO Box 583, Wilmington, NC 28402
PH: 910-431-4040 FX: 866-729-8212
Tracy Wilkinson thespygirl@spygirlproductions.biz
www.spygirlproductions.biz
Promotions, contract negotiations & drafting,
booking agent, publicity and marketing.

Stretch the Skies
770 Emerson St., Rochester, NY 14613
PH: 877-241-2613
info@stretchtheskies.com
www.stretchtheskies.com
Provides an all-encompassing system for artists to
rise through the levels of a career in the music
business.

Talent 2K
13618 N. 99th Ave. Sun City, AZ 85351
PH: 800-499-6395 FX: 623-875-5827
Dana contest@talent2k.com
www.talent2k.com
Independent A&R firm. We shop demos out to
different labels looking for recording contracts.

Team Clermont Promotion
191 E. Broad St. #310, Athens, GA 30601
PH: 706-548-6008 FX: 706-548-0094
prpeople@teamclermont.com
www.teamclermont.com
We get maximum exposure for the records we
promote.

Tinderbox Music
3148 Bryant Ave. S., Minneapolis, MN 55408
PH: 612-375-1113 FX: 612-341-3330
Krista Vilinskis krista@tinderboxmusic.com
www.tinderboxmusic.com
Music promotion and distribution company.

Thompson Entertainment Group
1300 Division St. #105, Nashville, TN 37203
PH: 615-742-8004 FX: 615-742-8014
info@thompsonentertainmentgroup.com
www.thompsonentertainmentgroup.com
Artist development, media/marketing and
management firm.

True Music And Songs
7 Wild Flower Dr. Kings Park, NY 11754
PH: 631-896-9800
David Whittaker
davidwhittaker@truemusicandsongs.com
www.truemusicandsongs.com
Helps artists get their music to the right people in
the music industry.

TwoShepsThatPass
476 Broome St. #5A, New York, NY 10013
PH: 646-613-1101 FX: 786-513-0692
Vera Sheps twoshepsthatpass@aol.com
www.twoshepsthatpass.com
Gives you a presence on and off the net.

Vigilant Promotions
PO Box 572, Princeton, MN 55371
Attn: Submissions
info@vigilantpromotions.com
www.vigilantpromotions.com
Using everything from street teams to radio
promotion, press to the web.

Wiselephant
PH: 888-625-9258
www.wiselephant.com
Marketing tools geared specifically to promote you.

Vendors and Labels

Most of the online vendors listed in this section
offer "non-exclusive" contracts. Non exclusive
means you are allowed to sign up with as many
of online vendors as you like without violating
any agreement. The fees and/or commissions
vary from site to site. I suggest you visit as
many as you can to find out which sites you get
a good feeling from. Be wary of large setup
fees!

N o r t h A m e r i c a

United States

4CDMusic.com
Mike Tobin mike@4cdmusic.com
4CDMusic.com
If your CD is available through a distributor, such
as the Orchard, then we should be able to get it in
our catalog, just let us know the UPC and we'll get
it listed.

AB-CD
www.ab-cd.com
We specialize in hard to find, rare and Indie music
and media.

ACMEnoise.com
www.acmerock.com
Offering a free place for artists to host as many
tracks as they like.

Allegro Corporation
Attn: Label Submissions, 14134 NE. Airport Way,
Portland, OR 97230-3443
www.allegro-music.com
One of the largest independent distributors of music
in the US. We work with labels that include no fewer
than 12 artists and/or 25 titles.

AmazingCDs
15213 N. Bonnett, Mead, WA 99021
info@amazingcds.com
www.amazingcds.com
All CDs are accepted - all styles of music.

amazon.com Advantage Program
orders@amazon.com
www.amazon.com/advantage
Lets millions of customers find, discover and buy
what you're selling.

Amp Camp
45 Main St. #516, Brooklyn, NY 11201
FX: 718-722-9203
info@ampcamp.com
www.ampcamp.com
Our review board of talented writers lets visitors
know the skinny on new releases.

Approachingstorm Records
PO Box 248134, Cleveland, OH 44124
PH: 216-376-0238
Dougless R. Esper
dougless@approachingstormrecords.com
www.approachingstormrecords.com
Dedicated to spreading quality music at an
affordable price to as many people as possible.

Artist1Stop
3650 Osage St., Denver, CO 80211
PH: 877-247-5046 FX: 303-433-8228
manager@artist1stop.com
www.artist1stop.com
Brick and mortar store CD distribution, online
distribution and digital distribution (iTunes, Napster
etc.).

awarestore.com
PH: 888-292-7301
info@awarerecords.com
www.awarestore.com
Indie CD and merchandise shop.

backstagecommerce.com
700 Freeport Pkwy. #100, Coppell, TX 75019
support@backstagecommerce.com
www.backstagecommerce.com
Sell your music goods on your website, our store
and your gigs.

BandMecca.com
6505 W. Park Blvd. #306-371, Plano, TX 75093
PH: 877-845-7864 FX: 240-384-2349
bands@bandmecca.com
www.bandmecca.com
We sell CDs and also have reviews of Indie music.

How to Promote Your Music Successfully on the Internet

Learn the promotion methods one musician uses to bring in over $5000 a month from the Internet!

A message from the author: The Internet is an *amazing* promotional tool for independent musicians. You can get radio play, grow a fan base, create a distribution channel, set up your own tour and sell your music all online. Wouldn't it be great if literally *thousands* of people from all over the world heard your music every day? What if you could use the Internet to sell *hundreds* of CDs and downloads every month? Guess what? It doesn't take a brain surgeon to make it happen, but it does take a *lot* of hard work – and you need to know what you're doing.

Therein lies the problem. Most musicians just have no idea where to start when it comes to online promotion and distribution. Some get as far as putting up a web site, but stop there. They aren't sure what the next step should be. That's where I can help.

Who am I? I am an independent musician just like you, with one difference: In the last year, I've used the Internet to generate **over $60,000 in income**. Hard to believe, isn't it? But it's true. Today I'm doing the "music business" full-time from my home in Springfield, Oregon. I now invest my time working on my music rather than spending 40-60 hours a week working for someone else. I'm truly an *independent* musician.

My intent with this book is to give you the information you need to begin promoting, selling, and distributing your own music successfully online. I'll give you *proven* ideas you can put to use *immediately*. It doesn't take a ton of money to get started either – that's another great benefit of living in this digital age. Simply put, I'll take you step by step through the same marketing strategies I've used over the last ten years (since 1995) to promote my own music on the Internet and run my music business on my own terms.

I know you're skeptical. I too am a skeptic by nature. Here are just a few of my many testimonials from readers....

"How to Promote Your Music Successfully on the Internet" is an incredible resource! It's not only the hundreds of techniques and tricks, it's how truly inspiring this book is. I sold more than 3000 copies of one of my CDs in 9 months as a result of reading this book." - Mihkel Raud

"I bought your book and I just want to say a big thank you for inspiring me so much. Before downloading the book we were doing well online, but it took a lot of trial and error which in turn took time. After reading your book, things are beginning to skyrocket for us. We have huge interest in our debut album which is released soon and have built up a sizeable fan base which is growing by the day. If I'd have paid 5 times what I did for the book, I would still be absolutely delighted with the results I've got from implementing your methods." - Liam

"I downloaded your book... initially I was skeptical (I am a fellow software type of guy & very analytical about things)... I just wanted to tell you that I LOVE it. Thanks a million - it's worth every penny." - Sheldon Schake

Want to know more? Visit my web site at www.promoteyourmusic.com . There you can read dozens of customer testimonials, get more detailed information, and even ask me questions if you like. LET ME TEACH YOU how to SUCCESSFULLY promote your music from my own life experience! Read all about it at....

www.promoteyourmusic.com

bandVillage
PO Box 2211, 32 Ellis Oaks Dr. Leicester,
NC 28748
PH: 828-398-4453
Peter Fleming peter.fleming@bandvillage.com
www.bandVillage.com
*Provides promotional services and consignment CD
sales for artists and labels, online and at festivals.*

Bathtub Music
14201 SE. Petrovitsky Rd. #A3-385, Renton,
WA 98058
PH: 425-226-7716
David Tieman info@bathtubmusic.com
bathtubmusic.com
*An online CD store dedicated to selling and
promoting all genres of independent music with
FREE SETUP for musicians.*

BCS Records
101 Forest Ln. Boulder City, NV 89005
PH: 702-293-0361 FX: 702-528-2602
Billy Shields bcsrecords@msn.com
bcsrecords.com
Worldwide distribution for all styles of CDs.

Beaucoup Records
145 Hudson St. #6C, New York, NY 10013
PH: 212-431-3999 FX: 212-431-7229
Ramin Mirshah
ramin.mirshah@beaucouprecords.com
www.beaucouprecords.com
*Created to provide artists artistic freedom and a
chance to share their music with the world.*

BETA Records
Box 48, Hollywood, CA 90028
PH: 877-232-2382
Christian office@betarecords.com
BetaRecords.com
*Providing artists with an internet platform to
showcase their talent.*

Blizzard Records
525 Hertel Ave. Buffalo, NY 14207
wm@blizzardrecords.com
www.blizzardrecords.com
*Represent artists by promoting them online and
allowing them to distribute their own CDs.*

Blue Monkey Records
2107 Starlight Ln. Independence, KY 41051
PH: 859-356-1918
Junette Gausman junettegausman@aim.com
www.myspace.com/blumonkeyrecords
*We offer representation, distribution, promotion etc.
We want to build long term, lasting relationships
with our artists and their fans.*

Boosweet Records
PO Box 451594, Los Angeles, CA 90045
PH: 310-613-3535 FX: 909-877-9199
Vernon Neilly VNeillyI@aol.com
www.boosweet.com
*Specializing in the recording and distribution of
major acts as well as up and coming artists. We will
promote and sell your products worldwide via the
internet. We can get any artist's material into the
major digital download stores as well.*

BrownJungle
PO Box 1143, Alameda, CA 94501-0117
customerservice@brownjungle.com
www.brownjungle.com
An online music store selling CDs for Indie artists.

Built On Strength Records
PO Box 560149, Rockledge, FL 32956
Cameron promotions@builtonstrength.com
www.builtonstrength.com
*We are always looking for fresh music to add to our
roster of bands. Send your CD to the above address.
We listen to everything!*

buythiscd.com
buythiscd.com
*There are great artists waiting to be heard. We want
people to hear them!*

Canadian American/Caprice International
PO Box 808, Lititz, PA 17543
PH: 717-627-4800
capricerecords@webtv.net
www.capricerecording.com
Will distribute your album worldwide. 25% cut.

Captiva Records
925 Hwy. 80 #195, San Marcos, TX 78666
PH: 512-322-9293 FX: 512-479-1805
Chris Perez cperez@captivagroup.com
www.captivarecords.com
Indie label with a focus on artist development.

CD Army
PO Box 225023, Dallas, TX 75222
PH: 214-943-7550 FX: 214-943-7550
www.cdarmy.com
*Independent musicians web hosting and worldwide
distribution of your music.*

CD Baby
5925 NE. 80th Ave. Portland, OR 97218-2891
PH: 503-595-3000 FX: 503-296-2370
cdbaby@cdbaby.com
www.cdbaby.com
*We will expose your CD to
10,000 customers a day. In
addition we have an
amazing digital distribution
service that is available to
all CD Baby members. CD
Baby will also make your
CD available to over 2400
CD stores worldwide
(mostly US).*

CD Palace
www.cdpalace.com
*Will sell your CD for you.
Accepts all genres.*

The CD Party
PO Box 281431, Nashville,
TN 37228
PH: 615-299-7035
thecdparty@
TheCDparty.com
www.TheCDparty.com
*We sell and promote Indie
music online and
worldwide, representing all
genres of music.*

CD Quest Music
feedback@cdquest.com
www.cdquest.com
*Reaches farther into the
independent world than any
other site.*

CDfuse.com
PO Box 9615, Austin, TX 78766
PH: 512-825-9108
Sal Silva III sal@cdfuse.com
cdfuse.com
*We represent the next level for listening, reviewing
and buying music online.*

CDpulse.com
38439 5th Ave. #1407, Zephyrhills, FL 33542
PH: 718-832-5507
Rob Pezzoli rob@cdpulse.com
www.cdpulse.com
Online retailer of music for independent artists and labels. Also provides album reviews and Soundscan reporting.

CDreview.com
30 Compton Way, Hamilton Square, NJ 08690
PH: 609-689-1711
info@CDreview.com
www.CDreview.com
Get 100% of your CD sale price. Type in the code "indiebible" to even waive the set up fee.

CDs-FROM-THE-ARTIST dot com
www.cdsfromtheartist.com
Harnesses the potential of the web to bring independent artists and music lovers from all over the world together.

Coach House Records
3503 S. Harbor Blvd. Santa Ana, CA 92704
PH: 714-545-2622 FX: 714-545-3490
www.coachhouserecords.com
Introduces Indie releases into the retail market.

Crafty Records
75 Earley St., Bronx, NY 10464
Dan Treiber craftydan@craftyrecords.net
www.craftyrecords.net
An independent, artist friendly record label.

Darla Records
2107 Camino Cantera, Vista, CA 92084
PH: 760-631-1731 FX: 760-454-1625
webmaster@darla.com
www.darla.com
Sells Indie CDs worldwide.

DigitalCuts.com
2940 Heather Stone Way, Lawrenceville, GA 30043
www.digitalcuts.com
Offers artists the opportunity to develop and promote their music .

Disgraceland Records
PO Box 10882, Knoxville, TN 37939
Paul Noe paul@disgraceland.com
www.disgraceland.com
Online record label.

Dubxpress On-Demand Music Publishing
146 A McKnight Cir. Pittsburgh, PA 15237
PH: 412-519-8250
Peter Sysko pete@dubxpress.com
www.dubxpress.com
Free manufacturing and distribution integration for artists that cannot afford to manufacture their own products.

DSV Records
1800 Pembrooke Dr. #300, Orlando, FL 32810
PH: 407-667-4759
Dan Santana dsv58@msn.com
www.dsvrecords.com
We're looking for the next DSV star!

Dynasonic
PMB 115, 4880 Lower Roswell Rd. #165, Marietta, GA 30068-4385
PH: 770-984-8104 FX: 770-984-8105
info@dynasonic.com
www.dynasonic.com
We can enable you to efficiently record and distribute your music at a minimal cost using new technology.

EvO:R
news@evor.com
www.evor.com
Online store. Works with Indie musicians around the world.

Friendly Fire Recordings
PMB #79, 302 Bedford Ave. Brooklyn, NY 11211
info@friendlyfirerecordings.com
www.friendlyfirerecords.com
We like demos. In fact, we love demos. We listen to everything we receive.

Gadfly Records
PO Box 5231, Burlington, VT 05402
PH: 802-865-2406
gadfly1@aol.com
www.gadflyrecords.com
We specialize in offbeat and unique projects.

GEMM
PO Box 4062, Palm Springs, CA 92263
PH: 760-318-6251 FX: 760-318-6251
seller@gemm.com
www.gemm.com
Worlds largest music catalog. Submit your CD.

GoJangle.com
simon@gojangle.com
www.gojangle.com
Dedicated to fans of music who want a single source solution for all new music.

Grape Soda Records
PO Box 229, Depew, NY 14043
PH: 716-698-8426
Timothy J. Finucane info@grapesodarecords.com
www.grapesodarecords.com
We are an open music record label always on the lookout for new talent.

Guitar Nine Records
8201 Hambledon Ct. Raleigh, NC 27615
PH: 561-423-0741 FX: 561-423-0741
www.guitar9.com
Guitar worship. New releases and demos wanted!

Halogen Records
163 State St., Montpelier, VT 05602
PH: 206-338-3478
info@halogenrecords.com
www.halogenrecords.com
Grassroots promotion, marketing, distribution and manufacturer.

Hammondbeat
11124 NE. Halsey #488, Portland, OR 97220
Kahlil Breithaupt hbinfo@hammondbeat.com
www.hammondbeat.com
Community and record label dedicated to bands and fans of the organ sound.

HotLocalMusic
PH: 800-988-6077
information@hotlocalmusic.com
hotlocalmusic.com
Empowers independent artists, venues, managers & labels with the tools and network interrelationships to reach music fans, build customer loyalty and increase profitability.

The Independent Artist Promotion Network
3160 Cadiz Cir. Atlanta, GA 30349
PH: 770-907-1358
Steven VanDyke savandyke@aol.com
www.The-Independent-Artist.com
Allows artists to sell their albums for a monthly subscription. Artists receive 100% revenue from their sales.

Independent Records
PO Box 510, Blairstown, NJ 07825
PH: 908-362-5524
Chris Midkiff customerservice@indierec.com
www.indierec.com
Imagine your CD sitting in your local record store display window! Think it's impossible? WRONG!!!!

IndepenDisc Music Club
PO Box 183, North Haven, CT 06473
feedback@independisc.com
www.independisc.com
We listen to every submittal for review, representation, & promotion, regardless of genre.

Indie Rhythm
160 Aztec Way SE., Acworth, GA 30102
PH: 678-574-6310
James McCullough sales@indierhythm.com
www.IndieRhythm.com
We are a CD megastore specializing in CDs by independent musicians.

INDIE Warehouse
PO Box 511, Louisville, KY 40201
PH: 502-593-9910
Matt Heitzmann matt@indiewarehouse.com
www.indiewarehouse.com
Devoted to connecting grassroots musicians to a world public eager to hear quality music.

Indie4Ever.com
www.indie4ever.com
Where you can sell your music without selling out!

IndieGate
304 Main Ave. PMB 287, Norwalk, CT 06851
PH: 203-483-1798
Noel Ramos MixxMag@InterMixx.com
www.indiegate.com
The coolest place on the internet to buy Indie music!

IndiePro.com
PO Box 507, North Uxbridge, MA 01538-0507
submissions@indiepro.com
www.indiepro.com
Submit your CD for review. Sell it online.

Indiespace
PO Box 5458, Santa Monica, CA 90409
PH: 310-399-4349 FX: 310-396-5489
editors@indiespace.com
www.indiespace.com
Indie artists can get their work out directly to their audience.

Insound
221 W. 17th St. 5th Fl. New York, NY 10011
PH: 212-777-8056 FX: 212-777-8059
patrick@insound.com
www.insound.com
Brings the best underground culture to the surface.

IROCK Entertainment
PO Box 691247, Hollywood, CA 90069
PH: 310-246-0040 FX: 310-246-1044
Monte Malone info@irock.com
www.irock.com
An Indie label with major promotion & distribution.

ItsAboutMusic.com
2169 Kimberton Rd. Phoenixville, PA 19460
PH: 610-415-1311
Dean Sciarra dean@itsaboutmusic.com
www.itsaboutmusic.com
Connects artist with fans worldwide.

PEACEWORK MUSIC NET
THE global distribution solution for independent artists and labels

Have an idea that you just can't seem to get down on paper? Let our talented staff turn your vision into cover art at a price that will amaze you. If you distribute through us, you'll receive a further discount and we'll even carry half your fees on account to be paid through your sales. Don't let the high cost of design work keep you from getting your music into the hands of music fans world wide!

Design

http://www.peaceworkmusic.net/

From cdr copies to full package manufacturing, you'll find us affordable and dependable with the fastest turnaround in the industry . . . never more than a week and usually 48 hours! As with all our services, if you distribute through us you'll recieve a discount and we'll carry half your fees on account to be paid through your sales. Don't let the high cost of manufacturing keep you from getting your music to music lovers world wide.

ibinquire@peaceworkmusic.net

Duplication

We have offices in five countries, including Ukraine and China! This allows you to sell your music directly to fans all over the world in their native language and they even pay in their own currency! This gives you the opportunity to be heard by folks that would otherwise never have the opportunity.

Our basic package includes a buypage that you can use to market your album and the only cost to you is what it costs to send us one copy of your cd for our archives. Yes, the basic distribution service is totally free! An email to ibinquire@peaceworkmusic.net will get you all the details and you could be online and ready for business within a week.

We also have a Platinum Package which includes a shorter url to your buypage, up to 1,500 words of promotional text and up to five pictures.

Distribution

PeaceWork Music Net officially launched on July 4, 2000 as a constant reminder to everyone that we're a new millennia company with the goal in mind to make the process of getting music from the artists' head to the ears of the public easy and affordable. The staff is 'composed' entirely of musicians and we truly understand on a personal level how much frustration and expense has been involved up till now. It is our mission, our way of doing business, that we make this process what it should have been all along. You make the music, you tell the fans where to buy your music and we give your music a home where you can send your fans. Email us today for the details, you'll be glad you did.

PEACEWORK MUSIC NET
The 21st Century Music Store

The Kitefishing Family
241 E. S. Temple #4, Salt Lake City, UT 84111
PH: 801-637-2828
admin@kitefishingfamily.com
www.kitefishingfamily.com
Dedicated to the promotion of all forms of independent art.

Lakeshore-Records
9268 W. 3rd St., Beverly Hills, CA 90210
PH: 310-867-8000 FX: 310-300-3015
info@lakeshore-records.com
www.lakeshore-records.com
Dedicated to finding and developing unique new talent in addition to releasing soundtrack albums not only from our films, but also from other independent films of merit and interest.

LightningCD Corporation
4707 Aurora Ave. N., Seattle, WA 98103
distribution@lightningcd.com
www.lightningcd.com
Supports Indie artists with national distribution of their CDs.

Locals Online
PH: 503-419-6402
sales@localsonline.com
www.localsonline.com
Global collection of local music.

LOL Records
PO Box 5148, Beverly Hills, CA 90209
PH: 310-790-5689 FX: 208-460-2903
Gerry Davies info@lolrecords.com
lolrecords.com
Releases music overlooked by commercial recording companies.

LOUiPiMPS
1217 Silver St., New Albany, IN 47150
andrew@louipimps.com
www.louipimps.com
Internationally distributed Indie record label.

Lucky Unicorn Records
4339 Rialto St. #1, San Diego, CA 92107
PH: 619-246-3195
Mark Saalwaechter mark@luckyunicorn.com
www.luckyunicorn.com
Very small, independent record label interested in offbeat yet wildly talented bands. CDs sell for $5, with $1 going back to the band.

Maple Island Records
19030 Dreaming River Dr. Terrace, MN 56334
PH: 320-278-3019
island@mapleislandrecords.com
www.mapleislandrecords.com
Independent record producer & label.

Matchbox Recordings USA
A&R Dept., PO Box 644, Chanhassen, MN 55317
Rob Kerr matchboxrecs@msn.com
British Indie label seeking quality CDs from all genres of Rock music. Send your demos to the above address.

Merch Girl
PO Box 51222, Phoenix, AZ 85076
PH: 602-413-6935
Mattx merchgirlaz@yahoo.com
store.themerchgirl.com
We sell ANYONES music, art or movies on consignment.

Milk Records
2767 Scott Ave. Lincoln, NE 68516
milk@milkrecords.com
milkrecords.com
Sell your Indie albums worldwide.

Moozikoo
PO Box 50322, Nashville, TN 37205-0322
Anthony Bates anthony@moozikoo.com
www.moozikoo.com
A bilingual (Russian and English) music Etailer. Our target market is the Russian-speaking community within the United States and consumers within the emerging markets of the former Soviet Union (especially Russia, Ukraine, Moldova and Belarus), as well as specific English-speaking consumer groups.

Morphius Records
100 E. 23rd St., Baltimore MD 21218
PH: 410-662-0112 FX: 410-662-0116
Simeon Walunas simeon@morphius.com
www.morphius.com
Over 13 years of great Pop, Rock, Punk & Hip Hop releases. Sell your CDs and MP3s!

Muse-Wrapped Records
staff@muse-wrapped.com
www.muse-wrapped.com
Our mission is to become a magnet for the world's most accomplished musicians and producers.

Music Distributors.com
PH: 916-338-6881 FX: 916-338-6882
info@themusicdistributors.com
www.musicdistributors.com
We cater to independent artists and labels.

Music Loft
1445 1st Ave. SE., Cedar Rapids, IA 52402
PH: 319-362-4208
www.music-loft.com
We will set up an individual page for your music which includes description and reviews, cover shot, audio clips and a link to your website. No setup fee!

Musictogousa.com
32 McKinley Ave. Bristol, CT 06010
PH: 860-490-0542
Bert Gagnon neonproductions@sbcglobal.net
www.musictogousa.com
CD retail, broadcasts, music products and services for musicians and music lovers.

Navigator Records
1300 Division St. #105, Nashville, TN 37203
PH: 615-742-5581 FX: 615-742-8014
Chuck Thompson info@navigatorrecords.com
www.navigatorrecords.com
For the new artist searching for a label deal, we have a loyal audience and a well-established touring base.

Net Spin
PO Box 6927, Folsom, CA 95763
www.netspin.com
The Indie superstore for movies, music and more!

NETUNES.com
3183 Airway Ave. Bldg. E, Costa Mesa, CA 92626
PH: 949-498-3600 FX: 949-498-6900
Kelly@NETunes.com
www.netunes.com
You get a distribution agreement regardless of genre.

New Artist Direct
600 Washington Ave. N. #102, Minneapolis, MN 55401
customerservice@newartistdirect.com
www.newartistdirect.com
Helping Indie artists make a living.

New Artists Online
PO Box 21437, Philadelphia, PA 19141
PH: 215-696-0598 FX: 215-548-9216
newartistsonline@newartistsonline.com
www.newartistsonline.com
Dedicated to featuring, showcasing and selling the CDs of independent artists.

Nine 12 Records
275 Cathy Dr. Newbury Park, CA 91320
PH: 805-368-2251
Sara theman@nine12records.com
www.nine12records.com
Independent record label based in LA area. Individualized contracts based on artist goals.

Not Lame
PO Box 2266, Fort Collins, CO 80522
FX: 970-407-0256
Bruce popmusic@notlame.com
www.notlame.com
A record label that focuses on 'Power Pop'/Melodic Rock and also an online record store dedicated to selling Indie releases from other melodically driven bands.

Number 3 Records
Toddrick Spalding toddrick@number3records.com
www.number3records.com
A diverse independent label formed from a true love of music. Also, the best records you never heard!

OneSource
PO Box 162, Skippack, PA 19474
PH: 215-661-1100 FX: 215-661-8959
onesource@pan.com
onesource.pan.com
Distribution system for the online sale of e-CDs.

Online Rock
2033 Ralston Ave. #50, Belmont, CA 94002
PH: 650-649-2304 FX: 650-649-2304
info@onlinerock.com
www.onlinerock.com
Bands can promote, distribute and sell their music online.

OnScene
21 Madera Ave. San Carlos, CA 94070
PH: 650-637-0763 FX: 650-637-0824
info@onscene.com
www.onscene.com
We'll proudly display your work and help you find a market.

Orange Recordings
801 S. Wells St. #401, Chicago, IL 60607
info2@orangerecordings.com
www.orangerecordings.com
Tell us why you're the shit ...why do you want to be on this label? Don't send any MP3s!

The Orchard
100 Park Ave. 17th Fl. New York, NY 10003
PH: 212-201-9280 FX: 212-201-9203
info@theorchard.com
www.theorchard.com
Supplier of independent music on the internet.

OutBoundMusic.com
7037 Hwy. 6 N. PO Box 145, Houston, TX 77095
PH: 281-859-6715
info@outboundmusic.com
www.outboundmusic.com
Distribution and promotion services for Indie artists.

PeaceWork Music
PO Box 25102, Rochester, NY 14625
info@peacework.com
www.peaceworkmusic.net
We have duplication services in the US which ships to all countries outside of Eastern Europe and China. We also have distributors in Eastern Europe and China which cover those needs.

peermusic
3260 Blume Dr. #405, Richmond, CA 94806
PH: 510-222-9678 FX: 510-222-9676
sfcorp@peermusic.com
www.peermusic.com
Promotion and development with a personal touch.

Peppermint CDs
1170 15th Ave. SE. #206, Minneapolis, MN 55414
PH: 800-633-7020 FX: 651-293-4421
peppermintcds@gmail.com
www.peppermintcds.com
Wants full-time musicians with at least 2 CDs released.

Perris Records
PO Box 841533 Houston, TX 77284
PH: 281-550-0988 FX: 775-719-4768
Tom Mathers perrisrecords@ev1.net
www.perrisrecords.com
80's Rock label, mail order & distribution company that sells worldwide. Perris is now accepting CDs or CDRs for possible label consideration and distribution deals worldwide.

Planet CD
PO Box 29742, Charlotte, NC 28229
PH: 704-560-2379
info@planetcd.com
www.PlanetCD.com
We provide 2 custom designed pages for your listing - an "Info / Bio" page to tell about your music, the artist, or whatever message you want to get across - and a "CD page" which features a scan of your CD cover, a list of tracks and audio samples.

Point Five Limey
7536 E. Warren Dr. #15-304, Denver, CO 80231
PH: 303-306-7602
James Gardiner info@pointfivelimeyrecords.com
www.pointfivelimeyrecords.com
An online art, music and culture website that strives to sell, promote and display a variety art and music from around the world.

Pop Sweatshop
PO Box 460954, Denver, CO 80246
PH: 303-525-5840
Chris Barber info@popsweatshop.com
www.popsweatshop.com
We work furiously, in sweatshop conditions, to make and distribute great Indie releases for bands.

Range Records
2730 E. County Line Rd. Ardmore, PA 19003
PH: 610-649-7100 FX: 610-649-7566
Rich Myers richm@rangeentertainment.com
www.rangeentertainment.com
Our expertise lies in artist development, recording, booking, management and promotion.

Realm of Records
236 DeKalb Ave.
Brooklyn, NY 11205
PH: 716-316-2438
Allen Farmelo
allenfarmelo@yahoo.com
www.realmofrecords.com
Releases albums from independent artists regardless of genre. Instead, musical creativity and beauty are the guiding principles.

Reason Y
747 Barnett St. NE. #4,
Atlanta, GA 30306
PH: 404-723-5098
Moe moe@reasonY.com
www.reasonY.com
Promotion and distribution for Indie bands of all genres.

THE REC(o)RD LINK
PO Box 647, Orange, NJ 07051
mail@TheRecordLink.com
www.therecordlink.com
Will promote your recordings on the internet.

Revolver USA Distribution
2745 16th St., San Francisco, CA 94103
FX: 415-241-9009
Bobo bobo@midheaven.com
www.midheaven.com
Labels/bands interested in having us distribute their music can mail samples to the above address.

RiPPYFiSH Records
1800 SW. Temple #317, Salt Lake City, UT 84115
PH: 801-487-7302 FX: 801-487-7304
Lisa Miller lisa@rippyfish.com
www.rippyfish.com
We are an open genre independent record label.

ROA Records
6014 Chenango Ln. Orlando, FL 32807
Monica Rabino monica@roarecords.com
roarecords.com
Independent music label by artists for artists.

Rock Ridge Music
info@rockridgemusic.com
www.rockridgemusic.com
Offers national distribution and online marketing services.

SCREACHEN
PO Box 16352, Phoenix, AZ 85011-6352
Al Harbison President@Screachen.com
www.screachen.com
Reviews, manages and produces local & national bands.

Shut Eye Records
1526 DeKalb Ave. #21, Atlanta, GA 30307
PH: 678-986-5110 FX: 404-584-5171
Pete Knapp knapp@shuteyerecords.com
www.shuteyerecords.com
Record label, publicity firm, CD manufacturing and more.

SignHere Online, Inc.
contact@signhereonline.net
www.signhereonline.net
Provides artists with an opportunity to promote original MP3 music and solicit recording contract offers.

Silk City Recording Company
PO Box 704, West Paterson, NJ 07424
PH: 973-599-0236 FX: 973-599-0236
silkcity@silkcitycd.com
www.silkcitycd.com
An online retail site that sells Indie products.

something sacred
PO Box 15533, San Luis Obispo, CA 93401
PH: 805-545-5887
Jon Broyles jon@somethingsacred.com
www.somethingsacred.com
Promotes Indie artists. Submit your material.

sonaBLAST!
115 W. 28th St. #1102, New York, NY 10001
PH: 212-963-9655
info@sonablast.com
www.sonablast.com
We are a label, management and publishing firm all wrapped into one.

SongRamp
531 Metroplex Dr. #115A, Nashville, TN 37211
PH: 615-333-7775 FX: 615-333-7728
admin@songramp.com
www.songramp.com
We offer independent artists an outlet to sell their CDs.

Sonic Garden
info@sonicgarden.com
www.sonicgarden.com
Free music, videos, tour info, song info and more!

Sonic Wave International
415 S. Maple #603, Oak Park, IL 60302
PH: 708-445-8373 FX: 847-577-9528
www.sonicwaveintl.com
Our goal is to find, promote and release GOOD music that people want to hear.

Squid Music
dschraub@mis.net
www.squidmusic.com
If your interested in selling you CD, please drop us a line. We'll be happy to put a page out there plus whatever promo you might like to provide.

Stompinground.com
www.stompinground.com
Global independent promotion for local bands.

Strange Vibes
16000 Harrison St., Livonia, MI 48154-3499
Tracy Farley tracy@strangevibes.com
www.strangevibes.com
A free CD distribution site for Indie musicians.

Sub Pop Records
2013 4th Ave. Seattle, WA 98121
PH: 206-441-8441 FX: 206-441-8245
info@subpop.com
www.subpop.com
We don't listen to demos every day, but periodically we go through a bunch of them. Please don't call or e-mail to follow up.

Sunlight of the Spirit Music
PO Box 60097, Nashville, TN 37206
PH: 615-403-8587
Gracie Vandiver gracie@mkbmedia.com
www.sunlightofthespiritmusic.com
Offering only the highest quality music that has been created by artists in recovery. Please contact us via our website for approval before submitting CDs.

Sunny Music
6019 Glitter Gold Ct. N., Las Vegas, NV 89031-7212
PH: 678-315-8753 FX: 770-252-5802
Chris S. Douglas csd@sunnymusic.us
www.myCDstore.net
The independent musician's choice for selling and distributing their CDs worldwide.

Toadfish
info@toadfishrecords.com
www.toadfish.org
A unique collaboration of independent artists, promoters and marketers designed to help get the word out.

Tone Box Records
2814 Azalea Pl. Nashville, TN 37204
PH: 615-301-1836
Jason Bradford jason.bradford@tone-box.com
www.tone-box.com
Indie record label giving Indie artists access to large digital distributors.

UnderCover Records
5500 S. Marginal Rd. #210, Cleveland, OH 44103
PH: 216-432-3201
info@undercoverrecords.com
www.undercoverrecords.com
A direct sales, distribution and marketing company dedicated to new and developing independent music.

Unfun Records
19144 Brookview Dr. Saratoga CA 95070
PH: 408-344-0402 FX: 408-253-1653
Johnny johnny@unfunrecords.com
www.unfunrecords.com
Music distributor, reviews, mixing studio and record label for independent bands.

United For Opportunity Music
133 W. 25th St. 5th Fl. New York, NY 10001
PH: 212-414-0505 FX: 212-414-0525
www.ufomusic.com
An organization of experienced, independent-thinking music industry activists that have come together to create a new model for a record label/music distribution company.

Vochella Records
info@vochellarecords.com
www.vochellarecords.com
Indie label and artist promotions co-op.

Wampus Multimedia
4 Weems Ln. #300, Winchester, VA 22601
Mark Doyon mail2@wampus.com
wampus.com
Record label, retail store, recording studio and marketing company.

Warranty Records
243 Elm St. #207, Everett, WA 98203
PH: 206-262-9237 FX: 425-303-9547
Mark Lutch wrecords@warrantyrecords.biz
www.warrantyrecords.biz
Looking for demos. All genres are welcome. Visit our website for more info.

Woodstock CD
PO Box 119, Ruby, NY 12475
info@woodstockcd.com
www.woodstockcd.com
Distribute your Indie CD here.

Xact Records
PO Box 1832, Bangor, ME 04402-1832
info@xactrecords.com
xactrecords.com
Promotes unsigned bands and sells their merchandise.

Canada

Promotional Services

Absolutely Music
19 Cowdy St., Kingston, ON K7K 3V8
PH: 613-531-8827
njgreig@absolutelymusic.on.ca
www.absolutelymusic.on.ca
A full service entertainment agency dedicated to serving the needs of Canadian musicians and to providing public and corporate clients with quality music for all occasions.

CatsAsk Music & Entertainment
PO Box 31029, Barrie, ON L4N 0B3
PH: 705-792-0394
Duss Rodgers info@catsask.com
www.catsask.com
Band consultation, bio assistance, song copyright assistance and monthly music reviews.

City Lights Entertainment
16 Wynford Ave. Ottawa, ON K2G 3Z4
PH: 613-265-9967
Michael Wood mike@citylightsent.com
www.citylightsentertainment.com
We do not promote artists directly. We offer consultation and guidance services among other things.

Danie Cortese Entertainment & Publicity
93 Dunoon Dr. Maple, ON L6A 1Z3
PH: 905-660-9898
Danie Cortese dcortese@platinum1.com
www.daniecortese.com
Publicity representing all talent. Management & consulting. Radio releases. Film & music division.

The Image Management
9332 63rd Ave. Edmonton, AB T6E 0G4
PH: 780-993-5530
Michelle Rogers
michelle@theimagemanagement.com
www.theimagemanagement.com
Works with artists to get them signed. We also help our artists to write hit songs and make the best music video possible.

Kindling Music
Attn: Demos, 411 Queen St. W. 3rd Fl. Toronto, ON M5V 2A5
PH: 416-506-9696 x1001
info@kindling.ca
www.kindlingmusic.com
Label for career artists: promotion, publicity, marketing, booking and tour support.

Last Tango Productions
29 Galley Ave. Toronto, ON M6R 1G9
PH: 416-538-1838 FX: 416-538-2633
Yvonne Valnea lastango@pathcom.com
www.lasttangoproductions.com
National publicity & radio tracking. Tour support and promotions.

LastJack Management
266 Charlotte St. #335, Peterborough, ON K9J 2V4
PH: 705-748-3596 FX: 705-748-3596
Michael Bates booking@weberbrothers.com
www.weberbrothers.com
Indie management firm looking to add Ontario bands & artists to their current roster.

MassiveRecordProductions.com
10 Royal Orchard Blvd. #53081, Thornhill, ON L3T 7R9
PH: 905-764-1246
Jerry Bader info@mrpwebmedia.com
MassiveRecordProductions.com
We produce and promote the music artists who want to take their fledgling careers to the next level.

MRPwebmedia
10 Royal Orchard Blvd. #53081, Thornhill, ON L3T 7R9
PH: 905-764-1246
Jerry Bader info@mrpwebmedia.com
mrpwebmedia.com
Providing artists with the promotional tools needed to create a buzz in the competitive music industry.

S.L. Feldman & Associates
200-1505 W. 2nd Ave. Vancouver, BC V6H 3Y4
Attn: Watchdog
Sarah Fenton fenton@watchdogmgt.com
www.slfa.com
Canada's leading full-service entertainment agency. Please note we do our best to listen to all demos we receive.

Stamm'ler International
200 N. Service Rd. W. Unit 1, #435, Oakville, ON L6M 2Y1
PH: 905-842-2822 FX: 905-842-2823
Ragna Stamm'ler ragna@bellnet.ca
www.stammlerinternational.com
Covers all marketing/promotion aspects for the arts.

TEA South
101 Burlington St., Toronto, ON M8V 3W1
PH: 416-251-1501
www.teasouth.com
We provide radio tracking / promotions, live showcases, press kits and press releases. Always free consultations!

Tenoseven Entertainment
#8-5901 57th St., Taber, AB T1G 1P7
PH: 403-223-0844 FX: 403-223-0844
Sharla Bauschke sharla@tenoseven.com
www.tenoseven.com
Artist development & management services including booking, promotions, tracking and more.

Toots Capital
PH: 416-488-9649 FX: 416-488-8173
Valerie Dooley val@tootscapital.com
tootscapital.com
Public relations firm that specializes in publicizing, promoting, producing and representing clients. Let US toot YOUR horn!

Vizou
610 rue Frenette, Joliette, PQ J6E 8X3
PH: 450-759-5498
Dana Whittle dana@vizou.com
www.vizou.com
Services include concept development, writing and content development, illustration, custom typography and digital photography.

White Eagle Music Promotions
122 - 250 The East Mall #1109, Toronto, ON M9B 6L3
(US address) 342 Broadway #101, New York, NY 10013
PH: 416-620-1231 FX: 416-620-5912
Maureen Smith maureen@whiteeaglerecords.ca
www.whiteeaglerecords.ca
Specializing in artist development, distribution, radio promotion campaigns, music conference promotion and licensing.

Vendors and Labels

Atomic Records
music@atomicrecords.com
www.atomicrecords.com
Assisting independent bands in the art of effective promotion.

BenT Music
32 Paul St., Toronto, ON M5A 3H3
bentmusic@bentmusic.ca
www.bentmusic.ca
Helps musicians get their music out to the public.

Betty Records
317 Adelaide St. W. #503, Toronto, ON M5V 1P9
PH: 416-598-8806 FX: 416-598-0884
info@bettyrecords.com
www.bettyrecords.com
Exposes you to a large audience from around the globe.

Byte Music
153 Tracy Rd. New London, NH 03257
PH: 604-630-2799
Jamie Cooper jamie@unibyte.com
www.bytemusic.ca
An online music store, digital download service and marketplace for music fans, artists and music retailers.

CANtunes.com
356 Ontario St. #311, Stratford, ON N5A 7X6
Stewart
mail@brittlestar.ca
www.cantunes.com/indiebible.php
Sell your independent CDs in Canada the easy way!

Crony Records
290 Bridge St. W., Waterloo, ON N2K 1L2
Brad Weber brad@cronyrecords.ca
www.cronyrecords.ca
Community based record label helping musicians promote each other through the label.

Cyclone Records
PO Box 71550, Aurora, ON L4G 6S9
PH: 416-738-5022 FX: 905-841-7463
Brad Trew info@cyclonerecords.ca
www.cyclonerecords.ca
Producer of high quality CD compilations at a local, regional, national and international level.

gigzter.com
230 Hampton Heath Rd. Burlington, ON L7L4P3
PH: 905-631-8302
Steve Bihari admin@gigzter.com
www.gigzter.com
Your source for independent artist profiles, quality original music, profiles, charts, playlists and more!

High 4 Records
256 Major St., Toronto, ON M5S 2L6
PH: 416-561-1271
Darrin Pfeiffer darrin@high4records.com
www.high4records.com
We wanted to start a label where the bands have a lot of creative control, where they'd feel safe and where they could grow as artists.

TuneVault.com
steve@tenvolt.com
www.tunevault.com
Reviews, news, calendar, artist pages and more. Sell your stuff!

Europe

Austria

TON 4 Music Group
+44 (0)20-81-33-63-33
Patrick F. Plank office@ton4music.com
www.ton4music.com
We're an European label/publisher and have specialized in world-wide digital distribution and radio promotion. Contact us for our mailing address.

Belgium

Kinky Star Records
Vlasmarkt 9 9000 Gent Belgium
PH: +32-9-223-48-45
Sebbe d'Hose sebbe@kinkystar.com
www.kinkystar.com
Rock, Surf, Hip Hop, Electro and Experimental releases.

Soundoo.com
Ave. Paul Deschanel 263, B - 1030 Brussels, Belgium
PH: +32 (0)2-242-72-99
publisher_support@soundoo.com
soundoo.com
An online CD store dedicated to independent music.

Czech Republic

Indies Records
Stefánikova 8, Brno 602 00, Czech Republic
PH: +420-549-245-610 FX: +420-545-212-209
Premysl Stepanek indies@indiesrec.cz
www.indiesrec.cz
Supporting many young talented artists.

France

Laani Music
23 rue Lecourbe, 75015 Paris, France
PH: +33-6-10-71-86-86
Alain Bouet contact@laani-music.com
www.laani-music.com
Sell your CDs in France and Europe!

Ocean-Music
2, place du Foirail, 81220 St Paul Cap de Joux, France
eole@ocean-music.com
www.ocean-music.com
Listens to demos and promotes Indie artists.

Germany

amazon.de
www.amazon.de
Sell your CD through our store.

CoArt-Music
Graf-Anton-Weg 10, 22459 Hamburg, Germany
PH: 0049-0-7646-913555
Uwe Ruthard ur@co-art.com
www.co-art-music.com
Offers non exclusive physical and digital distribution in Germany for independent music.

Music Marketing Service
c/o Arte Leon Ltd., Albinsuweg 5, 06679 Hohenmoelsen, Germany
PH: 0049-34441-21184 FX: 0049-941-59-92-21-184
Michael Thurm info@music-marketing-service.com
www.music-marketing-service.com
We offer bands distribution throughout Europe. CDs and digital distribution. We also do radio promotion!

music2deal.com
Agathenstrasse 11, 20357 Hamburg, Germany
PH: +49-40-6481745 FX: +49-40-6473336
usa@music2deal.com
music2deal.com
This international network gives you a unique
possibility to be promoted in different foreign
countries via the top 5 or the local newsletter.

NovaTune
Christian Wirsig info@novatune.de
www.novatune.de
German fair-trade-label with reasonable prices and
fair artist payments.

RockCity Hamburg
Neuer Kamp 32 / 2.OG, 20357 Hamburg, Germany
PH: 040-319-60-60 FX: 040-319-60-69
Claudia music@rockcity.de
www.rockcity.de
Resource for Indie musicians.

Scales Records
Im Drostebusch 29B, 48155 Münster, Germany
PH: +49 (0)251-316540 FX: +49 (0)251-381813
Joerg Pasler scales@gmx.net
www.scales.de
Label & distributor of Instrumental Electric Guitar
music from Heavy Metal to Jazz and beyond.

track4.de
PH: +49 (0) 511-270-07-56
FX: +49 (0) 511-270-07-58
www.track4.de
MP3s, news, charts etc.

TWE Promotion
Intückenweg 13, 44289 Dortmund, Germany
Torsten Wohlgemuth booking.twe@web.de
www.myspace.com/twepromotion
Do you need a distro or label in Europe? Ask us!
You want to promote your releases in Europe? Don't
hesitate to contact us!

UEBER Distribution
Strichweg 110, 27476 Cuxhaven, Germany
PH: +49 4721 666470 FX: +49 4721 666471
Oliver Lagemann Oliver@ueber.us
www.ueber.us
We are looking for finished products in Rock, Pop
and Indie. NO Rap, Hip Hop, Dance or Techno.

Gibraltar

Melodrift Productions
30 Halifax Ct. Gibraltar, Europe
PH: +34-636737428
Wesley contact@melodrift.com
www.melodrift.com
Offering artists promotional advertising and/or
music distribution, licensing deals etc.

Italy

Alma Music
Via Marovich 5, 30030 Chirignago, Venezia, Italy
PH: 041-5441558 FX: 041-5441588
ossigeno@o2pub.com
www.almamusic.it a
Promotes and sells independent music from Italy
and the rest of the world.

OmOm World
Piazza Euclide 21, 00197 Roma, Italy
PH/FX: 39-06-8070486
Robert Ruggeri info@omomworld.com
www.omomworld.com
Italian independent label.

RES - Registrazioni e Suoni
PO Box 292, 31100 Treviso Centrale, Italy
PH: +39-335-8409306 FX: +39-0422-235743
Joachim Thomas info@res-net.org
www.res-net.org
A record label always looking for new music.

The Netherlands

Dying Giraffe Recordings
St. Anthoniusplaats 9, 6511, TR, Nijmegen,
The Netherlands
Ingmar info@dyinggiraffe-recordings.com
www.dyinggiraffe-recordings.com
We listen to all the stuff that comes in. You can send
us some MP3 files by e-mail or mail a CD.

Norway

Abòn Records
Ruud, 2847 Kolbu, Norway
PH: +47-61-16-82-12
records@abon.info
www.abon.info
Dedicated to producing quality Alternative sound
recordings.

ChewinPine Records/ HormonMelon Prod.
Serli gt.8A 0577, Oslo, Norway
chewinpine@chewinpine.no
www.chewinpine.no
Issues on Indie labels, booking, promotion and
more.

Romania

Media Pro Music
Str. Bdul Pache Protopopescu, nr. 109, Bucuresti,
sector 2, Romania
PH: +40-31-82-50-366 FX: +40-31-82-50-299
office@mediapromusic.ro
www.mediapromusic.ro
Indie label promoting artists internationally.

Spain

ATIZA
PH: 93-247-82-76
Juan info@atiza.com
www.atiza.com
Música, noticias, bares y conciertos en Barcelona.

popchild.com
c/Joan Güell 184-188, 08028 Barcelona, Spain
PH: +34-93-444-17-69
popchild@popchild.com
www.popchild.com
Promotes Indie/unknown artists.

pop-page.com
C/ Málaga 11, 18230 Atarfe (Granada), Spain
www.pop-page.com
Un e-zine dedicado a la música menos convencional
(¿independiente, Alternativa?).

TheBorderlineMusic
PH: 678-667576
promociones@theborderlinemusic.com
www.theborderlinemusic.com
If you have a group or CD that you want to
promote, our service is an inexpensive and effective
way to reach your goals.

Sweden

Top Five Records
c/o Singfeldt, Rönnholmsgränd 41 BV, SE-127 42
Skärholmen, Sweden
Mattias Andersson info@top-five-records.com
www.top-five-records.com
We are a mail order company that is starting to
release records. Send us your demo. Indie, Alt. Rock,
Electro, Garage, Pop etc.

Zorch Productions
Klostergatan 7-9, s70361, Orebro, Sweden
info@zorchproductions.com
www.zorchproductions.com
Label that release the best unsigned stuff from
Scandinavia.

Switzerland

Brambus Records
Berghalde, CH-8874 Mühlehorn, Switzerland
PH: ++41-55-614-10-77 FX: ++41-55-614-10-77
Paul Rostetter brambus@smile.ch
www.brambus.com
An excellent source for great Singer/Songwriter and
Jazz/Blues CDs. Check it out!

United Kingdom
Promotional Services

Crunchy Frog Management.
Geoff Osborne cfrogmanagement@aol.com
cfm.moonfruit.com
We really don't have time to reply to any messages.
Just send your link. We WILL visit every link and
listen to the music.

Evil Twin Promotions
29 Stoneway Rd. Cleveleys, Lancs, FY5 3AU UK
PH: 07863-352539
info@eviltwinpromotions.com
www.eviltwinpromotions.com
Promotional agency catering to unsigned bands,
solo artists and freelance musicians for hire. We
offer a full range of promotional services covering
hundreds of companies, including live, recording
and film services.

Jonny Random Music Promotions
PH: 07723-056570
john@jonnyrandom.com
www.jonnyrandom.com
Supporting & promoting unsigned music - including
news, gigs, band pages, forum etc.

Mark Jones Management & PR
22 Oakfield Rd. Stourbridge, West Midlands,
DY9 9DL UK
PH: 07947-232477
Mark Jones info@mark-jones.info
www.markjones.tk
Recognized music PR and commercial adviser to
record labels. A & R consultant.

Mosquito Records
PO Box 39375, London, SE13 5WP UK
PH: 442088520433 FX: 442088520433
mail@mosquito-records.com
www.mosquito-records.com
Indie label promoting bands and solo artists.

---

panartist.com
PO Box 45502, London, NW1 2AX UK
www.panartist.com
A physical and digital music distribution service. We supply our physical catalogue to thousands of major retail and internet stores in the US, Canada and Europe.

Traffic Online
6 Stucley Pl. London, NW1 8NS UK
teams@trafficonline.net
trafficonline.net
Promotions, street teams and more for UK bands.

Urban Street
tim@movingwindows.com
www.urbanstreet.co.uk
Helping artists to promote their music and ultimately get work or sell music.

Vendors and Labels

25 Records
PO Box 3006, Poole, BH12 2HU UK
info@25records.com
www.25records.com
Discovers new and exciting bands and brings them to the world's attention.

amazon.co.uk
www.amazon.co.uk
Simple, direct and profitable way for sell your music.

Astral Records
PH: +61-3-9849-1484 FX: +61-3-9878-6277
Mike Puskas puskas@astralrecords.co.uk
www.astralrecords.co.uk
A boutique label that specialises in outsourcing, developing, packaging and shopping artists to third party labels and publishers.

Boomkat Online
Unit 101, Ducie House, 37 Ducie St., Manchester, M1 2JW UK
PH: +44 (0) 161-834-2569
FX: +44 (0) 161-236-3351
www.boomkat.com
Your independent music specialist!

CD Unsigned
PO Box 4462, Worthing, West Sussex, BN11 3YF UK
PH: 0871-8725324
www.cdunsigned.com
Specializing in CDs by new and emerging bands.

CD WOW! 'unsigned...AS YET!'
#2a, Gregories Ct. Gregories Rd. Beaconsfield, Bucks, HP9 1HQ UK
PH: 44-0-1494-683500
unsigned@cd-wow.com
www.cd-wow.com/unsigned
Sell your music and gain exposure.

Collaborator Records
PH: 01225-404445
Paul Corket colaborator@clara.co.uk
www.collaboratorrecords.com
Specialising in producing limited edition EPs - which feature studio recordings, demos and live versions of songs that will be re-recorded for the artist's first albums.

DiscoWeb
PO Box 85995, EC50 6AA UK
mail@discoweb.com
www.discoweb.com
International music mega store.

fierce panda records
PO Box 21441, London, N7 6WZ UK
ellie@fiercepanda.co.uk
www.fiercepanda.co.uk
Send all demos to the above address. The music should be tuneful, handsome and whacked-out.

GoodMusicCentre.com
1B Avenue Rd. London, N14 4BU UK
PH: 02082924975
Michael info@GoodMusicCentre.com
www.GoodMusicCentre.com
Sales of music CDs and digital downloads. Markets and distributes to other retail outlets in the UK and USA.

Human Recordings
PO Box 3, Huntingdon, Cambs, PE28 0QX UK
www.human-recordings.com
We're sick of hearing bands that just don't make the grade and so our standards are very high. If we don't 100% fall in love with a band's music, we won't sign them.

iMusic Stage
4, Crosspost Industrial Pk. Cowfold Rd.
Bolney, W. Sussex RH17 5QU UK
PH: +44 (0)1444-881300 FX: +44 (0)1444-881030
Customer.Service@iMusicStage.com
www.iMusicStage.com
We cater to bands of all genres who want to sell their merchandise online.

Kabukikore
6 Rosebery Rd. Anstey, Leicestershire, LE7 7EJ UK
fieldops@kabukikore.net
www.kabukikore.net
Record label specialising in tiny limited editions in hand made sleeves.

Kissy Music
19 Middlesex Ct. Clacton-on-Sea, Essex, CO15 6EF UK
PH: 0044-1206-304309
Silke silke@kissymusic.com
www.kissymusic.com
Independent label, publishing house & music management service.

Mohican Records
Gti, Navigation Park, Abercynon, CF45 4SN UK
PH: 0208-751-2244
Dave Mohican
davemohican@mohicanrecords.co.uk
www.mohicanrecords.co.uk
Be creative. Be inspired. Be part of Mohican Records.

Norman Records
#1 Armley Park Ct. Stanningley Rd. Leeds, LS12 2AE UK
PH: 0-0113-2311114
phil@normanrecords.com
www.normanrecords.com
Features Indie CDs from around the world.

Overplay
PO Box 11188, Sutton Coldfield, B76 1WX UK
PH: 0870-112-1382
service@overplay.co.uk
www.overplay.com
Provides a platform for artists/bands to get reviews and to sell their music.

Rhonddarecords-Wales.com
226, Pentyntyla, Penrhys, Rhondda, CF43 3RB UK
PH: 01443-732705
Ray Joseph rayjoseph05@aol.com
www.Rhonddarecords-Wales.com
Promotion of all musicians who share our ideals: peaceful, sustainable, fair development.

Rough Trade
130 Talbot Rd. London, W11 1JA UK
PH: 020-7229-8541 FX: 020-7221-1146
enquiries@roughtrade.com
www.roughtrade.com
Send us your music to get on our shelves.

RPM Records UK
PO Box 679, Doncaster, DN3 3WW UK
PH: 44-0-1302-371791 FX: 44-0-1302-371791
questions@rpmrecords.uk.com
www.rpmrecords.uk.com
Online Indie CD/memorabilia shop. All genres.

Solarise Records
PO Box 31104, London, E16 4UE UK
PH: 44-0-7980-453628
info@solariserecords.com
www.solariserecords.com
Showcases, promotes and sells CDs online from any genre.

Stolenwine Records
52 Mainwaring Dr. Wilmslow, SK9 2QU UK
info@stolenwine.co.uk
www.stolenwine.co.uk
Indie record label. Sells CDs at a low cost.

Supertonic CDs
12 Cavendish Ave. St. Johns Wood, London, NW8 9JE UK
PH: 07968-199-617
sales@supertoniccds.com
supertoniccds.com
Giving musicians the opportunity to sell their music internationally.

tap into MUSIC
www.tapintomusic.com
Stocking the best music from independent record labels, artists and bands.

Ultimatemix
ultimatemix@gmail.com
www.ultimatemix.i12.com
Contact us about being on our "New Talent" section.

Zen Music
Moss Bridge Rd. Rochdale, OL16 5EA UK
FX: 01706-715795
Caroline Taylor sales@zenmusic.co.uk
www.zenmusic.co.uk
Join to produce your own album.

ZYX Music
11 Cambridge Ct. 210 Shepherd's Bush Rd.
Hammersmith, London, W6 7NL UK
PH: +44-207-371-6969 FX: +44-207-371-668
info@zyx.de
www.zyx.de
Supports Indie music of all genres.

Sign up for The Indie Contact Newsletter
www.indiebible.com

Australia
Promotional Services

Apollos Lounge
PO Box 366, Collins St. W. VIC 8007 Australia
PH: 0407-365-215 FX: 03-9642-2573
Richard O'Brien richard@apolloslounge.com
www.apolloslounge.com
*Consulting and assistance in developing and
promoting of artists and their works, through advice,
databases and all A & R aspects.*

Australian Music Biz
PO Box 30, Chermside South, QLD 4032 Australia
PH: 07-3854-0945 FX: 07-3854-0734
mail@musicbiz.com.au
www.musicbiz.com.au
Promotes local Indie labels on a national level.

NewSouthFolk
POB 328, Moruya, NSW 2537 Australia
PH: 61-2 -4-742736 FX: 61-2-44-742736
Jim MacQuarrie marmac@newsouthfolk.com.au
www.newsouthfolk.com.au
*A booking agency for Australian and overseas
artists.*

Vendors and Labels

Automatic Distribution
PO Box 26, S. Melbourne, VIC 3205 Australia
PH: 613-9352-7878 FX: 613-8610-1039
info@automaticdistribution.com
www.automaticdistribution.com
*Independent music distribution and online shop.
PLEASE no MP3s!*

The CAN
PO Box 99, Sassafras Gully, VIC 3787 3000
Australia
PH: 03-8662-4223
Jessie Malignaggi jessiem@thecan.com.au
www.thecan.com.au
*An online retail and distribution resource for
independent artists.*

CD Suite
14 Urquhart St., Hawthorn, VIC 3122 Australia
PH: +61398192954 FX: +61398192954
Nathan nathan@cdsuite.com
www.cdsuite.com
*Online CD store distributing albums by independent
artists. Get your album heard and distributed
internationally.*

digisounds.com
268B Domain Rd. South Yarra, VIC 3141 Australia
info@digisounds.com
www.digisounds.com
Allows bands to sell music to a global market.

Groovetracks Records
Steve Cole info@groovetracksrecords.com
www.groovetracksrecords.com
Boosts your sales through radio airplay & internet.

Modern World Records
PO Box 422, New Lambton, NSW 2305 Australia
Craig Mitchell modernworld@hunterlink.net.au
www.modernworld.com.au
Online catalogue for Australian Indie CDs.

One World Music
PO Box 396, Camperdown, NSW 1450 Australia
PH: 61-2-9565-4522 FX: 61-2-9565-5677
info@oneworldmusic.com.au
www.oneworldmusic.com.au
*Independent record label for Chill-Out/World Beat
genres.*

Pure Pop Records
PH: 03-9525-5066
info@purepop.com.au
www.purepop.com.au
Licenses and distributes Indie Pop CDs in Australia.

Africa

Merchant Records
PO Box 1508, Stellenbosch 7599, South Africa
PH/FX: +27-21-8802026
alan@merchantrecords.com
www.merchantrecords.com
*Record label and publishing house. Produces
international standard music in all styles and
genres.*

Asia

CDJam
2-18-1-501 Kusagae, Chuo-ku, Fukuoka,
810-0045, Japan
PH/FX: 81-92-716-8848
Jeffrey and Mutsumi Martin jeff@cdjam.jp
www.cdjam.jp
*Helps artists promote and sell their music in the
Japanese market. We not only will sell your music,
we also promote it to local media.*

Fish the Music
2-19-630 Mizusawa Miyamae, Kawasaki,
Kanagawa 216-0012 Japan
Yamamiya info@fishthemusic.com
fishthemusic.com
*Our "Artist's Explosion in Japan" package will help
you to get exposure for your music in Japan.*

RB Records
15-8-312 Sakuragaokacho Shibuya-ku,
Tokyo 150-0031 Japan
order@rb-records.com
www.rb-records.com
Mixture, Rapcore, Rapmetal.

Blues

Alligator Records
New Material, PO Box 60234, Chicago, IL 60660
info@allig.com
www.alligator.com
*We will NOT accept inquiries or phone calls
regarding the receipt or status of submissions. Also,
do not send song files. Send a CD with 4 songs max.*

Blue Skunk Music
3 Yorkshire Ct. South Elgin, IL 60177
Joe Rutan jrutan@blueskunkmusic.com
www.blueskunkmusic.com
*We encourage you to send us a press kit, including
audio samples of your group.*

Bluebeat Music
PO Box 1645, Boulder Creek, CA 95006-1645
PH/FX: 831-338-4784
www.bluebeatmusic.com
*We have one of the largest selections of Blues CDs
on the internet. Over 10,000 different Blues titles.*

The Blues Loft
14115 NE. 2nd St., Bellevue, WA 98007
PH: 888-780-0296
alawrence@jazzloft.com
www.jazzloft.com/bluesloft
Sell your Blues CD.

BluesandJazzSounds.com
134 Overlook St., Mt. Vernon, NY 10552
Bob Putignano info@bluesandjazzsounds.com
www.bluesandjazzsounds.com
*Pays attention to detail and dedicates itself to its
clients' success. We tailor each campaign to the
project's specific requirements and the client's
individual needs.*

CrossCut Records
PO Box 106524, 28065 Bremen, Germany
PH: +49-4748-8216-55 FX: +49-4748-8216-59
blues@crosscut.de
www.crosscut.de
*Our roster of artists is not limited to a certain Blues
style or region. Most importantly, we believe in
honest and heartfelt music.*

Crossroads Blues Agency
PO Box 10168, 7301 GD Apeldoorn,
The Netherlands
PH: 31-55-5214757 FX: 31-55-5787815
www.crossroads.nl
Specializes in European tours of Blues artists.

Silk City Records
PO Box 704, West Paterson, NJ 07424
PH: 973-599-0237 FX: 973-599-0236
Andy Allu silkcity@silkcitycd.com
www.silkcitycd.com
*Provides recordings of the finest quality Blues, Folk,
Jazz, New Age and Roots artists, both established
and emerging.*

Stony Plain Records
PO Box 861, Edmonton, AB T5J 2L8
PH: 780-468-6423 FX: 780-465-8941
info@stonyplainrecords.com
www.stonyplainrecords.com
Canada's prominent Roots music label.

Topcat Records
info@topcatrecords.com
topcatrecords.com
The primo Texas Blues Indie label.

Children's

Kids' CDs and Tapes
Old Bank Chambers, 43 Woodlands Rd.
Lytham St Annes, Lancashire, FY8 1DA UK
PH: 01253-731234
info@crs-records.com
www.kidsmusicshop.co.uk
Specialist producers of Children's music.

Kidsmusic
The Fairway, Bush Fair, Harlow, Essex,
CM18 6LY UK
PH: 44-01279-444707 FX: 44-01279-445570
Mike Kitson mike@cypmusic.co.uk
www.cypmusic.co.uk
Marketing and distribution of Children's audio.

Music for Little People
PO Box 1460, Redway, CA 95560
PH: 800-346-4445
customerservice@musicforlittlepeople.com
www.musicforlittlepeople.com
Producer of Children's music.

Music4Kids Online
220 SW. G St., Grants Pass, OR 97526
PH: 541-956-8600
mail@music4kids.com
www.music4kidsonline.com
Sells Children's Indie music.

Rabbit Ranch Records
PO Box 5020, Champaign, IL 61825
info@rabbitranch.com
www.rabbitranch.com
A Christian Children's music company.

Christian
Promotional Services

Black Gospel Promo
45 E. Cityline Ave. #303, Bala Cynwyd, PA 19004
PH: 215-883-1000 FX: 240-220-8694
info@blackgospelpromo.com
blackgospelpromo.com
The Gospels source for marketing & publicity.

The BuzzPlant
317 Main St. #205, Franklin, TN 37064
PH: 615-550-2305
info@buzzplant.com
www.buzzplant.com
Marketing and promotion for Christian music.

Cross Movements
PO Box 5620, Deptford, NJ 08096
PH: 856-728-0500 FX: 856-728-5757
store@crossmovementrecords.com
www.crossmovement.com
Accepts demos and sells Gospel CDs.

Divine Design Creative Services
PH: 403-286-1235
Denise Hill divinedesign@shaw.ca
www.divinepresskits.ca
Christian company offering administrative support for musicians including domain name research, custom website design and internet marketing services.

First Choice Management & Artist Development
16781 Chagrin #158, Shaker Heights, OH 44137
PH: 216-659-3710 FX: 208-723-3636
Martin Johnson martin@firstchoiceonline.com
www.firstchoiceonline.com
A full service artist management corporation specializing in artist development and promotion of Gospel and Christian artists.

Light It Up! Publicity
141 New Rd. #1J, Parsippany, NJ 07009
PH: 973-486-0867
Armando Triana armando@sparkpublicity.com
www.LightItUpPublicity.com
A Christian music publicity firm aimed at enhancing the exposure of its artists using all available print and online media outlets.

Prodigal Son Entertainment
115 Penn Warren Dr. #300, Box 145,
Brentwood, TN 37027
PH: 615-377-0057
www.prodigalson-entertainment.com
Artist management & development. Indie & signed mainstream and Christian (no Rap/Urban).

Worship Music Group
Marcia distribution@wmgmusic.com
www.wmgmusic.com
We have 3 core divisions: Worship music, Worship Urban and WMG Distribution. Since inception, WMG has expanded its outreach with a growing and diverse family of artists, encompassing genres from Rap to Inspirational, Praise and Worship.

Vendors and Labels

2BlessedMusic.com
Attn: Artist Demo, PO Box 110518, Palm Bay,
FL 32911
info@2blessedmusic.com
www.2blessedmusic.com
A diverse Christian/Gospel label. Please send 2 CDs along with press kit and promotional material to the above address.

Araunah Music
2 Oxley Square Rd. Gaithersburg, MD 20877
PH: 240-696-6051
www.araunah.com
A Christian label that produces, promotes and distributes the best Christian Indies.

Awake Music Group
659 Barking Rd. Plaistow, London, E13 9EX UK
PH: 011-44-8-821-9597
www.awakemusicgroup.com
We provide distribution services for The UK & Europe, to Christian recording artists.

blackgospelmusic.com
2628 N. 23rd St. #32, Philadelphia, PA 19132
PH: 215-227-5026 FX: 215-893-4321
webminister@blackgospel.com
www.blackgospel.com
Resources for the Black Gospel music community.

Blastbeats.com
PO Box 1018, Little Elm, TX 75068
PH: 972-668-2489 FX: 972-668-2487
staff@blastbeats.com
www.blastbeats.com
Indie/Underground Christian music.

Blue Duck Records
54 Pond St., East Bridgewater, MA 02333
PH: 508-345-0525
Jason Ronan blueduckrecords@aol.com
www.blueduckrecords.com
A Christian Indie label looking for talented Christian bands/artists to sign. Send a CD with a press kit/bio (must include lyrics) to the above address.

By Faith Records
PO Box 431647, Pontiac, MI 48343
PH: 313-531-3808 FX: 313-531-3808
Anthony Frazier contact@byfaithrecords.com
www.byfaithrecords.com
We provide spiritual uplifting through music.

Christian Concert Authority
2234 Ahu Niu Pl. Honolulu, HI 96821
FX: 406-622-3845
Karla@ccauthority.com
www.ccauthority.com
Sells Christian CDs (all genres) online.

ChristianDiscs.com
2705 S. Pike Ave. Allentown, PA 18103
service@christiandiscs.com
www.christiandiscs.com
Sells Indie and mainstream Christian CDs.

Con-Trad Music Group
9203 Hwy. 6 S. #124-163, Houston, TX 77083
PH: 281-558-6057
James Sayles jamess@contradrecords.com
www.contradrecords.com
Supports independent and Traditional Gospel music artists.

Crossing Music
1905 W. Charles St., Muncie, IN 47303
PH: 765-286-7231
customerservice@crossingmusic.com
www.crossingmusic.com
Import and independent Christian music.

Do Love Gospel Records
123 NW. 14th Way, #1, Dania, FL 33004
PH: 954-209-5313
D.L. Gilbert
DoLoveGospelRecords@EmailAccount.com
www.DoLoveGospelRecords.com
An independent Gospel label based in South Florida.

Gospel Artist Network
3913 Brainerd Rd. #106, Chattanooga, TN 37411
PH: 423-622-9867 FX: 423-622-9861
info@gospelartistnetwork.com
www.gospelmusicmart.com
A site developed for all Gospel and Christian artists.

Holy Hip Hop
PO Box 1023, Pine Lake, GA 30072
PH: 404-893-5752
globaldistribution@holyhiphop.com
holyhiphop.com
Production, distribution and marketing for Christian Hip Hop music.

independentbands.com
4316 Main St. #130, The Colony, TX 75056
bandrelations@independentbands.com
www.independentbands.com
Site and service for Christian Indie bands.

Indie Heaven
PO Box 1628, Franklin, TN 37065
Keith Mohr info@indieheaven.com
www.indieheaven.com
Site for all Indie Christian artists.

indievisionmusic.com
PO Box 6305, Laguna Niguel, CA 92607
info@indievisionmusic.com
www.indievisionmusic.com
Source for Indie Christian artists/music.

Jacob's Well Records
PO Box 21370, Minneapolis, MN 55421
PH: 612-208-0300 FX: 612-208-0301
David Coleman dave@jacobswellrecords.com
www.jacobswellrecords.com
Independent Contemporary Christian record label with major distribution.

New World Music Store
PO Box 1126, Lithonia, GA 30058
PH: 888-571-3949
www.neworldmusic.net
A positive music store and news to the Holy Hip Hop culture.

PasteMusic.com
PO Box 1606, Decatur, GA 30031
Jeremy Williams jeremy@pastemusic.com
www.pastemusic.com
Promotes lesser-known Indie musicians of all genres.

The PGE Label Group
PO Box 631001, Irving, TX 75063
PH: 877-447-2233 FX: 214-350-6249
info@pgedist.com
www.pgedist.com
African American Christian distributor.

RAD ROCKERS
PO Box 207, Milan, MI 48160
PH: 734-439-7029
customer.service@radrockers.com
www.radrockers.com
Mothership of hard to find Christian music.

RGM Records, Inc.
1304 Leafy Hollow Cir. Mt. Airy, MD 21771
PH: 301-351-4345 FX: 301-829-4057
Bruce Ferber bruce@recklessgrace.com
www.recklessgrace.com
Christian record company. Accepts demos.

Rock Solid Music
3779 154 A St., Surrey, BC V3S 0V4
PH: 604-628-2400
info@rocksolidmusic.com
www.rocksolidmusic.com
Contemporary Christian music of all styles.

The Shepherd's Nook
1794 Marion-Waldo Rd. Marion, OH 43302
PH: 740-389-4000 FX: 740-389-6601
Tom Hypes tom@theshepherdsnook.com
www.shopthenook.com
Carries Christian Indie CDs on consignment.

Spirit Music
Meadow House, Kingcombe Rd. Toller Porcorum,
Dorchester, DT2 0DG UK
PH: 01300-321564
info@spiritmusic.co.uk
www.spiritmusic.co.uk
Worldwide supplier of contemporary Christian music.

vineyardonline.com
5721 E. Virginia St., Evansville, IN 47715
PH: 800-578-7984 FX: 812-479-8805
info@vineyardonline.com
www.vineyardonline.com
Everything Christian.

worshipmusic.com
2432 W. Peoria Ave. #1182, Phoenix, AZ 85029
www.productsubmit.com
Before we can review your CD you must complete the easy steps of our submission process.

Wounded Records
1145 Stierley Rd. N., Wadesville, IN 47638
PH: 812-985-5969 FX: 812-985-5969
Bryant & Tonja woundedr@woundedrecords.com
www.woundedrecords.com
Accepting demos with a positive message. All genres. From recording to production of your project, including distro and promotion, we are here for you.

**Direct traffic to your website.
www.indielinkexchange.com/ile**

Classical

North America

United States

Centaur Records
136 St. Joseph St., Baton Rouge, LA 70802
PH: 225-336-4877 FX: 225-336-9678
info@centaurrecords.com
www.centaurrecords.com
Accepts unsolicited submissions of Classical material.

Cliff's Classics
mail@cliffsclassics.com
www.cliffsclassics.com
Supports independent Classical musicians.

Eroica Classical Recordings
4501-D Carpinteria Ave. Carpinteria, CA 93013
PH: 805-684-6140 FX: 805-745-1812
Larry A. Russell cds@eroica.com
www.eroica.com
Sells and distributes Indie Classical music CDs.

Ivory Classics
PO Box 341068, Columbus, OH 43234-1068
PH: 614-761-8709 FX: 614-761-9799
michaeldavis@ivoryclassics.com
www.IvoryClassics.com
Independent Classical record label devoted to pianists.

Jeffrey James Arts Consulting
45 Grant Ave. Farmingdale, NY 11735
PH/FX: 516-586-3433
jamesarts@worldnet.att.net
www.jamesarts.com
Management and PR for Classical artists.

Music & Arts
PO Box 771, Berkeley, CA 94701
PH: 510-525-4853 FX: 510-524-2111
info@musicandarts.com
www.musicandarts.com
Independent Classical and Jazz label.

New Albion Records
Box 25, Elizaville, NY 12523
PH: 415-621-5757 FX: 415-621-4711
ergo@newalbion.com
www.newalbion.com
Develops, records and releases for Indie artists.

Phoenix USA
200 Winston Dr. Cliffside Park, NJ 07010
PH: 201-224-8318 FX: 201-224-7968
sales@Phoenixcd.com
www.phoenixcd.com
A label for recent Classical music.

Wildboar Records
2430 Bancroft Way, Berkeley, CA 94704
PH: 510-849-0211 FX: 510-849-9214
wildboar@musicaloffering.com
www.musicaloffering.com
Independent Classical CD store/label.

Telarc
23307 Commerce Park Rd. Cleveland, OH 44122
PH: 216-464-2313
artists@telarc.com
www.telarc.com
Submit your demo to sell music here.

Canada

early-music.com
7753, rue Tellier, Montréal, QC H1L 2Z5
PH: 514-355-1825 FX: 514-355-5628
info@early-music.com
www.early-music.com
Providing an international marketplace for world-class professionals involved in all aspects of Early music.

Marquis Classics/Marquis Records
30 Kenilworth Ave. Toronto, ON M4L 3S3
PH: 416-690-7662 FX: 416-690-7346
info@marquisclassics.com
www.marquisclassics.com
Accepts submissions from independent musicians in several genres.

Europe

Denmark

Danacord Records
Norregade 22, DK-1165 Copenhage, Denmark
PH: 45-33-15-17-16 FX: 45-33-12-15-14
distribution@danacord.dk
www.danacord.dk
Independent Classical record label.

Germany

FARAO Classics
Schwere-Reiter-Str. 35 Gbd. 20, 80797 Munchen,
Germany
PH: 49-89-30777616 FX: 49-89-30777617
www.farao-classics.de
Founded by professional musicians for musicians!

Pink Tontraeger
Munstertaler Str. 23, D-79219 Stuafen im Breisgau,
Germany
PH: 7633-7265 FX: 7633-50441
info@pink-tontraeger.de
www.pink-tontraeger.de
Sells CDs of Classical Indie musicians.

Italy

Stradivarius
valeriaelli@stradivarius.it
www.stradivarius.it
The leading Italian Classical music label.

United Kingdom

Chandos
1 Commerce Pk, Commerce Way, Colchester,
Essex CO2 8HX UK
PH: 44-1206-225200 FX: 22-1206-225201
enquiries@chandos.net
www.chandos.net
Independent Classical record company.

Divine Art Record Company
8 The Beeches, E. Harlsey, N. Yorkshire,
DL6 2DJ UK
PH: 44-0-1609-882062
Stephen Sutton sales@divine-art.com
www.divine-art.com
We deal in Classical/Experimental/Nostalgia music.

Hyperion
PO Box 25, London, SE9 1AX UK
PH: 44-0-20-8318-1234 FX: 44-0-20-8463-1230
info@hyperion-records.co.uk
www.hyperion-records.co.uk
Independent Classical label.

METIER Records
127 Stanford Cottages, Semley, Dorset,
SP7 9AT UK
PH: 44-0-1747-830979 FX: 44-0-1747-830979
info@metierrecords.co.uk
www.metierrecords.co.uk
Independent, full service Classical label.

tutti.co.uk
18 Hillfield Park, London, N10 3QS UK
PH: 44-0-20-8444-8587
sell@tutti.co.uk
www.tutti.co.uk
Source for independent Classical labels. Sell your music.

Australia

Move Records
1 Linton St., Ivanhoe, VIC 3084 Australia
PH: 03-9497-3105 FX: 03-9497-4426
Martin Wright move@move.com.au
www.move.com.au
Classical and Jazz CD label with own studio with grand piano.

Asia

ArtPro Artist Management
10 Pa'amoni St. #23, Tel Aviv 62918 Israel
PH: 972-3-6046690 FX: 972-3-6043016
UriZur@ArtPro.co.il
www.artpro.co.il
All artists are represented exclusively and worldwide.

Naxos.com
Level 11, Cyberport 1, 100 Cyberport Rd.
Hong Kong
PH: 852-2760-7818 FX: 852-2760-1962
Customer.service@naxos.com
www.naxos.com
Selling and distribution of Classical Indie music.

Country

United States

Promotional Services

Honky Tonkin Music
2334 CR 2265, Telephone, TX 75488
PH: 903-664-3741 FX: 903-664-3741
info@honkytonkin.com
www.HonkyTonkin.com
We offer a wide variety of independent music.

Miranda Promotions
733 Ruth St., Prattville AL 36067
PH: 334-361-9060 FX: 334-361-9060
Miranda Leake miranda@mirandapromotions.net
www.mirandapromotions.net
Country and Gospel artist promotion and management. Radio distribution and bookings.

Payne County Line Promotions
3333 E. 68th St., Stillwater, OK 74074
Stan Moffat stan@paynecountyline.com
www.paynecountyline.com
We welcome all genres of music and accepts gladly your demos, press packets, band news, events etc.

Publicity House/Wildfire Publicity
PO Box 558, Smyrna, TN 37167
PH: 615-825-0019 FX: 760-437-4633
Laura Claffey wildfirepublicity@comcast.net
www.wildfirepublicity.net
We schedule interviews and coordinate CD reviews with e-zines, print magazines, newspapers etc.

Q-Note Productions
PO Box 462, Garden Valley, CA 95633
PH/FX: 530-333-1018
Cindy Hayden cindy@qnoteproductions.com
qnoteproductions.com
Publicity services for the touring artist including press and radio advance work, press release writing and launch. We also specialize in CD releases!

Red Haired Girl Publicity
PO Box 939, Cherryville, PA 18035-0939
PH: 484-221-1026
Liz Winchester publicity@yahoo.com
www.RHGPublicity.com
PR firm specializing in publicity for independent musicians and Indie labels in the Americana & Texas music formats.

so much MOORE media
1819 Tula Pace Rd. Pleasant View, TN 37146
PH: 615-746-3994 FX: 615-746-2073
Martha E. Moore martha@somuchmoore.com
www.somuchmoore.com
I am a full -time entertainment publicist working with Indie artists in Country, Alt-Country and Americana genres for 18 years.

Western Heart Promotions
4557 W. Bloomfield Rd. Glendale, AZ 85304
PH: 602-896-9910 FX: 602-896-9919
Gary Bradshaw gbradshaw3@cox.net
www.gbww.com
Promotions company primarily promoting Country music to foreign countries.

Vendors and Labels

AmericanaMusicplace.com
PO Box 5202, Concord, NC 28027-5202
PH: 704-788-6789
Bill Gamble gamco@goamericana.com
www.AmericanaMusicplace.com
Featuring Bluegrass, Gospel and Old-Time music.

Bloodshot Records
3039 W. Irving Park Rd. Chicago IL 60618
PH: 773-604-5300 FX: 773-604-5019
bshq@bloodshotrecords.com
www.bloodshotrecords.com
Insurgent Country label. We absolutely DO NOT accept demos from third party lawyers or promotion companies shopping stuff for clients.

BluegrassAmericana.com
PO Box 5202, Concord, NC 28027-5202
PH: 704-788-6789
submissions@GoAmericana.com
www.bluegrassamericana.com
The sounds and happenings of Bluegrass, Gospel and Old-Time music.

CountySales.com
PH: 540-745-2001 FX: 540-745-2008
info@countysales.com
www.countysales.com
World's largest selection of Bluegrass music.

Flat Earth Records
PO Box 30497, Indianapolis, IN 46230
info@flatearthrecords.com
www.flatearthrecords.com
Indie label with a focus on Twang.

Miles of Music
7306 Coldwater Canyon #9, North Hollywood,
CA 91605
PH: 818-765-8836 FX: 818-759-0336
info@milesofmusic.com
www.milesofmusic.com
More music to the gallon!

Old 97 Wrecords
1400 Lexington Ave. Greensboro, NC 27403
PH/FX: 336-275-7286
info@old97wrecords.com
www.old97wrecords.com
A cooperative label celebrating the diverse sounds of Southern String Band music.

Old-Time Music Home Page
20 Battery Park Ave. Asheville, NC 28801
PH: 828-285-8850 FX: 828-285-8851
david@lynchgraphics.com
www.oldtimemusic.com
Sells Old-Time (traditional Southern string band) music CDs.

Sound Stop Music
PO Box 57, Callaway, VA 24067
PH: 540-483-3373 FX: 540-483-0161
David Cannaday soundstopmusic@aol.com
www.soundstopmusic.com
Independent CD sales and publishing for Bluegrass artists.

Germany

Glitterhouse Records
Gruner Weg 25 D-37688 Beverungen, Germany
PH: 49-0-5273-36360 FX: 49-0-5273-363637
info@glitterhouse.com
www.glitterhouse.de
The ultimate Mail-order for Americana, Roots, Alternative and Folk CDs.

United Kingdom

Hotdisc
Friars Mount, Friars, Jedburgh, TD8 6BN Scotland
PH: +44 (0) 1835-864833 FX: +44 (0) 1835-864688
country@hotdisc.net
www.hotdisc.net
The leading promotional company for Country music in Europe.

Australia

NfS Publicity
PO Box 475, Morayfield, QLD 4506 Australia
PH: 07-5428-7167 FX: 07-5428-7168
nfs@nfspublicity.com.au
www.nfspublicity.com.au
Dedicated to the promotion of Country music in Australia.

Dance and Electronic

Promotional Services

masspool Dj Association
30 Revere Beach Pkwy. Revere, MA 02151
PH: 781-485-1901 FX: 781-485-1902
Gary Cannavo masspool@masspool.com
www.masspool.com
One of the most highly regarded DJ record pools in the US.

Vendors and Labels

Artificial Bliss Recordings
12 Lucas Gardens, Luton, Bedfordshire,
LU3 4BE UK
PH: +44-8708147752
Simon Curry info@artificialbliss.com
www.artificialbliss.com
An Electronic music based label and community focusing on innovation and creativity.

BangingTunes.com
28 Church Rd. Burgess Hill, W. Sussex,
RH15 9AE UK
PH: +44-1444-250251
info@BangingTunes.com
www.bangingtunes.com
The UK Dance music store.

Click Pop Records
1220 N. State St., Bellingham, WA 98225-5016
PH: 360-527-1150
Dave Richards dave@clickpoprecords.com
www.clickpoprecords.com
Specializing in Techno, House, Down Tempo and Alternative music.

Freestylemusic.com
18565 SW. 104th Ave. Miami, FL 33157
PH: 305-234-8033
freestylemusic@mailcity.com
www.freestylemusic.com
Distribution network for independent artists and DJs.

Haywire
Studio A. 21 John Campbell Rd. London,
N16 8JY UK
PH/FX: +44 (0) 20-7503 3921
Amanda Burton info@haywire.co.uk
www.haywire.co.uk
We deal with artist management, live bookings & events. We also offer ALL the info on the local music scene.

Knob Records
216 E. 29th St. #3A, New York, NY 10016
PH: 917-449-5250
DJ Style style@knobrecords.com
www.knobrecords.com
Underground Progressive, Tribal House, Trance and Breaks.

Nilaihah Records
Attn: Demo Submission,
PO Box 82614, Columbus, OH 43202
nilaihah@nilaihah.com
www.nilaihah.com
Indie record label for Dance music.

Nubreaks.Net.Label
Leninskiy pr./117, 198207 Saint-Petersburg,
Russian Federation
PH: +7(921)314-0822 FX: +7(921)314-0822
Galimzhan Begimov begimov@gmail.com
www.nubreaks.net
A home for Russian Breakbeat fresh and talented artists. We are proud to have released some of the Russian finest tunes/EPs and artist albums.

Phuture Sole Recordings
227 Madison Ave. Clifton, NJ 07011
PH/FX: 973-614-0302
Sweet Sarah SweetS@PhutureSoleRecordings.com
www.PhutureSoleRecordings.com
We are an independent label specializing in soulful House Dance music.

Real Estate Records
2544 W. North Ave. #2B, Chicago, IL 60647
PH: 773-862-9652 FX: 773-862-9662
Veronica Beckman info@elephanthaus.com
www.realestaterecords.com
Indie Electronic label.

Tweekin Records
593 Haight St., San Francisco, CA 94117
PH: 415-626-6995 FX: 415-626-5206
Manny m3@tweekin.com
www.tweekin.com
San Francisco's premiere Dance record store.

Ubiquity Records
70 Latham Ln. Berkeley, CA 94708
PH: 949-764-9012 FX: 949-764-9013
Andrew Jervis AndrewJ@ubiquityrecords.com
www.ubiquityrecords.com
Send demos by mail only. Do NOT send MP3s!

Web-Records.com
Im Vogelsang 17, 71101 Schonaich, Germany
PH: 0180-5-555-701 FX: 0180-5-555-702
info@web-records.com
web-records.com
World's biggest internet shop for Club music.

Experimental

Acids Musicks
PO Box 32552, Santa FE, NM 87594
Erik Bonner erik@acidsoxx.com
www.acidsoxx.com
Indie label specializing in bedroom-Rockstar Psychopop.

Arthropoda Records
1223 Wilshire Blvd., #812, Santa Monica,
CA 90403
PH: 310-930-0990 FX: 310-315-8273
Craig Garner craig@arthropodarecords.com
www.arthropodarecords.com
Record label promoting original thinking.

Artoffact Records
PO Box 68039, Winnipeg, MB R3L 2V9
demos@artoffact.com
www.artoffact.com
Releasing and promoting Electronic music sounds.

BiP_HOp webzine
BP 64, 13192 Marseille 20, France
PH: 33-0-491-64-89-15 FX: 33-0-491-64-89-15
ip@bip-hop.com
www.bip-hop.com
Label spreading unconventional sound adventures.

c367 Records
PO Box 771, Estill Springs, TN 37330
PH: 931-588-3109
www.c367.com
An Electronic music label focusing on Ambient and laid back Experimental music.

eurock.com
Archie Patterson apatters@eurock.com
www.eurock.com
Music retailer that sells Electronic, Progressive and Space music.

Forced Exposure
219 Medford St., Malden, MA 02148
FX: 781-321-0321
mailorder@forcedexposure.com
www.forcedexposure.com
Sells Experimental, Techno, IDM and more.

Frog Peak Music
PO Box 1052, Lebanon, NH 03755
PH: 603-643-9037 FX: 603-643-9037
fp@frogpeak.org
www.frogpeak.org
An artist-run composers' collective dedicated to producing Experimental and unusual works by its members.

Helmet Room Recordings
1227 Perry St., Denver, CO 80204
PH: 720-221-8370
Randall Frazier randall@helmetroom.com
www.helmetroom.com
Artist-owned label specializing in Psychedelic, Progressive, Experimental and Drone.

Hypnos
PO Box 6868, Portland, OR 97228
mg@hypnos.com
hypnos.com
Source for Ambient, Space and Experimental music.

The Infinite Sector
info@infinitesector.org
www.infinitesector.org
Sharing and promoting Experimental music, Noise and Electronica.

Joyful Noise
PO Box 20109, Indianapolis, IN 46220
Karl info@joyfulnoiserecordings.com
www.joyfulnoiserecordings.com
Spiritually focused Experimental/Noise/Improv label.

The Kitefishing Family
241 E. South Temple #4, Salt Lake City, UT 84111
PH: 801-637-2828
admin@kitefishingfamily.com
www.kitefishingfamily.com
Dedicated to the promotion of all forms of independent art.

Oddball Musicworks
315 Front St., Upper New York, NY 10960-1407
PH: 845-358-0497 FX: 845-358-0323
David dtp@oddballmusicworks.com
www.oddballmusicworks.com
Signs, produces and promotes artists that fall outside of the mainstream.

ping things *Canada*
rik@pingthings.com
www.pingthings.com
We sell CDs of Experimental and Electronic sounds.

Postdawn Nurseries Recordings
PO Box 1456, Alamogordo, NM 88311
PH: 505-434-3234
Christopher Maples postdawn@hotmail.com
postdawn.atspace.com
Ambient record label dealing in beautiful and strange, exotic electronics and atmospheric Soundscapes.

Postunder Records
19 Haruv St., Alfe Menashe 44851 Israel
PH: 972544346705
Yaron Eshkar postunder@postunder.net
www.postunder.net
An Electronic music label offering both online MP3 releases and CD releases.

Solnze Records
PH: +7-495-917-88-23
Oleg Tarasov info@solnzerecords.com
www.solnzerecords.com
Label/distributor/booking agency for unusual music that's not mainstream.

Sonic Arts Network
171 Union St., London, SE1 0LN UK
PH: 44-0-20-7928-7337 FX: 44-0-20-7928-7338
david@sonicartsnetwork.org
www.sonicartsnetwork.org
Worldwide events, education and information resource.

Squidco
160 Bennett Ave. #6K, New York, NY 10040
PH: 917-535-0265
sales@squidco.com
www.squidco.com
We sell Improvisational, Experimental, Progressive, RIO and otherwise unusual music.

sursumcorda.com
5115 Excelsior Blvd. #235, Minneapolis, MN 55416
FX: 612-677-3272
info@sursumcorda.com
www.sursumcorda.com
Promotes Experimental art and music.

SynGate.net
Eibenweg 10, 53894 Mechernich, Germany
PH: 49-2443-903609
Lothar Lubitz mail@syngate.net
www.syngate.net
The gate to Synthesizer based music.

Tract Records
PO Box 28705, Columbus, OH 43228-9998
Thomas Heath thomas@tractrecords.com
www.tractrecords.com
Label specializing in Underground Folk, Alt-Country and Experimental. We release compilations on a semi-yearly label. We accept demos.

Tzadik
200 E. 10th St. PMB 126, New York, NY 10003
info@tzadik.com
www.tzadik.com
Avant-garde and Experimental music.

Film and TV

ANOTHER League
5419 Hollywood Blvd. # C, PMB 708, Los Angeles, CA 90099-8112
music@anotherleague.com
www.anotherleague.com
We work hard to place your instrumental songs in television shows and movies. This is an equal split with you - 50/50. Absolutely NO VOCALS!

Cinecall Soundtracks
PO Box 854, Red Bank, NJ 07701
PH: 732-450-8882 FX: 732-450-8884
mail@cinecall.com
www.cinecall.com
Avenue for songwriters to be able to get their songs heard.

Countdown Entertainment
110 W. 26th St. 3rd Fl. New York, NY 10001-6805
PH: 212-645-3068 FX: 212-989-6459
CountdownEnt@netzero.net
www.CountdownEntertainment.com
International artist management & consultant firm.

Crucial Music
www.crucialmusic.com
Gives creators of original music a direct path to those important gatekeepers who place music in film, commercials and television shows.

dBE.Music
info@digitalbear.com
www.dbemusic.com
Specializes in placement of Indie music in TV, film, advertising and other sound for picture uses.

dittybase
#102, 31 Bastion Sq. Victoria, BC V8W 1J1
PH: 250-381-8780 FX: 250-384-6761
sales@dittybase.com
www.dittybase.com
Helps music directors find the perfect track for any project.

Filmtracks
Christian Clemmensen tyderian@filmtracks.com
www.filmtracks.com
Get the score ...the true orchestral magic of Film music.

FlightSafe Music
Attn: Music Submission,
4621 Sandalwood Dr. Pleasanton, CA 94588
info@flightsafemusic.com
www.flightsafemusic.com
Generates music synchronization licenses for placement in films, documentaries, commercials and TV shows.

Fresh Sounds Music Competition
c/o Dreaming Tree Films, 1807 W. Sunnyside Ave. #2E, Chicago, IL 60640
www.fresh-films.com
A music platform to uncover local independent music talent across the nation.

Goodnight Kiss Music
10153½ Riverside Dr. #239, Toluca Lake, CA 91602
PH: 831-479-9993
www.goodnightkiss.com
You MUST be a subscriber to our newsletter before you do anything else. If you send in your music without your assigned "code" it will be thrown away.

Indie Film Composers
PH/FX: 208-730-8713
indifilm@earthlink.net
www.indifilm.com
Subcontracts compositions out to our worldwide affiliates.

Indy Hits
PO Box 4102, Hollywood, CA 90078
PH: 323-276-1000 FX: 323-276-1001
info@bandpromote.com
www.indyhits.com
Working with unsigned bands helping to secure record/publishing deals and film/TV placements.

INgrooves
539 Bryant St. #405, San Francisco, CA 94107
PH: 415-896-2100
info@ingrooves.com
www.ingrooves.com
Works with Indie artists and labels to license your music to the TV & film industry.

J2R Music
471 Old Eagle School Rd. Wayne, PA 19087
PH: 610-687-3553
info@j2rmusic.com
www.j2rmusic.com
Supplies high quality original music to clients in network and cable television and feature film production.

Jetset Sound
PH: 925-586-6877
victor@jetsetsound.com
www.jetsetsound.com
Specializes in ongoing film and television music licensing of extremely talented, as yet unknown artists.

LoveCat Music
PO Box 548, Ansonia Stn. New York, NY 10023-0548
FX: 212-874-2888
info@lovecatmusic.com
www.lovecatmusic.com
We offer film & TV placements, licensing and more.

Luke Hits
137 N. Larchmont Blvd. #555, Los Angeles, CA 90004
PH: 310-236-5853
andrea1@lukehits.com
lukehits.com
Links bands with high profile film/TV projects. Please READ our online demo submission policy BEFORE you send in your music.

Mother West *The Vault*
37 W. 20th St. #1006, New York, NY 10011
PH: 212-807-0405 FX: 212-741-7688
thevault@motherwest.com
motherwest.com
A vast music licensing library.

MovieMusicBank.com
465 S. Orange Ave. #212, Maitland, FL 32751
PH: 888-700-2463
info@moviemusicbank.com
www.moviemusicbank.com
A bridge between artists and film makers, TV producers and advertising directors.

The Music Broker Network
The Studio, Homefield Ct. Marston Magna, BA22 8DJ UK
support@themusicbroker.net
www.themusicbroker.net
Pitches unsigned bands, artists & songwriters to labels, publishers and film/TV studios.

Noteborn Music

PO Box 8171, Ann Arbor, MI 48107-8171
info@notebornmusic.com
www.notebornmusic.com
We hand pick quality music for use in movies, TV shows, advertising campaigns and for music producers. If you do not have a Sonicbids membership, your submission can be mailed ($15 per submission/3 songs).

Position Soundtrack Services

PO Box 25907, Los Angeles, CA 90025
PH: 310-442-8170 FX: 310-442-8180
Tyler Bacon tyler@positionmusic.com
www.positionmusic.com
Represents artists for the placement of their music in film, television, soundtrack albums, advertising and video games.

Pump Audio

Box 458, Trivoli, NY 12583
artists@pumpaudio.com
www.pumpaudio.com
We license your music to TV, film and advertising.

Rumblefish

919 SW. Taylor St. #300, Portland, OR 97205
PH: 503-248-0706 FX: 503-248-0714
www.rumblefish.com
We handpick music from all over the world, across all genres for our catalog. Our artist-members' songs are pre-cleared and ready to license for film, TV, internet, corporate, even samples and beats.

Song and Film

Josh Zandman josh@songandfilm.com
www.songandfilm.com
Leading music placement company for film and TV.

SongCatalog

Can: 200-23 W. Pender St., Vancouver,
BC V6B 6E3
PH: 604-642-2888 FX: 604-642-2889
US: 6255 Sunset Blvd. #1024, Hollywood,
CA 90028
PH: 310-272-6960
info@songcatalog.com
www.songcatalog.com
Music management, marketing and licensing initiatives.

SongLink

23 Belsize Cr. London, NW3 5QY UK
PH: 44-0-207-794-2540 FX: 44-0-207-794-7393
www.songlink.com
Music contacts across the globe.

TAXI

PH: 800-458-2111
www.taxi.com
Record and publishing deals, film & TV placement.

Toryumon

22 Upper Grosvenor St., London, W1K 7PE UK
PH/FX: +44 (0) 20-7495 3885
artistinfo@toryumon.co.uk
www.toryumon.co.uk
Has licensed music for adverts fashion shows, film soundtracks and virtual online DJ mixing.

Transition Music Corporation

11288 Ventura Blvd. #709, Studio City, CA 91604
PH: 323-860-7074 FX: 323-860-7986
info@transitionmusic.com
www.transitionmusic.com
We have successfully published more first-time writers (without record deals) than any other publisher. Please visit our website for submission details.

TruSonic

7825 Fay Ave. Ste. LL-A, La Jolla, CA 92037
PH: 858-362-2323 FX: 858-362-2324
artistsupport@trusonic.com
www.trusonic.com
Music and messaging service used by various businesses. We're always on the lookout for fresh upcoming acts with artistic vision and control of their own content.

Tunetrader

PO Box 647, Portsmouth, PO1 2ZT UK
PH: +44-845-2262162 (UK)
PH: 727-736-4755 (US)
Nick Hooper enquiries@tunetrader.com
www.tunetrader.com
Platform for independent artists to promote their music towards placement in film, television and advertising.

VersusMedia

556 S. Fair Oaks Ave. #245, Pasadena, CA 91105
PH: 877-633-8764 FX: 323-375-0430
www.versusmedia.com
Provider of publicity services and film music networking opportunities.

Folk

Acoustic Music Resource

PO Box 3518, Seal Beach, CA 90740
PH: 562-431-1608 FX: 562-598-5928
www.acousticmusicresource.com
For most of the titles we list here, this is the only place you will ever find them!

Camsco Music

28 Powell St., Greenwich, CT 06831
PH: 800-548-3655
dick@camsco.com
www.camsco.com
Your single source for all Folk recordings.

Crow & Wolf Music

911 Central Ave. Albany, NY 12206
PH: 866-544-4129
William Feagin info@crowolfmusic.com
www.crowolfmusic.com
Online Folk and World music shop. Buy and sell your music with us. New and independent artists and old time favorites.

Desert Highway Records

1015 Gayley Ave. #1115, Los Angeles, CA 90024
info@deserthighwayrecords.com
deserthighwayradio.com
America needs its Roots music and it probably needs your music.

DIG Music

1831 V St., Sacramento, CA 95818
PH: 916-442-5344 FX: 916-442-5382
Ben Lefever ben@digmusic.com
www.digmusic.com
Independent record label and artist management company. AAA, Roots/Americana, Singer/Songwriter.

efolk Music

201B N. Greensboro St., Carrboro, NC 27510
PH: 919-968-4810
Chris Frank chris@efolkMusic.org
www.efolkmusic.org
Making Indie music available to the world.

FOLK TRAX *Australia*

manager@folktrax.com
www.folktrax.com
If you have Acoustic music related merchandise that you are prepared to consign to us, we will offer it for sale on our site.

Folkadelica Booking Agency

2 Northwood Ter. Haverhill, MA 01830
PH: 978-373-9199 FX: 978-373-9359
Shawna Torres Shawna@folkadelica.com
folkadelica.com
Representing exceptional contemporary artists from Americana, Bluegrass, Folk, Roots and beyond.

FolkWeb

95 Kidder Ave. Somerville, MA 02144
PH: 617-497-2096 FX: 617-497-2116
Karen LeCompte karen@folkweb.com
folkweb.com
Selling Indie music to a larger audience.

Green Linnet

PO Box 1905, Danbury, CT 06813
PH: 203-730-0333 FX: 203-778-4443
webmaster@greenlinnet.com
www.greenlinnet.com
Promotes new Celtic music.

Trad&Now Music Shop

PO Box 532, Woy Woy, NSW 2256 Australia
PH: +61-2-4325-7369 FX: +61-2-4325-7362
info@tradandnow.com
www.tradandnow.com/shopping
Supporting independent creativity.

tradmusic.com

Ellangowan House, Cunninghame Ter. Newton Stewart, Dumfries & Galloway, Scotland
DG8 6DY UK
PH: 01671-401363
sales@tradmusic.com
www.tradmusic.com
Promotes traditional music artists throughout the world.

Village Records

PO Box 3216, Shawnee, KS 66203
PH: 913-631-4199 FX: 913-631-6369
sales@villagerecords.com
villagerecords.com
Folk discs, special orders, independent labels and more.

GLBT

Centaur Music

45 Main S. #707, Brooklyn, NY 11201
PH: 718-852-6777 FX: 718-852-8877
info@centaurmusic.com
www.centaurmusic.com
Our products are sold in stores across the U.S and Canada, from independent record stores to major chains.

Chainsaw Records

PO Box 11384, Portland, OR 97211
info@chainsaw.com
www.chainsaw.com
Queer/girl friendly record label.

Gay-MART Music Shop

1148 Davie St., Vancouver, BC V6E 1N1
PH: 604-681-3262 FX: 604-681-9397
info@gaymart.com
www.gaymart.com/shopmusc/shopmusc.html
A wide collection of music CDs by gay and lesbian artists.

StoneWall Society
info@stonewallsociety.com
www.stonewallsociety.com
Presents a place to sell and buy GLBT music and art. Submissions reviewed in the StoneWall Society E-newsletter.

Woobie Bear Music
woobiebearmusic@adelphia.net
www.woobiebearmusic.com
Features music by bears, music for bears. The latest news, reviews and happenings.

Goth
Promotional Services

Carpe Diem Promotions
Elizabeth Maycox carpediempromo@yahoo.co.uk
www.myspace.com/carpediempromotions
A free international promotion service for underground & unsigned bands/record labels/zines etc.

Darkcell Digital Music
www.darkcelldigitalmusic.net
Designed to provide Dark music artists with a wide range of release options as possible to sell and profile their music.

Raven Entertainment Promotions
Heather Burke
admin@ravenentertainmentpromotions.com
ravenentertainmentpromotions.com
Your success will be achieved more easily because we guide you every step of the way up the ladder to stardom.

Vendors and Labels

13thTrack.com
2351 S. Shore Cn. PO Box 141, Alameda, CA 94501-5723
Mark Harvey reviews@13thTrack.com
www.13thtrack.com
Carries all Halloween related music.

Alfa Matrix
90 rue Charles Degroux, 1040 Brussels, Belgium
PH/FX: 0032-2-732-14-81
info@alfa-matrix.com
www.alfa-matrix.com
We have become a trademark for innovative Electronic music.

DSBP *(Ditch Sex Buy Product)*
237 Cagua NE., Albuquerque, NM 87108
PH: 505-266-8274
dsbp@dsbp.cx
www.dsbp.cx
America's Hard Elektro / Harsh Industrial label.

Final Joy Records
392 E. Harrison St. Chandler, AZ 85225
info@finaljoyrecords.com
www.finaljoyrecords.com
We specialize in Gothic music. Send us your demo!

Gore Galore
12 Madison Ave. Evansville, IN 47713
PH: 812-424-5220 FX: 309-410-2893
info@gore-galore.com
www.gore-galore.com
Submit your music for review.

IsoTank
526 S. 5th St., Philadelphia, PA 19147
PH: 215-861-0313 FX: 215-925-9075
isotank@aol.com
www2.mailordercentral.com/isotank
CDs, videos and merchandise.

Latex Records
5857 Brookstone Walk, Acworth, GA 30101-8473
E. Minzenmayer latex@latexrecords.com
latexrecords.com
Specializing in Goth/Industrial and related genres.

Metropolis Records
PO Box 54307, Philadelphia, PA 19105
PH: 610-595-9940 FX: 610-595-9944
label@metropolis-records.com
www.metropolis-records.com
Home to Industrial, Gothic and Electronic artists.

MONSTAAR Records
1345 W. North Shore Ave. Chicago, IL 60626
PH: 773-343-9337
monstaar.com
Purveyors of Noise, Experimental, Darkwave, Goth and other cruel & unusual music.

Musicwerks
612 E. Pine St., Seattle, WA 98122
PH: 206-320-8933
musicwerks@musicwerks.org
www.musicwerks.org
Complete selection of Gothic and Industrial CDs.

Planet Mu
PO Box 276, Worcester, WR5 2XJ UK
Mike Paradinas mike@planet-mu.com
www.planet-mu.com
Exposure for new and already established musicians.

Shocklines
Matt Schwartz help@shocklines.com
shocklines.stores.yahoo.net
If you do horror music, we'd love to sell it.

Tetragram Records
31 S. McLean Blvd. #16, Memphis, TN 38104
PH: 901-219-5509
Dennis Sawyer dennis@tetragramrecords.com
www.tetragramrecords.com
Artist services and consulting covering the darker side of Indie. All genres with emphasis on Heavy Metal, Gothic, Industrial, Psychobilly, Hellbilly, Darkwave and Alternative.

Van Richter Records
100 S. Sunrise Way #219, Palm Springs, CA 92262
PH: 415-235-3373
manager@vr.dv8.net
www.vanrichter.net
Your Aggro-Industrial record label!

Vinema Records
PO Box 12228, Spring, TX 77391-2228
Chris demo@vinema.com
www.vinemarecords.com/contact.html
E-mail us a link where we can listen to your music.

Hip Hop
Promotional Services

211 Records
28112 Grant St., Saint Clair Shores, MI 48081
PH: 313-308-6071
J-Bone, Rich, or Gosty
mike@crossfireentertainment.com
www.211records.com
Recording, promotions, booking, production, marketing and more!

215 Execs Entertainment Consulting and Management
PO Box 4032, Capital Heights, MD 20743-9998
G. Mookie McClary gmcclary@215execs.com
www.215execs.com
Music consulting and management firm. Rap is something you do. Hip Hop is something you live!

4oNe1
info@4oNe1.info
www.4oNe1.info
Specializing in Urban marketing, distribution & syndication.

Bring Em Out Entertainment
13141 Rittenhouse Dr. Midlothian, VA 23112
PH: 804-601-2430
info@bring-em-out.com
www.bring-em-out.com
Specializing in marketing, promotions, management, event planning and public relations.

Buzzin' Bee Entertainment
3833 W. Ave. 42, #117, Los Angeles, CA 90065
PH: 323-381-0000
Monica "MoniBee" Busby info@thebuzzinbee.com
www.thebuzzinbee.com
All aspects of guerilla brand marketing, promotions, public relations, event planning/management and bookings.

C.E.D Entertainment Distribution
1035 S. Semoran Blvd. #1049, Winter Park, FL 32792
PH: 407-679-6900 FX: 407-679-6901
review.dept@cedentertainment.com
www.cedentertainment.com
We can offer distribution deals to labels who are promoting their CD but don't have national or regional distribution.

Crazy Pinoy
PO Box 46999, Seattle, WA 98146
PH: 206-860-4052
Gene Dexter Hiphop206@aol.com
www.CrazyPinoy.com
I can write and implement a national marketing plan, help create an artist's image and consult on their material, look and sound.

Cream Music Consultants
PO Box 416, Brice, OH 43109
PH: 614-579-6150 FX: 614-863-4953
Pamela Bennington creammusicgroup@yahoo.com
www.creammusicgroup.com
Consulting, career development, demo-shopping, artist management and promotions. Hip Hop, R&B, Gospel, Reggae and Pop.

Cwood56
4259 Macedo Pl. Santa Clara, CA 94035
PH: 408-230-9897 FX: 408-988-8833
Chris Underwood chrisunderwood@cwood56.com
www.Cwood56.com
We provide professional management and marketing to Hip Hop artists and producers.

djizm.com
PH/FX: 206-984-4357
info@djizm.com
We'll submit your single to our digital record pool consisting of DJs, radio and magazines that like to break new artists.

Heavyweights Record Pool
14731 Manecita Dr. La Mirada, CA 90638
PH: 888-998-2041
Truly OdD heavyweightsent@aol.com
www.heavyweights.org
An outlet for labels trying to get their records to the most predominant DJs who actually will play and promote your records.

HomeBase Promotions
PO Box 680784, San Antonio, TX 78268
PH: 210-764-4760 FX: 210-764-4761
Takeyla Calhoun
takeyla@homebasepromotions.com
www.homebasepromotions.com
Promotions company providing profile listings, press releases, reviews and event management. Specializing in Hip Hop/R&B music genres.

IndieStreet Entertainment
rico@indiestreetent.com
www.indiestreetent.com
Provides a platform and opportunities to gain experience, exposure and knowledge. Our magazine features articles, photo galleries, music, interviews and event coverage.

Last Word
7812 Waterford Lakes Dr. #1226, Charlotte, NC 28210
PH: 704-493-6499
Mehka (Mecca) mehka_1@hotmail.com
www.lastwordonline.com
We offer services such as press release distribution, business plans or publicity.

Q-York Entertainment
1133 Justin Ave. Ste 121, Glendale, CA 91201
PH: 917-567-4622 FX: 718-529-2900
Steven Yassin contact@q-york.com
www.q-york.com
Hip Hop artists, music, videos, online store.

Richh Kiddz Entertainment
1st Ave. at Port Imperial #1202, West New York, NJ 07093
PH: 404-394-0365 FX: 201-430-3842
Russ Downs promotions@richhkiddz.com
www.richhkiddz.com
A multifaceted entertainment and marketing company. We help develop, expose and manage independent artists who take the business of music seriously.

shocksoundpromotions.com
3840 E. Robinson Rd. #200, Amherst, NY 14228
PH: 716-578-0097
shocksoundpromo@yahoo.com
www.shocksoundpromotions.com
Promoting urban recording artists, events and products.

Vendors and Labels

United States

3A Records
PO Box 29593, Denver, CO 80229
hiphop3a@hiphop3a.com
www.hiphop3a.com
Helping artists produce their full talent.

A-N-B Records Inc.
12 Iroqios Dr. Galloway, NJ 08205
PH: 609-673-0277
info@anbrecords.com
www.anbrecords.com
R&B/Hip Hop independent record label.

ATAK Distribution
PO Box 1027, La Canada, CA 91012-1027
PH: 626-398-3229
www.truehiphop.com
Send a copy of whatever you want ATAK to sell. If it's the dopest thing EVER, it's in the catalog. If it's doo-doo, you might not ever hear from us again.

basically-hiphop
Max maxjeromeo@basically-hiphop.com
basically-hiphop.com
Playing Underground and mainstream Hip Hop.

Block Party Records
320 N. Canon Dr. Beverly Hills, CA 90210
PH: 310 927-9666 FX: 310 492-6111
Tony Hicks tony@blockpartyrecords.com
www.blockpartyrecords.com
Reviews all Hip Hop/Rap music of unsigned artists.

Boundless NY
143 Roebling St. 1B, Brooklyn, NY 11211
PH: 718-821-9690 FX: 718-821-7881
info@boundlessny.com
boundlessny.com
Promotes independent Hip Hop artists.

Brick Records
PO Box 281, Boston, MA 02117
PH: 888-513-3998
www.brickrecords.com
An independent Hip Hop record label.

Cellar Noise
CellarNoise902@aol.com
www.cellarnoise.com
We will gladly sell your CDs, mix-tapes, vinyl and videos.

DJcity.com
4041 Sepulveda Blvd. Culver City, CA 90230
PH: 310-737-9200 FX: 801-340-7618
info@djcity.com
www.djcity.com
We specialize in both the party-jammin' major label Hip Hop and R&B, as well as all the underground label cuts blowin' up round the corner.

freshntasty.com
1131 W. Warren #239 Detroit, MI 48201
PH: 313-407-6507
David Pittman dave@freshntasty.com
www.freshntasty.com
An online store specializing in independent Urban music.

FTB Records
Cato Kelly khato@ftbrecords.com
www.ftbrecords.com
Our goal and mission is to promote and give exposure to musicians and models all over the world. To find the best music from unsigned artist, DJ's, producers or independent record labels.

Get Real Records
PH: 803-652-8994
Marc Myers getreal@get-real-records.com
www.get-real-records.com
We help Hip Hop artists promote and distribute their music.

HeadBOB
130 Webster St. #105, Oakland, CA 94607
musician@headbob.com
www.headbob.com
Provides completely free distribution with artists receiving all of the royalties.

Headquarters Records
PMB 141, #102, 2200 Wilson Blvd. Arlington, VA 22201
PH: 703-912-1720 FX: 703-995-4913
Al Clipper ac@headquartersrecords.com
www.headquartersrecords.com
All about positive vibes that are not offensive.

JaThom Records
PO Box 1579, New York, NY 10025
J.Minor justthemusic@att.net
www.jathomrecords.netfirms.com
Label and distributor that specializes in working with independent artists.

K.O. Kid Records
Nick Macaluso nick@kokidrecords.com
www.kokidrecords.com
We offer the newest up and coming knock out artists in the Hip Hop, Rap and R&B scene.

Licorich Record$
PH: 818-687-8990
Jay Plot jayplot@licorichrecords.com
www.licorichrecords.com
Label that sells and promotes the hottest Hip Hop. Always accepting demos!

Mic Master Records
PO Box 1671, Clementon, NJ 08021
PH: 732-277-2169
Juan Aponte donjuan@micmasterrecords.com
www.micmasterrecords.com
Booking agent and independent label.

Noc On Wood Records
300 Fairview Ave. N., Seattle, WA 98109
PH: 800-253-8009
noconwood@noconwood.com
www.noconwood.com
A new breed of record label run by a team of smart, enterprising young executives.

Nomadic Wax
486 Jefferson Ave. Brooklyn, NY 11221
info@nomadicwax.com
www.nomadicwax.com
African and international Hip Hop production company and label.

Red Brick Records
807 N. Salina, Syracuse, NY 13208
PH: 315-476-8703
mchilds2@twcny.rr.com
www.redbrickrecords.com
Helps all Indie Hip Hop artists.

R.H.R. Real Hip-Hop Records
PH: 410-718-5265
Benito Brewer rhr@realhiphoprecords.com
www.realhiphoprecords.com
When we say independent we mean independent!

Rotation Music Entertainment
Attn: A&R, PO Box 4807, Laguna Beach CA 92652
PH: 949-510-3188
sales@rotationmusic.com
www.rotationmusic.com
Send your demos to this Indie Hip Hop label.

Sandbox Automatic
245 W. 29th St. 9th Fl. New York, NY 10001
Attn: Submissions
sandbox@pobox.com
www.sandboxautomatic.com
We will check your stuff out and if we are interested, we will contact you back with more instructions. You do not need to follow up on your submission request.

Starfleet Music Pool
3521 Mallard Cove Ct. Charlotte, NC 28269
PH: 704-599-6645 FX: 704-599-1863
Ronnie Matthews rmatthews@starfleetmusic.com
www.starfleetmusic.com
Helping labels break their new releases in every night club in every city that Starfleet covers!

StatiQ Records
11221 Grouse Ln. Hagerstwon, MD 21742
PH: 301-992-9889
Natasha A. Smith-Hazzard, COO/Publicist
tasha@statiqrecords.ws
www.statiqrecords.ws
Underground Hip Hop & Latino music. Video production, publishing and publicity.

Stones Throw Records
2658 Griffith Park Blvd. #504, Los Angeles, CA 90039-2520
info@stonesthrow.com
www.stonesthrow.com
Indie record label. Calendar, news, sell CDs etc.

Support Online Hip Hop
www.sohh.com
Hip Hop news, reviews, online sales and more.

UndagroundArtists
PO Box 260435, Queens, NY 11426-0435
Attn: Judge Mental
PH: 877-320-1938
info@undagroundartists.com
www.undagroundartists.com
Showcasing solid Indie Hip Hop talent.

UndergroundHipHop.com
PH: 617-364-4900
www.undergroundhiphop.com
Do NOT mail us your CD. Read our online submission policy, then send us an E-MAIL with all the information that we request.

Urban Ikon
Box 953, Dept. IB06, Wingdale, NY 12594
David urbanikon@aol.com
www.urbanikon.com
We supply every major chain store and thousands of mom-and-pop stores across the United States directly and through our one-stop distribution partners We're looking for new artists to sign. For consideration, mail a demo CD with a minimum of 4 original songs to the address above.

UrbanMelodies.com
9175 Kiefer Blvd. #249, Sacramento, CA 95828
PH: 916-265-5662 FX: 916-265-5662
info@urbanmelodies.com
www.urbanmelodies.com
We are a normal music store, with the exception that we NEVER close. We focus on six specific genres: Rap/Hip Hop, R&B, Gospel, Jazz/Blues, Spoken Word and Reggae.

Vocal Graffiti Records
PO Box 746, Red Bank, NJ 07701
PH: 908-693-4247 FX: 310-229-5313
DJ New York City Ken djnycken@vocalgraffiti.com
www.vocalgraffiti.com
Formed in by industry professionals who realized the need for a true representation of independent Hip Hop culture on the net.

Canada

Battleaxe Records
www.battleaxerecords.com
Canadian Indie record company searching for artists.

Camobear Records
21646-1424 Commercial Dr. Vancouver, BC V5l 3X9
info@camobear.ca
www.camobear.ca
An Indie record label distributing Hip Hop music to the people. We also book Hip Hop shows in the Vancouver area.

Germany

Rap.de
Blücherstr. 22, 10961 Berlin, Germany
PH: 030-695-972-10 FX: 030-695-972-40
Mischa Wetzel wetzel@styleheads.de
www.rap.de
Magazine, events calendar, online store & more.

The Netherlands

recordbuddy.com
Stationstraat 10, 9711 AS Groningen, The Netherlands
PH: +31628336304
info@recordbuddy.com
www.recordbuddy.com
Our aim is to support the upcoming talents by selling CDs / tapes / LPs of Hip Hop talents.

Switzerland

hiphopstore.ch
General Guisan-Str.1 Ch-5000 Aarau, Switzerland
PH: 41-62-834-40-00 FX: 41-62-834-40-09
info@hiphopstore.ch
www.hiphopstore.ch
Online distribution of Indie CDs.

United Kingdom

benzull1972
26 Well St., Great Yarmouth, Norfolk, NR30 1ER UK
PH: 07833337316
Benny Edgar benjamin.edgar1@ntlworld.com
www.benzull1972.com
Fast service with cheap prices on new DVDs and UK Hip Hop. We also promote new bands in the UK.

Rap and Soul Mail Order
PO Box 37163, London, E4 7WR UK
PH: 020-8523-9578 FX: 020-8523-9601
james@rapandsoulmailorder.com
www.rapandsoulmailorder.com
Will sell your CD online for a low cost.

Jam Band

Harmonized Records
6520 Oak Grove Church Rd. Mebane, NC 27302
PH: 919-304-9931
Brian Asplin asplin@homegrownmusic.net
www.harmonizedrecords.com
Our goal is to team up with talented hard-working musicians and help them build their careers through a realistic record label/artist relationship.

Home Grown Music Network
PO Box 340, Mebane, MN 27302
PH: 919-563-4923
leeway@homegrownmusic.net
www.homegrownmusic.net
Promotes the best Indie music being made today.

Sunshine Daydream CDs & Gifts
2027 E. Euclid Ave. Mt. Prospect, IL 60056
PH: 847-299-2622
Mark Paradise sales@sunshinedaydream.biz
www.sunshinedaydream.biz
New & used CD retail store that specializes in Jam Band music.

Jazz

4 on 6 Media
58 Karee Ct., South Kingstown, RI 02879
FX: 401-633-6376
music4on6@yahoo.com
www.4on6.com
Promotes independent Jazz musicians.

AppleJazz
10825 Wheaton Ct. Orlando, FL 32821
PH: 888-241-2464
info@applejazz.com
www.applejazz.com
Offering online sales of Jazz CDs for Indie artists.

Counterpoint Music
PO Box 25093, Fresno, CA 93729-5093
PH: 559-225-7801 FX: 559-225-7801
info@counterpoint-music.com
www.counterpoint-music.com
Specialists in Jazz CDs!

InterJazz
9 Ridge Way, Purdys, NY 10578
PH: 914-277-7775
support@interjazz.com
www.interjazz.com
Your online connection to everything Jazz.

Jazz CD Promotional Campaign
8947 Washington Ave. Jacksonville, FL 32208
PH: 904-264-4642 FX: 904-264-4667
Rachelle Bivins mailbox@abyssjazz.com
www.abyssjazz.com
A 12-month marketing tool offering just about everything an independent Jazz artist needs to kick start their promotion.

The Jazz Loft
PO Box 3454, Bellevue, WA 98009
PH: 425-646-6406 FX: 206-418-6551
info@jazzloft.com
www.jazzloft.com
Your online resource for truly independent Jazz!

Jazz Now Direct
PO Box 19266, Oakland, CA 94619-0266
PH: 510-531-9249
jazznow@sbcglobal.net
www.jazznow.com/jnd
Great independently produced music.

Jazzconnect.com
PH: 800-866-9068
www.jazzconnect.com
Websites, CD store, new releases and artist spotlights.

JAZZCORNER.com
245 W. 25th St., New York, NY 10001
lois@jazzcorner.com
www.jazzcorner.com
News, reviews, interviews, web hosting.

Kari-On Productions
PO Box 436, Evans, GA 30809
PH: 706-294-9996 FX: 706-210-9453
Kari Gaffney karionprod@knology.net
www.karigaffney.com/publicity.html
Publicity agency that represents, Jazz, Blues and World artists to obtain reviews in music publications.

Maximum Music
435 W. Hastings St., Vancouver, BC V6B 1L4
PH: 604-915-5356 FX: 604-915-9736
David Milner david.milner@maxmusic.ca
www.maxmusic.ca
An Indie record label with a strong roster of Jazz, Folk and Roots artists.

Playscape
64 Belleclaire Ave. Longmeadow, MA 01106
PH: 413-567-7967
www.playscape-recordings.com
Promotes Jazz artists and music.

ropeadope
PO Box 1021, Village Stn. New York, NY 10014
Jerome Brown info@ropeadope.com
www.ropeadope.com
If you'd like to submit artwork, videos, audio mixes, editorial, e-mail them to us.

Utopia Records
PO Box 660-100, Flushing, NY 11366
PH: 718-418-7200 FX: 718-418-5696
Alfonzo Blackwell interns@UtopiaRecordings.com
utopiarecordings.com
Releasing promising Jazz artists that will bring great music and a legacy that will last a lifetime.

Latin

Barrio Records
PO Box 230801, Boston, MA 02123
info@barriorecords.com
www.barriorecords.com
Source for Latin music. Accepts submissions.

Boogalu Productions
PH: 707-823-0369
www.boogalu.com
Promotes the creative work of artists involved in Cuban culture.

DESCARGA.com
328 Flathbush Ave. #180, Brooklyn, NY 11238
PH: 718-693-2966 FX: 718-693-1316
info@descarga.com
www.descarga.com
The ultimate source for Latin CDs.

Discuba
317 10th St. 3rd y 5th Miramar, Play,
Havana City, Cuba
PH: 537-24-0637 FX: 537-24-2033
Teresita teresita@soycubano.com
www.discuba.com
Cuban music shop.

Latin Cool Records
PH: 973-571-0848
David Wasserman latincool2@aol.com
www.latincool.com
Supports/sells Latin Indie music.

MaraRecords
www.mararecords.com
Brazilian LPs, Groove, Bossa, Jazz, Soul, Funk and rare records.

Musica360.com
PO Box 733, Pocono Summit, PA 18334
PH: 570-236-7034
www.musica360.com
Our focus is strictly on independent Latin music artists. We cater to customers looking to discover new music.

Tejanoclassics.com
PH: 281-355-0777
tejanoclassics@worldnet.att.net
www.tejanoclassics.com
An online music vendor for classic and current titles.

Tumi
8/9 New Bond St., Pl. Bath, BA1 1BH UK
PH: 44-0-1225-464736 FX: 44-0-1225-444870
info@tumimusic.com
www.tumimusic.com
Website and record label for Latin American and Caribbean music.

Metal

Promotional Services

Fixion Media
43 Samson Blvd. #322, Laval, QC H7X 3R8
PH: 450-689-7106 FX: 450-689-7106
Rob sales@fixionmedia.com
www.fixionmedia.com
Expose your band to 2 million monthly visitors! We represent the leading Heavy music sites.

Glass Onyon Promotions
PO Box 207, Carolina Beach, NC 28428-0207
PH: 910-395-8265 FX: 910-703-0650
William James glassonyonpr@cs.com
www.ant-bee.com/glassonyonpr.htm
Publicity company with expertise in the promotion of Hard, Classic and Progressive Rock, Heavy Metal, Alternative, Avant-garde, Blues and Country.

Impact Artist Promotions
PO Box 568, Gilbertsville, PA 19525
PH: 610-473-7377 FX: 610-369-7795
www.artistpromo.com
We provide strategies and tools for marketing your music.

Just Rock PR
2976 Washington Blvd. Cleveland Heights,
OH 44118
PH: 216-453-0771
Ren Scarab publicity@justrockpr.com
justrockpr.com
We are media professionals that know how and why things get into print.

Represent:Music
734 El Sur Ave. Salinas, CA 93906
PH: 831-794-1614
Jason Hobbs jasonpromos@hotmail.com
www.representmusic.com
Do you have an upcoming Rock CD or DVD release and want to hit hard when it comes out? We can help. We can help you get radio play, internet plays, downloads, chat room discussions ...

Risestar Promotion
Palmas de Mallorca #1126, La Reina,
Santiago, Chile
PH: +56-2-266-05-27 FX: +56-2-358-24-60
info@risestar.cl
www.risestar.cl
Promotes Hard Rock and Heavy Metal bands worldwide.

V.Q. Promotions
4415 W. Verdugo Ave. Ste. B, Burbank, CA 91505
PH: 818-848-6093 FX: 818-688-3198
Publicity@vqpr.com
www.vqpr.com
Promotions services for Indie Rock bands.

Vendors and Labels

Abaddon Records
179 Silver Lake Rd. Bucksport, ME 04416
PH: 207-478-5077
info@abaddonrecords.com
www.abaddonrecords.com
A Metal and Hardcore independent label.

THINK OF IT AS THE WORLD'S **LARGEST** MUSIC VENUE

FIXION MEDIA
The Fixion Media advertising network represents an audience of 5+ million monthly visitors through leading heavy metal & hard rock web sites. One invoice, great digital marketing!

Advertise on our network
Blabbermouth.net · HardRadio.com · MetalReview.com · SMNnews.com
Blistering.com · KingsOfAR.com · MetalStorm.ee · Ultimate-Guitar.com
BraveWords.com · MetalEater.com · PureGrainAudio.com · UnrestrainedMag.com
DirtbagMusic.com · MetalInjection.net · Rockdetector.com · ZRock.com

Reach us at 514.705.7106 or WWW.FIXIONMEDIA.COM

Beowolf Productions
PO Box 731, Phoenixville, PA 19460
Burt Wolf beowolfco@aol.com
www.beowolfproductions.com
Covers all styles of Extreme music.

Brutal Noise Music Co.
PO Box 6827, San Juan, Puerto Rico 00914-6827
PH: 787-525-4545 FX: 787-948-5851
John Rodriguez metalkid@metalweb.net
www.brutalnoise.com
Promoting bands and creating awareness in the difficult world of music business.

CDSmash
109 Poe Ave. Poteau, OK 74953
cdsmash.com
Selling the music of Rock and Metal artists. Note that any CD sold through CD Smash will get played on our station.

Chunksofmeat Records CD Store
4640 Demaree Ct. House Springs, MO 63051
PH: 636-262-2296
Lee info@chunksofmeat.com
www.chunksofmeatrecords.com
Online store selling CDs for independent musicians.

BlackMetal.Com Records
PO Box 12635, Casa Grande, AZ 85230
PH: 520-421-1208 FX: 520-421-1208
Elden M. support@blackmetal.com
www.blackmetal.com
Send promotional copies to the above address. For retail consideration (once the band or label's sample has been approved), our terms preferred are either consignment or trade against our label's own releases.

Emperor Multimedia
126 Martindale Ave. Oakville, ON L6H 4G7
skelmetal@sympatico.ca
rrca.diskery.com
Promotion, distribution and preservation of Rock music.

Great White North Records America
PO Box 65028, Pl. Longueuil, Longueuil,
QC J4K 5J4
PH: 450-677-5195
sales@gwnrecords.com
www.gwnrecords.com
Production, distribution, manufacturing, licensing for Metal, Hardcore and Grind releases.

Limited Access Records
Intückenweg 13, 44289 Dortmund, Germany
Torsten Wohlgemuth contact@la-records.com
www.la-records.com
Stands for timeless Rock and Metal releases.

Metal Mayhem
32 Lanthorne Rd. Monroe, CT 06468
PH: 203-261-9536
info@metalmayhem.com
www.metalmayhem.com
Indie Bands, send us your CDs!

Mondongo Canibale
PO Box 27106, 28080 Madrid, Spain
mondongo@mondongocanibale.com
www.mondongocanibale.com
Metal, Punk, HC and Rock distribution and record label. Please don't send MP3s!

Nightmare Records & Distribution
7751 Greenwood Dr. St. Paul, MN 55112
PH: 763-784-9654 FX: 763-784-7914
Lance King Lance@nightmare-records.com
www.nightmare-records.com
A label and distributor of Indie based Melodic Hard Rock.

Rock Detector
PO Box 7556, Coalville, Leics, LE67 4WR UK
info@rockdetector.com
www.Rockdetector.com
If you have an independent CD you can now sell it here on the world's biggest Rock & Metal website.

Screaming Ferret Wreckords
PO Box 56, Hillsboro, NH 03244
PH: 603-770-0648
info@screamingferret.com
www.screamingferret.com
Accepts all styles of Metal for review and sales.

Shoutweb.com
3272 Motor Ave. #I, Los Angeles, CA 90034
Jess Redmon jess@shoutweb.com
www.shoutweb.com
Submit your promotional package for review.

StreetTeam.net
124000 Ventura Blvd. #330, Studio City, CA 91604
jon@streetteam.net
streetteam.net
Looking for bands who are ready to go to the next level.

Z Records A&R
info@zrecords.net
www.zrecords.net
Europe's premier Melodic and Classic Hard Rock label.

ZCM Records
Am Kesselhaus 9, 79576 Weil am Rhein, Germany
PH/FX: +49 (0) 76-21-1-67-79-50
Shelley Slater shelley@zcmrecords.com
www.zcmrecords.com
Independent Metal/Punk/Hardcore label, distro and mail order.

New Age

At Peace Media
1117 E. Putnam Ave. #345, Riverside, CT 06878
PH: 203-698-3440 FX: 203-698-3441
John Gelb john@atpeacemedia.com
www.esalenmassagevideo.com
We distribute music to the spa and health communities.

Backroads Music
PH: 800-767-4748 FX: 415-924-0648
mail@backroadsmusic.com
www.backroadsmusic.com
6,000 titles of Ambient, New Age, Space, Tribal & Global sounds.

Etherean Music
PO Box 395, Hotchkiss, CO 81419
PH: 888-384-3732 FX: 303-988-1221
www.ethereanmusic.com
Providing the highest quality music since 1985.

GROOVE Unlimited
PO Box 2171, 8203 AD Lelystad, The Netherlands
PH: 31-0-320-219496 FX: 31-0-320-218910
info@groove.nl
www.groove.nl
We have a large diversity of New Age, Synth, Spacerock etc.

Hearts of Space
PO Box 5916, Sausalito, CA 94966
PH: 415-331-3200 FX: 415-331-3280
info@hos.com
www.hos.com
Submit material for the record label.

LuxMusica Records
5841 Overbrook Ave. Philadelphia, PA 19131
PH: 215-477-9985 FX: 215-879-1457
Jamey Reilly jreilly@virtualux.com
www.luxmusica.com
Peaceful heart, quiet mind. exceptional music from around the world that celebrates the light of eternal truth in its many forms.

Music "à la Carte"
1111 Coolamon Scenic Dr. Mullumbimby,
NSW 2482 Australia
PH: 61-2-66843143 FX: 61-2-66843144
info@musicalacarte.net
www.musicalacarte.net
International Indie music store for soothing sounds.

Music Design
Attn: New Title Dept. 4650 N. Port Washington Rd.
Milwaukee, WI 53212
PH: 414-961-8380 FX: 414-961-8681
order@musicdesign.com
www.musicdesign.com
The premier wholesaler of music and self-help recordings into non-traditional markets.

NewAgeMusic.com
8033 Sunset Blvd. #472, Hollywood, CA 90046
PH: 323-851-3355 FX: 323-851-7981
info@newagemusic.com
www.newagemusic.com
Production, packaging, marketing and promotion.

The Night Cafe
PH: 11-44-870-896-5779
Richard Haze sales@nightcafe.co.uk
www.nightcafe.co.uk
Distributor of relaxing late night music with a high "chill out" factor. We also sell CDs by independent artists covering most genres.

Silver Wave Records
PO Box 7943, Boulder, CO 80306
PH: 303-443-5617 FX: 303-443-0877
Allen Wollard, Director info@silverwave.com
www.silverwave.com
Independent label producing Native American, New Age and World music. Will consider other genres.

Progressive Rock

CD Inzane
PO Box 136, Albertville, MN 55301
www.cdinzane.com
Promotion is what makes a band "become" and we are here to help!!!

Kinesis CDs
1430 Wisp Ct. Hanover, MD 21076-1693
FX: 309-276-9506
info@kinesiscd.com
www.kinesiscd.com
A CD label and mail order specializing in Progressive, Symphonic and Art Rock.

InsideOut Music America

Attn: Submissions, 1601 Banksville Rd. 2nd Fl.
Pittsburgh, PA 15216
PH: 412-561-1100 FX: 412-561-5440
info@insideoutmusic.com
www.insideoutmusic.com
We are dedicated to developing Progressive music as a genre by developing the best acts that the genre has to offer.

InsideOut Music Europe

Kolpingstrasse 9-11, 47533 Kleve, Germany
FX: +49-(0)2821-9791240
contact@insideout.de
www.insideout.de

Punk
Promotional Services

Earshot Media

2629 Manhattan Ave. PO Box 301, Hermosa Beach, CA 90254-2447
Mike Cubillos info@earshotmedia.com
www.earshotmedia.com
Publicity company for Alternative, Indie, Punk and Metal music.

Vendors and Labels

United States

Big Beaver Music

Stephen Dyrgas steve@bigbeavermusic.com
www.bigbeavermusic.com
Featuring bands and labels from Canada, USA, Sweden, Australia and Scotland.

Blackened Distribution

PO Box 8722, Minneapolis, MN 55408
PH: 612-722-1134 FX: 612-722-1134
www.profaneexistence.com
Making Punk a threat again!

Double Crown Records

PO Box 4336, Bellingham, WA 98227-4336
Sean Berry records@dblcrown.com
www.dblcrown.com
Surf and Garage Rock label, with an online catalog.

Elevator Music

PO Box 628, Bronxville, NY 10708
PH: 914-509-5870
Viriato fernando@rcn.com
www.elevatormusic.com
Underground fire to light your way.

Epitaph Records

2798 Sunset Blvd. Los Angeles, CA 90026
PH: 213-413-7353
publicity@epitaph.com
www.epitaph.com
Post your link. Accepts demos. Keep it Punk!

Eyeball Records

PO Box 179, Kearny, NJ 07032
info@eyeballrecords.com
www.eyeballrecords.com
Please don't be afraid to send us any questions, but if they are stupid we're going to pass them around the office and make fun of you, so choose wisely.

Fall Records

PO Box 20886, Baltimore, MD 21209
info@fallrecords.com
www.fallrecords.com
An independent record label featuring Indie, Rock, Punk and so on.

Flying Monkey Records

1204 S. MacArthur Blvd. Springfield, IL 62704
Dave Baker dave@flyingmonkeyrecords.com
flyingmonkeyrecords.com
We list and sell independently released Punk tunes.

Hill Billy Stew Records

PO Box 82625, San Diego, CA 92138-2625
Lee xhillxbillyx@hotmail.com
www.hillbillystew.com
Record label that puts out music by Indie, Punk, Folk and Country artists.

Interpunk

PO Box 651328, Potomac Falls, VA 20165-1328
sales@interpunk.com
www.interpunk.com
Punk bands worldwide. Submit your CDs.

Lumberjack Mordam Music

5920 American Rd. E., Toledo, OH 43612
PH: 419-726-3930 FX: 419-726-3935
www.lumberjackmordam.com
We distribute labels. We don't work directly with artists.

Matchbox Records

198 E. Park Ave. Flushing, MI 48433
PH: 810-423-1711
info@matchboxrecords.com
www.matchboxrecords.com
An independent record label for Rock, Alt, Punk, Metal type genres.

Number One Music

259 W. 30th St. #12FR, New York, NY 10001
reclabels@numberonemusic.com
www.numberonemusic.com
Pages include your bands' profile, history, up to 10 songs and a 'shows' page to announce dates and venues.

Poppunk.com

PO Box 520, Cranbury, NY 08512
FX: 609-298-6566
Steve Neurotic steve@poppunk.com
www.poppunk.com
Exposure for Pop/Punk music. Accepts submissions.

Radical Records

77 Bleecker St. #C2-21, New York, NY 10012
PH: 212-475-1111 FX: 212-475-3676
keith@radicalrecords.com
www.radicalrecords.com
NYC Indie label seeks Punk, Hardcore bands and the like.

RevHQ.com

PO Box 5232, Huntington Beach, CA 92615-5232
PH: 714-842-7584
feedback@revhq.com
www.revhq.com
The best source for independent music.

Rumble Club Records

9 E. 15th St., Covington, KY 41011
PH: 859-491-2835
info@rumbleclubrecords.com
www.rumbleclubrecords.com
Independent record label specializing in Rockabilly, Psychobilly and Punk.

Slackertone Records

PO Box 5633, Salem, OR 97304
Casper Adams info@slackertone.com
www.slackertone.com
Focusing on Rock, Punk and Americana artists who aren't afraid to work and play hard. No slackers allowed!

Takeover Records

PO Box 41070, Long Beach, CA 90853-4107
PH: 661-333-5461
info@takeoverrock.com
www.takeoverrock.com
A highly active/involved Rock/Pop Punk/everything & anything melodic record label.

Unfun Records

PO Box 40307, Berkeley, CA 94704
PH: 408-344-0402 FX: 408-253-1653
unfunrecords.com
Label dealing with mainly Rock, Indie, Punk, Hardcore and Electronica genres. We offer distribution for non-label artists as well.

Vagrant Records

2118 Wilshire Blvd. #361, Santa Monica, CA 90403
info@vagrant.com
www.vagrant.com
Indie and Punk Rock record label.

Zero Youth Records

1975 S. Maple Tree Ln. Bolivar, MO 65613
PH: 417-326-8308
Matt Oldenburg info@zeroyouthrecords.com
www.zeroyouthrecords.com
Label that actively puts out CDs from bands in the Punk and Psychobilly genres ...but we're open to others.

Canada

Steel Capped Records

301-1670 Fort St., Victoria, BC V8R 1H9
PH: 250-514-8434
Chris Disregard
chrisdisregard@steelcappedrecords.com
www.steelcappedrecords.com
Independent label focusing on the Punk/Oi/Streetpunk scene.

Sunday League Records

287 Salem Ave. 2nd Fl. Toronto, ON M6H 3C8
PH: 416-533-0553 FX: 416-533-7793
info@sundayleaguerecords.com
www.sundayleaguerecords.com
Visit our site for submission guidelines. Please do not send MP3s or links to MP3s. CDs only!

Year of the Sun Enterprises

3-304 Stone Rd. W. #520, Guelph, ON N1G 4W4
PH: 519-830-9687
contact@yearofthesun.com
www.yearofthesun.com
Punk, Alternative and Metal. We're always looking to expand our roster with new and exciting bands and artists.

France

Walked in line Records

B.P 04-60840, Breuil le Sec, France
PH: 03-44-50-23-63
www.wilrecords.com
The French Underground label.

Germany

Ebus Music
Bottenhorner Weg 37, 60489 Frankfurt, Germany
PH: +49 (0) 69-787-113 FX: +49 (0) 69-789-58-70
Carsten Mr. Ebu Olbrich Mr.Ebu@ebusmusic.com
www.ebusmusic.com
Established on earth since 1988 - label - broadcasting - mailorder - artist's club in Frankfurt.

unterm durchschnitt
PO Box 19 04 71, D-50501 Köln, Germany
PH: +0049 (0) 2234-91-45-95
info@unterm-durchschnitt.de
www.unterm-durchschnitt.com
A DIY Indie Rock, Stoner, Grunge, Garage, Punk label .

Wolverine Records
Rochusstr.48, 40479 Düsseldorf, Germany
PH: 0211-719493 FX: 0211-713454
sascha@wolverine-records.de
www.wolverine-records.de
Germany's finest independent Punk, Ska and Swing label.

Norway

Plata Records
Innherredsveien 51A, 7043 Trondheim, Norway
PH: 47-93-02-41-83
Steinar H. Bohn contact@platarecords.no
www.platarecords.no
Norwegian record company that specializes in Extreme music.

Switzerland

Lux.-NOISE Productions
Steinengraben 30, CH-4058 Basel, Switzerland
PH: 41-61-271-39-05
Michael Hediger info@luxnoise.com
www.luxnoise.com
Record label & promotion company. Alternative/Garage-Rock! NO ELECTRONIC-stuff.

United Kingdom

FFRUK.com
PO Box 410, Margate, Kent, CT9 3RB UK
PH: 020-8826-5901
Steve fullfrontalrecords@hotmail.com
www.ffruk.com
Online Punk record label promoting music, selling CDs and merchandise for Electronic and Punk Rock music.

Jello Records
Mountfield, E. Sussex, TN32 5JN UK
PH: 44-1580-881310 FX: 44-1580-882032
Ray ray@jellorecords.com
www.jellorecords.com
An Indie music label that has been in existence since the 70's promoting Punk and Rock music.

ORG Records
19 Herbert Gardens, London, NW10 3BX UK
Sean organ@organart.demon.co.uk
www.organart.com
If your music is something that excites us then we'll be on the case. We're mostly interested in Punk/Metal/Alternative and Prog.

punkrockcds.com
PO Box 231, Dewsbury, WF13 4WW UK
mail@punkrockcds.com
www.punkrockcds.com
Punk, Oi and Hardcore.

Reggae

Black Roots Online
The Basement, 301 Southend Ln. Catford, London, SE6 3ND UK
PH: 07050135444
admin@blackroots.net
www.blackroots.net
We have been producing and retailing Reggae music for over 25 years. Our online store is rapidly becoming the most stocked on the web.

Black Style Production
Calandastrasse 6, CH-8048 Zürich, Switzerland
PH: 0041-78-856-18-01
Felix Karli info@blackstyleproduction.com
www.blackstyleproduction.com
Organization of concerts and some parties throughout Switzerland, as well as the booking and management of artists throughout Europe.

Cruise International Records
PH: 07970-182621
Michael Cruise info@cruiseinternational.co.uk
www.cruiseinternational.co.uk
We sell some of the best in Reggae music online along with other styles of music.

Dubroom
www.dubroom.org
MP3s, reviews, forums and much more!

reggaeCD.com
PO Box 100-887, Brooklyn, NY 11210-0887
PH: 718-362-1711 FX: 718-763-6241
customerservice@ejaness.com
www.reggaecd.com
Online Reggae CD, DVD, video, MP3, t-shirt and merchandise store.

Zionway Recordings
1027 Mahlon Ct. Lafayette, CO 80026
PH: 720-300-4264 FX: 303-443-8701
www.zionway.net
Record label, recording studio and producers of conscious Reggae and Hip Hop music.

Soul / R&B
Promotional Services

4Sight Media Relations
109 W. 38th St. #1200, New York, NY 10018
PH: 212-730-1177 FX: 212-730-1188
Jackie O. Asare publicist@4sightmedia.com
www.4sightmedia.com
A diversified public relations firm for projects that require unique music-based experience.

Black Rose Music Group
900 W. Jackson Blvd. #3 East, Chicago, IL 60607
PH: 312-948-5189 FX: 312-896-5994
Wendy Muhammad BlackRoseEnt00@aol.com
www.BlackRoseMusicGroup.com
Professional artist management, consulting and music distribution.

Creativity in Music
PO Box 3481, Bridgeport, CT 06605
PH: 203-331-9982
Gi Dussault & Joe Kelley npsfunk@optonline.net
www.creativityinmusic.com
Promoting independent musicians - helping them in spreading the word.

The Chittlin Circuit
2403 N. L St., Pensacola, FL 32501
PH: 850-433-1842 FX: 850-454-0014
www.chittlincircuit.com
We offer exposure and promotions to independently owned record labels, authors, entertainers, dancers, comedians, movies and actors.

Line Um' Up Entertainment
4771 NW. 10th Ct. #106, Plantation, FL 33313
PH: 954-562-9772 FX: 954-731-9978
Kendell Mauzon
lineumupentertainment@hotmail.com
www.lineumupentertainment.4t.com
Artist development and promotions.

Sounds In The Key of Gee
PO Box 2998, Southfield, MI 48037
PH: 313-549-7400
Gisele "Gee" Caver
gisele@soundsinthekeyofgee.com
www.soundsinthekeyofgee.com
Entertainment and event consultants who specialize in the promotion of independent artists.

Vendors and Labels
United States

Clefnote.com
PO Box 833728, Richardson, TX 75083
Dawn Hall-Jones dawn@nrntechnology.com
www.clefnote.com
A growing network of professional independent artists and musicians of every music genre. Sell your music downloads and CDs online.

Dusty Groove America
Attn: Buyer, 1120 N. Ashland Ave. Chicago, IL 60622
PH: 773-342-5800 FX: 773-342-2180
dga@dustygroove.com
www.dustygroove.com
We tend to only stock music we love and music that we feel fits into our rather narrow format.

Got Beats Records
PH: 313-304-2245
Gary Felton Jr. gotbeatsceo@yahoo.com
gotbeatsrecords.com
Independent record label based in Detroit. Always seeking new talent in all genres of music.

Groove Distribution
1164 N. Milwaukee Ave. Chicago, IL 60622-4019
PH: 773-435-0250 FX: 773-435-0252
www.groovedis.com
The main thing is that you must fit our kind of music (Loungey Dance music—with a Jazz or Soul influence) AND we have to think we can sell you —which means you have to be REALLY good. Singles are FAR easier to pick up than a full CD (and by single I do mean a 12" VINYL single not a CD single).

It's Soul Time! Records
PO Box 572, Ridgewood, NJ 07451-0572
andy@itssoultime.com
www.itssoultime.com
Focusing on Soul and R&B.

Quinn Records
PO Box 771693, St. Louis, MO 63177
PH: 314-802-7550 FX: 314-802-7550
Dwight Quinn dwight@quinnrecords.com
www.quinnrecords.com
Label and distributor of Blues, Gospel, Jazz and Soul music.

Sound Mindz Entertainment
702 2nd Ave. N., Birmingham, AL 35203
PH: 205-252-5587 FX: 205-397-0320
Tony Gideon soundmindz@soundmindzmusic.com
www.soundmindzmusic.com
We are a record company interested in R&B, Blues and Black Gospel.

Voice Distributions
1026 6th Ave. #301 S., New York, NY 10018
PH: 917-545-2169
Maurice mauricewatts@mauricewatts.com
www.VoiceDistributions.com
Home of the best R&B, Soul and Classic music.

Canada

SoMuchSoul Records
2397 Bridge Rd. Oakville, ON L6L 2G9
PH: 905-334-2527
info@somuchsoul.com
www.somuchsoul.com
Promotes great music from talented artists. Funk, Jazz, Soul Grooves, Rock ...we cover it all!

United Kingdom

Acid Jazz Records
146 Bethnal Green Rd. London, E2 6DG UK
PH: 020-7613-1100
info@acidjazz.co.uk
www.acidjazz.co.uk
Acid jazz is the new Soul, anything with its head and mind in the history and the feet to the dance floor, eyes to the future. Send demos to the above address.

Crazy Beat Records
87 Corbets Tey Rd. Upminster, Essex, RM14 2AH UK
PH: 01708-228678 FX: 01708-640946
sales@crazybeat.co.uk
www.crazybeat.co.uk
Are you an artist or a distributor that has something hot that you think we should be promoting, then please get in touch or better still send us a sample. We carry Soul, Jazz, Funk, House, Garage, Dance etc.

Soul Brother Records
1 Keswick Rd. E. Putney, London, SW15 2HL UK
PH: 020-8875-1018 FX: 020-8871-0180
soulbrother@btinternet.com
www.soulbrother.com
We're specialists for new independent Soul and Jazz CDs as well as a good source for rare original vinyl LP's and 12" singles.

Soundmob
PO Box 1137, Liverpool, L69 3ZZ UK
PH: 07766332511
info@soundmob.co.uk
www.soundmob.co.uk
Will create a music policy for your business, supply you with DJs, organise live events and make sure your musical identity is properly promoted through every appropriate media.

Underground Soul
PH: +44 (0) 77-17184914
Eleonora Cutaia eleonora@underground-soul.com
www.underground-soul.com
Specialising in online marketing, publicity, promotion and bookings for new soulful sounds.

Japan

Totown Records
Tamari 30-1, Kakegawa City, Shizuoka Prefecture, Japan 436-0011
PH/FX: 81-537-23-7585
Malcolm W. Adams info@totown.net
www.totown.net/totownrecords.htm
Originators of the Nu-Jazz-Funk. Dedicated to producing and marketing the highest quality world-class entertainment products in the Asia Pacific region.

Women In Music
Promotional Services

Cat Scratch Productions
PO Box 40891, Denver, CO 80204
PH: 303-775-4723
Kristine Berntsen
inquiries@catscratchproductions.com
www.catscratchproductions.com
Producing and promoting women's events & women musicians. Please send kit and recent tour info.

Power of Pink Promotions
64 Central St., Ipswich, MA 01938
PH: 617-851-7298
Lynn 'JULIAN'
PowerofPink@CookieCutterGirl.com
www.cookiecuttergirl.com
Cookie Cutter Girl, "The Queen of Internet Promotion," will put *HER* skills to work for *YOU*! Who better than a Pop Superhero to make *your* business FLY?

Warrior Girl Music
12115 Magnolia Blvd. #200, North Hollywood, CA 91607
PH: 818-442-9294
info@warriorgirlmusic.com
www.warriorgirlmusic.com
Recording, publishing and promotions company that is about developing artists.

Vendors and Labels

Benten Records
3F Ebisu West, 1-16-15, Ebisu-Nishi, Shibuya-ku, Tokyo 150-0021 Japan
benten@sister.co.jp
www.sister.co.jp/english
Japanese label specializing in female artists of many genres.

chicks on speed records
Rosenthaler Strasse 3, 10119, Berlin, Germany
PH: 0049-30-27-89-05-24 FX: 0049-30-27-89-05-25
promo@chicksonspeed-records.com
www.chicksonspeed.com
Promotes Electronic female musicians.

Daemon Records
PO Box 1207, Decatur, GA 30031 Attn: A&R
hello@daemonrecords.com
www.daemonrecords.com
Indie label covering Southeastern US.

Goldenrod Music
1310 Turner St., Lansing, MI 48906
PH: 517-484-1712 FX: 517-484-1771
music@goldenrod.com
www.goldenrod.com
Full service center for Indie artists with a focus on women.

GoGirls Music Records
PO Box 16940, Sugar Land, TX 77496-6940
PH: 281-455-2584
Georgia Moncrief info@gogirlsmusicrecords.com
www.gogirlsmusicrecords.com
Our goal is simple... get great "women in music" heard without the artist giving up their ownership or paying big bucks.

Harmony Ridge Music
123 Bonita, Moss Beach, CA 94018
PH: 650-563-9280 FX: 650-563-9266
hrmusic@hrmusic.com
www.hrmusic.com
Dedicated to female Singer/Songwriters.

Hip Gloss Productions
PO Box 11130, Cincinnati, OH 45211
PH: 513-476-3580
Amy amy@hipgloss.com
www.hipgloss.com
Provides services to female musicians in the genre's: Electronic, Experimental, Electro Clash, Trip Hop, Hip Hop, Soul and more.

Hippie Chick Twang Records
118 16th Ave. S. #210, Nashville, TN 37203
PH: 615-244-4422
Kim McLean kim@kimmclean.com
www.hippiechicktwangrecords.com
An all-chick record label of award winning singer/songwriter women.

Kill Rock Stars
120 NE. State Ave. PMB 418, Olympia, WA 98501
krs@killrockstars.com
www.killrockstars.com
Send us your demo tapes!!

Ladyslipper.org
PO Box 3124, Durham, NC 27715
PH: 800-634-6044 FX: 919-383-3525
info@ladyslipper.org
www.ladyslipper.org
Our purpose is to further new musical and artistic directions for women musicians.

On the Rag Records
PO Box 251, Norco, CA 92860-0251
PH: 909-273-1402 FX: 909-478-5208
webmistress@ontherag.net
www.ontherag.net
For females in the DIY music scene and activist scene.

panx
BP 15058-31033 Toulouse, France
PH: 33-0-561612145 FX: 33-0-561114895
infos@panx.net
www.panx.net
Hardcore, Punk, CyberThrash, Grindcore, TechnoBruit, Crades Mélodies.

Sonic Cathedral
PO Box 8505, Baltimore, MD 21234
info@soniccathedral.com
www.soniccathedral.com
Specializing in female vocal Metal.

World

African Allstars
4325 Roosevelt Hwy. College Park, GA 30349
PH: 404-684-9955
www.panafricanallstars.com
We feature the best African music on the web.

Atlas Music
625 Biltmore Way #106, Coral Gables, FL 33134
info@atlasmusic.biz
www.atlasmusic.biz
Fosters global musical culture awareness and understanding.

Deep Down Productions
3-182 Wright Ave. Toronto, ON M6R 1L2
PH: 416-535-5247
info@deepdownproductions.com
www.deepdownproductions.com
Promotes Traditional music from around the world.

Earth Vibe Music
PO Box 5007, Brighton, BN50 9DS UK
PH: 0870-350-9407 FX: 0871-661-5556
contact@earthvibemusic.com
www.earthvibemusic.com
Promoting music from Indie bands and musicians.

Kongoi Productions *Norway*
www.kongoi.com
African music, PR and publishing company.

Music Yogi
#98-98/1, 3rd Fl. S. P. Rd. Bangalore, India - 560 002
PH: 009-80-41224526
Aadarsh Hariharan content.my@gmail.com
www.musicyogi.com/asp/independents.asp
Online Store that features Indies from India. Users can sample their music and buy their CDs.

New World Music
PO Box 3090, Ashland, OR, 97520
PH: 800-771-0987
newworld@wrightful.com
www.newworldmusic.com
We only release a very few carefully selected albums every year. Please visit our site for submission details.

Onzou Records
2444 Benny Cres. #110, Montreal, QC H4B 2R3
PH/FX: 514-485-0728
info@onzou.com
www.onzou.com
Producing traditional West African music.

Putamayo World Music
411 Lafayette St. 4th Fl. New York, NY 10003
Jacob Edgar info@putumayo.com
www.putumayo.com
Music of other cultures.
Submit demos.

Rhyme Records
1 Jackson Dr. N.,
Poughkeepsie, NY 12603
PH: 845-462-3450
FX: 845-463-7664
Probir K. Ghosh
probir@rhymerecords.com
www.rhymerecords.com
Our focus is to promote the rich musical heritage of India.

rock paper scissors
216 W. Allen St. #137, Bloomington, IN 47403
PH: 812-339-1195 FX: 801-729-4911
Dmitri Vietze music@rockpaperscissors.biz
rockpaperscissors.biz
Publicity and marketing in the U.S. for World music and Reggae labels, artists, websites etc.

World Music Store
56 Browns Mill Rd. Montpelier, VT 05602
PH: 802-223-1294 FX: 802-229-1834
info@worldmusicstore.com
www.worldmusicstore.com
Traditional and Contemporary World music.

Zook Beat
info@zookbeat.com
www.zookbeat.com
Check out up and coming artists and all time favorites!!

SECTION FIVE: SITES THAT WILL ALLOW YOU TO UPLOAD YOUR MUSIC OR VIDEO FILES

"The Internet is a powerful force, still in its infancy, and shows no sign of letting up. If you want to get your music to where the action is, get online. This is one bus you don't want to miss." – **David Nevue, author of "How to Successfully Promote Your Music on the Internet"**

Digital Music Distributors

CD Baby Digital Distribution
5925 NE. 80 Ave. Portland, OR 97218-2891
PH: 503-595-3000
cdbaby@cdbaby.com
cdbaby.net/dd
You keep all the rights to your music. You just lend us the right to be your digital distributor: to get your music to legitimate music services like Apple iTunes, Rhapsody, Napster, MSN Music, MP3tunes, AOL's MusicNet, Yahoo MusicMatch and more!

FoxyMelody Digital Distribution
1610 W. 7th St. #312, Los Angeles, CA 90017
PH: 310-857-6686 FX: 408-676-0985
Jeremy Belcher j.belcher@foxymelody.com
www.foxymelody.com
Digital distribution for Indie labels/artists. Sell your music on the world's best online retailers.

HIP Video Promo
2 Draeger Pl., South River, NJ 08882
PH: 732-613-1779
Andy Gesner hipvideo@aol.com
www.hipvideopromo.com
We can get your video to the outlets most likely to share and appreciate your own musical and visual aesthetic.

Independent Digital Entertainment & Arts
IDEA
28 Locust St. #303, Brooklyn, NY 11206
Alfredo Cabeza contact@ideadistributors.com
www.ideadistributor.com
Music and video distribution to the leading online services such as iTunes, Napster, Rhapsody etc.

Indie Artist 411
6435 W. Jefferson Blvd. #125, Ft. Wayne, IN 46804
PH: 260-341-1137
Kris Marino admin@indieartist411.com
www.indieartist411.com
Promotion & digital distribution for independent artists.

INgrooves
539 Bryant St. #400, San Francisco, CA 94107
PH: 415-896-2100 FX: 415-896-2220
submissions@ingrooves.com
www.ingrooves.com
Signing content from the best established and emerging artists from around the world and serving as their digital record company (distribution, marketing, promotion, licensing).

IODA
539 Bryant St. #303, San Francisco, CA 94107
PH: 415-777-4632
Vivek info@IODAlliance.com
www.iodalliance.com
We distribute music from independent labels, but typically don't work with individual artists. Artists signed to independent labels should have their labels contact us.

The Orchard
100 Park Ave. 17th Fl. New York, NY 10003
PH: 212-201-9280 FX: 212-201-9203
info@theorchard.com
www.theorchard.com
Supplier for North American digital music as well as the leading European DMS providers.

TuneCore
(Main) 20 Jay St. #7A2, Brooklyn, NY 11201
(Rip Center) 871 Lyndale Ave. Bloomington, MN 55420
info@tunecore.com
www.tunecore.com
Distribution service that gets music you created up for sale on iTunes and Rhapsody without asking for your rights or taking any money from the sale.

Visual Image Marketing
PO Box 120576, Nashville, TN 37212
PH: 615-419-0886
Steve Baker steveb@visualimagemarketing.com
www.visualimagemarketing.com
Promotes & markets music videos to video outlets.

Vision Promotions
22 Upper Grosvenor St., London, W1K 7PE UK
PH: 44-0207-499-8024 FX: 44-0207-499-8032
Rob Dallison visionrob@btconnect.com
www.visionmusic.co.uk
A collection agent for a Japanese digital licensing company 'Toryumon'.

Digital Music Sites

Getting your music onto the sites listed in this section varies a great deal cost-wise. Many services will allow you to upload your files for free, while others charge a fee or percentage from each sale that you make. Be wary of large setup fees. Many of the Online Digital Stores deal only with Digital Distribution Services such as CD Baby or The Orchard to get their Indie Music. I have indicated which stores deal only with Distributors throughout this Section. There are also many MP3 Blog sites listed that will post your music (if they like it) for a week or two in order to help promote your music.

All Styles

North America

United States

96decibels.com
4700 Kearney Rd. NW., Bremerton, WA 98312
PH: 253-856-0927
support@96decibels.com
www.96decibels.com
We provide ICPs, labels and artists with value added tools that can easily be incorporated into their current web presence.

Acid Planet
PH: 608-256-5555 FX: 608-250-1745
www.acidplanet.com
Artist profile for uploading songs and writing reviews. Now featuring weekly podcasts.

amazon.com Digital Music Network
www.amazon.com/exec/obidos/subst/jungle/jungle-gateway.html
Upload your songs, info, lyrics, images and more.

American Idol Underground
5813-A Uplander Way, Culver City, CA 90230
info@idolunderground.com
idolunderground.com
An online community where emerging artists get their music heard and fans discover new music.

AOL MusicNow
aol.musicnow.com
Songs must be delivered through a Digital Music Distributor such as www.cdbaby.com or www.theorchard.com

Apple's iTunes Music
www.apple.com/itunes
Songs must be delivered through a Digital Music Distributor such as www.cdbaby.com or www.theorchard.com

Artistopia
PO Box 3538, Alexandria, VA 22302
PH: 540-967-9609 FX: 703-566-7500
Donna Liguria info@artistopia.com
www.artistopia.com
Professional presentation of the music artist to the music industry, with comprehensive profile and press kit building tools.

Artist Label
www.artistlabel.com
Offering free downloads of independent artists.

Artist Weekly
10740 N. 56th St. #195, Tampa, FL 33617
contactus@artistweekly.com
ArtistWeekly.com
Post as many original songs as you like for five bucks each and you will automatically be entered into our weekly contest.

ARTISTdirect
1601 Cloverfield Blvd. #400 S., Santa Monica, CA 90404
listen.artistdirect.com
Showcases downloads from independent bands.

ArtistNow.com
ArtistNow.com
Members can upload audio, video, images, job postings, e-mail, chat ...

ArtistServer.com
www.artistserver.com
Supporting independent music! ARTISTS, get involved, be heard, get feedback - we have the technology!

AT&T Wireless Ringtones
www.attwireless.com/personal/features/fun/music.jhtml
Songs must be delivered through a Digital Music Distributor such as www.theorchard.com..

Audio Lunchbox
1021 N. Sepulveda Blvd. #R, Manhattan Beach, CA 90266
PH: 310-946-1004
support@audiolunchbox.com
www.audiolunchbox.com
We accept music from labels, distributors and individual unsigned artists.

AudioCandy.com
www.audiocandy.com
Song files are supplied through LiquidAudio.com

AudioLaunch.com
contact@audiolaunch.com
www.audiolaunch.com
Legal MP3 music downloads from independent bands of various genres.

AudioStreet.net
5422 NW. 50th Ct. Coconut Creek, FL 33073
audiostreet.net
Offers MP3 hosting, full artist pages with bios, reviews, event listings and much more.

axecity.com
forums@axecity.com
www.axecity.com
Our "Band Profile" area has been made available for you to showcase your band and your music.

The Band Universe
www.banduniverse.com
A free promotion engine for artists. You can enter bio, roster, gigs, recordings and MP3 audio.

BandBreak.com
PO Box 118, Stormville, NY 12582
Brett Brett@bandbreak.com
www.bandbreak.com
Resource for independent musicians. Upload your music. We'll help you promote it!

BearShare
info@bearshare.com
www.bearshare.com
File sharing system that promotes solid independent artists.

BeatBuggy
info@BeatBuggy.com
www.BeatBuggy.com
Sell your songs, set up a personal web space, upload videos and much more.

BestBuy.com Digital Downloads
www.bestbuy.com
Songs must be delivered through the CD Baby Digital Music Distributor www.cdbaby.com

Beta Records Music Hosting
1343 N. McCadden Pl. Hollywood, CA 90028
PH: 323-469-2382 FX: 323-469-2383
Georg Van Handel georg@betarecords.com
www.betarecords.com
Free music hosting for bands. Promotional tools, e-mail management, event calendar and blogs.

The Big Ugly Review
490 2nd St. 2nd Fl. San Francisco, CA 94107
Elizabeth Bernstein music@biguglyreview.com
www.biguglyreview.com
In the music section we have downloadable songs of artists that visitors can listen to. Includes interviews.

Bitmunk
bitmunk.com
You set the amount of money you want to receive for each sale of your music, then different sellers can sell it for whatever price they want on top of that.

Broadjam Download Store
313 W. Beltline Hwy. #147, Madison, WI 53713
PH: 608-271-3633
customerservice@broadjam.com
www.broadjam.com
Exposure is everything and the more places you can sell your music the better, right?

BurnLounge
304 Hudson St. 7th Fl. New York, NY 10013
customersupport@burnlounge.com
www.burnlounge.com
Our focus is on rare, unsigned, geo-specific and independent artists.

BuyMusic.com
85 Enterprise #100, Aliso Viejo, CA 92656
www.buymusic.com
Great option for the independent community.

Buzzplay.com
2894 Rowena Ave. Los Angeles, CA 90039
PH: 323-664-2899
LJ Scott info@buzzplay.com
buzzplay.com
We do our best to give bands the chance to have their music and material heard by record labels and professional music reps.

Can You Hear Me TV
info@canyouhearme.tv
www.canyouhearme.tv
Free competitions in various cities give bands a shot to be on this show.

CDFreedom.com
47 Mellen St., Framingham, MA 01702
FX: 508-820-7920
www.cdfreedom.com
We take a smaller cut than most online distributors!

Cdigix
www.cdigix.com
Digital media provider to colleges and universities. Songs must be delivered through a Digital Music Distributor such as www.theorchard.com..

CDTV.NET
67 Wall St. 22nd Fl. New York, NY 10005
PH: 212-696-7890
support@cdtv.net
www.cdtv.net
Accepts demo CDs/music videos from all genres.

Clear Channel NEW Music Network
newmusicnetwork@clearchannel.com
clearchannelnewmusicnetwork.com
Share your music with your fans and music industry professionals who want to find new, promising acts.

Click4Musicians.com
PO Box 677, Cave Creek, AZ 85327
Cindy Carlier info@countrywesternbands.com
www.click4musicians.com
Accepting band material for our singles community playlist. Upload your MP3 and bio.

CollegeMusicRadio.com
management@collegemusicradio.com
CollegeMusicRadio.com
Visitors decide which songs get played on the our station. We want our listeners to have total control of the music.

cornerband.com
www.cornerband.com
Online musical forum for both independent and record-labeled musicians.

cStream
2 Deer Path, Gladstone, NJ 07934
PH: 617-974-3085
www.cstream.com
We believe that artists should have control over their own music.

culturedeluxe
www.culturedeluxe.com
News, views, reviews, abuse ...

CYBERMIDI.com
PO Box 120040, Staten Island, NY 10312
PH: 800-987-6434
cybermidi.com/community
We've got your favorite songs in MIDI the way they were meant to be heard. Feel free to send us some samples of your work and we can talk about including them at Shop CYBERMIDI.

DecentXposure.com
411@decentxposure.com
DecentXposure.com
An Indie magazine chock full of ringtones, downloads and other ways for fans and bands to get together.

DigitalSoundboard.net
support@digitalsoundboard.net
www.DigitalSoundboard.net
Delivers *paid-for* MP3s and FLAC digital music files.

DigiFreq Music Promotion
www.digifreq.com/digifreq/music.asp
Aims to help independent musicians gain some added exposure for their work. The title being submitted must be available for sale from either Amazon.com or CDBaby.com.

DigiPie
22647 Ventura Blvd. #145, Woodland Hills, CA 91364
PH: 818-713-1510
Max Davis artists@digipie.com
digipie.com
Offers creators/artists powerful tools to profit from their digital creations from A-Z built into our model and software.

DMusic
101 Greenwood Ave. #200, Jenkintown, PA 19046
PH: 215-885-3302 FX: 215-885-3303
www.dmusic.com
Get your music played on our broadcasts.

Download.com Music
music.download.com
A free artist upload and download site that is part of Download.com.

DreamMakersMP3.com
453 River Styx Rd. Hopatcong, NJ 070843
PH: 973-398-8540 FX: 973-398–8526
info@dreammakersmp3.com
DreamMakersMP3.com
Bridging the gap between your music and your fans by providing artist-friendly, professional services.

The Echo Music Video Show *KCSG*
6980 Roswell Rd. #O6, Atlanta, GA 30328
videos@unsignedmusicmag.com
www.unsignedmusicmag.com/videos.html
TV show featuring the best independent music videos.

Echoingwalls Music
571 Rock Pillar Rd. Clayton, NC 27520
PH: 877-505-0476 FX: 877-907-1941
Dexter Nelson artists@echoingwalls.com
www.echoingwalls.com
Aimed at helping new and struggling artists by providing resources.

Echospin
425 W. 14th St. #427-3F, New York, NY 10014
PH: 212-994-0307 FX: 800-786-7738
www.echospin.com
Enables artists to sell and deliver music directly to their customers via a wide variety of distribution channels.

epitonic.com
labels@epitonic.com
www.epitonic.com
We aspire to live up to our neologistic moniker, the center from which waves of disruptive purity emit.

FAIRCOPY
info@faircopy.com
www.faircopy.com
Sell your works on P2P networks and on the web.

Fake Science
PO Box 10823, Oakland, CA 94610
support@fakescience.com
www.fakescience.com
We are dedicated to making independent music available digitally and affordably.

FileFactory
www.filefactory.com
Free unlimited file hosting. Your file will remain on our servers forever, provided it has been downloaded at least once in the past 15 days.

Fresh New Media
Chris info@freshnewmedia.com
www.freshnewmedia.com
A free online exhibit featuring film, video, visual and digital arts, literature for anybody! Join for free and post your work online today!!!

Fresh Tracks Music
1609 N. Wolcott #305, Chicago, IL 60622
PH: 773-529-6733 FX: 773-529-6737
info@freshtracksmusic.com
www.freshtracksmusic.com
To submit to the Coke/FreshTracksmusic program, please visit www.sonicbids.com

funender.com
www.funender.com
Will review your songs and give you more plays.

Fuse
11 Penn Plaza, 15th Fl. New York, NY 10001
PH: 212-324-3400 FX: 212-324-3445
fuseinfo@fuse.tv
www.fuse.tv
Submit your music and band info.

Fuseboard
support@fuseboard.com
www.fuseboard.com
Exists to provide a platform for artists to expand their music through collaboration and networking with other artists.

Future Music Now
www.futuremusicnow.com
Free MP3 hosting. We provide a developing portal for artists to promote their music online for free.

garageband.com
1617 Boylston Ave. Seattle, WA 98122
artistmanager@garageband.com
www.garageband.com
Rewriting the rules about how the music industry operates.

Google Video
https://upload.video.google.com
In addition to televised content, we'll also host video from anyone who wants to upload content to us.

GorillaPop
gorilla@gorillapop.com
www.gorillapop.com
Artists, add your songs and find new fans.

Griffdog Records
17442 Apex Cir. Huntington Beach, CA 92647
PH: 714-375-6162
Thomas thomas@griffdogrecords.com
www.griffdogrecords.com
We are actively looking for new talent. Register on our website and make your music available for download.

Groove Mobile
www.groovemobile.net
Supplies full-length track downloads to some of Europe's leading mobile music services. Songs must be delivered through The Orchard's distribution service www.theorchard.com

Groupie Tunes
3100 Main St. #349, Dallas, TX 75226
PH: 214-760-9977 FX: 214-742-1245
customerservice@groupietunes.com
www.GroupieTunes.com
A mobile community dedicated to create a real-time, direct relationship for fans with their favorite artists.

Hightide Music
PH: 612-251-3327
Doug Kasper thuggishdougish@msn.com
www.hightidemusic.com
A referral site hosting MP3s of independent bands. Our mission is to bring a greater awareness to independent music.

HipTingle
djspy@spydigital.com
hiptingle.spydigital.com
Helps bands showcase and get feedback on their work and promote upcoming events.

Hollywood Music
admin@hollywoodmusic.tv
www.hollywoodmusic.tv
We're here to help all motivated and talented artists get the visibility they deserve. We offer artists the ability to upload their profile to our website.

HouseOfGigs.com
12157 W. Linebaugh #211, Tampa, FL 33626
PH: 888-260-3138 FX: 888-260-3138
houseofgigs@gmail.com
www.houseofgigs.com
Artists can set up gigs, post songs, buy and sell equipment, check out the latest music news and much more.

howsmymusic.com
12750 Sharon Hollow Rd. Manchester, MI 48158
Eric Moore talentscout@howsmymusic.com
www.howsmymusic.com
Online music contest with cash prizes. Winners voted by the public. Also has sales MP3 platform.

iamusic.com
44 Music Sq. E. #503, Nashville, TN 37203
PH: 615-335-3262 FX: 215-895-9672
add-your-music@iamusic.com
www.iamusic.com/add_your_music.php
For Instrumental music only!

iManifest
Mark McFarland artists@imanifest.biz
www.imanifest.biz
Service for musicians to expose their demos to music industry people looking for new artists.

SONGWRITERS
GET SUPPORT
GET HEARD
GET PROMOTED

CRITIQUE WORKSHOPS
ARTIST SHOWCASES
CD SAMPLER COMPILATIONS
ONLINE CRITIQUES
STUDIO RECORDING
RETREATS AND SONGCAMPS
INDUSTRY SEMINARS
FILM & TV SONG LEADS
WEBSITE ARTIST PAGE
SELL CDS AND PODCAST
TOUR THE WORLD
CONNECT WITH OTHERS
WEEKLY BIZ NEWSLETTER
SUPPORT AND COACHING

Songsalive!

www.songsalive.org

got songs?

www.songsalive.org

supporting and promoting songwriters and composers worldwide

Songsalive! is a non-profit organization dedicated to the nurturing, support and promotion of songwriters and composers worldwide. Founded in 1997 in Sydney Australia, Songsalive! is run by songwriters for songwriters and now has over 15 chapter cities around the world. It acts as an epicentre, a heart of the international songwriting community and music markets, bridging the gaps, tapping songwriters into the pulse of the business and at the same time giving them and their music the support they deserve. Through Songsalive!, songs and songwriters can be accessed by the whole world and when the hunt is on, Songsalive! is a one-stop song shop!

Songsalive! gives life to songs, provides opportunities for collaboration, creates awareness about original music, promotes and educates through an amazing network of programs providing access between songwriters and music business professionals - through workshops, showcases, CD Samplers, songcamps & retreats, live events and showcases, songwriter critique workshops, songleads & industry pitches; education seminars and Expos, artist development; studio production; informational resources and networking. On-line, Songsalive! is the source for great resources for songwriters and acts as a vehicle for discussion, promotion and retail for our members and their music.

Membership includes access to our programs, support , partner opportunities, community and resources.
Add on elite membership to get some buzz, including a member page online, interview, CD review and store links, plus songs on rotation in our podcast, special offers and pitch opportunities.
JOIN TODAY!

www.songsalive.org

groups.myspace.com/songsalive - free discussions
www.songsalive.org/enotes - free news

iMove Music
7814 Benton St., Huntsville, AL 35802
PH: 256-348-2472
Sandy sandy@imovemusic.com
www.imovemusic.com
We only accept great music that our visitors will love to hear. We limit the amount of artists so visitors have the time to hear it all!

iMuzic.com
2560 San Carlos Ave. Ste. A, Castro Valley, CA 94546
muzic@imuzic.com
www.imuzic.com
Back-end tracking letting you know what the fans think of your music.

In Real Time
POB 15371, Boston, MA 02215
PH: 617-233-7426
James McCaffrey info@inrealtime.com
www.inrealtime.com
Services to help musicians create and share their music and videos with the world through online digital distribution and promotion.

Independent Artists Company
admin@independentartistscompany.com
independentartistscompany.com
We combine the best features from the MP3 era with modern options such as digital singles sales.

Indiecore.com
12711 Ventura Blvd. #320 Studio City, CA 91604
PH: 818-508-5588 FX: 818-508-6203
Bob Downey bobby@indiecore.com
www.indiecore.com
Sign up and create a profile, sell ringtones, cell phone tools and MP3s. You may also receive nationwide exposure through our extensive network.

Indiepad.com
info@indiepad.com
indiepad.com
Complete our artist registration form and we will upload your songs free of charge!

indieTunes
1162 St. Georges Ave. #294, Avenel, NJ 07001
support@indietunes.com
www.indietunes.com
We offer a very modest subscription fee and pay 100% from each sale back to the artist.

IndyReview.net
artists@indyreview.net
www.indyreview.net
Our job is to attract visitors to the great variety of music online here!

Insomnia Radio: Resonate.TV
PO Box 132, Ripley, OH 45167
info@indiemusicproject.com
Jason Evangelho video@resonate.tv
www.resonate.tv
A music video show highlighting independent artists from around the world.

Insound
221 W. 17th St. 5th Fl. New York, NY 10011
PH: 212-777-8056 FX: 212-777-8059
Patrick patrick@insound.com
www.insound.com
Bringing the best underground culture to the surface.

iSOUND.COM
3140 Dyer St. #1500, Dallas, TX 75275
PH: 877-757-6863 FX: 214-965-9007
labels@isound.com
www.isound.com
Free place for bands to upload their music and gain exposure to our music community of over 1,000,000 visitors per month!

ItsFun.com
info@itsfun.com
www.ItsFun.com
Fans and professionals alike can access, not only cutting edge music from up and coming artists, but also bios, pictures, performance schedules and promotional materials.

Jabbertones
105 Forrest Ave. #26, Los Gatos, CA 95032
PH: 408-340-1993 FX: 408-868-9803
Scott Manthey jabbertones@gmail.com
www.jabbertones.com
Port your music in the form of ringtones to over 179 million US cellular customers! Paid revenue share per download.

Jamster
jamster.com
Selling and marketing ringtones to mobile customers around the world. Songs must be delivered through The Orchard's distribution service www.theorchard.com

JamVault
info@jamvault.com
www.jamvault.com
Indie music downloads, schedules and more!

Jookey
www.jookey.com
Provides a medium for artists and creative minds to network with others who share similar interests.

JukeBoxAlive
311 Montford Ave. Asheville, NC 28801
PH: 828-232-0016
Will Cumberland cumberland@jukeboxalive.com
jukeboxalive.com
Our Advanced Jukebox Player protects your music from being digitally downloaded, yet allows fans to hear your music online. This creates exciting possibilities for you to present yourself to new audiences without being ripped off.

JustEnough TV
PH: 831-624-9100 FX: 831-624-7878
info@justenough.net
justenoughtv.com
Your source for the latest news, independent videos and music instruction. We are a Microsoft partner and are able to offer Indie bands FREE exposure to 7.1 million viewers through our exclusive Indie Channel on MSN Video.

Kvibe.com
Khoi Le support@kvibe.com
www.kvibe.com
We offer artists/music seekers another means to find "ORIGINAL" quality music production for their demos or other purposes.

Latest Music Videos
PH: 0802-547-2535
Roy roy@latestmusicvideos.com
www.latestmusicvideos.com
Showcase for many artists and bands of the future.

ListenUp247.com
info@ListenUp247.com
www.listenup247.com
Featuring not only cutting edge music from up and coming artists, but also bios, pictures, performance schedules and promotional materials.

Livedigital
www.LiveDigital.com
A digital community that allows you to manage your entire digital lifestyle.

LocalTracks
info@localtracks.com
www.localtracks.com
You keep complete control of your digital content and set the price for each song.

The Ls.media Project
www.lsmedia.biz
An independent digital release portal. Our innovative project provides you to sell your releases in digital form without ANY file size or file type limitations.

Lulu.com
3131 RDU Ctr. #210, Morrisville, NC 27560
PH: 919-459-5858
support@lulu.com
www.lulu.com
Upload your music, set your royalty, customize & promote your Lulu storefront.

Magnatune
2070 Allston Way #102, Berkeley, CA 94704
PH: 510-684-4175 FX: 510-217-6374
magnatune.com
MP3 music and music licensing. Artists get a full 50% of the purchase price. We can also sell your CD for you.

ManiaTV
Submissions@ManiaTV.com
www.maniatv.com
Expose your band to a worldwide audience via live internet television.

Media Kinesis.com
mediakinesis.com
Get your own pro website, stream MP3 and WMV (video), events calendar, radio station and more.

MediaPal
6100 Hollywood Blvd. #305, Hollywood, FL 33024
PH: 954-889-5651
support@MediaPal.com
www.mediapal.com
Makes selling any type of digital content fast, safe and easy.

Mixposure
management@mixposure.com
www.mixposure.com
Music promotion, free MP3 downloads, band exposure, music forum. Rate and review.

The Mod Archive
mods@modarchive.com
www.modarchive.com
Songs on this site are provided for free download by the artists.

MOSIQ.COM
Mosiq.com
Provides musicians with an online presence designed to bring fans and bands together.

MP3 charts.com
www.mp3charts.com
Offers bands the highest possible visibility.

Mp3Allies
donc@mp3allies.com
www.mp3allies.com
The source for the best independent musicians on the internet!

MP3tunes
9333 Genesee Ave. #100, San Diego, CA 92121
www.MP3tunes.com
We use music from CD Baby's digital distribution program. High rev-share to artists, with artists keeping almost $6 of every CD sold and almost $.60 for each song.

MP3Unsigned.com
admin@mp3unsigned.com
www.mp3unsigned.com
The best MP3s from new and unsigned artists.

MPEG NATION
3100 Dundee Rd. #708, Northbrook, IL 60062
PH: 408-850-9658
info@digitalsilo.com
www.mpegnation.com
Our mission is to stream your video content and make it universally accessible and useful.

Mperia
www.mperia.com
You get your music on Mperia by signing up for a free artist account and uploading your songs. It's as simple as that.

MSN Music
music.msn.com
Songs must be delivered through a Digital Music Distributor such as www.cdbaby.com or www.theorchard.com

MSSVision
542 W. University Pkwy. Baltimore, MD 21210
www.mssvision.com
Webcasts your Indie music video.

Music Forte
11363 S. Churchill, Plainfield, IL 60585
PH: 888-659-2867
Greg Percifield support@musicforte.com
www.musicforte.com
Musicians - we're ready to start promoting your band and music and it won't cost you a cent!

Music Gorilla
12407 Mopac Expressway N. 100-312, Austin, TX 78758
PH: 512-918-8978 FX: 212-258-6394
Alexia info@musicgorilla.com
www.musicgorilla.com
Exposure to major labels, Indie labels, film studios and publishers.

Music Itch
222 N. Columbus Dr. #1907, Chicago, IL 60601
Will Barroso will@musicitch.com
www.musicitch.com
Exposes music aficionados to the ever-growing music catalog within the independent market. Our motto is, "If you have an Itch for Music we'll scratch it!"

The Music Oven Network
PH: 512-334-6270
editor@musicoven.com
www.musicoven.com
Provides free promotional services to independent artists. Submit your music ONLINE using our form.

Music Scene Online
admin@musicsceneonline.com
www.musicsceneonline.com
Dedicated to the promotion and distribution music from emerging artists.

The Music Tap
postmaster@themusictap.com
www.themusictap.com
Dedicated to helping musicians spread the word about their music.

Music Torch
PO Box 472, New Hampton, NY 10958
PH: 917-232-4624
www.musictorch.com
A digital music store for artists who are looking for a place to sell their music.

Musicane
www.musicane.com
The do it yourself e-commerce solution that enables artists and labels to sell digital downloads from their own website.

MUSICFREEDOM.com
info@musicfreedom.com
www.musicfreedom.com
No monthly fee. We only make money when you do!

MusicGiants
926 Incline Way, Incline Village, NV 89451
support@musicgiants.com
musicgiants.com
Combines a music player, a music store and your music collection.

MusicIP
605 E. Huntington Dr., #201, Monrovia, CA 91016
PH: 626-359-9702 FX: 626-359-9827
www.musicip.com
Somewhere in the world, there is an audience that is looking for your unique sound. We can get you explosive exposure by linking you directly to fans who will love and buy your music.

MusicNet AOL
www.musicnet.com
Songs must be delivered through a Digital Music Distributor such as www.cdbaby.com or www.theorchard.com

MusicNoyz.com
Falmouth, ME 04021
PH: 207-878-1722 FX: 207-878-1723
info@musictoyz.com
www.musicnoyz.com
Offers full service music hosting to artists who want to share their artistic vision online.

MusicSpawn.com
35 Village Walk, Covington, GA 30016
PH: 404-202-6344 FX: 770-786-2305
artistsupport@musicspawn.com
www.musicspawn.com
Downloads from new and upcoming artists.

MVspy
3435 Ocean Park Blvd. #106, Los Angeles, CA 90405
PH: 310-593-4873
Tim Scanlin info@mvspy.com
www.mvspy.com
A video on demand channel offering guaranteed exposure on television. $500.00 per video.

MyJonesMusic.com
234 9th Ave. N., Seattle, WA 98109
Chris King info@myjonesmusic.com
www.myjonesmusic.com
Jones Soda Co. has created this free for all Indie music site.

myMPO
www.mympo.com
Content for myMPO's main database must be delivered through a Digital Music Distributor such as www.theorchard.com..

MyOriginalMusic.Com
258 Neiger Hollow Rd. Barton, NY 13734
PH: 607-687-2381
Jay Hammond jhammond@myoriginalmusic.com
www.myoriginalmusic.com
Music server and promotion for independent artists, bands and songwriters.

MySongStore.com
mysongstore.com
Allows any musician to sell their downloads from any of their web pages - MySpace.com, PureVolume.com, HostBaby.com etc.

MyxerTags
www.myxertones.com
Allows bands to easily create and distribute mobile phone ringtones to their fans.

mZeus.com
admin@mzeus.com
mzeus.com
Register now & upload your tracks, videos, & pictures all for free!

Napster
artistrelations@napster.com
www.napster.com
Contact us to get your music featured.

Nareos PeerReach
8350 Wilshire Blvd. #200, Beverly Hills 90211
PH: 323-556-0666 FX: 323-556-0601
info@nareos.com
www.nareos.com
Enables legal music downloads on P2P networks.
Songs must be delivered through www.cdbaby.com

Nextposure.com
PH: 604-261-5026
Jan Cooper cooperjan@telus.net
www.nextposure.com
Online video network. We are seeking bands with
good videos who want worldwide exposure.

NextRadio Solutions
www.nextradiosolutions.com
Streaming music to hundreds of thousands of users.
Songs must be delivered through a Digital Music
Distributor such as www.theorchard.com..

NewBandTV
info@newbandtv.com
www.newbandtv.com
Featuring videos of the hottest new bands on the
planet!

NewHotMusic.com
PO Box 2877, Palm Beach, FL 33480
PH: 561-775-4561 FX: 561-775-4562
www.newhotmusic.com
Take advantage of our promotional network.

Number One Music
259 W. 30th St. #12FR, New York, NY 10001
reclabels@numberonemusic.com
www.NumberOneMusic.com
Creating a buzz for EVERY artist registered with us
and turning 'potential' fans into committed fans.

OMD Online Music Directory
1167 White Pine Dr. Wellington, FL 33414
PH: 561-422-7198 FX: 561-422-7198
John Horner Admin@UnSignedOMD.com
www.UnSignedOMD.com
Where independent artists are the stars! Easy to use
charts, stores, photos and video.

OneSource e-CD Distribution System
Perry Leopold onesource@pan.com
onesource.pan.com
Sell from your own website and get paid 100% of
the sale.

OSRecords
www.osrecords.com
Providing you with quality music from independent
artists, without the usual record industry hype.

OtherWorld Distractions
PO Box 27421, Los Angeles, CA 90027
nonews@otherw.com
www.otherw.com
An alternative to iTunes and Napster. Many of the
artists here are ones you won't find anywhere else.

passalong
www.passalong.com
Innovative p2pREVOLUTION™ platform and
massive song catalog to build your own custom
download store.

PassTheMic.com
4130 Heyward St., Cincinnati, OH 45205
PH: 718-213-4176
www.passthemic.com
Community for independent Hip Hop artists, by
choice!

PayLoadz
295 Park Ave. S. #6B, New York, NY 10010
payloadz.com
It works seamlessly with your PayPal account,
enabling you to offer digital music from your
website or online auctions.

payplay.fm
PH: 212-202-0220
Elliot Goykhman elliot@payplay.com
www.payplay.fm
Online Indie music download store. Visit our site to
learn how to submit your music.

phonector USA
41 Hausman St., Brooklyn, NY 11222
PH: 347-495-7878
info@phonector.com
www.phonector.com
We can help you sell your music via download
distribution and burned audio CD distribution.

Playgroundz.net
Kevin J. Farrell staytuned@playgroundz.net
www.playgroundz.net
Independent music & video hosting, artist pages,
charts, reviews, rankings and more.

PostYourMusic.com
PH: 949 679-9361
Tom postyourmusic@postyourmusic.com
postyourmusic.com
Working musicians (for hire) search engine. Upload
your MP3s & videos. Download ringtones.

Primetones.com
PO Box 101, Porter, TX 77365
PH: 281-354-7677 FX: 281-354-7677
info@primetones.com
www.primetones.com
Present your music as MP3 tracks and ringtones.

Prize Talent
www.prizetalent.com
Offers you the opportunity to get exposure to agents,
producers and industry media.

promosquad
info@promosquad.com
home.promosquad.com
Our website is separated into five main areas: The
Promosquad Jukebox (rate new music), Polls/
Interactive, Get Famous, The Prize Store and the
message boards.

Promotion West
484 Washington St. #106, Monterey, CA 93940
PH: 831 373-6627
www.promotionwest.com
MP3 music download site for unsigned artists.

Publik Music
PO Box 4076, Portland, ME 04101
PH: 207-772-6102 FX: 207-772-6106
info@publikmusic.com
www.publikmusic.com
Showcase artists in an intimate, interactive setting
while cost-effectively reaching and growing their
audiences.

pureVOLUME
119 Braintree St. #603, Boston, MA 02134
labels@purevolume.com
www.purevolume.com
The place for rising artists to promote their music
and shows.

QTRnote.com
PH: 901-487-0754
peter@qtrnote.com
www.qtrnote.com
Can work with accomplished composers.

Radio Radio
553 E. Main St., Jackson, TN 38301
PH: 615-986-9271 FX: 866-294-7843
RT Curtis webmaster@radioradio.us
www.radioradio.us
Create your own store to start selling music. All
music that you upload will be played on our radio
station.

Radiotakeover
32 Mill St., Mount Holly, NJ 08060
PH: 609-733-1046
info@radiotakeover.com
www.radiotakeover.com
Promotional services for Indie artists.

RateMyCreation
www.ratemycreation.com
Developed for musicians who want to know what
others think of their music.

Rate Our Band
thecrew@digitalwhammy.com
www.rateourband.com
Get the general public's opinion of your band's
music.

RateSumMusic.com
www.ratesummusic.com
An opportunity to be heard, discovered and
reviewed by the public and industry players.

ReadyToBreak.com
6725 Sunset Blvd. #420 Los Angeles, CA 90028
PH: 310-593-4172
Paula Moore management@readytobreak.com
www.ReadyToBreak.com
Comprehensive talent portal where emerging artists
upload samples of work for signing consideration.

RedDotNet
2052 Corte Del Nogal, Carlsbad, CA 92009
PH: 973-657-1558 FX: 760-931-8026
www.digitalon-demand.com
Our content is drawn from the All Media Guide.

ResearchMusic
michael@researchmusic.com
www.researchmusic.com
We can publish your song or broker your master
recording to a record label. Upload MP3 files for
review by our A&R team.

RHAPSODY
www.rhapsody.com
Songs must be delivered through a Digital Music
Distributor such as www.cdbaby.com or
www.theorchard.com

RiPPYFeST
PO Box 1964, Salt Lake City, UT 84110-1964
PH: 801-487-7302
Lisa info@rippyfest.com
rippyfest.com
Bands compete for visitor's votes in hopes of being
named RiPPYFeST's best.

RoadNoise
PO Box 1811, East Lansing, MI 48826
PH: 800-758-9267
K. Michael Babcock mail@road-noise.net
www.road-noise.net
Enables independent artists to bring their music to the world and music fans to bring the world of music to their fingertips.

Ruckus Network
www.ruckusnetwork.com
A subscription download service designed exclusively for colleges and universities. Songs must be delivered through a Digital Music Distributor such as www.cdbaby.com or www.theorchard.com

ShareNewYork.com
PH: 516-967-2795
Ed Bernstein ed@sharenewyork.com
sharenewyork.com
Weed storage $1/MB/year. 60 days free. Hear fans tell you what they like about your music.

SignHere Online
contact@signhereonline.net
www.signhereonline.net
Visitors listen to the available selections and provide feedback via electronic survey. These results are made available to interested record labels.

SizzleFizzle.com
editor@sizzlefizzle.com
www.sizzlefizzle.com/home_music.asp
Features contests where visitors vote on their favorite song and videos in each genre.

SNOCAP
128 Spear St. 2nd Fl. San Francisco, CA 94105
feedback@snocap.com
www.snocap.com
Content registry and clearinghouse that enables record labels, publishers and individual artists to sell their entire catalogs through peer-to-peer networks and online retailers.

SongCast.net
7770 Jacksboro Hwy. Fort Worth, TX 76135
PH: 817-238-6693
admin@songcast.net
www.songcast.net
Upload your audio and video tracks. You live by exposure and the more you get, the better you will do in this business.

SongCritic.com
J. Atkinson songcritic@comcast.net
www.SongCritic.com
A site where fans can download and listen to your song(s) and then post "reviews" of your tune.

Songfight.org
fightmaster@songfight.org
www.songfight.org
We post a title, people make songs for that title and compete.

SongPlanet.com
feedback@songplanet.com
www.songplanet.com
We offer free artist pages, forums and live chat.

SongScope.com
PO Box 948, Columbus, GA 31902
PH: 770-754-4543
writerinfo@songscope.com
SongScope.com
Enables writers to build an online catalog of their songs to pitch to record labels, publishing companies and producers.

Sony Connect
www.sonyconnect.com
Songs must be delivered through a Digital Music Distributor such as www.cdbaby.com or www.theorchard.com

SoundClick
support@soundclick.com
www.soundclick.com
You can sell single songs as MP3 downloads or multiple songs as MP3 albums.

Soundmetro.com
PH: 714-777-2361
Greg Yancy daddysylem@soundmetro.com
www.soundmetro.com
A place for artists to get their faces seen and their music heard. Includes free web space, MP3 uploads and more!

SoundSauce
general@soundsauce.net
www.soundsauce.net
Write music? Play or Sing in a band? Join now and upload your MP3s for free!

Starbucks Music Download Service
www.starbucks.com
Songs must be delivered through a Digital Music Distributor such as www.theorchard.com..

stimTVnetwork
4347 Raytheon Rd. Oxnard, CA 93033
PH: 805-271-2759
submissions@stimtv.com
www.stimtvmusic.com
Hosts an endless stream of music video clips. Submit your band's videos.

Sunset Online Store
customerservice@sunsetonlinestore.com
www.SunsetOnlineStore.com
Get your content in the DiscLogic download portal.

SwayThisWay.com
PO Box 50911, Los Angeles, CA 90050
PH: 323-254-1934
customersupport@swaythisway.com
www.SwayThisWay.com
We've taken the best internet technological breakthroughs and combined these to present our audience with a tool to listen, enjoy and purchase music.

TastyAudio
www.tastyaudio.com
An online music discovery system. Our goal is to promote artists and provide a new venue for listeners to hear your music.

Tap It
207 N. El Camino Real #172, San Clemente, CA 92672
PH: 949-369-5333 FX: 949-369-5333
Joey Jimenez talent@tapitfame.com
www.tapitfame.com
A digital distribution and discovery engine for independent talent. Built for artists by artists.

TheBeat.fm
www.thebeat.fm/jamroom
Upload, listen, share your songs. Create your personal online store and earn money for your music.

Tower Records Digital Downloads
www.towerrecords.com
Songs must be delivered through a Digital Music Distributor such as www.cdbaby.com..

tradebit
3422 Old Capitol Trail #717, Wilmington, DE 19808-6192
PH: 484-685-4535 FX: 480-275-3582
usa@tradebit.com
www.tradebit.com
Sell music, photos and ebooks using your own PayPal account or just host with us!

TrakHeadz.com
PO Box 1304, Teaneck, NJ 07666-1304
support@trakheadz.com
www.TrakHeadz.Com
When you upload a song it is distributed to the accounts of our DJs members. When a DJ logs into his/her account, your song will be waiting there for him/her to review.

TVU Music Television
PO Box 1887, Westerville, OH 43086
PH: 614-890-9977
www.tvulive.com
The music video channel that actually plays music videos!

Ultimate Band List
10900 Wilshire Blvd. #1400, Los Angeles CA 90024
info@ubl.com
ubl.com
The ultimate online destination for independent bands, their fans and the music lovers who want to discover them.

Unsigned Band Network
158 Wigwam Trail, Livingston, TX 77351-3551
PH: 936-465-7487
James Stetler unsignedbandnetwork@gmail.com
www.unsignedbandnetwork.com
Allows free uploading of music merchandise and ringtones. You can make your own ringtone or we can create one for you.

Unsigned Talents
PH: 818-785-2611 FX: 818-785-2611
contact@unsignedtalents.com
www.unsignedtalents.com
Sign up to give talent agents a chance to discover you.

Upto11.net
feedback@upto11.net
www.upto11.net
Music lovers visit our site, type a band name into the search box, press "Get Recommendations" and we provide them with a list of recommended bands that they might like.

Verizon Wireless V CAST
www.verizonwireless.com/music
Music catalog available for download on mobile phones. Songs must be delivered through a CD Baby's Digital Music Service www.cdbaby.com

Virgin Megastore Digital Downloads
VirginDigital.com
Songs must be delivered through a Digital Music Distributor such as www.cdbaby.com or www.theorchard.com

vSocial
www.vsocial.com
The fastest, easiest way to upload, watch and share your favorite video clips.

Wal-Mart Music Downloads
www.walmart.com/music
Artists must go through a distributor to get their music online such as www.theorchard.com..

Weed
content@weedshare.com
www.weedshare.com
Pays you to share music files.

WorldPhonic
info@worldphonic.com
www.worldphonic.com
An internet music distributor providing you an easy way to distribute and profit from your music.

Xrateit.com
4232 Balboa Ave. #9, San Diego, CA 92117
FX: 561- 431-0664
contact@xrateit.com
Xrateit.com
Upload your music for FREE! What's the catch? The music is rated which means, if it's BUNK, it's gone! If it's TIGHT it stays!

YOUMAKEMUSIC.COM
mail@youmakemusic.com
www.youmakemusic.com
Features a download shop (digital distribution) and an 'old fashioned' web shop (physical distribution).

YouTube
www.youtube.com
Broadcast yourself. Watch and share your videos worldwide!

ZeBox
no_spam@zebox.com
www.zebox.com
A great efficient music engine for Indie artists.

Canada

Apple iTunes Canada
www.apple.com/ca/itunes
Songs must be delivered through a Digital Music Distributor such as www.cdbaby.com or www.theorchard.com

Bluetracks.ca
5074 de Lanaudiere, Montreal, QC H2J 3R1
info@bluetracks.ca
bluetracks.ca
We offer visitors an independent music catalogue that is varied, innovative and in constant evolution.

Mp3room.com
Ste. B - 2306 Bedford Pl. Abbotsford, BC V2T 4A5
Jayson Lockyer jayson@mp3room.com
www.mp3room.com
Created to promote and showcase the music of independent bands.

Musicianmp3.com
Can: PO Box 1692, Grand Forks, BC V0H1H0
US: PO Box 244, Danville, WA 99121
PH: 250-442-0304
musicianmp3.com
MP3 hosting for independent musicians.

NoWhere Radio
Box 42065 Southland Crossing PO, Calgary, AB T2J 7A6
artists@nowhereradio.com
www.nowhereradio.com
Here to help promote independent musicians around the world.

Puretracks
www.puretracks.com
Songs must be delivered through a Digital Music Distributor such as www.cdbaby.com or www.theorchard.com

Tzomé
1161 Country Rd. #2 E., Brockville, ON K6V 5T1
info@Tzome.com
www.tzome.com
Features an online database of searchable music. Staffed by some incredibly talented Indie artists.

The Weed Files
3256 D'Amours, Sainte-Foy, QC G1X1M7
PH: 418-657-5039
Christopher Stewart contact@weed-files.com
www.weed-files.com
A DIY music store intended for artists who want to distribute their music in the Weed format.

zunior.com
283 Danforth Ave. #358, Toronto, ON M4K 1N2
Dave Ullrich dave@zunior.com
www.zunior.com
Artists pay only a 15% administrative fee to use zunior.com. The majority of this goes towards the merchant account, hosting and bandwidth fees.

South America

Opson-Web
c/ 36 Nª 828, Mercedes, Buenos Aires, Argentina
PH: 02324427265
Hernan Botta hernanbotta@yahoo.com
www.opson-web.com.ar
A site based in Argentina where you can upload your music and video files for free!

Search MP3
Av. Das America, 700 Bloco 03 Sala 112,
Rio de Janeiro, Brazil 22640-100
PH: 55-21-2132-7757
www.searchmpthree.com
Register to create your own homepage containing your songs.

Europe

Austria

Trackseller
Hollandstrasse 8/4, A - 1020 Wien, Austria
PH: 0043-1-218-34-76-26 FX: 0043-1-218-63-00-63
Marc Muncke shop@trackseller.com
www.trackseller.com
Manages paid music downloads for musicians of any kind and all around the world directly off their website.

Croatia

Technopop Music
Giuseppe Verdi 23, 51410 Opatija, Croatia
PH: +385-98-713-330
Dario Dzimbeg (kod Cicin-Sain)
info@technopopmusic.com
www.technopopmusic.com
A small independent label for FREE Technopop music placed throughout Europe and beyond.

Czech Republic

Poslouchej.net
redakce@poslouchej.net
www.poslouchej.net
Czech music website (all genres) with online radios and MP3 downloads. 5000+ daily visitors.

Finland

Mikseri
www.mikseri.net
Downloads covering all genres.

France

Apple iTunes France
www.apple.com/fr/itunes
Songs must be delivered through a Digital Music Distributor such as www.cdbaby.com or www.theorchard.com

Music75
cougniot@music75.com
www.music75.com
An online site designed to help you create, profile and promote original songs.

Germany

Apple iTunes Germany
www.apple.com/de/itunes
Songs must be delivered through a Digital Music Distributor such as www.cdbaby.com or www.theorchard.com

besonic.com
Hochstadenstr. 15, 50674 Koln, Germany
PH: 49-221-53097-51 FX: 49-221-53097-70
www.besonic.com
Music anytime, anywhere, tailored to the individual likes of users.

MP3.de
www.mp3.de
Germany's largest MP3 site.

Music4u
www.music4u.cc
Free service. Upload your pics and MP3s to our database.

phonector Europe
Gleimstr.60, D-10437 Berlin, Germany
PH: +49 (0)30-44032480
info@phonector.com
www.phonector.com
We can help you sell your music via download distribution and burned audio CD distribution.

Open Music Source
Ickstattstr. 1, 80469 München, Germany
PH: 49-89-255-519-110 FX: 49-89-255-519-258
info@openmusicsource.net
www.openmusicsource.net
Database system which stores music and videos from bands around the globe.

Pooltrax
www.pooltrax.de
MP3 kostenlos downloaden, Charts, news, software für musik & MP3, uvm. bei POOLTRAX.

Songs Wanted
Willhelm-Dull-Str. 9, 80638, Munich, Germany
PH: 089-157-32-50 FX: 089-157-50-36
ellie@songswanted.com
www.songswanted.com
Helping artists get recognition.

Soundlift.com
www.soundlift.com
A music community open for musicians and music lovers from all over the world sharing their music and videos.

web62.com
www.web62.com
Internet Television. Music coverage.

Weedis
Reinekestr 26 A, 81545 Munich, Germany
PH: 0049-89-452-477-00
Michael Folkmer michael@folkmer.de
www.weedis.com
A progressive platform enabling super distribution for music and video.

Italy

MP3.it
www.mp3.it
Italy's largest MP3 site.

Latvia

Music is Here!
info@musicishere.com
www.musicishere.com
Songs must be delivered through a Digital Music Distributor such as www.cdbaby.com

The Netherlands

Fabchannel.com
Weteringschans 6-8, 1017 SG Amsterdam,
The Netherlands
PH: +31 (0)20-796-00-73 FX: +31 (0)20-796-00-76
info@fabchannel.com
www.fabchannel.com
A wide variety of live music in sound and vision. From upcoming acts to big stars.

Legal Download
Postbus 240, 3500 AE Utrecht, The Netherlands
info@legaldownload.net
www.legaldownload.net
De demo's worden eerst geselecteerd door bekende artiesten die hun sporen reeds in de muziekwereld hebben verdiend.

MP3.nl
www.mp3.nl
Large database with information about tracks, albums and artists.

Norway

beAudible.com
Strandgaten 90, 5011 Bergen, Norway
PH: +4797149153 FX: +4755311197
Sigmund Elias Holm beaudible@beaudible.com
www.beaudible.com
A premier provider of digital music distribution systems using the Weed platform, developed by Shared Media Licensing.

Poland

MP3.pl
www.mp3.pl
Poland's largest MP3 site.

Russia

MP3.ru
www.mp3.ru
Russia's largest MP3 site.

RealMusic
info@realmusic.ru
realmusic.ru
Covers all genres of music.

Spain

MUSICDLD.COM
Pl. Julio Gonzalez 8, bajos, Barcelona 08005, Spain
PH: +34-932240117 FX: +34-932240118
contacto@musicdld.com
www.musicdld.com
A promotion & digital distribution music portal.

Sweden

Digfi
Lars Jämtelid lars.jamtelid@digfi.com
www.digfi.com
Publicize your music on the site for free. Download our online application form.

Klicktrack
Box 1336, SE-621 24 Visby, Sweden
info@klicktrack.com
www.klicktrack.com
Provides ready-made, fully operational music download stores.

MP3Lizard.com
mp3lizard.com
Promote your band for free!

Musicbrigade
PH: +46-771-545-545
support@musicbrigade.com
www.musicbrigade.com
For a small fee we will take your video, digitize it to our high quality specifications and put it on our site.

Soundation
Halsingegatan 9, Stockholm, Sweden
PH: 001-46-8-660-9910
Martha martha@powerfx.com
www.soundation.com
Sell your music directly from your website and MySpace pages (we don't take a percentage). Don't wait to be signed to a label - be your own e-label!

Switzerland

beatmaka.com
Manessestrasse 120, CH-8045 Zurich, Switzerland
Marc Hedinger marc@beatmaka.com
www.beatmaka.com
Our review panel checks each incoming track and assures that only the best ones get online.

EuropaMp3.org
helpmusiciens@europamp3.org
www.europamp3.org
Boosts the launch of new labels and musicians by remunerating its subscribers for the essential work that they carry out for the distribution of your music!

United Kingdom

Apple iTunes UK
www.apple.com/uk/itunes
Songs must be delivered through a Digital Music Distributor such as www.cdbaby.com or www.theorchard.com

Arkade
www.arkade.com
Secure sales of MP3s, CDs and merchandise for bands and artists.

Audigist
Studio Nyne, 75 Church St., Bonsall, Derbyshire
DE4 2AE UK
support@audigist.com
www.audigist.com
Take your music to a wider audience.

Beathut
labels@beathut.com
www.beathut.com
We focus on independent music from independent labels.

BeatPick
Unit 8, 2nd Fl. East Wing, Oslo House, Felstead St.,
London, E9 5LG UK
FX: 0044 (0) 2089867712
Frank Danieli info@beatpick.com
www.beatpick.com
FairPlay music label and music licensing (download music and license pre-cleared Indie music).

contactmusic.com
Gate House, Iron Row, Burley in Wharfdale,
Ilkley, LS29 7DB UK
PH: 44-0-1943-865111 FX: 44-0-1943-865222
hello@contactmusic.com
www.contactmusic.com
If you get a deal through our site, you'll get 100% of the royalties.

CPU.ie
c/o Loop Studios, Space 28, North Lotts,
Dublin 1, Ireland
PH: 00353-87-785-8572
www.cpu.ie
Dedicated to unsigned bands around the globe. Has Ireland's first download MP3 chart. Hundreds of artists have made their music available free of charge.

Cube-music
Albany Boathouse, Lower Ham Rd.
Kingston-upon-Thames, KT2 5BB UK
PH: 020-85471543 FX: 020-85471544
info@cube-music.com
www.cube-music.com
Promote your video or audio tracks to UK audiences.

Daddy Fresh Music
Metways, 55 Canning St., Brighton, BN2 0EF UK
downloads@daddyfreshmusic.com
www.daddyfreshmusic.com
We specialise in music publishing and A&R. We are a digital label and download store.

Downtune
downtune@iesys.net
music.downtune.com
Sell your music directly to your fans.

easyMusic.com
www.easyMusic.com
Our "Copyleft" section features music from unsigned artists, including music which can be downloaded for free.

Eat This Music!
PO Box 8479, Prestwick, Ayrshire,
Scotland KA9 2YR
FX: 01292-677918
admin@eatthismusic.com
www.eatthismusic.com
Unsigned bands can get their info out to venues, management companies, promoters etc.

eircom.net Music Club
www.eircom.net/music
Irish download site. Songs must be delivered through a Digital Music Distributor such as www.theorchard.com..

IntoMusic
support@intomusic.co.uk
www.intomusic.co.uk
Download music featuring independent musicians.

iowntheMUSIC
info@iownthemusic.com
www.iownthemusic.com
Listen and be heard ...for free!

Launch Music on Yahoo UK
uk.launch.yahoo.com
Songs must be delivered through a Digital Music Distributor such as www.theorchard.com..

Letstalkmusic.com
Post House, Fitzalan Rd. Arundel, W. Sussex, BN18 9JY UK
PH: 01273-424413
opps@letstalkmusic.com
www.letstalkmusic.com
Upload your music for review, enter the showcase CD and more.

Mean Fiddler Music
www.meanfiddler.com
Songs must be delivered through a Digital Music Distributor such as www.theorchard.com..

MetroTunes Music Store
www.metrotunes.co.uk
Songs must be delivered through a Digital Music Distributor such as www.theorchard.com..

Monkeys Who Dream
artist@monkeyswhodream.com
www.MonkeysWhoDream.com
A collective of independent artists that believe art has a place and purpose beyond entertainment.

MP3Songs
www.mp3songs.org.uk
Help for unsigned artists.

MTV UK
www.mtv.co.uk
Songs must be delivered through a Digital Music Distributor such as www.theorchard.com..

MyCokeMusic
mycokemusic.com
Songs must be delivered through a Digital Music Distributor such as www.theorchard.com..

Napster.co.uk
artistrelations@napster.com
www.napster.co.uk
Offers tracks by hundreds of independent and unsigned artists.

News of the Noise
PO Box 78, Swanley, BR8 9AA UK
colum1@newsofthenoise.com
www.newsofthenoise.com
You can send .mp3 or .wma files electronically or drop a CD in the post.

OIKZ.com
Pól pm@oIKz.com
www.oikz.com
Gives bands and songwriters the opportunity to easily sell their music.

Orange Music
www.orange.co.uk/music
Songs must be delivered through a Digital Music Distributor such as www.theorchard.com..

Packard Bell Music Station
www.packardbell.co.uk/products/playground/music.html
Songs must be delivered through a Digital Music Distributor such as www.theorchard.com..

peoplesound.com
20 Orange St., London, WC2H 7NN UK
PH: 44-0-207-766-4000 FX: 44-0-207-766-4001
www.peoplesound.com
Get your music heard. by millions of visitors.

poptones.co.uk
brandnewyrretro@aol.com
www.poptones.co.uk
New label with streaming webcast.

Project Overseer Productions
www.projectoverseer.biz
DJs & members play your music and add real time comments.

PutItOnline.com
PH: 07957474268
Chris Ogunsalu Chris.Ogunsalu@t-mobile.co.uk
www.putitonline.com
Distribution service geared towards helping unsigned artists sell their music and digital content worldwide.

SafeSell
Studio 6, 105 Boundary St., Liverpool, L5 9YJ UK
PH: +44 (0)151-482-5557
info@safesell.com
www.safesell.com
Lets musicians sell secure music downloads directly from their own websites. No setup fees, 70/30 split.

Shiny New Music
Florence shinynewmusic@hotmail.co.uk
www.florencep.co.uk
Free interactive music website where visitors can listen to & discuss the hottest unsigned bands. Submit your demo!

The Song Site
PO Box 22949, London, N10 3ZH UK
PH: 44-020-8444-0987
simon@thesongsite.com
www.thesongsite.com
Something for everyone, be you artist or label.

Songstuff UK
www.songstuff.co.uk
Post your songs for review, review other's songs, discuss technical, creative and music business issues, chat in our forum.

SONY Connect Europe
www.connect-europe.com
Songs must be delivered through a Digital Music Distributor such as www.cdbaby.com or www.theorchard.com

Soundlift.com
www.soundlift.com
Open for musicians and music lovers from all over the world sharing their music and videos.

Stayaround.com
25 Barnes Wallis Rd. Segensworth East, Fareham, PO15 5TT UK
PH: +44 (0)1489 889821 FX: +44 (0)1489 889887
info@stayaround.com
stayaround.com
We offer the hottest, freshest and most upfront music around and let you decide how to listen.

Tesco.com Downloads Store
www.tescodownloads.com
Songs must be delivered through a Digital Music Distributor such as www.theorchard.com..

Tiscali Music
www.tiscali.co.uk/music
Songs must be delivered through a Digital Music Distributor such as www.theorchard.com..

TuneTribe.com
50-52 Paul St., London, EC2A 4LB UK
PH: 020-7613-8200
unsigned@tunetribe.com
www.tunetribe.com
Send your CD and we will prepare it for inclusion on the site for free! You set the price per download.

UKscreen
www.ukscreen.com
A center for film and music making. From casting, networking and crewing to broadcasting and distribution.

Australia

Apple iTunes Australia
www.apple.com/au/itunes
Songs must be delivered through a Digital Music Distributor such as www.cdbaby.com or www.theorchard.com

Asylum TV
Peter Deske pd54@optusnet.com.au
www.asylumtv
TV program focusing on independent artists. Overseas submissions welcome.

Boost Digital
36 Emmett St., Crows Nest, NSW 2065 Australia
PH: +61-2 9959-4405 FX: +61-2-9460-0044
Ian MacRae newmusic@boostdigital.com
www.boostdigital.com
The search is on worldwide for video makers who are keen for their music to be not only heard but seen.

ChaosMusic
5 Harper St., Abbotsford, VIC 3067 Australia
PH: +61-3-9412-3596
info@chaosmusic.com
www.chaosmusic.com
Indie artists WANTED!!! Sell your CDs/sound files.

eChoonz.net
PO Box 2495, Fitzroy Business Ctr. Melbourne, VIC 3065 Australia
Kristo Beyrouthy administration@echoonz.net
www.echoonz.net
We accept tracks from any style of music.

HMV Australia
www.hmv.com.au
Songs must be delivered through a Digital Music Distributor such as www.theorchard.com..

Public Revolution

PO Box 3282, Helensvale Town Ctr. QLD 4212
Australia
PH: +61-7-5529-9331
info@publicrevolution.com
www.publicrevolution.com
You now have a chance to showcase your music to the world!

sanity.com.au

www.sanity.com.au
Songs must be delivered through a Digital Music Distributor such as www.theorchard.com..

Soundbuzz

www.Soundbuzz.com
A digital music service provider and the only provider with a regional focus on the Asia-Pacific markets.

Asia

Gone Fishing for Blue Skies

2-2-4-503, Azuma, Kashiwa, Chiba, 277-0014,
Japan
PH: 81-80-3278-2862
Big Foot bigfoot@gonefishingforblueskies.com
www.gonefishingforblueskies.com
On demand music streaming, introducing independent music from around the globe.

jammy.jp

www.jammy.jp
Japanese social networking service.

listen.co.jp

www.listen.co.jp
Specializes in Indie/mainstream music.

Orientaltunes.com

admin@orientaltunes.com
www.orientaltunes.com
Follows the modern trends in Oriental music.

PlanetMG

2 Int. Bus. Pk. #05-10, Tower 1, The Strategy,
Singapore 609930
FX: 65-6329-8520
admin@planetmg.com
www.planetmg.com
Downloadable music from mainstream & Indie artists.

recommuni.jp

info@recommuni.jp
recommuni.jp
Japanese social networking service with over 10,000 members.

Sweet Basil

www.omega.co.jp/sb-i
Japanese site featuring overseas Indie music.

MP3 Blogs

MP3 blogs vary in what they have to offer artists. Some do in-depth reviews of CDs and will post a few MP3s of your songs, while others simply post the songs with a few words about the band. Your songs are visible to visitors for up to 30 days. After that, visitors of the blog would have to search the archives to find your posts. Some blogs also post videos. Many also feature podcasts of music they like.

Most MP3 blogs feature what is called "podsafe music". To find out what podsafe music is, read the article in SECTION SEVEN of this book called "What is Podsafe Music?"

United States

3hive

PO Box 3778, Huntington Beach, CA 92605
suggestionbox@3hive.com
www.3hive.com
Promoting MP3s in hope that people will hear enough to buy the album, attend the live show, wear the t-shirt ...

4waystop

4waystop@gmail.com
www.4waystop.com
Helps new bands get exposure and exposes our listeners to new music.

A Plague of Angels

Molotov mikarr785@aol.com
plagueofangels.blogspot.com
Music mandated by activist judges.

Advance Copy

kmhopkin@juno.com
advancecopy.blogspot.com
This is what you want, this is what you get.

Adzuki Bean Stash

Cchang cchang@math.utexas.edu
adzukipod.blogspot.com
If you discover a musician/band on here that happens to take your fancy, please read up on them.

Aeki Tuesday

Jenny Francois aekituesday@gmail.com
www.aekituesday.com
Devoted to publishing music news, reviews, interviews with a small dosage of pop culture.

An Idiot's Guide to Dreaming

farmerglitch@gmail.com
loki23.blogspot.com
The blogging equivalent of an acid tattoo scare.

Arjan Writes

arjanwrites@gmail.com
www.arjanwrites.com
Original interviews, music reviews and exclusive reports from behind the scenes.

Ashcan Rantings

Charles & Leah email.ashcan@gmail.com
ashcanrantings.blogspot.com
A blog about music and the arts.

aurgasm

3 Ashford Ct. #1, Boston, MA 02134-2204
Paul Irish aurgasm@mac.com
aurgasm.us
An eclectic menagerie of aural pleasures. I scout out music you've never heard and deliver only the finest.

Banana Nutrament

nutramentmike@gmail.com
banananutrament.blogspot.com
Investigating new and old artists and music. We like to support artists making a living with their music.

Beat the Indie Drum

btidmatt@gmail.com
www.beattheindiedrum.com
News and music reviews.

Between Thought and Expression

DJMonsterMo BTandE@gmail.com
djmonstermo.blogspot.com
An eclectic guide to life's musical journey. Features Indie and Electronic MP3s, mash-ups and entertainment.

bigstereo

PO Box 5062. Portland, ME 04101
Travis promo@bigstereo.net
this.bigstereo.net
We try to work with artists and labels to provide content for our readers. Have a record we should hear?

The Big Ticket

mr.gilbert@mac.com
the-big-ticket.blogspot.com
News, opinions and MP3 reviews.

Bows + Arrows

555 Guava Ln. #9G, Davis, CA 95616
Brian Lum brian@bowsplusarrows.com
bowsplusarrows.com
I listen to absolutely everything I'm sent.

The Camera as Pen

mikejonze@gmail.com
thecameraaspen.blogspot.com
Profiling exciting music, new and old.

Can You See the Sunset From the Southside?

Eric canyouseethesunset@gmail.com
cystsfts.blogspot.com
Daily MP3s and occasional podcasts. A little left of the mainstream and that's the way I like it.

Catbirdseat

catbirdseat.org@gmail.com
www.catbirdseat.org
MP3 blog with news and reviews.

Clever Titles Are So Last Summer

Bethanne Siettas butcherthegirl@yahoo.com
clevertitlesaresolastsummer.blogspot.com
I do accept submissions on a case-by-case basis. Contact me for my mailing address.

clicky clicky

Jay jay.breitling@gmail.com
clickyclickymusic.com
News. reviews, opinion, fanboy excitation since 2003.

Coffee Snorter

coffeesnorter@gmail.com
coffeesnorter.blogspot.com
Created by an over caffeinated coffee zealot with a slight case of A.D.D. in music.

Come Pick Me Up

backtothesound@mac.com
cpmu.blogspot.com
I'm here to inform, not provide. If visitors dig the MP3s I post, I ask that they support the artist and purchase a CD.

Copy, Right?
bigfatprettyface@yahoo.com
copycommaright.blogspot.com
Posts cover tunes.

Culture Bully
Chris chris@culturebully.com
www.culturebully.com
With album reviews and other posts ranging from Indie Rock to Hip Hop to Electronica, you never know what we'll bring.

Daytrotter.com
info@daytrotter.com
www.daytrotter.com
We're giving you exclusive, re-worked, alternate versions of old songs and unreleased tracks by some of your favorite bands and by a lot of your next favorite bands.

The DIY Rockstar
Jeff diyrockstar@gmail.com
www.thediyrockstar.com
One of the main selling-points of this blog is that it features interviews with artists that are relevant to the independent music community and make music I love personally.

Dreams of Horses
Michael cassettetapes@gmail.com
dreamsofhorses.blogspot.com
If you'd like to see your band featured on my site, send me an MP3 and some info.

Each Note Secure
joe@eachnotesecure.com
www.eachnotesecure.com
MP3 blog created with the intent of promoting my favorite music.

EAR FARM
Matt earfarm@mac.com
earfarm.blogspot.com
If you send something to us and we like it, we'll feature it on our site.

EARVOLUTION
hilltownmedia@gmail.com
earvolution.com
Music news, reviews, interviews and notes.

Elbows
elbo.ws
A collection of great music blog posts and is meant to provide you a snapshot of what's going on in this new genre of blogging.

Everybody Cares, Everybody Understands
everybodycares@gmail.com
everybodycares.blogspot.com
I'm rather obsessed with finding good (free and legal) music to share with everybody.

Exitfare
exitfare@gmail.com
exitfare.blogspot.com
New music, shows, interviews, TV and club night fun!

extrawack!
extrawack@gmail.com
extrawack.blogspot.com
Featuring reviews and quality MP3s of new music.

Feed me Good Tunes
Silent K silentk@feedmegoodtunes.com
feedmegoodtunes.com
An opportunity for friends and strangers alike to uncover new music that may or may not blend into their music tastes.

Fine Fine Music
mail@finefinemusic.com
www.finefinemusic.com
We link to MP3s of bands that we like.

Fluxblog
Matthew Perpetua fluxblog@gmail.com
www.fluxblog.org
Reviews music and posts MP3s. Send MP3s to my e-mail address. Contact me for instructions on sending your CD.

Freeway Jam
freejam@gmail.com
freewayjam.blogspot.com
We have a new feature profiling artists who offer new music on the internet. Visit our website for submission details.

Funtime OK
ok@funtimeok.com
www.funtimeok.com
Feel free to contact us about albums, new bands, reviews ...whatever.

Good Weather For Airstrikes
DerekDavies@aol.com
www.goodweatherforairstrikes.com
A place for me to share info about up and coming bands.

gorilla vs. bear
Chris chrismc99@hotmail.com
gorillavsbear.blogspot.com
We never have a bad thing to say about anyone, even if they are lame.

Heart on a Stick
heartonastick@gmail.com
heartonastick.blog-city.com
News, photos, reviews etc.

Hello Gina
ginahello@gmail.com
hellogina.blogspot.com
Downloads and music news.

The House of Leaf and Lime
leafandlime@gmail.com
leafandlime.hobix.com
Updated several times weekly.

The Hype Machine
hype.non-standard.net
An experiment that keeps track of songs and discussion posted on the best blogs about music. Visitors listen, discover and buy songs that everyone is talking about!

I Am Fuel, You Are Friends
browneheather@gmail.com
www.fuelfriends.blogspot.com
Got something I should hear? E-mail me.

I Guess I'm Floating
contact.iguessimfloating@gmail.com
iguessimfloating.blogspot.com
Blog of the Rock n' Roll variety. If you're a band and would like to submit a demo, just e-mail us!

I Rock Cleveland
irockcleveland@gmail.com
irockcleveland.blogspot.com
Contact us if you want your band to be featured on our site.

Indie Don't Dance
indiedontdance@hotmail.com
indiedontdance.blogspot.com
I listen to amazing independent music and try my hardest not to dance.

Indoor Fireworks
The Vicar indoorfireworksonline@gmail.com
indoorfireworks.blogspot.com
Music news and MP3s.

Kingblind
Martin Lee info@kingblind.com
www.kingblind.com
Music news, album & concerts reviews, MP3s, videos, art / entertainment and much more!

Largehearted Boy
boy@largeheartedboy.com
blog.largeheartedboy.com
Featuring daily free and legal music downloads as well as news from the worlds of music, literature and pop culture.

The Listen
2046 Hillhurst Ave. #22, Los Angeles, CA 90027
tips@thelisten.net
www.thelisten.net
We can't promise that we'll post your submissions, but we will do our best to give every song submitted a spin.

marathonpacks
eric@marathonpacks.com
www.marathonpacks.com
I am very picky about what I post here, but you may make submission requests.

MOISTWORKS
moistworks@gmail.com
www.moistworks.com
We enjoy listening to new material and try to listen to everything sent our way.

Moroccan Role
hammmd@gmail.com
moroccanrole.blogspot.com
A totally killer music/MP3 blog.

Music For Kids Who Can't Read Good
7407 N. Windsor Ln. Peoria, IL 61614
musicforants@mac.com
musicforants.com
If you have music you'd like me to write about, e-mail me the MP3s or mail your CD.

music for robots
contact@music.for-robots.com
music.for-robots.com
Contact us if you think we'd be interested in your music.

My Mean Magpie
Five Seventeen five17@telus.net
www.mymeanmagpie.com
I'm always happy to receive free things. Check my site for submission details. Do NOT send attachments/MP3s with your e-mail.

My Old Kentucky Blog
8565 Scarsdale Dr. E., Indianapolis, IN 46256
dodge77@gmail.com
myoldkyhome.blogspot.com
You can e-mail MP3s or send materials to our mailing address.

MyselfMyself
www.myselfmyself.com
Downloads of music that we've come across that we want everyone else to enjoy.

Mystery & Misery
jason.wilder@gmail.com
www.mysteryandmisery.com
Devoted to independent and underground music. Music news, CD and MP3 reviews.

Needcoffee.com
wakeupyoubastards@needcoffee.com
www.needcoffee.com
You think you've got something that can keep us awake? Well? Do ya, punk? Bring that noise. We like it, we'll post it.

Noise for Toaster
noisefortoaster@gmail.com
noisefortoaster.blogspot.com
We'll drag you through concerts, websites, new music reviews and the same shit you read everywhere else.

the of mirror eye
ofmirroreye@gmail.com
blog.ofmirroreye.net
The songs I'm posting are some of my favorites for one reason or another.

the oh so quiet show
roboppy@gmail.com
music.diskobox.net
Send me MP3s or real CDs (ask for my shipping address) but I'm not obligated to write about anything unless I like it.

Out the Other
Janet Timmons outtheother@gmail.com
www.outtheother.com
A streaming archive of music to pay attention to. I also host a radio show on WRVU.

Pocket|Trax
pockettrax@gmail.com
www.pockettrax.com
We do not review music. What we do is collect and share artist info and sample tracks and leave the reviewing up to the readers/listeners.

PolloxNiner
Sunny Pollox9@aol.com
polloxniner.blogs.com
I write and edit for magazines, newspapers, websites and TV.

rbally
jennings@rbally.net
rbally.net
Features Acoustic songs.

Revolution in the Head
revolutionblogspot@yahoo.com
revolutioninthehead.blogspot.com
I show you the music I love. You agree. Or not. You tell me. Or not.

The Rich Girls Are Weeping
Cindy and Pinkie elegantfaker@gmail.com
therichgirlsareweeping.blogspot.com
Almost all of the content is dependent the vagaries of your hostess' weird tastes and whatever we're really into these days.

The Rawking Refuses to Stop!
David Greenwald davideg@ucla.edu
rawkblog.blogspot.com
If you are in a band or work for a label, I'd love to hear your stuff. Link me some MP3s or drop me an e-mail and I'll let you know where can you send me promos.

Scenestars
www.scenestars.net
Send event info and MP3s for us to review!

scissorkick.com
8801 Ridge Blvd. Brooklyn, NY 11209
steve@scissorkick.com
www.scissorkick.com
A blog used for the purpose of cultivating interest in musicians and their music.

Silence is a Rhythm Too
Michael djrez1@hotmail.com
siart.blogspot.com
I love music and I've always loved to share my favorite music. I like a lot of different things and hope you will too.

Sixeyes
alanlwilliamson@gmail.com
sixeyes.blogspot.com
An MP3 blog that posts music news, reviews and interviews.

skatterbrain
Matthew mortigi_tempo@verizon.net
blownbythewind.blogspot.com
Covering new and interesting Indie music spanning just about all genres. We update daily with news, band spotlights and exclusive MP3 posts.

Slave to the Details
team@slavetothedetails.net
slavetothedetails.net
All MP3s are up for a limited time and are for sampling purposes only.

songs:illinois
629 Belleforte St., Oak Park, IL 60302
Craig Bonnell cbonnell@gmail.com
www.songsillinoismp3.blogspot.com
Mostly music musings on new and old releases, current favs and live shows. MP3 downloads updated several times a week for evaluation purposes.

The Sound of Indie
kevin@thesoundofindie.com
www.thesoundofindie.com
One person's music collection laid forth for the world to hear.

Strawberry Fire
strawberryfirenyc@mac.com
www.strawberryfire.blogspot.com
Because you're going to hear about it sooner or later.

The Suburbs are Killing Us
suburbs@christopherporter.com
www.christopherporter.com
MP3s are here to promote love. They are removed after one week.

The Test Pilot
Jonathan jonathan@jonathanschmitt.com
thetestpilot.blogspot.com
I am using this site to put music out there that I think people don't know about and should try, so IF YOU LIKE IT, BUY IT and support the artist!

The Tofu Hut
316 York St., Top Apt. Jersey City, NJ 07302
forksclovetofu@gmail.com
tofuhut.blogspot.com
Music posted here is posted out of love, not with the intention for profit.

Torr.org
428 Hanbee St., Richardson, TX 75080
Torr Leonard torrleonard@gmail.com
torr.typepad.com/weblog
If you are interested in submitting music for plugging consideration, please send it to the above address.

Trigger Cut
Johnny Metro triggercut@crankautomotive.com
www.triggercut.com
Audio and video blog with occasional reviews.

Tuning
jaysniemann@sbcglobal.net
ggth.typepad.com/tng
Got a CD or band I should know about? Well then, why don't you flack yer tunes?

Two and 1/2 Pounds Of Bacon
fastbacker@haywoodnyc.com
fastbacker.blogspot.com
MP3 and video blog based out of Brooklyn.

Yeti Don't Dance
Jerry Yeti jerryyeti@gmail.com
noyetidance.blogspot.com
Blog posting music news and MP3s.

You Ain't No Picasso
thatkid42@gmail.com
youaintnopicasso.blogspot.com
Blog with interviews with artists and reviews of MP3s.

Canada

A Soundtrack for Everyone
asoundtrackforeveryone@gmail.com
tdot.blogspot.com
News and reviews. If you want to send some music my way, I'll happily check it out.

Checkerboard Chimes
breath_mint@hotmail.com
checkerboardchimes.blogspot.com
Feel free to send me stuff.

chromewaves.net
Frank frank@chromewaves.net
www.chromewaves.net
I write about stuff that I find interesting and noteworthy. Please check the site to see if your music fits before sending it in.

herohill.com
herohill@gmail.com
www.herohill.com
Music interviews, news, reviews and tracks.

i (heart) music
1276 Wellington Ave. 2ⁿᵈ Fl. Ottawa, ON K1Y 3A7
info@iheartmusic.net
www.iheartmusic.net
All the latest news, views, reviews and MP3s. We'll accept anything and everything, but can't guarantee a review.

Indie Launchpad
Colin Meeks colin@indielaunchpad.com
www.indielaunchpad.com
Showcasing some of the best in independent music. We also have a podcast that features tracks from the music we review.

Mocking Music
RR 1, Mountstewart, PE C0A 1T0
Casey Dorrell mockingmusic@gmail.com
www.mockingmusic.blogspot.com
E-mail us to make arrangements and we'll gladly review your music.

Muzak for Cybernetics
Sean muzakforcybernetics@gmail.com
www.indierockblog.com
Features Indie Rock, Electro, Hip Hop and other cool music from all over the world.

My Indie World
Hanson Ho hansonho@shaw.ca
www.myindieworld.com
Music geek and pop culture freak!

Popsheep
popsheep@gmail.com
popsheep.com
Reviews of MP3s and live shows. Contact us if you want to invite us to your show.

Pregnant Without Intercourse
3647 Ave. Henri-Julien, Montreal, QC H2X 3H4
Keith Serry fatcitizen@gmail.com
www.pwithouti.com
What we taught the world is that you can suck and still rule.

Rock Snob
Miss Valerie sheswiththeband@hotmail.com
therocksnob.blogspot.com
Because we're better and we know it!

Said the Gramophone
Jordan Himelfarb jordan@saidthegramophone.com
www.saidthegramophone.com
A daily sampler of really good songs. All tracks are posted out of love.

The Underground Express
40 Falling River Dr. Richmond Hill, ON L4S 2R1
Andrew Iliadis blew82@hotmail.com
theundergroundexpress.blogspot.com
Features music tracks and reviews.

Villains Always Blink
Kelly trillionmillion@hotmail.com
thetrainingground.blogspot.com
Indie music, reviews, hype, news, MP3s ...

Czech Republic

Getecho
getecho@hotmail.com
getecho.blogspot.com
Send me info, you can! I also appreciate all suggestions/tips and label/band news. I'm specially searching for new bands!

Denmark

Hits in the Car
Stytzer hits_in_the_car@yahoo.dk
stytzer.blogspot.com
It's all about music!

France

La Blogothèque
www.blogotheque.net
Le premier MP3 blog, audioblog en France.

Germany

Indie Surfer
Ziggy gpanic@gmail.com
indiesurfer.blogspot.com
Intended to popularize the music of independent artists and to give you the latest info on their activity.

Italy

Indie for Dummies
indiefordummies@gmail.com
www.indiefordummies.com
We help bands we like to be noticed in Italy.

Norway

For the Eardrums
eardrums@lindbjor.net
eardrums.blogspot.com
A focus on new and interesting music. Alternative artists from the world of Indie, Electronica, Experimental or Alt-Folk.

Spain

fuck me i'm twee
tweepopster@gmail.com
fuckmeimtwee.blogsome.com
News and music reviews.

United Kingdom

Another Form of Relief
PO Box 756, Gillingham, Kent, ME8 6WW UK
scrunty@gmail.com
www.theclerisy.com/afor
We'll listen to everything that we are sent and will write about anything that we like.

Black Country Grammar
jon@blackcountrygrammar.co.uk
grammardj.blogspot.com
If you have something for me to listen to, drop me a line.

headphone sex
PO Box 204, Slough, SL2 2QE UK
James Woodley james@headphonesex.co.uk
www.headphonesex.co.uk
Tracks are posted for one week. Send me music!

Indie MP3 - Keeping C86 Alive!
Tom blog@indie-mp3.co.uk
www.indie-mp3.co.uk
Working hard to keep the Indie Pop scene alive.

Let's kiss and Make up...
Colin c.r.clark@strath.ac.uk
letskissandmakeup.blogspot.com
I really should be using my limited spare time in a much more productive manner than this.

No Rock & Roll Fun
Simon simonb@gmail.com
xrrf.blogspot.com
Music news and reviews.

Nothing But Green Lights
mikesmithmikesmith@gmail.com
nothingbutgreenlights.net
Features fresh and exciting, legal MP3's from diverse artists and Pop acts from around the globe.

The Torture Garden
Shane thetorturegarden@gmail.com
thetorturegarden.blogspot.com
Downloads, news and interviews.

Children's

(sm)all ages
superclea@cox.net
smallages.blogspot.com
MP3 blog featuring Children's music.

Christian

ChristianMp3.com
info@christianmusicentertainmentgroup.com
www.christianmp3.com
We are dedicated to offering Christian music in modern formats including MP3, CDs and more.

ChristianWeed.com
PO Box 18895, Panama City Beach, FL 32417
FX: 707-549-4436
James Moore info@christianweed.com
christianweed.com
E-mail us (preferably with a link to samples of your material). If we feel your music is marketable, we'll reply with the paperwork you'll need to fill out and fax back to us.

Gospel Swap
info@gospelswap.com
www.gospelswap.com
Let us help you to promote and sell your original Gospel music!

Jamsline.com
www.jamsline.com
Get your singles to radio and other industry entities.

Triplestrandmp3.com
info@triplestrandmp3.com
www.triplestrandmp3.com
Supporting the works of emerging & unsigned Christian music artists.

Classical

ChoralNet
4230 Mary Dr. Rapid City, SD 57702
www.choralnet.org
Extensive resources for Choral artists.

Classic Cat
webmaster@classiccat.net
www.classiccat.net
A directory with links to over 2000 free to download Classical performances on the internet, sorted by composer and work.

The Classical Music Archives
200 Sheridan Ave. #403, Palo Alto, CA 94306
PH: 650-330-8050
www.classicalarchives.com
Submit your music to get exposure.

Classical.com

PO Box 31687, 18 Denbigh Rd. London,
W11 2UX UK
PH: +44-20-8816-8848
conductor@classical.com
www.classical.com
Online listening, downloads, custom CDs and more.

eClassical.com

Theres Svenssons gata 10, SE. 417 55 Göteborg,
Sweden
PH: +46-31-3608715
info@eclassical.com
www.eclassical.com
A completely virtual record label.

Impulse Classical Music

impulse@impulse-music.co.uk
www.impulse-music.co.uk
Provides personalized pages on performers and composers.

NetNewMusic

netnewmusic.net
A portal for the world of NON-Pop/Extreme Indie/Avant-whatever music.

OnClassical

Via Ca'Petofi 13 - (36022) Cassola, Vicenza, Italy
PH: +39-0424-533137 FX: +39-0424-533137
me@onclassical.com
www.OnClassical.com
Distributing high quality Classical music in MP3 or OGG formats. We are associated with kunstderfuge.com, the greatest resource of free MIDI files on the net.

Country

acousticfriends.com

www.acousticfriends.com
Enables Acoustic musicians to be seen and heard by posting their music, video and upcoming performance information, increasing their fan base.

Mandolin Cafe

eadg@mandolincafe.com
www.mandolincafe.com/mp3
Introduces new mandolin players.

Dance and Electronic

7161.com

www.7161.com
We are a non profit site run by musicians. We have free web space for artists to add their music for streaming. We also offer free homepage creation and other free tools.

Audiojelly

80 Hadley Rd. Barnet, Herts. EN5 5QR UK
PH: +44 (0) 208-440-0710
FX: +44 (0) 208-441-0163
info@audiojelly.com
www.audiojelly.com
It's only a matter of time now before this becomes the norm and going into a record shop to buy a CD becomes unusual.

Beatport

support@beatport.com
www.beatport.com
Designed to service the evolution of the Digital music culture, redefining how DJs and enthusiasts acquire their music.

BLEEP

PO Box 25378, London, NW5 1GL UK
info@bleep.com
www.bleep.com
Warp Records selection of downloadable Electronica.

ClubFreestyle.com

info@clubfreestyle.com
www.clubfreestyle.com
Worlds largest Freestyle music community.

Digibag.com

info@digibag.com
www.digibag.com
All CD-quality tracks as well as MP3s you can download in seconds, available now!

DJ SETS

6 Iliados Str. PC 54641, Thessaloniki, Greece
PH: +302310-843124
www.djsets.gr
A community where DJs can post their music files and have people rate them.

Electromancer *UK*

www.electromancer.com
We are a community of unsigned Electronic musicians and a resource where they can make their music available to visitors and other musicians.

Groovegate

Simrishamnsgatan 20a, SE-214 23 Malmoe, Sweden
PH: +46-(0) 40-972 273 FX: +46-850-593-986
www.groovegate.com
A one stop store for DJ's and end users alike where they can find all the latest grooves for their listening pleasures.

headstrong Dance music

info@headstrong-hq.com
www.headstrong-hq.com
Put your demos here to get exposure.

InternetDJ.com

17 State St. 14ᵗʰ Fl. New York, NY 10004
Michael Bordash mbordash@internetdj.com
www.internetdj.com
Hosts and plays MP3s from independent musicians.

Knobtweakers

www.knobtweakers.net
The world's leading free and legal Electronic music MP3 blog, established to support and promote Electronic music culture.

Music V2

US PH: 719-966-4322
UK PH: +44-020-7871-7440
musicv2@musicv2.com
www.musicv2.com
Free MP3 hosting, artist pages, DJ sets, free music downloads.

Pitch Adjust

Simrishamnsgatan 20a, SE-214 23 Malmoe, Sweden
PH: +46 (0)40-972-273 FX: +46-850-593-986
www.pitchadjust.com
Labels can find new talents, new talents can find a label and promoters can post info.

Play it tonight

#23 - 1917 W. 4ᵗʰ Ave. Vancouver, BC V6J 1M7
FX: 208-246-4676
info@playittonight.com
www.playittonight.com
If you would like to sell your music through our site, please contact us via e-mail.

SectionZ

2513 W. Superior St. 1ˢᵗ Fl. Chicago, IL 60612
www.sectionz.com
An artist only Electronica community. We strive to provide a platform for people who are interested in learning about the construction and philosophies of the electronic medium.

SMART-MUSIC.NET

Vogelsangstr. 30a, 70197 Stuttgart, Germany
PH: +49 (0)179-243-11-40
FX: 49 (0)1212-510-479-968
Bernd Drescher info@smart-music.net
www.smart-music.net
We only feature legal MP3s where the source can be easily identified and we only offer links to full-length, high quality files.

tribal mixes dot com

tribalmixes.com
Website for sharing live DJ mixes and live sets recorded in MP3 format.

Virgo Lounge

PO Box 4721, St. Louis, MO 63108
info@virgolounge.com
www.VirgoLounge.com
An online source for Dance music, industry networking and an event marketplace. Please send us your press release or info about your project or event.

WOMB

350 Lincoln Rd. #318, Miami Beach, FL 33139
PH: 305-673-9488 FX: 305-402-0839
digital@thewomb.com
www.thewomb.com
The first 24/7 worldwide radio & internet television broadcaster of live mixes & performances. We have launched the first all-in-one download shop for the digital culture.

Xpressbeats

Devonshire House, 223 Upper Richmond Rd.
London, SW15 6SQ UK
PH: +44 (0) 20-8780-0612
FX: +44 (0) 20-8789-8668
admin@xpressbeats.com
www.xpressbeats.com
We provide quality 'upfront' Dance music and an extensive catalogue of tracks for music lovers.

Experimental

Music For Maniacs

Mr. Fab mail@m-1.us
musicformaniacs.blogspot.com
MP3 blog dedicated to extremes in music. "Outsider" recordings and utterly unique sounds reviewed.

tapegerm

1478 Stetson Cir. Salt Lake City, UT 84104
PH: 801-972-2441 FX: 801-972-2443
feedback@tapegerm.com
www.tapegerm.com
A new and vibrant center for music creativity.

Folk

Cantaria

www.chivalry.com/cantaria
A library of "bardic" Folk songs, mostly from Ireland, Scotland and England.

efolk Music
201B N. Greensboro St., Carrboro, NC 27510
PH: 919-968-4810
artists@efolkMusic.org
www.efolkmusic.org
Independent Folk MP3 and CD source.

GLBT

Dyke TV
PO Box 170-163, Brooklyn, NY 11217
PH: 718-230-4770
Elizabeth Maynard staff@dyketv.org
www.dyketv.org
Lesbian cable access show that airs nation-wide. We do occasionally solicit or welcome music submissions.

Goth

SlagHuis MultiMedia
PO Box 190792, Miami Beach, FL 33119-0792
PH: 305-434-8651 FX: 305-531-5609
Sam Bradford support@slaghuis.net
www.slaghuismultimedia.com
Gothic, Darkwave & Industrial. Get heard. Get seen online, today!

Hip Hop

Drulz.com
www.drulz.com
Changing the way you download music!

Ear Fuzz
djmaru@earfuzz.com
www.earfuzz.com
A venue for music appreciation. Files are shared out of love and respect and is only meant to help expose and promote the featured artists.

Givemebeats.com
www.givemebeats.com
If you make beats and you want to sell them on the internet, this is the beat place to do so.

Hip Hop Palace.com
PO Box 158, Bowling Green Stn. New York, NY 10274
hiphoppalaceceo@yahoo.com
www.hiphoppalace.com
Upload your music and be on our radio show.

MP3 Rap Hip Hop
info.rap.hiphop@gmail.com
www.reohiphop.com.ar
Just good Latin Hip Hop underground Indie artists. MP3s, news, forums, photos ...

Notes from a Different Kitchen
ian@differentkitchen.com
differentkitchen.blogspot.com
MP3 blog featuring news, reviews, music etc.

Real-HipHop.com
info2@real-hiphop.com
www.real-hiphop.com
Real MC's, DJ's, fans, music, videos and more.

StreetCDs
7948 Winchester Rd. #109-300, Memphis, TN 38125
Jay Style Williams jaystyle@streetcds.com
www.streetcds.com
We intend to be the recognized digital music store for Street music.

UnderworldHipHop.com
PH: 416-333-2446
www.underworldhiphop.com
A free MP3 uploading service for Hip Hop artists. We also do reviews.

Unlimitedtracks.com
922 Hwy. 81 E. Box 315, McDonough, GA 30252
PH: 678-432-1229
sales@unlimitedtracks.com
www.unlimitedtracks.com
An online store for Urban musicians. Sell your tracks online for .99 cents per track. You can also sell your CD from our site.

Ya Heard
yaheard.bet.com
Unsigned artists upload your original songs and create your own web page.

Jam Band

bt.etree.org / BitTorrent
bt.e@etree.org
bt.etree.org
Provided by the etree.org community for sharing the live concert recordings of trade friendly artists. Please tell your friends and family about new bands that catch your ear and support these artists by going to see them live and buying their CDs!

etree.org
wiki.etree.org
An online community that uses an independent network of file (FTP) servers that host and distribute Shorten (SHN) audio files.

jambase.com
1 Zoe St., San Francisco, CA 94107
PH: 415-543-7000 FX: 415-543-7775
rhapsody@jambase.com
rhapsody.jambase.com
New, interactive digital music service. Promotes independent artists and bands from around the world.

LIVEDOWNLOADS
www.livedownloads.com
Offering an opportunity to listen to shows from a current tour very soon after they've happened, mastered directly from the soundboard.

nugs.net
web1.nugs.net
Artists can harness the demand for their live performances and studio recordings.

Jazz

Any Swing Goes
PO Box 721675, San Diego, CA 92172-1675
PH: 858-484-7716 FX: 801-382-6409
doug@anyswinggoes.com
www.anyswinggoes.com
Focuses on the revival of Big Band and Swing music.

Cjazz
8554 122nd Ave. NE. #120, Kirkland, WA 98022
PH: 425-827-5441 FX: 425-827-1170
Michele Abrams michele@cjazz.com
www.cjazz.com
Show the world who you are and what you can do.

Jazztronic
contact@jazztronic.com
Jazztronic.com
Our main interest is Electronic Jazz music. We think that Jazz spirit mixed to the new Electronic ways to play music is going to become a great thing.

No Idle Frets
Nick Carver noidlefrets@gmail.com
noidlefrets.blogspot.com
MP3 blog. Dedicated to podsafe Jazz guitar music.

Quiet FM
www.quietfm.com/jcblog
MP3 blog featuring a primarily instrumental blend. Jazz, New Age, Ambient/Electronic and World music.

Latin

FaroLatino.com
Conesa 960 dpto 1, Ciudad de Buenos Aires, BA 1426, Argentina
PH: +5411-4551-7527
administracion@farolatino.com
tienda.farolatino.com
"La Cocina del Arte" is a virtual space dedicated to promoting new bands. It offers an online space to bands to promote their products.

Latin Cool Now
www.latincoolnow.com
Sell your Indie music here.

Metal

Ear Assault
Jason admin@earassault.com
www.earassault.com
A place for Metal bands to upload MP3s and gain exposure.

EarAche.com
43 W. 38th St. 2nd Fl. New York, NY 10018
PH: 212-840-9090 FX: 212-840-4033
www.earache.com
Metal MP3s and videos.

metalvideo.com
www.metalvideo.com
Metal videos, MP3s and more.

Reality Check TV
PH: 415-831-2825
Ace Annese acespace@realitychecktv.com
www.realitychecktv.com
Connect to the Metal underground world. We accept submissions!

The Rocking Ape
Leubeweg 91, D-89134 Blaustein, Germany
PH: +49 (0) 7304-929289 FX: +49 (0) 7304-929386
info@rockingape.com
www.rockingape.de
Your independent music portal. Metal, Punk, Rock and Rock n' Roll.

Vicious Enterprises
Death Priest admin@viciousenterprises.net
www.viciousenterprises.net
Free MP3 downloads from undiscovered talent. You submit we post.

Punk

altsounds.com
www.altsounds.com
Free artist profiles allow you to host MP3s, WMA's or OGG files, upload photos, news, gigs plus much more.

BlankTV
361 Vine St., Glendale, CA 91204
PH: 818-242-3107
info@blanktv.com
www.BlankTV.com
Free exposure for your videos to a worldwide audience of Indie music lovers.

DirtbagMusic.com
webmaster@dirtbagmusic.com
www.dirtbagmusic.com
Sign up and upload your music, bio, news, tour dates and much more.

Download Punk
info@downloadpunk.com
www.DownloadPunk.com
We do accept submissions directly from unsigned artists, but we do request that they don't send demos, only pressed CDs.

Enough MP3s
PO Box 12 07 50, 68058 Mannheim, Germany
info@enoughfanzine.com
www.enoughfanzine.com
Feel free to upload your band's/label's MP3 files.

Reggae

Surforeggae
contato@surforeggae.com.br
www.surforeggae.com.br
Reggae MP3s, news, events and more.

Soul / R&B

Captain's Crate
Captain Planet charlie@bywayof.net
bywayof.net/captains_crate
An MP3 blog featuring rare, funky and soulful music.

Myonlinemusic.net
Keith sales@myonlinemusic.net
www.myonlinemusic.net
Dedicated to getting out the great music of Smooth Jazz and R&B artists.

Women In Music

blowupdoll
mordiblowupdoll@yahoo.co.uk
blow-up-doll.blogspot.com
MP3 blog featuring women artists.

International House Of Pussy
25 Woodhorn Farm, Newbiggin By The Sea, Northumberland, NE64 6AH UK
mp3@theinternationalhouseofpussy.co.uk
www.theinternationalhouseofpussy.co.uk
MP3 blog featuring mostly female artists.

Schlocker
Bruno transistorrythm@yahoo.com
schlocker.blogspot.com
MP3 blog featuring audio and video of European female artists.

Womenfolk
robbie@womenfolk.net
womenfolk.net
The song blog dedicated to women in music.

World

Aduna
regcontact@free.fr
aduna.free.fr
Blog audio dédié à la musique Afro d'hier, d'aujourd'hui et de demain ...

Benn loxo du taccu
Matt Yanchyshyn letters@mattgy.net
bennloxo.com
MP3 blog featuring African music for the masses.

Calabash Music
211 Pleasant St., Arlington, MA 02476
PH: 781-777-1109 FX: 617-507-7769
www.calabashmusic.com
A global marketplace for independent World music.

Worldly Disorientation
Peter peter@petermargasak.com
worldlydisorientation.blogs.com
MP3 blog with semi-coherent musings on the ephemeral cultural asteroids in my orbit.

SECTION SIX: HELPFUL RESOURCES FOR MUSICIANS AND SONGWRITERS

"If you can achieve one successful thing a day to help your music career then you are on the right track. Pick one thing, just one and do it today!" – **Chris Standring, Founder of A&R Online**

General Resources

335 Design
PO Box 29742, Charlotte, NC 28229
PH: 704-560-2379
contact@335.com
www.335.com
Not selling many CDs through your website? Let us help! We provide affordable, superior website design for musicians and music related businesses.

ArtistPromo Hotel Sponsorship
PO Box 685, Shutesbury, MA 01072
PH: 413-259-1227
Jaime Campbell Morton artspromo@artspromo.org
www.artspromo.org/hotelsponsor
The hotel donates the room in trade for a stage mention and I get a small fee for setting it up.

Babel Fish Language Translator
world.altavista.com
Ever get a music review in a foreign country and have no idea what they're saying?

Band Command
PH: 503-471-1304 FX: 971-223-4713
info@bandcommand.com
www.bandcommand.com
We can help you find current booking information on tons of live music venues!

Bandit A&R Newsletter
68-70 Lugley St., Newport, PO30 5ET UK
PH: +44-1983-524110
bandit@banditnewsletter.com
www.banditnewsletter.com
Helping ambitious bands target their demos to labels, publishers etc.

bandsforlabels.com
PH: 562-627-9251
info@bandsforlabels.com
www.bandsforlabels.com
A free band-label matchmaking site.

Bandzoogle
550 Jean d'Estrees, #901, Montreal, QC H3C 6W1
Keif keif@bandzoogle.com
www.bandzoogle.com
Lets you build a band website without any web programming knowledge.

The BardsCrier.com
PO Box 4067, Austin, TX 78765
www.bardscrier.com/articles
A free guerrilla music marketing ezine.

The Brink
350 W. Simpson St., Tucson, AZ 85701
PH: 646-213-0900 FX: 520-623-6395
Danny Vinik danny@brink.com
www.brink.com
An e-zine about life on the edge. Our passions are pop-culture, indie-film and travel. We think radically and play hard. Our users send us digital photos, films, music etc.

CCNow
www.ccnow.com
A low-risk way for small businesses to sell their product online.

Clear Channel Music - NEW!
new@clearchannel.com
www.clearchannelmusic.com/new
Unsigned artists, please submit music to www.garageband.com. Every three months we'll pick 50 NEW! independent artists from the top of the GarageBand charts.

Digital Music News
Paul Resnikoff paulr@digitalmusicnews.com
www.digitalmusicnews.com
Technology news for music industry professionals.

Downhill Battle
PH: 508-963-7832
contact@downhillbattle.org
www.downhillbattle.org
Creating a decentralized music business and a level playing field for independent musicians and labels.

Finding Your Path
Mark Maxey m-squared@m-squared.org
cnx.rice.edu/content/col10326/latest
This FREE course can help new and struggling bands with the information they need to be successful.

GetmySong.com
artists@getmysong.com
www.getmysong.com
Provides music business news, artist directories and music forums. To add your songs, photos and biography to our 'Artist Directory' e-mail us your material.

Flashrock
11669½ Vanowen St., North Hollywood, CA 91605
PH: 818-503-1404
flashrock.com
Loads of promotional tools for artists including webcasts that helps to bring exposure to bands.

getsigned.com
707 Miamisburg-Centerville Rd. #103, Dayton, OH 45459
Shawn Fields editor@getsigned.com
www.getsigned.com
EVERYTHING you ever wanted to know about the music biz.

Giglist.com
www.giglist.com
Add and update your gigs online!

GigMasters
460 Old Post Rd. Bedford, NY 10506
PH: 866-342-9794 FX: 209-370-9793
info@gigmasters.com
www.gigmasters.com
A complete entertainment booking agency.

GIGPAGE.com
PO Box 16940, Sugar Land, TX 77496-6940
PH: 281-541-0981
info@gigpage.com
www.gigpage.com
An easy, do-it-yourself calendar for your gigs!

HearUsPlay.com
webhost@hearusplay.com
www.hearusplay.com
Free utilities that can be utilized by bands that have a strong web presence.

Hostbaby
5925 NE. 80th Ave. Portland, OR 97218-2891
PH: 888-448-6369
hostbaby@hostbaby.com
www.hostbaby.com
The best place to host your website/domain!

House of Blues Entertainment *Ones to Watch*
Attn: Jesse Ervin / Ones To Watch,
6255 Sunset Blvd. 16th Fl. Hollywood, CA 90028
www.hob.com/artistfeatures/onestowatch
Introducing promising new talents that aren't even playing our stages yet. Send package to the above address (no calls or e-mails please).

I am the Next Idol
enquiries@iamthenextidol.com
www.iamthenextidol.com
We give you a free showcase to post your photos and music.

Indie Contact Newsletter
indiecontactnewsletter@rogers.com
www.bigmeteor.com/newsletter
Free monthly e-zine that lists radio shows, music magazines, labels etc. looking for new music.

Indie-Music.com Classifieds
www.indie-music.com/classifieds
You can list your CD release, gigs, equipment for sale, anything at all. Help us fill the store - please post an ad today!

International Country Calling Codes and World Time Zones
www.countrycallingcodes.com
Find the international dialing code or time zone for any country. Online tool will instantly show you ALL telephone prefixes needed to call from one area code to another.

The World's Leading
International Songwriting
Competition

The U.S.A.

Songwriting

Competition

WINNING SONGS GET RADIO AIRPLAY!
$50,000 TOP PRIZE & MORE!
EXPOSURE!

Top Industry Professionals Judging!
ENTER TODAY!

*Sponsored by Indie Bible, Sony, New Music Weekly, Keyboard Magazine, Sam Ash Music Stores, Ibanez Guitars, D'Addario Strings, Audio Technica, Peavey, IK Multimedia, AirplayONLY, Mixdown Media Network, Garitian Music Sofwatre, Loggins Promotion, Hear Technologies, Superdups, LiveWireMusician.com, Acoustic Café and XM Radio.

FREE INFO
www.songwriting.net

or Call toll free: 1-877-USA-SONG
outside US call: (954) 776-1577

IRLWebhost.com
1167 White Pine Dr. Wellington, FL 33414
PH: 561-422-7198 FX: 561-422-7198
John Horner Admin@IRLWebHost.com
www.IRLWebhost.com
Web hosting and domain registration for Indie artists. NO set up fees!

Jagermusic.com
20 Cedar St. #203, New Rochelle, NY 10801
bands@jagermusic.com
www.jagermusic.com
Sponsors bands and supplies them with giveaway items. We recommend that all interested bands send us an electronic press kit from www.sonicbids.com

The League of Rockers & The Rolling RocHaus
13318 31st Ave. NE., Seattle, WA 98125-4411
PH: 206-367-3584
James II therollingrochaus@hotmail.com
www.theleagueofrockers.com
Each is a licensed recording, publishing, motion picture & concert promotion company all wrapped into one!

Listen to Our Band
Heather Heather_Donovan@student.uml.edu
www.listentoourband.net
Music site dedicated to unsigned/Indie bands in need of free promotion and for music fans looking for new music — anything other than what is on MTV!

LiveJournal
www.livejournal.com
A journal community with powerful personal publishing ("blogging") tool, built on open source software.

Lost in the Grooves Sub-Publishing
PO Box 31227, Los Angeles, CA 90031
PH: 818-324-3152
www.lostinthegrooves.com/subpub
Helping bands/labels without publishing deals claim performance/sales/licensing royalties from overseas.

Market Wire
200 N. Sepulveda Blvd. #1050, El Segundo, CA 90245
PH: 310-846-3600 FX: 310-846-3700
www.marketwire.com
We post news released by small to large businesses worldwide.

Marketing Your Music
www.marketingyourmusic.com
An array of tips on how to call attention to your music.

Missingink
122 Industrial Dr.
PO Box 505,
White House, TN 37188
PH: 615-672-9368 x111
FX: 615-672-7225
www.missingink.com
With our online shop module and fulfillment services we have created a risk free solution for any band looking for an official online shop.

mojam
concertmaster@
mojam.com
www.mojam.com
Promote your upcoming events, add info to your artist page and more.

Music Biz Academy
David Nevue dnevue@rainmusic.com
www.musicbizacademy.com
We aim to teach musicians how to use the internet to their financial advantage and to arm musicians with all the information they need to move their music career forward in the 'real' world.

Music Biz Solutions
www.mbsolutions.com/articles
Articles to help musicians start and grow successful music businesses.

Music Industry News Network *(mi2n)*
1814 Astoria Blvd. Astoria, NY 11102
PH: 718-278-0662
Eric de Fontenay editor@mi2n.com
www.mi2n.com/submit_top.html
Submit your press releases for free.

Music Network USA
2118 Wilshire Blvd. #368, Santa Monica, CA 90403
Vic support@mnusa.com
www.mnusa.com
Features music business classifieds, newswire, artist video showcase and internet services.

The Music Pages
www.themusicpages.com
If your band needs a gig or if your club needs a band please visit our Gig Board.

Music Video Wire
www.mvwire.com
The resource for music video industry news, interviews and educational content.

MusicBizWebsitePro
PH: 615-781-9295
Julie Blake Julie@MusicBizWebsitePro.com
www.MusicBizWebsitePro.com
Build and update your own professional website. Point and click easy. NO programming skills needed. FREE 10-day trial (NO credit card required).

MusicBrainz
info@musicbrainz.org
www.musicbrainz.org
We are building an open-source database containing all the information you would ever want to know about songs, albums and artists.

Musician's Cyber Cooler
PH: 330-807-5236
Dave Jackson musicianscooler@gmail.com
www.jammindave.com
Promotional tools and resources for musicians.

Musician's Health
www.musicianshealth.com
Explanation of musician's injuries, along with guidelines regarding injury prevention, optimizing your musical performance and for achieving an optimum state of health.

MusiciansOnly.net
www.musiciansonly.net
A FREE musician classified system. The concept is similar to Craigslist but more tailored for musicians.

MusicPressReport.com
PO Box 79, Oak Lawn, IL 60454
PH: 708-499-4726 FX: 801-327-4735
Editor C.J. Chilvers amwp@amwp.org
www.MusicPressReport.com
A daily weblog featuring headlines, articles, links and resources for the music press. We're constantly looking for useful content and skillful writers.

MyMusicJob.com
www.mymusicjob.com
Providing assistance to those who make their living in the music industry.

New Music Weekly Magazine
26239 Senator Ave. Harbor City, CA 90710
PH: 310-325-9997 FX: 866-243-4357
editor@newmusicweekly.com
www.newmusicweekly.com
Covers the radio and music industry with its 24+ page weekly magazine. Has become the standard for tracking radio airplay nationwide.

New Music Tipsheet
scott@sperrymedia.com
www.newmusictipsheet.com
We do everything we can to turn on readers to up & coming artists.

Operation Gratitude
16444 Refugio Rd. Encino, CA 91436
cblashek@aol.com
www.opgratitude.com
Sends care packages and letters of support to soldiers deployed overseas. If you have excess inventory that you can donate to us, we would be delighted to include your CDs, DVDs, caps, t-shirts etc. in our packages.

PayPal
www.paypal.com
The world's largest online payment solution. No start-up fees, no monthly fees.

PR Web
PO Box 333, Ferndale, WA 98248
PH: 360-312-0892 FX: 360-380-9981
www.prweb.com
We have helped over 4,000 companies distribute their press releases.

Press Release Writing Tips
315 Fruitwood Ln. Knoxville, TN 37922
PH: 865-671-8366 FX: 865-671-8437
info@press-release-writing.com
www.press-release-writing.com
Contains free tips on writing good press releases.

The Reger Datablogging Platform
PH: 404-394-6102
Joe Reger info@reger.com
reger.com
You can create a blog and publish your first entry in minutes.

Rent My Band
admin@rentmyband.com
www.rentmyband.com
Online booking agent to help you find local & national gigs.

Rock-n-Roll Web Design and Hosting
PO Box 1922, Salisbury, MD 21802
PH: 410-835-8895
Audra Coldiron audra@rock-n-roll-design.com
www.rock-n-roll-design.com
We offer powerful hosting tools that give you complete control over all content on your site.

Savidetup Productions
PO Box 121626, Fort Worth, TX 76121-1626
PH: 817-737-3026
Tim Sisk tim@savidetup.com
www.savidetup.com
Services for the consumer, artist and business communities.

Sonicbids
580 Harrison Ave. 4th Fl. Boston, MA 02118
PH: 617-275-7222
Panos artists@sonicbids.com
www.sonicbids.com
Creator of the Electronic Press Kit (EPK™). It's an easy-to-use, web-based graphic interface that contains all the basic information of a musical act such as music, photos or date calendar.

spinme.com
Joe Taylor joetaylor@spinme.com
www.spinme.com
Daily news, tools & tips for working musicians.

StagePass News
www.stagepassnews.com
Whether you need to find sponsorship money for your band's tour or how to handle intellectual rights, there is plenty to read here.

starpolish
1 Irving Pl. #P8C, New York, NY 10003
FX: 212-477-5259
info2@starpolish.com
www.starpolish.com
Resources include an extensive library of business advice, self-management tools and strong exposure opportunities.

TheConcertChannel.com
PO Box 32017, Kansas City, MO 64171
PH: 913-384-9021
greg@theconcertchannel.com
www.theconcertchannel.com
Makes live shows more accessible to the public.

Topica
www.topica.com/channels/music
Browse through hundreds of newsletters on music related subjects.

TOURdatabase.com
support@tourdatabase.com
www.tourdatabase.com
The concept of TMS is to centralize your tour dates which makes your events accessible to any website.

USA Musicians Network
PO Box 133, Williamsville, NY 14231-0133
PH: 716-565-1969 FX: 716-565-9779
info@usamusician.com
usamusician.com
Promote your music and local gigs.

CD Duplication and Mastering

Abet Disc
1938 S. Myrtle Ave. 2nd Fl. Monrovia, CA 91016
PH: 626-303-4114 FX: 626-236-5591
info@abetdisc.com
www.abetdisc.com
Specializes in CD and DVD replication, short-run CD and DVD duplication, audio CD mastering, DVD authoring, CD graphic design, printing and packaging.

Acme Vinyl Corporation
187 Steelcase Rd. W. #15, Markham, ON L3R 2R9
PH: 905-470-2937 FX: 905-470-2856
www.acmevinyl.com
Created to address the declining capacity and quality of vinyl in North America.

CDman
4794 6th Ave. W., Vancouver, BC V6T 1C5
PH: 800-557-3347 FX: 604-261-3313
www.cdman.com
We know how to put the customer first. We are the print professional's choice for fast CD / DVD Duplication & CD / DVD replication services. Since 1991 our reputation has been one of honesty and integrity.

CD MASTERCOPY
800 Summer St. 2nd Fl. Stamford , CT 06901
PH: 888-443-3855
Renee Lunchana rlt@2000te.com
www.cdmastercopy.com
CD duplication services that cares about your project. Fast, easy, professional and 100% satisfaction!

CDRollout.com
4001 Pacific Coast Hwy. #104, Torrance, CA 90505
PH: 310-791-7624 FX: 310-791-7620
Mike Naylor info@cdrollout.com
www.cdrollout.com
We offer CD and DVD replication, manufacturing as well as a wide range of services to market and promote your project. It's our "one-stop-shop" convenience that sets us apart from other companies.

Crazy Daisy Productions
4257 Barger Dr. #171, Eugene, OR 97402
PH: 541-517-1458 FX: 425-790-0630
Erik Veach info@crazymastering.com
www.crazymastering.com
Our state-of-the-art CD mastering provides high-quality professional sound at a price anyone can afford. Have all the tracks you can fit on a single audio CD (up to 80 min) mastered for less than $250.

Crystal Clear Disc & Tape
10486 Brockwood Rd. Dallas, TX 75238
PH: 800-880-0073
Jim Cocke info@crystalclearcds.com
www.crystalclearcds.com
For over 35 years thousands of artists have trusted us to take their CD duplication projects from concept to finished product. We can do it all - from full-color art design and digital mastering and editing to professional "retail-ready" manufacturing and packaging.

DISC MAKERS
7905 N. Rte 130, Pennsauken, NJ 08110-1402
PH: 856-663-9030 FX: 856-661-3458
www.discmakers.com
The nation's leading CD / DVD duplicator, replicator and printer. When you're ready to make CDs, we're ready to make it happen. We're musicians too, so we know what you need to make it in this business: The best-looking product, the hottest-sounding audio and the most valuable (and free) promotional tools, including free distribution, a free UPC bar code and much more!

Moonlight Mastering
11022 SW. Oaks Dr. Austin, TX 78737
PH: 512-291-3083
Nancy Matter nmatter@earthlink.net
www.moonlightmastering.com
We specialize in major sound - minor budgets. 24-bit mastering. Package design and graphics services also available.

Music Manufacturing Services
Can: 25 Defries St., Toronto, ON M5A 3N4
PH: 416-364-1943
US: 20 W. 20th St. #302, New York, NY 10011
PH: 212-337-0252
Dave Larson dave@musicmanufacturing.com
musicmanufacturing.com
Since 1988, we have been the manufacturer of choice for thousands of musicians, bands and labels throughout North America.

MVD Distribution
422 Business Ctr. H-840 N. Circle Dr. Oaks, PA 19456
PH: 610-650-8200 FX: 610-650-9102
www.mvdb2b.com
A one-stop for music DVDs, carrying the best selection of the format in the world. We execute the physical fulfillment of our products servicing major chains, distributors, one-stops, online & independent retailers.

OASIS CD Manufacturing
12625 Lee Hwy. PO Box 214, Sperryville, VA 22740
PH: 888-296-2747 FX: 540-987-8812
info@oasisCD.com
www.oasiscd.com
We help you manufacture your CD or DVD project. We also help you package it creatively, promote and distribute it so it doesn't become just more clutter in your apartment.

Odds On Recording
14B Sunset Way, Henderson, NV 89014
PH: 877-633-7661 FX: 702-697-5341
Sheila Parham support@oddsonrecording.com
www.oddsonrecording.com
For the best in replication, mastering & recording! Odds On is a full service facility with an impressive customer list from major corporations to independent labels.

Play-It Productions
259 W. 30th St. 3rd Fl. New York, NY 10001
PH: 212-695-6530 FX: 212-695-4304
info@play-itproductions.net
www.play-itproductions.net
Founded in 1990 to provide local musicians and other content owners with a one stop solution for all of their duplication and graphic needs no matter the size of the project.

Sonarus Corporation
5 Vertical Dr. Cannonsburg, PA 15317
PH: 888-757-3472 FX: 724-746-0745
Derek info@sonarus.com
www.sonarus.com
Whether you need one copy or millions, we will produce the job on time and on budget. Our award winning Digital Cloning Laboratory(TM) thrives on CD replication service and DVD replication service perfection. You get exactly what you want, when you want it.

Tape & Disc Services
7570 Springhill Ct. Gladstone, OR 97027
PH: 888-655-2272 FX: 503-656-4742
info@tapeanddisc.com
www.tapeanddisc.com
A full-service CD duplication and replication company that also specializes in DVD replication and duplication.

Databases

Abbie's Open Mic Directory
Abbie abbie@abbiegardner.com
www.abbiegardner.com/mics.html
A comprehensive list of Open Mics, especially in the NE US.

All Media Guide
1168 Oak Valley Dr. Ann Arbor, MI 48108
www.allmusic.com
Massive database of CDs. Add yours!

allrecordlabels.com
324 8th St. E., Saskatoon, SK S7H 0P5
Peter Scott scottp@moondog.usask.ca
allrecordlabels.com
lights1.blogspot.com
A database of record label websites. I also announce new releases in my blog.

Bandname.com
Ryan Crowley information@bandname.com
www.bandname.com
A worldwide database of band and artist name activity. The service notifies artists and labels where potential name conflicts exist.

Celebrity Access
PO Box 817, Stonington, CT 06378-0817
PH: 860-536-5700 FX: 860-536-5713
sales@celebrityaccess.com
www.celebrityaccess.com
A database with contact info on agents, managers, record companies, talent buyers and venues.

CHaT Venues Database
chatmusic.com/venues.htm
Search engine with over 2000 venues throughout the US. Search by region, capacity, genres etc.

Coalition of Independent Music Stores
www.cimsmusic.com
A group of some of the best independent music stores in America. Contact the CIMS office to coordinate their efforts nationwide.

Daily Newspapers around the World
www.refdesk.com/paper.html
Links to hundreds of daily newspapers worldwide.

Discogs.com
www.discogs.com
A user-built database containing information on artists, labels and their recordings.

Festival Network Online
PO Box 18839, Asheville, NC 28814
PH: 800-200-3737 FX: 828-645-3374
info@festivalnet.com
festivalnet.com
Lists more than 7,000 events throughout the U.S. and Canada seeking performers, from local & regional to national & international.

FestivalFinder
music@festivalfinder.com
www.festivalfinder.com
Discover the latest details on more than 2,500 music festivals in North America.

Festivals.com
900 4th Ave. #3350, Seattle, WA 98164
PH: 206-621-7723 FX: 206-621-9399
www.festivals.com
Submit your festival photos and join our online communities.

GigNation
Chris Clang chrisclang1@adelphia.net
www.gignation.com
Connecting Indie bands with clubs, promoters, music fans and each other.

HitQuarters
www.hitquarters.com
Presents the world's top record company A&Rs, managers, publishers and producers, including their contact info & track records.

The Independent Artist Registry
Fallon Arenkiel fally@independentartistregistry.com
www.independentartistregistry.com
The labels and promoters who use the IAR are looking for the best artists who are regionally developed and have the talent to make it at the next level.

Indie Link Exchange
indielinkexchange@rogers.com
www.indielinkexchange.com/ile
Free service with listings of over 1500 Indie music sites that wish to exchange links with other music related sites.

Music Publishers Directory
mpa.org
A listing of contact information for publishers, both domestic and foreign and copyright administrating offices.

MusicClassifieds.us
mcwebmaster03@musicclassifieds.us
www.musicclassifieds.us
Features instant posting of ads, over 80 music categories and much more.

Newspaper and News Media Guide
www.abyznewslinks.com
Database of HUNDREDS of international newspapers.

POLLSTAR
www.pollstar.com
Submit your itineraries to our route book department.

record labels on the web
www.rlabels.com
5000+ links to record labels (Note: this website is no longer being updated).

SoundRangers.com
PH: 206-352-8818 FX: 206-374-8109
www.soundrangers.com
Royalty free music and sound effects download site.

studiofinder.com
www.studiofinder.com
Search for a studio by name, location, equipment, price and/or area of expertise.

Virtual-Festivals.com
4 Rowan Ct. 56 High St., Wimbledon, London, SW19 5EE UK
PH: +44 (0) 20-8605-2691
FX: +44 (0) 20-8605-2255
editor@virtualfestivals.com
www.virtualfestivals.com
Providing the most comprehensive and frequently updated coverage of the UK and global music festival scene.

Equipment, Merch and Software

ABC Pictures
1867 E. Florida St., Springfield, MO 65803-4583
PH: 417-869-3456 FX: 417-869-9185
www.abcpictures.com
Quality publicity picture reproduction, posters, 8x10's, head shots & composites for the entertainment industry.

Ace Products
11 5th St. #106, Petaluma, CA 94952
PH: 800-950-1095
info@aceproducts.com
www.kaces.com
Provides excellent gig bags, cases and accessories for percussion, electronic, guitar and orchestral instruments.

ALLPARTS
13027 Brittmoore Park Dr. Houston, TX 77041
PH: 713-466-6414 FX: 713-466-5803
allparts@allparts.com
www.allparts.com
America's premier guitar and bass parts supplier.

AUDIOCAL
PH: 828-232 0016
www.audiocal.com
An audio-video calendar maker with streaming MP3 audio and video for bands, clubs, concerts and live music promotion.

Busy Beaver Buttons
PO Box 87676, Chicago, IL 60680
Christen Carter buttongal@busybeaver.net
www.busybeaver.net
We make custom buttons good, fast and cheap!

CDstands.com
30 Compton Way, Hamilton Sq. NJ 08690
PH: 609-689-1711
info@cdreview.com
cdstands.com
We manufacture our own line of CD Boxes for artists to sell their music at shows or in stores.

Coll Audio
3595 St. Clair Ave. E. #2, Toronto, ON M1K 1L8
PH: 416-264-1188 FX: 416-264-1190
mail@collaudio.com
www.collaudio.com
Canada's leading source for backline musical instrument rentals.

Goombah
contact@goombah.com
www.goombah.com
A new efficient way for artists and labels to reach individuals who already like their style of music.

Gracenote CDDB
2000 Powell St. #1380, Emeryville, CA 94608
PH: 510-547-9680 FX: 510-547-9681
GracenoteSupport@gracenote.com
www.gracenote.com
The industry standard for music recognition services. Seamless handling of soundtracks and other compilations, expanded album and track fields, credits, genres and ISRC code.

Harris Musical Products
49 Rose St. Stoughton, MA 02072
PH: 781-341-0776 FX: 781-341-0778
Marc Harris info@picksbythepound.com
www.picksbythepound.com
For over 80 years, a manufacturer and distributor of musical instruments and accessories.

Indie Band Manager
620 Iroquois Dr. Fremont, MI 49412
PH: 215-825-6913
Charlie Cheney info@indiebandmanager.com
www.indiebandmanager.com
Database software for independent musicians.

Indie Office
620 Iroquois Dr. Fremont, MI 49412
PH: 215-825-6913
Charlie Cheney info@indieoffice.com
www.indieoffice.com
It prints mailing labels, letters, invoices, contracts, postcards, contact lists, accounts receivable reports, merge letters...you name it!

Jakprints
3133 Chester Ave. Cleveland, OH 44114
PH: 216-622-6360 FX: 216-622-6361
www.jakprints.com
We continually strive to help each and every customer big or small, to expand and promote their passion with the highest quality service and merchandise.

LiveWire Contacts
156 Hamilton St., Cambridge, MA 02139
support@LiveWireContacts.com
www.LiveWireContacts.com
A contact manager specifically designed for musicians.

Music Arsenal
12105 W. Center Rd. #280, Omaha, NE 68144
PH: 800-231-9273
Jimmy Winter info@musicarsenal.com
www.musicarsenal.com
A new way for record labels to organize, track and utilize their business information.

Muze
304 Hudson St. 8th Fl.
New York, NY 10013
PH: 212-824-0300
info@muze.com
www.muze.com
Our products and services are designed to drive commerce, enhance the consumer experience and increase customer loyalty.

MyNewsletterBuilder
comments@
mynewsletterbuilder.com
www.mynewsletterbuilder.com
A user-friendly, feature-rich, online newsletter management program for novices and professionals alike.

OnlineBandManager.com
Mike
info@onlinebandmanager.com
www.OnlineBandManager.com
Free contact manager + website four bands/acts. Forums, mailing list, gallery, news, calendar and more!

Onlinegigs
PO Box 6368, Delray Beach, FL 33482
PH: 888-595-3122
FX: 866-215-0034
Jay Flanzbaum
support@onlinegigs.com
www.onlinegigs.com
Automates the administration of booking and promoting your band. It is a centralized database of nationwide venues, colleges, festivals and media contacts.

Pick Guy
PO Box 70, Westfield, IN 46074
PH: 317-698-5141
Marty Camire pickguy@verizon.net
www.PickGuy.com
Offers custom printed guitar picks and personalized guitar straps. We provide quality products at affordable prices.

PowerGig
www.powergig.com
The power tool for finding, booking and promoting gigs.

Rock Star Promotions
PO Box 5867, Ft. Lauderdale, FL 33310
PH: 954-739-9205 FX: 801-740-6554
Aaron Schimmel servicedesk@rockstarpromos.com
www.rockstarpromos.com
Dedicated to helping everyone live like a rock star, even if you can't play a note!

Samplesense
www.samplesense.com
Here you can find a vast array of royalty free samples to load into your favourite sequencer, along with a selection of free VST plugins & demo software to help improve your music production.

Seatthole Shirts
PO Box 3137, Bellingham, WA 98227
PH: 360-733-2154
Django Bohren info@seatthole.com
seatthole.com
High-quality custom t-shirt screen printing and Rock n' Roll promotional items for your high-, medium-, low- or no-budget project.

Superscope Technologies
1508 Batavia Ave. Geneva, IL 60134
PH: 630-232-8900
www.superscope.net
Portable dual drive CD recorder for songwriting. Record yourself directly to CD. Play along to CD accompaniment and change key, change tempo, reduce vocals and set A-B repeat loops.

Vista Prints
www.vistaprint.com
Get 250 free business cards.

Westone Music Products
2235 Executive Cir. Colorado Springs, CO 80906
PH: 719-540-9333 FX: 719-540-9183
Paul Carhart music@westone.com
www.westone.com/music
In-ear musicians monitoring and hearing protection products.

youSENDit
www.yousendit.com
Allows you to e-mail files up to 100 mbs for free!

Sign up for The Indie Contact Newsletter at
www.indiebible.com

Legal Resources

American Bar Association
www.abanet.org/intelprop
The home page of the ABA Section of Intellectual Property Law.

The Better Business Bureau
bbb.org
Find a local BBB in the US and Canada serving the consumers and businesses in their areas.

BitLaw
www.bitlaw.com
Contains over 1,800 pages on patent, copyright, trademark and internet legal issues.

Copyright & Fair Use
fairuse.stanford.edu
Stanford U. information on copyright law.

Copyright Infringement and Piracy Watch
www.copynot.com
Devoted to the protection of copyright works, anti-piracy and promotion of legitimate music sources.

Copyright Kit
www.indie-music.com/free2.php
Free download of Copyright Kit.

Copyright Law in the United States
www.bitlaw.com/copyright
A discussion on the copyright laws.

The Copyright Website
www.benedict.com
Copyright registration and information resource.

Copyright Your Song
www.loc.gov/copyright/forms/formpai.pdf
The PDF form to file with the U.S. Copyright Office.

Copyright Your Sound Recording
www.loc.gov/copyright/forms/formsri.pdf
The PDF form to file with the U.S. Copyright Office.

Creative Commons
info@creativecommons.org
creativecommons.org
A nonprofit whose goal is to build a layer of reasonable, flexible copyright in the face of increasingly restrictive default rules.

Findlaw
www.findlaw.com
Provides information and links to resources on all areas of law, including copyright and entertainment law.

GS1 US *(Uniform Code Council)*
www.gs1us.org
Administers the U.P.C. bar code.

Independent Music Law Advice *UK*
Elliot Chalmers elliot@musiclawadvice.co.uk
www.musiclawadvice.co.uk
Providing accurate and up to date information on all issues related to music law.

Lawgirl.com
www.lawgirl.com
A free, interactive legal resource for those in the arts.

Music Law Offices
www.music-law.com
Free articles on copyright and music publishing.

MusicContracts.com
help@jsrlaw.net
www.musiccontracts.com
Sells downloadable copies of the most widely used music business contracts.

Negativland: Intellectual Property Issues
www.negativland.com/intprop.html
Lots of good articles relating to the music business & copyright issues.

Songfile
711 3rd Ave. New York, NY 10017
PH: 212-370-5330 FX: 646-487-6779
www.songfile.com
The Harry Fox Agency online search and mechanical licensing tool. HFA represents the song catalogs of almost 28,000 publishers for their U.S. licensing needs.

Trademark Search
www.uspto.gov/main/trademarks.htm
Valuable information on trademarks in the US.

United States Copyright Office
101 Independence Ave. SE., Washington, DC 20559-6000
PH: 202-707-3000
copyinfo@loc.gov
www.loc.gov/copyright
Key publications and the homepages of other copyright-related organizations.

United States Patent and Trademark Office
TrademarkAssistanceCenter@uspto.gov
www.uspto.gov
The official website.

Volunteer Lawyers for the Arts
6128 Delmar, St. Louis, MI 63112
PH: 314-863-6930 FX: 314-863-6932
vlaa@stlrac.org
www.vlaa.org/resources.asp
A variety of programs and services.

World Intellectual Property Organization
PO Box 18, CH-1211 Geneva 20, Switzerland
PH: +41-22-338-9111 FX: +41-22-733-54-28
www.wipo.org
Promoting the use and protection of works of the human spirit, through patents and copyright

Online Communities

Band Weblogs
Jenny May and Dave Tommo
info@bandweblogs.com
www.bandweblogs.com
Submit band press, reviews, links to MP3s, music videos, podcasts and more.

Bandwidth Discussion Group
launch.groups.yahoo.com/group/bandwidth
Discussion of web design as it relates to bands, labels and other music related sites.

BlogExplosion
www.blogexplosion.com
A blogging community where people can find and read your blog, get your blog reviewed or even chat with other bloggers all around the world!

cdmusicpage.com
www.cdmusicpage.com
Promoting independent music with text, images and audio.

Face-Pic.com
5 Viewpoint Office Village, Babbage Rd.
Stevenage, Herts, SG1 2EQ UK
PH: +44 (0)1438-356-764 FX: +44 (0)1438-724-115
David Ames dave@face-pic.com
www.face-pic.com
A UK social networking service (like MySpace) that allows unsigned acts to upload music.

F-Jam Online
fjam@cashette.com
fjam.zapto.org
Musical collaboration studio site featuring a tracks server, public forums, webring and more!

FormingBands.com / FormingBands.co.uk
80 Lawrence Moorings, Herts, Sawbridgeworth, CM21 9PE UK
Aidan team@formingbands.com
www.formingbands.com
www.formingbands.co.uk
We've developed this site to help you get in touch with musicians who want to play your type of music in your way at your level.

GAZZAG
www.gazzag.com
MySpace type community. Our intention is to make your social life and that of your friends, more active and interesting.

IndieMusicBox.com
1621 Haight St. PMB 9, San Francisco, CA 94117
gig@indiemusicbox.com
www.indiemusicbox.com
A distribution and job search service for the music and music video industry. Please create an account to post your web link and access the funding library.

Just Plain Folks
5327 Kit Dr. Indianapolis, IN 46237
jpnotes@aol.com
www.jpfolks.com
Organization that networks, promotes and educates musicians.

Loopwise.com
www.loopwise.com
A virtual internet collaboration system for serious recording artists.

MadHorns.com
205 Lee St. #503, Gaithersburg, MD 20877
PH: 240-683-8538
www.madhorns.com
Now, horn players that are into Pop, Rock and Funk have a place to call home too!

The MODE
brew@theMode.com
www.themode.com
Find band mates and network with other musicians.

MOG
www.mog.com
With dedicated pages for artists, albums and songs, MOG is a springboard for delving deeper into the music you love.

Music Highway
15030 Ventura Blvd. #843, Sherman Oaks, CA 91403
PH: 818-785-7144
Sheena Metal sheenametal@onemain.com
www.music-highway.com
An organization that specializes in supplying invaluable industry contacts, promotional resources and a support network for aspiring artists.

Music Talks Sessions
PH: 212-568-7506
David C. Knight info@musictalkssessions.com
www.musictalkssessions.com
Gives artists the opportunity to discuss, express and share their experiences about the music and recording industries among themselves.

Music Thoughts Discussion Group
musicthoughts-subscribe@egroups.com
launch.groups.yahoo.com/group/musicthoughts
All areas of music are discussed from promotion to tips on playing live.

Musicianzoo.com
artistservice@musicianzoo.com
www.musicianzoo.com
Promotes local bands, as well as major label artists.

MySpace Music
www.myspace.com/index.cfm?fuseaction=music
Upload your music for exposure, reviews and more.

New Artist Headquarters
92 Stirling Rd. Watchung, NJ 07069
PH: 215-219-8915
Dave ceo@newartisthq.com
www.newartisthq.com
Customized artist and company profiles, a special fan section called the Green Room, contests, free blogs, a gallery forum and more!

Newrust
www.newrust.com
Online community dedicated to promoting artists from all around the world.

Open Music Factory
PH: +390331461367 FX: +390331461367
thevolution music@thevolution.net
www.openmusicfactory.com
We offer a forum focused on music collaborations, a personal jam room and a store to sell your own original music CDs.

Soundshed.com
www.soundshed.com
A musicians classifieds service with over 10,000 registered members.

Sunnymead
PO Box 277, Waterloo, QC J0E 2N0
PH: 450-539-2098
FX: 450-539-5176
info@sunnymead.org
www.sunnymead.org
A virtual village of independent artists.

TagWorld.com
PH: 310-394-5164
FX: 310-394-5167
www.tagworld.com
Join for free and view profiles, connect with others, blog, upload music and much more!

TalentMatch.com
ms@talentmatch.com
www.talentmatch.com
Designed to help aspiring and accomplished bands, singers, musicians and writers easily gain support, share their talents and gain worldwide exposure.

Unsigned Band Web
www.unsignedbandweb.com
Trade reviews, ideas, find answers, get feedback.

Upcoming.org
upcoming.org
A social event calendar, completely driven by people like you. Manage your events, share events with friends and family and syndicate your calendar to your own site.

Yahoo! Music Related Groups
launch.dir.groups.yahoo.com/dir/Music
Share photos & files, plan events, send a newsletter and more.

YourSpins
Chris Leonard talk2us@yourspins.com
www.YourSpins.com
Online community where you share your mixes with others. Rate and comment on other mixes.

ZBands.com
Barbara White barb@zbands.com
ZBands.com
Musicians and venues can quickly & easily post their information and the general public can quickly & easily retrieve it.

Organizations

Creative Musicians Coalition
PO Box 6205, Peoria, IL 61601-6205
PH: 309-685-4843 FX: 309-685-4879
aimcmc@aol.com
www.aimcmc.com
A fellowship of artists and labels that share and network.

Future of Music Coalition
1325 13th St. NW. #34, Washington, DC 20005
PH: 202-518-4117
Jenny Toomey jenny@futureofmusic.org
www.futureofmusic.org
A voice for musicians and citizens in Washington.

Guild of International Songwriters and Composers
Sovereign House, 12 Trewartha Rd. Praa Sands, Penzance, Cornwall, TR20 9ST UK
PH: 01736-762826 FX: 01736-763328
songmag@aol.com
www.songwriters-guild.co.uk
International songwriters organization representing songwriters.

Indie Managers Association *(IMA)*
554 N. Frederick Ave. #218, Gaithersburg, MD 20877
PH: 240-638-5060 FX: 240-597-1330
info@indiemanagers.com
www.indiemanagers.com
Exists to promote, educate and connect managers with artists seeking representation.

International Association of African American Music
PO Box 382, Gladwyne, PA 19035
PH: 610-664-8292 FX: 610-664-5940
iaaam1@aol.com
www.iaaam.com
Promoting, perpetuating and preserving America's indigenous music.

International Songwriters Association
Ireland
jliddane@songwriter.iol.ie
www.songwriter.co.uk
Extensive information service for songwriters, lyric writers and music publishers.

Busy Beaver Buttons
CUSTOM BUTTONS SINCE 1995

1 INCH
black/white
100 for $25
500 for $100
full color
100 for $30
500 for $125

1.25 INCH
black/white
100 for $30
500 for $125
full color
100 for $35
500 for $150

1.5 INCH
black/white
50 for $23
100 for $35
500 for $150
full color
50 for $26
100 for $40
500 for $175

1.5 INCH SQUARE
black/white
50 for $28
100 for $40
500 for $190
full color
50 for $31
100 for $45
500 for $210

2.25 INCH
black/white
50 for $30
100 for $45
500 for $180
full color
50 for $35
100 for $50
500 for $210

All prices include ground postage!

BUSY BEAVER BUTTONS
P.O. Box 87676
Chicago IL 60680
buttongal@busybeaver.net
773 646 3359

ORDER BUTTONS DIRECTLY AT:
WWW.BUSYBEAVER.NET

OR JUST MAIL US YOUR ORDER:
1. your art 2. payment (check, money order, or cash)
3. your address & phone number

LIFEbeat
630 9th Ave. #1010, New York, NY 10036
PH: 212-459-2590
info@lifebeat.org
www.lifebeat.org
Mobilizes the music industry to raise awareness and to provide support for the AIDS community.

MusiCares
3402 Pico Blvd. Santa Monica, CA 90405
PH: 310-392-3777 FX: 310-399-3090
Dee Dee deedee@grammy.com
www.grammy.com/musicares
A place to turn in times of financial, medical or personal crisis.

Musicians On Call
1133 Broadway, #630, New York, NY 10010-8072
PH: 212-741-2709 FX: 212-741-3465
info@musiciansoncall.org
www.musiciansoncall.org
Using music to complement the healing process for patients in healthcare facilities.

MusicPro Insurance Agency
45 Crossways Park Dr. Woodbury, NY 11797-2002
PH: 800-605-3187 FX: 888-290-0302
insurance@MusicProInsurance.com
www.musicproinsurance.com
Affordable and convenient insurance for musicians, including instruments, equipment, studio, tour, composer's liability, travel accident and health.

Positive Music Association
4593 Maple Ct. Boulder, CO 80301
PH: 303-581-9083
www.positivemusicassociation.com
Established to promote positive music and those who create it and to establish a new musical genre called "Positive Music." It's about making the world a better place through music.

Recording Industry Association of America (RIAA)
webmaster@riaa.com
www.riaa.org
The trade group that represents the U.S. recording industry. Its mission is to foster a business and legal climate that supports and promotes our members' creative and financial vitality.

Society of Singers
6500 Wilshire Blvd. #640, Los Angeles, CA 90048
PH: 323-653-7672 FX: 323-653-7675
sos@singers.org
www.singers.org
Helps professional vocalists, worldwide, in times of crisis.

Performing Rights Societies

AFM & AFTRA Intellectual Property Rights Distribution Fund
12001 Ventura Pl. #500, Studio City, CA 91604
PH: 818-755-7780 FX: 818-755-7779
Jo-Anne McGettrick jmcgettrick@mpspf.org
www.raroyalties.org
Recording Artist Royalties Formed for the purpose of distributing royalties from various foreign territories and royalties established by government statute under U.S. Copyright Law.

American Federation of Television & Radio Artists (AFTRA)
5757 Wilshire Blvd. 9th Fl. Los Angeles,
CA 90036-3689
PH: 323-634-8100 FX: 323-634-8194
www.aftra.com
National labor union representing artists.

American Society of Composers, Authors and Publishers (ASCAP)
1 Lincoln Plaza, New York, NY 10023
PH: 212-621-6000 FX: 212-724-9064
info@ascap.com
www.ascap.com
A performing rights society that represents its members.

Australasian Mechanical Copyright Owners Society (AMCOS)
6-12 Atchison St., St Leonards, NSW 2065 Australia
PH: 02-9935-7900 FX: 02-9935-7999
www.apra.com.au
Represents music publishers in Australia and New Zealand.

British Academy of Composers & Songwriters
25-27 Berners St., London, W1T 3LR UK
PH: 020-7636-2929
info@britishacademy.com
www.britishacademy.com
Representing the interests of over 3,000 UK music writers.

British Music Rights
26 Berners St., London, W1T 3LR UK
PH: 44-0-20-7306-4446 FX: 44-0-20-7306-4449
britishmusic@bmr.org
www.bmr.org
Promotes the interests of composers, songwriters and music publishers .

Broadcast Music, Inc (BMI)
320 W. 57th St., New York, NY 10019-3790
PH: 212-586-2000
www.bmi.com
Collects license fees on behalf of those American creators it represents.

GEMA
Bayreuther St. 37, 10787, Berlin, Germany
PH: 030-21245-00 FX: 030-21245-950
gema@gema.de
www.gema.de
German performing rights society.

Irish Music Rights Organization (IMRO)
Pembroke Row, Lower Baggot St., Dublin 2, Ireland
PH: 353-1-661-4844 FX: 353-1-661-3789
info@imro.ie
www.imro.ie
Collects and distributes royalties arising from the public performance of copyright works.

Lost in the Grooves Sub-Publishing
PO Box 31227, Los Angeles, CA 90031
PH: 818-324-3152
Kim Cooper amscray@gmail.com
www.lostinthegrooves.com/subpub
Helping bands/labels without publishing deals claim performance/sales/licensing royalties from overseas.

Mechanical Copyright Protection Society
Elgar House, 41 Streatham High Rd. London,
SW16 1ER UK
classicalquery@mcps-prs-alliance.co.uk
www.mcps.co.uk
Licenses the recording and use of music in the UK.

Performing Arts Media Rights Association (PAMRA)
PO Box 4398, London, W1A 7RU UK
PH: 0207-534-1234 FX: 020-7543-1383
office@pamra.org.uk
www.pamra.org.uk
The UK's collecting society for performers.

SESAC
55 Music Sq. E., Nashville, TN 37203
PH: 615-320-0055 FX: 615-329-9627
www.sesac.com
Performing rights organization in the US.

Societa Italiana Degli Autori Ed Editori
Musica@siae.it
www.siae.it
Performing Rights Association of Italy.

Societe Des Auteurs Compositeurs Et Editeurs De Musique (SACEM)
225 ave. Charles de Gaulle 92528 Neuilly-sur-Seine, France
PH: 01-47-15-47-15
communication@sacem.fr
www.sacem.fr
An advocate for French performers.

Society of Composers, Authors and Music Publishers of Canada (SOCAN)
41 Valleybrook Dr. Toronto, ON M3B 2S6
PH: 416-445-8700 FX: 416-445-7108
www.socan.ca
We represent individuals who make their living creating music.

SoundExchange
1330 Connecticut Ave. NW. #330, Washington,
DC 20036
PH: 202-833-0120 FX: 202-833-2141
info@soundexchange.com
www.soundexchange.com
Distributes royalties from internet airplay (ie: XM, Sirius, Live365). If you have had airplay from any internet sources, you probably have some royalties waiting for you. Sign up today!

SoundScan
PH: 914-684-5525 FX: 914-684-5680
clientservices@soundscan.com
home.soundscan.com
An information system that tracks sales of music and music video products throughout the United States and Canada. Sales data from point-of-sale cash registers is collected weekly from over 14,000 retail, mass merchant and non-traditional (online stores, venues etc.) outlets.

Sweden Songs
PO Box 15210, SE-10465 Stockholm, Sweden
PH: +4686485762
Keith Almgren info@swedensongs.se
www.swedensongs.se
Music publishing service.

Songwriting Resources

Addicted-to-Songwriting
info@addicted-to-songwriting.com
www.addicted-to-songwriting.com
Your resource for songwriting information, articles, news, tips and more.

Circle of Songs
1223 Wilshire Blvd. #1610 Santa Monica,
CA 90403
PH: 310-458-7664 FX: 310-458-7663
Jenna Leigh jenna@circleofsongs.com
www.circleofsongs.com
Learn to build a lifetime career in music.

HitWriters.com
Anthony Martin anthony@hitwriters.com
hitwriters.com
Created to promote and give access to the best songwriters in the world.

Muse's Muse
jodi@musesmuse.com
www.musesmuse.com
Songwriting tips, tools, interactivities and opportunities to connect.

Pianocast - Anatomy of a Song Podcast
Todd Thalimer pianocast@gmail.com
www.thalimer.com
Creating a song from an idea so that listeners can hear how a song evolves as it created from the first musical notes, to the last lyric.

Singer/Songwriter Directory
FX: 561-760-0891
info@singer-songwriter.com
www.singer-songwriter.com
Lists new CD releases, featured CDs and "Site of the Week".

Singers U.K.
singers@singers-uk.org
www.singers-uk.net
Created to help promote professional singers on the internet.

The Singers' Workshop
4804 Laurel Canyon Blvd.
#123, Valley Village,
CA 91607
PH: 818-623-6668
Lis Lewis
lis@thesingersworkshop.com
www.thesingersworkshop.com
Provides valuable articles that singers need to know.

SingerUniverse
11684 Ventura Blvd. #975, Studio City, CA 91604
Dale info@singeruniverse.com
www.SingerUniverse.com
Features valuable, comprehensive information for pros and newcomers alike. We don't accept unsolicited material. Please contact us before submitting your music.

The Singing Spot
thesingingspot.com
Resource directory and forum for singers.

Songbridge
79 Frank St., PO Box 370, Campbellford,
ON K0L 1L0
PH: 705-653-2700 FX: 705-653-2709
Jana Lee Reid jana@thesongbridge.com
www.thesongbridge.com
Provides a weekly "pitch sheet" full of "song wanted" ads to its songwriting and publishing members.

Songsalive!
12115 Magnolia Blvd. #200, North Hollywood,
CA 91607
PH: 310-238-0359
usa@songsalive.org
www.songsalive.org
Non profit organization supporting and promoting songwriters and composers worldwide.

Songstuff
www.songstuff.com
Articles, reference material, artist pages, news and forums.

Songwriter Festivals
info@songfestivals.com
www.songfestivals.com
Podcasting, tips, tools, free artist pages, downloads, promotion and songwriting technique.

Songwriter101.com
contact@songwriter101.com
songwriter101.com
Everything about the business side of the songwriter's profession.

SongwriterPro.com
info@SongwriterPro.com
www.songwriterpro.com
Seeking to bring together like-minded songwriters, musicians, agents, producers, artists and music fans.

Songwriters Showcases of America
608 McIntosh Rd. Ormond Beach, FL 32174
PH: 386-672-3789 FX: 775-249-3127
showstage@aol.com
www.ssa.cc
Creates showcases for songwriters and original bands.

Songwriters Resource Network
PO Box 135, 6327-C Capitol Hill Hwy. Portland,
OR 97239
Steve Cahill info@songwritersresourcenetwork.com
www.songwritersresourcenetwork.com
A free online news and information resource.

Songwriter's Tip Jar
Robert Cote robert@songwriterstipjar.com
www.songwriterstipjar.com
FREE weekly ezine focused on helping craft a better song.

Songwriting.Org
www.songwriting.org
Post lyrics and audio links for critique and discussion.

Songwriting Contests
jodi@musesmuse.com
www.musesmuse.com/contests.html
Listing of all the best songwriting contests.

Songwriters Directory
swd@songwritersdirectory.com
www.songwritersdirectory.com
Listings database used by music fans and music industry executives.

Tunesmith
www.tunesmith.net
Provides info and networking opportunities. Our main goal is to offer our members helpful advice whenever we can, through seminars, message boards etc.

USA Songwriting Competition
Eddie Phoon info@songwriting.net
www.songwriting.net
The world's leading international songwriting event honors songwriters, composers, bands and recording artists everywhere.

Worldwide Songwriters Assc.
FX: 302-348-6409
contact@wwswa.com
www.wwswa.com
Here to assist and encourage songwriters in all genres of music. Members can now sell their CDs from our site.

Blues

Blues Festival Guide
info@bluesfestivalguide.com
www.bluesfestivalguide.com
An online directory of Blues festivals.

The Blues Foundation
49 Union Ave. Memphis, TN 38103
PH: 901-527-2583 FX: 901-529-4030
www.blues.org
Encourages and recognizes the achievements of Blues artists.

BluesFestivals.com
www.bluesfestivals.com
Searchable database for locating Blues festivals around the nation.

CD of the Week / Cornbreads Parking Lot
11469 Olive Blvd. #163, St. Louis, MO 63141
Cornbread@STLBlues.net
www.stlblues.net/parking_info.htm
*We get over 15,000 hits a day. A great way to
promote your CD!*

Mary4Music.com
Mary mary@mary4music.com
www.mary4music.com
*Blues, Indie & DIY music links, musician's
resources, reviews and band listings.*

Children's

Children's Music Network
PO Box 1341, Evanston, IL 60204-1341
PH: 847-733-8003
office@cmnonline.org
www.cmnonline.org
*Catalyst for education and community-building
through music.*

Children's Music Web
www.childrensmusic.org
Connecting families with great Children's music.

Children's Music Workshop
newman@childrensmusicworkshop.com
www.childrensmusicworkshop.com
*A music education resource for students, parents
and teachers.*

KiddieGifts
18 Tnuat Hameri St., Ramat Gan, Israel
PH: 972-3-6766122 FX: 972-57-7947115
Amos Barzel amos@kiddiegifts.co.il
www.kiddiegifts.co.il
*A production company producing musical programs
on CDs, DVDs and cassettes.*

Kids Music Web
webmaster@kidsmusicweb.com
www.kidsmusicweb.com
Contact to join the Kid's music artist listing.

KidScreen
366 Adelaide St. W. #500, Toronto, ON M5V 1R9
PH: 416-408-2300 FX: 416-408-0870
www.kidscreen.com
*Serving the information needs of children
entertainers.*

Music Musketeers
PO Box 804, Los Gatos, CA 95031
info@musicmusketeers.org
musicmusketeers.org
*Bringing music back to children, where budget cuts
have taken it away from them! Features "Artist of
the Week".*

Parents' Choice Awards
201 W. Padonia Rd. #203, Timonium, MD 21093
PH: 410-308-3858 FX: 410-308-3877
awards@parents-choice.org
www.parents-choice.org
Details and entry forms are available online.

Christian

Christian Country Music Association
PO Box 101336, Nashville, TN 37224
PH: 615-742-9210 FX: 615-248-8505
www.ccma.cc
Promoting Christian Country music.

Christian Indies
PH: 877-295-7049
www.christianindies.com
*Bringing you the best of Christian Indie bands
including the most concise databases of band and
venue information and resources.*

Christian Radio & Retail Weekly
5350 N. Academy Blvd. #200, Colorado Springs,
CO 80918
PH: 719-536-9000 FX: 719-598-7461
Dave Koch dave@christianradioweekly.com
www.christianradioweekly.com
*Publication featuring song rankings, news and
information for various genres of Christian music.*

ChristianIndieForums.com
Michael Eshom oldiesmann@oldiesmann.us
www.christianindieforums.com
*Artists can have their board hosted here, as well as
ask for reviews and critiques on their music while
meeting new fans and other artists.*

ChristianTuner.com
PO Box 147, Power Springs, GA 30127
submissions@christiantuner.com
www.christiantuner.com
*The most complete collection of live Christian radio
and TV stations, programs, MP3 downloads and
podcasting links on the internet.*

Creative Soul
PH: 615-400-3910
Eric Copeland ec@CreativeSoulOnline.com
www.CreativeSoulOnline.com
*Christian music resource designed for artists who
need to reach the next level of music ministry.*

Crossdogs
315 Edwards Rd. Circleville, OH 43113
info@crossdogs.com
www.Crossdogs.com
*We will help you get gigs! By enabling you to submit
your Electronic Dog Tag™ to venues looking for
your style of music.*

FindJesusFreaks.com
admin@findjesusfreaks.com
www.findjesusfreaks.com
*It's a database/network of free classifieds for
Christian musicians.*

Gospel Elevations
2710 Barth St., Flint, MI 48504
PH: 810-625-0992
James Robinson jrobin747@yahoo.com
www.gospelelevations.net
*A site where people can find out about Gospel
artists.*

Gospel Music Association
1205 Division St., Nashville, TN 37203
PH: 615-242-0303 FX: 615-254-9755
www.gospelmusic.org
*Promoting the development of all forms of Gospel
music.*

Gospel Music Workshop of America
www.gmwanational.org
Dedicated to the perpetuation of Gospel music.

GospelIndex.com
PO Box 1892, Lowell, MA 01853
PH: 978-590-4609
www.gospelindex.com
Independent and unsigned Gospel music talent.

Heaven's Metal
webmaster@heavensmetal.com
www.heavensmetal.com
Your CD is rated by visitors to the site.

HeavenSound
PH: 817-691-8840
info@heavensound.com
www.heavensound.com
*Offers concert database services to Gospel artists,
with the added benefit that music fans can easily
find hundreds of concerts for their area.*

IHearMusic-online.com
klmartinjr1@hotmail.com
www.ihearmusiconline.com
*Brings you up to date information on your favorite
Worship & Praise leaders & Gospel music artists.*

Independent Soul
Michael Nicholson staff@independent-soul.com
www.independent-soul.com
*A source for locating musical talent for events at a
low cost.*

Ministry Networks
ministrynetworks@sympatico.ca
www.ministrynetworks.rockofages.ca
*Known for having the most extensive database of
Christian radio stations and programs in Canada.*

MyMusicMission.com
www.mymusicmission.com
*Providing artists valuable career
management/promotion tools, resources, guidance
and support, as well as access to music industry
buyers and service providers.*

**National Association of Christian Rock
Radio**
nacrr@nacrr.org
www.nacrr.org
*Supports those struggling to work in this new and
progressive avenue of ministry.*

Really Big City Festivals
PO Box 1668, Franklin, TN 37065
PH: 615-714-1385
info@reallybigcity.com
www.reallybigcity.com
Excellent exposure for upcoming Christian bands!

Urban Gospel Alliance
PO Box 5211, Oakland, CA 94605
PH: 510-472-0177
info@urbangospelalliance.com
www.urbangospelalliance.com
Broadening Gospel music's reach into the streets.

USA Church
www.usachurch.com
*Christian resource that has an entertainment section
for most US cities. You can post gigs, music, news
etc.*

Classical

North America

United States

Afrocentric Voices in Classical Music
www.afrovoices.com/futurevoices.html
Focusing on African American performers.

American Composers Forum
332 Minnesota St. #145E, St. Paul, MN 55101-1300
PH: 651-228-1407 FX: 651-291-7978
www.composersforum.org
Supporting composers and developing new markets for their music.

American Guild of Musical Artists
1430 Broadway, 14th Fl. New York, NY 10018
PH: 212-265-3687 FX: 212-262-9088
www.musicalartists.org
Labor organization that represents Operatic, Choral and Dance artists.

American Harp Society
PO Box 38334, Los Angeles, CA 90038-0334
www.harpsociety.org
National society that promotes harpists.

American Music Center
30 W. 26th St. #1001, New York, NY 10010
PH: 212-366-5260 FX: 212-366-5265
www.amc.net
Encourages the composition of Contemporary (American) music.

American Pianists Association
www.americanpianists.org
Advancing the careers of American Classical and Jazz pianists.

American Viola Society
14070 Proton Rd. #100, Dallas, TX 75244
PH: 972-233-9107 x204
www.americanviolasociety.org
Promotion of viola performance and research.

Cadenza Musicians' Directory
PH: 206-202 3690
www.cadenza.org
Directory of performances and artists.

Center for the Promotion of Contemporary Composers
PO Box 631043, Nacogdoches, TX 75963
cpcc@under.org
www.under.org/cpcc
An internet-based service organization for composers.

Chamber Music America
305 7th Ave. 5th Fl. New York, NY 10001
PH: 212-242-2022 FX: 212-242-7955
www.chamber-music.org
Promotes artistic excellence and economic stability within the profession.

Chorus America
1156 15th St. NW. #310, Washington, DC 20005
PH: 202-331-7577
www.chorusamerica.org
Strengthens choruses and increases appreciation of Choral music.

classicOL.com
info@classicol.com
www.classicol.com
Get your free website specifically designed for Classical musicians.

ClassiQuest
29 Alscot Ln. Langhorne, PA 19047
PH: 215-891-0560 FX: 215-891-0561
David Osenberg Osenbergdd@aol.com
www.classiquest.com
FREE service for those in the music media.

Composers Concordance
PO Box 36-20548 PABT, New York, NY 10129
info@composersconcordance.org
www.composersconcordance.org
Created to increase awareness of the Concert music of our time.

Early Music America
2366 Eastlake Ave. E. #429, Seattle, WA 98102
PH: 206-720-6270 FX: 206-720-6290
earlymusic.org
Extensive resources for members.

earlyMusic.net
PO Box 854, Atlanta, GA 30301
PH: 770-638-7554 FX: 770-638-7554
www.earlymusic.net
Information and services about Early music.

hornplayer.net
www.hornplayer.net
Free classifieds and information archive.

International Horn Society
www.hornsociety.org
Preservation and promotion of the horn

International Society of Bassists
14070 Proton Rd. #100, Dallas, TX 75244
PH: 972-233-9107 x204 FX: 972-490-4219
www.ISBworldoffice.com
Inspiring public interest in the double bass.

International Trumpet Guild
www.trumpetguild.org
Promotes communication among trumpet players around the world.

International Tuba and Euphonium Association
www.iteaonline.org
Promotes performance of the euphonium and tuba.

Internet Bass Clarinet Society
www.new-music.org
Information about bass clarinet performances.

Internet Cello Society
www.cello.org
An international cyber-community of cellists.

Meet the Composer
75 9th Ave. 3R Ste. C, New York, NY 10011
PH: 212-645-6949 FX: 212-645-9669
hhitchens@meetthecomposer.org
www.meetthecomposer.org
Increases opportunities for composers.

Musical Chairs
features@musicalchairs.info
www.musicalchairs.info
List of worldwide orchestral jobs and competitions.

National Association of Composers
PO Box 49256, Barrington Stn. Los Angeles, CA 90049
www.music-usa.org/nacusa
Promotion and performance of American music.

New Directions Cello Association
501 Linn St., Ithaca, NY 14850
PH: 607-277-1686
www.newdirectionscello.com
Newsletter, interviews, events and more.

Opera Base
www.operabase.com
Extensive online resource for Opera artists.

Sax Talk
www.saxtalk.com
A central spot for sax players to meet, talk, buy and sell saxophones etc. Features an "Artist of the Month".

Society of Composers
PO Box 450, New York, NY 10113-0450
www.societyofcomposers.org
A professional society promoting new and contemporary music.

Viola Website
www.viola.com
Viola events and competitions, articles, resources and publishers.

Young Artists International
2430 Apollo Dr. Los Angeles, CA 90046-1628
PH: 310-281-3303 FX: 323-969-8742
info@youngartists.org
www.youngartists.org
Develops the careers of exceptionally gifted young musicians.

Young Concert Artists
250 W. 57th St. #1222, New York, NY 10019
PH: 212-307-6655 FX: 212-581-8894
yca@yca.org
www.yca.org
Discovering and launching the careers of extraordinary young musicians.

Europe

France

ConcertoNet.com
67 rue St. Jacques, 75005 Paris, France
concertonet@yahoo.com
www.concertonet.com
Providing information about Classical music worldwide.

La Lettre du Musicien
14 rue Violet, F.75015, Paris, France
PH: 33-01-56-77-04-00 FX: 33-01-56-77-04-09
info@lettre-musicien.fr
www.lettre-musicien.fr
News and information from the Classical music scene in Europe.

Italy

Operissimo
Via B. d'Alviano 71, IT-20146 Milano MI, Italy
PH: +39-02-415-62-26 FX: +39-02-415-62-29
parisi@operissimo.org
www.operissimo.com
Add your information to our database.

United Kingdom

Early Music Network
3 Onslow House, Castle Rd. Turnbridge Wells, Kent, TN4 8BY UK
PH: 44-0-1892-11652 FX: 44-0-1892-11652
www.earlymusic.org.uk
Provides personalised pages on performers and composers together with entries for record labels and affiliated organisations.

International Assoc. of Music Information Centres
www.iaml.info
Network of organizations promoting new music.

Muso
4th Fl. 117-119 Portland St., Manchester, M1 6ED UK
PH: 0161-236-9526 FX: 0161-247-7978
info@muso-online.com
www.muso-online.com
Designed for young professional musicians, students or music enthusiasts wanting to keep up with the latest news and gossip,

Country

All About Country
webmaster@allaboutcountry.com
www.allaboutcountry.com
THE website where Country labels & artists can reach radio decision makers. We carry the latest news and information.

Americana Music Association
411 E. Iris Dr. Ste. D, Nashville, TN 37204
PH: 615-386-6936 FX: 615-386-6937
www.americanamusic.org
Promotes awareness of this genre.

Country & Gospel Music Message Board
David W. Kelley
CountryMusicPromoter@webtv.net
community-2.webtv.net/CountryMusicPromoter/CheckoutOurCountry
A site where Country music DJs from around the world post their playlists.

The Euro Americana Chart
home.hetnet.nl/~noci48
Compiled by DJs, journalists, retailers, promoters and other people who are interested in Americana music from all over Europe. Every month they send in their top 6 CDs.

FiddleFork
PO Box 989, Chetwynd, BC V0C 1J0
PH: 250-401-303
info@fiddlefork.com
fiddlefork.com
One stop platform for anything fiddle related.

Indie World Country Record Report
PO Box 130, Brush Creek, TN 38547
PH: 615-683-8308
www.indieworldcountry.com
Designed to candidly alert the independent community, the general public and "major" industry about the growth development, aspirations and talents of new singers and songwriters worldwide.

International Bluegrass Music Association
2 Music Cir. S. #100, Nashville, TN 37203
PH: 888-438-4262
www.ibma.org
Promoting and expanding the success of Bluegrass music.

International Country Music Association
PO Box 291827, Nashville, TN 37229
www.radiocountry.org
Songwriter and artist pages.

National Traditional Country Music Association
PO Box 492, Anita, IA 50020
PH: 712-762-4363
www.oldtimemusic.bigstep.com
Preserving traditional Country and Bluegrass music.

The Rockabilly Hall of Fame
211 College St., Burns, TN 37029
PH: 615-740-7625
Bob Timmers bob@rockabillyhall.com
www.rockabillyhall.com
Great Rockabilly compilations and artists.

Rockabilly.info
www.rockabilly.info
Guide to the Rockabilly scene. Add an upcoming show.

Society for the Preservation of Bluegrass Music of America
PO Box 271, Kirksville, MO 63501
PH: 660-665-7172 FX: 660-655-7450
www.spbgma.com
Preserves traditional Bluegrass music.

Western Music Association
www.westernmusic.org
Promotes traditional and contemporary music of the Great American West.

Dance and Electronic

Dance Propaganda
www.dancepropaganda.com
Home of Indie Dance culture & community.

dancetech.com
www.dancetech.com
Offers 100% independent product reviews, newbie resources, gear listings + FREE online music-space & FREE artist/band/DJ homepages for all bands & musicians.

Electronic Music 411
www.em411.com
Giving Electronic musicians a place to discuss their tools and their craft.

Floorelevators.com
www.floorelevators.com/dancedjlinks
Dance music industry directory.

junglescene.com
junglescene.com
D n' B community. News, events, audio etc.

littledetroit.net
www.littledetroit.net
Techno and Electro music community.

quantum lounge
info@quantumlounge.net
www.quantumlounge.net
Created as an alternative musical outlet for discerning ears who won't settle for mainstream Top 40 or customary Dance culture.

SPRACI
PH: +61 (0) 415-802-648 FX: +61-1300-300-374
www.spraci.com
A worldwide resource site for parties/clubs/festivals etc.

Experimental

The 8bitpeoples
admin@8bitpeoples.com
www.8bitpeoples.com
A collective of artists sharing a common love for classic video games and an approach to music which reflected this obsession.

clan analogue
clananalogue.org
Indie record label that assists with promotional materials.

Electronic Music Foundation
PO Box 8748, Albany, NY 12208
PH: 518-434-4110 FX: 518-434-0308
www.emf.org
Increasing the public's understanding of Electronic music.

The Gas Station
15a George St., Bath, BA1 2EN UK
PH: 44-0-125-442546
nick@sonicstate.com
www.the-gas-station.com
The Electronic musician's knowledge base and number one discussion site.

Hometapes
PO Box 331547, Miami, FL 33233
info@home-tapes.com
www.home-tapes.com
Created to allow musical and visual artists a place to collaborate and experiment without the constraints, pressures and delays of traditional releases.

Other Minds
www.otherminds.org
A global New Music community where composers, students and listeners discover and learn about innovative music by composers from all over the world.

shift!
Choriner Strasse 50, D-10435 Berlin, Germany
PH: 49-030-693-7814 FX: 49-030-693-7844
info@shift.de
www.shift.de
Invites artists to create without compromise.

Society for Electro-Acoustic Music
1 Washington Sq. San Jose, CA 95192-0095
www.seamusonline.org
Represents every part of the country and virtually every musical style.

Film and TV

Film Music Magazine
5777 W. Century Blvd. #1550, Los Angeles, CA 90045
PH: 310-575-1820
www.filmmusicmag.com
Publication for professionals in the film and television music business.

The Film Music Network
www.filmmusic.net
Facilitates networking among professionals in the film music business.

Film Score Monthly
8503 Washington Blvd. Culver City, CA 90232
PH: 310-253-9595 FX: 310-253-9588
www.filmscoremonthly.com
Magazine about motion picture and television music.

Production Weekly
9669 Santa Monica Blvd. #1177, Beverly Hills, CA 90210-4303
PH: 800-284-2230 FX: 310-868-2594
www.productionweekly.com
Provides a comprehensive breakdown of projects in pre-production, preparation and development, for major studio, independent films and television films.

Society of Composers & Lyricists
400 S. Beverly Dr. #214, Beverly Hills, CA 90212
PH: 310-281-2812 FX: 310-284-4861
www.thescl.com
Focuses on the creative and business aspects of writing music and lyrics for film and television.

SoundtrackNet
12011 Rochester Ave. #7, Los Angeles, CA 90025
www.soundtrack.net
Articles, news, interviews and resources about film and television music. We do NOT do music placement.

Folk

FOLKDJ-L
www.folkradio.org
An electronic discussion group for DJs and other people interested in Folk-based music on the radio.

World Folk Music Association
PO Box 40553, Washington, DC 20016
PH: 202-362-2225
wfma.net
Interviews with artists and songwriters, CD and tape reviews and more.

GLBT

Herland Sister Resources
2312 NW. 39th St., Oklahoma City, OK 73112
PH: 405-521-9696
www.herlandsisters.org
Womanist organization with a strong lesbian focus.

The Lesbian and Gay Country Music Association
PO Box 190565, San Francisco, CA 94119
PH: 415-773-9482
www.lgcma.com
Created to organize and direct efforts to enlighten the mainstream culture by promoting and supporting openly lesbian and gay country performers.

OutMedia
285 5th Ave. #446, Brooklyn, NY 11215
PH: 718-789-1776 FX: 718-789-8007
www.outmedia.org
Our mission is to increase the positive visibility of LGBTQQA people and promote inclusive multiculturalism through the arts.

Outmusic
PO Box 376, Old Chelsea Stn. New York, NY 10113-0376
PH: 212-330-9197
www.outmusic.com
A network of gay, lesbian, bisexual and transgender musicians and supporters. Performers, producers, promoters and press/media.

OutVoice
PO Box 11135, Charleston, WV 25339
www.outvoice.net
Intersexed musician ranking chart and service network.

Goth

C8
stevvi@c8.com to c8.com
Resource which posts articles, interviews, reviews etc.

darksites.com
www.darksites.com
Post information - views, articles, interviews, reviews etc.

HellWire Industrial Music Underground
www.hellwire.com
Music charts offering exposure to artists in the Electronic / Goth / Industrial genres. Includes area to post reviews.

Hip Hop

HipHop-Network.Com
177 Stillman St., San Francisco, CA 94107
info@hiphop-network.com
www.hiphop-network.com
Represents Hip Hop and everyday life in the Hip Hop community.

HIPHOPDIRECTORY.COM
jamess@hiphopdirectory.com
hiphopdirectory.com
Largest directory of quality Hip Hop and Rap sites.

HipHopHotSpot.Com
PO Box 35534, RPO Strath Barton, Hamilton, ON L8H 7S6
www.hiphophotspot.com
Supports the growth of Hip Hop artists worldwide.

Ill Crew Universal
5551 W.29th St. #312, Greeley, CO 80634
PH: 707-778-1314
Steve B. steveb@illcrew.org
www.illcrew.org
A worldwide Hip Hop organization dedicated to the preservation, activism, empowerment, balance and unity of Hip Hop culture expressed in all of its elements.

IndependentHH.com
PH: 262-206-2597
www.independenthh.com
Provides up and coming Hip Hop artists with resources necessary to network, grow and reach the next level.

Listentomydemo.com
165 Courtland St. #A-203, Atlanta GA 30303
www.listentomydemo.com
Place your info online for others to see.

Spitkicker
45 W. 21st St. 5th Fl. New York, NY 10010
www.spitkickers.com
Submit your bio and music to become a featured artist.

TLA-PROnline.com
Robert administrator@tla-pronline.com
www.tla-pronline.com
A place where independent Rap, Hip Hop and Spoken Word artists are represented. We can help artists get noticed with interviews and press releases.

Urban Network
3255 Wilshire Blvd. #815, Los Angeles, CA 90010
PH: 213-388-4155 FX: 213-388-0034
Arthur Mitchell amitchell@urbanetwork.com
urbannetwork.com
The premier entertainment industry publication, online portal and multi-media company bridging the Urban entertainment community.

Jam Band

Beginners B&P Instructions
14222 29th Ave. SE., Mill Creek, WA 98012
PH: 425-379-0592 FX: 425-316-0999
www.mcnichol.com/bnp
Instructions for trading free live music on CD.

Coolmusicstuff.com
becky@coolmusicstuff.com
www.coolmusicstuff.com
A listing of hundreds of Jam band tour dates and festivals. If I dig what a band is doing, then I just might put them on the schedule.

Jam Band Meetup
jambands.meetup.com
Post information about your band.

JamBandDirectory.com
PH: 847-255-1946 FX: 847-890-6018
info@jambanddirectory.com
JamBandDirectory.com
Jam Band community featuring a variety of resources.

jamflower.org
info@jamflower.org
www.jamflower.org
We aim to be an important resource for the greater Jam music scene.

KindWeb
www.kindweb.com
A search engine, directory and online store specializing in music resources, band links and more.

TheJamZone
thejamzone.com
Press releases, band info, concert dates, classifieds and more!

Live Music Blog
Justin Ward vibes@livemusicblog.com
www.livemusicblog.com
A weblog dedicated to Indie/Jam Band music and all things great about live music.

Jazz

imuZZic
le Bourg, 69640 Montmelas-Saint-Sorlin, France
PH: 33 (0) 4-74-67-47-84
imuzzic@imuzzic.net
www.imuzzic.net
Supports the creation of trans-disciplinary projects, cause the emergence of national and international musical networks, seek the passages and the division of information.

Jazz Clubs Worldwide
www.jazz-clubs-worldwide.com
Contact information for hundreds of Jazz clubs.

The Jazz Vocal Coalition
www.jzvoc.org
Helping Jazz singers by educating, promoting and uniting them.

Jazzpedia the Internet Encyclopedia of Jazz
Peter Maguire pmaguire@jazz-clubs-worldwide.com
www.jazzpedia.org
Write whatever you choose to about Jazz, the music, musicians, the global Jazz scene. Share your knowledge, opinions, criticism, anecdotes, discography. The possibilities are endless.

JazzPolice
Don Berryman editor@jazzpolice.com
www.jazzpolice.com
Extensive coverage of the local Jazz scene in ALL major US cities.

The Jazzserver
info@jazzserver.org
www.jazzserver.org
Add your group, venue, festival or concerts to earth's coolest Jazz website for free!

JazzWeek
2117 Buffalo Rd. #317, Rochester, NY 14624
PH: 585-235-4685 FX: 775-878-7482
info@jazzweek.com
www.jazzweek.com
The definitive Jazz and Smooth Jazz national radio airplay chart.

The Polish Jazz Network
PO Box 40153, Long Beach, CA 90804
PH: 949-466-3517
info@polishjazz.com
www.polishjazz.com
The doorway to the world of improvised music from Poland. We offer the largest selection of material regarding Polish Jazz on the web.

Latin

AllBrazilianMusic
www.allbrazilianmusic.com
Aimed at providing news, information and critic reviews on Brazilian music.

Bocada Forte
www.bocada-forte.com.br
Matérias, ultimas notícias, colunistas.

Latin-Artists.com
11271 Ventura Blvd. #151, Studio City, CA 91604
PH: 310-360-5947
info@latin-artists.com
www.Latin-Artists.com
Connects record companies, up-and-coming stars, unsigned artists and fans.

PuroRock.com
PH: 408-386-1500 FX: 650-254-8907
Gabriel Meza gabriel@purorock.com
www.purorock.com
The premier Spanish portal in the US.

SalsaRoots.com
rita@salsacrazy.com
salsaroots.com
The heart and soul of Salsa. Articles, interviews, CD reviews ...

Metal

bandpromo.de
Schäfergraben 1, 91315 Höchstadt, Germany
PH: 09193/507860 FX: 09193/507861
www.bandpromo.de
Band promotion, band-shop und band-support.

Hard Radio
feedback@hardradio.com
www.hardradio.com
The Metal site with no Alternative aftertaste.

Heavycore.org
PO Box 4324, Bloomington, IL 61702
poserdisposer@heavycore.org
www.heavycore.org
Promotion for Heavy bands and musicians.

Metal HeadQuarters
www.metalheadquarters.com
Keeping Metal music alive.

Metal Map of Europe
metalmap.czweb.org

ZRock.com
www.ZRock.com
Join our FREE online community of rockers and help bring back the music!

New Age

Nuevas Músicas
PO Box 5352, Barcelona, Spain
Priscilla priscilla@yidneth.com
www.nuevasmusicas.org
Created to promote the music of New Age artists in Spain and the entire world. We also do CD reviews!

Progressive Rock

The Gibraltar Encyclopedia of Progressive Rock
Fred Trafton webmaster@gepr.net
www.gepr.net
Designed as a reference for visitors to discover bands that are unfamiliar and to broaden their listening horizons.

Heavy Harmonies
webmaster@heavyharmonies.com
heavyharmonies.com
Submit your CDs into our database.

Punk

Book Your Own Fucking Life
www.byofl.org
Guide for the Punk/Hardcore DIY community.

Grunnen Rocks scene
PO Box 6058, 9702 HB, Groningen,
The Netherlands
www.grunnenrocks.nl
News, reviews and more on the worldwide scene.

PunkRock.org
www.punkrock.org
News, upcoming gigs, blogs etc.

Reggae

IREGGAE
www.ireggae.com
Promoting the sound of Reggae music.

Irielion
maddoc@irielion.com
www.irielion.com
Irie Dutch/Belgian and Israeli Reggae/Ska concert agenda.

One Love Reggae
PO Box 2026, Sonoma, CA 95476
PH: 707-933-9790 FX: 707-933-9494
Bob Slayton onelove@humboldt.net
www.onelovereggae.com
West Coast calendar, clubs by state that do live music, festivals ...

Reggae Festival Guide Online
PO Box 50635, Reno, NV 89513
PH: 775-337-8344 FX: 775-337-6499
Kaati kaati@reggaefestivalguide.com
www.reggaefestivalguide.com
Find Reggae festivals around the world!

Skasummit.com
Ska Joe joe@ocska.com
www.skasummit.com
Great place for Ska bands from around the world to promote their shows and local scene.

USABB Reggae
info@ReggaeMusic.us
reggaemusic.us
Free service that lists all US based Reggae bands.

Soul / R&B

Amplified
amplified@amplified-online.co.uk
www.amplified-online.co.uk
Our mandate has always been the support and promotion of Black music not embraced by the mainstream yet loved by millions around the globe.

Goldsoul
latest@goldsoul.co.uk
www.soulnight.co.uk
Our Northern Soul night calendar provides up to the minute information on a selection of top nights throughout the UK. Please submit your events for free!

The Japan African-American Music Society
Tamari 30-1, Kakegawa City, Shizuoka Prefecture, Japan 436-0011
PH/FX: 81-537-23-7585
Malcolm W. Adams jams@totown.net
www.totown.net/jams.htm
An organization of professional musicians living and working in Japan. Our goal is to improve the economic status, social position and general welfare of our members.

soulportal.dk
Frank Ryle frank@soulportal.dk
www.soulportal.dk
Danish site featuring interviews and music charts.
Soul, Jazz, R&B and Hip Hop.

Soulful Kinda Music
Dave daverimmer1@btinternet.com
www.soulfulkindamusic.net
The definitive major reference site for Soul artists
discographies. If you have a discography that you
would like to see on the site, let me have a copy.

Soulwalking
www.soulwalking.co.uk
General resource with gigs, news, articles and more.

WFNK.com
20 E. Central Pkwy. #66, Cincinnati, OH 45202
wfnk@wfnk.com
www.wfnk.com
Welcome to Earth's Funk super site!

Women in Music

Angelic Music
PO Box 61, East Molesey, KT8 6BA UK
info@angelicmusic.co.uk
www.angelicmusic.co.uk
A meeting place to promote female artists and to
provide a place to make contact with each other for
help, support and advice.

Chick Singer Night
www.chicksingernight.com
All singers are welcome to submit demos and
perform. Check our website for the contact in your
city.

Chicks Rockfest
1915 Elm Ave. Cincinnati, OH 45212
PH: 513-404-0385
Jenny George-Schmidt jem@chicksrockfest.com
www.chicksrockfest.com
Annual festival for independent artists who feature
at least one girl in their band.

Christian D.I.V.A.s Network
www.christiandivas.net
Female Christian artists from around the country
who travel and perform in both secular and
Christian venues.

Drummergirl
2 E. Broadway, 4th Fl. New York, NY 10038
Happy Mazza dginfo@happymazza.com
www.drummergirl.com
For women who drum. News, gigs, articles etc.

FEMALE PRESSURE
info@femalepressure.net
www.femalepressure.net
International database for female DJs and/or
producers.

Indiegrrl
PO Box 1714, Dahlonega, GA 30533
PH: 770-561-5853
Vicki Blankenship vicki@indiegrrl.com
www.indiegrrl.com
A forum for information, networking and
conversation about independent music from a
female perspective.

IndieMusicCoach.com
Madalyn madalyn@gogirlsmusic.com
www.indiemusiccoach.com
Looking to elevate your music career? Would you
like to achieve a higher level of success with your
music? Sell more CDs? Attract more fans?

International Women in Jazz
PO Box 230015, Hollis, NY 11423
PH: 212-560-7553
www.internationalwomeninjazz.com
Supporting women Jazz artists.

Jazz Grrls
Jeannette Lambert nette@nette.ca
www.jazzgrrls.com
Celebrating the contributions made by women to
Jazz and improvised music in all its variations
worldwide.

The Kapralova Society
info@kapralova.org
www.kapralova.org
Dedicated to promoting women in the field of
Classical music.

MusiqQueen.com
PO Box 30337, Memphis, TN 38130
PH: 901-332-3504
Charla Littlejohn queen@musiqqueen.com
www.musiqqueen.com
Meet other women, gather resources and more.

The Other Side
Laura Lasley babydoclaz@aol.com
www.guitarnoise.com/otherside.php
Articles aimed at women who play the guitar.

Planet Woman
www.planetwoman.net
Provides concerts and workshops and particularly
aims to perform in areas or to groups, which
wouldn't otherwise receive a diverse range of
musical live acts.

Professional Women Singers Association
PO Box 884, New York, NY 10024
PH: 212-969-0590 FX: 928-395-2560
www.womensingers.org
Our performing members specialize in a variety of
Classical musical genres. Singers are selected by a
jury of voice teachers, coaches and directors.

Punk Girl *France*
infos@panx.net
www.panx.net/punkgirl
A cool Punk Rock girl photo gallery.

Rockin' Moms
PO Box 320988, Los Gatos, CA 95032
Tiffany Petrossi submit@rockinmoms.com
www.rockinmoms.com
Serves to highlight the careers and works of Moms
who rock. Songwriters, performers, musicians,
bands, teachers, promoters and other mothers who
work in the music industry.

Sign up for
The Indie Contact Newsletter
Every month you will receive
a new list of places to send your
music for review, radio play etc.

www.indiebible.con

Rocksie
Kultur Kooperative Ruhr, Guntherstr. 65, 44143
Dortmund, Germany
PH: 0231-557521-18 FX: 0231-557521-29
rocksie@rocksie.de
www.rocksie.de
European music network for Women.

SISTA Factory
sistafact@aol.com
www.sistafactory.com
Promotes and showcases diverse performing artists.

Women In the Arts
PO Box 1427, Indianapolis, IN 46206
PH: 317-713-1144
wiaonline.org
Produces and sponsors programs for women in the
arts.

Women in Jazz
2613 NE. MLK Jr. Blvd. Ste. B, Portland,
OR 97212
archive@jazzwomen.org
jazzwomen.org
Information about women in Jazz, both past and
present.

Women In Music National Network
PO Box 1925, El Cerrito, CA 94530
PH: 866-305-7963
www.womeninmusic.com
Supports the activities of women in all areas of
music.

Women in Music UK
7 Tavern St., Stowmarket, Suffollk, IP14 1PJ UK
PH: 01449-673990 FX: 01449-673994
www.womeninmusic.org.uk
Supports, encourages and enables women to make
music.

Women in Tune
23 High St., Lampeter, Ceredigion, SA48 7BH UK
PH: 01570-423-399
michele@womenintune.co.uk
womenintune.org.uk
A showcase for female musicians and a place of
encouragement and inspiration where women could
become involved in or learn about music with a
supportive atmosphere.

World Music

Cajun Zydeco Music & Dance
8255 Canning Ter. Greenbelt, MD 20770
PH: 301-345-3230
Gary Hayman ghayman@erols.com
users.erols.com/ghayman
Information, MP3s, events, festivals and
The ZydE-Zine magazine.

Local World Music Guides
www.worldmusiccentral.org/staticpages/index.php/
local_scenes
Guides for those who want to learn about the local
World music scenes throughout the globe.

Vimoksha
PH: 919-468-1723
www.vimoksha.com
Info on Indian Classical music. News, institutions,
teachers and artist profiles.

SECTION SEVEN: ARTICLES THAT WILL HELP YOU TO SUCCEED IN THE MUSIC BUSINESS

"Don't forget to applaud the little steps, as well as the big." – **Janet Fisher, Goodnight Kiss Music**

While creating The Indie Bible I have been fortunate enough to have met many of the most knowledgeable people in the Independent music industry. Successful authors, publicists, music reviewers, entertainment lawyers etc. I thought it would be a perfect fit if I presented several of their articles to help you gain insight on how to deal with the many twists and turns of this complicated industry. The articles in this section are sure to be helpful to musicians and songwriters, and especially to those that are just starting out. Every author I asked was kind enough to submit an article that will help you to move forward with your music career. Do yourself a favor, and put their experience to work for you!

o v e r v i e w

STAYING AHEAD OF THE CURVE: MUSIC MARKETING TRENDS YOU CAN COUNT ON

by Peter Spellman, MbSolutions.com
© 2007 All Rights Reserved. Used By Permission

The music biz stands at an historical crossroads – almost every aspect of the way people create, consume and listen to popular music is changing, dwarfing even the seismic shift in the 1880s when music lovers turned from sheet music and player pianos to wax cylinders and later, newfangled 78 rpm phonograph records.

The following highlights some of the most ground-shaking and, (in my opinion), enduring "metatrends" currently shaping the biz. The intent is to give guidelines to both musicians and industry careerists to help set their forward sails on this crazy ocean we call music.

METATREND 1: Empowered Music Consumers

Today may be the very best time to be a music fan, especially one looking for a connection to a favorite artist or guidance and access to the exotic or rare.

Be it the iPod, alluring satellite radio services such as XM, the fan-beloved minutiae posted on Web sites, the availability of live music performances on AOL, the esoteric music videos streaming off Launch.com or the self-tailored satisfaction of burning a homemade mix on CD at home, there is a singular zest to the modern fan experience today.

The public is now driving the market. The challenge to the industry is to respond positively in such a way as to secure the future of music while satisfying customer demand and providing choice.

It's becoming increasingly more difficult for companies to treat us like "mass market" ciphers. The trend is towards "mass customization" where consumers' unique needs are front and center. Some marketing gurus call this trend "The 1-to-1 Future" and the companies that can dance with this trend will prosper.

What You Can Do About It

- Get to know your fans. They are your chief asset going forward and the better you know them, the better you can communicate with them, build loyalty and enlist them in lending their support to you and your music projects.

- Involve them, empower them, mobilize them, let them co-create with you. None of us knows what all of us know. Build a community, a fan club, a subscription service and learn how to pool the wisdom of your following.

- Provide potential customers with as much choice as possible.

- Learn the technologies that will help you customize your communications with customers and fans.

METATREND 2: Music Product to Music as Service

Presenting music as a service, like radio or TV, would seem on the surface to be less profitable than selling millions of CDs, but actually, this change will be positive for the music industry. It will be able to sell more things associated with music. But the actual sale of music as a product will make less sense. It will be a move from transaction-based push to flat-fee pull.

Consumers have clicked, and they demand access to content by any means necessary. Just as AOL has gone from selling you five minutes of access to a take-whatever-you-want model, music too will move to a flat-fee model.

We're not there just yet. But in the next few years, the requisite technology will fall into place. Then most of us will carry a wireless Internet uber-gadget wherever we go – a unified cellphone/MP3 player/digital assistant/Blackberry/ camera/GPS locater/video recorder/co-pilot for life. This device will receive wireless Internet audio, a loose term I use to describe the various forms of streaming audio starting to appear on the Internet. With streaming audio, you can hear the music you love any time, anywhere.

The future isn't about a change in distribution, it's about the atrophy of distribution itself. Instead of distributing things, we'll get access. It's a critical difference.

The future isn't about downloading songs and burning CDs. It's about just-in-time customized delivery. Music as on-demand service not as industry-dictated product.

Just as in the early days of the record industry (c. 1900), music publishing will once again assume the primary role in the biz. Music will become available for diverse uses dictated by consumers and businesses.

How fast will the sun set on the compact disc? Quarter-size CDs that can float among compatible music players, computers, game devices, digital cameras and personal digital assistants are already developed.

Of course, a massive installed base of CD players means that the traditional recording industry markets are not going to disappear or even be impacted by digital distribution in the short term. But rising consumer interest in downloads and an increasingly multi-media business-to-business economy opens new opportunities for composers, editors, sound designers, and all forms of audio producer.

What You Can Do About It

- You should be figuring out how to distribute your work through digital music services now. The Net is your Open Mic to the world. Get yourself onto iTunes, Rhapsody and MusicNet. Learn the virtual ropes.

- As the industry moves away from physical product, it becomes increasingly important for musicians to learn the rules for licensing (read, 'renting') their music.

- Seek out users of music as well as buyers.

- Prepare for a multi-platform approach – value-added packages containing your music, artwork, DVDs, etc AND a container-less presentation using various online showcases, message boards and portals.

- Develop marketing plans for both your selected singles as well as for your full-length albums. 50% of current online music sales are in the singles format.

METATREND 3: The Next Music Companies

The writing is on the wall for traditional music companies. The record industry grew rapidly, matured, and is now in the throes of transformation. How successful this transformation will be depends on how creatively the musical industrial complex can dance with all the changes spiraling around it.

Unfortunately, so much of the music industry is beholden to corporate owners, itchy for quick profits, and driven by rigid corporate imperatives. This wreaks havoc with artist development; hell, it wreaks havoc with business development, and necessitates high turnover of both artists and employees. Major labels are also saddled with legacy problems regarding production and retail. Thus the geologic tempo of industry change.

But the same forces undoing the larger music companies are empowering individual musicians and micro-businesses.

As with most modern industries, a silent computer on a desk is the wildcard that makes so much tradition redundant. Perhaps the term "record company" itself is becoming outdated – "Music Services Company" might be more relevant. Many music biz execs echo the words of Steve Becket of Warp Records when he says, "I think we'll mutate into a new type of company – a mixture of artist management, publisher, marketing consultant, agent and promoter." "We're a communications company," agrees Marc Jones of Wall of Sound, "and that's what we're becoming more everyday. I don't think the model for a traditional record label will exist in this environment anymore."

But we don't have to solve the dilemma for the mainstream music business about which future to embrace. Indie artists are living the side-stream music movement that may inspire the majors but, God willing, will never be completely controlled by them.

Unlike mainstream commercial music, the farther you get out onto the fringes, the more helpful people become. The more participants, the greater the chances that something truly interesting will emerge from the collective rabble.

A new generation of music entrepreneurs is rising with a power in its corner it has never had before. The times are ripe for change and these creators are the spearhead.

What You Can Do About It

- The appetite for music only grows around the globe and you are the one who can satisfy it. You'll need to employ your maverick instincts over conventional "business rules", take fuller responsibility for your own success, and beware of "standard industry practices" that can chain your career.

- Concepts like "company", "work", "job" and "career" are morphing. The entire business economy is passing through a transition the likes of which haven't been seen since the industrial revolution. Rather than seeing your "career" as a ladder, think of it as a rouge wave full of rises, dips and switchbacks.

- It's time to think outside the normal channels of business and imagine new kinds of companies. Creative alliances and partnerships are the key. Combining good music, cheap, global distribution and business savvy almost guarantees success in today's music-hungry world.

METATREND 4: Segmenting Music Markets & Niche Music Cultures

I often hear musicians moaning about how consolidation and the monopolization of the media by companies like Clear Channel and Viacom threaten musical diversity, yet I can hear and obtain more interesting music today than I could ever hope to in the 1960s.

The menu of music choices and styles expands daily.

When the Grammys started in 1958 there were 28 categories of awards; last year there were 105. Check out the "Music Styles" page at the allmusic.com and you'll find over forty styles of music, each with a drop-down menu of several "sub-styles."

Even the pop charts, which have made room in recent months for PJ Harvey, Modest Mouse, Diana Krall and Franz Ferdinand, suggests there's an audience starving for something other than junk food.

The music market continues to segment and each segment is a "world", a portal, through which small companies can create value and success.

While good news for niche companies, this is bad news for the musical industrial complex. The major labels cannot justify going after these smaller markets because they are optimized instead for the larger, pop mainstream. These niche music cultures can't generate the sales needed to float the major label boat. While 20,000 unit sales are a cause to celebrate at a micro-label, they hardly register a blip on big company radar screens.

The times call for focus. Mass customization and a segmenting market encourage the development of products and services of a "niche" nature. Since few of us have the time, money or energy to mount national marketing campaigns, it is in our best interest to discover and concentrate on a niche, a segment, that we can explore towards successful enterprise. Whether your specialty is house, trance, bluegrass or neo-soul, learn to work that niche and scope out relationships and opportunities within it.

Micro-media targets the tributaries off the mainstream and if the artist occupies one of these "niche streams", they have an open and ready channel for exposure to their target audience. Each niche stream has its own burgeoning media culture and the smart combination of high-quality music, creative event-making, perseverance and strategic alliances gets people talking.

What You Can Do About It

- What is your niche? Maybe it's arranging music, or the history of rock, or the intricacies of music software. Whatever it is your niche will lie at the crossroads where your most compelling desires intersect with your background resources and current opportunities in the real world.

- What is your music's niche? If your music can be slotted into an established category, then master that area both musically and business-wise. Know the inlets and outlets for your music, become familiar with the influencers and tastemakers in that realm, and start communicating with them. If your music defies categorization then lead with that.

METATREND 5: The Next 'Big Thing' is Small

The analogy is television. 30 years ago, the three broadcast networks (ABC, CBS, and NBC) had a ninety percent share of the viewing audience. Today it's less than forty. Where's the other 50%? Watching cable channels. Though cable channels have miniscule ratings, they're profitable. Why? Because they've discovered and developed their niche.

And this is what smaller, indie labels do – the Americana sounds of New West Records, Red House Records' focus on singer/songwriters, the creative acid jazz of Instinct, and the deep reggae catalog of Trojan insures listeners they can expect quality discs from each company within their respective niche. Indie market share is on the rise!

Lacking vision beyond their own profit lines, major record companies fail to see that the revolution in music delivery occurred in reaction to the industry's mismanagement, not to mention its complicity in force-feeding the public a flavorless diet of sonic pabulum. With the increasingly conservative (read, "risk-averse") stance of the majors today, indie market niches become all the more important to the creative development of music.

The implosion of the musical industrial complex has also resulted in the availability of many formerly-signed artists and talented executives. The past ten years have seen veteran artists like The Pretenders, Rod Stewart, Foreigner, Aimee Mann, Sinead O'Connor, Carole King, Sammy Hagar, Dolly Parton, Hall & Oates, Hanson, Steve Vai, Sophie B. Hawkins and dozens of other either starting their own labels or signing on with smart indies.

What You Can Do About It

- The paternalisms of yesterday have given way to personal responsibility for your own success. The holy grail is NOT a record deal; it's waking up to your own power.

- Signing with a major label today in most cases is a career risk. These divisions-within-corporations are unstable and anti-art environments, and best avoided by aspiring recording artists.

- If you're up for it, start your own company and release your music through it. If you want to delegate the heavy lifting seek out a successful indie label to partner with. But only do so when you've achieved a level of success appealing to a business partner (that is, you're showing net profit for an extended period of time).

Record company bosses think society's top priority today must be restoring record-company revenue and profits. But music lovers and artists have a different perspective. They want to know how musicians can exploit the extraordinary technology of the Internet to expand the audience and enable more musicians to make a living doing what they love, and improve the quality of life of consumers.

In a sense musicians may be in a better place today than they've ever been before. Taking a cue from the cyber-bard John Perry Barlow, I believe we could be seeing a paradigm shift from the domination of the "music business" to that of the "musician business."

The more things go digital, the more we crave authentic, roots-based music; the more music that's available to us, the more we seek niches that provide meaning and navigation through all the choices; and the more worldwide radio shows through satellite radio, the more we desire shared cultural experience via local djs.

If we had to, all of these trends can be placed under one banner that reads: the larger the world economy the more powerful its smallest players.

Hey, we're talking about you.

Peter Spellman is Director of Career Development at Berklee College of Music, Boston and founder of Music Business Solutions, a training ground for music entrepreneurs. He's the author of The Self-Promoting Musician, Indie Power: A Business-Building Guide for Record Labels, Music Production Houses and Merchant Musicians and his newest, Indie Marketing Power: THE Guide for Maximizing Your Music Marketing. Find him at mbsolutions.com

radio airplay

GETTING RADIO AIRPLAY

by Lord Litter, host of Lord Litter's Radio Show
© 2007 All Rights Reserved. Used By Permission

It was the late 80's and I was doing freelance work for a commercial radio station. The first thing I discovered was an enormous heap of releases in the hallway. Here are some hints how to approach DJs. An important aspect of a release surely is that it can be used to promote the band/musician. If you don't take care of certain areas, your music *might* be on air, but no one will get to know who you are and where they can buy your music...so the whole promotional effect is lost.

Here are things that give me trouble and that I think may cause other DJs to NOT play the release:

1. Every item you send should have a clearly marked address. Info material will be separated from the CD, so if there is no address on the cover, then you'll get no play listing, your address will be not spread etc...

2. Since the CD became *the* medium of choice, some bands should send magnifying glasses with their releases. Sometimes covers look great but the writing is either much too small, or the use of colors make it impossible to read. Make sure it as *easy as possible* to identity the name of your band, the song order, and a contact address.

3. The more well known a DJ is, the better the promotional effect. It also means that a known DJ gets piles of releases every day. Therefore, the time to care about the individual release shrinks to almost seconds, leaving no time left to care about questions like: What the name of the band is, and what the title of the release is.

4. Give all of your material a professional approach. It is impossible to read ten pages to get the basic info about a band. Send a reduced informative version of your material with the offer to send more if interested. A link to your website is what I appreciate.

5. DJs are human beings - yes they are! Treat them like you want to be treated. No need to send endless letters, but a short "Hey, thanks - airplay really appreciated!" proves that you *care* about your music and about the one that *cares* about your music - the DJ.

6. The best way to get in touch is to check in before you send your music and say something like "We heard about your show from ... would you be interested in our music? If the DJ doesn't answer you can forget him/her anyway. You might not even get playlist later. The basic idea here is to keep it somehow personal. You'll discover that it creates a very positive effect - in some cases you might even find a friend!

7. If you send CDRs (I do broadcast these!) make sure they really work! I have one CD player that doesn't take badly burned CDs. So, if your CD (in the running order of the show) must be played on that player and it doesn't work, it will not be played.

The basic idea is: make it as easy as possible to handle your material. Before you finish your material, take it to the printer, if the required aspects are not clear, change it. I know it's a lot of work, but the alternative would be: become rich, hire a professional promoter and watch how your release will be thrown away with the others. The answer is always "somewhere in the middle" as we say in Germany.

Lord Litter has earned the reputation for producing and delivering what is arguably one of the world's best independent music programs. Since the early 1990s, Lord Litter has known the pulse of independent music, and today, indie musicians from all over the planet know that his program is one of the ultimate destinations for their music. Website: www.LordLitter.de

♦

RADIO AIRPLAY 101 - COMMERCIAL AIRPLAY MYTHS

by Bryan Farrish, Bryan Farrish Radio Promotion
© 2007 All Rights Reserved. Used By Permission

When talking to people who are launching their first couple of projects, invariably the same misunderstood points come up concerning commercial regular-rotation airplay. *Here are some common myths:*

DJ's play the records

This only applies to non-commercial radio, and specialty/mixshow radio. The majority of people in the U.S. listen to commercial regular-rotation radio, and on these stations, the DJs have no say at all in what is going to be played (unless, in the case of a smaller station, the DJ is also the PD). So, the biggest pitfall to avoid is asking a DJ at a commercial station "Can I give you my CD for possible rotation?" The DJ is not allowed to say "No", and he/she is probably not going to explain that only the PD can approve regular rotation. The DJ is just going to say "OK".

Why do they play it?

Good songs do not mystically spread to other stations. Every single song you hear (or every syndicated program you hear) on commercial regular-rotation radio is on that station because of layers of promotion and marketing. The song you hear was the one that made it, it beat out the other 300 songs that were going for adds that week. What you don't hear are the endless phone calls, faxes, trade ads, personal meetings, consultant recommendations, call-out research, and other things which went into getting the station to add the record. The station owners make it a requirement that DJs make it sound like they picked the music themselves.

College or specialty/mix-show will expand to commercial

Just because you do well on non-commercial or specialty/mixshow radio, it does not mean anything will happen on commercial regular-rotation radio. Nothing at all will happen at commercial unless a separate, higher-level campaign is put into place to take the record into regular rotation. The pitfall here is that a listener will hear something on college, and then a month later hear it on commercial, and conclude that the college caused the commercial to happen. The listener did not know that both campaigns were in place simultaneously, and the college simply went for adds a month earlier.

You have to be signed

Untrue, being signed is only a signal to the stations that the basic marketing practices are going to be done right. If you have the budget, you can duplicate the marketing practices of larger labels, provided you know how. The band *Creed* set a good example, of putting their $5 million marketing dollars into the right place.

Request calls will help

They won't hurt but your time is better spent doing other things, like inviting people to your gigs. Stations know which calls are real, and which are bands and their friends. Stations have consultants and seminars which cover this *one* topic.

I can't get airplay without distribution

It depends on the size of radio that you are going after. Smaller commercial regular-rotation stations in smaller markets won't make this too much of a sticking point, especially if you have a powerful radio campaign going, or if you are doing great gigs in their city, or if you have great college or specialty/mixshow results. But the larger stations... which you can't work anyway until you do the smaller ones... won't touch a project that has no distribution.

Airplay without gigs

Again, it depends on the size of radio that you are going after. Not being able to gig is a serious handicap at any station, but you can overcome it in smaller markets with intense radio promo, press, sales, and non-comm results.

Non-monitored stations are of no use

Non-monitored stations are of no use only on the *Billboard*, *R&R*, and the seven *Album Network* mag charts. But *FMQB*, *CMJ* and all specialty/mixshow charts are compiled manually. Since you need to start off on these smaller charts first, this works out just fine.

Bryan Farrish is an independent radio airplay promoter. He can be reached at 818-905-8038 or airplay@radio-media.com. Contact: and other articles found @ www.radio-media.com.

♦

INDEPENDENT RADIO PROMOTER CHECKLIST

by Bryan Farrish, Bryan Farrish Radio Promotion
© 2007 All Rights Reserved. Used By Permission

If you are hiring a promoter to push your artist to radio, here are a few things you can consider which will help you have the greatest chance of success (and when I say promoter, I mean an airplay promoter, not a club or booking promoter). The big concern with this process is, if you choose the wrong person(s) to promote your artist and end up with bad results, you can't just go back and do it over again. That's it for that CD (at those stations). That CD is now "an old project" at those stations, and you can't go back to them until you have a new release.

Part One: Overview

Using a friend: Non-experienced friends sometimes offer to promote artists to radio for free, or "a few dollars". This is fine as long as you use them for the right tasks, like helping with the mailing. If you are working college radio, in the 20-30 station range, then they could make some calls too. If they try to call *commercial* radio, they will probably stumble after just a couple of weeks. And forget about any capacity of doing reports or trade charts.

Moonlighter: Staff promoters at major labels sometimes offer to "help you out on the side" for a fee. On their days off, or on the weekend, they say they will "make some calls for you". What happens is that their company finds out and disallows it, or the person gets tied up on their days off, and can't do it. Either way, it is a conflict of interest for them.

Publicity: Public relations people sometimes offer to work an artist to radio for airplay. But don't, however, confuse PR with airplay. A real radio campaign has nothing to do with publicity. They are two separate techniques, with different contacts, lead times, terminology, call frequency, and so on. A person who is good at one is usually terrible at the other. This is why they are always separate departments at labels.

Station People: Station employees are sometimes recruited to work an artist, and will tell you that "they know what stations want." This sounds convincing, but in reality, taking the calls (which they do/did at the station), and making the calls, are very different. Until station people are trained (at a label or indie), they make poor promoters.

Big clients: The most-often used sales technique of promoters is to tell you they have worked "some big artist", and that this would benefit you. Ask them what they mean by "worked". Were they solely responsible for charting that artist? Probably not, more than likely, the promoter was probably just partnered with a label or another promoter, or worse, was just an assistant or sidekick. Again, they will NOT tell you they were not the only promoter. You will *have* to ask the artist or the artist's management directly.

Part Two: What to look for in a Promoter

Making contact: Some Indies are always there when you call, others are never there. The ones who never answer that is usually a *bad sign*. If you thought it was difficult reaching them before you hire them, just wait until *after* they get your money. Also be wary, if they say they give clients (and potential clients) a different phone number to call than the one they give the stations. It is more likely you will never get that person on the phone when you do need them.

Reports: Reports are a requirement that well-organized promoters provide to you. Without a report, there is no other way you are going to be able to understand what is going on with your airplay each week... much less someone else such as stores, papers, clubs etc.

Office: If the promoter does not have an office (even a small one), then you will be competing with things like the promoter's sleep, TV, neighbors, dinner, etc.

Assistants: If a promoter handles more than one genre of music at the same time, or if the promoter does college radio at all, then assistants are mandatory. The phone calls have to be made, and no one person can call more than 150 stations a week, do reports, faxes, emails *and* talk to you when you call!

College Radio: College should be considered for every campaign, even if you are doing high-level commercial radio. College radio is relatively inexpensive, and will allow you to create some good looking charts and reports to show retail, press and clubs.

Faxes: Serious promoters use faxes. Faxing is simply the fastest way to get a one-page synopsis of info to the stations... with pictures if needed. They are not cheap, but a good promoter should still include these faxes.

Emails: While you may get excited about email, remember that since email is free, stations get them from every artist on the planet. And all the emails look the same. So, in order to build a solid project, you must use faxes and phone calls, because most artists can't afford them (and that is why you will stand out.)

References: Any promoter worth consideration will have a list of past clients. What you are looking for, is a promoter with projects that are on your (independent) level. A list of "big" clients, doesn't necessarily better, since a promoter used to having massive help from major label staff promoters, national tours, retail promotions, advertising etc., will not have these with your project. You need a promoter who is set up to work with indie projects like yours.

Do your Homework: The "major label" promoter was actually not the promoter that worked the major projects in the first place. They were probably just assistants in the office, or were mail people, or more often than not, they were just outright lying. It happens all the time. Ask the artist directly to find out.

Bryan Farrish is an independent radio airplay promoter. He can be reached at 818-905-8038, or www.radio-media.com. Email for event info: meet@radio-media.com

INTERNET RADIO: THE AFFORDABLE ALTERNATIVE

by Nathan Fisher, live365.com
© 2007 All Rights Reserved. Used By Permission

Many people don't yet think that Internet radio is or could be a viable medium. This is simply not borne out by facts. Internet radio already has millions of listeners per month and is growing stronger by the day. Independent artists who recognize this opportunity have a decided advantage over those who would wait for years to make it on corporate FM radio, often unsuccessfully.

What is Internet radio?

In appearance and feel, Internet radio is similar to regular radio. Instead of turning a dial, you enter a URL. Anyone with a broadband Internet connection can hear CD-quality audio, better sound quality, in fact, than with traditional FM radio. Even dial-up users can get sound quality roughly analogous to AM radio. Another key difference is that under federal law, Internet radio stations are responsible for paying per-performance royalties for each track they play that they do not own the rights to. Regular radio stations are not responsible for per-performance royalties.

Internet radio operates on a different, radically decentralized model: individual DJs decide what music they like and what music to play. And music fans listen; they even pay a premium to listen to ad-free content.

Traditional radio is limited

Traditional radio suffers from play list homogeneity and an astonishing unwillingness to take risks on new artists. FCC regulations, licensing fees and scarce spectrum bandwidth make it virtually impossible for independent stations to exist unless they are run by colleges or are pirated. This is compounded by the deregulation of radio station ownership following the federal Telecommunications Act of 1996, which made it easier than ever for big industry players like Clear Channel and Infinity to own a nationwide empire that can offer a limited range of programming formats. Indeed, in 1996 Clear Channel was a small media company that owned thirty stations. With the benefits of deregulation, Clear Channel now owns over 1,200 stations. Together, Clear Channel and Infinity control forty-five percent of the American radio audience.

What the future holds

Though Internet radio currently gets fewer listener-hours than traditional radio, the number is steadily increasing and has the potential to experience exponential growth in the next few years as broadband connections become increasingly available in portable devices and automobiles. Plus, it's a good bet that the average Internet radio listener is more of a music fan than the average traditional radio listener.

Moreover, Internet radio makes it simple to track listening behavior, accurately gauge total listener-hours and gather demographic data on listeners. You can easily use Live365's Web site to see which stations are playing your music and how many listening-hours they have had over the past month. This is completely unlike traditional radio, whose ratings system is stuck in the proverbial dark ages.

The Live 365 lowdown

Live365 makes it easy for independent artists to get their tracks into broadcasters' hands and listeners' ears. The ever-expanding library www.live365.com/cgi-bin/library.cgi is a virtual record pool, (a secure service that lets all Live365 DJs preview and add your tracks directly into their stations' playlists.) You can also allow broadcasters and listeners to download your entire track, if you prefer. Live365 is licensed and pays royalties to ASCAP, BMI and SESAC.

Each week, Live365 reports its DJs' playlists to Radio and Records, College Music Journal, Billboard Online, New Age Reporter, and other web properties. With the help of Radiowave.com, Live365 also compiles and reports a run-of-site weekly airplay chart. As the largest Internet radio network, with thousands of active broadcasters and over 2 million unique listeners a month, Live365 provides independent artists with an unprecedented opportunity for large-scale radio exposure. You can also submit your album or track to Live365's editorial department for consideration to be listed, free of charge (www.live365.com/labelservices.)

Nathan Fisher is the Editor and Music Library Coordinator for Live365. He grew up in idyllic South Minneapolis, where he learned to implicitly mistrust the status quo. After graduating from Pomona College with a degree in Politics, he relocated to Oakland, CA, where he lives a vaguely bohemian lifestyle with several other roommates in their early twenties. For more information about what Live365 has to offer please visit them at www.live365.com.

♦

PODCASTS AS A PROMOTIONAL TOOL

by Colin Meeks, IndieLaunchPad.com
© 2007 All Rights Reserved. Used By Permission

In their simplest form, podcasts are audio files created on a computer or portable media device that are subscribed to by people interested in the content of the Podcast. These audio files are then transported across the Internet to the users computer. This can be done automatically using one of a myriad of podcast aggregators like Juice, Doppler or WinPodder. Podcast comes from the amalgamation of two words, iPod and broadcast. This has led to the common misconception that an iPod is required to listen to them, this is not the case. You can listen to a podcast on any computer, MP3 player or CD player if the podcast has been written to an audio CD. The early genesis of podcasting is commonly attributed to Adam Curry and Dave Winer. With Adam's drive to make it happen and Dave's RSS (Really Simple Syndication) to act as the kind transport layer to get the podcast out to all subscribers. Talking of subscribers, another common misconception is that you need to pay for the podcasts you download, after all you are a subscriber. While there are a few paid for podcasts, the vast majority are totally free. Podcasts have grown at a phenomenal rate and their popularity was launched into the stratosphere, when Apple decided to jump on the podcast wagon and allow people to subscribe to podcasts through iTunes. Like music before it, suddenly podcasts were available to the regular person, without requiring complex knowledge of RSS feeds and aggregator software.

With podcasts coming into their own in the latter half of 2004, suddenly there was a medium that was inexpensive and could reach the world over. Creating a podcast can be relatively cheap, but once the bug catches hold, it's not long before podcasters outgrow their modest hardware and strive for perfection with a new microphone and mixer. Another big issue for podcasters is bandwidth. Having a few dozen people download your podcast is fine, even though the average music podcast is around 20-30 megabytes, but just imagine what happens when you have thousands of people downloading. Many people find themselves with an expensive bill from their Internet provider. There are many services that alleviate this problem for a small fee and it's these hidden costs that most people, especially listeners are not aware of.

Adam Curry had his own podcast called the Daily Source Code. At the beginning of each show and occasionally within, he would play music often referred to as mashups. This was the fusion of two or more different songs into one. This sometimes resulted in some great songs, but it was also in direct violation of copyright. While many didn't think it to be a real problem, it wasn't long before the powers that be came knocking on Mr. Curry's door and he was forced to stop. In the latter half of 2005 however an artist from NY, USA stepped into the breech and gave Adam full permission to play his song Summertime on the Daily Source Code. This artist was Brother Love and it was the beginning of something quite special. It wasn't long after this, that bands began to see the potential of podcasts and either gave permission to podcasts to feature their music or to sometimes create podcasts themselves.

There are now literally thousands of podcasts, featuring a multitude of new bands and artists. Bands are now finding new audiences from around the world. Hollow Horse, a band from Glasgow, Scotland are one of the many bands with positive things to say about podcasts. Kenny Little from the band says "If it wasn't for the medium of podcasting we would probably have split up. As it is, we are now in the middle of recording our third album and, the strange sideline to all of this, is we now have friends and fans from all over the world.". After being first featured in a couple of podcasts, Kenny said "We have sold more copies of the album in America than we have in Scotland. How amazing is that". Many bands now have no intention of seeking a record label, preferring to handle everything themselves. With Podcasts, MySpace and a Myriad of other services available in your arsenal, it's now quite a feasible thing to do.

Colin Meeks is host and produce of the Indie Launchpad Podcast www.indielaunchpad.com which showcases some of the best in independent music.

◆

WHAT IS PODSAFE MUSIC?

by David Wimble, The Indie Bible
© 2007 All Rights Reserved. Used By Permission

As you visit the hundreds of music podcast and MP3 blog sites you'll notice that most them feature something called PODSAFE MUSIC. For this article I have gathered information from various internet sites in order to help clarify what podsafe music is and how it can become another helpful tool to place into your marketing utility belt.

Definition of podsafe music (from Wikipedia en.wikipedia.org)
Podsafe is a term created in the podcasting community to refer to any work which, through its licensing, specifically allows the use of the work in podcasting, regardless of restrictions the same work might have in other realms. For example, a song may be legal to use in podcasts, but may need to be purchased or have royalties paid for over-the-air radio use, television use, and possibly even personal use.

The effective definition of "podsafe" for a given work depends entirely on the contract through which the podcaster licenses the work; there is no single podsafe license. The concept of podsafety, in its true form, greatly favors the artist and the profitability of the artist's product, in exchange for only very limited concessions to the podcasting community.

While some works such as public domain works or works under some Creative Commons licenses are inherently podsafe, the only actual requirement for a work to be podsafe is that any licensing requirements it has, if applicable, allow for the work's free use (typical broadcast use in its original form, if in no other form, depending on the specific license) in a podcast or web broadcast. This gives specific favor to podcasts only, allowing the artist to impose more traditional constraints on everyone else. Podsafe licensing can, for example, continue to require non-podcast consumers to pay for the work, require royalties on derivative works, and profit significantly from the work's use in traditional radio, television, or film.

The licensor of any podsafe work must be legally capable of making it so. An artist cannot distribute his or her own work through a podsafe license if doing so would break any laws or breach any standing agreements (e.g. with the RIAA). The creator of a derivative work may also not claim this work podsafe without express permission from the original copyright holders. (PMN has more specific and stringent terms to this effect in its agreement.)

Another point of contention is that not all podcasts are non-commercial works; in fact, an increasing number of podcasts are taking on sponsors and looking to make a profit. In general, no significant distinction is yet made between podsafe for non-commercial use and podsafe for commercial use, but it could easily arise at any moment.

Motives for the podcaster to use podsafe music (from Wikipedia en.wikipedia.org)
As podcasting grows more and more popular, illegal use of heavily licensed music (as through the RIAA) becomes increasingly difficult to hide. This is in general of greater concern to podcasters than to the typical sharer of music, because podcasters usually produce their shows for and promote them to the public—a far more overt and traceable action.

Including such licensed music legally has its own set of caveats. Indeed, under many jurisdictions it's currently impossible, but the message from those in the know is that many licensing agencies, if they do intend to allow the use of their music on podcasts, will require not only the payment of royalties but also the use of DRM on the shows. (DRM, because of its proprietary, system-specific nature, would be destructive to the general openness and system independence of podcasts.)

Use of podsafe music instead of more stringently licensed material allows a podcaster to continue to produce an inexpensive, legal program with little hassle. Not least important for an independent podcaster is the promise of being able to avoid the confusing maze of licensing organisations.

Motives for the artist to use podsafe music (from Wikipedia en.wikipedia.org)
Conventional radio (and television) can present a difficult, and not always logical, barrier of entry for a musician or other media artist involving large sums of money and often a great deal of surrender in both ownership and creative freedom.

In contrast, podcasting, an increasingly popular medium for audio programs, is as a whole very receptive, indeed thirsty for artists and input. This is due in part to the creative and economic nature of the largely independent podcasting community and further fueled by its need to avoid repetition. While a conventional radio show may be able to risk replaying a large part of its music selection from day to day, there would be little point in downloading a music podcast whose selection did not vary significantly from a previous show. Podcasting is thus a voracious medium. With a growing and international audience podcasting is now becoming an effective means for inexpensive artist promotion often aimed squarely at the people most like to be interested in that type of music.

What is The Podsafe Music Network?
The Podsafe Music Network (music.podshow.com) is a comprehensive source for podsafe music. It was founded in 2005 by ex MTV VJ and current podcaster Adam Curry (Daily Source Code www.dailysourcecode.com). PMN brings a large group of podcasters together with a wide variety of all-podsafe music and the artists who produce it.

According to PMN, podsafe music is music that meets all of the following conditions:

1. Works submitted to the Podsafe Music Network are the property of the artist, and all rights to these works, including lyrics and music, are the property of the artist.

2. All works contain no recordings, lyrics, copyrights, or other elements that are the copyright of any other artist, except under the limited provisions of the Creative Commons License Agreement www.creativecommons.org

3. Despite any recording contracts with RIAA, ASCA, BMI or other recording industry entity, the artist retains ownership of the works and is free to distribute, broadcast, license or sell these works at the artist's discretion.

The licensing agreement between the artist and PMN: music.podshow.com/music/artistTerms.htm

What are Creative Commons Licenses?
(from www.creativecommons.org)
Creative Commons Licenses help you publish your work online while letting others know exactly what they can and can't do with your work. When you choose a licence, we provide you with tools and tutorials that let you add licence information to our own site or to one of several free hosting services that have incorporated Creative Commons.

1. Standard License
License your song under your terms. Our set of standard licenses will let you share music with fans while protecting your song from limits you put in place.

Or, choose a prepared license for audio works.

2. Sampling License
People can take and transform pieces of your work for any purpose other than advertising, which is prohibited. Copying and distribution of the entire work is also prohibited.

3. Share Music License
This license is aimed at the musician that wants to spread their music on web and filesharing networks legally for fans to download and share, while protecting the music from commercial use or remixing of any kind.

How does a Creative Commons license operate?
Creative Commons license are based on copyright. So it applies to all works that are protected by copyright law. The kinds of works that are protected by copyright law are books, websites, blogs, photographs, films, videos, songs and other audio & visual recordings, for example. Software programs are also protected by copyright but, as explained below, we do not recommend that you apply a Creative Commons license to software code or documentation.

Creative Commons licenses give you the ability to dictate how others may exercise your copyright rights—such as the right of others to copy your work, make derivative works or adaptations of your work, to distribute your work and/or make money from your work. They do not give you the ability to restrict
anything that is otherwise permitted by exceptions or limitations to copyright—including, importantly, fair use or fair dealing—nor do they give you the ability to control anything that is not protected by copyright law, such as facts and ideas.

Creative Commons licenses attach to the work and authorize everyone who comes in contact with the work to use it consistent with the license. This means that if Bob has a copy of your Creative Commons-licensed work, Bob can give a copy to Carol and Carol will be authorized to use the work consistent with the Creative Commons license. You then have a license agreement separately with both Bob and Carol.

Where are the forms that I have to fill out?
Creative Commons licenses are expressed in three different formats: the Commons Deed (human-readable code), the Legal Code (lawyer-readable code) and the metadata (machine readable code). You don't need to sign anything to get a CCL. Just select your license here: www.creativecommons.org/license

Hmmm …what if I change my mind?
This is an extremely important point for you to consider. Creative Commons licenses are **non-revocable**. This means that you cannot stop someone, who has obtained your work under a Creative Commons license, from using the work according to that license. You can stop offering your work under a Creative Commons license at any time you wish; but this will not affect the rights with any copies of your work already in circulation under a Creative Commons license. So you need to think carefully when choosing a Creative Commons license to make sure that you are happy for people to be using your work consistent with the terms of the license, even if you later stop distributing your work.

Before you do anything, make sure you have the rights!
Before applying a Creative Commons license to a work, you need to make sure you have the authority to do so. This means that you need to make sure that the person who owns the copyright in the work is happy to have the work made available under a Creative Commons license.

Where do podcasters find podsafe music? (from Dave's
Imaginary Sound Space soundblog.spaces.live.com)
Discovering new music and the ability to use it fairly without fear of copyright infringement is a key issue for podcasters and listeners alike. Artists, composers, producers and consumers can all benefit from clear, fair and flexible copyright licenses that embrace new technologies. 'Podsafe' means non-RIAA audio and video that can be used legally in podcast productions and freely distributed online for downloading.

Podsafe music can be found in many locations on the web including: artists websites, MP3 blogs, open source music communities, podcast directories, netlabels, P2P networks and BitTorrent hosts. A quick search for "podsafe" in a podcast directory like PodcastAlley.com reveals a rich and diverse array of productions featuring podsafe music. Unfortunately it becomes extremely time consuming for podcasters to source available music and listen to it. Recommendations by listeners and fans play an important part in the podcast production process.

The definitive list of podcasting safe music sites can be found here: www.soundblog.spaces.live.com/Blog/cns!1pXOS7l93k8mqeQ7FlEEmOSQ!907.entry

It's always about the music
For an artist just entering into the podcast/MP3 blog universe, the amount of information to take in can be overwhelming. It's not unlike a lifelong typist being plopped in front of a computer and asked to create a spreadsheet with colored charts.

As you watch the internet continue to explode with new technologies, it may feel like life has passed you by and left you lying in the dust. However, the truth is we're all still tightly bundled together. No one is *ever* left behind. The opportunity to move towards the cutting edge is available to anyone (my father-in-law has just learned how to use a computer at the age of 81). Don't let fear (and the excuses it can conjure up) lessen your attempts to succeed.

Remember, it has always been, and always will be about the music - that unique expression that *you* have to offer to the world. Podcasts, podsafe music, MP3 blogs, Creative Commons licenses and all that other bounce-off-the-head stuff is simply a collection of new and useful tools to help you get your music heard by more people.

Final thoughts
For the newbie, my suggestion would be to take it slow. Go to the Creative Commons site www.creativecommons.org and poke around. It's a very user-friendly website. They understand that musicians are not lawyers.

Once you're done that, then start checking out the various podcast and blog websites. You'll soon discover that bloggers and podcasters are simply human beings with a passion for music - a collection of music lovers that are ready and willing to help you get your songs heard by a new stream of potential fans.

♦

ALTERNATIVE RADIO TRENDS AND WHAT THEY MEAN TO YOU
by Liz Koch, Notorious Radio
© 2007 All Rights Reserved. Used By Permission

In January 2005, WHFS, a flagship station for the Modern Rock/ Alternative format in the Baltimore/DC market, flipped to Spanish programming. Mid-way through 2004 KHRO in El Paso, TX did the same. Even a year ago, two other flagship stations, KNDD "The End" in Seattle and WNNX "99X" in Atlanta, decided to drop the majority of the 'new music' on their playlists, opting instead to play more 'Alternative Gold' (aka Classic Rock for Gen X) with a few 'cool' and 'local' bands thrown in for flavor.

Meanwhile the trends for 2004 show Satellite Radio, which can be heard Nationally, gaining millions of new listeners last year between both XM and Sirius. Web Radio, which can be heard Globally, DOUBLED its listening base in just ONE year and is now listened to by 10% of the ENTIRE U.S. population!!! Whereas it's true technology and digital listening are on the rise, I think there's something much more important going on.

Let's break it down into simple terms: WHFS and KHRO flip, which means they no longer had the listener base to attract advertisers (because sadly that's what Commercial Radio is about: commercials). "The End" and "99X" changed up their formats for two reasons, the first being the above, the second being they saw the writing on the wall before it was too late. But why an 'Alternative Gold' and a 'cool'/local focus? Easy: the risk of losing the displaced Gen X listening community FOREVER, thus losing their base and therefore their advertisers. This group of loyal listeners, who made them what they are, have found themselves less and less able to relate to what was going on the radio. I know because I was one!

These stations also ran the risk of losing local band support, aka the TRUE music heads of the market. Playlists, over the past few years, have become increasingly less open to 'taking a chance'. Less bands got spun more, in the true Pop radio fashion. Also driving the local bands away was the fact that 9 out of 9 of the bands ON that tight playlist were on Major Labels, with Major Label dollars behind them: something most local bands could only dream about competing with, but realizing the reality.

Mix that all together, and what do you have? Disaffected music fans turning off their radios once and for all. The same group of people searching for alternate means to hear something different, something local, something tangible and, sadly, something more interesting.

Enter Web and Satellite radio with no commercials. Enter the displaced DJs and programmers who had either quit traditional radio out of frustration or were forced out for caring too much about the music. In most cases these folks programmed the New Music or 'Specialty' shows, which showcased different sounds from the station playlist, a lot of times playing local and unsigned bands. They did the radio that took the chances that made Radio exciting in the first place. They saw in Web and Satellite radio what had attracted them to Radio in the first place: turning people on to amazing new music. They saw in Web and Satellite radio the exact thing that has led to its rapid growth: the ability to deliver something different with less inane talk and no commercials. They saw the freedom that traditional radio had forgotten about.

So, what does this all mean for you, the indie band who wants to make themselves known? Simple: EVERYTHING!!! If more traditional radio stations embrace the format changes "The End" and "99X" have done, you will have more of a shot of getting heard on your local Commercial Alternative radio station. NOT just on the New Music or Specialty show...in regular rotation! But why only strive for local domination? The numbers show that you can easily gain a National audience by getting on Satellite radio. There is a channel, XM-Unsigned, that plays nothing but bands like yours day in and day out. Billy Zero (the channel's programmer) will even mention your band's website on the air, and link you from the XM website. From there you will see record sales in markets you didn't necessarily think would be into your music. And from THERE you can better focus your touring, marketing and promotional efforts.

But why settle for the US? Web Radio will give you exposure around the globe! It's becoming more and more common for me to hear about independent artists touring Scandinavia or Japan, simply because someone over there heard about the band via the internet and had the means or the contacts to bring the band over. Countries outside of the U.S., Canada, Australia and Britain have a MUCH broader taste in music, and the beauty part is: being "signed to a label" matters a LOT less over there. If your music is available for purchase and your site, etc. come off as legit (even if it's a self-release on your own fake label), you can sell a boatload of records!

Don't you see? It's finally happening! The American music buying public, aka your audience, don't want to be told what to listen to, like, or buy anymore. This mass exodus to new forms of music exposure, coupled with the technology being both more available as well as affordable, is the most important thing to happen in music in YEARS. If a station like Indie 103.1 in Los Angeles (a station who cares about the Music) can go up against the Mothership of the Alternative format, KROQ, and pull enough listeners to make KROQ broaden its playlist, the door is open. Get your foot in there now!

Liz was the Los Angeles/ Orange County Street Marketing Rep for 3 years @ EMI Records. During this period she also worked as Danny Elfman's personal assistant for two & a half years. After her first CMJ (College Music Journal) Convention in 1994, she KNEW that the Music Business was what she wanted to do & that New York City was where she wanted to do it. So, she got her Associates Degree, moved to NYC & began working at Tommy Boy Music in the Underground Rock Dept in 1997. She was at Tommy Boy for almost 5 years before the company folded in March 2002. She now works out of her home in Astoria, Queens, NYC. notorious@notoriousradio.com www.notoriousradio.com

◆

KNOWING THE DIFFERENCE BETWEEN GOOD PR AND BAD PR

by John Foxworthy, Garage Radio

Publicity and networking are the two most important parts of any successful music project. Unless you lack aspirations to venture beyond your local scene, your career risks stagnation without them. This is why it's important to get a handle on how to conduct yourself when interacting with radio, publications, labels or any other facet of the music business … otherwise you chance snuffing your credibility before you even get out of the gate.

Whether you work PR for your own act or someone else's, your role seems simple … create and maintain public interest; however, even the most marketable project and the most interesting press releases are hardly enough to achieve these goals. As with anything you do, there are unwritten laws of etiquette you must follow to function effectively as a publicist.

As the Chief Editor of a busy e-zine and Host of a widely listened radio show, bands, labels, publicists and other publications contact me regarding press and airplay on a regular basis. This correspondence is truly the backbone of what I do … it keeps me in the know on many levels and provides me the opportunity to make new contacts. On the other hand, it also aggravates and frustrates me more often than not. I'm learning that better than half of the folks taking responsibility for public relations are most likely shooting themselves in the foot.

Do your research

This is a point I just can't stress enough. In fact, I could write this entire article on just that subject. It requires a lot of work, but the rewards will come back ten-fold. There are so many source guides and directories out there that it's virtually impossible to keep up and these are great tools, but used unwisely they can actually work against you. Here's a scenario based on my own experience:

I host a Rock/Punk/Metal radio show that's clearly described as such on my web site, as well as every directory in which it appears. Yet, almost daily I get press releases and requests for airplay from artists who play anything but Rock, Punk or Metal. This probably wouldn't annoy me as much if I didn't also get the same, exact emails to my e-zine inbox.

You may ask me, "What's the problem? Why not just delete the email?"

That's a simple solution and often times I do, but this is the symptom of a behavior that's sure to thwart the efforts of the sender. Think about it … if they're doing it to me, they're doing it to their other contacts as well. It tells me that this is someone who uses the gum-at-the-wall approach and may not be worth looking into … plus they tend to go onto my SPAM list. I also stay in regular contact with my other colleagues in the biz, so they may even end up on a "blacklist" and could even get stonewalled press-wise in the future.

The solution? Take some time to find out to whom your email is going by doing a simple search to check out their site, show, magazine or whatever. It's even acceptable to send a preliminary email to introduce yourself and get a better idea of what they're looking for (or if they even want your correspondence) before you fire off that request. This is also a great way to make first contact, which makes for an appropriate segue into our next topic.

First contact

I leave my email address publicly accessible to make it easy for people to contact me. This also contributes to the amount of SPAM I receive … a necessary evil in my position … so I spend an average of eleven hours a week sifting through my new messages in an attempt to separate the SPAM from the news. Why? First of all, most people don't know how to effectively title the subject of their message. Secondly, it's first contact … I may not know who sent the email because I've never corresponded with them.

In the last eight years I've trained myself to tell the difference between South African bank scams and artists trying to get exposure for new releases. This doesn't mean I've trained myself to stop deleting messages based on the subject. Titles like, "WE REQUEST YOUR ATTENTION" or "THE NEXT BIG THING" equate to "GET THE LOWDOWN ON THE SMALLEST CAPS" and will quickly prompt most of your potential contacts to hit the delete button.

First contact is the most important contact. The old adage that you never get a second chance to make a first impression holds very true ... especially with the sensitive nature with which people have been conditioned regarding SPAM these days. So, the first lesson on the subject is to make sure your email says what it means before it's even opened.

"New Alternative Rock Band From NYC" is a simple, yet operative title for an email to a new contact. They'll get an idea of the message you're trying to get across and you'll notice it wasn't all capitalized, which could be another form of suicide!

Next, you'll want to make sure you tailor the body of your email to fit your expected recipient. Address them by name (if you have it), be cordial, introduce your act (or yourself) and get to the point. Proper grammar and punctuation play a big role here, so if you have no clue what I mean by that, you shouldn't be doing PR in the first place.

Your first email should be more of a request than a release. Remember, you're dealing with people that are busy, so summarizing a description of the music, adding a few stats (including CD sales) and press quotes is quite alright as long as you keep it to a minimum ... 3 short paragraphs will suffice. Then, you can include links and contact info for your recipients to explore further if they're interested. DO NOT, and I reiterate, DO NOT email MP3 files or other attachments. This is annoying and will piss your target off in a heartbeat.

After you've made your first contact, it's wise to set a waiting period before following up. Again, these people are busy and prone to a lot of email, so there is a fine line between correspondence and SPAM.

Follow-up

I'm one to appreciate diligence and I'll be the first to admit that some of my attempts to create steady contacts have backfired on me more than once. Now, finding myself on the receiving end, I see what I was doing wrong. A beleaguered ally can quickly become a foe ... and it's for this reason I find it essential to define the difference between follow-up and pestilence.

Let's disregard the preceding tips for a moment and imagine you've emailed your press release or a request for coverage to a few addresses. It's possible that a few of the folks you contacted have contacted you back, but there are some that haven't responded. Many of them may be preoccupied with current projects or might even be completely uninterested. You have no way of knowing where they stand, so how do you decide when (or if) to send a second email?

Five business days is a good rule, but hinges on when you sent your initial correspondence. Monday through Wednesday are the best days to get in touch with your potential outlets. Due to the fact that most schedules revolve around the standard workweek, it stands to reason that these are the best days to send your follow-ups. If you still get no responses, you'll be better to write these contacts off and continue your exchange with the responsive set.

Mailing lists

This falls more closely under the subject of "netiquette" than etiquette. Just because you have contact email addresses, doesn't mean you have contacts. The inventory of rules surrounding mailing lists is another that could be an entire handbook ... and could be one of the single most contributors to death in the press/play world, but I'll try to emphasize the biggest no-nos.

Never, never, NEVER add arbitrary email addresses to your list. There's no negotiating this rule ... here's why:

Out of hundreds of emails a day, only about 30% apply to my day-to-day dealings. Another 5%-10% are personal and the rest are just garbage. In my capacity, I have to consider every message as a possible contact ... even though I have a "strict" policy that defines how I want to communications to be sent.

My standards are such that I never post uninvited news to other sources and with that, I avoid accepting the same. I personally don't have time to sift through everything I get, so a great percentage is deleted out of constraint. What does this mean? I'm flat-out not interested in getting updates from unsolicited suppliers. It also implies that I'd like permission from people to be added to their mailing lists ... and I'm pretty sure there are a lot of people out there that feel exactly the same way.

Not separating your contact lists is another hugely horrific move. This is a chapter right out of "BE ORGANIZED!" Sending gig updates to radio shows or publications that specifically do CD reviews is a waste of time. Additionally, sending the next gig on the morning of your next gig is just plain stupid. Your fans may want to know this (even though they probably already do), but it does no good to inform anyone else that you'll be playing CBGB in seven hours. Plan out your itinerary and send a release with your calendar for the next month or so. If your target wants to announce it, they'll have time to get the word out.

It's best to separate the lists of publications, shows, and other entities by type ... and tailor your announcements accordingly. You'll never ruin a contact faster than if you send a daily barrage of so-called updates and/or messages containing your personal agenda.

Last, but NOT least is how to send to your lists. Your email program or web-based mail will have the fields "To" "CC," and "BCC." Forget all about the "CC" field when sending to multiple recipients ... and I mean FORGET IT! No matter your capacity in the biz, this line is bad MoJo. Every contact in this field can be seen by every other contact that receives the email. Use "BCC" and save yourself a bevy of pissed off contacts!

Is your news really news?

I get everything from updates on CD sales figures to reminders that bands will be playing venues ... the same venues ... several times a week. This goes back to a behaviorism, and a destructive one at that. I, and many in my position, are extremely turned off by this and are very likely to disregard further contact.

Constant updates are not a great way to keep your act in the forefront of our minds. We like to stay informed, but it's good form to save up the news. One release with the band's future happenings, or a retrospective of the last month or so will go a lot further than a daily barrage of minor occurrences ... no need to desensitize your awaiting public.

Press kits

Press kits are arguably the meat and potatoes of exposure for any act. This is a pretty easy subject, as you won't likely get an address which to send them without permission. For those that make their mailing info readily available, it's a good idea to look further and find an email contact. Make your target privy of the impending envelope and allow a week for it to arrive, but DO NOT follow up in a week!

One thing you must understand is that many of these folks get quite a few of these packages every day. I myself get 30 per week, so I really don't have the time I need to properly distribute and/or review them in seven days. In this case a good follow-up rule is probably 2 weeks ... even if you never heard back from your email.

These are the best tips I have without writing an entire book on public relations. My advice is a culmination of my experience and that of the professionals I work with every day. Following it can enhance your effectiveness as a publicist and help create your niche in the music world ... not following it may greatly reduce your chances of success in this fickle world we call the music biz.

In 2002 I co-founded Garage Radio, a site dedicated to the indie community, which has seen great success over the past couple of years. I also hosts a radio show called "The RoadRash Bash," a Rock and Metal extravaganza featuring indie bands and name bands that are on indie labels, but not getting the exposure they deserve. I work with the industry on every level these days and that experience has given me the insight and contacts I need to bring informative commentaries to the people who need them most ... the DIY and independent community.
Contact: www.garageradio.com broadrash@garageradio.com

HOW TO SUBMIT MUSIC FOR REVIEW

by Jodi Krangle, The Muse's Muse
© 2007 Jodi Krangle. All Rights Reserved. Used By Permission.

Getting the attention of music reviewers can be almost as difficult as breaking into a bank - and let's face it - sometimes far less profitable. But a good review is worth its weight in gold. So how does one go about getting reviewers to give your particular package the time of day? I receive quite a few of these packages myself, so while I'm no expert, I do have a few suggestions:

Be polite when making first contact

1. This may sound like it's too obvious to mention, but trust me - if you contact a potential reviewer by demanding their submissions address because you are simply the best thing that has happened to music since the microphone and the reviewer would be out of their mind to pass you up, you're likely to be disappointed at the response you receive.

2. Your initial contact should be polite and brief. A simple, "Hello, my name is (so and so) and I'm interested in a possible review in your (publication/web site). Would you be able to supply me with the proper contact information so that I can send you my CD?" will be kindly received. Even if it takes the reviewer a little while to get back to you - whether it's by regular mail, e-mail or through the feedback form of a web site - their reply will usually be helpful.

3. One last word on the subject of first contact: PLEASE don't send an e-mail with your web site address and only a "Check this out!" line for clarification. You don't want to know how much spam e-mail I receive in a day and messages like that simply make me feel as if I'm being asked to check out the latest in cheesy porn. I delete such messages on sight and I honestly don't know many reviewers who pay them any attention either.

Presentation

1. The presentation of the CD itself is probably the most important element of your package. It's that CD that will give the reviewer their initial impression of your music. That doesn't mean you have to have spent thousands of dollars on your presentation, a huge CD insert, a gorgeous color cover, etc. That just means that your "look" should be consistent.

Note: if you're not getting a professional printing of anything, a color inkjet printer creating your own letterhead along with a similarly designed CD covering sticker, will work quite nicely.

2. Simplicity is often the best way to go. Above all, avoid sending in a blank recordable CD with black marker written on it. Your contact information should be on the CD and the insert and/or cover. No matter what you do, make sure your contact information is easy to find.

3. The insert certainly doesn't need to be in color but there should be one, if at all possible. The insert is the perfect place to put contact information, credits (the reviewer is often fascinated by who did and wrote what), anecdotal information, etc - the things that make you special and different from the other folks the reviewer will be listening to. If there is a chance the CD might become separated from the rest of your work, you want the reviewer to be able to contact you from that CD alone.

Things to include in your package

- A brief cover letter addressing the reviewer by name (a MUST)
- A bio (1 page!)
- A CD, with an insert of some kind.

- Up to 3 reviews if you really feel you need them (try to keep this on one or two pages)
- Make sure your contact information is on everything.

Note: Keep in mind that if your CD itself is a nice little package all on its own including inserts, you may not need the bio or the reviews and could probably get away with just sending in the CD and a cover letter. If you have a web site and include the URL to that site in your cover letter, the reviewer can find out tons more information on you should they wish to.

Be patient

Remember to be patient, not that you shouldn't ever re-contact the reviewer. Remind the reviewer you're around! Just don't do it every day. Wait a couple of weeks between contacts. Reviewers have a lot of demands upon their time and are frequently several weeks - or even months behind in their reviews depending on the publication(s) they write for.

Be professional

The way in which you treat people will reflect upon your professionalism even more so than the look of your CD. It takes years to build up a good reputation and only a few minutes to completely destroy it. As with anything in the music business, you never know when someone you were kind to will be in a position to return that kindness. It's all about relationships. Make sure you're the sort of person who fosters good ones and it'll all come back to you.

Be pleasant; don't demand to know why your CD wasn't chosen for a review and/or spotlight if you are told that it wasn't - not unless you actually want to hear what the reviewer has to say. And if that reviewer *does* let you know why, let it be a lesson and move on. Try to keep in contact with the reviewer. It might be that a future release of yours will be better received. I hope these hints have helped. Meanwhile, good luck with your music!

Jodi Krangle is Proprietress of The Muse's Muse Songwriting Resource www.musesmuse.com Visit Jodi@www.musesmuse.com, to find out more about her free monthly e-zine.

♦

INSIDE THE HEAD OF A MUSIC REVIEWER

by Suzanne Glass, CEO Indie-Music.com
© 2007 All Rights Reserved. Used By Permission

What to send? When to follow up? What to say? Should you keep bugging a writer to review your material? What makes writers chose one CD over another to review? And most of all can you increase your chances of getting a published review when you submit a CD? Answer: Absolutely! By understanding a writer's mind, and following a few simple guidelines, you will substantially increase the likelihood your music will be chosen for a review or feature.

Indie-Music.com recently asked our writers; Heidi Drokelman, Jennifer Layton, Les Reynolds, and Erik Deckers, a series of questions designed to let musicians see inside writers' heads, and get a unique look at how the behind-the-scenes process works. After the Q&A, we give a quick checklist for getting your music reviewed successfully.

Q. What impresses you about an artist/musician/band?

A. *Heidi Drokelman:* Number one; the biggest impression is always the music, and the talent (however sometimes hidden it is) of songwriting. The versatility of all the members is important, and having an appreciation for good songwriting, no matter the genre, will always shine through in someone's work. Sure, clean production always sounds nice and makes a big impression when you're only listening to something a few times for review.... but I've been doing this [reviewing] for a long time now, and if the material is there (even in raw form), the first thing I forgive is production quality. When your songs stand out, even if you've recorded on the worst machine you can possibly find, then that's what counts. Even the worst material can't surpass a production snow job.

A. *Jennifer Layton:* There's no one thing. I've been impressed by so many different things. I'm impressed when I hear a musician doing something new that I've never heard before. I'm impressed when I hear a poetic folk song that expresses something so true; I feel it tugging at my heart. No matter what the press kits look like or how fancy the web site is, none of it matters if I'm not touched by the music in some way.

A. *Les Reynolds:* Real talent in at least one area (vocal, instrumental, lyrical) and especially when all those elements come together. Also, if they've got their s*** together —correspond in timely manner, not pushy about reviews, answer questions coherently and communicate well (even if this is through an agent, having the right agent who can do those things is crucial).

Q. What impresses you in a promo pack submission?

A. *Erik Deckers:* "Is the press kit complete? Does it have a bio and headshot or group photo? Are there other articles from other reviewers? If the answer is YES to these questions, then I am impressed. If the press kit contains a three-line bio, or vague and airy generalities discussing the metaphysics of the universe in relation to their music, I am decidedly unimpressed."

A. *Heidi Drokelman:* "Oh, this is a completely relative thing. I look at this part of the packaging after I've already listened to the music. If getting signed by a label is your goal, I'd much rather receive bio materials, a dated letter (it's really hard to separate the volume of mail that some of us receive, so including a dated letter from a band representative is a nice touch), a simple photo that expresses the personality of an artist or band, and on occasion, I enjoy a good piece of gag swag. Taking that extra step, and coming up with a creative piece of swag can push a pack to the top of the pile. However, please refrain from the offensive, even if it's meant in jest."

A. *Jennifer Layton:* "I take a different route with promo packs. I know those materials are expensive, and I have a small office and can't hang on to all the press materials I get each month. Which means that if I don't absolutely love the artist, the promo pack winds up in the trash after I write the review. I feel really guilty about that. So when an artist contacts me about submitting material, I tell them they don't have to bother with headshots or elaborate press kits — just a simple bio sheet that includes the web site address, telling me whatever they want me to know about them. What I'm really interested in is the music."

A. *Les Reynolds:* "It looks like the artist/band took time and care in preparing it and it "fits" with the image and overall music style. Quality photos, if included, also get my attention. While I won't use the pix (except to decorate my pod at work!), it says something about the artist — I can get a "vibe" or feel off that. I am also just impressed with quality photography since I used to be a photographer."

Q. How can bands get your attention?

A. *Erik Deckers:* "Write a personalized note to me, not a generalized form letter."

A. *Heidi Drokelman:* "Bands can get my attention fairly easily, but holding it can be another story altogether. I am all about helping out quality bands and artists, and will take extra steps to make sure that I am doing all I can without showing blatant favoritism (although I AM known for that as well), so some of the ways to do this are: Be courteous: I should clarify because I despise kiss asses just as much as the repeat offender rudeness. I'm not asking for special treatment, just a bit of humanity. Don't be overly pushy. I don't mind the follow-up to check in on the status of a review, but DO NOT expect to get a review every time you send in material. Some pushiness is good, but use common sense to know where the line has been drawn."

A. *Les Reynolds:* "Contact me directly. Keep the lines of communication open, and don't tell me to just go to your MP3 site. I hate that! It's become the universal cop-out (besides —what if the computer is malfunctioning or the internet is down?) Also: if they can describe their music accurately in a sentence— that shows they know who they are and have read my Indie-Music.com bio blurb."

Q. What do bands do which wastes their money, when they send submissions?

A. *Erik Deckers:* "Send crappy press kits. If I don't have much background information on the band, I can't write a good review. If I can't write a good review, then it doesn't help the band much."

A. *Heidi Drokelman:* "If they're unsolicited, it's a huge waste of money in general. Don't just blindly send your discs out to everyone you think has an inkling of interest in your work. Make sure that you contact someone and at least use the proper procedure. I'm sure this may sound lame to you, but the procedure we use is built to enhance our reviews, not to bring you down. On another note, photos, postcards, stickers, bio write-ups, and discs are not a waste of money. Just plan your priorities and work up to the full packet."

A. *Jennifer Layton:* "I hate to see bands spend money by sending me glossy headshots and other expensive materials. While I'm impressed by their professionalism, I'm not a label rep or someone who will have a major influence on their career — I'm just an indie writer. Also, I tell artists not to waste money by sending their submissions by Federal Express. Regular old mail will do fine.

A. *Les Reynolds:* Sending tons of press clippings - one sheet is enough. Sending all sorts of odd-shaped stickers and things that, by themselves — once away from the package — mean nothing. Most
Press kits are guilty of overkill."

Q. How can bands improve their submissions?

A. *Heidi Drokelman:* "Solicit your submissions for review – it will ultimately benefit you more to do some research and look into different publications and specific writers, than it will to blindly send things out. Quality is key - you're looking for someone to thoughtfully review your material, to respect it, and cultivate new contacts for publicity and marketing purposes. Do what you can presently afford, and the rest will fall into place."

A. *Jennifer Layton:* "I think they can tone down their bios a little. I'm aware that most artists write their own bio sheets, so I have to laugh when I read stuff like "This is the most amazing rock band on the music scene today. No one has ever come close to matching their talent and energy." Also, be sure to run your press materials through a spell- checker! One of the funniest bio sheets I ever got was from a folk artist who called himself a great intellectual songwriter, and the word "intellectual" was misspelled."

A. *Les Reynolds:* "Unwrap those CDs - Pleeeze!!! Send quality materials that won't fall apart immediately. Send good quality CDs (occasionally defective ones or discs produced in an odd format is received, and they won't play.)"

Q. How do you deal with your personal music preferences when reviewing? Do you review styles you would not normally listen to/buy?

A. *Erik Deckers:* "It's actually a little harder for an artist to impress me when they're in a genre I already like, because I have some definite ideas about what I enjoy and what I don't. But that means that if an artist CAN impress me, then they've done an excellent job. I do review styles that I normally don't listen to, so if an artist can create something that I enjoy (i.e. country music), then they also get a good review."

A. *Heidi Drokelman:* "Actually, I may be one of the few reviewers that will instantly admit that I use my personal music preference as a barometer for my reviews. I believe that it is almost impossible to take that out of the mix, especially when considering first impressions and different "trends". But this can be a very positive tool, especially when considering things like generational preferences (determining who this music will appeal to), and regional trends."

A. *Jennifer Layton:* "That's been an interesting issue for me. Over the past three years, I've learned not to rule out styles of music I don't normally listen to. I thought I hated all folk music before I started writing for Indie-Music.com, and now I am completely in love with acoustic folk/rock music. The only thing I can't review is rap. I'm a middle-class white girl who still listens to Barry Manilow and the Carpenters occasionally – I have ZERO credibility when it comes to rap and hip-hop."

Q. What do you most enjoy about reviewing indie music?

A. *Erik Deckers:* "It's not the same old schlock I hear on commercial radio. In most cases, it's better.

A. *Heidi Drokelman:* I'm still amazed, after all these years, at the quality and talent that's out there. The best thing about reviewing indie music is the sheer unpredictability of it all."

A. *Jennifer Layton:* "I know this sounds dramatic, but writing about indie music for the past three years has changed my life. I'm a lot more open-minded about so many things because I've learned to be more open-minded about the music I listen to. I've met several of the artists I've reviewed and am so happy that I've been able to encourage them by contributing positive reviews to their press kits. I've become such a fan of indie music that I flew up to NYC for my birthday last year to see performances by some of the artists I'd written about."

A. *Les Reynolds:* "The fact that there's an unlimited amount of real talent out there and it keeps coming and won't ever stop. I've heard stuff I would have never heard otherwise, met musicians I'd never even dreamed existed. And the cream is when a real connection is made... that's worth everything."

Q. What most irritates you in writing reviews?

A. *Erik Deckers:* "Getting unsolicited reviews. I'm pretty busy to begin with, and so I have to be selective about whose reviews I undertake. When I get one that I didn't ask for, I don't look favorably upon that artist. If I do manage to get around to doing their review, they've got a bigger hurdle to clear in that I'm already annoyed with them."

A. *Heidi Drokelman:* "The only thing that ever gets me is the volume of the mailings that I get. Making the commitment to give advice, constructive criticism, and deliver it in a way that isn't cruel, disconcerting, or rude is never easy. I may have harped a little about bands realizing that the reviewers are human, but remembering how personal the work is to others keeps me in check when delivering my honest opinion about their work."

A. *Jennifer Layton:* "What drives me NUTS is when artists or labels put me on their mailing lists when I didn't ask them to. Some artists have even put me on their lists before they've even sent me the CD for review. The worst was after I wrote a positive review of one band, and then their label put me on the mailing list of every single artist on their roster. That's one of the reasons I don't deal with labels or PR people anymore. If I love an artist's work, I'll ask to be put on the mailing list. And I have done that many times."

A. *Les Reynolds:* "Bad (inaccurate/incomplete) information on liner notes (it happens) or if the info is not legible — that stuff is very helpful and often necessary (in my opinion) in writing reviews. That, and wishing I had nothing to do but write, because most of these artists deserve a timely review."

Review check list

1. Communicate professionally - Use standard grammar and punctuation, proofread, and use a spell checker. You don't have to write a business letter like you learned in 8th Grade Grammar class, the letter could be creative, but make sure it is identifiable as a business communication and not junk mail. Make sure to directly state you are looking for a review. Don't send mass mailings, it's obvious to the recipient. On the phone, leave useful messages designed to make it easy to call you back (spell your name, and repeat your phone number twice to make copying easy for the listener).

2. Follow submission guidelines - Guidelines exist for a reason, which is to help an organization handle a large flow of music submissions in an efficient manner. Each publication does it differently, but if you choose not to follow the guidelines, expect your submission to be late, lost, or worse.

3. Send a cohesive promo pack - Writers have differing preferences on what they like to receive as part of a promo pack. Most writers, though, like to read a band biography and a few press clips (it helps in writing a review to know more about an artist), and many also like to see a band photo. If you are unsure what a writer requires, err on the side of sending too MUCH rather than not enough. If you choose not to include photos and graphics, make sure they are easily available on your website, in case the reviewer plans to publish your review with pictures.

4. Give contact information - When your review goes up, nothing would be dumber than to make your CD hard to find. Many artists, though, forget to include full contact information including mailing address, phone, email, and website URL.

5. Identify your genre - When people read reviews, they want to know, upfront, whether it's their "style" or not. So even if you simply say "a cross of rock, folk, and punk", that is much better than saying "we cannot be categorized". Better to categorize yourself than let a writer do it for you. Many writers are not musicians, and do not know precisely how to describe your genre just by listening. Help them.

6. Write a meaningful bio - Drop the lines that say you are "incredible", "changing the face of music", or "talented beyond belief etc.,

7. Make the writer's job easy - Since writers are, at the basic level, just people doing their job, it only makes sense that if you can make their job easier, they will like you and try to return the favor. That's just human nature. Include everything the writer needs, be sensitive to their schedule, and provide graphics or answers to any questions promptly.

8. Follow up courteously - Writers vary greatly in how they respond to follow-ups. Some people will respond promptly, keeping you up to date at each step of the process. Other writers ignore follow-ups completely. Your best bet is learning each writer personally. As a general rule, follow up about 2-4 weeks after your submission should have arrived with a short note. If you hear nothing, try again in another two weeks. If you again hear nothing, try waiting a month. Don't threaten or chastise the writers, just ask if a decision has been made about your review yet.

9. Don't argue with the reviewer - You can't win. If you don't like the review, you can pass on that reviewer with your next CD. Or you can submit again and see if their opinion has changed. Either way picking a fight about something the reviewer wrote is a waste of your time. If there is a factual error, fine, ask the writer to correct it. But don't argue, "Our choruses are NOT boring! They are complex and emotive". Since the characterization of your choruses as "boring" is only the reviewer's opinion, you are not going to change it. You might, however, piss off the writer for life.

10. Keep the connection - You need to cultivate your relationships with writers. Check in with them periodically between CDs, read their other work, let them know if you have news, and send thank-you notes - even if you did not get reviewed. Your goal is to build a relationship. You never know when that relationship may help you out - but you can be sure it will work in your favor if you present yourself as nice, interested, and understanding.

Suzanne Glass is the founder of Indie-Music.com, All the reviewers featured in this piece write for Indie-music. For more information please contact: www.indie-music.com.

◆

WHY MOST DEMO RECORDINGS ARE REJECTED
by Christopher Knab author of "Music Is Your Business"
© 2007 All Rights Reserved. Used By Permission

"Getting a deal" has long been the goal of many would-be artists and bands. For mostly naive reasons, most new talent feel that by securing a recording contract with a significant major or independent label, success will be guaranteed. (Talk about naiveté.) To get this 'belief system' up and running, many musicians figure all they have to do is send off their music to a label, and a recording contract will come their way shortly.

How to improve your odds

The following list of 10 Reasons Why Demo Are Rejected was gathered together after years of listening to comments made by Record Label A&R reps at music industry conferences and workshops, as well as from personal interviews with reps, and from many interviews A&R reps have given to the press. The purpose of providing you with this information is to at least improve the odds that your music will get listened to when you submit your demos. This list will look at the most common mistakes musicians make when either shopping for a record deal, or trying to get the attention of A&R Reps with their demo recordings.

10 reasons why demos are rejected

1. No Contact Information on CDR and/or CDR container: Put your name, address, email, and phone number on both.

2. Lack of Originality: Just because you can record, doesn't mean your music is worth recording.

3. The Music Is Good, But The Artist Doesn't Play Live: This applies to all genres of music except electronica and experimental music.

4. Poorly Recorded Material: So you bought Pro-Tools ... so what!

5. Best songs are not identified or highlighted on the CDR: Give the folks a break. For demos-send only 3 or 4 songs and highlight the best ones.

6. Sending Videos In Place Of CDRs: Keep it simple, in the demo mode. All anyone wants is to check out your songwriting and musicianship.

7. Sending Unsolicited Recordings: You sent them, but they never asked for them.

8. Sending The Wrong Music To The Wrong Label: You didn't do your research to find out what labels put out what kind of music.

9. Musicians Can't Play Their Instruments Competently: This is so basic, but you would be astounded at how incompetent most start-up musicians are.

10. The Music Sucks: This criticism is as old as music itself. You may think your music is the greatest thing since frappacinos, but most demo recordings the industry receives are as bad as the first round contestants on American Idol.

Christopher Knab is a music business Consultant, Author and Lecturer. He was recently honored by Seattle's Rocket magazine as "One of the Most Influential People in the Northwest Music Industry." Visit his website at: www.4frontmusic.com or contact him personally at: Chris@Knab.com

tools

WHAT ARE PERFORMANCE RIGHTS ORGANIZATIONS?

by Jer Olsen, CEO MusicBootCamp.com
© 2007 All Rights Reserved. Used By Permission.

Performance rights organizations like BMI, ASCAP and SESAC all perform a similar task but in slightly different ways. Essentially, they all perform the duty of collecting royalties for non-dramatic performances of intellectual property. In simpler terms, they collect the income from radio stations, TV stations, programming companies, Internet marketers and any other entity where music and related intellectual property is used. These royalties are then, in turn, paid to the various publishers and authors associated with a particular recording or performance.

Why do we need them?

The fundamental reason behind the birth of these organizations is the simple fact that individual artists and song writers can't possibly devote the time, attention and research required to collect royalties from the plethora of companies that use their music, even though by law they are entitled to those royalties. Artists depend on these performance rights organizations to do the hunting and collecting for them—a small price to pay for a piece of a much, much bigger pie! There's a saying, "50% of everything is a whole lot better than 100% of nothing!" Well, we don't know exactly how much money these organizations charge for their services, but we can be certain it covers their time and energy (similar to how music publishers earn money for getting music played in movies, TV shows, or recorded by other artists, etc.) The truth is, performance rights organizations are a necessary and helpful tool for musicians and publishers. The toughest decision is choosing which one to align with.

Which one to choose?

Please visit the page of each organization to find on-line information about joining as well as a ton of other terrific resources. Compare and make a decision on which one best suits you. If you don't, you can practically assure yourself of never being paid for airplay.

United States
BMI—Broadcast Music, Inc (www.bmi.com)
ASCAP—The American Society of Composers Authors and Publishers (www.ascap.com),
SESAC (www.sesac.com)
Canada
SOCAN—The Society of Composers Authors and Music Publishers of Canada (www.socan.ca)
The UK
PAMRA—Performing Arts Media Rights Association (www.pamra.org.uk)
PRS—The Performing Right Society (www.prs.co.uk)
MCPS—The British Mechanical Copyright Protection Society Limited (www.mcps.co.uk)
France
SACEM—Societe Des Auteurs Compositeurs Et Editeurs De Musique (www.sacem.fr)
CISAC—Confédération Internationale des Sociétés d'Auteurs et Compositeurs (www.cisac.org)
Germany
GEMA—The German Society For Musical Performing Rights And Mechanical Reproduction Rights (www.gema.de)
Italy
SIAE—Societa Italiana Degli Autori ed Editori (www.siae.it)
Spain
SGAE—Sociedad General de Autores y Editores (www.sgae.es)
Sweden
STIM—Svenska Tonsattares Internationella Musikbyra (www.stim.se)
Australia
APRA-The Australasian Performing Right Association Limited (www.apra.com.au)

Note: If you are looking for information on how to start your own publishing company, inquire on each site or call each company on how to obtain membership as a publisher. Becoming a publisher is not as nearly as difficult as performing the duties of a publishing company since a publisher's main task is exposing compositions and recordings to as many profitable opportunities as possible. Many of the duties of publishing companies can be effectively performed through a membership with the *Harry Fox Agency* (www.harryfox.com).

Jer Olsen is the founder and CEO of MusicBootCamp.com, home of "Dirt-Cheap CD Replication and FREE Music Business Training!" This article is a sample of the many free resources available on the Web site. Jer is also an accomplished musician and producer with several top 20 Billboard hit remixes to his credit. www.MusicBootCamp.com

♦

UPC & BARCODES FOR PENNIES AND SENSE
by Lygia Ferra, LAMusicGuide.com

With all the details that go into making a CD it is easy to put off making certain decisions, especially if there is cost involved or contradictory information.

So what exactly is a barcode?
Bar codes are also called UPC Symbols (generated by the Uniform Code Council (www.uc-council.org.) They are the small black and white lines that correspond to a unique 12 digit number used to track sales of CD's, while Sound scan correlates the information with your barcode in their database. Unless you are planning on starting a record label and putting out a number of releases with several artists, the $750 expense isn't really necessary.

Soundscan
Since Soundscan (www.soundscan.com) has a direct influence on placement in Billboard and CMJ music charts and other forms of recognition, payola has all been obliterated. It is a tracking system that did away with the potentially subjective reports of radio programmers and store managers prior to 1991. Sound Scan's records are not public, so the only way to access their data is open an account at a minimum price of several thousand dollars per year. The only ones checking are the larger labels and bigger companies. If you want to impress, you would need to sell more than 1,000 units to catch their eye.

Why do you need one?
One reason why you may need a barcode at all is that most stores and online retailers require an UPC code on every product they sell. So sparing the $750 expense, you can acquire one through Oasis or Discmakers for "free" when you replicate your discs, or through *CD Baby* for a modest $20 fee.

In the case of CD Baby the agreement does not bind you to the company in any way, other than having them listed as your "Parent Label" in Sound Scan's database. They provide you with the code as an electronic image, and you can include it in any cover art as appropriate.

How do you get credit for sales?
To ensure you are properly credited for all record sales as in the case of Discmakers you fax the necessary forms to Soundscan (914-328-0234), you will need a separate form for each release. Any independent artist or band can have their retail sales tracked through Sound scan, though only a label with two or more acts can take part in their Venue Sales Reporting Procedure. You must also have been in business two years or more, with a $500 fee.

It's never too late
You can always purchase one afterwards and have them printed on stickers. If you do it yourself make sure your printer is at least 720 dpi so they will read correctly. You can easily download a shareware barcode. A simple search for "UPC Barcode" @ http://shareware.cnet.com, or www.download.com will yield many results.

Alternatives
You can also go through a company (usually with a minimum order of 1,000 stickers) they will print them out for you, saving you the hassle of doing it yourself. If you are only going to sell your product at gigs or through alternative means, you really do not need a barcode at all. But for a mere $20, CD baby will save you all the worry and give you many more possibilities to sell your product.

Sources:
The Uniform Code Council: 1-800-543-8137 www.uc-council.org
Soundscan: (914) 684-5525 www.soundscan.com, clientservices@soundscan.com
Note: If you do decide to bite the bullet and purchase a barcode through the Uniform Code Council the process can take a number of weeks so allow for that extra time.

Independent Records: 1000 stickers Single Format Registration, Price: $55.00 - www.indierec.com/s-barcodes-register.html
Bar Codes Talk, Inc: 888-728-4009 Florida $30.00 shipping included.

Lygia Ferra is a Singer/Songwriter, Producer and Entrepreneur based in Los Angeles, Ca. In addition to helping with the IMB, she is actively involved with developing the La Music Guide site (where this article originally appeared) (www.lamusicguide.com). Please visit www.lygiaferra.com, for more info.

◆

BAND AND PRESS KIT ESSENTIALS
by Richard V. Tuttell, Daily News

Destiny's Mother-in-Law may not be the best local band in town — or even the loudest, but they know how to attract attention. The heavy metal group's marketing plan included an obvious first contact for any promotion — their hometown newspaper. Many bands overlook this option when promoting their CDs and gigs. What may seem stuffy and low-tech, however, is a golden opportunity for getting publicity and building a local following.

In the case of Destiny, a power trio based in eastern North Carolina, the first step was a phone call to the editor to introduce the band, gauge interest and find out the preferred method of submitting information. A press kit containing, a press release, photo and CD followed this.

Press release
This is the most important piece of the promotion program. It should answer six questions: who (the name of the band and its members), what (the style of music, gigs, or recording being promoted), where (the location of the performance or where the recordings are available, when (the time and date of the show), why and how (is the show a benefit, then for whom, why should people want to hear the band and how can people get advance tickets or find the club or other venue?) Leave the detailed back-story, how the lead singer while working at the Citgo station met the guitarist when he drove in with a flat, for a later full-blown feature.

Format is just as important as content. A sloppy presentation reflects a lack of professionalism and reduces the chances the release will run as written, or at all. Type the release on standard letter-size sheets or submit it as a digital text file on diskette or by email. Use plain text, which is compatible with most computer programs and operating systems used by newspapers. Not everybody has a copy of Microsoft Word around. If you email your release, paste the text of the release into the body of the message because editors are wary of opening attachments from strangers. Write in narrative form with complete sentences (use both lowercase and uppercase letters) rather than sending a flyer, (because it gives the band a better shot at controlling how the information will be printed.) Be sure to include contact information (names, phone numbers and email addresses), just in case.

Photos
Destiny's Mother-In-Law sent a standard 8x10 black and white print, which was fine for our paper, but I would suggest sending color prints. It leaves open the opportunity of it being used on a feature front. If the image is to go on an inside page a color photo can still be scanned as grayscale. Many papers are using digital cameras and will accept digital images with a resolution of at least 2 MPs. Submit a jpeg or tiff file on a diskette or by email. It's helpful to provide a paper printout to show what the digital image looks like. You can also refer to a Web site from which the photo can be downloaded.

Don't print a digital image on your inkjet, submit it on a sheet of copy paper and expect it to be published. The quality just won't be acceptable. Also avoid Polaroids that usually have poor production quality. Spend a few bucks for a professional portrait or get a friend with a decent camera and an eye for composition to help you out. Keep the shot tight with members grouped closely together to avoid dead space. Filling the viewfinder to the max allows you to decide how the photo should be cropped rather than a photo editor.

Always attach caption information to the photo on a piece of paper taped the back or bottom of the print. Name everyone in the photo, identifying each person. Even if that information is already on the accompanying press release put in the caption. Photos and releases are often separated.

Recordings

Including a CD showcasing your talent is a nice touch with a press release, but is more important when requesting a music review or feature story. Some newspapers prefer to experience the band live and others may accept MP3 files. Do not send your only master copy of your sure-fire hit, because there's often no guarantee that it will be returned.

Don't be discouraged if the big metro paper rejects your submission. For every daily paper there are about nine weeklies or other non- daily publications, and they depend on local content

Daily newspaper editor Richard Tuttell is the author of Good Press: An Insider's Guide to Publicizing Business and Community News, available from Barnesandnoble.com, Amazon.com and other on-line booksellers. This article originally appeared in Disc Makers Fast Forward newsletter. For a free one-year subscription, call 1-800-468-9353, or visit www.discmakers.com.

◆

SO, WHAT'S THE SCOOP WITH ELECTRONIC PRESS KITS?

by Panos Panay, CEO Sonic Bids

It seems that the big buzz out there in the music word today is all about Electronic Press Kits (EPK™). Should independent musicians use an EPK™ or a traditional press kit when approaching club promoters, festival organizers, radio programmers or record label A&R representatives? Do they work as well as regular press kits or should one stick with the tried and true method of snail mail kits? Are industry insiders even using them?

Electronic press kit, why is it important?

The answer is simple: like every other major innovation over the years ranging from the Compact Disc to the MP3, the industry was slow to initially accept it but it's fast becoming the ubiquitous standard that everyone from up-and-coming independent artists to word-renown festival directors is using to send and receive information about bands and artists from around the globe.

An EPK™ is like a virtual passport that you can use again and again to gain entry into hundreds of conferences, festivals, clubs, music competitions, colleges, or to even get your songs played on radio or reviewed by record companies or music producers. It contains everything your regular press kit contains and more: music samples, high-resolution photos, bio, press reviews, and even an up-to-date gig calendar (try that with a regular press kit). What's great about an EPK™ is that it takes literally 20 minutes to create one online and you can put it to use and start saving money almost immediately. For the cost of little more than sending out two regular press kits, you can sign up for an account, create an electronic press kit, and email it out to anyone, anywhere, at anytime. It not only communicates all the information that is found in your average press kit or web site, but it does so more quickly, more efficiently and far more effectively. Think how mind-blowing it is to be able to email someone everything they need to know about you or your band as soon as you get off the phone with them (or better yet, while you are even still talking with them).

Cost effective solution

Think of the implications of this innovation for the average up-and-coming artist. For the first time in history, there is no direct link between how many people you can reach and the cost of reaching them. For example, with a traditional press kit there is a vast cost difference between sending out 10, 100, or 1,000 of them. This means that even though today an independent artist has access to an unprecedented amount of information, the ability to

take full advantage of this has, until now, been limited (consider the cost involved in sending a regular press kit to every single possible contact in this guide.)

The Electronic Press Kit has changed all this. Every day there are artists that are sending out their EPK™ to say, 100, or 200 college promoters at practically zero cost. These artists are receiving offers from people that normally they would have had to spend way too much money to reach (and often paying way more in reaching them than the actual fee they receive). The cost and effort of emailing an EPK™ to all these promoters is a small fraction of the corresponding investment in regular press kits – not to mention the benefits of the fact that communication is practically immediate (versus waiting for a week or so to get a press kit in the mail).

Conclusion

Does all this mean that you can go ahead and recycle all your physical kits right after you finish reading this article? Well, my prediction is that "hard" copy press kits are going the way of the vinyl and the cassette tape but like any other new technology, adoption takes a while — and there are still the technology laggards. Traditional press kits and CDs still have their place (for now) but my advice is to save your money and send them to the increasingly fewer people that specifically ask for them after they review your electronic press kit. Then you at least know that these are high prospects that are worth spending an extra $20 in trying to communicate with them.

Panos Panay is the founder and CEO of Sonicbids, the online pioneer of the Electronic Press Kit (EPK™) platform. The service currently has over 70,000 registered artist members and 6,000 active promoter members who actively use EPK's to connect and communicate with each other on a daily basis.

◆

WRITING A BAND BIO

by Suzanne Glass, Indie-Music.com

Having a little trouble coming up with a decent band bio? Check out these suggestions:

1. Don't worry about writing a book. One page or even a few paragraphs is fine. In fact, most people don't want to read any more than that.

2. Do emphasize your strong points while minimizing areas where you lack. If you have played gigs with well known bands, be sure to list it. If you haven't played many gigs, don't bother mentioning the fact. Go on to your recording, or your other musical experience. Also, while it's OK to "hype" a little bit, never tell any out-and- out lies or make a boast you might not be able to come through on. It will come back to haunt you, and then you will lose all credibility in the reader's eyes. Not to mention these music people talk to each other...and HOW!

3. Do use your band's letterhead to write it on. (You DO have a logo and letterhead, right?) Be consistent in your entire promo package with the image, logo, etc.

4. Don't say your band's music is "not able to be classified". Aside from the fact that a million other bands say the same thing, the music industry contact reading your bio wants and NEEDS to know who you are comparable to. For instance, if someone recommends a movie to you, you probably need to know if it's a horror flick, a romance or whatever before you decide if you want to see it.

5. Do use humor or slight sarcasm if it fits your band's image. But avoid the temptation to go overboard. A bit of humor can make a low budget press kit seem better. Too much is a loser. Also, some types of bands fit into a niche that is more open to humor. Just make sure what you say will not offend anyone.

6. Don't, repeat, DO NOT say you are the coolest, best, or greatest band around, or anything even remotely close to it. Music Industry people want to decide for themselves if you are good or not. Avoid the flowery adjectives.

7. Do list the band's major musical influences. This goes along with trying to give the person an idea of what you sound like. It can work great to come up with a unique description of your music. For instance, Indiana guitarist Michael Kelsey describes his music as "Progressive, aggressive acoustic music".

8. Unless your band has former members of Aerosmith and Van Halen in it, it's probably not a good idea to do one of those story bios. "John was playing in Joe's band until the singer quit. Then John met Steve, who was playing with the Nobodys. They formed a band called The Losers. When the drummer quit, they changed their name to The New Losers", etc. This is irrelevant and, well, boring. Not to mention it shows your lack of ability to keep a band together. It is OK to use an interesting line or two about how the band got started, or how songs are written. It's also OK to add any interesting facts, like maybe your band donates all proceeds from their cassette sales to charity.

9. Of course you want to list all your major accomplishments. Any recordings, awards, education, or whatever.

10. A quick concise listing of each member is good. Sometimes you can do fun things with this like a listing of each members' favorite drink, or other non-relevant stuff. But make sure it works. Nobody really cares what your favorite anything is, so it has to be part of a humorous image. If any members have played in well known bands, it's good to mention it here, but don't make a big deal out of it.

11. You may use a different version of your bio depending on who will be receiving it. For instance, a record label and a club booking agent might need different info to decide if you interest them. A record label wants to know you have it all together: music, business, a fan base, songwriting, etc. A club agent is mostly concerned with whether you have a following that will bring paying business to his club.

12. Do make absolutely sure you have your address and phone number (and your e-mail and website URL, if applicable) listed prominently. This goes for all items in your press kit. Name, address, and number on EVERYTHING. (Demo tape included!)

13. Read other bands' bios. Compare and rewrite. Have other people read and comment on what you write. Make sure it is grammatically correct, with no typos. If you really feel yourself lacking in this area, consider hiring someone to write your bio for you. A good bio is part of the press kit that forms the first impression of your band. Don't mess it up.

Suzanne Glass is the founder of Indie-Music.com, an online magazine that reviews dozens of independent artists each month, includes music charts, audio & internet radio, and how-to-succeed articles for musicians, all at no cost. A paid members option gets your music in rotation with streaming audio, radio, multimedia advertising AND full access to our DIY music industry database with over 7000 venues. www.indie-music.com

♦

WHY MAILING LISTS ARE SO IMPORTANT
by Vivek J. Tiwary, CEO StarPolish.com
© 2007 All Rights Reserved. Used By Permission

The very first piece of business you should attend to is starting and maintaining a mailing list. Your mailing list will be your most direct and personal link to your fans and entertainment industry contacts— in many ways, the mailing list can be considered the "business lifeblood" of a developing artist.

Where to begin
Keep your mailing list on computer, using any good database program. I have found Microsoft Access to be very versatile and easy to use, but any good database software should suffice. Remember to back up your mailing list by keeping identical copies on both your hard drive and a removable disk. You will want to keep the following information about each member of your mailing list: name, snail-mail (i.e. regular postal) address, email

address, and perhaps telephone number. Other fields you may want to consider including are company affiliation and job title (if applicable) or school address (if applicable and if your act does/will appeal to a college fan base).

Start your mailing list by personally adding all the folks you think would support your act, and all your entertainment industry contacts you want to keep posted on any new developments. As a test, in addition to your industry contacts, your list should include everyone who would come to a show or would buy/download your music. In other words, if your grandmother who lives in another state would buy a CD, she very much belongs on the mailing list. You will find that apart from industry contacts, these early members are mostly friends and family— that's both normal and acceptable. Don't think that because they're close to you or your band they somehow "don't count." In your early days, where else do you expect to get your support? Remember this important piece of advice; every single name on the mailing list makes a difference.

Building your list
If you are a band, I suggest that one band member maintain the mailing list and that once a week, every band member must submit 10 new names to the mailing list until you exhaust your collective resources of appropriate friends, family, contacts, etc. Be aggressive about your mailing list. Whenever you bump into an old friend or acquaintance on the street and they ask you what's new, tell them about your act and ask them for their information to include on your mailing list. You'll find that as you grow busier with your musical career, your mailing list becomes a good way to keep in touch with people, especially those folks you don't see often.

You must also solicit new names for your mailing list after shows. Prepare one or more clipboards, each loaded with several signup sheets. Each signup sheet should have sections clearly marked for name, address, and email. Space permitting, it may be useful to include a section on "comments" to see what new fans thought of your act. Remember that people may be filling out these sheets in a dark bar or venue and will therefore need to write in big letters, so don't put too many signup boxes on each sheet, and make sure there is plenty of space for each entry— I recommend no more than four new signups per sheet. Make each signup sheet look professional and presentable— have them designed on computer, or if they're hand-made, be extremely neat. Adding artwork or some other creative presentation can never hurt, but remember that the most important thing with the signup sheets is that they are easy to use.

Creative ideas
Provide potential fans with thick, dark-colored pens, again keeping in mind that they may be writing in a dark bar or venue. If possible, go the extra step and bring a penlight with you to make it even easier for them to fill out the form.

At the risk of sounding like a sexist asshole, I'm going to offer the following piece of advice because no one else may tell it to you, and it can quite literally be the difference between 100 and 600 names on your mailing list in the early days of your career. I recommend that an attractive and friendly/personable woman walk around with each clipboard and solicit additions to your mailing list. It is actually a statistically proven fact that audience members— both male and female— are more likely to fill out a mailing list signup form when asked by a friendly/personable woman. I'm not exactly sure why that is, but it's definitely a truth I have observed through years of experience. Try it and see for yourself.

You or any band member can also assist with soliciting names for the mailing list, because potential fans may want to say hello and that can be a good opportunity to solicit signup. You may find it is more ideal to have a friend of the band deal with the mailing list, and have band members selling merchandise behind a table where they can still say hello to their friends while generating and controlling customer traffic.

Mailing list and beyond…
Your mailing list is your lifeline to your fans, supporters, and industry contacts. You should use it regularly to keep in touch with list members and let them know what you've been up to. Even if it has been a fairly inactive period for your act, let the list members know that you're still around but taking some time off from the public eye. One common mistake many developing artists make is using their mailing list only to

promote an upcoming show. Your mailing list should be an informational source, like a regular newsletter, informing list members not only about your shows, but new CD releases, new additions to your website, new career developments, funny stories from the road (if you're on tour), etc. On average, you should send a mailing to your list about once a month.

Sending snail-mail or regular postal mailings to a large mailing list can be very expensive— the cost of producing mass flyers and newsletters in addition to the costs of mass postage can add up to depleting your budget. Don't be surprised if in your early days, the money you make from your shows barely covers the cost of mailing announcements about those same shows to your list. Depending on the size of your mailing list, it may be cost-effective to sign up for U.S. Bulk Mail Service, which gives you a per-letter/postcard discount on very large mailings.

Remember that email is free. There is no reason why you can't send at least one email a month to your entire list in newsletter format. But keep these emails on the shorter side, noting the most pertinent details up front— most folks don't like to receive and wade through lengthy emails.

Your information lifeline

If you can afford it, also send monthly postal mailings to bolster your emails (the regular mail pieces can be more lengthy and informative than the emails). But if you can't afford it, focus on the emails and only use the regular post to announce very special events or developments, (An important upcoming show or CD release.) Remember that if you are promoting a concert, you need to mail your postal mailings 10-14 days in advance so they arrive well before the upcoming show date. While mailings/emails are important don't over due it.

Apart from being a lifeline to your fans and contacts, your mailing list is one of your most valuable calling card to the entertainment industry: People who work in the industry— from A & R talent scouts to club owners— are always impressed with large mailing lists. In the same way they are impressed with a large number of CDs sold, your mailing list is a quantifiable way of noting how popular you are. Once you've built a large mailing list, mention its existence and the total number of people on it in appropriate business cover letters.

Every name counts

Lastly never remove a name from your mailing list unless you are confident that each address attached to that name is outdated. While every name may count, if someone asks to be removed from the mailing list, be professional and remove him or her immediately. Never forget that a large mailing list is both an important tool and an impressive asset.

Vivek J. Tiwary is the founder and President/CEO of both StarPolish and The Tiwary Entertainment Group, a multi-faceted entertainment ventures focusing on artist management, marketing consultation, and project production. Contact www.starpolish.com

◆

THE "T" IN TOUR MERCHANDISE STANDS FOR T-SHIRT

by Gigi Swanson, M.G. Incentives Inc.
© 2007 All Rights Reserved. Used By Permission

When you think of tour merchandise you might envision major label artists playing large arenas and selling everything from tie-dye t-shirts, bumper stickers, embroidered baseball caps and in the case of the Rolling Stone's famed Voodoo Lounge tour—a custom motorcycle.

But even if you are an independent artist you can run your business like the big acts by utilizing an added revenue stream source—custom merchandise. As an artist/performer you are selling an experience and fans will buy a souvenir of that experience in the form of a CD, clothing, buttons, posters, etc. As music fans we have all come home with something more tangible than a ticket stub and it's usually something we can wear.

The custom wearables market has plenty to choose from, but let's focus on the long held wardrobe staple—the t-shirt. What better promotion is there than a walking billboard to advertise who you are and what you do. It's generally inexpensive to produce and if made with good-quality materials it can last a very long time. But better than that, there is a

healthy margin of profit in the sales of wearables, which can at least offset or even cover your travel expenses.

You can package CDs with a T –shirt for an "added value" sales incentive such as offering them "half off" with a CD purchase. You can use them as door prizes or as a thank you for the sound guy or the waitress at the clubs you play. The same applies for coffeehouse, church and house concert gigs. Even when you play for free you can earn money and build goodwill and name recognition.

Don't think selling T- shirts is for more visible and established acts. If you are playing out and selling CDs you can sell shirts. But before you jump in, here are a few pointers to make your promotional dollars work for you.

The most popular T- shirt is the basic crew neck. Not only is it low in cost, it's a style people are familiar with. As far as color options are concerned, the sky is the limit with the least expensive being the standard white, then the heathers/naturals, and then the darker colors. Besides the basic tee, you can branch out with different styles such as '70s retro ringer tees, baseball raglan tees and new styles made for women such as scoop necks, baby-doll tees, and the new layered looks.

I prefer 100% cotton heavyweight Tees in the 6.0 oz range for long term durability. Brands such as Gildan, Hanes, and Jerzees have been common favorites for years. Heavier fabric is knitted tighter which enables a better screen print, especially when using detail and four color process. Plus they are typically cut larger and hold up better with multiple washings. But you must think of the tastes of the end user and the image you are trying to promote. That's where fashion often comes in. Knowing your audience is key.

For example, one of my Rap group clients goes for the extra large size heavier weight tees, whereas a rock group client sells mostly light weight, smaller tight fitting "alternative" tees. They cost more but the look they achieve supports their brand image. Check out the on-line stores of different recording artists to get a sense of what fans are buying and to see what might work with your audience.

What makes your t-shirt sell isn't the style, its size or color but its logo design. Logo art needs to be readable and convey the image you want to promote, but keep in mind it should be something a person will want to wear.

When it comes to printing logos, you can opt for gel, sugar-glitter, suede, reflective, metallic, glow in the dark, and ink in one color and up to 12 colors.

Screen printing using one color ink in one position on the shirt is the most economical. You have to pay for an art screen with each color you use as well as for any extra handling of the shirt. That includes flipping it over to print on a different side. Some artwork may require added film screens to replicate more complicated designs. So keep it simple if you can. If you have to go with a certain "look" make sure you get a thorough quote before you proceed.

Your logo art needs to be in a graphic format generally saved as an eps file. Many imprinters charge an hourly rate to prepare art that isn't standard or isn't vector art for more complicated designs. Most printers carry standard Pantone Colors but also offer color-matching inks for an added charge.

How many T shirts should you buy? The real price breakpoints in the industry start at 144 units, but that amount isn't practical for everyone. You can find reasonable shirts at the 72-unit range or even less if you plan it right. Funds still short? I know of some bands that purchased co-op shirts with another band or with a sponsor such as a local nightclub. They basically sold space on the shirt to share or subsidize the cost and helped promote their partners at the same time.

If you can get your shirts for under $5 and sell them in the $10-15 range you will see a quick return on your investment. When I taught music business classes, I used to illustrate the power of selling tour merchandise to my students this way: A typical major label recording artist might make a little over $1 off the sale of a CD . He would have to sell five CDs or more to make the same margin off the sale of one basic T- shirt. That's why some of the major labels have affiliated merchandise companies as an added revenue stream for themselves.

Tour or gig merchandise can be incorporated in your overall marketing plan. It fits right in with preparing press kits, driving traffic to your website, getting people in the door and selling CDs. The right product will promote you long after the gig.

Keep an eye out for future articles on more promotional products. Trucker hats anyone?

Gigi Swanson started an entertainment division three years ago when she left her teaching and administrative duties as director of the music business program at McNally Smith College of Music located in the Twin Cities. She commutes between the company's Minneapolis and St. Petersburg offices and recently opened a satellite office in Nashville. M.G. Incentives, Inc., a company that specializes in promotional products. The company has worked with advertising firms and corporations for over 15 years.

♦

HOW TO MAKE THE MOST OUT OF A MUSIC CONFERENCE

by Valerie DeLaCruz, Musician/Songwriter
© 2007 All Rights Reserved. Used By Permission.

OK, so you've decided to take a positive step toward your goal as a songwriter or artist; you want to check out that music conference you keep getting brochures or email blasts about. It's time to take the plunge, whether you are a seasoned veteran and have attended them before, or a "newbie" hoping nobody at the conference notices!

How you get the most out of the experience

1. Review the promotional materials to determine what the main focus of the conference is; i.e.: songwriting, legal issues, performance, and make sure that this is an area you are interested in.

2. Define your goals. Are you going to strengthen some qualities you already have? Gain more knowledge about something technical or legal? To network with others at you're level and hopefully move up a notch in your field of expertise? Write them down and refer to them as you determine your schedule. Often, panels or workshops are taking place at the same time and you have to choose between them. If you go with a friend, you can split up and compare notes and resources later.

3. Figure out the overall cost including travel, accommodations, conference fees, etc. Start saving up and realize this is an investment in your profession. You may be able to interest a friend to go and share the expenses of a room.

4. There is almost always the opportunity to showcase at these events, and usually, if you are selected to showcase, you can attend the conference at a reduced fee or for FREE. This is certainly worth doing as you will get to show the industry professionals and potential collaborators what you can do. Be realistic about the costs involved in bringing your band to the conference. You may elect to do a solo or duo acoustic set to cut costs if that presents your material well. If not, again it may be a worthwhile investment to perform a showcase, always more fun than a bar gig and in a concert setting where people actually listen. We'll touch on the showcase preparation further on.

5. Send in the application. Many times there is a reduced "early bird" registration fee and this is great if you can take advantage of it. If you are also applying for a showcase slot, tailor your presentation materials to the theme of the conference to better your chances of being selected. Remember that professional presentations, or something that stands out, will cut through the many, many packages that the organizers will be receiving.

6. Reserve your room and travel arrangements. Often the conference will have blocks of rooms reserved for the conference at a reduced rate. It is always better to spend a little more and stay right at the hotel where the conference is taking place. A great deal of the networking and connections that take place are during casual times between seminars, and you don't want to waste time in a taxi getting back and forth. You may need to run back up to your room to get another package or CD to give out. They usually have special airfare rates, too. I use www.expedia.com for the best rates and schedules.

7. Now that you are set to go, you need to prepare the materials you will need. Make a checklist and give yourself a few weeks to gather them. Once I left printing out lyric sheets and bios 'til the last minute, and of course, the cartridge on my printer started to act up on a Sunday evening when there were no stores open! I also email things like the bio file and one-sheets to myself so that in a pinch, I can download them at Kinko's or forward them to someone I meet. They are up there in my virtual file cabinet wherever I go.

What's in a package?

Bring 5-10 full packages that include: Bios, photos, a one-sheet of several of your reviews and critics' quotations, photocopies of great press if you had a photo in print or if it is from a major publication like Billboard. Use the magazine's actual heading on your press sheet to get attention and gain credibility. Also don't forget your business card and CONTACT INFORMATION (the most important thing, seemingly obvious, right?)

The packages should be set up so that your name (or band name) and photo are on the front. If you have a CD, using the CD cover on the front of your folder looks very professional too. You want them to quickly identify you when they are digging through a huge pile of packages. Inside, have something visually compelling like a color copy or photo on one side and your bio immediately available on the other. Insert a CD or demo into one of the pockets. I hate to say this, but it's time to bite the bullet if you are still using cassettes and get a CD burner so you can make CD demos tailored to the audience you are trying to reach.

Note: Have extras of all of the above materials in case you need to throw together more packages or don't want the expense of handing out an entire package when selected materials will do.

Promotional tools

Have flyers of your performance time and venue if you are showcasing to hand out and leave all over the place. Have a stack of business cards. It is worth it to spend a little extra on these, as they are truly your calling card, and will remind someone of whom you are. I always like to have a photo on it, and color stands out. An unusual layout is important, and if you are a band, have a graphic designer (not your cousin's girlfriend) design a logo that will identify you. The most important thing here is to make it legible! A card that you need a magnifying glass to read already makes your contact frustrated.

Plaster your website on all of your materials. Everything you hand out should have all your contact information. This seems obvious, but how many CDs have ended up in the trash can because no one could find the envelope or cover it came in? A website is the most important business tool you can have. Busy industry people are inundated with wanna-be and would-be artists. They love to check out your site in the privacy of their own office/home and get the important info at their own leisure. Remember a slow-loading site is one that will not be viewed as they go on to the next one.

Check in

Take advantage of early check-in, arrive the night before so you are rested and don't have to fight a crowd. I always plan to stay one more day if possible, so that I can really enjoy the last day and night, which is when you are really feeling connected to the other participants and start making plans to get together for follow ups or collaborations. Get the materials upon registration and go back to your room and plot out your schedule. Leave time for regrouping; non-stop seminars can be exhausting.

Network

Networking is the name of the game. You will meet so many people that you won't remember them all when you leave, and the same for them remembering you. The single most important thing you can do is exchange and collects business cards. Write a note to yourself about what you talked about, and whether or not you told the person you would like to follow up. Don't just start handing out packages to the panelists after their presentation. Instead collect their card and ask if you can send it along in a week or two. This again separates out your stuff from the crowd. But use your judgment; seize the moment. If you have the opportunity to hand deliver a package to the producer you never thought you'd be lucky enough to meet, take it! Practice remembering names; it will go a long way to be able to address someone you met by their name. Everyone wants to feel valued.

Other important tips

1. Find out where everyone is hanging out after the sessions. Definitely go to the "mixers" to talk to people in a more casual atmosphere. Sometimes there are informal "jams" or guitar-pulls late into the night where you hear some of the most compelling music. I ended up booking someone to share a bill with me after being astonished at her beautiful song during one of these sessions.

2. In the question-and-answer session that normally follows a presentation, be conscious of not wasting the time of the panelists or other attendees with your personal request. (I heard recently and saw many eyes roll when a participant used his chance at the microphone to go into microscopic detail about the steps he had taken to get his demo played on radio). Ask yourself if the question you have would benefit everyone, or if it would be better to talk to the speaker later privately.

3. Take advantage of signing up for one-on-one critique sessions. These are invaluable and educational, not to mention making a personal connection with someone in the industry that may be able to help you. Even if there is an extra charge for this, sign up for at least one. Here is where you can pick the brains of the experts. And if you ask for a critique, take it graciously; don't challenge the reviewer's advice or become defensive. This is how we learn and progress. You may not agree entirely with them (it is, after all, one person's opinion), but there is probably a grain of truth in there.

4. If you showcase, prepare a great and tight set list that shows what you have that is different than everyone else. Better a fantastic five-song set than two hours in a bar where no one pays attention. Have only one ballad, and close with another fantastic up-tempo song.

5. If they can't get a flavor of your style, in five songs, then you have not focused on a genre, and you will have a lot of problems anyway. It's good to start with a strong, driving, up tempo song. Try for a smooth transition. Don't stand around onstage while you and the band are trying to decide the next song; this looks unprofessional. Be flexible though if you think a different song would maintain your momentum; just be well rehearsed and prepared for this possibility if you do it.

6. Have your cards and demo CDs at the stage readily available for people to take. You never know when Miles Copeland will be in the audience!

When you get home, the real work begins, unless you were signed to a recording contract right on the spot! Follow up with thank you notes to all your contacts. Start by organizing the business cards you collected and assign action steps to them. Put the packages together and send them within a week or ten days while it is still fresh. To stay organized, keep a log of your contacts, and what you did to follow up. Then call in about two weeks to follow up on the packages you sent out. Lastly schedule those co-writing or demo sessions, and order the publications and/or resources that you discovered.

Valerie is one of the 60 original Just Plain Folks members and her passionate career pursuit and professionalism has been a model for other grassroots artists. Through hard work and persistence (and talent!) she's continued to prosper in the industry. This article originally appeared in the Just Plain Notes! Newsletter July 3, 2002 Contact: www.valeriedelacruz.com.

♦

BUILDING A MUSIC SITE THAT SELLS: PROMOTE YOUR CD, NOT YOURSELF

by Mihkel Raud, author of "How to Build a Music Website that Sells"
© 2007 All Rights Reserved. Used By Permission.

Marketing your CD on the Internet isn't really that different from marketing any other product on the Net – be it some fancy million dollar mansion in the Hollywood Hills, a how-to-get-divorced-in-less-than-ten-days consulting service, a super-cheap DVD player, or a subscription to some kind of porno website...whatever....it's the same game. To play any game, you have to know the rules.

Break all the rules

When it comes to music, I encourage people to get as crazy as they can. Break all the rules you've ever heard of. Try new! Don't think just of radio! Forget about what anyone else may or may not think of your music! Be yourself! Do what you want to do! And do it now! You have to dare to do!

Still, marketing your music – be it on the Internet or offline – is a totally different ballgame. You need to use some rational sense if you want to see results.

I know that it's pretty uncomfortable to think of your CD as a piece of merchandise. After all, music is supposed to be art, right? It is. Tell the opposite and I'd be the first to protest. Your CD is just as much of a product as a bottle of beer. Your CD is a product that everybody should "need."

This concept of "need" is exactly what sooooo many musicians fail to understand. Almost every band or singer/songwriter website that I have seen concentrates on the artist.

Basic elements to a site

- Biography
- Photo gallery
- News
- Gigs
- Sound samples

Think outside the box

There are many possibilities of what to include on your site. Some bands post lyrics, or have discussion boards and chat rooms. The most commonly used concept in the music business is still to build the website around the artist.

So what's wrong with that approach? Nothing really, except that it's so common. And the artist approach will not sell your CDs. You ask... how is that true? Let's look at an example. Let's say you're planning to buy a Mesa Boogie amp. You want to get yourself the best full stack in the world. Visit Mesa (www.mesaboogie.com) and take a close look at what's on that site. Are you being bombarded by raves about just how great a guy Randall Smith is? He's the mastermind behind Mesa amplifiers. Do you see any Smith family snapshots on the front page? Or "better" yet, is there a guest book form asking you to leave Randall an "I love you" message? Nope. None of that "person" stuff is on the Mesa Boogie amp website. Why? Because it's the product you're after, not touchy feely with its inventor. Why on earth should your website be any different?

If you really want to succeed, you need to stand out. In order to beat that competition, you will have to use The Billion Dollar Baby Website Concept, as I have ironically titled the concept (if you know the Alice Cooper song, you know what I mean!) In other words, create a website that is solely focused on your product – the CD.

Your CD as the spotlight

That's right. The only hero of your movie should be your cool-sounding-Grammy-winning-absolutely-fabulous CD. Every other detail of your website has to serve the same master - your CD. Nothing is more important than that music that you want to sell. If you use The Billion Dollar Baby Website Concept, you can turn the whole internet music game upside down. And you will win. It's as simple as that! OK, this may hurt your ego a little bit. I understand perfectly. After all, you wrote the songs. You spent hours singing them in perfect tune. Heck, you may even have produced the CD all by yourself and that's no easy task. But now I'm asking you to spotlight the CD instead of yourself?

Remember this important point. I'm NOT telling you to shut down your existing artist website. On the contrary, it's smart to have one. In fact, you can have a bunch of them…. the more, the merrier. You can have your loyal fans create them for you. However, on your Billion Dollar Baby Concept Website you are going to play a supporting role. Your CD will be the main player.

A separate website?

It is absolutely essential to have a separate website for your CD only. And when the time comes, for your next CD…. plan a separate website for it too. Every time you put out a new CD, you will build a new website designed just for it. My concept demands a lot of time and dedication, and is directly from my own experience. It's loads of work, and is expensive, but is another way to be a success.

I found a medieval music band from Estonia and produced a record of Black Sabbath songs in the 14th Century style of music. "War Pigs" sung in Latin. "The Wizard" played on Gothic harp and a fiddle (www.sabbatum.com.) I sold well over 1000 copies in the first few months. I sold 1000 copies entirely on the Internet with no marketing funds whatsoever. I did it all from my small apartment in Tallinn, Estonia. Now, if I could do it, so will you.

Mihkel Raud is the author of "How To Build A Music Website That Sells". To order your copy, please go to: www.musicpromotiontips.com

technical

STREAMING YOUR MP3 FILES
by Luke Sales, GlassWing Media
© 2007 All Rights Reserved. Used By Permission.

So you want to stream your MP3s? No problem! What follows is a brief tutorial about streaming your MP3s online. There are two major parts to play in streaming MP3 files: serving up the files correctly and configuring your computer to receive them. If you are running your own website, you only need to worry about serving the files, but you should know how to receive them too. How else will you be able to test that the streaming works?

Serving up the MP3s

1. There are several different ways to serve up streaming MP3s. First, you must encode your MP3s at a low bit rate, so that listeners will be able to hear the music without having to stop and download. A good compression setting for most listeners is 32kbps Mono. The audio quality at this setting is fairly low, since we are trying to accommodate listeners with slow Internet connections. You may wish to make two different versions of your music - one at 32kbps mono (for modem users) and another at 128kbps for broadband.

2. Name the MP3 files appropriately (ending with '. MP3') and uploads the files to your web server. Figure out what the address of the files is. For example, http://yourserver.com/mymusic.MP3, where 'yourserver.com' is the name of your server and 'mymusic.MP3' is the name of the MP3 file.

3. Now create a plain text ".m3u" playlist file containing the address of the MP3 file you wish to stream. This file should be a plain text document that contains only one line. (Use a program like Notepad to create this file). Using the example above, the file would only say http://yourserver.com/mymusic.MP3

4. Save text file as 'mymusic.m3u', where 'mymusic' is the name of the song. Upload this file to your server. Now just create a link to this file from somewhere on your web site. This sample HTML link would

display 'click here to stream' and would link directly to the .m3u file above:

<a href = "/mymusic.m3u">click here to stream</a>

If the listener's computer is configured correctly, all they need to do is click on this link and their MP3 player should pop up and begin to stream. How does a person set themselves up to hear streaming MP3s?

Receiving and listening to an MP3 stream

If your computer is not set up for MP3 streaming, it will not know what to do with the .m3u playlist file. To solve this problem, install a streaming-capable MP3 player. Here are some good ones: Windows: Winamp, Kjofol, Sonique, Windows Media Player, or Real Player. Mac: Soundjam, Macamp, or Audion.

Online resources:

www.webmonkey.com contains many great tutorials about all aspects of web development (including streaming).

Internet radio? Check out www.shoutcast.com, a free technology that makes it easy to run an MP3 radio station. If you just want something easy, go to live365.com - you have to pay, but they do all the work.

Create an .m3u play list that contains the address of the MP3 you want to stream. Create a link to this file. That's it - Have fun streaming!

Luke Sales is a trumpet player/programmer/web dude who works for GlassWing Media in Portland. GlassWing will assist no matter how small your projects, assisting with CD-ROMs, DVDs, web sites, and guitar tuning. Contact: www.glasswing.com.

◆

CD DUPLICATION TIPS
by Hadas, Eric Mueller, Oliver Gos, Recordpressing.com
© 2007 All Rights Reserved. Used By Permission

There are many different variables involved in creating an effective package to market yourself and your music. The artistic element of your release, the cover art and promotional materials, are important as they introduce a new dimension to your aesthetic identity. Flipping through endless racks of CDs and records, it is the artwork that can instantly spark an interest for an otherwise unknown release. The hidden element involved in providing your release this opportunity is a well-developed understanding of the options offered by the printing and media manufacturing industry. The manufacturing process can be extremely frustrating, confusing, and financially straining for musicians and record labels (novices and veterans alike), but with sufficient research and eventually a well-established relationship with the right company, you can make virtually any vision come to life and fit within your budget.

The CD format

It is first essential to determine the medium(s) that will best deliver your message to its intended audience. If you choose to release your music in CD format, the following will assist in the process:

1. Where to go. Find an independent operation that offers high quality work at reasonable prices and turnaround times, and most importantly cares about its customers.

2. Glass mastering. Confirm that you are getting glass mastered replicated CDs rather than duplicated CD's, to insure the integrity of your product all the way through your entire pressing.

3. Quality. Choose a company that offers the best print quality for the booklets, tray card, and CD face. (The use of offset printing results in the most professional print quality, and usually involves a turnkey filmless process that yields much higher line screen than silk-screening and thus better detail on the print work. This is particularly true on the CD face.)

4. Extra charges. Please make sure to ask about film charges, as some

manufacturers won't mention them until after you have committed to the project. In some cases, films can cost as much as $300, so WATCH OUT. Film charges are normal for the CD face, but avoid going with a company that charges for any films beyond that. There are a host of other options available to make your CD release unique.

5. Enhanced CDs. Ask if the manufacturer can make your CD an enhanced CD; Adding a video or links to your photos or website only strengthens your release in the eyes of fans or industry people, and a good manufacturer will gladly do this at little or no extra cost.

6. How to stand out. Other options to make your CD stand out include making it a dye cut shaped, clear, or even scratch-n-sniff CD. Something utilizing some interesting artwork that takes advantage of the various printed cardboard cases, jackets, and sleeves offered throughout the industry as more hip packaging options for CD's and DVD's. Regardless, find a company who can give you some options to work with, so there is no chance of stifling your potential, or that of your graphic artists'.

What about vinyl?

Many people opt to release their music on vinyl records as well, as this is still a very popular choice for DJ's and collectors of various musical genres. Should you choose to release your music on vinyl, there are some extremely important things to look and listen for.

The finer points are

Find a company that can provide you with the highest level of versatility and quality in terms of sound quality and packaging options. There are only a few companies that still press quality vinyl records, and even fewer who also provide in-house printing and packaging. Manufacturing the packaging and vinyl record at the same facility saves shipping charges and hassle.

Look for a company that uses more modern equipment, like DMM (direct to metal mastering) equipment. DMM processing essentially cuts out one whole generation of the replicating process, reducing the overall cost of making vinyl, while at the same time yielding a wider potential sound range, and significantly reducing the ambient noise, pops, crackles, and hisses that are too often present on cheap vinyl.

Make sure to get 100% virgin vinyl, not partially recycled compound, as next to mastering this is the most important factor in getting audiophile quality records.

Ensure that your records are manufactured heavy enough so that you do not receive warped records when they arrive at your door. A good weight for a 12" record pressing is 140g or above, and for a 7" record pressing 40g and above. A few companies will even record pressing much heavier than this.

Asking the right questions and really comparing apples to apples can be difficult when researching vinyl manufacturing, but it is vital in order to get the most for your money. Vinyl is a great promotional tool, and when designed and manufactured well, can capture the attention of DJ's, collectors, and labels as well, if not better than any other medium.

Make financial sense

It is understood that releasing music independently is financially draining, and many people cut corners left and right because of this. Depending on the stage you're at, a few cut corners might be okay, but there is also a general understanding that professional looking and sounding packages will certainly have a marked advantage at piquing the interest of A&R folks, writers, publishers, booking agents, DJs and club owners. There are ways to cut costs in the manufacturing of your art and music; sacrificing the integrity and quality of your product is not one of these ways. Do the best you can within whatever budget you find yourself working with, and make sure you DO YOUR RESEARCH. Get what you want and pay a reasonable price for it, and if at all possible, keep it independent.

In summary

Definitely find yourself a reputable independent company that can fulfill ALL of your manufacturing needs. Choose a company that is not too small to handle all your needs, and not too big so that you'll find yourself lost in the corporate red tape shuffle. Do your homework as far as pricing goes,

and remember cheaper is not necessarily better, and going with a company that promises whistles and bells such as online distribution posters will also increase your bill significantly. Build and maintain a mutually beneficially relationship with a capable company whom you enjoy working with. In the long run it will benefit you much more than the dollar you'd save here and there constantly shopping and bouncing around solely for the cheapest price.

Hadas, Eric Mueller, and Oliver Goss, respectively Marketing Director, General Manager, and President of Recordpressing.com contributed this article. Recordpressing.com is an independent source for high quality CD, DVD, vinyl record, and promotional material manufacturing. If you have questions or comments regarding this article, contact Recordpressing.com at help@recordpressing.com.

◆

PODCAST PRIMER: A MUSICIAN'S QUICK REFERENCE GUIDE

by Andre Calilhanna, Disc Makers
© 2007 All Rights Reserved. Used By Permission

What's a podcast?

Most simply, a podcast is the digital delivery of an audio or video file. In many ways, podcasts are to the internet what "on-demand" cable is to television. With podcasting, music and video content is available by subscription download. Once downloaded, it can be viewed or heard at the user's command.

A computer program, dubbed a "podcatcher," is required to listen to or view a podcast. Contrary to what the name suggests, podcasts don't have to be heard or viewed on an iPod. The iPod is the most popular digital audio player in the world, but various other players can be used, either portable or on a computer.

The technology that makes podcasts possible is cutting-edge, but the model is fairly basic. A podcaster will assemble a show – many resemble a radio show – and post it online with an RSS (Really Simple Syndication) file that enables it to be distributed via podcast. Users use software like iTunes to subscribe and download the content. Once downloaded, the files are ready to be listened to on the user's digital audio/video player of choice.

A majority of the content available as podcasts is free, and podcasting software makes it easy to keep up with the latest contribution from your favorite podcasters. In fact, the software is constantly seeking updates and new programs once you subscribe to a podcast.

Here's an example: Let's say you go online to the iTunes directory and subscribe to a free audio podcast from IndieFeed. You can then download any or all of the individual songs they've archived for podcasting. And since you're now a subscriber, iTunes will constantly (invisibly to you) check for new episodes from IndieFeed. When new songs are posted, they are automatically available for you to download.

This model is fairly consistent across the spectrum of material offered as podcasts, which is as varied as the internet itself. Business coaching, music videos, animated shorts, sermons, sporting events… it's all out there waiting to be podcasted. So is a ton of independent music.

Podcasting independent music

iTunes alone has over 150 different independent music podcasts available, and there are other directories out there that list hundreds more. If you're a user looking for indie music, the problem becomes, "How do I find the good stuff?" As an indie musician, the problem is, "How do I get my music heard?"

There are a number of independent music podcasts that solicit music from artists, including IndieFeed and Insomnia Radio. Browse through the directories included at the end of this article and you'll find dozens more. Most screen and hand-pick the songs for inclusion, so there's no guarantee your music will be podcasted. In many ways, these podcasts are analogous to college radio ten years ago: they are indie friendly, but getting in takes some luck and requires someone on the listening end appreciating your art.

Typically, all you need to submit for podcasting is an MP3 of your music, though many podcasters also ask for information about your act, like a short bio and URL to list in the event that they play your music.

Getting your music played on one of these podcasts is a viral means of reaching a fan base you wouldn't have reached before. As the medium gains momentum, more and more users are using podcasters as their gatekeepers. Landing a track on a popular podcast is almost like landing a song on a TV show or a soundtrack. It's all about getting more ears to hear your music.

Creating your own podcast

Another possibility is to create your own podcast. It can be just about anything you want it to, but for the sake of example, let's say you want to combine a music track with a voice-over. You can talk about the meaning or the inspiration for the song, go on a political rant, tell stories from the road – whatever you think might make your podcast more enjoyable and relevant.

It's fairly easy to do. You'll need:

- A computer
- An MP3 file to podcast
- Music editing/recording software
- Text-editing software
- An RSS text file
- Somewhere online to post your files

Let's assume you already have an original song saved as an MP3 file on your computer. You'll then want to add a voice-over track to complete the "show." With free audio software like Audacity, you can quickly record and edit voice-over elements right on your computer. If you have any kind of home studio, you can easily create a more elaborate recording.

Once compiled and edited, save the new file as an MP3 (if you're using Audacity, you'll need the LAME MP3 Encoder). To make your file ready to podcast, there is specific ID and naming protocol you need to follow. Yahoo! Has an easy tutorial at http://podcasts.yahoo.com/publish/1, and there's another great step-by-step explanation at www.podcastingnews.com/articles/How-to-Podcast.html. Then you need to FTP your file to your own web site, or use a hosting service like Yahoo! Geocities.

What sets podcasting apart from the simple hosting of MP3 files is that subscribers automatically get updates as soon as you post new shows. To make that possible, you have to create an RSS feed for your podcast. The RSS feed alerts subscribers' podcatchers to your updates and allows them to be downloaded immediately.

This article originally appeared in Disc Makers' Fast Forward monthly e-newsletter. Visit www.discmakers.com/music/ffwd to get a free subscription.

l e g a l

HOW TO COPYRIGHT YOUR MUSIC
by Nancy Falkow, Ask Nancy

Sometimes musicians think every song written needs to be immediately copywritten, but this isn't always true! Copyrighting, registers your music so that if a situation arises that someone is stealing your music, your registration of copyright is on file, which protects you. So, if you're singing these songs in your living room for your family, you don't need to run to Washington, DC!

What can be copy written?

Literary works; musical works, including any accompanying words, dramatic works, including any accompanying music, pantomimes and choreographic works, pictorial, graphic, and sculptural works, motion pictures and other audiovisual works, sound recordings and architectural works.

Library of Congress

If you plan on distributing your music through the web you should copyright your songs. Go to the *US Copyright Registration site* and download the forms you need. Each situation is different, read all of the information, and figure out which best applies to you. Put your music and lyrics on tape or CD, fill out the appropriate forms and write the check. It takes up to 6 weeks to receive all the paperwork and registrations.

Internet: www.loc.gov/copyright
Phone: 202/707-3000 (this is NOT a toll-free number)
Write: U.S. Copyright Office, Library of Congress, 101 Independence Avenue, S.E, Washington DC 20559-6000

The forms

What you need is a properly completed application form, a nonrefundable filing fee ($30) for each application and a non returnable deposit of the work being registered (A tape, CD, and/or lyric). You can copyright more than one song on one tape or CD by sending it in as an anthology. In short, you put your songs on one format, give it a name like "Greatest Hits" and send it in. This is the best way to save money. Instead of copyrighting each song for $30, you're copyrighting an entire batch for $30. Remember it's always important to protect yourself and your songs. Good luck!

Nancy Falkow is known throughout the Philadelphia area for writing catchy and melodic pop-folk songs with dynamics and soul. She still finds time to play bass and sing background vocals in an all girl rock band called The Dirty Triplets. Contact: www.nancyfalkow.com

◆

HOW TO TRADEMARK YOUR BAND NAME
by Derek Sivers, CEO CD Baby

Anytime you are promoting, you are also promoting your name - so make sure it's yours!

I'm giving you some unofficial advice here from my own experience. There are attorneys and specialists that can help you much more. I recommend a book called "*Trademark Legal Care for Your Business & Product Name*" by Stephen Elias (Nolo Press). It covers everything, and even includes the forms you'll need to register. For basic trademark advice, go to my web page of reprints from Nolo Press: (www.hitme.net/useful/c.html)

Research to make sure no one else has your name

Check the PhonoLog at your nearest record store. If you can, check *Billboard's Talent Directory*. (It IS expensive to buy however). If you've got $$, hire a search firm (attorneys) - this is the most reliable, but it will set you back $300-$500. I also heard CompuServe has a trademark research center.

The library is free

Call the nearest largest Public Library and ask if they have a "*Federal Trademark Register CD-Rom*". (Each state has between 1-3 libraries that will have one). You can go in, and they'll even show you how to do a search. Search for your full band name, then each word individually. *Example*: my band "Hit Me": search "Hit Me" then search "HIT" then search "ME". The reason is there may be a band called "Kick Me" or "Hit Us" that could be a conflict. If you can think of other similar words to search, try those, too. You can also get a printout of all this. If there's nothing even remotely similar, you're doing OK. If someone, even a clothing company, is using your name, then you should consult an attorney.

Trademark & Servicemark

1. Make sure you search the Federal Register, then the Pending Register. These are for the names that have been applied for, but not completed yet. Call Washington, DC: (703)308-HELP and ask for the book "Basic Facts about Registering a Trademark".

2. Trademark covers a product, while a Servicemark covers a service. As a musical act, we are a service. If ALL you do is make CDs and tapes, but never play live, maybe your name only applies to a product. For most of us, it's a service first, then a product second. It's all the same form, just a technicality. Note: You can still use the ® [little (R) in a circle] when you are registered.

3. You can start using "TM" or "SM" after your name now. It means you have *intent* to register, or are claiming legal ownership of that name. You can use the ® *after* and only after the whole registration is complete.

How much does it cost?

Each registration class costs $245. When I called the office help line, they said if you register your Servicemark, that's plenty of protection for now. That is until you start selling loads of t-shirts, hats, action figures! Make sure you get the new forms, since the older forms have $200. A Servicemark for a musical act, you will want to file a "CLASS 41". The description of product/services is: "Entertainment Services in the nature of Musical Performance." Don't forget to do this NOW, or all the work you're doing to promote your act will be wasted.

Derek Sivers is the President of the extremely popular online music store, CD Baby. In the first week of 2006 alone, CD Baby artists were paid $429,023!! As of the end of 2005, CD Baby paid over $23 million directly to their musicians for over 2.1 million CDs sold. To get your music online, visit www.CDBaby.com

♦

TRADEMARKING YOUR LOGO

by Vivek J. Tiwary and Gary L. Kaplan, StarPolish.com
© 2007 All Rights Reserved. Used By Permission

A good logo is an invaluable tool in the imaging and marketing of a developing artist. That is why it's important to design a logo immediately after you have settled on your name. But unlike your name, it's more acceptable to change your logo over the years without losing or confusing fans. *311* and *The Rolling Stones* are great examples of bands that have either changed or modified their logos to adapt with changing times or the themes of certain albums or tours.

Not every artist has a logo, but a logo can only help. Remember that your name simply and consistently printed in a certain standard font can be a fine logo (e.g. Cheap Trick). I personally like logos that are minimal, easy to remember, tied into the artist's name, and easily reproduced. Like your name, your logo should somehow also be in line with the vibe of your act.

How do you get one?

A band member or friend designing your logo may assure a genuine and intimate connection between the logo and the band. If no one you know is talented in the visual arts, you can seek help from local design companies. Be careful though, as some of these companies can be expensive. Alternately, you can solicit help from local design schools, whose students may be willing to design a logo for free in order to gain working experience and build up their own design portfolios. Try putting flyers/posters up in the schools or posts on school bulletin boards announcing that you are a local band/songwriter looking for a logo designer.

Be seen

Once you have a logo that you are satisfied with, put it on everything— all over your website, your merchandise, your CD, your letterhead, etc. Make stickers and always keep a small stack of your logo stickers on hand. Stick them on everything and everywhere. Consistency and repetition are critical marketing keys. The more times people see the same logo, the more they will remember it and your act.

Register your logo

Register with the *U.S. Patent and Trademark Office* (or comparable body

if you are based in another country). Much like with your name, you acquire rights to your logo when it is publicly used in commerce. This means that when you sell your merchandise, or play a show where your logo is displayed, you automatically obtain some common law rights in that logo. Registering your logo as a trademark, however, will provide you with important additional rights:

Do a search

Assuming that you are the first to use this logo, registering your logo will help secure your right to use it, and prevent others from using the same or a similar logo. Because of the extremely subjective nature of the trademark analysis for logos, it might not be worthwhile to perform a search. It is not with certainty you will discover the same or similar logo being used by another band. If you choose to perform a search, you can try *Thomson & Thomson*, or the folks at (*www.tradename.com*) A lawyer can take care of the whole thing, since the analysis is so touchy, that only an experienced trademark attorney will be able to offer sound advice.

The good news is it's not quite as disastrous, if you are forced to change your logo. It might not be what you'd ideally like to do, but it pales comparison to having to change your name. If you can afford to hire an attorney to assist you, go ahead and trademark your logo. If your problem is that you're strapped for cash, try to register your trademark yourself by using the website of the U.S. Patent and Trademark Office (www.uspto.gov.)

Vivek J. Tiwary is the founder and President/CEO of both StarPolish and The Tiwary Entertainment Group, a multi-faceted entertainment venture focusing on artist management, marketing consultation, and project production. Vivek has 10 years experience in the arts and entertainment industries, Prior to joining StarPolish.com, Gary L. Kaplan spent three years at Skadden, Arps, Slate, Meagher & Flom, one of the world's preeminent law firms. Gary was a member of Skadden's Intellectual Property Department, focusing on patent litigation. Contact: www.starpolish.com

♦

ENTERTAINMENT INDUSTRY LAWYERS: WHO, WHERE AND HOW MUCH?!

by Wallace Collins, Entertainment Lawyer
© 2007 All Rights Reserved. Used By Permission.

As a creative artist in the entertainment industry you do not need to know everything about the business in order to succeed, but you should hire people who do. When I was a teenage recording artist back in the late 70's, I can remember being intimidated by the "suits". Now that I am on the other side of the desk, I have a broader perspective. I am here to tell you that those "suits" can help you; provided, however, that like any other aspect of your life, you use your instincts in making your selection.

The team

The best place for you to start building your "team" of representatives is with a competent lawyer who specializes in entertainment law, which is a combination of contract, intellectual property (copyright, trademark and patent) and licensing law. Eventually, your team could possibly include a personal manager, a booking agent and a business manager/accountant. Your lawyer can assist you in assembling your team. He may then function as the linchpin in coordinating the activities of your team and insuring that these people are acting in your best interests.

The lawyer

A good lawyer will navigate you safely through the minefield that is the entertainment industry. Record contracts, publishing agreements and licensing arrangements can be extremely complicated. Proper negotiating and drafting requires superior legal skills as well as knowledge of entertainment business and intellectual property practice. Your lawyer can explain the concepts of copyrights, trademark and patents to you and assist you in securing proper protection for your work. In addition to structuring and documenting a deal to maximize the benefits to you, some lawyers also actively solicit deals for their clients.

What to look for

When looking for a lawyer take the time to interview a few before retaining one. Some lawyers are with large firms, but many are solo practitioners. Lawyers have various personalities and legal skills and you should seek out a situation where the "vibe" is right. It is not necessary that your lawyer like or even understand your creation. It is more important that you feel he or she is a trustworthy and competent advisor.

When do I pay?

Keep in mind that a lawyer with other big name clients is not necessarily the best lawyer for you; if it comes down to taking your calls or those of a superstar, which do you think will get preference? A lawyer, much like a doctor, is selling services, so if you go to him for advice you should expect to pay. With the odds of success in this business being what they are, very few lawyers will agree to work for you and wait for payment until you are successful and can pay your bills. You may also find someone who will work on a contingency basis.

The cost

1. A lawyer specializing in the entertainment field usually charges an hourly fee or a percentage of the money value of your deal. Hourly rates generally run from $200 and up. Percentages are based on the "reasonable value of services rendered" and generally run around 5% of the deal. A few lawyers may charge a set fee, such as $1,000 or $1,500, to review and negotiate certain documents. Check around to see if the fee arrangement proposed is competitive.

2. Most lawyers will require a payment of money in advance or "retainer", which can range anywhere from $1,000 to $10,000. Even those who take a percentage of the deal as a fee may require that you pay a retainer. In addition to the hourly fee or percentage, you are usually required to reimburse your lawyer for his out-of-pocket costs, including long distance telephone calls, photocopies, postage, fax, etc.

3. You should realize that in retaining a lawyer you are making a contract even if your agreement is not written. In return for a fee, the lawyer promises to render legal services on your behalf. However, some lawyers may want a fee arrangement in writing (specifically in connection with a percentage deal) and/or a payment direction letter. A cautious lawyer will advise you that you have the right to seek the advice of another lawyer as to the propriety of a percentage fee arrangement.

As a general rule

You need a lawyer if you are asked to sign anything other than an autograph. Too many aspiring creative artists want to get a deal so badly they will sign almost anything that promises them a chance to do it. Even successful careers have a relatively short life span, especially in the music, movie and television business. Therefore, it is important for you to get maximum returns in the good years and not sign away rights to valuable income.

Never sign anything without having your own lawyer review it first! Do not rely on anyone else (or even their lawyer) to tell you what your contract says. Do not let anyone rush you or pressure you into signing any agreement. There is really no such thing as a standard "form" contract. Any such contract was drafted by that party's attorney to protect that party's interests; your lawyer can help negotiate more favorable terms for you.

Wallace Collins is an entertainment lawyer with the New York law firm of Serling Rooks & Ferrara, LLP. He was a recording artist for Epic Records before attending Fordham Law School. Contact: (212) 245-7300, www.wallacecollins.com

♦

ROYALTIES IN THE MUSIC BUSINESS

by Joyce Sydnee Dollinger, Entertainment Lawyer

What is a royalty? In the real world, the word royalty is synonymous with the power or rank of a king and queen. In the music world, the word royalty is synonymous with *money*. Royalties are the most important entitlements of the musician. These entitlements warrant them to receive money from their craft - the craft of MAKING MUSIC.

Royalties

There are many types of royalties. The list is constantly growing because of the new technology, but here are some to name a few: Artist Royalties, Mechanical (Publishing) Royalties, US Performance Royalties Synchronization Royalties, Grand Rights Royalties, Foreign Royalties for record sells and performances, Lyric Reprint Royalties.

General definition

Artist Royalties, in a nutshell, are monies paid to the recording artist from the record company. They are the share of the proceeds from the sale of the artist's records paid directly to the artist after the artist records material for the record company. This, in turn, gives the record company permission to exploit the musical work in the marketplace.

Recording contracts

In artist recording contracts, artist royalties are usually negotiated in points. When record label business affairs attorneys use that terminology, they are referring to the percentage points the record company will pay an artist on each album sold. For example, if an artist gets 10 points, it usually means that the artist receives 10% of the retail cost of each record sold.

1. **Superstar Deals**

   Royalties usually are:
   - 16%-20% of retail of top-line records plus escalations
   - 18-20% is quite high and the artist must sell a lot of records - usually more than 5 million
   - 100% CD rate and can receive new configuration royalties
   - 12-14% of singles + escalations receive increased royalties when contract options are exercised

2. **Mid-Level Deals**

   Royalties usually are:
   - 14%-16% of retail top-line records plus escalations (escalations usually based on genre)
   - 16% is high and the artist must sell a lot of records
   - 85-90% CD rate and new configurations
   - 12-13% of singles or 3/4 of LP rate receives increased royalties when contract options are exercised

3. **New Artist Deals**

   Royalties usually are:
   - 11%-13% of retail top-line records
   - 75-85% CD rate and new configurations
   - 10-11% of singles

When to renegotiate

If the artist sells a ton of records, the artist can usually re-negotiate with the record label and try to receive increased royalty rates.
- Increase net royalty rates on remaining LPs in the contract increase rate for each successive LP include escalations for attaining sales plateaus
- Receive the increase royalty rate on future sales of past LPs improve the royalty computations increase foreign rates, the CD rate, the new technology rate, licensing fees and free goods
- Reduce the recoupment percentages

Record royalty formula

The record royalty formula is usually based upon a percentage of records that are sold. In using the formula, the record company looks to the retail price of the commercial top-line records and standard deductions that every record company takes from the gross income from the sales of those records. Some of the deductions are: recording costs of the records, packaging, returns and reserves, discounted military sales, video costs, tour support, promotional records and free goods. Please note: records on which royalties are paid are quite different from deductions from gross royalties.

Joyce Sydnee Dollinger is an attorney admitted in New York and Florida. She is also the Vice President of 2 Generations SPA Music Management, Inc., and involved with 2generations.com and SPA Records, Inc. Contact: www.sparecords.com.

◆

ARTIST-MANAGEMENT CONTRACTS

by Richard P. Dieguez, Entertainment Lawyer
© 2007 All Rights Reserved. Used By Permission.

Next to a record label deal, the artist management contract is the most exciting agreement an artist will sign. As with any legal document, a contract shouldn't be signed without the advice of a music attorney. Let your lawyer take the blame for "asking too much" or for being such a "tough negotiator" that is what they are being paid to do. Here are the fine points to negotiate:

*   How long will the agreement be in effect?
*   How much will the manager get paid during the agreement?
*   How much will the manager get paid after the agreement has ended?

The art of negotiation

1. It is likely you and your manager are each likely to have a legitimate difference of opinion as to the amount of time for which the contract will be binding. Whatever the reason, you don't want to get locked in with a loser for the next seven years. On the flipside nothing can be more frustrating for a manager than to have her budding artists go to another manager, where they then make it to the big time.

2. Depending on the particular circumstances of the parties, the negotiation will center on a contract term ranging from as short as six months to as long as several years. What length of time is fair really depends on what you and your manager are each bringing to the relationship you wish to form. For example, let's say that neither of you has too much experience in the music business. In this situation, you're both probably better off with a short-term contract, (6-12months) so that you can check each other out without getting locked in. You can always enter into another agreement if it turns out, at the end of the contract, that you have a future together.

The time and money equation

What happens if you can't agree to a fixed amount of time? Well, to satisfy both parties, the attorneys can always try to hammer out a compromise: a short-term contract with the potential of being converted into a long-term contract. For example, the parties could agree to a one-year contract. Part of the agreement, however, would be that the manager must meet certain conditions during this one-year period — such as getting you a record deal, a publishing deal or even guaranteeing that you earn a minimum amount of income. If the manager fails to meet the conditions, then the contract ends when the year is up. If, however, the manager is successful in meeting the conditions, then he has the right to automatically extend the contract for an additional period of time, say for another year.

Commission

The custom is for the manager to work on a commission. In other words, the manager gets compensated for his efforts by taking a percentage of whatever income you earn as an artist. Obviously, your attorney is going to try to negotiate for as small a percentage as possible. You'll argue that the manager simply manages, and without your talent, there is nothing to sell to the labels or to the publishers. The manager's attorney is going to negotiate for as high a commission as possible. Their position will be that there is a lot of talent out there — especially in the major music centers like California and New York.

Money talks

So what's the range of the amount of the commission? It can generally be anywhere from 10% to 25% of your gross income. The amount that is settled on may very well depend on the circumstances. Again, the art of compromise may bring new life to a negotiation that is at a deadlock on the issue of the commission amount. Regardless of the particulars, the concept here is that the lower percentage rate should be satisfactory to you, while the manager is also given an incentive to make a bigger percentage if he can get you to earn in excess of a certain amount of gross income. And, of course, getting you over that amount, whether it's $25,000.00 or whatever, will be to your benefit as well.

The manager

Your manager will likely try to apply their commission to every conceivable entertainment-related activity from which you could possibly earn an income. Examples of such money-making activities would be live performances, record sales and the sale of promotional merchandise such as t-shirts, posters, buttons, programs and pictures. If you feel that the commission rate the manager is asking for is too high, you can try to compromise by proposing that you'll accept the commission rate, but only if certain activities are excluded from the commission.

After the contract ends

Another touchy subject is whether the commission on gross income earned by the artist continues after the contract has ended. Your response will probably be "of course not!" After all, once the contract is over, neither party has any further obligation to the other. Once the contract is over, there should be a clean break, but it is not always so clear-cut

You may be fortunate enough to have signed some money-making deals. As agreed, the manager gets his percentage and you keep the rest. But it may be that your money-making contracts will still be in effect for quite some time after your management contract has ended. Since you will continue to profit from a deal he helped you obtain, the manager may feel that he should also continue to profit even after the artist-manager relationship legally ends.

When you get a new manager

If you enter into a contract with a new manager, that new manager will probably be no different from your former manager on the question of compensation. The new manager's attorney will probably demand that the commission apply to every conceivable entertainment- related activity from which you could possibly earn an income. And this would include the money pouring in from deals your former manager obtained! You wouldn't want to be stuck paying two commissions on the same money.

Conclusion

There are many aspects of the artist management contract that will be subject to negotiation. An issue may be made of as to who collects the income: the manager, you or maybe a third party like a business manager or accountant. Another traditional sticky point is the extent of the manager's authority to sign contracts on your behalf. There may even be some negotiating points that to you and the manager don't seem crucial, but to the attorneys seem to mean everything. The personal circumstances surrounding any given artist management contract can be so unique, that the art of compromise expands the parameters of the so-called "standard" contract.

An NYU Law graduate, Richard P. Dieguez has over 16 years experience in entertainment law. He has represented hundreds of clients across the U.S. and several nations in music, film, television, publishing etc., Mr. Dieguez is also the founder of The Circle, a monthly music industry seminar held in New York City. Contact: www.RPDieguez.com

THE WRITTEN AGREEMENT AMONGST BAND MEMBERS

by John Tormey III, Entertainment Lawyer

AABM

I have seen references to the above-mentioned document as both "Inter-Band Agreement", and "Intra-Band Agreement". Rather than initiate any argument with grammarians as to which term is correct -let's simply call this all-important document the "Agreement Amongst Band Members"; or, "AABM", for short. If one is a musician playing in a multi-member band, is an AABM needed? *Absolutely*, yes!

The agreement

There are some parallels to an agreement amongst band members, and a pre-nuptial agreement between prospective spouses. But I actually find the case for having an *AABM* more compelling than a pre-nup. A marriage should be a function of love. A band formation, on the other hand, is often a commercial exercise.

Written agreements should be required for any collaborative commercial endeavor between 2 or more people. Maybe it seems easier NOT to make it official, but no band member should skip the *AABM,* if the band member takes his or her band or career seriously. It may not be realistic to operate on blind trust, in place of a good written agreement.

If the band formation is not viewed as a commercial exercise, then I suppose the band members can simply agree on a handshake, and then gig for free in the subways. However, the majority of bands that I hear from, are concerned about their financial, as well as their artistic, futures. Many are trying to find a way to become economically self- sufficient on music alone, while preparing to quit their "day jobs". It is best to have an agreement in hand, rather than, to put it off.

When to begin?

No one wants to be required to negotiate and close the AABM once the band is already successful, or once the band has already been furnished with a proposed recording agreement. The optimal time to close the *AABM* is while the band is just being formed or while it is still struggling. A good *AABM* should also be flexible enough to contemplate future changes, such as changes in personnel and, Artistic direction. It is also likely one of the members may have more of a hand in the writing of the words or the music of the band's original songs, all the more reason for creating the *AABM* as early as possible.

Band members

In the average 4-person band, each member may play a different instrument. Some may have been in the band longer than others, or more experienced in the business of music. Maybe one of you has "connections" to clubs and labels, or more free time to invest in the running of the band's business. Each member can perform a different function in business.

Why a contract?

The real value of a contract - any contract, including the *AABM* - is as a dispute-resolution and dispute-avoidance tool. By dealing with things ahead of time, it may be best to discuss things now; and put the results on paper. Resolve things before having to pay litigators thousands upon thousands of dollars to do it in the courts later.

What happens if…

All of those "what if" questions, may not be the focus at the beginning. Band members may not want to think about, what *may* happen if the bass player departs to raise kids in Maui, or the singer-songwriter front man decides to join the Air Force. If all the other band members all value their investment of time, sweat and money in the band, then they should know and have fully thought through - in advance - the answers to these types of questions. Who owns and administrates the copyrights in the songs? Who is responsible for storing the masters? Who has final say in the hiring and firing of a manager? If the band breaks up, which member or members, if

any, may keep using the band's name? And these are just *some* of the questions that should come up.

When to get a lawyer

Every band's situation is different, and the lists of questions to consider will be as different as there are different band personalities and different band members. The band may be better off, if a lawyer prepares the AABM. In a perfect world, all band members would be separately represented by a different attorney, but that is not realistic.

Should all these considerations prevent a band from creating a good AABM? Absolutely not, the band should at least try to resolve amongst its own members, the answers to all of the "what if" questions that will likely come up in the life cycle of any band. The band can try to resolve these questions on paper. Thereafter when affordable, one of the band members may decide to consult with an attorney to review and revise the band's starting-point document - (typically, this turns out in practice to be the band member with the most at stake in the outcome).

Be aware that one attorney may well not be able, or be allowed to represent all band members simultaneously. This is due to concerns about possible conflicts of interest, (especially if different band members have different percentage investments at stake in the band's commercial endeavors.)

It is best to draft some kind of written agreement between band members, since doing so now can save a lot of heartache and expense down the road in the future.

John Tormey III is a New York lawyer who handles general commercial, transactional, and corporate matters. John is also admitted to practice law in California, and in Washington, D.C. John's focus is in the area of entertainment, arts, and media, including endeavors to market artistic material to professional entertainment industry recipients. Please contact: www.tormey.org

♦

HOW TO LEGALLY SELL DOWNLOADS OF COVER SONGS

by Derek Sivers, CD Baby

Please note that the below is not official legal advice. It is ONLY for the U.S.A. We are not your lawyers, and you should always contact your attorney before entering into any contract such as a license.

If you have recorded a cover version of someone else's song, and you plan to make that recording available over the Internet, the following information applies to you. You must follow these steps BEFORE you make your recording available for distribution to the public!

If you record a cover version of a song, (meaning your performance of a song that has been released in the U.S. with consent of the copyright owner), you are entitled by law to release your recording commercially, and the owner of the copyright to the song cannot prevent you from doing so.

The Copyright Act provides for what is called a "Compulsory License" for downloads and CD sales, which means that if you follow the steps set forth by statute, you can distribute your recording of that song on a CD or over the internet. This Compulsory License is only available for sales in the United States. Other uses of masters, such as streaming, conditional downloads, and the like, are not subject to a Compulsory License. A separate license from the publisher is needed in those cases.

The following details the procedure for individuals to obtain a compulsory license to digitally distribute cover songs over the Internet to end users in the United States.

Identify the Copyright Owner - the publisher

The first step is to identify the owner(s) of the copyright to the song. The publisher. The easiest way to do this is to search the songwriter/publisher databases, here:

BMI (bmi.com)
ASCAP (ascap.com)
SESAC (sesac.com)

Harry Fox (songfile.com)
U.S. Copyright Office (copyright.gov)

Keep in mind that the owner of these rights is typically a publisher, and that the owner of the rights in the song is not the same as the owner of the rights to any particular recording of the song. In other words, Record Labels are almost never the owners of the copyright to the musical composition - they typically own only sound recordings. You should be looking for the name of a publisher (or in some cases an individual).

Be careful to identify the exact song you want, as there are many songs with the same names. If you cannot find the owner through these websites, search the records of the Copyright Office online.

If you cannot find the copyright holder(s) after a thorough search, you can send the letter to the Copyright Office, along with a small filing fee, currently $12.00. See the Copyright Office website for the proper address and current filing fees if you are going to be sending the letter of intent to them.

Instructions on how to do that are on "Circular 73" from the U.S. Copyright Office, on a PDF file, here: copyright.gov/circs/circ73.pdf

WE STRONGLY RECOMMEND DOWNLOADING AND READING THIS FILE, because it carries the essence of this entire article.

Send a Letter of Intent - EXACTLY like this

You must send one letter for each song for which you seek a compulsory license 30 days before you begin distribution of your downloads. The letter must be sent by registered or certified mail and contain the following:

1. A clear subject line/title that says "Notice of Intention to Obtain a Compulsory License for Making and Distributing Phonorecords"

2. Your full legal name

3. All fictitious/assumed names (stage name, band name) used

4. The names of each individual owning a 25% interest or more in the distribution of the song (band members, if you split your sales income)

5. Your fiscal year (usually January 1st - December 31st)

6. Your full physical address - P.O. boxes are unacceptable, unless that is the only option for addresses in your geographic region

7. The title of the song

8. Name(s) of the author(s) of that song

9. The type of configuration expecting to be made (a music file distributed over the Internet is called a "Digital Phonorecord Delivery" (DPD))

10. The expected first date of distribution

11. The name of the performer/band doing the cover

12. Your signature.

If there is more than one publisher listed, sending a letter to one of them is sufficient for the compulsory mechanical license; however, if one or more of the copyright holders is not from the United States, it is best to send the notice to all copyright holders.

Send royalty statements and pay royalties

Once you begin distributing the song over the Internet, you must send monthly statements of royalties on or before the 20th of each month, and pay the royalties.

The monthly statement must be sent by registered or certified mail and include:

1. A clear title that says "Monthly Statement of Account Under Compulsory License for Making and Distributing Phonorecords"

2. The period (month and year) covered by the statement

3. Your full legal name

4. All fictitious/assumed names (stage name, band name) used

5. The names of each individual owning a 25% interest or more in the distribution of the song (band members, if you split your sales income)

6. Your full physical address - P.O. boxes are unacceptable, unless that is the only option for addresses in your geographic region

7. The title of the song

8. Name(s) of the author(s) of that song

9. the name of the performer/band doing the cover

10. The playing time (length) of your recording of the song (minutes:seconds)

11. The number of DPDs made, i.e. how many times your recording was downloaded

12. The number of DPDs that were never delivered due to a failed transmission

13. The number of DPDs that were retransmitted in order to complete/replace an incomplete/failed delivery

14. The total royalty payable (number of total DPDs, not counting ones never delivered multiplied by the statutory royalty rate (see below))

15. The following statement: "I certify that I have examined this Monthly Statement of Account and that all statements of fact contained herein are true, complete, and correct to the best of my knowledge, information, and belief, and are made in good faith"

16. Your signature

You must also send an Annual Statement of Account at the end of each calendar year, which is virtually identical in content to the Monthly Statements, but must be certified by a licensed Certified Public Accountant (CPA).

Statutory royalty rates

The current (2006) statutory rate for royalties is 9.1¢ for every copy sold if the playing time for the song is under five minutes. If the playing time for the song is longer than five minutes, the rate is 1.75¢ per minute, rounding up to the next minute.

under 5 minutes = 9.1¢ per copy

5 to 5:59 minutes = 10.5¢ per copy (6 minutes x 1.75¢)

6 to 6:59 minutes = 12.25¢ per copy (7 minutes x 1.75¢)

7 to 7:59 minutes = 14¢ per copy (8 minutes x 1.75¢) etc.

The Copyright Office can always keeps the most up to date information concerning statutory royalty rates at this link: www.copyright.gov/carp/m200a.html

IMPORTANT notes

The publisher may tell you to that they don't deal with compulsories, and that you should contact the Harry Fox Agency. Though the Harry Fox Agency can handle mechanical licenses for DPDs for most publishers, you still have right to obtain a compulsory license by following the directions, above.

Remember the law is on your side. You are entitled to a compulsory license by law. You have permission - (a compulsory license) - as soon as you send the notice, described above, to the proper publisher. As long as your notice complies with Copyright Section 115, (described above), the publisher need do nothing other than receive the royalty payments. You don't even need to wait for their reply.

Other notes

You may be able to negotiate a better deal for yourself, either with lower royalty rates or less frequent statements of account. If terms are negotiated which deviate from the standard Section 115 then a mechanical license will be issued by the publisher or HFA.

If you wish to distribute physical copies (e.g., CDs) of a cover song, you must obtain a similar compulsory license, available for most popular songs through the Harry Fox Agency at harryfox.com. If you plan on distributing between 500 and 2500 physical copies, you can obtain a compulsory license through the Harry Fox Agency online at songfile.com.

For more information on compulsory licenses for all forms of distribution, please refer to the Copyright Office's web site, at copyright.gov, and contact your attorney.

Helpful publications available through the Copyright Office include Circular 73 (Compulsory License for Making and Distributing Phonographs), Circular 75 (The Licensing Division of the Copyright Office), and M-200 (Checklists under Section 115 of Title 17).

If you have been distributing a cover song without a compulsory license or an agreement with the copyright owner, you are ineligible to obtain a compulsory license for that recording (!), and you may be subject to civil and/or criminal penalties for copyright infringement.

Be careful to follow the steps exactly as described above, in order to be legal.

Download and print/save these files

How to Investigate the Copyright Status of a Work
www.copyright.gov/circs/circ22.pdf

Compulsory License For Making and Distributing Phonorecords
www.copyright.gov/circs/circ73.pdf

Notice of intention to obtain a compulsory license
www.loc.gov/cgi-bin/formprocessor/copyright/cfr.pl?&urlmiddle=1.0.2.6.1.0.175.17&part=201&section=18&prev=17&next=19

Royalties and statements of account under compulsory license
www.loc.gov/cgi-bin/formprocessor/copyright/cfr.pl?&urlmiddle=1.0.2.6.1.0.175.18&part=201&section=19&prev=18&next=20

Checklists of Required Information
www.copyright.gov/carp/m-200.pdf

These and more available at the U.S. Copyright Office website:
www.copyright.gov

Derek Sivers is the President of the extremely popular online music store, CD Baby. In the first week of 2006 alone, CD Baby artists were paid $429,023!! As of the end of 2005, CD Baby paid over $23 million directly to their musicians for over 2.1 million CDs sold. To get your music online, visit www.CDBaby.com

marketing and promotion

CREATING AN INDIE BUZZ

by Daylle Deanna Schwartz, author of "I Don't Need a Record Deal! Your Survival Guide for the Indie Music Revolution"
© 2007 All Rights Reserved. Used By Permission

People won't buy your music or come to shows if they don't know about it. By working the media, you can create a foundation for your career. Artists ask, "Why would someone write about an unknown artist or play their music?" Lose that mentality if you want to create a buzz around you and your music! If you've got THE GOODS, the potential is there. Once you believe your music is worthy of media exposure, you can work to inform others.

Build your story one press clip and one radio show at a time. Take baby steps up the ladder from teeny publications and local radio stations to larger ones. As your story builds, so will opportunities to increase it even more! According to Dalis Allen, producer of the Kerrville Folk Festival, "Having your record reviewed in [local magazines] may not propel your career to the degree that you want it to end up. But every one of those things adds up. If I see a review of someone's record in Performing Songwriter and then hear their name somewhere else and then see their package, I've seen their name over and over again. It doesn't matter if it's

not the most important thing that you're going to do. It's one more step in what you're going to do."

Let people know about you and your music through the media. It may feel useless if your hard work doesn't pay off immediately. Don't lose hope! Every CD that goes out is another chance for progress. Indie artist Jennie DeVoe says, "I give CDs to radio and anyone else who should have it. It's like planting seeds." Plant your own seeds once you have something to pass out. It takes time, but if your music moves people, your career can sprout by means of reviews, radio play and other exposure that builds your foundation.

If you plant enough, you have a better chance for a lovely blooming garden. Indie artist Canjoe John says, "The business of music requires public awareness and major marketing in order to sell. Major labels have major money to market with. Independents must get publicity in order to survive. I send well-written press releases out on a regular basis. I look for every opportunity to get in the news, TV, radio, newspapers, magazines. If I'm in a new town, I call newsrooms to try and get a story. I've been very successful at this and consider getting major free press as much an art as performing major stages." Exposure builds your story!

Start by creating what's known as a one-sheet. It should be a summary of your story on one sheet of paper. Include whatever ammo you have – a short bio, a track listing, tour dates and past venues, radio play, short press quotes and any other notable info. Design the info on your one-sheet in an organized way. Send your one-sheet with a CD to publications for reviews, radio for airplay, venues, potential agents, managers, distributors and almost anyone else you want to get interested in you and your music. Call first to see if they want a full press kit or just a one-sheet with a link to your website.

Check out daily and weekly papers, alternative publications, trade magazines and even papers from schools. Be creative about where you can fit it into publications. If you have a good story or technique relating to your guitar playing, pitch a guitar magazine. If you've made savvy business moves, pitch a business magazine or the biz section of a local paper. Do research at stores with big magazine sections. Find an angle about you or your music and look for music and general publications that might write about it.

Create a good electronic press kit on your website that people can go to for more info and a selection of photos (least 300dpi in quality) that they can download without having to deal with you. Include a private page with full songs and send media people the URL so they can hear your music. Organize a street team of fans who can help you create your buzz. They can make follow-up calls to press and radio stations in their regions. Fanpower combined with your own hard work can create a buzz that will get you to bigger publications and radio stations, which leads to better venues. This can lead to the day you quit your day job because you've created a full time income from your music!

This is a sample from Daylle Deanna Schwartz's newest book, I Don't Need a Record Deal! Your Survival Guide for the Indie Music Revolution (Billboard Books). Daylle is the best-selling author of Start & Run Your Own Record Label and The Real Deal: How to Get Signed to a Record Label. She also presents music industry seminars, does phone consulting for musicians and record labels, and publishes Daylle's News & Resources, a free industry newsletter. She recently launched her new website www.IDontNeedaRecordDeal.com . daylle@daylle.com www.daylle.com

◆

HOW TO BE YOUR OWN PUBLICIST

by Ariel Hyatt, Ariel Publicity
© 2007 All Rights Reserved. Used By Permission

For this article, I interviewed several entertainment writers from across the country. Their comments and advice are included throughout. Writers who will come up throughout are: Mike Roberts (*The Denver Westword*), Jae Kim (*The Chicago Sun Times*), Silke Tudor (*The SF Weekly*).

MYTH: A Big Fat Press Kit Will Impress a Writer.

TRUTH: Writers will only become exasperated by a press kit that is not succinct and to the point. A bio, a photo and 6-8 articles double-sided on white paper is a good sized kit. If a writer wants to read more than that he will contact you for further information. If you don't have any articles, don't worry, this will soon change.

The first step in your journey is to create a press kit, which consists of four parts — the Bio, the Photo, the Articles and the CD.

Jae Kim: "The ultimate press kit is a very basic press kit which includes: a CD, a photo with band members' names labeled on it — not a fuzzy, arty photo — a clear black and white, a bio, and press clips — 10 at most, one or two at least. 40 are way too much."

PART 1: The bio
Write a one-page band bio that is succinct and interesting to read. I strongly advise avoiding vague clichés such as: melodic, brilliant harmonies, masterful guitar playing, tight rhythm section, etc. These are terms that can be used to describe any type of music. Try to make your description stand out. Create an introduction that sums up your sound, style and attitude in a few brief sentences. This way if a writer is pressed for time, she can simply take a sentence or two from your bio and place it directly in the newspaper. If you try to make a writer dig deeply for the gist, that writer will most likely put your press kit aside and look to one of the other 30 press kits that arrived that week.

TIP: Try to create a bio with the assumption that a vast majority of music writers may never get around to listening to your CD (500 new releases come out in the United States each week). Also, writers are usually under tight deadlines to produce copy — so many CD's fall by the wayside.

Q. Whose press materials stand out in your memory?

A. *Jae Kim:* "Action shots of bands. Blur has had a few great photos, and Mariah's are always very pretty. Also, Mary Cutrufello on Mercury has a great photo — enigmatic with a mysterious quality. Her picture was honest and intelligent, just like her music."

A. *Silke Tudor:* "The Slow Poisoners — a local SF band who are very devoted to their presentation. They have a distinct style and everything leads in to something else. Photos are dangerous. If the band looks young and they're mugging you have a pretty safe idea of what they're going to sound like."

PART 2: The photo
It is very tough to create a great band photo. In the thousands that I have encountered only a few have had creativity and depth. I know it can seem cheesy to arrange a photo shoot but if you take this part seriously you will deeply benefit from it in the long run.

Create a photo that is clear, light, and attention grabbing. Five musicians sitting on a couch is not interesting. If you have a friend who knows how to use PhotoShop, I highly recommend you enroll him or her to help you do some funky editing. Mike Roberts tends to gravitate towards: "Any photos that are not four guys standing against a wall. Also, a jazz musician doesn't always have to be holding a horn."

MYTH: Photos Cost a Fortune to Process in 8 x10 Format.

TRUTH: Photos do not have to be expensive. There a few places to have photos printed for a great price. My personal favorite is ABC Pictures in Springfield, MO. They will print 500 photos (with layout and all shipping) for $80. Click the link to check out their web site or telephone 888.526.5336. Another great resource is a company called 1-800-POSTCARD, (www.1800postcards.com) which will print 5000 full-color, double-sided postcards for $250. Extra postcards not used in press kits can be sent to people on your mailing list, or you can sell them or give them away at gigs

PART 3: The articles
Getting that first article written about you can be quite a challenge. Two great places to start are your local town papers (barring you don't live in Manhattan or Los Angeles), and any local fanzine, available at your favorite indie record store. Use this book as a resource for CD reviews. Find music that is similar to your band's type of music and then send your CD's to those reviewers. As your touring and effort swell, so will the amount of articles written about your band.

PART 4: The CD
The CD artwork, like the press kit, must be well thought out. You should customize your press kits so that they look in sync with your CD. This way when a writer opens up a package the press kit and the CD look like they go together. Put your phone number and contact info in the CD so if it gets separated from the press kit, the writer knows how to contact you. I asked Eric Rosen, the VP of Radical Records, how he oversees the development of product. He had a few things to say about stickering CD's (placing an extra sticker on the cover to spark the interest of a writer).

"If you are going to sticker your product, be unique in the way you present it — try to be clever about it — plain white stickers are boring." He went on to say that "Recommended Tracks" stickers are great for the press (suggesting no more than two or three selections). Eric does not think that stickers are too advantageous in CD stores, because then "You are just covering up your artwork."

TIP: Don't waste precious CD's! Keep in mind that 500 new CD's come out every week in the United States. Unless you are sure a writer actually writes CD reviews (many are not given the space to run them) don't waste your hard-earned dollars sending that writer a CD. Again, ask the promoter which writers like to receive CD's for review and which ones don't need them.

Q. What do writers like?

A. *Silke Tudor:* "When people personalize things and use casual words. If an envelope is hand-addressed, I will notice it right away and I always open things that people put together themselves. Hand-written stuff gets read first . . .The bands that do PR for themselves are the ones that stand out for me"

A. *Mike Roberts:* "Include the name, show date, time, ticket price, place, and who you are playing with. If I don't see the contact number I have 69 other kits to get to."

Q. What do writers hate?

A. *Jae Kim:* "I hate those padded envelopes that get gray flaky stuff all over you — I feel like its asbestos." She also dislikes "When I get a package with glitter or confetti in it — it gets all over my desk." "I [also] don't like Q & A sheets" — She prefers to come up with questions herself rather than receive answers pre-fabricated for her and spoon-fed.

A. *Silke Tudor* similarly reports: "I never open anything over my computer."

A. *Mike Roberts:* "I don't have much interest in gimmicks like hard candy. If I tried to eat it, it might kill me. Also you can't expect a writer to shove something in the paper at the last minute. Please give as much lead time as possible."

Q. What do writers throw in the garbage immediately?

A. *Mike Roberts:* "Anything past deadline."

A. *Jae Kim:* "Pictures of women's butts or profanity that is degrading to women."

A. *Silke Tudor:* "If I already know the band and I know that I don't like it."

Getting your press materials out there
Once you have a press kit together try to start planning PR for any tour 6-8 weeks before you hit the road. As soon as a gig is booked, ask the promoter for the club's press list (most clubs have one.) Promoters are dependent on this local press to help sell tickets. Have the list faxed or e-mailed to you. Don't be shy — you are working with the promoter to make the show happen and promoters love it when the show is well

publicized. Also be sure to ask the promoter who his or her favorite writers are and which ones will like your style of music. When you do call those writers, don't be afraid to say which promoter recommended them and invite them to the show.

If the local promoter has a publicist, let that publicist do his or her job. Pack everything up and mail it to the promoters. Make sure you ask the promoters how many posters they would like and send them along with the press kits. After a few days it's best to call and verify that the material was received. If you can't afford to send kits to everyone, ask the promoters in each area which three or four writers would most likely cover a band that plays your style of music. Also, ask the promoters where the clubs run strip ads (these ads will be in the papers that cover music and inform people in the area about club happenings.)

Publications

If you are servicing press yourself, and the club does not have a press list, pick up The Musician's Atlas, or The Musician's Guide To Touring. Both of these guides are packed with a wealth of information on publicity outlets across the country, as well as venues, record stores, labels, etc. I recommend sending materials 4-6 weeks prior to the gig. Beware of monthly publications — if you are not at least six weeks out, don't bother sending to them.

Call the writers

Most of the time you will be leaving messages on voice mail. Be polite, get right to the point, and be brief!! 9 times out of 10 writers will not call you back.

Persevere

If you are a totally new band and you are worried because a paper did not cover you the first time around, keep sending that paper information every time you play in the area. I have never met a writer that ignores several press kits from the same band sent over and over again. It may take a few passes through in each market, but the more a writer sees over time, the more likely he will be to write about you.

Don't let all that all that voice mail discourage you

I have placed hundreds of articles, mentions, and photos without ever speaking to the writer.

Writers are more responsive to e-mail

It's free for them and does not take too long to respond to. If you are sending e-mail follow-ups, put a link to your site, or the club's site if you don't have one. You can also send a sound clip if you have the capability. IMPORTANT NOTE: Don't bother sending out materials a few days before the gig. Writers are usually way past their deadlines by then and they won't be able to place your band.

Posters

Posters are a great form of PR and they don't have to cost you a fortune. The most cost-effective way to make posters is to buy 11x17 colored paper from your local paper store (approx. $7 per ream of 500) and run off copies at the copy shop (approx. 7 cents each). Make several white copies and include these with your colored posters — this way the promoter can make extras, if needed. For higher quality posters, I recommend a copy process called docutech. These cost a penny or so more apiece, but they are computer-generated and look better than regular copies. Have whoever designed your poster also design small lay-ups to send out as fliers and ad-mats. Make sure your logo is included on them so the promoter can use them for strip or display advertising.

Have patience

The first few times you play a market, you may not get any press. PR is a slow moving vehicle that can take time to get results. I have worked with some bands that have needed to go through a market 3-4 times before any results started showing up in the press. When sending materials on repeated occasions, include a refresher blurb to remind the writer of your style. Always include the following information: date, show time, ages, ticket price, club name and address, time, and who is on the bill. Don't make

writers hunt around for the event info. Make their job as easy as possible by providing as much information. Also keep in mind that some writers will probably not write about you over and over again. If you hit the same markets continually, a great tactic is to change your photo every few months and write "New Band Photo" on the outside of the envelope.

Field staff

Try to enroll a fan to be on your field staff in each market you visit. In exchange for a few tickets to your show, have this person put up posters, hand out fliers, and talk to the college newspaper about writing a feature or the local radio station about spinning your CD. To get a field staff started, include a sign up column on your mailing list and on your web site. If they sign up, they are the people for you! With a bit of planning and focus, you can spin your own publicity wheel. All it takes is foresight and organization. A band that plans well is a band that receives the most PR.

Your website

If you don't already have one — get on it!! Websites can be easy and inexpensive to design — you can buy software that can take you through it step by step. Better yet, have a friend or a fan help you design a site. Your site should include your upcoming tour dates, as most people will visit it to find out when you are coming through town. Another great place to post all of your dates is tourdates.com it's free, and you can also put your bio and photo up as well. More advanced sites include merch as well as CD sales. This is a great idea if you are at the point where you're selling a lot of merchandise. If you're for your own site, at least be sure to link your site to a place where fans can order your CD.

Ariel Hyatt is the President of Ariel Publicity, Artist Relations, and Cyber Promotions, in NYC. For the past five years she has worked closely publicizing a diverse family of touring and developing indie bands including Sally Taylor, Leftover Salmon, K-Floor, and The Stone Coyotes. Contact: www.arielpublicity.com

♦

SELLING YOUR MUSIC ONLINE - A REALITY CHECK

by David Nevue, author of "How to Promote Your Music Successfully on the Internet"

I am often asked how much money a person can really make selling music online. I hear both extremes, both from artists who think they'll use the Internet to make it rich, and others who don't believe anyone can make any money online selling music. The truth is somewhere in between.

What follows is a brief, edited excerpt from the introductory chapter of my book, How to Promote Your Music Successfully on the Internet.

Will you make millions?

Let's get real for a moment. Promoting your music successfully on the Internet is hard work. Don't ever forget that. I've spent years doing this. The Internet is not a shortcut to success — it's simply another tool, one that can be very effective in the hands of someone who knows how to use it. Still, it's important to have realistic expectations before investing your time and money marketing your music online. You're going to face some very heated competition. There literally tens of thousands of musicians out there who already have web pages on the Internet (as of this writing there are over 98,000 artists registered with CDBaby.com alone). How can you compete with all those musicians? They are just the tip of the iceberg, though. Once you embark upon your promotional journey, you are, in a very real sense, competing with every other web page out there. How can you possibly stand out in that crowd? Pretty daunting, isn't it?

According to the Neilsen Netratings web site, there are over 299 million people actively using the Internet. A Georgia Tech survey of actual buyers provided some very interesting statistics: 70% of all buyers searched for the item they bought, 16% searched for a topic related to what they bought, and 4% searched for the name of another product which led them to the final product they purchased. Adding it up, 90% of all buyers used the Internet as a modern-day, digital Yellow Pages. So the question is, what does this tell you about selling your music on the Net?

Quite simply, it means that creating a web page to sell your music is not enough. That's something I discovered very early on. Even if you submit your site to the search engines, you're not likely to see a significant traffic increase. Think about it. If 90% of the buyers out there already know what they are looking for and are searching the Internet for that particular item, how will they find you, someone whose music they have likely never heard of? If they are not looking for you, they won't find you. So, what ARE they looking for? Therein lies the key.

Here's the slap-in-the-face reality: In my experience, the average musician sells between two and five CDs a year from their web site. Sales that low do not justify the expense of putting your music online. Can you do better than five CDs a year? Yes, you can do much, much better, but only if you have a quality product people care about and market it properly. Let me be up front with you. To succeed on the Internet, you must prepare yourself for the long haul and prepare to work hard. Success on the Internet won't come overnight.

As you read on, keep the following questions in the back of your mind. They hold the key to successful online music promotion:

1) What is unique about my music?

2) What general style of music are my fans most interested in?

3) What other artists do my fans compare my music to?

and most importantly...

4) Who is my target customer?

5) What kind of information is my *target* customer searching for on the Internet?

6) How can I use that information to bring that target customer to my web site?

To answer the question I posed at the beginning of this article, no, you are not likely to make millions on the Internet doing just music. But you can bring in a good, steady income. In 2004, I was able to generate an average of about $6,000 per month in total sales just from the Internet (that doesn't include gigs and CD sales at gigs). This income comes not only from CD sales, but sheet music sales (of my own music), book sales, partnerships, advertising revenue, and other sources. But every single thing I do online is related to the music business I love.

It's not just about the money...

There is still the question of using the Internet to advance your music career, and that's something the Internet can help you do also. I've been able to generate a lot of publicity for my music online, and as a result not only do I sell CDs, but I often receive requests to have my music used in independent film and media projects. I've negotiated three distribution deals overseas as a result of someone finding my music online. One company is using my music on an internationally distributed DVD series that raises funds for various charities. Even NBC contacted me to inquire about using my music in a made for TV film. Finally, I'm playing a lot more gigs in a lot more places as a direct result of marketing my music online and as you know, the more you play live, the more doors get opened up for you. You, like me, can use the Internet to create a huge amount of exposure for your music. The more exposure you generate, the more likely you are to gain new fans, sell more music get more gigs and of course, make those contacts you want to make within the music industry.

David Nevue is the founder of The Music Biz Academy, an online resource for musicians at www.musicbizacademy.com. He is also a professional pianist, recording artist, full-time musician, and author of the book, "How to Promote Your Music Successfully on the Internet" which you can read about at www.promoteyourmusic.com

♦

MUSIC MARKETING STRATEGIES
by Derek Sivers, CEO CD Baby
© 2007 Derek Sivers. Reprinted with permission.

Call the destination, and ask for directions

Work backwards. Define your goal (your final destination) - then contact someone who's there, and ask how to get there. If you want to be in Rolling Stone magazine, pick up the phone, call their main office in New York City, and when the receptionist answers, say "Editorial, please." Ask someone in the editorial department which publicists they recommend. Then call each publicist, and try to get their attention. (Hint: Don't waste Rolling Stone's time asking for the publicist's phone number. You can find it elsewhere; get off the phone as soon as possible.)

If you want to play at the biggest club in town, bring a nice box of fancy German cookies to the club booker, and ask for just 5 minutes of their advice. Ask them what criteria must be met in order for them to take a chance on an act. Ask what booking agents they recommend, or if they recommend using one at all. Again, keep your meeting as short as possible. Get the crucial info, and then leave them alone. (Until you're back, headlining their club one day!)

I know an artist manager of a small-unsigned act, who over the course of a year, met with the managers of U2, REM, and other top acts. She asked them for their advice, coming from the top, and got great suggestions that she's used with big results.

Put your fans to work

You know those loyal few people who are in the front row every time you perform? You know those people that sat down to write you an Email to say how much they love your music? The guy that said, "Hey if you ever need anything - just ask!" Put them all to work!

Often, people who reach out like that are looking for a connection in this world. Looking for a higher cause. They want to feel they have some other purpose than their stupid accounting job. You may be the best thing in their life. You can break someone out of their drab life as an assistant sales rep for a manufacturing company. You might be the coolest thing that ever happened to a teenager going through an unpopular phase. You can give them a mission!

Gather a few interested fans for pizza, and spend a night doing a mailing to colleges. Anyone wanting to help have them post flyers, or drive a van full of friends to your gig an hour away. Have the guts to ask that "email fan" if she'd be into going through the *Indie Contact Bible* and sending your press kit to 20 magazines a week. Eventually, as you grow, these people can be the head of "street teams" of 20 people in a city that go promote you like mad each time you have a concert or a new CD.

Go where the filters are

Have you been filtered? If not, you should start now. People in the music biz get piles of CDs in the mail everyday from amateurs. Many of them aren't very good. How do you stand out? Filters allow the best of the best pass through. It will also weed out the "bad music", or the music that isn't ready. I worked at Warner Brothers for 3 years. I learned why they never accept unsolicited demos: It helps weed out the people that didn't do enough research to know they have to go meet managers or lawyers or David Geffen's chauffeur *first* in order to get to the "big boys. If you *really* believe in your music, than have the confidence to put yourself into those places where most people get rejected. (Radio, magazines, big venues, agents, managers, record labels, promoters...)

Have someone work on the inside

I prefer to ignore the music industry. Maybe that's why you don't see me on the cover of Rolling Stone. One of my only regrets about my own band was that we toured and got great reviews, toured and got lots of air play, toured and booked some great-paying gigs. BUT... nobody was working the inside of the music business. Nobody was connecting with the "gatekeepers" to bring us to the next level. We just kept doing the same gigs. Maybe you're happy on the outside of the biz. (I know I am.) But if what you want is to tour with major-label artists, be on the cover of *Spin*, heard on the airwaves, or get onto MTV, You're going to have to have someone working the inside of the biz, Someone who loves it. Someone persuasive who gets things done 10 times faster than you ever could, and who's excited enough about it, that they would never be discouraged. Find someone who's passionate about the business side of music, and particularly the business side of YOUR music.

Be a novice marketer not an expert

Get to the point of being a novice marketer/promoter/agent. Then hand it to an expert. Moby, the famous techno artist, says the main reason for his success was that he found experts to do what they're best at, instead of trying to do it himself. (Paraphrased:) "Instead of trying to be a booking agent, publicist, label, and manager, I put my initial energy into finding and impressing the best agent.... I just kept making lots of the best music I could."

If you sense you are becoming an expert, figure out what your real passions in life are and act accordingly. Maybe you're a better publicist than bassist. Maybe you're a better bassist than publicist. Maybe it's time to admit your weakness as a booking agent, and hand it off to someone else. Maybe it's time to admit your genius as a booking agent, and commit to it full- time.

Reach them like you would want to be reached

Reach people like *you* would want to be reached. Would you rather have someone call you up in a dry business monotone, and start speaking a script like a telemarketer? Or would you rather have someone be a cool person, a real person?

When you contact people, no matter how it's done (phone, email, mail, face-to-face) - show a little spunk. If it sounds like they have a moment and aren't in a major rush, entertain them a bit. Ask about their day and expect a real answer. Talk about something non-business for a minute or two. If they sound hectic, skip the long introduction. Know what you want to say ahead of time, just in case.

Every contact with the people around your music (fans and industry) is an extension of your art. If you make depressing, morose, acoustic music, maybe you should send your fans a dark brown-and-black little understated flyer that's depressing just to look at. Set the tone. Pull in those people who love that kind of thing. Proudly alienate those that don't. If you're an in your face, tattooed, country-metal-speedpunk band, have the guts to call a potential booking agent and scream, "Listen you fucking motherfucker. If they like that introduction, you've found a good match. Don't be afraid to be different.

What has worked on you?

Any time you're trying to influence people to do something, think what has worked on YOU in the past. Are you trying to get people to buy your CD? Write down the last 20 CDs you bought, then for each one, write down what made you buy it. Did you ever buy a CD because of a matchbook, postcard, or 30-second web sound clip? What DID work? (Reviews, word-of-mouth, live show?) Write down your top 10 favorite artists of all time, and a list of what made you discover each one and become a fan.

This goes beyond music. Which TV ads made you buy something? What anonymous Emails made you click a link and check out a website? Which flyers or radio ads made you go see a live show by someone you had never heard?

Have the confidence to target

Bad Target Example: Progressive Rocker Targeting Teeny Bopper. On CD Baby, there is a great musician who made an amazing heavy-progressive-metal record. When we had a "search keywords" section, asking for three artists he sounds like, he wrote, "britney spears, ricky martin, jennifer lopez, backstreet boys, MP3, sex, free" What the hell was he thinking? He just wanted to turn up in people's search engines, at any cost. For what, and who? Did he really want a Britney Spears fan to get "tricked" into finding his dark-progressive-metal record? Would that 13-year-old girl actually spend the 25 minutes to download his 10 minute epic, "Confusing Mysteries of Hell"? If she did, would she buy his CD? I suggested he instead have the confidence to target the REAL fans of his music. He put three semi-obscure progressive artists into the search engine, and guess what? He's selling more CDs than ever! He found his true fans.

If you don't say whom you sound like, you won't make any fans

A person asks you, "What kind of music do you do?" Musicians say, "All styles. Everything." That person then asks, "So who do you sound like?" Musicians say, "Nobody. We're totally unique. Like nothing you've ever heard before." What does that person do? Nothing. They might make a vague promise to check you out sometime. Then they walk on, and forget about you! Why??? You didn't arouse their curiosity! You violated a HUGE rule of self-promotion! Bad bad bad!

What if you had said, "It's 70's porno-funk music being played by men from Mars." Or... "This CD is a delicate little kiss on your earlobe from a pink-winged pixie. Or... "We sound like a cross between *AC/DC* and *Tom Jones*." Any one of these, and you've got their interest.

Get yourself a magic key phrase that describes what you sound like. Try out a few different ones, until you see which one always gets the best reaction from strangers. Have it ready at a moment's notice. It doesn't have to narrow what you do at all. Any of those three examples I use above could sound like anything. And that's just the point - if you have a magic phrase that describes your music in curious but vague terms, you can make total strangers start wondering about you.

Touch as many senses of theirs as you can

The more senses you touch in someone, the more they'll remember you. BEST: a live show, with you sweating right on top of someone, the PA system pounding their chest, the smell of the smoky club, the flashing lights and live-in-person performance. WORST: an email, a single web page, or a review in a magazine with no photo.

Whenever it is possible, try to reach as many senses as possible. Have an amazing photo of yourself or your band, and convince every reviewer to put that photo next to the review of your album. Send videos with your press kit. Play live shows often. Understand the power of radio to make people hear your music instead of just hearing about it. Get onto any TV shows you can. Scent your album with patchouli oil. Make your songs and productions truly emotional instead of merely catchy.

Be an extreme version of yourself

Define yourself. Show your weirdness. Bring out all your quirks. Your public persona, the image you show to the world, should be an extreme version of yourself.

A good biz plan wins no matter what happens

In doing this test marketing you should make a plan that will make you a success even if nobody comes along with his or her magic wand. Start now. Don't wait for a "deal". Don't just record a "demo" that is meant only for record companies.

You have all the resources you need to make a finished CD that thousands of people would want to buy. If you need more money, get it from anyone except a record company. And if, as you're following your great business plan, selling hundreds, then thousands of CDs, selling out small, then larger venues, getting on the cover of magazines... you'll be doing so well that you won't need a record deal. If you get an offer you'll be in the position of taking it or leaving it. There's nothing more attractive to an investor than someone who doesn't need his or her money. Make the kind of business plan that will get you to a good sustainable level of success, even without a big record deal.

Don't be afraid to ask for favors

Some people *like* doing favors. It's like asking for directions in New York City. People's egos get stroked when they know the answer to something you're asking. They'll gladly answer to show off their knowledge.

One bold musician I know called me up one day and said, "I'm coming to New York in 2 months. Can you give me a list of all the important contacts you think I should meet?" I ended doing a search in my database, E-mailing him a list of 40 people he should call, and mention my name.

Maybe you need to find something specific: a video director for cheap, a PA system you can borrow for a month, a free rehearsal studio. Call up everyone you know and ask! This network of friends you are creating will have everything you want in life. Some rare and lucky folks (perhaps on your "band mailing list") have time on their hands and would rather help you do something, than sit at home in front of the TV another night. Need help doing flyers, or help getting equipment to a show? Go ahead and ask!

Keep in touch!
Sometimes the difference between success and failure is just a matter of keeping in touch! There are some AMAZING musicians who have sent a CD to CD Baby, and when I heard it, I flipped. In a few cases, I've stopped what I was doing at that moment, picked up the phone and called them wherever they were to tell them I thought they were a total genius. (Believe me - this is rare. Maybe 1 in 500.) Often I get an answering machine, and guess what... they don't call back!! What success-sabotaging kind of thing is that to do? 2 weeks later I've forgotten about their CD as new ones came in.

The lesson: If they would have just called back, and kept in touch, they may have a fan like no other at the head of one of the largest distributors of independent music on the web. A fan that would go out on a limb to help their career in ways others just dream of. But they never kept in touch and now I can't remember their names. Some others whose CDs didn't really catch my attention the first time around, just keep in touch so well that I often find myself helping them more as a friend than a fan.

A short description - 10 Seconds or less
Most of the world has never heard your music. Most of the world WON'T hear your music, unless you do a good job describing it. It's like a Hollywood screenplay. You not only have to write a great screenplay, but you have to have a great description of it that you can say in 10 seconds or less, in order to catch people's attention. Find a way to describe your music that would catch anyone's attention, and describe it accurately.

Read about new music
Go get a magazine like CMJ, Magnet, or Alternative Press. You'll read about (and see pictures of) dozens of artists who you've never heard of before. Out of that whole magazine, only one or two will really catch your attention. WHY? I don't have the answer. Only you do. Ask yourself why a certain headline or photo or article caught your attention. What was it exactly that intrigued you? Adapt those techniques to try writing a headline or article about your music.

Derek Sivers is the Founder of CD Baby. Derek has been a full-time musician for 8 years, and toured the world as a guitarist sideman with some famous folks. He also ran a recording studio, and worked inside the industry at Warner/Chappell Music for 3 years. Derek cracked the college market and got hired by 400 colleges, and sold a few thousand CD's.

♦

43 MILLION COMPELLING REASONS TO USE MYSPACE.COM
by Andre Calilhanna, Discmakers

The indie music universe is constantly waning and expanding: new bands emerge, old ones dissolve, conferences come and go, new web sites pop up as older ones fall out of fashion. As with any other industry or business model, these indie music offerings fail and succeed with their ability to create and meet market demand for their service.

Enter MySpace.com. Incorporating successful elements of MP3.com and IUMA, and eclipsing PureVolume and Friendster as the place to be online, MySpace is the epitome of what an online community can be. In it's short life it has adapted and evolved to meet the evolving needs of its user base, and it has expanded to a network of over 43 million users in the process. Thanks, in large part, to the bands.

Billionaire Boys Club, from Jersey City, NJ, boast the distinction of being the first band ever to grace the front page of MySpace. Through good timing and good tunes, BBC caught the attention of MySpace co-founder Tom Anderson and ushered in a new wrinkle in the MySpace universe. The band is still listed as one of Anderson's MySpace favorites.

Fireflight, from Orlando, FL, recently signed to Flicker Records, and attribute a lot of their growing fan base to their efforts and presence on MySpace. Through their page on MySpace, the band sees continuous growth and interest, which should only increase as they release their album in July and start playing a full regimen of shows.

We sat down with these two indie music veterans and gleaned some insights into the finer points of MySpace marketing. Here's our list of five phenomenal reasons to use MySpace!

1. Super-targeted viral marketing.
2. Communication runs both ways.
3. Motivated fans.
4. Crossover marketing opportunities.
5. Free marketing is the best marketing ever!

Super-targeted viral marketing
One of the tenets of good marketing is to target your market. You wouldn't pitch your Crunk Speed-Metal band with an ad in Today's Grandparent magazine. The idea is to figure out who your market is, find out where they are, develop your message, then figure out how to get that message in front of the people who might want to buy what you're selling.

MySpace delivers this in spades. Pockets and niches of users, called "friends," gather around each other and share info on bands they like. For instance, let's say you like My Chemical Romance. You can go check out their site, listen to their music, and read their blog. Then, if you want to find bands with a similar sound, you can check out the band's friends, which include a host of other bands. Presumably, these are bands that have something in common with My Chemical Romance, so you go and check them out.

There are also fans listed as friends, and they typically have a bunch of bands on their pages. So someone into My Chemical Romance will have a number of other bands posted. You might be interested in checking some of them out. It's viral marketing in its purest form, and the friend network is what really sets MySpace apart from other band sites.

It's also why Isac Walter, who does marketing and programming for MySpace, says major labels are clamoring to get their bands on the site. "With 43 million users, it's almost better than going to TV, what with the way people watch TV nowadays. People come to this site to discover new music, and what better way to expose an artist than to leak a band to this audience?"

As a band, this works the other way, too. Once you start developing a fan base, you can communicate to them when you have a show or a news event to broadcast. MySpace provides a service where you can target the friends you contact by region.

Billionaire Boys Club, from Jersey City, NJ
"They added this feature," says Leigh Nelson of BBC, "where you can set up an event, and you can say I want to invite all my friends in a radius of x number of miles from this zip code. So we'll do a show in New York and set up an invitation and invite all of our friends within 50 or 100 miles of the city. So we're directly targeting that audience, where with email you end up sending show announcements to people in Germany. These are things that get added one little bit at a time. Tom really seems to get how people are using MySpace and what they want to do with it, and they're always adding functionality based on that."

Communication runs both ways
The internet has completely changed the way we communicate, particularly in terms of marketing. Take something as simple as a band mailing list, for instance. In the early 90's, that meant printing post cards, labeling them, putting stamps on them, and lugging it all to the post office weeks before the gig. It sounds like the Dark Ages, doesn't it? It cost a bunch of money, and fans could only communicate by seeing you at a show or writing a letter. Email changed all that. Now it's free to email your announcement, fans can immediately reply, and you don't need to plan your promotion months in advance.

MySpace has taken that even further. MySpace not only allows you to communicate with your fans quickly and cost effectively, but it allows them to communicate with you and each other.

Fans can tell you what they think of everything on your page – a picture, a song, a blog entry – and their response is posted immediately. They can then spread your news to their friends with a couple of keystrokes. It's an amazing development, and there are many ways to take advantage of it to create drama and stir up a buzz.

Fireflight, from Orlando, FL

"We started leaking the news about our signing to Flicker on MySpace because we knew people were going to be reading our blog," says Justin Cox of Fireflight, "but we got way more response than we thought we would. That generated more interest in our page than anything had in a long time. You could see us singing a contract but you didn't know with who, and that blog is the most visited we have. We put it on our regular site, too, but we don't have it set up where people can comment, so it's cool to know that so many people were keeping track and were genuinely interested."

There are examples of bands booking shows to meet the demand of their MySpace fans, tells Walter. "There's this band Cut Copy from Australia who did the Franz Ferdinand tour, and when they played Los Angeles they had enough people on MySpace saying, 'Oh I wish you were playing your own show!' So they booked a show at a smaller club called The Echo and gave discounts to their MySpace friends and sold the place out. Bands like that who keep in contact and get a little more personal with their audience can really have success."

And Nelson explains that opportunities are coming to them by way of MySpace. "We used to get a decent amount of fan email, but now all those comments are pretty much coming exclusively from MySpace. Also coming in are show offers, booking people who are interested, soundtracks who are interested in songs… a lot of that comes via MySpace. It makes us more likely to follow up, too, because we can get a better idea of who these people are by looking at their page."

Motivated fans who find you and help promote you

Indie bands need help. It's a lot of work to do promotion, book gigs, sell merch, rehearse, write, and do the hundreds of little details involved with a band. Street teams and helpful fans have been the solution to much of that, though not always easy to assemble and coordinate. MySpace, with its younger demographic and infectious network qualities, makes it easier to find folks ready to jump on and paint your bandwagon. Sometimes, the band doesn't even know it happening.

"We have this banner on our MySpace page," explains Cox. "I was surprised to find that people who were our friends were taking it and posting it on other people's MySpace pages, trying to drive traffic to us. So let's say there was no MySpace and you had a web site, and you had that same banner. It's cool, but what are people going to do with it? Now that we've got MySpace, they take those banners and post them as comments on other people's pages and blogs, and people read the blogs and then automatically they're going to your site for no other reason than that it's there."

Finding where your MySpace fans are coming from can lead to unexpected market research, like expanding your gig radius based on fan input. "I can search for BBC across the whole site and see how many people have added us and said we're one of their favorite bands," says Nelson. "It's really cool to see fans crop up in markets we've never even been to. All of a sudden we see there are a lot of friends in upstate New York, we get in touch with them and find out where we should play and then go do some shows. In the past there was no way to find that kind of information."

Crossover marketing

At its best, one marketing endeavor feeds another, and spills into your other efforts. As Walter says, "The bands who promote their MySpace pages become the biggest bands on MySpace, hands down." By linking from your regular web site, adding your MySpace URL to all your stickers, t-shirts, etc., you drive people to your site, and more likely broadcast to all those MySpace users that you're on there, too.

It also works in reverse. MySpace traffic drives traffic to your regular web site, and people to your shows. "Traffic on our site has increased drastically as well," says Cox, "and I'm sure that has something to do with MySpace because it's been a steady ramp since we've been on there."

"I can also remember instances specifically where people have come up to me at a show and say they heard us on MySpace and decided to come check us out, which to me is the best. It's just a big network and a big word of mouth kind of thing and you can't get that kind of exposure unless you're playing shows every night. It's just been this awesome marketing tool."

Free marketing is the best marketing ever!

Sounds obvious, and it is! But it can't be understated or undervalued. Many of the band web sites out there offer great services, and there's no reason not to be on every site you can get to. MySpace has the unique distinction, though, of offering just about everything you could imagine wanting all under one roof: a potential fan base, an opportunity to broadcast your music, a place to hang your photos, a web presence with a decent amount of customization… the list goes on. Not to mention the features and functions that allow you to be a smart marketer.

"The thing that sets MySpace apart from sites that are just for bands," touts Nelson, "is people sign onto MySpace every day, just to check their messages, read, and communicate. I use it every day, to check in and see what's going on, look for any bulletins from bands, figure out what's going on tonight in the city. So just by putting your journal or show dates or advertisements and songs up there, you're simply going to get a lot more exposure than people just randomly checking your web site. People spend more time on it than anywhere else. I guess credit to Tom there, for setting it up in such a way that makes it so addictive!"

This article originally appeared in Disc Makers' Fast Forward monthly e-newsletter. Visit www.discmakers.com/music/ffwd to get a free subscription.

d i s t r i b u t i o n

PREPARING FOR DISTRIBUTION

by Daylle Deanna Schwartz, author of "The Real Deal"

© 2007 Revenge Productions. Reprinted with permission.

People who want to press up their music in order to sell it are most concerned about getting distribution. Your focus if you want to make money from your music, is to first take yourself seriously as a business. Whether you like it or not, outside of your circle of fans, you and your music are looked upon as products. If you prefer being idealistic, create and perform music for fun. But, if earning a living from your music is an eventual goal, developing a *business attitude* is critical.

What's necessary?

Read books on the biz and attend seminars if you can. Get a good picture of how the music industry operates. Network as much as possible to create a support system of folks you can call on for resources, advice and encouragement. While you shouldn't negotiate your own contracts, you should know enough to discuss the terms of one with your lawyer. Don't be one of those musicians who tell their lawyer, publisher, manager, etc., "Whatever you say." Gather enough knowledge so you can make informed decisions based on input from your representatives. Think of yourself as a professional. Even if you're only pressing up your own music, you're a record label. Act like one! Being responsible will max your chances of others wanting to work with you.

Getting distribution

Getting distribution isn't always a guarantee. You can ship 500 pieces and get them all back if you haven't been able to promote your product to a target audience. Distributors get records into stores. Most don't promote them. Stores tell me that records sell because people know the artist. Before taking in your product, distributors need to see that you have a market already interested in buying it. Creating a demand is what sells records. Distributors want you to have a handle on promotion before they work with your label. Once you have that, they'll want your product.

Do the groundwork

Until you identify your potential market and develop strategies for letting them know about your music, having distribution won't sell CDs. The most important thing you can do first is to target the group who might buy your product and figure out how to reach them. Distributors want product that will sell, and will *want* to work with labels that have artists with a buzz going. They don't care how good the music is if nobody knows about it.

It still amazes me how many folks come to me for consultations and aren't sure who is most likely to buy their music. They tell me since it's good music, everyone will buy. That usually means they have no clue and don't want to bother to figure it out. If you can't target your audience, play your music for people who work in record stores or other music related folks and ask for their honest feedback.

Your audience

Anyone may buy your CD, but promote it to the group more likely to appreciate it. Is it college students? Young adults? Teens? Baby boomers? Once you know that, what kinds of promotion will you do to make them want to buy your record? Figuring this out sounds simple at first but if it was, there would be a lot more records making big money independently. It is more than the music being great, for people to buy your CD. They need to hear your music to be enticed to buy it. How will you reach their ears? What will make them buy it? Figuring out a marketing plan can be the hardest part of putting out your music. Distribution is easy once you get this in place.

Create a demand

The best way to get your product into stores is to develop a story around your act first. Focus your energy on getting reviews, getting radio play (college and public radio are best to start with), selling product on your own, and increasing your fan base by touring. Create a demand, and then put together a one-page synopsis of the artist's story, known as a one-sheet. This has the artist's story - reviews and stories in the media (include quotes), radio play, gigs, direct sales, internet presence, etc, as well as details about the record itself. Include anything that shows the act is marketable, concisely on one sheet of paper. A small photo of the act and/or the album cover should be on the sheet too.

How to get in stores

Send you're one-sheet to potential distributors. Don't send a sample of the music until they request it. The story is more important than the music. Some distributors take calls if you want to try that first. But if their interest is piqued, they'll ask you to fax them a one-sheet. Be prepared. Don't approach distributors until you have a good foundation. Make them take you seriously the first time! Distributors are in the business of selling records. If they think yours will sell, they'll carry it. It's that simple. Start with a local distributor until your buzz gets stronger and you prove you can sell product on a wider scale. Then work your way up to larger ones.

Daylle Deanna Schwartz is the author of Start & Run Your Own Record Label and The Real Deal: How to Get Signed to a Record Label from A to Z, both on Billboard Books. She also teaches full day seminars and does consulting on these topics. Contact: www.outersound.com/revenge

◆

25 THINGS TO REMEMBER ABOUT RECORD DISTRIBUTION

by Christopher Knab, author of "Music Is Your Business".
© 2007 All Rights Reserved. Used By Permission

1. Distributors will usually only work with labels that have been in business for at least 3 years, or have at least 3 previous releases that have sold several thousand copies each.

2. Distributors get records into retail stores, and record labels get customers into retail stores through promotion and marketing tactics.

3. Make sure there is a market for your style of music. Prove it to distributors by showing them how many records you have sold through live sales, internet sales, and any other alternative methods.

4. Be prepared to sign a written contract with your distributor because there are no 'handshake deals' anymore.

5. Distributors want 'exclusive' agreements with the labels they choose to work with. They usually want to represent you exclusively.

6. You will sell your product to a label for close to 50% of the retail list price.

7. When searching for a distributor find out what labels they represent, and talk to some of those labels to find out how well the distributor did getting records into retailers.

8. Investigate the distributor's financial status. Many labels have closed down in recent years, and you cannot afford to get attached to a distributor that may not be able to pay its invoices.

9. Find out if the distributor has a sales staff, and how large it is. Then get to know the sales reps.

10. What commitment will the distributor make to help get your records into stores?

11. Is the distributor truly a national distributor, or only a regional distributor with ambitions to be a national distributor? Many large chain stores will only work with national distributors.

12. Expect the distributor to request that you remove any product you have on consignment in stores so that they can be the one to service retailers.

13. Make sure that your distributor has the ability to help you setup various retail promotions such as: coop advertising (where you must be prepared to pay the costs of media ads for select retailers), in-store artist appearances, in-store listening station programs, and furnishing POP's (point of purchase posters and other graphics).

14. Be aware that as a new label you will have to offer a distributor 100% on returns of your product.

15. You must bear all the costs of any distribution and retail promotions.

16. Furnish the distributor with hundreds of 'Distributor One Sheets' (Attractively designed summary sheets describing your promotion and marketing commitments. Include barcodes, list price, picture of the album cover, and catalog numbers of your product too.

17. Distributors may ask for hundreds of free promotional copies of your release to give to the buyers at the retail stores.

18. Make sure all promotional copies have a hole punched in the barcode, and that they are not shrink-wrapped. This will prevent any unnecessary returns of your product.

19. Don't expect a distributor to pay your invoices in full or on time. You will always be owed something by the distributor because of the delay between orders sent, invoices received, time payment schedules (50-120 days per invoice) and whether or not your product has sold through, or returns are pending.

20. Create a relationship that is a true partnership between your label and the distributor.

21. Keep the distributor updated on any and all promotion and marketing plans and results, as they develop.

22. Be well financed. Trying to work with distributors without a realistic budget to participate in promotional opportunities would be a big mistake.

23. Your distributor will only be as good as your marketing plans to sell the record. Don't expect them to do your work for you, remember all they do is get records into the stores.

24. Read the trades, especially Billboard for weekly news on the health of the industry, and/or the status of your distributor.

25. Work your product relentlessly on as many fronts as possible… commercial and non commercial airplay, internet airplay and sales campaigns, on and offline publicity ideas, and touring…eternally touring!

Christopher Knab is a music business Consultant, Author and Lecturer. He was recently honored by Seattle's Rocket magazine as "One of the Most Influential People in the Northwest Music Industry." Contact: www.4frontmusic.com, Chris@Knab.com

◆

SUCCEEDING WITHOUT A LABEL

by Bernard Baur, Music Connection Magazine
© 2007 All Rights Reserved. Used By Permission

DIY

Music Connection set out to see how realistic the independent route is, and if artists can find success on their own. We found that independent artists are very popular with music fans; and, that acts like *The Dave Matthews Band*, *Godsmack*, *Nickelback* and *The White Stripes* didn't depend on a record company to break them. They did it themselves and sold thousands of records, which naturally attracted hundreds of labels. Moreover, those who enjoyed independent success negotiated deals that were superior to the average deal most artists are offered.

To find out what it takes, MC contacted a variety of artists who took the "Do It Yourself" approach and are making it work. They are self-sufficient artists who found that they didn't need a label to live their dream. They prove that the DIY option is not only viable; it may also be the best course of action. After all, who wouldn't like to call their own shots in a market that's up for grabs?

Choosing the road less traveled

Sitting in a label president's office suite can be surreal, especially when he's explaining what an artist needs to do to get signed. The list is so long (covering a variety of areas) so, you can't help but ask, " If an artist did all of that, why the hell would they need you?"

Well, some artists don't think they need an established label at all. Award winning artist, Aimee Mann, has had three major record deals but now says, "I can't recommend signing a label deal. Why should you give them all the power? Really, it's frustrating. You think labels are supposed to sell records, but they don't always do what they're supposed to so, why deal with them?" In response, Mann formed her own company, *Super Ego Records*, and became a poster girl for DIY success thanks to her Oscar-nominated song from the film *"Magnolia"* and the 200,000 units sold of her *"Bachelor No. 2"* album. Today, she claims to be happier than she ever was at a major. "Now, I have the freedom to do what I want, when I want. And, if any mistakes are made, I get to make them myself rather than have someone make them for me."

The independent mindset

It seems simple. You don't have to be signed to release a record. In fact, if you wait to be signed it could be a very long time according to Tim Sweeney, a consultant who specializes in independent artists. He not only presents workshops on DIY, but has also written books about it. Sweeney maintains, "Less acts are being signed nowadays, and of those that do get a deal only 1-3% will make it beyond a record or two before they get dumped."

DIY avoids that scenario, but artists need to be a special breed to do it right. According to Pat McKeon, former owner of *Dr. Dream Records* and general manager at *Ranell Records,* states, "An independent artist will have to wear more than one hat. When they first start out, they'll probably be doing everything themselves, and not every artist can handle that."

It is also important to understand how much work DIY truly is. K.K. Martin, an indie artist who survived several label deals intimated, "You have to learn about the business and pay attention to it. If you can't do that, find someone you trust, or you'll never progress."

Keeping' it real

If you want DIY success, you have to have realistic expectations. Nearly every artist dreams of playing The Forum or appearing on MTV. Unfortunately, that doesn't even happen to major label acts unless they have a hit and are extremely successful. Most independent artists have to set their sights a little lower. That's not to say it could never happen, because it does. But, the fact is you'd have to have fantastic connections or enjoy phenomenal success to reach that level.

"Keeping your goals realistic is essential for all independents," Moon points out. "If you don't do that, you're going to be disappointed." Moon suggests keeping it real and at a level you can achieve. "Set up small goals on a monthly, quarterly and yearly basis. Then, evaluate the results. If you reached your goals, move on – if not, figure out why."

Perhaps the greatest state of mind independent artists need is patience. Angus Richardson, of the band Brother, has known phenomenal success, selling over 150,000 records and playing almost 250 dates a year. Nevertheless, even Brother had to suck it up. " When we didn't get a quick record deal, it would have been easy to get discouraged," Richardson reveals. "But, we believed in our music, our fans and ourselves. And, the fact is," he stresses, "if you get hurt every time you're rejected in this business, you're going to have a lot of scars. Just look around at all the bands that have disappeared"

Touring is key

The most important part of the plan is playing live. Everything, including radio, promotions, distribution and marketing, should revolve around that, it's the way you sell records. Of course, you're going to need a recording, but according to Moon, it need not be up to industry standards. "Even a live recording will do," she says. "Your fans want to hear your songs, not the production."

Most artists have booked themselves before, so this area should be familiar. The difference is that you have to book gigs beyond your backyard. Sweeney suggests that artists should start by looking 2-3 hours in each direction. "That will only cost $30-40 in gas, and you should be able to make that in sales," he says. "If an act is based in Los Angeles, they can look as far as San Diego and Santa Barbara. Eventually, increase the drive time and even look at neighboring states. But, he warns, "don't try to do it all at once."

Naturally, when it comes to touring solo artists have it the easiest. Moon, Malone and Martin only occasionally bring a full band along. "It's a matter of economics as well as personal dynamics," Martin maintains. "Traveling in a van with five other guys can challenge your patience." To cut costs, Malone, who toured eight times across the country in three years, established a network of musicians he hires in each city. "That way," he says, "I only have to pay them for the gig."

Expenses on the road

If you're a real band, expenses become a concern. Tina Broad, Bother's manager, relates that their merchandise table is a critical part of their financial success. "If we didn't have product to sell we couldn't do it. Our merchandise sales (CDs and goods) have a dramatic impact on our ability to tour. Traditionally, we make 2 to 3 times more from our merchandise than we do from tour guarantees or ticket sales." Broad also advises bands to take a serious look at their hospitality riders. "Include things that you need (towels, water, food, backline, etc) so that you have fewer things to deal with, and insist on a 50% deposit so that you're not shouldering all the cash flow until the performance check clears."

Your bank

Touring, recordings, and merchandise obviously require money, and artists should be ready to dip into their own pockets. Sweeney contends that if artists aren't willing to invest in themselves, he questions how serious they are about a career. "However, if resources are severely limited, you just have to start smaller and think smarter," he says. "Find a sponsor to help with costs. Play free shows for them and put their name on your CD. " Moon suggests doing your own artwork or finding a friend who's talented. In fact, every independent artist who is successful uses a network of resources to help them defray costs.

Some, such as *Skywind*, a Minneapolis band who tours over 100 days a year and plays before 1000 or more fans, got their family and friends to loan them seed money. Bill Berry, their manager, indicates, "Everyone got paid back in just over a year. And since then," he relates, "We've been able to pick up sponsorships and lines of credit." Each band member contributes to pay off loans and, by doing this; Skywind has been able buy a van and tour three states.

The bottom line is that you're going to need a budget, so that you know what you can do. Indeed, Brother's manager, Broad advises artists to be realistic about costs. "If you don't know what your real expenses are," she informs, " you're going to be operating in a vacuum."

Art meets commerce

If you want to be an independent artist who's self-sufficient, don't deceive yourself: you are in business, and there are two parts to business – the legal side and the practical side. Legally, you must protect your interests and follow the law. Everyone agrees that you should consult with counsel when setting things up. You may need a band contract, a business license, and an assortment of other things that make you a legal entity.

On the practical side, keep accurate records of all your sales and income. Sweeney informs us that you can simply pay the tax on your sales, to obtain a verifiable record. These figures are all important if you hope to convince anyone – including a label, a distributor or a lender – to work with you. Indeed, Broad says it still makes her guts churn to think that Brother neglected to register the sales from their 2001 Summer Tour. "That was 15,000 unverifiable sales," she sighs. "We've got manufacturing records, but it's not the same."

Marketing & promotion

Mann contends that marketing and promotion is always a challenge, whether you're on a label or not. "It was my biggest cause for concern with every deal I had," she reports. "At least, now, I have the freedom and control to do it the way I want." But, when you're independent, you have to think outside the box. You cannot compete with the majors, so you have to do things differently.

McKeon points out, "All independent promotions must revolve around live gigs. That has to be your focus because it's your moneymaker. After booking gigs, you can contact press, radio and retail." Of all of them, radio is usually the most difficult, but persistence pays off.

Skywind's Berry relates that they maintained a two-year relationship with a local station before their songs were played. "We bought advertising time late at night because it's cheaper and played radio events for free. After they got to know us, they put our songs in rotation." Sweeney suggests attending station concerts and handing out free CDs. "It gets your music to their audience," he says.

Artists should also learn to cooperate with each other. Sweeney advises, "Artists should work towards a common goal, book shows together, share expenses and even buy commercial time on cable TV. Cable companies will sell 30-60 seconds for less than $100 and you can promote your act on MTV. If you run a few commercials a week before your show, you'll see tremendous results."

The distribution monster

Distribution is one of the biggest issues facing all independent artists. You need to stock your CDs wherever you play, but getting distribution isn't easy. For some artists, consignments may be the way to go. Many record stores will accept your CDs on spec and if they sell, will order more. "You might start with only 10-20 in a store, but if they move the orders will increase," Martin explains. "The only problem with consignment is that you have to keep on top of it on a regular basis."

Other artists, like Nashville songwriter, Hal Bynum, have found alternative markets. He reveals, "I've been a songwriter for 50 years, and it's still not easy to get distribution." So, Bynum created a unique package – a book and CD – that Barnes & Noble will carry. "I agreed to make in-store appearances and they agreed to promote me."

Start an organization or join one

Some artists set up their own organization. With the help of her New York manager, Michael Hausman, Aimee Mann founded *"United Musicians,"* a sort of cooperative for artists. Hausman explains, "We found that distributors don't like to work with a single artist. They want product every few months, so we set up *United Musicians* for other artists who may be in the same boat. *R.E.D.* agreed to distribute our records and we're sharing our contacts with artists."

If you're not quite to that stage yet, there are services to meet your needs. The independent network is full of companies that cater to independent artists, and one of the newest and most intriguing *is 101 Distribution.* Damon Evans, 101's executive director, describes his

company as an alternative solution to traditional distribution. "We service over 2100 retail stores across the country and into Europe." Essentially, 101 take the work out of consignments. They give stores product on consignment, collect revenue and pay artists every 30 days. Their split with artists is generous (70-80% of wholesale) and they will handle promotions and marketing, unlike other distributors.

The ultimate reward

Of course, for some, whose music may not be mainstream, independence is their only choice; while for others it's by design. But, regardless of whether you're a maverick or an act still seeking a deal, the same rules apply. If you want success, you have to work for it. While DIY may be a lot of work, it can be very rewarding. "It is time consuming and takes a lot of patience but," Gilli Moon concludes, " there's nothing quite like having control over your own destiny. You can be as big or as small as you want and go at your own pace."

Ten steps to success for the independent artist

(All the artists profiled are self-sufficient. They make a living "solely" with their music. This list was compiled from their interviews.)

1. **Believe in yourself**
   You must believe in yourself. Realize that you don't need a label to be a success. Don't be egotistical, but be confident. Be optimistic – believe you are good enough and can get what you want. If you don't have faith in yourself – no one else will.

2. **Be realistic**
   Do research – Get objective opinions - Identify your market. Know that you're going to have to tour. Know when to ask for help. Accept the fact that you probably won't become a star or get on MTV, but that you can make a living playing music.

3. **Make a wish list**
   Create a Wish List – What do you ultimately want and how do you plan to get it? What are the things you need to do and how long will it take? Set reasonable goals and break your Plan into phases: 3 months – 6 months – 1 year – 3 years, etc…

4. **Know your budget**
   If you're serious about a career, you're going to have to invest in yourself. Itemize your expenses and add 20%. Approach Sponsors with a detailed plan. Negotiate deals that take care of the basics: travel, food, lodging, backline, etc… And, don't forget manufacturing and promotional costs.

5. **Take care of business**
   Remember – it is the music "business." Network as much as possible; organize a team, with each person responsible for a specific area. If you're solo, manage your time wisely. Get your own Bar Code. Seek professional advice to set up your business entities. Pay attention to licenses and tax implications. When you tour, get insurance.

6. **Market yourself**
   Think creatively. Make time for "personal appearances" before your gigs. Set up cross-promotions with radio stations, sponsors, venues, and retail stores. Make sure you have enough products to sell – both CDs and merchandise. Offer promotional contests. Play Special Events. Work your mailing list and keep in touch with your fans at least once a month.

7. **Keep records**
   Keep books that reflect income and expenses. Accurately account for sales. Register and report to SoundScan. Maintain tax records. Record your draw – note the venue/locale that draws best. Keep updating your mailing list.

8. **Adapt & adjust**
   Evaluate results: What works – What doesn't? Revise your plan and adjust your approach accordingly. Find ways to increase your fan base and make a profit. What can be done better?

9. **Keep the faith**

No matter how hard you work, there will be frustrating times. Keep the faith and don't let it deter you. Everyone experiences setbacks. Those that persevere will prevail.

10. **Make it fun**

If it's not fun anymore – don't do it. Reward yourself (and your team) whenever possible. Acknowledge a job well done. Take a break – enjoy life – then, get back to work.

Bernard Baur is the Review Editor & Feature Writer for Music Connection Magazine. Contact: www.musicconnection.com, Tel: 818-755-0101 Ext.519 EqxManLtd@aol.com

t o u r i n g

THE BASICS OF BOOKING YOUR OWN TOURS

by Jay Flanzbaum, Onlinegigs.com
© 2007 All Rights Reserved. Used By Permission

To be able to book gigs successfully you'll need a ton of persistence and even better organization. Whether you are booking locally, regionally or nationally you will essentially need the same skills and tools to be effective. Independent bands and agents, by definition, tend to lack the nationwide connections necessary to make the idea of booking an extended tour possible. As a result the ones that are most successful are generally the same ones that understand how to gather, and effectively manage, all of their business related contacts. We've all seen some pretty lousy bands with some damn good gigs, so talent isn't always the main issue.

Data collection

If you haven't already, you are going to have to start collecting contact information for the people that can help you achieve your goals. If your goal is to have a touring career in the music industry then you better find some venues, colleges, festivals, record companies, managers, record stores and media contacts, to do business with. It is never too early to start this process. You should start today even if your CD won't be ready for another 3 years and you don't have a full time drummer yet. Every person you meet and every possible gig that you hear about will need to be recalled at a later date. There are many sources that a beginner, or even a veteran, can turn to for gathering this type of information.

Printed music industry directories like the Indie Contact Bible can have an incredible amount of information to get you started. Alternative news weeklies like the Village Voice or the Boston Phoenix are a great source of local music venues, festivals and college listings. Most major markets in the country have an independent weekly publication; some of them can be found online at www.awn.org. Online music communities like are also an ideal place to find where bands of a similar style are playing.

Data Management

Once you start gleaning contact information from printed directories, online communities, newspapers and other bands, you will soon realize that you need a good way to organize and access all of this data. You most likely have pages full of notes, emails with venue referrals and spreadsheets covered with names and numbers. The key now is to be able to effectively organize all of your new found contacts in a way that maximizes your opportunity with each one of them.

Software or web based contact managers like Outlook, Act, Maximizer or Onlinegigs, are all efforts to help you centralize your business related messages, tasks and contact information. It doesn't make sense to dig thru multiple email boxes on different computers to find important messages. Anymore than it would to be unable to find an important phone number because you left your address book in Spokane, WA. Whatever application or method you choose, be sure to get as many of the following features as would apply to your specific needs.

- Complete and total access to all of your important contact and business information in one location
- Multiple, archived backups of your information in case of data loss or equipment failure
- Reminder system for upcoming activities and tasks
- Integrated email & fax messaging with message tracking and searching
- Customizable for your specific industry
- Remotely accessible from any internet connection
- Ability to easily share information with others

Importance of contracts

After a few months of working your task list religiously and following up on every CD in a consistent and professional manner, you should be ready to start booking some gigs. After all the work you have just gone through to find contacts and reach out to each one of them, it would be a shame to lose out on a gig at the last minute. Admittedly, last minute cancellations and double bookings can and will occur. The story usually goes like this:

You sent out your CD in January; to finally book a gig in April for your upcoming August tour. It's just a Tuesday night for 100% of the door, rooms and food; but it's a needed stop-over between Colorado and Nevada. You call a week before the gig from somewhere in Texas and the club has never heard of you. What's worse, there is another band booked on that night and the other band has a confirmed written agreement. In a toss up situation between the band with no proof and the band with a contract, the band with the contract usually wins.

For gigs that are low-dough or no-dough deals, you should still send a written agreement. A written agreement is your only line of defense after all of the work you have gone thru to secure the gig, not to mention the work you will need to do for properly promoting it. Email is the easiest method because you can easily send the same message over and over until you get confirmation. Faxing is also relatively easy, however having to send a snail mail agreement over and over can be a pretty big hassle. Your goal here is to constantly remind the talent buyer of your agreement and put all of the details in front of them. The higher the dollar value on the agreement the more diligent you should be about insisting on a signed, hard-copy version of the agreement.

Getting ready for the road

Putting a group of people on the road for any amount of time comes with responsibilities. There are many people who will need detailed information about your schedule in order for your tour to be effective, safe and organized. Band members and their families, your manager, a publicist and even your fans all need to have access to different information about your trip. At a minimum all of your shows should be listed on your website as soon as they are confirmed. Ideally you would also list set times, the venue's address, phone number, website and any other bands on the bill with you.

The Tour Itinerary however is really the best way to be sure your trip is error free. Everyone on your team should have a chronological listing of each of your tour dates with as much or as little detail as they need. But the master itinerary for you and your band members should list all of the contact info for each venue, set times, payment details, venue capacity, ticket price, age limits and step by step directions from one gig to the next. This is your bible for the trip and the more copies you make the less likely you will be lost in Lincoln, Nebraska without the buyer's phone number or any sense of direction.

The Tour Itinerary is also a crucial tool in satisfying your greatest responsibility as a touring band: Advancing Your Shows. If you want your journey to free of surprises, then you will advance all of your shows. This simply means contacting the venue a week or so before the gig to confirm performance details, get important load in information and find out about any last minute changes. Out of your entire organization of band members, managers, agents, tour managers and interns, there needs to be one person who can assume this role.

Properly promoting your shows

If you have never played before in a particular market, then most likely nobody in that town has any idea who you are. And why would anyone come out to see you play if they have no idea that you are even playing. What you really need is some press or at a minimum just a listing with the local radio and print music calendars.

Your first step is to put together all of the contact names, fax numbers, email addresses etc. for the local media outlets in a 30-60 mile radius of each of your gigs. Then you will have to prepare a professional and concise press release. A good release should be able to convey all of the pertinent information on one page. Radio stations and newspapers get flooded everyday with hundreds of releases, they do not have time to read numerous pages that outline your band's Zen philosophy or each of your bass player's numerous influences. Keep it to the point or they will not read it all. Keep your layout clean; do not use multiple fonts and font sizes or too many colors and graphics.

Make sure your release has a section with the performance details that is easy to pick out and includes: Performance Date, Band Name, Venue Name, Full Address, Phone, Website, Ticket Price, Set Times, Age Limit and any other bands on the bill. Also be sure to include your personal contact information: Contact Name, Phone, Email, and Website. If someone needs to get in touch for a photo or an interview, you will want them to be able to track you down quickly and easily.

Here is where your Contact Management program really comes in handy. You could take the time to create numerous, personalized press releases for each press contact you have found. This would probably take you days depending on the size of the market. If we are talking about New York City, it could take you months. But if you have the proper tools like I mentioned in the section above, you should be able to create one template and send personally addressed releases, by fax or email to hundreds of media contacts all at once.

The dance

You should think of every band outing as a well choreographed dance. All of the administration needs to happen with precision for you to grow each new market. Put a check list in place and follow it like a religion for every gig and pretty soon it will become second nature to you and your band members. Organization alone is not going to make you a success but the sooner you get the basics in place the sooner you can spend time enjoying your music. In today's music marketplace, exposure for independent acts is generally limited to touring. If you want to be heard outside of your local market you are going to have get your band some gigs outside of your local market! Put a solid plan in place and achieve your goals.

Jay Flanzbaum of Onlinegigs got his start as a booking agent putting together national and regional tours for independent bands. Those years running a boutique agency inspired the creation of Onlinegigs, an incredibly powerful booking and promotional tool for independent bands and agents.

♦

TO TOUR OR NOT TO TOUR...THAT IS THE QUESTION!

by Sheena Metal, Music Highway
© Copyright, 2007, Revenge Productions. Reprinted with permission.

It's every musician's fantasy. The tour bus rolls up to the arena (full of groupies, beer and pizza). Fans are crowded out front hoping to catch a glimpse of America's hottest band. The group is escorted to their dressing room (full of more groupies, beer and pizza). They enjoy the various pleasures of stardom while roadies set up the stage. It's show time. The artists take the stage. The crowd is screaming. The lights are glaring. The amps are humming. The drummer clicks off the first song and...

You wake up in the back of your PT Cruiser. Your bass player's elbow is in your ear and the drummer's asleep on your foot. You've eaten nothing for the last week but corn dogs and frozen burritos. This is not the tour you imagined. This is not your Lilith Faire. This is not your Lollapalooza. This is not your Warped Tour. This...sucks.

Every musician dreams of touring. Getting out of their same boring town. Trying their tunes out on new crowds, in new areas, for fresh faces. Bonding on road, writing new tunes in the motel room, free food, free drinks, getting paid, getting laid...living the life.

But the music biz is full of touring horror stories. Bands stuck on the road with no money to come home. Musicians not eating for days. Clubs canceling gigs the night of with no warning. Negative reactions from bar patrons and local bands. The list goes on.

So, how do you make sure that your touring experience is a positive one? What can you, as musicians do, to eliminate potentially negative experiences and create positive ones.

The following are a few tips that add success to your touring experience

Don't plan a tour because you're unhappy at home

Just as an affair will not fix the problems in a marriage, a tour is not the cure for: problems within the band, problems in the band members' lives, or a general malaise for your local scene. A tour is strain and stress and loads of work. You should be excited, and enthusiastic and positive when planning.

Over prepare before you leave

You can never plan too much or take too many precautions. At home is the time to rethink ever scenario and arrange accordingly. Get the van tuned up. Pack extra emergency money. Bring a list of additional clubs in the area in case your gigs fall through. Pack extra strings and sticks. Bring a backup guitar. Pack extra merchandise. Bring emergency food/water. Pack extra batteries and power cords. Bring cell phones.

Be humble and thankful

You're in a strange town and a new club, act like a guest. Nothing ticks off a club owner/promoter who's taken a chance on an unknown band more than out-of-towners swaggering into a club like Paris Hilton in an episode of "The Simple Life." No matter how cool you are in your own town, this is unproven ground and your first impression is important. Ask, don't demand. Set up quickly. Play at an appropriate volume. Clean up after yourselves. Be friendly and courteous. Say "please" and "thank you". Unless you're booking in Jerkville USA, this positive attitude could set you well on your way to a repeat booking with better perks and more local support.

Seize every opportunity

If you're going to take the time away from work, family, and the buzz you've built in your own music community to head out into the great beyond and conquer unknown lands...you might as well come back with something other than lovely memories and an out-of-state parking ticket. You're in a new place and the possibilities are endless. Sell CDs. Sell T-shirts. Get new names on your mailing list. Solicit local reviews, interviews, and radio. Introduce yourself to other club owners for future bookings. Find out who books local festivals. Play an impromptu house party after your gig. Make new friends that can street team for you next time. Think of something I haven't even written here and do it!

Don't expect to conquer the world in one tour

Rome wasn't built in a day and neither will your touring empire be. Have fun. Enjoy each trip and using it as a building block to make each tour to that particular place better and more elaborate. Play your cards right, and after a few trips you may be making terrific money, have secured lodging (either new friends let you crash or a club pays for a motel), get food and drinks comped, and guaranteed press and radio coverage.

In short, touring can be the best thing that ever happened to your band if you work hard, play it smart, and follow through correctly. But no matter how much you love to tour, always remember to keep your foot in the door locally. It's the great work that you do at home that makes other clubs excited about you bringing your show to their town.

Sheena Metal is a radio host, producer, promoter, music supervisor, consultant, columnist, journalist and musician. Her syndicated radio program, Music Highway Radio, airs on over 700 affiliates to more than 126 million listeners. Her musicians' assistance program, Music Highway, boasts over 10,000 members. She currently promotes numerous live shows weekly in the Los Angeles Area, where she resides. For more info: www.sheena-metal.com.

10 KEY BUSINESS PRINCIPLES

by Diane Rapaport, author of "A Music Business Primer"
© 2007 Reprinted with permission.

Given two bands (or two businesses) that have equal talent, the one that incorporates the business principles below will often have a competitive edge.

Business principles to follow

1. Get to know the people you work with personally. Go out of your way to meet them.

2. Make it easy to for people to associate with your business.
   • Show up for gigs and appointments on time
   • Keep promises you make
   • Phone people back in a timely manner
   • Have a positive attitude
   • Pay your bills on time. If you cannot, call people up and explain your situation.
   • Be nice to secretaries and receptionists. Often the "gatekeepers" for access to their bosses.
   • Develop long-term relationships with service vendors.
   • Key business people have few minutes to listen. State what you want succinctly and politely.
   • Say thank you. Forgive easily. Anyone can make a mistake.

3. Treat your employees courteously, pay them a fair wage, be appreciative of their good work, and when you can afford it, reward them with bonuses and other benefits. They'll repay you with loyalty and good work. Retraining a new employee costs time and money.

4. Listen to the needs of the people and businesses you work with. Find out what is important to them.

5. Do every job and every gig as though it mattered.

6. Provide value added to people you do business with. This can mean everything from playing an extra encore, having special prices for CDs for fans who buy them at gigs; sending out a free newsletter once a month; providing one free CD for every ten a customer buys; and sending favored vendors free goods.

7. Keep track of your money. Negotiate for better rates. Keep business debt to a minimum. Pay your loans on time.

8. Cultivate a good reputation. Be principled in your dealings. Leadership in ethics and good conduct will be rewarded many times over in loyalty, in people speaking well of your business, and, perhaps most importantly, of people you do business with dealing fairly and ethically with you. If you examine the histories of people who are constantly being taken advantage of or stolen from, you will almost invariably find that their business conduct invited it.

9. Good advice is invaluable, and, often freely given. Learn to invite advice. Feedback is important, even when it is negative. Receive criticism with neutrality and graciousness.

10. When you are successful, give something back to the industry that has served you. Share information with other bands. Donate time or profits to a nonprofit organization.

This article is from Diane Rapaport's book, "A Music Business Primer", published by Prentice Hall (Pearson Education). Diane Rapaport is also the author of How to Make and Sell Your Own Recording. Her company, Jerome Headlands Press, designs and produces The Musician's Business and Legal Guide; and The Acoustic Musician's Guide to Sound Reinforcement and Live Recording by Mike Sokol. Contact: jhpress@sedona.net

◆

LOOKING FOR AN AGENT

by Jeri Goldstein, author of "How to Be Your Own Booking Agent and Save Thousands of Dollars"
© 2007 All Rights Reserved. Used By Permission

You have reached that point in your career development when adding an agent to your team would be a logical next step. Before you pick up the phone and start calling around, I suggest you do the following:

Get a clear picture

Take inventory and create an overview of your career position to date. This process and information will help you present a clear picture of your career for yourself and assist you in making a more powerful pitch to any agent you are considering.

Taking inventory includes re-evaluating your past two year's growth. I would include a list of all your past performance venues, the fees you actually received, the capacity of the venue and the number of seats you sold. If you haven't been keeping track of this information, it is not too soon to begin. Along with these details, I would also list the merchandise sales you had for each venue. All of this information helps assess your growth from year to year and venue to venue especially when you play a specific venue a number of times during the year. If your numbers increase each time, there is good indication you are building a following. This is exactly the type of information a booking agent wants to know when determining whether they will invest their time and money to add you to their roster. When you present an organized evaluation of your career development to an agent along with your promotional package, you immediately set yourself above most scouting for an agent.

Define your goals

Create a set of career goals, timelines and projections. Most artists are looking for an agent to relieve them of work they dislike doing for themselves-making calls to book gigs. Look for an agent to help you raise the level of your performance dates and increase the number of dates and the performance fees. Set career goals for the types of venues you would like to play and present this to prospective agents. Determine a specific time line in which you would like to have these goals accomplished. Then based on the kind of concrete information you've gathered from your evaluation (step 1 above), you can make some realistic projections about what percentage of increase you foresee in the next two years. For example, based on last year's information, you are able to determine that your bookings, fees and merchandise will increase by 20% during the next year and 20% the year after. When you present an agent with hard numbers they can more effectively evaluate whether or not it is worth their involvement.

Research

The final step before making phone calls is to do some research. It doesn't matter how well organized you are or how talented you are, if you are calling the wrong type of agent, you are wasting your time. There are many different databases or agency listing one can review. You may need to purchase some of these directories, but it will be well worth the expense when you begin calling appropriate agencies Some resources with agency listings are: Pollstar (www.pollstar.com), The Musician's Atlas (www.MusiciansAtlas.com) and Music Review (www.musreview.com).

Some agents book specific genres music or styles of performance. When researching agencies, determine if the genre of music or the type of performance is compatible with your own. Check their roster of artists to see if you recognize anyone. There may be some acts for which you might open-when finally speaking with someone at the agency, mention that. Create a list of appropriate agencies and make sure you get the names of one or two or the head of the agency if it is a small company. If you know any acts who are working with a specific agent with whom you might be compatible, ask that act if they would mind sharing some information about their agent. You may get some insider information regarding whether or not it is a good time to make your pitch based on whom the agent just signed or if they are looking for new acts to add.

Go to conferences

Another method of researching agents is to attend booking and showcasing conferences. Agents often use these conferences to scout for new talent. Seeing acts in live performance help agents get a sense of audience reaction as well as getting a better picture of what they might potentially be selling. The other great benefit to attending booking conferences is that you can walk around the exhibit hall and meet all the agents who are representing their acts. View their booths to see who is on their roster as well as examining how the agency presents their artists with their booth display. You can get a sense of the agent's organization and creativity by the manner in which they represent the talent. Stand by and listen to the way they pitch their artists to prospective buyers.

With these three tasks under your belt, you can confidently present yourself to appropriate agencies when you feel you are ready to make a pitch. You will present a much more professional overview of your act with a clear evaluation of your past performance and a realistic projection of your future.

Jeri Goldstein is the author of, How To Be Your Own Booking Agent - A Performing Artist's Guide to a Successful Touring Career. She had been an agent and artist's manager for 20 years. Currently she consults with artists, agents, managers through her consultation program Manager-In-A-Box and presents The Performing Biz, seminars and workshops at conferences, universities, arts councils and to organizations. Her book and information about her other programs is available at www.nmtinc.com or phone 1-888-550-6827 toll free.

◆

STOP BURNING BRIDGES…OR YOUR CAREER MIGHT GO UP IN FLAMES!

by Sheena Metal, Music Highway
© 2007 All Rights Reserved. Used By Permission

Hey, nobody said the music business was going to be easy. It truly is a jungle out there filled with: snakes, rats, rabid carnivores, sharks…well, you get the picture. In the course of your musical journey, there will be confrontations, arguments, misunderstandings, and miscommunications. You'll get jerked around, screwed over, ripped off and disrespected. So, you want to be a rockstar? Welcome to your nightmare.

But this is also a business of good people, who'll give you opportunities and chances and help you out when you least expect it. That's why it's so important that you, as musicians and as a band, act professionally and respectfully regardless of the behavior of those you encounter. You don't have to be a pushover and of course, you have a right to defend yourself against the questionable actions of others, but the music community can be a very small town and the behavior you exhibit will follow you throughout your musical career.

On the flipside of that, there are musicians out there who, either knowingly or unknowingly bring negativity on themselves through their own actions. Short temperedness, egocentricism, brazen entitlement, compulsive lying and just plain old psychotic behavior can brand your band as troublemakers and deprive you of important opportunities that you need to move forward in this business.

So, how can you make sure that you're doing onto others as you wish they would do onto you? What can you, as musicians do, to eliminate aspects of your personality that may be causing bad blood between you and the people you run across on your way to superstardom?

The following are a few tips that may help you to make sure you're exhibiting professional behavior at all times.

Be timely and courteous

Whether you're playing out live or emailing booking inquiries from home, there is never a substitute for courteously or timeliness. At gigs, show up when you're supposed to, be friendly, treat others with respect, set up quickly, end your set on time, break down quickly, be mindful of other bands on stage, compliment those around you and don't forget simple things like, "please" and "thank you." When you leave a positive impression in people's minds, you'll be high on their list when it comes time to fill an open booking slot, recommend a band for a review, etc.

Make sure your actions match your words

It's such a simple thing but you'd be surprised how many musicians seem incapable to doing what they say they're going to. If you book a gig, show up and play. If you say you're going to bring twenty friends and fans to your gig, do it. If you reserve an ad in a local music magazine, pay for it. If you write a check, make sure that it doesn't bounce. If you say you're going to send out a press package or a CD, mail it. It is true that many people in the music business are distrustful of bands that they don't know, and with good reason in many instances. Build your good reputation in the industry by proving that you will do what you've promised. Start small. Once you've gain people's trust, you'll see more and more doors opening up for your band.

Take the high road

It may be tough but there's nothing to be gained from returning someone's improper behavior with a heap-load of your own. That doesn't mean that you need to let every industry slime-bag from New York to LA ride roughshod all over your music project but there are ways to deal with the negative behavior in this business without branding yourself with a label equally as negative. Sending firm yet professional letters, making intelligent and informed phone inquiries and, if need be, taking legal action against those who have acted inappropriately are ways to handle unpleasant situations without drawing negative attention to yourself. Public scenes, yelling and screaming, long-winded and ranting emails, threats and accusations and spiteful actions may make you feel vindicated but it may chase away the good people as well as the bad and that just sets your band back.

You can't undo what you've already done

It's much harder to undo past bad behaviors, or reverse negative reputations than it is to foster positive ones. It's best when starting out to avoid acting rash as a rule. If you have a band member that is incapable of keeping his or her cool, perhaps it's time to rethink his or her place in your group. The entertainment industry has a long memory and a spiteful tongue. Make sure when people speak of you, they're speaking well.

This may all seem like such common sense that it isn't even worth mentioning but you'd be surprised how many shows, interviews, tours, and record deals have never materialized because of burned bridges. You may have talent and great tunes, but if your attitude sucks you'll get passed over time and again. No one wants to work with rage-aholics, egomaniacs or crazies. Don't let anyone think that's what your band is about. Sure it's important to be creative geniuses but if no one likes you, you'll be performing your masterpieces in the garage for grandma and her Pomeranian. Get smart and treat people right and you may find yourself rockin' all the way to the bank.

Sheena Metal is a radio host, producer, promoter, music supervisor, consultant, columnist, journalist and musician. Her syndicated radio program, Music Highway Radio, airs on over 700 affiliates to more than 126 million listeners. Her musicians' assistance program, Music Highway, boasts over 10,000 members. She currently promotes numerous live shows weekly in the Los Angeles Area, where she resides. For more info: www.sheena-metal.com

◆

FINDING A SPONSOR

by Bronson Herrmuth, author of "100 Miles To A Record Deal"
© 2007 All Rights Reserved. Used By Permission

Success in the music business is about separating yourself from the pack. One of the quickest and most effective ways to do this as an artist is to find sponsors. Unless you live in some unpopulated remote region of the world, then you are probably surrounded by plenty of potential sponsors for your music. Basically any individual, company or corporation doing business in your area is a possible sponsor. All it really takes is them wanting to sponsor you, and then you feeling good about promoting whatever the product is that they make, sell, or distribute. In a nutshell that is how a sponsorship works. Your sponsor "supports" you and in return you promote their product.

How does a sponsor support?

A sponsor can support you in many different ways, depending on their product and how active they are in promoting it. To give you a real-life example, my band once had a sponsorship with Budweiser through a regional distributor who we met through a club owner friend after we played his club. We were invited to this distributors warehouse where we were given t-shirts, ball caps, fancy mugs, stickers, etc., all kinds of Budweiser merchandise including several cases of their beer. They paid to have a big banner made with our logo on it, done very professionally and to our satisfaction. We would hang it up behind us whenever we performed. In one corner of the banner it said "Budweiser presents" with their logo and then our logo, much bigger and more prominent. None of this cost us a dime and being sponsored by Budweiser definitely gave us an edge up on our competition when it came time to get gigs in the clubs.

How do you find a sponsor for your music?

1. Target the businesses that actively promote their product on your local radio stations or TV, the ones that are already showing their desire and ability to promote their product effectively in your area, city or town.

2. Call or just stop by their location and meet them. Do your homework first to find out who are in charge, then make an appointment and go meet them. Chances are you may already know them if you live in a small town or city. Maybe someone you know, like a friend or a family member, already has a relationship with him or her. Use any and all connections you have to get started.

3. If they run radio spots and you have original music already professionally recorded, see if they are open to using your music for the background music "bed" in their radio promotions.

4. If you are a songwriter, write them a song. This can be tremendously effective as a starting point to approaching a potential sponsor. Walk in and play them a song you wrote about them and their product.

5. Car dealerships are great places to start looking. Many bands are riding down the road right now in a vehicle that was provided by their sponsor. Good chance that there name or logo is professionally painted on that vehicle too, along with their sponsor's. Car dealerships also do lots of promotions and events where they have live music for their customers. Even if you approach them for a sponsorship and they decline, making them aware of you and your music can turn into some great paying gigs on a consistent, long-term basis.

6. Radio stations can be awesome sponsors. Many radio stations produce and promote concerts and in most cases use local or area talent to open these concerts, not to mention all the free radio exposure you can get if they sponsor you, or even if they just like you. If you have a record out, having a radio station for a sponsor can really help you get exposed in your immediate area quickly. Approach the ones that play your style of music.

Bronson Herrmuth is author of the new book "100 Miles To A Record Deal". For more details please visit him @ www.iowahomegrown.com, or www.songrepair.com

m o t i v a t i o n a l   a r t i c l e s

DEALING WITH REJECTION IN THE MUSIC BUSINESS

by Suzanne Glass, CEO Indie-Music.com
© 2007 All Rights Reserved. Used By Permission

Being a musician, by and large, is a rewarding thing. We get to indulge our muse, spend time with other artistic types, and hear a lot of great sounds. When it comes to jobs, being a musician is great work if you can get it. Unfortunately, it's not all roses. The tremendous amount of competition makes it likely that we will sometimes lose a gig, get fired from a band, or be turned down for a songwriting award. Most of us handle the rejections pretty well most of the time. However, problems can start to occur if you

have a run of too many rejections in too short a time. Musicians may begin to doubt their talent, commitment, and even sanity when repeatedly slapped with "no's".

Tips to help you through the hard times:

1. Believe in your music and yourself. People tell you this all the time, and you need to take it seriously. Many mega-hit songs were repeatedly rejected before someone decided to release them to become #1 hits. Believe that your talent is unique, and continue to pursue your own musical path.

2. If you hear the same type of rejection often, ("You need to pick up your choruses" or "Work on your pitch"), you may want to look into the criticism. Having an open mind may help you improve your craft.

3. If you get down on music, take some time out. Go to the beach, the mountains, or your backyard, and do something enjoyable that has nothing to do with music.

4. Give yourself the freedom to quit. This may sound contradictory, though by giving you a mental "out", it can help diffuse the pressure when nothing is going right. Chances are you won't quit, but you will know you have a choice.

5. Go jam with some musician friends who do it just for fun, and forget the business. People who strictly do music as a hobby sometimes have a positive energy that will help your jaded, negative energy slip away, and bring you back to the joy of playing music.

6. If you are in a situation where you can't find a band to jam with, and have excess creative energy, consider another type of art or craft. Doing something creative, even though it's not music, will keep your creative juices flowing. Painting, carving, candle making - activities like these may also open your creative flow and inspire you musically.

7. If the problem is due to a conflict in your band, talk it out honestly with the people involved instead of keeping it to yourself and becoming cynical. Conflicts are common in bands (and every other kind of group), and surviving them means the difference between success and failure, since most bands will break up if the unresolved conflicts are not addressed. It will NOT be a pleasant experience.

8. Write a song about it. Who knows, it might be a masterpiece.

9. Think back on all your successes and good times in music, and focus on that energy. Try to balance the current bad times by realizing it's all part of the flow.

10. If you can't kick the down feelings in a few weeks, don't hesitate to talk to your doctor. Artists are known to have high rates of depression and stress-related illnesses, and today there are many new treatments. Make sure you follow a healthy diet and get some exercise.

Getting through those periods when "music sucks" is an experience all musicians have been through at one time or another. Those that master the down times go on to have productive musical careers. Those that get bogged down in the problems and become bitter are doomed to less happy - and maybe less musical - futures.

Suzanne Glass is the founder of Indie-Music.com, one of the Internet's premier musician websites. The company offers thousands of resources and contacts to achieve success in the music industry, including venues, labels, radio, media, studios, and band listings, plus articles, interviews, and reviews of indie music. Contact: www.indie-music.com

♦

THE PROCESS AND POWER OF PERSISTENCE

by Brian Austin Whitney, Founder of the Just Plain Folks Music Organization

If you speak with successful people in nearly any business, especially those with an artistic bent, one common factor you'll find among nearly all of them is that they were persistent. Whether it was in the face of competition, lack of understanding or acceptance among their peers, or their family asking when they were going to get a day job, those who persist through the ups and downs seem to last the longest and do the best. There is more than just relentlessness to that formula. While being persistent, you need to evolve and develop while staying focused on your goals. To do this you will need a plan in order to progress.

Guide markers to help you along the way:

1. Keep Learning

One of the things that persistence offers is an ongoing education. You learn by doing and you learn by trial and error. You also learn by reading books and taking advantage of various resources surrounding the music community. But you have to keep doing it. It never stops and you never know everything there is, and even if you did, it changes.

2. Keep making friends

It really is about whom you know and how well they like you. Sure talent matters, but there is a lot of talent out there. Being friends with the right people is always the tiebreaker, and in a business filled with so many worthy talents, you need the tiebreaker on your side. But that doesn't just mean the well-known stars and the already successful industry figures. In fact, the most important friends you can make are those who are also on their way up or are developing their own network of connections. One of my most important music industry allies is someone I met when I was 22 and he was 15 and we played in a band together in a small town in the middle of nowhere Indiana. Now I run the one of the world's largest music organizations and he is a key player with Virgin's Internet Radio Division. You can never have too many friends and one enemy often turns out to be one too many.

3. Be sincere and honest

Don't exaggerate your skills. Don't falsely praise other's either. Find your real strengths and emphasize those. Admit those things you need help with and do the same for your peers. It's an old cliché, but if you always tell the truth, you never have to remember your lies. If you are always sincere, people will support you even when you make a mistake or are wrong. And if you DO make a mistake, the quicker you admit it and take full responsibility for it, the quicker others will forgive and forget and in some cases rally to your side to help. Denial of the truth is the biggest downfall of politicians and one of the biggest weaknesses an artist can possess. The best artists are those who are the most honest in both their business and their art.

4. Reinvent yourself

Few, if any of us get it right the first time. As we mature as artists or performers, we need to take that new knowledge and allow it to adjust the way we write or perform. Being persistent doesn't mean being rigid and unchanging. It means constant motion forward. Traveling to a destination is never a completely straight line. Your style, technique, presentation and approach shouldn't try to be a straight line either.

5. Create your art for yourself, market it for everyone else

Some artists will insist that your art should only concern yourself, and no one else. This is partially true. But it is also partially deadly to your long-term career. You SHOULD create the art that is true to yourself, true to your vision and true to your heart. But once you bring it to life, you must shift gears and concern yourself with everyone else. Find out who your audience is, what they want and how you can market your art to them. Are you mainstream? Are you part of a small niche? Learn who you are through the eyes of your potential audience and plan your marketing accordingly. This means lose the attitude about being in a genre or sounding like another artist. Being able to categorize yourself and your music makes it easier for your audience to buy your music, see your show, and become your fan. And that is what it needs to be about. Your job is to remove any barrier between you and the music consuming public at large on their terms, not yours.

6. Help others along the way

Small-minded people think they can succeed by the failures of their peers. Good business people understand that a strong peer makes for a larger and more vigorous market for your work as well. Retailers often build near similar rivals so that customers get used to going to a particular shopping area to buy that product. They use the marketing efforts of their competitors to bring people within their grasp. The same holds true with musicians. If there are bands with similar fan bases and niches as you, it is always in your best interest to work with them and share the limelight and double the spotlight that your combined efforts will bring on the music you all make. Help your fellow bands get gigs. Not only will they return the favor but the music fan base will begin to expect more live music and will start associating all the cooperative bands with the others, and will begin to support all of you instead of just one of you.

7. Get out of your basement and into your community

Even if you are a solo writer who doesn't perform, get out into your community and participate. See other bands. Attend area songwriter and music organization meetings. Spend a few hours at the local music store and get to know the people working there (they are usually the most in touch with who is active in your community musically). Get to know the people at the local recording studios and ask if you can watch some recording sessions now and then. Being out in your community not only networks you with others but it will keep you up on the area industry gossip and goings on. It will also keep you hip to trends and styles and what is working for some and not working for others.

8. Seize the day

Make positive progress every single day. Even if that progress is tiny. If you are performing, *always* give it your best, even if you are performing for 3 people at an open stage at 1 AM. If you are a performer, then treat every performance as if it is *the* pivotal one. Treat every audience member as if THEY hold the key to the rest of your career. If you do that, one day they will. Industry people and those they know come in all shapes and sizes. Never underestimate the impact a great performance by you will have on any audience. Also, never assume that a small opportunity isn't worthy of your best effort. You are creating music because you love it, so give it your all.

9. Perform every chance you get. Co-Write every chance you get

If you are a writer or performer, you probably feel the need and desire to do it at every chance. If you don't feel this desire, it might not be the right career path after all. If you do, it's possible that you can never get your fill of it and struggle to find opportunities, especially if you don't have a band, don't know other writers and so on. Getting out there also means sitting in with others at open stages, singing back up, or playing an instrument for other bands. The same goes for writing. If you hear something interesting by a local writer, suggest co-writing. Challenge yourself to write with folks who write differently or within another genre completely. Stretch your artistic perspective, by performing with different artists doing different types of music. This will only improve your chops, not to mention expose you to a larger audience.

10 Always remember, the persistent journey IS the thing. Not the destination

Your life isn't about the destination. The same is true for your musical life. It is all about your development, your successes and failures, and all the things you do along the way. From the people you will meet, the songs you write and pure joy of the creative effort enjoy it all and learn from it. Succeed on your terms. The journey begins with our first creative step forward and keeps going until we let it.

Sometimes reaching a goal earlier than planned is a great achievement as it shows you have worked hard, pushed ahead and made it happen. However, sometimes reaching a goal far past your original deadline is an even greater achievement. This shows you persisted and never gave up, due to adversity, deficit, criticism and those little life detours that end many dreams and goals. In many ways, this is a reason for even more pride!

Brian Austin Whitney is the Founder of the Just Plain Folks Music Organization, which is one of the largest groups of artists, writers and industry professionals in the world (over 40,000 artists). To become a member, or learn more about all the organization has to offer, visit their website at www.jpfolks.com

♦

BABY STEPS AND THE ROAD TO SUCCESS

By Chris Standring, A&R Online
© 2007 All Rights Reserved. Used By Permission

"If you can achieve one successful thing a day to help your music career on the right path then you are on the right track".

It's very easy to sit at home and get frustrated with the apparent lack of forward movement in your music career. Especially when you know in your heart that you have what it takes to succeed. It's very easy to get discouraged, for the simple reason that it seems "you are only as good as your last event". Musicians and actors are similar in that we like the highs that our performances give us. We thrive on the exhilaration. It's like a drug. When it goes away we want it again.

All about perception

Gearing up to a live event is exciting. We can talk it up to friends and fans, promote it the best way we know how and enjoy the thrill of the performance itself. Then it is over and there may be a lull between events. It can seem like your career is going nowhere. It's very easy to feel that. However, other people's perception may be entirely different and probably is.

The music business is all about perception. It is based on hype and salesmanship ability. I wish it was different but it is not and will never ever be. If your band is perceived to be doing well then people will talk. If your band is perceived to be on the way out then people will also talk. If your band is doing nothing, nobody will talk! It is therefore extremely important that you keep the hype factor up. This is one of the things you need to be focusing on between events. Sit back and think about what you clearly have achieved so far in your career. Think about the things that were absolutely in your control.

Take baby steps

We are constantly bombarded with new creative marketing ideas, most of them excellent, inventive and effective. However, the ideas that you personally will primarily adopt are those ideas that you are totally comfortable with. These are the things that you will make a priority. It's too easy to get overwhelmed with new promotional ideas so we put them off and resort to the things we know we can do. I have two words to give you. BABY STEPS.

How not to get overwhelmed

It's just too damn hard to do every new promotional idea to get your band to the next level at the same time. This is especially true, if you don't have a team of people working with you. Start by doing just one thing today. If you can achieve one successful thing a day to help your music career on the right path then you are on the right track. So the key is to pick one thing, and do it today!

Increase your fan-base

The only way you can get successful as an independent artist is by letting people know you exist. So ask yourself for example, "What can I do today to expand my fan-base?" Well, there are infinite possibilities. Let's say you want to increase your e-mail database. Think about the most effective ways

you can do that. The most effective ways to build a database, (but more importantly get those people to be fans and come to shows), is to personally get to know them. So start with friends, have them refer their friends, and so on. Hand out flyers and sample CD's or tapes to everyone you know. (Make sure you have a good stack in your car.) Grab business cards of all the people you meet and get their e-mail addresses. Send them a very personal e-mail asking them if they would be interested to know about your band.

An overview

Be creative, DO something that you know you can personally do, to expand other people's awareness of you. It takes a good amount of time but you can help yourself by really being active and productive.

Read everything you can about promoting your own shows and do the things that you are most comfortable doing, the things that you know you can be effective at. Then, step out and try something new.

Do one thing a day to help get to where you want to be, and at the end of each week think about what you have achieved. There is nothing that fuels drive, more than drive itself. There's nothing that fuels lethargy more than sitting at home wishing you were successful and doing little about it!

It can be extremely overwhelming when there seems such a long way to go. So take it one step at a time. That's all truly successful people ever did.

Chris Standring is the CEO and founder of A&R Online www.aandronline.com). He is also a contemporary jazz guitarist presently signed to Mesa/Bluemoon Records. The music is marketed at NAC and Urban AC radio. For more info visit Chris @ www.chrisstandring.com

♦

SO HOW DO WE MAKE OUR DREAM BECOME REALITY?

by Janet Fisher, Director of Goodnight Kiss Music
© 2007 All Rights Reserved. Used By Permission

Define the dream

What is it you are actually trying to do? Be the world's best writer? Become a megastar performer? Lead the church choir? Own a record label that records other acts? You would not believe how many writer/artists come to me, saying they just want to do "something" in the Music Industry. Sorry, you have to specialize a bit more than that!

Sit down with paper and pen. Define EXACTLY what it is in your heart that you dream of. (Hint, the bigger the dream, the harder to achieve... but as long as you are prepared to give what it takes, you'll find a place in the scheme of things.

Research the dream

Let's say you decided that you want to be a great writer, who is successfully cut on the charts, and makes a lot of money. Do you know what the real charts are? Who's on them currently? What labels are consistently charted? What are the styles of the top ten successes been in the last two years?

Do you know what the actual elements of a great standard song are? Can you name the top sellers of all time in your genre, or the top sellers of the current year? How did they attain success? Do you hone your skills and knowledge whenever you have a chance? Can you make the presentation of your art a commercial reality? Not just WILL you, CAN you?

Practice the dream

Go do 150 sit ups without practice. Go write a great song without practice. You have to practice (i.e., actually write) everyday, just like you would with any improvement program. If the newest song you are showing is old, you are not competing as a writer.

Rewrite the dream

If something doesn't go the exact direction you thought it should have, rewrite the situation. If it's the song that has flaws, rewrite it until they are gone. If it's the voice, get some training.

If it's the gig, create one that works for you (when I was playing gigs in KCMO, I went to the Plaza, to nice places that DIDN'T have entertainment. I'd offer the owner a free evening of music, if he liked it, I'd work X amount of weekends for X amount per night. I almost always got the gig, partly because I was prepared, partly because few can resist something for nothing and not sense some obligatory return. (Most wanted entertainment, but had no idea they could afford it. For me, it was a way to go).

If you find that you thought you wanted the big dream, but then you realize that your dream didn't include all the nonsense that goes along with one of those in exchange for your "other dream(s)", (perhaps your family or job?), it is TOTALLY alright to adapt your dreams to accommodate each other. Unfortunately, some dreams require 24 hour dedication to maintain (ask any professional who is a megastar in their field.)

Pursue the dream

Don't give up. That's the first thing anyone successful who is giving advice says, so it MUST be true. Take advantage of all opportunities, work, work, and work at it!

Live the dream

Remember that each time you sing, play, write, perform, discuss, pitch, etc., you are creating a reality that supports your dream. Don't forget to applaud the little steps, as well as the big. You write a birthday song for your sister-in-law, and it makes her cry with your kindness. Your song is used in a campaign for adoption, and though it didn't earn a dime, it was perfect, and said so much to so many. A peer complimented your writing at a recent song pitch. You were the hit of the community musical. It all matters. All these things make us more professional, and give us the reasons for doing the work. They are as important as the royalties, and enrich our life of music. Don't overlook them.

Appreciate your dream

Did you know that most of your little steps are someone else's big dream? Some people would give a great deal to have the opportunity to perform ONE karaoke song in front of an audience, or have anyone use a song for any reason. Appreciate the skills and opportunities you have been blessed with, and that you might even *have* a dream.

Janet Fisher is Managing Director of Goodnight Kiss Music (BMI) www.goodnightkiss.com, along with its sister company, Scene Stealer Music (ASCAP). Both are Music Publishers dedicated to supplying the Entertainment Industries with perfect material for any musical need. Janet is also an author in, and the editor of "Music horror Stories", a collection of gruesome, true tales as told by innocent victims seeking a career in the music business". Contact: janet@goodnightkiss.com

EVEN MORE Radio & XM Satellite exposure, free website and a NO-OBLIGATION FREE CD just for inquiring!

You've probably already heard about the best place to manufacture your disc

So c'mon—give us a call!

You've more than likely already heard—from your fellow musicians, the BBB, and independent reviewers—that Oasis offers the most reliable and innovative CD and DVD manufacturing and marketing services.

So isn't it time for you to give us a call?

We think it is—if you've put your heart and soul into your project. And you want the discs and packaging you send out into the world to truly reflect (or even improve upon) your original vision. And you need help with the crucial task of getting people out there to actually hear your music.

Because if that describes your situation, may we suggest what it calls for?

It calls for Oasis.

www.**oasisCD.com**/indiebible
(866) 381-7017
info@oasisCD.com

Oasis is the only national disc manufacturing company certified by both The Better Business Bureau and BBBonline.

INCLUDED WITH YOUR CD or DVD PROJECT—THE OASIS TOP™ TOOLS OF PROMOTION:

Your Music on an OasisSampler™ Distributed to Radio Nationwide	Galaris/Oasis CD-ROM with 14,000+ Music Industry Contacts	Distribution for your CD/DVD: **iTunes Music Store** amazon.com cdbaby.com TOWER.COM BORDERS.com Waldenbooks.com	A **Full Year** of Electronic Press Kit® Service and Exclusive Live Performance Opportunities: sonicbids	SoundScan®, Music-Career Software, Retail Cases, Barcodes	**FREE Website** with the features musicians need!